THE
MODERN
AGE

THE MODERN AGE

LITERATURE

THIRD EDITION

LEONARD LIEF • JAMES F. LIGHT

Herbert H. Lehman College of The City University of New York

HOLT, RINEHART AND WINSTON

New York Chicago San Francisco Atlanta Dallas Montreal Toronto

Library of Congress Cataloging in Publication Data

Lief, Leonard, comp.
  The modern age.

  1. American literature—20th century. 2. English literature—20th century. 3. American literature—19th century. 4. English literature—19th century. I. Light, James F., joint comp. II. Title.
PS535.5.L5   1976   820'.8   75–31558
ISBN: 0–03–089801–3

Max Beerbohm. "Self-Caricature 1897" from *Max's Nineties: Drawings 1892–1899* by Max Beerbohm. Copyright © 1958 by Elisabeth Beerbohm. Published in the United States by J. B. Lippincott Company. Canadian rights held by Rupert Hart-Davis.

John Held, Jr. "Flapper." Culver Pictures.

Cartoon by Colos, *The New York Times,* January 11, 1971. © by The New York Times Company. Reprinted by permission.

Boris Artzybasheff. "We Are Getting to the Bottom of It," copyright 1948, Time, Inc.

Drawing by Chas. Addams; © 1975 The New Yorker Magazine, Inc.

Boris Artzybasheff. "The Triumph of Wit," reproduced by permission of the estate of Boris Artzybasheff.

"Terror of War" reprinted by permission of WIDE WORLD PHOTOS.

Photograph of Astronaut Edwin E. Aldrin, Jr., NASA.

Paul Freeman. "Concentration Camp," *The New York Times Book Review,* May 29, 1966. © 1966 by The New York Times Company. Reprinted by permission of The New York Times Company and the artist.

Bill Mauldin. "Fresh, spirited American troops, flushed with victory, are bringing in thousands of hungry, ragged, battle-weary prisoners . . ." © 1945 United Feature Syndicate and Bill Mauldin.

Cartoon by Jules Feiffer. © 1967 Jules Feiffer. Courtesy Publishers-Hall Syndicate.

PREFACE

This third edition of *The Modern Age* is designed, as were the earlier editions, for use in First-Year English and Introduction to Literature courses that require examples of expository writing as well as of fiction, poetry, and drama. The success of the earlier editions has encouraged our belief in the appeal and the usefulness of a text that attempts, as we said earlier, "to provide a coherent intellectual adventure by illuminating some of the primary events and dilemmas of Anglo-American civilization of the recent past as these have been pondered by important writers." In order to achieve depth and focus we have confined our selections (with the exception of those by Marx, Engels, and Freud) to the work of Anglo-American writers.

Like the earlier editions of *The Modern Age*, the present edition is divided into three chronological segments. As in the second edition, the largest division is the third chronological unit ("Under the Volcano"). Thus, while suggesting important aspects of the recent past, we have stressed the variety and excitement of contemporary Anglo-American life and literature, particularly the shifting social, sexual, and ethnic relationships that absorb modern consciousness.

The basic emphasis of the text is historical, but an alternative table of contents has been provided for instructors who prefer to emphasize theme. For those who prefer a genre approach, there is a genre table of contents in the *Instructor's Manual*. Whatever the approach, we believe each selection speaks to the present generation, all the more because numerous selections illuminate specific events (such as the assassination of Malcolm X) that are part of the living past or (like "Tin Lizzie") depict people or movements that changed forever the quality of Anglo-American life. What we are today is a result of what we were yesterday. Accordingly, the selections in *The Modern Age* illuminate the continuity of past and present.

The selections also emphasize the dilemmas of our own times—our relationship to our fellow human beings, to our state, to our God (or gods), to our increasingly urban, mechanized environment, and to the world community fraught with wars and the terrifying question of destruction or survival. In addition the selections manifest the influence of three intellectual giants of the modern era—Charles Darwin, Karl Marx, and Sigmund Freud—for no understanding of the present can pretend to intelligence without an awareness of their pervasive influence. Finally, as expressions of the human spirit, the selections capture the eternal joys, agonies, and aspirations of youth. Topics with which students identify and to which they most often respond—sex, love, marriage, rebellion, alienation—are fully represented.

In this third edition of *The Modern Age* we have attempted to ameliorate what one reviewer of the second edition called "the relentless pursuit of an historical theme." We have eliminated selections included earlier primarily or solely for their historical significance. We have also omitted some selections that, whatever their literary merit, have failed empirically the test of the classroom. In their place we have represented certain writers more fully—Stephen Crane, William Faulkner, and Flannery O'Connor, for example; have added other writers—from Robert Browning to William Carlos Williams to Philip Levine; have included one major full-length play by Tennessee Williams; have given greater attention to the problems of literary composition by including the essays of Mark Twain, George Orwell, and Edwin Newman; and have devoted more space to the concerns of women and ethnic minorities.

The expository sections are divided, somewhat arbitrarily, into exposition and argument. The sections on exposition progress from essays that are largely narrative or descriptive to essays that concentrate on ideas; the argumentative selections progress from the relatively objective to those that are made emotionally persuasive by the use of narration, description, and imaginative devices. The fiction and drama sections have been organized on the general principle of progression from the basically realistic and traditional to the symbolic, impressionistic, and experimental. The poetry is grouped as narrative and dramatic poetry, lyric poetry, and poetry of wit and satire, but for teaching purposes a few special poetic forms have also been presented. As in the earlier editions, the teaching apparatus of *The Modern Age* remains modest and appears in the Appendix.

. . .

We are pleased to thank Professor Richard S. Beal of Boston University for his advice. We wish also to express our gratitude to the following readers of the manuscript for their valuable suggestions and constructive criticism: Professor Chris Antonides, Lansing Community College; Professor Jack Campbell, Oklahoma State University; Professor Larry S. Champion, North Carolina State University (Raleigh); Professor Paul Davis, University of New Mexico; Professor Robert C. Frazier, Arizona State University; Professor Celia Millwood, Boston University; Professor Eric Nicolet, Ventura College.

Bronx, New York   L.L
January 1976   J.F.L.

CONTENTS

2 THE LONG ARMISTICE, 1918-1939

3 UNDER THE VOLCANO, 1939-1976

Appendix

Index   785

THEMATIC CONTENTS

Man, Science, and the Machine: or Who's in Charge Here?

A Complex of Ids and Egos: or the Writer as Analyst

Ethnic Voices

Man and His God (or Gods)

War

The Writer and the Writer's Art

EXPOSITION AND ARGUMENT

POETRY

Credos

FICTION

POETRY

1
INFLUENTIAL VOICES
1848-1917

INTRODUCTION

One might argue that the modern age begins with Nicolaus Copernicus, the sixteenth-century astronomer whose observations led him to believe that the sun, rather than the earth, was the center of the planetary system. His observations shook the medieval faith that the heavens had been created expressly for God's creature, man. Since Copernicus, scientific observation has continued to reveal man's insignficance. In an ever-expanding universe of awesome forces, it is hard to believe that man, once the center of creation, is more than a cosmic accident. For that reason, man's need to matter in his world is now largely unsatisfied, and few men today really believe that they are numbered among God's best beloved.

One might also argue that the modern age begins with the first atomic bomb, which exploded in Alamogordo, New Mexico, on July 16, 1945. The two subsequent explosions over Hiroshima and Nagasaki, which killed 152,000 and injured thousands more, haunt modern man with the horror of mass annihilation. Although everyday life continues in America, Russia, and China, the modern age might well be called the age of terror.

Whatever its beginning, the modern age reflects the part of the past that has molded people toward thinking and writing as they do today. Among the influential voices that shaped and pervaded the thought of the present are those of Karl Marx and Friedrich Engels, who in 1848 stated the principles of "Scientific Socialism" (or Communism) in *The Communist Manifesto*. There they posited an economic interpretation of history, proclaimed the necessity of class struggle, and asserted the inevitable revolution of the proletariat against the capitalists. Their manifesto to the workers of the world—"unite; you have nothing to lose but your chains"—inspired such later proclamations as that of the American Communist and labor leader, Joe Hill, who, before his execution, pleaded of his followers: "Don't mourn for me. Organize!"

Another nineteenth-century thinker, Charles Darwin, with the publication of his *On the Origin of the Species* (1859), precipitated a long debate between religion and science. After Darwin such religious men as Gerard Manley Hopkins could cling to the concept of God's grandeur, but Darwin's doctrine of evolution and the survival of the fittest led many thinking men to despair; led them to feel, as Thomas Hardy put it, "God-forgotten"; and led them to seek a viable faith—such as that implied in Matthew Arnold's cry in "Dover Beach": "Ah, love, let us be true to one another"—to replace the lost God of their fathers. Nietzsche's statement "God is dead" only affirmed the conviction of less learned men. Similarly, Stephen Crane's declaration in "The Open Boat" of man's insignificance in a world where chance, not justice, determines who survives and who does not, anticipated, long before the theories of existentialist philosophy became formalized, the absurdity of man's condition in a universe he neither made nor understands. Even to the common existentialist credo that man should matter, at least to himself, and therefore must act as if his choices have meaning, Crane gave one answer through the "supplicant" in "The Open Boat," who pleads, "Yes, but I love myself." To that solipsism nature answers by silence: "A high cold star on a winter's night is the word he feels that she says to him." Modern man still struggles to retain moral convictions in a universe that on the weight of considerable objective evidence seems governed less by absolute ethical law than by haphazard accident or by the "natural" law of brute force.

Other forces for change moved relentlessly onward in nineteenth-century England and America. In "Recessional" Rudyard Kipling mourned the decline of the English empire—"Lo, all our pomp of yesterday/Is one with Nineveh and Tyre"—while Stephen Crane in "The Bride Comes to Yellow Sky" lamented the loss of a way of life that was passing with the decline of the American frontier. Although imperialism reached its peak in the nineteenth century (see Kipling's poem "The White Man's Burden"), it bred its own opponents. Henry David Thoreau's passionate appeal in "Civil Disobedience" to a higher law than force has been followed by a century of voices vehemently protesting imperialistic exploitation and the immorality of war. Yet, not only in the Mexican-American war to which Thoreau specifically objected, but also in the holocaust that began in 1914, innumerable young men such as Wilfred Owen kept their rendezvous with death. Despite modern man's heightened consciousness of one world and the mutual problems its citizens must solve, nations persist in greed and violence.

The irrational in human conduct has caused some writers (often called realists) to turn to common sense and social justice for the solution of man's problems. Though they spoke in unique tongues, Mark Twain and Finley Peter Dunne both satirized violations of reason and justice, political corruption, artistic irrationality, religious superstition, educational absurdities, and the folly as well as the cruelty of slavery. The same concern for common sense and social justice pervades Booker T. Washington's search for identity in his autobiography *Up from Slavery*. Although Washington condemns slavery on moral grounds, his fundamental contention is that the peculiar institution was harmful to both black and white because it lessened the "usefulness" of both races. Throughout the volume Washington voiced the frustrations and aspirations of Black Americans, and though the eloquence of his cry for the dignity and freedom of his people was largely ignored in his time, it speaks ever more loudly to Americans of all colors in our time. In addition to this appeal for social justice, innumerable writers in England and America propounded the virtues of socialism. George Bernard Shaw, for example, a lifelong advocate of socialism and an iconoclast and dramatist, satirized the hypocrisy of alleged Christians and the "morality" of the ruling class.

Late-nineteenth- and early-twentieth-century writers in England and America also sought emancipation from puritan morality and conventional artistic forms. Walt Whitman may not have sought to destroy institutions, or so he claimed, but in his identification with democracy and the common man, and in the "barbaric yawp" of his poetry (the raw "free verse" that was to revolutionize twentieth-century poetry), Whitman belongs to the modern age as much as Allen Ginsberg, the guru of contemporary poetry. Rudyard Kipling shed poetic conventions for colloquial diction and realism. Robert Browning's variations in the dramatic monologue and Gerard Manley Hopkins' innovations in metrics and language expanded the boundaries of poetic form for future artistic exploration. Thomas Hardy and Stephen Crane, anticipating mid-century poets, presented in vivid images, ironic contrasts, and startling comparisons the universe as absurd. The familiar meters of the poetry of Matthew Arnold and A. E. Housman belie the modernity of their knowledge: that while old values and standards are dying, no new ones take their place. The complex wit, wordplay, half-rhymes, and stunning conceits of Emily Dickinson foreshadow by half a century T. S. Eliot's formulation of the objective correlative and MacLeish's dictum that a poem "should not mean, but be."

Though Victorian compromises and gentility lingered into the twentieth century, novelists as well as poets assaulted the artistic preconceptions and genteel sensibilities of their readers. Because they offended Victorian notions of decency, the works of D. H. Lawrence were originally banned. Even more daring than his linguistic innovation was his exploration of the Freudian unconscious, his revolt against rationalism, and his exaltation of the mystical. He dramatized the secret urges, agonies, and joys that attend the discovery and the loss of love. Perhaps the greatest creative emancipator of our time, however, was the Irishman James Joyce. In his short stories he captured the "epiphanies" (moments that blindingly reveal inward truths) that modern writers desperately strive to conceive and illuminate. With his weapons of "silence, exile, and cunning" he made his life a symbolic dedication to art. His novel *Ulysses* (written between 1914 and 1921 and first published in Paris in its complete form in 1922) gained immediate notoriety for its "obscenity" and "blasphemy." It was banned in the United States until 1933 but has steadily gained fame. *Ulysses* in its stream-of-consciousness technique, its multiple levels of meaning, its erudition and evocative wordplay (especially its puns in a variety of languages), its labyrinthian structure, and its dramatization of the trials of a representative modern man (the outcast Irish Jew, Leopold Bloom) in a representative modern city (Dublin) on a single day (June 16, 1904) taught innumerable writers some of the ways to enter the modern age in literature.

The spirit of innovation that has characterized the modern age bequeaths to the artist today the freedom to be bound by nothing but the expressive needs of his material. He may dispense not only with rhyme and meter, chapters and verses, heroes and villains, but with conventional spelling, punctuation, even syntax. The need to be new in order to be modern may compel him to risk obscenity and narrow his audience by the demands he makes. It is likely, however, that the artist of genuine merit, like James Joyce, will be clarified, not obscured, by time.

EXPOSITION AND ARGUMENT

Charles Darwin (1809–1882)

NATURAL SELECTION

How will the struggle for existence . . . act in regard to variation? Can the principle of selection, which we have seen is so potent in the hands of man, apply under nature? I think we shall see that it can act most efficiently. Let the endless number of slight variations and individual differences occurring in our domestic productions, and, in a lesser degree, in those under nature, be borne in mind; as well as the strength of the hereditary tendency. Under domestication, it may be truly said that the whole organization becomes in some degree plastic. But the variability, which we almost universally meet with in our domestic productions, is not directly produced, as Hooker and Asa Gray have well remarked, by man; he can neither originate varieties, nor prevent their occurrency; he can preserve and accumulate such as do occur. Unintentionally he exposes organic beings to new and changing conditions of life, and variability ensues; but similar changes of conditions might and do occur under nature. Let it also be borne in mind how infinitely complex and close-fitting are the mutual relations of all organic beings to each other and to their physical conditions of life; and consequently what infinitely varied diversities of structure might be of use to each being under changing conditions of life. Can it, then, be thought improbable, seeing that variations useful to man have undoubtedly occurred, that other variations useful in some way to each being in the great and complex battle of life, should occur in the course of many successive generations? If such do occur, can we doubt (remembering that many more individuals are born than can possibly survive) that individuals having any advantage, however, slight, over others, would have the best chance of surviving and procreating their kind? On the other hand, we may feel sure that any variation in the least degree injurious would be rigidly destroyed. This preservation of favourable individual differences and variations, and the destruction of those which are injurious, I have called Natural Selection, or the Survival of the Fittest. Variations neither useful nor injurious would not be affected by natural selection, and would be left either a fluctuating element, as perhaps we see in certain polymorphic species, or would ultimately become

From *On the Origin of Species*, 1859.

5

fixed, owing to the nature of the organism and the nature of the conditions.

Several writers have misapprehended or objected to the term Natural Selection. Some have even imagined that natural selection induces variability, whereas it implies only the preservation of such variations as arise and are beneficial to the being under its conditions of life. No one objects to agriculturists speaking of the potent effects of man's selection; and in this case the individual differences given by nature, which man for some object selects, must of necessity first occur. Others have objected that the term selection implies conscious choice in the animals which become modified; and it has even been urged that, as plants have no volition, natural selection is not applicable to them! In the literal sense of the word, no doubt, natural selection is a false term; but who ever objected to chemists speaking of the elective affinities of the various elements?—and yet an acid cannot strictly be said to elect the base with which it in preference combines. It has been said that I speak of natural selection as an active power or Deity; but who objects to an author speaking of the attraction of gravity as ruling the movements of the planets? Every one knows what is meant and is implied by such metaphorical expressions; and they are almost necessary for brevity. So again it is difficult to avoid personifying the word Nature; but I mean by Nature, only the aggregate action and product of many natural laws, and by laws the sequence of events as ascertained by us. With a little familiarity such superficial objections will be forgotten.

We shall best understand the probable course of natural selection by taking the case of a country undergoing some slight physical change, for instance, of climate. The proportional numbers of its inhabitants will almost immediately undergo a change, and some species will probably become extinct. We may conclude, from what we have seen of the intimate and complex manner in which the inhabitants of each country are bound together, that any change in the numerical proportions of the inhabitants, independently of the change of climate itself, would seriously affect the others. If the country were open on its borders, new forms would certainly immigrate, and this would likewise seriously disturb the relations of some of the former inhabitants. Let it be remembered how powerful the influence of a single introduced tree or mammal has been shown to be. But in the case of an island, or of a country partly surrounded by barriers, into which new and better adapted forms could not freely enter, we should then have places in the economy of nature which would assuredly be better filled up, if some of the original inhabitants were in some manner modified; for, had the area been open to immigration, these same places would have been seized on by intruders. In such cases, slight modifications, which in any way favored the individuals of any species, by better adapting them to their altered conditions, would tend to be preserved; and natural selection would have free scope for the work of improvement.

We have good reason to believe . . . that changes in the conditions of life give a tendency to increased variability; and in the foregoing cases the conditions have changed, and this would manifestly be favourable to natural selection, by affording a better chance of the occurrence of profitable variations. Unless such occur, natural selection can do nothing. Under the term of "variations," it must never be forgotten that mere individual differences are included. As man can produce a great result with his domestic animals and plants by adding up in any given direction individual differences, so could natural selection, but far more easily from having incomparably longer time for action. Nor do I believe that any great physical change, as of climate, or any unusual degree of isolation to check immigration, is necessary in order that new and unoccupied places should be left, for natural selection to fill up by improving some of the varying inhabitants. For as all the inhabitants of each country are struggling together with nicely balanced forces, extremely slight modifications in the structure or habits of one species would often give it an advantage over others; and still further modifications of the same kind would often still further increase the advantage, as long as the species continued under the same conditions of life and profited by similar means of subsistence and defence. No country can be named in which all the native inhabitants are now so perfectly adapted to each other and to the physical conditions under which they live, that none of them could be still better adapted or improved; for in all countries, the natives have been so far conquered by naturalised productions, that they have allowed some foreigners to take firm possession of the land. And as foreigners have thus in every country beaten some of the natives, we may safely conclude that the natives might have been modified with advantage, so as to have better resisted the intruders.

As man can produce, and certainly has produced, a great result by his methodical and unconscious means of selection, what may not natural selection effect? Man can act only on external and visible characters: Nature, if I may be allowed to personify the nature preservation of survival of the fittest, cares nothing for appearances, except in so far as they are useful to any being. She can act on every internal organ, on every shade of constitutional difference, on the whole machinery of life. Man selects only for his own good: Nature only for that of the being which she tends. Every selected character is fully exercised by her, as is implied by the fact of their selection. Man keeps the natives of many climates in the same country; he seldom exercises each selected character in some peculiar and fitting manner; he feels a long- and a short-beaked pigeon on the same food; he does not exercise a long-backed or long-legged quadruped in any peculiar manner; he exposes sheep with long and short wool to the same climate. He does not allow the most vigorous males to struggle for the females. He does not rigidly destroy all inferior animals, but protects during each varying season, as far as lies in his power, all his productions. He often begins his selection by some half-monstrous form; or at least by some modification prominent enough to catch the eye or to be plainly useful to him. Under nature, the slightest differences of structure or constitution may well turn the nicely balanced scale in the struggle for life, and so be preserved. How fleeting are the wishes and efforts of man! how short his time! and consequently how poor will be his results, compared with those accumulated by Nature during whole geological periods! Can we wonder, then, that Nature's productions should be far "truer" in character than man's productions; that they should be infinitely better adapted to the most complex conditions of life, and should plainly bear the stamp of far higher workmanship?

It may metaphorically be said that natural selection is daily and hourly scrutinising, throughout the world, the slightest variations; rejecting those that are bad, preserving and adding up all that are good; silently and insensibly working, *whenever and wherever opportunity offers*, at the improvement of each organic being in relation to its organic and inorganic conditions of life. We see nothing of these slow changes in progress, until the hand of time has marked the lapse of ages, and then so imperfect is our view into long-past geological ages, that we see only that the forms of life are now different from what they formerly were. . . .

Karl Marx (1818–1883) and Friedrich Engels (1820–1895)

THE COMMUNIST MANIFESTO

A spectre is haunting Europe, the spectre of Communism. All the powers of old Europe have entered into a holy alliance to exorcise this spectre; Pope and Czar, Metternich and Guizot, French Radicals and German police-spies.

Where is the party in opposition that has not been decried as communistic by its opponents in power? Where is the Opposition that has not hurled back the branding reproach of Communism, against the more advanced opposition parties, as well as against its reactionary adversaries?

Two things result from this fact:

1. Communism is already acknowledged by all European powers to be itself a power.
2. It is high time that Communists should openly, in the face of the whole world, publish their views, their aims, their tendencies, and meet this nursery tale of the spectre of Communism with a manifesto of the party itself.

To this end, Communists of various nationalities have assembled in London, and sketched the following manifesto, to be published in the English, French, German, Italian, Flemish, and Danish languages.

I. BOURGEOIS AND PROLETARIANS

The history of all hitherto existing society is the history of class struggles.

Freeman and slave, patrician and plebeian, lord and serf, guild-master and journeyman, in a word, oppressor and oppressed, stood in constant opposition to one another, carried on an uninterrupted, now hidden, now open fight, a fight that each time ended either in a revolutionary reconstitution of society at large, or in the common ruin of the contending classes.

In the earlier epochs of history, we find almost everywhere a complicated arrangement of society into various orders, a manifold gradation of social rank. In ancient Rome we have patricians, knights, plebeians, slaves; in the Middle Ages, feudal lords, vassals, guild-masters, journeymen, apprentices, serfs; in almost all of these classes, again, subordinate gradations.

The modern bourgeois society that has sprouted from the ruins of feudal society has not done away with class antagonisms. It has but established new classes, new conditions of oppression, new forms of struggle in place of the old ones.

Our epoch, the epoch of the bourgeoisie, possesses, however, this distinctive feature; it has simplified the class antagonisms. Society as a whole is more and more splitting up into two great hostile camps, into two great classes directly facing each other: Bourgeoisie and Proletariat.

. . .

In proportion as the bourgeoisie, i.e., capital, is developed, in the same proportion is the proletariat, the modern working-class, developed, a class of laborers, who live only so long as they find work, and who find work only so long as their labor increases capital. These laborers, who must sell themselves piecemeal, are a commodity, like every other article of commerce, and are consequently exposed to all the vicissitudes of competition, to all the fluctuations of the market.

Owing to the extensive use of machinery and to division of labor, the work of the proletarians has lost all individual character, and, consequently, all charm for the workman. He becomes an appendage of the machine, and it is only the most simple, most monotonous, and most easily acquired knack that is required of him. Hence, the cost of production of a workman is restricted, almost entirely, to the means of subsistence that he requires for his maintenance, and for the propagation of his race. But the price of a commodity, and also of labor, is equal to its cost of production. In proportion, therefore, as the repulsiveness of the work increases, the wage decreases. Nay more, in proportion as the use of machinery and division of labor increases, in the same proportion the burden of toil also increases, whether by prolongation of the working hours, by increase of the work enacted in a given time, or by increased speed of the machinery, etc.

Modern industry has converted the little workshop of the patriarchal master into the great factory of the industrial capitalist. Masses of laborers, crowded into the factory, are organized like soldiers. As privates of the industrial army they are placed under the command of a perfect hierarchy of officers and sergeants. Not only are they the slaves of the bourgeois class, and of the bourgeois State, they are daily and hourly enslaved by the machine, by the overlooker, and, above all, by the individual bourgeois manufacturer himself. The more openly this despotism proclaims gain to be its end and aim, the more petty, the more hateful and the more embittering it is.

The less the skill and exertion or strength implied in manual labor, in other words, the more modern industry becomes developed, the more is the labor of men superseded by that of women. Differences of age and sex have no longer any distinctive social validity for the working class. All are instruments of labor, more or less expensive to use, according to their age and sex.

No sooner is the exploitation of the laborer by the manufacturer, so far at an end, and he receives his wages in cash, than he is set upon by the other portions of the bourgeoisie, the landlord, the shopkeeper, the pawnbroker, etc.

The lower strata of the middle class, the small tradespeople, shopkeepers, and retired tradesmen generally, the handicraftsmen and peasants, all these sink gradually into the proletariat, partly because their diminutive capital does not suffice for the scale on which Modern Industry is carried on, and is swamped in the competition with the large capitalists, partly because their specialized skill is rendered worthless by new methods of production. Thus the proletariat is recruited from all classes of the population.

        • • •

Of all the classes that stand face to face with the bourgeoisie today, the proletariat alone is a really revolutionary class. The other classes decay and finally disappear in the face of modern industry; the proletariat is its special and essential product.

The lower middle-class, the small manufacturer, the shopkeeper, the artisan, the peasant, all these fight against the bourgeoisie, to save from extinction their existence as fractions of the middle class. They are, therefore, not revolutionary, but conservative. Nay more, they are reactionary, for they try to roll back the wheel of history. If by chance they are revolutionary, they are so, only in view of their impending transfer into the proletariat; they thus defend not their present, but their future interests, they desert their own standpoint to place themselves at that of the proletariat.

The "dangerous class," the social scum, that passively rotting mass thrown off by the lowest layers of old society, may, here and there, be swept into the movement by a proletarian revolution; its conditions of life, however, prepare it far more for the part of a bribed tool of reactionary intrigue.

In the conditions of the proletariat, those of old society at large are already virtually swamped. The proletarian is without property; his relation to his wife and children has no longer anything in common with the bourgeois family relations; modern industrial labor, modern subjection to capital, the same in England as in France, in America as in Germany, has stripped him of every trace of national character. Law, morality, religion, are to him so many bourgeois prejudices, behind which lurk in ambush just as many bourgeois interests. All the preceding classes that got the upper hand sought to fortify their already acquired status by subjecting society at large to their conditions of appropriation. The proletarians cannot become masters of the productive forces of society, except by abolishing their own previous mode of appropriation, and thereby also every other previous mode of appropriation. They have nothing of their own to secure and to fortify; their mission is to destroy all previous securities for, and insurances of, individual property.

All previous historical movements were movements of minorities, or in the interest of minorities. The proletarian movement is the self-conscious, independent movement of the immense majority, in the interest of the immense majority. The proletariat, the lowest stratum of our present society, cannot stir, cannot raise itself up, without the whole superincumbent strata of official society being sprung into the air.

Though not in substance, yet in form, the struggle of the proletariat with the bourgeoisie is at first a national struggle. The proletariat of each country must first of all settle matters with its bourgeoisie. In depicting the most general phases of the development of the proletariat, we traced the more or less veiled civil war, raging within existing society, up to the point where the war breaks out into open revolution, and where the violent overthrow of the bourgeoisie, lays the foundation for the sway of the proletariat.

Hitherto, every form of society has been based, as we have already seen, on the antagonism of oppressing and oppressed classes. But in order to oppress a class, certain conditions must be assured to it under which it can, at least, continue its slavish existence. The serf, in the period of serfdom, raised himself to membership in the commune, just as the petty bourgeois, under the yoke of feudal absolution, managed to develop into a bourgeois. The modern laborer, on the contrary, instead of rising with the progress of industry, sinks deeper and deeper below the conditions of existence of his own class. He becomes a pauper, and pauperism develops more rapidly than population and wealth. And here it becomes evident that the bourgeoisie is unfit any longer to be the ruling class in society, and to impose its conditions of existence upon society, as and overriding law. It is unfit to rule, because it is incompetent to assure an existence to its slave within his slavery, because it cannot help letting him sink into such a state that it has to feed him. Society can no longer live under this bourgeoisie, in other words, its existence is no longer compatible with society. The essential condition for the existence, and for the sway of the bourgeois class, is the formation and augmentation of capital; the condition for capital is wage-labor. Wage-labor rests exclusively on competition between the laborers. The advance of industry, whose involuntary promoter is the bourgeoisie, replaces the isolation of the laborers, due to competition, by their involuntary combination, due to association. The development of Modern Industry therefore cuts from under its feet the very foundation on which the bourgeoisie produces and appropriates products. What the bourgeoisie therefore produces, above all, are its own gravediggers. Its fall and the victory of the proletariat are equally inevitable.

II. PROLETARIANS AND COMMUNISTS

In what relation do the Communists stand to the proletarians as a whole?

The Communists do not form a separate party opposed to other working-class parties.

They have no interests separate and apart from those of the proletariat as a whole.

They do not set up any sectarian principles of their own, by which to shape and mould the proletarian movement.

The communists are distinguished from the other working-class parties by this only: 1. In the national struggles of the proletarians of the different countries they point out and bring to the front the common interests of the entire proletariat independently of all nationality. 2. In the various stages of development which the struggle of the working class against the bourgeoisie has to pass through, they always and everywhere represent the interests of the movement as a whole.

The Communists, therefore, are on the one hand practically the most advanced and resolute section of the working-class parties of every country, that section which pushes forward all others; on the other hand, theoretically, they have over the great mass of the proletariat the advantage of clearly understanding the line of march, the conditions, and the ultimate general results of the proletarian movement.

The immediate aim of the Communists is the same as that of all the other proletarian parties: formation of the proletariat into a class, overthrow of the bourgeois supremacy, conquest of political power by the proletariat.

The theoretical conclusions of the Communists are in no way based on ideas or principles that have been invented, or discovered, by this or that would-be universal reformer.

They merely express, in general terms, actual relations springing from an existing class struggle, from an historical movement going on under our very eyes. The abolition of existing property relations is not at all a distinctive feature of Communism. All property relations in the past have continually been subject to historical change consequent upon the change in historical conditions.

. . .

You are horrified at our intending to do away with private property. But in your existing society, private property is already done away with for nine-tenths of the population; its existence for the few is solely due to it non-existence in the hands of those nine-tenths. You reproach us, therefore, with intending to do away with a form of property, the necessary condition for whose existence is the non-existence of any property for the immense majority of society. In a word, you reproach us with intending to do away with your property. Precisely so; that is just what we intend.

. . .

The selfish misconception that induces you to transform into eternal laws of nature and of reason, the social forms springing from your present mode of production and form of property, historical relations that rise and disappear in the progress of production, this misconception you share with every ruling class that has preceded you. What you see clearly in the case of ancient property, what you admit in the case of feudal property, you are of course forbidden to admit in the case of your own bourgeois form of property.

Abolition of the family! Even the

most radical flare up at this infamous proposal of the Communists.

On what foundation is the present family, the bourgeois family, based? On capital, on private gain. In its completely developed form this family exists only among the bourgeoisie. But this state of things finds its complement in the practical absence of the family among the proletarians, and in public prostitution.

The bourgeois family will vanish as a matter of course when its complement vanishes, and both will vanish with the vanishing of capital.

Do you charge us with wanting to stop the exploitation of children by their parents? To this crime we plead guilty.

But, you will say, we destroy the most hallowed of relations, when we replace home education by social. And your education! Is not that also social, and determined by the social conditions under which you educate, by the intervention, direct or indirect, of society by means of school, etc.? The Communists have not invented the intervention of society in education; they do but seek to alter the character of that intervention, and to rescue education from the influence of the ruling class.

The bourgeois clap-trap about the family and education, about the hallowed co-relation of parent and child, becomes all the more disgusting, the more, by the action of Modern Industry, all family ties among the proletarians are torn asunder, and their children transformed into simple articles of commerce and instruments of labor.

But you Communists would introduce community of women, screams the whole bourgeoisie in chorus. The bourgeois sees in his wife a mere instrument of production. He hears that the instruments of production are to be exploited in common, and, naturally, can come to no other conclusion than that the lot of being common to all will likewise fall to the women.

He has not even a suspicion that the real point aimed at is to do away with the status of women as the mere instruments of production in society. For the rest, nothing is more ridiculous than the virtuous indignation of our bourgeois at the community of women which, they pretend, is to be openly and officially established by the Communists. The Communists have no need to introduce community of women; it has existed almost from time immemorial.

Our bourgeois, not content with having the wives and daughters of their proletarians at their disposal, not to speak of the common prostitutes, take the greatest pleasure in seducing each others' wives. Bourgeois marriage is in reality a system of wives in common and thus, at the most, what the Communists might possibly be reproached with, is that they desire to introduce, in substitution for a hypocritically concealed, an openly legalized community of women. For the rest, it is self-evident that the abolition of the present system of production must bring with it the abolition of the community of women springing from that system, i.e., of prostitution both public and private.

The Communists are further reproached with desiring to abolish countries and nationalities.

The working men have no country. We cannot take from them what they have not got. Since the proletariat must first of all acquire political supremacy, must rise to be the leading class of the nation, must constitute itself the nation, it is, so far, itself national, though not in the bourgeois sense of the word.

The national differences and antagonisms between peoples are daily more and more vanishing, owing to the development of the bourgeoisie, to freedom of commerce, to the world-market, to uniformity in the mode of production and in the conditions of life corresponding thereto.

The supremacy of the proletariat will cause them to vanish still faster. United action, of the leading civilized countries at least, is one of the first conditions for the emancipation of the proletariat.

In proportion as the exploitation of one individual by another is put an end to, the exploitation of one nation by another will also be put an end to. In proportion as the antagonism between classes within the nation vanishes, the hostility of one nation to another will come to an end.

The charges against Communism made from a religious, a philosophical, and generally, from an ideological standpoint, are not deserving of serious examination.

Does it require deep intuition to comprehend that man's ideas, views, and conceptions, in one word, man's consciousness, changes with every change in the conditions of his material existence, in his social relations and in his social life?

What else does the history of ideas prove, than that intellectual production changes in character in proportion as material production is changed? The ruling ideas of each age have ever been the ideas of its ruling class.

When people speak of ideas that revolutionize society, they do but express the fact, that within the old society, the elements of a new one have been created, and that the dissolution of the old ideas keeps even pace with the dissolution of the old conditions of existence.

When the ancient world was in its last throes, the ancient religions were overcome by Christianity. When Christian ideas succumbed in the 18th century to rationalist ideas, feudal society fought its death battle with the then revolutionary bourgeoisie. The ideas of religious liberty and freedom of conscience, merely gave expression to the sway of free competition within the domain of knowledge. "Undoubtedly," it will be said, "religious, moral, philosophical and juridical ideas have been modified in the course of historical de-

velopment. But religion, morality, philosophy, political science, and law, constantly survived this change.

"There are, besides, eternal truths, such as Freedom, Justice, etc., that are common to all states of society. But Communism abolishes eternal truths, it abolishes all religion, and all morality, instead of constituting them on a new basis; it therefore acts in contradiction to all past historical experience."

What does this accusation reduce itself to? The history of all past society has consisted in the development of class antagonisms, antagonisms that assumed different forms at different epochs.

But whatever form they may have taken, one fact is common to all past ages, viz., the exploitation of one part of society by the other. No wonder, then, that the social consciousness of past ages, despite all the multiplicity and variety it displays, moves within certain common forms, or general ideas, with the total disappearance of class antagonisms.

The Communist revolution is the most radical rupture with traditional property relations; no wonder its development involves the most radical rupture with the traditional ideas of all of the bourgeoisie. But let us have done with the bourgeois objections to Communism.

We have seen above, that the first step in the revolution by the working class, is to raise the proletariat to the position of ruling class, to win the battle of democracy.

The proletariat will use its political supremacy to wrest, by degrees, all capital from the bourgeoisie, to centralize all instruments of production in the hands of the State, i.e., of the proletariat organized as the ruling class, and to increase the total of productive forces as rapidly as possible.

Of course, in the beginning, this cannot be effected except by means of despotic inroads on the rights of property, and on the conditions of bourgeois production; by means of measures, therefore, which appear economically insufficient and untenable, but which, in the course of the movement, outstrip themselves, necessitate further inroads upon the old social order, and are unavoidable as a means of entirely revolutionizing the mode of production.

These measures will of course be different in different countries.

Nevertheless in the most advanced countries the following will be found pretty generally applicable:

1. Abolition of property in land and application of all rents of land to public purposes.
2. A heavy progressive or graduated income tax.
3. Abolition of all right of inheritance.
4. Confiscation of property of emigrants and rebels.
5. Centralization of credit in the hands of the State, by means of a national bank with State capital and an exclusive monopoly.
6. Centralization of the means of communication and transport in the hands of the State.
7. Extension of factories and instruments of production owned by the State; the bringing into cultivation of waste lands, and the improvement of the soil generally in accordance with a common plan.
8. Equal liability of all to labor. Establishment of industrial armies, especially for agriculture.
9. Combination of agriculture with manufacturing industries; gradual abolition of the distinction between town and country, by a more equitable distribution of population over the country.
10. Free education for all children in public schools. Abolition of children's factory labor in its present form. Combination of education with industrial production, etc., etc.

When, in the course of development, class distinctions have disappeared, and all production has been concentrated in the hands of a vast association of the whole nation, the public power will lose its political character. Political power, properly so called, is merely the organized power of one class for oppressing another. If the proletariat during its contest with the bourgeoisie is compelled, by the force of circumstances, to organize itself as a class, if, by means of a revolution, it makes itself the ruling class, and, as such, sweeps away by force the old conditions of production, then it will, along with these conditions, have swept away the conditions for the existence of class antagonisms, and of classes generally, and will thereby have abolished its own supremacy as a class.

In place of the old bourgeois society, with its classes and class antagonisms, we shall have an association, in which the free development of each is the condition for the free development of all. . . .

Henry David Thoreau (1817–1862)
CIVIL DISOBEDIENCE

I heartily accept the motto,—"The government is best which governs least"; and I should like to see it acted up to more rapidly and systematically. Carried out, it finally amounts to this, which also I believe,—"That government is best which governs not at all"; and when men are prepared for it, that will be the kind of government which they will have. Government is at best but an expedient; but most governments are usually, and all governments are sometimes, inexpedient. The objections which have been brought against a standing army, and they are many and weighty, and deserve to prevail, may also at last be brought against a standing government. The standing army is only an arm of the standing government. The government itself, which is only the mode which the people have chosen to execute their will, is equally liable to be abused and perverted before the people can act through it. Witness the present Mexican war, the work of comparatively a few individuals using the standing government as their tool; for, in the outset, the people would not have consented to this measure.

This American government,—what is it but a tradition, though a recent one, endeavoring to transmit itself unimpaired to posterity, but each instant losing some of its integrity? It has not the vitality and force of a single living man; for a single man can bend it to his will. It is a sort of wooden gun to the people themselves. But it is not the less necessary for this; for the people must have some complicated machinery or other, and hear its din, to satisfy that idea of government which they have. Governments show thus how successfully men can be imposed on, even impose on themselves, for their own advantage. It is excellent, we must all allow. Yet this government never of itself furthered any enterprise, but by the alacrity with which it got out of its way. *It* does not keep the country free. *It* does not settle the West. *It* does not educate. The character inherent in the American people has done all that has been accomplished; and it would have done somewhat more, if the government had not sometimes got in its way. For government is an expedient by which men would fain succeed in letting one another alone; and, as has been said, when it is most expedient, the governed are most let alone by it. Trade and commerce, if they were not made of india-rubber, would never manage to bounce over the obstacles which legislators are continually putting in their way; and, if one were to judge these men wholly by the effects of their actions and not partly by their intentions, they would deserve to be classed and punished with those mischievous persons who put obstructions on the railroads.

But, to speak practically and as a citizen, unlike those who call themselves no-government men, I ask for, not at once no government, but *at once* a better government. Let every man make known what kind of government would command his respect, and that will be one step toward obtaining it.

After all, the practical reason why, when the power is once in the hands of the people, a majority are permitted, and for a long period continue, to rule is not because they are most likely to be in the right, nor because this seems fairest to the minority, but because they are physically the strongest. But a government in which the majority rule in all cases cannot be based on justice, even as far as men understand it. Can there not be a government in which majorities do not virtually decide right and wrong, but conscience?—in which majorities decide only those questions to which the rule of expediency is applicable? Must the citizen ever for a moment, or in the least degree, resign his conscience to the legislator? Why has every man a conscience, then? I think that we should be men first, and subjects afterward. It is not desirable to cultivate a respect for the law, so much as for the right. The only obligation which I have a right to assume is to do at any time what I think right. It is truly enough said that a corporation has no conscience; but a corporation of conscientious men is a corporation *with* a conscience. Law never made men a whit more just; and, by means of their respect for it, even the well-disposed are daily made the agents of injustice. A common and natural result of an undue respect for law is, that you may see a file of soldiers, colonel, captain, corporal, privates, powder-monkeys, and all, marching in admirable order over hill and dale to the wars, against their wills, ay, against their common sense and consciences, which makes it very steep marching indeed, and produces a palpitation of the heart. They have no doubt that it is a damnable business in which they are concerned; they are all peaceably inclined. Now, what are they? Men at all? or small movable forts and magazines, at the service of some unscrupulous man in power? Visit the Navy-Yard, and behold a marine, such a man as an American government can make, or such as it can make a man with its black arts,—a mere shadow and reminiscence of humanity, a man laid out alive and standing, and already, as one may say, buried under arms with funeral accompaniments, though it may be,—

"Not a drum was heard, not a funeral
  note,
As his corpse to the rampart we
  hurried;
Not a soldier discharged his farewell
  shot
O'er the grave where our hero we
  buried."

The mass of men serve the state thus, not as men mainly, but as machines, with their bodies. They are the standing army, and the militia, jailers, constables, *posse comitatus,* etc. In most cases there is no free exercise whatever of the judgment or of the moral sense; but they put themselves on a level with wood and earth and stones; and wooden men can perhaps be manufactured that will serve the purpose as well. Such command no more respect than men of straw or a lump of dirt. They have the same sort of worth only as horses and dogs. Yet such as these even are commonly esteemed good citizens. Others— as most legislators, politicians, lawyers, ministers, and office-holders—serve the state chiefly with their heads; and, as they rarely make any moral distinctions, they are as likely to serve the devil, without *intending* it, as God. A very few,—as heroes, patriots, martyrs, reformers in the great sense, and *men*— serve the state with their consciences also, and so necessarily resist it for the most part; and they are commonly treated as enemies by it. A wise man will only be useful as a man, and will not submit to be "clay," and "stop a hole to keep the wind away," but leave that office to his dust at least:—

"I am too high-born to be propertied,
To be a secondary at control,
Or useful serving-man and instrument
To any sovereign state throughout the
  world."

He who gives himself entirely to his fellow-men appears to them useless and selfish; but he who gives himself partially to them is pronounced a benefactor and philanthropist.

How does it become a man to behave toward this American government today? I answer, that he cannot without disgrace be associated with it. I cannot for an instant recognize that political organization as *my* government which is the *slave's* government also. . . .

Unjust laws exist: shall we be content to obey them, or shall we endeavor to amend them, and obey them until we have succeeded, or shall we transgress them at once? Men generally, under such a government as this, think that they ought to wait until they have persuaded the majority to alter them. They think that, if they should resist, the remedy would be worse than the evil. But it is the fault of the government itself that the remedy *is* worse than the evil. *It* makes it worse. Why is it not more apt to anticipate and provide for reform? Why does it not cherish its wise minority? Why does it cry and resist before it is hurt? Why does it not encourage its citizens to be on the alert to point out its faults, and *do* better than it would have them? Why does it always crucify Christ, and excommunicate Copernicus and Luther, and pronounce Washington and Franklin rebels?

One would think, that a deliberate and practical denial of its authority was the only offense never contemplated by government; else, why has it not assigned its definite, its suitable and proportionate penalty? If a man who has no property refuses but once to earn nine shillings for the State, he is put in prison for a period unlimited by any law that I know, and determined only by the discretion of those who placed him there; but if he should steal ninety times nine shillings from the State, he is soon permitted to go at large again.

If the injustice is part of the necessary friction of the machine of government, let it go, let it go: perchance it will wear smooth,—certainly the machine will wear out. If the injustice has a spring, or a pulley, or a rope, or a crank, exclusively for itself, then perhaps you may consider whether the remedy will not be worse than the evil, but if it is of such a nature that it requires you to be the agent of injustice to another, then, I say, break the law. Let your life be a counter friction to stop the machine. What I have to do is to see, at any rate, that I do not lend myself to the wrong which I condemn.

As for adopting the ways which the State has provided for remedying the evil, I know not of such ways. They take too much time, and a man's life will be gone. I have other affairs to attend to. I came into this world, not chiefly to make this a good place to live in, but to live in it, be it good or bad. A man has not everything to do, but something; and because he cannot do *everything,* it is not necessary that he should do *something* wrong. It is not my business to be petitioning the Governor or

the Legislature any more than it is theirs to petition me; and if they should not hear my petition, what should I do then? But in this case the State has provided no way: its very Constitution is the evil. This may seem to be harsh and stubborn and unconciliatory; but it is to treat with the utmost kindness and consideration the only spirit that can appreciate or deserve it. So is all change for the better, like birth and death, which convulse the body.

I do not hesitate to say, that those who call themselves Abolitionists should at once effectually withdraw their support, both in person and property, from the government of Massachusetts, and not wait till they constitute a majority of one, before they suffer the right to prevail through them. I think that it is enough if they have God on their side, without waiting for that other one. Moreover, any man more right than his neighbors constitutes a majority of one already.

I meet this American government, or its representative, the State government, directly, and face to face, once a year— no more—in the person of its tax-gatherer; this is the only mode in which a man situated as I am necessarily meets it; and it then says distinctly, Recognize me; and the simplest, the most effectual, and, in the present posture of affairs, the indispensablest mode of treating with it on this head, of expressing your little satisfaction with and love for it, is to deny it then. My civil neighbor, the tax-gatherer, is the very man I have to deal with,—for it is, after all, with men and not with parchment that I quarrel,—and he has voluntarily chosen to be an agent of the government. How shall he ever know well what he is and does as an officer of the government, or as a man, until he is obligated to consider whether he shall treat me, his neighbor, for whom he has respect, as a neighbor and well-disposed man, or as a maniac and disturber of the peace, and see if he can get over this obstruction to his neighborliness without a ruder and more impetuous thought or speech corresponding with his action. I know this well, that if one thousand, if one hundred, if ten men whom I could name,—if ten *honest* men only,—ay, if *one* HONEST man, in this State of Massachusetts, *ceasing to hold slaves,* were actually to withdraw from this copartnership, and be locked up in the county jail therefor, it would be the abolition of slavery in America. For it matters not how much the beginning may seem to be: what is once well done is done forever. But we love better to talk about it: that we say is our mission. Reform keeps many scores of newspapers in its service, but not one man. If my esteemed neighbor, the State's ambassador, who will devote his days to the settlement of the question of human rights in the Council Chamber, instead of being threatened with the prisons of Carolina, were to sit down the prisoner of Massachusetts, that State which is so anxious to foist the sin of slavery upon her sister,—though at present she can discover only an act of inhospitality to be the ground of a quarrel with her,—the Legislature would not wholly waive the subject the following winter.

Under a government which imprisons any unjustly, the true place for a just man is also a prison. The proper place to-day, the only place which Massachusetts has provided for her freer and less desponding spirits, is in her prisons, to be put out and locked out of the State by her own act, as they have already put themselves out by their principles. It is there that the fugitive slave, and the Mexican prisoner on parole, and the Indian come to plead the wrongs of his race should find them; on that separate, but more free and honorable ground, where the State places those who are not *with* her, but *against* her,—the only house in a slave State in which a free man can abide with honor. If any think that their influence would be lost there, and their voices no longer afflict the ear

of the State, that they would not be as an enemy within its walls, they do not know by how much truth is stronger than error, nor how much more eloquently and effectively he can combat injustice who has experienced a little in his own person. Cast your whole vote, not a strip of paper merely, but your whole influence. A minority is powerless while it conforms to the majority; it is not even a minority then; but it is irresistible when it clogs by its whole weight. If the alternative is to keep all just men in prison, or give up war and slavery, the State will not hesitate which to choose. If a thousand men were not to pay their tax-bill this year, that would not be a violent and bloody measure, as it would be to pay them, and enable the State to commit violence and shed innocent blood. This is, in fact, the definition of a peaceable revolution, if any such is possible. If the tax-gatherer, or any other public officer, asks me, as one has done, "But what shall I do?" my answer is, "If you really wish to do anything, resign your office." When the subject has refused allegiance, and the officer has resigned his office, then the revolution is accomplished. But even suppose blood should flow. Is there not a sort of blood shed when the conscience is wounded? Through this wound a man's real manhood and immortality flow out, and he bleeds to an everlasting death. I see this blood flowing now.

I have contemplated the imprisonment of the offender, rather than the seizure of his goods,—though both will serve the same purpose,—because they who assert the purest right, and consequently are most dangerous to a corrupt State, commonly have not spent much time in accumulating property. To such the State renders comparatively small service, and a slight tax is wont to appear exorbitant, particularly if they are obliged to earn it by a special labor with their hands. If there were one who lived wholly without the use of money, the State itself would hesitate to demand it of him. But the rich man—not to make any invidious comparison—is always sold to the institution which makes him rich. Absolutely speaking, the more money, the less virtue; for money comes between a man and his objects, and obtains them for him; and it was certainly no great virtue to obtain it. It puts to rest many questions which he would otherwise be taxed to answer; while the only new question which it puts is the hard but superfluous one, how to spend it. Thus his moral ground is taken from under his feet. The opportunities of living are diminished in proportion as what are called the "means" are increased. The best thing a man can do for his culture when he is rich is to endeavor to carry out those schemes which he entertained when he was poor. Christ answered the Herodians according to their condition. "Show me the tribute-money," said he;—and took one penny out of his pocket;—if you use money which has the image of Caesar on it and which he has made current and valuable, that is, *if you are men of the State,* and gladly enjoy the advantages of Caesar's government, then pay him back some of his own when he demands it. "Render therefore to Caesar that which is Caesar's, and to God those things which are God's"—leaving them no wiser than before as to which was which; for they did not wish to know.

When I converse with the freest of my neighbors, I perceive that, whatever they may say about the magnitude and seriousness of the question, and their regard for the public tranquillity, the long and the short of the matter is, that they cannot spare the protection of the existing government, and they dread the consequences to their property and families of disobedience to it. For my own part, I should not like to think that I ever rely on the protection of the State. But, if I deny the authority of the State when it presents its tax-bill, it will soon take and waste all my property,

and so harass me and my children without end. This is hard. This makes it impossible for a man to live honestly, and at the same time comfortably, in outward respects. It will not be worth the while to accumulate property; that would be sure to go again. You must hire or squat somewhere, and raise but a small crop, and eat that soon. You must live within yourself, and depend upon yourself always tucked up and ready for a start, and not have many affairs. A man may grow rich in Turkey even, if he will be in all respects a good subject of the Turkish government. Confucius said: "If a state is governed by the principles of reason, poverty and misery are subjects of shame; if a state is not governed by the principles of reason, riches and honors are the subjects of shame." No: until I want the protection of Massachusetts to be extended to me in some distant Southern port, where my liberty is endangered, or until I am bent solely on building up an estate at home by peaceful enterprise, I can afford to refuse allegiance to Massachusetts, and her right to my property and life. It costs me less in every sense to incur the penalty of disobedience to the State than it would to obey. I should feel as if I were worth less in that case.

Some years ago, the State met me in behalf of the Church, and commanded me to pay a certain sum toward the support of a clergyman whose preaching my father attended, but never I myself. "Pay," it said, "or be locked up in the jail." I declined to pay. But, unfortunately, another man saw fit to pay it. I did not see why the schoolmaster should be taxed to support the priest, and not the priest the schoolmaster; for I was not the State's schoolmaster, but I supported myself by voluntary subscription. I did not see why the lyceum should not present its tax-bill, and have the State to back its demand, as well as the Church. However, at the request of the selectmen, I condescended to make some such statement as this in writing:—"Know all men by these presents, that I, Henry Thoreau, do not wish to be regarded as a member of any incorporated society which I have not joined." This I gave to the town clerk; and he has it. The State, having thus learned that I did not wish to be regarded as a member of that church, has never made a like demand on me since; though it said that it must adhere to its original presumption that time. If I had known how to name them, I should then have signed off in detail from all the societies which I never signed on to; but I did not know where to find a complete list.

I have paid no poll-tax for six years. I was put into a jail once on this account, for one night; and, as I stood considering the walls of solid stone, two or three feet thick, the door of wood and iron, a foot thick, and the iron grating which strained the light, I could not help being struck with the foolishness of that institution which treated me as if I were mere flesh and blood and bones, to be locked up. I wondered that it should have concluded at length that this was the best use it could put me to, and had never thought to avail itself of my services in some way. I saw that, if there was a wall of stone between me and my townsmen, there was a still more difficult one to climb or break through before they could get to be as free as I was. I did not for a moment feel confined, and the walls seemed a great waste of stone and mortar. I felt as if I alone of all my townsmen had paid my tax. They plainly did not know how to treat me, but behaved like persons who are underbred. In every threat and in every compliment there was a blunder; for they thought that my chief desire was to stand the other side of that stone wall. I could not but smile to see how industriously they locked the door on my meditations, which followed them out again without let or hindrance, and *they* were really all that was dangerous. As they could not reach me, they had resolved to punish my body;

just as boys, if they cannot come at some person against whom they have a spite, will abuse his dog. I saw that the State was half-witted, that it was timid as a lone woman with her silver spoons, and that it did not know its friends from its foes, and I lost all my remaining respect for it, and pitied it.

Thus the State never intentionally confronts a man's sense, intellectual or moral, but only his body, his senses. It is not armed with superior wit or honesty, but with superior physical strength. I was not born to be forced. I will breathe after my own fashion. Let us see who is the strongest. What force has a multitude? They only can force me who obey a higher law than I. They force me to become like themselves. I do not hear of *men* being *forced* to live this way or that by masses of men. What sort of life were that to live? When I meet a government which says to me, "Your money or your life," why should I be in haste to give it my money? It may be in a great strait, and not know what to do: I cannot help that. It must help itself; do as I do. It is not worth the while to snivel about it. I am not responsible for the successful working of the machinery of society. I am not the son of the engineer. I perceive that, when an acorn and a chestnut fall side by side, the one does not remain inert to make way for the other, but both obey their own laws, and spring and grow and flourish as best they can, till one, perchance, overshadows and destroys the other. If a plant cannot live according to its nature, it dies; and so a man.

The night in prison was novel and interesting enough. The prisoners in their shirt-sleeves were enjoying a chat and the evening air in the doorway, when I entered. But the jailer said, "Come, boys, it is time to lock up;" and so they dispersed, and I heard the sound of their steps returning into the hollow apartments. My room-mate was introduced to me by the jailer as "a first-rate fellow and a clever man." When the door was locked, he showed me where to hang my hat, and how he managed matters there. The rooms were white-washed once a month; and this one, at least, was the whitest, most simply furnished, and probably the neatest apartment in the town. He naturally wanted to know where I came from, and what brought me there; and, when I had told him, I asked him in my turn how he came there, presuming him to be an honest man, of course; and, as the world goes, I believe he was. "Why," said he, "they accuse me of burning a barn: but I never did it." As near as I could discover, he had probably gone to bed in a barn when drunk, and smoked his pipe there; and so a barn was burnt. He had the reputation of being a clever man, had been there some three months waiting for his trial to come on, and would have to wait as much longer; but he was quite domesticated and contented, since he got his board for nothing, and thought that he was well treated.

He occupied one window, and I the other; and I saw that if one stayed there long, his principal business would be to look out the window. I had soon read all the tracts that were left there, and examined where former prisoners had broken out, and where a grate had been sawed off, and heard the history of the various occupants of that room; for I found that even here there was a history and a gossip which never circulated beyond the walls of the jail. Probably this is the only house in the town where verses are composed, which are afterward printed in circular form, but not published. I was shown quite a long list of verses which were composed by some young men who had been detected in an attempt to escape, who avenged themselves by singing them.

I pumped my fellow-prisoner as dry as I could, for fear I should never see him again; but at length he showed me which was my bed, and left me to blow out the lamp.

It was like traveling into a far country, such as I had never expected to be-hold, to lie there for one night. It seemed to me that I never had heard the town clock strike before, nor the evening sounds of the village; for we slept with the windows open, which were inside the grating. It was to see my native village in the light of the Middle Ages, and our Concord was turned into a Rhine stream, and visions of knights and castles passed before me. They were the voices of old burghers that I heard in the streets. I was an involuntary spectator and auditor of whatever was done and said in the kitchen of the adjacent village-inn,—a wholly new and rare experience to me. It was a closer view of my native town. I was fairly inside of it. I never had seen its institutions before. This is one of the peculiar institutions; for it is a shire town. I began to comprehend what its inhabitants were about.

In the morning, our breakfasts were put through the hole in the door, in small oblong-square tin pans, made to fit, and holding a pint of chocolate, with brown bread, and an iron spoon. When they called for the vessels again, I was green enough to return what bread I had left; but my comrade seized it, and said that I should lay that up for lunch or dinner. Soon after he was let out to work at haying in a neighboring field, whither he went every day, and would not be back till noon; so he bade me good-day, saying that he doubted if he should see me again.

When I came out of prison,—for some one interfered, and paid that tax,—I did not perceive that great changes had taken place on the common, such as he observed who went in a youth and emerged a tottering and gray-headed man; and yet a change had to my eyes come over the scene,—the town, and State, and country,—greater than any that mere time could effect. I saw yet more distinctly the State in which I lived. I saw to what extent the people among whom I lived could be trusted as good neighbors and friends; that their friendship was for summer weather only; that they did not greatly propose to do right; that they were a distinct race from me by their prejudices and superstitions, as the Chinamen and Malays are; that in their sacrifices to humanity they ran no risks, not even to their property; that after all they were not so noble but they treated the thief as he had treated them, and hoped, by a certain outward observance and a few prayers, and by walking in a particular straight though useless path from time to time, to save their souls. This may be to judge my neighbors harshly; for I believe that many of them are not aware that they have such an institution as the jail in their village.

It was formerly the custom in our village, when a poor debtor came out of jail, for his acquaintances to salute him, looking through their fingers, which were crossed to represent the grating of a jail window, "How do ye do?" My neighbors did not thus salute me, but first looked at me, and then at one another, as if I had returned from a long journey. I was put into jail as I was going to the shoemaker's to get a shoe which was mended. When I was let out the next morning, I proceeded to finish my errand, and, having put on my mended shoe, joined a huckleberry party, who were impatient to put themselves under my conduct; and in half an hour,—for the horse was soon tackled,—was in the midst of a huckleberry field, on one of our highest hills, two miles off, and then the State was nowhere to be seen.

This is the whole history of "My Prisons."

I have never declined paying the highway tax, because I am as desirous of being a good neighbor as I am of being a bad subject; and as for supporting schools, I am doing my part to educate my fellow countrymen now. It is for no particular item in the tax-bill that I refuse to pay it. I simply wish to refuse allegiance to the State, to withdraw and stand aloof from it effectually. I do not care to trace the course of my dollar, if I could, till it buys a man or a musket to shoot one with,—the dollar is innocent,—but I am concerned to trace the effects of my allegiance. In fact, I quietly declare war with the State, after my fashion, though I will still make what use and get what advantage of her I can, as is usual in such cases.

If others pay the tax which is demanded for me, from a sympathy with the State, they do but what they have already done in their own case, or rather they abet injustice to a greater extent than the State requires. If they pay the tax from a mistaken interest in the individual taxed, to save his property, or prevent his going to jail, it is because they have not considered wisely how far they let their private feelings interfere with the public good.

This, then, is my position at present. But one cannot be too much on his guard in such a case, lest his action be biased by obstinacy or an undue regard for the opinions of men. Let him see that he does only what belongs to himself and to the hour.

I think sometimes, Why, this people mean well, they are only ignorant; they would do better if they knew how: why give your neighbors this pain to treat you as they are not inclined to? But I think again, This is no reason why I should do as they do, or permit others to suffer much greater pain of a different kind. Again, I sometimes say to myself, When many millions of men, without heat, without ill will, without personal feeling of any kind, demand of you a few shillings only, without the possibility, such is their constitution, of retracting or altering their present demand, and without the possibility, on your side, of appeal to any other millions, why expose yourself to this overwhelming brute force? You do not resist cold and hunger, the winds and the waves, thus obstinately; you quietly submit to a thousand similar necessities.

You do not put your head into the fire. But just in proportion as I regard this as not wholly a brute force, but partly a human force, and consider that I have relations to those millions as to so many millions of men, and not of mere brute or inanimate things, I see that appeal is possible, first and instantaneously, from them to the Maker of them, and, secondly, from them to themselves. But if I put my head deliberately into the fire, there is no appeal to fire or to the Maker of fire, and I have only myself to blame. If I could convince myself that I have any right to be satisfied with men as they are, and to treat them accordingly, and not according, in some respects, to my requisitions and expectations of what they and I ought to be, then, like a good Mussulman and fatalist, I should endeavor to be satisfied with things as they are, and say it is the will of God. And, above all, there is this difference between resisting this and a purely brute or natural force, that I can resist this with some effect; but I cannot expect, like Orpheus, to change the nature of the rocks and trees and beasts.

I do not wish to quarrel with any man or nation. I do not wish to split hairs, to make fine distinctions, or set myself up as better than any neighbors. I seek rather, I may say, even an excuse for conforming to the laws of the land. I am but too ready to conform to them. Indeed, I have reason to suspect myself on this head; and each year, as the tax-gatherer comes round, I find myself disposed to review the acts and position of the general and State governments, and the spirit of the people, to discover a pretext for conformity.

"We must affect our country as our parents,
And if at any time we alienate
Our love or industry from doing it honor,
We must respect effects and teach the soul
Matter of conscience and religion,
And not desire of rule or benefit."

I believe that the State will soon be able to take all my work of this sort out of my hands, and then I shall be no better a patriot than my fellow-countrymen. Seen from a lower point of view, the Constitution, with all its faults, is very good; the law and the courts are very respectable; even this State and this American government are, in many respects, very admirable, and rare things, to be thankful for, such as a great many have described them; but seen from a point of view a little higher, they are what I have described them; seen from a higher still, and the highest, who shall say what they are, or that they are worth looking at or thinking of at all?

However, the government does not concern me much, and I shall bestow the fewest possible thoughts on it. It is not many moments that I live under a government, even in this world. If a man is thought-free, fancy-free, imagination-free, that which *is not* never for a long time appearing *to be* to him, unwise rulers or reformers cannot fatally interrupt him.

I know that most men think differently from myself; but those whose lives are by profession devoted to the study of these or kindred subjects content me as little as any. Statesmen and legislators, standing so completely within the institution, never distinctly and nakedly behold it. They speak of moving society, but have no resting-place without it. They may be men of a certain experience and discrimination, and have no doubt invented ingenious and even useful systems, for which we sincerely thank them; but all their wit and usefulness lie within certain not very wide limits. They are wont to forget that the world is not governed by policy and expediency. Webster never goes behind government, and so cannot speak with authority about it. His words are wisdom to those legislators who contemplate no essential reform in the existing government; but for thinkers, and those who legislate for all time, he never once glances at the subject. I know of those whose serene and wise speculations on this theme would soon reveal the limits of his mind's range and hospitality. Yet, compared with the cheap professions of most reformers, and the still cheaper wisdom and eloquence of politicians in general, his are almost the only sensible and valuable words, and we thank Heaven for him. Comparatively, he is always strong, original, and, above all, practical. Still, his quality is not wisdom, but prudence. The lawyer's truth is not Truth, but consistency or a consistent expediency. Truth is always in harmony with herself, and is not concerned chiefly to reveal the justice that may consist with wrong-doing. He well deserves to be called, as he has been called, the Defender of the Constitution. There are really no blows to be given by him but defensive ones. He is not a leader, but a follower. His leaders are the men of '87. "I have never made an effort," he says, "and never propose to make an effort; I have never countenanced an effort, and never mean to countenance an effort, to disturb the arrangement as originally made, by which the various States came into the Union." Still thinking of the sanction which the Constitution gives to slavery, he says, "Because it was a part of the original compact,—let it stand." Notwithstanding his special acuteness and ability, he is unable to take a fact out of its merely political relations, and behold it as it lies absolutely to be disposed of by the intellect,—what, for instance, it behooves a man to do here in America to-day with regard to slavery,—but ventures, or is driven, to make some such desperate answer as the following, while professing to speak absolutely, and as a private man,— from which what new and singular code of social duties might be inferred? "The manner," says he, "in which the governments of those States where slavery exists are to regulate it is for their own consideration, under their responsibility to their constituents,

to the general laws of propriety, humanity, and justice, and to God. Associations formed elsewhere, springing from a feeling of humanity, or any other cause, have nothing whatever to do with it. They have never received any encouragement from me, and they never will."

They who know of no purer sources of truth, who have traced up its stream no higher, stand, and wisely stand, by the Bible and the Constitution, and drink at it there with reverence and humility; but they who behold where it comes trickling into this lake or that pool, gird up their loins once more, and continue their pilgrimage toward its fountain-head.

No man with a genius for legislation has appeared in America. They are rare in the history of the world. There are orators, politicians, and eloquent men, by the thousands; but the speaker has not yet opened his mouth to speak who is capable of settling the much-vexed questions of the day. We love eloquence for its own sake, and not for any truth which it may utter, or any heroism it may inspire. Our legislators have not yet learned the comparative value of free trade and of freedom, of union, and of rectitude, to a nation. They have no genius or talent for comparatively humble questions of taxation and finance, commerce and manufactures and agriculture. If we were left solely to the wordy wit of legislators in Congress for our guidance, uncorrected by the seasonable experience and the effectual complaints of the people, America would not long retain her rank among the nations. For eighteen hundred years, though perchance I have no right to say it, the New Testament has been written; yet where is the legislator who has wisdom and practical talent enough to avail himself of the light which it sheds on the science of legislation?

The authority of government, even such as I am willing to submit to,—for

I will cheerfully obey those who know and can do better than I, and in many things even those who neither know nor can do so well,—is still an impure one: to be strictly just, it must have the sanction and consent of the governed. It can have no pure right over my person and property but what I concede to it. The progress from an absolute to a limited monarchy, from a limited monarchy to a democracy, is a progress toward a true respect for the individual. Even the Chinese philosopher was wise enough to regard the individual as the basis of the empire. Is a democracy, such as we know it, the last improvement possible in government? Is it not possible to take a step further towards recognizing and organizing the rights of man? There will never be a really free and enlightened State until the State comes to recognize the individual as a higher and independent power, from which all its own power and authority are derived, and treats him accordingly. I please myself with imagining a State at last which can afford to be just to all men, and to treat the individual with respect as a neighbor; which even would not think it inconsistent with its own repose if a few were to live aloof from it, not meddling with it, nor embraced by it, who fulfilled all the duties of neighbors and fellow-men. A State which bore this kind of fruit, and suffered it to drop off as fast as it ripened, would prepare the way for a still more perfect and glorious State, which also I have imagined, but not yet anywhere seen.

Thomas Henry Huxley (1825–1895)
THE METHOD OF SCIENTIFIC INVESTIGATION

The method of scientific investigation is nothing but the expression of the necessary mode of working of the human mind. It is simply the mode at which all phenomena are reasoned about, rendered precise and exact. There is no more difference, but there is just the same kind of difference, between the mental operations of a man of science and those of an ordinary person as there is between the operations and methods of a baker or of a butcher weighing out his goods in common scales and the operations of a chemist in performing a difficult and complex analysis by means of his balance and finely graduated weights. It is not that the action of the scales in the one case and the balance in the other differ in the principles of their construction or manner of working; but the beam of one is set on an infinitely finer axis than the other and of course turns by the addition of a much smaller weight.

You will understand this better, perhaps, if I give you some familiar example. You have all heard it repeated, I dare say, that men of science work by means of induction and deduction, and that by the help of these operations they, in a sort of sense, wring from nature certain other things which are called natural laws and causes, and that out of these, by some cunning skill of their own, they build up hypotheses and theories. And it is imagined by many that the operations of the common mind can be by no means compared with these processes and that they have to be acquired by a sort of special apprenticeship to the craft. To hear all these large words you would think that the mind of a man of science must be constituted differently from that of his fellow men; but if you will not be frightened by terms, you will discover that you are quite wrong and that all these terrible apparatus are being used by yourselves every day and every hour of your lives.

There is a well-known incident in one of Molière's plays where the author makes the hero express unbounded delight on being told that he had been talking prose during the whole of his life. In the same way I trust that you will take comfort and be delighted with yourselves on the discovery that you have been acting on the principles of inductive and deductive philosophy during the same period. Probably there is not one here who has not in the course of the day had occasion to set in motion a complex train of reasoning of the very same kind, though differing of course in degree, as that which a scientific man goes through in tracing the causes of natural phenomena.

A very trivial circumstance will serve to exemplify this. Suppose you go into a fruiterer's shop, wanting an apple. You take up one, and on biting it you find it is sour; you look at it and see that it is hard and green. You take up another one, and that too is hard, green, and sour. The shopman offers you a third; but before biting it you examine it and find that it is hard and green, and you immediately say that you will not have it, as it must be sour like those that you have already tried.

Nothing can be more simple than what you think, but if you will take the trouble to analyze and trace out into its logical elements what has been done by the mind, you will be greatly surprised. In the first place you have performed the operation of induction. You found that in two experiences hardness and greenness in apples go together with sourness. It was so in the first case, and it was confirmed by the second. True, it is a very small basis, but still it is

enough to make an induction from; you generalize the facts, and you expect to find sourness in apples where you get hardness and greenness. You found upon that a general law that all hard and green apples are sour; and that, so far as it goes, is a perfect induction. Well, having got your natural law in this way, when you are offered another apple which you find is hard and green, you say, "All hard and green apples are sour; this apple is hard and green; therefore this apple is sour." That train of reasoning is what logicians call a syllogism and has all its various parts and terms—its major premise, its minor premise, and its conclusion. And by the help of further reasoning, which if drawn out would have to be exhibited in two or three other syllogisms, you arrive at your final determination, "I will not have that apple." So that, you see, you have, in the first place, established a law by induction, and upon that you have founded a deduction and reasoned out the special conclusion of the particular case. Well now suppose, having got your law that at some time afterwards you are discussing the qualities of apples with a friend. You will say to him, "It is a very curious thing, but I find that all hard and green apples are sour!" Your friend says to you, "But how do you know that?" You at once reply, "Oh, because I have tried them over and over again and have always found them to be so." Well, if we were talking science instead of common sense, we should call that an experimental verification. And if still opposed you go further and say, "I have heard from the people in Somersetshire and Devonshire, where a large number of apples are grown, that they have observed the same thing. It is also found to be the case in Normandy and in North America. In short, I find it to be the universal experience of mankind wherever attention has been directed to the subject." Whereupon, your friend, unless he is a very unreasonable man, agrees with you and is convinced that you are quite right in the conclusion you have drawn. He believes, although perhaps he does not know he believes it, that the more extensive verifications are, that the more frequently experiments have been made and results of the same kind arrived at, that the more varied the conditions under which the same results have been attained the more certain is the ultimate conclusion, and he disputes the question no further. He sees that the experiment has been tried under all sorts of conditions as to time, place, and people with the same result; and he says with you, therefore, that the law you have laid down must be a good one and he must believe it.

In science we do the same thing: the philosopher exercises precisely the same faculties, though in a much more delicate manner. In scientific inquiry it becomes a matter of duty to expose a supposed law to every possible kind of verification, and to take care, moreover, that this is done intentionally and not left to mere accident as in the case of the apples. And in science, as in common life, our confidence in a law is in exact proportion to the absence of variation in the result of our experimental verifications. For instance, if you let go your grasp of an article you may have in your hand, it will immediately fall to the ground. That is a very common verification of one of the best established laws of nature, that of gravitation. The method by which men of science established the existence of that law is exactly the same as that by which we have established the trivial proposition about the sourness of hard and green apples. But we believe it in such an extensive, thorough, and unhesitating manner because the universal experience of mankind verifies it, and we can verify it ourselves at any time; and that is the strongest possible foundation on which any natural law can rest.

So much by way of proof that the method of establishing laws in science is exactly the same as that pursued in common life. Let us now turn to another matter (though really it is but another phase of the same question), and that is the method by which from the relations of certain phenomena we prove that some stand in the position of causes towards the others.

I want to put the case clearly before you, and I will therefore show you what I mean by another familiar example. I will suppose that one of you, on coming down in the morning to the parlor of your house, finds that a teapot and some spoons which had been left in the room on the previous evening are gone; the window is open, and you observe the mark of a dirty hand on the windowframe; and perhaps, in addition to that, you notice the impress of a hobnailed shoe on the gravel outside. All these phenomena have struck your attention instantly, and before two seconds have passed you say, "Oh, somebody has broken open the window, entered the room, and run off with the spoons and the teapot!" That speech is out of your mouth in a moment. And you will probably add, "I know there has; I am quite sure of it." You mean to say exactly what you know; but in reality what you have said has been the expression of what is, in all essential particulars, an hypothesis. You do not *know* it at all; it is nothing but an hypothesis rapidly framed in your own mind! And it is an hypothesis founded on a long train of inductions and deductions.

What are those inductions and deductions, and how have you got at this hypothesis? You have observed, in the first place, that the window is open; but by a train of reasoning involving many inductions and deductions, you have probably arrived long before at the general law—and a very good one it is— that windows do not open of themselves; and you therefore conclude that something has opened the window. A second general law that you have arrived at in the same way is that teapots and spoons do not go out of a window spontaneously, and you are satisfied that, as they are not now where you left them, they have been removed. In the third place, you look at the marks on the window and the shoe marks outside, and you say that in all previous experience the former kind of mark has never been produced by anything else but the hand of a human being; and the same experience shows that no other animal but man at present wears shoes with hobnails on them such as would produce the marks in the gravel. I do not know, even if we could discover any of those "missing links" that are talked about, that they would help us to any other conclusion! At any rate the law which states our present experience is strong enough for my present purpose. You next reach the conclusion that as these kinds of marks have not been left by any other animal than man, or are liable to be formed in any other way than by a man's hand and shoe, the marks in question have been formed by a man in that way. You have, further, a general law founded on observation and experience, and that too is, I am sorry to say, a very universal and unimpeachable one—that some men are thieves; and you assume at once from all these premises—and that is what constitutes your hypothesis—that the man who made the marks outside and on the window sill opened the window, got into the room, and stole your teapot and spoons. You have now arrived at a *vera causa;* you have assumed a cause which it is plain is competent to produce all the phenomena you have observed. You can explain all these phenomena only by the hypothesis of a thief. But that is an hypothetical conclusion of the practice of which you have no absolute proof at all, it is only rendered highly probable by a series of inductive and deductive reasonings.

I suppose your first action, assuming that you are a man of ordinary common sense and that you have established this hypothesis to your own satisfaction, will very likely be to go off for the police and set them on the track of the burglar with the view to the recovery of your property. But just as you are starting with this object, some person comes in and on learning what you are about says, "My good friend, you are going on a great deal too fast. How do you know that the man who really made the marks took the spoons? It might have been a monkey that took them, and the man may have merely looked in afterwards." You would probably reply, "Well, that is all very well, but you see it is contrary to all experience of the way teapots and spoons are abstracted; so that, at any rate, your hypothesis is less probable than mine." While you are talking the thing over in this way, another friend arrives, one of that good kind of people that I was talking of a little while ago.

And he might say, "Oh, my dear sir, you are certainly going on a great deal too fast. You are most presumptuous. You admit that all these occurrences took place when you were fast asleep, at a time when you could not possibly have known anything about what was taking place. How do you know that the laws of nature are not suspended during the night? It may be that there has been some kind of supernatural interference in this case." In point of fact, he declares that your hypothesis is one of which you cannot at all demonstrate the truth and that you are by no means sure that the laws of nature are the same when you are asleep as when you are awake.

Well, now, you cannot at the moment answer that kind of reasoning. You feel that your worthy friend has you somewhat at a disadvantage. You will feel perfectly convinced in your own mind, however, that you are quite right, and you will say to him, "My good friend, I can only be guided by the natural probabilities of the case, and if you will be kind enough to stand aside and permit me to pass I will go and fetch the police." Well, we will suppose that your journey is successful and that by good luck you meet with a policeman; that eventually the burglar is found with your property on his person and the marks correspond to his hand and to his boots. Probably any jury would consider those facts a very good experimental verification of your hypothesis touching the cause of the abnormal phenomena observed in your parlor, and would act accordingly.

Now, in this supposititious case I have taken phenomena of a very common kind in order that you might see what are the different steps in an ordinary process of reasoning, if you will only take the trouble to analyze it carefully. All the operations I have described, you will see, are involved in the mind of any man of sense in leading him to a conclusion as to the course he should take in order to make good a robbery and punish the offender. I say that you are led, in that case, to your conclusion by exactly the same train of reasoning as that which a man of science pursues when he is endeavoring to discover the origin and laws of the most occult phenomena. The process is, and always must be, the same; and precisely the same mode of reasoning was employed by Newton and Laplace in their endeavors to discover and define the causes of the movements of the heavenly bodies as you with your own common sense would employ to detect a burglar. The only difference is that, the nature of the inquiry being more abstruse, every step has to be most carefully watched so that there may not be a single crack or flaw in your hypothesis. A flaw or crack in many of the hypotheses of daily life may be of little or no moment as affecting the general correctness of the conclusions at which we may arrive; but in a scientific inquiry a fallacy, great or small, is always of importance and is sure to be in the long run constantly productive of mischievous if not fatal results.

Do not allow yourselves to be misled by the common notion that any hypothesis is untrustworthy simply because it is an hypothesis. It is often urged in respect to some scientific conclusion that, after all, it is only an hypothesis. But what more have we to guide us in nine-tenths of the most important affairs of daily life than hypotheses, and often very ill-based ones? So that in science, where the evidence of an hypothesis is subjected to the most rigid examination, we may rightly pursue the same course. You may have hypotheses and hypotheses. A man may say, if he likes, that the moon is made of green cheese; that is an hypothesis. But another man, who has devoted a great deal of time and attention to the subject and availed himself of the most powerful telescopes and the results of the observations of others, declares that in his opinion it is probably composed of materials very similar to those of which our own earth is made up; and that is also only an hypothesis. But I need not tell you that there is an enormous difference in the value of the two hypotheses. That one which is based on sound scientific knowledge is sure to have a corresponding value; and that which is a mere hasty random guess is likely to have but little value. Every great step in our progress in discovering causes has been made in exactly the same way as that which I have detailed to you. A person observing the occurrence of certain facts and phenomena asks, naturally enough, what kind of operation known to occur in nature applied to the particular case, will unravel and explain the mystery. Hence you have the scientific hypothesis; and its value will be proportionate to the care and completeness with which its basis has been tested and verified. It is in these matters as in the commonest affairs of practical life: the guess of the fool will be folly, while the guess of the wise man will contain wisdom. In all cases you see that the value of the result depends on the patience and faithfulness with which the investigator applies to his hypothesis every possible kind of verification.

Mark Twain (1835–1910)
FENIMORE COOPER'S LITERARY OFFENSES

The Pathfinder and *The Deerslayer* stand at the head of Cooper's novels as artistic creations. There are others of his works which contain parts as perfect as are to be found in these, and scenes even more thrilling. Not one can be compared with either of them as a finished whole.

The defects in both of these tales are comparatively slight. They were pure works of art.—*Prof. Lounsbury.*

The five tales reveal an extraordinary fulness of invention.

. . . One of the very greatest characters in fiction, Natty Bumppo. . . .

The craft of the woodsman, the tricks of the trapper, all the delicate art of the forest, were familiar to Cooper from his youth up.—*Prof. Brander Matthews.*

Cooper is the greatest artist in the domain of romantic fiction yet produced by America.—*Wilkie Collins.*

It seems to me that it was far from right for the Professor of English Literature in Yale, the Professor of English Literature in Columbia, and Wilkie Collins to deliver opinions on Cooper's literature, without having read some of it. It would have been much more decorous to keep silent and let persons talk who have read Cooper.

Cooper's art has some defects. In one place in *Deerslayer,* and in the restricted space of two-thirds of a page, Cooper has scored 114 offenses against literary art of a possible 115. It breaks the record.

There are nineteen rules governing literary art in the domain of romantic fiction—some say twenty-two. In *Deerslayer* Cooper violated eighteen of them. . . .

The reader will find some examples of Cooper's high talent for inaccurate observation in the account of the shooting-match in *The Pathfinder.*

> "A common wrought nail was driven lightly into the target, its head having been first touched with paint."

The color of the paint is not stated—an important omission, but Cooper deals freely in important omissions. No, after all, it was not an important omission; for this nailhead is a *hundred yards from* the marksmen, and could not be seen by them at that distance, no matter what its color might be. How far can the best eyes see a common house-fly? A hundred yards? It is quite impossible. Very well; eyes that cannot see a house-fly that is a hundred yards away cannot see an ordinary nail head at that distance, for the size of the two objects is the same. It takes a keen eye to see a fly or a nail-head at fifty yards—one hundred and fifty feet. Can the reader do it?

The nail was lightly driven, its head painted, and game called. Then the Cooper miracles began. The bullet of the first marksman chipped an edge of the nail-head; the next man's bullet drove the nail a little way into the target—and removed all the paint. Haven't the miracles gone far enough now? Not to suit Cooper; for the purpose of this whole scheme is to show off his prodigy, Deerslayer-Hawkeye-Long-Rifle - Leather - Stocking - Pathfinder - Bumppo before the ladies.

" 'Be all ready to clench it, boys!' cried out Pathfinder, stepping into his friend's tracks the instant they were vacant. 'Never mind a new nail; I can see that, though the paint is gone, and what I can see I can hit at a hundred yards, though it were only a mosquito's eye. Be ready to clench!'
"The rifle cracked, the bullet sped its way, and the head of the nail was buried in the wood, covered by the piece of flattened lead."

There, you see, is a man who could hunt flies with a rifle, and command a ducal salary in a Wild West show today if we had him back with us.

The recorded feat is certainly surprising just as it stands; but it is not enough for Cooper. Cooper adds a touch. He has made Pathfinder do this miracle with another man's rifle; and not only that, but Pathfinder did not have even the advantage of loading it himself. He. had everything against him, and yet he made that impossible shot; and not only made it, but did it with absolute confidence, saying, "Be ready to clench." Now a person like that would have undertaken that same feat with a brickbat, and with Cooper to help he would have achieved it, too.

Pathfinder showed off handsomely that day before the ladies. His very first feat was a thing which no Wild West show can touch. He was standing with the group of marksmen, observing—a hundred yards from the target, mind; one

Jasper raised his rifle and drove the center of the bull's-eye. Then the Quartermaster fired. The target exhibited no result this time. There was a laugh. "It's a dead miss," said Major Lundie. Pathfinder waited an impressive moment or two; then said, in that calm, indifferent know-it-all way of his, "No, Major, he has cover Jasper's bullet, as will be seen if anyone will take the trouble to examine the target."

Wasn't it remarkable! How *could* he see that little pellet fly through the air and enter that distant bullet-hole? Yet that is what he did; for nothing is impossible to a Cooper person. Did any of those people have any deep-seated doubts about this thing? No; for that would imply sanity, and these were all Cooper people.

"The respect for Pathfinder's skill and for his *quickness and accuracy of sight*" (the italics are mine) "was so profound and general, that the instant he made this declaration the spectators began to distrust their own opinions, and a dozen rushed to the target in order to ascertain the fact. There, sure enough, it was found that the Quartermaster's bullet had gone through the hole made by Jasper's, and that, too, so accurately as to require a minute examination to be certain of the circumstances, which, however, was soon clearly established by discovering one bullet over the other in the stump against which the target was placed."

They made a "minute" examination; but never mind, how could they know there were two bullets in that hole without digging the latest one out? for neither probe nor eyesight could prove the presence of any more than one bullet. Did they dig? No; as we shall see. It is the Pathfinder's turn now; he steps out before the ladies, takes aim, and fires.

But, alas! here is a disappointment; an incredible, an unimaginable disappointment—for the target's aspect is unchanged; there is nothing there but that same old bullet-hole!

> " 'If one dared to hint at such a thing,' cried Major Duncan, "I should say that the Pathfinder has also missed the target!' "

As nobody had missed it yet, the "also" was not necessary; but never mind about that, for the Pathfinder is going to speak.

> " 'No, no, Major; said he confidently, 'that *would* be a risky declaration. I didn't load the piece, and can't say what was in it; but if it was lead, you will find the bullet driving down those of the Quartermaster and Jasper, else is not my name Pathfinder.'
> "A shout from the target announced the truth of this assertion."

Is the miracle sufficient as it stands? Not for Cooper. The Pathfinder speaks again, as he "now slowly advances towards the stage occupied by the females":

> " 'That's not all, boys, that's not all; if you find the target touched at all, I'll own to a miss. The Quartermaster cut the wood, but you'll find no wood cut by that last messenger.' "

The miracle is at last complete. He knew—doubtless *saw*—at the distance of a hundred yards—that his bullet had passed into the hole *without fraying the edges*. There were now three bullets in that one hole—three bullets embedded processionally in the body of the stump back of the target. Everybody knew this—somehow or other—and yet nobody had dug any of them out to make sure. Cooper is not a close observer, but he is interesting. He is certainly always that, no matter what happens. And he is more interesting when he is not noticing what he is about than when he is. This is a considerable merit.

The conversations in the Cooper books have a curious sound in our modern ears. To believe that such talk really ever came out of people's mouths would be to believe that there was a time when time was of no value to a person who thought he had something to say; when it was the custom to spread a two-minute remark out to ten; when a man's mouth was a rolling-mill, and busied itself all day long in turning four-foot pigs of thought into thirty-foot bars of conversational railroad iron by attention; when subjects were seldom faithfully stuck to, but the talk wandered all around and arrived nowhere; when conversations consisted mainly of irrelevancies, with here and there a relevancy, a relevancy with an embarrassed look, as not being able to explain how it got there.

Cooper was certainly not a master in the construction of dialogue. Inaccurate observation defeated him here as it defeated him in so many other enterprises of his. He even failed to notice that the man who talks corrupt English six days in the week must and will talk it on the seventh, and can't help himself. In the *Deerslayer* story he lets Deerslayer talk the showiest kind of book-talk sometimes, and at other times the basest of base dialects. For instance, when someone asks him if he has a sweetheart, and if so, where she abides, this is his majestic answer:

> " 'She's in the forest—hanging from the boughs of the trees, in a soft rain—in the dew on the open grass—the clouds that float about in the blue heavens—the birds that sing in the woods—the sweet springs where I slake my thirst—and in all the other glorious gifts that comes from God's Providence!' "

And he preceded that, a little before, with this:

> " 'It consarns me as all things that touches a fri'nd consarns a fri'nd.' "

And this is another of his remarks:

> " 'If I was Injin born, now, I might tell of this, or carry in the scalp and

boast of the expl'ite afore the whole tribe; or if my inimy had only been a bear' "—and so on.

We cannot imagine such a thing as a veteran Scotch Commander-in-Chief comporting himself in the field like a windy melodramatic actor, but Cooper could. On one occasion Alice and Cora were being chased by the French through a fog in the neighborhood of their father's fort:

" *'Point de quartier aux coquins!'* cried an eager pursuer, who seemed to direct the operations of the enemy.
" 'Stand firm and be ready, my gallant 60ths!' suddenly exclaimed a voice above them! 'wait to see the enemy; fire low, and sweep the glacis.'
" 'Father! father!' exclaimed a piercing cry from out the mist; 'it is I! Alice! thy own Elsie! spare, O! save your daughters!'
" 'Hold!' shouted the former speaker, in the awful tones of parental agony, the sound reaching even to the woods, and rolling back in solemn echo. ' 'Tis she! God has restored me my children! Throw open the sally-port; to the fields, 60ths, to the field, pull not a trigger, lest ye kill my lambs! Drive off these dogs of France with your steel!' "

Cooper's word-sense was singularly dull. When a person has a poor ear for music he will flat and sharp right along without knowing it. He keeps near the tune, but it is *not* the tune. When a person has a poor ear for words, the result is a literary flatting and sharping; you perceive what he is intending to say, but you also perceive that he doesn't *say* it. This is Cooper. He was not a word-musician. His ear was satisfied with the *approximate* word. I will furnish some circumstantial evidence in support of this charge. My instances are gathered from half a dozen pages of the tale called *Deerslayer*. He uses "verbal," for "oral"; "precision," for "facility"; "phenomena," for "marvels"; "necessary," for "predetermined"; "unsophisticated," for "primitive"; "preparation,"

for "expectantcy"; "rebuked," for "subdued"; "dependent on," for "resulting from"; "fact," for "condition"; "fact," for "conjecture"; "precaution," for "caution"; "explain," for "determine"; "mortified," for "disappointed"; "meretricious," for "factitious"; "materially," for "considerably"; "decreasing," for "deepening"; "increasing," for "disappearing"; "embedded," for "enclosed"; "treacherous," for "hostile"; "stood," for "stooped"; "softened," for "replaced"; "rejoined," for "remarked"; "situation," for "condition"; "different," for "differing"; "insensible," for "unsentient"; "brevity," for "celerity"; "distrusted," for "suspicious"; "mental imbecility," for "imbecility"; "eyes," for "sight"; "counteracting," for "opposing"; "funeral obsequies," for "obsequies."

There have been daring people in the world who claimed that Cooper could write English, but they are all dead now—all dead but Lounsbury. I don't remember that Lounsbury makes the claim in so many words, still he makes it, for he says that *Deerslayer* is a "pure work of art." Pure, in that connection, means faultless—faultless in all details—and language is a detail. If Mr. Lounsbury had only compared Cooper's English with the English which he writes himself—but it is plain that he didn't; and so it is likely that he imagines until this day that Cooper's is as clean and compact as his own. Now I feel sure, deep down in my heart, that Cooper wrote about the poorest English that exists in our language, and that the English of *Deerslayer* is the very worst that even Cooper ever wrote.

I may be mistaken, but it does seem to me that *Deerslayer* is not a work of art in any sense; it does seem to me that it is destitute of every detail that goes to the making of a work of art; in truth, it seems to me that *Deerslayer* is just simply a literary *delirium tremens*.

A work of art? It has no invention; it has no order, system, sequence, or result; it has no lifelikeness, no thrill, no stir, no seeming of reality; its characters are confusedly drawn, and by their acts and words they prove that they are not the sort of people the author claims that they are; its humor is pathetic; its pathos is funny; its conversations are—oh! indescribable; its love-scenes odious; its English a crime against the language.

Counting these out, what is left is Art. I think we must all admit that.

THREE LETTERS

TO J. H. BURROUGH

Hartford, November 1, 1876.
MY DEAR BURROUGH:

As you describe me I can picture myself as I was 22 years ago. The portrait is correct. You think I have grown some; upon my word there was room for it. You have described a callow fool, a self-sufficient ass, a mere human tumble-bug, stern in air, heaving at his bit of dung and imagining he is remolding the world and is entirely capable of doing it right. Ignorance, intolerance, egotism, self-assertion, opaque perception, dense and pitiful chuckle-headedness—and an almost pathetic unconsciousness of it all. That is what I was at 19-20, and that is what the average Southerner is at 60 today. Northerners too, of a certain grade. It is of children like this that voters are made. And such is the primal source of our government! A man hardly knows whether to swear or cry over it. . . .

Yes, Will Bowen and I have exchanged letters now and then for several years but I suspect that I made him mad with my last—shortly after you saw him in St. Louis, I judge. There is one thing which I can't stand, and *won't* stand from many people. That is sham sentimentality—the kind a school-girl puts into her graduating composition; the sort that makes up the Original Poetry column of a country newspaper; the rot that deals in "the happy days of yore," "the sweet yet melancholy past," with its "blighted hopes" and its "vanished dreams"—and all that sort of drivel. Will's were *always* of this stamp. I stood it years. When I get a letter like that from a grown man and he a widower with a family, it gives me the bowel complaint. And I just told Will Bowen so, last summer. I told him to stop being 16 at 40; told him to stop drooling about the sweet yet melancholy past and take a pill. I said there was but one solitary thing about the past worth remembering and that was the fact that it *is* the past—can't be restored. Well, I exaggerated some of these truths a little—but only a little—but my idea was to kill his nasty sham sentimentality once and forever and so make a good fellow of him again. I went to the unheard of trouble of re-writing the letter and saying the same harsh things softly, so as to sugar-coat the anguish and make it a little more endurable, and I asked him to write and thank me honestly for doing him the best and kindliest favor that any friend ever *had* done him—but he hasn't done it yet. Maybe he will some time. I am grateful to God that I got that letter off before he was married (I get that news from you), else he would just have slobbered all over me and drowned me when the event happened. . . .

Your old friend
SAML L. CLEMENS

TO ANDREW LANG

[early 1890]

. . . The critic assumes every time that if a book doesn't meet the cultivated-class standard, it isn't valuable. Let us apply his law all around: for if it is sound in the case of novels, narratives, pictures, and such things, it is certainly sound and applicable to all the steps which lead up to culture and make culture possible. It condemns the spelling book, for a spelling book is of no use to a person of culture; it condemns all school books and all schools which lie between the child's primer and Greek, and between the infant school and the university; it condemns all the rounds of art which lie between the cheap terra cotta groups and the Venus de Medici, and between the chromo and the Transfiguration; it requires Whitcomb Riley to sing no more till he can sing like Shakespeare, and it forbids all amateur music and will grant its sanction to nothing below the "classic."

Is this an extravagant statement? No, it is a mere statement of fact. It is the fact itself that is extravagant and grotesque. And what is the result? This, and it is sufficiently curious: the critic has actually imposed upon the world the superstition that a painting by Raphael is more valuable to the civilizations of the earth than is a chromo; and the august opera than the hurdy-gurdy and the villagers' singing society; and Homer than the little everybody's-poet whose rhymes are in all mouths to-day and will be in nobody's mouth next generation; and the Latin classics than Kipling's far-reaching bugle-note; and Jonathan Edwards than the Salvation Army; and the Venus di Medici than the plaster-cast peddler; the superstition, in a word, that the vast and awful comet that trails its cold lustre through the remote abysses of space once a century and interests and instructs a cultivated handful of astronomers is worth more to the world than the sun which warms and cheers all the nations every day and makes the crops to grow.

If a critic should start a religion it would not have any object but to convert angels, and they wouldn't need it. The thin top crust of humanity—the cultivated—are worth pacifying, worth pleasing, worth coddling, worth nourishing and preserving with dainties and delicacies, it is true; but to be caterer to that little faction is no very dignified or valuable occupation, it seems to me; it is merely feeding the over-fed and there must be small satisfaction in that. It is not that little minority who are already saved that are best worth lifting at, I should think, but the mighty mass of the uncultivated who are underneath. That mass will never see the Old Masters—that sight is for the few; but the chromo maker can lift them all one step upward toward appreciation of art; they cannot have the opera, but the hurdy-gurdy and the singing class lift them a little way toward that far height; they will never know Homer, but the passing rhymester of their day leaves them higher than he found them; they may never even hear of the Latin classics but they will strike step with Kipling's drum-beat, and they will march; for all Jonathan Edward's help they would die in their slums, but the Salvation Army will beguile some of them up to pure air and a cleaner life; they know no sculpture, the Venus is not even a name to them, but they are a grade higher in the scale of civilization by the ministrations of the plaster-cast than they were before it took its place upon their mantel and made it beautiful to their unexacting eyes.

Indeed I have been misjudged from the very first. I have never tried in even one single little instance to help cultivate the cultivated classes. I was not equipped for it, either by native gifts or training. And I never had any ambition in that direction, but always hunted for bigger game—the masses. I have seldom deliberately tried to instruct them but have done my best to entertain them. To simply amuse them would have satisfied my dearest ambition at any time; for they could get instruction elsewhere and I had two chances to help to the teacher's one: for amusement is a good preparation for study and a good healer of fatigue after it. My audience is dumb, it has no voice in print, and so I cannot know whether I have won its approbation or only got its censure.

Yes, you see, I have always catered for the Belly and the Members but have been served like the others—criticized from the culture-standard—to my sorrow and pain; because, honestly, I never cared what became of the cultured classes; they could go to the theatre and the opera, they had no use for me and the melodeon.

And now at last I arrive at my object and tender my petition, making supplication to this effect: that the critics adopt a rule recognizing the Belly and the Members and formulate a standard whereby work done for them shall be judged. Help me, Mr. Lang; no voice can reach further than yours in a case of this kind, or carry greater weight of authority.

TO THE REVEREND
J. H. TWICHELL

May, 1892.

DEAR JOE:

. . . The dogs of the Campagna (they watch sheep without human assistance) are big and warlike, and are terrible creatures to meet in those lonely expanses. Two young Englishmen—one of them a friend of mine—were away out there yesterday, with a peasant guide of the region who is a simple-hearted and very devout Roman Catholic. At one point the guide stopped and said they were now approaching a spot where two especially ferocious dogs were accustomed to herd sheep: that it would be well to go cautiously and be prepared to retreat if they saw the dogs. So then they started on but presently came suddenly upon the dogs. The immense brutes came straight for them, with death in their eyes. The guide said in a voice of horror, "Turn your backs, but for God's sake don't stir—I will pray—I will pray the Virgin to do a miracle and save us; she will hear me, oh, my God she surely will." And straightway he began to pray. The Englishmen stood quaking with fright, and wholly without faith in the man's prayer. But all at once the furious snarling of the dogs ceased— at three steps distant—and there was dead silence. After a moment my friend, who could no longer endure the awful suspense, turned—and there was the miracle, sure enough: the gentleman dog had mounted the lady dog and both had forgotten their solemn duty in the ecstasy of a higher interest!

The strangers were saved and they retired from that place with thankful hearts. The guide was in a frenzy of pious gratitude and exultation, and praised and glorified the Virgin without stint; and finally wound up with, "But you—you are Protestants; she would not have done it for you; she did it for me—only me—praised be she for evermore! and I will hang a picture of it in the church and it shall be another proof that her loving care is still with her children who humbly believe and adore."

By the time the dogs got unattached the men were five miles from there.

Booker T. Washington (1856–1915)
from UP FROM SLAVERY: A SLAVE AMONG SLAVES

I was born a slave on a plantation in Franklin County, Virginia. I am not quite sure of the exact place or exact date of my birth, but at any rate I suspect I must have been born somewhere and at some time. As nearly as I have been able to learn, I was born near a cross-roads post-office called Hale's Ford, and the year was 1858 or 1859. I do not know the month or the day. The earliest impressions I can now recall are of the plantation and the slave quarters—the latter being the part of the plantation where the slaves had their cabins.

My life had its beginning in the midst of the most miserable, desolate, and discouraging surroundings. This was so, however, not because my owners were especially cruel, for they were not, as compared with many others. I was born in a typical log cabin, about fourteen by sixteen feet square. In this cabin I lived with my mother and a brother and sister till after the Civil War, when we were all declared free.

Of my ancestry I know almost nothing. In the slave quarters, and even later, I heard whispered conversations among the coloured people of the tortures which the slaves, including, no doubt, my ancestors on my mother's side, suffered in the middle passage of the slave ship while being conveyed from Africa to America. I have been unsuccessful in securing any information that would throw any accurate light upon the history of my family beyond my mother. She, I remember, had a half-brother and a half-sister. In the days of slavery not very much attention was given to family history and family records—that is,

black family records. My mother, I suppose, attracted the attention of a purchaser who was afterward my owner and hers. Her addition to the slave family attracted about as much attention as the purchase of a new horse or cow. Of my father I know even less than of my mother. I do not even know his name. I have heard reports to the effect that he was a white man who lived on one of the near-by plantations. Whoever he was, I never heard of his taking the least interest in me or providing in any way for my rearing. But I do not find especial fault with him. He was simply another unfortunate victim of the institution which the Nation unhappily had engrafted upon it at that time.

The cabin was not only our living-place, but was also used as the kitchen for the plantation. My mother was the plantation cook. The cabin was without glass windows; it had only openings in the side which let in the light, and also the cold, chilly air of winter. There was a door to the cabin—that is, something that was called a door—but the uncertain hinges by which it was hung, and the large cracks in it, to say nothing of the fact that it was too small, made the room a very uncomfortable one. In addition to these openings there was, in the lower right-hand corner of the room, the "cat-hole,"—a contrivance which almost every mansion or cabin in Virginia possessed during the antebellum period. The "cat-hole" was a square opening, about seven by eight inches, provided for the purpose of letting the cat pass in and out of the house at will during the night. In the case of our particular cabin I could never understand the necessity for this convenience, since there were at least a half-dozen other places in the cabin that would have accommodated the cats. There was no wooden floor in our cabin, the naked earth being used as a floor. In the centre of the earthen floor there was a large, deep opening covered with boards, which was used as a place in which to store sweet potatoes during the winter. An impression of this potato-hole is very distinctly engraved upon my memory, because I recall that during the process of putting the potatoes in or taking them out I would often come into possession of one or two, which I roasted and thoroughly enjoyed. There was no cooking-stove on our plantation, and all the cooking for the whites and slaves my mother had to do over an open fire place, mostly in pots and "skillets." While the poorly built cabin caused us to suffer with cold in the winter, the heat from the open fireplace in summer was equally trying.

The early years of my life, which where spent in the little cabin, were not very different from those of thousands of other slaves. My mother, of course, had little time in which to give attention to the training of her children during the day. She snatched a few moments for our care in the early morning before her work began, and at night after the day's work was done. One of my earliest recollections is that of my mother cooking a chicken late at night, and awakening her children for the purpose of feeding them. How or where she got it I do not know. I presume, however, it was procured from our owner's farm. Some people may call this theft. If such a thing were to happen now, I should condemn it as theft myself. But taking place at the time it did, and for the reason that it did, no one could ever make me believe that my mother was guilty of thieving. She was simply a victim of the system of slavery. I cannot remember having slept in a bed until after our family was declared free by the Emanicipation Proclamation.

Three children—John, my older brother, Amanda, my sister, and myself—had a pallet on the dirt floor, or, to be more correct, we slept in and on a bundle of filthy rags laid upon the dirt floor.

I was asked not long ago to tell something about the sports and pastimes that I engaged in during my youth. Until that question was asked it had never occurred to me that there was no period of my life that was devoted to play. From the time that I can remember anything, almost every day of my life has been occupied in some kind of labour; though I think I would now be a more useful man if I had had time for sports. During the period that I spent in slavery I was not large enough to be of much service, still I was occupied most of the time in cleaning the yards, carrying water to the men in the fields, or going to the mill, to which I used to take the corn, once a week, to be ground. The mill was about three miles from the plantation. This work I always dreaded. The heavy bag of corn would be thrown across the back of the horse, and the corn divided about evenly on each side; but in some way, almost without exception, on the trips, the corn would so shift as to become unbalanced and would fall off the horse, and often I would fall with it. As I was not strong enough to reload the corn upon the horse, I would have to wait, sometimes for many hours, till a chance passer-by came along who would help me out of my trouble. The hours while waiting for some one were usually spent in crying. The time consumed in this way made me late in reaching the mill, and by the time I got my corn ground and reached home it would be far into the night. The road was a lonely one, and often led through dense forests. I was always frightened. The woods were said to be full of soldiers who had deserted from the army, and I had been told that the first thing a deserter did to a Negro boy when he found him alone was to cut off his ears. Besides, when I was late in getting home I knew I would always get a severe scolding or a flogging.

I had no schooling whatever while I was a slave, though I remember on several occasions I went as far as the schoolhouse door with one of my young mistresses to carry her books. The picture of several dozen boys and girls in a schoolroom engaged in study made a deep impression upon me, and I had the feeling that to get into a schoolhouse and study in this way would be about the same as getting into paradise.

So far as I can now recall, the first knowledge that I got of the fact that we were slaves, and that freedom of the slaves was being discussed, was early one morning before day, when I was awakened by my mother kneeling over her children and fervently praying that Lincoln and his armies might be successful, and that one day she and her children might be free. In this connection I have never been able to understand how the slaves throughout the South, completely ignorant as were the masses so far as books or newspapers were concerned, were able to keep themselves so accurately and completely informed about the great National questions that were agitating the country. From the time that Garrison, Lovejoy, and others began to agitate for freedom, the slaves throughout the South kept in close touch with the progress of the movement. Though I was a mere child during the preparation for the Civil War and during the war itself, I now recall the many late-at-night whispered discussions that I heard my mother and the other slaves on the plantation indulge in. These discussions showed that they understood the situation, and that they kept themselves informed of events by what was termed the "grape-vine" telegraph.

During the campaign when Lincoln was first a candidate for the Presidency, the slaves on our far-off plantation, miles from any railroad or large city or daily newspapers, knew what the issues involved were. When war was begun between the North and the South, every slave on our plantation felt and knew that, though other issues were discussed, the primal one was that of slavery. Even the most ignorant members of my race on the remote plantations felt in their hearts, with a certainty that admitted of no doubt, that the freedom of the slaves would be the one great result of the war, if the Northern armies conquered. Every success of the Federal armies and every defeat of the Confederate forces was watched with the keenest and most intense interest. Often the slaves got knowledge of the results of great battles before the white people received it. This news was usually gotten from the coloured man who was sent to the post-office for the mail. In our case the post-office was about three miles from the plantation, and the mail came once or twice a week. The man who was sent to the office would linger about the place long enough to get the drift of the conversation from the group of white people who naturally congregated there, after receiving their mail, to discuss the latest news. The mail-carrier on his way back to our master's house would as naturally retail the news that he had secured among the slaves, and in this way they often heard of important events before the white people at the "big house," as the master's house was called.

I cannot remember a single instance during my childhood or early boyhood when our entire family sat down to the table together, and God's blessing was asked, and the family ate a meal in a civilized manner. On the plantation in Virginia, and even later, meals were gotten by the children very much as dumb animals get theirs. It was a piece of bread here and a scrap of meat there. It was a cup of milk at one time and some potatoes at another. Sometimes a portion of our family would eat out of the skillet or pot, while some one else would eat from a tin plate held on the knees, and often using nothing but the hands with which to hold the food. When I had grown to a sufficient size, I was required to go to the "big house" at mealtimes to fan the flies from the table by means of a large set of paper fans operated by a pulley. Naturally much of the conversation of the white people turned upon the subject of freedom and the war, and I absorbed a good deal of it. I remember that at one time I saw two of my young mistresses and some lady visitors eating ginger-cakes, in the yard. At that time those cakes seemed to me to be absolutely the most tempting and desirable things that I had ever seen; and I then and there resolved that, if I ever got free, the height of my ambition would be reached if I could get to the point where I could secure and eat ginger-cakes in the way that I saw those ladies doing.

Of course as the war was prolonged the white people, in many cases, often found it difficult to secure food for themselves. I think the slaves felt the deprivation less than the whites, because the usual diet for the slaves was corn bread and pork, and these could be raised on the plantation; but coffee, tea, sugar, and other articles which the whites had been accustomed to use could not be raised on the plantation, and the conditions brought about by the war frequently made it impossible to secure these things. The whites were often in great straits. Parched corn was used for coffee, and a kind of black molasses was used instead of sugar. Many times nothing was used to sweeten the so-called tea and coffee.

The first pair of shoes that I recall wearing were wooden ones. They had rough leather on the top, but the bottoms, which were about an inch thick, were of wood. When I walked they made a fearful noise, and besides this they were very inconvenient, since there was no yielding to the natural pressure of the foot. In wearing them one presented an exceedingly awkward appearance. The most trying ordeal that I was forced to endure as a slave boy, however, was the wearing of a flax shirt. In the portion of Virginia where I lived it was common to use flax as part of the clothing for the slaves. That part of the flax from which our clothing was made was largely the refuse, which of course was the cheapest and roughest part. I can scarcely imagine any torture, except, perhaps, the pulling of a tooth, that is equal to that caused by putting on a new flax shirt for the first time. It is almost equal to the feeling that one would experience if he had a dozen or more chestnut burrs, or a hundred small pinpoints, in contact with his flesh. Even to this day I can recall accurately the tortures that I underwent when putting on one of these garments. The fact that my flesh was soft and tender added to the pain. But I had no choice. I had to wear the flax shirt or none; and had it been left to me to choose, I should have chosen to wear no covering. In connection with the flax shirt, my brother John, who is several years older than I am, performed one of the most generous acts that I ever heard of one slave relative doing for another. On several occasions when I was being forced to wear a new flax shirt, he generously agreed to put it on in my stead and wear it for several days, till it was "broken in." Until I had grown to be quite a youth this single garment was all that I wore.

One may get the idea, from what I have said, that there was bitter feelings toward the white people on the part of my race, because of the fact that most of the white population was away fighting in a war which would result in keeping the Negro in slavery if the South was successful. In the case of the slaves on our place this was not true, and it was not true of any large portion of the slave population in the South where the Negro was treated with anything like decency. During the Civil War one of my young masters was killed, and two were severely wounded. I recall the feeling of sorrow which existed among the slaves when they heard of the death of "Mars' Billy." It was no sham sorrow, but real. Some of the slaves had nursed "Mars' Billy"; others had played with him when he was a child. "Mars' Billy" had begged for mercy in the case of others when the overseer or master was thrashing them. The sorrow in the slave quarter was only second to that in the "big house." When the two young masters were brought home wounded, the sympathy of the slaves was shown in many ways. They were just as anxious to assist in the nursing as the family relatives of the wounded. Some of the slaves would even beg for the privilege of sitting up at night to nurse their wounded masters. This tenderness and sympathy on the part of those held in bondage was a result of their kindly and generous nature. In order to defend and protect the women and children who where left on the plantations when the white males went to war, the slaves would have laid down their lives. The slave who was selected to sleep in the "big house" during the absence of the males was considered to have the place of honour. Any one attempting to harm "young Mistress" or "old Mistress" during the night would have had to cross the dead body of the slave to do so. I do not know how many have noticed it, but I think that it will be found to be true that there are few instances, either in slavery or freedom, in which a member of my race has been known to betray a specific trust.

As a rule, not only did the members of my race entertain no feelings of bitterness against the whites before and during the war, but there are many instances of Negroes tenderly caring for their former masters and mistresses who for some reason have become poor and dependent since the war. I know of instances where the former masters of slaves have for years been supplied with money by their former slaves to keep them from suffering. I have known of still other cases in which the former slaves have assisted in the education of the descendants of their former owners. I know of a case on a large plantation in the South in which a young white man, the son of the former owner of the estate, has become so reduced in purse and self-control by reason of drink that he is a pitiable creature; and yet, notwithstanding the poverty of the coloured people themselves on this plantation, they have for years supplied this young white man with the necessities of life. One sends him a little coffee or sugar, another a little meat, and so on. Nothing that the coloured people possess is too good for the son of "old Mars' Tom," who will perhaps never be permitted to suffer while any remain on the place who knew directly or indirectly of "old Mars' Tom."

I have said that there are few instances of a member of my race betraying a specific trust. One of the best illustrations of this which I know of is in the case of an ex-slave from Virginia whom I met not long ago in a little town in the state of Ohio. I found that this man had made a contract with his master, two or three years previous to the Emancipation Proclamation, to the effect that the slave was to be permitted to buy himself, by paying so much per year for his body; and while he was paying for himself, he was to be permitted to labour where and for whom he pleased. Finding that he could secure better wages in Ohio, he went there. When freedom came, he was still in debt to his master some three hundred dollars. Notwithstanding that the Emancipation Proclamation freed him from any obligation to his master, this black man walked the greater portion of the distance back to where the old master lived in Virgina, and placed the last dollar, with interest, in his hands. In talking to me about this, the man told me that he knew that he did not have to pay the debt, but that he had given his word to his master, and his word he had never broken. He felt that he could not enjoy freedom till he had fulfilled his promise.

From some things that I have said one may get the idea that some of the slaves did not want freedom. This is not true. I have never seen one who did not want to be free, or one who would return to slavery.

I pity from the bottom of my heart any nation or body of people that is so unfortunate as to get entangled in the net of slavery. I have long since ceased to cherish any spirit of bitterness against the Southern white people on account of the enslavement of my race. No one section of our country was wholly responsible for its introduction, and, besides, it was recognized and protected for years by the General Government. Having once got its tentacles fastened on to the economic and social life of the Republic, it was no easy matter for the country to relieve itself of the institution. Then, when we rid ourselves of prejudice, or racial feeling, and look facts in the face, we must acknowledge that, notwithstanding the cruelty and moral wrong of slavery, the ten million Negroes inhabiting this country, who themselves or whose ancestors went through the school of American slavery, are in a stronger and more hopeful condition, materially, intellectually, morally, and religiously, than is true of an equal number of black people in any other portion of the globe. This is so to such an extent that Negroes in this country, who themselves or whose forefathers went through the school of slavery, are constantly returning to Africa as missionaries to enlighten those who remained in the fatherland. This I say, not to justify slavery—on the other hand, I condemn it as an institution, as we all know that in America it was established for selfish and financial reasons, and not from a missionary motive—but to call attention to a fact, and to show how Providence so often uses men and institutions to accomplish a purpose. When persons ask me in these days how, in the midst of what sometimes seem hopelessly dscouraging conditions, I can have such faith in the future of my race in this country, I remind them of the wilderness through which and out of which, a good Providence has already led us.

Ever since I have been old enough to think for myself, I have entertained the idea that, notwithstanding the cruel wrongs inflicted upon us, the black man got nearly as much out of slavery as the white man did. The hurtful influences of the institution were not by any means confined to the Negro. This was fully illustrated by the life upon our own plantation. The whole machinery of slavery was so constructed as to cause labour, as a rule, to be looked upon as a badge of degradation, of inferiority. Hence labour was something that both races on the slave plantation sought to escape. The slave system on our place, in a large measure, took the spirit of self-reliance and self-help out of the white people. My old master had many boys and girls, but not one, so far as I know, ever mastered a single trade or special line of productive industry. The girls were not taught to cook, sew, or to take care of the house. All of this was left to the slaves. The slaves, of course, had little personal interest in the life of the plantation, and their ignorance prevented them from learning how to do things in the most improved and thorough manner. As a result of the system, fences were out of repair, gates were hanging half off the hinges, doors creaked, window-panes were out, plastering had fallen but was not replaced, weeds grew in the yard. As a rule, there was food for whites and blacks, but inside the house, and on the dining-room table, there was wanting that delicacy and refinement of touch and finish which can make a home the most convenient, comfortable, and attractive place in the world. Withal there was a waste of food and other materials which was sad. When freedom came, the slaves were almost as well fitted to begin life anew as the master, except in the matter of book-learning and ownership of property. The slave owner and his sons had mastered no special industry. They unconsciously had imbibed the feeling that manual labour was not the proper thing for them. On the other hand, the slaves, in many cases, had mastered some handicraft, and none were ashamed, and few unwilling, to labour.

Finally the war closed, and the day of freedom came. It was a momentous and eventful day to all upon our plantation. We had been expecting it. Freedom was in the air, and had been for months. Deserting soldiers returning to their homes were to be seen every day. Others who had been discharged, or whose regiments had been paroled, were constantly passing near our place. The "grapevine telegraph" was kept busy night and day. The news and mutterings of great events were swiftly carried from one plantation to another. In the fear of "Yankee" invasions, the silverware and other valuables were taken from the "big house," buried in the woods, and guarded by trusted slaves. Woe be to any one who would have attempted to disturb the buried treasure. The slaves would give the Yankee soldiers food, drink, clothing—anything but that which had been specifically intrusted to their care and honour. As the great day drew nearer, there was more singing in the slave quarters than usual. It was bolder, had more ring, and lasted later into the nights. Most of the verses of the plantation songs had some reference to freedom. True, they had sung those same verses before, but they had been careful to explain that the "freedom" in these songs referred to the next world, and had no connection with life in this world. Now they gradually threw off the mask, and were not afraid to let it be

known that the "freedom" in their songs meant freedom of the body in this world. The night before the eventful day, word was sent to the slave quarters to the effect that something unusual was going to take place at the "big house" the next morning. There was little, if any, sleep that night. All was excitement and expectancy. Early the next morning word was sent to all the slaves, old and young, to gather at the house. In company with my mother, brother, and sister, and a large number of other slaves, I went to the master's house. All of our master's family were either standing or seated on the veranda of the house, where they could see what was to take place and hear what was said. There was a feeling of deep interest, or perhaps sadness, on their faces, but not bitterness. As I now recall the impression they made upon me, they did not at the moment seem to be sad because of the loss of property, but rather because of parting with those whom they had reared and who were in many ways very close to them. The most distinct thing that I now recall in connection with the scene was that some man who seemed to be a stranger (United States officer, I presume) made a little speech and then read a rather long paper—the Emancipation Proclamation, I think. After the reading we were told that we were all free, and could go when and where we pleased. My mother, who was standing by my side, leaned over and kissed her children, while tears of joy ran down her checks. She explained to us what it all meant, that this was the day for which she had been so long praying, but fearing that she would never live to see.

For some minutes there was great rejoicing, and thanksgiving, and wild scene of ecstasy. But there was no feeling of bitterness. In fact, there was pity among the slaves for our former owners. The wild rejoicing on the part of the emancipated coloured people lasted but for a brief period, for I noticed that by the time they returned to their cabins there was a change in their feelings. The great responsibility of being free, of having charge of themselves, of having to think and plan for themselves and their children, seemed to take possession of them. It was very much like suddenly turning a youth of ten or twelve years out into the world to provide for himself. In a few hours the great questions with which the Anglo-Saxon race had been grappling for centuries had been thrown upon these people to be solved. These were the questions of a home, a living, the rearing of children, education, citizenship, and the establishment and support of churches. Was it any wonder that within a few hours the wild rejoicing ceased and a feeling of deep gloom seemed to pervade the slave quarters? To some it seemed that, now that they were in actual possession of it,

freedom was a more serious thing than they had expected to find it. Some of the slaves were seventy or eighty years old; their best days were gone. They had no strength with which to earn a living in a strange place and among strange people, even if they had been sure where to find a new place of abode. To this class the problem seemed especially hard. Besides, deep down in their hearts there was a strange and peculiar attachment to "old Master" and "old Missus," and to their children, which they found it hard to think of breaking off. With these they had spent in some cases nearly a half-century, and it was no light thing to think of parting. Gradually, one by one, stealthily at first, the older slaves began to wander from the slave quarters back to the "big house" to have a whispered conversation with their former owners as to the future.

Finley Peter Dunne (1867–1936)

MR. DOOLEY ON THE EDUCATION OF THE YOUNG

"If ye had a boy wud ye sind him to colledge?" asked Mr. Hennessy.
"Well," said Mr. Dooley, "at th' age whin a boy is fit to be in colledge I wudden't have him around th' house."

*   *   *

The troubled Mr. Hennessy had been telling Mr. Dooley about the difficulty of making a choice of schools for Packy Hennessy, who at the age of six was at the point where the family must decide his career.

"'Tis a big question," said Mr. Dooley, "an' wan that seems to be worryin' th' people more thin it used to whin ivry boy was designed f'r th' priesthood, with a full undherstandin' be his parents that th' chances was in favor iv a brick yard. Nowadays they talk

about th' edycation iv th' child befure they choose th' name. 'Tis: "Th' kid talks in his sleep. 'Tis th' fine lawyer he'll make.' Or, 'Did ye notice him admirin' that photygraph? He'll be a gr-reat journalist.' Or, 'Look at him fishin' in Uncle Tim's watch pocket. We must thrain him f'r a banker.' Or, 'I'm afraid he'll niver be sthrong enough to wurruk. He must go into th' church.' Befure he's baptized too, d'ye mind. 'Twill not be long befure th' time comes whin th' soggarth'll christen th' infant: 'Judge Pathrick Aloysius Hinnissy, iv th'

Northern District iv Illinye,' or 'Profissor P. Aloysius Hinnissy, LL.D., S.T.D., P.G.N., iv th' faculty iv Northre Dame.' Th' innocent child in his cradle, wondherin' what ails th' mist iv him an' where he got such funny lookin' parents fr'm, has thim to blame that brought him into the wurruld if he dayvilops into a sicond story man befure he's twinty-wan an' is took up be th' polis. Why don't you lade Packy down to th' occylist an' have him fitted with a pair iv eye-glasses? Why don't ye put goloshes on him, give him a blue umbrelly an' call him a doctor at wanst an' be done with it?

"To my mind, Hinnissy, we're wastin' too much time thinkin' iv th' future iv our young, an' thryin' to larn thim early what they oughtn't to know till they've growed up. We sind th' childher to school as if 'twas a summer garden where they go to be amused instead iv a pinitinchry where they're sint f'r original sin. Whin I was a la-ad I was put at me ah-bee abs, th' first day I set fut in th' school behind th' hedge an' me head was sore inside an' out befure I wint home. Now th' first thing we larn th' future Mark Hannas an' Jawn D. Gateses iv our naytion is waltzin', singin', an' cuttin' pitchers out iv a book. We'd be much betther teachin' thim th' sthrangle hold, f'r that's what they need in life.

"I know what'll happen. Ye'll sind Packy to what th' Germans call a Kindygarten, an' 'tis a good thing f'r Germany, because all a German knows is what some wan tells him, and his grajation papers is a certyficate that he don't need to think annymore. But we've inthrajooced it into this counthry, an' whin I was down seein' if I cud injooce Rafferty, th' Janitor iv th' Isaac Muggs Grammar School, f'r to vote f'r Riordan—an' he's goin' to—I dhropped in on Cassidy's daughter, Mary Ellen, an' see her kindygartnin'. Th' childher was settin' ar-round on th' flure an' some was moldin' dachshunds out iv mud an'

wipin' their hands on their hair, an' some was carvin' figures iv a goat out iv paste-board an' some was singin' an some was sleepin' an' a few was dancin' an' wan la-ad was pullin' another la-ad's hair. 'Why don't ye take th' coal shovel to that little barbaryan, Mary Ellen?' says I. 'We don't believe in corporeal punishment,' says she. 'School shud be made pleasant f'r childher,' she says. 'Th' child who's hair is bein' pulled is larnin' patience,' she says, 'an' th' child that's pullin' th' hair is discoverin' th' footility iv human indeavor,' says she. 'Well, oh, well,' says I, 'times has changed since I was a boy,' I says. 'Put thim through their exercises,' says I 'Tommy,' says I, 'spell cat,' I says. 'Go to th' divvle,' says th' cheerub. 'Very smartly answered,' says Mary Ellen. 'Ye shud not ask thim to spell,' she says. 'They don't larn that till they get to colledge,' she says, 'an',' she says, 'sometimes not even thin,' she says. 'An' what do they larn?' says I. 'Rompin,' she says, 'an' dancin',' she says, 'an' indepindance iv speech, an' beauty songs, an' sweet thoughts, an' how to make home homelike,' she says. 'Well,' says I, 'I didn't take anny iv thim things at colledge, so ye needn't unblanket thim,' I says. 'I won't put thim through anny exercise to-day,' I says. 'But whisper, Mary Ellen,' says I, 'Don't ye niver feel like bastin' the seeraphims?' 'Th' teachin's iv Freebull and Pitzotly is conthrary to that,' she says. 'But I'm goin' to be marrid an' lave th' school on Choosdah, th' twintysicond iv Janooary,' she says, 'an' on Mondah, th' twinty-first, I'm goin' to ask a few iv th' little darlin's to th' house an',' she says, 'stew thim over a slow fire,' she says. Mary Ellen is not a German, Hinnissy.

"Well, afther they have larned in school what they ar're licked f'r larnin' in th' back yard—that is squashin' mud with their hands—they're conducted up through a channel iv free an' beautiful thought till they're r-ready f'r colledge. Mamma packs a few doylies an' tidies into son's bag, an' some silver to be used in case iv throuble wit th' landlord, an' th' la-ad throts off to th' siminary. If he's not sthrong enough to look f'r high honors as a middleweight pugilist he goes into th' thought departmint. Th' prisidint takes him into a Turkish room, gives him a cigareet an' says: 'Me dear boy, what special branch iv larnin' wud ye like to have studied f'r ye be our compitint profissors? We have a chair iv Beauty an' wan iv Puns an' wan iv Pothry on th' Changin' Hues iv th' Settin' Sun, an' wan on Platonic Love, an' wan on Non-sense Rhymes, an' wan on Sweet Thoughts, an' wan on How Green Grows th' Grass, an' wan on th' Relation iv Ice to th' Greek Idee iv God,' he says. 'This is all ye'll need to equip ye f'r th' perfect life, onless,' he says, 'ye intind bein' a dintist, in which case,' he says, 'we won't think much iv ye, but we have a good school where ye can larn that disgraceful thrade,' he says. An' th' la-ad makes his choice, an' ivry mornin' whin he's up in time he takes a whiff iv hasheesh an' goes off to hear Profissor Maryanna tell him that "if th' dates iv human knowledge must be rejicted as subjictive, how much more must they be subjicted as rejictive if, as I think, we keep our thoughts fixed upon th' inanity iv th' finite in comparison with th' onthinkable truth with th' ondivided an' onimaginable reality. Boys, ar-re ye with me?' . . ."

"I don't undherstand a wurrud iv what ye'r sayin'," said Mr. Hennessy.

"No more do I," said Mr. Dooley, "But I believe 'tis as Father Kelly says: 'Childher shuddn't be sint to school to larn, but to larn how to larn. I don't care what ye larn thim so long as 'tis onpleasant to thim.' 'Tis thrainin' they need, Hinnissy. That's all. I niver cud make use iv what I larned in colledge about thrigojoomethry an'—an'—grammar an' th' welts I got on th' skull fr'm th' schoolmaster's cane I have niver been able to turn to anny account in th' business, but 'twas th' bein' there an' havin' to get things to heart without askin' th' meanin' iv thim an' goin' to school cold an' comin' home hungry, that made th' man iv me ye see befure ye."

"That's why th' good woman's throubled about Packy," said Hennessy.

"Go home," said Mr. Dooley.

FICTION

Stephen Crane (1871–1900)

THE BRIDE COMES TO YELLOW SKY

I

The great Pullman was whirling onward with such dignity of motion that a glance from the window seemed simply to prove that the plains of Texas were pouring eastward. Vast flats of green grass, dull-hued spaces of mesquit and cactus, little groups of frame houses, woods of light and tender trees, all were sweeping into the east, sweeping over the horizon, a precipice.

A newly married pair had boarded this coach at San Antonio. The man's face was reddened from many days in the wind and sun, and a direct result of his new black clothes was that his brick-colored hands were constantly performing in a most conscious fashion. From time to time he looked down respectfully at his attire. He sat with a hand on each knee, like a man waiting in a barber's shop. The glances he devoted to other passengers were furtive and shy.

The bride was not pretty, nor was she very young. She wore a dress of blue cashmere, with small reservations of velvet here and there, and with steel buttons abounding. She continually twisted her head to regard her puff sleeves, very stiff, straight, and high. They embarrassed her. It was quite apparent that she had cooked, and that she expected to cook, dutifully. The blushes caused by the careless scrutiny of some passengers as she had entered the car were strange to see upon this plain, under-class countenance, which was drawn in placid, almost emotionless lines.

They were evidently very happy. "Ever been in a parlor-car before?" he asked, smiling with delight.

"No," she answered; "I never was. It's fine, ain't it?"

"Great! And then after a while we'll go forward to the diner, and get a big lay-out. Finest meal in the world. Charge a dollar."

"Oh, do they?" cried the bride. "Charge a dollar? Why, that's too much—for us—ain't it, Jack?"

"Not this trip, anyhow," he answered bravely. "We're going to go the whole thing."

Later he explained to her about the trains. "You see, it's a thousand miles from one end of Texas to the other; and this train runs right across it, and never stops but four times." He had the pride of an owner. He pointed out to her the dazzling fittings of the coach; and in truth her eyes opened wider as she contemplated the sea-green figured velvet, the shining brass, silver, and glass, the wood that gleamed as darkly brilliant as the surface of a pool of oil. At one end a bronze figure sturdily held a support for a separated chamber, and at convenient places on the ceiling were frescos in olive and silver.

To the minds of the pair, their surroundings reflected the glory of their marriage that morning in San Antonio; this was the environment of their new estate; and the man's face in particular beamed with an elation that made him appear ridiculous to the negro porter. This individual at times surveyed them from afar with an amused and superior grin. On other occasions he bullied them with skill in ways that did not make it exactly plain to them that they were being bullied. He subtly used all the manners of the most unconquerable kind of snobbery. He oppressed them; but of this oppression they had small knowledge, and they speedily forgot that infrequently a number of travellers covered them with stares of derisive enjoyment. Historically there was supposed to be something infinitely humorous in their situation.

"We are due in Yellow Sky at 3:42," he said, looking tenderly into her eyes.

"Oh, are we?" she said, as if she had not been aware of it. To evince surprise at her husband's statement was part of her wifely amiability. She took from a pocket a little silver watch; and as she held it before her, and stared at it with a frown of attention, the new husband's face shone.

"I bought it in San Anton' from a friend of mine," he told her gleefully.

"It's seventeen minutes past twelve," she said, looking up at him with a kind of shy and clumsy coquetry. A passenger, noting this play, grew excessively sardonic, and winked at himself in one of the numerous mirrors.

At last they went to the dining-car. Two rows of negro waiters, in glowing white suits, surveyed their entrance with the interest, and also the equanimity, of men who had been forewarned. The pair fell to the lot of a waiter who happened to feel pleasure in steering them through their meal. He viewed them with the manner of a fatherly pilot, his countenance radiant with benevolence. The patronage, entwined with the ordinary deference, was not plain to them. And yet, as they returned to their coach, they showed in their faces a sense of escape.

To the left, miles down a long purple slope, was a little ribbon of mist where moved the keening Rio Grande. The train was approaching it at an angle, and the apex was Yellow Sky. Presently it was apparent that, as the distance from Yellow Sky grew shorter, the husband became commensurately restless. His brick-red hands were more insistent in their prominence. Occasionally he was even rather absent-minded and far-away when the bride leaned forward and addressed him.

As a matter of truth, Jack Potter was beginning to find the shadow of a deed weigh upon him like a leaden slab. He, the town marshall of Yellow Sky, a man known, liked, and feared in his corner, a prominent person, had gone to San Antonio to meet a girl he believed he loved, and there, after the usual prayers, had actually induced her to marry him, without consulting Yellow Sky for any part of the transaction. He was now bringing his bride before an innocent and unsuspecting community.

Of course people in Yellow Sky married as it pleased them, in accordance with a general custom; but such was Potter's thought of his duty to his friends, or of their idea of his duty, or of an unspoken form which does not control men in these matters, that he felt he was heinous. He had committed an extraordinary crime. Face to face with this girl in San Antonio, and spurred by his sharp impulse, he had gone headlong over all the social hedges. At San Antonio he was like a man hidden in the dark. A knife to sever any friendly duty, and form, was easy to his hand in that remote city. But the hour of Yellow Sky—the hour of daylight—was approaching.

He knew full well that his marriage was an important thing to his town. It could only be exceeded by the burning of the new hotel. His friends could not forgive him. Frequently he had reflected on the advisability of telling them by telegraph, but a new cowardice had been upon him. He feared to do it. And now the train was hurrying him toward a scene of amazement, glee, and reproach. He glanced out of the window at the line of haze swinging slowly in toward the train.

Yellow Sky had a kind of brass band, which played painfully, to the delight of the populace. He laughed without heart as he thought of it. If the citizens could dream of his prospective arrival with his bride, they would parade the band at the station and escort them, amid cheers and laughing congratulations, to his adobe home.

He resolved that he would use all the devices of speed and plains-craft in making the journey from the station to his house. Once within that safe citadel, he could issue some sort of vocal bulletin, and then not go among the citizens until they had time to wear off a little of their enthusiasm.

The bride looked anxiously at him. "What's worrying you, Jack?"

He laughed again. "I'm not worrying, girl; I'm only thinking of Yellow Sky."

She flushed in comprehension.

A sense of mutual guilt invaded their minds and developed a finer tenderness. They look at each other with eyes softly aglow. But Potter often laughed the same nervous laugh; the flush upon the bride's face seemed quite permanent.

The traitor to the feelings of Yellow Sky narrowly watched the speeding landscape. "We're nearly there," he said.

Presently the porter came and announced the proximity of Potter's home. He held a brush in his hand, and, with all his airy superiority gone, he brushed Potter's new clothes as the latter slowly turned this way and that way. Potter fumbled out a coin and gave it to the porter, as he had seen others do. It was a heavy and muscle-bound business, as that of a man shoeing his first horse.

The porter took their bag, and as the train began to slow they moved forward to the hooded platform of the car. Presently the two engines and their long string of coaches rushed into the station of Yellow Sky.

"They have to take water here," said Potter, from a constricted throat and in mournful cadence, as one announcing death. Before the train stopped his eye had swept the length of the platform, and he was glad and astonished to see there was none upon it but the station-agent, who, with a slightly hurried and anxious air, was walking toward the water-tanks. When the train had halted, the porter alighted first, and placed in position a little temporary step.

"Come on, girl," said Potter, hoarsely. As he helped her down they each laughed on a false note. He took the bag from the negro, and bade his wife cling to his arm. As they slunk rapidly away, his hang-dog glance perceived that they were unloading the two trunks, and also that the station-agent, far ahead near the baggage-car, had turned and running toward him, making gestures. He laughed, and groaned as he laughed, when he noted his first effect of his marital bliss upon Yellow Sky. He gripped his wife's arm firmly to his side, and they fled. Behind them the porter stood, chuckling fatuously.

II

The California express on the Southern Railway was due at Yellow Sky in twenty-two minutes. There were six men at the bar of the Weary Gentleman saloon. One was a drummer who talked a great deal and rapidly; three were Texans who did not care to talk at that time; and two were Mexican sheep-herders, who did not talk as a general practice in the Weary Gentleman saloon. The barkeeper's dog lay on the board walk that crossed in front of the door. His head was on his paws, and he glanced drowsily here and there with the constant vigilance of a dog that is kicked on occasion. Across the sandy street were some vivid green grass-plots, so wonderful in appearance, amid the sands that burned near them in a blazing sun, that they caused a doubt in the mind. They exactly resembled the grass mats used to represent lawns on the stage. At the cooler end of the railway station, a man without a coat sat in a tilted chair and smoked his pipe. The fresh-cut bank of the Rio Grande circled near the town, and there could be seen beyond it a great plum-colored plain of mesquit.

Save for the busy drummer and his companions in the saloon, Yellow Sky was dozing. The new-comer leaned gracefully upon the bar, and recited many tales with the confidence of a bard who has come upon a new field.

"—and at the moment that the old man fell downstairs with the bureau in his arms, the old woman was coming up with two scuttles of coal, and of course—"

The drummer's tale was interrupted by a young man who suddenly appeared in the open door. He cried: "Scratchy Wilson's drunk, and has turned loose with both hands." The two Mexicans at once sat down their glasses and faded out of the rear entrance of the saloon.

The drummer, innocent and jocular, answered: "All right, old man. S'pose he has? Come in and have a drink, anyhow."

But the information had made an obvious cleft in every skull in the room that the drummer was obliged to see its importance. All had become instantly solemn. "Say," said he, mystified, "what is this?" His three companions made the introductory gesture of eloquent speech; but the young man at the door forestalled them.

"It means, my friend," he answered, as he came into the saloon, "that for the next two hours this town won't be a health resort."

The barkeeper went to the door, and locked and barred it; reaching out of the window, he pulled in heavy wooden shutters, and barred them. Immediately a solemn, chapel-like gloom was upon the place. The drummer was looking from one to another.

"But say," he cried, "what is this, anyhow? You don't mean there is going to be a gun-fight?"

"Don't know whether there'll be a fight or not," answered one man, grimly; "but there'll be some shootin'—some good shootin'."

The young man who had warned them waved his hand. "Oh, there'll be a fight fast enough, if any one wants it. Anybody can get a fight out there in the street. There's a fight just waiting."

The drummer seemed to be swayed between the interest of a foreigner and a perception of personal danger.

"What did you say his name was?" he asked.

"Scratchy Wilson," they answered in chorus.

"And will he kill anybody? What are you going to do? Does this happen often? Does he rampage around like this once a week or so? Can he break in that door?"

"No; he can't break down that door," replied the barkeeper. "He's tried it three times. But when he comes you'd better lay down on the floor, stranger. He's dead sure to shoot at it, and a bullet may come through."

Thereafter the drummer kept a strict eye upon the door. The time had not yet been called for him to hug the floor, but, as a minor precaution, he sidled near to the wall. "Will he kill anybody?" he said again.

The men laughed low and scornfully at the question.

"He's out to shoot, and he's out for trouble. Don't see any good in experimentin' with him."

"But what do you do in a case like this? What do you do?"

A man responded: "Why, he and Jack Potter—"

"But," in chorus the other men interrupted, "Jack Potter's in San Anton'."

"Well, who is he? What's he got to do with it?"

"Oh, he's the town marshal. He goes out and fights Scratchy when he gets on one of these tears."

"Wow!" said the drummer, mopping his brow. "Nice job he's got."

The voices had toned away to mere whisperings. The drummer wished to ask further questions, which were born of an increasing anxiety and bewilderment; but when he attempted them, the men merely looked at him in irritation and motioned him to remain silent. A tense waiting hush was upon them. In the deep shadows of the room their eyes shone as they listened for sounds from the street. One man made three gestures at the barkeeper; and the latter, moving like a ghost, handed him a glass and a bottle. The man poured a full glass of whiskey, and set down the bottle noiselessly. He gulped the whiskey in a swallow, and turned again toward the door in immovable silence. The drummer saw that the barkeeper, without a sound, had taken a Winchester from beneath the bar. Later he saw this individual beckoning to him, so he tiptoed across the room.

"You better come with me back of the bar."

"No, thanks," said the drummer, perspiring; "I'd rather be where I can make a break for the back door."

Whereupon the man of bottles made a kindly but peremptory gesture. The drummer obeyed it, and, finding himself seated on a box with his head below the level of the bar, balm was laid upon his soul at sight of various zinc and copper fittings that bore a resemblance to armor-plate. The barkeeper took a seat comfortably upon an adjacent box.

"You see," he whispered, "this here Scratchy Wilson is a wonder with a gun—a perfect wonder; and when he goes on the war-trail, we hunt our holes—naturally. He's about the last one of the old gang that used to hang out along the river here. He's a terror when he's drunk. When he's sober he's all right—kind of simple—wouldn't hurt a fly—nicest fellow in town. But when he's drunk—whoo!"

There were periods of stillness. "I wish Jack Potter was back from San Anton'," said the barkeeper. "He shot Wilson up once—in the leg—and he would sail in and pull out the kinks in this thing."

Presently they heard from a distance the sound of a shot, followed by three wild yowls. It instantly removed a bond from the men in the darkened saloon. There was a shuffling of feet. They looked at each other. "Here he comes," they said.

III

A man in a maroon-colored flannel shirt, which had been purchased for purposes of decoration, and made principally by some Jewish woman on the East Side of New York, rounded a corner and walked into the middle of the main street of Yellow Sky. In either hand the man held a long, heavy, blue-black revolver. Often he yelled, and these cries ran through a semblance of a deserted village, shrilly flying over the roofs in a volume that seemed to have no relation to the ordinary vocal strength of a man. It was as if the surrounding stillness formed the arch of a tomb over him. These cries of ferocious challenge rang against walls of silence. And his boots had red tops with gilded imprints, of the kind beloved in winter by little sledding boys on the hillsides of New England.

The man's face flamed in a rage begot of whiskey. His eyes, rolling, and yet keen for ambush, hunted the still doorways and windows. He walked with the creeping movement of the midnight cat. As it occurred to him, he roared menacing information. The long revolvers in his hands were as easy as straws; they were moved with an electric swiftness. The little fingers of each hand played sometimes in a musician's way.

Plain from the low collar of the shirt, the cords of his neck straightened and sank, straightened and sank, as passion moved him. The only sounds were his terrible invitations. The calm adobes preserved their demeanor at the passing of this small thing in the middle of the street.

There was no offer of fight—no offer of fight. The man called to the sky. There were no attractions. He bellowed and fumed and swayed his revolvers here and everywhere.

The dog of the barkeeper of the Weary Gentleman saloon had not appreciated the advance of events. He yet lay dozing in front of his master's door. At sight of the dog, the man paused and raised his revolver humorously. At sight of the man, the dog sprang up and walked diagonally away, with a sullen head, and growling. The man yelled, and the dog broke into a gallop. As it was about to enter an alley, there was a loud noise, a whistling, and something spat the ground directly before it. The dog screamed, and, wheeling in terror, galloped headlong in a new direction. Again there was a noise, a whistling, and sand was kicked viciously before it. Fear-stricken, the dog turned and flurried like an animal in a pen. The man stood laughing, his weapons at his hips.

Ultimately the man was attracted by the closed door of the Weary Gentleman saloon. He went to it and, hammering with a revolver, demanded drink.

The door remaining imperturbable, he picked a bit of paper from the walk, and nailed it to the framework with a knife. He then turned his back contemptuously upon this popular resort and, walking to the opposite side of the street and spinning there on his heel quickly and lithely, fired at the bit of paper. He missed it by a half-inch. He swore at himself, and went away. Later he comfortably fusilladed the windows of his most intimate friend. The man was playing with this town; it was a toy for him.

But still there was no offer of fight. The name of Jack Potter, his ancient antagonist, entered his mind, and he concluded that it would be a glad thing if he should go to Potter's house, and by bombardment induce him to come out and fight. He moved in the direction of his desire, chanting Apache scalp-music.

When he arrived at it, Potter's house presented the same still front as had the other adobes. Taking up a strategic position, the man howled a challenge. But this house regarded him as might a great stone god. It gave no sign. After a decent wait, the man howled further challenges, mingling with them wonderful epithets.

Presently there came the spectacle of a man churning himself into deepest rage over the immobility of a house. He fumed at it as the winter wind attacks a prairie cabin in the North. To the distance there should have gone the sound of a tumult like the fighting of two hundred Mexicans. As necessity bade him, he paused for breath or to reload his revolvers.

IV

Potter and his bride walked sheepishly and with speed. Sometimes they laughed together shamefacedly and low.

"Next corner, dear," he said finally.

They put forth the efforts of a pair walking bowed against a strong wind. Potter was about to raise a finger to point the first appearance of the new home when, as they circled the corner, they came face to face with a man in a maroon-colored shirt, who was feverishly pushing cartridges into a large revolver. Upon the instant the man dropped his revolver to the ground and, like lightning, whipped another from its holster. The second weapon was aimed at the bridegroom's chest.

There was a silence. Potter's mouth seemed to be merely a grave for his tongue. He exhibited an instinct to at once loosen his arm from the women's grip, and he dropped his bag to the sand. As for the bride, her face had gone as yellow as old cloth. She was a slave to hideous rites, gazing at the apparitional snake.

The two men faced each other at a distance of three paces. He of the revolver smiled with a new and quiet ferocity.

"Tried to sneak up on me," he said. "Tried to sneak up on me!" His eyes grew more baleful. As Potter made a slight movement, the man thrust his revolver venomously forward. "No; Don't you move a finger toward a gun just yet. Don't you move an eyelash. The time has come for me to settle with you, and I'm goin' to do it my own way, and loaf along with no interferin'. So if you don't want a gun bent on you, just mind what I tell you."

Potter looked at his enemy, "I ain't got a gun on me, Scratchy," he said. "Honest, I ain't." He was stiffening and steadying, but yet somewhere at the back of his mind a vision of the Pullman floated: the sea-green figured velvet, the shining brass, silver, and glass, the wood that gleamed as darkly brilliant as the surface of a pool of oil— all the glory of the marriage, the environment of the new estate. "You know I fight when it comes to fighting, Scratchy Wilson; but I ain't got a gun on me. You'll have to do all the shootin' yourself."

His enemy's face went livid. He stepped forward, ad lashed his weapon to and fro before Potter's chest. "Don't you tell me you ain't got no gun on you, you whelp. Don't tell me no lie like that. There ain't a man in Texas ever seen you without no gun. Don't take me for no kid." His eyes blazed with light, and his throat worked like a pump.

"I ain't takin' you for no kid," an-

swered Potter. His heels had not moved an inch backward. "I'm takin' you for a damn fool. I tell you I ain't got a gun, and I ain't. If you're goin' to shoot me up, you better begin now; you'll never get a chance like this again."

So much enforced reasoning had told on Wilson's rage; he was calmer. "If you ain't got a gun, why ain't you got a gun?" he sneered. "Been to Sunday-school?"

"I ain't got a gun because I've just come from San Anton' with my wife. I'm married," said Potter. "And if I'd thought there was going to be any galoots like you prowling around when I brought my wife home, I'd had a gun, and don't you forget it."

"Married!" said Scratchy, not at all comprehending.

"Yes, married. I'm married," said Potter, distinctly.

"Married?" said Scratchy. Seemingly for the first time, he saw the drooping, drowning woman at the other man's side. "No!" he said. He was like a creature allowed a glimpse of another world. He moved a pace backward, and his arm, with the revolver, dropped to his side. "Is this the lady?" he asked.

"Yes; this is the lady," answered Potter.

There was another period of silence.

"Well," said Wilson at last, slowly, "I s'pose it's all off now."

"It's all off if you say so, Scratchy. You know I didn't make the trouble," Potter lifted his valise.

"Well, I 'low it's off, Jack," said Wilson. He was looking at the ground. "Married!" He was not a student of chivalry; it was merely that in the presence of this foreign condition he was a simple child of the earlier plains. He picked up his starboard revolver, and, placing both weapons in their holsters, he went away. His feet made funnel-shaped tracks in the heavy sand.

THE OPEN BOAT

A Tale Intended to be after the Fact: Being the Experience
of Four Men from the Sunk Steamer "COMMODORE"

I

None of them knew the color of the sky. Their eyes glanced level, and were fastened upon the waves that swept toward them. These waves were of the hue of slate, save for the tops, which were of foaming white, and all of the men knew the colors of the sea. The horizon narrowed and widened, and dipped and rose, and at all times its edge was jagged with waves that seemed thrust up in points like rocks.

Many a man ought to have a bathtub larger than the boat which here rode upon the sea. These waves were most wrongfully and barbarously abrupt and tall, and each froth-top was a problem in small-boat navigation.

The cook squatted in the bottom, and looked with both eyes at the six inches of gunwale which separated him from the ocean. His sleeves were rolled over his fat forearms, and the two flaps of his unbuttoned vest dangled as he bent to bail out the boat. Often he said, "Gawd! that was a narrow clip." As he remarked it he invariably gazed eastward over the broken sea.

The oiler, steering with one of the two oars in the boat, sometimes raised himself suddenly to keep clear of water that swirled in over the stern. It was a thin little oar, and it seemed often ready to snap.

The correspondent, pulling at the other oar, watched the waves and wondered why he was there.

The injured captain, lying in the bow, was at this time buried in that profound dejection and indifference which comes, temporarily at least, to even the bravest and most enduring when, willy-nilly, the firm fails, the army loses, the ship goes down. The mind of the master of a vessel is rooted deep in the timbers of her, though he command for a day or a decade; and this captain had on him the stern impression of a scene in the grays of dawn of seven turned faces, and later a stump of a topmast with a white ball on it, that slashed to and fro at the waves, went low and lower, and down. Thereafter there was something strange in his voice. Although steady, it was deep with mourning, and a quality beyond oration or tears.

"Keep'er a little more south, Billie," said he.

"A little more south, sir," said the oiler in the stern.

A seat in this boat was not unlike a seat upon a bucking broncho, and by the same token a broncho is not much smaller. The craft pranced and reared and plunged like an animal. As each wave came, and she rose for it, she seemed like a horse making at a fence outrageously high. The manner of her scramble over these walls of water is a mystic thing, and, moreover, at the top of them were ordinarily these problems in white water, the foam racing down from the summit of each wave requiring a new leap, and a leap from the air. Then, after scornfully bumping a crest, she would slide and race and splash down a long incline, and arrive bobbing and nodding in front of the next menace.

A singular disadvantage of the sea

lies in the fact that after successfully surmounting one wave you discover that there is another behind it just as important and just as nervously anxious to do something effective in the way of swamping boats. In a ten-foot dinghy one can get an idea of the resources of the sea in the line of waves that is not probable to the average experience, which is never at sea in a dinghy. As each slaty wall of water approached, it shut all else from the view of the men in the boat, and it was not difficult to imagine that this particular wave was the final outburst of the ocean, the last effort of the grim water. There was a terrible grace in the move of the waves, and they came in silence, save for the snarling of the crests.

In the wan light the faces of the men must have been gray. Their eyes must have glinted in strange ways as they gazed steadily astern. Viewed from a balcony, the whole thing would, doubtless, have been weirdly picturesque. But the men in the boat had no time to see it, and if they had had leisure, there were other things to occupy their minds. The sun swung steadily up the sky, and they knew it was broad day because the color of the sea changed from slate to emerald-green streaked with amber lights, and the foam was like tumbling snow. The process of the breaking day was unknown to them. They were aware only of the effect upon the color of the waves that rolled toward them.

In disjointed sentences the cook and the correspondent argued as to the difference between a life-saving station and a house of refuge. The cook had said: "There's a house of refuge just north of the Mosquito Inlet Light, and as soon as they see us they'll come off in their boat and pick us up."

"As soon as who sees us?" said the correspondent.

"The crew," said the cook.

"Houses of refuge don't have crews," said the correspondent. "As I understand them, they are only places where clothes and grub are stored for the benefit of shipwrecked people. They don't carry crews."

"Oh, yes, they do," said the cook.

"No, they don't," said the correspondent.

"Well, we're not there yet, anyhow," said the oiler, in the stern.

"Well," said the cook, "perhaps it's not a house of refuge that I'm thinking of as being near Mosquito Inlet Light; perhaps it's a life-saving station."

"We're not there yet," said the oiler in the stern.

II

As the boat bounced from the top of each wave the wind tore through the hair of the hatless men, and as the craft plopped her stern down again the spray splashed past them. The crest of each of these waves was a hill, from the top of which the men surveyed for a moment a broad tumultuous expanse, shining and wind-riven. It was probably splendid, it was probably glorious, this play of the free sea, wild with lights of emerald and white and amber.

"Bully good thing it's an on-shore wind," said the cook. "If not, where would we be? Wouldn't have a show."

"That's right," said the correspondent.

The busy oiler nodded his assent.

Then the captain, in the bow, chuckled in a way that expressed humor, contempt, tragedy, all in one. "Do you think we've got much of a show now, boys?" said he.

Whereupon the three were silent, save for a trifle of hemming and hawing. To express any particular optimism at this time they felt to be childish and stupid, but they all doubtless possessed this sense of the situation in their minds. A young man thinks doggedly at such times. On the other hand, the ethics of their condition was decidedly against any open suggestion of hopelessness. So they were silent.

"Oh, well," said the captain, soothing his children, "we'll get ashore all right."

But there was that in his tone which made them think; so the oiler quoth, "Yes! if this wind holds."

The cook was bailing. "Yes! if we don't catch hell in the surf."

Canton flannel gulls flew near and far. Sometimes they sat down on the sea, near patches of brown seaweed that rolled over the waves with a movement like carpets on a line in a gale. The birds sat comfortably in groups, and they were envied by some in the dinghy, for the wrath of the sea was no more to them than it was to a covey of prairie chickens a thousand miles inland. Often they came very close and stared at the men with black bead-like eyes. At these times they were uncanny and sinister in their unblinking scrutiny, and the men hooted angrily at them, telling them to be gone. One came, and evidently decided to alight on the top of the captain's head. The bird flew parallel to the boat and did not circle, but made short sidelong jumps in the air in chicken fashion. His black eyes were wistfully fixed upon the captain's head. "Ugly brute," said the oiler to the bird. "You look as if you were made with a jackknife." The cook and the correspondent swore darkly at the creature. The captain naturally wished to knock it away with the end of the heavy painter, but he did not dare do it, because anything resembling an emphatic gesture would have capsized this freighted boat; and so, with his open hand, the captain gently and carefully waved the gull away. After it had been discouraged from the pursuit the captain breathed easier on account of his hair, and others breathed easier because the bird struck their minds at this time as being somehow gruesome and ominous.

In the meantime the oiler and the correspondent rowed; and also they rowed. They sat together in the same seat, and each rowed an oar. Then the oiler took both oars; then the correspondent took both oars, then the oiler; then the correspondent: They rowed and they rowed. The very ticklish part of the business was when the time came for the reclining one in the stern to take his turn at the oars. By the very last star of truth, it is easier to steal eggs from under a hen than it was to change seats in the dinghy. First the man in the stern slid his hand along the thwart and moved with care, as if he were of Sèvres. Then the man in the rowing-seat slid his hand along the other thwart. It was all done with the most extraordinary care. As the two sidled past each other, the whole party kept watchful eyes on the coming wave, and the captain cried: "Look out, now! Steady, there!"

The brown mats of seaweed that appeared from time to time were like islands, bits of earth. They were travelling, apparently, neither one way nor the other. They were, to all intents, stationary. They informed the men in the boat that it was making progress slowly toward the land.

The captain, rearing cautiously in the bow after the dinghy soared on a great swell, said that he had seen the lighthouse at Mosquito Inlet. Presently the cook remarked that he had seen it. The correspondent was at the oars then, and for some reason he too wished to look at the lighthouse; but his back was toward the far shore, and the waves were important, and for some time he could not seize an opportunity to turn his head. But at last there came a wave more gentle than the others, and when at the crest of it he swiftly scoured the western horizon.

"See it?" said the captain.

"No," said the correspondent, slowly; "I didn't see anything."

"Look again," said the captain. He pointed. "It's exactly in that direction."

At the top of another wave the correspondent did as he was bid, and this time his eyes chanced on a small, still thing on the edge of the swaying horizon. It was precisely like the point of a pin. It took an anxious eye to find a lighthouse so tiny.

"Think we'll make it, Captain?"

"If this wind holds and the boat don't swamp, we can't do much else," said the captain.

The little boat, lifted by each towering sea and splashed viciously by the crests, made progress that in the absence of seaweed was not apparent to those in her. She seemed just a wee thing wallowing, miraculously top up, at the mercy of five oceans. Occasionally a great spread of water, like white flames, swarmed into her.

"Bail her, cook," said the captain, serenely.

"All right, Captain," said the cheerful cook.

III

It would be difficult to describe the subtle brotherhood of men that was here established on the seas. No one said that it was so. No one mentioned it. But it dwelt in the boat, and each man felt it warm him. They were a captain, an oiler, a cook, and a correspondent, and they were friends—friends in a more curiously iron-bound degree than may be common. The hurt captain, lying against the water-jar in the bow, spoke always in a low voice and calmly; but he could never command a more ready and swiftly obedient crew than the motley three of the dinghy. It was more than a mere recognition of what was best for the common safety. There was surely in it a quality that was personal and heart-felt. And after this devotion to the commander of the boat, there was this comradeship, that the correspondent, for instance, who had been taught to be cynical of men, knew even at the time was the best experience of his life. But no one said that it was so. No one mentioned it.

"I wish we had a sail," remarked the captain. "We might try my overcoat on the end of an oar, and give you two boys a chance to rest." So the cook and the correspondent held the mast and spread wide the overcoat; the oiler steered; and the little boat made good way with her new rig. Sometimes the oiler had to scull sharply to keep a sea from breaking into the boat, but otherwise sailing was a success.

Meanwhile the lighthouse had been growing slowly larger. It had now almost assumed color, and appeared like a little gray shadow on the sky. The man at the oars could not be prevented from turning his head rather often to try for a glimpse of this little gray shadow.

At last, from the top of each wave, the men in the tossing boat could see land. Even as the lighthouse was an upright shadow on the sky, this land seemed but a long black shadow on the sea. It certainly was thinner than paper. "We must be about opposite New Smyrna," said the cook, who had coasted this shore often in schooners. "Captain, by the way, I believe they abandoned that life-saving station there about a year ago."

"Did they?" said the captain.

The wind slowly died away. The cook and the correspondent were not now obliged to slave in order to hold high the oar. But the waves continued their old impetuous swooping at the dinghy, and the little craft, no longer under way, struggled woundily over them. The oiler or the correspondent took the oars again.

Shipwrecks are *apropos* of nothing. If men could only train for them and have them occur when the men had reached pink condition, there would be less drowning at sea. Of the four in the dinghy none had slept any time worth mentioning for two days and two nights previous to embarking in the dinghy, and in the excitement of clambering about the deck of a foundering ship they had also forgotten to eat heartily.

For these reasons, and for others, neither the oiler nor the correspondent was fond of rowing at this time. The correspondent wondered ingenuously how in the name of all that was sane could there be people who thought it amusing to row a boat. It was not an amusement; it was a diabolical punishment, and even a genius of mental aberrations could never conclude that it was anything but a horror to the muscles and a crime against the back. He mentioned to the boat in general how the amusement of rowing struck him, and the weary-faced oiler smiled in full sympathy. Previously to the foundering, by the way, the oiler had worked a double watch in the engineroom of the ship.

"Take her easy now, boys," said the captain. "Don't spend yourselves. If we have to run a surf you'll need all your strength, because we'll sure have to swim for it. Take your time."

Slowly the land arose from the sea. From a black line it became a line of black and a line of white—trees and sand. Finally the captain said that he could make out a house on the shore. "That's the house of refuge, sure," said the cook. "They'll see us before long, and come out after us."

The distant lighthouse reared high. "The keeper ought to be able to make us out now, if he's looking through a glass," said the captain. "He'll notify the life-saving people."

"None of those other boats could have got ashore to give word of this wreck," said the oiler, in a low voice, "else the lifeboat would be out hunting us."

Slowly and beautifully the land loomed out of the sea. The wind came again. It had veered from the northeast to the southeast. Finally a new sound struck the ears of the men in the boat. It was the low thunder of the surf on the shore. "We'll never be able to make the lighthouse now," said the captain. "Swing her head a little more north, Billie."

"A little more north, sir," said the oiler.

Whereupon the little boat turned her nose once more down the wind, and all but the oarsman watched the shore grow. Under the influence of this expansion doubt and direful apprehension were leaving the minds of the men. The management of the boat was still most absorbing, but it could not prevent a quiet cheerfulness. In an hour, perhaps, they would be ashore.

Their backbones had become thoroughly used to balancing in the boat, and they now rode this wild colt of a dinghy like circus men. The correspondent thought that he had been drenched to the skin, but happening to feel in the top pocket of his coat, he found therein eight cigars. Four of them were soaked with sea-water; four were perfectly scatheless. After a search, somebody produced three dry matches; and thereupon the four waifs rode impudently in their little boat and, with an assurance of an impending rescue shining in their eyes, puffed at the big cigars, and judged well and ill of all men. Everybody took a drink of water.

IV

"Cook," remarked the captain, "there don't seem to be any signs of life about your house of refuge."

"No," replied the cook. "Funny they don't see us!"

A broad stretch of lowly coast lay before the eyes of the men. It was of low dunes topped with dark vegetation. The roar of the surf was plain, and sometimes they could see the white lip of waves as it spun up the beach. A tiny house was blocked out black upon the sky. Southward, the slim lighthouse lifted its little gray length.

Tide, wind, and waves were swinging the dinghy northward. "Funny they don't see us," said the men.

The surf's roar was here dulled, but its tone was nevertheless thunderous and mighty. As the boat swam over the great rollers the men sat listening to this roar. "We'll swamp sure," said everybody.

It is fair to say here that there was not a life-saving station within twenty miles in either direction; but the men did not know this fact, and in consequence they made dark and opprobrious remarks concerning the eyesight of the nation's lifesavers. Four scowling men sat in the dinghy and surpassed records in the invention of epithets.

"Funny they don't see us."

The light-heartedness of a former time had completely faded. To their sharpened minds it was easy to conjure pictures of all kinds of incompetency and blindness and, indeed, cowardice. There was the shore of the populous land, and it was bitter and bitter to them that from it came no sign.

"Well," said the captain, ultimately, "I suppose we'll have to make a try for ourselves. If we stay out here too long, we'll none of us have strength left to swim after the boat swamps."

And so the oiler, who was at the oars, turned the boat straight for the shore. There was a sudden tightening of muscles. There was some thinking.

"If we don't all get ashore," said the captain—"if we don't all get ashore, I suppose you fellows know where to send news of my finish?"

They then briefly exchanged some addresses and admonitions. As for the reflections of the men, there was a great deal of rage in them. Perchance they might be formulated thus: "If I am going to be drowned—if I am going to be drowned—if I am going to be drowned, why, in the name of the seven mad gods who rule the sea, was I allowed to come thus far and contemplate sand and trees? Was I brought here merely to have my nose dragged away as I was about to nibble the sacred cheese of life? It is preposterous. If this old ninny-woman, Fate, cannot do better than this, she should be deprived of the management of men's fortunes. She is an old hen who knows not her intention. If she has decided to drown me, why did she not do it in the beginning and save me all this trouble? The whole affair is absurd. . . . But no; she cannot mean to drown me. She dare not drown me. She cannot drown me.

Not after all this work." Afterward the man might have had an impulse to shake his fist at the clouds. "Just you drown me, now, and then hear what I call you!"

The billows that came at this time were more formidable. They seemed always just about to break and roll over the little boat in a turmoil of foam. There was a preparatory and long growl in the speech of them. No mind unused to the sea would have concluded that the dinghy could ascend these sheer heights in time. The shore was still afar. The oiler was a wily surfman. "Boys," he said swiftly, "she won't live three minutes more, and we're too far out to swim. Shall I take her to sea again, Captain!"

"Yes; go ahead!" said the captain.

This oiler, by a series of quick miracles and fast and steady oarsmanship, turned the boat in the middle of the surf and took her safely to sea again.

There was a considerable silence as the boat bumped over the furrowed sea to deeper water. Then somebody in gloom spoke: "Well, anyhow, they must have seen us from the shore by now."

The gulls went in slanting flight up the wind toward the gray, desolate east. A squall, marked by dinghy clouds and clouds brick-red, like smoke from a burning building, appeared from the southeast.

"What do you think of those lifesaving people? Ain't they peaches?"

"Funny they haven't seen us."

"Maybe they think we're out here for sport! Maybe they think we're fishin'. Maybe they think we're damned fools."

It was a long afternoon. A changed tide tried to force them southward, but wind and wave said northward. Far ahead, where coast-line, sea, and sky formed their mighty angle, there were little dots which seemed to indicate a city on the shore.

"St. Augustine?"

The captain shook his head. "Too near Mosquito Inlet."

And the oiler rowed, and then the

correspondent rowed; then the oiler rowed. It was a weary business. The human back can become the seat of more aches and pains than are registered in books for the composite anatomy of a regiment. It is a limited area, but it can become the theater of innumerable muscular conflicts, tangles, wrenches, knots, and other forts.

"Did you ever like to row, Billie?" asked the correspondent.

"No," said the oiler; "hang it!"

When one exchanged the rowing-seat for a place in the bottom of the boat, he suffered a bodily depression that caused him to be careless of everything save an obligation to wiggle one finger. There was cold sea-water swashing to and fro in the boat, and he lay in it. His head, pillowed on a thwart, was within an inch of the swirl of a wave-crest, and sometimes a particularly obstreperous sea came inboard and drenched him once more. But these matters did not annoy him. It is almost certain that if the boat had capsized he would have tumbled comfortably out upon the ocean as if he felt sure that it was a great soft mattress.

"Look! There's a man on the shore!"

"Where?"

"There! See 'im? See 'im!"

"Yes, sure! He's walking along."

"Now he's stopped. Look! He's facing us!"

"He's waving at us!"

"So he is! By thunder!"

"Ah, now we're all right! Now we're all right! There'll be a boat out here for us in half an hour."

"He's going on. He's running. He's going up to that house there."

The remote beach seemed lower than the sea, and it required a searching glance to discern the little black figure. The captain saw a floating stick, and they rowed to it. A bath towel was by some weird chance in the boat, and, tying this on the stick, the captain waved it. The oarsman did not dare turn his head, so he was obliged to ask questions.

"What's he doing now!"

"He's standing still again. He's looking, I think. . . . There he goes again—toward the house. . . . Now he's stopped again."

"Is he waving at us?"

"No, not now; he was, though."

"Look! There comes another man!"

"He's running."

"Look at him go, would you!"

"Why, he's on a bicycle. Now he's met the other man. They're both waving at us. Look!"

"There comes something up the beach."

"What the devil is that thing?"

"Why, it looks like a boat."

"Why, certainly, it's a boat."

"No; it's on wheels."

"Yes, so it is. Well, that must be the life-boat. They drag them along shore on a wagon."

"That's the life-boat, sure."

"No, by God, it's—it's an omnibus."

"I tell you it's a life-boat."

"It is not! It's an omnibus. I can see it plain. See? One of these big hotel omnibuses."

"By thunder, you're right. It's an omnibus, sure as fate. What do you suppose they are doing with an omnibus? Maybe they are going around collecting the life-crew, hey?"

"That's it, likely. Look! There's a fellow waving a little black flag. He's standing on the steps of the omnibus. There come those other two fellows. Now they're all talking together. Look at the fellow with the flag. Maybe he ain't waving it!"

"That ain't a flag, is it? That's his coat. Why, certainly, that's his coat."

"So it is; it's his coat. He's taken it off and is waving it around his head. But would you look at him swing it!"

"Oh, say, there isn't any life-saving station there. That's just a winter-resort hotel omnibus that has brought over some of the boarders to see us drown."

"What's that idiot with the coat mean? What's he signaling, anyhow?"

"It looks as if he were trying to tell

us to go north. There must be a life-saving station up there."

"No; he thinks we're fishing. Just giving us a merry hand. See? Ah, there, Willie!"

"Well, I wish I could make something out of those signals. What do you suppose he means?"

"He don't mean anything; he's just playing."

"Well, if he'd signal us to try the surf again, or to go to sea and wait, or go north, or go south, or go to hell, there would be some reason in it. But look at him! He just stands there and keeps his coat revolving like a wheel. The ass!"

"There come more people."

"Now there's quite a mob. Look! Isn't that a boat?"

"Where? Oh, I see where you mean. No, that's no boat."

"That fellow is still waving his coat."

"He must think we like to see him do that. Why don't he quit it! It don't mean anything."

"I don't know. I think he is trying to make us go south. It must be that there's a life-saving station there somewhere."

"Say, he ain't tired yet. Look at 'im wave!"

"Wonder how long he can keep that up. He's been revolving his coat ever since he caught sight of us. He's an idiot. Why aren't they getting men to bring a boat out? A fishing-boat—one of those big yawls—could come out here all right. Why don't he do something?"

"Oh, it's all right now."

"They'll have a boat out here for us in less than no time, now that they've seen us."

A faint yellow tone came into the sky over the low land. The shadows on the sea slowly deepened. The wind bore coldness with it, and the men began to shiver.

"Holy smoke!" said one, allowing his voice to express his impious mood, "if we keep on monkeying out here! If we've got to flounder out here all night!"

"Oh, we'll never have to stay here all night! Don't you worry. They've seen us now, and it won't be long before they'll come chasing out after us."

The shore grew dusky. The man waving a coat blended gradually into this gloom, and it swallowed in the same manner the omnibus and the group of people. The spray, when it dashed uproariously over the side, made the voyagers shrink and swear like men who were being branded.

"I'd like to catch the chump who waved the coat. I feel like socking him one, just for luck."

"Why? What did he do?"

"Oh, nothing, but then he seemed so damned cheerful."

In the meantime the oiler rowed, and then the corresponpondent rowed, and then the oiler rowed. Gray-faced and bowed forward, they mechanically, turn by turn, plied the leaden oars. The form of the lighthouse had vanished from the southern horizon, but finally a pale star appeared, just lifting from the sea. The streaked saffron in the west passed before the all-merging darkness, and the sea to the east was black. The land had vanished, and was expressed only by the low and drear thunder of the surf.

"If I am going to be drowned—if I am going to be drowned—if I am going to be drowned, why, in the name of the seven mad gods who rule the sea, was I allowed to come thus far and contemplate sand and trees? Was I brought here merely to have my nose dragged away as I was about to nibble the sacred cheese of life?"

The patient captain, drooped over the water-jar, was sometimes obliged to speak to the oarsman.

"Keep her head up! Keep her head up!"

"Keep her head up, sir." The voices were weary and low.

This was surely a quiet evening. All save the oarsman lay heavily and listlessly in the boat's bottom. As for him, his eyes were just capable of noting the tall black waves that swept forward in a most sinister silence, save for an occasional subdued growl of a crest.

The cook's head was on a thwart, and he looked without interest at the water under his nose. He was deep in other scenes. Finally he spoke. "Billie," he murmured, dreamfully, "what kind of pie do you like best?"

V

"Pie!" said the oiler and the correspondent, agitatedly. "Don't talk about those things, blast you!"

"Well," said the cook, "I was just thinking about ham sandwiches, and—"

A night on the sea in an open boat is a long night. As darkness settled finally, the shine of the light, lifting from the sea in the south, changed to full gold. On the northern horizon a new light appeared, a small bluish gleam on the edge of the waters. These two lights were the furniture of the world. Otherwise there was nothing but waves.

Two men huddled in the stern, and distances were so magnificent in the dinghy that the rower was enabled to keep his feet pretty warm by thrusting them under his companions. Their legs indeed extended far under the rowing-seat until they touched the feet of the captain forward. Sometimes, despite the efforts of the third oarsman, a wave came piling into the boat, an icy wave of the night, and the chilling water soaked them anew. They would twist their bodies for a moment and groan, and sleep the dead sleep once more, while the water in the boat gurgled about them as the craft rocked.

The plan of the oiler and the correspondent was for one to row until he lost the ability, and then arouse the other from his sea-water couch in the bottom of the boat.

The oiler plied the oars until his head drooped forward and the overpowering sleep blinded him; and he rowed yet afterward. Then he touched a man in the bottom of the boat, and called his name. "Will you spell me for a little while?" he said meekly.

"Sure, Billie," said the correspondent, awaking and dragging himself to a sitting position. They exchanged places carefully, and the oiler, cuddling down in the sea-water at the cook's side, seemed to go to sleep instantly.

The particular violence of the sea had ceased. The waves came without snarling. The obligation of the man at the oars was to keep the boat headed so that the tilt of the rollers would not capsize her, and to preserve her from filling when the crests rushed past. The black waves were silent and hard to be seen in the darkness. Often one was almost upon the boat before the oarsman was aware.

In a low voice the correspondent addressed the captain. He was not sure that the captain was awake, although this iron man seemed to be always awake. "Captain, shall I keep her making for the light north, sir?"

The same steady voice answered him. "Yes. Keep it about two points off the port bow."

The cook had tied a life-belt around himself in order to get even the warmth which this clumsy cork contrivance could donate, and he seemed almost stove-like when a rower, whose teeth invariably chattered wildly as soon as he ceased his labor, dropped down to sleep.

The correspondent, as he rowed, looked down at the two men sleeping underfoot. The cook's arm was around the oiler's shoulders, and, with their fragmentary clothing and haggard faces, they were the babes of the sea—a grotesque rendering of the old babes in the wood.

Later he must have grown stupid at his work, for suddenly there was a growling of water, and a crest came with a roar and a swash into the boat, and it was a wonder that it did not set the cook affoat in his life-belt. The cook continued to sleep, but the oiler sat up, blinking his eyes and shaking with the new cold.

"Oh, I'm awfully sorry, Billie," said the correspondent, contritely.

"That's all right, old boy," said the oiler, and lay down again and was asleep.

Presently it seemed that even the captain dozed, and the correspondent thought that he was the one man afloat on all the ocean. The wind had a voice as it came over the waves, and it was sadder than the end.

There was a long, loud swishing astern of the boat, and a gleaming trail of phosphorescence, like blue flame, was furrowed on the black waters. It might have been made by a monstrous knife.

Then there came a stillness, while the correspondent breathed with open mouth and looked at the sea.

Suddenly there was another swish and another long flash of bluish light, and this time it was alongside the boat, and might almost have been reached with an oar. The correspondent saw an enormous fin speed like a shadow through the water, hurling the crystalline spray and leaving the long glowing trail.

The correspondent looked over his shoulder at the captain. His face was hidden, and he seemed to be asleep. He looked at the babes of the sea. They certainly were sleep. So, being bereft of sympathy, he leaned a little way to one side and swore softly into the sea.

But the thing did not then leave the vicinity of the boat. Ahead or astern, on one side or the other, at intervals long or short, fled the long sparkling streak, and there was to be heard the *whirroo* of the dark fin. The speed and power of the thing was greatly to be admired. It cut the water like a gigantic and keen projectile.

The presence of this biding thing did not affect the man with the same horror that it would if he had been a picnicker.

He simply looked at the sea dully and swore in an undertone.

Nevertheless, it is true that he did not wish to be alone with the thing. He wished one of his companions to awake by chance and keep him company with it. But the captain hung motionless over the water-jar, and the oiler and the cook in the bottom of the boat were plunged in slumber.

VI

"If I am going to be drowned—if I am going to be drowned—if I am going to be drowned, why, in the name of the seven mad gods who rule the sea, was I allowed to come thus far and contemplate sand and trees?"

During this dismal night, it may be remarked that a man would conclude that it was really the intention of the seven mad gods to drown him, despite the abdominal injustice of it. For it was certainly an abdominal injustice to drown a man who had worked so hard, so hard. The man felt it would be a crime most unnatural. Other people had drowned at sea since galleys swarmed with painted sails, but still—

When it occurs to a man that nature does not regard him as important, and that she feels she would not maim the universe by disposing of him, he at first wishes to throw bricks at the temple, and he hates deeply the fact that there are no bricks and no temples. Any visible expression of nature would surely be pelleted with his jeers.

Then, if there be no tangible thing to hoot, he feels, perhaps, the desire to confront a personification and indulge in pleas, bowed to one knee, and with hands supplicant, saying, "Yes, but I love myself.

A high cold star on a winter's night is the word he feels that she says to him. Thereafter he knows the pathos of his situation.

The men in the dinghy had not discussed these matters, but each had, no doubt, reflected upon them in silence and according to his mind. There was seldom any expression upon their faces save the general one of complete weariness. Speech was devoted to the business of the boat.

To chime the notes of his emotion, a verse mysteriously entered the correspondent's head. He had even forgotten that he had forgotten this verse, but it suddenly was in his mind.

A soldier of the Legion lay dying in Algiers;
There was lack of women's nursing, there was dearth of woman's tears;!
But a comrade stood beside him, and he took that comrade's hand,
And he said, "I never more shall see my own, my native land."

In his childhood the correspondent had been made acquainted with the fact that a soldier of the Legion lay dying in Algiers, but he had never regarded it as important. Myriads of his schoolfellows had informed him of the soldier's plight, but the dinning had naturally ended by making him perfectly indifferent. He had never considered it his affair that a soldier of the Legion lay dying in Algiers, nor had it appeared to him as a matter for sorrow. It was less to him than the breaking of a pencil's point.

Now, however, it quaintly came to him as a human, living thing. It was no longer merely a picture of a few throes in the breast of a poet, meanwhile drinking tea and warming his feet at the grate; it was an actuality—stern, mournful, and fine.

The correspondent plainly saw the soldier. He lay on the sand with his feet out straight and still. While his pale left hand was upon his chest in an attempt to thwart the going of his life, the blood came between his fingers. In the far Algerian distance, a city of low square forms was set against a sky that was faint with the last sunset hues. The correspondent, plying the oars and dreaming of the slow and slower move-

ments of the lips of the soldier, was moved by a profound and perfectly impersonal comprehension. He was sorry for the soldier of the Legion who lay dying in Algiers.

The thing which had followed the boat and waited had evidently grown bored at the delay. There was no longer to be heard the slash of the cut-water, and there was no longer the flame of the long trail. The light in the north still glimmered, but it was apparently no nearer to the boat. Sometimes the boom of the surf rang in the correspondent's ears, and he turned the craft seaward then and rowed harder. Southward, some one had evidently built a watch-fire on the beach. It was too low and too far to be seen, but it made a shimmering, roseate reflection upon the bluff in back of it, and this could be discerned from the boat. The wind came stronger, and sometimes a wave suddenly raged out like a mountain-cat, and there was to be seen the sheen and sparkle of a broken crest.

The captain, in the bow, moved on his water-jar and sat erect. "Pretty long night," he observed to the correspondent. He looked at the shore. "Those life-saving people take their time."

"Did you see that shark playing around?"

"Yes, I saw him. He was a big fellow, all right."

"Wish I had known you were awake."

Later the correspondent spoke into the bottom of the boat. "Billie!" There was a slow and gradual disentanglement. "Billie, will you spell me?"

"Sure," said the oiler.

As soon as the correspondent touched the cold, comfortable sea-water in the bottom of the boat and had huddled close to the cook's life-belt he was deep in sleep, despite the fact that his teeth played all the popular airs. This sleep was so good to him that it was a moment before he heard a voice call his name in a tone that demonstrated the last stages of exhaustion. "Will you spell me?"

"Sure, Billie."

The light in the north had mysteriously vanished, but the correspondent took his course from the wide-awake captain.

Later in the night they took the boat farther out to sea, and the captain directed the cook to take one oar at the stern and keep the boat facing the seas. He was to call out if he should hear the thunder of the surf. This plan enabled the oiler and the correspondent to get respite together. "We'll give those boys a chance to get into shape again," said the captain. They curled down and, after a few preliminary chatterings and trembles, slept once more the dead sleep. Neither knew they had bequeathed to the cook the company of another shark, or perhaps the same shark.

As the boat caroused on the waves, spray occasionally bumped over the side and gave them a fresh soaking, but this had no power to break their repose. The ominous slash of the wind and the water affected them as it would have affected mummies.

"Boys," said the cook, with the notes of every reluctance in his voice, "she's drifted in pretty close. I guess one of you had better take her to sea again." The correspondent, aroused, heard the crash of the toppled crests.

As he was rowing, the captain gave him some whiskey-and-water, and this steadied the chills out of him. "If I ever get ashore and anybody shows me even a photograph of an oar—"

At last there was a short conversation.

"Billie! . . . Billie, will you spell me?"

"Sure," said the oiler.

VII

When the correspondent again opened his eyes, the sea and the sky were each of the gray hue of the dawning. Later, carmine and gold was painted upon the waters. The morning appeared finally, in its splendor, with a sky of pure blue, and the sunlight flamed on the tips of the waves.

On the distant dunes were set many little black cottages, and a tall white windmill reared above them. No man, nor dog, nor bicycle appeared on the beach. The cottages might have formed a deserted village.

The voyagers scanned the shore. A conference was held in the boat. "Well," said the captain, "if no help is coming, we might better try a run through the surf right away. If we stay out here much longer we will be too weak to do anything for ourselves at all." The others silently acquiesced in this reasoning. The boat was headed for the beach. The correspondent wondered if none ever ascended the tall wind-tower, and if then they never looked seaward. This tower was a giant, standing with its back to the plight of the ants. It represented in a degree, to the correspondent, the serenity of nature amid the struggles of the individual—nature in the wind, and nature in the vision of men. She did not seem cruel to him then, nor beneficent, nor treacherous, nor wise. But she was indifferent, flatly indifferent. It is, perhaps, plausible that a man in this situation, impressed with the unconcern of the universe, should see the innumerable flaws of his life, and have them taste wickedly in his mind, and wish for another chance. A distinction between right and wrong seems absurdly clear to him, then, in this new ignorance of the grave-edge, and he understands that if he were given another opportunity he would mend his conduct and his words, and be better and brighter during an introduction or at a tea.

"Now, boys," said the captain, "she is going to swamp sure. All we can do is to work her in as far as possible, and then when she swamps, pile out and scramble for the beach. Keep cool now, and don't jump until she swamps sure."

The oiler took the oars. Over his shoulders he scanned the surf. "Captain," he said, "I think I'd better bring her about and keep her head-on to the seas and back her in."

"All right, Billie," said the captain. "Back her in." The oiler swung the boat then, and, seated in the stern, the cook and the correspondent were obliged to look over their shoulders to contemplate the lonely and indifferent shore.

The monstrous inshore rollers heaved the boat high until the men were again enabled to see the white sheets of water scudding up the slanted beach. "We won't get in very close," said the captain. Each time a man could wrest his attention from the rollers, he turned his glance toward the shore, and in the expression of the eyes during this contemplation there was a singular quality. The correspondent, observing the others, knew that they were not afraid, but the full meaning of their glances was shrouded.

As for himself, he was too tired to grapple fundamentally with the fact. He tried to coerce his mind into thinking of it, but the mind was dominated at this time by the muscles, and the muscles said they did not care. It merely occurred to him that if he should drown it would be a shame.

There were no hurried words, no pallor, no plain agitation. The men simply looked at the shore. "Now, remember to get well clear of the boat when you jump," said the captain.

Seaward the crest of a roller suddenly fell with a thunderous crash, and the long white comber came roaring down upon the boat.

"Steady now," said the captain. The men were silent. They turned their eyes from the shore to the comber and waited. The boat slid up the incline, leaped at the furious top, bounced over it, and swung down the long back of the wave. Some water had been shipped, and the cook bailed it out.

But the next crest crashed also. The tumbling, boiling flood of white water caught the boat and whirled it almost perpendicular. Water swarmed in from all sides. The correspondent had his hands on the gunwale at this time, and when the water entered at that place he swiftly withdrew his fingers, as if he objected to wetting them.

The little boat, drunken with this weight of water, reeled and snuggled deeper into the sea.

"Bail her out, cook! Bail her out!" said the captain.

"All right, Captain," said the cook.

"Now boys, the next one will do for us sure," said the oiler. "Mind to jump clear of the boat."

The third wave moved forward, huge, furious, implacable. It fairly swallowed the dinghy, and almost simultaneously the men tumbled into the sea. A piece of life-belt had lain in the bottom of the boat, and as the correspondent went overboard he held this to his chest with his left hand.

The January water was icy, and he reflected immediately that it was colder than he had expected to find it off the coast of Florida. This appeared to his dazed mind as a fact important enough to be noted at the time. The coldness of the water was sad; it was tragic. This fact was somehow mixed and confused with his opinion of his own situation, so that it seemed almost a proper reason for tears. The water was cold.

When he came to the surface he was conscious of little but the noisy water. Afterward he saw his companions in the sea. The oiler was ahead in the race. He was swimming strongly and rapidly. Off to the correspondent's left, the cook's great white and corked back bulged out of the water, and in the rear the captain was hanging with his one good hand to the keel of the overturned dinghy.

There is a certain immovable quality to a shore, and the correspondent wondered at it amid the confusion of the sea.

It seemed also very attractive; but the correspondent knew that it was a long journey, and he paddled leisurely. The piece of life-preserver lay under him, and sometimes he whirled down the incline of a wave as if he were on a handsled.

But finally he arrived at a place in the sea where travel was beset with difficulty. He did not pause swimming to inquire what manner of current had caught him, but there his progress ceased. The shore was set before him like a bit of scenery on a stage, and he looked at it and understood with his eyes each detail of it.

As the cook passed, much farther to the left, the captain was calling to him, "Turn over on your back, cook! Turn over on your back and use the oar."

"All right, sir." The cook turned on his back, and, paddling with an oar, went ahead as if he were a canoe.

Presently the boat also passed to the left of the correspondent, with the captain clinging with one hand to the keel. He would have appeared like a man raising himself to look over a board fence if it were not for the extraordinary gymnastics of the boat. The correspondent marveled that the captain could still hold to it.

They passed on nearer to shore—the oiler, the cook, the captain—and following them went the water-jar, bouncing gaily over the seas.

The correspondent remained in the grip of this strange new enemy, a current. The shore, with its white slope of sand and its green bluff topped with little silent cottages, was spread like a picture before him. It was very near to him then, but he was impressed as one who, in a gallery, looks at a scene from Brittany or Algiers.

He thought: "I am going to drown? Can it be possible? Can it be possible? Can it be possible?" Perhaps an individual must consider his own death to be the final phenomenon of nature.

But later a wave perhaps whirled him out of this small deadly current, for he found suddenly that he could again make progress toward the shore. Later

still he was aware that the captain, clinging with one hand to the keel of the dinghy, had his face turned away from the shore and toward him, and was calling his name. "Come to the boat! Come to the boat!"

In his struggle to reach the captain and the boat, he reflected that when one gets properly wearied drowning must really be a comfortable arrangement—a cessation of hostilities accompanied by a large degree of relief; and he was glad of it, for the main thing in his mind for some moments had been horror of the temporary agony; he did not wish to be hurt.

Presently he saw a man running along the short. He was undressing with most remarkable speed. Coat, trousers, shirt, everything flew magically off him.

"Come to the boat!" called the captain.

"All right, Captain." As the correspondent paddled, he saw the captain let himself down to bottom and leave the boat. Then the correspondent performed his one little marvel of the voyage. A large wave caught him and flung him with ease and supreme speed completely over the boat and far beyond it. It struck him even then as an event in gymnastics and a true miracle of the sea. An overturned boat in the surf is not a plaything to a swimming man.

The correspondent arrived in water that reached only to his waist, but his condition did not enable him to stand for more than a moment. Each wave knocked him into a heap, and the undertow pulled at him.

Then he saw the man who had been running and undressing, and undressing and running, come bounding into the water. He dragged ashore the cook, and then waded toward the captain; but the captain waved him away and sent him to the correspondent. He was naked—naked as a tree in winter; but a halo was about his head, and he shone like a saint. He gave a strong pull, and a long drag, and a bully heave at the correspondent's hand. The correspondent, schooled in the minor formulae, said, "Thanks, old man." But suddenly the man cried, "What's that?" He pointed a swift finger. The correspondent said, "Go."

In the shallows, face downward, lay the oiler. His forehead touched sand that was periodically, between each wave, clear of the sea.

The correspondent did not know all that transpired afterward. When he achieved safe ground he fell, striking the sand with each particular part of his body. It was as if he had dropped from a roof, but the thud was grateful to him.

It seemed that instantly the beach was populated with men with blankets, clothes, and flasks, and women with coffee-pots and all the remedies sacred to their minds. The welcome of the land to the men from the sea was warm and generous; but a still and dripping shape was carried slowly up the beach, and the land's welcome for it could only be the different and sinister hospitality of the grave.

When it came night, the white waves paced to and fro and the moonlight, and the wind brought the sound of the great sea's voice to the men on the shore, and they felt that they could then be interpreters.

James Joyce (1882–1941)

A LITTLE CLOUD

Eight years before he had seen his friend off at the North Wall and wished him godspeed. Gallaher had got on. You could tell that at once by his travelled air, his well-cut tweed suit, and fearless accent. Few fellows had talents like his and fewer still could remain unspoiled by such success. Gallaher's heart was in the right place and he had deserved to win. It was something to have a friend like that.

Little Chandler's thoughts ever since lunchtime had been of his meeting with Gallaher, of Gallaher's invitation and of the great city London where Gallaher lived. He was called Little Chandler because, though he was but slightly under the average stature, he gave one the idea of being a little man. His hands were white and small, his frame was fragile, his voice was quiet and his manners were refined. He took the greatest care of his fair silken hair and moustache and used perfume discreetly on his handkerchief. The half-moons of his nails were perfect and when he smiled you caught a glimpse of a row of childish white teeth.

As he sat at his desk in the King's Inns he thought what changes those eight years had brought. The friend whom he had known under a shabby and necessitous guise had become a brilliant figure on the London Press. He turned often from his tiresome writing to gaze out of the office window. The glow of a late autumn sunset covered the grass plots and walks. It cast a shower of kindly golden dust on the untidy nurses and decrepit old men who drowsed on the benches; it flickered upon all the moving figures—on the children who ran screaming along the gravel paths and on everyone who passed through the gardens. He watched the scene and thought of life; and (as always happened when he thought of life) he became sad. A gentle melancholy took possession of him. He felt how useless it was to struggle against fortune, this being the burden of wisdom which the ages had bequeathed to him.

He remembered the books of poetry upon his shelves at home. He had bought them in his bachelor days and many an evening, as he sat in the little room off the hall, he had been tempted to take one down from the bookshelf and read out something to his wife. But shyness had always held him back; and so the books remained on their shelves. At times he repeated lines to himself and this consoled him.

When his hour had struck he stood up and took leave of his desk and of his fellow-clerks punctiliously. He emerged from under the feudal arch of the King's Inns, a neat modest figure, and walked swiftly down Henrietta Street. The golden sunset was waning and the air had grown sharp. A horde of grimy children populated the street. They stood or ran in the roadway or crawled up the steps before the gaping doors or squatted like mice upon the thresholds. Little Chandler gave them no thought. He picked his way deftly through all that minute vermin-like life and under the shadow of the gaunt spectral mansions in which the old nobility of Dublin had roystered. No memory of the past touched him, for his mind was full of a present joy.

He had never been in Corless's but he knew the value of the name. He knew that people went there after the theatre to eat oysters and drink liqueurs; and he had heard that the waiters there spoke French and German. Walking swiftly by at night he had seen cabs drawn up before the door and richly dressed ladies, escorted by cavaliers, alight and enter quickly. They wore noisy dresses and many wraps. Their faces were powdered and they caught up their dresses, when they touched earth, like alarmed Atalantas. He had always passed without turning his head to look. It was his habit to walk swiftly in the street even by day and whenever he found himself in the city late at night he hurried on his way apprehensively and excitedly. Sometimes, however, he courted the causes of his fear. He chose the darkest and narrowest streets and, as he walked boldly forward, the silence that was spread about his footsteps troubled him, the wandering, silent figures troubled him; and at times a sound of low fugitive laughter made him tremble like a leaf.

He turned to the right towards Capel Street. Ignatius Gallaher on the London Press! Who would have thought it possible eight years before? Still, now that he reviewed the past, Little Chandler could remember many signs of future greatness in his friend. People used to say that Ignatius Gallaher was wild. Of course he did mix with a rakish set of fellows at that time, drank freely and borrowed money on all sides. In the end he had got mixed up in some shady affair, some money transaction: at least, that was one version of his flight. But nobody denied him talent. There was always a certain . . . something in Ignatius Gallaher that impressed you in spite of yourself. Even when he was out at elbows and at his wits' end for money he kept up a bold face. Little Chandler remembered (and the remembrance brought a slight flush of pride to his cheek) one of Ignatius Gallaher's sayings when he was in a tight corner:

"Half time now boys," he used to say lightheartedly. "Where's my considering cap?"

That was Ignatius Gallaher all out; and, damn it, you couldn't but admire him for it.

Little Chandler quickened his pace. For the first time in his life he felt himself superior to the people he passed. For the first time his soul revolted against the dull inelegance of Capel Street. There was no doubt about it: if you wanted to succeed you had to go away. You could do nothing in Dublin. As he crossed Grattan Bridge he looked down the river towards the lower quays and pitied the poor stunted houses. They seemed to him a band of tramps, huddled together along the river-banks, their old coats covered with dust and soot, stupefied by the panorama of sunset and waiting for the first chill of night to bid them arise, shake themselves and be gone. He wondered whether he could write a poem to express his idea. Perhaps Gallaher might be able to get it into some London paper for him. Could he write something original? He was not sure what idea he wished to express but the thought that a poetic moment had touched him took life within him like an infant hope. He stepped onward bravely.

Every step brought him nearer to London, farther from his own sober inartistic life. A light began to tremble on the horizon of his mind. He was not so old—thirty-two. His temperament might be said to be just at the point of maturity. There were so many different moods and impressions that he wished to express in verse. He felt them within him. He tried to weigh his soul to see if it was a poet's soul. Melancholy was the dominant note of his temperament, he thought, but it was a melancholy tempered by recurrences of faith and resignation and simple joy. If he could give expression to it in a book of poems perhaps men would listen. He would never be popular: he saw that. He could not sway the crowd but he might appeal to a little circle of kindred minds. The English critics, perhaps, would recognize him as one of the Celtic school by reason of the melancholy tone of his poems; besides that, he would put in allusions. He began to invent sentences and phrases from the notice which his

book would get. *"Mr. Chandler has the gift of easy and graceful verse."* . . . *"A wistful sadness pervades these poems."* . . . *"The Celtic note."* It was a pity his name was not more Irish-looking. Perhaps it would be better to insert his mother's name before the surname: Thomas Malone Chandler, or better still: T. Malone Chandler. He would speak to Gallaher about it.

He pursued his revery so ardently that he passed his street and had to turn back. As he came near Corless's his former agitation began to overmaster him and he halted before the door in indecision. Finally he opened the door and entered.

The light and noise of the bar held him at the doorway for a few moments. He looked about him, but his sight was confused by the shining of many red and green wine-glasses. The bar seemed to him to be full of people and he felt that the people were observing him curiously. He glanced quickly to right and left (frowning slightly to make his errand appear serious), but when his sight cleared a little he saw that nobody had turned to look at him: and there, sure enough, was Ignatius Gallaher leaning with his back against the counter and his feet planted far apart.

"Hallo, Tommy, old hero, here you are! What is it to be? What will you have? I'm taking whisky: better stuff than we get across the water. Soda? Lithia? No mineral? I'm the same. Spoils the flavour. . . . Here, *garçon*, bring us two halves of malt whisky, like a good fellow. . . . Well, and how have you been pulling along since I saw you last? Dear God, how old we're getting! Do you see any signs of aging in me—eh, what? A little grey and thin on the top—what?"

Ignatius Gallaher took off his hat and displayed a large closely cropped head. His face was heavy, pale and clean-shaven. His eyes which were of bluish slate-colour, relieved his unhealthy pallor and shone out plainly above the vivid orange tie he wore. Between these rival features the lips appeared very long and shapeless and colourless. He bent his head and felt with two sympathetic fingers the thin hair at the crown. Little Chandler shook his head as a denial. Ignatius Gallaher put on his hat again.

"It pulls you down," he said, "press life. Always hurry and scurry, looking for copy and sometimes not finding it: and then, always to have something new in your stuff. Damn proofs and printers, I say, for a few days. I'm deuced glad, I can tell you, to get back to the old country. Does a fellow good, a bit of a holiday. I feel a ton better since I landed again in dear dirty Dublin. . . . Here you are, Tommy. Water? Say when."

Little Chandler allowed his whisky to be very much diluted.

"You don't know what's good for you, my boy," said Ignatius Gallaher. "I drink mine neat."

"I drink very little as a rule," said Little Chandler modestly. "An odd half-one or so when I meet any of the old crowd: that's all."

"Ah, well," said Ignatius Gallaher, cheerfully, "here's to us and to old times and old acquaintance."

They clinked glasses and drank the toast.

"I met some of the old gang today," said Ignatius Gallaher. "O'Hara seems to be in a bad way. What's he doing?"

"Nothing," said Little Chandler. "He's gone to the dogs."

"But Hogan has a good sit, hasn't he?"

"Yes; he's in the Land Commission."

"I met him one night in London and he seemed to be very flush. . . . Poor O'Hara! Boose, I suppose?"

"Other things, too," said Little Chandler shortly.

Ignatius Gallaher laughed.

"Tommy," he said, "I see you haven't changed an atom. You're the very same serious person that used to lecture me on Sunday mornings when I had a sore head and a fur on my tongue. You'd want to knock about a bit in the world. Have you never been anywhere even for a trip?"

"I've been to the Isle of Man," said Little Chandler.

Ignatius Gallaher laughed.

"The Isle of Man!" he said. "Go to London or Paris: Paris, for choice. That'd do you good."

"Have you seen Paris?"

"I should think I have! I've knocked about there a little."

"And is it really so beautiful as they say?" asked Little Chandler.

He sipped a little of his drink while Ignatius Gallaher finished his boldly.

"Beautiful?" said Ignatius Gallaher, pausing on the word and on the flavour of his drink. "It's not so beautiful, you know. Of course, it is beautiful. . . . But it's the life of Paris; that's the thing. Ah, there's no city like Paris for gaiety, movement, excitement. . . ."

Little Chandler finished his whisky and, after some trouble, succeeded in catching the barman's eye. He ordered the same again.

"I've been to the Moulin Rouge," Ignatius Gallaher continued when the barman had removed their glasses, "and I've been to all the Bohemian cafés. Hot stuff! Not for a pious chap like you, Tommy."

Little Chandler said nothing until the barman returned with two glasses: then he touched his friend's glass lightly and reciprocated the former toast. He was beginning to feel somewhat disillusioned. Gallaher's accent and way of expressing himself did not please him. There was something vulgar in his friend which he had not observed before. But perhaps it was only the result of living in London amid the bustle and competition of the Press. The old personal charm was still there under this new gaudy manner. And, after all, Gallaher had lived, he had seen the world. Little Chandler looked at his friend enviously.

"Everything in Paris is gay," said Ignatius Gallaher. "They believe in enjoying life—and don't you think they're right? If you want to enjoy yourself properly you must go to Paris. And, mind you, they've a great feeling for the Irish there. When they heard I was from Ireland they were ready to eat me, man."

Little Chandler took four or five sips from his glass.

"Tell me," he said, "is it true that Paris is so . . . immoral as they say?"

Ignatius Gallaher made a catholic gesture with his right arm.

"Every place is immoral," he said. "Of course you do find spicy bits in Paris. Go to one of the students' balls, for instance. That's lively, if you like, when the *cocottes* begin to let themselves loose. You know what they are, I suppose?"

"I've heard of them," said Little Chandler.

Ignatius Gallaher drank off his whisky and shook his head.

"Ah," he said, "you may say what you like. There's no woman like the Parisienne—for style, for go."

"Then it is an immoral city," said Little Chandler, with timid insistence—"I mean, compared with London or Dublin?"

"London!" said Ignatius Gallaher. "It's six of one and half-a-dozen of the other. You ask Hogan, my boy. I showed him a bit about London when he was over there. He'd open your eye. . . . I say, Tommy, don't make punch of that whisky: liquor up."

"No, really. . . ."

"Oh, come on, another one won't do you any harm. What is it? The same again, I suppose?"

"Well . . . all right."

"*François*, the same again. . . . Will you smoke, Tommy?"

Ignatius Gallaher produced his cigarcase. The two friends lit their cigars and puffed at them in silence until their drinks were served.

"I'll tell you my opinion," said Ignatius Gallaher, emerging after some time from the clouds of smoke in which he had taken refuge, "it's a rum world. Talk of immortality! I've heard of cases—what am I saying?—I've known them: cases of . . . immorality. . . ."

Ignatius Gallaher puffed thoughtfully at his cigar and then, in a calm historian's tone, he proceeded to sketch for his friend some pictures of the corruption which was rife abroad. He summarised the vices of many capitals and seemed inclined to award the palm to Berlin. Some things he could not vouch for (his friends had told him), but of others he had had personal experience. He spared neither rank nor caste. He revealed many of the secrets of religious houses on the Continent and described some of the practices which were fashionable in high society and ended by telling, with details, a story about an English duchess—a story which he knew to be true. Little Chandler was astonished.

"Ah, well," said Ignatius Gallaher, "here we are in old jog-along Dublin where nothing is known of such things."

"How dull you must find it," said Little Chandler, "after all the other places you've seen!"

"Well," said Ignatius Gallaher, "it's a relaxation to come over here, you know. And, after all, it's the old country, as they say, isn't it? You can't help having a certain feeling for it. That's human nature. . . . But tell me something about yourself. Hogan told me you had . . . tasted the joys of connubial bliss. Two years ago, wasn't it?"

Little Chandler blushed and smiled.

"Yes," he said. "I was married last May twelve months."

"I hope it's not too late in the day to offer my best wishes," said Ignatius

Gallaher. "I didn't know your address or I'd have done so at the time."

He extended his hand, which Little Chandler took.

"Well, Tommy," he said, "I wish you and yours every joy in life, old chap, and tons of money, and may you never die till I shoot you. And that's the wish of a sincere friend, and old friend. You know that?"

"I know that," said Little Chandler.

"Any youngsters?" said Ignatius Gallaher.

Little Chandler blushed again.

"We have one child," he said.

"Son or daughter?"

"A little boy."

Ignatius Gallaher slapped his friend sonorously on the back.

"Bravo," he said, "I wouldn't doubt you, Tommy."

Little Chandler smiled, looked confusedly at his glass and bit his lower lip with three childishly white front teeth.

"I hope you'll spend an evening with us," he said, "before you go back. My wife will be delighted to meet you. We can have a little music and—"

"Thanks awfully, old chap," said Ignatius Gallaher, "I'm sorry we didn't meet earlier. But I must leave tomorrow night."

"Tonight perhaps, . . . ?"

"I'm awfully sorry, old man. You see I'm over here with another fellow, clever young chap he is too, and we arranged to go to a little card-party. Only for that. . . ."

"O, in that case. . . ."

"But who knows?" said Ignatius Gallaher considerably. "Next year I may take a little skip over here now that I've broken the ice. It's only a pleasure deferred."

"Very well," said Little Chandler, "the next time you come we must have an evening together. That's agreed now, isn't it?"

"Yes, that's agreed," said Ignatius Gallaher. "Next year if I come, *parole d'honneur*."

"And to clinch the bargain," said Little Chandler, "we'll just have one more now."

Ignatius Gallaher took out a large gold watch and looked at it.

"Is it to be the last?" he said. "Because you know, I have an a.p."

"O, yes, positively," said Little Chandler.

"Very well, then," said Ignatius Gallaher, "let us have another one as a *deoc an dorius*—that's good vernacular for a small whisky I believe."

Little Chandler ordered the drinks. The blush which had risen to his face a few moments before was establishing itself. A trifle made him blush at any time: and now he felt warm and excited. Three small whiskies had gone to his head and Gallaher's strong cigar had confused his mind, for he was a delicate and abstinent person. The adventure of meeting Gallaher after eight years, of finding himself with Gallaher in Corless's surrounded by lights and noise, of listening to Gallaher's stories and of sharing for a brief space Gallaher's vagrant and triumphant life, upset the equipoise of his sensitive nature. He felt acutely the contrast between his own life and his friend's, and it seemed to him unjust. Gallaher was his inferior in birth and education. He was sure that he could do something better than his friend had ever done, or could ever do, something higher than mere tawdry journalism if he only got the chance. What was it that stood in his way? His unfortunate timidity! He wished to vindicate himself in some way, to assert his manhood. He saw behind Gallaher's refusal of his invitation. Gallaher was only patronising him by his friendliness just as he was patronising Ireland by his visit.

The barman brought their drinks. Little Chandler pushed one glass towards his friend and took up the other boldly.

"Who knows?" he said, as they lifted their glasses. "When you come next year I may have the pleasure of wishing long life and happiness to Mr. and Mrs. Ignatius Gallaher."

Ignatius Gallaher in the act of drinking closed one eye expressively over the rim of his glass. When he had drunk he smacked his lips decisively, set down his glass and said:

"No blooming fear of that, my boy. I'm going to have my fling first and see a bit of life and world before I put my head in the sack—if I ever do."

"Some day you will," said Little Chandler calmly.

Ignatius Gallaher turned his orange tie and slate-blue eyes full upon his friend.

"You think so?" he said.

"You'll put your head in the sack," repeated Little Chandler stoutly, "like everyone else if you can find the girl."

He had slightly emphasised his tone and he was aware that he had betrayed himself; but, though the colour had heightened in his cheek, he did not flinch from his friend's gaze. Ignatius Gallaher watched him for a few moments and then said:

"If ever it occurs, you may bet your bottom dollar there'll be no mooning and spooning about it. I mean to marry money. She'll have a good fat account at the bank or she won't do for me."

Little Chandler shook his head.

"Why, man alive," said Ignatius Gallaher, vehemently, "do you know what it is? I've only to say the word and to-morrow I can have the woman and the cash. You don't believe it? Well, I know it. There are hundreds—what am I saying?—thousands of rich Germans and Jews, rotten with money, that'd only be too glad. . . . You wait a while, my boy. See if I don't play my cards properly. When I go about a thing I mean business, I tell you. You just wait."

He tossed his glass to his mouth, finished his drink and laughed loudly. Then he looked thoughtfully before him and said in a calmer tone:

"But I'm in no hurry. They can wait. I don't fancy tying myself up to one woman, you know."

He imitated with his mouth the act of tasting and made a wry face.

"Must get a bit stale, I should think," he said.

．．．

Little Chandler sat in the room off the hall, holding a child in his arms. To save money they kept no servant but Annie's young sister Monica came for an hour or so in the morning and an hour or so in the evening to help. But Monica had gone home long ago. It was a quarter to nine. Little Chandler had come home late for tea and, moreover, he had forgotten to bring Annie home the parcel of coffee from Bewley's. Of course she was in a bad humour and gave him short answers. She said she would do without any tea but when it came near the time at which the shop at the corner closed she decided to go out herself for a quarter of a pound of tea and two pounds of sugar. She put the sleeping child deftly in his arms and said:

"Here. Don't waken him."

A little lamp with a white china shade stood upon the table and its light fell over a photograph which was enclosed in a frame of crumpled horn. It was Annie's photograph. Little Chandler looked at it, pausing at the thin tight lips. She wore the pale blue summer blouse which he had brought her home as a present one Saturday. It had cost him ten and elevenpence; but what an agony of nervousness it had cost him! How he had suffered that day, waiting at the shop door until the shop was empty, standing at the counter and trying to appear at his ease while the girl piled ladies' blouses before him, paying at the desk and forgetting to take up the odd penny of his change, being called back by the cashier, and finally, striving to hide his blushes as he left the shop by examining the parcel to see if it were securely tied. When he brought the blouse home Annie kissed him and said it was very pretty and stylish; but when she heard the price she threw the blouse on the table and said it was a regular swindle to charge ten and elevenpence for it. At first she wanted to take it back but when she tried it on she was delighted with it, especially with the make of the sleeves, and kissed him and said he was very good to think of her.

Hm! . . .

He looked coldly into the eyes of the photograph and they answered coldly. Certainly they were pretty and the face itself was pretty. But he found something mean in it. Why was it so unconscious and ladylike? The composure of the eyes irritated him. They repelled him and defied him: there was no passion in them, no rapture. He thought of what Gallaher had said about rich Jewesses. Those dark Oriental eyes, he thought, how full they are of passion, of voluptuous longing! . . . Why had he married the eyes in the photograph?

He caught himself up at the question and glanced nervously around the room. He found something mean in the pretty furniture which he had bought for his house on the hire system. Annie had chosen it herself and it reminded him of her. It too was prim and pretty. A dull resentment against his life awoke within him. Could he not escape from his little house? Was it too late for him to try to live bravely like Gallaher? Could he go to London? There was the furniture still to be paid for. If he could only write a book and get it published, that might open the way for him.

A volume of Byron's poems lay before him on the table. He opened it cautiously with his left hand lest he should waken the child and began to read the first poem in the book:

Hushed are the winds and still the
    evening gloom,
  Not e'en a Zephyr wanders through
    the grove,

Whilst I return to view my Margaret's
    tomb
  And scatter flowers on the dust I
    love.

He paused. He felt the rhythm of the verse about him in the room. How melancholy it was! Could he, too, write like that, express the melancholy of his soul in verse? There were so many things he wanted to describe: his sensation of a few hours before on Grattan Bridge, for example. If he could get back again into that mood. . . .

The child awoke and began to cry. He turned from the page and tried to hush it: but it would not be hushed. He began to rock it to and fro in his arms but its wailing cry grew keener. He rocked it faster while his eyes began to read the second stanza:

Within this narrow cell reclines her
    clay,
  That clay where once . . .

It was useless. He couldn't read. He couldn't do anything. The wailing of the child pierced the drum of his ear. It was useless! He was a prisoner for life. His arms trembled with anger and suddenly bending to the child's face he shouted: "Stop!"

The child stopped for an instant, had a spasm of freight and began to scream. He jumped up from his chair and walked hastily up and down the room with the child in his arms. It began to sob piteously, losing its breath for four or five seconds, and then bursting out anew. The thin walls of the room echoed the sound. He tried to soothe it but it sobbed more convulsively. He looked at the contracted and quivering face of the child and began to be alarmed. He counted seven sobs without a break between them and caught the child to his breast in fright. If it died! . . .

The door was burst open and a young woman ran in, panting.

"What is it? What is it?" she cried.

The child, hearing its mother's voice, broke out into a paroxysm of sobbing.

"It's nothing, Annie . . . it's nothing. . . . He began to cry . . ."

She flung her parcels on the floor and snatched the child from him.

"What have you done to him?" she cried, glaring into his face.

Little Chandler sustained for one moment the gaze of her eyes and his heart closed together as he met the hatred in them. He began to stammer:

"It's nothing. . . . He . . . began to cry. . . . I couldn't . . . I didn't do anything. . . . What?"

Giving no heed to him she began to walk up and down the room, clasping the child tightly in her arms and murmuring:

"My little man! My little mannie! Was 'ou frightened, love? . . . There now, love. There now! . . . Lambabaun! Mamma's little lamb of the world! . . . There now!"

Little Chandler felt his cheeks suffused with shame and he stood back out of the lamplight. He listened while the paroxysm of the child's sobbing grew less and less; and tears of remorse started to his eyes.

D. H. Lawrence (1885–1930)
THE HORSE DEALER'S DAUGHTER

"Well, Mabel, and what are you going to do with yourself?" asked Joe, with foolish flippancy. He felt quite safe himself. Without listening for an answer, he turned aside, worked a grain of tobacco to the tip of his tongue, and spat it out. He did not care about anything, since he felt safe himself.

The three brothers and the sister sat round the desolate breakfast table, attempting some sort of desultory consultation. The morning's post had given the final tap to the family fortune, and all was over. The dreary dining-room itself, with its heavy mahogany furniture, looked as if it were waiting to be done away with.

But the consultation amounted to nothing. There was a strange air of ineffectuality about the three men, as they sprawled at table, smoking and reflecting vaguely on their own condition. The girl was alone, a rather short, sullen-looking young woman of twenty-seven. She did not share the same life as her brothers. She would have been good-looking, save for the impassive fixity of her face, "bull-dog," as her brothers called it.

There was a confused tramping of horses' feet outside. The three men all sprawled round in their chairs to watch. Beyond the dark holly-bushes that separated the strip of lawn from the highroad, they could see a cavalcade of shire horses swinging out of their own yard, being taken for exercise. This was the last time. These were the last horses that would go through their hands. The young men watched with critical, callous look. They were all frightened at the collapse of their lives, and the sense of disaster in which they were involved left them no inner freedom.

Yet they were three fine, well-set fellows enough. Joe, the eldest, was a man of thirty-three, broad and handsome in a hot, flushed way. His face was red, he twisted his black moustache over a thick finger, his eyes were shallow and restless. He had a sensual way of uncovering his teeth when he laughed, and his bearing was stupid. Now he watched the horses with a glazed look of helplessness in his eyes, a certain stupor of downfall.

The great draught-horses swung past. They were tied head to tail, four of them, and they heaved along to where a lane branched off from the highroad, planting their great hoofs floutingly in the fine black mud, swinging their great rounded haunches sumptuously, and trotting a few sudden steps as they were led into the lane, round the corner. Every movement showed a massive, slumbrous strength, and a stupidity which held them in subjection. The groom at the head looked back, jerking the leading rope. And the cavalcade moved out of sight up the lane, the tail of the last horse, bobbed up tight and stiff, held out taut from the swinging great haunches as they rocked behind the hedges in a motion like sleep.

Joe watched with glazed hopeless eyes. The horses were almost like his own body to him. He felt he was done for now. Luckily he was engaged to a woman as old as himself, and therefore her father, who was steward of a neighbouring estate, would provide him with a job. He would marry and go into harness. His life was over, he would be a subject animal now.

He turned uneasily aside, the retreating steps of the horses echoing in his ears. Then, with foolish restlessness, he reached for the scraps of bacon-rind from the plates, and making a faint whistling sound, flung them to the terrier that lay against the fender. He watched the dog swallow them, and waited till the creature looked into his eyes. Then a faint grin came on his face, and in a high, foolish voice he said:

"You won't get much more bacon, shall you, you little bitch?"

The dog faintly and dismally wagged its tail, then lowered its haunches, circled round, and lay down again.

There was another helpless silence at the table. Joe sprawled uneasily in his seat, not willing to go till the family conclave was dissolved. Fred Henry, the second brother, was erect, clean-limbed, alert. He had watched the passing of the horses with more sang-froid. If he was an animal, like Joe, he was an animal which controls, not one which is controlled. He was master of any horse, and he carried himself with a well-tempered air of mastery. But he was not master of the situations of life. He pushed his coarse brown moustache upwards, off his lip, and glanced irritably at his sister, who sat impassive and inscrutable.

"You'll go and stop with Lucy for a bit, shan't you?" he asked. The girl did not answer.

"I don't see what else you can do," persisted Fred Henry.

"Go as a skivvy," Joe interpolated laconically.

The girl did not move a muscle.

"If I was her, I should go in for training for a nurse," said Malcolm, the youngest of them all. He was the baby of the family, a young man of twenty-two, with a fresh, jaunty *museau*.

But Mabel did not take any notice of him. They had talked at her and round her for so many years, that she hardly heard them at all.

The marble clock on the mantelpiece softly chimed the half-hour, the dog rose uneasily from the hearthrug and looked at the party at the breakfast table. But still they sat on in inffectual conclave.

"Oh, all right," said Joe suddenly, apropos of nothing. "I'll get a move on."

He pushed back his chair, straddled his knees with a downward jerk, to get them free, in horsey fashion, and went to the fire. Still he did not go out of the room; he was curious to know what the others would do or say. He began to charge his pipe, looking down at the dog and saying, in a high, affected voice:

"Going wi' me? Going wi' me are ter? Tha'rt goin' further tha that counts on just now, dost hear?"

The dog faintly wagged its tail, the man struck out his jaw and covered his pipe with his hands, and puffed intently, losing himself in the tobacco, looking down all the while at the dog with an absent brown eye. The dog looked up at him in mournful distrust. Joe stood with his knees stuck out, in real horsey fashion.

"Have you had a letter from Lucy?" Fred Henry asked of his sister.

"Last week," came the neutral reply.

"And what does she say?"

There was no answer.

"Does she *ask* you to go and stop there?" persisted Fred Henry.

"She says I can if I like."

"Well, then, you'd better. Tell her you'll come on Monday."

This was received in silence.

"That's what you'll do then, is it?" said Fred Henry, in some exasperation.

But she made no answer. There was a silence of futility and irritation in the room. Malcolm grinned fatuously.

"You'll have to make up your mind between now and next Wednesday," said Joe loudly, "or else find yourself lodgings on the kerbstone."

The face of the young woman darkened, but she sat on immutable.

"Here's Jack Fergusson!" exclaimed Malcolm, who was looking aimlessly out of the window.

"Where?" exclaimed Joe, loudly.

"Just gone past."

"Coming in?"

Malcolm craned his neck to see the gate.

"Yes," he said.

There was a silence. Mabel sat on like one condemned, at the head of the table. Then a whistle was heard from the kitchen. The dog got up and barked sharply. Joe opened the door and shouted:

"Come on."

After a moment a young man entered. He was muffled up in overcoat and a purple woollen scarf, and his tweed cap, which he did not remove, was pulled down on his head. He was of medium height, his face was rather long and pale, his eyes looked tired.

"Hello, Jack! Well, Jack!" exclaimed Malcolm and Joe. Fred Henry merely said, "Jack."

"What's doing?" asked the newcomer, evidently addressing Fred Henry.

"Same. We've got to be out by Wednesday. Got a cold?"

"I have—got it bad, too."

"Why don't you stop in?"

"*Me* stop in? Why I can't stand on my legs, perhaps I shall have a chance." The young man spoke huskily. He had a slight Scotch accent.

"It's a knock-out, isn't it," said Joe, boisterously, "if a doctor goes round croaking with a cold. Looks bad for the patients, doesn't it?"

The young doctor looked at him slowly.

"Anything the matter with *you*, then?" he asked sarcastically.

"Not as I know of. Damn your eyes, I hope not. Why?"

"I thought you were very concerned about the patients, wondered if you might be one yourself."

"Damn it, no, I've never been patient to no flaming doctor, and hope I never shall be," returned Joe.

At this point Mabel rose from the table, and they all seemed to become aware of her existence. She began putting the dishes together. The young doctor looked at her, but did not address her. He had not greeted her. She went out of the room with the tray, her face impassive and unchanged.

"When are you off then, all of you?" asked the doctor.

"I'm catching the eleven-forty," replied Malcolm. "Are you goin' down wi' th' trap, Joe?"

"Yes, I've told you I'm going down wi' th' trap, haven't I?"

"We'd better be getting her in then. So long, Jack, if I don't see you before I go," said Malcolm, shaking hands.

He went out, followed by Joe, who seemed to have his tail between his legs.

"Well, this is the devil's own," exclaimed the doctor, when he was left alone with Fred Henry. "Going before Wednesday, are you?"

"That's the orders," replied the other.

"Where, to Northampton?"

"That's it."

"The devil!" exclaimed Ferguson, with quiet chagrin.

And there was silence between the two.

"All settled up, are you?" asked Fergusson.

"About."

There was another pause.

"Well, I shall miss yer, Freddy, boy," said the young doctor.

"And I shall miss thee, Jack," returned the other.

"Miss you like hell," mused the doctor.

Fred Henry turned aside. There was nothing to say. Mabel came in again, to finish clearing the table.

"What are *you* going to do, then, Miss Pervin?" asked Fergusson. "Going to your sister's, are you?"

Mabel looked at him with her steady, dangerous eyes, that always made him uncomfortable, unsettling his superficial ease.

"No," she said.

"Well, what in the name of fortune *are* you going to do? Say what you mean to do," cried Fred Henry, with futile intensity.

But she only averted her head, and continued her work. She folded the white table-cloth, and put on the chenille cloth.

"The sulkiest bitch that ever trod!" muttered her brother.

But she finished her task with perfectly impassive face, the young doctor watching her interestedly all the while. Then she went out.

Fred Henry stared after her, clenching his lips, his blue eyes fixing in sharp antagonism, as he made a grimace of sour exasperation.

"You could bray her into bits, and that's all you'd get out of her," he said in a small, narrowed tone.

The doctor smiled faintly.

"What's she *going* to do, then?" he asked.

"Strike me if *I* know!" returned the other.

There was a pause. Then the doctor stirred.

"I'll be seeing you to-night, shall I?" he said to his friend.

"Ay—where's it to be? Are we going over to Jessdale?"

"I don't know. I've got a cold on me. I'll come round to the Moon and Stars, anyway."

"Let Lizzie and May miss their night for once, eh?"

"That's it—if I feel as I do now."

"All's one—"

The two young men went through the passage and down to the back door together. The house was large, but it was servantless now, and desolate. At the back was a small bricked house-yard, and beyond that a big square, gravelled fine and red, and having stables on two sides. Sloping, dank, winter-dark fields stretched away on the open sides.

But the stables were empty. Joseph Pervin, the father of the family, had been a man of no education, who had become a fairly large horse dealer. The stables had been full of horses, there was a great turmoil and come-and-go of horses and of dealers and grooms. Then the kitchen was full of servants. But of late things had declined. The old man had married a second time, to retrieve his fortunes. Now he was dead and everything was gone to the dogs, there was nothing but debt and threatening.

For months, Mabel had been servantless in the big house, keeping the home together in penury for her ineffectual brothers. She had kept house for ten years. But previously it was with unstinted means. Then, however brutal and coarse everything was, the sense of money had kept her proud, confident. The men might be foulmouthed, the women in the kitchen might have bad reputations, her brothers might have illegitimate children. But so long as there was money, the girl felt herself established, and brutally proud, reserved.

No company came to the house, save dealers and coarse men. Mabel had no associates of her own sex, after her sister went away. But she did not mind. She went regularly to church, she attended to her father. And she lived in the memory of her mother, who had died when she was fourteen, and whom she had loved. She had loved her father, too, in a different way, depending upon him, and feeling secure in him, until at the age of fifty-four he married again. And then she had set hard against him. Now he had died and left them all hopelessly in debt.

She had suffered badly during the period of poverty. Nothing, however, could shake the curious sullen, animal pride that dominated each member of the family. Now, for Mabel, the end had come. Still she would not cast about her. She would follow her own way just the same. She would always hold the keys of her own situation. Mindless and persistent, she endured from day to day. Why should she think? Why should she answer anybody? It was enough that this was the end, and there was no way out. She need not pass any more darkly along the main street of the small town, avoiding every eye. She need not demean herself any more going into the shops and buying the cheapest food. This was at an end. She thought of nobody, not even of herself. Mindless and persistent, she seemed in a sort of ecstasy to be coming nearer to her fulfillment, her own glorification, approaching her dead mother, who was glorified.

In the afternoon she took a little bag, with shears and sponge and a small scrubbing brush, and went out. It was a grey, wintery day, with saddened, dark green fields and an atmosphere blackened by the smoke of foundries not far off. She went quickly, darkly along the causeway, heeding nobody, through the town to the churchyard.

There she always felt secure, as if no one could see her, although as a matter of fact she was exposed to the stare of every one who passed along under the churchyard wall. Nevertheless, once under the shadow of the great looming church, among the graves, she felt immune from the world, reserved within the thick churchyard wall as in another country.

Carefully she clipped the grass from the grave, and arranged the pinky white, small chrysanthemums in the tin cross. When this was done, she took an empty jar from a neighbouring grave, brought water, and carefully, most scrupulously sponged the marble headstone and the coping-stone.

It gave her sincere satisfaction to do this. She felt in immediate contact with the world of her mother. She took minute pains, went through the park in a state bordering on pure happiness, as if in performing this task she came into a subtle, intimate connection with her mother. For the life she followed here in the world was far less real than the world of death she inherited from her mother.

The doctor's house was just by the Church. Fergusson, being a mere hired assistant, was slave to the country-side. As he hurried now to attend to the outpatients in the surgery, glancing across the grave yard with his quick eye, he saw the girl at her task at the grave. She seemed so intent and remote, it was like looking into another world. Some mystical element was touched in him. He slowed down as he walked, watching her as if spell-bound.

She lifted her eyes, feeling him looking. Their eyes met. And each looked away again at once, each feeling, in some way, found out by the other. He lifted his cap and passed on down the road. There remained distinct in his consciousness, like a vision, the memory of her face, lifted from the tombstone in the churchyard, and looking at him with slow, large, portentous eyes. It *was* portentous, her face. It seemed to mesmerize him. There was a heavy power in her eyes which laid hold of his whole being, as if he had drunk some powerful drug. He had been feeling weak and done before. Now the life came back into him, he felt delivered from his own fretted, daily self.

He finished his duties at the surgery as quickly as might be, hastily filling up the bottle of the waiting people with cheap drugs. Then, in perpetual haste, he set off again to visit several cases in another part of his round, before tea-time. At all times he preferred to walk if he could, but particularly when he was not well. He fancied the motion restored him.

The afternoon was falling. It was grey, deadened, and wintry, with a slow, moist, heavy coldness sinking in and deadening all the faculties. But why should he think or notice? He hastily climbed the hill and turned across the dark green fields, following the black cinder-track. In the distance, across a shallow dip in the country, the small town was clustered like smouldering ash, a tower, a spire, a heap of low, raw, extinct houses. And on the nearest fringe of the town, sloping into the dip, was Oldmeadow, the Pervins' house. He could see the stables and the out-buildings distinctly, as they lay towards him on the slope. Well, he would not go there many more times! Another resource would be lost to him, another

place gone: the only company he cared for in the alien, ugly little town he was losing. Nothing but work, drudgery, constant hastening from dwelling to dwelling among the colliers and the iron-workers. It wore him out, but at the same time he had a craving for it. It was a stimulant to him to be in the homes of the working people, moving as it were through the innermost body of their life. His nerves were excited and gratified. He could come so near, into the very lives of the rough, inarticulate, powerfully emotional men and women. He grumbled, he said he hated the hellish hole. But as a matter of fact it excited him, the contact with the rough, strongly-feeling people was a stimulant applied direct to his nerves.

Below Oldmeadow, in the green, shallow, soddened hollow of fields, lay a square, deep pond. Roving across the landscape, the doctor's quick eye detected a figure in black passing through the gate of the field, down towards the pond. He looked again. It would be Mabel Pervin. His mind suddenly became alive and attentive.

Why was she going down there? He pulled up on the path on the slope above, and stood staring. He could just make sure of the small black figure moving in the hollow of the failing day. He seemed to see her in the midst of such obscurity, that he was like a clairvoyant, seeing rather with the mind's eye than with ordinary sight. Yet he could see her positively enough, whilst he kept his eye attentive. He felt, if he looked away from her, in the thick, ugly falling dusk, he would lose her altogether.

He followed her minutely as she moved, direct and intent, like something transmitted rather than stirring in voluntary activity, straight down the field towards the pond. There she stood on the bank for a moment. She never raised her head. Then she waded slowly into the water.

He stood motionless as the small black figure walked slowly and deliberately towards the centre of the pond, very slowly, gradually moving deeper into the motionless water, and still moving forward as the water got up to her breast. Then he could see her no more in the dusk of the dead afternoon.

"There!" he exclaimed. "Would you believe it?"

And he hastened straight down, running over the wet, soddened fields, pushing through the hedges, down into the depression of callous wintry obscurity. It took him several minutes to come to the pond. He stood on the bank, breathing heavily. He could see nothing. His eyes seemed to penetrate the dead water. Yes, perhaps that was the dark shadow of her black clothing beneath the surface of the water.

He slowly ventured into the pond. The bottom was deep, soft clay, he sank in, and the water clasped dead cold round his legs. As he stirred he could smell the cold, rotten clay that fouled up into the water. It was objectionable in his lungs. Still, repelled and yet not heeding, he moved deeper into the pond. The cold water rose over his thighs, over his loins, upon his abdomen. The lower part of his body was all sunk in the hideous cold element. And the bottom was so deeply soft and uncertain he was afraid of pitching with his mouth underneath. He could not swim, and was afraid.

He crouched a little, spreading his hands under the water and moving them round, trying to feel for her. The dead cold pond swayed upon his chest. He moved again, a little deeper, and again, with his hands underneath, he felt all around under the water. And he touched her clothing. But it evaded his fingers. He made a desperate effort to grasp it.

And so doing he lost his balance and went under, horribly, suffocating in the foul earthy water, struggling madly for a few moments. At last, after what seemed an eternity, he got his footing, rose again into the air and looked around. He gasped, and knew he was in the world. Then he looked at the water. She had risen near him. He grasped her clothing, and drawing her nearer, turned to take his way to land again.

He went very slowly, carefully, absorbed in the slow progress. He rose higher, climbing out of the pond. The water was now only about his legs; he was thankful, full of relief to be out of the clutches of the pond. He lifted her and staggered on to the bank, out of the horror of wet, grey clay.

He laid her down on the bank. She was quite unconscious and running with water. He made the water come from her mouth, he worked to restore her. He did not have to work very long before he could feel the breathing begin again in her; she was breathing naturally. He worked a little longer. He could feel her live beneath his hands; she was coming back. He wiped her face, wrapped her in his overcoat, looked round into the dim, dark grey world, then lifted her and staggered down the bank and across the fields.

It seemed an unthinkably long way, and his burden so heavy he felt he would never get to the house. But at last he was in the stable-yard, and then in the houseyard. He opened the door and went into the house. In the kitchen he laid her down on the hearthrug, and called. The house was empty. But the fire was burning in the grate.

Then again he kneeled to attend to her. She was breathing regularly, her eyes were wide open and as if conscious, but there seemed something missing in her look. She was conscious in herself, but unconscious of her surroundings.

He ran upstairs, took blankets from a bed, and put them before the fire to warm. Then he removed her saturated, earthy-smelling clothing, rubbed her dry with a towel, and wrapped her naked in the blankets. Then he went into the dining-room, to look for spirits. There was a little whisky. He drank a gulp himself, and put some into her mouth.

The effect was instantaneous. She looked full into his face, as if she had been seeing him for some time, and yet had only just become conscious of him.

"Dr. Fergusson?" she said.

"What?" he answered.

He was divesting himself of his coat, intending to find some dry clothing upstairs. He could not bear the smell of the dead, clayey water, and he was mortally afraid of his own health.

"What did I do?" she asked.

"Walked into the pond," he replied. He had begun to shudder like one sick, and could hardly attend to her. Her eyes remained full on him, he seemed to be going dark in his mind, looking back at her helplessly. The shuddering became quieter in him, his life came back in him, dark and unknowing, but strong again.

"Was I out of my mind?" she asked, while her eyes were fixed on him all the time.

"Maybe, for the moment," he replied. He felt quiet, because his strength had come back. The strange fretful strain had left him.

"Am I out of my mind now?" she asked.

"Are you?" he reflected a moment. "No," he answered truthfully, "I don't see that you are." He turned his face aside. He was afraid now, because he felt dazed, and felt dimly that her power was stronger than his, in this issue. And she continued to look at him fixedly all the time. "Can you tell me where I shall find some dry things to put on?" he asked.

"Did you dive into the pond for me?" she asked.

"No," he answered. "I walked in. But I went in overhead as well."

There was silence for a moment. He hesitated. He very much wanted to go upstairs to get into dry clothing. But there was another desire in him. And she seemed to hold him. His will

seemed to have gone to sleep, and left him, standing there slack before her. But he felt warm inside himself. He did not shudder at all, though his clothes were sodden on him.

"Why did you?" she asked.

"Because I didn't want you to do such a foolish thing," he said.

"It wasn't foolish," she said, still gazing at him as she lay on the floor, with a sofa cushion under her head. "It was the right thing to do. *I* knew best, then."

"I'll go and shift these wet things," he said. But still he had not the power to move out of her presence, until she sent him. It was as if she had the life of his body in her hands, and he could not extricate himself. Or perhaps he did not want to.

Suddenly she sat up. Then she became aware of her own immediate condition. She felt the blankets about her, she knew her own limbs. For a moment it seemed as if her reason were going. She looked round, with wild eye, as if seeking something. He stood still with fear. She saw her clothing lying scattered.

"Who undressed me?" she asked, her eyes resting full and inevitable on his face.

"I did," he replied, "to bring you round."

For some moments she sat and gazed at him awfully, her lips parted.

"Do you love me, then?" she asked.

He only stood and stared at her, fascinated. His soul seemed to melt.

She shuffled forward on her knees, and put her arms round him, round his legs, and he stood there, pressing her breasts against his knees and thighs, clutching him with strange, convulsive certainty, pressing his thighs against her, drawing him to her face, her throat, as she looked up at him with flaring, humble eyes of transfiguration, triumphant in first possession.

"You love me," she murmured, in strange transport, yearning and triumphant and confident. "You love me. I know you love me, I know."

And she was passionately kissing his knees, through the wet clothing, passionately and indiscriminately kissing his knees, his legs, as if unaware of everything.

He looked down at the tangled wet hair, the wild, bare, animal shoulders. He was amazed, bewildered, and afraid. He had never thought of loving her. He had never wanted to love her. When he rescued her and restored her, he was a doctor, and she was a patient. He had had no single personal thought of her. Nay, this introduction of the personal element was very distasteful to him, a violation of his professional honour. It was horrible to have her there embracing his knees. It was horrible. He revolted from it, violently. And yet—and yet—he had not the power to break away.

She looked at him again, with the same supplication of powerful love, and the same transcendent, frightening light of triumph. In view of the delicate flame which seemed to come from her face like a light, he was powerless. And yet he had never intended to love her. He had never intended. And something stubborn in him could not give way.

"You love me," she repeated, in a murmur of deep, rhapsodic assurance. "You love me."

Her hands were drawing him, drawing him down to her. He was afraid, even a little horrified. For he had, really, no intention of loving her. Yet her hands were drawing him towards her. He put out his hand quickly to steady himself, and grasped her bare shoulder. A flame seemed to burn the hand that grasped her soft shoulder. He had no intention of loving her; his whole will was against his yielding. It was horrible. And yet wonderful was the touch of her shoulders, beautiful the shining of her face. Was she perhaps mad? He had a horror of yielding to her. Yet something in him ached also.

He had been staring away at the door, away from her. But his hand remained on her shoulder. She had gone suddenly very still. He looked down at her. Her eyes were now wide with fear, with doubt, the light was dying from her face, a shadow of terrible greyness was returning. He could not bear the touch of her eyes' question upon him, and the look of death behind the question.

With an inward groan he gave way. and let his heart yield towards her. A sudden gentle smile came on his face. And her eyes, which never left his face, slowly, slowly filled with tears. He watched the strange water rise in her eyes, like some slow fountain coming up. And his heart seemed to burn and melt away in his breast.

He could not bear to look at her any more. He dropped on his knees and caught her head with his arms and pressed her face against his throat. She was very still. His heart, which seemed to have broken, was burning with a kind of agony in his breast. And he felt her slow, hot tears wetting his throat. But he could not move.

He felt the hot tears wet his neck and the hollows of his neck, and he remained motionless, suspended through one of man's eternities. Only now it had become indispensable to him to have her face pressed close to him; he could never let her go again. He could never let her head go away from the close clutch of his arm. He wanted to remain like that for ever, with his heart hurting him in a pain that was also life to him. Without knowing, he was looking down on her damp, soft brown hair.

Then, as it were suddenly, he smelt the horrid stagnant smell of that water. And at the same moment she drew away from him and looked at him. Her eyes were wistful and unfathomable. He was afraid of them, and he fell to kissing her, not knowing what he was doing. He wanted her eyes not to have that terrible, wistful, unfathomable look.

When she turned her face to him again, a faint delicate flush was glowing, and there was again dawning that terrible shining of joy in her eyes, which really terrified him, and yet which he now wanted to see, because he feared the look of doubt still more.

"You love me?" she said, rather faltering.

"Yes." The word cost him a painful effort. Not because it wasn't true. But because it was too newly true, the *saying* seemed to tear open again his newly-torn heart. And he hardly wanted it to be true, even now.

She lifted her face to him, and he bent forward and kissed her on the mouth, gently, with the one kiss that is an eternal pledge. And as he kissed her his heart strained again in his breast. He never intended to love her. But now it was over. He had crossed over the gulf to her, and all that he had left behind had shrivelled and become void.

After the kiss, her eyes again slowly filled with tears. She sat still, away from him, with her face drooped aside, and her hands folded in her lap. The tears fell very slowly. There was complete silence. He too sat there motionless and silent on the hearthrug. The strange pain of his heart that was broken seemed to consume him. That he should love her? That this was love! That he should be ripped open in this way! Him, a doctor! How they would all jeer if they knew! It was agony to him to think they might know.

In the curious naked pain of the thought he looked again to her. She was sitting there drooped into a muse. He saw a tear fall, and his heart flared hot. He saw for the first time that one of her shoulders was quite uncovered, one arm bare, he could see one of her small breasts; dimly, because it had become almost dark in the room.

"Why are you crying!" he asked, in an altered voice.

She looked up at him, and behind her tears the consciousness of her situation for the first time brought a dark look of shame to her eyes.

"I'm not crying, really," she said, watching him half frightened.

He reached his hand, and softly closed it on her bare arm.

"I love you! I love you!" he said in a soft, low vibrating voice, unlike himself.

She shrank, and dropped her head. The soft, penetrating grip of his hand on her arm distressed her. She looked up at him.

"I want to go," she said. "I want to go and get you some dry things."

"Why?" he said. "I'm all right."

"But I want to go," she said. "And I want you to change your things."

He released her arm, and she wrapped herself in the blanket, looking at him rather frightened. And still she did not rise.

"Kiss me," she said wistfully.

He kissed her, but briefly, half in anger.

Then, after a second, she rose nervously, all mixed up in the blanket. He watched her in her confusion, as she tried to extricate herself and wrap herself up so that she could walk. He watched her relentlessly, as she knew. And as she went, the blanket trailing, and as he saw a glimpse of her feet and her white leg, he tried to remember her as she was when he had wrapped her in the blanket. But then he didn't want to remember, because she had been nothing to him then, and his nature revolted from remembering her as she was when she was nothing to him.

A tumbling, muffled noise from within the dark house startled him. Then he heard her voice:—"There are clothes." He rose and went to the foot of the stairs, and gathered up the garments she had thrown down. Then he came back to the fire, to rub himself down and dress. He grinned at his own appearance when he had finished.

The fire was sinking, so he put on coal. The house was now quite dark, save for the light of a streetlamp that shone in faintly from beyond the holly trees. He lit the gas with matches he found on the mantlepiece. Then he emptied the pockets of his own clothes, and threw all his wet things in a heap into the scullery. After which he gathered up her sodden clothes, gently, and put them in a separate heap on the copper-top in the scullery.

It was six o'clock on the clock. His own watch had stopped. He ought to go back to the surgery. He waited, and still she did not come down. So he went to the foot of the stairs and called:

"I shall have to go."

Almost immediately he heard her coming down. She had on her best dress of black voile, and her hair was tidy, but still damp. She looked at him—and in spite of herself, smiled.

"I don't like you in those clothes," she said.

"Do I look a sight?" he answered.

They were shy of one another.

"I'll make you some tea," she said.

"No, I must go."

"Must you?" And she looked at him again with the wide, strained, doubtful eyes. And again, from the pain of his breast, he knew how he loved her. He went and bent to kiss her, gently, passionately, with his heart's painful kiss.

"And my hair smells so horrible," she murmured in distraction. "And I'm so awful, I'm so awful! Oh, no, I'm too awful." And she broke into bitter, heartbroken sobbing. "You can't want to love me, I'm horrible."

"Don't be silly, don't be silly," he said, trying to comfort her, kissing her, holding her in his arms. "I want you, I want to marry you, we're going to be married, quickly, quickly—tomorrow if I can."

But she only sobbed terribly, and cried:

"I feel awful, I feel awful, I feel I'm horrible to you."

"No, I want you, I want you," was all he answered, blindly, with that terrible intonation which frightened her almost more than her horror lest he should *not* want her.

DRAMA

George Bernard Shaw (1856–1950)

MAJOR BARBARA

CHARACTERS

SIR ANDREW UNDERSHAFT

LADY BRITOMART UNDERSHAFT, *his wife*

BARBARA, *his elder daughter, a Major in the Salvation Army*

SARAH, *his younger daughter*

STEPHEN, *his son*

ADOLPHUS CUSINS, *a professor of Greek in love with Barbara*

CHARLES LOMAX, *young-man-about-town engaged to Sarah*

MORRISON, *Lady Britomart's butler*

BRONTERRE O'BRIEN ["Snobby"] PRICE, *a cobbler-carpenter down on his luck*

MRS ROMOLA ["Rummy"] MITCHENS, *a worn-out lady who relies on the Salvation Army worker*

JENNY HILL, *a young Salvation Army worker*

PETER SHIRLEY, *an unemployed coal-broker*

BILL WALKER, *a bully*

MRS BAINES, *Commissioner in the Salvation Army*

BILTON, *a foreman at Perivale St. Andrews*

The action of the play occurs within several days in January, 1906.

ACT I *The Library of Lady Britomart's house in Wilton Crescent, fashionable London suburb.*

ACT II *The yard of the Salvation Army shelter in West Ham, an industrial suburb in London's East End.*

ACT III *The library in Lady Britomart's house; a parapet overlooking Perivale St. Andrews, a region in Middlesex northwest of London.*

Act I

It is after dinner in January 1906, in the library in LADY BRITOMART UNDERSHAFT'S *house in Wilton Crescent. A large and comfortable settee is in the middle of the room, upholstered in dark leather. A person sitting on it {it is vacant at present} would have, on his right,* LADY BRITOMART'S *writing-table, with the lady herself busy at it; a smaller writing-table behind him on his left; the door behind him on* LADY BRITO-

MART'S *side; and a window with a window-seat directly on his left. Near the window is an armchair.*

LADY BRITOMART *is a women of fifty or thereabouts, well dressed and yet careless of her dress, well bred and quite reckless of her breeding, well mannered and yet appallingly outspoken and indifferent to the opinion of her interlocutors, amiable and yet peremptory, arbitrary, and high-tempered to the last bearable degree, and withal a very typical managing matron of the upper class, treated as a naughty child until she grew into a scolding mother, and finally settling down with plenty of practical ability and worldly experience, limited in the oddest way with domestic and class limitations, conceiving the universe exactly as if it were a large house in Wilton Crescent, though handling her corner of it very effectively on the assumption, and being quite enlightened and liberal as to the books in the library, the pictures on the wall, the music in the portfolios, and the articles in the papers.*
Her son, STEPHEN, *comes in. He is a gravely correct young man under 25, taking himself very seriously, but still in some awe of his mother, from childish habit and bachelor shyness rather than from any weakness of character.*

STEPHEN: What's the matter?

LADY BRITOMART: Presently, Stephen. [STEPHEN *submissively walks to the settee and sits down. He takes up a liberal weekly called* The Speaker]

LADY BRITOMART: Don't begin to read, Stephen. I shall require all your attention.

STEPHEN: It was only while I was waiting—

LADY BRITOMART: Don't make excuses, Stephen. {He *puts down* The Speaker] Now! {She *finishes her writing, rises; and comes to the settee}* I have not kept you waiting very long, I think.

STEPHEN: Not at all, mother.

LADY BRITOMART: Bring me my cushion. {He *takes the cushion from the chair at the desk and arranges it for her as she sits down on the settee}* Sit down. {He *sits down and fingers his tie nervously}* Don't fiddle with your tie, Stephen: there is nothing the matter with it.

STEPHEN: I beg your pardon. {He *fiddles with his watch chain instead}*

LADY BRITOMART: Now are you attending to me, Stephen?

STEPHEN: Of course, mother.

LADY BRITOMART: No: it's not of course. I want something much more than your everyday matter-of-course attention. I am going to speak to you very seriously, Stephen. I wish you to let that chain alone.

STEPHEN: {Hastily *relinquishing the chain}* Have I done anything to annoy you, mother? If so, it was quite unintentional.

LADY BRITOMART: {Astonished} Nonsense! {With *some remorse}* My poor boy, did you think I was angry with you?

STEPHEN: What is it, then, mother? You are making me very uneasy.

LADY BRITOMART: {Squaring *herself at him rather aggressively}* Stephen: may I ask how soon you intend to realize that you are a grown-up man, and that I am only a woman?

STEPHEN: {Amazed} Only a—

LADY BRITOMART: Don't repeat my words, please: it is a most aggravating habit. You must learn to face life seriously, Stephen. I really cannot bear the whole burden of our family affairs any longer. You must advise me: you must assume the responsibility.

STEPHEN: I!

LADY BRITOMART: Yes, you, of course. You were twenty-four last June. You've been at Harrow and Cambridge. You've been to India and Japan. You must know a lot of things, now; unless you have wasted your time most scandalously. Well, advise me.

STEPHEN: {Much *perplexed}* You

know I have never interfered in the household—

LADY BRITOMART: No: I should think not. I don't want you to order the dinner.

STEPHEN: I mean in our family affairs.

LADY BRITOMART: Well, you must interfere now; for they are getting quite beyond me.

STEPHEN: *{Troubled}* I have thought sometimes that perhaps I ought; but really, mother, I know so little about them; and what I do know is so pain ful—it is so impossible to mention some things to you—*{He stops, ashamed}*

LADY BRITOMART: I suppose you mean your father.

STEPHEN: *{Almost inaudibly}* Yes.

LADY BRITOMART: My dear: we can't go on all our lives not mentioning him. Of course you were quite right not to open the subject until I asked you to; but you are old enough now to be taken into my confidence, and to help me to deal with him about the girls.

STEPHEN: But the girls are all right. They are engaged.

LADY BRITOMART: *{Complacently}* Yes. I have made a very good match for Sarah. Charles Lomax will be a millionaire at thirty-five. But that is ten years ahead; and in the meantime his trustees cannot under the terms of his father's will allow him more than £800 a year.

STEPHEN: But the will says also that if he increases his income by his own exertions, they may double the increase.

LADY BRITOMART: Charles Lomax's exertions are much more likely to decrease his income than to increase it. Sarah will have to find at least another £800 a year for the next ten years; and even then they will be as poor as church mice. And what about Barbara? I thought Barbara was going to make the most brilliant career of all of you. And what does she do? Joins the Salvation Army; discharges her maid; lives on a pound a week; and walks in one evening with a professor of Greek whom she has picked up in the street, and who pretends to be a Salvationist, and actually plays the big drum for her in public because he has fallen head over ears in love with her.

STEPHEN: I was certainly rather taken aback when I heard they were engaged. Cusins is a very nice fellow, certainly: nobody would ever guess that he was born in Australia; but—

LADY BRITOMART: Oh, Adolphus Cusins will make a very good husband. After all, nobody can say a word against Greek: it stamps a man at once as an educated gentleman. And my family, thank Heaven, is not a pigheaded Tory one. We are Whigs, and believe in liberty. Let snobbish people say what they please: Barbara shall marry, not the man they like, but the man *I* like.

STEPHEN: Of course I was thinking only of his income. However, he is not likely to be extravagant.

LADY BRITOMART: Don't be too sure of that, Stephen. I know your quiet, simple, refined, poetic people like Adolphus—quite content with the best of everything! They cost more than your extravagant people, who are always as mean as they are second rate. No: Barbara will need at least £2000 a year. You see it means two additional households. Besides, my dear, you must marry soon. I don't approve of the present fashion of philandering bachelors and late marriages; and I am trying to arrange something for you.

STEPHEN: It's very good of you, mother; but perhaps I had better arrange that for myself.

LADY BRITOMART: Nonsense! you are much too young to begin match-making: you would be taken in by some pretty little nobody. Of course I don't mean that you are not to be consulted: you know that as well as I do. [STEPHEN *closes his lips and is silent}* Now don't sulk, Stephen.

STEPHEN: I am not sulking, mother. What has all this got to do with—with—with my father?

LADY BRITOMART: My dear Stephen:

where is the money to come from? It is easy enough for you and the other children to live on my income as long as we are in the same house; but I can't keep four families in four separate houses. You know how poor my father is: he has barely seven thousand a year now; and really, if he were not the Earl of Stevenage, he would have to give up society. He can do nothing for us. He says, naturally enough, that it is absurd that he should be asked to provide for the children of a man who is rolling in money. You see, Stephen, your father must be fabulously wealthy, because there is always a war going on somewhere.

STEPHEN: You need not remind me of that, mother. I have hardly ever opened a newspaper in my life without seeing our name in it. The Undershaft torpedo! The Undershaft quick firers! The Undershaft ten inch! The Undershaft disappearing rampart gun! The Undershaft submarine! and now the Undershaft aerial battleship! At Harrow they called me the Woolwich Infant. At Cambridge it was the same. A little brute at King's who was always trying to get up revivals, spoilt my Bible— your first birthday present to me—by writing under my name, "Son and heir to Undershaft and Lazarus, Death and Destruction Dealers: address, Christendom and Judea." But that was not so bad as the way I was kowtowed to everywhere because my father was making millions by selling cannons.

LADY BRITOMART: It is not only the cannons, but the war loans that Lazarus arranges under cover of giving credit for the cannons. You know, Stephen, it's perfectly scandalous. Those two men, Andrew Undershaft and Lazarus, positively have Europe under their thumbs. That is why your father is able to behave as he does. He is above the law. Do you think Bismarck or Gladstone or Disraeli could have openly defied every social and moral obligation all their lives as your father has? They simply wouldn't have dared. I asked Gladstone to take it up. I asked *The Times* to take it up. I asked the Lord Chamberlain to take it up. But it was just like asking them to declare war on the Sultan. They wouldn't. They said they couldn't touch him. I believe they were afraid.

STEPHEN: What could they do? He does not actually break the law.

LADY BRITOMART: Not break the law! He is always breaking the law. He broke the law when he was born: his parents were not married.

STEPHEN: Mother! Is that true?

LADY BRITOMART: Of course it's true: that was why we separated.

STEPHEN: He married without letting you know this!

LADY BRITOMART: {Rather taken aback by this inference} Oh no. To do Andrew justice, that was not the sort of thing he did. Besides, you know the Undershaft motto: Unashamed. Everybody knew.

STEPHEN: But you said that was why you separated.

LADY BRITOMART: Yes, because he was not content with being a foundling himself: he wanted to disinherit you for another foundling. That was what I couldn't stand.

STEPHEN: {Ashamed} Do you mean for—for—for—

LADY BRITOMART: Don't stammer, Stephen. Speak distinctly.

STEPHEN: But this is so frightful to me, mother. To have to speak to you about such things!

LADY BRITOMART: It's not pleasant for me, either, especially if you are still so childish that you must make it worse by a display of embarrassment. It is only in the middle classes, Stephen, that people get into a state of dumb helpless horror when they find that there are wicked people in the world. In our class, we have to decide what is to be done with wicked people; and nothing should disturb our self-possession. Now ask your question properly.

STEPHEN: Mother: you have no consideration for me. For Heaven's sake either treat me as a child, as you always do, and tell me nothing at all; or tell me everything and let me take it as best I can.

LADY BRITOMART: Treat you as a child! What do you mean? It is most unkind and ungrateful of you to say such a thing. You know I have never treated any of you as children. I have always made you my companions and friends, and allowed you perfect freedom to do and say whatever you liked, so long as you liked what I could approve of.

STEPHEN: {Desperately} I daresay we have been the very imperfect children of a very perfect mother; but I do beg of you to let me alone for once, and tell me about this horrible business of my father wanting to set me aside for another son.

LADY BRITOMART: {Amazed} Another son! I never said anything of the kind. I never dreamt of such a thing. This is what comes of interrupting me.

STEPHEN: But you said—

LADY BRITOMART: {Cutting him short} Now be a good boy, Stephen, and listen to me patiently. The Undershafts are descended from a foundling in the parish of St Andrew Undershaft in the city. That was long ago, in the reign of James the First. Well, this foundling was adopted by an armorer and gunmaker. In the course of time the foundling succeeded to the business; and from some notion of gratitude, or some vow or something, he adopted another foundling, and left the business to him. And that foundling did the same. Ever since that, the cannon business has always been left to an adopted foundling named Andrew Undershaft.

STEPHEN: But did they never marry? Were there no legitimate sons?

LADY BRITOMART: Oh yes: they married just as your father did; and they were rich enough to buy land for their own children and leave them well provided for. But they always adopted and trained some foundling to succeed them in the business; and of course they always quarreled with their wives furiously over it. Your father was adopted in that way; and he pretends to consider himself bound to keep up the tradition and adopt somebody to leave the business to. Of course I was not going to stand that. There may have been some reason for it when the Undershafts could only marry women in their own class, whose sons were not fit to govern great estates. But there could be no excuse for passing over my son.

STEPHEN: {Dubiously} I am afraid I should make a poor hand of managing a cannon foundry.

LADY BRITOMART: Nonsense! you could easily get a manager and pay him a salary.

STEPHEN: My father evidently had no great opinion of my capacity.

LADY BRITOMART: Stuff, child! you were only a baby: it had nothing to do with your capacity. Andrew did it on principle, just as he did every perverse and wicked thing on principle. When my father remonstrated, Andrew actually told him to his face that history tells us of only two successful institutions: one the Undershaft firm, and the other the Roman Empire under the Antonines. That was because the Antonine emperors all adopted their successors. Such rubbish! The Stevenages are as good as the Antonines, I hope; and you are a Stevenage. But that was Andrew all over. There you have the man! Always clever and unanswerable when he was defending nonsense and wickedness: always awkward and sullen when he had to behave sensibly and decently.

STEPHEN: Then it was on my account that your home life was broken up, mother. I am sorry.

LADY BRITOMART: Well, dear, there were other differences. I really cannot bear an immoral man. I am not a Pharisee, I hope; and I should not have minded his merely doing wrong things: we are none of us perfect. But your father didn't exactly do wrong things:

he said them and thought them: that was what was so dreadful. He really had a sort of religion of wrongness. Just as one doesn't mind men practicing immorality so long as they own that they are in the wrong by preaching morality; so I couldn't forgive Andrew for preaching immorality while he practiced morality. You would all have grown up without principles, without any knowledge of right and wrong, if he had been in the house. You know, my dear, your father was a very attractive man in some ways. Children did not dislike him; and he took advantage of it to put the wickedest ideas into their heads, and make them quite unmanageable. I did not dislike him myself: very far from it; but nothing can bridge over moral disagreement.

STEPHEN: All this simply bewilders me, mother. People may differ about matters of opinion, or even about religion; but how can they differ about right and wrong? Right is right; and wrong is wrong; and if a man cannot distinguish them properly, he is either a fool or a rascal: that's all.

LADY BRITOMART: *{Touched}* That's my own boy! *{She pats his cheek}* Your father never could answer that: he used to laugh and get out of it under cover of some affectionate nonsense. And now that you understand the situation, what do you advise me to do?

STEPHEN: Well, what can you do?

LADY BRITOMART: I must get the money somehow.

STEPHEN: We cannot take money from him. I had rather go and live in some cheap place like Bedford Square or even Hampstead than take a farthing of his money.

LADY BRITOMART: But after all, Stephen, our present income comes from Andrew.

STEPHEN: *{Shocked}* I never knew that.

LADY BRITOMART: Well, you surely didn't suppose your grandfather had anything to give me. The Stevenages could not do everything for you. We gave you social position. Andrew had to contribute something. He had a very good bargain, I think.

STEPHEN: *{Bitterly}* We are utterly dependent on him and his cannons, then?

LADY BRITOMART: Certainly not: the money is settled. But he provided it. So you see it is not a question of taking money from him or not: it is simply a question of how much. I don't want any more for myself.

STEPHEN: Nor do I.

LADY BRITOMART: But Sarah does; and Barbara does. That is, Charles Lomax and Adolphus Cusins will cost them more. So I must put my pride in my pocket and ask for it, I suppose. That is your advise, Stephen, is it not?

STEPHEN: No.

LADY BRITOMART: *{Sharply}* Stephen!

STEPHEN: Of course if you are determined—

LADY BRITOMART: I am not determined: I ask your advice; and I am waiting for it. I will not have all the responsibility thrown on my shoulders.

STEPHEN: *{Obstinately}* I would die sooner than ask him for another penny.

LADY BRITOMART: *{Resignedly}* You mean that *I* must ask him. Very well, Stephen: it shall be as you wish. You will be glad to know that your grandfather concurs. But he thinks I ought to ask Andrew to come here and see the girls. After all he must have some natural affection for them.

STEPHEN: Ask him here! ! !

LADY BRITOMART: Do not repeat my words, Stephen. Where else can I ask him?

STEPHEN: I never expected you to ask him at all.

LADY BRITOMART: Now don't tease, Stephen. Come! you see that it is necessary that he should pay us a visit, don't you?

STEPHEN: *{Reluctantly}* I suppose so, if the girls cannot do without his money.

LADY BRITOMART: Thank you,

Stephen: I knew you would give me the right advice when it was properly explained to you. I have asked your father to come this evening. [STEPHEN *bounds from his seat}* Don't jump, Stephen: it fidgets me.

STEPHEN: *{In utter consternation}* Do you mean to say that my father is coming here to-night—that he may be here at any moment?

LADY BRITOMART: *{Looking at her watch}* I said nine. *{He gasps. She rises}* Ring the bell, please. [STEPHEN *goes to the smaller writing table; presses a button on it; and sits at it with his elbows on the table and his head in his hands, outwitted and overwhelmed}* It is ten minutes to nine yet; and I have to prepare the girls. I asked Charles Lomax and Adolphus to dinner on purpose that they might be here. Andrew had better see them in case he should cherish any delusions as to their being capable of supporting their wives. *{The butler enters: LADY BRITOMART goes behind the settee to speak to him}* Morrison: go up to the drawing-room and tell everybody to come down here at once. [MORRISON *withdraws.* LADY BRITOMART *turns to* STEPHEN] Now remember, Stephen: I shall need all your countenance and authority. *{He rises and tries to recover some vestige of these attributes}* Give me a chair, dear. *{He pushes a chair forward from the wall to where she stands, near the smaller writing table. She sits down; and he goes to the armchair, into which he throws himself}* I don't know how Barbara will take it. Ever since they made her a major in the Salvation Army she has developed a propensity to have her own way and order people about which quite cows me sometimes. It's not ladylike: I'm sure I don't know where she picked it up. Anyhow, Barbara shan't bully me; but still it's just as well that your father should be here before she has time to refuse to meet him or make a fuss. Don't look nervous, Stephen: it will only encourage Barbara to make difficulties. *I* am nervous enough, goodness knowns; but I don't shew it.

[SARAH *and* BARBARA *come in with their respective young men,* CHARLES LOMAX *and* ADOLPHUS CUSINS. SARAH *is slender, bored, and mundane.* BARBARA *is robuster, jollier, much more energetic.* SARAH *is fashionably dressed:* BARBARA *is in Salvation Army uniform.* LOMAX, *a young man about town, is like many other young men about town. He is afflicted with a frivolous sense of humor which plunges him at the most inopportune moments into paroxysms of imperfectly suppressed laughter.* CUSINS *is a spectacled student, slight, thin haired, and sweet voiced, with a more complex form of* LOMAX's *complaint. His sense of humor is intellectual and subtle, and is complicated by an appalling temper. The life-long struggle of a benevolent temperament and a high conscience against impulses of inhuman ridicule and fierce impatience has set up a chronic strain which has visibly wrecked his constitution. He is a most implacable, determined, tenacious, intolerant person who by mere force of character presents himself as—and indeed actually is— considerate, gentle, explanatory, even mild and apologetic, capable possibly of murder, but not of cruelty or coarseness. By the operation of some instinct which is not merciful enough to blind him with the illusions of love, he is obstinately bent on marrying* BARBARA. LOMAX *likes* SARAH *and thinks it will be rather a lark to marry her. Consequently he has not attempted to resist* LADY BRITOMART's *arrangements to that end.*

All four look as if they had been having a good deal of fun in the drawing room. The girls enter first, leaving the swains outside. SARAH *comes to the settee.* BARBARA *comes in after her and stops at the door}*

BARBARA: Are Cholly and Dolly to come in?

LADY BRITOMART: *{Forcibly}* Barbara: I will not have Charles called

Cholly: the vulgarity of it positively makes me ill.

BARBARA: It's all right, mother: Cholly is quite correct nowadays. Are they to come in?

LADY BRITOMART: Yes, if they will behave themselves.

BARBARA: *{Through the door}* Come in, Dolly; and behave yourself. [BARBARA *comes to her mother's writing table.* CUSINS *enters smiling, and wanders towards* LADY BRITOMART]

SARAH: *{Calling}* Come in, Cholly. [LOMAX *enters, controlling his features very imperfectly, and places himself vaguely between* SARAH *and* BARBARA]

LADY BRITOMART: *{Peremptorily}* Sit down, all of you. *{They sit.* CUSINS *crosses to the window and seats himself there.* LOMAX *takes a chair.* BARBARA *sits at the writing table and* SARAH *on the settee}* I don't in the least know what you are laughing at, Adolphus. I am surprised at you, though I expected nothing better from Charles Lomax.

CUSINS: *{In a remarkably gentle voice}* Barbara has been trying to teach me the West Ham Salvation March.

LADY BRITOMART: I see nothing to laugh at in that; nor should you if you are really converted.

CUSINS: *{Sweetly}* You were not present. It was really funny, I believe.

LOMAX: Ripping.

LADY BRITOMART: Be quiet, Charles. Now listen to me, children. Your father is coming here this evening. *{General stupefaction.* LOMAX, SARAH, *and* BARBARA *rise:* SARAH *scared, and* BARBARA *amused and expectant}*

LOMAX: *{Remonstrating}* Oh I say!

LADY BRITOMART: You are not called on to say anything, Charles.

SARAH: Are you serious, mother?

LADY BRITOMART: Of course I am serious. It is on your account, Sarah, and also on Charles's. *{Silence.* SARAH *sits, with a shrug.* CHARLES *looks painfully unworthy}* I hope you are not going to object, Barbara.

BARBARA: I! why should I? My father

has a soul to be saved like anybody else. He's quite welcome as far as I am concerned. *{She sits on the table, and softly whistles "Onward, Christian Soldiers"}*

LOMAX: *{Still remonstrant}* But really, don't you know! Oh I say!

LADY BRITOMART: *{Frigidly}* What do you wish to convey, Charles?

LOMAX: Well, you must admit that this is a bit thick.

LADY BRITOMART: *{Turning with ominous suavity to* CUSINS] Adolphus: you are a professor of Greek. Can you translate Charles Lomax's remarks into reputable English for us?

CUSINS: *{Cautiously}* If I may say so, Lady Brit, I think Charles has rather happily expressed what we all feel. Homer, speaking to Autolycus, uses the same phrase. πυκινὸν δόμον ἐλθεῖν means a bit thick.

LOMAX: *{Handsomely}* Not that I mind, you know, if Sarah don't *{He sits}*

LADY BRITOMART: *{Crushingly}* Thank you. Have I your permission, Adolphus, to invite my own husband to my own house?

CUSINS: *{Gallantly}* You have my unhesitating support in everything you do.

LADY BRITOMART: Tush! Sarah: have you nothing to say?

SARAH: Do you mean that he is coming regularly to live here?

LADY BRITOMART: Certainly not. The spare room is ready for him if he likes to stay for a day or two and see a little more of you; but there are limits.

SARAH: Well, he can't eat us, I suppose. *I* don't mind.

LOMAX: *{Chuckling}* I wonder how the old man will take it.

LADY BRITOMART: Much as the old woman will, no doubt, Charles.

LOMAX: *{Abashed}* I didn't mean—at least—

LADY BRITOMART: You didn't think, Charles. You never do; and the result is you never mean anything. And now please attend to me, children. Your father will be quite a stranger to us.

LOMAX: I suppose he hasn't seen Sarah since she was a little kid.

LADY BRITOMART: Not since she was a little kid, Charles, as you express it with that elegance of diction and refinement of thought that seem never to desert you. Accordingly—er— {*Impatiently*} Now I have forgotten what I was going to say. That comes of your proviking me to be sarcastic, Charles. Adolphus: will you kindly tell me where I was.

CUSINS: {*Sweetly*} You were saying that as Mr. Undershaft has not seen his children since they were babies, he will form his opinion of the way you have brought them up from their behavior tonight, and that therefore you wish us all to be particularly careful to conduct ourselves well, especially Charles.

LADY BRITOMART: {*With emphatic approval*} Precisely.

LOMAX: Look here, Dolly: Lady Brit didn't say that.

LADY BRITOMART: {*Vehemently*} I did, Charles. Adolphus's recollection is perfectly correct. It is most important that you should be good; and I do beg you for once not to pair off into opposite corners and giggle and whisper while I am speaking to your father.

BARBARA: All right, mother. We'll do you credit. {*She comes off the table, and sits in her chair with ladylike elegance*}

LADY BRITOMART: Remember Charles, that Sarah will want to feel proud of you instead of ashamed of you.

LOMAX: Oh I say! there's nothing to be exactly proud of, don't you know.

LADY BRITOMART: Well, try and look as if there was. [MORRISON, *pale and dismayed, breaks into the room in unconcealed disorder*}

MORRISON: Might I speak a word to you, my lady?

LADY BRITOMART: Nonsense! Shew him up.

MORRISON: Yes, my lady. {*He goes*}

LOMAX: Does Morrison know who it is?

LADY BRITOMART: Of course. Morrison has always been with us.

LOMAX: It must be a regular corker for him, don't you know.

LADY BRITOMART: Is this a moment to get on my nerves, Charles, with your outrageous expressions?

LOMAX: But this is something out of the ordinary, really—

MORRISON: {*At the door*} The—er— Mr. Undershaft. {*He retreats in confusion.* ANDREW UNDERSHAFT *comes in. All rise.* LADY BRITOMART *meets him in the middle of the room behind the settee.*

ANDREW *is, on the surface a stoutish, easy-going elderly man, with kindly patient manners, and an engaging simplicity of character. But he has a watchful, deliberate, waiting, listening face, and formidable reserves of power, both bodily and mental, in his capacious chest and long head. His gentleness is partly that of a strong man who has learnt by experience that his natural grip hurts ordinary people unless he handles them very carefully, and partly the mellowness of age and success. He is also a little shy in his present very delicate situation*}

LADY BRITOMART: Good evening, Andrew.

UNDERSHAFT: How do'ye do, my dear.

LADY BRITOMART: You look a good deal older.

UNDERSHAFT: {*Apologetically*} I am somewhat older. {*Taking her hand with a touch of courtship*} Time has stood still with you.

LADY BRITOMART: {*Throwing away his hand*} Rubbish! This is your family.

UNDERSHAFT: {*Surprised*} Is it so large? I am sorry to say my memory is failing very badly in some things. {*He offers his hand with paternal kindness to* LOMAX}

LOMAX: {*Jerkily shaking his hand*} Ahdedoo.

UNDERSHAFT: I can see you are my eldest. I am very glad to meet you again, my boy.

LOMAX: {*Remonstrating*} No, but

look here don't you know—*{Overcome}* Oh I say!

LADY BRITOMART: *{Recovering from momentary speechlessness}* Andrew: do you mean to say that you don't remember how many children you have?

UNDERSHAFT: Well, I am afraid I— They have grown so much—er. Am I making any ridiculous mistake? I may as well confess: I recollect only one son. But so many things have happened since, of course—er—

LADY BRITOMART: *{Decisively}* Andrew: you are talking nonsense. Of course you have only one son.

UNDERSHAFT: Perhaps you will be good enough to introduce me, my dear.

LADY BRITOMART: That is Charles Lomax, who is engaged to Sarah.

UNDERSHAFT: My dear sir, I beg your pardon.

LOMAX: Notatall. Delighted, I assure you.

LADY BRITOMART: This is Stephen.

UNDERSHAFT: *{Bowing}* Happy to make your acquaintance, Mr. Stephen. Then *{Going to* CUSINS] you must be my son. *{Taking* CUSINS' *hands in his}* How are you, my young friend? *{To* LADY BRITOMART] He is very like you, my love.

CUSINS: You flatter me, Mr. Undershaft. My name is Cusins: engaged to Barbara. *{Very explicitly}* That is Major Barbara Undershaft, of the Salvation Army. That is Sarah, your second daughter. This is Stephen Undershaft, your son.

UNDERSHAFT: My dear Stephen, I beg your pardon.

STEPHEN: Not at all.

UNDERSHAFT: Mr. Cusins: I am indebted to you for explaining so precisely. *{Turning to* SARAH] Barbara, my dear—

SARAH: *{Prompting him}* Sarah.

UNDERSHAFT: Sarah, of course. *{They shake hands. He goes over to* BARBARA] Barbara—I am right this time, I hope.

BARBARA: Quite right. *{They shake hands}*

LADY BRITOMART: *{Resuming command}* Sit down, all of you. Sit down, Andrew. *{She comes forward and sits on the settee.* CUSINS *also brings his chair forward on her left.* BARBARA *and* STEPHEN *resume their seats.* LOMAX *gives his chair to* SARAH *and goes for another}*

UNDERSHAFT: Thank you, my love.

LOMAX: *{Conversationally, as he brings a chair forward between the writing table and the settee, and offers it to* UNDERSHAFT] Takes you some time to find out exactly where you are, don't it?

UNDERSHAFT: *{Accepting the chair, but remaining standing}* That is not what embarrasses me, Mr. Lomax. My difficulty is that if I play the part of a father, I shall produce the effect of an intrusive stranger; and if I play the part of a discreet stranger, I may appear a callous father.

LADY BRITOMART: There is no need for you to play any part at all, Andrew. You had much better be sincere and natural.

UNDERSHAFT: *{Submissively}* Yes, my dear: I daresay that will be best. *{He sits down comfortably}* Well, here I am. Now what can I do for you all?

LADY BRITOMART: You need not do anything, Andrew. You are one of the family. You can sit with us and enjoy yourself. *{A painfully conscious pause.* BARBARA *makes a face at* LOMAX, *whose too long suppressed mirth immediately explodes in agonized neighings}*

LADY BRITOMART: *{Outraged}* Charles Lomax: if you can behave yourself, behave yourself. If not, leave the room.

LOMAX: I'm awfully sorry, Lady Brit; but really, you know, upon my soul! *{He sits on the settee between* LADY BRITOMART *and* UNDERSHAFT, *quite overcome}*

BARBARA: Why don't you laugh if you want to, Cholly? It's good for your inside.

LADY BRITOMART: Barbara: you have

had the education of a lady. Please let your father see that; and don't talk like a street girl.

UNDERSHAFT: Never mind me, my dear. As you know, I am not a gentleman; and I was never educated.

LOMAX: *{Encouragingly}* Nobody'd know it, I assure you. You look all right, you know.

CUSINS: Let me advise you to study Greek, Mr. Undershaft. Greek scholars are privileged men. Few of them know Greek; and none of them know anything else; but their position is unchallengeable. Other languages are the qualifications of waiters and commercial travellers: Greek is to a man of position what the hallmark is to silver.

BARBARA: Dolly: don't be insincere. Cholly: fetch your concertina and play something for us.

LOMAX: *{Jumps up eagerly, but checks himself to remark doubtfully to* UNDERSHAFT]* Perhaps that sort of thing isn't in your line, eh?

UNDERSHAFT: I am particularly fond of music.

LOMAX: *{Delighted}* Are you? Then I'll get it. *{He goes upstairs for the instrument}*

UNDERSHAFT: Do you play, Barbara?

BARBARA: Only the tambourine. But Cholly's teaching me the concertina.

UNDERSHAFT: Is Cholly also a member of the Salvation Army?

BARBARA: No: he says it's bad form to be a dissenter. But I don't despair of Cholly. I made him come yesterday to a meeting at the dock gates, and take the collection in his hat.

UNDERSHAFT: *{Looks whimsically at his wife}*!!

LADY BRITOMART: It is not my doing, Andrew. Barbara is old enough to take her own way. She has no father to advise her.

BARBARA: Oh yes she has. There are no orphans in the Salvation Army.

UNDERSHAFT: Your father there has a great many children and plenty of experience, eh?

BARBARA: *{Looking at him with quick interest and nodding}* Just so. How did you come to understand that? [LOMAX *is heard at the door trying the concertina}*

LADY BRITOMART: Come in, Charles. Play us something at once.

LOMAX: Righto! *{He sits down in his former place, and preludes}*

UNDERSHAFT: One moment, Mr. Lomax, I am rather interested in the Salvation Army. Its motto might be my own: Blood and Fire.

LOMAX: *{Shocked}* But not your sort of blood and fire, you know.

UNDERSHAFT: My sort of blood cleanses: my sort of fire purifies.

BARBARA: So do ours. Come down tomorrow to my shelter—the West Ham shelter—and see what we're doing. We're going to march to a great meeting in the Assembly Hall at Mile End. Come and see the shelter and then march with us: it will do you a lot of good. Can you play anything?

UNDERSHAFT: In my youth I earned pennies, and even shillings occasionally, in the streets and in public house parlors by my natural talent for stepdancing. Later on, I became a member of the Undershaft orchestral society, and performed passably on the tenor trombone.

LOMAX: *{Scandalized—putting down the concertina}* Oh I say!

BARBARA: Many a sinner has played himself into heaven on the trombone, thanks to the Army.

LOMAX: *{To* BARBARA, *still rather shocked}* Yes; but what about the cannon business, don't you know? *{To* UNDERSHAFT]* Getting into heaven is not exactly in your line, is it?

LADY BRITOMART: Charles ! ! !

LOMAX: Well; but it stands to reason, don't it? The cannon business may be necessary and all that: we can't get on without cannons; but it isn't right, you know. On the other hand, there may be a certain amount of tosh about the Salvation Army—I belong to the Established Church myself—but still you can't deny that it's religion; and you can't go against religion, can you? At least unless you're downright immoral, don't you know.

UNDERSHAFT: You hardly appreciate my position, Mr. Lomax—

LOMAX: *{Hastily}* I'm not saying anything against you personally—

UNDERSHAFT: Quite so, quite so. But consider for a moment. Here I am, a profiteer in mutilation and murder. I find myself in a specially amiable humor just now because, this morning, down at the foundry, we blew twenty-seven dummy soldier into fragments with a gun which formerly destroyed only thirteen.

LOMAX: *{Leniently}* Well, the more destructive war becomes, the sooner it will be abolished, eh?

UNDERSHAFT: Not at all. The more destructive war becomes, the more fascinating we find it. No, Mr. Lomax: I am obliged to you for making the usual excuse for my trade; but I am not ashamed of it. I am not one of those men who keep their morals and their business in watertight compartments. All the spare money my trade rivals spend on hospitals, cathedrals, and other receptacles for conscience money, I devote to experiments and researches in improved methods of destroying life and property. I have always done so; and I always shall. Therefore your Christmas card moralities of peace on earth and goodwill among men are of no use to me. Your Christianity, which enjoins you to resist not evil, and to turn the other cheek, would make me a bankrupt. My morality—my religion—must have a place for cannons and torpedoes in it.

STEPHEN: *{Coldly—almost sullenly}* You speak as if there were half a dozen moralities and religions to choose from, instead of one true morality and one true religion.

UNDERSHAFT: For me there is only one true morality; but it might not fit you, as you do not manufacture aerial battleships. There is only one true morality for every man; but every man has not the same true morality.

LOMAX: *{Overtaxed}* Would you mind saying that again? I didn't quite follow it.

CUSINS: It's quite simple. As Euripides says, one man's meat is another man's poison morally as well as physically.

UNDERSHAFT: Precisely.

LOMAX: Oh, that. Yes, yes, yes. True. True.

STEPHEN: In other words, some men are honest and some are scoundrels.

BARBARA: Bosh. There are no scoundrels.

UNDERSHAFT: Indeed? Are there any good men?

BARBARA: No. Not one. There are neither good men nor scoundrels: there are just children of one Father; and the sooner they stop calling one another names the better. You needn't talk to me: I know them. I've had scores of them through my hands: scoundrels, criminals, infidels, philanthropists, missionaries, county councillors, all sorts. They're all just the same sort of sinner; and there's the same salvation ready for them all.

UNDERSHAFT: May I ask have you ever saved a maker of cannons?

BARBARA: No. Will you let me try?

UNDERSHAFT: Well, I will make a bargain with you. If I go to see you tomorrow in your Salvation Shelter, will you come the day after to see me in my cannon works?

BARBARA: Take care. I may end in your giving up the cannons for the sake of the Salvation Army.

UNDERSHAFT: Are you sure it will not end in your giving up the Salvation Army for the sake of cannons?

BARBARA: I will take my chance of that.

UNDERSHAFT: And I will take my chance of the other. *{They shake hands on it}* Where is your shelter?

BARBARA. In West Ham. At the sign of the cross. Ask anybody in Canning Town. Where are your works?

UNDERSHAFT: In Perivale St Andrews. At the sign of the sword. Ask anybody in Europe.

LOMAX: Hadn't I better play something?

BARBARA: Yes. Give us "Onward, Christian Soldiers."

LOMAX: Well, that's rather a strong order to begin with, don't you know. Suppose I sing "Thou're passing hence, my brother." It's much the same tune.

BARBARA: It's too melancholy. You get saved, Cholly; and you'll pass hence, my brother, without making such a fuss about it.

LADY BRITOMART: Really, Barbara, you go on as if religion were a pleasant subject. Do have some sense of propriety.

UNDERSHAFT: I do not find it an unpleasant subject, my dear. It is the only one that capable people really care for.

LADY BRITOMART: *{Looking at her watch}* Well, if you are determined to have it, I insist on having it in a proper and respectable way. Charles: ring for prayers. *{General amazement.* STEPHEN *rises in dismay}*

LOMAX: *{Rising}* Oh I say!

UNDERSHAFT: *{Rising}* I am afraid I must be going.

LADY BRITOMART: You cannot go now, Andrew: it would be most improper. Sit down. What will the servants think?

UNDERSHAFT: My dear: I have conscientious scruples. May I suggest a compromise? If Barbara will conduct a little service in the drawing room, with Mr. Lomax as organist, I will attend it willingly. I will even take part, if a trombone can be procured.

LADY BRITOMART: Don't mock, Andrew.

UNDERSHAFT: *{Shocked—to* BARBARA] You don't think I am mocking, my love, I hope.

BARBARA: No, of course not; and it

wouldn't matter if you were: half the Army came to their first meeting for a lark. *{Rising}* Come along. *{She throws her arm around her father and sweeps him out, calling to the others from the threshold}* Come, Dolly. Come, Cholly. [CUSINS *rises}*

LADY BRITOMART: I will not be disobeyed by everybody. Adolphus: sit down. *{He does not}* Charles: you may go. You are not fit for prayers: you cannot keep your contenance.

LOMAX: Oh I say! *{He goes out}*

LADY BRITOMART: *{Continuing}* But you, Adolphus, can behave yourself if you choose to. I insist on your staying.

CUSINS: My dear Lady Brit: there are things in the family prayer book that I couldn't bear to hear you say.

LADY BRITOMART: What things, pray?

CUSINS: Well, you would have to say before all the servants that we have done things we ought not to have done, and left undone things we ought to have done, and that there is no health in us. I cannot bear to hear you doing yourself such an injustice, and Barbara such an injustice. As for myself, I flatly deny it: I have done my best. I shouldn't dare to marry Barbara—I couldn't look you in the face—if it were true. So I must go to the drawing room.

LADY BRITOMART: *{Offended}* Well, go. *{He starts for the door}* And remember this, Adolphus *{He turns to listen}* I have a strong suspicion that you went to the Salvation Army to worship Barbara and nothing else. And I quite appreciate the clever way in which you systematically humbug me. I have found you out. Take care Barbara doesn't. That's all.

CUSINS: *{With unruffled sweetness}* Don't tell on me. *{He steals out}*

LADY BRITOMART: Sarah: if you want to go, go. Anything's better than to sit there as if you wished you were a thousand miles away.

SARAH: *{Languidly}* Very well,

mamma. *{She goes}* [LADY BRITOMART, *with a sudden flounce, gives way to a little gust of tears}*

STEPHEN: *{Going to her}* Mother: what's the matter?

LADY BRITOMART: *{Swishing away her tears with her handkerchief}* Nothing, Foolishness. You can go with him, too, if you like, and leave me with the servants.

STEPHEN: Oh, you mustn't think that, mother. I—I don't like him.

LADY BRITOMART: The others do. That is the injustice of a woman's lot. A woman has to bring up her children; and that means to restrain them, to deny them things they want, to set them tasks, to punish them when they do wrong, to do all the unpleasant things. And then the father, who has nothing to do but pet them and spoil them, comes in when all her work is done and steals their affection from her.

STEPHEN: He has not stolen our affection from you. It is only curiosity.

LADY BRITOMART: *{Violently}* I won't be consoled, Stephen. There is nothing the matter with me. *{She rises and goes towards the door}*

STEPHEN: Where are you going, mother?

LADY BRITOMART: To the drawing room, of course. *{She goes out. "Onward, Christian Soldiers," on the concertina, with tambourine accompaniment, is heard when the door opens}* Are you coming, Stephen?

STEPHEN: No. Certainly not. *{She goes. He sits down on the settee, with compressed lips and an expression of strong dislike}*

END OF ACT I

Act II

The yard of the West Ham shelter of the Salvation Army is a cold place on a January morning. The building itself, an old warehouse, is newly whitewashed. Its gabled end projects into the yard in the middle, with a door on the ground floor, and another in the loft above it without any balcony or ladder, but with a pulley rigged over it for hoisting sacks. Those who come from this central gable end into the yard have the gateway leading to the street on their left, with a stone horsetrough just beyond it, and, on the right, a penthouse shielding a table from the weather. There are forms at the table; and on them are seated a man and a woman, both much down on their luck, finishing a meal of bread (one thick slice each, with margarine and golden syrup) and diluted milk.

The man, a workman out of employment, is young, agile, a talker, a poser, sharp enough to be capable of anything in reason except honesty or altruistic considerations of any kind. The woman is a commonplace old bundle of poverty and hardworn humanity. She looks sixty and probably is forty-five. If they were rich people, gloved and muffed and well wrapped up in furs and overcoats, they would be numbed and miserable; for it is a grindingly cold, raw, January day; and a glance at the background of grimy warehouses and leaden sky visible over the whitewashed walls of the yard would drive any idle rich person straight to the Mediterranean. But these two, being no more troubled with visions of the Mediterranean than of the moon, and being compelled to keep more of their clothes in the pawnshop, and less on their persons, in winter than in summer, are not depressed by the cold: rather are they stung into vivacity, to which their meal has just now given an almost jolly turn. The man takes a pull at his mug, and then gets up and moves about the yard with his hands deep in his pockets, occasionally breaking into a stepdance.

THE WOMAN: Feel better arter your meal, sir?

THE MAN: No. Call that a meal! Good enough for you, p'raps; but wot is it to me, an intelligent workin' man?

THE WOMAN: Workin' man! Wot are you?

THE MAN: Painter.

THE WOMAN: {Skeptically} Yus, I dessay.

THE MAN: Yus, you dessay! I know. Every loafer that can't do nothink calls 'isself a painter. Well, I'm a real painter: grainer, finisher, thirty-eight bob a week when I can get it.

THE WOMAN: Then why don't you go and get it?

THE MAN: I'll tell you why. Fust: I'm intelligent—fffff! it's rotten cold here {He dances a step or two}—yes; intelligent beyond the station o' life into which it has pleased the capitalists to call me; and they don't like a man that sees through 'em. Second, an intelligent bein' needs a doo share of 'appiness; so I drink somethink cruel when I get the chawnce. Third, I stand by my class and do as little as I can so's to leave 'arf the job for me fellow workers. Fourth, I'm fly enough to know wot's inside the law and wot's outside it; and inside it I do as the capitalists do: pinch wot I can lay me 'ands on. In a proper state of society I am sober, industrious, and honest: in Rome, so to speak, I do as the Romans do. Wot's the consequence? When trade is bad—and it's rotten bad just now—and the employers 'az to sack 'arf their men, they generally start on me.

THE WOMAN: What's your name?

THE MAN: Price. Bronterre O'Brien Price. Usually called Snobby Price, for short.

THE WOMAN: Snobby's a carpenter, ain't it? You said you was a painter.

PRICE: Not that kind of snob, but the genteel sort. I'm too uppish, owing to my intelligence, and my father being a Chartist and a reading, thinking man: a stationer, too. I'm none of your common hewers of wood and drawers of water; and don't you forget it. {He returns to his seat at the table, and takes up his mug} Wot's your name?

THE WOMAN: Rummy Mitchens, sir.

PRICE: {Quaffing the remains of his milk to her} Your 'elth, Miss Mitchens.

RUMMY: {Correcting him} Missis Mitchens.

PRICE: Wot! Oh Rummy, Rummy! Respectable married woman, Rummy, gittin' rescued by the Salvation Army by pretendin' to be a bad un. Same old game!

RUMMY: What am I to do? I can't starve. Them Salvation lasses is dear good girls; but the better you are, the worse they likes to think you were before they rescued you. Why shouldn't they 'av a bit o' credit, poor loves? they're worn to rags by their work. And where would they get the money to rescue us if we was to let on we're no worse than other people? You know what ladies and gentlemen are.

PRICE: Thievin' swine! Wish I 'ad their job, Rummy, all the same. Wot does Rummy stand for? Pet name p'raps?

RUMMY: Short for Romola.

PRICE: For wot!?

RUMMY: Romola. It was out of a new book. Somebody me mother wanted me to grow up like.

PRICE: We're companions in misfortune, Rummy. Both of us got names that nobody cawn't pronounce. Consequently I'm Snobby and you're Rummy because Bill and Sally wasn't good enough for our parents. Such is life!

RUMMY: Who saved you, Mr. Price? Was it Major Barbara?

PRICE: No: I come here on my own. I'm goin' to be Bronterre O'Brien Price, the converted painter. I know wot they like. I'll tell 'em how I blasphemed and gambled and wopped my poor old mother—

RUMMY: {Shocked} Used you to beat your mother?

PRICE: Not likely. She used to beat me. No matter: you come and listen to the converted painter, and you'll hear how she was a pious woman that taught me me prayers at 'er knee, an' how I used to come home drunk and drag her out o' bed be 'er snow-white 'airs, an' lam into 'er with the poker.

RUMMY: That's what's so unfair to us women. Your confessions is just as big lies as ours: you don't tell what you really done no more than us; but you men can tell your lies right out at the meetin's and be made much of for it; while the sort o' confessions we 'az to make 'az to be whispered to one lady at a time. It ain't right, spite of all their piety.

PRICE: Right! Do you s'pose the Army'd be allowed if it went and did right? Not much. It combs our 'air and makes us good little blokes to be robbed and put upon. But I'll play the game as good as any of 'em. I'll see somebody struck by lightnin', or hear a voice sayin' "Snobby Price: where will you spend eternity?" I'll 'ave a time of it, I tell you.

RUMMY: You won't be let drink, though.

PRICE: I'll take it out in gorspellin', then. I don't want to drink if I can get fun enough any other way. [JENNY HILL, *a pale, overwrought, pretty Salvation lass of eighteen, comes in through the yard gate, leading* PETER SHIRLEY, *a half hardened, half worn-out elderly man, weak with hunger*]

JENNY: *{Supporting him}* Come! pluck up. I'll get you something to eat. You'll be all right then.

PRICE: *{Rising and hurrying officiously to take the old man off* JENNY's *hands}* Poor old man! Cheer up, brother: you'll find rest and peace and 'appiness 'ere. Hurry up with the food, miss: 'e's fair done. (JENNY *hurries into the shelter}* 'Ere, buck up, daddy! she's fetchin' y'a thick slice o' bread'n treacle, an' a mug o' skyblue. *{He seats him at the corner of the table}*

RUMMY: *{Gaily}* Keep up your old 'art! Never say die!

SHIRLEY: I'm not an old man. I'm only forty-six. I'm as good as ever I was. The grey patch come in my hair before I was thirty. All it wants is three pennorth o' hair dye: am I to be turned on the streets to starve for it? Holy God! I've worked ten to twelve hours a day since I was thirteen, and paid my way all through; and now am I to be thrown into the gutter and my job given to a young man that can do it no better than me because I've black hair that goes white at the first change?

PRICE: *{Cheerfully}* No good jawrin' about it. You're only a jumped-up, jerked-off, 'orspittle-turned-out incurable of a ole workin' man: who cares about you? Eh? Make the thievin' swine give you a meal: they've stole many a one from you. Get a bit o' your own back. [JENNY *returns with the usual meal}* There you are, brother. Awsk a blessin' an' tuck that into you.

SHIRLEY: *{Looking at it ravenously but not touching it, and crying like a child}* I never took anything before.

JENNY: *{Petting him}* Come, come! the Lord sends it to you: he wasn't above taking bread from his friends; and why should you be? Besides, when we find you a job you can pay us for it if you like.

SHIRLEY: *{Eagerly}* Yes, yes: that's true. I can pay you back: it's only a loan. *{Shivering}* Oh Lord! oh Lord! *{He turns to the table and attacks the meal ravenously}*

JENNY: Well, Rummy, are you more comfortable now?

RUMMY: God bless you, lovey! you've fed my body and saved my soul, haven't you? [JENNY, *touched, kisses her}* Sit down and rest a bit: you must be ready to drop.

JENNY: I've been going hard since morning. But there's more work than we can do. I mustn't stop.

RUMMY: Try a prayer for just two minutes. You'll work all the better after.

JENNY: *{Her eyes lighting up}* Oh isn't it wonderful how a few minutes prayer revives you! I was quite light-headed at twelve o'clock, I was so tired; but Major Barbara just sent me to pray for five minutes; and I was able to go on as if I had only just begun. *{To* PRICE*}* Did you have a piece of bread?

PRICE: *{With unction}* Yes, miss; but I've got the piece that I value more; and that's the peace that passeth hall hannerstennin.

RUMMY: *{Fervently}* Glory Halle-lujah! (BILL WALKER, *a rough customer of about 25, appears at the yard gate and looks malevolently at* JENNY*}*

JENNY: That makes me so happy. When you say that, I feel wicked for loitering here. I must get to work again. *{She is hurrying to the shelter, when the newcomer moves quickly up to the door and intercepts her. His manner is so threatening that she retreats as he comes at her truculently, driving her down the yard}*

BILL: Aw knaow you. You're the one that took aw'y maw girl. You're the one that set 'er agen me. Well, I'm gowin' to 'ev 'er aht. Not that Aw care a carse for 'er or you: see? But Aw'll let 'er knaow; and Aw'll let you knaow. Aw'm gowin' to give her a doin' that'll teach 'er to cat aw'y from me. Nah in wiv you and tell 'er to cam aht afore Aw cam in and kick 'er aht. Tell 'er Bill Walker wants 'er. She'll knaow wot thet means; and if she keeps me witin' it'll be worse. You stop to jawr beck at me; and Aw'll stawt on you: d'ye 'eah? There's your w'y. In you gow. *{He takes her by the arm and slings her towards the door of the shelter. She falls on her hand and knee.* RUMMY *helps her up again}*

PRICE: *{Rising, and venturing ir-resolutely towards* BILL*}* Easy there, mate. She ain't doin' you no 'arm.

BILL: 'Oo are you callin' mite? *{Stand-ing over him threateningly}* Youre go-win' to stend up for 'er, aw yer? Put ap your 'ends.

RUMMY: *{Running indignantly to* him to scold him*}* Oh, you great brute —*{He instantly swings his left hand back against her face. She screams and reels back to the trough, where she sits down, covering her bruised face with her hands and rocking herself and moaning with pain}*

JENNY: *{Going to her}* Oh, God for-give you! How could you strike an old woman like that?

BILL: *{Seizing her by the hair so violently that she also screams, and tear-ing her away from the old woman}* You Gawd forgimme again and Aw'll Gawd forgive you one on the jawr thet'll stop you pryin' for a week. *{Holding her and turning fiercely on* PRICE*}* 'Ev you ennything to s'y agen it?

PRICE: *{Intimidated}* No, matey: she ain't anything to do with me.

BILL: Good job for you! Aw'd pat two meals into you and fawt you with one finger arter, you stawved cur. *{To* JENNY*}* Nah are you gowin' to fetch aht Mog Ebbijem; or em Aw to knock your fice off you and fetch her meself?

JENNY: *{Writhing in his grasp}* Oh, please, someone go in and tell Major Barbara— *{She screams again as he wrenches her head down; and* PRICE *and* RUMMY *flee into the shelter}*

BILL: You want to gow in and tell your Mijor of me, do you?

JENNY: Oh, please, don't drag my hair. Let me go.

BILL: Do you or down't you? *{She stifles a scream}* Yus or nao?

JENNY: God give me strength—

BILL: *{Striking her with his fist in the face}* Gow an' shaow her thet, and tell her if she wants one lawk it to cam and interfere with me. [JENNY, *crying with pain, goes into the shed. He goes to the form and addresses the old man}* 'Eah: finish your mess; and git aht o' maw w'y.

SHIRLEY: *{Springing up and facing him fiercely, with the mug in his hand}* You take a liberty with me, and I'll smash you over the face with the mug and cut your eye out. Ain't you satisfied —young whelps like you—with takin' the bread out o' the mouths of your elders that have brought you up and slaved for you, but you must come shovin' and cheekin' and bullyin' in here, where the bread o' charity is sickenin' in our stummicks?

BILL: *{Contemptuously, but backing a little}* Wot good are you, you aold palsy mag? Wot good are you?

SHIRLEY: As good as you and better. I'll do a· day's work agen you or any fat young soaker of your age. Go and take my job at Horrockses, where I worked for ten year. They want young men there: they can't afford to keep men over forty-five. They're very sorry—give you a character and happy to help you to get anything suited to your years— sure a steady man won't be long out of a job. Well, let 'em try you. They'll find the differ. What do you know? Not as much as how to beeyave yourself— layin' your dirty fist across the mouth of a respectable woman!

BILL: Downt provowk me to l'ye it acrost yours: d'ye 'eah?

SHIRLEY: *{With blighting contempt}* Yes: you like an old man to hit, don't you, when you've finished with the women. I ain't seen you hit a young one yet.

BILL: *{Stung}* You loy, you aold soup-kitchener, you. There was a yang menn 'eah. Did aw offer to 'itt him or did Aw not?

SHIRLEY: Was he starvin' or was he not? Was he a man or only a crosseyed thief an' a loafer? Would you hit my son-in-law's brother?

BILL: 'Oo's 'ee?

SHIRLEY: Todger Fairmile o' Balls Pond. Him that won £20 off the Japanese wrastler at the music hall by standin' out 17 minutes 4 seconds agen him.

BILL: *{Sullenly}* Aw'm nao music 'awl wrastler. Ken he box?

SHIRLEY: Yes: an' you can't.

BILL: Wot! Aw cawn't, cawn't Aw? Wot's they you s'y? *{Threatening him}*

SHIRLEY: *{Not budging an inch}* Will you box Todger Fairmile if I put him on to you? Say the word.

BILL: *{Subsiding with a slouch}* Aw'll stend ap to enny menn alawv, if he was ten Todger Fairmawls. But Aw down't set ap to be a perfeshnal.

SHIRLEY: *{Looking down on him with unfathomable disdain}* You box! Slap an old woman with the back o' your hand! You hadn't even the sense to hit her where a magistrate couldn't see the mark of it, you silly young lump of conceit and ignorance. Hit a girl in the jaw an on'y make her cry! If Todger Fairmile'd done it, she wouldn't 'a got up inside o' ten minutes, no more than you would if he got on to you. Yah! I'd set about you myself if I had a week's feedin' in me instead o' two months' starvation. *{He turns his back on him and sits down moodily at the table}*

BILL: *{Following him and stooping over him to drive the taunt in}* You loy! you've the bread and treacle in you that you cam 'eah to beg.

SHIRLEY: *{Bursting into tears}* Oh God! it's true: I'm only an old pauper on the scrap heap. *{Furiously}* But you'll come to it yourself; and then you'll know. You'll come to it sooner than a teetotaller like me, fillin' yourself with gin at this hour o' the mornin!

BILL: Aw'm nao gin drinker, you oald lawr; bat wen Aw want to give my girl a bloomin' good' awdin' Aw lawk to 'ev a bit o' devil in me: see? An' 'eah Aw emm, talking to a rotten aold blawter like you stead o' given' 'er wot for. *{Working himself into a rage}* Aw'm gowin' in there to fetch her aht. *{He makes vengefully for the shelter door}*

SHIRLEY: You're goin' to the station on a stretcher, more likely; and they'll take the gin and the devil out of you there when they get you inside. You mind what you're about: the major here is the Earl o' Stevenage's granddaughter.

BILL: *{Checked}* Garn!

SHIRLEY: You'll see.

BILL: {*His resolution oozing*} Well, Aw ain't dan nathin' to 'er.

SHIRLEY: S'pose she said you did! who'd believe you?

BILL: {*Very uneasy, skulking back to the corner of the penthouse*} Gawd! there's no jastice in this cantry. To think wot them people can do! Aw'm as good as 'er.

SHIRLEY: Tell her so. It's just what a fool like you would do. [BARBARA, *brisk and businesslike, comes from the shelter with a note book, and addresses herself to* SHIRLEY. BILL, *cowed, sits down in the corner on a form, and turns his back on them*]

BARBARA: Good morning.

SHIRLEY: {*Standing up and taking off his hat*} Good morning, miss.

BARBARA: Sit down: make yourself at home. {*He hesitates; but she puts a friendly hand on his shoulder and makes him obey*} Now then! since you've made friends with us, we want to know all about you. Names and addresses and trades.

SHIRLEY: Peter Shirley. Fitter. Chucked out two months ago because I was too old.

BARBARA: {*Not at all surprised*} You'd pass still. Why didn't you dye your hair?

SHIRLEY: I did. Me age come out at a coroner's inquest on me daughter.

BARBARA: Steady?

SHIRLEY: Teetotaller. Never out of a job before. Good worker. And sent to the knackers like an old orse!

BARBARA: No matter: if you did your part God will do his.

SHIRLEY: {*Suddenly stubborn*} My religion's no concern of anybody but myself.

BARBARA: {*Guessing*} I know. Secularist?

SHIRLEY: {*Hotly*} Did I offer to deny it?

BARBARA: Why should you? My own father's a Secularist, I think. Our Father —yours and mine—fulfils himself in many ways; and I daresay he knew what

he was about when he made a Secularist of you. So buck up, Peter! we can always find a job for a steady man like you. [SHIRLEY, *disarmed and a little bewildered, touches his hat. She turns from him to* BILL] What's your name?

BILL: {*Insolently*} Wot's thet to you?

BARBARA: {*Calmly making a note*} Afraid to give his name. Any trade?

BILL: 'Oo's afride to give 'is nime? {*Doggedly, with a sense of heroically defying the House of Lords in the person of Lord Stevenage*} If you want to bring a chawge agen me, bring it. {*She waits, unruffled*} Moy nime's Bill Walker.

BARBARA: {*As if the name were familiar: trying to remember how*} Bill Walker? {*Recollecting*} Oh, I know: you're the man that Jenny Hill was praying for inside just now. {*She enters his name in her note book*}

BILL: 'Oo's Jenny 'ill? And wot call 'as she to pr'y for me?

BARBARA: I don't know. Perhaps it was you that cut her lip.

BILL: {*Defiantly*} Yus, it was me that cat her lip. Aw ain't afride o' you.

BARBARA: How could you be, since you're not afraid of God? You're a brave man, Mr Walker. It takes some pluck to do our work here; but none of us dare lift our hand against a girl like that, for fear of her father in heaven.

BILL: {*Suddenly*} I want nan o' your kentin' jawr. I spowse you think Aw cam 'eah to beg from you, like this demmiged lot 'eah. Not me. Aw down't want your bread and scripe and ketlep. Aw don't b'live in your Gawd, no more than you do yourself.

BARBARA: {*Sunnily apologetic and ladylike, as on a new footing with him*} Oh, I beg your pardon for putting your name down, Mr Walker. I didn't understand. I'll strike it out.

BILL: {*Taking this as a slight, and deeply wounded by it*} 'Eah! you let maw nime alown. Ain't it good enaff to be in your book?

BARBARA: {*Considering*} Well, you see, there's no use putting down your name unless I can do something for you, is there? What's your trade?

BILL: {Still smarting} Thets nao concern o' yours.

BARBARA: Just so. {Very businesslike} I'll put you down as {Writing} the man who—struck—poor little Jenny Hill—in the mouth.

BILL: {Rising threateningly} See 'eah. Awve 'ed enaff o' this.

BARBARA: {Quite sunny and fearless} What did you come to us for?

BILL: Aw cam for maw gel, see? Aw came to tike her aht o' this and to brike 'er jawr for 'er.

BARBARA: {Complacently} You see I was right about your trade. [BILL, on the point of retorting furiously, finds himself, to his great shame and terror, in danger of crying instead. He sits down again suddenly} What's her name?

BILL: {Dogged} 'Er nime's Mog Ebbijem: thet's wot her nime is.

BARBARA: Mog Habbijam! Oh, she's gone to Canning Town, to our barracks there.

BILL: {Fortified by his resentment of MOG's perfidy} Is she? {Vindictively} Then Aw'm gowin' to Kennintahn arter her. {He crosses to the gate; hesitates; finally comes back at BARBARA] Are you loyin' to me to git shat o' me?

BARBARA: I don't want to get shut of you. I want to keep you here and save your soul. You'd better stay: you're going to have a bad time today, Bill.

BILL: 'Oo's gowin to give it to me? You, p'reps?

BARBARA: Someone you don't believe in. But you'll be glad afterwards.

BILL: {Slinking off} Aw'll gow to Kennintahn to be aht o' reach o' your tangue. {Suddenly turning on her with intense malice} And if Aw down't fawnd Mog there, Aw'll cam back and do two years for you, s'elp me Gawd if Aw downt!

BARBARA: {A shade kindlier, if possible} It's no use, Bill. She's got another bloke.

BILL: Wot!

BARBARA: One of her own converts. He fell in love with her when he saw her with her soul saved, and her face clean, and her hair washed.

BILL: {Surprised} Wottud she wash it for, the carroty slat? It's red.

BARBARA: It's quite lovely now, because she wears a new look in her eyes with it. It's a pity you're too late. The new bloke has put your nose out of joint, Bill.

BILL: Aw'll put his nowse aht o' joint for him. Not that Aw care a carse for 'er, mawnd thet. But Aw'll teach her to drop me as if Aw was dirt. And Aw'll teach him to meddle with maw judy. Wots 'iz bleedin' nime?

BARBARA: Sergeant Todger Fairmile.

SHIRLEY: {Rising with grim joy} I'll go with him, miss. I want to see them two meet. I'll take him to the infirmary when it's over.

BILL: {To SHIRLEY, with undissembled misgiving} Is thet 'im you was speakin' on?

SHIRLEY: That's him.

BILL: 'Im that wrastled in the music 'awl?

SHIRLEY: The competitions at the National Sportin' Club was worth nigh a hundred a year to him. He's gev 'em up now for religion; so he's a bit fresh for want of the exercise he was accustomed to. He'll be glad to see you. Come along.

BILL: Wot's 'is wight?

SHIRLEY: Thirteen four. [BILL's last hope expires}

BARBARA: Go and talk to him, Bill. He'll convert you.

SHIRLEY: He'll convert your head into a mashed potato.

BILL: {Sullenly} Aw ain't afride of 'im. Aw ain't afride of ennybody. Bat 'e can lick me. She's dan me. {He sits down moodily on the edge of the horse trough}

SHIRLEY: You ain't goin'. I thought not. {He resumes his seat}

BARBARA: {Calling} Jenny!

JENNY: *{Appearing at the shelter door with a plaster on the corner of her mouth}* Yes, Major.

BARBARA: Send Rummy Mitchens out to clear away here.

JENNY: I think she's afraid.

BARBARA: *{Her resemblance to her mother flashing out for a moment}* Nonsense! she must do as she's told.

JENNY: *{Calling into the shelter}* Rummy: the Major says you must come. [JENNY *comes to* BARBARA, *purposely keeping on the side next* BILL, *lest he should suppose that she shrank from him or bore malice}*

BARBARA: Poor little Jenny! Are you tired? *{Looking at the wounded cheek}* Does it hurt?

JENNY: No: it's all right now. It was nothing.

BARBARA: *{Critically}* It was as hard as he could hit, I expect. Poor Bill! You don't feel angry with him, do you?

JENNY: Oh no, no, no: indeed I don't, Major, bless his poor heart! [BARBARA *kisses her; and she runs away merrily into the shelter.* BILL *writhes with an agonizing return of his new and alarming symptoms, but says nothing.* RUMMY MITCHENS *comes from the shelter}*

BARBARA: *{Going to meet* RUMMY] Now Rummy, bustle. Take in those mugs and plates to be washed; and throw the crumbs about for the birds. [RUMMY *takes the three plates and mugs; but* SHIRLEY *takes back his mug from her, as there is still some milk left in it}*

RUMMY: There ain't any crumbs. This ain't a time to waste good bread on birds.

PRICE: *{Appearing at the shelter door}* Gentleman come to see the shelter, Major. Says he's your father.

BARBARA: All right. Coming [SNOBBY *goes back into the shelter, followed by* BARBARA]

RUMMY: *{Stealing across to* BILL *and addressing him in a subdued voice, but with intense conviction}* I'd 'av the lor

of you, you flat eared pignosed pot-walloper, if she'd let me. You're no gentleman, to hit a lady in the face. [BILL, *with greater things moving in him, takes no notice}*

SHIRLEY: *{Following her}* Here! in with you and don't get yourself into more trouble by talking.

RUMMY: *{With hauteur}* I ain't 'ad the pleasure o' being hintroduced to you, as I can remember. *{She goes into the shelter with the plates}*

SHIRLEY: That's the—

BILL: *{Savagely}* Downt you talk to me, d'ye 'eah? You lea' me alown, or Aw'll do you a mischief. Aw'm not dirt under your feet, ennywy.

SHIRLEY: *{Calmly}* Don't you be afeerd. You ain't such prime company that you need expect to be sought after. *{He is about to go into the shelter when* BARBARA *comes out, with* UNDERSHAFT *on her right}*

BARBARA: Oh, there you are, Mr Shirley! *{Between them}* This is my father: I told you he was a Secularist, didn't I? Perhaps you'll be able to comfort one another.

UNDERSHAFT: *{Startled}* A Secularist! Not the least in the world: on the contrary, a confirmed mystic.

BARBARA: Sorry, I'm sure. By the way, papa, what is your religion? in case I have to introduce you again.

UNDERSHAFT: My religion? Well, my dear, I am a Millionaire. That is my religion.

BARBARA: Then I'm afraid you and Mr Shirley won't be able to comfort one another after all. You're not a Millionaire, are you, Peter?

SHIRLEY: No; and proud of it.

UNDERSHAFT: *{Gravely}* Poverty, my friend, is not a thing to be proud of.

SHIRLEY: *{Angrily}* Who made your millions for you? Me and my like. What's kep' us poor? Keepin' you rich. I wouldn't have your conscience, not for all your income.

UNDERSHAFT: I wouldn't have your

income, not for all your conscience, Mr Shirley. *{He goes to the penthouse and sits down on a form}*

BARBARA: *{Stopping* SHIRLEY *adroitly as he is about to retort}* You wouldn't think he was my father, would you, Peter? Will you go into the shelter and lend the lasses a hand for a while: we're worked off our feet.

SHIRLEY: *{Bitterly}* Yes: I'm in their debt for a meal, ain't I?

BARBARA: Oh, not because you're in their debt, but for love of them, Peter, for love of them. *{He cannot understand, and is rather scandalized}* There! don't stare at me. In with you; and give that conscience of yours a holiday. *{Bustling him into the shelter}*

SHIRLEY: *{As he goes in}* Ah! it's a pity you never was trained to use your reason, miss. You'd have been a very taking lecturer on Secularism. [BARBARA *turns to her father}*

UNDERSHAFT: Never mind me, my dear. Go about your work; and let me watch it for a while.

BARBARA: All right.

UNDERSHAFT: For instance, what's the matter with that outpatient over there?

BARBARA: *{Looking at* BILL, *whose attitude has never changed, and whose expression of brooding wrath has deepened}* Oh, we shall cure him in no time. Just watch. *{She goes over to* BILL *and waits. He glances up at her and casts his eyes down again, uneasy, but grimmer than ever}* It would be nice to just stamp on Mog Habbijam's face, wouldn't it, Bill?

BILL: *{Starting up from the trough in consternation}* It's a loy: Aw never said so. *{She shakes her head}* 'Oo taold you wot was in moy mawnd?

BARBARA: Only your new friend.

BILL: Wot new friend?

BARBARA: The devil, Bill. When he gets round people they get miserable, just like you.

BILL: *{With a heartbreaking attempt at devil-may-care cheerfulness}* Aw ain't

miserable. *{He sits down again, and stretches his legs in an attempt to seem indifferent}*

BARBARA: Well, if you're happy, why don't you look happy, as we do?

BILL: *{His legs curling back in spite of him}* Aw'm 'eppy enaff, Aw tell you. Woy cawn't you lea' me alown? Wot 'ev I dan to you? Aw ain't smashed your fice, 'ev Aw?

BARBARA: *{Softly: wooing his soul}* It's not me that's getting at you, Bill.

BILL: 'Oo else is it?

BARBARA: Somebody that doesn't intend you to smash women's faces, I suppose. Somebody or something that wants to make a man of you.

BILL: *{Blustering}* Mike a menn o' me! Ain't Aw a menn? eh? 'Oo sez Aw'm not a menn?

BARBARA: There's a man in you somewhere, I suppose. But why did he let you hit poor little Jenny Hill? That wasn't very manly of him, was it?

BILL: *{Tormented}* 'Ev dan wiv it, Aw tell you. Chack it. Aw'm sick o' your Jenny 'Ill and 'er silly little fice.

BARBARA: They why do you keep thinking about it? Why does it keep coming up against you in your mind? You're not getting converted, are you?

BILL: *{With conviction}* Not ME. Not lawkly.

BARBARA: That's right, Bill. Hold out against it. Put out your strength. Don't let's get you cheap. Todger Fairmile said he wrestled for three nights against his salvation harder than he ever wrestled with the Jap at the music hall. He gave in to the Jap when his arm was going to break. But he didn't give in to his salvation until his heart was going to break. Perhaps you'll escape that. You havn't any heart, have you?

BILL: Wot d'ye mean? Woy ain't Aw got a 'awt the sime as ennybody else?

BARBARA: A man with a heart wouldn't have bashed poor little Jenny's face, would he?

BILL: *{Almost crying}* Ow, will you lea' me alown? 'Ev Aw ever offered to meddle with you, that you cam neggin' and provowkin' me lawk this? *{He writhes convulsively from his eyes to his toes}*

BARBARA: *{With a steady soothing hand on his arm and a gentle voice that never lets go}* It's your soul that's hurting you, Bill, and not me. We've been through it all ourselves. Come with us, Bill. *{He looks wildly round}* To brave manhood on earth and eternal glory in heaven. *{He is on the point of breaking down}* Come. *{A drum is heard in the shelter; and* BILL, *with a gasp, escapes from the spell as* BARBARA *turns quickly.* ADOLPHUS *enters from the shelter with a big drum}* Oh! there you are, Dolly. Let me introduce a new friend of mine, Mr Bill Walker. This is my bloke, Bill: Mr Cusins. [CUSINS *salutes with his drumstick}*

BILL: Gowing to merry 'im?

BARBARA: Yes.

BILL: *{Fervently}* Gawd 'elp 'im! Gaw-aw-aw-awd 'elp 'im!

BARBARA: Why? Do you think he won't be happy with me?

BILL: Awve aony 'ed to stend it for a mawnin': 'e'll 'ev to stend it for a lawftawn.

CUSINS: That is a frightful reflection, Mr Walker. But I can't tear myself away from her.

BILL: Well, Aw ken. *{To* BARBARA*}* 'Eah! do you knaow where Aw'm gowin' to, and wot Aw'm gowin' to do?

BARBARA: Yes: you're going **to** heaven; and you're coming back **here** before the week's out to tell me so.

BILL: You loy. Aw'm gowin to Kennintahn, to spit in Todger Fairmawl's eye. Aw beshed Jenny 'Ill's fice; an nar Aw'll git me aown fice beshed and cam beck and shaow it to 'er. 'Ee'll 'itt me 'ardern Aw 'itt 'er. That'll mike us square. *{To* ADOLPHUS*}* Is that fair or is it not? You're a genlm'n: you oughter knaow.

BARBARA: Two black eyes won't make one white one, Bill.

BILL: Aw didn't awst you. Cawnt you never keep your mahth shat? Oy awst the genlm'n.

CUSINS: *{Reflectively}* Yes: I think you're right, Mr Walker. Yes: I should do it. It's curious: it's exactly what an ancient Greek would have done.

BARBARA: But what good will it do?

CUSINS: Well, it will give Mr Fairmile some exercise; and it will satisfy Mr Walker's soul.

BILL: Rot! there ain't nao sach a thing as a saoul. Ah kin you tell wevver Aw've a saoul or not? You never seen it.

BARBARA: I've seen it hurting you when you went against it.

BILL: *{With compressed aggravation}* If you was maw gel and took the word aht o' me mahth lawk thet, Aw'd give you sathink you'd feel 'urtin, Aw would. *{To* ADOLPHUS*]* You like maw tip, mite. Stop 'er jawr; or you'll doy afoah your tawm. *{With intense expression}* Wore aht: thet's you'll be: wore aht. *{He goes away through the gate}*

CUSINS: *{Looking after him}* I wonder!

BARBARA: Dolly! *{Indignant, in her mother's manner}*

CUSINS: Yes, my dear, it's very wearing to be in love with you. If it lasts, I quite think I shall die young.

BARBARA: Should you mind?

CUSINS: Not at all. *{He is suddenly softened, and kisses her over the drum, evidently not for the first time, as people cannot kiss over a big drum without practice.* UNDERSHAFT *coughs}*

BARBARA: It's all right, papa, we've not forgotten you. Dolly: explain the place to papa: I havn't time. *{She goes busily into the shelter.* UNDERSHAFT *and* ADOLPHUS *now have the yard to themselves.* UNDERSHAFT, *seated on a form, and still keenly attentive, looks hard at* ADOLPHUS. ADOLPHUS *looks hard at him}*

UNDERSHAFT: I fancy you guess something of what is in my mind, Mr Cusins. [CUSINS *flourishes his drumsticks as if in the act of beating a lively rataplan, but makes no sound}* Exactly so. But suppose Barbara finds you out!

CUSINS: You know, I do not admit that I am imposing on Barbara. I am quite genuinely interested in the views of the Salvation Army. The fact is, I am a sort of collector of religions; and the curious thing is that I find I can believe them all. By the way, have you any religion?

UNDERSHAFT: Yes.

CUSINS: Anything out of the common?

UNDERSHAFT: Only that there are two things necessary to Salvation.

CUSINS: *{Disappointed, but polite}* Ah, the Church Catechism. Charles Lomax also belongs to the Established Church.

UNDERSHAFT: The two things are—

CUSINS: Baptism and—

UNDERSHAFT: No. Money and gunpowder.

CUSINS: *{Surprised, but interested}* That is the general opinion of our governing classes. The novelty is in hearing any man confess it.

UNDERSHAFT: Just so.

CUSINS: Excuse me: is there any place in your religion for honor, justice, truth, love, mercy and so forth?

UNDERSHAFT: Yes: they are the graces and luxuries of a rich, strong, and safe life.

CUSINS: Suppose one is forced to choose between them and money or gunpowder?

UNDERSHAFT: Choose money and gunpowder; for without enough of both you cannot afford the others.

CUSINS: That is your religion?

UNDERSHAFT: Yes. *{The cadence of this reply makes a full close in the conversation.* CUSINS *twists his face dubiously and contemplates* UNDERSHAFT. UNDERSHAFT *contemplates him}*

CUSINS: Barbara won't stand that. You will have to choose between your religion and Barbara.

UNDERSHAFT: So will you, my friend. She will find out that that drum of yours is hollow.

CUSINS: Father Undershaft: you are mistaken: I am a sincere Salvationist. You do not understand the Salvation Army. It is the army of joy, of love, of courage: it has banished the fear and remorse and despair of the old hell-ridden evangelical sects: it marches to fight the devil with trumpet and drum, with music and dancing, with banner and palm, as becomes a sally from heaven by its happy garrison. It picks the waster out of the public house and makes a man of him: it finds a worm wriggling in a back kitchen, and lo! a woman! Men and women of rank too, sons and daughters of the Highest. It takes the poor professor of Greek, the most artificial and self-suppressed of human creatures, from his meal of roots, and lets loose the rhapsodist in him; reveals the true worship of Dionysos to him; sends him down the public street drumming dithyrambs. *{He plays a thundering flourish on the drum}*

UNDERSHAFT: You will alarm the shelter.

CUSINS: Oh, they are accustomed to these sudden ecstasies of piety. However, if the drum worries you—*{He pockets the drumsticks; unhooks the drum; and stands it on the ground opposite the gateway}*

UNDERSHAFT: Thank you.

CUSINS: You remember what Euripides says about your money and gunpowder?

UNDERSHAFT: No.

CUSINS: *{Declaiming}*

> One and another
> In money and guns may outpass his
>   brother;
> And men in their millions float and
>   flow
> And seethe with a million hopes as
>   leaven;
> And they win their will; or they miss
>   their will;
> And their hopes are dead or are pined
>   for still;
>   But whoe'er can know
>   As the long days go
> That to live is happy, has found his
>   heaven.

My translation: what do you think of it?

UNDERSHAFT: I think, my friend, that if you wish to know, as the long days go, that to live is happy, you must first acquire money enough for a decent life, and power enough to be your own master.

CUSINS: You are damnably discouraging. *{He resumes his declamation}*

Is it so hard a thing to see
That the spirit of God—whate'er it be—
The law that abides and changes not, ages long,
The Eternal and Nature-born: these things be strong?
What else is Wisdom? What of Man's endeavor,
Or God's high grace so lovely and so great?
To stand from fear set free? to breathe and wait?
To hold a hand uplifted over Fate?
And shall not Barbara be loved for ever?

UNDERSHAFT: Euripides mentions Barbara, does he?

CUSINS: It is a fair translation. The word means Loveliness.

UNDERSHAFT: May I ask—as Barbara's father—how much a year she is to be loved for ever on?

CUSINS: As Barbara's father, that is more your affair than mine. I can feed her by teaching Greek: that is about all.

UNDERSHAFT: Do you consider it a good match for her?

CUSINS: *{With polite obstinacy}* Mr Undershaft: I am in many ways a weak, timid, ineffectual person; and my health is far from satisfactory. But whenever I feel that I must have anything, I get it, sooner or later. I feel that way about Barbara. I don't like marriage: I feel intensely afraid of it; and I don't know what I shall do with Barbara or what she will do with me. But I feel that I and nobody else must marry her. Please regard that as settled—Not that I wish to be arbitrary; but why should I waste

your time in discussing what is inevitable?

UNDERSHAFT: You mean that you will stick at nothing: not even the conversion of the Salvation Army to the worship of Dionysos.

CUSINS: The business of the Salvation Army is to save, not to wrangle about the name of the pathfinder. Dionysos or another: what does it matter?

UNDERSHAFT: *{Rising and approaching him}* Professor Cusins: you are a young man after my own heart.

CUSINS: Mr Undershaft: you are, as far as I am able to gather, a most infernal old rascal; but you appeal very strongly to my sense of ironic humor. [UNDERSHAFT *mutely offers his hand. They shake}*

UNDERSHAFT: *{Suddenly concentrating himself}* And now to business.

CUSINS: Pardon me. We were discussing religion. Why go back to such an uninteresting and unimportant subject as business?

UNDERSHAFT: Religion is our business at present, because it is through religion alone that we can win Barbara.

CUSINS: Have you, too, fallen in love with Barbara?

UNDERSHAFT: Yes, with a father's love.

CUSINS: A father's love for a grown-up daughter is the most dangerous of all infatuations. I apologize for mentioning my own pale, coy, mistrustful fancy in the same breath with it.

UNDERSHAFT: Keep to the point. We have to win her; and we are neither of us Methodists.

CUSINS: That doesn't matter. The power Barbara wields here—the power that wields Barbara herself—is not Calvinism, not Presbyterianism, not Methodism—

UNDERSHAFT: Not Greek Paganism either, eh?

CUSINS: I admit that. Barbara is quite original in her religion.

UNDERSHAFT: *{Triumphantly}* Aha! Barbara Undershaft would be. Her inspiration comes from within herself.

CUSINS: How do you suppose it got there?

UNDERSHAFT: *{In towering excitement}* It is the Undershaft inheritance. I shall hand on my torch to my daughter. She shall make my converts and preach my gospel—

CUSINS: What! Money and gunpowder!

UNDERSHAFT: Yes, money and gunpowder; freedom and power; command of life and command of death.

CUSINS: *{Urbanely: trying to bring him down to earth}* This is extremely interesting, Mr Undershaft. Of course you know that you are mad.

UNDERSHAFT: *{With redoubled force}* And you?

CUSINS: Oh, mad as a hatter. You are welcome to my secret since I have discovered yours. But I am astonished. Can a madman make cannons?

UNDERSHAFT: Would anyone else than a madman make them? And now *{With surging energy}* question for question. Can a sane man translate Euripides?

CUSINS: No.

UNDERSHAFT: *{Seizing him by the shoulder}* Can a sane woman make a man of a waster or a woman of a worm?

CUSINS: *{Reeling before the storm}* Father Colossus—Mammoth Millionaire—

UNDERSHAFT: *{Pressing him}* Are there two mad people or three in this Salvation shelter to-day?

CUSINS: You mean Barbara is as mad as we are?

UNDERSHAFT: *{Pushing him lightly off and resuming his equanimity suddenly and completely}* Pooh, Professor! let us call things by their proper names. I am a millionaire; you are a poet; Barbara is a savior of souls. What have we three to do with the common mob of slaves and idolators? *{He sits down with a shrug of contempt for the mob}*

CUSINS: Take care! Barbara is in love with the common people. So am I. Have you never felt the romance of that love?

UNDERSHAFT: *{Cold and sardonic}* Have you ever been in love with Poverty, like St Francis? Have you ever been in love with Dirt, like St Simeon? Have you ever been in love with disease and suffering, like our nurses and philanthropists? Such passions are not virtues, but the most unnatural of all the vices. This love of the common people may please an earl's granddaughter and a university professor; but I have been a common man and a poor man; and it has no romance for me. Leave it to the poor to pretend that poverty is a blessing: leave it to the coward to make a religion of his cowardice by preaching humility: we know better than that. We three must stand together above the common people: how else can we help their children to climb up beside us? Barbara must belong to us, not to the Salvation Army.

CUSINS: Well, I can only say that if you think you will get her away from the Salvation Army by talking to her as you have been talking to me, you don't know Barbara.

UNDERSHAFT: My friend: I never ask for what I can buy.

CUSINS: *{In a white fury}* Do I understand you to imply that you can buy Barbara?

UNDERSHAFT: No; but I can buy the Salvation Army.

CUSINS: Quite impossible.

UNDERSHAFT: You shall see. All religious organizations exist by selling themselves to the rich.

CUSINS: Not the Army. That is the Church of the poor.

UNDERSHAFT: All the more reason for buying it.

CUSINS: I don't think you quite know what the Army does for the poor.

UNDERSHAFT: Oh, yes, I do. It draws their teeth: that is enough for me—as a man of business—

CUSINS: Nonsense! It makes them sober—

UNDERSHAFT: I prefer sober workmen. The profits are larger.

CUSINS: —honest—

UNDERSHAFT: Honest workmen are the most economical.

CUSINS: —attached to their homes—

UNDERSHAFT: So much the better: they will put up with anything sooner than change their shop.

CUSINS: —happy—

UNDERSHAFT: An invaluable safeguard against revolution.

CUSINS: —unselfish—

UNDERSHAFT: Indifferent to their own interests, which suits me exactly.

CUSINS: —with their thoughts on heavenly things—

UNDERSHAFT: {Rising} And not on Trade Unionism nor Socialism. Excellent.

CUSINS: {Revolted} You really are an infernal old rascal.

UNDERSHAFT: {Indicating PETER SHIRLEY, *who has just come from the shelter and strolled dejectedly down the yard between them}* And this is an honest man!

SHIRLEY: Yes; and what 'av I got by it? {*He passes on bitterly and sits on the form, in the corner of the penthouse.* SNOBBY PRICE, *beaming sanctimoniously, and* JENNY HILL, *with a tambourine full of coppers, come from the shelter and go to the drum, on which* JENNY *begins to count the money}*

UNDERSHAFT: {*Replying to* SHIRLEY] Oh, your employers must have got a good deal by it from first to last. {*He sits on the table, with one foot on the side form.* CUSINS, *overwhelmed, sits down on the same form nearer the shelter.* BARBARA *comes from the shelter to the middle of the yard. She is excited and a little overwrought}*

BARBARA: We've just had a splendid experience meeting at the other gate in Cripp's Lane. I've hardly ever seen them so much moved as they were by your confession, Mr Price.

PRICE: I could almost be glad of my past wickedness if I could believe that it would 'elp to keep hathers stright.

BARBARA: So it will, Snobby. How much, Jenny?

JENNY: Four and tenpence, Major.

BARBARA: Oh, Snobby, if you had given your poor mother just one more kick, we should have got the whole five shillings!

PRICE: If she heard you say that, Miss, she'd be sorry I didn't. But I'm glad. Oh what a joy it will be to her when she hears I'm saved!

UNDERSHAFT: Shall I contribute the odd twopence, Barbara? The millionaire's mite, eh? {*He takes a couple of pennies from his pocket}*

BARBARA: How did you make that twopence?

UNDERSHAFT: As usual. By selling cannons, torpedoes, submarines, and my new patent Grand Duke hand grenade.

BARBARA: Put it back in your pocket. You can't buy your Salvation here for twopence: you must work it out.

UNDERSHAFT: Is twopence not enough? I can afford a little more, if you press me.

BARBARA: Two million millions would not be enough. There is bad blood on your hands; and nothing but good blood can cleanse them. Money is no use. Take it away. {*She turns to* CUSINS] Dolly: you must write another letter for me to the papers. {*He makes a wry face}* Yes: I know you don't like it; but it must be done. The starvation this winter is beating us: everybody is unemployed. The General says we must close this shelter if we can't get more money. I force the collections at the meetings until I am ashamed: don't I, Snobby?

PRICE: It's a fair treat to see you work it, Miss. The way you got them up from three-and-six to four-and-ten with that hymn, penny by penny and verse by verse, was a caution. Not a Cheap Jack on Mile End Waste could touch you at it.

BARBARA: Yes; but I wish we could do without it. I am getting at last to think more of the collection than of the people's souls. And what are those hatfuls of pence and halfpence? We want thousands! tens of thousands! hundreds of thousands! I want to convert people, not to be always begging for the Army in a way I'd die sooner than beg for myself.

UNDERSHAFT: *{In profound irony}* Genuine unselfishness is capable of anything, my dear.

BARBARA: *{Unsuspectingly, as she turns away to take the money from the drum and put it in a cash bag she carries}* Yes, isn't it? [UNDERSHAFT *looks sardonically at* CUSINS]

CUSINS: *{Aside to* UNDERSHAFT*}* Mephistopheles! Machiavelli!

BARBARA: *{Tears coming into her eyes as she ties the bag and pockets it}* How are we to feed them? I can't talk religion to a man with bodily hunger in his eyes. *{Almost breaking down}* It's frightful.

JENNY: *{Running to her}* Major, dear—

BARBARA: *{Rebounding}* No: don't comfort me. It will be all right. We shall get the money.

UNDERSHAFT: How?

JENNY: By praying for it, of course. Mrs Baines says she prayed for it last night; and she has never prayed for it in vain: never once. *{She goes to the gate and looks out into the street}*

BARBARA: *{Who has dried her eyes and regained her composure}* By the way, dad, Mrs Baines has come to march with us to our big meeting this afternoon; and she is very anxious to meet you, for some reason or other. Perhaps she'll convert you.

UNDERSHAFT: I shall be delighted, my dear.

JENNY: *{At the gate: excitedly}* Major! Major! here's that man back again.

BARBARA: What man?

JENNY: The man that hit me. Oh, I hope he's coming back to join us. [BILL WALKER, *with frost on his packet, comes through the gate, his hands deep in his pockets and his chin sunk between his shoulders, like a cleaned-out gambler. He halts between* BARBARA *and the drum}*

BARBARA: Hullo, Bill! Back already!

BILL: *{Nagging at her}* Bin talkin' ever sence, 'ev you?

BARBARA: Pretty nearly. Well, has Todger paid you out for poor Jenny's jaw?

BILL: Nao 'e ain't.

BARBARA: I thought your jacket looked a bit snowy.

BILL: Sao it is snaowy. You want to knaow where the snaow cam from, down't you?

BARBARA: Yes.

BILL: Well, it cam from orf the grahnd in Pawkinses Corner in Kennintahn. It got rabbed orf be maw shaoulders: see?

BARBARA: Pity you didn't rub some off with your knees, Bill! That would have done you a lot of good.

BILL: *{With sour mirthless humor}* Aw was savin' anather menn's knees at the tawm. 'E was kneelin' on moy 'ed, 'e was.

JENNY: Who was kneeling on your head?

BILL: Todger was. 'E was pryin' for me: pryin' camfortable wiv me as a cawpet. Sow was Mog. Sao was the aol bloomin' meetin'. Mog she sez "Ow Lawd brike is stabborn sperrit; bat down't 'urt is dear 'art." Thet was wot she said. "Down't 'urt is dear 'art"! An 'er blowk—thirteen stun four!—kneelin' wiv all is wight on me. Fanny, ain't it?

JENNY: Oh no. We're so sorry, Mr Walker.

BARBARA: *{Enjoying it frankly}* Nonsense! of course it's funny. Served you right, Bill! You must have done something to him first.

BILL: *{Doggedly}* Aw did wot Aw said Aw'd do. Aw spit in 'is eye. 'E looks ap at the skoy and sez, "Ow that Aw should be fahnd worthy to be spit upon for the gospel's sike!" 'e sez; an Mog sez "Gloary 'Allelloolier"; an' then 'e called me Braddher, and dahned me as if Aw was a kid and 'e was me mather worshin' me a Setterda nawt. Aw 'ednt jast nao shaow wiv 'im at all. 'Arf the street pr'yed; and the tather 'arf larfed fit to split theirselves. {*To* BARBARA} There! are you sattisfawd nah?

BARBARA: {*Her eyes dancing*} Wish I'd been there, Bill.

BILL: Yus: you'd 'a got in a hextra bit 'o talk on me, wouldn't you?

JENNY: I'm so sorry, Mr Walker.

BILL: {*Fiercely*} Down't you gow bein' sorry for me: you've no call. Listen 'eah. Aw browk your pawr.

JENNY: No, it didn't hurt me: indeed it didn't, except for a moment. It was only that I was frightened.

BILL: Aw down't want to be forgive be you, or be ennybody. Wot Aw did Aw'll p'y for. Aw trawd to gat me aown jawr browk to settisfaw you—

JENNY: {*Distressed*} Oh no—

BILL: {*Impatiently*} Tell y' Aw did: cawnt you listen to wot's bein' taold you? All Aw got be it was being mide a sawt of in the pablic street for me pines. Well, if Aw cawnt settisfaw you one wy, Aw ken anather. Listen 'eah! Aw 'ed two quid sived agen the frost; an Aw've a pahnd of it left. A mite o' mawn last week 'ed words with the judy 'e's gowin to merry. 'E give 'er wotfor; and 'e's bin fawnd fifteen bob. 'E 'ed a rawt to 'itt 'er cause they was gowin to be merrid; but Aw 'ednt nao rawt to 'itt you; sao put anather fawv bob on an cal it a pahnd's worth. {*He produces a sovereign*} 'Eahs the manney. Tike it; and let's 'ev no more o' your forgivin' an' pryin' and your Mijor jawrin' me. Let wot dan be dan an' pide for; and let there be a end of it.

JENNY: Oh, I couldn't take it, Mr Walker. But if you would give a shilling or two to poor Rummy Mitchens! you really did hurt her; and she's old.

BILL: {*Contemptuously*} Not lawkly. Aw'd give her anather as soon as look at 'er. Let her 'ev the lawr o' me as she threatened! She ain't forgiven me: not mach. Wot Aw dan to 'er is not on me mawnd—wot she {*Indicating* BARBARA} mawt call on me conscience—no more than stickin' a pig. It's this Christian gime o' yours that Aw wown't 'ev

pl'yed agen me: this bloomin' forgivin' an neggin' an jawrin' that mikes a menn thet sore that 'iz lawf's a burden to 'im. Aw wown't 'ev it, Aw tell you! sao tike your manney and stop thraowin' your silly beshed fice hap agen me.

JENNY: Major: may I take a little of it for the Army?

BARBARA: No: the Army is not to be bought. We want your soul, Bill; and we'll take nothing less.

BILL: {*Bitterly*} Aw knaow. Me an' maw few shillin's is not good enaff for you. You're a earl's grendorter, you are. Nathink less than a 'andered pahnd for you.

UNDERSHAFT: Come, Barbara! you could do a great deal of good with a hundred pounds. If you will set this gentleman's mind at ease by taking his pound, I will give the other ninety-nine. [BILL, *dazed by such opulence, instinctively touches his cap*]

BARBARA: Oh, you're too extravagant, papa. Bill offers twenty pieces of silver. All you need offer is the other ten. That will make the standard price to buy anybody who's for sale. I'm not; and the Army's not. {*To* BILL} You'll never have another quiet moment, Bill, until you come around to us. You can't stand out against your salvation.

BILL: {*Sullenly*} Aw cawnt stend aht agen music 'awl wrastlers and awtful tangued women. Aw've offered to p'y. Aw can do no more. Tike it or leave it. There it is. {*He throws the sovereign on the drum, and sits down on the horse trough. The coin fascinates* SNOBBY PRICE, *who takes an early opportunity of dropping his cap on it.* MRS BAINES *comes from the shelter. She is dressed as a Salvation Army Commissioner. She is an earnest looking woman of about forty, with a caressing, urgent voice, and an appealing manner*}

BARBARA: This is my father, Mrs Baines. [UNDERSHAFT *comes from the table, taking his hat off with marked civility*} Try what you can do with him. He won't listen to me, because he remembers what a fool I was when I was a baby. *{She leaves them together and chats with* JENNY*}*

MRS BAINES: Have you been shewn over the shelter, Mr Undershaft? You know the work we're doing, of course.

UNDERSHAFT: *{Very civilly}* The whole nation knows it, Mrs Baines.

MRS BAINES: No, sir: the whole nation does not know it, or we should not be crippled as we are for want of money to carry our work through the length and breadth of the land. Let me tell you that there would have been rioting this winter in London but for us.

UNDERSHAFT: You really think so?

MRS BAINES: I know it. I remember 1886, when you rich gentlemen hardened your hearts against the cry of the poor. They broke the windows of your clubs in Pall Mall.

UNDERSHAFT: *{Gleaming with approval of their method}* And the Mansion House Fund went up the next day from thirty thousand pounds to seventy-nine thousand! I remember quite well.

MRS BAINES: Well, won't you help me to get at the people? They won't break windows then. Come here, Price. Let me shew you to this gentleman. *[*PRICE *comes to be inspected}* Do you remember the window breaking?

PRICE: My ole father thought it was the revolution, ma'am.

MRS BAINES: Would you break windows now?

PRICE: Oh no ma'am. The windows of 'eaven 'av bin opened to me. I know now that the rich man is a sinner like myself.

RUMMY: *{Appearing above at the loft door}* Snobby Price!

SNOBBY: Wot is it?

RUMMY: Your mother's askin' for you at the other gate in Crippses Lane. She's heard about your confession. *[*PRICE *turns pale}*

MRS BAINES: Go, Mr Price; and pray with her.

JENNY: You can go through the shelter, Snobby.

PRICE: *{To* MRS BAINES*]* I couldn't face her now, ma'am, with all the weight of my sins fresh on me. Tell her she'll find her son at 'ome, waitin' for her in prayer. *{He skulks off through the gate, incidentally stealing the sovereign on his way out by picking up his cap from the drum}*

MRS BAINES: *{With swimming eyes}* You see how we take the anger and bitterness against you out of their hearts, Mr Undershaft.

UNDERSHAFT: It is certainly most convenient and gratifying to all large employers of labor, Mrs Baines.

MRS BAINES: Barbara: Jenny: I have good news: most wonderful news. *[*JENNY *runs to her}* My prayers have been answered. I told you they would, Jenny, didn't I?

JENNY: Yes, yes.

BARBARA: *{Moving nearer to the drum}* Have we got money enough to keep the shelter open?

MRS BAINES: I hope we shall have enough to keep all the shelters open. Lord Saxmundham has promised us five thousand pounds—

BARBARA: Hooray!

JENNY: Glory!

MRS BAINES: —if—

BARBARA: "If!" If what?

MRS BAINES: —if five other gentlemen will give a thousand each to make it up to ten thousand.

BARBARA: Who is Lord Saxmundham? I never heard of him.

UNDERSHAFT: *{Who has pricked up his ears at the peer's name, and is now watching* BARBARA *curiously}* A new creation my dear. You have heard of Sir Horace Bodger?

BARBARA: Bodger! Do you mean the distiller? Bodger's whisky!

UNDERSHAFT: That is the man. He is oue of the greatest of our public benefactors. He restored the cathedral at Hakington. They made him a baronet for that. He gave half a million to the funds of his party: they made him a baron for that.

SHIRLEY: What will they give him for the five thousand?

UNDERSHAFT: There is nothing left to give him. So the five thousand, I should think, is to save his soul.

MRS BAINES: Heaven grant it may! Oh Mr Undershaft, you have some very rich friends. Can't you help us towards the other five thousand? We are going to hold a great meeting this afternoon at the Assembly Hall in the Mile End Road. If I could only announce that one gentleman had come forward to support Lord Saxmundham, others would follow. Don't you know somebody? couldn't you? wouldn't you? {Her eyes fill with tears} oh, think of those poor people, Mr Undershaft: think of how much it means to them, and how little to a great man like you.

UNDERSHAFT: {Sardonically gallant} Mrs Baines: you are irresistible. I can't disappoint you; and I can't deny myself the satisfaction of making Bodger pay up. You shall have your five thousand pounds.

MRS BAINES: Thank God!

UNDERSHAFT: You don't thank me?

MRS BAINES: Oh sir, don't try to be cynical: don't be ashamed of being a good man. The Lord will bless you abundantly; and our prayers will be like a strong fortification round you all the days of your life. {With a touch of caution} You will let me have the cheque to shew at the meeting, won't you? Jenny: go in and fetch a pen and ink. [JENNY runs to the shelter door}

UNDERSHAFT: Do not disturb Miss Hill: I have a fountain pen. [JENNY halts. He sits at the table and writes the cheque. CUSINS rises to make room for him. They all watch him silently}

BILL: {Cynically, aside to BARBARA, his voice and accent horribly debased} Wot prawce Selvytion nah?

BARBARA: Stop. [UNDERSHAFT stops writing: they all turn to her in surprise} Mrs Baines: are you really going to take this money?

MRS BAINES: {Astonished} Why not, dear?

BARBARA: Why not! Do you know what my father is? Have you forgotten that Lord Saxmundham is Bodger the whisky man? Do you remember how we implored the County Council to stop him from writing Bodger's whisky in letters of fire against the sky; so that the poor drink-ruined creatures on the Embankment would not wake up from their snatches of sleep without being reminded of their deadly thirst by that wicked sky sign? Do you know that the worst thing I have had to fight here is not the devil, but Bodger, Bodger, Bodger, with his whisky, his distilleries, and his tied houses? Are you going to make our shelter another tied house for him, and ask me to keep it?

BILL: Rotten dranken whisky it is too.

MRS BAINES: Dear Barbara: Lord Saxmundham has a soul to be saved like any of us. If heaven has found the way to make a good use of his money, are we to set ourselves up against the answer to our prayers?

BARBARA: I know he has a soul to be saved. Let him come down here; and I'll do my best to help him to his salvation. But he wants to send his cheque down to buy us, and go on being as wicked as ever.

UNDERSHAFT: {With a reasonableness which CUSINS alone perceives to be ironical} My dear Barbara: alcohol is a very necessary article. It heals the sick—

BARBARA: It does nothing of the sort.

UNDERSHAFT: Well, it assists the doctor: that is perhaps a less questionable way of putting it. It makes life bearable to millions of people who could not endure their existence if they were quite sober. It enables Parliament to do things at eleven at night that no sane person would do at eleven in the morning. Is it Bodger's fault that this inestimable gift is deplorably abused by less than one per cent of the poor? {He turns again to the table; signs the cheque; and crosses it}

MRS BAINES: Barbara: will there be less drinking or more if all those poor souls we are saving come tomorrow and find the doors of our shelters shut in their faces? Lord Saxmundham gives us the money to stop drinking—to take his own business from him.

CUSINS: {Impishly} Pure self-sacrifice on Bodger's part, clearly! Bless dear Bodger! [BARBARA almost breaks down as Adolphus, too, fails her}

UNDERSHAFT: {Tearing out the cheque and pocketing the book as he rises and goes past CUSINS to MRS BAINES] I also, Mrs Baines, may claim a little disinterestedness. Think of my business; think of the widows and orphans! the men and lads torn to pieces with shrapnel and poisoned with lyddite! [MRS BAINES shrinks; but he goes on remorselessly} the oceans of blood, not one drop of which is shed in a really just cause! the ravaged crops! the peaceful peasants forced, women and men, to till their fields under the fire of opposing armies on pain of starvation! the bad blood of the fierce little cowards at home who egg on others to fight for the gratification of their national vanity! All this makes money for me: I am never richer, never busier than when the papers are full of it. Well, it is your work to preach peace on earth and goodwill to men. [MRS BAINES's face lights up again} Every convert you make is a vote against war. {Her lips move in prayer} Yet I give you this money to help you to hasten my own commercial ruin. {He gives her the cheque}

CUSINS: {Mounting the form in an ecstasy of mischief} The millennium will be inaugurated by the unselfishness of Undershaft and Bodger. Oh be joyful! {He takes the drumsticks from his pocket and flourishes them}

MRS BAINES: {Taking the cheque} The longer I live the more proof I see that there is an Infinite Goodness that turns everything to the work of salvation sooner or later. Who would have thought that any good could have come out of war and drink? And yet their profits are brought today to the feet of salvation to do its blessed work. {She is affected to tears}

JENNY: {Running to MRS BAINES and throwing her arms around her} Oh dear! how blessed, how glorious it all is!

CUSINS: {In a convulsion of irony} Let us seize this unspeakable moment. Let us march to the great meeting at once. Excuse me just an instant. {He rushes into the shelter. JENNY takes her tambourine from the drum head}

MRS BAINES: Mr Undershaft: have you ever seen a thousand people fall on their knees with one impulse and pray? Come with us to the meeting. Barbara shall tell them that the Army is saved, and saved through you.

CUSINS: {Returning impetuously from the shelter with a flag and a trombone, and coming between MRS BAINES and UNDERSHAFT] You will carry the flag down the first street, Mrs Baines. {He gives her the flag} Mr Undershaft is a gifted trombonist: he shall intone an Olympian diapason to the West Ham Salvation March. {Aside to UNDERSHAFT, as he forces the trombone on him} Blow, Machiavelli, blow.

UNDERSHAFT: {Aside to him, as he takes the trombone} The trumpet in Zion! [CUSINS rushes to the drum, which he takes up and puts on. UNDERSHAFT continues aloud} I will do my best. I could vamp a bass if I knew the tune.

CUSINS: It is a wedding chorus from one of Donizetti's operas; but we have converted it. We convert everything to good here, including Bodger. You remember the chorus. "For thee immense rejoicing—immenso giubilo—immenso giubilo." {With drum obligato} Rum tum ti tum tum, tum tum ti ta—

BARBARA: Dolly: you are breaking my heart.

CUSINS: What is a broken heart more or less here? Dionysos Undershaft has descended. I am possessed.

MRS BAINES: Come, Barbara: I must have my dear Major to carry the flag with me.

JENNY: Yes, yes, Major darling. [CUSINS snatches the tambourine out of JENNY's hand and mutely offers it to BARBABA]

BARBARA: {*Coming forward a little as she puts the offer behind her with a shudder, whilst* CUSINS *recklessly tosses the tambourine back to* JENNY *and goes to the gate}* I can't come.

JENNY: Not come!

MRS BAINES: {*With tears in her eyes}* Barbara: do you think I am wrong to take the money?

BARBARA: {*Impulsively going to her and kissing her}* No, no: God help you, dear, you must: you are saving the Army. Go; and may you have a great meeting!

JENNY: But arn't you coming?

BARBARA: No. {*She begins taking off the silver S brooch from her collar}*

MRS BAINES: Barbara: what are you doing?

JENNY: Why are you taking your badge off? You can't be going to leave us, Major.

BARBARA: {*Quietly}* Father: come here.

UNDERSHAFT: {*Coming to her}* My dear! {*Seeing that she is going to pin the badge on his collar, he retreats to the penthouse in some alarm}*

BARBARA: {*Following him}* Don't be frightened. {*She pins the badge on and steps back towards the table, shewing him to the others}* There! It's not much for £5000, is it?

MRS BAINES: Barbara: if you won't come and pray with us, promise me you will pray for us.

BARBARA: I can't pray now. Perhaps I shall never pray again.

MRS BAINES: Barbara!

JENNY: Major!

BARBARA: {*Almost delirious}* I can't bear any more. Quick march!

CUSINS: {*Calling to the procession in the street outside}* Off we go. Play up, there! *Immenso giubilo.* {*He gives the time with his drum; and the band strikes up the march, which rapidly becomes more distant as the procession moves briskly away}*

MRS BAINES: I must go, dear. You're overworked: you will be all right to-morrow. We'll never lose you. Now

Jenny: step out with the old flag. Blood and Fire! {*She marches out through the gate with her flag}*

JENNY: Glory Hallelujah! {*Flourishing her tambourine and marching}*

UNDERSHAFT: {*To* CUSINS, *as he marches out past him easing the slide of his trombone}* "My ducats and my daughter"!

BARBARA: Drunkenness and Murder! My God: why hast thou forsaken me? {*She sinks on the form with her face buried in her hands. The march passes away into silence.* BILL WALKER *steals across to her}*

BILL: {*Taunting}* Wot prawce selvytion nah?

SHIRLEY: Don't you hit her when she's down.

BILL: She 'itt me wen aw wiz dahn. Waw shouldn't Aw git a bit o' me aown beck?

BARBARA: {*Raising her head}* I didn't take your money, Bill. {*She crosses the yard to the gate and turns her back on the two men to hide her face from them}*

BILL: {*Sneering after her}* Naow, it warn't enaff for you. {*Turning to the drum, he misses the money}* 'Ellow! If you ain't took it sammun else 'ez. Were's it gorn? Bly me if Jenny 'Ill didn't tike it arter all!

RUMMY: {*Screaming at him from the loft}* You lie, you dirty blackguard! Snobby Price pinched it off the drum when he took up his cap. I was up here all the time an see 'im do it.

BILL: Wot! Stowl maw money! Waw didn't you call thief on him, you silly aold macker you?

RUMMY: To serve you aht for 'ittin me across the face. It's cost y'pahnd, that 'az {*Raising a paean of squalid triumph}* I done you. I'm even with you. I've 'ad it aht o'y—[BILL *snatches up* SHIRLEY's *mug and hurls it at her. She slams the loft door and vanishes. The mug smashes against the door and falls in fragments}*

BILL: {*Beginning to chuckle}* Tell us, aol menn, wot o'clock this mawnin' was it wen 'im as they call Snobby Prawce was sived?

BARBARA: *{Turning to him more composedly, and the unspoiled sweetness}* About half past twelve, Bill. And he pinched your pound at a quarter to two. *I* know. Well, you can't afford to lose it. I'll send it to you.

BILL: *{His voice and accent suddenly improving}* Not if Aw wiz to stawve for it. Aw ain't to be bought.

SHIRLEY: Ain't you? You'd sell yourself to the devil for a pint o' beer; only there ain't no devil to make the offer.

BILL: *{Unashamed}* Sao Aw would, mite, and often 'ev, cheerful. But she cawn't baw me. *{Approaching* BARBARA] You wanted maw saoul, did you? Well, you ain't got it.

BARBARA: I nearly got it, Bill. But we've sold it back to you for ten thousand pounds.

SHIRLEY: And dear at the money!

BARBARA: No, Peter: it was worth more than money.

BILL: *{Salvationproof}* It's nao good: you cawn't get rahnd me nah. Aw down't b'lieve in it; and Aw've seen tod'y that Aw was rawt. *{Going}* Sao long, aol soup-kitchener! Ta, ta, Mijor Earl's Grendorter! *{Turning at the gate}* Wot prawce selvytion nah? Snobby Prawce! Ha! Ha!

BARBARA: *{Offering her hand}* Goodbye, Bill.

BILL: *{Taken aback, half plucks his cap off; then shoves it on again de-* *fiantly}* Git aht. [BARBARA *drops her hand, discouraged. He has a twinge of remorse}* But thet's aw rawt, you knaow. Nathink pasn'l. Naow mellice. Sao long, Judy. *{He goes}*

BARBARA: No malice. So long, Bill.

SHIRLEY: *{Shaking his head}* You make too much of him, Miss, in your innocence.

BARBARA: *{Going to him}* Peter: I'm like you now. Cleaned out, and lost my job.

SHIRLEY: You've youth and hope. That's two better than me.

BARBARA: I'll get you a job, Peter. That's hope for you: the youth will have to be enough for me. *{She counts her money}* I have just enough left for two teas at Lockharts, a Rowton doss for you, and my tram and bus home. *{He frowns and rises with offended pride. She takes his arm}* Don't be proud, Peter: it's sharing between friends. And promise me you'll talk to me and not let me cry. *{She draws him towards the gate}*

SHIRLEY: Well, I'm not accustomed to talk to the like of you—

BARBARA: *{Urgently}* Yes, yes: you must talk to me. Tell me about Tom Paine's books and Bradlaugh's lectures. Come along.

SHIRLEY: Ah, if you would only read Tom Paine in the proper spirit, Miss! *{They go out through the gate together}*

END OF ACT II

Act III

Next day after lunch LADY BRITOMART *is writing in the library in Wilton Crescent.* SARAH *is reading in the armchair near the window.* BARBARA, *in ordinary fashionable dress, pale and brooding, is on the settee.* CHARLES LOMAX *enters. He starts on seeing* BARBARA *fashionably attired and in low spirits.*

LOMAX: You've left off your uniform! [BARBARA *says nothing; but an expression of pain passes over her face}* LADY BRITOMART: *{warning him in low tones to be careful}* Charles!

LOMAX: *{Much concerned, coming* behind the settee and bending sympathetically over BARBARA] I'm awfully sorry, Barbara. You know I helped you all I could with the concertina and so forth. *{Momentously}* Still, I have never shut my eyes to the fact that there is a certain amount of tosh about the Salvation Army. Now the claims of the Church of England—

LADY BRITOMART: That's enough, Charles. Speak of something suited to your mental capacity.

LOMAX: *But surely the Church of England is suited to all our capacities.*

BARBARA: {*Pressing his hand*} Thank you for your sympathy, Cholly. Now go and spoon with Sarah.

LOMAX: {*Dragging a chair from the writing table and seating himself affectionately by* SARAH's *side*} How is my ownest today?

SARAH: I wish you wouldn't tell Cholly to do things, Barbara. He always comes straight and does them. Cholly: we're going to the works this afternoon.

LOMAX: What works?

SARAH: The cannon works.

LOMAX: What? Your governor's shop!

SARAH: Yes.

LOMAX: Oh I say! [CUSINS *enters in poor condition. He also starts visibly when he sees* BARBARA *without her uniform*}

BARBARA: I expected you this morning, Dolly. Didn't you guess that?

CUSINS: {*Sitting down beside her*} I'm sorry. I have only just breakfasted.

SARAH: But we've just finished lunch.

BARBARA: Have you had one of your bad nights?

CUSINS: No: I had rather a good night: in fact, one of the most remarkable nights I have ever passed.

BARBARA: The meeting?

CUSINS: No: after the meeting.

LADY BRITOMART: You should have gone to bed after the meeting. What were you doing?

CUSINS: Drinking.

LADY BRITOMART:	Adolphus!
SARAH:	Dolly!
BARBARA:	Dolly!
LOMAX:	Oh I say!

LADY BRITOMART: What were you drinking, may I ask?

CUSINS: A most devilish kind of Spanish burgundy, warranted free from added alcohol: a Temperance burgundy in fact. Its richness in natural alcohol made any addition superfluous.

BARBARA: Are you joking, Dolly?

CUSINS: {*Patiently*} No. I have been making a night of it with the nominal head of this household: that is all.

LADY BRITOMART: Andrew made you drunk!

CUSINS: No: he only provided the wine. I think it was Dionysos who made me drunk. {*To* BARBARA] I told you I was possessed.

LADY BRITOMART: You're not sober yet. Go home to bed at once.

CUSINS: I have never before ventured to reproach you, Lady Brit; but how could you marry the Prince of Darkness?

LADY BRITOMART: It was much more excusable to marry him than to get drunk with him. That is a new accomplishment of Andrew's, by the way. He usen't to drink.

CUSINS: He doesn't now. He only sat there and completed the wreck of my moral basis, the rout of my convictions, the purchase of my soul. He cares for you, Barbara. That is what makes him so dangerous to me.

BARBARA: That has nothing to do with it, Dolly. There are larger loves and diviner dreams than the fireside ones. You know that, don't you?

CUSINS: Yes: that is our understanding. I know it. I hold to it. Unless he can win me on that holier ground he may amuse me for a while; but he can get no deeper hold, strong as he is.

BARBARA: Keep to that; and the end will be right. Now tell me what happened at the meeting?

CUSINS: It was an amazing meeting. Mrs Baines almost died of emotion. Jenny Hill simply gibbered with hysteria. The Prince of Darkness played his trombone like a madman: its brazen roarings were like the laughter of the damned. 117 conversions took place then and there. They prayed with the most touching sincerity and gratitude for Bodger, and for the anonymous donor of the £5000. Your father would not let his name be given.

LOMAX: That was rather fine of the old man, you know. Most chaps would have wanted the advertisement.

CUSINS: He said the charitable institutions would be down on him like kites on a battle field if he gave his name.

LADY BRITOMART: That's Andrew all over. He never does a proper thing without giving an improper reason for it.

CUSINS: He convinced me that I have all my life been doing improper things for proper reasons.

LADY BRITOMART: Adolphus: now that Barbara has left the Salvation Army, you had better leave it too. I will not have you playing that drum in the streets.

CUSINS: Your orders are already obeyed, Lady Brit.

BARBARA: Dolly: were you ever really in earnest about it? Would you have joined if you had never seen me?

CUSINS: *{Disingenuously}* Well—er—well, possibly, as a collector of religions—

LOMAX: *{Cunningly}* Not as a drummer, though, you know. You are a very clearheaded brainy chap, Dolly; and it must have been apparent to you that there is a certain amount of tosh about—

LADY BRITOMART: Charles: if you must drivel, drivel like a grown-up man and not like a schoolboy.

LOMAX: *{Out of countenance}* Well, drivel is drivel, don't you know, whatever a man's age.

LADY BRITOMART: In good society in England, Charles, men drivel at all ages by repeating silly formulas with an air of wisdom. Schoolboys make their own formulas out of slang, like you. When they reach your age, and get political private secretaryships and things of that sort, they drop slang and get their formulas out of *The Spectator* or *The*

Times. You had better confine yourself to *The Times*. You will find that there is a certain amount of tosh about *The Times*; but at least its language is reputable.

LOMAX: *{Overwhelmed}* You are so awfully strong-minded, Lady Brit—

LADY BRITOMART: Rubbish! {MORRISON *comes in}* What is it?

MORRISON: If you please, my lady, Mr Undershaft has just drove up to the door.

LADY BRITOMART: Well, let him in. {MORRISON *hesitates}* What's the matter with you?

MORRISON: Shall I announce him, my lady; or is he at home here, so to speak, my lady?

LADY BRITOMART: Announce him.

MORRISON: Thank you, my lady. You won't mind my asking, I hope. The occasion is in a manner of speaking new to me.

LADY BRITOMART: Quite right. Go and let him in.

MORRISON: Thank you, my lady. {He *withdraws}*

LADY BRITOMART: Children: go and get ready. [SARAH *and* BARBARA *go upstairs for their out-of-door wraps}* Charles: go and tell Stephen to come down here in five minutes: you will find him in the drawing room. [CHARLES *goes}* Adolphus: tell them to send round the carriage in about fifteen minutes. [ADOLPHUS *goes}*

MORRISON: *{At the door}* Mr Undershaft. [UNDERSHAFT *comes in.* MORRISON *goes out}*

UNDERSHAFT: Alone! How fortunate!

LADY BRITOMART: *{Rising}* Don't be sentimental, Andrew. Sit down. *{She sits on the settee: he sits down beside her, on her left. She comes to the point before he has time to breathe}* Sarah must have £800 a year until Charles Lomax comes into his property. Barbara will need more, and need it permanently, because Adolphus hasn't any property.

UNDERSHAFT: *{Resignedly}* Yes, my

dear: I will see to it. Anything else? for yourself, for instance?

LADY BRITOMART: I want to talk to you about Stephen.

UNDERSHAFT: *{Rather wearily}* Don't, my dear. Stephen doesn't interest me.

LADY BRITOMART: He does interest me. He is our son.

UNDERSHAFT: Do you really think so? He has induced us to bring him into the world; but he chose his parents very incongruously, I think. I see nothing of myself in him, and less of you.

LADY BRITOMART: Andrew: Stephen is an excellent son, and a most steady, capable, highminded young man. You are simply trying to find an excuse for disinheriting him.

UNDERSHAFT: My dear Biddy: the Undershaft tradition disinherits him. It would be dishonest of me to leave the cannon foundry to my son.

LADY BRITOMART: It would be most unnatural and improper of you to leave it to anyone else, Andrew. Do you suppose this wicked and immoral tradition can be kept up for ever? Do you pretend that Stephen could not carry on the foundry just as well as all the other sons of the big business houses?

UNDERSHAFT: Yes: he could learn the office routine without understanding the business, like all the other sons; and the firm would go on by its own momentum until the real Undershaft— probably an Italian or a German— would invent a new method and cut him out.

LADY BRITOMART: There is nothing that any Italian or German could do that Stephen could not do. And Stephen at least has breeding.

UNDERSHAFT: The son of a foundling! Nonsense!

LADY BRITOMART: My son, Andrew! And even you may have good blood in your veins for all you know.

UNDERSHAFT: True. Probably I have. That is another argument in favor of a foundling.

LADY BRITOMART: Andrew: don't be aggravating. And don't be wicked. At present you are both.

UNDERSHAFT: This conversation is part of the Undershaft tradition, Biddy. Every Undershaft's wife has treated him to it ever since the house was founded. It is mere waste of breath. If the tradition be ever broken it will be for an abler man than Stephen.

LADY BRITOMART: *{Pouting}* Then go away.

UNDERSHAFT: *{Deprecatory}* Go away!

LADY BRITOMART: Yes: go away. If you will do nothing for Stephen, you are not wanted here. Go to your foundling, whoever he is; and look after him.

UNDERSHAFT: The fact is, Biddy—

LADY BRITOMART: Don't call me Biddy. I don't call you Andy.

UNDERSHAFT: I will not call my wife Britomart: it is not good sense. Seriously, my love, the Undershaft tradition has landed me in a difficulty. I am getting on in years; and my partner Lazarus has at last made a stand and insisted that the succession must be settled one way or the other; and of course he is quite right. You see, I haven't found a fit successor yet.

LADY BRITOMART: *{Obstinately}* There is Stephen.

UNDERSHAFT: That's just it: all the foundlings I can find are exactly like Stephen.

LADY BRITOMART: Andrew!

UNDERSHAFT: I want a man with no relations and no schooling: that is, a man who would be out of the running altogether if he were not a strong man. And I can't find him. Every blessed foundling nowadays is snapped up in his infancy by Bernardo homes or School Board officers, or Boards of Guardians; and if he shews the least ability, he is fastened on by schoolmasters; trained to win scholarships like a racehorse; crammed with secondhand ideas; drilled and disciplined in docility and what they call good taste; and lamed for life so that he is fit for nothing but teaching. If you want to keep the foundry in the family, you had better find an eligible foundling and marry him to Barbara.

LADY BRITOMART: Ah! Barbara! Your pet! You would sacrifice Stephen to Barbara.

UNDERSHAFT: Cheerfully. And you, my dear, would boil Barbara to make soup for Stephen.

LADY BRITOMART: Andrew: this is not a question of our likings and dislikings: it is a question of duty. It is your duty to make Stephen your successor.

UNDERSHAFT: Just as much as it is your duty to submit to your husband. Come, Biddy! these tricks of the governing class are of no use with me. I am one of the governing class myself; and it is waste of time giving tracts to a missionary. I have the power in this matter; and I am not to be humbugged into using it for your purposes.

LADY BRITOMART: Andrew: you can talk my head off; but you can't change wrong into right. And your tie is all on one side. Put it straight.

UNDERSHAFT: {Disconcerted} It won't stay unless it's pinned—{He fumbles at it with childish grimaces. STEPHEN comes in}

STEPHEN: {At the door} I beg your pardon. {About to retire}

LADY BRITOMART: No: come in, Stephen. [STEPHEN comes forward to his mother's writing table}

UNDERSHAFT: {Not very cordially} Good afternoon.

STEPHEN: {Coldly} Good afternoon.

UNDERSHAFT: {To LADY BRITOMART] He knows all about the tradition, I suppose?

LADY BRITOMART: Yes. {To STEPHEN] It is what I told you last night, Stephen.

UNDERSHAFT: {Sulkily} I understand you want to come into the cannon business.

STEPHEN: I go into trade! Certainly not.

UNDERSHAFT: {Opening his eyes, greatly eased in mind and manner} Oh! in that case—

LADY BRITOMART: Cannons are not trade, Stephen. They are enterprise.

STEPHEN: I have no intention of becoming a man of business in any sense. I have no capacity for business and no taste for it. I intend to devote myself to politics.

UNDERSHAFT: {Rising} My dear boy: this is an immense relief to me. And I trust it may prove an equally good thing for the country. I was afraid you would consider yourself disparaged and slighted. {He moves towards STEPHEN as if to shake hands with him}

LADY BRITOMART: {Rising and interposing} Stephen: I cannot allow you to throw away an enormous property like this.

STEPHEN: {Stiffly} Mother: there must be an end of treating me as a child, if you please. [LADY BRITOMART recoils, deeply wounded by his tone} Until last night I did not take your attitude seriously, because I did not think you meant it seriously. But I find now that you left me in the dark as to matters which you should have explained to me years ago. I am extremely hurt and offended. Any further discussion of my intentions had better take place with my father, as between one man and another.

LADY BRITOMART: Stephen! {She sits down again, her eyes filling with tears}

UNDERSHAFT: {With grave compassion} You see, my dear, it is only the big men who can be treated as children.

STEPHEN: I am sorry, mother, that you have forced me—

UNDERSHAFT: {Stopping him} Yes, yes, yes, yes: that's all right, Stephen. She won't interfere with you any more: your independence is achieved: you have won your watchkey. Don't rub it in; and above all, don't apologize. {He resumes his seat} Now what about your future, as between one man and another—I beg your pardon, Biddy: as between two men and a woman.

LADY BRITOMART: *{Who has pulled herself together strongly}* I quite understand, Stephen. By all means go your own way if you feel strong enough. [STEPHEN *sits down magisterially in the chair at the writing table with an air of affirming his majority*]

UNDERSHAFT: It is settled that you do not ask for the succession to the cannon business.

STEPHEN: I hope it is settled that I repudiate the cannon business.

UNDERSHAFT: Come, come! don't be so devilishly sulky: it's boyish. Freedom should be generous. Besides, I owe you a fair start in life in exchange for disinheriting you. You can't become prime minister all at once. Haven't you a turn for something? What about literature, art, and so forth?

STEPHEN: I have nothing of the artist about me, either in faculty or character, thank Heaven!

UNDERSHAFT: A philosopher, perhaps? Eh?

STEPHEN: I make no such ridiculous pretension.

UNDERSHAFT: Just so. Well, there is the army, the navy, the Church, the Bar. The Bar requires some ability. What about the Bar?

STEPHEN: I have not studied law. And I am afraid I have not the necessary push—I believe that is the name barristers give to their vulgarity—for success in pleading.

UNDERSHAFT: Rather a difficult case, Stephen. Hardly anything left but the stage, is there? [STEPHEN *makes an impatient movement}* Well, come! is there anything you know or care for?

STEPHEN: *{Rising and looking at him steadily}* I know the difference between right and wrong.

UNDERSHAFT: *{Hugely tickled}* You don't say so! What! no capacity for business, no knowledge of law, no sympathy with art, no pretension to philosophy; only a simple knowledge of the secret that has puzzled all the philosophers, baffled all the lawyers, muddled all the men of business, and ruined most of the artists: the secret of right and wrong. Why, man, you're a genius, a master of masters, a god! At twenty-four, too!

STEPHEN: *{Keeping his temper with difficulty}* You are pleased to be facetious. I pretend to nothing more than any honorable English gentleman claims as his birthright. *{He sits down angrily}*

UNDERSHAFT: Oh, that's everybody's birthright. Look at poor little Jenny Hill, the Salvation lassie! She would think you were laughing at her if you asked her to stand up in the street and teach grammar or geography or mathematics or even drawing room dancing; but it never occurs to her to doubt that she can teach morals and religion. You are all alike, you respectable people. You can't tell me the bursting strain of a ten-inch gun, which is a very simple matter; but you all think you can tell me the bursting strain of a man under temptation. You daren't handle high explosives; but you're all ready to handle honesty and truth and justice and the whole duty of man, and kill one another at that game. What a country! What a world!

LADY BRITOMART: *{Uneasily}* What do you think he had better do, Andrew?

UNDERSHAFT: Oh, just what he wants to do. He knows nothing and he thinks he knows everything. That points clearly to a political career. Get him a private secretaryship to someone who can get him an Under Secretaryship; and then leave him alone. He will find his natural and proper place in the end on the Treasury Bench.

STEPHEN: *{Springing up again}* I am sorry, sir, that you force me to forget the respect due to you as my father. I am an Englishman and I will not hear the Government of my country insulted. *{He thrusts his hands in his pockets, and walks angrily across to the window}*

UNDERSHAFT: *{With a touch of brutality}* The government of your country! *I* am the government of your country: I, and Lazarus. Do you suppose that you and half a dozen amateurs like you, sitting in a row in that foolish gabble shop, can govern Undershaft and Lazarus? No, my friend: you will do what pays us. You will make war when it suits us, and keep peace when it doesn't. You will find out that trade requires certain measures when we have decided on those measures. When I want anything to keep my dividends up, you will discover that my want is a national need. When other people want something to keep my dividends down, you will call out the police and military. And in return you shall have the support and applause of my newspapers, and the delight of imagining that you are a great statesman. Government of your country! Be off with you, my boy, and play with your caucuses and leading articles and historic parties and great leaders and burning questions and the rest of your toys. *I* am going back to my counting house to pay the piper and call the tune.

STEPHEN: *{Actually smiling, and putting his hand on his father's shoulder with indulgent patronage}* Really, my dear father, it is impossible to be angry with you. You don't know how absurd all this sounds to me. You are very properly proud of having been industrious enough to make money; and it is greatly to your credit that you have made so much of it. But it has kept you in circles where you are valued for your money and deferred to for it, instead of in the doubtless very old-fashioned and behind-the-times public school and university where I formed my habits of mind. It is natural for you to think that money governs England; but you must allow me to think I know better.

UNDERSHAFT: And what does govern England, pray?

STEPHEN: Character, father, character.

UNDERSHAFT: Whose character? Yours or mine?

STEPHEN: Neither yours nor mine, father, but the best elements in the English national character.

UNDERSHAFT: Stephen: I've found your profession for you. You're a born journalist. I'll start you with a hightoned weekly review. There! *{Before* STEPHEN *can reply* SARAH, BARBARA, LOMAX, *and* CUSINS *come in ready for walking.* BARBARA *crosses the room to the window and looks out.* CUSINS *drifts amiably to the armchair.* LOMAX *remains near the door, whilst* SARAH *comes to her mother.*

STEPHEN *goes to the smaller writing table and busies himself with his letters}*

SARAH: Go and get ready, mamma: the carriage is waiting. [LADY BRITOMART *leaves the room}*

UNDERSHAFT: *{To* SARAH] Good day, my dear. Good afternoon, Mr Lomax.

LOMAX: *{Vaguely}* Ahdedoo.

UNDERSHAFT: *{To* CUSINS] Quite well after last night, Euripides, eh?

CUSINS: As well as can be expected.

UNDERSHAFT: That's right. *{To* BARBARA] So you are coming to see my death and devastation factory, Barbara?

BARBARA: *{At the window}* You came yesterday to see my salvation factory. I promised you a return visit.

LOMAX: *{Coming forward between* SARAH *and* UNDERSHAFT] You'll find it awfully interesting. I've been through the Woolwich Arsenal; and it gives you a ripping feeling of security, you know, to think of the lot of beggars we could kill if it came to fighting. *{To* UNDERSHAFT, *with sudden solemnity}* Still, it must be rather an awful reflection for you, from the religious point of view as it were. You're getting on, you know, and all that.

SARAH: You don't mind Cholly's imbecility, papa, do you?

LOMAX: *{Much taken aback}* Oh I say!

UNDERSHAFT: Mr Lomax looks at the matter in a very proper spirit, my dear.

LOMAX: Just so. That's all I meant, I assure you.

SARAH: Are you coming, Stephen?

STEPHEN: Well, I am rather busy— er— *{Magnanimously}* Oh well, yes: I'll come. That is, if there is room for me.

UNDERSHAFT: I can take two with me

in a little motor I am experimenting with for field use. You won't mind its being rather unfashionable. It's not painted yet; but it's bullet proof.

LOMAX: *{Appalled at the prospect of confronting Wilton Crescent in an unpainted motor}* Oh I say!

SARAH: The carriage for me, thank you. Barbara doesn't mind what she's seen in.

LOMAX: I say, Dolly old chap: do you really mind the car being a guy? Because of course if you do I'll go in it. Still—

CUSINS: I prefer it.

LOMAX: Thanks awfully, old man. Come, my ownest. *{He hurries out to secure his seat in the carriage.* SARAH *follows him}*

CUSINS: *{Moodily walking across to* LADY BRITOMART's *writing table}* Why are we two coming to this Works Department of Hell? that is what I ask myself.

BARBARA: I have always thought of it as a sort of pit where lost creatures with blackened faces stirred up smoky fires and were driven and tormented by my father. Is it like that, dad?

UNDERSHAFT: *{Scandalized}* My dear! It is a spotlessly clean and beautiful hillside town.

CUSINS: With a Methodist chapel? Oh do say there's a Methodist chapel.

UNDERSHAFT: There are two: a Primitive one and a sophisticated one. There is even an Ethical Society; but it is not much patronized, as my men are all strongly religious. In the High Explosives Sheds they object to the presence of Agnostics as unsafe.

CUSINS: And yet they don't object to you!

BARBARA: Do they obey all your orders?

UNDERSHAFT: I never give them any orders. When I speak to one of them it is "Well, Jones, is the baby doing well? and has Mrs Jones made a good recovery?" "Nicely, thank you, sir." And that's all.

CUSINS: But Jones has to be kept in order. How do you maintain discipline among your men?

UNDERSHAFT: I don't. They do. You see, the one thing Jones won't stand is any rebellion from the man under him, or any assertion of social equality between the wife of the man with 4 shillings a week less than himself, and Mrs Jones! Of course they all rebel against me, theoretically. Practically, every man of them keeps the man just below him in his place. I never meddle with them. I never bully them. I don't even bully Lazarus. I say that certain things are to be done; but I don't order anybody to do them. I don't say, mind you, that there is no ordering about and snubbing and even bullying. The men snub the boys and order them about; the carmen snub the sweepers; the artisans snub the unskilled laborers; the foremen drive and bully both the laborers and artisans; the assistant engineers find fault with the foremen; the chief engineers drop on the assistants; the departmental managers worry the chiefs; and the clerks have tall hats and hymnbooks and keep up the social tone by refusing to associate on equal terms with anybody. The result is a colossal profit, which comes to me.

CUSINS: *{Revolted}* You really are a —well, what I was saying yesterday.

BARBARA: What was he saying yesterday?

UNDERSHAFT: Never mind, my dear. He thinks I have made you unhappy. Have I?

BARBARA: Do you think I can be happy in this vulgar silly dress? I! who have worn the uniform. Do you understand what you have done to me? Yesterday I had a man's soul in my hand. I set him in the way of life with his face to salvation. But when we took your money he turned back to drunkenness and derision. *{With intense conviction}* I will never forgive you that. If I had a child, and you destroyed its body with your explosives—if you murdered Dolly with your horrible guns—I could forgive you if my forgiveness would open the gates of heaven to you. But to take a human soul from me, and turn it into the soul of a wolf! that is worse than any murder.

UNDERSHAFT: Does my daughter despair so easily? Can you strike a man to the heart and leave no mark on him?

BARBARA: {Her face lighting up} Oh, you are right: he can never be lost now: where was my faith?

CUSINS: Oh, clever clever devil!

BARBARA: You may be a devil; but God speaks through you sometimes. {She takes her father's hands and kisses them} You have given me back my happiness: I feel it deep down now, though my spirit is troubled.

UNDERSHAFT: You have learnt something. That always feels at first as if you had lost something.

BARBARA: Well, take me to the factory of death; and let me learn something more. There must be some truth or other behind all this frightful irony. Come, Dolly. {She goes out}

CUSINS: My guardian angel! {To UNDERSHAFT} Avaunt! {He follows BARBARA}

STEPHEN: {Quietly, at the writing table} You must not mind Cusins, father. He is a very amiable good fellow; but he is a Greek scholar and naturally a little eccentric.

UNDERSHAFT: Ah, quite so. Thank you, Stephen. Thank you. {He goes out. STEPHEN smiles patronizingly; buttons his coat responsibly; and crosses the room to the door. LADY BRITOMART, dressed for out-of-doors, opens it before he reaches it. She looks around for the others; looks at STEPHEN; and turns to go without a word}

STEPHEN: {Embarrassed} Mother—

LADY BRITOMART: Don't be apologetic, Stephen. And don't forget that you have outgrown your mother. {he goes out}

{Perivale St Andrews lies between two Middlesex hills, half climbing the northern one. It is an almost smokeless town of white walls, roofs of narrow green slates or red tiles, tall trees, domes, campaniles, and slender chimney shafts, beautifully situated and beautiful in itself. The best view of it is obtained from the crest of a slope about half a mile to the east, where the high explosives are dealt with. The foundry lies hidden in the depths between, the tops of its chimneys sprouting like huge skittles into the middle distance. Across the crest runs an emplacement of concrete, with a firestep, and a parapet which suggests a fortification, because there is a huge cannon of the obsolete Woolwich Infant pattern peering across it at the town. The cannon is mounted on an experimental gun carriage: possibly the original model of the Undershaft disappearing rampart gun alluded to by Stephen. The firestep, being a convenient place to sit, is furnished here and there with straw disc cushions; and at one place there is the additional luxury of a fur rug.

BARBARA is standing on the firestep, looking over the parapet towards the town. On her right is the cannon; on her left the end of a shed raised on piles, with a ladder of three or four steps up to the door, which opens outwards and has a little wooden landing at the threshold, with a fire bucket in the corner of the landing. Several dummy soldiers more or less mutilated, with straw protruding from their gashes, have been shoved out of the way under the landing. A few others are nearly upright against the shed; and one has fallen forward and lies, like a grotesque corpse, on the emplacement. The parapet stops short of the shed, leaving a gap which is the beginning of the path down the hill through the foundry to the town. The rug is on the firestep near this gap. Down on the emplacement behind the cannon is a trolley carrying a huge conical bombshell with a red band painted on it. Further to the right is the door of an office, which, like the sheds, is of the lightest possible construction. CUSINS arrives by the path from the town}

BARBARA: Well?

CUSINS: Not a ray of hope. Everything perfect! wonderful! real! It only needs a cathedral to be a heavenly city instead of a hellish one.

BARBARA: Have you found out whether they have done anything for old Peter Shirley?

CUSINS: They have found him a job as gatekeeper and timekeeper. He's frightfully miserable. He calls the timekeeping brainwork, and says he isn't used to it; and his gate lodge is so splendid that he's ashamed to use the rooms, and skulks in the scullery.

BARBARA: Poor Peter! [STEPHEN *arrives from the town. He carries a field-glass}*

STEPHEN: *{Enthusiastically}* Have you two seen the place? Why did you leave us?

CUSINS: I wanted to see everything I was not intended to see; and Barbara wanted to make the men talk.

STEPHEN: Have you found anything discreditable?

CUSINS: No. They call him Dandy Andy and are proud of his being a cunning old rascal; but it's all horribly frightfully, immorally, unanswerably perfect. [SARAH *arrives}*

SARAH: Heavens! what a place! *{She crosses to the trolley}* Did you see the nursing home! *{She sits down on the shell}*

STEPHEN: Did you see the libraries and schools?

SARAH: Did you see the ball room and the banqueting chamber in the Town Hall?

STEPHEN: Have you gone into the insurance fund, the pension fund, the building society, the various applications of cooperation!? [UNDERSHAFT *comes from the office, with a sheaf of telegrams in his hand}*

UNDERSHAFT: Well, have you seen everything? I'm sorry I was called away. *{Indicating the telegrams}* Good news from Manchuria.

STEPHEN: Another Japanese victory?

UNDERSHAFT: Oh, I don't know.

Which side wins does not concern us here. No: the good news is that the aerial battleship is a tremendous success. At the first trial it has wiped out a fort with three hundred soldiers in it.

CUSINS: *{From the platform}* Dummy soldiers?

UNDERSHAFT: *{Striding across to* STEPHEN *and kicking the prostrate dummy brutally out of his way}* No: the real thing. [CUSINS *and* BARBARA *exchange glances. Then* CUSINS *sits on the step and buries his face in his hands.* BARBARA *gravely lays her hand on his shoulder. He looks up at her in whimsical desperation}*

UNDERSHAFT: Well, Stephen, what do you think of the place?

STEPHEN: Oh, magnificent. A perfect triumph of modern industry. Frankly, my dear father, I have been a fool: I had no idea of what it all meant: of the wonderful forethought, the power of organization, the administrative capacity, the financial genius, the colossal capital it represents. I have been repeating to myself as I came through your streets "Peace hath her victories no less renowned than War." I have only one misgiving about it all.

UNDERSHAFT: Out with it.

STEPHEN: Well, I cannot help thinking that all this provision for every want of your workmen may sap their independence and weaken their sense of responsibility. And greatly as we enjoyed our tea at that splendid restaurant —how they gave us all that luxury and cake and jam and cream for threepence I really cannot imagine!—still you must remember that restaurants break up home life. Look at the continent, for instance! Are you sure so much pampering is really good for the men's characters?

UNDERSHAFT: Well you see, my dear boy, when you are organizing civilization you have to make up your mind whether trouble and anxiety are good things or not. If you decide that they are, then, I take it, you simply don't organize civilization; and there you are, with trouble and anxiety enough to make us all angels! But if you decide the other way, you may as well go through with it. However, Stephen, our characters are safe here. A sufficient dose of anxiety is always provided by the fact that we may be blown to smithereens at any moment.

SARAH: By the way, papa, where do you make the explosives?

UNDERSHAFT: In separate little sheds, like that one. When one of them blows up, it costs very little; and only the people quite close to it are killed. [STEPHEN, *who is quite close to it, looks at it rather scaredly, and moves away quickly to the cannon. At the same moment the door of the shed is thrown abruptly open; and a foreman in overalls and list slippers comes out on the little landing and holds the door for* LOMAX, *who appears in the doorway}*

LOMAX: *{With studied coolness}* My good fellow: you needn't get into a state of nerves. Nothing's going to happen to you; and I suppose it wouldn't be the end of the world if anything did. A little bit of British pluck is what you want, old chap. *{He descends and strolls across to* SARAH]

UNDERSHAFT: *{To the foreman}* Anything wrong, Bilton?

BILTON: *{With ironic calm}* Gentleman walked into the high explosives shed and lit a cigaret, sir: that's all.

UNDERSHAFT: Ah, quite so. *{Going over to* LOMAX] Do you happen to remember what you did with the match?

LOMAX: Oh come! I'm not a fool. I took jolly good care to blow it out before I chucked it away.

BILTON: The top of it was red hot inside, sir.

LOMAX: Well, suppose it was! I didn't chuck it into any of your messes.

UNDERSHAFT: Think no more of it, Mr Lomax. By the way, would you mind lending me your matches?

LOMAX: *{Offering his box}* Certainly.

UNDERSHAFT: Thanks. *{He pockets the matches}*

LOMAX: *{Lecturing to the company generally}* You know, these high explosives don't go off like gunpowder, except when they're in a gun. When they're spread loose, you can put a match to them without the least risk: they just burn quietly like a bit of paper. *{Warming to the scientific interest of the subject}* Did you know that, Undershaft? Have you ever tried?

UNDERSHAFT: Not on a large scale, Mr Lomax. Bilton will give you a sample of gun cotton when you are leaving if you ask him. You can exeperiment with it at home. [BILTON *looks puzzled}*

SARAH: Bilton will do nothing of the sort, papa. I suppose it's your business to blow up the Russians and Japs; but you might really stop short of blowing up poor Cholly. [BILTON *gives it up and retires into the shed}*

LOMAX: My ownest, there is no danger. *{He sits beside her on the shell;* LADY BRITOMART *arrives from the town with a bouquet}*

LADY BRITOMART: *{Impetuously}* Andrew: you shouldn't have let me see this place.

UNDERSHAFT: Why, my dear?

LADY BRITOMART: Never mind why: you shouldn't have: that's all. To think of all that *{Indicating the town}* being yours! and that you have kept it to yourself all these years!

UNDERSHAFT: It does not belong to me. I belong to it. It is the Undershaft inheritance.

LADY BRITOMART: It is not. Your ridiculous cannons and that noisy banging foundry may be the Undershaft inheritance; but all that plate and linen, all that furniture and those houses and orchards and gardens belong to us. They belong to me: they are not a man's business. I won't give them up. You must be out of your senses to throw them all away; and if you persist in such folly, I will call in a doctor.

UNDERSHAFT: *{Stooping to smell the bouquet}* Where did you get the flowers my dear?

LADY BRITOMART: Your men presented them to me on your William Morris Labor Church.

CUSINS: Oh! It needed only that. A Labor Church! *{He mounts the firestep distractedly, and leans with his elbows on the parapet, turning his back to them}*

LADY BRITOMART: Yes, with Morris's words in mosaic letters ten feet high round the dome. NO MAN IS GOOD ENOUGH TO BE ANOTHER MAN'S MASTER. The cynicism of it!

UNDERSHAFT: It shocked the men at first, I am afraid. But now they take no more notice of it than of the ten commandments in church.

LADY BRITOMART: Andrew: you are trying to put me off the subject of the inheritance by profane jokes. Well, you shan't. I don't ask it any longer for Stephen: he has inherited far too much of your perversity to be fit for it. But Barbara has rights as well as Stephen. Why should not Adolphus succeed to the inheritance? I could manage the town for him; and he can look after the cannons, if they are really necessary.

UNDERSHAFT: I should ask nothing better if Adolphus were a foundling. He is exactly the sort of new blood that is wanted in English business, But he's not a foundling; and there's an end of it. *{He makes for the office door}*

CUSINS: *{Turning to them}* Not quite. *{They all turn and stare at him}* I think— Mind! I am not committing myself in any way as to my future course —but I think the foundling difficulty can be got over. *{He jumps down to the emplacement}*

UNDERSHAFT: *{Coming back to him}* What do you mean?

CUSINS: Well, I have something to say which is in the nature of a confession.

SARAH:
LADY BRITOMART:
BARBARA: } Confession!
STEPHEN:
LOMAX: Oh I say!

CUSINS: Yes, a confession. Listen, all. Until I met Barbara I thought myself in the main an honorable, truthful man, because I wanted the approval of my conscience more than I wanted anything else. But the moment I saw Barbara, I wanter her far more than the approval of my conscience.

LADY BRITOMART: Adolphus!

CUSINS: It is true. You accused me yourself, Lady Brit, of joining the Army to worship Barbara; and so I did. She bought my soul like a flower at a street corner; but she bought it for herself.

UNDERSHAFT: What! Not for Dionysos or another?

CUSINS: Dionysos and all the others are in herself. I adored what was divine in her, and was therefore a true worshipper. But I was romantic about her too. I thought she was a woman of the people, and that a marriage with a professor of Greek would be far beyond the wildest social ambitions of her rank.

LADY BRITOMART: Adolphus!!

CUSINS: When I learnt the horrible truth—

LADY BRITOMART: What do you mean by the horrible truth, pray?

CUSINS: That she was enormously rich; that her grandfather was an earl; that her father was the Prince of Darkness—

UNDERSHAFT: Chut!

CUSINS: —and that I was only an adventurer trying to catch a rich wife, then I stooped to deceive her about my birth.

BARBARA: *{Rising}* Dolly!

LADY BRITOMART: Your birth! Now Adolphus, don't dare to make up a wicked story for the sake of these wretched cannons. Remember: I have seen photographs of your parents; and the Agent General for South Western Australia knows them personally and has assured me that they are most respectable married people.

CUSINS: So they are in Australia; but here they are outcasts. Their marriage is legal in Australia, but not in England.

My mother is my father's deceased wife's sister; and in this island I am consequently a foundling. *{Sensation}*

BARBARA: Silly! *{She climbs to the cannon, and leans, listening, in the angle it makes with the parapet}*

CUSINS: Is the subterfuge good enough, Machiavelli?

UNDERSHAFT: *{Thoughtfully}* Biddy: this may be a way out of the difficulty.

LADY BRITOMART: Stuff! A man can't make cannons any the better for being his own cousin instead of his proper self. *{She sits down on the rug with a bounce that expresses her downright contempt for their casuistry}*

UNDERSHAFT: *{To CUSINS}* You are an educated man. That is against the tradition.

CUSINS: Once in ten thousand times it happens that the schoolboy is a born master of what they try to teach him. Greek has not destroyed my mind: it has nourished it. Besides, I did not learn it at an English public school.

UNDERSHAFT: Hm! Well, I cannot afford to be too particular: you have cornered the foundling market. Let it pass. You are eligible, Euripides: you are eligible.

BARBARA: Dolly: yesterday morning, when Stephen told us all about the tradition, you became very silent; and you have been strange and excited ever since. Were you thinking about your birth then?

CUSINS: When the finger of Destiny suddenly points at a man in the middle of his breakfast, it makes him thoughtful.

UNDERSHAFT: Aha! You have had your eye on the business, my young friend, have you?

CUSINS: Take care! There is an abyss of moral horror between me and your accursed aerial battleships.

UNDERSHAFT: Never mind the abyss for the present. Let us settle the practical details and leave your final decision open. You know that you will have to change your name. Do you object to that?

CUSINS: Would any man named Adolphus—any man called Dolly!—object to be called something else?

UNDERSHAFT: Good. Now, as to money! I propose to treat you handsomely from the beginning. You shall start at a thousand a year.

CUSINS: *{With sudden heat, his spectacles twinkling with mischief}* A thousand! You dare offer a miserable thousand to the son-in-law of a millionaire! No, by Heavens, Machiavelli! you shall not cheat me. You cannot do without me; and I can do without you. I must have two thousand five hundred a year for two years. At the end of that time, if I am a failure, I go. But if I am a success, and stay on, you must give me the other five thousand.

UNDERSHAFT: What other five thousand?

CUSINS: To make the two years up to five thousand a year. The two thousand five hundred is only half pay in case I should turn out a failure. The third year I must have ten per cent of the profits.

UNDERSHAFT: *{Taken aback}* Ten per cent! Why, man, do you know what my profits are?

CUSINS: Enormous, I hope: otherwise I shall require twenty-five per cent.

UNDERSHAFT: But, Mr Cusins, this is a serious matter of business. You are not bringing any capital into the concern.

CUSINS: What! no capital! Is my mastery of Greek no capital? Is my access to the subtlest thought, the loftiest poetry yet attained by humanity, no capital? My character! my intellect! my life! my career! what Barbara calls my soul! are these no capital? Say another word; and I double my salary.

UNDERSHAFT: Be reasonable—

CUSINS: *{Peremptorily}* Mr Undershaft: you have my terms. Take them or leave them.

UNDERSHAFT: *{Recovering himself}* Very well. I note your terms; and I offer you half.

CUSINS: *{Disgustedly}* Half!

UNDERSHAFT: *{Firmly}* Half.

CUSINS: You call yourself a gentleman; and you offer me half!!

UNDERSHAFT: I do not call myself a gentleman; but I offer you half.

CUSINS: This to your future partner! your successor! your son-in-law!

BARBARA: You are selling your own soul, Dolly, not mine. Leave me out of the bargain, please.

UNDERSHAFT: Come! I will go a step further for Barbara's sake. I will give you three fifths; but this is my last word.

CUSINS: Done!

LOMAX: Done in the eye! Why, I get only eight hundred, you know.

CUSINS: By the way, Mac, I am a classical scholar, not an arithmetical one. Is three fifths more than half or less?

UNDERSHAFT: More, of course.

CUSINS: I would have taken two hundred and fifty. How you can succeed in business when you are willing to pay all that money to a University don who is obviously not worth a junior clerk's wages!—well! What will Lazarus say?

UNDERSHAFT: Lazarus is a gentle romantic Jew who cares for nothing but string quartets and stalls at fashionable theatres. He will be blamed for your rapacity in money matters, poor fellow! as he has hitherto been blamed for mine. You are a shark of the first order, Euripides. So much the better for the firm!

BARBARA: Is the bargain closed, Dolly? Does your soul belong to him now?

CUSINS: No: the price is settled: that is all. The real tug of war is still to come. What about the moral question?

LADY BRITOMART: There is no moral question in the matter at all, Adolphus. You must simply sell cannons and weapons to people whose cause is right and just, and refuse them to foreigners and criminals.

UNDERSHAFT: {*Determinedly*} No: none of that. You must keep the true faith of an Armorer, or you don't come in here.

CUSINS: What on earth is the true faith of an Armorer?

UNDERSHAFT: To give arms to all men who offer an honest price for them, without respect of persons or principles: to aristocrat and republican, to Nihilist and Tsar, to Capitalist and Socialist, to Protestant and Catholic, to burglar and policeman, to black man, white man and yellow man, to all sorts and conditions, all nationalities, all faiths, all follies, all causes and all crimes. The first Undershaft wrote up in his shop IF GOD GAVE THE HAND, LET NOT MAN WITHHOLD THE SWORD. The second wrote up ALL HAVE THE RIGHT TO FIGHT: NONE HAVE THE RIGHT TO JUDGE. The third wrote up TO MAN THE WEAPON: TO HEAVEN THE VICTORY. The fourth had no literary turn; so he did not write up anything; but he sold cannons to Napoleon under the nose of George the Third. The fifth wrote up PEACE SHALL NOT PREVAIL SAVE WITH A SWORD IN HER HAND. The sixth, my master, was the best of all. He wrote up NOTHING IS EVER DONE IN THIS WORLD UNTIL MEN ARE PREPARED TO KILL ONE ANOTHER IF IT IS NOT DONE. After that, there was nothing left for the seventh to say. So he wrote up, simply UNASHAMED.

CUSINS: My good Machiavelli, I shall certainly write something up on the wall; only as I shall write it in Greek, you won't be able to read it. But as to your Armorer's faith, if I take my neck out of the noose of my own morality I am not going to put it into the noose of yours. I shall sell cannons to whom I please and refuse them to whom I please. So there!

UNDERSHAFT: From the moment when you become Andrew Undershaft, you will never do as you please again. Don't come here lusting for power, young man.

CUSINS: If power were my aim I should not come here for it. You have no power.

UNDERSHAFT: None of my own, certainly.

CUSINS: I have more power than you, more will. Yo do not drive this place; it drives you. And what drives the place?

UNDERSHAFT: *{Enigmatically}* A will of which I am a part.

BARBARA: *{Startled}* Father! Do you know what you are saying; or are you laying a snare for my soul?

CUSINS: Don't listen to his metaphysics, Barbara. The place is driven by the most rascally part of society, the money hunters, the pleasure hunters, the military promotion hunters; and he is their slave.

UNDERSHAFT: Not necessarily. Remember the Armorer's Faith. I will take an order from a good man as cheerfully as from a bad one. If you good people prefer teaching and shirking to buying my weapons and fighting the rascals, don't blame me. I cannot make courage and conviction. Bah! you tire me, Euripides, with your morality mongering. Ask Barbara: she understands. *{He suddenly reaches up and takes* BARBARA's *hands, looking powerfully into her eyes}* Tell him, my love, what power really means.

BARBARA: *{Hypnotized}* Before I joined the Salvation Army, I was in my own power; and the consequence was that I never knew what to do with myself. When I joined it, I had not time enough for all the things I had to do.

UNDERSHAFT: *{Approvingly}* Just so. And why was that, do you suppose?

BARBARA: Yesterday I should have said, because I was in the power of God. *{She resumes her self-possession, withdrawing her hands from his with a power equal to his own}* But you came and shewed me that I was in the power of Bodger and Undershaft. Today I feel —oh! how can I put it into words? Sarah: do you remember the earthquake at Cannes, when we were little children? —how little the surprise of the first shock mattered compared to the dread and horror of waiting for the second? That is how I feel in this place today. I stood on the rock I thought eternal; and without a word of warning it reeled and crumbled under me. I was safe with an infinite wisdom watching me, an army marching to Salvation with me; and in a moment, at a stroke of your pen in a cheque book, I stood alone; and the heavens were empty. That was the first shock of the earthquake: I am waiting for the second.

UNDERSHAFT: Come, come, my daughter! don't make too much of your little tinpot tragedy. What do we do here when we spend years of work and thought and thousands of pounds of solid cash on a new gun or an aerial battle ship that turns out just a hairbreadth wrong after all? Scrap it. Scrap it without wasting another hour or another pound on it. Well, you have made for yourself something that you call a morality or a religion or what not. It doesn't fit the facts. Well, scrap it. Scrap it and get one that does fit. That is what is wrong with the world at present. It scraps its obsolete steam engines and dynamos; but it won't scrap its old prejudices and its old moralities and its old religions and its old political constitutions. What's the result? In machinery it does very well; but in morals and religion and politics it is working at a loss that brings it nearer bankruptcy every year. Don't persist in that folly. If your old religion broke down yesterday, get a newer and a better one for tomorrow.

BARBARA: Oh how gladly I would take a better one to my soul! But you offer me a worse one. *{Turning on him with sudden vehemence}* Justify yourself: shew me some light through the darkness of this dreadful place, with its beautifully clean workshops, and respectable workmen, and model homes.

UNDERSHAFT: Cleanliness and respectability do not need justification, Barbara; they justify themselves. I see no darkness here, no dreadfulness. In your Salvation shelter I saw poverty, misery, cold and hunger. You gave them bread and treacle and dreams of heaven.

I give them thirty shilling a week to twelve thousand a a year. They find their own dreams; but I look after the drainage.

BARBARA: And their souls?

UNDERSHAFT: I save their souls just as I saved yours.

BARBARA: *{Revolted}* You saved my soul! What do you mean?

UNDERSHAFT: I fed you and clothed you and housed you. I took care that you should have money enough to live handsomely—more than enough; so that you could be wasteful, careless, generous. That saved your soul from the seven deadly sins.

BARBARA: *{Bewildered}* The seven deadly sins!

UNDERSHAFT: Yes, the deadly seven. *{Counting on his fingers}* Food, clothing, firing, rent, taxes, respectability and children. Nothing can lift those seven millstones from Man's neck but money; and the spirit cannot soar until the millstones are lifted. I lifted them from your spirit. I enabled Barbara to become Major Barbara; and I saved her from the crime of poverty.

CUSINS: Do you call poverty a crime?

UNDERSHAFT: The worst of crimes. All the other crimes are virtues beside it: all the other dishonors are chivalry itself by comparison. Poverty blights whole cities; spreads horrible pestilences; strikes dead the very souls of all who come within sight, sound or smell of it. What you call crime is nothing: a murder here and a theft there, a blow now and a curse then: what do they matter? they are only the accidents and illnesses of life: there are not fifty genuine professional criminals in London. But there are millions of poor people, abject people, dirty people, ill fed, ill clothed people. They poison us morally and physically: they kill the happiness of society: they force us to do away with our own liberties and to organize unnatural cruelties for fear they should rise against us and drag us down into their abyss. Only fools fear crime: we all fear poverty. Pah! *{Turning on* BARBARA*}* you talk of your half-saved ruffian in West Ham: you accuse me of dragging his soul back to perdition. Well, bring him to me here; and I will drag his soul back again to salvation for you. Not by words and dreams; but by thirty-eight shilling a week, a sound house in a handsome street, and a permanent job. In three weeks he will have a fancy waistcoat; in three months a tall hat and a chapel sitting; before the end of the year he will shake hands with a duchess at a Primrose League meeting, and join the Conservative Party.

BARBARA: And will he be the better for that?

UNDERSHAFT: You know he will. Don't be a hypocrite, Barbara. He will be better fed, better housed, better clothed, better behaved; and his children will be pounds heavier and bigger. That will be better than an American cloth mattress in a shelter, chopping firewood, eating bread and treacle, and being forced to kneel down from time to time to thank heaven for it: knee drill, I think you call it. It is cheap work converting starving men with a Bible in one hand and a slice of bread in the other. I will undertake to convert West Ham to Mahometanism on the same terms. Try your hand on my men: their souls are hungry because their bodies are full.

BARBARA: And leave the east end to starve?

UNDERSHAFT: *{His energetic tone dropping into one of bitter and brooding remembrance}* I was an east ender. I moralized and starved until one day I swore that I would be a full-fed free man at all costs—that nothing should stop me except a bullet, neither reason nor morals nor the lives of other men. I said "Thou shalt starve ere I starve"; and with that word I became free and great. I was a dangerous man until I had my will: now I am a useful, beneficient, kindly person. That is the history of most self-made millionaires, I fancy. When it is the history of every Englishman we shall have an England worth living in.

LADY BRITOMART: Stop making speeches, Andrew. This is not the place for them.

UNDERSHAFT: {Punctured} My dear: I have no other means of conveying my ideas.

LADY BRITOMART: Your ideas are nonsense. You got on because you were selfish and unscrupulous.

UNDERSHAFT: Not at all. I had the strongest scruples about poverty and starvation. Your moralists are quite unscrupulous about both: they make virtues of them. I had rather be a thief than a pauper. I had rather been a murderer than a slave. I don't want to be either; but if you force the alternative on me, then, by Heaven, I'll choose the braver and more moral one. I hate poverty and slavery worse than any other crimes whatsoever. And let me tell you this. Poverty and slavery have stood up for centuries to your sermons and leading articles: they will not stand up to my machine guns. Don't preach at them: don't reason with them. Kill them.

BARBARA: Killing. Is that your remedy for everything?

UNDERSHAFT: It is the final test of conviction, the only lever strong enough to overturn a social system, the only way of saying Must. Let six hundred and seventy fools loose in the streets; and three policemen can scatter them. But huddle them together in a certain house in Westminster; and let them go through certain ceremonies and call themselves certain names until at last they get the courage to kill; and your six hundred and seventy fools become a government. Your pious mob fills up ballot papers and imagines it is governing its masters; but the ballot paper that really governs is the paper that has a bullet wrapped up in it.

CUSINS: That is perhaps why, like most intelligent people, I never vote.

UNDERSHAFT: Vote! Bah! When you vote, you only change the names of the cabinet. When you shoot, you pull down governments, inaugurate new epochs, abolish old orders and set up new. Is that historically true, Mr Learned Man, or is it not?

CUSINS: It is historically true. I loathe to having to admit it. I repudiate your sentiments. I abhor your nature. I defy you in every possible way. Still, it is true. But it ought not to be true.

UNDERSHAFT: Ought! ought! ought! ought! ought! Are you going to spend your life saying ought, like the rest of our moralists? Turn your oughts into shalls, man. Come and make explosives with me. Whatever can blow men up can blow society up. The history of the world is the history of those who had courage enough to embrace this truth. Have you the courage to embrace it, Barbara?

LADY BRITOMART: Barbara, I positively forbid you to listen to your father's abominable wickedness. And you, Adolphus, ought to know better than to go about saying that wrong things are true. What does it matter whether they are true if they are wrong?

UNDERSHAFT: What does it matter whether they are wrong if they are true?

LADY BRITOMART: {Rising} Children: come home instantly. Andrew: I am exceedingly sorry I allowed you to call on us. You are wickeder than ever. Come at once.

BARBARA: {Shaking her head} It's no use running away from wicked people, mamma.

LADY BRITOMART: It is every use. It shews your disapprobation of them.

BARBARA: It does not save them.

LADY BRITOMART: I can see that you are going to disobey me. Sarah: are you coming home or are you not?

SARAH: I daresay it's very wicked of papa to make cannons; but I don't think I shall cut him on that account.

LOMAX: {Pouring oil on the troubled waters} The fact is, you know, there is a certain amount of tosh about this notion of wickedness. It doesn't work. You must look at the facts. Not that I would say a word in favor of anything wrong; but then, you see, all sorts of chaps are always doing all sorts of things; and we have to fit them in somehow, don't you know. What I mean is that you can't go cutting everybody; and that's about what it comes to. *{Their rapt attention to his eloquence makes him nervous}* Perhaps I don't make myself clear.

LADY BRITOMART: You are lucidity itself, Charles. Because Andrew is successful and has plenty of money to give to Sarah, you will flatter him and encourage him in his wickedness.

LOMAX: *{Unruffled}* Well, where the carcase is, there will the eagles be gathered, don't you know. *{To UNDERSHAFT}* Eh? What?

UNDERSHAFT: Precisely. By the way, may I call you Charles?

LOMAX: Delighted. Cholly is the usual ticket.

UNDERSHAFT: *{To LADY BRITOMART}* Biddy—

LADY BRITOMART: *{Violently}* Don't dare call me Biddy. Charles Lomax: you are a fool. Adolphus Cusins: you are a Jesuit. Stephen: you are a prig. Barbara: you are a lunatic. Andrew: you are a vulgar tradesman. Now you all know my opinion; and my conscience is clear, at all events. *{She sits down with a vehemence that the rug fortunately softens}*

UNDERSHAFT: My dear: you are the incarnation of morality. *{She snorts}* Your conscience is clear and your duty done when you have called everybody names. Come, Euripides! it is getting late; and we all want to go home. Make up your mind.

CUSINS: Understand this, you old demon—

LADY BRITOMART: Adolphus!

UNDERSHAFT: Let him alone, Biddy. Proceed, Euripides.

CUSINS: You have me in a horrible dilemma. I want Barbara.

UNDERSHAFT: Like all young men, you greatly exaggerate the difference between one young woman and another.

BARBARA: Quite true, Dolly.

CUSINS: I also want to avoid being a rascal.

UNDERSHAFT: *{With biting contempt}* You lust for personal righteousness, for self-approval, for what you call a good conscience, for what Barbara calls salvation, for what I call patronizing people who are not so lucky as yourself.

CUSINS: I do not: all the poet in me recoils from being a good man. But there are things in me that I must reckon with. Pity—

UNDERSHAFT: Pity! The scavenger of misery.

CUSINS: Well, love.

UNDERSHAFT: I know. You love the needy and the outcast: you love the oppressed races, the negro, the Indian ryot, the underdog everywhere. Do you love the Japanese? Do you love the French? Do you love the English?

CUSINS: No. Every true Englishman detests the English. We are the wickedest nation on earth; and our success is a moral horror.

UNDERSHAFT: That is what comes of your gospel of love, is it?

CUSINS: May I not love even my father-in-law?

UNDERSHAFT: Who wants your love, man? By what right do you take the liberty of offering it to me? I will have your due heed and respect, or I will kill you. But your love! Damn your impertinence!

CUSINS: *{Grinning}* I may not be able to control my affections, Mac.

UNDERSHAFT: You are fencing, Euripides. You are weakening: your grip is slipping. Come! try your last weapon. Pity and love have broken in your hand: forgiveness is still left.

CUSINS: No: forgiveness is a beggar's refuge. I am with you there: we must pay our debts.

UNDERSHAFT: Well said. Come! you will suit me. Remember the words of Plato.

CUSINS: *{Starting}* Plato! You dare quote Plato to me!

UNDERSHAFT: Plato says, my friend,

that society cannot be saved until either the Professors of Greek take to making gunpowder, or else the makers of gunpowder become Professors of Greek.

CUSINS: Oh, tempter, cunning tempter!

UNDERSHAFT: Come! choose, man, choose.

CUSINS: But perhaps Barbara will not marry me if I make the wrong choice.

BARBARA: Perhaps not.

CUSINS: *{Desperately perplexed}* You hear!

BARBARA: Father: do you love nobody?

UNDERSHAFT: I love my best friend.

LADY BRITOMART: And who is that, pray?

UNDERSHAFT: My bravest enemy. That is the man who keeps me up to the mark.

CUSINS: You know, the creature is really a sort of poet in his way. Suppose he is a great man, after all!

UNDERSHAFT: Suppose you stop talking and make up your mind, my young friend.

CUSINS: But you are driving me against my nature. I hate war.

UNDERSHAFT: Hatred is the coward's revenge for being intimidated. Dare you make war on war? Here are the means: my friend Mr Lomax is sitting on them.

LOMAX: *Springing up}* Oh I say! You don't mean that this thing is loaded, do you? My ownest: come off it.

SARAH: *{Sitting placidly on the shell}* If I am to be blown up, the more thoroughly it is done the better. Don't fuss, Cholly.

LOMAX: *{To UNDERSHAFT, strongly remonstrant}* Your own daughter, you know.

UNDERSHAFT: So I see. *{To CUSINS]* well, my friend, may we expect you here at six tomorrow morning?

CUSINS: *{Firmly}* Not on any account. I will see the whole establishment blown up with its own dynamite before I will get up at five. My hours are healthy, rational hours: eleven to five.

UNDERSHAFT: Come when you please:

before a week you will come at six and stay until I turn you out for the sake of your health. *{Calling}* Bilton! *{He turns to LADY BRITOMART, who rises}* My dear: let us leave these two young people to themselves for a moment. [BILTON *comes from the shed}* I am going to take you through the gun cotton shed.

BILTON: *{Barring the way}* You can't take anything explosive in here, sir.

LADY BRITOMART: What do you mean? Are you alluding to me?

BILTON: *{Unmoved}* No, ma'am. Mr Undershaft has the other gentleman's matches in his pocket.

LADY BRITOMART: *{Abruptly}* Oh! I beg your pardon. *{She goes into the shed}*

UNDERSHAFT: Quite right, Bilton, quite right: here you are. *{He gives BILTON the box of matches}* Come, Stephen. Come, Charles. Bring Sarah. *{He passes into the shed. BILTON opens the box and deliberately drops the matches into the fire-bucket}*

LOMAX: Oh I say! [BILTON *stolidly hands him the empty box}* Infernal nonsense! Pure scientific ignorance! *{He goes in}*

SARAH: Am I all right, Bilton?

BILTON: You'll have to put on list slippers, miss: that's all. We've got 'em inside. *{She goes in}*

STEPHEN: *{Very seriously to CUSINS]* Dolly, old fellow, think. Think before you decide. Do you feel that you are a sufficiently practical man? It is a huge undertaking, an enormous responsibility. All this mass of business will be Greek to you.

CUSINS: Oh, I think it will be much less difficult than Greek.

STEPHEN: Well, I just want to say this before I leave you to yourselves. Don't let anything I have said about right and wrong prejudice you against this great chance in life. I have satisfied myself that the business is one of the highest character and a credit to our country. *{Emotionally}* I am very proud of my father. I— *{Unable to proceed, he presses CUSINS' hand and goes hastily* *into the shed, followed by* BILTON. BARBARA *and* CUSINS, *left alone together, look at one another silently}*

CUSINS: Barbara: I am going to accept this offer.

BARBARA: I thought you would.

CUSINS: You understand, don't you, that I had to decide without consulting you. If I had thrown the burden of the choice on you, you would sooner or later have despised me for it.

BARBARA: Yes: I did not want you to sell your soul for me any more than for this inheritance.

CUSINS: It is not the sale of my soul that troubles me: I have sold it too often to care about that. I have sold it for a professorship. I have sold it for an income. I have sold it to escape being imprisoned for refusing to pay taxes for hangmen's ropes and unjust wars and things that I abhor. What is all human conduct but the daily and hourly sale of our souls for trifles? What I am now selling it for is neither money nor position nor comfort, but for reality and for power.

BARBARA: You know that you will have no power, and that he has none.

CUSINS: I know. It is not for myself alone. I want to make power for the world.

BARBARA: I want to make power for the world too; but it must be spiritual power.

CUSINS: I think all power is spiritual: these cannons will not go off by themselves. I have tried to make spiritual power by teaching Greek. But the world can never be really touched by a dead language and a dead civilization. The people must have power; and the people cannot have Greek. Now the power that is made here can be wielded by all men.

BARBARA: Power to burn women's houses down and kill their sons and tear their husbands to pieces.

CUSINS: You cannot have power for good without having power for evil too. Even mother's milk nourishes murderers as well as heroes. This power which only tears men's bodies to pieces has never been so horribly abused as the intellectual power, the imaginative power, the poetic, religious power that can enslave men's souls. As a teacher of Greek I gave the intellectual man weapons against the common man. I now want to give the common man weapons against the intellectual man. I love the common people. I want to arm them against the lawyers, the doctors, the priests, the literary men, the professors, the artists, and the politicians, who, once in authority, are more disastrous and tyrannical than all the fools, rascals, and imposters. I want a power simple enough for common man to use, yet strong enough to force the intellectual oligarchy to use its genius for the general good.

BARBARA: Is there no higher power than that? *{Pointing to the shell}*

CUSINS: Yes; but that power can destroy the higher powers just as a tiger can destroy a man: therefore Man must master that power first. I admitted this when the Turks and Greeks were last at war. My best pupil went out to fight for Hellas. My parting gift to him was not a copy of Plato's *Republic*, but a revolver and a hundred Undershaft cartridges. The blood of every Turk he shot—if he shot any—is on my head as well as on Undershaft's. That act committed me to this place for ever. Your father's challenge has beaten me. Dare I make war on war? I dare. I must. I will. And now, is it all over between us?

BARBARA: *{Touched by his evident dread of her answer}* Silly baby Dolly! How could it be!

CUSINS: *{Overjoyed}* Then you—you—you—— Oh for my drum! *{He flourishes imaginary drumsticks}*

BARBARA: *{Angered by his levity}* Take care, Dolly, take care. Oh, if only I could get away from you and from father and from it all! if I could have the wings of a dove and fly away to heaven!

CUSINS: And leave me!

BARBARA: Yes, you, and all the other

naughty mischievous children of men. But I can't. I was happy in the Salvation Army for a moment. I escaped from the world into a paradise of enthusiasm and prayer and soul saving; but the moment our money ran short, it all came back to Bodger: it was he who saved our people: he, and the Prince of Darkness, my papa. Undershaft and Bodger: their hands stretch everywhere: when we feed a starving fellow creature: it is with their bread, because there is no other bread; when we tend the sick, it is in the hospitals they endow; if we turn from the churches they build, we must kneel on the stones of the streets they pave. As long as that lasts, there is no getting away from them. Turning our backs on Bodger and Undershaft is turning our backs on life.

CUSINS: I though you were determined to turn your back on the wicked side of life.

BARBARA: There is no wicked side: life is all one. And I never wanted to shirk my share in whatever evil must be endured, whether it be sin or suffering. I wish I could cure you of middle-class ideas, Dolly.

CUSINS: {*Gasping*} Middle cl—! A snub! A social snub to me; from the daughter of a foundling!

BARBARA: That is why I have no class, Dolly: I come straight out of the heart of the whole people. If I were middle-class I should turn my back on my father's business; and we should both live in an artistic drawing room, with you reading the reviews in one corner, and I in the other at the piano, playing Schumann: both very superior persons, and neither of us a bit of use. Sooner than that, I would sweep out the gun-cotton shed, or be one of Bodger's barmaids. Do you know what would have happened if you had refused papa's offer?

CUSINS: I wonder!

BARBARA: I should have given you up and married the man who accepted it. After all, my dear old mother has more

sense than any of you. I felt like her when I saw this place—felt that I must have it—that never, never, never, could I let it go; only she thought it was the houses and the kitchen ranges and the linen and china, when it was really all the human souls to be saved: not weak souls in starved bodies, sobbing with gratitude for a scrap of bread and treacle, but fullfed, quarrelsome, snob-bish, uppish creatures, all standing on their little rights and dignities, and thinking that my father ought to be greatly obliged to them for making so much money for him—and so he ought. That is where salvation is really wanted. My father shall never throw it in my teeth again that my converts were bribed with bread. {*She is transfigured*} I have got rid of the bribe of bread. I have got rid of the bribe of heaven. Let God's work be done for its own sake: the work he had to create us to do because it cannot be done except by living men and women. When I die, let him be in my debt, not I in him; and let me forgive him as becomes a woman of my rank.

CUSINS: Then the way of life lies through the factory of death?

BARBARA: Yes, through the raising of hell to heaven and of man to God, through the unveiling of an eternal light in the Valley of The Shadow. {*Seizing him with both hands*} Oh, did you think my courage would never come back? did you believe that I was a deserter? that I, who have stood in the streets, and taken my people to my heart, and talked of the holiest and greatest things with them, could ever turn back and chatter foolishly to fashionable people about nothing in a drawing room? Never, never, never, never: Major Barbara will die with colors. Oh! and I have my dear little Dolly boy still; and he has found me my place and my work. Glory Hallelujah! {*She kisses him*}

CUSINS: My dearest: consider my delicate health. I cannot stand as much happiness as you can.

BARBARA: Yes: it is not easy work being in love with me, is it? But it's good for you. *{She runs to the shed, and calls, childlike}* Mamma! Mamma! [BILTON *comes out of the shed, followed by* UNDERSHAFT] I want mamma.

UNDERSHAFT: She is taking off her list slippers, dear. *{He passes on to* CUSINS} Well? What does she say?

CUSINS: She has gone right up into the skies.

LADY BRITOMART: *{Coming from the shed and stopping on the steps, obstructing* SARAH, *who follows with* LOMAX. BARBARA *clutches like a baby at her mother's skirt}* Barbara: when will you learn to be independent and to act and think for yourself? I know as well as possible what that cry of "Mamma, Mamma," means. Always running to me!

SARAH: *{Touching* LADY BRITOMART's *ribs with her finger tips and imitating a bicycle horn}* Pip! pip!

LADY BRITOMART: *{Highly indignant}* How dare you say Pip! pip! to me, Sarah? You are both very naughty children. What do you want, Barbara?

BARBARA: I want a house in the village to live in with Dolly. *{Dragging at the skirt}* Come and tell me which one to take.

UNDERSHAFT: *{To* CUSINS} Six o'clock tomorrow morning, Euripides.

CURTAIN

POETRY

Robert Browning (1812–1889)

SOLILOQUY OF THE SPANISH CLOISTER

Gr-r-r—there go, my heart's abhorrence!
 Water your damned flowerpots, do!
If hate killed men, Brother Lawrence,
 God's blood, would not mine kill you!
What? your myrtle bush wants trimming?
 Oh, that rose had prior claims—
Needs its leaden vase filled brimming?
 Hell dry you up with its flames!

At the meal we sit together:
 Salve tibi! I must hear   10
Wise talk of the kind of weather,
 Sort of season, time of year:
Not a plenteous cork crop: scarcely
 Dare we hope oak-galls, I doubt:
What's the Latin name for "parsley"?
 What's the Greek name for Swine's Snout?

Whew! We'll have our platter burnished,
 Laid with care on our own shelf!
With a fire-new spoon we're furnished,
 And a goblet for ourself,   20
Rinsed like something sacrificial
 Ere 'tis fit to touch our chaps—
Marked with L. for our initial!
 (He-he! There his lily snaps!)

Saint, forsooth! While brown Dolores
 Squats outside the Convent bank
With Sanchicha, telling stories,
 Steeping tresses in the tank,
Blue-black, lustrous, thick like horsehairs,
 —Can't I see his dead eye glow,   30
Bright as 'twere a Barbary corsair's?
 (That is, if he'd let it show!)

142

When he finishes refection,
        Knife and fork he never lays
Cross-wise, to my recollection,
        As do I, in Jesu's praise.
I the Trinity illustrate,
        Drinking watered orange pulp—
In three sips the Arian frustrate;
        While he drains his at one gulp.   40

Oh, those melons? If he's able
        We're to have a feast! so nice!
One goes to the Abbot's table,
        All of us get each a slice.
How go on your flowers? None double?
        Not one fruit-sort can you spy?
Strange!—And I, too, at such trouble,
        Keep them close-nipped on the sly!

There's a great text in Galatians,
        Once you trip on it, entails   50
Twenty-nine distinct damnations,
        One sure, if another fails:
If I trip him just a-dying,
        Sure of heaven as sure can be,
Spin him round and send him flying
        Off to hell, a Manichee?

Or, my scrofulous French novel
        On gray paper with blunt type!
Simply glance at it, you grovel
        Hand and foot in Belial's gripe: 60
If I double down its pages
        At the woeful sixteenth print,
When he gathers his greengages,
        Ope a sieve and slip it in't?

Or, there's Satan!—one might venture
        Pledge one's soul to him, yet leave
Such a flaw in the indenture
        As he'd miss till, past retrieve,
Blasted lay that rose-acacia
        We're so proud of! *Hy, Zy, Hine* . . .   70
St, there's Vespers! *Plena gratiá*
        Ave, Virgo! Gr-r-r—you swine!

MY LAST DUCHESS

That's my last Duchess painted on the wall,
Looking as if she were alive. I call
That piece a wonder, now; Frà Pandolf's hands
Worked busily a day, and there she stands.
Will 't please you sit and look at her? I said
"Frà Pandolf" by design, for never read
Strangers like you that pictured countenance,
The depth and passion of its earnest glance,
But to myself they turned (since none puts by
The curtain I have drawn for you, but I)   10
And seemed as they would ask me, if they durst,
How such a glance came there; so, not the first
Are you to turn and ask thus. Sir, 'twas not
Her husband's presence only, called that spot
Of joy into the Duchess' cheek; perhaps
Frà Pandolf chanced to say, "Her mantle laps
Over my lady's wrist too much," or "Paint
Must never hope to reproduce the faint
Half-flush that dies along her throat." Such stuff
Was courtesy, she thought, and cause enough   20
For calling up that spot of joy. She had
A heart—how shall I say?—too soon made glad,
Too easily impressed; she liked whate'er
She looked on, and her looks went everywhere.
Sir, 'twas all one! My favor at her breast,
The dropping of the daylight in the West,
The bough of cherries some officious fool
Broke in the orchard for her, the white mule
She rode with round the terrace—all and each
Would draw from her alike that approving speech,   30
Or blush, at least. She thanked men—good! but thanked
Somehow—I know not how—as if she ranked
My gift of a nine-hundred-years-old name
With anybody's gift. Who'd stoop to blame
This sort of trifling? Even had you skill
In speech—which I have not—to make your will
Quite clear to such an one, and say, "Just this
Or that in you disgusts me; here you miss,
Or there exceed the mark"—and if she let
Herself be lessoned so, nor plainly set   40
Her wits to yours, forsooth, and made excuse—
E'en then would be some stooping; and I choose
Never to stoop. Oh, sir, she smiled, no doubt,
Whene'er I passed her; but who passed without

Much the same smile? This grew; I gave commands;
Then all smiles stopped together. There she stands
As if alive. Will 't please you rise? We'll meet
The company below, then. I repeat,
The Count your master's known munificence
Is ample warrant that no just pretense   50
Of mine for dowry will be disallowed;
Though his fair daughter's self, as I avowed
At starting, is my object. Nay, we'll go
Together down, sir. Notice Neptune, though,
Taming a sea-horse, thought a rarity,
Which Claus of Innsbruck cast in bronze for me!

Walt Whitman (1819–1892)

I HEAR IT WAS CHARGED AGAINST ME

I hear it was charged against me that I sought to destroy institutions,
But really I am neither for or against institutions,
(What indeed have I in common with them? or what with the destruction of them?)
Only I will establish in the Mannahatta and in every city of these States inland and
    seaboard,
And in the fields and woods, and above every keel little or large that dents the
    water,   5
Without edifices or rules or trustees or any argument,
The institution of the dear love of comrades.

THE COMMONPLACE

The commonplace I sing;
How cheap is health! how cheap nobility!
Abstinence, no falsehood, no gluttony, lust;
The open air I sing, freedom, toleration,
(Take here the mainest lesson—less from books—less from the schools,)   5
The common day and night—the common earth and waters,
Your farm—your work, trade, occupation,
The democratic wisdom underneath, like solid ground for all.

WHEN I HEARD THE LEARN'D ASTRONOMER

When I heard the learn'd astronomer,
When the proofs, the figures, were ranged in columns before me,
When I was shown the charts and diagrams, to add, divide, and measure them,
When I sitting heard the astronomer where he lectured with much applause in the
    lecture-room,
How soon unaccountable I became tired and sick,   5
Till rising and gliding out I wander'd off by myself,
In the mystical moist night-air, and from time to time,
Look'd up in perfect silence at the stars.

A SIGHT IN CAMP IN THE DAYBREAK
GRAY AND DIM

A sight in camp in the daybreak gray and dim,
As from my tent I emerge so early sleepless,
As slow I walk in the cool fresh air the path near by the hospital tent,
Three forms I see on stretchers lying, brought out there untended lying,
Over each the blanket spread, ample brownish woolen blanket,   5
Gray and heavy blanket, folding, covering all.

Curious I halt and silent stand,
Then with light fingers I from the face of the nearest the first just lift the blanket;
Who are you elderly man so gaunt and grim, with well-gray'd hair, and flesh all
    sunken about the eyes?
Who are you my dear comrade?   10

Then to the second I step—and who are you my child and darling?
Who are you sweet boy with cheeks yet blooming?

Then to the third—a face nor child nor old, very calm, as of beautiful yellow-white
    ivory;
Young man I think I know you—I think this face is the face of Christ himself,
Dead and divine and brother of all, and here again he lies.   15

A NOISELESS PATIENT SPIDER

A noiseless patient spider,
I mark'd where on a little promontory it stood isolated,
Mark'd how to explore the vacant vast surrounding,
It launch'd forth filament, filament, filament out of itself,
Ever unreeling them, ever tirelessly speeding them.   5

And you O my soul where you stand,
Surrounded, detached, in measureless oceans of space,
Ceaselessly musing, venturing, throwing, seeking the spheres to connect them,
Till the bridge you will need be form'd, till the ductile anchor hold,
Till the gossamer thread you fling catch somewhere, O my soul.   10

Matthew Arnold (1822–1888)
DOVER BEACH

The sea is calm to-night.
The tide is full, the moon lies fair
Upon the straits;—on the French coast the light
Gleams and is gone; the cliffs of England stand
Glimmering and vast, out in the tranquil bay.   5

Come to the window, sweet is the night-air!
Only, from the long line of spray
Where the sea meets the moon-blanch'd land,
Listen, you hear the grating roar
Of pebbles which the waves draw back, and fling,   10
At their return, up the high strand,
Begin, and cease, and then again begin,
With tremulous cadence slow, and bring
The eternal note of sadness in.

Sophocles long ago   15
Heard it on the Ægean, and it brought
Into his mind the turbid ebb and flow,
Of human misery; we
Find also in the sound a thought,
Hearing it by this distant northern sea.   20

The Sea of Faith
Was once, too, at the full, and round earth's shore
Lay like the folds of a bright girdle furl'd.
But now I only hear
Its melancholy, long, withdrawing roar,   25
Retreating, to the breath
Of the night-wind, down the vast edges drear
And naked shingles of the world.

Ah, love, let us be true
To one another! for the world, which seems   30
To lie before us like a land of dreams,
So various, so beautiful, so new,
Hath really neither joy, nor love, nor light,
Nor certitude, nor peace, nor help for pain;
And we are here as on a darkling plain   35
Swept with confused alarms of struggle and flight,
Where ignorant armies clash by night.

Emily Dickinson (1830–1886)

I LIKE TO SEE IT LAP THE MILES

I like to see it lap the miles,
And lick the valleys up,
And stop to feed itself at tanks;
And then, prodigious, step

Around a pile of mountains,   5
And, supercilious, peer
In shanties by the sides of roads;
And then a quarry pare

To fit its sides, and crawl between,
Complaining all the while   10
In horrid, hooting stanza;
Then chase itself down hill

And neigh like Boanerges;
Then, punctual as a star,
Stop—docile and omnipotent—   15
At its own stable door.

BECAUSE I COULD NOT STOP FOR DEATH

Because I could not stop for Death,
He kindly stopped for me;
The carriage held but just ourselves
And Immortality.

We slowly drove, he knew no haste,   5
And I had put away
My labor, and my leisure too,
For his civility.

We passed the school where children
played,
Their lessons scarcely done;   10
We passed the fields of gazing grain,
We passed the setting sun.

We paused before a house that seemed
A swelling on the ground;
The roof was scarcely visible,   15
The cornice but a mound.

Since then 'tis centuries; but each
Feels shorter than the day
I first surmised the horses' heads
Were toward eternity.   20

WHAT SOFT, CHERUBIC CREATURES

What soft, cherubic creatures
 These gentlewomen are!
One would as soon assault a plush
 Or violate a star.

Such dimity convictions,   5
 A horror so refined
Of freckled human nature,
 Of Deity ashamed,—

It's such a common glory,
 A fisherman's degree!   10
Redemption, brittle lady,
 Be so ashamed of thee.

I TASTE A LIQUOR NEVER BREWED

I taste a liquor never brewed,
From tankards scooped in pearl;
Not all the vats upon the Rhine
Yield such an alcohol!

Inebriate of air am I,   5
And debauchee of dew,
Reeling, through endless summer days,
From inns of molten blue.

When landlords turn the drunken bee
Out of the foxlove's door,   10
When butterflies renounce their drams,
I shall but drink the more!

Till seraphs swing their snowy hats,
And saints to windows run,
To see the little tippler   15
Leaning against the sun!

A NARROW FELLOW IN THE GRASS

A narrow fellow in the grass
Occasionally rides;
You may have met him,—did you not?
His notice sudden is.

The grass divides as with a comb,   5
A spotted shaft is seen;
And then it closes at your feet
And opens further on.

He likes a boggy acre,
A floor too cool for corn,   10
Yet when a boy, and barefoot,
I more than once, at morn,

Have passed, I thought, a whip-lash
Unbraiding in the sun,—
When, stooping to secure it,   15
It wrinkled, and was gone.

Several of nature's people
I know, and they know me;
I feel for them a transport
Of cordiality;   20

But never met this fellow,
Attended or alone,
Without a tighter breathing,
And zero at the bone.

Thomas Hardy (1840–1928)

GOD-FORGOTTEN

I towered far, and lo! I stood within
The presence of the Lord Most High,
Sent thither by the sons of Earth, to win
    Some answer to their cry.

—"The Earth, sayest thou? The
    Human race?   5
By Me created? Sad its lot?
Nay: I have no remembrance of such
    place:
    Such world I fashioned not."—

—"O Lord, forgive me when I say
Thou spakest the word that made it
    all."—   10
"The Earth of men—let them bethink
    me. . . . Yea!
    I dimly do recall

"Some tiny sphere I built long back
(Mid millions of such shapes of
    mine)
So named . . . It perished, surely—not a
    wrack   15
    Remaining, or a sign?

"It lost my interest from the first,
My aims therefore succeeding ill;
Haply it died of doing as it durst?"—
    "Lord, it existeth still."—   20

"Dark, then, its life! For not a cry
Of aught it bears do I now hear;
Of its own act the threads were snapt
    whereby
    Its plaints had reached mine ear.

"It used to ask for gifts of good,   25
Till came its severance, self-entailed,
When sudden silence on that side
    ensued,
    And has till now prevailed.

"All other orbs have kept in touch;
    Their voicings reach me speedily: 30
Thy people took upon them overmuch
    In sundering them from me!

"And it is strange—though sad
    enough—
Earth's race should think that one
    whose call
Frames, daily, shining spheres of
    flawless stuff   35
    Must heed their tainted ball! . . .

"But sayest it is by pangs distraught,
And strife, and silent suffering?—
Sore grieved am I that injury should be
    wrought
    Even on so poor a thing!   40

"Thou shouldst have learnt that *Not
to Mend*
For Me could mean but *Not to Know:*
Hence, Messengers! and straightway put
an end
To what men undergo." . . .

Homing at dawn, I thought to see 45
One of the Messengers standing by.
—Oh, childish thought! . . . Yet often it
comes to me
When trouble hovers nigh.

THE DARKLING THRUSH

I leant upon a coppice gate
  When Frost was specter-gray,
And Winter's dregs made desolate
  The weakening eye of day.
The tangled bine-stems scored the
  sky   5
  Like strings of broken lyres,
And all mankind that haunted nigh
  Had sought their household fires.

The land's sharp features seemed to be
  The Century's corpse outleant,   10
His crypt the cloudy canopy,
  The wind his death-lament.
The ancient pulse of germ and birth
  Was shrunken hard and dry,
And every spirit upon earth   15
  Seemed fervorless as I.

At once a voice arose among
  The bleak twigs overhead
In a fullhearted evensong
  Of joy illimited;   20
An aged thrush, frail, gaunt, and small,
  In blast-beruffled plume,
Had chosen thus to fling his soul
  Upon the growing gloom.

So little cause for carolings   25
  Of such ecstatic sound
Was written on terrestrial things
  Afar or nigh around,
That I could think there trembled
  through
His happy good-night air   30
Some blessed Hope, whereof he knew
  And I was unaware.

THE CONVERGENCE OF THE TWAIN
(Lines on The Loss of The "TITANIC")

  In a solitude of the sea
  Deep from human vanity,
And the Pride of Life that planned her, stilly couches she.

  Steel chambers, late the pyres
  Of her salamandrine fires,   5
Cold currents thrid, and turn to rhythmic tidal lyres.

  Over the mirrors meant
  To glass the opulent
The sea worm crawls—grotesque, slimed, dumb, indifferent.

Jewels in joy designed   10
  To ravish the sensuous mind
Lie lightless, all their sparkles bleared and black and blind.

  Dim moon-eyed fishes near
  Gaze at the gilded gear
And query: "What does this vaingloriousness down here?" . . .   15

  Well: while was fashioning
  This creature of cleaving wing,
The Immanent Will that stirs and urges everything

  Prepared a sinister mate
  For her—so gaily great—   20
A Shape of Ice, for the time far and dissociate.

  And as the smart ship grew
  In stature, grace, and hue,
In shadowy silent distance grew the Iceberg too.

  Alien they seemed to be: 25
  No mortal eye could see
The intimate welding of their later history,

  Or sign that they were bent
  By paths coincident
On being anon twin halves of one august event,   30

  Till the Spinner of the Years
  Said "Now!" And each one hears,
And consummation comes, and jars two hemispheres.

IN TIME OF "THE BREAKING OF NATIONS"

1

Only a man harrowing clods
  In a slow silent walk
With an old horse that stumbles and
    nods
  Half asleep as they stalk.

2

Only thin smoke without flame   5
  From the heaps of couch-grass;
Yet this will go onward the same
  Though Dynasties pass.

3

Yonder a maid and her wight
  Come whispering by;   10
War's annals will cloud into night
  Ere their story die.

Gerard Manley Hopkins (1844–1889)
GOD'S GRANDEUR

The world is charged with the grandeur of God.
  It will flame out, like shining from shook foil;
  It gathers to a greatness, like the ooze of oil
Crushed. Why do men then now not reck his rod?   4
Generations have trod, have trod, have trod;
  And all is seared with trade; bleared, smeared with toil; ,
  And wears man's smudge and shares man's smell: the soil
Is bare now, nor can foot feel, being shod.   8

And for all this, nature is never spent;
  There lives the dearest freshness deep down things;
And though the last lights off the black West went
  Oh, morning, at the brown brink eastward, springs—
Because the Holy Ghost over the bent
  World broods with warm breast and with ah! bright wings.   14

PIED BEAUTY

Glory be to God for dappled things—
  For skies of couple-color as a brinded cow;
    For rose-moles all in stipple upon trout that swim;
Fresh-firecoal chestnut-falls; finches' wings;
  Landscape plotted and pieced—fold, fallow, and plow;   5
    And all trádes, their gear and tackle and trim.
All things counter, original, spare, strange;
  Whatever is fickle, freckled (who knows how?)
    With swift, slow; sweet, sour; adazzle, dim;
He fathers-forth whose beauty is past change: 10
               Praise him.

THE WINDHOVER

TO CHRIST OUR LORD

I caught this morning morning's minion, king-
  dom of daylight's dauphin, dapple-dawn-drawn Falcon, in his riding
  Of the rolling level underneath him steady air, and striding
High there, how he rung upon the rein of a wimpling wing
In his ecstasy! then off, off forth on swing,
  As a skate's heel sweeps smooth on a bow-bend: the hurl and gliding
  Rebuffed the big wind. My heart in hiding
Stirred for a bird,—the achieve of, the mastery of the thing!   7

Brute beauty and valor and act, oh, air, pride, plume, here
  Buckle! and the fire that breaks from thee then, a billion
Times told lovelier, more dangerous, O my chevalier!

  No wonder of it: shéer plód makes plow down sillion
Shine, and blue-bleak embers, ah my dear,
  Fall, gall themselves, and gash gold-vermilion.   13

A. E. Housman (1859–1936)
LOVELIEST OF TREES

Loveliest of trees, the cherry now
Is hung with bloom along the bough,
And stands about the woodland ride
Wearing white for Eastertide.

Now, of my threescore years and ten,   5
Twenty will not come again,
And take from seventy springs a score,
It only leaves me fifty more.

And since to look at things in bloom
Fifty springs are little room,   10
About the woodlands I will go
To see the cherry hung with snow.

TO AN ATHLETE DYING YOUNG

The time you won your town the race
We chaired you through the
  marketplace;
Man and boy stood cheering by,
And home we brought you shoulder-
  high.

To-day, the road all runners come,   5
Shoulder-high we bring you home,
And set you at your threshold down,
Townsman of a stiller town.

Smart lad, to slip betimes away
From fields where glory does not
  stay   10
And early though the laurel grows
It withers quicker than the rose.

Eyes the shady night has shut
Cannot see the record cut,
And silence sounds no worse than
  cheers   15
After earth has stopped the ears:

Now you will not swell the rout
Of lads that wore their honours out,
Runners whom renown outran
And the name died before the man.   20

So set, before its echoes fade,
The fleet foot on the sill of shade,
And hold to the low lintel up
The still-defended challenge-cup.

And round that early-laurelled head   25
Will flock to gaze the strengthless dead,
And find unwithered on its curls
The garland briefer than a girl's.

TERENCE, THIS IS STUPID STUFF

'Terence, this is stupid stuff:
You eat your victuals fast enough;
There can't be much amiss, 'tis clear,
To see the rate you drink your beer.
But oh, good Lord, the verse you
  make,   5
It gives a chap the belly-ache.
The cow, the old cow, she is dead;
It sleeps well, the horned head:
We poor lads, 'tis our turn now
To hear such tunes as killed the
  cow.   10
Pretty friendship 'tis to rhyme
Yours friends to death before their time
Moping melancholy mad:
Come, pipe a tune to dance to, lad.'

Why, if 'tis dancing you would
  be,   15
There's brisker pipes than poetry.
Say, for what were hop-yards meant,
Or why was Burton built on Trent?
Oh many a peer of England brews
Livelier liquor than the Muse,   20
And malt does more than Milton can
To justify God's ways to man.
Ale, man, ale's the stuff to drink
For fellows whom it hurts to think:
Look into the pewter pot   25
To see the world as the world's not.
And faith, 'tis pleasant till 'tis past:
The mischief is that 'twill not last.
Oh I have been to Ludlow fair

And left my necktie God knows
   where,   30
And carried half-way home, or near,
Pints and quarts of Ludlow beer:
Then the world seemed none so bad,
And I myself a sterling lad;
And down in lovely muck I've lain, 35
Happy till I woke again.
Then I saw the morning sky:
Heigho, the tale was all a lie;
The world, it was the old world yet,
I was I, my things were wet, 40
And nothing now remained to do
But begin the game anew.
   Therefore, since the world has still
Much good, but much less good than ill,
And while the sun and moon
   endure   45
Luck's a chance, but trouble's sure,
I'd face it as a wise man would,
And train for ill and not for good.
'Tis true, the stuff I bring for sale
Is not so brisk a brew as ale: 50
Out of a stem that scored the hand
I wrung it in a weary land.
But take it: if the smack is sour,

The better for the embittered hour;
It should do good to heart and head 55
When your soul is in my soul's stead;
And I will friend you, if I may,
In the dark and cloudy day.

   There was a king reigned in the East:
There, when kings will sit to feast, 60
They get their fill before they think
With poisoned meat and poisoned
   drink.
He gathered all that springs to birth
From the many-venomed earth;
First a little, thence to more, 65
He sampled all her killing store;
And easy, smiling, seasoned sound,
Sate the king when healths went round.
They put arsenic in his meat
And stared aghast to watch him eat; 70
They poured strychnine in his cup
And shook to see him drink it up:
They shook, they stared as white's their
   shirt:
Them it was their poison hurt.
—I tell the tale that I heard told. 75
Mithridates, he died old.

Rudyard Kipling (1865–1936)

TOMMY

I went into a public-'ouse to get a pint o' beer,
The publican 'e up an' sez, "We serve no red-coats here."
The girls be'ind the bar they laughed an' giggled fit to die,
I outs into the street again, an' to myself sez I:
   O it's Tommy this, an' Tommy that, an' "Tommy go away";   5
   But it's "Thank you, Mister Atkins," when the band begins to play,
   The band begins to play, my boys, the band begins to play,
   O it's "Thank you, Mister Atkins," when the band begins to play.

I went into a theatre as sober as could be,
They give a drunk civilian room, but 'adn't none for me;   10
They sent me to the gallery or round the music-'alls,
But when it comes to fightin', Lord! they'll shove me in the stalls.

"Tommy," "Recessional," and "The White Man's Burden" from *Rudyard Kilpling's Verse: Definitive Edition* (Doubleday) and *Barrack-Room Ballads* (The Macmillan Co. of Canada). Reprinted by permission of Mrs. George Bambridge, Doubleday & Company, Inc., and the Macmillan Co. of Canada Ltd.

For it's Tommy this, and Tommy that, an' "Tommy wait outside";
But it's "Special train for Atkins," when the trooper's on the tide,
The troopships on the tide, my boys, etc.   15

O makin' mock o' uniforms that guard you wile you sleep
Is cheaper than them uniforms, an' they're starvation cheap;
An' hustlin' drunken sodgers when they're goin' large a bit
Is five times better business than paradin' in full kit.
    Then it's Tommy this, and Tommy that, an' "Tommy 'ow's yer soul?"   20
    But it's "Thin red lines of 'eroes" when the drums begin to roll,
    The drums begin to roll, my boys, etc.

We aren't no thin red 'eroes, nor we aren't no blackguards too,
But single men in barracks, most remarkable like you;
An' if sometimes our conduck isn't all your fancy paints,   25
Why, single men in barracks don't grow into plaster saints.
    While it's Tommy this, and Tommy that, an' "Tommy fall be'ind";
    But it's "Please to walk in front, sir," when there's trouble in the wind,
    There's trouble in the wind, my boys, etc.

You talk o' better food for us an' schools, an' fires, an' all: 30
We'll wait for extra rations if you treat us rational.
Don't mess about the cook-room slops, but prove it to our face
The Widow's uniform is not the soldier-man's disgrace.
    But it's Tommy this, an' Tommy that, an' "Chuck him out, the brute!"
    But it's "Saviour of 'is country" when the guns begin to shoot;   35
    An' it's Tommy this, an' Tommy that, an' anything you please;
    An' Tommy ain't a bloomin' fool—you bet that Tommy sees!

RECESSIONAL

God of our fathers, known of old,
   Lord of our far-flung battle-line,
Beneath whose awful hand we hold
   Dominion over palm and pine—
Lord God of Hosts, be with us yet,   5
Lest we forget—lest we forget!

The tumult and the shouting dies;
   The captains and the kings depart:
Still stands Thine ancient sacrifice,
   An humble and a contrite heart.   10
Lord God of Hosts, be with us yet,
Lest we forget—lest we forget!

Far-called, our navies melt away;
   On dune and headland sinks the fire:
Lo, all our pomp of yesterday   15
   Is one with Nineveh and Tyre!

Judge of the Nations, spare us yet,
Lest we forget—lest we forget!

If, drunk with sight of power, we loose
   Wild tongues that have not Thee in
      awe,   20
Such boastings as the Gentiles use,
   Or lesser breeds without the Law—
Lord God of Hosts, be with us yet,
Lest we forget—lest we forget!

For heathen heart that puts her trust   25
   In reeking tube and iron shard,
All valiant dust that builds on dust,
   And, guarding, calls not Thee to
      guard
For frantic boast and foolish word—
Thy Mercy on Thy People, Lord!   30

THE WHITE MAN'S BURDEN

Take up the White Man's burden—
  Send forth the best ye breed—
Go bind your sons to exile
  To serve your captives' need;

To wait in heavy harness,   5
  On fluttered folk and wild—
Your new-caught, sullen peoples,
  Half-devil and half-child.

Take up the White Man's burden—
  In patience to abide,   10
To veil the threat of terror
  An check the show of pride;
By open speech and simple,
  An hundred times made plain,
To seek another's profit,   15
  And work another's gain.

Take up the White Man's burden—
  The savage wars of peace—
Fill full the mouth of Famine
  And bid the sickness cease;   20
And when your goal is nearest
  The end for others sought,
Watch Sloth and heathen Folly
  Bring all your hope to nought.

Take up the White Man's burden—   25
  No tawdry rule of kings,
But toil of serf and sweeper—
  The tale of common things.

The ports ye shall not enter,
  The roads ye shall not tread,   30
Go make them with your living,
  And mark them with your dead.

Take up the White Man's burden—
  And reap his old reward:
The blame of those ye better,   35
  The hate of those ye guard—
The cry of hosts ye humor
  (Ah, slowly!) toward the light:—
"Why brought ye us from bondage,
  Our loved Egyptian night?"   40

Take up the White Man's burden—
  Ye dare not stoop to less—
Nor call too loud on Freedom
  To cloak your weariness;
By all ye cry or whisper,   45
  By all ye leave or do,
The silent sullen peoples
  Shall weigh your Gods and you.

Take up the White Man's burden—
  Have done with childish days—   50
The lightly proffered laurel,
  The easy, ungrudged praise.
Come now, to search your manhood
  Through all the thankless years,
Cold, edged with dear-bought
    wisdom,   55
  The judgment of your peers!

Edwin Arlington Robinson (1869–1935)
LUKE HAVERGAL

Go to the western gate, Luke Havergal,
There where the vines cling crimson on
the wall,
And in the twilight wait for what will
come.
The leaves will whisper there of her,
and some,
Like flying words, will strike you as
they fall;   5
But go, and if you listen, she will call.
Go to the western gate, Luke
Havergal—
Luke Havergal.

No, there is not a dawn in eastern skies
To rift the fiery night that's in your
eyes;   10
But there, where western glooms are
gathering,
The dark will end the dark, if anything:
God slays himself with every leaf that
flies,
And hell is more than half of paradise.
No, there is not a dawn in eastern
skies—   15
In eastern skies.

Out of a grave I come to tell you this,
Out of a grave I come to quench the
kiss
That flames upon your forehead with a
glow
That blinds you to the way that you
must go.   20
Yes, there is yet one way to where she
is,
Bitter, but one that faith may never
miss.
Out of a grave I come to tell you this—
To tell you this.

There is the western gate, Luke
Havergal,   25
There are the crimson leaves upon the
wall.
Go, for the winds are tearing them
away,—
Nor think to riddle the dead words they
say,
Nor any more to feel them as they fall;
But go, and if you trust her she will
call.   30
There is the western gate, Luke
Havergal—
Luke Havergal.

RICHARD CORY

Whenever Richard Cory went down
  town,
We people on the pavement looked at
  him:
He was a gentleman from sole to crown,
Clean favored, and imperially slim.

And he was aways quietly arrayed,   5
And he was always human when he
  talked;
But still he fluttered pulses when he
  said,
"Good-morning," and he glittered when
  he walked.

And he was rich,—yes, richer than a
  king,—
And admirably schooled in every
  grace: 10
In fine, we thought that he was
  everything
To make us wish that we were in his
  place.

So on we worked, and waited for the
  light,
And went without the meat, and cursed
  the bread;
And Richard Cory, one calm summer
  night,   15
Went home and put a bullet through
  his head.

Stephen Crane (1871–1900)

A MAN SAID TO THE UNIVERSE

A man said to the universe:
"Sir, I exist!"
"However," replied the universe,
"The fact has not created in me
A sense of obligation."   5

THE TREES IN THE GARDEN RAINED FLOWERS

The trees in the garden rained flowers.
Children ran there joyously.
They gathered the flowers
Each to himself.
Now there were some   5
Who gathered great heaps—
Having opportunity and skill—
Until, behold, only chance blossoms

Remained for the feeble,
Then a little spindling tutor   10
Ran importantly to the father, crying:
"Pray, come hither!
See this unjust thing in your garden!"
But when the father had surveyed,
He admonished the tutor: 15
"Not so, small sage!

This thing is just.
For, look you,
Are not they who possess the flowers
Stronger, bolder, shrewder   20
Than they who have none?
Why should the strong—
The beautiful strong—

Why should they not have the
     flowers?"
Upon reflection, the tutor bowed to the
     ground,   25
"My Lord," he said,
"The stars are displaced
By this towering wisdom."

GOD FASHIONED THE SHIP OF THE WORLD CAREFULLY

God fashioned the ship of the world carefully.
With the infinite skill of an All-Master
Made He the hull and the sails,
Held He the rudder
Ready for adjustment.   5
Erect stood He, scanning His work proudly.
Then—at fateful time—a wrong called,
And God turned, heeding.
Lo, the ship, at this opportunity, slipped slyly,
Making cunning noiseless travel down the ways,   10
So that, for ever rudderless, it went upon the seas
Going ridiculous voyages,
Making quaint progress,
Turning as with serious purpose
Before stupid winds.   15
And there were many in the sky
Who laughed at this thing.

DO NOT WEEP, MAIDEN, FOR WAR IS KIND

Do not weep, maiden, for war is kind.
Because your lover threw wild hands toward the sky
And the affrighted steed ran on alone,
Do not weep.
War is kind.   5

     Hoarse, booming drums of the regiment,
     Little souls who thirst for fight,
     These men were born to drill and die.
     The unexplained glory flies above them,
     Great is the battle-god, great, and his kingdom— 10
     A field where a thousand corpses lie.

Do not weep, babe, for war is kind.
Because your father tumbled in the yellow trenches,
Raged at his breast, gulped and died,
Do not weep.   15
War is kind.

> Swift blazing flag of the regiment,
> Eagle with crest of red and gold,
> These men were born to drill and die.
> Point for them the virtue of slaughter,   20
> Make plain to them the excellence of killing
> And a field where a thousand corpses lie.

Mother whose heart hung humble as a button
On the bright splendid shroud of your son,
Do not weep.   25
War is kind.

Siegfried Sassoon (1886–1967)
BASE DETAILS

If I were fierce and bald and short of
   breath,
   I'd live with scarlet Majors at the
   Base,
And spread glum heroes up the line of
   death.
   You'd see me with my puffy petulant
   face,
Guzzling and gulping in the best
   hotel,   5
Reading the Roll of Honor. "Poor
   young chap,"
I'd say—"I used to know his father well.
   Yes, we've lost heavily in this last
   scrap."
And when the war is done and youth
   stone dead,
I'd toddle safely home and die—in
   bed.   10

DREAMERS

Soldiers are citizens of death's gray
  land,
   Drawing no dividend from time's
   tomorrows.
In the great hour of destiny they stand,
   Each with his feuds, and jealousies,
   and sorrows.
Soldiers are sworn to action; they must
   win   5
   Some flaming, fatal climax with their
   lives.
Soldiers are dreamers; when the guns
   begin
   They think of firelit homes, clean
   beds, and wives.

I see them in foul dug-outs, gnawed by
   rats,
   And in the ruined trenches, lashed
   with rain,   10
Dreaming of things they did with balls
   and bats,
   And mocked by hopeless longing to
   regain
Bank-holidays, and picture shows, and
   spats,
   And going to the office in the train.

ATTACK

At dawn the ridge emerges massed and
   dun
In the wild purple of the glowering sun
Smoldering through spouts of drifting
   smoke that shroud
The menacing scarred slope; and, one
   by one,
Tanks creep and topple forward to the
   wire.   5
The barrage roars and lifts. Then,
   clumsily bowed
With bombs and guns and shovels and
   battle-gear,

Men jostle and climb to meet the
   bristling fire.
Lines of gray, muttering faces, masked
   with fear,
They leave their trenches, going over
   the top,   10
While time ticks bland and busy on
   their wrists,
And hope, with furtive eyes and
   grappling fists,
Flounders in mud. O Jesu, make it stop!

DOES IT MATTER?

Does it matter?—losing your legs? . . .
For people will always be kind,
And you need not show that you mind
When the others come in after hunting
To gobble their muffins and eggs.   5

Does it matter?—losing your sight? . . .
There's such spendid work for the
  blind;
And people will always be kind,
As you sit on the terrace remembering
And turning your face to the light. 10

Do they matter?—those dreams from
  the pit? . . .
You can drink and forget and be glad,
And people won't say that you're mad;
For they'll know that you've fought for
  your country,
And no one will worry a bit.   15

Wilfred Owen (1893–1918)

ARMS AND THE BOY

Let the boy try along this bayonet-blade
How cold steel is, and keen with hunger
  of blood;
Blue with all malice, like a madman's
  flash;
And thinly drawn with famishing for
  flesh.

Lend him to stroke these blind, blunt
  bullet-heads   5
Which long to nuzzle in the heart of
  lads,

Or give him cartridges of fine zinc
  teeth,
Sharp with the sharpness of grief and
  death.

For his teeth seem for laughing round
  an apple.
There lurk no claws behind his fingers
  supple;   10
And god will grow no talons at his
  heels,
Nor antlers through the thickness of his
  curls.

ANTHEM FOR DOOMED YOUTH

What passing-bells for these who die as
  cattle?
Only the monstrous anger of the guns.
Only the stuttering rifles' rapid rattle
Can patter out their hasty orisons.
No mockeries for them; no prayers nor
  bells,   5
Nor any voice of mourning save the
  choirs,—
The shrill, demented choirs of wailing
  shells;
And bugles calling for them from sad
  shires.

What candles may be held to speed
  them all?
Not in the hands of boys, but in their
  eyes   10
Shall shine the holy glimmers of good-
  byes.
The pallor of girls' brows shall be their
  pall;
Their flowers the tenderness of patient
  minds,
And each slow dusk a drawing-down of
  blinds.

GREATER LOVE

Red lips are not so red
  As the stained stones kissed by the
    English dead.
Kindness of wooed and wooer
Seems shame to their love pure.
O Love, your eyes lose lure   5
  When I behold eyes blinded in my
    stead!

Your slender attitude
  Trembles not exquisite like limbs
    knife-skewed,
Rolling and rolling there
Where God seems not to care;   10
Till the fierce love they bear
  Cramps them in death's extreme
    decrepitude.

Your voice sings not so soft,—
  Though even as wind murmuring
    through raftered loft,—
Your dear voice is not clear,   15
Gentle, and evening clear,
As theirs whom none now hear
  Now earth has stopped their piteous
    mouths that coughed.

Heart, you were never hot,
  Nor large, nor full like hearts made
    great with shot;   20
And though your hand be pale,
Paler are all which trail
Your cross through flame and hail:
  Weep, you may weep, for you may
    touch them not.

DULCE ET DECORUM EST

Bent double, like old beggars under sacks,
Knock-kneed, coughing like hags, we cursed through sludge,
Till on the haunting flares we turned our backs
And towards our distant rest began to trudge.   5
Men marched asleep. Many had lost their boots
But limped on, blood-shod. All went lame; all blind;
Drunk with fatigue; deaf even to the hoots
Of tired, outstripped Five-Nines that dropped behind.

Gas! GAS! Quick, boys!—An ecstasy of fumbling,
Fitting the clumsy helmets just in time;   10
But someone still was yelling out and stumbling
And flound'ring like a man in fire or lime . . .
Dim, through the misty panes and thick green light,
As under a green sea, I saw him drowning.

In all my dreams, before my helpless sight,   15
He plunges at me, guttering, choking, drowning.

If in some smothering dreams you too could pace
Behind the wagon that we flung him in,
And watch the white eyes writhing in his face,
His hanging face, like a devil's sick of sin;   20
If you could hear, at every jolt, the blood
Come gargling from the froth-corrupted lungs,
Obscene as cancer, bitter as the cud
Of vile, incurable sores on innocent tongues,—
My friend, you would not tell with such high zest   25
To children ardent for some desperate glory,
The old Lie: Dulce et decorum est
Pro patria mori.

"The trouble with you boys to-day is you have no imagination!"
"Well, girlie, nowadays we don't need imagination."

2
THE LONG ARMISTICE
1918-1939

INTRODUCTION

The Long Armistice between November 11, 1918 and November 1, 1939 was turbulent. The idealistic hopes of Woodrow Wilson, who dreamt of making peace with honor, soon lapsed into the disillusioned conviction that World War I had been fought less to save the world for democracy than to increase corporate profits. That despair was deepened by the implications of Freudian and behavioristic psychology, which suggested that man was at the mercy of drives he could neither understand nor control, and by some interpretations of the new physics, which seemed to imply, by the law of entropy, that the earth's supply of available energy was limited and the universe was inevitably doomed. The stock market crash of 1929 lent credence to Marx's economic predictions, and the Great Depression lured many men to envision a political system that might provide greater security than capitalistic democracy.

The prospect of a second world war grew ever more certain. The seeds for that conflict were planted in innumerable ways: in the division of the spoils of war at the Treaty of Versailles in 1919; in the American isolationism that led Congress, in 1919, to reject membership in the League of Nations; in the irresponsible boom and bust psychology of the 1920's; in the diminution of the British Empire; in the territorial ambitions of Japan, Italy, and Germany which spawned aggression respectively in China, Ethiopia, and Europe; in the Nazi violence against Jews and other minority groups; and in the Spanish Civil War, the dress rehearsal for World War II. By the time Neville Chamberlain, the British prime minister, flew to Munich in March, 1939, to make his futile attempt to appease Hitler—a trip from which Chamberlain returned with the ironic promise of

"peace in our time"—the Long Armistice was nearly over.

Economic and political changes were vast. The Bolshevist Revolution of 1917, inspired by the doctrines of Karl Marx, established a communist state, abolished most private property, and proclaimed the Soviet Union the international champion of the labor class. After the death of Lenin in 1924, Joseph Stalin substituted personal dictatorship for the "dictatorship of the proletariat" and intense nationalism for the goal of international revolution. He demanded immense sacrifice and absolute obedience of all Soviet citizens. The purges of the 1930s, in which Stalin "liquidated" every vestige of opposition to his authority, revealed the potential of the modern totalitarian state to control every aspect of its citizens' lives. Though Stalinist tyranny disillusioned some Marxists, others in England, America, and elsewhere continued to look to Russia for leadership in the class struggle.

In Germany, Adolf Hitler returned from World War I with an Iron Cross for bravery and a fanatic dream to unify and glorify the German fatherland. The skillful demagogue, Hitler founded the National Socialist (or Nazi) Party and captured power in Germany by terror and propaganda. With the aid of his brown-shirted storm troops he intimidated opposition, and after the blood purges of 1934 proclaimed himself "Der Fuehrer" and prescribed "Heil Hitler" as the official German salutation. His doctrine of racial differences extolled the supremacy of Aryan peoples—the master race—and demanded the extermination or subordination of inferior "races." The "final solution" of the Jewish question was to be accomplished in such notorious death camps as Dachau and Auschwitz. His messianic purpose was not contained within German boundaries. Ostensibly in quest of "lebensraum," German forces invaded and conquered the Rhineland in 1936, Austria in 1938, and Czechoslovakia in the same year— conquests that England and France were too weak or intimidated to oppose. Hitler's alliance with the Italian dictator, Benito Mussolini, was made explicit by cooperative efforts, from 1936 till 1939, to assist General Francisco Franco, the rebel leader in the Spanish war, and was consolidated in 1939 by the Berlin-Rome Axis (later to include Tokyo). With the Russo-German nonaggression pact of August 9, 1939, Hitler secured Russian neutrality, and, on September 1, he ordered the invasion of Poland. Chamberlain's dream of "peace in our time" had lasted less than six months.

In America, the interim between the wars began with the dreams of President Woodrow Wilson and ended with the pragmatism of President Franklin Delano Roosevelt. On November 11, 1918 when the war ended, Wilson proclaimed that "everything for which America fought has been accomplished," but in the light of history that affirmation is more pathetic than ironic. The American Congress refused to approve the work of the "four old men" who dominated the peace conference of 1919 at Versailles, and Congress firmly rejected membership in the League of Nations. By its actions, the Congress derided Wilson's declaration: "We cannot turn back. We can only go forward, with lifted eyes and freshened spirit, to follow the vision." His declaration reflected the idealism and illusions with which the War had been fought. Now, however, such utopian slogans of Wilson as "A war to end war" were replaced by the kind of cynicism that Hemingway expressed in *A Farewell to Arms* in 1929: "I was always embarrassed by the words *sacred, glorious,*

sacrifice and the expression *in vain....* I had seen nothing sacred, and the things that were glorious had no glory and the sacrifices were like the stockyards at Chicago if nothing was done with the meat except to bury it."

From Wilson's aspirations and the vainglory of foreign intervention, America was lured by Warren Harding's promise of "a full dinner pail" to elect a president who promised, in his inaugural address, nothing more venturesome than a "return to normalcy." The Roaring Twenties, the Jazz Age, the Big Boom, and the Lost Generation are epithets applied to the postwar decade, a period of material prosperity, monetary inflation, restless morality, governmental ineptness and corruption, reckless lawlessness (stimulated in part by the folly of prohibition), extreme philistinism, and intellectual disillusionment. The "new" jazz, cacophonous and savage to older ears, blared everywhere, and new dances such as the Charleston and the Black Bottom replaced the waltz. Henry Ford's Tin Lizzie filled the highways and altered living habits, and movies, radio, and organized sport became national passions. "Flappers" and "bob-haired bandits" talked a great deal about sex and its prophet Dr. Freud, bound their breasts tightly in an effort to become just one of the boys, and asserted their newfound sophistication by cursing, drinking, and smoking. Everywhere young people were rootless and restless. Many of them would have agreed with Amory Blaine, the hero of F. Scott Fitzgerald's novel *This Side of Paradise*, that they had "grown up to find all Gods dead, all wars fought, all faiths in man shaken...."

The period ended with a bang on Black Thursday, October 24, 1929, the day the stock market crashed. Its plunge ushered in the Great Depression. General Electric, a typical blue-chip stock, fell from a high of 396¼ on September 3, 1929 to 197¼ on November 13, 1929 to 34 in 1936. Although the Depression was worldwide, it was most severe in America. Banks failed; unemployment spread; hunger and starvation were common; bewilderment and fear bred murmurs of chaos and communism. The unkempt veterans, the Bonus Army of 1932, marching on Washington to plead for a veteran's bonus, seemed a portent of imminent revolution.

If the name of President Woodrow Wilson dominated the early part of the period, and if the collapse of his utopian dreams into a carnival of sensuous, restless escapism reflected the intellectual disillusionment of the twenties, the name of Franklin Delano Roosevelt dominated the period from 1930 until the beginning of World War II. With his election as president in 1932, Roosevelt promised a "New Deal"; he and a "Brain Trust" of intellectuals set about shuffling the cards. It was about time, for the Depression had left Americans of all classes bewildered by a catastrophe they could not comprehend. Traditional authority had been weakened. Paternal status had been undermined by unemployment, and free enterprise had been reduced to a set of economic imponderables. Business leaders were as confused as their employees. Charles N. Schwab, a United States Steel tycoon, confessed: "I'm afraid, every man is afraid. I don't know, we don't know, whether the values we have are going to be real next month or not." As Robert and Helen Lynd concluded in their study, of the average town, which they dubbed Middletown: ". . . the great knife of the Depression had cut down impartially through the entire population cleaving open lives and hopes of rich as well as poor. . . . it has approached in its elemental shock the primary experience of birth and death."

Instead of merely promising, like his predecessor Herbert Hoover, that prosperity was "just around the corner," Roosevelt acted; and although the projects of the New Deal—such as the TVA, CWA, WPA, CCC, and the NYA—did not solve all economic ills, they gave hope to millions of Americans and may well have averted revolution. Although he avoided the dictatorial course of Stalin, Hitler and Mussolini, Roosevelt greatly expanded the powers of the federal government. *Laissez-faire* had proved an insufficient guarantor of prosperities; since Roosevelt's administration governmental regulation of private enterprise has increased rather than disappeared.

In America, as in England, the internal problems posed by the Depression were so extreme that most national leaders (England's Winston Churchill was a notable exception) were reluctant to face the unspeakable horrors of the German regime and the threat of the Nazi military juggernaut. That terror loomed over the thirties, and its images—of Nazi troops, goose-stepping in ostentatious parade, of the black Nazi insignia and the rigid Nazi salute, of the balcony harangues of Der Feuhrer as he roared "Only force rules . . . force is the first law"—remain etched in the modern consciousness.

The literature of the period reflects its moods and contradictions. Although William Butler Yeats in "A Prayer for My Daughter" looked to the stability and order of an earlier time, and although Robert Frost used traditional poetic forms, simple diction, and spoken language rhythms to paint rural scenes and to suggest personal and universal religious tensions, most writers of the twenties were radically experimental. A poetic renaissance began in 1912 with the founding in America of Harriet Monroe's *Poetry: A Magazine of Verse*; among its contributors were a group of Imagists, with whom Ezra Pound and Carl Sandburg were originally associated. The Imagists strove to evoke emotional response to verbal images. In seeking to liberate poetry from its traditional form and subject matter, they often abandoned meter and rhyme in favor of more natural rhythms; they sought the simplicity and naturalness of real speech and everyday life; they relied on imaginative association rather than conventional syntax; and they insisted on the freedom to go beyond typically "poetic" subjects.

Many writers in the twenties, preoccupied with the physical and psychic wounds left by World War I, created poetically a sterile, loveless, godless wasteland, where shell-shocked creatures clung to a precarious mental balance and stoically stifled their fears. Faulkner's "Death Drag," for instance, dramatizes the psychic death of those aviators of World War I who came back unfitted for prosaic civilian existence. Ernest Hemingway deifies stoicism in a world where, as he wrote his friend F. Scott Fitzgerald, "we are all bitched from the start." In the simple diction and deliberate understatement of "In Another Country" he reveals his suspicion of complex ideas and dramatizes, through the actions and reactions of two wounded soldiers, the grammar of courage by the actions of one who knows the language well—but still cannot "resign" himself—and another who has yet to grasp the total grammar but is slowly learning it in his bones. Hemingway's suspicion of the intellect, like that of D. H. Lawrence and E. E. Cummings, implies a postwar disillusionment with the rational and the scientific. In both style and attitude, Hemingway became a model for his contemporaries.

T. S. Eliot, an intellectual aristocrat unlike Hemingway, dictated poetic sensibility in the postwar decade. Like his creature, J. Alfred Prufrock, Eliot was bored by the triviality of polite society and offended by the crudities of "men in shirt sleeves." In his view, man was not a tragic hero but a pathetic fool, dead, yet yearning to be born. That awareness Eliot raised to a metaphor of the human condition in "The Hollow Men": the hollow men desire to pray, to believe, but can only begin, never complete, an act of devotion. Paralyzed by indecision, they engage in empty rituals: "Here we go round the prickly pear/At five o'clock in the morning."

Perhaps even more important than his ideas, however, were Eliot's poetic strategies. The indirection and obscurity of his poetry (much like that of his early teacher Ezra Pound) anticipate much of modern poetry. Eliot's sophistication and intellectualism, his recondite and at times private allusions, his dry wit and omnipresent irony, his contrast of this brass age with an earlier golden one, his complex symbolism, his psychological leaps (which result in the lack of logical transitions so common in his poetry), and his disgust with the vulgarity of modern man and his milieu —all these qualities were so overwhelming that not until the late 1950s did there begin to be a serious revolt against the "tryanny" of Eliot's influence.

Save for the furor aroused by the trial and execution of two poor anarchists, Sacco and Vanzetti, the twenties was a time more concerned with individual problems—especially spiritual emptiness—than with practical politics or social justice. The Great Depression, however, lured many writers to preach radical ideology in such lyrical phrases as those of Stephen Spender's "The Express," or in such challenges as that of John Dos Passos (in his trilogy *USA*): "all right we are two nations." And always, in the late thirties, the stench of the Nazi concentration camps pervaded the air, not only throughout Germany, but in England and America. In his long poem "Autumn Journal" Louis

MacNeice captures the despair and paralysis of those months in 1939 when the world waited to reap the whirlwind sown by clever, greedy, and irresponsible men.

With the thirties the mood of artistic experimentation declined. Instead of looking inward, most artists looked outward, and what they saw led them to cry out for social reform. Though the influence of Freud did not diminish greatly, Marx became the dominant prophet of the age. To assert their artistic independence, artists were often content to proclaim, in conventional forms, the rottenness of the capitalistic system, and innumerable writers created propagandistic novels with such titles as those of Jack Conroy's "The Disinherited" (a powerful cry for the union of the oppressed against their capitalistic exploiters) and "A World to Win" (inspired by the concluding peroration of *The Communist Manifesto:* "Workers of the World unite; you have nothing to lose but your chains; you have a world to win!"). Richard Wright for a time was lured by the Marxist ideal, but in his novel *Native Son* and his autobiography *Black Boy* he speaks far more poignantly of the dreams of black youth, the humiliation of black lives, and the rage of black men—with all of which America would soon have to reckon. That day of reckoning William Faulkner also foresaw, not only stemming from the treatment of blacks but also from the thoughtless exploitation of the land. In "Delta Autumn" he dramatizes the sins and the guilt of past generations, and implies the necessity of new, more cooperative and more Christian modes of life and thought. By such protest many writers outraged conventional society but soothed their own indignation. The painter Rivera, who so offended Nelson Rockefeller by questioning the right of wealth to dictate the terms of art (and of whom E. B. White writes in "I Paint What I See"), was a common phenomenon among artists in the thirties.

Though there is little doubt that the period between the wars is split at the beginning of the Great Depression, some artistic obsessions cover the entire era. Throughout the period, creative writers reflect the theories of the subconscious posed by Freud and dramatize the ideas of behaviorist psychologists such as John Watson, which seem to reduce men to mere fleshly machines responding automatically to appropriate stimuli. In the course of his career Freud gradually emphasized the use of dreams and the free association of ideas as methods of psychiatric analysis. Constantly he explored man's subconscious fears and fantasies, the conflicts between id, ego, and superego, and insistently he stated the importance of sexual drives (especially repressed sexual urges) in the understanding of personality and its malformation. Among the numerous theories of Freud that have become folklore, none have become more widespread than those of the oedipal and electra complex (the oedipal imagery of Eugene O'Neill's *Desire under the Elms* becomes painfully obvious today), and much of modern literature dramatizes such concepts. Because of the influence of such men as Freud and Watson, many of the characters in the fiction and the drama of the times seem grotesque, to use a favorite word of Sherwood Anderson, and it is in opposition to the grotesqueness of such beings that John Collier asserts the existence of a world of mystery, beyond natural, scientific explanation, in "Thus I Refute Beelzy."

Almost as omnipresent is the fascination with, and the fear of, the machines by which man continued to transform his environment and social habits. The distaste with which E. M. Forster in *The Machine Stops* contemplated the progress of man toward sluggish, loveless, dehumanization under the tyranny of the machine is paralleled by Stephen Vincent Benét's satire in "Nightmare Number Three." In Benét's poem, the human narrator dreams, after the revolt and victory of the machines, "Oh, it's going to be jake. /There won't be so much real difference —honest, there won't—." But Benét knew there would be. And we are today increasingly finding out the quality of the difference.

EXPOSITION AND ARGUMENT

Sigmund Freud (1856–1940)

from THE INTERPRETATION OF DREAMS

According to my already extensive experience, parents play a leading part in the infantile psychology of all persons who subsequently become psychoneurotics. Falling in love with one parent and hating the other forms part of the permanent stock of the psychic impulses which arise in early childhood, and are of such importance as the material of the subsequent neurosis. But I do not believe that psychoneurotics are to be sharply distinguished in this respect from other persons who remain normal—that is, I do not believe that they are capable of creating something absolutely new and peculiar to themselves. It is far more probable—and this is confirmed by incidental observations of normal children—that in their amorous or hostile attitude toward their parents, psychoneurotics do not more than reveal to us, by magnification, something that occurs less markedly and intensively in the minds of the majority of children. Antiquity has furnished us with legendary matter which corroborates this belief, and the profound and universal validity of the old legends is explicable only by an equally universal validity of the above-mentioned hypothesis of infantile psychology.

I am referring to the legend of King Oedipus and the *Oedipus Rex* of Sophocles. Oedipus, the son of Laius, king of Thebes, and Jocasta, is exposed as a suckling, because an oracle had informed the father that his son, who was still unborn, would be his murderer. He is rescued, and grows up as a king's son at a foreign court, until, being uncertain of his origin he, too, consults the oracle, and is warned to avoid his native place, for he is destined to become the murderer of his father and the husband of his mother. On the road leading away from his supposed home he meets King Laius, and in a sudden quarrel strikes him dead. He comes to Thebes, where he solves the riddle of the Sphinx, who is barring the way to the city, whereupon he is elected king by the grateful Thebans, and is rewarded with the hand of Jocasta. He reigns for many years in peace and honour, and begets two sons and two daughters upon his unknown mother, until at last a plague breaks out—which causes the Thebans to consult the oracle anew. Here Sophocles' tragedy begins. The messengers bring the reply that the plague will stop as soon as the murderer of Laius is driven from the country. But where is he?

"Where shall be found,
Faint, and hard to be known, the trace
    of the ancient guilt?"

The action of the play consists simply in the disclosure, approached step by step and artistically delayed (and comparable to the work of a psychoanalysis) that Oedipus himself is the murderer of Laius, and that he is the son of the murdered man and Jocasta. Shocked by the abominable crime which he has unwittingly committed, Oedipus blinds himself, and departs from his native city. The prophecy of the oracle has been fulfilled. . . .

If the *Oedipus Rex* is capable of moving a modern reader or playgoer no less powerfully than it moved the contemporary Greeks, the only possible explanation is that the effect of the Greek tragedy does not depend upon the conflict between fate and human will, but upon the peculiar nature of the material by which this conflict is revealed. There must be a voice within us which is prepared to acknowledge the compelling power of fate in the *Oedipus* . . . And there actually is a motive in the story of King Oedipus which explains the verdict of this inner voice. His fate moves us only because it might have been our own, because the oracle laid upon us before our birth the very curse which rested upon him. It may be that we were all destined to direct our first sexual impulses toward our mothers, and our first impulses of hatred and violence toward our fathers; our dreams convince us that we were. King Oedipus, who slew his father Laius and wedded his mother Jocasta, is nothing more or less than a wish-fulfillment—the fulfilment of the wish of our childhood. But we, more fortunate than he, in so far as we have not become psychoneurotics, have since our childhood succeeded in withdrawing our sexual impulses from our mothers, and in forgetting our jealousy of our fathers. We recoil from the person for whom this primitive wish of our childhood has been fulfilled with all the force of the repression which these wishes have undergone in our minds since childhood. As the poet brings the guilt of Oedipus to light by his investigation, he forces us to become aware of our inner selves, in which the same impulses are still extant, even though they are suppressed. The antithesis with which the chorus departs:—

". . . Behold this is Oedipus,
Who unravelled the great riddle, and
    was first in power,
Whose fortune all the townsmen
    praised and envied:
See in what dread adversity he sank!"

—this admonition touches us and our own pride, us who since the years of our childhood have grown so wise and so powerful in our own estimation. Like Oedipus, we live in ignorance of the desires that offend morality, the desires that nature has forced upon us and after their unveiling we may well prefer to avert our gaze from the scenes of our childhood.

In the very text of Sophocles' tragedy there is an unmistakable reference to the fact that the Oedipus legend had its source in dream-material of immemorial antiquity, the content of which was the painful disturbance of the child's relations to its parents caused by the first impulses of sexuality. Jocasta comforts Oedipus,—who is not yet enlightened, but is troubled by the recollection of the oracle—by an allusion, to a dream which is often dreamed, though it cannot, in her opinion, mean anything:—

"For many a man hath seen himself in
    dreams
His mother's mate, but he who gives
    no heed
To suchlike matters bears the easier
    life . . ."

Another of the great poetic tragedies, Shakespeare's Hamlet, is rooted in the same soil as *Oedipus Rex*. But the whole difference in the psychic life of the two widely separated periods of civilization, and the progress, during the course of time, of repression in the emotional life of humanity, is manifested in the differing treatment of the same material. In *Oedipus Rex* the basic wish-phantasy of the child is brought to light and realized as it is in dreams; in Hamlet it remains repressed, and we learn of its existence—as we discover the relevant facts in a neurosis—only through the inhibitory effects which proceed from it . . . The play is based upon Hamlet's hesitation in accomplishing the task of revenge assigned to him; the text does not give the cause or the motive of this hesitation, nor have the manifold attempts at interpretation succeeded in doing so. According to the still prevailing conception, a conception for which Goethe was first responsible, Hamlet represents the type of man whose active energy is paralysed by excessive intellectual activity: "Sicklied o'er with the pale cast of thought." According to another conception, the poet has endeavoured to portray a morbid, irresolute character, on the verge of neurasthenia. The plot of the drama, however, shows us that Hamlet is by no means intended to appear as a character wholly incapable of action. On two separate occasions we see him assert himself: once in a sudden outburst of rage, when he stabs the eavesdropper behind the arras, and on the other occasion when he deliberately, and even craftily, with the complete unscrupulousness of a prince of the Renaissance, sends the two courtiers to the death which was intended for himself. What is it, then, that inhibits him in accomplishing the task which his father's ghost has laid upon him? Here the explanation offers itself that it is the peculiar nature of this task. Hamlet is able to do anything but take vengeance upon the man who did away with his father and has taken his father's place with his mother—the man who shows him in realization the repressed desires of his own childhood. The loathing which should have driven him to revenge is thus replaced by self-reproach, by conscientious scruples, which tell him that he himself is no better than the murderer whom he is required to punish. I have here translated into consciousness what had to remain unconscious in the mind of the hero; if anyone wishes to call Hamlet an hysterical subject I cannot but admit that this is the deduction to be drawn from my interpretation. The sexual aversion which Hamlet expresses in conversation with Ophelia is perfectly consistent with this deduction— the same sexual aversion during the next few years was increasingly to take possession of the poet's soul, until it found its supreme utterance in *Timon of Athens*. It can, of course, be only the poet's own psychology with which we are confronted in *Hamlet*; and in a work on Shakespeare by Georg Brandes (1896) I find the statement that the drama was composed immediately after the death of Shakespeare's father (1601)—that is to say, when he was still mourning his loss, and during a revival, as we may fairly assume, of his own childish feelings in respect of his father. It is known, too, that Shakespeare's son, who died in childhood, bore the name of Hamnet (identical with Hamlet). . . .

F. Scott Fitzgerald (1896–1940)
EARLY SUCCESS

Seventeen years ago this month I quit work or, if you prefer, I retired from business. I was through—let the Street Railway Advertising Company carry along under its own power. I retired, not on my profits, but on my liabilities, which included debts, despair, and a broken engagement and crept home to St. Paul to "finish a novel."

That novel, begun in a training camp late in the war, was my ace in the hole. I had put it aside when I got a job in New York, but I was as constantly aware of it as of the shoe with cardboard in the sole, during all one desolate spring. It was like the fox and goose and the bag of beans. If I stopped working to finish the novel, I lost the girl.

So I struggled on in a business I detested and all the confidence I had garnered at Princeton and in a haughty career as the army's worst aide-de-camp melted gradually away. Lost and forgotten, I walked quickly from certain places—from the pawn shop where one left the field glasses, from prosperous friends whom one met when wearing the suit from before the war—from restaurants after tipping with the last nickle, from busy cheerful offices that were saving the jobs for their own boys from the war.

Even having a first story accepted had not proved very exciting. Dutch Mount and I sat across from each other in a car-card slogan advertising office, and the same mail brought each of us an acceptance from the same magazine—the old *Smart Set.*

"My check was thirty—how much was yours?"

"Thirty-five."

The real blight, however, was that my story had been written in college two years before, and a dozen new ones hadn't even drawn a personal letter. The implication was that I was on the downgrade at twenty-two. I spent the thirty dollars on a magenta feather fan for a girl in Alabama.

My friends who were not in love or who had waiting arrangements with "sensible" girls, braced themselves patiently for a long pull. Not I—I was in love with a whirlwind and I must spin a net big enough to catch it out of my head, a head full of trickling nickels and sliding dimes, the incessant music box of the poor. It couldn't be done like that, so when the girl threw me over I went home and finished my novel. And then, suddenly, everything changed, and this article is about that first wild wind of success and the delicious mist it brings with it. It is a short and precious time—for when the mist rises in a few weeks, or a few months, one finds that the very best is over.

It began to happen in the autumn of 1919 when I was an empty bucket, so mentally blunted with the summer's writing that I'd taken a job repairing car roofs at the Northern Pacific shops. Then the postman rang, and that day I quit work and ran along the streets, stopping automobiles to tell friends and acquaintances about it—my novel *This Side of Paradise* was accepted for publication. That week the postman rang and rang, and I paid off my terrible small debts, bought a suit, and woke up every morning with a world of ineffable top-loftiness and promise.

While I waited for the novel to appear, the metamorphosis of amateur into professional began to take place— a sort of stitching together of your whole life into a pattern of work, so that the end of one job is automatically the beginning of another. I had been an amateur before; in October, when I strolled with a girl among the stones of a southern graveyard, I was a professional and my enchantment with certain things that she felt and said was already paced by an anxiety to set them down in a story—it was called *The Ice Palace* and it was published later. Similarly, during Christmas week in St. Paul, there was a night when I had stayed home from two dances to work on a story. Three friends called up during the evening to tell me I had missed some rare doings: a well-known man-about-town had disguised himself as a camel and, with a taxi-driver as the rear half, managed to attend the wrong party. Aghast with myself for not being there, I spent the next day trying to collect the fragments of the story.

"Well, all I can say is it was funny when it happened." "No, I don't know where he got the taxi-man." "You'd have to know him well to understand how funny it was."

In despair I said:

"Well, I can't seem to find out exactly what happened but I'm going to write about it as if it was ten times funnier than anything you've said." So I wrote it, in twenty-two consecutive hours, and wrote it "funny," simply because I was so emphatically told it was funny. *The Camel's Back* was published and still crops up in the humorous anthologies.

With the end of the winter set in another pleasant pumped-dry period, and, while I took a little time off, a fresh picture of life in America began to form before my eyes. The uncertainties of 1919 were over—there seemed little doubt about what was going to happen—America was going on the greatest, gaudiest spree in history and there was going to be plenty to tell about it. The whole golden boom was in the air —its splendid generosities, its outrageous corruptions and the tortuous death struggle of the old America in prohibition. All the stories that came into my head had a touch of disaster in them—the lovely young creatures in my novels went to ruin, the diamond mountains of my short stories blew up, my millionaries were as beautiful and damned as Thomas Hardy's peasants. In life these things hadn't happened yet, but I was pretty sure living wasn't the reckless, careless business these people thought—this generation just younger than me.

For my point of vantage was the dividing line between the two generations, and there I sat—somewhat self-consciously. When my first big mail came in—hundreds and hundreds of letters on a story about a girl who bobbed her hair—it seemed rather absurd that they should come to me about it. On the other hand, for a shy man it was nice to be somebody except oneself again: to be "the Author" as one had been "the Lieutenant." Of course one wasn't really an author any more than one had been an army officer, but nobody seemed to guess behind the false face.

All in three days I got married and the presses were pounding out *This Side of Paradise* like they pound out extras in the movies.

With its publication I had reached a stage of manic depressive insanity. Rage and bliss alternated hour by hour. A lot of people thought it was a fake, and perhaps it was, and a lot of others thought it was a lie, which it was not. In a daze I gave out an interview—I told what a great writer I was and how I'd achieved the heights. Heywood Broun, who was on my trail, simply quoted it with the comment that I seemed to be a very self-satisfied young man, and for some days I was notably poor company. I invited him to lunch and in a kindly way told him that it was too bad he had let his life slide away without accomplishing anything. He had just turned thirty and it was about then that I wrote a line which certain people will not let me forget: "She was a faded but still lovely woman of twenty-seven."

In a daze I told the Scribner Company that I didn't expect my novel to sell more than twenty thousand copies and when the laughter died away I was told that a sale of five thousand was excellent for a first novel. I think it was a week after publication that it passed the twenty thousand mark, but I took myself so seriously that I didn't even think it was funny.

These weeks in the clouds ended abruptly a week later when Princeton turned on the book—not undergraduate Princeton but the black mass of faculty and alumni. There was a kind of reproachful letter from President Hibben, and a room full of classmates who suddenly turned on me with condemnation. We had been part of a rather gay party staged conspicuously in Harvey Firestone's car of robin's-egg blue, and in the course of it I got an accidental black eye trying to stop a fight. This was magnified into an orgy and in spite of a delegation of undergraduates who went to the board of Governors, I was suspended from my club for a couple of months. The *Alumni Weekly* got after my book and only Dean Gauss had a good word to say for me. The unctuousness and hypocrisy of the proceedings was exasperating and for seven years I didn't go to Princeton. Then a magazine asked me for an article about it and when I started to write it, I found I really loved the place and that the experience of one week was a small item in the total budget. But on that day in 1920

most of the joy went out of my success.

But one was now a professional—and the new world couldn't possibly be presented without bumping the old out of the way. One gradually developed a protective hardness against both praise and blame. Too often people liked your things for the wrong reasons or people liked them whose dislike would be a compliment. No decent career was ever founded on a public and one learned to go ahead without precedents and without fear. Counting the bag, I found that in 1919 I had made $800 by writing, that in 1920 I had made $18,000, stories, picture rights and book. My story price had gone from $30 to $1,000. That's a small price to what was paid later in the Boom but what it sounded like to me couldn't be exaggerated.

The dream had been early realized and the realization carried with it a certain bonus and a certain burden. Premature success gives one an almost mystical conception of destiny as opposed to will power—at its worst the Napoleonic delusion. The man who arrives young believes that he exercises his will because his star is shining. The man who only asserts himself at thirty has a balanced idea of what will power and fate have each contributed, the one who gets there at forty is liable to put the emphasis on will alone. This comes out when the storms strike your craft.

The compensation of a very early success is a conviction that life is a romantic matter. In the best sense one stays young. When the primary objects of love and money could be taken for granted and a shaky eminence had lost its fascination, I had fair years to waste, years that I can't honestly regret, in seeking the eternal Carnival by the Sea. Once in the middle twenties I was driving along the High Corniche Road through the twilight with the whole French Riviera twinkling on the sea below. As far ahead as I could see was Monte

Carlo, and though it was out of season and there were no Grand Dukes left to gamble and E. Phillips Oppenheim was a fat industrious man in my hotel, who lived in a bathrobe—the very name was so incorrigibly enchanting that I could only stop the car and like the Chinese whisper: "Ah me! Ah me!" It was not Monte Carlo I was looking at. It was back into the mind of the young man with cardboard soles who had walked the streets of New York. I was him again—for an instant I had the good fortune to share his dreams, I who had no more dreams of my own. And there are still times when I creep up on him, surprise him on an autumn morning in New York or a spring night in Carolina when it is so quiet that you can hear a dog barking in the next county. But never again as during that all too short period when he and I were one person, when the fulfilled future and the wistful past were mingled in a single gorgeous moment—when life was literally a dream.

John Dos Passos (1896–1970)
TIN LIZZIE

"Mr. Ford the automobileer," the feature-writer wrote in 1900,

"Mr. Ford the automobileer began by giving his steed three or four sharp jerks with the lever at the righthand side of the seat; that is, he pulled the level up and down sharply in order, as he said, to mix air with gasoline and drive the charge into the exploding cylinder. . . . Mr. Ford slipped a small electric switch handle and there followed a puff, puff, puff. . . . The puffing of the machine assumed a higher key. She was flying along about eight miles an hour. The ruts in the road were deep, but the machine certainly went with a dreamlike smoothness. There was none of the bumping common even to a streetcar. . . . By this time the boulevard had been reached, and the automobileer, letting a lever fall a little, let her out. Whiz! She picked up speed with infinite rapidity. As she ran on there was a clattering behind, the new noise of the automobile."

For twenty years or more,

ever since he'd left his father's farm when he was sixteen to get a job in a Detroit machineshop, Henry Ford had been nuts about machinery. First it was watches, then he designed a steamtractor, then he built a horseless carriage with an engine adapted from the Otto gas-engine he'd read about in *The World of Science*, then a mechanical buggy with a onecylinder fourcyle motor, that would run forward but not back;

at last, in ninetyeight, he felt he was far enough along to risk throwing up his job with the Detroit Edison Company, where he'd worked his way up from night fireman to chief engineer, to put all his time into working on a new gasoline engine,

(in the late eighties he'd met Edison at a meeting of electriclight employees in Atlantic City. He'd gone up to Edison after Edison had delivered an address and asked him if he thought gasoline was practical as a motor fuel. Edison had said yes. If Edison said it, it was true. Edison was the great admiration of Henry Ford's life);

and in driving his mechanical buggy, sitting there at the lever jauntily dressed in a tightbuttoned jacket and a high collar and a derby hat, back and forth over the level illpaved streets of Detroit,

scaring the big brewery horses and the skinny trotting horses and the sleek-rumped pacers with the motor's loud explosions,

looking for men scatterbrained enough to invest money in a factory for building automobiles.

He was the eldest son of an Irish immigrant who during the Civil War had married the daughter of a prosperous Pennsylvania Dutch farmer and settled down to farming near Dearborn in Wayne County, Michigan;

like plenty of other Americans, young Henry grew up hating the endless sogging through the mud about the chores, the hauling and pitching manure, the kerosene lamps to clean, the irk and sweat and solitude of the farm.

He was a slender, active youngster, a good skater, clever with his hands; what he liked was to tend the machinery and let the others do the heavy work. His mother had told him not to drink, smoke, gamble or go into debt, and he never did.

When he was in his early twenties his father tried to get him back from Detroit, where he was working as mechanic and repairman for the Drydock Engine Company that built engines for steamboats, by giving him forty acres of land.

Young Henry built himself an uptodate square white dwelling-house with a false mansard roof and married and settled down on the farm,

but he let the hired men do the farming;

he bought himself a buzzsaw and rented a stationary engine and cut the timber off the woodlots.

He was a thrifty young man who never drank or smoked or gambled or coveted his neighbor's wife, but he couldn't stand living on the farm.

He moved to Detroit, and in the brick barn behind his house tinkered for years in his spare time with a mechanical buggy that would be light enough to run over the clayey wagonroads of Wayne County, Michigan.

By 1900 he had a practicable car to promote.

He was forty years old before the Ford Motor Company was started and production began to move.

Speed was the first thing the early automobile manufacturers went after. Races advertised the makes of cars.

Henry Ford himself hung up several records at the track at Grosse Pointe and on the ice on Lake St. Clair. In his 999 he did the mile in thirtynine and fourfifths seconds.

But it had always been his custom to hire others to do the heavy work. The speed he was busy with was speed in production, the records were records in efficient output. He hired Barney Oldfield, a stunt bicyclerider from Salt Lake City, to do the racing for him.

Henry Ford had ideas about other things than the designing of motors, carburetors, magnetos, jigs and fixtures, punches and dies; he had ideas about sales,

that the big money was in economical quantity production, quick turnover, cheap interchangeable easilyreplaced standardized parts;

it wasn't until 1909, after years of arguing with his partners, that Ford put out the first Model T.

Henry Ford was right.

That season he sold more than ten thousand tin lizzies, ten years later he was selling almost a million a year.

In these years the Taylor Plan was stirring up plantmanagers and manufacturers all over the country. Efficiency was the word. The same ingenuity that went into improving the performance of a machine could go into improving the performance of the workmen producing the machine.

In 1913 they established the assemblyline at Ford's. That season the profits were something like twentyfive million dollars, but they had trouble in keeping the men on the job, machinists didn't seem to like it at Ford's.

Henry Ford had ideas about other things than production.

He was the largest automobile manufacturer in the world; he paid high wages; maybe if the steady workers thought they were getting a cut (a very small cut) in the profits, it would give trained men an inducement to stick to their jobs,

wellpaid workers might save enough money to buy a tin lizzie; the first day Ford's announced that cleancut properly-married American workers who wanted jobs had a chance to make five bucks a day (of course it turned out that there were strings to it; always there were strings to it)

such an enormous crowd waited outside the Highland Park plant

all through the zero January night

that there was a riot when the gates were opened; cops broke heads, jobhunters threw bricks; property, Henry Ford's own property, was destroyed. The company dicks had to turn on the fire-hose to beat back the crowd.

The American Plan; automotive prosperity seeping down from above; it turned out there were strings to it.

But that five dollars a day

paid to good, clean American workmen

who didn't drink or smoke cigarettes or read or think,

and who didn't commit adultery

and whose wives didn't take in boarders,

made America once more the Yukon of the sweated workers of the world;

made all the tin lizzies and the automotive age, and incidentally,

made Henry Ford, the automobileer, the admirer of Edison, the birdlover, the great American of his time.

But Henry Ford had ideas about other things beside assemblylines and the livinghabits of his employees. He was full of ideas. Instead of going to the city to make his fortune, here was a country boy who'd made his fortune by bringing the city out to the farm. The precepts he'd learned out of McGuffey's Reader, his mother's prejudices and preconceptions, he had preserved clean and unworn as freshprinted bills in the safe in a bank.

He wanted people to know about his ideas, so he bought the *Dearborn Independent* and started a campaign against cigarettesmoking.

When war broke out in Europe, he had ideas about that too. (Suspicion of armymen and soldiering were part of the midwest farm tradition, like thrift, stickativeness, temperance and sharp practice in money matters.) Any intelligent American mechanic could see that if the Europeans hadn't been a lot of ignorant underpaid foreigners who drank, smoked, were loose about women and wasteful in their methods of production, the war could never have happened.

When Rosika Schwimmer broke through the stockade of secretaries and servicemen who surrounded Henry Ford and suggested to him that he could stop the war,

he said sure they'd hire a ship and go over and get the boys out of the trenches by Christmas.

He hired a steamboat, the *Oscar II*, and filled it up with pacifists and socialworkers,

to go over to explain to the princelings of Europe

that what they were doing was vicious and silly.

It wasn't his fault that Poor Richard's commonsense no longer rules the world and that most of the pacifists were nuts,

goofy with headlines.

When William Jennings Bryan went over to Hoboken to see him off, somebody handed William Jennings Bryan a squirrel in a cage; William Jennings Bryan made a speech with the squirrel under his arm. Henry Ford threw American Beauty roses to the crowd. The band played *I Didn't Raise My Boy to Be a Soldier*. Practical jokers let loose more squirrels. An eloping couple was married by a platoon of ministers in the saloon, and Mr. Zero, the flophouse humanitarian who reached the dock too late to sail,

dove into the North River and swam after the boat.

The *Oscar II* was described as a floating Chautauqua; Henry Ford said it felt like a middlewestern village, but by the time they reached Christiansand in Norway, the reporters had kidded him so that he had gotten cold feet and gone to bed. The world was too crazy outside of Wayne County, Michigan. Mrs. Ford and the management sent an Episcopal dean after him who brought him home under wraps,

and the pacifists had to speechify without him.

Two years later Ford's was manufacturing munitions, Eagle boats; Henry Ford was planning oneman tanks, and oneman submarines like the one tried out in the Revolutionary War. He announced to the press that he'd turn over his war profits to the government,

but there's no record that he ever did.

One thing he brought back from his trip

was the Protocols of the Elders of Zion.

He started a campaign to enlighten the world in the *Dearborn Independent*;

the Jews were why the world wasn't like Wayne County, Michigan, in the old horse and buggy days;

the Jews had started the war. Bolshevism, Darwinism, Marxism, Nietzsche, short skirts and lipstick. They were behind Wall Street and the international bankers, and the whiteslave traffic and the movies and the Supreme Court and ragtime and the illegal liquor business.

Henry Ford denounced the Jews and ran for senator and sued the *Chicago Tribune* for libel,

and was the laughingstock of the kept metropolitan press;

but when the metropolitan bankers tried to horn in on his business

he thoroughly outsmarted them.

In 1918 he had borrowed on notes to buy out his minority stockholders for the picayune sum of seventyfive million dollars.

In February, 1920, he needed cash to pay off some of these notes that were coming due. A banker is supposed to have called on him and offered him every facility if the bankers' representative could be made a member of the board of directors. Henry Ford handed the banker his hat,

and went about raising the money in his own way:

he shipped every car and part he had in his plant to his dealers and demanded immediate cash payment. Let the other fellow do the borrowing had always been a cardinal principle. He shut down production and canceled all orders from the supplyfirms. Many dealers were ruined, many supplyfirms, failed, but when he reopened his plant,

he owned it absolutely,

the way a man owns an unmortgaged farm with the taxes paid up.

In 1922 there started the Ford boom for President (high wages, waterpower, industry scattered to the small towns) that was skillfully pricked behind the scenes by another crackerbarrel philosopher, Calvin Coolidge,

but in 1922 Henry Ford sold one million three hundred and thirtytwo thousand two hundred and nine tin lizzies; he was the richest man in the world.

Good roads had followed the narrow ruts made in the mud by the Model T. The great automotive boom was on. At Ford's production was improving all the time; lest waste, more spotters, straw-bosses, stoolpigeons (fifteen minutes for lunch, three minutes to go to the toilet, the Taylorized speedup everywhere, reach under, adjust washer, screw down bolt, shove in cotterpin, reachunder adjustwasher, screwdown bolt, reachunderadjustscrewdownreachunderadjust until every ounce of life was sucked off into production and at night the workmen went home grey shaking husks).

Ford owned every detail of the process from the ore in the hills until the car rolled off the end of the assemblyline under its own power, the plants were rationalized to the last tenthousandth of an inch as measured by the Johansen scale;

in 1926 the production cycle was reduced to eightyone hours from the ore in the mine to the finished salable car proceeding under its own power,

but the Model T was obsolete.

New Era prosperity and the American Plan

(there were strings to it, always there were strings to it)

had killed Tin Lizzie

Ford's was just one of many automobile plants.

When the stockmarket bubble burst,

Mr. Ford the crackerbarrel philosopher said jubilantly,

"I told you so.

Serves you right for gambling and getting in debt.

The country is sound."

But when the country on cracked shoes, in frayed trousers, belts tightened over hollow bellies,

idle hands cracked and chapped with the cold of that coldest March day of 1932,

started marching from Detroit to Dearborn, asking for work and the American Plan, all they could think of at Ford's was machineguns.

The country was sound, but they mowed the marchers down.

They shot four of them dead.

Henry Ford was an old man

is a passionate antiquarian,

(lives besieged on his father's farm embedded in an estate of thousands of millionaire acres, protected by an army of servicemen, secretaries, secret agents, dicks under orders of an English ex-prizefighter,

always afraid of the feet in broken shoes on the roads, afraid the gangs will kidnap his grandchildren,

that a crank will shoot him,

that Change and the idle hands out of work will break through the gates and the high fences;

protected by a private army against

the new America of starved children and hollow bellies and cracked shoes stamping on souplines,

that has swallowed up the old thrifty farmlands

of Wayne County, Michigan,

as if they had never been).

Henry Ford as an old man

is a passionate antiquarian.

He rebuilt his father's farmhouse and put it back exactly in the state he remembered it in as a boy. He built a village of museums for buggies, sleighs, coaches, old plows, waterwheels, obsolete models of motorcars. He scoured the country for fiddlers to play old-fashioned squaredances.

Even old taverns he bought and put back into their original shape, as well as Thomas Edison's early laboratories.

When he bought the Wayside Inn

near Sudbury, Massachusetts, he had the new highway where the newmodel cars roared and slithered and hissed oilily past *(the new noise of the automobile)*,

moved away from the door,
put back the old bad road,
so that everything might be
the way it used to be,
in the days of horses and buggies.

THE CAMERA EYE (50)

They have clubbed us off the streets they are stronger   they are rich they hire and fire the politicians the newspapereditors the old judges the small men with reputations the collegepresidents the wardheelers (listen businessmen collegepresidents judges   America will not forget her betrayers) they hire the men with guns   the uniforms the policecars the patrolwagons

all right you have won   you will kill the brave men our friends tonight

there is nothing left to do   we are beaten   we the beaten crowd together in these old dingy schoolrooms on Salem Street   shuffle up and down the gritty creaking stairs sit hunched with bowed heads on benches and hear the old words of the haters of oppression   made new in sweat and agony tonight

our work is over   the scribbled phrases   the nights typing releases the smell of the printshop the sharp reek of newprinted leaflets the rush for Western Union stringing words into wires the search for stinging words to make you feel who are your oppressors America

America our nation has been beaten by strangers who have turned our language inside out who have taken the clean words our fathers spoke and made them slimy and foul

their hired men sit on the judge's bench they sit back with their feet on the tables under the dome of the State House they are ignorant of our beliefs they have the dollars the guns the armed forces the powerplants

they have built the electricchair and hired the executioner to throw the switch

all right we are two nations

America our nation has been beaten by strangers who have bought the laws and fenced off the meadows and cut down the woods for pulp and turned our pleasant cities into slums and sweated the wealth out of our people and when they want to they hire the executioner to throw the switch

but do they know that the old words of the immigrants are being renewed in blood and agony tonight do they know that the old American speech of the haters of oppression is new tonight in the mouth of an old woman from Pittsburgh of a husky boilermaker from Frisco who hopped freights clear from the Coast to come here in the mouth of a Back Bay socialworker in the mouth of an Italian printer of a hobo from Arkansas   the language of the beaten nation is not forgotten in our ears tonight

the men in the deathhouse made the old words new before they died

If it had not been for these things, I might have lived out my life talking at streetcorners to scorning men. I might

have died unknown, unmarked, a fail-
ure. This is our career and our triumph.
Never in our full life can we hope to
do such work for tolerance, for justice,
for man's understanding of man as now
we do by an accident.

now their work is over   the immigrants haters of oppression lie quiet
in black suits in the little undertaking
parlor in the North End   the city is
quiet   the men of the conquering
nation are not to be seen on the streets

they have won why are they scared
to be seen on the streets?   on the
streets you see only the downcast faces
of the beaten nation   all the way to
the cemetery where the bodies of the
immigrants are to be burned   we line
the curbs in the drizzling rain we crowd
the wet sidewalks elbow to elbow silent
pale looking with scared eyes at the
coffins

we stand defeated America

George Orwell (1903–1950)
SHOOTING AN ELEPHANT

In Moulmein, in Lower Burma, I was
hated by large numbers of people—the
only time in my life that I have been
important enough for this to happen to
me. I was sub-divisional police officer
of the town, and in an aimless, petty
kind of way anti-European feeling was
very bitter. No one had the guts to
raise a riot, but if a European woman
went through the bazaars alone somebody would probably spit betel juice
over her dress. As a police officer I was
an obvious target and was baited whenever it seemed safe to do so. When a
nimble Burman tripped me up on the
football field and the referee (another
Burman) looked the other way, the
crowd yelled with hideous laughter.
This happened more than once. In the
end the sneering yellow faces of young
men that met me everywhere, the insults hooted after me when I was at a
safe distance, got badly on my nerves.
The young Buddhist priests were the
worst of all. There were several thousands of them in the town and none of
them seemed to have anything to do except stand on street corners and jeer
at Europeans.

All this was perplexing and upsetting.
For at that time I had already made
up my mind that imperialism was an
evil thing and the sooner I chucked up
my job and got out of it the better.
Theoretically—and secretly, of course
—I was all for the Burmese and all
against their oppressors, the British. As
for the job I was doing, I hated it more
bitterly than I can perhaps make clear.
In a job like that you see the dirty work
of Empire at close quarters. The
wretched prisoners huddling in the
stinking cages of the lock-ups, the grey,
cowed faces of the long-term convicts,
the scarred buttocks of the men who
had been flogged with bamboos—all
these oppressed me with an intolerable
sense of guilt. But I could get nothing
into perspective. I was young and ill-
educated and I had had to think out my

From *Shooting an Elephant and Other Essays*, by George Orwell, copyright 1945, 1946,
1949, 1950 by Sonia Brownell Orwell. Reprinted by permission of Harcourt Brace Jovanovich,
Inc., Miss Sonia Brownell and Secker & Warburg Ltd.

problems in the utter silence that is imposed on every Englishman in the East. I did not even know that the British Empire is dying, still less did I know that it is a great deal better than the younger empires that are going to supplant it. All I knew was that I was stuck between my hatred of the empire I served and my rage against the evil-spirited little beasts who tried to make my job impossible. With one part of my mind I thought of the British Raj as an unbreakable tyranny, as something clamped down, in *saecula saeculorum*, upon the will of prostrate peoples; with another part I thought that the greatest joy in the world would be to drive a bayonet into a Buddhist priest's guts. Feelings like these are the normal byproducts of imperialism; ask any Anglo-Indian official, if you can catch him off duty.

One day something happened which in a roundabout way was enlightening. It was a tiny incident in itself, but it gave me a better glimpse than I had had before of the real nature of imperialism —the real motives for which despotic governments act. Early one morning the sub-inspector at a police station the other end of the town rang me up on the 'phone and said that an elephant was ravaging the bazaar. Would I please come and do something about it? I did not know what I could do, but I wanted to see what was happening and I got on to a pony and started out. I took my rifle, an old .44 Winchester and much too small to kill an elephant, but I thought the noise might be useful *in terrorem*. Various Burmans stopped me on the way and told me about the elephant's doings. It was not, of course, a wild elephant, but a tame one which had gone "must." It had been chained up, as tame elephants always are when their attack of "must" is due, but on the previous night it had broken its chain and escaped. Its mahout, the only person who could manage it when it was in that state, had set out in pursuit, but had taken the wrong direction and was now twelve hours' journey away, and in the morning the elephant had suddenly reappeared in the town. The Burmese population had no weapons and were quite helpless against it. It had already destroyed somebody's bamboo hut, killed a cow and raided some fruit-stalls and devoured the stock; also it had met the municipal rubbish van and, when the driver jumped out and took to his heels, had turned the van over and inflicted violences upon it.

The Burmese sub-inspector and some Indian constables were waiting for me in the quarter where the elephant had been seen. It was a very poor quarter, a labyrinth of squalid bamboo huts, thatched with palm-leaf, winding all over a steep hillside. I remember that it was a cloudy, stuffy morning at the beginning of the rains. We began questioning the people as to where the elephant had gone and, as usual, failed to get any definite information. That is invariably the case in the East, a story always sounds clear enough at a distance, but the nearer you get to the scene of events the vaguer it becomes. Some of the people said that the elephant had gone in one direction, some said that he had gone in another, some professed not even to have heard of any elephant. I had almost made up my mind that the whole story was a pack of lies, when we heard yells a little distance away. There was a loud, scandalized cry of "Go away, child! Go away this instant!" and an old woman with a switch in her hand came round the corner of a hut, violently shooing away a crowd of naked children. Some more women followed, clicking their tongues and exclaiming; evidently there was something that the children ought not to have seen. I rounded the hut and saw a man's dead body sprawling in the mud. He was an Indian, a black Dravidian coolie, almost naked, and he could not have been dead many minutes. The people said that the elephant had come suddenly upon him round the corner of the hut, caught him with its trunk, put its foot on his back and ground him into the earth. This was the rainy season and the ground was soft, and his face had scored a trench a foot deep and a couple of yards long. He was lying on his belly with arms crucified and head sharply twisted to one side. His face was coated with mud, the eyes wide open, the teeth bared and grinning with an expression of unendurable agony. (Never tell me, by the way, that the dead look peaceful. Most of the corpses I have seen looked devilish.) The friction of the great beast's foot had stripped the skin from his back as neatly as one skins a rabbit. As soon as I saw the dead man I sent an orderly to a friend's house nearby to borrow an elephant rifle. I had already sent back the pony, not wanting it to go mad with fright and throw me if it smelt the elephant.

The orderly came back in a few minutes with a rifle and five cartridges, and meanwhile some Burmans had arrived and told us that the elephant was in the paddy fields below, only a few hundred yards away. As I started forward practically the whole population of the quarter flocked out of the houses and followed me. They had seen the rifle and were all shouting excitedly that I was going to shoot the elephant. They had not shown much interest in the elephant when he was merely ravaging their homes, but it was different now that he was going to be shot. It was a bit of fun to them, as it would be to an English crowd; besides they wanted the meat. It made me vaguely uneasy. I had no intention of shooting the elephant—I had merely sent for the rifle to defend myself if necessary—and it is always unnerving to have a crowd following you. I marched down the hill, looking and feeling a fool, with the rifle over my shoulder and an ever-growing army of people jostling at my heels. At the bottom, when you got away from the huts, there was a metalled road and beyond that a miry waste of paddy fields a thousand yards across, not yet ploughed but soggy from the first rains and dotted with coarse grass. The elephant was standing eight yards from the road, his left side towards us. He took not the slightest notice of the crowd's approach. He was tearing up bunches of grass, beating them against his knees to clean them and stuffing them into his mouth.

I had halted on the road. As soon as I saw the elephant I knew with perfect certainty that I ought not to shoot him. It is a serious matter to shoot a working elephant—it is comparable to destroying a huge and costly piece of machinery—and obviously one ought not to do it if it can possibly be avoided. And at that distance, peacefully eating, the elephant looked no more dangerous than a cow. I thought then and I think now that his attack of "must" was already passing off; in which case he would merely wander harmlessly about until the mahout came back and caught him. Moreover, I did not in the least want to shoot him. I decided that I would watch him for a little while to make sure that he did not turn savage again, and then go home.

But at that moment I glanced round at the crowd that had followed me. It was an immense crowd, two thousand at the least and growing every minute. It blocked the road for a long distance on either side. I looked at the sea of yellow faces above the garish clothes— faces all happy and excited over this bit of fun, all certain that the elephant was going to be shot. They were watching me as they would watch a conjurer about to perform a trick. They did not like me, but with the magical rifle in my hands I was momentarily worth watching. And suddenly I realized that I should have to shoot the elephant after all. The people expected it of me and I had got to do it; I could feel their two thousand wills pressing me forward, irresistibly. And it was at this moment, as I stood there with the rifle in my hands, that I first grasped the hollowness, the futility of the white man's dominion in the East. Here was I, the white man with his gun, standing in front of the unarmed native crowd—seemingly the leading actor of the piece; but in reality I was only an absurd puppet pushed to and fro by the will of those yellow faces behind. I perceived in this moment that when the white man turns tyrant it is his own freedom that he destroys. He becomes a sort of hollow, posing dummy, the conventionalized figure of a sahib. For it is the condition of his rule that he shall spend his life in trying to impress the "natives," and so in every crisis he has got to do what the "natives" expect of him. He wears a mask; and his face grows to fit it. I had got to shoot the elephant. I had committed myself to doing it when I sent for the rifle. A sahib has got to act like a sahib; he has got to appear resolute, to know his own mind and do definite things. To come all that way, rifle in hand, with two thousand people marching at my heels, and then to trail feebly away, having done nothing—no, that was impossible. The crowd would laugh at me. And my whole life, every white man's life in the East, was one long struggle not to be laughed at.

But I did not want to shoot the elephant. I watched him beating his bunch of grass against his knees, with that preoccupied grandmotherly air that elephants have. It seemed to me that it would be murder to shoot him. At that age I was not squeamish about killing animals, but I had never shot an elephant and never wanted to. (Somehow it always seems worse to kill a *large* animal.) Besides, there was the beast's owner to be considered. Alive, the elephant was worth at least a hundred pounds; dead, he would only be worth the value of his tusks, five pounds, possibly. But I had got to act quickly. I turned to some experienced-looking Burmans who had been there when we arrived, and asked them how the elephant had been behaving. They all said the same thing: he took no notice of you if you left him alone, but he might charge if you went too close to him.

It was perfectly clear to me what I ought to do. I ought to walk up to within, say, twenty-five yards of the elephant and test his behavior. If he charged, I could shoot; if he took no notice of me, it would be safe to leave him until the mahout came back. But also I knew that I was going to do no such thing. I was a poor shot with a rifle and the ground was soft mud into which one would sink at every step. If the elephant charged and I missed him, I should have about as much chance as a toad under a steam-roller. But even then I was not thinking particularly of my own skin, only of the watchful yellow faces behind. For at that moment, with the crowd watching me, I was not afraid in the ordinary sense, as I would have been if I had been alone. A white man mustn't be frightened in front of "natives"; and so, in general, he isn't frightened. The sole thought in my mind was that if anything went wrong those two thousand Burmans would see me pursued, caught, trampled on and reduced to a grinning corpse like that Indian up the hill. And if that happened it was quite probable that some of them would laugh. That would never do. There was only one alternative. I shoved the cartridges into the magazine and lay down on the road to get a better aim.

The crowd grew very still, and a deep, low, happy sigh, as of people who see the theatre curtain go up at last, breathed from innumerable throats. They were going to have their bit of fun after all. The rifle was a beautiful German thing with cross-hair sights. I did not then know that in shooting an elephant one would shoot to cut an imaginary bar running from ear-hole to ear-hole. I ought, therefore, as the elephant was sideways on, to have aimed straight at his ear-hole; actually I aimed several inches in front of this, thinking the brain would be further forward.

When I pulled the trigger I did not hear the bang or feel the kick—one never does when a shot goes home—but I heard the devilish roar of glee that went up from the crowd. In that instant, in too short a time, one would have thought, even for the bullet to get there, a mysterious, terrible change had come over the elephant. He neither stirred nor fell, but every line of his body had altered. He looked suddenly stricken, shrunken, immensely old, as though the frightful impact of the bullet had paralysed him without knocking him down. At last, after what seemed a long time —it might have been five seconds, I dare say—he sagged flabbily to his knees. His mouth slobbered. An enormous senility seemed to have settled upon him. One could have imagined him thousands of years old. I fired again into the same spot. At the second shot he did not collapse but climbed with desperate slowness to his feet and stood weakly upright, with legs sagging and head drooping. I fired a third time. That was the shot that did for him. You could see the agony of it jolt his whole body and knock the last remnant of strength from his legs. But in falling he seemed for a moment to rise, for as his hind legs collapsed beneath him he seemed to tower upward like a huge rock toppling, his trunk reaching skywards like a tree. He trumpeted, for the first and only time. And then down he came, his belly towards me, with a crash that seemed to shake the ground even where I lay.

I got up. The Burmans were already racing past me across the mud. It was obvious that the elephant would never rise again, but he was not dead. He was breathing very rhythmically with long rattling gasps, his great mound of a side painfully rising and falling. His mouth was wide open—I could see far down into caverns of pale pink throat. I waited a long time for him to die, but his breathing did not weaken. Finally I fired my two remaining shots into the spot where I thought his heart must be. The thick blood welled out of him like red velvet, but still he did not die. His body did not even jerk when the shots hit him, the tortured breathing continued without a pause. He was dying, very slowly and in great agony, but in some world remote from me where not even a bullet could damage him further. I felt that I had got to put an end to that dreadful noise. It seemed dreadful to see the great beast lying there, powerless to move and yet powerless to die, and not even to be able to finish him. I sent back for my small rifle and poured shot after shot into his heart and down his throat. They seemed to make no impression. The tortured gasps continued as steadily as the ticking of a clock.

In the end I could not stand it any longer and went away. I heard later that it took him half an hour to die. Burmans were bringing dahs and baskets even before I left, and I was told they had stripped his body almost to the bones by the afternoon.

Afterwards, of course, there were endless discussions about the shooting of the elephant. The owner was furious, but he was only an Indian and could do nothing. Besides, legally I had done the right thing, for a mad elephant has to be killed, like a mad dog, if its owner fails to control it. Among the Europeans opinion was divided. The older men said I was right, the younger men said it was a damn shame to shoot an elephant for killing a coolie, because an elephant was worth more than any damn Coringhee coolie. And afterwards I was very glad that the coolie had been killed; it put me legally in the right and it gave me a sufficient pretext for shooting the elephant. I often wondered whether any of the others grasped that I had done it solely to avoid looking a fool.

POLITICS AND THE ENGLISH LANGUAGE

Most people who bother with the matter at all would admit that the English language is in a bad way, but it is generally assumed that we cannot by conscious action do anything about it. Our civilization is decadent and our language—so the argument runs—must inevitably share in the general collapse. It follows that any struggle against the abuse of language is a sentimental archaism, like preferring candles to electric light or hansom cabs to aeroplanes. Underneath this lies the half-conscious belief that language is a natural growth and not an instrument which we shape for our own purposes.

Now, it is clear that the decline of a language must ultimately have political and economic causes: it is not due simply to the bad influence of this or that individual writer. But an effect can become a cause, reinforcing the original cause and producing the same effect in an intensified form, and so on indefinitely. A man may take to drink because he feels himself to be a failure, and then fail all the more completely because he drinks. It is rather the same thing that is happening to the English language. It becomes ugly and inaccurate because our thoughts are foolish, but the slovenliness of our language makes it easier for us to have foolish thoughts. The point is that the process is reversible. Modern English, especially written English, is full of bad habits which spread by imitation and which can be avoided if one is willing to take the necessary trouble. If one gets rid of these habits one can think more clearly, and to think clearly is a necessary first step towards political regener-ation: so that the fight against bad English is not frivolous and is not the exclusive concern of professional writers. I will come back to this presently, and I hope that by that time the meaning of what I have said here will have become clearer. Meanwhile, here are five specimens of the English language as it is now habitually written.

These five passages have not been picked out because they are especially bad—I could have quoted far worse if I had chosen—but because they illustrate various of the mental vices from which we now suffer. They are a little below the average, but are fairly representative samples. I number them so that I can refer back to them when necessary:

(1) I am not, indeed, sure whether it is not true to say that the Milton who once seemed not unlike a seventeenth-century Shelley had not become, out of an experience ever more bitter in each year, more alien {sic} to the founder of that Jesuit sect which nothing could induce him to tolerate.

Professor Harold Laski
(Essay in *Freedom of Expression*).

(2) Above all, we cannot play ducks and drakes with a native battery of idioms which prescribes such egregious collocations of vocables as the Basic *put up with* for *tolerate* or *put at a loss* for *bewilder*.

Professor Lancelot Hogben
(*Interglossa*).

(3) On the one side we have the free personality: by definition it is not neurotic, for it has neither conflict nor dream. Its desires, such as they are, are transparent, for they are just what in-

stitutional approval keeps in the fore-front of consciousness; another insti-tutional pattern would alter their num-ber and intensity; there is little in them that is natural, irreducible, or culturally dangerous. But *on the other side,* the social bond itself is nothing but the mutual reflection of these self-secure integrities. Recall the definition of love. Is not this the very picture of a small academic? Where is there a place in this hall of mirrors for either per-sonality or fraternity?

Essay on psychology in *Politics* (New York).

(4) All the "best people" from the gentlemen's clubs, and all the frantic fascist captains, united in common hatred of Socialism and bestial horror of the rising tide of the mass revolu-tionary movement, have turned to acts of provocation, to foul incendiarism, to medieval legends of poisoned wells, to legalize their own destruction of pro-letarian organizations, and rouse the agitated petty-bourgeoisie to chau-vinistic fervor on behalf of the fight against the revolutionary way out of the crisis.

Communist pamphlet.

(5) If a new spirit *is* to be infused into this old country, there is one thorny and contentious reform which must be tackled, and that is the human-ization and galvanization of the B.B.C. Timidity here will bespeak canker and atrophy of the soul. The heart of Britain may be sound and of strong beat, for instance, but the British lion's roar at present is like that of Bottom in Shakespeare's *Midsummer Night's Dream*—as gentle as any sucking dove. A virile new Britain cannot continue indefinitely to be traduced in the eyes or rather ears, of the world by the effete languors of Langham Place, brazenly masquerading as "standard English." When the Voice of Britain is heard at nine o'clock, better far and infinity less ludicrous to hear aitches honestly dropped than the present prig-gish, inflated, inhibited, school-ma'amish arch braying of blameless bashful mewing maidens!

Letter in *Tribune*

Each of these passages has faults of its own, but, quite apart from avoidable ugliness, two qualities are common to all of them. The first is staleness of imagery; the other is lack of precision. The writer either has a meaning and cannot express it, or he inadvertently says something else, or he is almost in-different as to whether his words mean anything or not. This mixture of vague-ness and sheer incompetence is the most marked characteristic of modern Eng-lish prose, and especially of any kind of political writing. As soon as certain topics are raised, the concrete melts in-to the abstract and no one seems able to think of turns of speech that are not hackneyed: prose consists less and less of *words* chosen for the sake of their meaning, and more and more of *phrases* tacked together like the sections of a prefabricated hen-house. I list below, with notes and examples, various of the tricks by means of which the work of prose-construction is habitually dodged:

Dying metaphors. A newly invented metaphor assists thought by evoking a visual image, while on the other hand a metaphor which is technically "dead" (e.g. *iron resolution*) has in effect re-verted to being an ordinary word and can generally be used without loss of vividness. But in between these two classes there is a huge dump of worn-out metaphors which have lost all evocative power and are merely used because they save people the trouble of inventing phrases for themselves. Ex-amples are: *Ring the changes on, take up the cudgels for, toe the line, ride roughshod over, stand shoulder to shoulder with, play into the hands of, no axe to grind, grist to the mill, fish-ing in troubled waters, on the order of the day, Achilles' heel, swan song, hot-bed.* Many of these are used without knowledge of their meaning (what is a "rift," for instance?), and incompatible metaphors are frequently mixed, a sure sign that the writer is not interested in what he is saying. Some metaphors now current have been twisted out of their original meaning without those who use them even being aware of the fact. For example, *toe the line* is sometimes written *tow the line*. Another example is *the hammer and the anvil,* now always used with the implication that the anvil gets the worst of it. In real life it is always the anvil that breaks the hammer, never the other way about: a writer who stopped to think what he was saying would be aware of this, and would avoid perverting the original phrase.

Operators or *verbal false limbs.* These save the trouble of picking out appropriate verbs and nouns, and at the same time pad each sentence with extra syllables which give it an appearance of symmetry. Characteristic phrases are *render inoperative, militate against, make contact with, be subjected to, give rise to, give grounds for, have the effect of, play a leading part (role) in, make itself felt, take effect, exhibit a tendency to, serve the purpose of, etc., etc.* The keynote is the elimination of simple verbs. Instead of being a single word, such as *break, stop, spoil, mend, kill,* a verb becomes a *phrase,* made up of a noun or adjective tacked on to some general-purposes verb such as *prove, serve, form, play, render.* In addition, the passive voice is wherever possible used in preference to the active, and noun constructions are used instead of gerunds (*by examination of* instead of *by examining*). The range of verbs is further cut down by means of the *-ize* and *de-* formations, and the banal statements are given an appearance of profundity by means of the *not un-* formation. Simple conjunctions and prepositions are replaced by such phrases as *with respect to, having regard to, the fact that, by dint of, in view of, in the interests of, on the*

hypothesis that; and the ends of sentences are saved by anticlimax by such resounding common-places as *greatly to be desired, cannot be left out of account, a development to be expected in the near future, deserving of serious consideration, brought to a satisfactory conclusion,* and so on and so forth.

Pretentious diction. Words like *phenomenon, element, individual* (as noun), *objective, categorical, effective, virtual, basic, primary, promote, constitute exhibit, exploit, utilize, eliminate, liquidate,* are used to dress up simple statement and give an air of scientific impartiality to biased judgments. Adjectives like *epoch-making, epic, historic, unforgettable, triumphant, age-old, inevitable, inexorable, veritable,* are used to dignify the sordid processes of international politics, while writing that aims at glorifying war usually takes on an archaic color, its characteristic words being: *realm, throne, chariot, mailed fist, trident, sword, shield, buckler, banner, jackboot, clarion.* Foreign words and expressions such as *cul de sac, ancien régime, deus ex machina, mutatis mutandis, status quo, gleichschaltung, weltanschauung,* are used to give an air of culture and elegance. Except for the useful abbreviations *i.e., e.g.,* and *etc.,* there is no real need for any of the hundreds of foreign phrases now current in English. Bad writers, and especially scientific, political and sociological writers, are nearly always haunted by the notion that Latin or Greek words are grander than Saxon ones, and unnecessary words like *expedite, ameliorate, predict, extraneous, deracinated, clandestine, subaqueous* and hundreds of others constantly gain ground from their Anglo-Saxon opposite numbers.[1] The jargon peculiar to Marxist writing (*hyena, hangman, cannibal,*

---

[1] An interesting illustration of this is the way in which the English flower names which were in use till very recently are being ousted by Greek ones, *snapdragon* becoming *antirrhinum,* *forget-me-not* becoming *myositis,* etc. It is hard to see any practical reason for this change of fashion: it is probably due to an instinctive turning-away from the more homely word and a vague feeling that the Greek word is scientific.

petty bourgeois, these gentry, lacquey, flunkey, mad dog, White Guard, etc.) consists largely of words and phrases translated from Russian, German or French; but the normal way of coining a new word is to use a Latin or Greek root with the appropriate affix and, where necessary, the size formation. It is often easier to make up words of this kind (*deregionalize, impermissible, extramarital, non-fragmentary* and so forth) than to think up the English words that will cover one's meaning. The result, in general, is an increase in slovenliness and vagueness.

Meaningless words. In certain kinds of writing, particularly in art criticism and literary criticism, it is normal to come across long passages which are almost completely lacking in meaning.[2] Words like *romantic, plastic, values, human, dead, sentimental, natural, vitality,* as used in art criticism, are strictly meaningless, in the sense that they not only do not point to any discoverable object, but are hardly ever expected to do so by the reader. When one critic writes, "The outstanding feature of Mr. X's work is its living quality," while another writes, "The immediately striking thing about Mr. X's work is its peculiar deadness," the reader accepts this as a simple difference of opinion. If words like *black* and *white* were involved, instead of the jargon words *dead* and *living,* he would see at once that language was being used in an improper way. Many political words are similarly abused. The word *Fascism* has now no meaning except in so far as it signifies "something not desirable." The words *democracy, socialism, freedom, patriotic, realistic, justice,* have each of them several different meanings which cannot be reconciled with one

another. In the case of a word like *democracy,* not only is there no agreed definition, but the attempt to make one is resisted from all sides. It is almost universally felt that when we call a country democratic we are praising it: consequently the defenders of every kind of régime claim that it is a democracy, and fear that they might have to stop using the word if it were tied down to any one meaning. Words of this kind are often used in a consciously dishonest way. That is, the person who uses them has his own private definition, but allows his hearer to think he means something quite different. Statements like *Marshal Pétain was a true patriot, The Soviet Press is the freest in the world, The Catholic Church is opposed to persecution,* are almost always made with intent to deceive. Other words used in variable meanings, in most cases more or less dishonestly, are: *class, totalitarian, science, progressive, reactionary, bourgeois, equality...*

Now that I have made this catalogue of swindles and perversions, let me give another example of the kind of writing that they lead to. This time it must of its nature be an imaginary one. I am going to translate a passage of good English into modern English of the worst sort. Here is a well-known verse from *Ecclesiastes*:

> I returned and saw under the sun, that the race is not to the swift, nor the battle to the strong, neither yet bread to the wise, nor yet riches to men of understanding, nor yet favour to men of skill; but time and chance happeneth to them all.

Here it is in modern English:

> Objective considerations of contemporary phenomena compels the conclusion that success or failure in com-

---

[2] Example: "Comforts catholicity of perception and image, strangly Whitmanesque in range, almost the exact opposite in aesthetic compulsion, continues to evoke that trembling atmospheric accumulative hinting at a cruel, an inexorably serene timelessness. . . . Wrey Gardiner scores by aiming at simple bull's-eyes with precision. Only they are not so simple, and through this contented sadness runs more than the surface bitter-sweet of resignation." (*Poetry Quarterly.*)

petition activities exhibits no tendency to be commensurate with innate capacity, but that a considerable element of the unpredictable must invariably be taken into account.

This is a parody, but not a very gross one. Exhibit (3), above, for instance, contains several patches of the same kind of English. It will be seen that I have not made a full translation. The beginning and ending of the sentence follow the original meaning fairly closely, but in the middle the concrete illustrations—race, battle, bread—dissolve into the vague phrase "success or failure in competitive activities." This had to be so, because no modern writer of the kind I am discussing—no one capable of using phrases like "objective consideration of contemporary phenomena"—would ever tabulate his thoughts in that precise and detailed way. The whole tendency of modern prose is away from *concreteness*. Now analyse these two sentences a little more closely. The first contains forty-nine words but only sixty syllables, and all its words are those of everyday life. The second contains thirty-eight words of ninety syllables: eighteen of its words are from Latin roots, and one from Greek. The first sentence contains six vivid images, and only one phrase ("time and chance") that could be called vague. The second contains not a single fresh, arresting phrase, and in spite of its ninety syllables it gives only a shortened version of the meaning contained in the first. Yet without a doubt it is the second kind of sentence that is gaining ground in modern English. I do not want to exaggerate. This kind of writing is not yet universal, and outcrops of simplicity will occur here and there in the worst-written page. Still, if you or I were told to write a few lines on the uncertainty of human fortunes, we should probably come much nearer to my imaginary sentence than to the one from *Ecclesiastes*.

As I have tried to show, modern writing at its worst does not consist in picking out words for the sake of their meaning and inventing images in order to make the meaning clearer. It consists in gumming together long strips of words which have already been set in order by someone else, and making the results presentable by sheer humbug. The attraction of this way of writing is that it is easy. It is easier—even quicker, once you have the habit—to say *In my opinion it is not an unjustifiable assumption that* than to say *I think*. If you use ready-made phrases, you not only don't have to hunt about for words; you also don't have to bother with the rhythms of your sentences, since these phrases are generally so arranged as to be more or less euphonious. When you are composing in a hurry—when you are dictating to a stenographer, for instance, or making a public speech—it is natural to fall into a pretentious, Latinized style. Tags like *a consideration which we should do well to bear in mind* or *a conclusion to which all of us would readily assent* will save many a sentence from coming down with a bump. By using stale metaphors, similes and idioms, you save much mental effort, at the cost of leaving your meaning vague, not only for your reader but for yourself. This is the significance of mixed metaphors. The sole aim of a metaphor is to call up a visual image. When these images clash—as in *The Fascist octopus has sung its swan song, the jackboot is thrown into the melting pot*—it can be taken as certain that the writer is not seeing a mental image of the objects he is naming; in other words he is not really thinking. Look again at the examples I gave at the beginning of this essay. Professor Laski (1) uses five negatives in fifty-three words. One of these is superfluous, making nonsense of the whole passage, and in addition there is the slip *alien* for akin, making further nonsense, and several avoidable pieces of clumsiness which increase the general vagueness. Professor Hogben (2) plays ducks and drakes with a battery which is able to write prescriptions, and, while disapproving of the everyday phrase *put up with*, is unwilling to look *egregious* up in the dictionary and see what it means; (3), if one takes an uncharitable attitude towards it, is simply meaningless: probably one could work out its intended meaning by reading the whole of the article in which it occurs. In (4), the writer knows more or less what he wants to say, but an accumulation of stale phrases chokes him like tea leaves blocking a sink. In (5), words and meaning have almost parted company. People who write in this manner usually have a general emotional meaning—they dislike one thing and want to express solidarity with another—but they are not interested in the detail of what they are saying. A scrupulous writer, in every sentence that he writes, will ask himself at least four questions, thus: What am I trying to say? What words will express it? What image or idiom will make it clearer? Is this image fresh enough to have an effect? And he will probably ask himself two more: Could I put it more shortly? Have I said anything that is avoidably ugly? But you are not obliged to go to all this trouble. You can shirk it by simply throwing your mind open and letting the ready-made phrases come crowding in. They will construct your sentences for you—even think your thoughts for you, to a certain extent—and at need they will perform the important service of partially concealing your meaning even from yourself. It is at this point that the special connection between politics and the debasement of language becomes clear.

In our time it is broadly true that political writing is bad writing. Where it is not true, it will generally be found that the writer is some kind of rebel, expressing his private opinions and not a "party line." Orthodoxy, of whatever color, seems to demand a lifeless, imitative style. The political dialects to be found in pamphlets, leading articles, manifestos, White Papers and the speeches of under-secretaries do, of course, vary from party to party, but they are all alike in that one almost never finds in them a fresh, vivid, home-made turn of speech. When one watches some tired hack on the platform mechanically repeating the familiar phrases —*bestial atrocities, iron heel, blood-stained tyranny, free peoples of the world, stand shoulder to shoulder*—one often has a curious feeling that one is not watching a live human being but some kind of dummy: a feeling which suddenly becomes stronger at moments when the light catches the speaker's spectacles and turns them into blank discs which seem to have no eyes behind them. And this is not altogether fanciful. A speaker who uses that kind of phraseology has gone some distance towards turning himself into a machine. The appropriate noises are coming out of his larynx, but his brain is not involved as it would be if he were choosing his words for himself. If the speech he is making is one that he is accustomed to make over and over again, he may be almost unconscious of what he is saying, as one is when one utters the responses in church. And this reduced state of consciousness, if not indispensable, is at any rate favorable to political conformity.

In our time, political speech and writing are largely the defence of the indefensible. Things like the continuance of British rule in India, the Russian purges and deportations, the dropping of the atom bombs on Japan, can indeed be defended, but only by arguments which are too brutal for most people to face, and which do not square with the professed aims of political parties. Thus political language has to consist largely of euphemism, question-begging and sheer cloudy vagueness. Defenceless villages are bombarded from the air, the inhabitants driven out into the countryside, the cattle machine-gunned, the huts set on fire with incendiary bullets: this is called *pacification.* Millions of peasants are robbed of their farms and sent trudging along the roads with no more than they can carry: this is called *transfer of population* or *rectification of frontiers.* People are imprisoned for years without trial, or shot in the back of the neck or sent to die of scurvy in Arctic lumber camps: this is called *elimination of unreliable elements.* Such phraseology is needed if one wants to name things without calling up mental pictures of them. Consider for instance some comfortable English professor defending Russian totalitarianism. He cannot say outright, "I believe in killing off your opponents when you can get good results by doing so." Probably, therefore, he will say something like this:

> While freely conceding that the Soviet regime exhibits certain features which the humanitarian may be inclined to deplore, we must, I think, agree that a certain curtailment of the right to political opposition is an unavoidable concomitant of transitional periods, and that the rigors which the Russian people have been called upon to undergo have been amply justified in the sphere of concrete achievement.

The inflated style is itself a kind of euphemism. A mass of Latin words falls upon the facts like soft snow, blurring the outlines and covering up all the details. The great enemy of clear language is insincerity. When there is a gap between one's real and one's declared aims, one turns as it were instinctively to long words and exhausted idioms, like a cuttlefish squirting out ink. In our age there is no such thing as "keeping out of politics." All issues are political issues, and politics itself is a mass of lies, evasions, folly, hatred and schizophrenia. When the general atmosphere is bad, language must suffer. I should expect to find—this is a guess which I have not sufficient knowledge to verify —that the German, Russian and Italian languages have all deteriorated in the last ten or fifteen years, as a result of dictatorship.

But if thought corrupts language, language can also corrupt thought. A bad usage can spread by tradition and imitation, even among people who should and do know better. The debased language that I have been discussing is in some ways very convenient. Phrases like *a not unjustifiable assumption, leaves much to be desired, would serve no good purpose, a consideration which we should do well to bear in mind,* are a continuous temptation, a packet of aspirins always at one's elbow. Look back through this essay, and for certain you will find that I have again and again committed the very faults I am protesting against. By this morning's post I have received a pamphlet dealing with conditions in Germany. The author tells me that he "felt impelled" to write it. I open it at random, and here is almost the first sentence that I see: "[The Allies] have an opportunity not only of achieving a radical transformation of Germany's social and political structure in such a way as to avoid a nationalistic reaction in Germany itself, but at the same time of laying the foundations of a co-operative and unified Europe." You see, he "feels impelled" to write—feels, presumably, that he has something new to say—and yet his words, like cavalry horses answering the bugle, group themselves automatically into the familiar dreary pattern. This invasion of one's mind by ready-made phrases (*lay the foundations, achieve a radical transformation*) can only be prevented if one is constantly on guard against them, and every such phrase anaesthetizes a portion of one's brain.

I said earlier that the decadence of

our language is probably curable. Those who deny this would argue, if they produced an argument at all, that language merely reflects existing social conditions, and that we cannot influence its development by any direct tinkering with words and constructions. So far as the general tone or spirit of a language goes, this may be true, but it is not true in detail. Silly words and expressions have often disappeared, not through any evolutionary process but owing to the conscious action of a minority. Two recent examples were *explore every avenue* and *leave no stone unturned,* which were killed by the jeers of a few journalists. There is a long list of fly-blown metaphors which could similarly be got rid of if enough people would interest themselves in the job; and it should also be possible to laugh the *not un-* formation out of existence,[3] to reduce the amount of Latin and Greek in the average sentence, to drive out foreign phrases and strayed scientific words, and, in general, to make pretentiousness unfashionable. But all these are minor points. The defence of the English language implies more than this, and perhaps it is best to start by saying what it does *not* imply.

To begin with it has nothing to do with archaism, with the salvaging of obsolete words and turns of speech, or with the setting up of a "standard English" which must never be departed from. On the contrary, it is especially concerned with the scrapping of every word or idiom which has outworn its usefulness. It has nothing to do with correct grammar and syntax, which are of no importance so long as one makes one's meaning clear, or with the avoidance of Americanisms, or with having what is called a "good prose style." On the other hand it is not concerned with faked simplicity and the attempt to make written English colloquial. Nor

does it even imply in every case preferring the Saxon word to the Latin one, though it does imply using the fewest and shortest words that will cover one's meaning. What is above all needed is to let the meaning choose the word, and not the other way about. In prose, the worst thing one can do with words is to surrender to them. When you think of a concrete object, you think wordlessly, and then, if you want to describe the thing you have been visualizing you probably hunt about till you find the exact words that seem to fit it. When you think of something abstract you are more inclined to use words from the start, and unless you make a conscious effort to prevent it, the existing dialect will come rushing in and do the job for you, at the expense of blurring or even changing your meaning. Probably it is better to put off using words as long as possible and get one's meaning as clear as one can through pictures or sensations. Afterwards one can choose—not simply *accept*—the phrases that will best cover the meaning, and then switch round and decide what impression one's words are likely to make on another person. This last effort of the mind cuts out all stale or mixed images, all prefabricated phrases, needless repetitions, and humbug and vagueness generally. But one can often be in doubt about the effect of a word or a phrase, and one needs rules that one can rely on when instinct fails. I think the following rules will cover most cases:

(i) Never use a metaphor, simile or other figure of speech which you are used to seeing in print.

(ii) Never use a long word where a short one will do.

(iii) If it is possible to cut a word out, always cut it out.

(iv) Never use the passive where you can use the active.

(v) Never use a foreign phrase, a

---

[3] One can cure oneself of the *not un-* formation by memorizing this sentence: *A not unblack dog was chasing a not unsmall rabbit across a not ungreen field.*

scientific word or a jargon word if you can think of an everyday English equivalent.

(vi) Break any of these rules sooner than say anything outright barbarous.

These rules sound elementary, and so they are, but they demand a deep change of attitude in anyone who has grown used to writing in the style now fashionable. One could keep all of them and still write bad English, but one could not write the kind of stuff that I quoted in those five specimens at the beginning of this article.

I have not here been considering the literary use of language, but merely language as an instrument of expressing and not for concealing or preventing thought. Stuart Chase and others have come near to claiming that all abstract words are meaningless, and have used this as a pretext for advocating a kind of political quietism. Since you don't know what Fascism is, how can you struggle against Fascism? One need not swallow such absurdities as this, but

one ought to recognize that the present political chaos is connected with the decay of language, and that one can probably bring about some improvement by starting at the verbal end. If you simplify your English, you are freed from the worst follies of orthodoxy. You cannot speak any of the necessary dialects, and when you make a stupid remark its stupidity will be obvious, even to yourself. Political language— and with variations this is true of all political parties, from Conservatives to Anarchists—is designed to make lies sound truthful and murder respectable, and to give an appearance of solidity to pure wind. One cannot change this all in a moment, but one can at least change one's own habits, and from time to time one can even, if one jeers loudly enough, send some worn-out and useless phrase—some *jackboot, Achilles' heel, hotbed, melting pot, acid test, veritable inferno* or other lump of verbal refuse—into the dustbin where it belongs.

Richard Wright (1908–1960)
from BLACK BOY

One morning I arrived early at work and went into the bank lobby where the Negro porter was mopping. I stood at a counter and picked up the Memphis *Commercial Appeal* and began my free reading of the press. I came finally to the editorial page and saw an article dealing with one H. L. Mencken. I knew by hearsay that he was the editor of the *American Mercury*, but aside from that I knew nothing about him. The article was a furious denunciation of Mencken, concluding with one, hot, short sentence: Mencken is a fool.

I wondered what on earth this Mencken had done to call down upon him the scorn of the South. The only people I had ever heard denounced in the South were Negroes, and this man was not a Negro. Then what ideas did Mencken hold that made a newspaper like the *Commercial Appeal* castigate him publicly? Undoubtedly he must be advocating ideas that the South did not like. Were there, then, people other than Negroes who criticized the South? I knew that during the Civil War the South had hated northern whites, but I had not encountered such hate during my life. Knowing no more of Mencken than I did at that moment, I felt a vague sympathy for him. Had not the South, which had assigned me the role of a non-man, cast at him its hardest words?

Now, how could I find out about this Mencken? There was a huge library near the riverfront, but I knew that Negroes were not allowed to patronize its shelves any more than they were the parks and playgrounds of the city. I had gone into the library several times to get books for the white men on the job. Which of them would now help me to get books? And how could I read them without causing concern to the white men with whom I worked? I had so far been successful in hiding my thoughts and feelings from them, but I knew that I would create hostility if I went about this business of reading in a clumsy way.

I weighed the personalities of the men on the job. There was Don, a Jew; but I distrusted him. His position was not much better than mine and I knew that he was uneasy and insecure; he had always treated me in an offhand, bantering way that barely concealed his contempt. I was afraid to ask him to help me to get books; his frantic desire to demonstrate a racial solidarity with the whites against Negroes might make him betray me.

Then how about the boss? No, he was a Baptist and I had the suspicion that he would not be quite able to comprehend why a black boy would want to read Mencken. There were other white men on the job whose attitudes showed clearly that they were Kluxers or sympathizers, and they were out of the question.

There remained only one man whose attitude did not fit into an anti-Negro category, for I had heard the white men refer to him as a "Pope lover." He was an Irish Catholic and was hated by the white Southerners. I knew that he read books, because I had got him volumes from the library several times. Since he, too, was an object of hatred, I felt that he might refuse me but would hardly betray me. I hesitated, weighing and balancing the imponderable realities.

One morning I paused before the Catholic fellow's desk.

"I want to ask you a favor," I whispered to him.

"What is it?"

"I want to read. I can't get books from the library. I wonder if you'd let me use your card?"

He looked at me suspiciously.

"My card is full most of the time," he said.

"I see," I said and waited, posing my question silently.

"You're not trying to get me into trouble, are you, boy?" he asked, staring at me.

"Oh, no sir."

"What books do you want?"

"A book by H. L. Mencken."

"Which one?"

"I don't know. Has he written more than one?"

"He has written several."

"I didn't know that."

"What makes you want to read Mencken?"

"Oh, I just saw his name in the newspaper," I said.

"It's good of you to want to read," he said. "But you ought to read the right things."

I said nothing. Would he want to supervise my reading?

"Let me think," he said. "I'll figure out something."

I turned from him and he called me back. He stared at me quizzically.

"Richard, don't mention this to the other white men," he said.

"I understand," I said. "I won't say a word."

A few days later he called me to him.

"I've got a card in my wife's name," he said. "Here's mine."

"Thank you, sir."

"Do you think you can manage it?"

"I'll manage fine," I said.

"If they suspect you, you'll get in trouble," he said.

"I'll write the same kind of notes to the library that you wrote when you sent me for books," I told him. "I'll sign your name."

He laughed.

"Go ahead. Let me see what you get," he said.

That afternoon I addressed myself to forging a note. Now, what were the names of books written by H. L. Mencken? I did not know any of them. I finally wrote what I thought would be a foolproof note: *Dear Madam: Will you please let this nigger boy*—I used the word "nigger" to make the librarian feel that I could not possibly be the author of the note—*have some books by H. L. Mencken?* I forged the white man's name.

I entered the library as I had always done when on errands for whites, but I felt that I would somehow slip up and betray myself. I doffed my hat, stood a respectful distance from the desk, looked as unbookish as possible, and waited for the white patrons to be taken care of. When the desk was clear of people, I still waited. The white librarian looked at me.

"What do you want, boy?"

As though I did not possess the power of speech, I stepped forward and simply handed her the forged note, not parting my lips.

"What books by Mencken does he want?" she asked.

"I don't know, ma'am," I said, avoiding her eyes.

"Who gave you this card?"

"Mr. Falk," I said.

"Where is he?"

"He's at work, at the M——Optical Company," I said. "I've been in here for him before."

"I remember," the woman said. "But he never wrote notes like this."

Oh, God, she's suspicious. Perhaps she would not let me have the books? If she had turned her back at that mo-ment, I would have ducked out the door and never gone back. Then I thought of a bold idea.

"You can call him up, ma'am," I said, my heart pounding.

"You're not using these books, are you?" she asked pointedly.

"Oh, no, ma'am. I can't read."

"I don't know what he wants by Mencken," she said under her breath.

I knew now that I had won; she was thinking of other things and the race question had gone out of her mind. She went to the shelves. Once or twice she looked over her shoulder at me, as though she was still doubtful. Finally she came forward with two books in her hand.

"I'm sending him two books," she said. "But tell Mr. Falk to come in next time, or send me the names of the books he wants. I don't know what he wants to read."

I said nothing. She stamped the card and handed me the books. Not daring to glance at them, I went out of the library, fearing that the woman would call me back for further questioning. A block away from the library I opened one of the books and read a title: *A Book of Prefaces.* I was nearing my nineteenth birthday and I did not know how to pronounce the word "preface." I thumbed the pages and saw strange words and strange names. I shook my head, disappointed. I looked at the other book; it was called *Prejudices.* I knew what that word meant; I had heard it all my life. And right off I was on guard against Mencken's books. Why would a man want to call a book *Prejudices?* The word was so stained with all my memories of racial hate that I could not conceive of anybody using it for a title. Perhaps I had made a mistake about Mencken? A man who had prejudices must be wrong.

When I showed the books to Mr. Falk, he looked at me and frowned.

"That librarian might telephone you," I warned him.

"That's all right," he said. "But when

you're through reading those books, I want you to tell me what you get out of them."

That night in my rented room, while letting the hot water run over my can of pork and beans in the sink, I opened *A Book of Prefaces* and began to read. I was jarred and shocked by the style, the clear, clean, sweeping sentences. Why did he write like that? And how did one write like that? I pictured the man as a raging demon, slashing with his pen, consumed with hate, denouncing everything American, extolling everything European or German, laughing at the weaknesses of people, mocking God, authority. What was this? I stood up, trying to realize what reality lay behind the meaning of the words . . . Yes, this man was fighting, fighting with words. He was using words as a weapon, using them as one would use a club. Could words be weapons? Well, yes, for here they were. Then, maybe, perhaps, I could use them as a weapon? No. It frightened me. I read on and what amazed me was not what he said, but how on earth anybody had the courage to say it.

Occasionally I glanced up to reassure myself that I was alone in the room. Who were these men about whom Mencken was talking so passionately? Who was Anatole France? Joseph Conrad? Sinclair Lewis, Sherwood Anderson, Dostoevski, George Moore, Gustave Flaubert, Maupassant, Tolstoy, Frank Harris, Mark Twain, Thomas Hardy, Arnold Bennett, Stephen Crane, Zola, Norris, Gorky, Bergson, Ibsen, Balzac, Bernard Shaw, Dumas, Poe, Thomas Mann, O. Henry, Dreiser, H. G. Wells, Gogol, T. S. Eliot, Gide, Baudelaire, Edgar Lee Masters, Stendhal, Turgenev, Huneker, Nietzsche, and scores of others? Were these men real? Did they exist or had they existed? And how did one pronounce their names?

I ran across many words whose meanings I did not know, and I either looked them up in a dictionary or, be-fore I had a chance to do that, encountered the word in a context that made its meaning clear. But what strange word was this? I concluded the book with the conviction that I had somehow overlooked something terribly important in life. I had once tried to write, had once reveled in feeling, had let my crude imagination roam, but the impulse to dream had been slowly beaten out of me by experience. Now it surged up again and I hungered for books, new ways of looking and seeing. It was not a matter of believing or disbelieving what I read, but of feeling something new, of being affected by something that made the look of the world different.

As dawn broke I ate my pork and beans, feeling dopey, sleepy. I went to work, but the mood of the book would not die; it lingered, coloring everything I saw, heard, did. I now felt that I knew what the white men were feeling. Merely because I had read a book that had spoken of how they lived and thought, I identified myself with that book. I felt vaguely guilty. Would I, filled with bookish notions, act in a manner that would make the whites dislike me?

I forged more notes and my trips to the library became frequent. Reading grew into a passion. My first serious novel was Sinclair Lewis's *Main Street*. It made me see my boss, Mr. Gerald, and identify him as an American type. I would smile when I saw him lugging his golf bags into the office. I had always felt a vast distance separating me from the boss, and now I felt closer to him, though still distant. I felt now that I knew him, that I could feel the very limits of his narrow life. And this had happened because I had read a novel about a mythical man called George F. Babbitt.

The plots and stories in the novels did not interest me so much as the point of view revealed. I gave myself over to each novel without reserve, without trying to criticize it; it was enough for me to see and feel something different. And for me, everything was something different. Reading was like a drug, a dope. The novels created moods in which I lived for days. But I could not conquer my sense of guilt, my feeling that the white men around me knew that I was changing, that I had begun to regard them differently.

Whenever I brought a book to the job, I wrapped it in newspaper—a habit that was to persist for years in other cities and under other circumstances. But some of the white men pried into my packages when I was absent and they questioned me.

"Boy, what are you reading those books for?"

"Oh, I don't know, sir."

"That's deep stuff you're reading, boy."

"I'm just killing time, sir."

"You'll addle your brains if you don't watch out."

I read Dreiser's *Jennie Gerhardt* and *Sister Carrie* and they revived in me a vivid sense of my mother's suffering; I was overwhelmed. I grew silent, wondering about the life around me. It would have been impossible for me to have told anyone what I derived from these novels, for it was nothing less than a sense of life itself. All my life had shaped me for the realism, the naturalism of the modern novel, and I could not read enough of them.

Steeped in new moods and ideas, I bought a ream of paper and tried to write; but nothing would come, or what did come was flat beyond telling. I discovered that more than desire and feeling were necessary to write and I dropped the idea. Yet I still wondered how it was possible to know people sufficiently to write about them? Could I ever learn about life and people? To me, with my vast ignorance, my Jim Crow station in life, it seemed a task impossible of achievement. I now knew

what being a Negro meant. I could endure the hunger. I had learned to live with hate. But to feel that there were feelings denied me, that the very breath of life itself was beyond my reach, that more than anything else hurt, wounded me. I had a new hunger.

In buoying me up, reading also cast me down, made me see what was possible, what I had missed. My tension returned, new, terrible, bitter, surging, almost too great to be contained. I no longer *felt* that the world about me was hostile, killing; I *knew* it. A million times I asked myself what I could do to save myself, and there were no answers. I seemed forever condemned, ringed by walls.

I did not discuss my reading with Mr. Falk, who had lent me his library card; it would have meant talking about myself and that would have been too painful. I smiled each day, fighting desperately to maintain my old behavior, to keep my disposition seemingly sunny. But some of the white men discerned that I had begun to brood.

"Wake up there, boy!" Mr. Olin said one day.

"Sir!" I answered for the lack of a better word.

"You act like you've stolen something," he said.

I laughed in the way I knew he expected me to laugh, but I resolved to be more conscious of myself, to watch my every act, to guard and hide the new knowledge that was dawning within me.

If I went north, would it be possible for me to build a new life then? But how could a man build a life upon vague, unformed yearnings? I wanted to write and I did not even know the English language. I bought English grammars and found them dull. I felt that I was getting a better sense of the language from novels than from grammars. I read hard, discarding a writer as soon as I felt that I had grasped his point of view. At night the printed page stood before my eyes in sleep.

Mrs. Moss, my landlady, asked me one Sunday morning:

"Son, what is this you keep on reading?"

"Oh, nothing. Just novels."

"What you get out of 'em?"

"I'm just killing time," I said.

"I hope you know your own mind," she said in a tone which implied that she doubted if I had a mind.

I knew of no Negroes who read the books I liked and I wondered if any Negroes ever thought of them. I knew that there were Negro doctors, lawyers, newspapermen, but I never saw any of them. When I read a Negro newspaper I never caught the faintest echo of my preoccupation in its pages. I felt trapped and occasionally, for a few days, I would stop reading. But a vague hunger would come over me for books, books that opened up new avenues of feeling and seeing, and again I would forge another note to the white librarian. Again I would read and wonder as only the naïve and unlettered can read and wonder, feeling that I carried a secret, criminal burden about with me each day.

That winter my mother and brother came and we set up housekeeping, buying furniture on the installment plan, being cheated and yet knowing no way to avoid it. I began to eat warm food and to my surprise found that regular meals enabled me to read faster. I may have lived through many illnesses and survived them, never suspecting that I was ill. My brother obtained a job and we began to save toward the trip north, plotting our time, setting tentative dates for departure. I told none of the white men on the job that I was planning to go north; I knew that the moment they felt I was thinking of the North they would change toward me. It would have made them feel that I did not like the life I was living, and because my life was completely conditioned by what they said or did, it would have been tantamount to challenging them.

I could calculate my chances for life in the South as a Negro fairly clearly now.

I could fight the southern whites by organizing with other Negroes, as my grandfather had done. But I knew that I could never win that way; there were many whites and there were but few blacks. They were strong and we were weak. Outright black rebellion could never win. If I fought openly I would die and I did not want to die. News of lynchings were frequent.

I could submit and live the life of a genial slave, but that was impossible. All of my life had shaped me to live by my own feelings and thoughts. I could make up to Bess and marry her and inherit the house. But that, too, would be the life of a slave; if I did that, I would crush to death something within me, and I would hate myself as much as I knew the whites already hated those who had submitted. Neither could I ever willingly present myself to be kicked, as Shorty had done. I would rather have died than do that.

I could drain off my restlessness by fighting with Shorty and Harrison. I had seen many Negroes solve the problem of being black by transferring their hatred of themselves to others with a black skin and fighting them. I would have to be cold to do that, and I was not cold and I could never be.

I could, of course, forget what I had read, thrust the whites out of my mind, forget them; and find release from anxiety and longing in sex and alcohol. But the memory of how my father had conducted himself made that course repugnant. If I did not want others to violate my life, how could I voluntarily violate it myself?

I had no hope whatever of being a professional man. Not only had I been so conditioned that I did not desire it, but the fulfillment of such an ambition was beyond my capabilities. Well-to-do Negroes lived in a world that was almost as alien to me as the world inhabited by whites.

What, then, was there? I held my life in my mind, in my consciousness each day, feeling at times that I would stumble and drop it, spill it forever. My reading had created a vast sense of distance between me and the world in which I lived and tried to make a living, and that sense of distance was increasing each day. My days and nights were one long, quiet, continuously contained dream of terror, tension, and anxiety. I wondered how long I could bear it.

FICTION

Sherwood Anderson (1876–1941)

SEEDS

He was a small man with a beard and was very nervous. I remember how the cords of his neck were drawn taut.

For years he had been trying to cure people of illness by the method called psychoanalysis. The idea was the passion of his life. "I came here because I am tired," he said dejectedly. "My body is not tired but something inside me is old and worn-out. I want joy. For a few days or weeks I would like to forget men and women and the influences that make them the sick things they are."

There is a note that comes into the human voice by which you may know real weariness. It comes when one has been trying with all his heart and soul to think his way along some difficult road of thought. Of a sudden he finds himself unable to go on. Something within him stops. A tiny explosion takes place. He bursts into words and talks, perhaps foolishly. Little side currents of his nature he didn't know were there run out and get themselves expressed. It is at such times that a man boasts, uses big words, makes a fool of himself in general.

And so it was the doctor became shrill. He jumped up from the steps where he had been sitting, talking, and walked about. "You come from the West. You have kept away from people. You have preserved yourself—damn you! I haven't—" His voice had indeed become shrill. "I have entered into lives. I have gone beneath the surface of the lives of men and women. Women especially I have studied—our own women, here in America."

"You have loved them?" I suggested.

"Yes," he said. "Yes—you are right there. I have done that. It is the only way I can get at things. I have to try to love. You see how that is? It's the only way. Love must be the beginning of things with me."

I began to sense the depths of his weariness. "We will go swim in the lake," I urged.

"I don't want to swim or do any damn plodding thing. I want to run and shout," he declared. "For a while, for a few hours, I want to be like a dead leaf blown by the winds over these hills. I have one desire and one only—to free myself."

We walked in a dusty country road. I wanted him to know that I thought I understood, so I put the case in my own way.

When he stopped and stared at me I talked. "You are no more and no better than myself," I declared. "You are

From *The Triumph of the Egg* by Sherwood Anderson. Reprinted by permission of Harold Ober Associates, Inc. Copyright © 1918 by Eleanor Copenhaver Anderson, renewed.

a dog that has rolled in offal, and because you are not quite a dog you do not like the smell of your own hide."

In turn my voice became shrill. "You blind fool," I cried impatiently. "Men like you are fools. You cannot go along that road. It is given to no man to venture far along the road of lives."

I became passionately in earnest. "The illness you pretend to cure is the universal illness," I said. "The thing you want to do cannot be done. Fool—do you expect love to be understood?"

We stood in the road and looked at each other. The suggestion of a sneer played about the corners of his mouth. He put a hand on my shoulder and shook me. "How smart we are—how aptly we put things!"

He spat the words out and then turned and walked a little away. "You think you understand, but you don't understand," he cried. "What you say can't be done can be done. You're a liar. You cannot be so definite without missing something vague and fine. You miss the whole point. The lives of people are like young trees in a forest. They are being choked by climbing vines. The vines are old thoughts and beliefs planted by dead men. I am myself covered by crawling creeping vines that choke me."

He laughed bitterly. "And that's why I want to run and play," he said. "I want to be a leaf blown by the wind over hills. I want to die and be born again, and I am only a tree covered with vines and slowly dying. I am, you see, weary and want to be made clean. I am an amateur venturing timidly into lives," he concluded. "I am weary and want to be made clean. I am covered by creeping crawling things."

A woman from Iowa came here to Chicago and took a room in a house on the west-side. She was about twenty-seven years old and ostensibly she came to the city to study advanced methods for teaching music.

A certain young man also lived in the west-side house. His room faced a long hall on the second floor of the house and the one taken by the woman was across the hall facing his room.

In regard to the young man—there is something very sweet in his nature. He is a painter but I have often wished he would decide to become a writer. He tells things with understanding and he does not paint brilliantly.

And so the woman from Iowa lived in the west-side house and came home from the city in the evening. She looked like a thousand other women one sees in the streets every day. The only thing that at all made her stand out among the women in the crowds was that she was a little lame. Her right foot was slightly deformed and she walked with a limp. For three months she lived in the house—where she was the only woman except the landlady—and then a feeling in regard to her began to grow up among the men of the house.

The men all said the same thing concerning her. When they met in the hallway at the front of the house they stopped, laughed and whispered. "She wants a lover," they said and winked. "She may not know it but a lover is what she needs." One knowing Chicago and Chicago men would think that an easy want to be satisfied. I laughed when my friend—whose name is Le-Roy—told me the story, but he did not laugh. He shook his head. "It wasn't so easy," he said. "There would be no story were the matter that simple."

LeRoy tried to explain. "Whenever a man approached her she became alarmed," he said. Men kept smiling and speaking to her. They invited her to dinner and to the theatre, but nothing would induce her to walk in the streets with a man. She never went into the streets at night. When a man stopped and tried to talk with her in the hallway she turned her eyes to the floor and then ran into her room. Once a young drygoods clerk who lived there induced her to sit with him on the steps before the house.

He was a sentimental fellow and took hold of her hand. When she began to cry he was alarmed and arose. He put a hand on her shoulder and tried to explain, but under the touch of his fingers, her whole body shook with terror. "Don't touch me," she cried, "don't let your hands touch me!" She began to scream and people passing in the streets stopped to listen. The drygoods clerk was alarmed and ran upstairs to his own room. He bolted the door and stood listening. "It is a trick," he declared in a trembling voice. "She is trying to make trouble. I did nothing to her. It was an accident and anyway what's the matter? I only touched her arm with my fingers."

Perhaps a dozen times LeRoy has spoken to me of the experience of the Iowa woman in the west-side house. The men there began to hate her. Although she would have nothing to do with them she would not let them alone. In a hundred ways she continually invited approaches that when made she repelled. When she stood naked in the bathroom facing the hallway where the men passed up and down she left the door slightly ajar. There was a couch in the living room downstairs, and when men were present she would sometimes enter and without saying a word throw herself down before them. On the couch she lay with lips drawn slightly apart. Her eyes stared at the ceiling. Her whole physical being seemed to be waiting for something. The sense of her filled the room. The men standing about pretended not to see. They talked loudly. Embarrassment took possession of them and one by one they crept quietly away.

One evening the woman was ordered to leave the house. Someone, perhaps the drygoods clerk, had talked to the landlady and she acted at once. "If you leave tonight I shall like it that much better," LeRoy heard the elder woman's voice saying. She stood in the hallway before the Iowa woman's room. The landlady's voice rang through the house.

LeRoy the painter is tall and lean and his life has been spent in devotion to ideas. The passions of his brain have consumed the passions of his body. His income is small and he has not married. Perhaps he has never had a sweetheart. He is not without physical desire but he is not primarily concerned with desire.

On the evening when the Iowa woman was ordered to leave the west-side house, she waited until she thought the landlady had gone downstairs, and then went into LeRoy's room. It was about eight o'clock and he sat by a window reading a book. The woman did not knock but opened the door. She said nothing but ran across the floor and knelt at his feet. LeRoy said that her twisted foot made her run like a wounded bird, that her eyes were burning and that her breath came in little gasps. "Take me," she said, putting her face down upon his knees and trembling violently. "Take me quickly. There must be a beginning to things. I can't stand the waiting. You must take me at once."

You may be quite sure LeRoy was perplexed by all this. From what he has said I gathered that until that evening he had hardly noticed the woman. I suppose that of all the men in the house he had been the most indifferent to her. In the room something happened. The landlady followed the woman when she ran to LeRoy, and the two women confronted him. The woman from Iowa knelt trembling and frightened at his feet. The landlady was indignant. LeRoy acted on impulse. An inspiration came to him. Putting his hand on the kneeling woman's shoulder he shook her violently. "Now behave yourself," he said quickly. "I will keep my promise." He turned to the landlady and smiled. "We have been engaged to be married," he said. "We have quarreled. She came here to be near me. She has been unwell and excited. I will take her away. Please don't let yourself be annoyed. I will take her away."

When the woman and LeRoy got out of the house she stopped weeping and put her hand into his. Her fears had all gone away. He found a room for her in another house and then went with her into a park and sat on a bench.

Everything LeRoy has told me concerning this woman strengthens my belief in what I said to the man that day in the mountains. You cannot venture along the road of lives. On the bench he and the woman talked until midnight and he saw and talked with her many times later. Nothing came of it. She went back, I suppose, to her place in the West.

In the place from which she had come the woman had been a teacher of music. She was one of four sisters, all engaged in the same sort of work and, LeRoy says, all quiet capable women. Their father had died when the eldest girl was not yet ten, and five years later the mother died also. The girls had a house and a garden.

In the nature of things I cannot know what the lives of the women were like but of this one may be quite certain—they talked only of women's affairs, thought only of women's affairs. No one of them ever had a lover. For years no man came near the house.

Of them all only the youngest, the one who came to Chicago, was visibly affected by the utterly feminine quality of their lives. It did something to her. All day and every day she taught music to young girls and then went home to the women. When she was twenty-five she began to think and to dream of men. During the day and through the evening she talked with women of women's affairs, and all the time she wanted desperately to be loved by a man. She went to Chicago with that hope in mind. LeRoy explained her attitude in the matter and her strange behavior in the west-side house by saying she had thought too much and acted too little. "The life force within her became decentralized," he declared. "What she wanted she could not achieve. The living force within could not find expression. When it could not get expressed in one way it took another. Sex spread itself out over her body. It permeated the very fibre of her being. At the last she was sex personified, sex become condensed and impersonal. Certain words, the touch of a man's hand, sometimes even the sight of a man passing in the street did something to her."

Yesterday I saw LeRoy and he talked to me again of the woman and her strange and terrible fate.

We walked in the park by the lake. As we went along the figure of the woman kept coming into my mind. An idea came to me.

"You might have been her lover," I said. "That was possible. She was not afraid of you."

LeRoy stopped. Like the doctor who was so sure of his ability to walk into lives he grew angry and scolded. For a moment he stared at me and then a rather odd thing happened. Words said by the other man in the dusty road in the hills came to LeRoy's lips and were said over again. The suggestion of a sneer played about the corners of his mouth. "How smart we are. How aptly we put things," he said.

The voice of the young man who walked with me in the park by the lake in the city became shrill. I sensed the weariness in him. Then he laughed and said quietly and softly, "It isn't so simple. By being sure of yourself you are in danger of losing all of the romance of life. You miss the whole point. Nothing in life can be settled so definitely. The woman—you see—was like a young tree choked by a climbing vine.

The thing that wrapped her about had shut out the light. She was as grotesque as many trees in the forest are grotesque. Her problem was such a difficult one that thinking of it has changed the whole current of my life. At first I was like you. I was quite sure. I thought I would be her lover and settle the matter."

LeRoy turned and walked a little away. Then he came back and took hold of my arm. A passionate earnestness took possession of him. His voice trembled. "She needed a lover, yes, the men in the house were quite right about that," he said. "She needed a lover and at the same time a lover was not what she needed. The need of a lover was, after all, a quite secondary thing. She needed to be loved, to be long and quietly and patiently loved. To be sure she is grotesque, but then all the people in the world are grotesque. We all need to be loved. What would cure her would cure the rest of us also. The disease she had is, you see, universal. We all want to be loved and the world has no plan for creating our lovers."

LeRoy's voice dropped and he walked beside me in silence. We turned away from the lake and walked under trees. I looked closely at him. The cords of his neck were drawn taut. "I have seen under the shell of life and I am afraid," he mused. "I am myself like the woman. I am covered with creeping crawling vine-like things. I cannot be a lover. I am not subtle or patient enough. I am paying old debts. Old thoughts and beliefs—seeds planted by dead men—spring up in my soul and choke me."

For a long time we walked and LeRoy talked, voicing the thoughts that came into his mind. I listened in silence. His mind struck upon the refrain voiced by the man in the mountains. "I would like to be a dead dry thing," he muttered looking at the leaves scattered over the grass. "I would like to be a leaf blown away by the wind." He looked up and his eyes turned to where among the trees we could see the lake in the distance. "I am weary and want to be made clean. I am a man covered by creeping crawling things. I would like to be dead and blown by the wind over limitless waters," he said. "I want more than anything else in the world to be clean."

E. M. Forster (1879–1970)
THE MACHINE STOPS

PART I: THE AIR-SHIP

Imagine, if you can, a small room, hexagonal in shape, like the cell of a bee. It is lighted neither by window nor by lamp, yet it is filled with a soft radiance. There are no apertures for ventilation, yet the air is fresh. There are no musical instruments, and yet, at the moment that my meditation opens, this room is throbbing with melodious sounds. An arm-chair is in the center, by its side a reading-desk—that is all the furniture. And in the arm-chair there sits a swaddled lump of flesh—a woman, about five feet high, with a face as white as a fungus. It is to her that the little room belongs.

An electric bell rang.

The woman touched a switch and the music was silent.

"I suppose I must see who it is," she thought, and set her chair in motion. The chair, like the music, was worked by machinery, and it rolled her to the other side of the room, where the bell still rang importunately.

"Who is it?" she called. Her voice was irritable, for she had been interrupted often since the music began. She knew several thousand people; in certain directions human intercourse had advanced enormously.

But when she listened into the receiver, her white face wrinkled into smiles, and she said:

"Very well. Let us talk, I will isolate myself. I do not expect anything important will happen for the next five minutes—for I can give you fully five minutes, Kuno. Then I must deliver my lecture on 'Music during the Australian Period.' "

She touched the isolation knob, so that no one else could speak to her. Then she touched the lighting apparatus, and the little room was plunged into darkness.

"Be quick!" she called, her irritation returning. "Be quick, Kuno; here I am in the dark wasting my time."

But it was fully fifteen seconds before the round plate that she held in her hands began to glow. A faint blue light shot across it, darkening to purple, and presently she could see the image of her son, who lived on the other side of the earth, and he could see her.

"Kuno, how slow you are."

He smiled gravely.

"I really believe you enjoy dawdling."

"I have called you before, mother, but you were always busy or isolated. I have something particular to say."

"What it is, dearest boy? Be quick. Why could you not send it by pneumatic post?"

"Because I prefer saying such a thing. I want—"

"Well?"

"I want you to come and see me."

Vashti watched his face in the blue plate.

"But I can see you!" she exclaimed. "What more do you want?"

"I want to see you not through the Machine," said Kuno. "I want to speak to you not through the wearisome Machine."

"Oh, hush!" said his mother, vaguely shocked. "You mustn't say anything against the Machine."

"Why not?"

"One mustn't."

"You talk as if a god had made the Machine," cried the other. "I believe that you pray to it when you are unhappy. Men made it, do not forget that. Great men, but men. The Machine is much, but it is not everything. I see something like you in this plate, but I do not see you. I hear something like you through this telephone, but I do not hear you. That is why I want you to come. Come and stop with me. Pay me a visit, so that we can meet face to face, and talk about the hopes that are in my mind."

She replied that she could scarcely spare the time for a visit.

"The air-ship barely takes two days to fly between me and you."

"I dislike air-ships."

"Why?"

"I dislike seeing the horrible brown earth, and the sea, and the stars when it is dark. I get no ideas in an air-ship."

"I do not get them anywhere else."

"What kind of ideas can the air give you?"

He paused for an instant.

"Do you not know four big stars that form an oblong, and three stars close together in the middle of the oblong, and hanging from these stars, three other stars?"

"No, I do not. I dislike the stars. But did they give you an idea? How interesting; tell me."

"I had an idea that they were like a man."

"I do not understand."

"The four big stars are the man's shoulders and his knees. The three stars in the middle are his belts that men wore once, and the three stars hanging are like a sword."

"A sword?"

"Men carried swords about with them, to kill animals and other men."

"It does not strike me as a very good idea, but it is certainly original. When did it come to you first?"

"In the air-ship—" He broke off, and she fancied that he looked sad. She could not be sure, for the Machine did not transmit nuances of expression. It only gave a general idea of people— an idea that was good enough for all practical purposes, Vashti thought. The imponderable bloom, declared by a discredited philosophy to be the actual essence of intercourse, was rightly ignored by the Machine, just as the imponderable bloom of the grape was ignored by the manufacturers of artificial fruit. Something "good enough" had long since been accepted by our race.

"The truth is," he continued, "that I want to see these stars again. They are curious stars. I want to see them not from the air-ship, but from the surface of the earth, as our ancestors did, thousands of years ago. I want to visit the surface of the earth."

She was shocked again.

"Mother you must come, if only to explain to me what is the harm of visiting the surface of the earth."

"No harm," she replied, controlling herself. "But no advantage. The surface of the earth is only dust and mud, no life remains on it, and you would need

a respirator, or the cold of the outer air would kill you. One dies immediately in the outer air."

"I know; of course I shall take all precautions."

"And besides—"

"Well?"

She considered, and chose her words with care. Her son had a queer temper, and she wished to dissuade him from the expedition.

"It is contrary to the spirit of the age," she asserted.

"Do you mean by that, contrary to the Machine?"

"In a sense, but—"

His image in the blue plate faded.

"Kuno!"

He had isolated himself.

For a moment Vashti felt lonely.

Then she generated the light, and the sight of her room, flooded with radiance and studded with electric buttons and switches everywhere—buttons to call for food, for music, for clothing. There was the hotbath button, by pressure of which a basin of (imitation) marble rose out of the floor, filled to the brim with a warm deodorized liquid. There was the cold-bath button. There was the button that produced literature. And there were of course the buttons by which she communicated with her friends. The room, though it contained nothing, was in touch with all that she cared for in the world.

Vashti's next move was to turn off the isolation-switch and all the accumulations of the last three minutes burst upon her. The room was filled with the noise of bells, and speaking-tubes. What was the new food like? Could she recommend it? Had she had any ideas lately? Might one tell her one's own ideas? Would she make an engagement to visit the public nurseries at an early date?—say this day month.

To most of these questions she replied with irritation—a growing quality in that accelerated age. She said that the new food was horrible. That she could not visit the public nurseries through press of engagements. That she had no ideas of her own but had just been told one—that four stars and three in the middle were like a man: She doubted there was much in it. Then she switched off her correspondents, for it was time to deliver her lecture on Australian music.

The clumsy system of public gatherings had been long since abandoned; neither Vashti nor her audience stirred from their rooms. Seated in her armchair she spoke, while they in their armchairs heard her, fairly well, and saw her, fairly well. She opened with a humorous account of music in the pre-Mongolian epoch, and went on to describe the great outburst of song that followed the Chinese conquest. Remote and primeval as were the methods of I-San-So and the Brisbane school, she yet felt (she said) that study of them might repay the musician of today; they had freshness; they had, above all, ideas.

Her lecture, which lasted ten minutes, was well received, and at its conclusion she and many of her audience listened to a lecture on the sea; there were ideas to be got from the sea; the speaker had donned a respirator and visited it lately. Then she fed, talked to many friends, had a bath, talked again, and summoned her bed.

The bed was not to her liking. It was too large, and she had a feeling for a small bed. Complaint was useless, for beds were of the same dimension all over the world, and to have had an alternative size would have involved vast alterations in the Machine. Vashti isolated herself—it was necessary, for neither day nor night existed under the ground—and reviewed all that had happened since she had summoned the bed last. Ideas? Scarcely any. Events—was Kuno's invitation an event?

By her side, on the little reading-desk, was a survival from the ages of litter—one book. This was the Book of the Machine. In it were instructions against every possible contingency. If she was hot or cold or dyspeptic or at loss for a word, she went to the Book, and it told her which button to press. The Central Committee published it. In accordance with a growing habit, it was richly bound.

Sitting up in the bed, she took it reverently in her hands. She glanced round the glowing room as if some one might be watching her. Then, half ashamed, half joyful, she murmured, "O Machine! O Machine!" and raised the volume to her lips. Thrice she kissed it, thrice inclined her head, thrice she felt the delirium of acquiescence. Her ritual performed, she turned to page 1367, which gave the times of the departure of the air-ships from the island in the southern hemisphere, under whose soil she lived, to the island in the northern hemisphere, whereunder lived her son.

She thought, "I have not the time."

She made the room dark and slept; she awoke and made the room light; she ate and exchanged ideas with her friends, and listened to music and attended lectures; she made the room dark and slept. Above her, beneath her, and around her, the Machine hummed eternally; she did not notice the noise, for she had been born with it in her ears. The earth, carrying her, hummed as it sped through silence, turning her now to the invisible sun, now to the invisible stars. She awoke and made the room light.

"Kuno!"

"I will not talk to you," he answered, "until you come."

"Have you been on the surface of the earth since we spoke last?"

His image faded.

Again she consulted the Book. She became very nervous and lay back in her chair palpitating. Think of her as without teeth or hair. Presently she directed the chair to the wall, and pressed an unfamiliar button. The wall swung apart slowly. Through the opening she saw a tunnel that curved slightly, so that its goal was not visible. Should she go to see her son, here was the beginning of the journey.

Of course she knew all about the communication-system. There was nothing mysterious in it. She would summon a car and it would fly with her down the tunnel until it reached the lift that communicated with the airship station: the system had been in use for many, many years, long before the universal establishment of the Machine. And of course she had studied the civilization that had immediately preceded her own—the civilization that had mistaken the functions of the system, and had used it for bringing people to things, instead of for bringing things to people. Those funny old days, when men went for change of air instead of changing the air in their rooms! And yet—she was frightened of the tunnel: she had not seen it since her last child was born. It curved—but not quite as brilliant as a lecturer had suggested. Vashti was seized with the terrors of direct experience. She shrank back into the room, and the wall closed up again.

"Kuno," she said, "I cannot come to see you. I am not well."

Immediately an enormous apparatus fell on to her out of the ceiling, a thermometer was automatically inserted between her lips, a stethoscope was automatically laid upon her heart. She lay powerless. Cool pads soothed her forehead. Kuno had telegraphed to her doctor.

So the human passions still blundered up and down in the Machine. Vashti drank the medicine that the doctor projected into her mouth, and the machinery retired into the ceiling. The voice of Kuno was heard asking how she felt.

"Better." Then with irritation: "But why do you not come to me instead?"

"Because I cannot leave this place."

"Why?"

"Because, any moment, something tremendous may happen."

"Have you been on the surface of the earth yet?"

"Not yet."

"Then what is it?"

"I will not tell you through the Machine."

She resumed her life.

But she thought of Kuno as a baby, his birth, his removal to the public nurseries, her one visit to him there, his visits to her—visits which stopped when the Machine had assigned him a room on the other side of the earth. "Parents, duties of," said the Book of the Machine, "cease at the moment of birth. P. 422327483." True, but there was something special about Kuno—indeed there had been something special about all her children—and, after all, she must brave the journey if he desired it. And "something tremendous might happen." What did he mean? The nonsense of a youthful man, no doubt, but she must go. Again she pressed the unfamiliar button, again the wall swung back, and she saw the tunnel that curved out of sight. Clasping the Book, she rose, tottered onto the platform, and summoned the car. Her room closed behind her: the journey to the northern hemisphere had begun.

Of course it was perfectly easy. The car approached and in it she found armchairs exactly liked her own. When she signaled, it stopped, and she tottered into the lift. One other passenger was in the lift, the first fellow creature she had seen face to face for months. Few traveled in these days, for, thanks to the advance of science, the earth was exactly alike all over. Rapid intercourse, from which the previous civilization had hoped so much, had ended by defeating itself. What was the good of going to Pekin when it was just like Shrewsbury? Why return to Shrewsbury when it would be just like Pekin? Men seldom moved their bodies; all unrest was concentrated in the soul.

The air-ship service was a relic from the former age. It was kept up, because it was easier to keep it up than to stop it or to diminish it, but it now far exceeded the wants of the population. Vessel after vessel would rise from the vomitories of Rye or of Christchurch (I use the antique names), would sail into the crowded sky, and would draw up at the wharves of the south—empty. So nicely adjusted was the system, so independent of meteorology, that the sky, whether calm or cloudy, resembled a vast kaleidoscope whereon the same patterns periodically recurred. The ship on which Vashti sailed started now at sunset, now at dawn. But always, as it passed above Rheims, it would neighbor the ship that served between Helsingfors and the Brazils, and every third time it surmounted the Alps, the fleet of Palermo would cross its track behind. Night and day, wind and storm, tide and earthquake, impeded man no longer. He had harnessed Leviathan. All the old literature, with its praise of Nature, and its fear of Nature, rang false as the prattle of a child.

Yet as Vashti saw the vast flank of the ship, stained with exposure to the outer air, her horror of direct experience returned. It was not quite like the air-ship in the cinematophote. For one thing it smelt—not strongly or unpleasantly, but it did smell, and with her eyes shut she should have known that a new thing was close to her. Then she had to walk to it from the lift, had to submit to glances from the other passengers. The man in front dropped his Book—no great matter, but it disquieted them all. In the rooms, if the Book was dropped, the floor raised it mechanically, but the gangway to the air-ship was not so prepared, and the sacred volume lay motionless. They stopped—the thing was unforeseen—and the man, instead of picking up his property, felt the muscles of his arm to see how they had failed him. Then someone actually said with direct utterance: "We shall be late"—and they trooped on board, Vashti treading on the pages as she did so.

Inside, her anxiety increased. The arrangements were old-fashioned and rough. There was even a female attendant, to whom she would have to announce her wants during the voyage. Of course a revolving platform ran the length of the boat, but she was expected to walk from it to her cabin. Some cabins were better than others, and she did not get the best. She thought the attendant had been unfair, and spasms of rage shook her. The glass valves had closed, she could not go back. She saw, at the end of the vestibule, the lift in which she had ascended going quietly up and down, empty. Beneath those corridors of shining tiles were rooms, tier below tier, reaching far into the earth, and in each room there sat a human being, eating, or sleeping, or producing ideas. And buried deep in the hive was her own room. Vashti was afraid.

"O Machine! O Machine!" she murmured, and caressed her Book, and was comforted.

Then the sides of the vestibule seemed to melt together, as do the passages that we see in dreams, the life vanished, the Book that had been dropped slid to the left and vanished, polished tiles rushed by like a stream of water, there was a slight jar, and the air-ship, issuing from its tunnel, soared above the waters of a tropical ocean.

It was night. For a moment she saw the coast of Sumatra edged by the phosphorescence of waves, and crowned by light-houses, still sending forth their disregarded beams. They also vanished, and only the stars distracted her. They were not motionless, but swayed to and fro above her head, thronging out of one sky-light into another, as if the universe and not the air-ship was careening. And, as often happens on clear nights, they seemed now to be in perspective, now on a plane; now piled tier beyond tier into the infinite heavens, now concealing infinity, a roof limiting for ever the visions of men. In either case they seemed intolerable. "Are we to travel in the dark?" called the passengers angrily, and the attendant, who had been careless, generated the light, and pulled down the blinds of pliable metal. When the air-ships had been built, the desire to look direct at things still lingered in the world. Hence the extraordinary number of skylights and windows, and the proportionate discomfort to those who were civilized and refined. Even in Vashti's cabin one star peeped through a flaw in the blind, and after a few hours' uneasy slumber, she was disturbed by an unfamiliar glow, which was the dawn.

Quick as the ship had sped westwards, the earth had rolled eastwards quicker still, and had dragged back Vashti and her companions towards the sun. Science could prolong the night, but only for a little, and those high hopes of neutralizing the earth's diurnal revolution had passed, together with hopes that were possibly higher. To "keep pace with the sun," or even to outstrip it, had been the aim of the civilization preceding this. Racing aeroplanes had been built for the purpose, capable of enormous speed, and steered by the greatest intellects of the epoch. Round the globe they went, round and round, westward, westward, round and round, amidst humanity's applause. In vain. The globe went eastward quicker still, horrible accidents occurred, and the Committee of the Machine, at the time rising into prominence, declared the pursuit illegal, unmechanical, and punishable by Homelessness.

Of Homelessness more will be said later.

Doubtless the Committee was right. Yet the attempt to "defeat the sun" aroused the last common interest that our race experienced about the heavenly bodies, or indeed about anything. It was the last time that men were compacted by thinking of a power outside the world. The sun had conquered, yet it was the end of his spiritual dominion. Dawn, midday, twilight, the zodiacal path, touched neither men's lives nor their hearts, and science retreated into the ground, to concentrate herself upon problems that she was certain of solving.

So when Vashti found her cabin invaded by a rosy finger of light, she was annoyed, and tried to adjust the blind. But the blind flew up altogether, and she saw through the skylight small pink clouds, swaying against a background of blue, and as the sun crept higher, its radiance entered direct, brimming down the wall, like a golden sea. It rose and fell with the air-ship's motion, just as waves rise and fall, but it advanced steadily as a tide advances. Unless she was careful, it would strike her face. A spasm of horror shook her and she rang for the attendant. The attendant too was horrified, but she could do nothing; it was not her place to mend the blind. She could only suggest that the lady should change her cabin, which she accordingly prepared to do.

People were almost exactly alike all over the world, but the attendant of the air-ship, perhaps owing to her exceptional duties, had grown a little out of the common. She had often to address passengers with direct speech, and this had given her a certain roughness and originality of manner. When Vashti swerved away from the sunbeams with a cry, she behaved barbarically—she put out her hand to steady her.

"How dare you!" exclaimed the passenger. "You forget yourself!"

The woman was confused, and apologized for not having let her fall. People never touched one another. The custom had become obsolete, owing to the Machine.

"Where are we now?" asked Vashti haughtily.

"We are over Asia," said the attendant, anxious to be polite.

"Asia?"

"You must excuse my common way of speaking. I have got into the habit of calling places over which I pass by their unmechanical names."

"Oh, I remember Asia. The Mongols came from it."

"Beneath us, in the open air, stood a city that was once called Simla."

"Have you ever heard of the Mongols and of the Brisbane school?"

"No."

"Brisbane also stood in the open air."

"Those mountains to the right—let me show you them." She pushed back a metal blind. The main chain of the Himalayas was revealed. "They were once called the Roof of the World, those mountains."

"What a foolish name!"

"You must remember that, before the dawn of civilization, they seemed to be an impenetrable wall that touched the stars. It was supposed that no one but the gods could exist above their summits. How we have advanced, thanks to the Machine!"

"How we have advanced, thanks to the Machine!" said Vashti.

"How we have advanced, thanks to the Machine!" echoed the passenger who had dropped his Book the night before, and who was standing in the passage.

"And that white stuff in the cracks? —what is it?"

"I have forgotten its name."

"Cover the window, please. These mountains give me no ideas."

The northern aspect of the Himalayas was in deep shadow: on the Indian slope the sun had just prevailed. The forests had been destroyed during the literature epoch for the purpose of making newspaper-pulp, but the snows were awakening to their morning glory, and clouds still hung on the breasts of Kinchinjunga. In the plain were seen the ruins of cities, with diminished rivers creeping by their walls, and by the sides of these were sometimes the signs of vomitories, marking the cities of today. Over the whole prospect air-ships rushed, crossing and intercrossing with incredible aplomb, and rising nonchalantly when they desired to escape the perturbations of the lower atmosphere and to traverse the Roof of the World.

"We have indeed advanced, thanks to the Machine," repeated the attendant, and hid the Himalayas behind a metal blind.

The day dragged wearily forward. The passengers sat each in his cabin, avoiding one another with an almost physical repulsion and longing to be once more under the surface of the earth. There were eight or ten of them, mostly young males, sent out from the public nurseries to inhabit the rooms of those who had died in various parts of the earth. The man who had dropped his Book was on the homeward journey. He had been sent to Sumatra for the purpose of propagating the race. Vashti alone was traveling by her private will.

At midday she took a second glance at the earth. The air-ship was crossing another range of mountains, but she could see little, owing to clouds. Masses of black rock hovered below her, and merged indistinctly into gray. Their shapes were fantastic; one of them resembled a prostrate man.

"No ideas here," murmured Vashti, and hid the Caucasus behind a metal blind.

In the evening she looked again. They were crossing a golden sea, in which lay many small islands and one peninsula.

She repeated, "No ideas here," and hid Greece behind a metal blind.

PART II: THE MENDING APPARATUS

By a vestibule, by a lift, by a tubular railway, by a platform, by a sliding door—by reversing all the steps of her departure did Vashti arrive at her son's room, which exactly resembled her own. She might well declare that the visit was superfluous. The buttons, the knobs, the reading-desk with the Book, the temperature, the atmosphere, the illumination—all were exactly the same. And if Kuno himself, flesh of her flesh, stood close beside her at last, what profit was there in that? She was too well-bred to shake him by the hand.

Averting her eyes, she spoke as follows:

"Here I am. I have had the most terrible journey and greatly retarded the development of my soul. It is not worth it, Kuno, it is not worth it. My time is too precious. The sunlight almost touched me, and I have met with the rudest people. I can only stop a few minutes. Say what you want to say, and then I must return."

"I have been threatened with Homelessness, and I could not tell you such a thing through the Machine."

Homelessness means death. The victim is exposed to the air, which kills him.

"I have been outside since I spoke to you last. The tremendous thing has happened, and they have discovered me."

"But why shouldn't you go outside!" she exclaimed. "It is perfectly legal, perfectly mechanical, to visit the surface of the earth. I have lately been to a lecture on the sea; there is no objection to that; one simply summons a respirator and gets an Egression-permit. It is not the kind of thing that spiritually-minded people do, and I begged you not to do it, but there is no legal objection to it."

"I did not get an Egression-permit."

"Then how did you get out?"

"I found out a way of my own."

The phrase conveyed no meaning to her, and he had to repeat it.

"A way of your own?" she whispered. "But that would be wrong."

"Why?"

The question shocked her beyond measure.

"You are beginning to worship the Machine," he said coldly. "You think it irreligious of me to have found out a way of my own. It was just what the Committee thought, when they threatened me with Homelessness."

At this she grew angry. "I worship nothing!" she cried. "I am most advanced. I don't think you irreligious, for there is no such thing as religion left. All the fear and the superstition that existed once have been destroyed by the Machine. I only meant that to find out a way of your own was—Besides, there is no new way out."

"So it is always supposed."

"Except through the vomitories, for which one must have an Egression-permit, it is impossible to get out. The Book says so."

"Well, the Book's wrong, for I have been out on my feet."

For Kuno was possessed of a certain physical strength.

By these days it was a demerit to be muscular. Each infant was examined at birth, and all who promised undue strength were destroyed. Humanitarians may protest, but it would have been no true kindness to let an athlete live; he would never have been happy in that state of life to which the Machine had called him; he would have yearned for trees to climb, rivers to bathe in, meadows and hills against which he might measure his body. Man must be adapted to his surroundings, must he not? In the dawn of the world our weakly must be exposed on Mount Taygetus, in its twilight our strong will suffer Euthanasia, that the Machine may progress, that the Machine may progress, that the Machine may progress eternally.

"You know that we have lost the sense of space. We say 'space is annihilated,' but we have annihilated not space, but the sense thereof. We have lost a part of ourselves. I determined to recover it, and I began by walking up and down the platform of the railway outside my room. Up and down, until I was tired, and so did recapture the meaning of 'Near' and 'Far.' 'Near' is a place to which I can get quickly *on my feet*, not a place to which the train or the air-ship will take me quickly. 'Far' is a place to which I cannot get quickly on my feet; the vomitory is 'far,' though I could be there in thirty-eight seconds by summoning the train. Man is the measure. That was my first lesson. Man's feet are the measure for distance, his hands are the measure for ownership, his body is the measure for all that is lovable and desirable and strong. Then I went further: it was then that I called to you for the first time, and you would not come.

"This city, as you know, is built deep beneath the surface of the earth, with only the vomitories protruding. Having paced the platform outside my own room, I took the lift to the next platform and paced that also, and so with each in turn, until I came to the topmost, above which begins the earth. All the platforms were exactly alike, and all that I gained by visiting them was to develop my sense of space and my muscles. I think I should have been content with this—it is not a little thing— but as I walked and brooded, it occurred to me that our cities had been built in the days when men still breathed the outer air and that there had been ventilation shafts for the workmen. I could think of nothing but these ventilation shafts. Had they been destroyed by all the food-tubes and medicine-

tubes and music-tubes that the Machine had evolved lately? Or did traces of them remain? One thing was certain. If I came upon them anywhere, it would be in the railway-tunnels of the topmost story. Everywhere else, all space was accounted for.

"I am telling my story quickly, but don't think that I was not a coward or that your answers never depressed me. It is not the proper thing, it is not mechanical, it is not decent to walk along a railway-tunnel. I did not fear that I might tread upon a live rail and be killed. I feared something far more intangible—doing what was not contemplated by the Machine. Then I said to myself, 'Man is the measure,' and I went, and after many visits I found an opening.

"The tunnels, of course, were lighted. Everything is light, artificial light; darkness is the exception. So when I saw a black gap in the tiles, I knew that it was an exception, and rejoiced. I put in my arm—I could put in no more at first—and waved it round and round in ecstasy. I loosened another tile, and put in my head, and shouted into the darkness: 'I am coming, I shall do it yet,' and my voice reverberated down endless passages. I seemed to hear the spirits of those dead workmen who had returned each evening to the starlight and to their wives, and all the generations who had lived in the open air called back to me, 'You will do it yet, you are coming.' "

He paused, and, absurd as he was, his last words moved her. For Kuno had lately asked to be a father, and his request had been refused by the Committee. His was not a type that the Machine desired to hand on.

"Then a train passed. It brushed by me, but I thrust my head and arms into the hole. I had done enough for one day, so I crawled back to the platform, went down in the lift, and summoned my bed. Ah, what dreams! And again I called you, and again you refused."

She shook her head and said:

"Don't. Don't talk of these terrible things. You make me miserable. You are throwing civilization away."

"But I had got back the sense of space and a man cannot rest then. I determined to get in at the hole and climb the shaft. And so I exercised my arms. Day after day I went through ridiculous movements, until my flesh ached, and I could hang by my hands and hold the pillow of my bed outstretched for many minutes. Then I summoned a respirator, and started.

"It was easy at first. The mortar had somehow rotted, and I soon pushed some more tiles in, and clambered after them into the darkness, and the spirits of the dead comforted me. I don't know what I mean by that. I just say what I felt. I felt, for the first time, that a protest had been lodged against corruption, and that even as the dead were comforting me, so I was comforting the unborn. I felt that humanity existed, and that it existed without clothes. How can I possibly explain this? It was naked, humanity seemed naked, and all these tubes and buttons and machineries neither came into the world with us, nor will they follow us out, nor do they matter supremely while we are here. Had I been strong, I would have torn off every garment I had, and gone out into the outer air unswaddled. But this is not for me, nor perhaps for my generation. I climbed with my respirator and my hygienic clothes and my dietetic tabloids! Better thus than not at all.

"There was a ladder, made of some primeval metal. The light from the railway fell upon its lowest rungs, and I saw that it led straight upwards out of the rubble at the bottom of the shaft. Perhaps our ancestors ran up and down it a dozen times daily, in their building. As I climbed, the rough edges cut through my gloves so that my hands bled. The light helped me for a little, and then came darkness and, worse still, silence which pierced my ears like a sword. The Machine hums! Did you know that? Its hum penetrates our blood, and may even guide our thoughts. Who knows! I was getting beyond its power. Then I thought: 'This silence means that I am doing wrong.' But I heard voices in the silence, and again they strengthened me." He laughed. "I had need of them. The next moment I cracked my head against something."

She sighed.

"I had reached one of those pneumatic stoppers that defend us from the outer air. You may have noticed them on the air-ship. Pitch dark, my feet on the rungs of an invisible ladder, my hands cut; I cannot explain how I lived through this part, but the voices still comforted me, and I felt for fastenings. The stopper, I suppose, was about eight feet across. I passed my hand over it as far as I could reach. It was perfectly smooth. I felt it almost to the center. Not quite to the center, for my arm was too short. Then the voice said: 'Jump. It is worth it. There may be a handle in the center, and you may catch hold of it and so come to us your own way. And if there is no handle so that you may fall and are dashed to pieces—it is still worth it; you will still come to us your own way.' So I jumped. There was a handle, and—"

He paused. Tears gathered in his mother's eyes. She knew that he was fated. If he did not die today he would die tomorrow. There was not room for such a person in the world. And with her pity disgust mingled. She was ashamed at having borne such a son, she who had always been so respectable and so full of ideas. Was he really the little boy to whom she had taught the use of his stops and buttons, and to whom she had given his first lessons in the Book? The very hair that disfigured his lip showed that he was reverting to some savage type. On atavism the Machine can have no mercy.

"There was a handle, and I did catch

it. I hung tranced over the darkness and heard the hum of these workings as the last whisper in a dying dream. All the things I had cared about and all the people I had spoken to through tubes appeared infinitely little. Meanwhile the handle revolved. My weight had set something in motion and I spun slowly, and then—

"I cannot describe it. I was lying with my face to the sunshine. Blood poured from my nose and ears and I heard a tremendous roaring. The stopper, with me clinging to it, had simply been blown out of the earth, and the air that we make down here was escaping through the vent into the air above. It burst up like a fountain. I crawled back to it—for the upper air hurts—and, as it were, I took great sips from the edge. My respirator had flown goodness knows where, my clothes were torn. I just lay with my lips close to the hole, and I sipped until the bleeding stopped. You can imagine nothing so curious. This hollow in the grass—I will speak of it in a minute,—the sun shining into it, not brilliantly but through marbled clouds,—the peace, the nonchalance, the sense of space, and, brushing my cheek, the roaring fountain of our artificial air! Soon I spied my respirator, bobbing up and down in the current high above my head, and higher still were many air-ships. But no one ever looks out of air-ships, and in my case they could not have picked me up. There I was, stranded. The sun shone a little way down the shaft, and revealed the topmost rung of the ladder, but it was hopeless trying to reach it. I should either have been tossed up again by the escape, or else have fallen in, and died. I could only lie on the grass, sipping and sipping, and from time to time glancing around me.

"I knew that I was in Wessex, for I had taken care to go to a lecture on the subject before starting. Wessex lies above the room in which we are talking now. It was once an important

state. Its kings held all the southern coast from the Andredswald to Cornwall, while the Wansdyke protected them on the north, running over the high ground. The lecturer was only concerned with the rise of Wessex, so I do not know how long it remained an international power, nor would the knowledge have assisted me. To tell the truth I could do nothing but laugh, during this part. There was I, with a pneumatic stopper by my side and a respirator bobbing over my head, imprisoned, all three of us, in a grass-grown hollow that was edged with fern."

Then he grew grave again.

"Lucky for me that it was a hollow. For the air began to fall back into it and to fill it as water fills a bowl. I could crawl about. Presently I stood. I breathed a mixture, in which the air that hurts predominated whenever I tried to climb the sides. This was not so bad. I had not lost my tabloids and remained ridiculously cheerful, and as for the Machine, I forgot about it altogether. My one aim now as to get to the top, where the ferns were, and to view whatever objects lay beyond.

"I rushed the slope. The new air was still too bitter for me and I came rolling back, after a momentary vision of something gray. The sun grew very feeble, and I remembered that he was in Scorpio—I had been to a lecture on that too. If the sun is in Scorpio and you are in Wessex, it means that you must be as quick as you can, or it will get too dark. (This is the first bit of useful information I have ever got from a lecture, and I expect it will be the last.) It made me try frantically to breathe the new air, and to advance as far as I dared out of my pond. The hollow filled so slowly. At times I thought that my fountain played with less vigor. My respirator seemed to dance nearer the earth; the roar was decreasing."

He broke off.

"I don't think this is interesting you. The rest will interest you even less.

There are no ideas in it, and I wish that I had not troubled you to come. We are too different, mother."

She told him to continue.

"It was evening before I climbed the bank. The sun had very nearly slipped out of the sky by this time, and I could not get a good view. You, who have just crossed the Roof of the World, will not want to hear an account of the little hills that I saw—low colorless hills. But to me they were living and the turf that covered them was a skin, under which their muscles rippled, and I felt that those hills had called with incalculable force to men in the past, and that men had loved them. Now they sleep—perhaps forever. They commune with humanity in dreams. Happy the man, happy the woman, who awakes the hills of Wessex. For though they sleep, they will never die."

His voice rose passionately.

"Cannot you see, cannot all your lecturers see, that it is we who are dying, and that down here the only thing that really lives is the Machine? We created the Machine, to do our will, but we cannot make it do our will now. It has robbed us of the sense of space and of the sense of touch, it has blurred every human relation and narrowed down love to a carnal act, it has paralyzed our bodies and our wills, and now it compels us to worship it. The Machine develops—but not to our goal. We only exist as the blood corpuscles that course through its arteries, and if it could work without us, it would let us die. Oh, I have no remedy—or, at least, only one —to tell men again and again that I have seen the hills of Wessex as Aelfrid saw them when he overthrew the Danes.

"So the sun set. I forgot to mention that a belt of mist lay between my hill and other hills, and that it was the color of pearl."

He broke off for the second time.

"Go on. Nothing that you say can distress me now. I am hardened."

"I had meant to tell you the rest, but I cannot: I know that I cannot: goodby."

Vashti stood irresolute. All her nerves were tingling with his blasphemies. But she was also inquisitive.

"This is unfair," she complained. "You have called me across the world to hear your story, and hear it I will. Tell me—as briefly as possible, for this is a disastrous waste of time—tell me how you returned to civilization."

"Oh,—that!" he said, starting. "You would like to hear about civilization. Certainly. Had I got to where my respirator fell down?"

"No—but I understand everything now. You put on your respirator, and managed to walk along the surface of the earth to a vomitory, and there your conduct was reported to the Central Committee."

"By no means."

He passed his hand over his forehead, as if dispelling some strong impression. Then, resuming his narrative, he warmed to it again.

"My respirator fell about sunset. I had mentioned that the fountain seemed feebler, had I not?"

"Yes."

"About sunset, it let the respirator fall. As I said, I had entirely forgotten about the Machine, and I paid no great attention at the time, being occupied with other things. I had my pool of air, into which I could dip when the outer keenness became intolerable, and which would possibly remain for days, provided that no wind sprang up to disperse it. Not until it was too late, did I realize what the stoppage of the escape implied. You see—the gap in the tunnel had been mended; the Mending Apparatus, the Mending Apparatus, was after me.

"One other warning I had, but I neglected it. The sky at night was clearer than it had been in the day, and the moon, which was about half the sky behind the sun, shone into the dell at moments quite brightly. I was in my usual place—on the boundary between the two atmospheres—when I thought I saw something dark move across the bottom on the dell, and vanish into the shaft. In my folly, I ran down. I bent over and listened, and I thought I heard a faint scraping noise in the depths.

"At this—but it was too late—I took alarm. I determined to put on my respirator and to walk right out of the dell. But my respirator had gone. I knew exactly where it had fallen—between the stopper and the aperture—and I could even feel the mark that it had made in the turf. It had gone, and I realized that something evil was at work, and I had better escape to the other air, and, if I must die, die running towards the cloud that had been the color of a pearl. I never started. Out of the shaft—it is too horrible. A worm, a long white worm, had crawled out of the shaft and was gliding over the moonlit grass.

"I screamed. I did everything that I should not have done, I stamped upon the creature instead of flying from it, and it fought. The worm let me run all over the dell, but edged up my leg as I ran. 'Help!' I cried. (That part is too awful. It belongs to the part that you will never know.) 'Help!' I cried. (Why cannot we suffer in silence?) 'Help!' I cried. Then my feet were wound together, I fell, I was dragged away from the dear ferns and the living hills, and past the great metal stopper (I can tell you this part), and I thought it might save me again if I caught hold of the handle. It also was enwrapped, it also. Oh, the whole dell was full of the things. They were searching it in all directions, they were denuding it, and the white snouts of others peeped out of the hole, ready if needed. Everything that could be moved they brought—brushwood, bundles of fern, everything, and down we all went intertwined into

hell. The last things that I saw, ere the stopper closed after us, were certain stars, and I felt that a man of my sort lived in the sky. For I did fight, I fought till the very end, and it was only my head hitting against the ladder that quieted me. I woke up in this room. The worms had vanished. I was surrounded by artificial air, artificial light, artificial peace, and my friends were calling to me down speaking-tubes to know whether I had come across any new ideas lately."

Here his story ended. Discussion of it was impossible, and Vashti turned to go.

"It will end in Homelessness," she said quietly.

"I wish it would," retorted Kuno.

"The Machine has been most merciful."

"I prefer the mercy of God."

"By that superstitious phrase, do you mean that you could live in the outer air?"

"Yes."

"Have you ever seen, round the vomitories, the bones of those who were extruded after the Great Rebellion?"

"Yes."

"They were left where they perished for our edification. A few crawled away, but they perished, too—who can doubt it? And so with the Homeless of our own day. The surface of the earth supports life no longer."

"Indeed."

"Ferns and a little grass may survive, but all higher forms have perished. Has any air-ship detected them?"

"No."

"Has any lecturer dealt with them?"

"No."

"Then why this obstinacy?"

"Because I have seen them," he exploded.

"Seen *what?*"

"Because I have seen her in the twilight—because she came to my help when I called—because she, too, was entangled by the worms, and, luckier than I, was killed by one of them piercing her throat."

He was mad. Vashti departed, nor, in the troubles that followed, did she ever see his face again.

PART III: THE HOMELESS

During the years that followed Kuno's escapade, two important developments took place in the Machine. On the surface they were revolutionary, but in either case men's minds had been prepared beforehand, and they did but express tendencies that were latent already.

The first of these was the abolition of respirators.

Advanced thinkers, like Vashti, had always held it foolish to visit the surface of the earth. Air-ships might be necessary, but what was the good of going out for mere curiosity and crawling along for a mile or two in a terrestrial motor? The habit was vulgar and perhaps faintly improper; it was unproductive of ideas, and had no connection with the habits that really mattered. So respirators were abolished, and with them, of course, the terrestrial motors, and except for a few lecturers, who complained that they were debarred access to their subject-matter, the development was accepted quietly. Those who still wanted to know what the earth was like had after all only to listen to some gramophone, or to look into some cinematophote. And even the lecturers acquiesced when they found that a lecture on the sea was none the less stimulating when compiled out of other lectures that had already been delivered on the same subject. "Beware of first-hand ideas!" exclaimed one of the most advanced of them. "First-hand ideas do not really exist. They are but the physical impressions produced by love and fear, and on this gross foundation who could erect a philosophy? Let your

ideas be second-hand, and if possible tenth-hand, for then they will be far removed from that disturbing element—direct observation. Do not learn anything about this subject of mine—the French Revolution. Learn instead what I think that Enichamon thought Urizen thought Gutch thought Ho-Yung thought Chi-Bo-Sing though Lafcadio Hearn thought Carlyle thought Mirabeau said about the French Revolution. Through the medium of these eight great minds, the blood that was shed at Paris and the windows that were broken at Versailles will be clarified to an idea which you may employ most profitably in your daily lives. But be sure that the intermediates are many and varied, for in history one authority exists to counteract another. Urizen must counteract the skepticism of Ho-Yung and Enicharmon, I must myself counteract the impetuosity of Gutch. You who listen to me are in a better position to judge about the French Revolution than I am. Your descendants will be even in a better position than you, for they will learn what you think I think, and yet another intermediate will be added to the chain. And in time"—his voice rose —"there will come a generation that has got beyond facts, beyond impressions, a generation absolutely colorless, a generation

> seraphically free
> From taint of personality,

which will see the French Revolution not as it happened, nor as they would like it to have happened, but as it would have happened, had it taken place in the days of the Machine."

Tremendous applause greeted this lecture, which did but voice a feeling already latent in the minds of men—a feeling that terrestrial facts must be ignored, and that the abolition of respirators was a positive gain. It was even suggested that air-ships should be abolished too. This was not done, because air-ships had somehow worked themselves into the Machine's system. But year by year they were used less, and mentioned less by thoughtful men.

The second great development was the re-establishment of religion.

This, too, had been voiced in the celebrated lecture. No one could mistake the reverent tone in which the peroration had concluded, and it awakened a responsive echo in the heart of each. Those who had long worshiped silently, now began to talk. They described the strange feeling of peace that came over them when they handled the Book of the Machine, the pleasure that it was to repeat certain numerals out of it, however little meaning those numerals conveyed to the outward ear, the ecstasy of touching a button, however unimportant, or of ringing an electric bell, however superfluously.

"The Machine," they exclaimed, "feeds us and clothes us and houses us; through it we speak to one another, through it we see one another, in it we have our being. The Machine is the friend of ideas and the enemy of superstition: the Machine omnipotent, eternal; blessed is the Machine." And before long this allocution was printed on the first page of the Book, and in subsequent editions the ritual swelled into a complicated system of praise and prayer. The word "religion" was sedulously avoided, and in theory the Machine was still the creation and the implement of man. But in practice all, save a few retrogrades, worshiped it as divine. Nor was it worshiped in unity. One believer would be chiefly impressed by the blue optic plates, through which he saw other believers; another by the Mending Apparatus, which sinful Kuno had compared to worms; another by the lifts, another by the Book. And each would pray to this or to that, and ask it to intercede for him with the Machine as a whole. Persecution—that also was present. It did not break out, for reasons that will be set forward shortly. But it was latent, and all who did not accept the minimum known as "undenominational Mechanism" lived in danger of Homelessness, which means death, as we know.

To attribute these two great developments to the Central Committee, is to take a very narrow view of civilization. The Central Committee announced the developments, it is true, but they were no more the cause of them than were the kings of the imperialistic period the cause of war. Rather did they yield to some invincible pressure, which came no one knew whither, and which, when gratified, was succeeded by some new pressure equally invincible. To such a state of affairs it is convenient to give the name of progress. No one confessed the Machine was out of hand. Year by year it was served with increased efficiency and decreased intelligence. The better a man knew his own duties upon it, the less he understood the duties of his neighbor, and in all the world there was not one who understood the monster as a whole. Those master brains had perished. They had left full directions, it is true, and their successors had each of them mastered a portion of those directions. But Humanity, in its desire for comfort, had over-reached itself. It had exploited the riches of nature too far. Quietly and complacently, it was sinking into decadence, and progress had come to mean the progress of the Machine.

As for Vashti, her life went peacefully forward until the final disaster. She made her room dark and slept; she awoke and made the room light. She lectured and attended lectures. She exchanged ideas with her innumerable friends and believed she was growing more spiritual. At times a friend was granted Euthanasia, and left his or her room for the homelessness that is beyond all human conception. Vashti did not much mind. After an unsuccessful lecture, she would sometimes ask for Euthanasia herself. But the death-rate was not permitted to exceed the birth-rate, and the Machine had hitherto refused it to her.

The troubles began quietly, long before she was conscious of them.

One day she was astonished at receiving a message from her son. They never communicated, having nothing in common, and she had only heard indirectly that he was still alive, and had been transferred from the northern hemisphere, where he had behaved so mischievously, to the southern—indeed, to a room not far from her own.

"Does he want me to visit him?" she thought. "Never again, never. And I have not the time."

No, it was madness of another kind.

He refused to visualize his face upon the blue plate, and speaking out of the darkness with solemnity said:

"The Machine stops."

"What do you say?"

"The Machine is stopping. I know it, I know the signs."

She burst into a peal of laughter. He heard her and was angry, and they spoke no more.

"Can you imagine anything more absurd?" she cried to a friend. "A man who was my son believes that the Machine is stopping. It would be impious if it was not mad."

"The Machine is stopping?" her friend replied. "What does that mean? The phrase conveys nothing to me."

"Nor to me."

"He does not refer, I suppose, to the trouble there has been lately with the music?"

"Oh, no, of course not. Let us talk about music."

"Have you complained to the authorities?"

"Yes, and they say it wants mending, and referred me to the Committee of the Mending Apparatus. I complained of those curious gasping sighs that disfigure the symphonies of the Brisbane school. They sound like someone in pain. The Committee of the Mending Apparatus say that it shall be remedied shortly."

Obscurely worried, she resumed her life. For one thing, the defect in the music irritated her. For another thing, she could not forget Kuno's speech. If he had known that the music was out of repair—he could not know it, for he detested music—if he had known that it was wrong, "the Machine stops" was exactly the venomous sort of remark he would have made. Of course he had made it at a venture, but the coincidence annoyed her, and she spoke with some petulance to the Committee of the Mending Apparatus.

They replied, as before, that the defect would be set right shortly.

"Shortly! At once!" she retorted. "Why should I be worried by imperfect music? Things are always put right at once. If you do not mend it at once, I shall complain to the Central Committee."

"No personal complaints are received by the Central Committee," the Committee of the Mending Apparatus replied.

"Through whom am I to make my complaint, then?"

"Through us."

"I complain then."

"Your complaint shall be forwarded in its turn."

"Have others complained?"

This question was unmechanical, and the Committee of the Mending Apparatus refused to answer it.

"It is too bad!" she exclaimed to another of her friends. "There never was such an unfortunate woman as myself. I can never be sure of my music now. It gets worse and worse each time I summon it."

"I too have my troubles," the friend replied. "Sometimes my ideas are interrupted by a slight jarring noise."

"What is it?"

"I do not know whether it is inside my head, or inside the wall."

"Complain, in either case."

"I have complained, and my complaint will be forwarded in its turn to the Central Committee."

Time passed, and they resented the defects no longer. The defects had not been remedied, but the human tissues in the latter day had become so subservient, that they readily adapted themselves to every caprice of the Machine. The sigh at the crisis of the Brisbane symphony no longer irritated Vashti; she accepted it as part of the melody. The jarring noise, whether in the head or in the wall, was no longer resented by her friend. And so with the moldy artificial fruit, so with the bath water that began to stink, so with the defective rhymes that the poetry machine had taken to emit. All were bitterly complained of at first, and then acquiesced in and forgotten. Things went from bad to worse unchallenged.

It was otherwise with the failure of the sleeping apparatus. That was a more serious stoppage. There came a day when over the whole world—in Sumatra, in Wessex, in the innumerable cities of Courland and Brazil—the beds, when summoned by their tired owners, failed to appear. It may seem a ludicrous matter, but from it we may date the collapse of humanity. The Committee responsible for the failure was assailed by complainants, whom it referred, as usual, to the Committee of the Mending Apparatus, who in its turn assured them that their complaints would be forwarded to the Central Committee. But the discontent grew, for mankind was not yet sufficiently adaptable to do without sleeping.

"Someone is meddling with the Machine—" they began.

"Someone is trying to make himself king, to reintroduce the personal element."

"Punish that man with Homelessness."

"To the rescue! Avenge the Machine! Avenge the Machine!"

"War! Kill the man!"

But the Committee of the Mending Apparatus now came forward, and allayed the panic with well-chosen words. It confessed that the Mending Apparatus was itself in need of repair.

The effect of this frank confession was admirable.

"Of course," said a famous lecturer —he of the French Revolution, who gilded each new decay with splendor— "of course we shall not press our complaints now. The Mending Apparatus has treated us so well in the past that we all sympathize with it, and will wait patiently for its recovery. In its own good time it will resume its duties. Meanwhile let us do without our beds, our tabloids, our other little wants. Such, I feel sure, would be the wish of the Machine."

Thousands of miles away his audience applauded. The Machine still linked them. Under the sea, beneath the roots of the mountains, ran the wires through which they saw and heard, the enormous eyes and ears that were their heritage, and the hum of many workings clothed their thoughts in one garment of subserviency. Only the old and the sick remained ungrateful, for it was rumored that Euthanasia, too, was out of order, and that pain had reappeared among men.

It became difficult to read. A blight entered the atmosphere and dulled its luminosity. At times Vashti could scarcely see across her room. The air, too, was foul. Loud were the complaints, impotent the remedies, heroic the tone of the lecturer as he cried: "Courage, courage! What matter so long as the Machine goes on? To it the darkness and the light are one." And though things improved again after a time, the old brilliancy was never recaptured, and humanity never recovered from its entrance into twilight. There was an hysterical talk of "measures," of "provisional dictatorship," and the inhabitants of Sumatra were asked to familiarize themselves with the workings of the central power station, the said power station being situated in France. But for the most part panic reigned, and men spent their strength praying to their Books, tangible proofs of the Machine's omnipotence. There were gradations of terror—at times came rumors of hope —the Mending Apparatus was almost mended—the enemies of the Machine had been got under—new "nerve-centers" were evolving, which would do the work even more magnificently than before. But there came a day when, without the slightest warning, without any previous hint of feebleness, the entire communication-system broke down, all over the world, and the world, as they understood it, ended.

Vashti was lecturing at the time and her earlier remarks had been punctuated with applause. As she proceeded the audience became silent, and at the conclusion there was no sound. Somewhat displeased, she called to a friend who was a specialist in sympathy. No sound: doubtless the friend was sleeping. And so with the next friend whom she tried to summon, and so with the next, until she remembered Kuno's cryptic remark, "The Machine stops."

The phrase still conveyed nothing. If Eternity was stopping it would of course be set going shortly.

For example, there was still a little light and air—the atmosphere had improved a few hours previously. There was still the Book, and while there was the Book there was security.

Then she broke down, for with the cessation of activity came an unexpected terror—silence.

She had never known silence, and the coming of it nearly killed her—it did kill many thousands of people outright.

Ever since her birth she had been surrounded by the steady hum. It was to the ear what artificial air was to the lungs, and agonizing pains shot across her head. And scarcely knowing what she did, she stumbled forward and pressed the unfamiliar button, the one that opened the door of her cell.

Now the door of the cell worked on a simple hinge of its own. It was not connected with the central power station, dying far away in France. It opened, rousing immoderate hopes in Vashti, for she thought that the Machine had been mended. It opened, and she saw the dim tunnel that curved far away towards freedom. One look, and then she shrank back. For the tunnel was full of people—she was almost the last in that city to have taken alarm.

People at any time repelled her, and these were nightmares from her worst dreams. People were crawling about, people were screaming, whimpering, gasping for breath, touching each other, vanishing in the dark, and ever and anon being pushed off the platform onto the live rail. Some were fighting round the electric bells, trying to summon trains which could not be summoned. Others were yelling for Euthanasia or for respirators, or blaspheming the Machine. Others stood at the doors of their cells fearing, like herself, either to stop in them or to leave them. And behind all the uproar was silence— the silence which is the voice of the earth and of the generations who have gone.

No—it was worse than solitude. She closed the door again and sat down to wait for the end. The disintegration went on, accompanied by horrible cracks and rumbling. The valves that restrained the Medical Apparatus must have been weakened, for it ruptured and hung hideously from the ceiling. The floor heaved and fell and flung her from her chair. A tube oozed towards her serpent fashion. And at last the final horror approached—light began to ebb, and she knew that civilizations' long day was closing.

She whirled round, praying to be saved from this, at any rate, kissing the Book, pressing button after button. The uproar outside was increasing, and even penetrated the wall. Slowly the brilliancy of her cell was dimmed, the reflections faded from her metal switches. Now she could not see the reading-stand, now not the Book, though she held it in her hand. Light followed the flight of sound, air was following light, and the original void returned to the cavern from which it had been so long excluded. Vashti continued to whirl, like the devotees of an earlier religion, screaming, praying, striking at the buttons with bleeding hands.

It was thus that she opened her prison and escaped—escaped in the spirit: at least so it seems to me, ere my meditation closes. That she escapes in the body—I cannot perceive that. She struck, by chance, the switch that released the door, and the rush of foul air on her skin, the loud throbbing whispers in her ears, told her that she was facing the tunnel again, and that tremendous platform on which she had seen men fighting. They were not fighting now. Only the whispers remained, and the little whimpering groans. They were dying by hundreds out in the dark.

She burst into tears.

Tears answered her.

They wept for humanity, those two, not for themselves. They could not bear that this should be the end. Ere silence was completed their hearts were opened, and they knew what had been important on the earth. Man, the flower of all flesh, the noblest of all creatures visible, man who had once made god in his image, and had mirrored his strength on the constellations, beautiful naked man was dying, strangled in the garments that he had woven. Century after century had he toiled, and here was his reward. Truly the garment had

seemed heavenly at first, shot with the colors of culture, sewn with the threads of self-denial. And heavenly it had been so long as it was a garment and no more, so long as man could shed it at will and live by the essence that is his soul, and the essence, equally divine, that is his body. The sin against the body—it was for that they wept in chief; the centuries of wrong against the muscles and nerves, and those five portals by which we can alone apprehend—glozing it over with talk of evolution, until the body was white pap, the home of ideas as colorless, last sloshy stirrings of a spirit that had grasped the stars.

"Where are you?" she sobbed.

His voice in the darkness said, "Here."

"Is there any hope, Kuno?"

"None for us."

"Where are you?"

She crawled towards him over the bodies of the dead. His blood spurted over her hands.

"Quicker," he gasped, "I'm dying—but we touch, we talk, not through the Machine."

He kissed her.

"We have come back to our own. We die, but we have recaptured life, as it was in Wessex, when Aelfrid overthrew the Danes. We know what they know outside, they who dwelt in the cloud that is the color of a pearl."

"But, Kuno, is it true? Are there still men on the surface of the earth? Is this—this tunnel, this poisoned darkness—really not the end?"

He replied:

"I have seen them, spoken to them, loved them. They are hiding in the mist and the ferns until our civilization stops. Today they are the Homeless—tomorrow—"

"Oh, tomorrow—some fool will start the Machine again, tomorrow."

"Never," said Kuno, "never. Humanity has learnt its lesson."

As he spoke, the whole city was broken like a honey-comb. An air-ship had sailed in through the vomitory into a ruined wharf. It crashed downwards, exploding as it went, rending gallery after gallery with its wings of steel. For a moment they saw the nations of the dead, and, before they joined them, scraps of the untainted sky.

William Faulkner

DELTA AUTUMN

Soon now they would enter the Delta. The sensation was familiar to him. It had been renewed like this each last week in November for more than fifty years—the last hill, at the foot of which the rich unbroken alluvial flatness began as the sea began at the base of its cliffs, dissolving away beneath the unhurried November rain as the sea itself would dissolve away.

At first they had come in wagons: the guns, the bedding, the dogs, the food, the whisky, the keen heart-lifting anticipation of hunting; the young men who could drive all night and all the following day in the cold rain and pitch a camp in the rain and sleep in the wet blankets and rise at daylight the next morning and hunt. There had been bear then. A man shot a doe or a fawn as quickly as he did a buck, and in the afternoons they shot wild turkey with pistols to test their stalking skill and markmanship, feeding all but the breast to the dogs. But that time was gone now. Now they went in cars, driving faster and faster each year because the roads were better and they had farther and farther to drive, the territory in which game still existed drawing yearly inward as his life was drawing inward, until now he was the last of those who had once made the journey in wagons without feeling it and now those who accompanied him were the sons and grandsons of the men who had ridden for twenty-four hours in the rain or sleet behind the steaming mules. They called him 'Uncle Ike' now, and he no longer told anyone how near eighty he actually was because he knew as well as they did that he no longer had any business making such expeditions, even by car.

In fact, each time now, on that first night in camp, lying aching and sleepless in the harsh blankets, his blood only faintly warmed by the single thin whisky-and-water which he allowed himself, he would tell himself that this would be his last. But he would stand that trip—he still shot almost as well as he ever had, still killed almost as much of the game he saw as he ever killed; he no longer even knew how many deer had fallen before his gun— and the fierce long heat of the next summer would renew him. Then November would come again, and again in the car with two of the sons of his old companions, whom he had taught not only how to distinguish between the prints· left by a buck or a doe but between the sound they made in moving, he would look ahead past the jerking arc

of the windshield wiper and see the land flatten suddenly and swoop, dissolving away beneath the rain as the sea itself would dissolve, and he would say, "Well, boys, there it is again."

This time though, he didn't have time to speak. The driver of the car stopped it, slamming it to a skidding halt on the greasy pavement without warning, actually flinging the two passengers forward until they caught themselves with their braced hands against the dash. "What the hell, Roth!" the man in the middle said. "Cant you whistle first when you do that? Hurt you, Uncle Ike?"

"No," the old man said. "What's the matter?" The driver didn't answer. Still leaning forward, the old man looked sharply past the face of the man between them, at the face of his kinsman. It was the youngest face of them all, aquiline, saturnine, a little ruthless, the face of his ancestor too, tempered a little, altered a little, staring sombrely through the streaming windshield across which the twin wipers flicked and flicked.

"I didn't intend to come back in here this time," he said suddenly and harshly.

"You said that back in Jefferson last week," the old man said. "Then you changed your mind. Have you changed it again? This aint a very good time to——"

"Oh, Roth's coming," the man in the middle said. His name was Legate. He seemed to be speaking to no one, as he was looking at neither of them. "If it was just a buck he was coming all this distance for, now. But he's got a doe in here. Of course a old man like Uncle Ike cant be interested in no doe, not one that walks on two legs—when she's standing up, that is. Pretty light-colored too. The one he was after them nights last fall when he said he was coon-hunting, Uncle Ike. The one I figured maybe he was still running when he was gone all that month last January. But of course a old man like Uncle Ike aint got no interest in nothing like that." He chortled, still looking at no one, not completely jeering.

"What?" the old man said. "What's that?" But he had not even so much as glanced at Legate. He was still watching his kinsman's face. The eyes behind the spectacles were the blurred eyes of an old man, but they were quite sharp too; eyes which could still see a gun-barrel and what ran beyond it as well as any of them could. He was remembering himself now: how last year, during the final stage by motor boat in to where they camped, a box of food had been lost overboard and how on the next day his kinsman had gone back to the nearest town for supplies and had been gone overnight. And when he did return, something had happened to him. He would go into the woods with his rifle each dawn when the others went, but the old man, watching him, knew that he was not hunting. "All right," he said. "Take me and Will on to shelter where we can wait for the truck, and you can go on back."

"I'm going in," the other said harshly, "Dont worry. Because this will be the last of it."

"The last of deer hunting, or of doe hunting?" Legate said. This time the old man paid no attention to him even by speech. He still watched the young man's savage and brooding face.

"Why?" he said.

"After Hitler gets through with it? Or Smith or Jones or Roosevelt or Willkie or whatever he will call himself in this country?"

"We'll stop him in this country," Legate said. "Even if he calls himself George Washington."

"How?" Edmonds said. "By singing God bless America in bars at midnight and wearing dime-store flags in our lapels?"

"So that's what's worrying you," the old man said. "I aint noticed this country being short of defenders yet, when it needed them. You did some of it yourself twenty-odd years ago, before you were a grown man even. This country is a little mite stronger than any one man or group of men, outside of it or even inside of it either. I reckon, when the time comes and some of you have done got tired of hollering we are whipped if we dont go to war and some more are hollering we are whipped if we do, it will cope with one Austrian paper-hanger, no matter what he will be calling himself. My pappy and some other better men than any of them you named tried once to tear it in two with a war, and they failed."

"And what have you got left?" the other said. "Half the people without jobs and half the factories closed by strikes. Half the people on public dole that wont work and half that couldn't work even if they would. Too much cotton and corn and hogs, and not enough for people to eat and wear. The country full of people to tell a man how he cant raise his own cotton whether he will or wont, and Sally Rand with a sergeant's stripes and not even the fan couldn't fill the army rolls. Too much not-butter and not even the guns——"

"We got a deer camp—if we ever get to it," Legate said. "Not to mention does."

"It's a good time to mention does," the old man said. "Does and fawns both. The only fighting anywhere that ever had anything of God's blessing on it has been when men fought to protect does and fawns. If it's going to come to fighting, that's a good thing to mention and remember too."

"Haven't you discovered in—how many years more than seventy is it?— that women and children are one thing there's never any scarcity of?" Edmonds said.

"Maybe that's why all I am worrying about right now is that ten miles of river we still have got to run before we can make camp," the old man said. "So let's get on."

They went on. Soon they were going

fast again, as Edmonds always drove, consulting neither of them about the speed just as he had given neither of them any warning when he slammed the car to stop. The old man relaxed again. He watched, as he did each recurrent November while more than sixty of them passed, the land which he had seen change. At first there had been only the old towns along the River and the old towns along the hills, from each of which the planters with their gangs of slaves and then of hired laborers had wrested from the impenetrable jungle of water-standing cane and cypress, gum and holly and oak and ash, cotton patches which as the years passed became fields and then plantations. The paths made by deer and bear became roads and then highways, with towns in turn springing up along them and along the rivers Tallahatchie and Sunflower which joined and became the Yazoo, the River of the Dead of the Choctaws—the thick, slow, black, unsunned streams almost without current, which once each year ceased to flow at all and then reversed, spreading, drowning the rich land and subsiding again, leaving it still richer.

Most of that was gone now. Now a man drove two hundred miles from Jefferson before he found wilderness to hunt in. Now the land lay open from the cradling hills on the East to the rampart of levee on the West, standing horseman-tall with cotton for the world's looms—the rich black land, imponderable and vast, fecund up to the very doorsteps of the negroes who worked it and of the white men who owned it; which exhausted the hunting life of a dog in one year, the working life of a mule in five and of a man in twenty—the land in which neon flashed past them from the little countless towns and countless shining this-year's automobiles sped past them on the broad plumb-ruled highways, yet in which the only permanent mark of man's occupation seemed to be the tre-

mendous gins, constructed in sections of sheet iron and in a week's time though they were, since no man, millionaire though he be, would build more than a roof and walls to shelter the camping equipment he lived from when he knew that once each ten years or so his house would be flooded to the second storey and all within it ruined; —the land across which there came now no scream of panther but instead the long hooting of locomotives: trains of incredible length and drawn by a single engine, since there was no gradient anywhere and no elevation save those raised by forgotten aboriginal hands as refuges from the yearly water and used by their Indian successors to sepulchre their fathers' bones, and all that remained of that old time were the Indian names on the little towns and usually pertaining to water—Aluschaskuna, Tillatoba, Homochitto, Yazoo.

By early afternoon, they were on water. At the last little Indian-named town at the end of pavement they waited until the other car and the two trucks—the one carrying the bedding and tents and food, the other the horses —overtook them. They left the concrete and, after another mile or so, the gravel too. In caravan they ground on through the ceaselessly dissolving afternoon, with skid-chains on the wheels now, lurching and splashing and sliding among the ruts, until presently it seemed to him that the retrograde of his remembering had gained an inverse velocity from their own slow progress, that the land had retreated not in minutes from the last spread of gravel but in years, decades, back toward what it had been when he first knew it: the road they now followed once more the ancient pathway of bear and deer, the diminishing fields they now passed once more scooped punily and terrifically by axe and saw and mule-drawn plow from the wilderness' flank, out of the brooding and immemorial tangle, in place of ruthless mile-wide parallelograms wrought by ditching the dyking machinery.

They reached the river landing and unloaded, the horses to go overland down stream to a point opposite the camp and swim the river, themselves and the bedding and food and dogs and guns in the motor launch. It was himself, though no horseman, no farmer, not even a countryman save by his distant birth and boyhood, who coaxed and soothed the two horses, drawing them by his own single frail hand until, backing, filling, trembling a little, they surged, halted, then sprang scrambling down from the truck, possessing no affinity for them as creatures, beasts, but being merely insulated by his years and time from the corruption of steel and oiled moving parts which tainted the others.

Then, his old hammer double gun which was only twelve years younger than he standing between his knees, he watched even the last puny marks of man—cabin, clearing, the small and irregular fields which a year ago were jungle and in which the skeleton stalks of this year's cotton stood almost as tall and rank as the old cane had stood, as if man had had to marry his planting to the wilderness in order to conquer it —fall away and vanish. The twin banks marched with wilderness as he remembered it—the tangle of brier and cane impenetrable even to sight twenty feet away, the tall tremendous soaring of oak and gum and ash and hickory which had rung to no axe save the hunter's, had echoed to no machinery save the beat of oldtime steam boats traversing it or to the snarling of launches like their own of people going into it to dwell for a week or two weeks because it was still wilderness. There was some of it left, although now it was two hundred miles from Jefferson when once it had been thirty. He had watched it, not being conquered, destroyed, so much as retreating since its purpose was served now and its time an outmoded time, retreating southward through this in-verted-apex, this ▽-shaped section of earth between hills and River until what was left of it seemed now to be gathered and for the time arrested in one tremendous density of brooding and inscrutable impenetrability at the ultimate funneling tip.

They reached the site of their last-year's camp with still two hours left of light. "You go on over under that driest tree and set down," Legate told him. "—if you can find it. Me and these other young boys will do this." He did neither. He was not tired yet. That would come later. *Maybe it wont come at all this time*, he thought, as he had thought at this point each November for the last five or six of them. *Maybe I will go out on stand in the morning too;* knowing that he would not, not even if he took the advice and sat down under the driest shelter and did nothing until camp was made and supper cooked. Because it would not be the fatigue. It would be because he would not sleep tonight but would lie instead wakeful and peaceful on the cot amid the tent-filling snoring and the rain's whisper as he always did on the first night in camp; peaceful, without regret or fretting, telling himself that was all right too, who didn't have so many of them left as to waste one sleeping.

In his slicker he directed the unloading of the boat—the tents, the stove, bedding, the food for themselves and the dogs until there should be meat in camp. He sent two of the negroes to cut firewood; he had the cook-tent raised and the stove up and a fire going and supper cooking while the big tent was still being staked down. Then in the beginning of dusk he crossed in the boat to where the horses waited, backing and snorting at the water. He took the lead-ropes and with no more weight than that and his voice, he drew them down into the water and held them beside the boat with only their heads above the surface, as though they actually were suspended from his frail and strengthless old man's hands, while the boat recrossed and each horse in turn lay prone in the shallows, panting and trembling, its eyes rolling in the dusk, until the same weightless hand and unraised voice gathered it surging upward, splashing and thrashing up the bank.

Then the meal was ready. The last of light was gone now save the thin stain of it snared somewhere between the river's surface and the rain. He had the single glass of thin whisky-and-water, then, standing in the churned mud beneath the stretched tarpaulin, he said grace over the fried slabs of pork, the hot soft shapeless bread, the canned beans and molasses and coffee in iron plates and cups,—the town food, brought along with them—then covered himself again, the others following. "Eat," he said. "Eat it all up. I dont want a piece of town meat in camp after breakfast tomorrow. Then you boys will hunt. You'll have to. When I first started hunting in this bottom sixty years ago with old General Compson and Major de Spain and Roth's grandfather and Will Legate's too, Major de Spain wouldn't allow but two pieces of foreign grub in his camp. That was one side of pork and one ham of beef. And not to eat for the first supper and breakfast neither. It was to save until along toward the end of camp when everybody was so sick of bear meat and coon and venison that we couldn't even look at it."

"I thought Uncle Ike was going to say the pork and beef was for the dogs," Legate said, chewing. "But that's right; I remember. You just shot the dogs a mess of wild turkey every evening when they got tired of deer guts."

"Times are different now," another said. "There was game here then."

"Yes," the old man said quietly. "There was game here then."

"Besides, they shot does then too," Legate said. "As it is now, we aint got but one doe-hunter in——"

"And better men hunted it," Edmonds said. He stood at the end of the rough plank table, eating rapidly and steadily as the others ate. But again the old man looked sharply across at the sullen, handsome, brooding face which appeared now darker and more sullen still in the light of the smoky lantern. "Go on. Say it."

"I didn't say that," the old man said. "There are good men everywhere, at all times. Most men are. Some are just unlucky, because most men are a little better than their circumstances give them a chance to be. And I've known some that even the circumstances couldn't stop."

"Well, I wouldn't say—" Legate said.

"So you've lived almost eighty years," Edmonds said. "And that's what you finally learned about the other animals you lived among. I suppose the question to ask you is, where have you been all the time you were dead?"

There was a silence; for the instant even Legate's jaw stopped chewing while he gaped at Edmonds. "Well, by God, Roth—" the third speaker said. But it was the old man who spoke, his voice still peaceful and untroubled and merely grave:

"Maybe so," he said. "But if being what you call alive would have learned me any different, I reckon I'm satisfied, wherever it was I've been."

"Well, I wouldn't say that Roth—" Legate said.

The third speaker was still leaning forward a little over the table looking at Edmonds. "Meaning that it's only because folks happen to be watching him that a man behaves at all," he said. "Is that it?"

"Yes," Edmonds said. "A man in a blue coat, with a badge on it watching him. Maybe just the badge."

"I deny that," the old man said. "I dont——"

The other two paid no attention to him. Even Legate was listening to them for the moment, his mouth still full of food and still open a little, his knife with another lump of something balanced on the tip of the blade arrested halfway to his mouth. "I'm glad I dont have your opinion of folks," the third speaker said. "I take it you include yourself."

"I see," Edmonds said. "You prefer Uncle Ike's opinion of circumstances. All right. Who makes the circumstances?"

"Luck," the third said. "Chance. Happen-so. I see what you are getting at. But that's just what Uncle Ike said: that now and then, maybe most of the time, man is a little better than the net result of his and his neighbors' doings, when he gets the chance to be."

This time Legate swallowed first. He was not to be stopped this time. "Well, I wouldn't say that Roth Edmonds can hunt one doe every day and night for two weeks and was a poor hunter or a unlucky one neither. A man that still have the same doe left to hunt on again next year——"

"Have some meat," the man next to him said.

"—aint so unlucky—What?" Legate said.

"Have some meat." The other offered the dish.

"I got some," Legate said.

"Have some more," the third speaker said. "You and Roth Edmonds both. Have a heap of it. Clapping your jaws together that way with nothing to break the shock." Someone chortled. Then they all laughed, with relief, the tension broken. But the old man was speaking, even into the laughter, in that peaceful and still untroubled voice:

"I still believe. I see proof everywhere. I grant that man made a heap of his circumstances, him and his living neighbors between them. He even inherited some of them already made, already almost ruined even. A while ago Henry Wyatt there said how there used to be more game here. There was. So much that we even killed does. I seem to remember Will Legate mentioning that too—" Someone laughed, a single guffaw, stillborn. It ceased and

they all listened, gravely, looking down at their plates. Edmonds was drinking his coffee, sullen, brooding, inattentive.

"Some folks still kill does," Wyatt said. "There wont be just one buck hanging in this bottom tomorrow night without any head to fit it."

"I didn't say all men," the old man said. "I said most men. And not just because there is a man with a badge to watch us. We probably wont even see him unless maybe he will stop here about noon tomorrow and eat dinner with us and check our licenses——"

"We dont kill does because if we did kill does in a few years there wouldn't even be any bucks left to kill, Uncle Ike," Wyatt said.

"According to Roth yonder, that's one thing we wont never have to worry about," the old man said. "He said on the way here this morning that does and fawns—I believe he said women and children—are two things this world aint ever lacked. But that aint all of it," he said. "That's just the mind's reason a man has to give himself because the heart dont always have time to bother with thinking up words that fit together. God created man and He created the world for him to live in and I reckon He created the kind of world He would have wanted to live in if He had been a man—the ground to walk on, the big woods, the trees and the water, and the game to live in it. And maybe He didn't put the desire to hunt and kill game in man but I reckon He knew it was going to be there, that man was going to teach it to himself, since he wasn't quite God himself yet——"

"When will he be?" Wyatt said.

"I think that every man and woman, at the instant when it dont even matter whether they marry or not, I think that whether they marry then or afterward or dont never, at that instant the two of them together were God."

"Then there are some Gods in this world I wouldn't want to touch, and with a damn long stick," Edmonds said.

He set his coffee cup down and looked at Wyatt. "And that includes myself, if that's what you want to know. I'm going to bed." He was gone. There was a general movement among the others. But it ceased and they stood again about the table, not looking at the old man, apparently held there yet by his quiet and peaceful voice as the heads of the swimming horses had been held above the water by his weightless hand. The three negroes—the cook and his helper and old Isham—were sitting quietly in the entrance of the kitchen tent, listening too, the three faces dark and motionless and musing.

"He put them both here: man, and the game he would follow and kill, foreknowing it. I believe He said, 'So be it.' I reckon He even foreknew the end. But He said, 'I will give him his chance. I will give him warning and foreknowledge too, along with the desire to follow and the power to slay. The woods and fields he ravages and the game he devastates will be the consequence and signature of his crime and guilt, and his punishment.'—Bed time," he said. His voice and inflection did not change at all. "Breakfast at four o'clock, Isham. We want meat on the ground by sunup time."

There was a good fire in the sheet-iron heater; the tent was warm and was beginning to dry out, except for the mud underfoot. Edmonds was already rolled into his blankets, motionless, his face to the wall. Isham had made up his bed too—the strong, battered iron cot, the stained mattress which was not quite soft enough, the worn, often-washed blankets which as the years passed were less and less warm enough. But the tent was warm; presently, when the kitchen was cleaned up and readied for breakfast, the young negro would come in to lie down before the heater, where he could be roused to put fresh wood into it from time to time. And then, he knew now he would not sleep tonight anyway; he no longer

needed to tell himself that perhaps he would. But it was all right now. The day was ended now and night faced him, but alarmless, empty of fret. *Maybe I came for this,* he thought: *Not to hunt, but for this. I would come anyway, even if only to go back home tomorrow.* Wearing only his bagging woolen underwear, his spectacles folded away in the worn case beneath the pillow where he could reach them readily and his lean body fitted easily into the old worn groove of mattress and his eyes closed while the others undressed and went to bed and the last of the sporadic talking died into snoring. Then he opened his eyes and lay peaceful and quiet as a child, looking up at the motionless belly of rain-murmured canvas upon which the glow of the heater was dying slowly away and would fade still further until the young negro, lying on two planks before it, would sit up and stoke it and lie back down again.

They had a house once. That was sixty years ago, when the Big Bottom was only thirty miles from Jefferson and old Major de Spain, who had been his father's cavalry commander in '61 and '2 and '3 and '4, and his cousin (his older brother; his father too) had taken him into the woods for the first time. Old Sam Fathers was alive then, born in slavery, son of a Negro slave and a Chickasaw chief, who had taught him how to shoot, not only when to shoot but when not to; such a November dawn as tomorrow would be and the old man led him straight to the great cypress and he had known the buck would pass exactly there because there was something running in Sam Fathers' veins which ran in the veins of the buck too, and they stood there against the tremendous trunk, the old man of seventy and the boy of twelve, and there was nothing save the dawn until suddenly the buck was there, smoke-colored out of nothing, magnificent with speed: and Sam Fathers said, 'Now.

Shoot quick and shoot slow:' and the gun levelled rapidly without haste and crashed and he walked to the buck lying still intact and still in the shape of that magnificent speed and bled it with Sam's knife and Sam dipped his hands into the hot blood and marked his face forever while he stood trying not to tremble, humbly and with pride too though the boy of twelve had been unable to phrase it then: *I slew you; my bearing must not shame your quitting life. My conduct forever onward must become your death*; marking him for that and for more than that: that day and himself and McCaslin juxtaposed not against the wilderness but against the tamed land, the old wrong and shame itself, in repudiation and denial at least of the land and the wrong and shame even if he couldn't cure the wrong and eradicate the shame, who at fourteen when he learned of it had believed he could do both when he became competent and when at twenty-one he became competent he knew that he could do neither but at least he could repudiate the wrong and shame, at least in principle, and at least the land itself in fact, for his son at least: and did, thought he had: then (married then) in a rented cubicle in a back-street stock-traders' boarding-house, the first and last time he ever saw her naked body, himself and his wife juxtaposed in their turn against that same land, that same wrong and shame from whose regret and grief he would at least save and free his son and, saving and freeing his son, lost him. They had the house then. That roof, the two weeks of each November which they spent under it, had become his home. Although since that time they had lived during the two fall weeks in tents and not always in the same place two years in succession and now his companions were the sons and even the grandsons of them with whom he had lived in the house and for almost fifty years now the house itself had not even existed, the conviction, the sense and feeling of home, had been merely transferred into the canvas. He owned a house in Jefferson, a good house though small, where he had had a wife and lived with her and lost her, ay, lost her even though he had lost her in the rented cubicle before he and his old clever dipsomaniac partner had finished the house for them to move into it: but lost her, because she loved him. But women hope for so much. They never live too long to still believe that anything within the scope of their passionate wanting is likewise within the range of their passionate hope: and it was still kept for him by his dead wife's widowed niece and her children and he was comfortable in it, his wants and needs and even the small trying harmless crochets of an old man looked after by blood at least related to the blood which he had elected out of all the earth to cherish. But he spent the time within those walls waiting for November, because even this tent with its muddy floor and the bed which was not wide enough nor soft enough nor even warm enough, was his home and these men, some of whom he only saw during these two November weeks and not one of whom even bore any name he used to know— De Spain and Compson and Ewell and Hogganbeck—were more his kin than any. Because this was his land——

The shadow of the youngest negro loomed. It soared, blotting the heater's dying glow from the ceiling, the wood billets thumping into the iron maw until the glow, the flame, leaped high and bright across the canvas. But the negro's shadow still remained, by its length and breadth, standing, since it covered most of the ceiling, until after a moment he raised himself on one elbow to look. It was not the negro, it was his kinsman; when he spoke the other turned sharp against the red firelight the sullen and ruthless profile.

"Nothing," Edmonds said. "Go on back to sleep."

"Since Will Legate mentioned it," McCaslin said, "I remember you had some trouble sleeping in here last fall too. Only you called it coon-hunting then. Or was it Will Legate called it that?" The other didn't answer. Then he turned and went back to his bed. McCaslin, still propped on his elbow, watched until the other's shadow sank down the wall and vanished, became one with the mass of sleeping shadows. "That's right," he said. "Try to get some sleep. We must have meat in camp tomorrow. You can do all the setting up you want to after that." He lay down again, his hands crossed again on his breast, watching the glow of the heater on the canvas ceiling. It was steady again now, the fresh wood accepted, being assimilated; soon it would begin to fade again, taking with it the last echo of that sudden upflare of a young man's passion and unrest. Let him lie awake for a little while, he thought; He will lie still some day for a long time without even dissatisfaction to disturb him. And lying awake here, in these surroundings, would soothe him if anything could, if anything could soothe a man just forty years old. Yes, he thought; Forty years old or thirty, or even the trembling and sleepless ardor of a boy; already the tent, the rain-murmured canvas globe, was once more filled with it. He lay on his back, his eyes closed, his breathing quiet and peaceful as a child's, listening to it— that silence which was never silence but was myriad. He could almost see it, tremendous, primeval, looming, musing downward upon this puny evanescent clutter of human sojourn which after a single brief week would vanish and in another week would be completely healed, traceless in the unmarked solitude. Because it was his land, although he had never owned a foot of it. He had never wanted to, not even after he saw plain its ultimate doom, watching it retreat year by year before the onslaught of axe and saw and log-lines and then dynamite and tractor plows, because it belonged to no man. It belonged to all; they had only to use it

well, humbly and with pride. Then suddenly he knew why he had never wanted to own any of it, arrest at least that much of what people called progress, measure his longevity at least against that much of its ultimate fate. It was because there was just exactly enough of it. He seemed to see the two of them —himself and the wilderness—as co-evals, his own span as a hunter, a woodsman not contemporary with his first breath but transmitted to him, assumed by him gladly, humbly, with joy and pride, from that old Major de Spain and that old Sam Fathers who had taught him to hunt, the two spans running out together, not toward oblivion, nothingness, but into a dimension free of both time and space where once more the untreed land warped and wrung to mathematical squares of rank cotton for the frantic old-world people to turn into shells to shoot at one another, would find ample room for both—the names, the faces of the old men he had known and loved and for a little while outlived, moving again among the shades of tall unaxed trees and sightless brakes where the wild strong immortal game ran forever before the tireless belling immortal hounds, falling and rising phoenix-like to the soundless guns.

He had been asleep. The lantern was lighted now. Outside in the darkness the oldest negro, Isham, was beating a spoon against the bottom of a tin pan and crying, "Raise up and get yo foa clock coffy. Raise up and get yo foa clock coffy," and the tent was full of low talk and of men dressing, and Legate's voice, repeating: "Get out of here now and let Uncle Ike sleep. If you wake him up, he'll go out with us. And he aint got any business in the woods this morning."

So he didn't move. He lay with his eyes closed, his breathing gentle and peaceful, and heard them one by one leave the tent. He listened to the breakfast sounds from the table beneath the tarpaulin and heard them depart—the horses, the dogs, the last voice until it died away and there was only the sounds of the negroes clearing breakfast away. After a while he might possibly even hear the first faint clear cry of the first hound ring through the wet woods from where the buck had bedded, then he would go back to sleep again—The tent-flap swung in and fell. Something jarred sharply against the end of the cot and a hand grasped his knee through the blanket before he could open his eyes. It was Edmonds, carrying a shotgun in place of his rifle. He spoke in a harsh, rapid voice:

"Sorry to wake you. There will be a——"

"I was awake," McCaslin said. "Are you going to shoot that shotgun today?"

"You just told me last night you want meat," Edmonds said. "There will be a——"

"Since when did you start having trouble getting meat with your rifle?"

"All right," the other said, with that harsh, restrained, furious impatience. Then McCaslin saw in his hand a thick oblong: an envelope. "There will be a message here some time this morning, looking for me. Maybe it wont come. If it does, give the messenger this and tell h—say I said No."

"A what?" McCaslin said. "Tell who?" He half rose onto his elbow as Edmonds jerked the envelope onto the blanket, already turning toward the entrance, the envelope striking solid and heavy and without noise and already sliding from the bed until McCaslin caught it, divining by feel through the paper as instantaneously and conclusively as if he had opened the envelope and looked, the thick sheaf of banknotes. "Wait," he said. "Wait:"—more than the blood kinsman, more even than the senior in years, so that the other paused, the canvas lifted, looking back, and McCaslin saw that outside it was already day. "Tell her No," he said. "Tell her." They stared at one another —the old face, wan, sleep-raddled above the tumbled bed, the dark and sullen younger one at once furious and cold. "Will Legate was right. This is what you called coon-hunting. And now this." He didn't raise the envelope. He made no motion, no gesture to indicate it. "What did you promise her that you haven't the courage to face her and retract?"

"Nothing!" the other said. "Nothing! This is all of it. Tell her I said No." He was gone. The tent flap lifted on an inwaft of faint light and the constant murmur of rain, and fell again, leaving the old man still half-raised onto one elbow, the envelope clutched in the other shaking hand. Afterward it seemed to him that he had begun to hear the approaching boat almost immediately, before the other could have got out of sight even. It seemed to him that there had been no interval whatever: the tent flap falling on the same out-waft of faint and rain-filled light like the suspiration and expiration of the same breath and then in the next second lifted again—the mounting snarl of the outboard engine, increasing, nearer and nearer and louder and louder then cut short off, ceasing with the absolute instantaneity of a blown-out candle, into the lap and plop of water under the bows as the skiff slid in to the bank, the youngest negro, the youth, raising the tent flap beyond which for that instant he saw the boat—a small skiff with a negro man sitting in the stern beside the up-slanted motor—then the woman entering, in a man's hat and a man's slicker and rubber boots, carrying the blanket-swaddled bundle on one arm and holding the edge of the unbuttoned raincoat over it with the other hand: and bringing something else, something intangible, an effluvium which he knew he would recognise in a moment because Isham had already told him, warned him, by sending the young negro to the tent to announce the visitor instead of coming himself, the flap falling at last on the young negro and they were alone—the face indistinct and as yet only young and with dark eyes, queerly colorless but not ill and not that of a country woman despite the garments she wore, looking down at him where he sat upright on the cot now, clutching the envelope, about him and the twisted blankets huddled about his hips.

"Is that his?" he cried. "Dont lie to me!"

"Yes," she said. "He's gone."

"Yes. He's gone. You wont jump him here. Not this time. I dont reckon even you expected that. He left you this. Here." He fumbled at the envelope. It was not to pick it up, because it was still in his hand; he had never put it down. It was as if he had to fumble somehow to co-ordinate physically his heretofore obedient hand with what his brain was commanding of it, as if he had never performed such an action before, extending the envelope at last, saying again, "Here. Take it. Take it:" until he became aware of her eyes, or not the eyes so much as the look, the regard fixed now on his face with that immersed contemplation, that bottomless and intent candor, of a child. If she had ever seen either the envelope or his movement to extend it, she did not show it.

"You're Uncle Isaac," she said.

"Yes," he said. "But never mind that. Here. Take it. He said to tell you No." She looked at the envelope, then she took it. It was sealed and bore no superscription. Nevertheless, even after she glanced at the front of it, he watched her hold it in the one free hand and tear the corner off with her teeth and manage to rip it open and tilt the neat sheaf of bound notes onto the blanket without even glancing at them and look into the empty envelope and take the edge between her teeth and tear it completely open before she crumpled and dropped it.

"That's just money," she said.

"What did you expect? What else did you expect? You have known him long enough or at least often enough to have got that child, and you dont know him any better than that?"

"Not very often. Not very long. Just that week here last fall, and in January he sent for me and we went West, to New Mexico. We were there six weeks, where I could at least sleep in the same apartment where I cooked for him and looked after his clothes—"

"But not marriage," he said. "Not marriage. He didn't promise you that. Dont lie to me. He didn't have to."

"No. He didn't have to. I didn't ask him to. I knew what I was doing. I knew that to begin with, long before honor I imagine he called it told him the time had come to tell me in so many words what his code I suppose he would call it would forbid him forever to do. And we agreed. Then we agreed again before he left New Mexico, to make sure. That that would be all of it. I believed him. No, I dont mean that; I mean I believed myself. I wasn't even listening to him anymore by then because by that time it had been a long time since he had had anything else to tell me for me to have to hear. By then I wasn't even listening enough to ask him to please stop talking. I was listening to myself. And I believed it. I must have believed it. I dont see how I could have helped but believe it, because he was gone then as we had agreed and he didn't write as we had agreed, just the money came to the bank in Vicksburg in my name but coming from nobody as we had agreed. So I must have believed it. I even wrote him last month to make sure again and the letter came back unopened and I was sure. So I left the hospital and rented myself a room to live in until the deer season opened so I could make sure myself and I was waiting beside the road yesterday when your car passed and he saw me and so I was sure."

"Then what do you want?" he said. "What do you want? What do you expect?"

"Yes," she said. And while he glared at her, his white hair awry from the pillow and his eyes, lacking the spectacles to focus them, blurred and irisless and apparently pupilless, he saw again that grave, intent, speculative and detached fixity like a child watching him. "His great great—Wait a minute.—great great *great* grandfather was your grandfather. McCaslin. Only it got to be Edmonds. Only it got to be more than that. Your cousin McCaslin was there that day when your father and Uncle Buddy won Tennie from Mr. Beauchamp for the one that had no name but Terrel so you called him Tomey's Terrel, to marry. But after that it got to be Edmonds." She regarded him, almost peacefully, with that unwinking and heatless fixity—the dark wide bottomless eyes in the face's dead and toneless pallor which to the old man looked anything but dead, but young and incredibly and even ineradicably alive—as though she were not only not looking at anything, she was not even speaking to anyone but herself. "I would have made a man of him. He's not a man yet. You spoiled him. You, and Uncle Lucas and Aunt Mollie. But mostly you."

"Me?" he said. "Me?"

"Yes. When you gave to his grandfather that land which didn't belong to him, not even half of it by will or even law."

"And never mind that too," he said. "Never mind that too. You," he said. "You sound like you have been to college even. You sound almost like a Northerner even, not like the draggle-tailed women of these Delta peckerwoods. Yet you meet a man on the street one afternoon just because a box of groceries happened to fall out of a boat. And a month later you go off with him and live with him until he got a child on you: and then, by your own statement, you sat there while he took his hat and said goodbye and walked out. Even a Delta peckerwood would look after even a draggle-tail better

than that. Haven't you got any folks at all?"

"Yes," she said. "I was living with one of them. My aunt, in Vicksburg. I came to live with her two years ago when my father died; we lived in Indianapolis then. But I got a job, teaching school here in Aluschaskuna, because my aunt was a widow, with a big family, taking in washing to sup——"

"Took in what?" he said. "Took in washing?" He sprang, still seated even, flinging himself backward onto one arm, awry-haired, glaring. Now he understood what it was she had brought into the tent with her, what old Isham had already told him by sending the youth to bring her in to him—the pale lips, the skin pallid and dead-looking yet not ill, the dark and tragic and foreknowing eyes. *Maybe in a thousand or two thousand years in America*, he thought. *But not now! Not now!* He cried, not loud, in a voice of amazement, pity, and outrage: "You're a nigger!"

"Yes," she said. "James Beauchamp—you called him Tennie's Jim though he had a name—was my grandfather. I said you were Uncle Isaac."

"And he knows?"

"No," she said. "What good would that have done?"

"But you did," he cried. "But you did. Then what do you expect here?"

"Nothing."

"Then why did you come here? You said you were waiting in Aluschaskuna yesterday and he saw you. Why did you come this morning?"

"I'm going back North. Back home. My cousin brought me up the day before yesterday in his boat. He's going to take me on to Leland to get the train."

"Then go," he said. Then he cried again in that thin not loud and grieving voice: "Get out of here! I can do nothing for you! Cant nobody do nothing for you!" She moved; she was not looking at him again, toward the entrance. "Wait," he said. She paused again, obediently still, turning. He took up the sheaf of banknotes and laid it on the blanket at the foot of the cot and drew his hand back beneath the blanket. "There," he said.

Now she looked at the money, for the first time, one brief blank glance, then away again. "I dont need it. He gave me money last winter. Besides the money he sent to Vicksburg. Provided. Honor and code too. That was all arranged."

"Take it," he said. His voice began to rise again, but he stopped it. "Take it out of my tent." She came back to the cot and took up the money; whereupon once more he said, "Wait:" although she had not turned, still stooping, and he put out his hand. But, sitting, he could not complete the reach until she moved her hand, the single hand which held the money, until he touched it. He didn't grasp it, he merely touched it—the gnarled, bloodless, bone-light bone-dry old man's fingers touching for a second the smooth young flesh where the strong old blood ran after its long lost journey back to home. "Tennie's Jim," he said. "Tennie's Jim." He drew the hand back beneath the blanket again: he said harshly now: "It's a boy, I reckon. They usually are, except that one that was its own mother too."

"Yes," she said. "It's a boy." She stood for a moment longer, looking at him. Just for an instant her free hand moved as though she were about to lift the edge of the raincoat away from the child's face. But she did not. She turned again when once more he said Wait and moved beneath the blanket.

"Turn your back," he said. "I am going to get up. I aint got my pants on." Then he could not get up. He sat in the huddled blanket, shaking, while again she turned and looked down at him in dark interrogation. "There," he said harshly, in the thin and shaking old man's voice. "On the nail there. The tent-pole."

"What?" she said.

"The horn!" he said harshly. "The horn." She went and got it, thrust the money into the slicker's side pocket as if it were a rag, a soiled handkerchief, and lifted down the horn, the one which General Compson had left him in his will, covered with the unbroken skin from a buck's shank and bound with silver.

"What?" she said.

"It's his. Take it."

"Oh," she said. "Yes. Thank you."

"Yes," he said, harshly, rapidly, but not so harsh now and soon not harsh at all but just rapid, urgent, until he knew that his voice was running away with him and he had neither intended it nor could stop it: "That's right. Go back North. Marry: a man in your own race. That's the only salvation for you—for a while yet, maybe a long while yet. We will have to wait. Marry a black man. You are young, handsome, almost white; you could find a black man who would see in you what it was you saw in him, who would ask nothing of you and expect less and get even still less than that, if it's revenge you want. Then you will forget all this, forget it ever happened, that he ever existed—" until he could stop it at last and did, sitting there in his huddle of blankets during the instant when, without moving at all, she blazed silently down at him. Then that was gone too. She stood in the gleaming and still dripping slicker, looking quietly down at him from under the sodden hat.

"Old man," she said, "have you lived so long and forgotten so much that you dont remember anything you ever knew or felt or even heard about love?"

Then she was gone too. The waft of light and the murmur of the constant rain flowed into the tent and then out again as the flap fell. Lying back once more, trembling, panting, the blanket huddled to his chin and his hands crossed on his breast, he listened to the pop and snarl, the mounting then fading whine of the motor until it died away and once again the tent held only silence and the sound of rain. And cold too: he lay shaking faintly and steadily in it, rigid save for the shaking. This Delta, he thought: This Delta. *This land which man has deswamped and denuded and deriverred in two generations so that white men can own plantations and commute every night to Memphis and black men own plantations and ride in jim crow cars to Chicago to live in millionaires' mansions on Lakeshore Drive, where white men rent farms and live like niggers and niggers crop on shares and live like animals, where cotton is planted and grows man-tall in the very cracks of the sidewalks, and usury and mortgage and bankruptcy and measureless wealth, Chinese and African and Aryan and Jew, all breed and spawn together until no man has time to say which one is which nor cares. . . .* No wonder the ruined woods I used to know dont cry for retribution! he thought: The people who have destroyed it will accomplish its revenge.

The tent flap jerked rapidly in and fell. He did not move save to turn his head and open his eyes. It was Legate. He went quickly to Edmonds' bed and stooped, rummaging hurriedly among the still-tumbled blankets.

"What is it?" he said.

"Looking for Roth's knife," Legate said. "I come back to get a horse. We got a deer on the ground." He rose, the knife in his hand, and hurried toward the entrance.

"Who killed it?" McCaslin said. "Was it Roth?"

"Yes," Legate said, raising the flap.

"Wait," McCaslin said. He moved, suddenly, onto his elbow. "What was it?" Legate paused for an instant beneath the lifted flap. He did not look back.

"Just a deer, Uncle Ike," he said impatiently. "Nothing extra." He was gone; again the flap fell behind him, wafting out of the tent again the faint light and the constant and grieving rain. McCaslin lay back down, the blanket once more drawn to his chin, his crossed hands once more weightless on his breast in the empty tent.

"It was a doe," he said.

Ernest Hemingway (1898–1961)

IN ANOTHER COUNTRY

In the fall the war was always there, but we did not go to it any more. It was cold in the fall in Milan and the dark came very early. Then the electric lights came on, and it was pleasant along the streets looking in the windows. There was much game hanging outside the shops, and the snow powdered in the fur of the foxes and the wind blew their tails. The deer hung stiff and heavy and empty, and small birds blew in the wind and the wind turned their feathers. It was a cold fall and the wind came down from the mountains.

We were all at the hospital every afternoon, and there were different ways of walking across the town through the dusk to the hospital. Two of the ways were alongside canals, but they were long. Always, though, you crossed a bridge across a canal to enter the hospital. There was a choice of three bridges. On one of them a woman sold roasted chestnuts. It was warm, standing in front of her charcoal fire, and the chestnuts were warm afterward in your pocket. The hospital was very old and very beautiful, and you entered through a gate on the other side. There were usually funerals starting from the courtyard. Beyond the old hospital were the new brick pavilions, and there we met every afternoon and were all very polite and interested in what was the matter, and sat in the machines that were to make so much difference.

The doctor came up to the machine where I was sitting and said: "What did you like best to do before the war? Did you practise a sport?"

I said: "Yes, football."

"Good," he said. "You will be able to play football again better than ever."

My knee did not bend and the leg dropped straight from the knee to the ankle without a calf, and the machine was to bend the knee and make it move as in riding a tricycle. But it did not bend yet, and instead the machine lurched when it came to the bending part. The doctor said: "That will all pass. You are a fortunate young man. You will play football again like a champion."

In the next machine was a major who had a little hand like a baby's. He winked at me when the doctor examined his hand, which was between two leather straps that bounced up and down and flapped the stiff fingers, and said: "And will I too play football, captain-doctor?" He had been a very great fencer, and before the war the greatest fencer in Italy.

The doctor went to his office in a back room and brought a photograph which showed a hand that had been withered almost as small as the major's, before it had taken a machine course, and after was a little larger. The major held the photograph with his good hand and looked at it very carefully. "A wound?" he asked.

"An industrial accident," the doctor said.

"Very interesting, very interesting," the major said, and handed it back to the doctor.

"You have confidence?"

"No," said the major.

There were three boys who came each day who were about the same age I was. They were all three from Milan, and one of them was to be a lawyer, and one was to be a painter, and one had intended to be a soldier, and after we were finished with the machines, sometimes we walked back together to the Café Cova, which was next door to the Scala. We walked the short way through the communist quarter because we were four together. The people hated us because we were officers, and from a wine-shop some one called out, "A basso gli ufficiali!" as we passed. Another boy who walked with us sometimes and made us five wore a black silk handkerchief across his face because he had no nose then and his face was to be rebuilt. He had gone out to the front from the military academy and been wounded within an hour after he had gone into the front line for the first time. They rebuilt his face, but he came from a very old family and they could never get the nose exactly right. He went to South America and worked in a bank. But this was a long time ago, and then we did not any of us know how it was going to be afterward. We only knew then that there was always the war, but that we were not going to it any more.

We all had the same medals, except the boy with the black silk bandage across his face, and he had not been at the front long enough to get any medals. The tall boy with a very pale face who was to be a lawyer had been a lieutenant of Arditi and had three medals of the sort we each had only one of. He had lived a very long time with death and was a little detached. We were all a little detached, and there was nothing that held us together except that we met every afternoon at the hospital. Although, as we walked to the Cova through the tough part of town, walking in the dark, with light and singing coming out of the wine-shops, and sometimes having to walk into the street when the men and women would crowd together on the sidewalk so that we would have had to jostle them to get by, we felt held together by there being something that had happened that they, the people who disliked us, did not understand.

We ourselves all understood the Cova, where it was rich and warm and not too brightly lighted, and noisy and smoky at certain hours, and there were always girls at the tables and the illustrated papers on a rack on the wall. The girls at the Cova were very patriotic, and I found that the most patriotic people in Italy were the café girls—and I believe they are still patriotic.

The boys at first were very polite about my medals and asked me what I had done to get them. I showed them the papers, which were written in very beautiful language and full of *fratellanza* and *abnegazione*, but which really said, with the adjectives removed, that I had been given the medals because I was an American. After that their manner changed a little toward me, although I was their friend against outsiders. I was a friend, but I was never really one of them after they had read the citations, because it had been different with them and they had done very different things to get their medals. I had been wounded, it was true; but we all knew that being wounded, after all, was really an accident. I was never ashamed of the ribbons, though, and sometimes, after the cocktail hour, I would imagine myself having done all the things they had done to get their medals; but walking home at night through the empty streets with the cold wind and all the shops closed, trying to keep near the street lights, I knew that I would never have done such things, and I was very much afraid to die, and often lay in bed at night by myself, afraid to die and wondering how I would be when I went back to the front again.

The three with the medals were like hunting-hawks; and I was not a hawk, although I might seem a hawk to those who had never hunted; they, the three, knew better and so we drifted apart. But I stayed good friends with the boy who had been wounded his first day at the front, because he would never know now how he would have turned out; so he could never be accepted either, and I liked him because I thought perhaps he would not have turned out to be a hawk either.

The major, who had been the great fencer, did not believe in bravery, and spent much time while we sat in the machines correcting my grammar. He had complimented me on how I spoke Italian, and we talked together very easily. One day I had said that Italian seemed such an easy language to me that I could not take a great interest in it; everything was so easy to say. "Ah, yes," the major said. "Why, then, do you not take up the use of grammar?" So we took up the use of grammar, and soon Italian was such a difficult language that I was afraid to talk to him until I had the grammar straight in my mind.

The major came very regularly to the hospital. I do not think he ever missed a day, although I am sure he did not believe in the machines. There was a time when none of us believed in the machines, and one day the major said it was all nonsense. The machines were new then and it was we who were to prove them. It was an idiotic idea, he said, "a theory, like another." I had not learned my grammar, and he said I was a stupid impossible disgrace, and he was a fool to have bothered with me. He was a small man and he sat straight up in his chair with his right hand thrust into the machine and looked straight ahead at the wall while the straps thumped up and down with his fingers in them.

"What will you do when the war is over if it is over?" he asked me. "Speak grammatically!"

"I will go to the States."

"Are you married?"

"No, but I hope to be."

"The more of a fool you are," he said. He seemed very angry. "A man must not marry."

"Why, Signor Maggiore?"

"Don't call me 'Signor Maggiore.'"

"Why must not a man marry?"

"He cannot marry. He cannot marry," he said angrily. "If he is to lose everything, he should not place himself in a position to lose that. He should not place himself in a position to lose. He should find things he cannot lose."

He spoke very angrily and bitterly, and looked straight ahead while he talked.

"But why should he necessarily lose it?"

"He'll lose it," the major said. He was looking at the wall. Then he looked down at the machine and jerked his little hand out from between the straps and slapped it hard against his thigh. "He'll lose it," he almost shouted. "Don't argue with me!" Then he called to the attendant who ran the machines. "Come and turn this damned thing off."

He went back into the other room for the light treatment and the massage. Then I heard him ask the doctor if he might use his telephone and he shut the door. When he came back into the room, I was sitting in another machine. He was wearing his cape and had his cap on, and he came directly toward my machine and put his arm on my shoulder.

"I am so sorry," he said, and patted me on the shoulder with his good hand. "I would not be rude. My wife has just died. You must forgive me."

"Oh—" I said, feeling sick for him. "I am *so* sorry."

He stood there biting his lower lip. "It is very difficult," he said. "I cannot resign myself."

He looked straight past me and out through the window. Then he began to cry. "I am utterly unable to resign myself," he said and choked. And then crying, his head up looking at nothing, carrying himself straight and soldierly, with tears on both his cheeks and biting his lips, he walked past the machines and out the door.

The doctor told me that the major's wife, who was very young and whom he had not married until he was definitely invalided out of the war, had died of pneumonia. She had been sick only a few days. No one expected her to die. The major did not come to the hospital for three days. Then he came at the usual hour, wearing a black band on the sleeve of his uniform. When he came back, there were large framed photographs around the wall, of all sorts of wounds before and after they had been cured by the machines. In front of the machine the major used were three photographs of hands like his that were completely restored. I do not know where the doctor got them. I always understood we were the first to use the machines. The photographs did not make much difference to the major because he only looked out of the window.

Katherine Anne Porter (1890–   )
A DAY'S WORK

The dull scrambling like a giant rat in the wall meant the dumb-waiter was on its way up, the janitress below hauling on the cable. Mrs. Halloran paused, thumped her iron on the board, and said, "There it is. Late. You could have put on your shoes and gone around the corner and brought the things an hour ago. I can't do everything."

Mr. Halloran pulled himself out of the chair, clutching the arms and heaving to his feet slowly, looking around as if he hoped to find crutches standing near. "Wearing out your socks, too," added Mrs. Halloran. "You ought either go barefoot outright or wear your shoes over your socks as God intended," she said. "Sock feet. What's the good of it, I'd like to know? Neither one thing nor the other."

She unrolled a salmon-colored chiffon nightgown with cream-colored lace and broad ribbons on it, gave it a light flirt in the air, and spread it on the board. "God's mercy, look at that indecent thing," she said. She thumped the iron again and pushed it back and forth over the rumpled cloth. "You might just set the things in the cupboard," she said, "and not leave them around on the floor. You might just."

Mr. Halloran took a sack of potatoes from the dumb-waiter and started for the cupboard in the corner next the icebox. "You might as well take a load," said Mrs. Halloran. "There's no need on earth making a half-dozen trips back and forth. I'd think the poorest sort of man could well carry more than five pounds of potatoes at one time. But maybe not."

Her voice tapped on Mr. Halloran's ears like wood on wood. "Mind your business, will you?" he asked, not speaking to her directly. He carried on the argument with himself. "Oh, I couldn't do that, Mister Honey," he answered in a dull falsetto. "Don't ever ask me to think of such a thing, even. It wouldn't be right," he said, standing still with his knees bent, glaring bitterly over the potato sack at the scrawny strange woman he had never liked, that one standing there ironing clothes with a dirty look on her whole face like a suffering saint. "I may not be much good any more," he told her in his own voice, "but I still have got wits enough to take groceries off a dumb-waiter, mind you."

"That's a miracle," said Mrs. Halloran. "I'm thankful for that much."

"There's the telephone," said Mr. Halloran, sitting in the armchair again and taking his pipe out of his shirt pocket.

"I heard it as well," said Mrs. Halloran, sliding the iron up and down over the salmon-colored chiffon.

"It's for you, I've no further business in this world," said Mr. Halloran. His little greenish eyes glittered; he exposed his two sharp dogteeth in a grin.

"You could answer it. It could be the wrong number again or for somebody downstairs," said Mrs. Halloran, her flat voice going flatter, even.

"Let it go in any case," decided Mr. Halloran, "for my own part, that is."

He struck a match on the arm of his chair, touched off his pipe, and drew in his first puff while the telephone went on with its nagging.

"It might be Maggie again," said Mrs. Halloran.

"Let her ring, then," said Mr. Halloran, settling back and crossing his legs.

"God help a man who won't answer the telephone when his own daughter calls up for a word," commented Mrs. Halloran to the ceiling. "And she in deep trouble, too, with her husband treating her like a dog about the money, and sitting out late nights in saloons with that crowd from the Little Tammany Association. He's getting into politics now with the McCorkery gang. No good will come of it, and I told her as much."

"She's no troubles at all, her man's a sharp fellow who will get ahead if she'll let him alone," said Mr. Halloran. "She's nothing to complain of, I could tell her. But what's a father?" Mr. Halloran cocked his head toward the window that opened on the brick-paved areaway and crowed like a rooster, "What's a father these days and who would heed his advice?"

"You needn't tell the neighbors, there's disgrace enough already," said Mrs. Halloran. She set the iron back on the gas ring and stepped out to the telephone on the first stair landing. Mr. Halloran leaned forward, his thin, red-haired hands hanging loosely between his knees, his warm pipe sending up its good decent smell right into his nose. The woman hated the pipe and the smell; she was a woman born to make any man miserable. Before the depression, while he still had a good job and prospects of a raise, before he went on relief, before she took in fancy washing and ironing, in the Good Days Before, God's pity, she didn't exactly keep her mouth shut, there wasn't a word known to man she couldn't find an answer for, but she knew which side her bread was buttered on, and put up with it. Now she was, you might say, buttering her own bread and she never forgot it for a minute. And it's her own fault we're not riding round today in a limousine with ash trays and a speaking tube and a cut-glass vase for flowers in it. It's what a man gets for marrying one of these holy women. Gerald McCorkery had told him as much, in the beginning.

"There's a girl will spend her time holding you down," Gerald had told him. "You're putting your head in a noose will strangle the life out of you. Heed the advice of one who wishes you well," said Gerald McCorkery. This was after he had barely set eyes on Lacey Mahaffy one Sunday morning in Coney Island. It was like McCorkery to see that in a flash, born judge of human nature that he was. He could look a man over, size him up, and there was an end to it. And if the man didn't pass muster, McCorkery could ease him out in a way that man would never know how it happened. It was the secret of McCorkery's success in the world.

"This is Rosie, herself," said Gerald that Sunday in Coney Island. "Meet the future Mrs. Gerald J. McCorkery." Lacey Mahaffy's narrow face had gone sour as whey under her big straw hat. She barely nodded to Rosie, who gave Mr. Halloran a look that fairly undressed him right there. Mr. Halloran had thought, too, that McCorkery was picking a strange one; she was good-looking all right, but she had the smell of a regular little Fourteenth Street hustler if Halloran knew anything about women. "Come on," said McCorkery, his arm around Rosie's waist, "let's all go on the roller coaster." But Lacey would not. She said, "No, thank you. We didn't plan to stay, and we must go now." On the way home Mr. Halloran said, "Lacey, you judge too harshly. Maybe that's a nice girl at heart; hasn't had your opportunities."

Lacey had turned upon him a face ugly as an angry cat's, and said, "She's a loose, low woman, and 'twas an insult to introduce her to me." It was a good while before the pretty fresh face that Mr. Halloran had fallen in love with returned to her.

Next day in Billy's Place, after three drinks each, McCorkery said, "Watch your step, Halloran; think of your future. There's a straight good girl I don't doubt, but she's no sort of mixer. A man getting into politics needs a wife who can meet all kinds. A man needs a woman knows how to loosen her corsets and sit easy."

Mrs. Halloran's voice was going on in the hall, a steady dry rattle like old newspapers blowing on a park bench. "I told you before it's no good coming to me with your troubles now. I warned you in time but you wouldn't listen. . . . I told you just how it would be, I tried my best. . . . No, you couldn't listen, you always knew better than your mother. . . . So now all you've got to do is stand by your married vows and make the best of it. . . . Now listen to me, if you want himself to do right you have to do right first. The woman has to do right first, and then if the man won't do right in turn it's no fault of hers. You do right whether he does wrong or no, just because he does wrong is no excuse for you."

"Ah, will you hear that?" Mr. Halloran asked the areaway in an awed voice. "There's a holy terror of a saint for you."

". . . the woman has to do right first, I'm telling you," said Mrs. Halloran into the telephone, "and then if he's a devil in spite of it, why she has to do right without any help from him." Her voice rose so the neighbors could get an earful if they wanted. "I know you from old, you're just like your father. You must be doing something wrong yourself or you wouldn't be in this fix. You're doing wrong this minute, calling over the telephone when you ought to be getting your work done. I've got an iron on, working over the dirty nightgowns of a kind of woman I wouldn't soil my foot on if I'd had a man to take care of me. So now you do up your housework and dress yourself and take a walk in the fresh air. . . ."

"A little fresh air never hurt anybody," commented Mr. Halloran loudly through the open window. "It's the gas gets a man down."

"Now listen to me, Maggie, that's not the way to talk over the public wires. Now you stop that crying and go and do your duty and don't be worrying me any more. And stop saying you're going to leave your husband, because where will you go, for one thing? Do you want to walk the streets or set up a laundry in your kitchen? You can't come back here, you'll stay with your husband where you belong. Don't be a fool, Maggie. You've got your living, and that's more than many a woman better than you has got. Yes, your father's all right. No, he's just sitting here, the same. God knows what's to become of us. But you know how he is, little he cares. . . . Now remember this, Maggie, if anything goes wrong with your married life it's your own fault and you needn't come here for sympathy. . . . I can't waste any more time on it. Good-by."

Mr. Halloran, his ears standing up for fear of missing a word, thought how Gerald J. McCorkery had gone straight on up the ladder with Rosie; and for every step the McCorkerys took upward, he, Michael Halloran, had taken a step downward with Lacey Mahaffy. They had started as greenhorns with the same chances at the same time and the same friends, but McCorkery had seized all his opportunities as they came, getting in steadily with the Big Shots in ward politics, one good thing leading to another. Rosie had known how to back him up and push him onward. The McCorkerys for years had invited him and Lacey to come over to the house and be sociable with the crowd, but Lacey would not.

"You can't run with that fast set and drink and stay out nights and hold your job," said Lacey, "and you should know better than to ask your wife to associate with that woman." Mr. Halloran had got into the habit of dropping around by himself, now and again, for McCorkery still liked him, was still willing to give him a foothold in the right places, still asked him for favors at election time. There was always a good lively crowd at the McCorkerys, wherever they were; for they moved ever so often to a better place, with more furniture. Rosie helped hand around the drinks, taking a few herself with a gay word for everybody. The player piano or the victrola would be going full blast, with everybody dancing, all looking like ready money and a bright future. He would get home late these evenings, back to the same little cold-water walk-up flat, because Lacey would not spend a dollar for show. It must all go into savings against old age, she said. He would be full of good food and drink, and find Lacey, in a bungalow apron, warming up the fried potatoes once more, cross and bitterly silent, hanging her head and frowning at the smell of liquor on his breath. "You might at least eat the potatoes when I've fried them and waited all this time," she would say. "Ah, eat them yourself, they're none of mine," he would snarl in his disappointment with her, and with the life she was leading him.

He had believed with all his heart for years that he would one day be manager of one of the G. and I. chain grocery stores he worked for, and when that hope gave out there was still his pension when they retired him. But two years before it was due they fired him, on account of the depression, they said. Overnight he was on the sidewalk, with no place to go with the news but home. "Jesus," said Mr. Halloran, still

remembering that day after nearly seven years of idleness.

The depression hadn't touched McCorkery. He went on and on up the ladder, giving beefsteaks and beanfests and beer parties for the boys in Billy's Place, standing in with the right men and never missing a trick. At last the Gerald J. McCorkery Club chartered a whole boat for a big excursion up the river. It was a great day, with Lacey sitting at home sulking. After election Rosie had her picture in the papers, smiling at McCorkery; not fat exactly, just a fine figure of a woman with flowers pinned on her spotted fur coat, her teeth as good as ever. Oh, God, there was a girl for any man's money. Mr. Halloran saw out of his eye-corner the bony stooped back of Lacey Mahaffy, standing on one foot to rest the other like a tired old horse, leaning on her hands waiting for the iron to heat.

"That was Maggie, with her woes," she said.

"I hope you gave her some good advice," said Mr. Halloran. "I hope you told her to take up her hat and walk out on him."

Mrs. Halloran suspended the iron over a pair of pink satin panties. "I told her to do right and leave wrong-doing to the men," she said, in her voice like a phonograph record running down. "I told her to bear with the trouble God sends as her mother did before her."

Mr. Halloran gave a loud groan and knocked out his pipe on the chair arm. "You would ruin the world, woman, if you could, with your wicked soul, treating a new-married girl as if she had no home and no parents to come to. But she's no daughter of mine if she sits there peeling potatoes, letting a man run over her. No daughter of mine and I'll tell her so if she—"

"You know well she's your daughter, so hold your tongue," said Mrs. Halloran, "and if she heeded you she'd be walking the streets this minute. I brought her up an honest girl, and an honest woman she's going to be or I'll take her over my knee as I did when she was little. So there you are, Halloran."

Mr. Halloran leaned far back in his chair and felt along the shelf above his head until his fingers touched a half-dollar he had noticed there. His hand closed over it, he got up instantly and looked about for his hat.

"Keep your daughter, Lacey Mahaffy," he said, "she's none of mine but the fruits of your long sinning with the Holy Ghost. And now I'm off for a little round and a couple of beers to keep my mind from dissolving entirely."

"You can't have that dollar you just now sneaked off the shelf," said Mrs. Halloran. "So you think I'm blind besides? Put it back where you found it. That's for our daily bread."

"I'm sick of bread daily," said Mr. Halloran, "I need beer. It was not a dollar, but a half-dollar as you know well."

"Whatever it was," said Mrs. Halloran, "it stands instead of a dollar to me. So just drop it."

"You've got tomorrow's potatoes sewed up in your pocket this minute, and God knows what sums in that black box wherever you hide it, besides the life savings," said Mr. Halloran. "I earned this half-dollar on relief, and it's going to be spent properly. And I'll not be back for supper, so you'll save on that, too. So long, Lacey Mahaffy, I'm off."

"If you never come back, it will be all the same," said Mrs. Halloran, not looking up.

"If I came back with a pocket full of money, you'd be glad to see me," said Mr. Halloran.

"It would want to be a great sum," said Mrs. Halloran.

Mr. Halloran shut the door behind him with a fine slam.

He strolled out into the clear fall weather, a late afternoon sun warming his neck and brightening the old red-brick, high-stooped houses of Perry Street. He would go after all these years to Billy's Place, he might find some luck there. He took his time, though, speaking to the neighbors as he went. "Good afternoon, Mr. Halloran." "Good afternoon to you, Missis Caffery." . . . "It's fine weather for the time of year, Mr. Gogarty." "It is indeed, Mr. Halloran." Mr. Halloran thrived on these civilities, he loved to flourish his hat and give a hearty good day like a man who has nothing on his mind. Ah, there was the young man from the G. and I. store around the corner. He knew what kind of job Mr. Halloran once held there. "Good day, Mr. Halloran." "Good day to you, Mr. McInerny, how's business holding up with you?" "Good for the times, Mr. Halloran, that's the best I can say." "Things are not getting any better, Mr. McInerny." "It's the truth we are all hanging on by the teeth now, Mr. Halloran."

Soothed by this acknowledgment of man's common misfortune Mr. Halloran greeted the young cop at the corner. The cop, with his quick eyesight, was snatching a read from a newspaper on the stand across the sidewalk. "How do you do, Young O'Fallon," asked Mr. Halloran, "is your business lively these days?"

"Quiet as the tomb itself on this block," said Young O'Fallon. "But that's a sad thing about Connolly, now." His eyes motioned toward the newspaper.

"Is he dead?" asked Mr. Halloran; "I haven't been out until now, I didn't see the papers."

"Ah, not yet," said Young O'Fallon, "but the G-men are after him, it looks they'll get him surely this time."

"Connolly in bad with the G-men? Holy Jesus," said Mr. Halloran, "who will they go after next? The meddlers."

"It's that numbers racket," said the cop. "What's the harm, I'd like to know? A man must get his money from somewhere when he's in politics. They oughta give him a chance."

"Connolly's a great fellow, God bless him, I hope he gives them the slip," said Mr. Halloran, "I hope he goes right through their hands like a greased pig."

"He's smart," said the cop. "That Connolly's a smooth one. He'll come out of it."

Ah, will he though? Mr. Halloran asked himself. Who is safe if Connolly goes under? Wait till I give Lacey Mahaffy the news about Connolly, I'll like seeing her face the first time in twenty years. Lacey kept saying, "A man is a down-right fool must be a crook to get rich. Plenty of the best people get rich and do no harm by it. Look at the Connollys now, good practical Catholics with nine children and more to come if God sends them, and Mass every day, and they're rolling in wealth richer than your McCorkerys with all their wickedness." So there you are, Lacey Mahaffy, wrong again, and welcome to your pious Connollys. Still and all it was Connolly who had given Gerald McCorkery his start in the world; McCorkery had been publicity man and then campaign manager for Connolly, in the days when Connolly had Tammany in the palm of his hand and the sky was the limit. And McCorkery had begun at the beginning, God knows. He was running a little basement place first, rent almost nothing, where the boys of the Connolly Club and the Little Tammany Association, just the mere fringe of the district, you might say, could drop in for quiet evenings for a game and a drink along with the talk. Nothing low, nothing but what was customary, with the house taking a cut on the winnings and a fine profit on the liquor, and holding the crowd together. Many was the big plan hatched there came out well for everybody. For everybody but myself, and why was that? And when

McCorkery says to me, "You can take over now and run the place for the McCorkery Club," ah, there was my chance and Lacey Mahaffy wouldn't hear of it, and with Maggie coming on just then it wouldn't do to excite her.

Mr. Halloran went on, following his feet that knew the way to Billy's Place, head down, not speaking to passersby any more, but talking it out with himself again, again. What a track to go over seeing clearly one by one the crossroads where he might have taken a different turn that would have changed all his fortunes; but no, he had gone the other way and now it was too late. She wouldn't say a thing but "It's not right and you know it, Halloran," so what could a man do in all? Ah, you could have gone on with your rightful affairs like any other man, Halloran, it's not the woman's place to decide such things; she'd have come round once she saw the money, or a good whack on the backsides would have put her in her place. Never had mortal woman needed a good walloping worse than Lacey Mahaffy, but he could never find it in his heart to give it to her for her own good. That was just another of your many mistakes, Halloran. But there was always the life-long job with the G. and I. and peace in the house more or less. Many a man envied me in those days I remember, and I was resting easy on the savings and knowing with that and the pension I could finish out my life with some little business of my own. "What came of that?" Mr. Halloran inquired in a low voice, looking around him. Nobody answered. You know well what came of it, Halloran. You were fired out like a delivery boy, two years before your time was out. Why did you sit there watching the trick being played on others before you, knowing well it could happen to you and never quite believing what you saw with your own eyes? G. and I. gave me my start, when I was green in this country, and they were my own kind or I thought so. Well, it's done now. Yes, it's done now, but there was all the years you could have cashed in on the numbers game with the best of them, helping collect the protection money and taking your cut. You could have had a fortune by now in Lacey's name, safe in the bank. It was good quiet profit and none the wiser. But they're wiser now, Halloran, don't forget; still it's a lump of grief and disappointment to swallow all the same. The game's up with Connolly, maybe; Lacey Mahaffy had said, "Numbers is just another way of stealing from the poor, and you weren't born to be a thief like that McCorkery." Ah, God, no, Halloran, you were born to rot on relief and maybe that's honest enough for her. That Lacey— A fortune in her name would have been no good to me whatever. She's got all the savings tied up, such as they are, she'll pinch and she'll starve, she'll wash dirty clothes first, she won't give up a penny to live on. She has stood in my way, McCorkery, like a skeleton rattling its bones, and you were right about her, she has been my ruin. "Ah, it's not too late yet, Halloran," said McCorkery, appearing plain as day inside Mr. Halloran's head with the same old face and way with him. "Never say die, Halloran. Elections are coming on again, it's a busy time for all, there's work to be done and you're the very man I'm looking for. Why didn't you come to me sooner, you know I never forget an old friend. You don't deserve your ill fortune, Halloran," McCorkery told him; "I said so to others and I say it now to your face, never did man deserve more of the world than you, Halloran, but the truth is, there's not always enough good luck to go round; but it's your turn now, and I've got a job for you up to your abilities at last. For a man like you, there's nothing to it at all, you can toss it off with one hand tied, Halloran, and good money in it. Organization work, just

among your own neighbors, where you're known and respected for a man of your word and an old friend of Gerald McCorkery. Now look, Halloran," said Gerald McCorkery, tipping him the wink, "do I need to say more? It's voters in large numbers we're after, Halloran, and you're to bring them in, alive or dead. Keep your eye on the situation at all times and get in touch with me when necessary. And name your figure in the way of money. And come up to the house sometimes, Halloran, why don't you? Rosie has asked me a hundred times, 'Whatever went with Halloran, the life of the party?' That's the way you stand with Rosie, Halloran. We're in a two-story flat now with green velvet curtains and carpets you can sink to your shoetops in, and there's no reason at all why you shouldn't have the same kind of place if you want it. With your gifts, you were never meant to be a poor man."

Ah, but Lacey Mahaffy wouldn't have it, maybe. "Then get yourself another sort of woman, Halloran, you're a good man still, find yourself a woman like Rosie to snuggle down with at night." Yes, but McCorkery, you forget that Lacey Mahaffy had legs and hair and eyes and a complexion fit for a chorus girl. But would she do anything with them? Never. Would you believe there was a woman wouldn't take off all her clothes at once even to bathe herself? What a hateful thing she was with her evil mind thinking everything was a sin, and never giving a man a chance to show himself a man in any way. But she's faded away now, her mean soul shows out all over her, she's ugly as sin itself now, McCorkery. "It's what I told you would happen," said McCorkery, "but now with the job and the money you can go your ways and let Lacey Mahaffy go hers." I'll do it, McCorkery. "And forget about Connolly. Just remember I'm my own man and always was. Connolly's finished, but I'm not. Stronger than ever, Halloran, with

Connolly out of the way. I saw this coming long ever ago, Halloran, I got clear of it. They don't catch McCorkery with his pants down, Halloran. And I almost forgot . . . Here's something for the running expenses to start. Take this for the present, and there's more to come. . . ."

Mr. Halloran stopped short, a familiar smell floated under his nose: the warm beer-and-beefsteak smell of Billy's Place, sawdust and onions, like any other bar maybe, but with something of its own besides. The talk within him stopped also as if a hand had been laid on his mind. He drew his fist out of his pocket almost expecting to find green money in it. The half dollar was in his palm. "I'll stay while it lasts and hope McCorkery will come in."

The moment he stepped inside his eye lighted on McCorkery standing at the bar pouring his own drink from the bottle before him. Billy was mopping the bar before him idly, and his eye, swimming toward Halloran, looked like an oyster in its own juice. McCorkery saw him too. "Well, blow me down," he said, in a voice that had almost lost its old County Mayo ring, "if it ain't my old sidekick from the G. and I. Step right up, Halloran," he said, his poker-face as good as ever, no man ever saw Gerald McCorkery surprised at anything. "Step up and name your choice."

Mr. Halloran glowed suddenly with the warmth around the heart he always had at the sight of McCorkery, he couldn't put a name on it, but there was something about the man. Ah, it was Gerald all right, the same, who never forgot a friend and never seemed to care whether a man was rich or poor, with his face of granite and his eyes like blue agates in his head, a rock of a man surely. There he was, saying "Step right up," as if they had parted only yesterday; portly and solid in his expensive-looking clothes, as always; his hat a darker gray than his suit, with a

devil-may-care roll to the brim, but nothing sporting, mind you. All first-rate, well made, and the right thing for him, more power to him. Mr. Halloran said, "Ah, McCorkery, you're the one man on this round earth I hoped to see today, but I says to myself, maybe he doesn't come round to Billy's Place so much nowadays."

"And why not?" asked McCorkery, "I've been coming around to Billy's Place for twenty-five years now, it's still headquarters for the old guard of the McCorkery Club, Halloran." He took in Mr. Halloran from head to foot in a flash of a glance and turned toward the bottle.

"I was going to have a beer," said Mr. Halloran, "but the smell of that whiskey changes my mind for me." McCorkery poured a second glass, they lifted the drinks with an identical crook of the elbow, a flick of the wrist at each other.

"Here's to crime," said McCorkery, and "Here's looking at you," said Mr. Halloran, merrily. Ah, to hell with it, he was back where he belonged, in good company. He put his foot on the rail and snapped down his whiskey, and no sooner was his glass on the bar than McCorkery was filling it again. "Just time for a few quick ones," he said, "before the boys get here." Mr. Halloran downed that one, too, before he noticed that McCorkery hadn't filled his own glass. "I'm ahead of you," said McCorkery, "I'll skip this one."

There was a short pause, a silence fell around them that seemed to ooze like a fog from somewhere deep in McCorkery, it was suddenly as if he had not really been there at all, or hadn't uttered a word. Then he said outright: "Well, Halloran, let's have it. What's on your mind?" And he poured two more drinks. That was McCorkery all over, reading your thoughts and coming straight to the point.

Mr. Halloran closed his hand round his glass and peered into the little pool of whiskey. "Maybe we could sit down," he said, feeling weak-kneed all at once. McCorkery took the bottle and moved over to the nearest table. He sat facing the door, his look straying there now and then, but he had a set, listening face as if he was ready to hear anything.

"You know what I've had at home all these years," began Mr. Halloran, solemnly, and paused.

"Oh, God, yes," said McCorkery with simple good-fellowship. "How is herself these days?"

"Worse than ever," said Mr. Halloran, "but that's not it."

"What is it, then, Halloran?" asked McCorkery, pouring drinks. "You know well you can speak out your mind to me. Is it a loan?"

"No," said Mr. Halloran. "It's a job."

"Now that's a different matter," said McCorkery. "What kind of a job?"

Mr. Halloran, his head sunk between his shoulders, saw McCorkery wave a hand and nod at half a dozen men who came in and ranged themselves along the bar. "Some of the boys," said McCorkery. "Go on." His face was tougher, and quieter, as if the drink gave him a firm hold on himself. Mr. Halloran said what he had planned to say, had said already on the way down, and it still sounded reasonable and right to him. McCorkery waited until he had finished, and got up, putting a hand on Mr. Halloran's shoulder. "Stay where you are, and help yourself," he said, giving the bottle a little push, "and anything else you want, Halloran, order it on me. I'll be back in a few minutes, and you know I'll help you out if I can."

Halloran understood everything but it was through a soft warm fog, and he hardly noticed when McCorkery passed him again with the men, all in that creepy quiet way like footpads on a dark street. They went into the back room, the door opened on a bright light and closed again, and Mr. Halloran reached for the bottle to help himself

wait until McCorkery should come again bringing the good word. He felt comfortable and easy as if he hadn't a bone or muscle in him, but his elbow slipped off the table once or twice and he upset his drink on his sleeve. Ah, McCorkery, is it the whole family you're taking on with the jobs? For my Maggie's husband is in now with the Little Tammany Association. "There's a bright lad will go far and I've got my eye on him, Halloran," said the friendly voice of McCorkery in his mind, and the brown face, softer than he remembered it, came up clearly behind his closed eyes.

"Ah, well, it's like myself beginning all over again in him," said Mr. Halloran, aloud, "besides my own job that I might have had all this time if I'd just come to see you sooner."

"True for you," said McCorkery in a merry County Mayo voice, inside Mr. Halloran's head, "and now let's drink to the gay future for old times' sake and be damned to Lacey Mahaffy." Mr. Halloran reached for the bottle but it skipped sideways, rolled out of reach like a creature, and exploded at his feet. When he stood up the chair fell backward from under him. He leaned on the table and it folded up under his hands like cardboard.

"Wait now, take it easy," said McCorkery, and there he was, real enough, holding Mr. Halloran braced on the one side, motioning with his hand to the boys in the back room, who came out quietly and took hold of Mr. Halloran, some of them, on the other side. Their faces were all Irish, but not an Irishman Mr. Halloran knew in the lot, and he did not like any face he saw. "Let me be," he said with dignity, "I came here to see Gerald J. McCorkery, a friend of mine from old times, and let not a thug among you lay a finger upon me."

"Come on, Big Shot," said one of the younger men, in a voice like a file grating, "come on now, it's time to go."

"That's a fine low lot you've picked to run with, McCorkery," said Mr. Halloran, bracing his heels against the slow weight they put upon him toward the door, "I wouldn't trust one of them far as I could throw him by the tail."

"All right, all right, Halloran," said McCorkery. "Come on with me. Lay off him, Finnegan." He was leaning over Mr. Halloran and pressing something into his right hand. It was money, a neat little roll of it, good smooth thick money, no other feel like it in the world, you couldn't mistake it. Ah, he'd have an argument to show Lacey Mahaffy would knock her off her feet. Honest money with a job to back it up. "You'll stand by your given word, McCorkery, as ever?" he asked, peering into the rock-colored face above him, his feet weaving a dance under him, his heart ready to break with gratitude.

"Ah, sure, sure," said McCorkery in a loud hearty voice with a kind of curse in it. "Crisakes, get on with him, do." Mr. Halloran found himself eased into a taxicab at the curb, with McCorkery speaking to the driver and giving him money. "So long, Big Shot," said one of the thug faces, and the taxicab door thumped to. Mr. Halloran bobbed about on the seat for a while, trying to think. He leaned forward and spoke to the driver. "Take me to my friend Gerald J. McCorkery's house," he said, "I've got important business. Don't pay any attention to what he said. Take me to his house."

"Yeah?" said the driver, without turning his head. "Well, here's where you get out, see? Right here." He reached back and opened the door. And sure enough, Mr. Halloran was standing on the sidewalk in front of the flat in Perry Street, alone except for the rows of garbage cans, the taxicab hooting its way around the corner, and a cop coming toward him, plainly to be seen under the street light.

"You should cast your vote for McCorkery, the poor man's friend,"

Mr. Halloran told the cop, "McCorkery's the man who will get us all off the spot. Stands by his old friends like a maniac. Got a wife named Rosie. Vote for McCorkery," said Mr. Halloran, working hard at his job, "and you'll be Chief of the Force when Halloran says the word."

"To hell with McCorkery, that stooge," said the cop, his mouth square and sour with the things he said and the things he saw and did every night on that beat. "There you are drunk again, Halloran, shame to you, with Lacey Mahaffy working her heart out over the washboard to buy your beer."

"It wasn't beer and she didn't buy it, mind you," said Mr. Halloran, "and what do you know about Lacey Mahaffy?"

"I knew her from old when I used to run errands for St. Veronica's Altar Society," said the cop, "and she was a great one, even then. Nothing good enough."

"It's the same today," said Mr. Halloran, almost sober for a moment.

"Well, go on up now and stay up till you're fit to be seen," said the cop, censoriously.

"You're Johnny Maginnis," said Mr. Halloran, "I know you well."

"You should know me by now," said the cop.

Mr. Halloran worked his way upstairs partly on his hands and knees, but once at his own door he stood up, gave a great blow on the panel with his fist, turned the knob and surged in like a wave after the door itself, holding out the money toward Mrs. Halloran, who had finished ironing and was at her mending.

She got up very slowly, her bony hand over her mouth, her eyes starting out at what she saw. "Ah, did you steal it?" she asked. "Did you kill somebody for that?" the words grated up from her throat in a dark whisper. Mr. Halloran glared back at her in fear.

"Suffering Saints, Lacey Mahaffy," he

shouted until the whole houseful could hear him, "haven't ye any mind at all that you can't see your husband has had a turn of fortune and a job and times are changed from tonight? Stealing, is it? That's for your great friends the Connollys with their religion. Connolly steals, but Halloran is an honest man with a job in the McCorkery Club, and money in pocket."

"McCorkery, is it?" said Mrs. Halloran, loudly too. "Ah, so there's the whole family, young and old, wicked and innocent, taking their bread from McCorkery, at last. Well, it's no bread of mine, I'll earn my own as I have, you can keep your dirty money to yourself, Halloran, mind you I mean it."

"Great God, woman," moaned Mr. Halloran, and he tottered from the door to the table, to the ironing board, and stood there, ready to weep with rage, "haven't you a soul even that you won't come along with your husband when he's riding to riches and glory on the Tiger's back itself, with everything for the taking and no questions asked?"

"Yes, I have a soul," cried Mrs. Halloran, clenching her fists, her hair flying. "Surely I have a soul and I'll save it yet in spite of you. . . ."

She was standing there before him in a kind of faded gingham winding sheet, with her dead hands upraised, her dead eyes blind but fixed upon him, her voice coming up hollow from the deep tomb, her throat thick with grave damp. The ghost of Lacey Mahaffy was threatening him, it came nearer, growing taller as it came, the face changing to a demon's face with a fixed glassy grin. "It's all that drink on an empty stomach," said the ghost, in a hoarse growl. Mr. Halloran fetched a yell of horror right out of his very boots, and seized the flatiron from the board. "Ah, God damn you, Lacey Mahaffy, you devil, keep away, keep away," he howled, but she advanced on air, grinning and growling. He raised the flatiron and hurled it without aiming, and the specter, whoever it was, whatever it was, sank and was gone. He did not look, but broke out of the room and was back on the sidewalk before he knew he had meant to go there. Maginnis came up at once. "Hey there now, Halloran," he said, "I mean business this time. You get back upstairs or I'll run you in. Come along now, I'll help you get there this time, and that's the last of it. On relief the way you are, and drinking your head off."

Mr. Halloran suddenly felt calm, collected; he would take Maginnis up and show him just what had happened. "I'm not on relief any more, and if you want any trouble, just call on my friend, McCorkery. He'll tell you who I am."

"McCorkery can't tell me anything about you I don't know already," said Maginnis. "Stand up there now." For Halloran wanted to go up again on his hands and knees.

"Let a man be," said Mr. Halloran, trying to sit on the cop's feet. "I killed Lacey Mahaffy at last, you'll be pleased to hear," he said, looking up into the cop's face. "It was high time and past. But I did not steal the money."

"Well, ain't that just too bad," said the cop, hauling him up under the arms. "Chees, why'n't you make a good job while you had the chance? Stand up now. Ah, hell with it, stand up or I'll sock you one."

Mr. Halloran said, "Well, you don't believe it so wait and see."

At that moment they both glanced upward and saw Mrs. Halloran coming downstairs. She was holding to the rail, and even in the speckled hall-light they could see a great lumpy clout of flesh standing out on her forehead, all colors. She stopped, and seemed not at all surprised.

"So there you are, Officer Maginnis," she said. "Bring him up."

"That's a fine welt you've got over your eye this time, Mrs. Halloran," commented Officer Maginnis, politely.

"I fell and hit my head on the ironing board," said Mrs. Halloran. "It comes of overwork and worry, day and night. A dead faint, Officer Maginnis. Watch your big feet there, you thriving, natural fool," she added to Mr. Halloran. "He's got a job now, you mightn't believe it, Officer Maginnis, but it's true. Bring him on up, and thank you."

She went ahead of them, opened the door, and led the way to the bedroom through the kitchen, turned back the covers, and Officer Maginnis dumped Mr. Halloran among the quilts and pillows. Mr. Halloran rolled over with a deep groan and shut his eyes.

"Many thanks to you, Officer Maginnis," said Mrs. Halloran.

"Don't mention it, Mrs. Halloran," said Officer Maginnis.

When the door was shut and locked, Mrs. Halloran went and dipped a large bath towel under the kitchen tap. She wrung it out and tied several good hard knots in one end and tried it out with a whack on the edge of the table. She walked in and stood over the bed and brought the knotted towel down in Mr. Halloran's face with all her might. He stirred and muttered, ill at ease. "That's for the flatiron, Halloran," she told him, in a cautious voice as if she were talking to herself, and whack, down came the towel again. "That's for the half-dollar," she said, and whack, "that's for your drunkenness—" Her arm swung around regularly, ending with a heavy thud on the face that was beginning to squirm, gasp, lift itself from the pillow and fall back again, in a puzzled kind of torment. "For your sock feet," Mrs. Halloran told him, whack, "and your laziness, and this is for missing Mass and"—here she swung half a dozen times—"that is for your daughter and your part in her...."

She stood back breathless, the lump on her forehead burning in its furious colors. When Mr. Halloran attempted to rise, shielding his head with his arms, she gave him a push and he fell back again. "Stay there and don't give me a word," said Mrs. Halloran. He pulled the pillow over his face and subsided again, this time for good.

Mrs. Halloran moved about very deliberately. She tied the wet towel around her head, the knotted end hanging over her shoulder. Her hand ran into her apron pocket and came out again with the money. There was a five-dollar bill with three one-dollar bills rolled in it, and the half-dollar she had thought spent long since. "A poor start, but something," she said, and opened the cupboard door with a long key. Reaching in, she pulled a loosely fitted board out of the wall, and removed a black-painted metal box. She unlocked this, took out one five-cent piece from a welter of notes and coins. She then placed the new money in the box, locked it, put it away, replaced the board, shut the cupboard door and locked that. She went out to the telephone, dropped the nickel in the slot, asked for a number, and waited.

"Is that you, Maggie? Well, are things any better with you now? I'm glad to hear it. It's late to be calling, but there's news about your father. No, no, nothing of that kind, he's got a job. I said a *job*. Yes, at last, after all my urging him onward. . . . I've got him bedded down to sleep it off so he'll be ready for work tomorrow. . . . Yes, it's political work, toward the election time, with Gerald McCorkery. But that's no harm, getting votes and all, he'll be in the open air and it doesn't mean I'll have to associate with low people, now or ever. It's clean enough work, with good pay; if it's not just what I prayed for, still it beats nothing, Maggie. After all my trying . . . it's like a miracle. You see what can be done with patience and doing your duty, Maggie. Now mind you do as well by your own husband."

John Collier (1901–)
THUS I REFUTE BEELZY

"There goes the tea bell," said Mrs. Carter. "I hope Simon hears it."

They looked out from the window of the drawing-room. The long garden, agreeably neglected, ended in a waste plot. Here a little summer-house was passing close by beauty on its way to complete decay. This was Simon's retreat: it was almost completely screened by the tangled branches of the apple tree and the pear tree, planted too close together, as they always are in suburban gardens. They caught a glimpse of him now and then, as he strutted up and down, mouthing and gesticulating, performing all the solemn mumbo-jumbo of small boys who spend long afternoons at the forgotten ends of long gardens.

"There he is, bless him," said Betty.

"Playing his game," said Mrs. Carter.

"He won't play with the other children any more. And if I go down there—the temper! And comes in tired out."

"He doesn't have his sleep in the afternoons?" asked Betty.

"You know what Big Simon's ideas are," said Mrs. Carter. " 'Let him choose for himself,' he says. That's what he chooses, and he comes in as white as a sheet."

"Look. He's heard the bell," said Betty. The expression was justified, though the bell had ceased ringing a full minute ago. Small Simon stopped in his parade exactly as if its tinny dingle had at that moment reached his ear. They watched him perform certain ritual sweeps and scratchings with his little stick, and come lagging over the hot and flaggy grass towards the house.

Mrs. Carter led the way down to the play-room, or garden-room, which was also the tea-room for hot days. It had been the huge scullery of this tall Georgian house. Now the walls were cream-washed, there was coarse blue net in the windows, canvas-covered armchairs on the stone floor, and a reproduction of Van Gogh's *Sunflowers* over the mantelpiece.

Small Simon came drifting in, and accorded Betty a perfunctory greeting. His face was an almost perfect triangle, pointed at the chin, and he was paler than he should have been. "The little elf-child!" cried Betty.

Simon looked at her. "No," said he.

At that moment the door opened, and Mr. Carter came in, rubbing his hands. He was a dentist, and washed them before and after everything he did. "You!" said his wife. "Home already!"

"Not unwelcome, I hope," said Mr. Carter, nodding to Betty. "Two people cancelled their appointments: I decided to come home. I said, I hope I am not unwelcome."

"Silly!" said his wife. "Of course not."

"Small Simon, are you sorry to see me at tea with you?"

"No, Daddy."

"No, what?"

"No, Big Simon."

"That's right. Big Simon and Small Simon. That sounds more like friends, doesn't it? At one time little boys had to call their father 'sir!' If they forgot—a good spanking. On the bottom, Small Simon! On the bottom!" said Mr. Carter, washing his hands once more with his invisible soap and water.

The little boy turned crimson with shame or rage.

"But now, you see," said Betty, to help, "you can call your father whatever you like."

"And what," asked Mr. Carter, "has Small Simon been doing this afternoon? While Big Simon has been at work."

"Nothing," muttered his son.

"Then you have been bored," said Mr. Carter. "Learn from experience, Small Simon. Tomorrow, do something amusing, and you will not be bored. I want him to learn from experience, Betty. That is my way, the new way."

"I have learned," the boy said, speaking like an old, tired man, as little boys often do.

"It would hardly seem so," said Mr. Carter, "if you sit on your behind all the afternoon, doing nothing. Had *my* father caught me doing nothing, I should not have sat very comfortably."

"He played," said Mrs. Carter.

"A bit," said the boy, shifting on his chair.

"Too much," said Mrs. Carter. "He comes in all nervy and dazed. He ought to have his rest."

"He is six," said her husband. "He is a reasonable being. He must choose for himself. But what game is this, Small Simon, that is worth getting nervy and dazed over? There are very few games as good as all that."

"It's nothing," said the boy.

"Oh, come," said his father. "We are friends, are we not? You can tell me. I was a Small Simon once, just like you, and played the same games you play. Of course there were no aeroplanes in those days. With whom do you play this fine game? Come on, we must all answer civil questions, or the world would never go round. With whom do you play?"

"Mr. Beelzy," said the boy, unable to resist.

"Mr. Beelzy?" said the father, raising his eyebrows inquiringly at his wife.

"It's a game he makes up," said she.

"Not makes up!" cried the boy. "Fool!"

"That is telling stories," said his mother. "And rude as well. We had better talk of something different."

"No wonder he is rude," said Mr. Carter, "if you say he tells lies, and then insist on changing the subject. He tells you his fantasy: you implant a guilt feeling. What can you expect? A defence mechanism. Then you get a real lie."

"Like in *These Three*," said Betty. "Only different, of course. *She* was an unblushing little liar."

"I would have made her blush," said Mr. Carter, "in the proper part of her anatomy. But Small Simon is in the fantasy stage. Are you not, Small Simon? You just make things up."

"No, I don't," said the boy.

"You do," said the father. "And because you do, it is not too late to reason with you. There is no harm in a fantasy, old chap. There is no harm in a bit of make-believe. Only you have to know the difference between day dreams and real things, or your brain will never grow. It will never be the brain of a Big Simon. So come on. Let us hear about this Mr. Beelzy of yours. Come on. What is he like?"

"He isn't like anything," said the boy.

"Like nothing on earth?" said his father. "That's a terrible fellow."

"I'm not frightened of him," said the child, smiling. "Not a bit."

"I should hope not," said his father. "If you were, you would be frightening yourself. I am always telling people, older people than you are, that they are just frightening themselves. Is he a funny man? Is he a giant?"

"Sometimes he is," said the little boy.

"Sometimes one thing, sometimes another," said his father. "Sounds pretty vague. Why can't you tell us just what he's like?"

"I love him," said the small boy. "He loves me."

"That's a big word," said Mr. Carter. "That might be better kept for real things, like Big Simon and Small Simon."

"He is real," said the boy, passionately, "He's not a fool. He's real."

"Listen," said the father. "When you go down the garden there's nobody there. Is there?"

"No," said the boy.

"Then you think of him, inside your head, and he comes."

"No," said Small Simon. "I have to do something with my stick."

"That doesn't matter."

"Yes, it does."

"Small Simon, you are being obstinate," said Mr. Carter. "I am trying to explain something to you. I have been longer in the world than you have, so naturally I am older and wiser. I am explaining that Mr. Beelzy is a fantasy of yours. Do you hear? Do you understand?"

"Yes, Daddy."

"He is a game. He is a let's-pretend."

The little boy looked down at his plate, smiling resignedly.

"I hope you are listening to me," said his father. "All you have to do is to say, 'I have been playing a game of let's-pretend. With someone I make up, called Mr. Beelzy.' Then no one will say you tell lies, and you will know the difference between dreams and reality. Mr. Beelzy is a day dream."

The little boy still stared at his plate.

"He is sometimes there and sometimes not there," pursued Mr. Carter. "Sometimes he's like one thing, sometimes another. You can't really see him. Not as you see me. I am real. You can't touch him. You can touch me. I can touch you." Mr. Carter stretched out his big, white, dentist's hand, and took his little son by the shoulder. He stopped speaking for a moment and tightened his hand. The little boy sank his head still lower.

"Now you know the difference," said Mr. Carter, "between a pretend and a real thing. You and I are one thing; he is another. Which is the pretend? Come on. Answer me. Which is the pretend?"

"Big Simon and Small Simon," said the little boy.

"Don't!" cried Betty, and at once put her hand over her mouth, for why should a visitor cry "Don't!" when a father is explaining things in a scientific and modern way?

"Well, my boy," said Mr. Carter, "I have said you must be allowed to learn from experience. Go upstairs. Right up to your room. You shall learn whether it is better to reason, or to be perverse and obstinate. Go up. I shall follow you."

"You are not going to beat the child?" cried Mrs. Carter.

"No," said the little boy. "Mr. Beelzy won't let him."

"Go on up with you!" shouted his father.

Small Simon stopped at the door. "He said he wouldn't let anyone hurt me," he whimpered. "He said he'd come like a lion with wings on, and eat them up."

"You'll learn how real he is!" shouted his father after him. "If you can't learn it at one end, you shall learn it at the other. I'll have your breeches down. I shall finish my cup of tea first, however," said he to the two women.

Neither of them spoke. Mr. Carter finished his tea, and unhurriedly left the room, washing his hands with his invisible soap and water.

Mrs. Carter said nothing. Betty could think of nothing to say. She wanted to be talking: she was afraid of what they might hear.

Suddenly it came. It seemed to tear the air apart. "Good God!" she cried "What was that? He's hurt him." She sprang out of her chair, her silly eyes flashing behind her glasses. "I'm going up there!" she cried, trembling.

"Yes, let us go up," said Mrs. Carter. "Let us go up. That was not Small Simon."

It was on the second-floor landing that they found the shoe, with the man's foot still in it, like that last morsel of a mouse which sometimes falls from the jaws of a hasty cat.

"We are getting to the bottom of it."

Graham Greene (1904–   )

THE BASEMENT ROOM

1

When the front door had shut them out and the butler Baines had turned back into the dark heavy hall, Philip began to live. He stood in front of the nursery door, listening until he heard the engine of the taxi die out along the street. His parents were gone for a fortnight's holiday; he was "between nurses," one dismissed and the other not arrived; he was alone in the great Belgravia house with Baines and Mrs. Baines.

He could go anywhere, even through the green baize door to the pantry or down the stairs to the basement living-room. He felt a stranger in his home because he could go into any room and all the rooms were empty.

You could only guess who had once occupied them: the rack of pipes in the smoking-room beside the elephant tusks, the carved wood tobacco jar; in the bedroom the pink hangings and pale perfumes and the three-quarter finished jars of cream which Mrs. Baines had not yet cleared away; the high glaze on the never-opened piano in the drawing-room, the china clock, the silly little tables and the silver: but here Mrs. Baines was already busy, pulling down the curtains, covering the chairs in dust-sheets.

"Be off out of here, Master Philip," and she looked at him with her hateful peevish eyes, while she moved round, getting everything in order, meticulous and loveless and doing her duty.

Philip Lane went downstairs and pushed at the baize door; he looked into the pantry, but Baines was not there, then he set foot for the first time on the stairs to the basement. Again he had the sense: this is life. All his seven nursery years vibrated with the strange, the new experience. His crowded busy brain was like a city which feels the earth tremble at a distant earthquake shock. He was apprehensive, but he was happier than he had ever been. Everything was more important than before.

Baines was reading a newspaper in his shirtsleeves. He said: "Come in, Phil, and make yourself at home. Wait a moment and I'll do the honours," and going to a white cleaned cupboard he brought out a bottle of ginger-beer and half a Dundee cake. "Half-past eleven in the morning," Baines said. "It's opening time, my boy," and he cut the cake and poured out the ginger-beer. He was more genial than Philip had ever known him, more at his ease, a man in his own home.

"Shall I call Mrs. Baines?" Philip asked, and he was glad when Baines said no. She was busy. She liked to be busy, so why interfere with her pleasure?

"A spot of drink at half-past eleven," Baines said, pouring himself out a glass of ginger-beer, "gives an appetite for chop and does no man any harm."

"A chop?" Philip asked.

"Old Coasters," Baines said, "call all food chop."

"But it's not a chop?"

"Well, it might be, you know, cooked with palm oil. And then some paw-paw to follow."

Philip looked out of the basement window at the dry stone yard, the ash-can and the legs going up and down beyond the railings.

"Was it hot there?"

"Ah, you never felt such heat. Not a nice heat, mind, like you get in the park on a day like this. Wet," Baines said, "corruption." He cut himself a slice of cake. "Smelling of rot," Baines said, rolling his eyes round the small basement room, from clean cupboard to clean cupboard, the sense of bare-ness, of nowhere to hide a man's se-crets. With an air of regret for some-thing lost he took a long draught of ginger-beer.

"Why did father live out there?"

"It was his job," Baines said, "same as this is mine now. And it was mine then too. It was a man's job. You wouldn't believe it now, but I've had forty niggers under me, doing what I told them to."

"Why did you leave?"

"I married Mrs. Baines."

Philip took the slice of Dundee cake in his hand and munched it round the room. He felt very old, independent and judicial; he was aware that Baines was talking to him as man to man. He never called him Master Philip as Mrs. Baines did, who was servile when she was not authoritative.

Baines had seen the world; he had seen beyond the railings, beyond the tired legs of typists, the Pimlico parade to and from Victoria. He sat there over his ginger pop with the resigned dignity of an exile; Baines didn't complain; he had chosen his fate; and if his fate was Mrs. Baines he had only himself to blame.

But today, because the house was almost empty and Mrs. Baines was up-stairs and there was nothing to do, he allowed himself a little acidity.

"I'd go back tomorrow if I had the chance."

"Did you ever shoot a nigger?"

"I never had any call to shoot," Baines said. "Of course I carried a gun. But you didn't need to treat them bad. That just made them stupid. Why," Baines said, bowing his thin grey hair with embarrassment over the ginger pop, "I loved some of those damned niggers. I couldn't help loving them. There they'd be, laughing, holding hands; they liked to touch each other; it made them feel fine to know the other fellow was round.

"It didn't mean anything we could understand; two of them would go about all day without loosing hold, grown men; but it wasn't love; it didn't mean anything we could understand."

"Eating between meals," Mrs. Baines said. "What would your mother say, Master Philip?"

She came down the steep stairs to the basement, her hands full of pots of cream and salve, tubes of grease and paste. "You oughtn't to encourage him, Baines," she said, sitting down in a wick-er armchair and screwing up her small ill-humoured eyes at the Coty lipstick, Pond's cream, the Leichner rouge and Cyclax powder and Elizabeth Arden astringent.

She threw them one by one into the wastepaper basket. She saved only the cold cream. "Telling the boy stories," she said. "Go along to the nursery, Master Philip, while I get lunch."

Philip climbed the stairs to the baize door. He heard Mrs. Baines's voice like the voice in a nightmare when the small Price light has gutted in the saucer and the curtains move; it was sharp and shrill and full of malice, louder than people ought to speak, exposed.

"Sick to death of your ways, Baines, spoiling the boy. Time you did some work about the house," but he couldn't hear what Baines said in reply. He pushed open the baize door, came up like a small earth animal in his grey flannel shorts into a wash of sunlight on a parquet floor, the gleam of mirrors dusted and polished and beautified by Mrs. Baines.

Something broke downstairs, and Philip sadly mounted the stairs to the nursery. He pitied Baines; it occurred to him how happily they could live together in the empty house if Mrs. Baines were called away. He didn't want to play with his Meccano sets; he wouldn't take out his train or his soldiers; he sat at the table with his chin on his hands: this is life; and suddenly he felt responsible for Baines, as if he were the master of the house and Baines an ageing servant who deserved to be cared for. There was not much one could do; he decided at least to be good.

He was not surprised when Mrs. Baines was agreeable at lunch; he was used to her changes. Now it was "another helping of meat, Master Philip," or "Master Philip, a little more of this nice pudding." It was a pudding he liked, Queen's pudding with a perfect meringue, but he wouldn't eat a second helping lest she might count that a victory. She was the kind of woman who thought that any injustice could be counterbalanced by something good to eat.

She was sour, but she liked making sweet things; one never had to complain of a lack of jam or plums; she ate well herself and added soft sugar to the meringue and the strawberry jam. The half light through the basement window set the motes moving above her pale hair like dust as she sifted the sugar, and Baines crouched over his plate saying nothing.

Again Philip felt responsibility. Baines had looked forward to this, and Baines was disappointed: everything was being spoilt. The sensation of disappointment was one which Philip could share; knowing nothing of love or jealousy or passion, he could understand better than anyone this grief, something hoped for not happening,

something promised not fulfilled, something exciting turning dull. "Baines," he said, "will you take me for a walk this afternoon?"

"No," Mrs. Baines said, "no. That he won't. Not with all the silver to clean."

"There's a fortnight to do it in," Baines said.

"Work first, pleasure afterwards." Mrs. Baines helped herself to some more meringue.

Baines suddenly put down his spoon and fork and pushed his plate away, "Blast," he said.

"Temper," Mrs. Baines said softly, "temper. Don't you go breaking any more things, Baines, and I won't have you swearing in front of the boy. Master Philip, if you've finished you can get down." She skinned the rest of the meringue off the pudding.

"I want to go for a walk," Philip said.

"You'll go and have a rest."

"I will go for a walk."

"Master Philip," Mrs. Baines said. She got up from the table, leaving her meringue unfinished, and came towards him, thin, menacing, dusty in the basement room. "Master Philip, you do as you're told." She took him by the arm and squeezed it gently; she watched him with a joyless passionate glitter and above her head the feet of the typists trudged back to the Victoria offices after the lunch interval.

"Why shouldn't I go for a walk?" But he weakened; he was scared and ashamed of being scared. This was life; a strange passion he couldn't understand moving in the basement room. He saw a small pile of broken glass swept into a corner by the wastepaper basket. He looked to Baines for help and only intercepted hate; and sad hopeless hate of something behind bars.

"Why shouldn't I?" he repeated.

"Master Philip," Mrs. Baines said, "you've got to do as you're told. You mustn't think just because your father's away there's nobody here to—"

"You wouldn't dare," Philip cried,

and was startled by Baines's low interjection, "There's nothing she wouldn't dare."

"I hate you," Philip said to Mrs. Baines. He pulled away from her and ran to the door, but she was there before him; she was old, but she was quick.

"Master Philip," she said, "you'll say you're sorry." She stood in front of the door quivering with excitement. "What would your father do if he heard you say that?"

She put a hand out to seize him, dry and white with constant soda, the nails cut to the quick, but he backed away and put the table between them, and suddenly to his surprise she smiled; she became again as servile as she had been arrogant. "Get along with you, Master Philip," she said with glee. "I see I'm going to have my hands full till your father and mother come back."

She left the door unguarded and when he passed her she slapped him playfully. "I've got too much to do today to trouble about you. I haven't covered half the chairs," and suddenly even the upper part of the house became unbearable to him as he thought of Mrs. Baines moving round shrouding the sofas, laying out the dust-sheets.

So he wouldn't go upstairs to get his cap but walked straight out across the shining hall into the street, and again, as he looked this way and looked that way, it was life he was in the middle of.

2

It was the pink sugar cakes in the window on a paper doily, the ham, the slab of mauve sausage, the wasps driving like small torpedoes across the pane that caught Philip's attention. His feet were tired by pavements; he had been afraid to cross the road, had simply walked first in one direction, then in the other. He was nearly home now; the square was at the end of the street; this was a shabby outpost of Pimlico,

and he smudged the pane with his nose, looking for sweets, and saw between the cakes and ham a different Baines. He hardly recognized the bulbous eyes, the bald forehead. It was a happy, bold and buccaneering Baines, even though it was, when you looked closer, a desperate Baines.

Philip had never seen the girl. He remembered Baines had a niece and he thought that this might be her. She was thin and drawn, and she wore a white mackintosh; she meant nothing to Philip; she belonged to a world about which he knew nothing at all. He couldn't make up stories about her, as he could make them up about withered Sir Hubert Reed, the Permanent Secretary, about Mrs. Wince-Dudley who came up once a year from Penstanley in Suffolk with a green umbrella and an enormous black handbag, as he could make them up about the upper servants in all the houses where he went to tea and games. She just didn't belong; he thought of mermaids and Undine; but she didn't belong there either, nor to the adventures of Emil, nor to the Bastables. She sat there looking at an iced pink cake in the detachment and mystery of the completely disinherited, looking at the half-used pots of powder which Baines had set out on the marble-topped table between them.

Baines was urging, hoping, entreating, commanding, and the girl looked at the tea and the china pots and cried. Baines passed his handkerchief across the table, but she wouldn't wipe her eyes; she screwed it in her palm and let the tears run down, wouldn't do anything, wouldn't speak, would only put up a silent despairing resistance to what she dreaded and wanted and refused to listen to at any price. The two brains battled over the tea-cups loving each other, and there came to Philip outside, beyond the ham and wasps and dusty Pimlico pane, a confused indication of the struggle.

He was inquisitive and he didn't understand and he wanted to know. He went and stood in the doorway to see better, he was less sheltered than he had ever been; other people's lives for the first time touched and pressed and moulded. He would never escape that scene. In a week he had forgotten it, but it conditioned his career, the long austerity of his life; when he was dying he said: "Who is she?"

Baines had won; he was cocky and the girl was happy. She wiped her face, she opened a pot of powder, and their fingers touched across the table. It occurred to Philip that it would be amusing to imitate Mrs. Baines's voice and call "Baines" to him from the door.

It shrivelled them; you couldn't describe it in any other way; it made them smaller, they weren't happy any more and they weren't bold. Baines was the first to recover and trace the voice, but that didn't make things as they were. The sawdust was spilled out of the afternoon; nothing you did could mend it, and Philip was scared. "I didn't mean. . ." He wanted to say that he loved Baines, that he had only wanted to laugh at Mrs. Baines. But he had discovered that you couldn't laugh at Mrs. Baines. She wasn't Sir Hubert Reed, who used steel nibs and carried a pen-wiper in his pocket; she wasn't Mrs. Wince-Dudley; she was darkness when the night-light went out in a draught; she was the frozen blocks of earth he had seen one winter in a graveyard when someone said, "They need an electric drill"; she was the flowers gone bad and smelling in the little closet room at Penstanley. There was nothing to laugh about. You had to endure her when she was there and forget about her quickly when she was away, suppress the thought of her, ram it down deep.

Baines said, "It's only Phil," beckoned him in and gave him the pink iced cake the girl hadn't eaten, but the afternoon was broken, the cake was like dry bread in the throat. The girl left them at once; she even forgot to take the powder; like a small blunt icicle in her white mackintosh she stood in the doorway with her back to them, then melted into the afternoon.

"Who is she?" Philip asked. "Is she your niece?"

"Oh, yes," Baines said, "that's who she is; she's my niece," and poured the last drops of water on to the coarse black leaves in the teapot.

"May as well have another cup," Baines said.

"The cup that cheers," he said hopelessly, watching the bitter black fluid drain out of the spout.

"Have a glass of ginger pop, Phil?"

"I'm sorry. I'm sorry, Baines."

"It's not your fault, Phil. Why, I could believe it wasn't you at all, but her. She creeps in everywhere." He fished two leaves out of his cup and laid them on the back of his hand, a thin soft flake and a hard stalk. He beat them with his hand: "Today," and the stalk detached itself, "tomorrow, Wednesday, Thursday, Friday, Saturday, Sunday," but the flake wouldn't come, stayed where it was, drying under his blows, with a resistance you wouldn't believe it to possess. "The tough one wins," Baines said.

He got up and paid the bill and out they went into the street. Baines said, "I don't ask you to say what isn't true. But you needn't mention to Mrs. Baines you met us here."

"Of course not," Philip said, and catching something of Sir Hubert Reed's manner, "I understand, Baines." But he didn't understand a thing; he was caught up in other people's darkness.

"It was stupid," Baines said. "So near home, but I hadn't time to think, you see. I'd got to see her."

"Of course, Baines."

"I haven't time to spare," Baines said. "I'm not young. I've got to see that she's all right."

"Of course you have, Baines."

"Mrs. Baines will get it out of you if she can."

"You can trust me, Baines," Philip

said in a dry important Reed voice; and then, "Look out. She's at the window watching." And there indeed she was, looking up at them, between the lace curtains, from the basement room, speculating. "Need we go in, Baines?" Philip asked, cold lying heavy on his stomach like too much pudding; he clutched Baines's arm.

"Careful," Baines said softly, "careful."

"But need we go in, Baines? It's early. Take me for a walk in the park."

"Better not."

"But I'm frightened, Baines."

"You haven't any cause," Baines said. "Nothing's going to hurt you. You just run along upstairs to the nursery. I'll go down by the area and talk to Mrs. Baines." But even he stood hesitating at the top of the stone steps pretending not to see her, where she watched between the curtains. "In at the front door, Phil, and up the stairs."

Philip didn't linger in the hall; he ran, slithering on the parquet Mrs. Baines had polished, to the stairs. Through the drawing-room doorway on the first floor he saw the draped chairs; even the china clock on the mantel was covered like a canary's cage; as he passed it, it chimed the hour, muffled and secret under the duster. On the nursery table he found his supper laid out: a glass of milk and a piece of bread and butter, a sweet biscuit, and a little cold Queen's pudding without the meringue. He had no appetite; he strained his ears for Mrs. Baines's coming, for the sound of voices, but the basement held its secrets; the green baize door shut off that world. He drank the milk and ate the biscuit, but he didn't touch the rest, and presently he could hear the soft precise footfalls of Mrs. Baines on the stairs: she was a good servant, she walked softly; she was a determined woman, she walked precisely.

But she wasn't angry when she came in; she was ingratiating as she opened the night nursery door—"Did you have a good walk, Master Philip?"—pulled

down the blinds, laid out his pyjamas, came back to clear his supper. "I'm glad Baines found you. Your mother wouldn't have liked your being out alone." She examined the tray. "Not much appetite, have you, Master Philip? Why don't you try a little of this nice pudding? I'll bring you up some more jam for it."

"No, no, thank you, Mrs. Baines," Philip said.

"You ought to eat more," Mrs. Baines said. She sniffed round the room like a dog. "You didn't take any pots out of the wastepaper basket in the kitchen, did you, Master Philip?"

"No," Philip said.

"Of course you wouldn't. I just wanted to make sure." She patted his shoulder and her fingers flashed to his lapel; she picked off a tiny crumb of pink sugar. "Oh, Master Philip," she said, "that's why you haven't any appetite. You've been buying sweet cakes. That's not what your pocket money's for."

"But I didn't," Philip said. "I didn't."

She tasted the sugar with the tip of her tongue.

"Don't tell lies to me, Master Philip. I won't stand for it any more than your father would."

"I didn't, I didn't," Philip said. "They gave it me. I mean Baines," but she had pounced on the word "they." She had got what she wanted; there was no doubt about that, even when you didn't know what it was she wanted. Philip was angry and miserable and disappointed because he hadn't kept Baines's secret. Baines oughtn't to have trusted him; grown-up people should keep their own secrets, and yet here was Mrs. Baines immediately entrusting him with another.

"Let me tickle your palm and see if you can keep a secret." But he put his hand behind him; he wouldn't be touched. "It's a secret between us, Master Philip, that I know all about them. I suppose she was having tea with him," she speculated.

"Why shouldn't she?" he said, the responsibility for Baines weighing on his spirit, the idea that he had got to keep her secret when he hadn't kept Baines's making him miserable with the unfairness of life. "She was nice."

"She was nice, was she?" Mrs. Baines said in a bitter voice he wasn't used to.

"And she's his niece."

"So that's what he said," Mrs. Baines struck softly back at him like the clock under the duster. She tried to be jocular. "The old scoundrel. Don't you tell him I know, Master Philip." She stood very still between the table and the door, thinking very hard, planning something. "Promise you won't tell. I'll give you that Meccano set, Master Philip. . . ."

He turned his back on her; he wouldn't promise, but he wouldn't tell. He would have nothing to do with their secrets, the responsibilities they were determined to lay on him. He was only anxious to forget. He had received already a larger dose of life than he had bargained for, and he was scared. "A 2A Meccano set, Master Philip." He never opened his Meccano set again, never built anything, never created anything, died, the old dilettante, sixty years later with nothing to show rather than preserve the memory of Mrs. Baines's malicious voice saying good night, her soft determined footfalls on the stairs to the basement, going down, going down.

3

The sun poured in between the curtains and Baines was beating a tattoo on the water-can. "Glory, glory," Baines said. He sat down on the end of the bed and said, "I beg to announce that Mrs. Baines has been called away. Her mother's dying. She won't be back till tomorrow."

"Why did you wake me up so early?" Philip said. He watched Baines with uneasiness; he wasn't going to be drawn in; he'd learnt his lesson. It wasn't right for a man of Baines's age to be so merry. It made a grown person human in the same way that you were human. For if a grown-up could behave so childishly, you were liable to find yourself in their world. It was enough that it came at you in dreams: the witch at the corner, the man with a knife. So "It's very early," he complained, even though he loved Baines, even though he couldn't help being glad that Baines was happy. He was divided by the fear and the attraction of life.

"I want to make this a long day," Baines said. "This is the best time." He pulled the curtains back. "It's a bit misty. The cat's been out all night. There she is, sniffing round the area. They haven't taken in any milk at 59. Emma's shaking out the mats at 63." He said, "This was what I used to think about on the Coast: somebody shaking mats and the cat coming home. I can see it today," Baines said, "just as if I was still in Africa. Most days you don't notice what you've got. It's a good life if you don't weaken." He put a penny on the washstand. "When you've dressed, Phil, run and get a *Mail* from the barrow at the corner. I'll be cooking the sausages."

"Sausages?"

"Sausages," Baines said. "We're going to celebrate today. A fair bust." He celebrated at breakfast, reckless, cracking jokes, unaccountably merry and nervous. It was going to be a long, long day, he kept on coming back to that: for years he had waited for a long day, he had sweated in the damp Coast heat, changed shirts, gone down with fever, lain between the blankets and sweated, all in the hope of this long day, that cat sniffing round the area, a bit of mist, the mats beaten at 63. He propped the *Mail* in front of the coffee-pot and read pieces aloud. He said, "Cora Down's been married for the fourth time." He was amused, but it wasn't his idea of a long day. His long day was the Park, watching the riders in the Row, seeing Sir Arthur Stillwater pass beyond the rails ("He dined with us once in Bo; up from Freetown; he was governor there"), lunch at the Corner House for Philip's sake (he'd have preferred himself a glass of stout and some oysters at the York bar), the Zoo, the long bus ride home in the last summer light: the leaves in the Green Park were beginning to turn and the motors nuzzled out of Berkeley Street with the low sun gently glowing on their wind-screens. Baines envied no one, not Cora Down, or Sir Arthur Stillwater, or Lord Sandale, who came out on to the steps of the Army and Navy and then went back again because he hadn't got anything to do and might as well look at another paper. "I said don't let me see you touch that black again." Baines had led a man's life; everyone on top of the bus pricked their ears when he told Philip all about it.

"Would you have shot him?" Philip asked, and Baines put his head back and tilted his dark respectable man-servant's hat to a better angle as the bus swerved round the artillery memorial.

"I wouldn't have thought twice about it. I'd have shot to kill," he boasted, and the bowed figure went by, the steel helmet, the heavy cloak, the downturned rifle and the folded hands.

"Have you got the revolver?"

"Of course I've got it," Baines said. "Don't I need it with all the burglaries there've been?" This was the Baines whom Philip loved: not Baines singing and carefree, but Baines responsible, Baines behind barriers, living his man's life.

All the buses streamed out from Victoria like a convoy of aeroplanes to bring Baines home with honour. "Forty blacks under me," and there waiting near the area steps was the proper conventional reward, love at lighting-up time.

"It's your niece," Philip said, recognizing the white mackintosh, but not the

happy sleepy face. She frightened him like an unlucky number; he nearly told Baines what Mrs. Baines had said; but he didn't want to bother, he wanted to leave things alone.

"Why, so it is," Baines said. "I shouldn't wonder if she was going to have a bite of supper with us." But he said they'd play a game, pretend they didn't know her, slip down the area steps, "and here," Baines said, "we are," lay the table, put out the cold sausages, a bottle of beer, a bottle of ginger pop, a flagon of harvest burgundy. "Everyone his own drink," Baines said. "Run upstairs, Phil, and see if there's been a post."

Philip didn't like the empty house at dusk before the lights went on. He hurried. He wanted to be back with Baines. The hall lay there in quiet and shadow prepared to show him something he didn't want to see. Some letters rustled down and someone knocked. "Open in the name of the Republic." The tumbrils rolled, the head bobbed in the bloody basket. Knock, knock, and the postman's footsteps going away. Philip gathered the letters. The slit in the door was like the grating in a jeweller's window. He remembered the policeman he had seen peer through. He had said to his nurse, "What's he doing?" and when she said, "He's seeing if everything's all right," his brain immediately filled with images of all that might be wrong. He ran to the baize door and the stairs. The girl was already there and Baines was kissing her. She leant breathless against the dresser.

"This is Emmy, Phil."

"There's a letter for you, Baines."

"Emmy," Baines said, "it's from her." But he wouldn't open it. "You bet she's coming back."

"We'll have supper, anyway," Emmy said. "She can't harm that."

"You don't know her," Baines said. "Nothing's safe. Damn it," he said, "I was a man once," and he opened the letter.

"Can I start?" Philip asked, but Baines didn't hear; he presented in his stillness and attention an example of the importance grown-up people attached to the written word: you had to write your thanks, not wait and speak them, as if letters couldn't lie. But Philip knew better than that, sprawling his thanks across a page to Aunt Alice who had given him a doll he was too old for. Letters could lie all right, but they made the lie permanent: they lay as evidence against you; they made you meaner than the spoken word.

"She's not coming back till tomorrow night," Baines said. He opened the bottles, he pulled up the chairs, he kissed Emmy again against the dresser.

"You oughtn't to," Emmy said, "with the boy here."

"He's got to learn," Baines said, "like the rest of us," and he helped Philip to three sausages. He only took one himself; he said he wasn't hungry; but when Emmy said she wasn't hungry either he stood over her and made her eat. He was timid and rough with her; he made her drink the harvest burgundy because he said she needed building up; he wouldn't take no for an answer, but when he touched her his hands were light and clumsy too, as if he were afraid to damage something delicate and didn't know how to handle anything so light.

"This is better than milk and biscuits, eh?"

"Yes," Philip said, but he was scared, scared for Baines as much as for himself. He couldn't help wondering at every bite, at every draught of the ginger pop, what Mrs. Baines would say if she ever learnt of this meal; he couldn't imagine it, there was a depth of bitterness and rage in Mrs. Baines you couldn't sound. He said, "She won't be coming back tonight?" but you could tell by the way they immediately understood him that she wasn't really away at all; she was there in the basement with them, driving them to longer drinks and louder talk, biding her time for the right cutting word. Baines wasn't really happy; he was only watching happiness from close to instead of from far away.

"No," he said, "she'll not be back till late tomorrow." He couldn't keep his eyes off happiness; he'd played around as much as other men, he kept on reverting to the Coast as if to excuse himself for his innocence; he wouldn't have been so innocent if he'd lived his life in London, so innocent when it came to tenderness. "If it was you, Emmy," he said, looking at the white dresser, the scrubbed chairs, "this'd be like a home." Already the room was not quite so harsh; there was a little dust in corners, the silver needed a final polish, the morning's paper lay untidily on a chair. "You'd better go to bed, Phil; it's been a long day."

They didn't leave him to find his own way up through the dark shrouded house; they went with him, turning on lights, touching each other's fingers on the switches; floor after floor they drove the night back; they spoke softly among the covered chairs; they watched him undress, they didn't make him wash or clean his teeth, they saw him into bed and lit his night-light and left his door ajar. He could hear their voices on the stairs, friendly like the guests he heard at dinner-parties when they moved down the hall, saying good night. They belonged; wherever they were they made a home. He heard a door open and a clock strike, he heard their voices for a long while, so that he felt they were not far away and he was safe. The voices didn't dwindle, they simply went out, and he could be sure that they were still somewhere not far from him, silent together in one of the many empty rooms, growing sleepy together as he grew sleepy after the long day.

He had just time to sigh faintly with satisfaction, because this too perhaps had been life, before he slept and the inevitable terrors of sleep came round him: a man with a tricolour hat beat at the door on His Majesty's service, a bleeding head lay on the kitchen table in a basket, and the Siberian wolves crept closer. He was bound hand and foot and couldn't move; they leapt round him breathing heavily; he opened his eyes and Mrs. Baines was there, her gray untidy hair in threads over his face, her black hat askew. A loose hairpin fell on pillow and one musty thread brushed his mouth. "Where are they?" she whispered. "Where are they?"

4

Philip watched her in terror. Mrs. Baines was out of breath as if she had been searching all the empty rooms, looking under loose covers.

With her untidy grey hair and her black dress buttoned to her throat, her gloves of black cotton, she was so like the witches of his dreams that he didn't dare to speak. There was a stale smell in her breath.

"She's here," Mrs. Baines said; "you can't deny she's here." Her face was simultaneously marked with cruelty and misery; she wanted to "do things" to people, but she suffered all the time. It would have done her good to scream, but she daren't do that: it would warn them. She came ingratiatingly back to the bed where Philip lay rigid on his back and whispered, "I haven't forgotten the Meccano set. You shall have it tomorrow, Master Philip. We've got secrets together, haven't we? Just tell me where they are."

He couldn't speak. Fear held him as firmly as any nightmare. She said, "Tell Mrs. Baines, Master Philip. You love your Mrs. Baines, don't you?" That was too much; he couldn't speak; but he could move his mouth in terrified denial, wince away from her dusty image.

She whispered, coming closer to him, "Such deceit. I'll tell your father. I'll settle with you myself when I've found them. You'll smart; I'll see you smart." Then immediately she was still, listening. A board had creaked on the floor below, and a moment later, while she stooped listening above his bed, there came the whispers of two people who were happy and sleepy together after a long day. The night-light stood beside the mirror and Mrs. Baines could see bitterly there her own reflection, misery and cruelty wavering in the glass, age and dust and nothing to hope for. She sobbed without tears, a dry, breathless sound; but her cruelty was a kind of pride which kept her going; it was her best quality, she would have been merely pitiable without it. She went out of the door on tiptoe, feeling her way across the landing, going so softly down the stairs that no one behind a shut door could hear her. Then there was complete silence again; Philip could move; he raised his knees; he sat up in bed; he wanted to die. It wasn't fair, the walls were down again between his world and theirs; but this time it was something worse than merriment that the grown people made him share; a passion moved in the house he recognized but could not understand.

It wasn't fair, but he owed Baines everything: the Zoo, the ginger pop, the bus ride home. Even the supper called on his loyalty. But he was frightened; he was touching something he touched in dreams: the bleeding head, the wolves, the knock, knock, knock. Life fell on him with savagery; you couldn't blame him if he never faced it again in sixty years. He got out of bed, carefully from habit put on his bedroom slippers, and tiptoed to the door: it wasn't quite dark on the landing below because the curtains had been taken down for the cleaners and the light from the street came in through the tall windows. Mrs. Baines had her hand on the glass doorknob; she was very carefully turning it; he screamed: "Baines, Baines."

Mrs. Baines turned and saw him cowering in his pyjamas by the banister; he was helpless, more helpless even than Baines, and cruelty grew at the sight of him and drove her up the stairs. The nightmare was on him again and he couldn't move; he hadn't any more courage left for ever; he'd spent it all, had been allowed no time to let it grow, no years of gradual hardening; he couldn't even scream.

But the first cry had brought Baines out of the best spare bedroom and he moved quicker than Mrs. Baines. She hadn't reached the top of the stairs before he'd caught her round the waist. She drove her black cotton gloves at his face and he bit her hand. He hadn't time to think, he fought her savagely like a stranger, but she fought back with knowledgeable hate. She was going to teach them all and it didn't really matter whom she began with; they had all deceived her; but the old image in the glass was by her side, telling her she must be dignified, she wasn't young enough to yield her dignity; she could beat his face, but she mustn't bite; she could push, but she mustn't kick.

Age and dust and nothing to hope for were her handicaps. She went over the banisters in a flurry of black clothes and fell into the hall; she lay before the front door like a sack of coals which should have gone down the area into the basement. Philip saw; Emmy saw; she sat down suddenly in the doorway of the best spare bedroom with her eyes open as if she were too tired to stand any longer. Baines went slowly down into the hall.

It wasn't hard for Philip to escape; they'd forgotten him completely; he went down the back, the servants' stairs, because Mrs. Baines was in the hall; he didn't understand what she was doing lying there; like the startling pictures in a book no one had read to him, the things he didn't understand terrified him. The whole house had been turned over to the grown-up world; he wasn't safe in the night nursery; their passions had flooded it. The only thing he could do was to get away, by the back stair, and up through the area, and never come back. You didn't think of the cold, of the need of food and sleep; for an hour it would seem quite possible to escape from people for ever.

He was wearing pyjamas and bedroom slippers when he came up into the square, but there was no one to see him. It was that hour of the evening in a residential district when everyone is at the theatre or at home. He climbed over the iron railings into the little garden: the plane-trees spread their large pale palms between him and the sky. It might have been an illimitable forest into which he had escaped. He crouched behind a trunk and the wolves retreated; it seemed to him between the little iron seat and the tree-trunk that no one would ever find him again. A kind of embittered happiness and self-pity made him cry; he was lost; there wouldn't be any more secrets to keep; he surrendered responsibility once and for all. Let grown-up people keep to their world and he would keep to his, safe in the small garden between the plane-trees. "In the lost childhood of Judas Christ was betrayed"; you could almost see the small unformed face hardening into the deep dilettante selfishness of age.

Presently the door of 48 opened and Baines looked this way and that; then he signalled with his hand and Emmy came; it was as if they were only just in time for a train, they hadn't a chance of saying good-bye; she went quickly by, like a face at a window swept past the platform, pale and unhappy and not wanting to go. Baines went in again and shut the door; the light was lit in the basement, and a policeman walked round the square, looking into the areas. You could tell how many families were at home by the lights behind the first-floor curtains.

Philip explored the garden: it didn't take long: a twenty-yard square of bushes and plane-trees, two iron seats and a gravel path, a padlocked gate at either end, a scuffle of old leaves. But he couldn't stay: something stirred in the bushes and two illuminated eyes peered out at him like a Siberian wolf, and he thought how terrible it would be if Mrs. Baines found him there. He'd have no time to climb the railings; she'd seize him from behind.

He left the square at the unfashionable end and was immediately among the fish-and-chip shops, the little stationers selling Bagatelle, among the accommodation addresses and the dingy hotels with open doors. There were few people about because the pubs were open, but a blowsy woman carrying a parcel called out to him across the street and the commissionaire outside a cinema would have stopped him if he hadn't crossed the road. He went deeper: you could go farther and lose yourself more completely here than among the plane-trees. On the fringe of the square he was in danger of being stopped and taken back: it was obvious where he belonged: but as he went deeper he lost the marks of his origin. It was a warm night: any child in those free-living parts might be expected to play truant from bed. He found a kind of camaraderie even among grown-up people; he might have been a neighbour's child as he went quickly by, but they weren't going to tell on him, they'd been young once themselves. He picked up a protective coating of dust from the pavements, of smuts from the trains which passed along the backs in a spray of fire. Once he was caught in a knot of children running away from something or somebody, laughing as they ran; he was whirled with them round a turning

and abandoned, with sticky fruit-drop in his hand.

He couldn't have been more lost; but he hadn't the stamina to keep on. At first he feared that someone would stop him; after an hour he hoped that someone would. He couldn't find his way back, and in any case he was afraid of arriving home alone; he was afraid of Mrs. Baines, more afraid than he had ever been. Baines was his friend, but something had happened which gave Mrs. Baines all the power. He began to loiter on purpose to be noticed, but no one noticed him. Families were having a last breather on the doorsteps, the refuse bins had been put out and bits of cabbage stalks soiled his slippers. The air was full of voices, but he was cut off; these people were strangers and would always now be strangers; they were marked by Mrs. Baines and he shied away from them into a deep class-consciousness. He had been afraid of policemen, but now he wanted one to take him home; even Mrs. Baines could do nothing against a policeman. He sidled past a constable who was directing traffic, but he was too busy to pay him any attention. Philip sat down against a wall and cried.

It hadn't occurred to him that that was the easiest way, that all you had to do was to surrender, to show you were beaten and accept kindness. . . . It was lavished on him at once by two women and a pawnbroker. Another policeman appeared, a young man with a sharp incredulous face. He looked as if he noted everything he saw in pocketbooks and drew conclusions. A woman offered to see Philip home, but he didn't trust her: she wasn't a match for Mrs. Baines immobile in the hall. He wouldn't give his address; he said he was afraid to go home. He had his way; he got his protection. "I'll take him to the station," the policeman said, and holding him awkwardly by the hand (he wasn't married; he had his career to make) he led him round the corner, up the stone stairs into the little bare overheated room where Justice waited.

5

Justice waited behind a wooden counter on a high stool; it wore a heavy moustache; it was kindly and had six children ("three of them nippers like yourself"); it wasn't really interested in Philip, but it pretended to be, it wrote the address down and sent a constable to fetch a glass of milk. But the young constable was interested; he had a nose for things.

"Your home's on the telephone, I suppose," Justice said. "We'll ring them up and say you are safe. They'll fetch you very soon. What's your name, sonny?"

"Philip."

"Your other name."

"I haven't got another name." He didn't want to be fetched; he wanted to be taken home by someone who would impress even Mrs. Baines. The constable watched him, watched the way he drank the milk, watched him when he winced away from questions.

"What made you run away? Playing truant, eh?"

"I don't know."

"You oughtn't do it, young fellow. Think how anxious your father and mother will be."

"They are away."

"Well, your nurse."

"I haven't got one."

"Who looks after you, then?" That question went home. Philip saw Mrs. Baines coming up the stairs at him, the heap of black cotton in the hall. He began to cry.

"Now, now, now," the sergeant said. He didn't know what to do; he wished his wife were with him; even a policewoman might have been useful.

"Don't you think it's funny," the constable said, "that there hasn't been an inquiry?"

"They think he's tucked up in bed."

"You are scared, aren't you?" the constable said. "What scared you?"

"I don't know."

"Somebody hurt you?"

"No."

"He's had bad dreams," the sergeant said. "Thought the house was on fire, I expect. I've brought up six of them. Rose is due back. She'll take him home."

"I want to go home with you," Philip said; he tried to smile at the constable, but the deceit was immature and unsuccessful.

"I'd better go," the constable said. "There may be something wrong."

"Nonsense," the sergeant said. "It's a woman's job. Tact is what you need. Here's Rose. Pull up your stockings, Rose. You're a disgrace to the Force. I've got a job of work for you." Rose shambled in: black cotton stockings drooping over her boots, a gawky Girl Guide manner, a hoarse hostile voice. "More tarts, I suppose."

"No, you've got to see this young man home." She looked at him owlishly.

"I won't go with her," Philip said. He began to cry again. "I don't like her."

"More of that womanly charm, Rose," the sergeant said. The telephone rang on his desk. He lifted the receiver. "What? What's that?" he said. "Number 48? You've got a doctor?" He put his hand over the telephone mouth. "No wonder this nipper wasn't reported," he said. "They've been too busy. An accident. Woman slipped on the stairs."

"Serious?" the constable asked. The sergeant mouthed at him; you didn't mention the word death before a child (didn't he know? he had six of them), you made noises in the throat, you grimaced, a complicated shorthand for a word of only five letters anyway.

"You'd better go, after all," he said,

"and make a report. The doctor's there."

Rose shambled from the stove; pink apply-dapply cheeks, loose stockings. She stuck her hands behind her. Her large morgue-like mouth was full of blackened teeth. "You told me to take him and now just because something interesting . . . I don't expect justice from a man . . ."

"Who's at the house?" the constable asked.

"The butler."

"You don't think," the constable said, "he saw . . ."

"Trust me," the sergeant said. "I've brought up six. I know 'em through and through. You can't teach me anything about children."

"He seemed scared about something."

"Dreams," the sergeant said.

"What name?"

"Baines."

"This Mr. Baines," the constable said to Philip, "you like him, eh? He's good to you?" They were trying to get something out of him; he was suspicious of the whole roomful of them; he said "yes" without conviction because he was afraid at any moment of more responsibilities, more secrets.

"And Mrs. Baines?"

"Yes."

They consulted together by the desk; Rose was hoarsely aggrieved; she was like a female impersonator, she bore her womanhood with an unnatural emphasis even while she scorned it in her creased stockings and her weather-exposed face. The charcoal shifted in the stove; the room was overheated in the mild late summer evening. A notice on the wall described a body found in the Thames, or rather the body's clothes: wool vest, wool pants, wool shirt with blue stripes, size ten boots, blue serge suit worn at the elbows, fifteen and a half celluloid collar. They couldn't find anything to say about the body, except its measurements, it was just an ordinary body.

"Come along," the constable said. He was interested, he was glad to be going, but he couldn't help being embarrassed by his company, a small boy in pyjamas. His nose smelt something, he didn't know what, but he smarted at the sight of the amusement they caused: the pubs had closed and the streets were full again of men making as long a day of it as they could. He hurried through the less frequented streets, chose the darker pavements, wouldn't loiter, and Philip wanted more and more to loiter, pulling at his hand, dragging with his feet. He dreaded the sight of Mrs. Baines waiting in the hall: he knew now that she was dead. The sergeant's mouthings had conveyed that; but she wasn't buried, she wasn't out of sight; he was going to see a dead person in the hall when the door opened.

The light was on in the basement, and to his relief the constable made for the area steps. Perhaps he wouldn't have to see Mrs. Baines at all. The constable knocked on the door because it was too dark to see the bell, and Baines answered. He stood there in the doorway of the neat bright basement room and you could see the sad complacent plausible sentence he had prepared wither at the sight of Philip; he hadn't expected Philip to return like that in the policeman's company. He had to begin thinking all over again; he wasn't a deceptive man; if it hadn't been for Emmy he would have been quite ready to let the truth lead him where it would.

"Mr. Baines?" the constable asked.

He nodded; he hadn't found the right words; he was daunted by the shrewd knowing face, the sudden appearance of Philip there.

"This little boy from here?"

"Yes," Baines said. Philip could tell that there was a message he was trying to convey, but he shut his mind to it. He loved Baines, but Baines had involved him in secrets, in fears he didn't understand. The glowing morning thought "This is life" had become under Baines's tutelage the repugnant memory "That was life": the musty hair across the mouth, the breathless cruel tortured inquiry "Where are they?," the heap of black cotton tipped into the hall. That was what happened when you loved: you got involved; and Philip extricated himself from life, from love, from Baines with a merciless egotism.

There had been things between them, but he laid them low, as a retreating army cuts the wires, destroys the bridges. In the abandoned country you may leave much that is dear—a morning in the Park—an ice at a corner house, sausages for supper—but more is concerned in the retreat than temporary losses. There are old people who, as the tractors wheel away, implore to be taken, but you can't risk the rearguard for their sake: a whole prolonged retreat from life, from care, from human relationships is involved.

"The doctor's here," Baines said. He nodded at the door, moistened his mouth, kept his eyes on Philip, begging for something like a dog you can't understand. "There's nothing to be done. She slipped on these stone basement stairs. I was in here. I heard her fall." He wouldn't look at the notebook, at the constable's tiny spidery writing which got a terrible lot on one page.

"Did the boy see anything?"

"He can't have done. I thought he was in bed. Hadn't he better go up? It's a shocking thing. Oh," Baines said, losing control, "it's a shocking thing for a child."

"She's through there?" the constable asked.

"I haven't moved her an inch," Baines said.

"He better then—"

"Go up the area and through the hall," Baines said and again he begged dumbly like a dog: one more secret, keep this secret, do this for old Baines, he won't ask another.

"Come along," the constable said. "I'll see you up to bed. You're a gentleman; you must come in the proper way through the front door like the master should. Or will you go along with him, Mr. Baines, while I see the doctor?"

"Yes," Baines said, "I'll go." He came across the room to Philip, begging, begging, all the way with his soft old stupid expression: this is Baines, the old Coaster; what about a palm-oil chop, eh?; a man's life; forty niggers; never used a gun; I tell you I couldn't help loving them: it wasn't what we call love, nothing we could understand. The messages flickered out from the last posts at the border, imploring, beseeching, reminding: this is your old friend Baines; what about an eleven's; a glass of ginger pop won't do you any harm; sausages; a long day. But the wires were cut, the messages just faded out into the enormous vacancy of the neat scrubbed room in which there had never been a place where a man could hide his secrets.

"Come along, Phil, it's bedtime. We'll just go up the steps . . ." Tap, tap, tap, at the telegraph; you may get through, you can't tell, somebody may mend the right wire. "And in at the front door."

"No," Philip said, "no. I won't go. You can't make me go. I'll fight. I won't see her."

The constable turned on them quickly. "What's that? Why won't you go?"

"She's in the hall," Philip said. "I know she's in the hall. And she's dead. I won't see her."

"You moved her then?" the constable said to Baines. "All the way down here? You've been lying, eh? That means you had to tidy up. . . . Were you alone?"

"Emmy," Philip said, "Emmy." He wasn't going to keep any more secrets: he was going to finish once and for all with everything, with Baines and Mrs.

Baines and the grown-up life beyond him; it wasn't his business and never, never again, he decided, would he share their confidences and companionship. "It was all Emmy's fault," he protested with a quaver which reminded Baines that after all he was only a child; it had been hopeless to expect help there; he was a child; he didn't understand what it all meant; he couldn't read this short-hand of terror; he'd had a long day and he was tired out. You could see him dropping asleep where he stood against the dresser, dropping back into the comfortable nursery peace. You couldn't blame him. When he woke in the morning, he'd hardly remember a thing.

"Out with it," the constable said, addressing Baines with professional ferocity, "who is she?" just as the old man sixty years later startled his secretary, his only watcher, asking, "Who is she? Who is she?" dropping lower and lower into death, passing on the way perhaps the image of Baines: Baines hopeless, Baines letting his head drop, Baines "coming clean."

DRAMA

Eugene O'Neill (1887–1953)

DESIRE UNDER THE ELMS

CHARACTERS

EPHRAIM CABOT

SIMEON \
PETER } *His sons* \
EBEN /

ABBIE PUTNAM

Young Girl, Two Farmers, The Fiddler, A Sheriff, and other folk from the neighboring farms.

The action of the entire play takes place in, and immediately outside of, the Cabot farmhouse in New England, in the year 1850. The south end of the house faces front to a stone wall with a wooden gate at center opening on a country road. The house is in good condition but in need of paint. Its walls are a sickly grayish, the green of the shutters faded. Two enormous elms are on each side of the house. They bend their trailing branches down over the roof. They appear to protect and at the same time subdue. There is a sinister maternity in their aspect, a crushing, jealous absorption. They have developed from their intimate contact with the life of man in the house an appalling humaneness. They brood oppressively over the house. They are like exhausted women resting their sagging breasts and hands and hair on its roof, and when it rains their tears trickle down monotonously and rot on the shingles.

There is a path running from the gate around the right corner of the house to the front door. A narrow porch is on this side. The end wall facing us has two windows in its upper story, two larger ones on the floor below. The two upper are those of the father's bedroom and that of the brothers. On the left, ground floor, is the kitchen—on the right, the parlor, the shades of which are always drawn down.

Part I

SCENE ONE

Exterior of the Farmhouse. It is sunset of a day at the beginning of summer in the year 1850. There is no wind and everything is still. The sky above the roof is

282

suffused with deep colors, the green of the elms glows, but the house is in shadow, seeming pale and washed out by contrast.

A door opens and EBEN CABOT *comes to the end of the porch and stands looking down the road to the right. He has a large bell in his hand and this he swings mechanically, awakening a deafening clangor. Then he puts his hands on his hips and stares up at the sky. He sighs with a puzzled awe and blurts out with halting appreciation.*

EBEN: God! Purty! *{His eyes fall and he stares about him frowningly. He is twenty-five, tall and sinewy. His face is well-formed, good-looking, but its expression is resentful and defensive. His defiant, dark eyes remind one of a wild animal's in captivity. Each day is a cage in which he finds himself trapped but inwardly unsubdued. There is a fierce repressed vitality about him. He has black hair, mustache, a thin curly trace of beard. He is dressed in rough farm clothes.*

He spits on the ground with intense disgust, turns and goes back into the house.

SIMEON *and* PETER *come in from their work in the fields. They are tall men, much older than their half-brother {*SIMEON *is thirty-nine and* PETER *thirty-seven}, built on a squarer, simpler model, fleshier in body, more bovine and homelier in face, shrewder and more practical. Their shoulders stoop a bit from years of farm work. They clump heavily along in their clumsy thick-soled boots caked with earth. Their clothes, their faces, hands, bare arms and throats are earth-stained. They smell of earth. They stand together for a moment in front of the house and, as if with the one impulse, stare dumbly up at the sky, leaning on their hoes. Their faces have a compressed, unresigned expression. As they look upward, this softens}*

SIMEON: *{grudgingly}* Purty.

PETER: Ay-eh.

SIMEON: *{suddenly}* Eighteen years ago.

PETER: What?

SIMEON: Jenn. My woman. She died.

PETER: I'd fergot.

SIMEON: I rec'lect—now an' agin. Makes it lonesome. She'd hair long's a hoss' tail—an' yaller like gold!

PETER: Waal—she's gone. *{This with indifferent finality—then after a pause}* They's gold in the West, Sim.

SIMEON: *{still under the influence of sunset—vaguely}* In the sky?

PETER: Waal—in a manner o' speakin'—thar's the promise. *{Growing excited}* Gold in the sky—in the West—Golden Gate—Californi-a!—Goldest West!—fields o' gold!

SIMEON: *{excited in his turn}* Fortunes layin' just atop o' the ground waitin' t' be picked! Solomon's mines, they says! *{For a moment they continue looking up at the sky—then their eyes drop}*

PETER: *{with sardonic bitterness}* Here—it's stones atop o' the ground—stones atop o' makin' stone walls—year atop o' year—him 'n' yew 'n' me 'n' then Eben—makin' stone walls fur him to fence us in!

SIMEON: We've wuked. Give our strength. Give our years. Plowed 'em under in the ground,—*{he stamps rebelliously}*—rottin'—makin' soil for his crops! *{A pause}* Waal—the farm pays good for hereabouts.

PETER: If we plowed in Californi-a, they'd be lumps o' gold in the furrow!

SIMEON: Californi-a's t'other side o' earth, a'most. We got t' calc'late—

PETER: *{after a pause}* 'Twould be hard fur me, too, to give up what we've 'arned here by our sweat. *{A pause.* EBEN *sticks his head out of the dining-room window, listening}*

SIMEON: Ay-eh. *{A pause}* Mebbe—he'll die soon.

PETER: *{doubtfully}* Mebbe.

SIMEON: Mebbe—fur all we knows —he's dead now.

PETER: Ye'd need proof.

SIMEON: He's been gone two months with no word.

PETER: Left us in the fields an evenin' like this. Hitched up an' druv off in the West. That's plum onnateral. He hain't never been off this farm 'ceptin' t' the village in thirty year or more, not since he married Eben's maw. *{A pause. Shrewdly}* I calc'late we might git him declared crazy by the court.

SIMEON: He skinned 'em too slick. He got the best o' all on 'em. They'd never b'lieve him crazy. *{A pause}* We got t' wait—till he's under ground.

EBEN: *{with a sardonic chuckle}* Honor thy father! *{They turn, startled, and stare at him. He grins, then scowls}* I pray he's died. *{They stare at him. He continues matter-of-factly}* Supper's ready.

SIMEON *and* PETER: *{together}* Ay-eh.

EBEN: *{gazing up at the sky}* Sun's downin' purty.

SIMEON *and* PETER: *{together}* Ay-eh. They's gold in the West.

EBEN: Ay-eh. *{Pointing}* Yonder atop o' the hill pasture, ye mean?

SIMEON *and* PETER: *{together}* In Californi-a!

EBEN: Hunh? *{Stares at them indifferently for a second, then drawls}* Waal—supper's gettin' cold. *{He turns back into kitchen}*

SIMEON: *{startled—smacks his lips}* I air hungry!

PETER: *{sniffing}* I smells bacon!

SIMEON: *{with hungry appreciation}* Bacon's good!

PETER: *{in same tone}* Bacon's bacon! *{They turn, shouldering each other, their bodies bumping and rubbing together as they hurry clumsily to their food, like two friendly oxen toward their evening meal. They disappear around the right corner of house and can be heard entering the door}*

CURTAIN

SCENE TWO

The color fades from the sky. Twilight begins. The interior of the kitchen is now visible. A pine table is at center, a cookstove in the right rear corner, four rough wooden chairs, a tallow candle on the table. In the middle of the rear wall is fastened a big advertising poster with a ship in full sail and the word "California" in big letters. Kitchen utensils hang from nails. Everything is neat and in order but the atmosphere is of a men's camp kitchen rather than that of a home.

Places for three are laid. EBEN *takes boiled potatoes and bacon from the stove and puts them on the table, also a loaf of bread and a crock of water.* SIMEON *and* PETER *shoulder in, slump down in their chairs without a word.* EBEN *joins them. The three eat in silence for a moment, the two elder as naturally unrestrained as beasts of the field,* EBEN *picking at his food without appetite, glancing at them with a tolerant dislike.*

SIMEON: *{suddenly turns to* EBEN*}* Looky here! Ye'd oughtn't t' said that, Eben.

PETER: 'Twa'n't righteous.

EBEN: What?

SIMEON: Ye prayed he'd died.

EBEN: Waal—don't yew pray it? *{A pause}*

PETER: He's our Paw.

EBEN: *{violently}* Not mine!

SIMEON: *{dryly}* Ye'd not let no one else say that about yer Maw! Ha! *{He gives one abrupt sardonic guffaw.* PETER *grins}*

EBEN: *{very pale}* I meant—I hain't his'n—I hain't like him—he hain't me!

PETER: *{dryly}* Wait till ye've growed his age!

EBEN: *{intensely}* I'm Maw—every drop o' blood! *{A pause. They stare at him with indifferent curiosity}*

PETER: *{reminiscently}* She was good t' Sim 'n' me. A good Stepmaw's scurse.

SIMEON: She was good t' everyone.

EBEN: *{greatly moved, gets to his feet and makes an awkward bow to each of them—stammering}* I be thankful t' ye. I'm her—her heir. *{He sits down in confusion}*

PETER: *{after a pause—judicially}* She was good even t' him.

EBEN: *{fiercely}* An' fur thanks he killed her!

SIMEON: *{after a pause}* No one never kills nobody. It's allus somethin'. That's the murderer.

EBEN: Didn't he slave Maw t' death?

PETER: He's slaved himself t' death. He's slaved Sim 'n' me 'n' yew t' death —on'y none o' us hain't died—yit.

SIMEON: It's somethin'—drivin' him —t' drive us!

EBEN: *{vengefully}* Waal—I hold him t' jedgment! *{Then scornfully}* Somethin'! What's somethin'?

SIMEON: Dunno.

EBEN: *{sardonically}* What's drivin' yew to Californi-a, mebbe? *{They look at him in surprise}* Oh, I've heerd ye! *{Then, after a pause}* But ye'll never go t' the gold fields!

PETER: *{assertively}* Mebbe!

EBEN: Whar'll ye git the money?

PETER: We kin walk. It's an a'mighty ways—Californi-a—but if yew was t' put all the steps we've walked on this farm end t' end we'd be in the moon!

EBEN: The Injuns'll skulp ye on the plains.

SIMEON: *{with grim humor}* We'll mebbe make 'em pay a hair fur a hair!

EBEN: *{decisively}* But t'aint that. Ye won't never go because ye'll wait here fur yer share o' the farm, thinkin' allus he'll die soon.

SIMEON: *{after a pause}* We've a right.

PETER: Two-thirds belongs t'us.

EBEN: *{jumping to his feet}* Ye've no right! She wa'n't yewr Maw! It was her farm! Didn't he steal it from her? She's dead. It's my farm.

SIMEON: *{sardonically}* Tell that t' Paw—when he comes! I'll bet ye a dollar he'll laugh—fur once in his life. Ha! *{He laughs himself in one single mirthless bark}*

PETER: *{amused in turn, echoes his brother}* Ha!

SIMEON: *{after a pause}* What've ye got held agin us, Eben? Year arter year it's skulked in yer eye—somethin'.

PETER: Ay-eh.

EBEN: Ay-eh. They's somethin'. *{Suddenly exploding}* Why didn't ye never stand between him 'n' my Maw when he was slavin' her to her grave—t' pay her back fur the kindness she done t' yew? *{There is a long pause. They stare at him in surprise}*

SIMEON: Waal—the stock'd got t' be watered.

PETER: 'R they was woodin' t' do.

SIMEON: 'R plowin'.

PETER: 'R hayin'.

SIMEON: 'R spreadin' manure.

PETER: 'R weedin'.

SIMEON: 'R prunin'.

PETER: 'R milkin'.

EBEN: *{breaking in harshly}* An' makin' walls—stone atop o' stone— makin' walls till yer heart's a stone ye heft up out o' the way o' growth onto a stone wall t' wall in yer heart!

SIMEON: *{matter-of-factly}* We never had no time t' meddle.

PETER: *{to EBEN}* Yew was fifteen afore yer Maw died—an' big fur yer age. Why didn't ye never do nothin'?

EBEN: *{harshly}* They was chores t' do, wa'n't they? *{A pause—then slowly}* It was on'y arter she died I come to think o' it. Me cookin'—doin' her work —that made me know her, suffer her sufferin'—she'd come back t'help—come back t' bile potatoes—come back t' fry bacon—come back t' bake biscuits— come back all cramped up t' shake the fire, an' carry ashes, her eyes weepin' an' bloody with smoke an' cinders same's they used t' be. She still comes back—stands by the stove thar in the evenin'—she can't find it nateral sleepin' an' restin' in peace. She can't git used t' bein' free—even in her grave.

SIMEON: She never complained none.

EBEN: She'd got too tired. She'd got too used t' bein' too tired. That was what he done. *{With vengeful passion}* An' sooner'r later, I'll meddle. I'll say the thin's I didn't say then t' him! I'll yell 'em at the top o' my lungs. I'll see t' it my Maw gits some rest an' sleep in her grave! *{He sits down again, relapsing into a brooding silence. They look at him with a queer indifferent curiosity}*

PETER: *{after a pause}* Whar in tarnation d'ye s'pose he went, Sim?

SIMEON: Dunno. He druv off in the buggy, all spick an' span, with the mare all breshed an' shiny, druv off clackin' his tongue an' wavin' his whip. I remember it right well. I was finishin' plowin', it was spring an' May an' sunset, an' gold in the West, an' he druv off into it. I yells "Whar ye goin', Paw?" an' he hauls up by the stone wall a jiffy. His old snake's eyes was glitterin' in the sun like he'd been drinkin' a jugful an' he says with a mule's grin: "Don't ye run away till I come back!"

PETER: Wonder if he knowed we was wantin' fur Californi-a?

SIMEON: Mebbe. I didn't say nothin' and he says, lookin' kinder queer an' sick: "I been hearin' the hens cluckin' an' the roosters crowin' all the durn day. I been listenin' t' the cows lowin' an' everythin' else kickin' up till I can't stand it no more. It's spring an' I'm feelin' damned," he says. "Damned like an old bare hickory tree fit on'y fur burnin'," he says. An' then I calc'late I must've looked a mite hopeful, fur he adds real spry and vicious: "But don't git no fool idee I'm dead. I've sworn t' live a hundred an' I'll do it, if on'y t' spite yer sinful greed! An' now I'm rid-

in' out t' learn God's message t' me in the spring, like the prophets done. An' yew git back t' yer plowin'," he says. An' he druv off singin' a hymn. I thought he was drunk—'r I'd stopped him goin'.

EBEN: *{scornfully}* No, ye wouldn't! Ye're scared o' him. He's stronger—inside—than both o' ye put together!

PETER: *{sardonically}* An' yew—be yew Samson?

EBEN: I'm gittin' stronger. I kin feel it growin' in me—growin' an' growin' —till it'll bust out—! *{He gets up and puts on his coat and hat. They watch him, gradually breaking into grins.* EBEN *avoids their eyes sheepishly}* I'm goin' out fur a spell—up the road.

PETER: T' the village?

SIMEON: T' see Minnie?

EBEN: *{defiantly}* Ay-eh!

PETER: *{jeeringly}* The Scarlet Woman!

SIMEON: Lust—that's what's growin' in ye!

EBEN: Waal—she's purty!

PETER: She's been purty fur twenty year!

SIMEON: A new coat o' paint'll make a heifer out of forty.

EBEN: She hain't forty!

PETER: If she hain't, she's teeterin' on the edge.

EBEN: *{desperately}* What d'yew know—

PETER: All they is . . . Sim knew her—an' then me arter—

SIMEON: An' Paw kin tell yew somethin' too! He was fust!

EBEN: D'ye mean t' say he . . .?

SIMEON: *{with a grin}* Ay-eh! We air his heirs in everythin'!

EBEN: *{intensely}* That's more to it! That grows on it! It'll bust soon! *{Then violently}* I'll go smash my fist in her face! *{He pulls open the door in rear violently}*

SIMEON: *{with a wink at* PETER—*drawlingly}* Mebbe—but the night's wa'm—purty—by the time ye git thar mebbe ye'll kiss her instead!

PETER: Sart'n he will! *{They both roar with coarse laughter.* EBEN *rushes out and slams the door—then the outside front door—comes around the corner of the house and stands still by the gate, staring up at the sky.}*

SIMEON: *{looking after him}* Like his Paw.

PETER: Dead spit an' image!

SIMEON: Dog'll eat dog!

PETER: Ay-eh. *{Pause. With yearning}* Mebbe a year from now we'll be in Californi-a.

SIMEON: Ay-eh. *{A pause. Both yawn}* Let's git t'bed. *{He blows out the candle. They go out door in rear.* EBEN *stretches his arms up to the sky—rebelliously}*

EBEN: Waal—thar's a star, an' somewhar's they's him, an' here's me, an' thar's Min up the road—in the same night. What if I does kiss her? She's like t'night, she's soft 'n' wa'm, her eyes kin wink like a star, her mouth's wa'm, her arms're wa'm, she smells like a wa'm plowed field, she's purty . . . Ay-eh! By God A'mighty she's purty, an' I don't give a damn how many sins she's sinned afore mine or who's she's sinned 'em with, my sin's as purty as any one on 'em *{He strides off down the road to the left}*

SCENE THREE

It is the pitch darkness just before dawn. EBEN *comes in from the left and goes around to the porch, feeling his way, chuckling bitterly and cursing half-aloud to himself.*

EBEN: The cussed old miser! *{He can be heard going in the front door. There is a pause as he goes upstairs, then a loud knock on the bedroom door of the brothers}* Wake up!

SIMEON: *{startedly}* Who's thar?

EBEN: *{pushing open the door and coming in, a lighted candle in his hand. The bedroom of his brothers is revealed. Its ceiling is the sloping roof. They can stand upright only close to the center dividing wall of the upstairs.* SIMEON *and* PETER *are in a double bed front.* EBEN's *cot is to the rear.* EBEN *has a mixture of silly grin and vicious scowl on his face}* I be!

PETER: *{angrily}* What in hell's fire . . .?

EBEN: I got news fur ye! Ha! *{He gives one abrupt sardonic guffaw}*

SIMEON: *{angrily}* Couldn't ye hold it 'til we'd got our sleep?

EBEN: It's nigh sunup. *{Then explosively}* He's gone an' married agen!

SIMEON *and* PETER: *{explosively}* Paw?

EBEN: Got himself hitched to a female 'bout thirty-five—an' purty, they says . . .

SIMEON: *{aghast}* It's a durn lie!

PETER: Who says?

SIMEON: They been stringin' ye!

EBEN: Think I'm a dunce, do ye? The hull village says. The preacher from New Dover, he brung the news—told it t'our preacher—New Dover, that's whar the old loon got himself hitched—that's whar the woman lived—

PETER: *{no longer doubting—stunned}* Waal . . . !

SIMEON: *{the same}* Waal . . . !

EBEN: *{sitting down on a bed—with vicious hatred}* Ain't he a devil out o' hell? It's just t' spite us—the damned old mule!

PETER: *{after a pause}* Everythin'll go t' her now.

SIMEON: Ay-eh. *{A pause—dully}* Waal—if it's done—

PETER: It's done us. *{Pause—then persuasively}* They's gold in the fields o' Californi-a, Sim. No good a-stayin' here now.

SIMEON: Jest what I was a-thinkin'. *{Then with decision}* S'well fust's last! Let's light out and git this mornin'.

PETER: Suits me.

EBEN: Ye must like walkin'.

SIMEON: *{sardonically}* If ye'd grow wings on us we'd fly thar!

EBEN: Ye'd like ridin' better—on a boat, wouldn't ye? *{Fumbles in his pocket and takes out a crumpled sheet of foolscap}* Waal, if ye sign this ye kin ride on a boat. I've had it writ out an' ready in case ye'd ever go. It says fur three hundred dollars t' each ye agree yewr shares o' the farm is sold t' me. *{They look suspiciously at the paper. A pause}*

SIMEON: *{wonderingly}* But if he's hitched agen—

PETER: An' whar'd yew git that sum o' money, anyways?

EBEN: *{cunningly}* I know whar it's hid. I been waitin'—Maw told me. She knew whar it lay fur years, but she was waitin' . . . It's her'n—the money he hoarded from her farm an' hid from Maw. It's my money by rights now.

PETER: Whar's it hid?

EBEN: *{cunningly}* Whar yew won't never find it without me. Maw spied on him—'r she'd never knowed. *{A pause. They look at him suspiciously, and he at them}* Waal, is it fa'r trade?

SIMEON: Dunno.

PETER: Dunno.

SIMEON: *{looking at window}* Sky's grayin'.

PETER: Ye better start the fire, Eben.

SIMEON: An' fix some vittles.

EBEN: Ay-eh. *{Then with a forced jocular heartiness}* I'll git ye a good one. If ye're startin t' hoof it t' Californi-a ye'll need somethin' that'll stick t' yer ribs. *{He turns to the door, adding meaningly}* But ye kin ride on a boat if ye'll swap. *{He stops at the door and pauses. They stare at him}*

SIMEON: *{suspiciously}* Whar was ye all night?

EBEN: *{defiantly}* Up t' Min's. *{Then slowly}* Walkin' thar, fust I felt's if I'd kiss her; then I got a-thinkin' o' what ye'd said o' him an' her an' I says, I'll bust her nose fur that! Then I got t' the village an' heerd the news an' I got madder'n hell an' run all the way t' Min's not knowin' what I'd do—*{He pauses—then sheepishly but more defiantly}* Waal—when I seen her, I didn't hit her—nor I didn't kiss her nuther—I begun t' beller like a calf an' cuss at the same time, I was so durn mad—an' she got scared—an' I jest grabbed holt an' tuk her! *{Proudly}* Yes, siree! I tuk her. She may've been his'n—an' your'n, too —but she's mine now!

SIMEON: *{dryly}* In love, air yew?

EBEN: *{with lofty scorn}* Love! I don't take no stock in sech slop!

PETER: *{winking at SIMEON}* Mebbe Eben's aimin' t' marry, too.

SIMEON: Min'd make a true faithful he'pmeet! *{They snicker}*

EBEN: What do I care fur her—'ceptin' she's round an' wa'm? The p'int is she was his'n—an' now she b'longs t' me! *{He goes to the door—and turns—rebelliously}* An' Min hain't sech a bad un. They's worse'n Min in the world, I'll bet ye! Wait'll we see this cow the Old Man's hitched t'! She'll beat Min, I got a notion! *{He starts to go out}*

SIMEON: *{suddenly}* Mebbe ye'll try t' make her your'n, too?

PETER: Ha! *{He gives a sardonic laugh of relish at this idea}*

EBEN: *{spitting with disgust}* Her—here—sleepin' with him—stealin' my Maw's farm! I'd as soon pet a skunk 'r kiss a snake! *{He goes out. The two stare after him suspiciously. A pause. They listen to his steps receding}*

PETER: He's startin' the fire.

SIMEON: I'd like t' ride t' Californi-a —but—

PETER: Min might o' put some scheme in his head.

SIMEON: Mebbe it's all a lie 'bout Paw marryin'. We'd best wait an' see the bride.

PETER: An' don't sign nothin' till we does!

SIMEON: Nor till we've tested it's good money! *{Then with a grin}* But if Paw's hitched we'd be sellin' Eben somethin' we'd never git nohow!

PETER: We'll wait an' see. *{Then with sudden vindictive anger}* An' till he comes, let's yew 'n' me not wuk a lick, let Eben tend to thin's if he's a mind t', let's us jest sleep an' eat an' drink likker, an' let the hull damned farm go t' blazes!

SIMEON: *{excitedly}* By God, we've 'arned a rest! We'll play rich fur a change. I hain't a-going to stir outa bed till breakfast's ready.

PETER: An' on the table!

SIMEON: *{after a pause—thoughtfully}* What d'ye calc'late she'll be like —our new Maw? Like Eben thinks?

PETER: More'n' likely.

SIMEON: *{vindictively}* Waal—I hope she's a she-devil that'll make him wish he was dead an' livin' in the pit o' hell fur comfort!

PETER: *{fervently}* Amen!

SIMEON: *{imitating his father's voice}* "I'm ridin' out t' learn God's message t' me in the spring like the prophets done," he says. I'll bet right then an' thar he knew plumb well he was goin' whorin', the stinkin' old hypocrite!

SCENE FOUR

Same as Scene Two—shows the interior of the kitchen with a lighted candle on table. It is gray dawn outside. SIMEON *and* PETER *are just finishing their breakfast.* EBEN *sits before his plate of untouched food, brooding frowningly.*

PETER: *{glancing at him rather irritably}* Lookin' glum don't help none.

SIMEON: *{sarcastically}* Sorrowin' over his lust o' the flesh!

PETER: *{with a grin}* Was she yer fust?

EBEN: *{angrily}* None o' yer business. *{A pause}* I was thinkin' o' him. I got a notion he's gettin' near—I kin feel him comin' on like yew kin feel malaria chill afore it takes ye.

PETER: It's too early yet.

SIMEON: Dunno. He'd like t' catch us nappin'—jest t' have somethin' t' hoss us 'round over.

PETER: *{mechanically gets to his feet. SIMEON does the same}* Waal—let's git t' wuk. *{They both plod mechanically toward the door before they realize. Then they stop short}*

SIMEON: *{grinning}* Ye're a cussed fool, Pete—and I be wuss! Let him see we hain't wukin'! We don't give a durn!

PETER: *{as they go back to the table}* Not a damned durn! It'll serve t' show him we're done with him. *{They sit down again.* EBEN *stares from one to the other with surprise}*

SIMEON: *{grins at him}* We're aimin' t' start bein' lilies o' the field.

PETER: Nary a toil 'r spin 'r lick o' wuk do we put in!

SIMEON: Ye're sole owner—till he comes—that's what ye wanted. Waal, ye got t' be sole hand, too.

PETER: The cows air bellerin'. Ye better hustle at the milkin'.

EBEN: *{with excited joy}* Ye mean ye'll sign the paper?

SIMEON: *{dryly}* Mebbe.

PETER: Mebbe.

SIMEON: We're considerin' *{Peremptorily}* Ye better git t' wuk.

EBEN: *{with queer excitement}* It's Maw's farm agen! It's my farm! Them's my cows! I'll milk my durn fingers off fur cows o' mine. *{He goes out door in rear, they stare after him indifferently}*

SIMEON: Like his Paw.

PETER: Dead spit 'n' image!

SIMEON: Waal—let dog eat dog! *{EBEN comes out of front door and around the corner of the house. The sky is beginning to grow flushed with sunrise.* EBEN *stops by the gate and stares around him with glowing, possessive eyes. He takes in the whole farm with his embracing glance of desire}*

EBEN: It's purty! It's damned purty! It's mine! *{He suddenly throws his head back boldly and glares with hard, defiant eyes at the sky}* Mine, d'ye hear? Mine! *{He turns and walks quickly off left, rear, toward the barn. The two brothers light their pipes}*

SIMEON: *{putting his muddy boots up*

on the table, tilting back his chair, and puffing defiantly} Waal—this air solid comfort—fur once.

PETER: Ay-eh. *{He follows suit. A pause. Unconsciously they both sigh}*

SIMEON: *{suddenly}* He never was much o' a hand at milkin', Eben wa'n't.

PETER: *{with a snort}* His hands air like hoofs! *{A pause}*

SIMEON: Reach down the jug thar! Let's take a swaller. I'm feelin' kind o' low.

PETER: Good idee! *{He does so—gets two glasses—they pour out drinks of whisky}* Here's t' the gold in Cali-forni-a!

SIMEON: An' luck t' find it! *{They drink—puff resolutely—sigh—take their feet down from the table}*

PETER: Likker don't pear t' sot right.

SIMEON: We hain't used t' it this early. *{A pause. They become very restless}*

PETER: Gittin' close in this kitchen.

SIMEON: *{with immense relief}* Let's git a breath o' air. *{They arise briskly and go out rear—appear around house and stop by the gate. They stare up at the sky with a numbed appreciation}*

PETER: Purty!

SIMEON: Ay-eh. Gold's t' the East now.

PETER: Sun's startin' with us fur the Golden West.

SIMEON: *{staring around the farm, his compressed face tightened, unable to conceal his emotion}* Waal—it's our last mornin'—mebbe.

PETER: *{the same}* Ay-eh.

SIMEON: *{stamps his foot on the earth and addresses it desperately}* Waal—ye've thirty year o' me buried in ye—spread out over ye—blood an' bone an' sweat—rotted away—fertilizin' ye—richin' yer soul—prime manure, by God, that's what I been t' ye!

PETER: Ay-eh! An' me!

SIMEON: An' yew, Peter. *{He sighs —then spits}* Waal—no use'n cryin' over spilt milk.

PETER: They's gold in the West—an' freedom, mebbe. We been slaves t' stone walls here.

SIMEON: *{defiantly}* We hain't no-body's slaves from this out—nor nothin's slaves nuther. *{A pause—restlessly}* Speakin' o' milk, wonder how Eben's managin'?

PETER: I s'pose he's managin'.

SIMEON: Mebbe we'd ought t' help —this once.

PETER: Mebbe. The cows knows us.

SIMEON: An' likes us. They don't know him much.

PETER: An' the hosses, an' pigs, an' chickens. They don't know him much.

SIMEON: They knows us like brothers —an' likes us! *{Proudly}* Hain't we raised 'em t' be fust-rate, number one prize stock?

PETER: We hain't—not no more.

SIMEON: *{dully}* I was fergettin'. *{Then resignedly}* Waal, let's go help Eben a spell an' git waked up.

PETER: Suits me. *{They are starting off down left, rear, for the barn when* EBEN *appears from there hurrying toward them, his face excited}*

EBEN: *{breathlessly}* Waal—har they be! The old mule an' the bride! I seen 'em from the barn down below at the turnin'.

PETER: How could ye tell that far?

EBEN: Hain't I as far-sight as he's near-sight? Don't I know the mare 'n' buggy, an' two people settin' in it? Who else . . . ? An' I tell ye I kin feel 'em a-comin', too! *{He squirms as if he had the itch}*

PETER: *{beginning to be angry}* Waal—let him do his own unhitchin'!

SIMEON: *{angry in his turn}* Let's hustle in an' git our bundles an' be a-goin' as he's a-comin'. I don't want never t' step inside the door agen arter he's back. *{They both start back around the corner of the house.* EBEN *follows them}*

EBEN: *{anxiously}* Will ye sign it afore ye go?

PETER: Let's see the color o' the old

skinflint's money an' we'll sign. *{They disappear left. The two brothers clump upstairs to get their bundles.* EBEN *appears in the kitchen, runs to window, peers out, comes back and pulls up a strip of flooring in under stove, takes out a canvas bag and puts it on table, then sets the floorboard back in place. The two brothers appear a moment after. They carry old carpet bags}*

EBEN: *{puts his hand on bag guardingly}* Have ye signed?

SIMEON: *{shows paper in his hand}* Ay-eh. *{Greedily}* Be that the money?

EBEN: *{opens bag and pours out pile of twenty-dollar gold pieces}* Twenty-dollar pieces—thirty on 'em. Count 'em. *{*PETER *does so, arranging them in stacks of five, biting one or two to test them}*

PETER: Six hundred. *{He puts them in bag and puts it inside his shirt carefully}*

SIMEON: *{handing paper to* EBEN*}* Har ye be.

EBEN: *{after a glance, folds it carefully and hides it under his shirt—gratefully}* Thank yew.

PETER: Thank yew fur the ride.

SIMEON: We'll send ye a lump o' gold fur Christmas. *{A pause.* EBEN *stares at them and they at him}*

PETER: *{awkwardly}* Waal—we're a-goin'.

SIMEON: Comin' out t' the yard?

EBEN: No. I'm waitin' in here a spell. *{Another silence. The brothers edge awkwardly to door in rear—then turn and stand}*

SIMEON: Waal—good-by.

PETER: Good-by.

EBEN: Good-by. *{They go out. He sits down at the table, faces the stove and pulls out the paper. He looks from it to the stove. His face, lighted up by the shaft of sunlight from the window, has an expression of trance. His lips move. The two brothers come out to the gate}*

PETER: *{looking off toward barn}* Thar he be—unhitchin'.

SIMEON: *{with a chuckle}* I'll bet ye he's riled!

PETER: An' thar she be.

SIMEON: Let's wait 'n' see what our new Maw looks like.

PETER: *{with a grin}* An' give him our partin' cuss!

SIMEON: *{grinning}* I feel like raisin' fun. I feel light in my head an' feet.

PETER: Me, too. I feel like laffin' till I'd split up the middle.

SIMEON: Reckon it's the likker?

PETER: No. My feet feel itchin' t' walk an' walk—an' jump high over thin's—and'. . . .

SIMEON: Dance? *{A pause}*

PETER: *{puzzled}* It's plumb onnateral.

SIMEON: *{a light coming over his face}* I calc'late it's 'cause school's out. It's holiday. Fur once we're free!

PETER: *{dazedly}* Free?

SIMEON: The halter's broke—the harness is busted—the fence bars is down —the stone walls air crumblin' an' tumblin'! We'll be kickin' up an' tearin' away down the road!

PETER: *{drawing a deep breath—oratorically}* Anybody that wants this stinkin' old rock-pile of a farm kin hev it. T'ain't our'n, no siree!

SIMEON: *{takes the gate off its hinges and puts it under his arm}* We harby 'bolishes shet gates, an' open gates, an' all gates, by thunder!

PETER: We'll take it with us fur luck an' let 'er sail free down some river.

SIMEON: *{as a sound of voices comes from left, rear}* Har they comes! *{The two brothers congeal into two stiff, grim-visaged statues.* EPHRAIM **CABOT** *and* ABBIE **PUTNAM** *come in.* CABOT *is seventy-five, tall and gaunt, with great, wiry, concentrated power, but stoop-shouldered from toil. His face is as hard as if it were hewn out of a boulder, yet there is a weakness in it, a petty pride in its own narrow strength. His eyes are small, close together, and extremely near-sighted, blinking continually in the effort to focus on objects, their stare having a straining, ingrowing quality. He is dressed in his dismal black Sunday suit.*

ABBIE *is thirty-five, buxom, full of vitality. Her round face is pretty but marred by its rather gross sensuality. There is strength and obstinacy in her jaw, a hard determination in her eyes, and about her whole personality the same unsettled, untamed, desperate quality which is so apparent in* EBEN]

CABOT: *{as they enter—a queer strangled emotion in his dry cracking voice}* Har we be t' hum, Abbie.

ABBIE: *{with lust for the word}* Hum! *{Her eyes gloating on the house without seeming to see the two stiff figures at the gate}* It's purty—purty! I can't b'lieve it's r'ally mine.

CABOT: *{sharply}* Yewr'n? Mine! *{He stares at her penetratingly. She stares back. He adds relentingly}* Our'n— mebbe! It was lonesome too long. I was growin' old in the spring. A hum's got t' hev a woman.

ABBIE: *{her voice taking possession}* A woman's got t' hev a hum!

CABOT: *{nodding uncertainly}* Ay-eh. *{Then irritably}* Whar be they? Ain't thar nobody about—'r wukin'—'r nothin'?

ABBIE: *{sees the brothers. She returns their stare of cold appraising contempt with interest—slowly}* Thar's two men loafin' at the gate an' starin' at me like a couple o' strayed hogs.

CABOT: *{straining his eyes}* I kin see 'em—but I can't make out. . . .

SIMEON: It's Simeon.

PETER: It's Peter.

CABOT: *{exploding}* Why hain't ye wukin'?

SIMEON: *{dryly}* We're waitin' t' welcome ye hum—yew an' the bride!

CABOT: *{confusedly}* Huh? Waal— this be yer new Maw, boys. *{She stares at them and they at her}*

SIMEON: *{turns away and spits contemptuously}* I see her!

PETER: *{spits also}* An' I see her!

ABBIE: *{with the conqueror's conscious superiority}* I'll go in an' look at *my* house. *{She goes slowly around to porch}*

SIMEON: *{with a snort}* Her house!

PETER: *{calls after her}* Ye'll find Eben inside. Ye better not tell him it's *yewr* house.

ABBIE: *{mouthing the name}* Eben. *{Then quietly}* I'll tell Eben.

CABOT: *{with a contemptuous sneer}* Ye needn't heed Eben. Eben's a dumb fool—like his Maw—soft an' simple!

SIMEON: *{with his sardonic burst of laughter}* Ha! Eben's a chip o' yew— spit 'n' image—hard 'n' bitter's a hickory tree! Dog'll eat dog. He'll eat ye yet, old man!

CABOT: *{commandingly}* Ye git t' wuk!

SIMEON: *{as* ABBIE *disappears in house—winks at* PETER *and says tauntingly}* So that thar's our new Maw, be it? Whar in hell did ye dig her up? *{He and* PETER *laugh}*

PETER: Ha! Ye'd better turn her in the pen with the other sows. *{They laugh uproariously, slapping their thighs}*

CABOT: *{so amazed at their effrontery that he stutters in confusion}* Simeon! Peter! What's come over ye? Air ye drunk?

SIMEON: We're free, old man—free o' yew an' the hull damned farm! *{They grow more and more hilarious and excited}*

PETER: An' we're startin' out fur the gold fields o' Californi-a!

SIMEON: Ye kin take this place an' burn it!

PETER: An' bury it—fur all we cares!

SIMEON: We're free, old man! *{He cuts a caper}*

PETER: Free! *{He gives a kick in the air}*

SIMEON: *{in a frenzy}* Whoop!

PETER: Whoop! *{They do an absurd Indian war dance about the old man who is petrified between rage and the fear that they are insane}*

SIMEON: We're free as Injuns! Lucky we don't skulp ye!

PETER: An' burn yer barn an' kill the stock!

SIMEON: An' rape yer new woman! Whoop! *{He and* PETER *stop their* *dance, holding their sides, rocking with wild laughter}*

CABOT: *{edging away}* Lust fur gold —fur the sinful, easy gold o' Californi-a! It's made ye mad!

SIMEON: *{tauntingly}* Wouldn't ye like us to send ye back some sinful gold, ye old sinner?

PETER: They's gold besides what's in Californi-a! *{He retreats back beyond the vision of the old man and takes the bag of money and flaunts it in the air above his head, laughing}*

SIMEON: And sinfuller, too!

PETER: We'll be voyagin' on the sea! Whoop! *{He leaps up and down}*

SIMEON: Livin' free! Whoop! *{He leaps in turn}*

CABOT: *{suddenly roaring with rage}* My cuss on ye!

SIMEON: Take our'n in trade fur it! Whoop!

CABOT: I'll hev ye both chained up in the asylum!

PETER: Ye old skinflint! Good-by!

SIMEON: Ye old blood sucker! Good-by!

CABOT: Go afore I . . . !

PETER: Whoop! *{He picks a stone from the road. SIMEON does the same}*

SIMEON: Maw'll be in the parlor.

PETER: Ay-eh! One! Two!

CABOT: *{frightened}* What air ye . . . ?

PETER: Three! *{They both throw, the stones hitting the parlor window with a crash of glass, tearing the shade}*

SIMEON: Whoop!

PETER: Whoop!

CABOT: *{in a fury now, rushing toward them}* If I kin lay hands on ye —I'll break yer bones fur ye! *{But they beat a capering retreat before him, SIMEON with the gate still under his arm. CABOT comes back, panting with impotent rage. Their voices as they go off take up the song of the gold-seekers to the old tune of "Oh, Susannah!"}*

I jumped aboard the Liza ship,
And traveled on the sea,
And every time I thought of home
I wished it wasn't me!

Oh! Californi-a,
That's the land fur me!
I'm off to Californi-a!
With my wash bowl on my knee.

{In the meantime, the window of the upper bedroom on right is raised and ABBIE sticks her head out. She looks down at CABOT—with a sigh of relief}

ABBIE: Waal—that's the last o' them two, hain't it? *{He doesn't answer. Then in possessive tones}* This here's a nice bedroom, Ephraim. It's a r'al nice bed. Is it my room, Ephraim?

CABOT: *{grimly—without looking up}* Our'n! *{She cannot control a grimace of aversion and pulls back her head slowly and shuts the window. A sudden horrible thought seems to enter CABOT's head}* They been up to somethin'! Mebbe—mebbe they've pizened the stock—'r somethin'! *{He almost runs off down toward the barn. A moment later the kitchen door is slowly pushed open and ABBIE enters. For a moment she stands looking at EBEN. He does not notice her at first. Her eyes take him in penetratingly with a calculating appraisal of his strength as against hers. But under this her desire is dimly awakened by his youth and good looks. Suddenly he becomes conscious of her presence and looks up. Their eyes meet. He leaps to his feet, glowering at her speechlessly}*

ABBIE: *{in her most seductive tones which she uses all through this scene}* Be you—Eben? I'm Abbie—*{She laughs}* I mean, I'm yer new Maw.

EBEN: *{viciously}* No, damn ye!

ABBIE: *{as if she hadn't heard—with a queer smile}* Yer Paw's spoke a lot o' yew. . . .

EBEN: Ha!

ABBIE: Ye mustn't mind him. He's an old man. *{A long pause. They stare at each other}* I don't want t' pretend playin' Maw t' ye, Eben. *{Admiringly}* Ye're too big an' too strong fur that. I want t' be frens with ye. Mebbe with me fur a fren ye'd find ye'd like livin' here better. I kin make it easy fur ye with him, mebbe. *{With a scornful sense* *of power}* I calc'late I kin git him t' do most anythin' fur me.

EBEN: *{with bitter scorn}* Ha! *{They stare again,* EBEN *obscurely moved, physically attracted to her—in forced stilted tones}* Yew kin go t' the devil!

ABBIE: *{calmly}* If cussin' me does ye good, cuss all ye've a mind t'. I'm all prepared t' have ye agin me—at fust. I don't blame ye nuther. I'd feel the same at any stranger comin' t' take my Maw's place. *{He shudders. She is watching him carefully}* Yew must've cared a lot fur yewr Maw, didn't ye? My Maw died afore I'd growed. I don't remember her none. *{A pause}* But yew won't hate me long, Eben. I'm not the wust in the world—an' yew an' me've got a lot in common. I kin tell that by lookin' at ye. Waal—I've had a hard life, too—oceans o' trouble an' nuthin' but wuk fur reward. I was a orphan early an' had t' wuk fur others in other folks' hums. Then I married an' he turned out a drunken spreer an' so he had to wuk fur others an' me too agen in other folks' hums, an' the baby died, an' my husband got sick an' died too, an' I was glad sayin' now I'm free fur once, on'y I diskivered right away all I was free fur was t' wuk agen in other folks' hums, doin' other folks' wuk till I'd most give up hope o' ever doin' my own wuk in my own hum, an' then your Paw come.... [CABOT *appears returning from the barn. He comes to the gate and looks down the road the brothers have gone. A faint strain of their retreating voices is heard: "Oh, Californi-a! That's the place for me." He stands glowering, his fist clenched, his face grim with rage}*

EBEN: *{fighting against his growing attraction and sympathy—harshly}* An' bought yew—like a harlot! *{She is stung and flushes angrily. She has been sincerely moved by the recital of her troubles. He adds furiously}* An' the price he's payin' ye—this farm—was my Maw's, damn ye!—an' mine now!

ABBIE: *{with a cool laugh of confidence}* Yewr'n? We'll see 'bout that!

{Then strongly} Waal—what if I did need a hum? What else'd I marry an old man like him fur.

EBEN: *{maliciously}* I'll tell him ye said that!

ABBIE: *{smiling}* I'll say ye're lyin' a-purpose—an' he'll drive ye off the place!

EBEN: Ye devil!

ABBIE: *{defying him}* This be my farm—this be my hum—this be my kitchen—!

EBEN: *{furiously, as if he were going to attack her}* Shut up, damn ye!

ABBIE: *{walks up to him—a queer coarse expression of desire in her face and body—slowly}* An' upstairs—that be my bedroom—an my bed! *{He stares into her eyes, terribly confused and torn. She adds softly}* I hain't bad nor mean —'ceptin' fur an enemy—but I got t' fight fur what's due me out o' life, if I ever 'spect t' git it. *{Then putting her hand on his arm—seductively}* Let's yew 'n' me be frens, Eben.

EBEN: *{stupidly—as if hypnotized}* Ay-eh. *{Then furiously flinging off her arm}* No, ye durned old witch! I hate ye! *{He rushes out the door}*

ABBIE: *{looks after him smiling satisfiedly—then half to herself, mouthing the word}* Eben's nice. *{She looks at the table, proudly}* I'll wash up *my* dishes now. [EBEN *appears outside, slamming the door behind him. He comes around corner, stops on seeing his father, and stands staring at him with hate}*

CABOT: *{raising his arms to heaven in the fury he can no longer control}* Lord God o' Hosts, smite the undutiful sons with Thy wust cuss!

EBEN: *{breaking in violently}* Yew 'n' yewr God! Allus cussin' folks—allus naggin' 'em.

CABOT: *{oblivious to him—summoningly}* God o' the old! God o' the lonesome!

EBEN: *{mockingly}* Naggin' His sheep t' sin! T' hell with yewr God! [CABOT *turns. He and* EBEN *glower at each other}*

CABOT: *{harshly}* So it's yew. I

might've knowed it. *{Shaking his finger threateningly at him}* Blasphemin' fool! *{Then quickly}* Why hain't ye t' wuk?

EBEN: Why hain't yew? They've went. I can't wuk it all alone.

CABOT: *{contemptuously}* Nor noways! I'm wuth ten o' ye yit, old's I be!

Ye'll never be more'n half a man! *{Then, matter-of-factly}* Waal—let's git t' the barn. *{They go. A last faint note of the "Californi-a" song is heard from the distance.* ABBIE *is washing her dishes}*

CURTAIN

Part II

SCENE ONE

The exterior of the farmhouse, as in Part One—a hot Sunday afternoon two months later. ABBIE, *dressed in her best, is discovered sitting in a rocker at the end of the porch. She rocks listlessly, enervated by the heat, staring in front of her with bored, half-closed eyes.*

EBEN *sticks his head out of his bedroom window. He looks around furtively and tries to see—or hear—if anyone is on the porch, but although he has been careful to make no noise,* ABBIE *has sensed his movement. She stops rocking, her face grows animated and eager, she waits attentively.* EBEN *seems to feel her presence, he scowls back his thoughts of her and spits with exaggerated disdain—then withdraws back into the room.* ABBIE *waits, holding her breath as she listens with passionate eagerness for every sound within the house.*

EBEN *comes out. Their eyes meet. His falter, he is confused, he turns away and slams the door resentfully. At this gesture,* ABBIE *laughs tantalizingly, amused but at the same time piqued and irritated. He scowls, strides off the porch to the path and starts to walk past her to the road with a grand swagger of ignoring her existence. He is dressed in his store suit, spruced up, his face shines from soap and water.* ABBIE *leans forward on her chair, her eyes hard and angry now, and, as he passes her, gives a sneering, taunting chuckle.*

EBEN: *{stung—turns on her furiously}* What air yew cacklin' 'bout?

ABBIE: *{triumphantly}* Yew!

EBEN: What about me?

ABBIE: Ye look all slicked up like a prize bull.

EBEN: *{with a sneer}* Waal—ye hain't so durned purty yerself, be ye? *{They stare into each other's eyes, his held by hers in spite of himself, hers glowingly possessive. Their physical attraction becomes a palpable force quivering in the hot air}*

ABBIE: *{softly}* Ye don't mean that, Eben. Ye may think ye mean it, mebbe, but ye don't. Ye can't. It's agin nature, Eben. Ye been fightin' yer nature ever since the day I come—tryin' t' tell yerself I hain't purty t'ye. *{She laughs a low humid laugh without taking her eyes*

from his. A pause—her body squirms desirously—she murmurs languorously} Hain't the sun strong an' hot? Ye kin feel it burnin' into the earth—Nature—makin' thin's grow—bigger 'n' bigger—burnin' inside ye—makin' ye want to grow—into somethin' else—till ye're jined with it—an' it's your'n—but it owns, ye, too—an' makes ye grow bigger —like a tree—like them elums—*{She laughs again softly, holding his eyes. He takes a step toward her, compelled against his will}* Nature'll beat ye, Eben. Ye might's well own up t' it fust 's last.

EBEN: *{trying to break from her spell —confusedly}* If Paw'd hear ye goin' on. . . . *{Resentfully}* But ye've made such a damned idjit out o' the old devil . . . ! *{*ABBIE *laughs}*

ABBIE: Waal—hain't it easier fur yew with him changed softer?

EBEN: *{defiantly}* No. I'm fightin' him—fightin' yew—fightin' fur Maw's rights t' her hum! *{This breaks her spell for him. He glowers at her}* An' I'm onto ye. Ye hain't foolin' me a mite. Ye're aimin' t' swaller up everythin' an' make it your'n. Waal, you'll find I'm a heap sight bigger hunk nor yew kin chew! *{He turns from her with a sneer}*

ABBIE: *{trying to regain her ascendancy—seductively}* Eben!

EBEN: Leave me be! *{He starts to walk away}*

ABBIE: *{more commandingly}* Eben!

EBEN: *{stops—resentfully}* What d'ye want?

ABBIE: *{trying to conceal a growing excitement}* Whar air ye goin'?

EBEN: *{with malicious nonchalance}* Oh—up the road a spell.

ABBIE: T' the village?

EBEN: *{airily}* Mebbe.

ABBIE: *{excitedly}* T' see that Min, I s'pose?

EBEN: Mebbe.

ABBIE: *{weakly}* What d'ye want t' waste time on her fur?

EBEN: *{revenging himself now—grinning at her}* Ye can't beat Nature, didn't ye say? *{He laughs and again starts to walk away}*

ABBIE: *{bursting out}* An ugly old hake!

EBEN: *{with a tantalizing sneer}* She's purtier'n yew be!

ABBIE: That every wuthless drunk in the country has. . . .

EBEN: *{tauntingly}* Mebbe—but she's better'n yew. She owns up fa'r 'n' squar' t' her doin's.

ABBIE: *{furiously}* Don't ye dare compare. . . .

EBEN: She don't go sneakin' an' stealin'—what's mine.

ABBIE: *{savagely seizing on his weak point}* Your'n? Yew mean—my farm?

EBEN: I mean the farm yew sold yerself fur like any other old whore—my farm!

ABBIE: *{stung—fiercely}* Ye'll never live t' see the day when even a stinkin' weed on it 'll belong 't ye! *{Then in a scream}* Git out o' my sight! Go on t' yer slut—disgracin' yer Paw 'n' me! I'll git yer Paw t' horsewhip ye off the place if I want t'! Ye're only livin' here 'cause I tolerate ye! Git along! I hate the sight o' ye! *{She stops, panting and glaring at him}*

EBEN: *{returning her glance in kind}* An' I hate the sight o' yew! *{He turns and strides off up the road. She follows his retreating figure with concentrated hate. Old* CABOT *appears coming up from the barn. The hard, grim expression of his face has changed. He seems in some queer way softened, mellowed. His eyes have taken on a strange, incongruous dreamy quality. Yet there is no hint of physical weakness about him— rather he looks more robust and younger.* ABBIE *sees him and turns away quickly with unconcealed aversion. He comes slowly up to her}*

CABOT: *{mildly}* War yew an' Eben quarrelin' agen?

ABBIE: *{shortly}* No.

CABOT: Ye was talkin' a'mighty loud. *{He sits down on the edge of porch}*

ABBIE: *{snappishly}* If ye heerd us they hain't no need askin' questions.

CABOT: I didn't hear what ye said.

ABBIE: *{relieved}* Waal—it wa'n't nothin' t' speak on.

CABOT: *{after a pause}* Eben's queer.

ABBIE: *{bitterly}* He's the dead spit 'n' image o' yew!

CABOT: *{queerly interested}* D'ye think so, Abbie? *{After a pause, ruminatingly}* Me 'n' Eben's allus fit 'n' fit. I never could b'ar him noways. He's so thunderin' soft—like his Maw.

ABBIE: *{scornfully}* Ay-eh! 'Bout as soft as yew be!

CABOT: *{as if he hadn't heard}* Mebbe I been too hard on him.

ABBIE: *{jeeringly}* Waal—ye're gittin' soft now—soft as slop! That's what Eben was sayin'.

CABOT: *{his face instantly grim and ominous}* Eben was sayin'? Waal, he'd best not do nothin' t' try me 'r he'll soon diskiver. . . . *{A pause. She keeps her face turned away. His gradually softens. He stares up at the sky}* Purty, hain't it?

ABBIE: *{crossly}* I don't see nothin' purty.

CABOT: The sky. Feels like a wa'm field up thar.

ABBIE: *{sarcastically}* Air yew aimin' t' buy up over the farm too? *{She snickers contemptuously}*

CABOT: *{strangely}* I'd like t' own my place up thar. *{A pause}* I'm gittin' old, Abbie. I'm gittin' ripe on the bough. *{A pause. She stares at him mystified. He goes on}* It's allus lonesome cold in the house—even when it's bilin' hot outside. Hain't yew noticed?

ABBIE: No.

CABOT: It's wa'm down t' the barn—nice smellin' an' warm—with the cows. *{A pause}* Cows is queer.

ABBIE: Like yew?

CABOT: Like Eben. *{A pause}* I'm gittin t' feel resigned t' Eben—jest as I got t' feel 'bout his Maw. I'm gettin' t' learn to b'ar his softness—jest like her'n. I calc'late I c'd a'most take t' him—if he wa'n't sech a dumb fool! *{A pause}* I s'pose it's old age a-creepin' in my bones.

ABBIE: *{indifferently}* Waal—ye hain't dead yet.

CABOT: *{roused}* No, I hain't, yew bet—not by a hell of a sight—I'm sound 'n' tough as hickory! *{Then moodily}* But arter three score and ten the Lord warns ye t' prepare. *{A pause}* That's why Eben's come in my head. Now that his cussed sinful brothers is gone their path t' hell, they's no one left but Eben.

ABBIE: *{resentfully}* They's me, hain't they? *{Agitatedly}* What's all this sudden likin' ye've tuk to Eben? Why don't ye say nothin' 'bout me? Hain't I yer lawful wife?

CABOT: *{simply}* Ay-eh. Ye be. *{A pause—he stares at her desirously—his eyes grow avid—then with a sudden movement he seizes her hands and squeezes them, declaiming in a queer camp meeting preacher's tempo}* Yew air my Rose o' Sharon! Behold, yew air fair; yer eyes air doves; yer lips air like scarlet; yer two breasts air like two fawns; yer navel be like a round goblet; yer belly be like a heap o' wheat. . . . *{He covers her hand with kisses. She does not seem to notice. She stares before her with hard angry eyes}*

ABBIE: *{jerking her hands away—harshly}* So ye're plannin' t' leave the farm t' Eben, air ye?

CABOT: *{dazedly}* Leave. . . .? *{Then with resentful obstinacy}* I hain't a-given' it t' no one!

ABBIE: *{remorselessly}* Ye can't take it with ye.

CABOT: *{thinks a moment—then reluctantly}* No, I calc'late not. *{After a pause—with a strange passion}* But if I could, I would, by the Etarnal! 'R if I could, in my dyin' hours, I'd set it afire an' watch it burn—this house an' every ear o' corn an' every tree down t' the last blade o' hay! I'd sit and know it was all a-dying with me and no one else'd ever own what was mine, what I'd made out o' nothin' with my own sweat 'n' blood! *{A pause—then he adds with a queer affection}* 'Ceptin' the cows. Them I'd turn free.

ABBIE: *{harshly}* An' me?

CABOT: *{with a queer smile}* Ye'd be turned free, too.

ABBIE: *{furiously}* So that's the thanks I git fur marryin' ye—t' have ye change kind to Eben who hates ye, an' talk o' turnin' me out in the road.

CABOT: *{hastily}* Abbie! Ye know I wa'n't. . . .

ABBIE: *{vengefully}* Just let me tell ye a thing or two 'bout Eben! Whar's he gone? T' see that harlot, Min! I tried fur t' stop him. Disgracin' yew an' me —on the Sabbath, too!

CABOT: *{rather guiltily}* He's a sinner —nateral-born. It's lust eatin' his heart.

ABBIE: *{enraged beyond endurance—wildly vindictive}* An' his lust fur me! Kin ye find excuses fur that?

CABOT: *{stares at her—after a dead pause}* Lust—fur yew?

ABBIE: *{defiantly}* He was tryin' t'

make love t' me—when ye heerd us quarrelin'.

CABOT: *{stares at her—then a terrible expression of rage comes over his face —he springs to his feet shaking all over}* By the A'mighty God—I'll end him!

ABBIE: *{frightened now for Eben}* No! Don't ye!

CABOT: *{violently}* I'll git the shot-gun an' blow his soft brains t' the top o' them elums!

ABBIE: *{throwing her arms around him}* No, Ephraim!

CABOT: *{pushing her away violently}* I will, by God!

ABBIE: *{in a quieting tone}* Listen, Ephraim. 'Twa'n't nothin' bad—on'y a boy's foolin'—Twa'n't meant serious— jest jokin' an teasin'. . . .

CABOT: Then why did ye say—lust?

ABBIE: It must hev sounded wusser'n I meant. An' I was mad at thinkin'— ye'd leave him the farm.

CABOT: *{quieter but still grim and cruel}* Waal then, I'll horsewhip him off the place if that much'll content ye.

ABBIE: *{reaching out and taking his hand}* No. Don't think o' me! Ye must-n't drive him off. 'Tain't sensible. Who'll ye get to help ye on the farm? They's no one hereabouts.

CABOT: *{considers this—then nodding his appreciation}* Ye got a head on ye. *{Then irritably}* Waal, let him stay. *{He sits down on the edge of the porch. She sits beside him. He murmurs contemp-tuously}* I oughtn't t' git riled so—at that 'ere fool calf. *{A pause}* But har's the p'int. What son o' mine'll keep on here t' the farm—when the Lord does call me? Simeon an' Peter air gone t' hell—an' Eben's follerin' 'em.

ABBIE: They's me.

CABOT: Ye're on'y a woman.

ABBIE: I'm yewr wife.

CABOT: That hain't me. A son is me —my blood—mine. Mine ought t' git mine. An' then it's still mine—even though I be six foot under. D'ye see?

ABBIE: *{giving him a look of hatred}* Ay-eh. I see. *{She becomes very thought-

ful, her face growing shrewd, her eyes studying CABOT craftily}*

CABOT: I'm gittin' old—ripe on the bough. *{Then with a sudden forced reassurance}* Not but what I hain't a hard nut t' crack even yet—an' fur many a year t' come! By the Etarnal, I kin break most o' the young feller's backs at any kind o' work any day o' the year!

ABBIE: *{suddenly}* Mebbe the Lord'll give *us* a son.

CABOT: *{turns and stares at her eagerly}* Ye mean—a son—t' me 'n' yew?

ABBIE: *{with cajoling smile}* Ye're a strong man yet, hain't ye? 'Tain't no-ways impossible, be it? We know that. Why d'ye stare so? Hain't ye never thought o' that afore? I been thinkin' o' it all along. Ay-eh—an' I been prayin' it'd happen, too.

CABOT: *{his face growing full of joy-ous pride and a sort of religious ecstasy}* Ye been prayin', Abbie?—fur a son— t' us?

ABBIE: Ay-eh. *{With a grim resolu-tion}* I want a son now.

CABOT: *{excitedly clutching both of her hands in his}* It'd be the blessin' o' God, Abbie—the blessin' o' God A'-mighty on me—in my old age—in my lonesomeness! They hain't nothin' I wouldn't do fur ye then, Abbie. Ye'd hev on'y t' ask it—anythin' ye'd a mind t'!

ABBIE: *{interrupting}* Would ye will the farm t' me then—t' me an' it. . . ?

CABOT: *{vehemently}* I'd do anythin' ye axed, I tell ye! I swar it! May I be everlastin' damned t' hell if I wouldn't! *{He sinks to his knees pulling her down with him. He trembles all over with the fervor of his hopes}* Pray t' the Lord agen, Abbie. It's the Sabbath! I'll jine ye! Two prayers air better nor one. "An' God hearkened unto Rachel"! An' God hearkened unto Abbie! Pray, Abbie! Pray fur him to hearken! *{He bows his head, mumbling. She pretends to do like-wise but gives him a side glance of scorn and triumph}*

SCENE TWO

About eight in the evening. The interior of the two bedrooms on the top floor is shown. EBEN *is sitting on the side of his bed in the room on the left. On account of the heat he has taken off everything but his undershirt and pants. His feet are bare. He faces front, brooding moodily, his chin propped on his hands, a desperate expression on his face.*

In the other room CABOT *and* ABBIE *are sitting side by side on the edge of their bed, an old four-poster with feather mattress. He is in his night shirt, she in her nightdress. He is still in the queer, excited mood into which the notice of a son has thrown him. Both rooms are lighted dimly and flickeringly by tallow candles.*

CABOT: The farm needs a son.

ABBIE: I need a son.

CABOT: Ah-eh. Sometimes ye air the farm an' sometimes the farm be yew. That's why I clove t' ye in my lonesomeness. {*A pause. He pounds his knee with his fist*} Me an' the farm has got t' beget a son!

ABBIE: Ye'd best go t' sleep. Ye're gittin' thin's all mixed.

CABOT: {*with an impatient gesture*} No, I hain't. My mind's clear's a well. Ye don't know me, that's it. {*He stares hopelessly at the floor*}

ABBIE: {*indifferently*} Mebbe. {*In the next room* EBEN *gets up and paces up and down distractedly.* ABBIE *hears him. Her eyes fasten on the intervening wall with concentrated attention.* EBEN *stops and stares. Their hot glances seem to meet through the wall. Unconsciously he stretches out his arms for her and she half rises. Then aware, he mutters a curse at himself and flings himself face downward on the bed, his clenched fists above his head, his face buried in the pillow.* ABBIE *relaxes with a faint sigh but her eyes remain fixed on the wall; she listens with all her attention for some movement from* EBEN]

CABOT: {*suddenly raises his head and looks at her—scornfully*} Will ye ever know me—'r will any man 'r woman? {*Shaking his head*} No. I calc'late 't wa'n't t' be. {*He turns away.* ABBIE *looks at the wall. Then, evidently unable to keep silent about his thoughts, without looking at his wife, he puts out his hand and clutches her knee. She starts violently, looks at him, sees he is not watching her, concentrates again on the wall and pays no attention to what he says*} Listen, Abbie. When I come here fifty odd year ago—I was jest twenty an' the strongest an' hardest ye ever seen—ten times as strong an' fifty times as hard as Eben. Waal—this place was nothin' but fields o' stones. Folks laughed when I tuk it. They couldn't know what I knowed. When ye kin make corn sprout out o' stones, God's livin' in yew! They wa'n't strong enuf fur that! They reckoned God was easy. They laughed. They don't laugh no more. Some died hereabouts. Some went West an' died. They're all under ground—fur follerin' arter an easy God. God hain't easy. {*He shakes his head slowly*} An' I growed hard. Folks kept allus sayin' he's a hard man like 'twas sinful t' be hard, so's at last I said back at 'em: Waal then, by thunder, ye'll git me hard an' see how ye like it! {*Then suddenly*} But I give in t' weakness once. 'Twas arter I'd been here two year. I got weak—despairful —they was so many stones. They was a party leavin', given' up, goin' West. I jined 'em. We tracked on 'n on. We come t' broad medders, plains, whar the soil was black an' rich as gold. Nary a stone. Easy. Ye'd on'y to plow an' sow an' then set an' smoke yer pipe an' watch thin's grow. I could o' been a rich man—but somethin' in me fit an' fit me—the voice o' God sayin': "This hain't wuth nothin' t' Me. Git ye back t' hum!" I got afeerd o' that voice an' I lit out back t' hum here, leavin' my claim an' crops t' whoever'd a mind t' take 'em. Ay-eh. I actoolly give up what was rightful mine! God's hard, not easy! God's in the stones! Build my church on a rock—out o' stones an' I'll be in them! That's what He meant t' Peter! {He sighs heavily—a pause} Stones. I picked 'em up an' piled 'em into walls. Ye kin read the years o' my life in them walls, every day a hefted stone, climbin' over the hills up and down, fencin' in the fields that was mine, whar I'd made thin's grow out o' nothin'—like the will o' God, like the servant o' His hand. It wa'n't easy. It was hard an' He made me hard fur it. {He pauses} All the time I kept gittin' lonesomer. I tuk a wife. She bore Simeon an' Peter. She was a good woman. She wuked hard. We was married twenty year. She never knowed me. She helped but she never knowed what she was helpin'. I was allus lonesome. She died. After that it wa'n't so lonesome fur a spell. {A pause} I lost count o' the years. I had no time t' fool away countin' 'em. Sim an' Peter helped. The farm growed. It was all mine! When I thought o' that I didn't feel lonesome. {A pause} But ye can't hitch yer mind t' one thin' day an' night: I tuk another wife—Eben's Maw. Her folks was contestin' me at law over my deeds t' the farm—my farm! That's why Eben keeps a-talkin' his fool talk o' this bein' his Maw's farm. She bore Eben. She was purty—but soft. She tried t' be hard. She couldn't. She never knowed me nor nothin'. It was lonesomer 'n hell with her. After a matter o' sixteen odd years, she died. {A pause} I lived with the boys. They hated me 'cause I was hard. I hated them 'cause they was soft. They coveted the farm without knowin' what it meant. It made me bitter 'n wormwood. It aged me—them coveting what I'd made fur mine. Then this spring the call come—the voice o' God cryin' in my wilderness, in my lonesomeness—t' go out an' seek an' find! {Turning to her with strange passion} I sought ye an'

I found ye! Yew air my Rose o' Sharon! Yer eyes air like. . . . {She has turned a blank face, resentful eyes to his. He stares at her for a moment—then harshly} Air ye any the wiser fur all I've told ye?

ABBIE: {confusedly} Mebbe.

CABOT: {pushing her away from him—angrily} Ye don't know nothin'—nor never will. If ye don't hev a son t' redeem ye. . . . {This is a tone of cold threat}

ABBIE: {resentfully} I've prayed, hain't I?

CABOT: {bitterly} Pray agen—fur understandin'!

ABBIE: {a veiled threat in her tone} Ye'll have a son out o' me, I promise ye.

CABOT: How kin ye promise?

ABBIE: I got second-sight mebbe. I kin foretell. {She gives a queer smile}

CABOT: I believe ye have. Ye give me the chills sometimes. {He shivers} It's cold in this house. It's oneasy. They's thin's pokin' about in the dark—in the corners. {He pulls on his trousers, tucking in his night shirt, and pulls on his boots}

ABBIE: {surprised} Whar air ye goin'?

CABOT: {queerly} Down whar it's restful—whar it's warm—down t' the barn. {Bitterly} I kin talk t' the cows. They know. They know the farm an' me. They'll give me peace. {He turns to go out the door}

ABBIE: {a bit frightenedly} Air ye ailin' tonight, Ephraim?

CABOT: Growin'. Growin' ripe on the bough. {He turns and goes, his boots clumping down the stairs. EBEN sits up with a start, listening. ABBIE is conscious of his movement and stares at the wall. CABOT comes out of the house around the corner and stands by the gate, blinking at the sky. He stretches up his hands in a tortured gesture} God A'mighty, call from the dark! {He listens as if expecting an answer. Then his arms drop, he shakes his head and plods off toward the barn. EBEN and ABBIE stare at each other through the wall. EBEN sighs heavily and ABBIE echoes it. Both become terribly *nervous, uneasy. Finally* ABBIE *gets up and listens, her ear to the wall. He acts as if he saw every move she was making, he becomes resolutely still. She seems driven into a decision—goes out the door in rear determinedly. His eyes follow her. Then as the door of his room is opened softly, he turns away, waits in an attitude of strained fixity.* ABBIE *stands for a second staring at him, her eyes burning with desire. Then with a little cry she runs over and throws her arms about his neck, she pulls his head back and covers his mouth with kisses. At first, he submits dumbly; then he puts his arms about her neck and returns her kisses, but finally, suddenly aware of his hatred, he hurls her away from him, springing to his feet. They stand speechless and breathless, panting like two animals}*

ABBIE: *{at last—painfully}* Ye shouldn't, Eben—ye shouldn't—I'd make ye happy!

EBEN: *{harshly}* I don't want t' be happy—from yew!

ABBIE: *{helplessly}* Ye do, Eben! Ye do! Why d'ye lie?

EBEN: *{viciously}* I don't take t'ye. I tell ye! I hate the sight o' ye!

ABBIE: *{with an uncertain troubled laugh}* Waal, I kissed ye anyways—an' ye kissed back—yer lips was burnin'— ye can't lie 'bout that! *{Intensely}* If ye don't care, why did ye kiss me back— why was yer lips burnin'?

EBEN: *{wiping his mouth}* It was like pizen on 'em. *{Then tauntingly}* When I kissed ye back, mebbe I thought 'twas someone else.

ABBIE: *{wildly}* Min?

EBEN: Mebbe.

ABBIE: *{torturedly}* Did ye go t' see her? Did ye r'ally go? I thought ye mightn't. Is that why ye throwed me off jest now?

EBEN: *{sneeringly}* What if it be?

ABBIE: *{raging}* Then ye're a dog, Eben Cabot!

EBEN: *{threateningly}* Ye can't talk that way t' me!

ABBIE: *{with a shrill laugh}* Can't I?

Did ye think I was in love with ye—a weak thin' like yew? Not much! I on'y wanted ye fur a purpose o' my own— an' I'll hev ye fur it yet 'cause I'm stronger'n yew be!

EBEN: *{resentfully}* I knowed well it was on'y part o' yer plan t' swaller everythin'!

ABBIE: *{tauntingly}* Mebbe!

EBEN: *{furious}* Git out o' my room!

ABBIE: This air my room an' ye're on'y hired help!

EBEN: *{threateningly}* Git out afore I murder ye!

ABBIE: *{quite confident now}* I hain't a mite afeerd. Ye want me, don't ye? Yes, ye do! An' yer Paw's son'll never kill what he wants! Look at yer eyes! They's lust fur me in 'em, burnin' 'em up! Look at yer lips now! They're tremblin' an' longin' t' kiss me, an' yer teeth t' bite! *{He is watching her now with a horrible fascination. She laughs a crazy triumphant laugh}* I'm a-goin' t' make all o' this hum my hum! They's one room hain't mine yet, but it's a-goin' t' be tonight. I'm a-goin' down now an' light up! *{She makes him a mocking bow}* Won't ye come courtin' me in the best parlor, Mister Cabot?

EBEN: *{staring at her—horribly confused—dully}* Don't ye dare! It hain't been opened since Maw died an' was laid out thar! Don't ye. . . ! *{But her eyes are fixed on his so burningly that his will seems to wither before hers. He stands swaying toward her helplessly}*

ABBIE: *{holding his eyes and putting all her will into her words as she backs out the door}* I'll expect ye afore long, Eben.

EBEN: *{stares after her for a while, walking toward the door. A light appears in the parlor window. He murmurs}* In the parlor? *{This seems to arouse connotations for he comes back and puts on his white shirt, collar, half ties the tie mechanically, puts on coat, takes his hat, stands barefooted looking about him in bewilderment, mutters wonderingly}* Maw! Whar air yew? *{Then goes slowly toward the door in rear}*

SCENE THREE

A few minutes later. The interior of the parlor is shown. A grim, repressed room like a tomb in which the family has been interred alive. ABBIE sits on the edge of the horsehair sofa. She has lighted all the candles and the room is revealed in all its preserved ugliness. A change has come over the woman. She looks awed and frightened now, ready to run away.

The door is opened and ELEN appears. His face wears an expression of obsessed confusion. He stands staring at her, his arms hanging disjointedly from his shoulders, his feet bare, his hat in his hand.

ABBIE: *{after a pause—with a nervous, formal politeness}* Won't ye set?

EBEN: *{dully}* Ay-eh. *{Mechanically he places his hat carefully on the floor near the door and sits stiffly beside her on the edge of the sofa. A pause. They both remain rigid, looking straight ahead with eyes full of fear}*

ABBIE: When I fust come in—in the dark—they seemed somethin' here.

EBEN: *{simply}* Maw.

ABBIE: I kin still feel—somethin'. . . .

EBEN: It's Maw.

ABBIE: At fust I was feered o' it. I wanted t' yell an' run. Now—since yew come—seems like it's growin' soft an' kind t' me. *{Addressing the air—queerly}* Thank yew.

EBEN: Maw allus loved me.

ABBIE: Mebbe it knows I love yew, too. Mebbe that makes it kind t' me.

EBEN: *{dully}* I dunno. I should think she'd hate ye.

ABBIE: *{with certainty}* No. I kin feel it don't—not no more.

EBEN: Hate ye fur stealin' her place —here in her hum—settin' in her parlor whar she was laid—*{He suddenly stops, staring stupidly before him}*

ABBIE: What is it, Eben?

EBEN: *{in a whisper}* Seems like Maw didn't want me t' remind ye.

ABBIE: *{excitedly}* I knowed, Eben! It's kind t' me! It don't b'ar me no grudges fur what I never knowed an' couldn't help!

EBEN: Maw b'ars him a grudge.

ABBIE: Waal, so does all o' us.

EBEN: Ay-eh. *{With passion}* I does, by God!

ABBIE: *{taking one of his hands in hers and patting it}* Thar! Don't git riled thinkin' o' him. Think o' yer Maw who's kind t' us. Tell me about yer Maw, Eben.

EBEN: They hain't nothin' much. She was kind. She was good.

ABBIE: *{putting one arm over his shoulder. He does not seem to notice— passionately}* I'll be kind an' good t' ye!

EBEN: Sometimes she used t' sing fur me.

ABBIE: I'll sing fur ye!

EBEN: This was her hum. This was her farm.

ABBIE: This is my hum! This is my farm!

EBEN: He married her t' steal 'em. She was soft an' easy. He couldn't 'preciate her.

ABBIE: He can't 'preciate me!

EBEN: He murdered her with his hardness.

ABBIE: He's murderin' me!

EBEN: She died. *{A pause}* Sometimes she used to sing fur me. *{He bursts into a fit of sobbing}*

ABBIE: *{both her arms around him— with wild passion}* I'll sing fur ye! I'll die fur ye! *{In spite of her overwhelming desire for him, there is a sincere maternal love in her manner and voice —a horribly frank mixture of lust and mother love}* Don't cry, Eben! I'll take yer Maw's place! I'll be everythin' she was t' ye! Let me kiss ye, Eben! *{She pulls his head around. He makes a bewildered pretense of resistance. She is tender}* Don't be afeered! I'll kiss ye pure, Eben—same 's if I was a Maw t' ye — an' ye kin kiss me back 's if yew was my son—my boy—sayin' good-night t' me! Kiss me, Eben. *{They kiss in restrained fashion. Then suddenly wild passion overcomes her. She kisses him lustfully again and again and he flings his arms about her and returns her kisses. Suddenly, as in the bedroom, he frees himself from her violently and springs to his feet. He is trembling all over, in a strange state of terror.* ABBIE *strains her arms toward him with fierce pleading}* Don't ye leave me, Eben! Can't ye see it hain't enuf—lovin' ye like a Maw—can't ye see it's got t' be that an' more—much more—a hundred times more—fur me t' be happy—fur yew t' be happy?

EBEN: *{to the presence he feels in the room}* Maw! Maw! What d'ye want? What air ye tellin' me?

ABBIE: She's tellin' ye t' love me. She knows I love ye an' I'll be good t' ye. Can't ye feel it? Don't ye know? She's tellin' ye t' love me, Eben!

EBEN: Ay-eh. I feel—mebbe she—but—I can't figger out—why—when ye've stole her place—here in her hum—in the parlor whar she was—

ABBIE: *{fiercely}* She knows I love ye!

EBEN: *{his face suddenly lighting up with a fierce, triumphant grin}* I see it! I sees why. It's her vengeance on him—so's she kin rest quiet in her grave!

ABBIE: *{wildly}* Vengeance o' God on the hull o' us! What d'we give a durn? I love ye, Eben! God knows I love ye! *{She stretches out her arms for him}*

EBEN: *{throws himself on his knees beside the sofa and grabs her in his arms—releasing all his pent-up passion}* An' I love yew, Abbie!—now I kin say it! I been dyin' fur want o' ye—every hour since ye come! I love ye! *{Their lips meet in a fierce, bruising kiss}*

SCENE FOUR

Exterior of the farmhouse. It is just dawn. The front door at right is opened and EBEN *comes out and walks around to the gate. He is dressed in his working clothes. He seems changed. His face wears a bold and confident expression, he is grinning to himself with evident satisfaction. As he gets near the gate, the window of the parlor is heard opening and the shutters are flung back and* ABBIE *sticks her head out. Her hair tumbles over her shoulders in disarray, her face is flushed, she looks at* EBEN *with tender, languorous eyes and calls softly}*

ABBIE: Eben. *{As he turns—playfully}* Jest one more kiss afore ye go. I'm goin' to miss ye fearful all day.

EBEN: An' me yew, ye kin bet! *{He goes to her. They kiss several times. He draws away, laughingly}* Thar. That's enuf, hain't it? Ye won't hev none left fur next time.

ABBIE: I got a million o' 'em left fur yew! *{Then a bit anxiously}* D'ye r'ally love me, Eben?

EBEN: *{emphatically}* I like ye better'n any gal I ever knowed! That's gospel!

ABBIE: Likin' hain't lovin'.

EBEN: Waal then—I love ye. Now air yew satisfied?

ABBIE: Ay-eh, I be. *{She smiles at him adoringly}*

EBEN: I better git t' the barn. The old critter's liable t' suspicion an' come sneakin' up.

ABBIE: *{with a confident laugh}* Let him! I kin allus pull the wool over his eyes. I'm goin' t' leave the shutters open and let in the sun 'n' air. This room's been dead long enuf. Now it's goin' t' be my room!

EBEN: *{frowning}* Ay-eh.

ABBIE: *{hastily}* I meant—our room.

EBEN: Ay-eh.

ABBIE: We made it our'n last night, didn't we? We give it life—our lovin' did. *{A pause}*

EBEN: *{with a strange look}* Maw's gone back t' her grave. She kin sleep now.

ABBIE: May she rest in peace! *{Then*

tenderly rebuking} Ye oughtn't t' talk o' sad thin's—this mornin'.

EBEN: It jest come up in my mind o' itself.

ABBIE: Don't let it. *{He doesn't answer. She yawns}* Waal, I'm a-goin' t' steal a wink o' sleep. I'll tell the Old Man I hain't feelin' pert. Let him git his own vittles.

EBEN: I see him comin' from the barn. Ye better look smart an git upstairs.

ABBIE: Ay-eh. Good-by. Don't ferget me. *{She throws him a kiss. He grins— then squares his shoulders and awaits his father confidently.* CABOT *walks slowly up from the left, staring up at the sky with a vague face}*

EBEN: *{jovially}* Mornin', Paw. Stargazin' in daylight?

CABOT: Purty, hain't it?

EBEN: *{looking around him possessively}* It's a durned purty farm.

CABOT: I mean the sky.

EBEN: *{grinning}* How d'ye know? Them eyes o' your'n can't see that fur. *{This tickles his humor and he slaps his thigh and laughs}* Ho-ho! That's a good un!

CABOT: *{grimly sarcastic}* Ye're feelin' right chipper, hain't ye? Whar'd ye steal the likker?

EBEN: *{good-naturedly}* 'Tain't likker. Jest life. *{Suddenly holding out his hand—soberly}* Yew 'n' me is quits. Let's shake hands.

CABOT: *{suspiciously}* What's come over ye?

EBEN: Then don't. Mebbe it's jest as well. *{A moment's pause}* What's come over me? *{Queerly}* Didn't ye feel her passin'—goin' back t' her grave?

CABOT: *{dully}* Who?

EBEN: Maw. She kin rest now an' sleep content. She's quits with ye.

CABOT: *{confusedly}* I rested. I slept good—down with the cows. They know how t' sleep. They're teachin' me.

EBEN: *{suddenly jovial again}* Good fur the cows! Waal—ye better git t' work.

CABOT: *{grimly amused}* Air yew bossin' me, ye calf?

EBEN: *{beginning to laugh}* Ay-eh! I'm bossin' yew! Ha-ha-ha! See how ye like it! Ha-ha-ha! I'm the prize rooster o' this roost. Ha-ha-ha! *{He goes off toward the barn laughing}*

CABOT: *{looks after him with scornful pity}* Soft-headed. Like his Maw. Dead spit 'n' image. No hope in him! *{He spits with contemptuous disgust}* A born fool! *{Then matter-of-factly}* Waal—I'm gittin' peckish. *{He goes toward door}*

CURTAIN

Part III

SCENE ONE

A night in late spring the following year. The kitchen and the two bedrooms upstairs are shown. The two bedrooms are dimly lighted by a tallow candle in each. EBEN *is sitting on the side of the bed in his room, his chin propped on his fists, his face a study of the struggle he is making to understand his conflicting emotions. The noisy laughter and music from below where a kitchen dance is in progress annoy and distract him. He scowls at the floor.*

In the next room a cradle stands beside the double bed.

In the kitchen all is festivity. The stove has been taken down to give more room to the dancers. The chairs, with wooden benches added, have been pushed back against the walls. On these are seated, squeezed in tight against one another, farmers and their wives and their young folks of both sexes from the neighboring farms. They are all chattering and laughing loudly. They evidently have some secret joke in common. There is no end of winking, of nudging, of meaning nods of the head toward CABOT *who, in a state of extreme hilarious excitement increased by the amount he has drunk, is standing near the rear door where there is a small keg of whisky and serving drinks to all the men. In the left corner, front, dividing the attention with her husband,* ABBIE *is sitting in a rocking chair, a shawl wrapped about her shoulders. She is very pale, her face is thin and drawn, her eyes are fixed anxiously on the open door in rear as if waiting for someone.*

The musician is tuning up his fiddle, seated in the far right corner. He is a lanky young fellow with a long, weak face. His pale eyes blink incessantly and he grins about him slyly with a greedy malice.

ABBIE: *{suddenly turning to a young girl on her right}* Whar's Eben?

YOUNG GIRL: *{eyeing her scornfully}* I dunno, Mrs. Cabot. I hain't seen Eben in ages. *{Meaningly}* Seems like he's spent most o' his time t' hum since yew come.

ABBIE: *{vaguely}* I tuk his Maw's place.

YOUNG GIRL: Ay-eh. So I've heerd. *{She turns away to retail this bit of gossip to her mother sitting next to her.* ABBIE *turns to her left to a big stoutish middle-aged man whose flushed face and starting eyes show the amount of "likker" he has consumed}*

ABBIE: Ye hain't seen Eben, hev ye?

MAN: No, I hain't. *{Then he adds with a wink}* If yew hain't, who would?

ABBIE: He's the best dancer in the county. He'd ought t' come an' dance.

MAN: *{with a wink}* Mebbe he's doin' the dutiful an' walkin' the kid t' sleep. It's a boy, hain't it?

ABBIE: *{nodding vaguely}* Ay-eh— born two weeks back—purty's a picter.

MAN: They all is—t' their Maws. *{Then in a whisper, with a nudge and a leer}* Listen, Abbie—if ye ever git tired o' Eben, remember me! Don't fergit now! *{He looks at her uncomprehending face for a second—then grunts disgustedly}* Waal—guess I'll likker agin. *{He goes over and joins* CABOT *who is arguing noisily with an old farmer over cows. They all drink}*

ABBIE: *{this time appealing to nobody in particular}* Wonder what Eben's a-doin'? *{Her remark is repeated down the line with many a guffaw and titter until it reaches the fiddler. He fastens his blinking eyes on* ABBIE]

FIDDLER: *{raising his voice}* Bet I kin tell ye, Abbie, what Eben's doin'! He's down t' the church offerin' up prayers o' thanksgivin'. *{They all titter expectantly}*

A MAN: What fur? *{Another titter}*

FIDDLER: 'Cause unto him a—*{He hesitates just long enough}* brother is born! *{A roar of laughter. They all look from* ABBIE *to* CABOT. *She is oblivious, staring at the door.* CABOT, *although he hasn't heard the words, is irritated by the laughter and steps forward, glaring about him. There is an immediate silence}*

CABOT: What're ye all bleatin' about —like a flock o' goats? Why don't ye dance, damn ye? I axed ye here t' dance —t' eat, drink an' be merry—an' thar ye set cacklin' like a lot o' wet hens with the pip! Ye've swilled my likker an' guzzled my vittles like hogs, hain't ye? Then dance fur me, can't ye? That's fa'r an' squar', hain't it? *{A grumble of resentment goes around but they are all evidently in too much awe of him to express it openly}*

FIDDLER: *{Slyly}* We're waitin' fur Eben. *{A suppressed laugh}*

CABOT: *{with a fierce exultation}* T'hell with Eben! Eben's done fur now! I got a new son! *{His mood switching with drunken suddenness}* But ye needn't t' laugh at Eben, none o' ye! He's my blood, if he be a dumb fool. He's better nor any o' yew! He kin do a day's work a'most up t' what I kin—an' that'd put any o' yew pore critters t' shame!

FIDDLER: An' he kin do a good night's work, too! *{A roar of laughter}*

CABOT: Laugh, ye damn fools! Ye're right jist the same, Fiddler. He kin work day an' night too, like I kin, if need be!

OLD FARMER: *{from behind the keg where he is weaving drunkenly back and forth—with great simplicity}* They hain't many t' touch ye, Ephraim—a son at seventy-six. That's a hard man fur ye! I be on'y sixty-eight an' I couldn't do it. *{A roar of laughter in which CABOT joins uproariously}*

CABOT: *{slapping him on the back}* I'm sorry fur ye, Hi. I'd never suspicion sech weakness from a boy like yew!

OLD FARMER: An' I never reckoned yew had it in ye nuther, Ephraim. *{There is another laugh}*

CABOT: *{suddenly grim}* I got a lot in me—a hell of a lot—folks don't know on. *{Turning to the fiddler}* Fiddle 'er up, durn ye! Give 'em somethin' t' dance t'! What air ye, an ornament? Hain't this a celebration? Then grease yer elbow an' go it!

FIDDLER: *{seizes a drink which the OLD FARMER holds out to him and downs it}* Here goes! *{He starts to fiddle "Lady of the Lake." Four young fellows and four girls form in two lines and dance a square dance. The FIDDLER shouts directions for the different movements, keeping his words in the rhythm of the music and interspersing them with jocular personal remarks to the dancers themselves. The people seated along the walls stamp their feet and clap their hands in unison. CABOT is especially active in this respect. Only ABBIE remains apathetic, staring at the door as if she were alone in a silent room}*

FIDDLER: Swing your partner t' the right! That's it, Jim! Give her a b'ar hug! Her Maw hain't lookin'. *{Laughter}* Change partners! That suits ye, don't it, Essie, now ye got Reub afore ye? Look at her redden up, will ye? Waal, life is short an' so's love, as the feller says. *{Laughter}*

CABOT: *{excitedly, stamping his foot}* Go it, boys! Go it, gals!

FIDDLER: *{with a wink at the others}* Ye're the spryest seventy-six ever I sees, Ephraim! Now if ye'd on'y good eyesight . . . ! *{suppressed laughter. He gives CABOT no chance to retort but roars}* Promenade! Ye're walkin' like a bride down the aisle, Sarah! Waal, while they's life they's allus hope, I've heerd tell. Swing your partner to the left! Gosh A'mighty, look at Johnny Cook high-steppin'! They hain't goin' t'be much strength left fur howin' in the corn lot t'morrow. *{Laughter}*

CABOT: Go it! Go it! *{Then suddenly, unable to restrain himself any longer, he prances into the midst of the dancers, scattering them, waving his arms about wildly}* Ye're all hoofs! Git out o' my road! Give me room! I'll show ye dancin'. Ye're all too soft! *{He pushes them roughly away. They crowd back toward the walls, muttering, looking at him resentfully}*

FIDDLER: *{jeeringly}* Go it, Ephraim! Go it! *{He starts "Pop Goes the Weasel," increasing the tempo with every verse until at the end he is fiddling crazily as fast as he can go}*

CABOT: *{starts to dance, which he does very well and with tremendous vigor. Then he begins to improvise, cuts incredibly grotesque capers, leaping up and cracking his heels together, prancing around in a circle with body bent in an Indian war dance, then suddenly straightening up and kicking as high as he can with both legs. He is like a monkey on a string. And all the while he intersperses his antics with shouts and derisive comments}* Whoop! Here's dancin' fur ye! Whoop! See that! Seventy-six, if I'm a day! Hard as iron yet! Beatin' the young 'uns like I allus done! Look at me! I'd invite ye t' dance on my hundredth birthday on'y ye'll all be dead by then. Ye're a sickly generation! Yer hearts air pink, not red! Yer veins is full o' mud an' water! I be the on'y man in the county! Whoop! See that! I'm a Injun!

I've killed Injuns in the West afore ye was born—an' skulped 'em too! They's a arrer wound on my backside I c'd show ye! The hull tribe chased me. I outrun 'em all—with the arrer stuck in me! An' I tuk vengeance on 'em. Ten eyes fur an eye, that was my motter! Whoop! Look at me! I kin kick the ceilin' off the room! Whoop!

FIDDLER: *{stops playing—exhaustedly}* God A'mighty, I got enuf. Ye got the devil's strength in ye.

CABOT: *{delightedly}* Did I beat yew, too? Wa'al, ye played smart. Hev a swig. *{He pours whisky for himself and FIDDLER. They drink. The others watch CABOT silently with cold, hostile eyes. There is a dead pause. The FIDDLER rests. CABOT leans against the keg, panting, glaring around him confusedly. In the room above, EBEN gets to his feet and tiptoes out the door in rear, appearing a moment later in the other bedroom. He moves silently, even frightenedly, toward the cradle and stands there looking down at the baby. His face is as vague as his reactions are confused, but there is a trace of tenderness, of interested discovery. At the same moment that he reaches the cradle, ABBIE seems to sense something. She gets up weakly and goes to CABOT]*

ABBIE: I'm goin' up t' the baby.

CABOT: *{with real solicitation}* Air ye able fur the stairs? D'ye want me t' help ye, Abbie?

ABBIE: No. I'm able. I'll be down agen soon.

CABOT: Don't ye git wore out! He needs ye, remember—our son does! *{He grins affectionately, patting her on the back. She shrinks from his touch}*

ABBIE: *{dully}* Don't—tech me. I'm goin'—up. *{She goes. CABOT looks after her. A whisper goes around the room. CABOT turns. It ceases. He wipes his forehead streaming with sweat. He is breathing pantingly}*

CABOT: I'm a-goin' out t' git fresh air. I'm feelin' a mite dizzy. Fiddle up thar! Dance, all o' ye! Here's likker fur them as wants it. Enjoy yerselves. I'll be back. *{He goes, closing the door behind him}*

FIDDLER: *{sarcastically}* Don't hurry none on our account! *{A suppressed laugh. He imitates* ABBIE] Whar's Eben? *{More laughter}*

A WOMAN: *{loudly}* What's happened in this house is plain as the nose on yer face! [ABBIE *appears in the doorway upstairs and stands looking in surprise and adoration at* EBEN *who does not see her}*

A MAN: Ssshh! He's li'ble t' be listenin' at the door. That'd be like him. *{Their voices die to an intensive whispering. Their faces are concentrated on this gossip. A noise as of dead leaves in the wind comes from the room. CABOT has come out from the porch and stands by the gate, leaning on it, staring at the sky blinkingly. ABBIE comes across the room silently. EBEN does not notice her until quite near}*

EBEN: *{starting}* Abbie!

ABBIE: Ssshh! *{She throws her arms around him. They kiss—then bend over the cradle together}* Ain't he purty?— dead spit 'n' image o' yew!

EBEN: *{pleased}* Air he? I can't tell none.

ABBIE: E-zactly like!

EBEN: *{frowningly}* I don't like this. I don't like lettin' on what's mine's his'n. I been doin' that all my life. I'm gittin' t' the end of b'arin' it!

ABBIE: *{putting her finger on his lips}* We're doin' the best we kin. We got t' wait. Somethin's bound t' happen. *{She puts her arms around him}* I got t' go back.

EBEN: I'm goin' out. I can't b'ar it with the fiddle playin' an' the laughin'.

ABBIE: Don't git feelin' low. I love ye, Eben. Kiss me. *{He kisses her. They remain in each other's arms}*

CABOT: *{at the gate, confusedly}* Even the music can't drive it out—somethin'. Ye kin feel it droppin' off the elums, climbin' up the roof, sneakin' down the chimney, pokin' in the corners! They's no peace in houses, they's no rest livin' with folks. Somethin's always livin' with ye. *{With a deep sigh}* I'll go t' the barn an' rest a spell. *{He goes wearily toward the barn}*

FIDDLER: *{tuning up}* Let's celebrate the old skunk gittin' fooled! We kin have some fun now he's went. *{He starts to fiddle "Turkey in the Straw." There is real merriment now. The young folks get up to dance}*

SCENE TWO

*A half hour later—Exterior—*EBEN *is standing by the gate looking up at the sky, an expression of dumb pain bewildered by itself on his face.* CABOT *appears, returning from the barn, walking wearily, his eyes on the ground. He sees* EBEN *and his whole mood immediately changes. He becomes excited, a cruel, triumphant grin comes to his lips, he strides up and slaps* EBEN *on the back. From within comes the whining of the fiddle and the noise of stamping feet and laughing voices.*

CABOT: So har ye be!

EBEN: *{startled, stares at him with hatred for a moment—then dully}* Ay-eh.

CABOT: *{surveying him jeeringly}* Why hain't ye been in t' dance? They was all axin' fur ye.

EBEN: Let 'em ax!

CABOT: They's a hull passel o' purty gals.

EBEN: T' hell with 'em!

CABOT: Ye'd ought t' be marryin' one o' 'em soon.

EBEN: I hain't marryin' no one.

CABOT: Ye might 'arn a share o' a farm that way.

EBEN: *{with a sneer}* Like yew did, ye mean? I hain't that kind.

CABOT: *{stung}* Ye lie! 'Twas yer Maw's folks aimed t' steal my farm from me.

EBEN: Other folks don't say so. *{After a pause—defiantly}* An' I got a farm, anyways!

CABOT: *{derisively}* Whar?

EBEN: *{stamps a foot on the ground}* Har!

CABOT: *{throws his head back and laughs coarsely}* Ho-ho! Ye hev, hev ye? Waal, that's a good un!

EBEN: *{controlling himself—grimly}* Ye'll see!

CABOT: *{stares at him suspiciously, trying to make him out—a pause—then with scornful confidence}* Ay-eh. I'll see. So'll ye. It's ye that's blind—blind as a mole underground. [EBEN *suddenly laughs, one short sardonic bark: "Ha."* A pause. CABOT *peers at him with renewed suspicion}* Whar air ye hawin' 'bout? [EBEN *turns away without answering.* CABOT *grows angry}* God A'mighty, yew air a dumb dunce! They's nothin' in that thick skull o' your'n but noise—like a empty keg it be! [EBEN *doesn't seem to hear.* CABOT's *rage grows}* Yewr farm! God A'mighty! If ye wa'n't a born donkey ye'd know ye'll never own stick nor stone on it, specially now arter him bein' born. It's his'n, I tell ye—his'n arter I die—but I'll live a hundred jest t' fool ye all—an' he'll be growed then—yewr age a'most! [EBEN *laughs again his sardonic "Ha." This drives* CABOT *into a fury}* Ha? Ye think ye kin git 'round that someways, do ye? Waal, it'll be her'n, too—Abbie's —ye won't git 'round her—she knows yer tricks—she'll be too much fur ye— she wants the farm her'n—she was afeerd o' ye—she told me ye was sneakin' 'round tryin' t' make love t' her t' get her on yer side . . . ye . . . ye mad fool, ye! *{He raises his clenched fists threateningly}*

EBEN: *{is confronting him choking with rage}* Ye lie, ye old skunk! Abbie never said no sech thing!

CABOT: *{suddenly triumphant when he sees how shaken* EBEN *is}* She did. An' I says, I'll blow his brains t' the top o' them elums—an' she says no, that hain't sense, who'll ye git t'help ye on the farm in his place—an' then she says yew'n me ought t' have a son—I know we kin, she says—an' I says, if we do, ye kin have anythin' I've got ye've a mind t'. An' she says, I wants Eben cut off so's this farm'll be mine when ye die! *{With terrible gloating}* An' that's what's happened, hain't it? An the farms her'n! An' the dust o' the road— that's you'rn! Ha! Now who's hawin'?

EBEN: *{has been listening, petrified with grief and rage—suddenly laughs wildly and brokenly}* Ha-ha-ha! So that's her sneakin' game—all along!—like I suspicioned at fust—t' swaller it all— an' me, too . . . ! *{Madly}* I'll murder her! *{He springs toward the porch but* CABOT *is quicker and gets in between}*

CABOT: No, ye don't!

EBEN: Git out o' my road! *{He tries to throw* CABOT *aside. They grapple in what becomes immediately a murderous struggle. The old man's concentrated strength is too much for* EBEN. CABOT *gets one hand on his throat and presses him back across the stone wall. At the same moment,* ABBIE *comes out on the porch. With a stifled cry she runs toward them}*

ABBIE: Eben! Ephraim! *{She tugs at the hand on* EBEN's *throat}* Let go, Ephraim! Ye're chokin him!

CABOT: *{removes his hand and flings* EBEN *sideways full length on the grass, gasping and choking. With a cry,* ABBIE *kneels beside him, trying to take his head on her lap, but he pushes her away.* CABOT *stands looking down with fierce triumph}* Ye needn't t've fret, Abbie, I wa'n't aimin' t' kill him. He hain't wuth hangin' fur—not by a hell of a sight! *{More and more triumphantly}* Seventy-six an' him not thirty yit—an' look whar he be fur thinkin' his Paw was easy! No, by God, I hain't easy! An' him upstairs, I'll raise him t' be like me! *{He turns to leave them}* I'm goin' in an' dance!— sing an' celebrate! *{He walks to the porch—then turns with a great grin}* I don't calc'late it's left in him, but if he

gits pesky, Abbie, ye jest sing out. I'll come a-runnin' an' by the Etarnal, I'll put him across my knee an' birch him! Ha-ha-ha! *{He goes into the house laughing. A moment later his loud "whoop" is heard}*

ABBIE: *{tenderly}* Eben. Air ye hurt? *{She tries to kiss him but he pushes her violently away and struggles to a sitting position}*

EBEN: *{gaspingly}* T'hell—with ye!

ABBIE: *{not believing her ears}* It's me, Eben—Abbie—don't ye know me?

EBEN: *{glowering at her with hatred}* Ay-eh—I know ye—now! *{He suddenly breaks down, sobbing weakly}*

ABBIE: *{fearfully}* Eben—What's happened t' ye—why did ye look at me 's if ye hated me?

EBEN: *{violently, between sobs and gasps}* I do hate ye! Ye're a whore—a damn trickin' whore!

ABBIE: *{shrinking back horrified}* Eben! Ye don't know what ye're sayin'!

EBEN: *{scrambling to his feet and following her—accusingly}* Ye're nothin' but a stinkin' passel o' lies! Ye've been lyin' t' me every word ye spoke, day an' night, since we fust—done it. Ye've kept sayin' ye loved me. . . .

ABBIE: *{frantically}* I do love ye! *{She takes his hand but he flings hers away}*

EBEN: *{unheeding}* Ye've made a fool o' me—a sick, dumb fool—a-purpose! Ye've been on'y playin' yer sneakin', stealin' game all along—gittin' me t' lie with ye so's ye'd hev a son he'd think was his'n, an' makin' him promise he'd give ye the farm and let me eat dust, if ye did git him a son! *{Staring at her with anguished, bewildered eyes}* They must be a devil livin' in ye! T'ain't human t' be as bad as that be!

ABBIE: *{stunned—dully}* He told yew . . . ?

EBEN: Hain't it true? It ain't no good in yew lyin'.

ABBIE: *{pleadingly}* Eben, listen—ye must listen—it was long ago—afore we done nothin'—yew was scornin' me— goin' t' see Min—when I was lovin' ye an' I said it t' him t' git vengeance on ye!

EBEN: *{unheedingly. With tortured passion}* I wish ye was dead! I wish I was dead along with ye afore this come! *{Ragingly}* But I'll git my vengeance too! I'll pray Maw t' come back t' help me—t' put her cuss on yew an' him!

ABBIE: *{brokenly}* Don't ye, Eben! Don't ye! *{She throws herself on her knees before him, weeping}* I didn't mean t' do bad t'ye! Fergive me, won't ye?

EBEN: *{not seeming to hear her— fiercely}* I'll git squar' with the old skunk —an' yew! I'll tell him the truth 'bout the son he's so proud o'! Then I'll leave ye here t' pizen each other—with Maw comin' out o' her grave at nights—an' I'll go t' the gold fields o' Californi-a whar Sim an' Peter be!

ABBIE: *{terrified}* Ye won't—leave me? Ye can't!

EBEN: *{with fierce determination}* I'm a-goin', I tell ye! I'll git rich thar an' come back an' fight him fur the farm he stole—an' I'll kick ye both out in the road—t' beg an' sleep in the woods—an' yer son along with ye—t' starve an' die! *{He is hysterical at the end}*

ABBIE: *{with a shudder—humbly}* He's yewr son, too, Eben.

EBEN: *{torturedly}* I wish he never was born! I wish he'd die this minit! I wish I'd never sot eyes on him! It's him —yew havin' him—a-purpose t' steal— that's changed everythin'!

ABBIE: *{gently}* Did ye believe I loved ye—afore he come?

EBEN: Ay-eh—like a dumb ox!

ABBIE: An' ye don't believe no more?

EBEN: B'lieve a lyin' thief! Ha!

ABBIE: *{shudders—then humbly}* An' did ye r'ally love me afore?

EBEN: *{brokenly}* Ah-eh—an' ye was trickin' me!

ABBIE: An' ye don't love me now!

EBEN: *{violently}* I hate ye, I tell ye!

ABBIE: An' ye're truly goin' West—

goin' t' leave me—all account o' him being born?

EBEN: I'm a-goin' in the mornin'—or may God strike me t' hell!

ABBIE: *{after a pause—with a dreadful cold intensity—slowly}* If that's what his comin's done t' me—killin' yewr love—takin' yew away—my on'y joy— the on'y joy I ever knowed—like heaven t' me—purtier'n heaven—then I hate him, too, even if I be his Maw!

EBEN: *{bitterly}* Lies! Ye love him! He'll steal the farm fur ye! *{Brokenly}* But t'ain't the farm so much—not no more—it's yew foolin' me—gittin' me t' love ye—lyin' yew loved me—jest t' git a son t' steal!

ABBIE: *{distractedly}* He won't steal! I'd kill him fust! I do love ye! I'll prove t' ye. . . !

EBEN: *{harshly}* T'aint no use lyin' no more. I'm deaf t' ye! *{He turns away}* I hain't seein' ye agen. Good-by!

ABBIE: *{pale with anguish}* Hain't ye even goin' t' kiss me—not once—arter all we loved?

EBEN: *{in a hard voice}* I hain't wantin' t' kiss ye never agen! I'm wantin' t' forgit I ever sot eyes on ye!

ABBIE: Eben!—ye mustn't—wait a spell—I want t' tell ye. . . .

EBEN: I'm a-goin' in t' git drunk. I'm a-goin' t' dance.

ABBIE: *{clinging to his arm—with passionate earnestness}* If I could make it—'s if he'd never come up between us—if I could prove t' ye I wa'n't schemin' t' steal from ye—so's everythin' could be jest the same with us, lovin' each other jest the same, kissin' an' happy the same's we've been happy afore he come —if I could do it—ye'd love me agen, wouldn't ye? Ye'd kiss me agen? Ye wouldn't never leave me, would ye?

EBEN: *{moved}* I calc'late not. *{Then shaking her hand off his arm—with a bitter smile}* But ye hain't God, be ye?

ABBIE: *{exultantly}* Remember ye've promised! *{Then with strange intensity}*

Mebbe I kin take back one thin' God does!

EBEN: *{peering at her}* Ye're gittin' cracked, hain't ye? *{Then going towards door}* I'm a-goin' t' dance.

ABBIE: *{calls after him intensely}* I'll prove t' ye! I'll prove I love ye better'n. . . . *{He goes in the door, not seeming to hear. She remains standing where she is, looking after him—then she finishes desperately}* Better'n everythin' else in the world!

SCENE THREE

Just before dawn in the morning—shows the kitchen and CABOT's *bedroom. In the kitchen, by the light of a tallow candle on the table,* EBEN *is sitting, his chin propped on his hands, his drawn face blank and expressionless. His carpetbag is on the floor beside him. In the bedroom, dimly lighted by a small whale-oil lamp,* CABOT *lies asleep.* ABBIE *is bending over the cradle, listening, her face full of terror yet with an undercurrent of desperate triumph. Suddenly, she breaks down and sobs, appears about to throw herself on her knees beside the cradle; but the old man turns restlessly, groaning in his sleep, and she controls herself, and, shrinking away from the cradle with a gesture of horror, backs swiftly toward the door in rear and goes out. A moment later she comes into the kitchen and, running to* EBEN, *flings her arms about his neck and kisses him wildly. He hardens himself, he remains unmoved and cold, he keeps his eyes straight ahead.*

ABBIE: *{hysterically}* I done it, Eben! I told ye I'd do it! I've proved I love ye—better'n everythin'—so's ye can't never doubt me no more!

EBEN: *{dully}* Whatever ye done, it hain't no good now.

ABBIE: *{wildly}* Don't ye say that! Kiss me, Eben, won't ye? I need ye t' kiss me arter what I done! I need ye t' say ye love me!

EBEN: *{kisses her without emotion—dully}* That's fur good-by. I'm a-goin' soon.

ABBIE: No! No! Ye won't go—not now!

EBEN: *{going on with his own thoughts}* I been a-thinkin'—an' I hain't goin' t' tell Paw nothin'. I'll leave Maw t' take vengeance on ye. If I told him, the old skunk'd jest be stinkin' mean enuf to take it out on that baby. *{His voice showing emotion in spite of him}* An' I don't want nothin' bad t' happen t' him. He hain't t' blame fur yew. *{He adds with a certain queer pride}* An' he looks like me! An' by God, he's mine! An' some day I'll be a-comin' back an' . . . !

ABBIE: *{too absorbed in her own thoughts to listen to him—pleadingly}* They's no cause fur ye t' go now—they's no sense—it's all the same's it was—they's nothin' come b'tween us now—arter what I done!

EBEN: *{something in her voice arouses him. He stares at her a bit frightenedly}* Ye look mad, Abbie. What did ye do?

ABBIE: I—I killed him, Eben.

EBEN: *{amazed}* Ye killed him?

ABBIE: *{dully}* Ay-eh.

EBEN: *{recovering from his astonishment—savagely}* An' serves him right! But we got t' do somethin' quick t' make it look s'if the old skunk'd killed himself when he was drunk. We kin prove by 'em all how drunk he got.

ABBIE: *{wildly}* No! No! Not him! *{Laughing distractedly}* But that's what I ought t' done, hain't it? I oughter killed him instead! Why didn't ye tell me?

EBEN: *{appalled}* Instead? What d'ye mean?

ABBIE: Not him.

EBEN: *{his face grown ghastly}* Not —not that baby!

ABBIE: {dully} Ay-eh!

EBEN: {falls to his knees as if he'd been struck—his voice trembling with horror} Oh, God A'mighty! A'mighty God! Maw, whar was ye, why didn't ye stop her?

ABBIE: {simply} She went back t' her grave that night we fust done it, remember? I hain't felt her about since. {A pause. EBEN hides his head in his hands, trembling all over as if he had the ague. She goes on dully} I left the piller over his little face. Then he killed himself. He stopped breathin'. {She begins to weep softly}

EBEN: {rage beginning to mingle with grief} He looked like me. He was mine, damn ye!

ABBIE: {slowly and brokenly} I didn't want t' do it. I hated myself fur doin' it. I loved him. He was so purty—dead spit 'n' image o' yew. But I loved yew more —an' yew was goin' away—far off whar I'd never see ye agen, never kiss ye, never feel ye pressed agin me agen—an' ye said ye hated me fur havin' him— ye said ye hated him an' wished he was dead—ye said if it hadn't been fur him comin' it'd be the same's afore between us.

EBEN: {unable to endure this, springs to his feet in a fury, threatening her, his twitching fingers seeming to reach out for her throat} Ye lie! I never said—I never dreamed ye'd—I'd cut off my head afore I'd hurt his finger!

ABBIE: {piteously, sinking on her knees} Eben, don't ye look at me like that—hatin' me—not after what I done fur ye—fur us—so's we could be happy agen—

EBEN: {furiously now} Shut up, or I'll kill ye! I see yer game now—the same old sneakin' trick—ye're aimin' t' blame me fur the murder ye done!

ABBIE: {moaning—putting her hands over her ears} Don't ye, Eben! Don't ye! {She grasps his legs}

EBEN: {his mood suddenly changing to horror, shrinks away from her} Don't ye tech me! Ye're pizen! How could ye —t' murder a pore little critter—Ye must've swapped yer soul t' hell! {Suddenly raging} Ha! I kin see why ye done it! Not the lies ye jest told—but 'cause ye wanted t' steal agen—steal the last thin' ye'd left me—my part o' him— no, the hull o' him—ye saw he looked like me—ye knowed he was all mine— an' ye couldn't b'ar it—I know ye! Ye killed him fur bein' mine! {All this has driven him almost insane. He makes a rush past her for the door—then turns— shaking both fists at her, violently} But I'll take vengeance now! I'll git the Sheriff! I'll tell him everythin'! Then I'll sing "I'm off to Californi-a!" an' go— gold—Golden Gate—gold sun—fields o' gold in the West! {This last he half shouts, half croons incoherently, suddenly breaking off passionately} I'm a-goin' fur the Sheriff t' come an' git ye! I want ye tuk away, locked up from me! I can't stand t' luk at ye! Murderer an' thief 'r not, ye still tempt me! I'll give ye up t' the Sheriff! {He turns and runs out, around the corner of house, panting and sobbing, and breaks into a swerving sprint down the road}

ABBIE: {struggling to her feet, runs to the door, calling after him} I love ye, Eben! I love ye! {She stops at the door weakly, swaying, about to fall} I don't care what ye do—if ye'll on'y love me agen—{She falls limply to the floor in a faint}

SCENE FOUR

About an hour later. Same as Scene Three. Shows the kitchen and CABOT's *bedroom. It is after dawn. The sky is brilliant with the sunrise. In the kitchen,* ABBIE *sits at the table, her body limp and exhausted, her head bowed down over her arms, her face hidden. Upstairs,* CABOT *is still asleep but awakens with a start. He looks toward the window and gives a snort of surprise and irritation—throws back the covers and begins hurriedly pulling on his clothes. Without looking behind him, he begins talking to* ABBIE *whom he supposes beside him.*

CABOT: Thunder 'n' lightnin', Abbie! I hain't slept this late in fifty year! Look 's if the sun was full riz a'most. Must've been the dancin' an' likker. Must be gittin' old. I hope Eben's t' wuk. Ye might've tuk the trouble t' rouse me, Abbie. *{He turns—sees no one there—surprised}* Waal—whar air she? Gittin' vittles, I calc'late. *{He tiptoes to the cradle and peers down—proudly}* Mornin', sonny. Purty's a picter! Sleepin' sound. He don't beller all night like most o' 'em. *{He goes quietly out the door in rear—few moments later enters kitchen—sees* ABBIE—*with satisfaction}* So thar ye be. Ye got any vittles cooked?

ABBIE: *{without moving}* No.

CABOT: *{coming to her, almost sympathetically}* Ye feelin' sick?

ABBIE: No.

CABOT: *{pats her on shoulder. She shudders}* Ye'd best lie down a spell. *{Half jocularly}* Yer son'll be needin' ye soon. He'd ought t' wake up with a gnashin' appetite, the sound way he's sleepin'.

ABBIE: *{shudders—then in a dead voice}* He hain't never goin' t' wake up.

CABOT: *{jokingly}* Takes after me this mornin'. I hain't slept so late in . . .

ABBIE: He's dead.

CABOT: *{stares at her—bewilderedly}* What. . . .

ABBIE: I killed him.

CABOT: *{stepping back from her—aghast}* Air ye drunk—'r crazy—'r . . . !

ABBIE: *{suddenly lifts her head and turns on him—wildly}* I killed him, I tell ye! I smothered him. Go up an' see if ye don't b'lieve me! [CABOT *stares at her a second, then bolts out the rear door, can be heard bounding up the stairs, and rushes into the bedroom and over to the cradle.* ABBIE *has sunk back lifelessly into her former position.* CABOT *puts his hand down on the body in the crib. An expression of fear and horror comes over his face}*

CABOT: *{shrinking away—tremblingly}* God A'mighty! God A'mighty. *{He stumbles out the door—in a short while returns to the kitchen—comes to* ABBIE, *the stunned expression still on his face —hoarsely}* Why did ye do it? Why? *{As she doesn't answer, he grabs her violently by the shoulder and shakes her}* I ax ye why ye done it! Ye'd better tell me 'r . . . !

ABBIE: *{gives him a furious push which sends him staggering back and springs to her feet—with wild rage and hatred}* Don't ye dare tech me! What right hev ye t' question me 'bout him? He wa'n't yewr son! Think I'd have a son by yew? I'd die fust! I hate the sight o' ye an' allus did! It's yew I should've murdered, if I'd had good sense! I hate ye! I love Eben. I did from the fust. An' he was Eben's son—mine an' Eben's— not your'n!

CABOT: *{stands looking at her dazedly—a pause—finding his words with an effort—dully}* That was it—what I felt—pokin' round the corners—while ye lied—holdin' yerself from me—sayin' ye'd a'ready conceived—*{He lapses into crushed silence—then with a strange emotion}* He's dead, sart'n. I felt his heart. Pore little critter! *{He blinks back one tear, wiping his sleeve across his nose}*

ABBIE: *{hysterically}* Don't ye! Don't ye! *{She sobs unrestrainedly}*

CABOT: *{with a concentrated effort that stiffens his body into a rigid line and hardens his face into a stony mask —through his teeth to himself}* I got t' be—like a stone—a rock o' jedgment! *{A pause. He gets complete control over himself—harshly}* If he was Eben's, I be glad he air gone! An' mebbe I suspicioned it all along. I felt they was somethin' onnateral—somewhars—the house got so lonesome—an' cold— drivin' me down t' the barn—t' the beasts o' the field. . . . Ay-eh. I must've suspicioned—somethin'. Ye didn't fool me—not altogether, leastways—I'm too old a bird—growin' ripe on the bough. . . . *{He becomes aware he is wandering, straightens again, looks at* ABBIE *with a cruel grin}* So ye'd liked t' hev murdered me 'stead o' him, would ye? Waal, I'll live to a hundred! I'll live t' see ye hung! I'll deliver ye up t' the jedgment o' God an' the law! I'll git the Sheriff now. *{Starts for the door}*

ABBIE: *{dully}* Ye needn't. Eben's gone fur him.

CABOT: *{amazed}* Eben—gone fur the Sheriff?

ABBIE: Ay-eh.

CABOT: T' inform agen ye?

ABBIE: Ay-eh.

CABOT: *{considers this—a pause—then in a hard voice}* Waal, I'm thankful fur him savin' me the trouble. I'll git t' wuk. *{He goes to the door—then turns—in a voice full of strange emotion}* He'd ought t' been my son, Abbie. Ye'd ought t' loved me. I'm a man. If ye'd loved me, I'd never told no Sheriff on ye no matter what ye did, if they was t' brile me alive!

ABBIE: *{defensively}* They's more to it nor yew know, makes him tell.

CABOT: *{dryly}* Fur yewr sake, I hope they be. *{He goes out—comes around to the gate—stares up at the sky. His control relaxes. For a moment he is old and weary. He murmurs despairingly}* God A'mighty, I be lonesomer'n ever! *{He hears running footsteps from the left, immediately is himself again.* EBEN *runs in, panting exhaustedly, wild-eyed and mad looking. He lurches through the gate.* CABOT *grabs him by the shoulder.* EBEN *stares at him dumbly}* Did ye tell the Sheriff?

EBEN: *{nodding stupidly}* Ay-eh.

CABOT: *{gives him a push away that sends him sprawling—laughing with withering contempt}* Good fur ye! A prime chip o' yer Maw ye be! *{He goes toward the barn, laughing harshly.* EBEN *scrambles to his feet. Suddenly* CABOT *turns—grimly threatening}* Git off this farm when the Sheriff takes her—or,

by God, he'll have t' come back an' git me fur murder, too! *{He stalks off.* EBEN *does not appear to have heard him. He runs to the door and comes into the kitchen.* ABBIE *looks up with a cry of anguished joy.* EBEN *stumbles over and throws himself on his knees beside her—sobbing brokenly}*

EBEN: Fergive me!

ABBIE: *{happily}* Eben! *{She kisses him and pulls his head over against her breast}*

EBEN: I love ye! Fergive me!

ABBIE: *{ecstatically}* I'd fergive ye all the sins in hell fur sayin' that! *{She kisses his head, pressing it to her with a fierce passion of possession}*

EBEN: *{brokenly}* But I told the Sheriff. He's comin' fur ye!

ABBIE: I kin b'ar what happens t' me now!

EBEN: I woke him up. I told him. He says, wait 'til I git dressed. I was waiting. I got to thinkin' o' yew. I got to thinkin' how I'd loved ye. It hurt like somethin' was bustin' in my chest an' head. I got t' cryin'. I knowed sudden I loved ye yet, an' allus would love ye!

ABBIE: *{caressing his hair—tenderly}* My boy, hain't ye?

EBEN: I begun t' run back. I cut across the fields an' through the woods. I thought ye might have time t' run away—with me—an' . . .

ABBIE: *{shaking her head}* I got t' take my punishment—t' pay fur my sin.

EBEN: Then I want t' share it with ye.

ABBIE: Ye didn't do nothin'.

EBEN: I put it in yer head. I wisht he was dead! I as much as urged ye t' do it!

ABBIE: No. It was me alone!

EBEN: I'm as guilty as yew be! He was the child o' our sin.

ABBIE: *{lifting her head as if defying God}* I don't repent that sin! I hain't askin' God t' fergive that!

EBEN: Nor me—but it led up t' the other—an' the murder ye did, ye did 'count o' me—an' it's my murder, too, I'll tell the Sheriff—an' if ye deny it, I'll say we planned it t'gether—an' they'll all b'lieve me, fur they suspicion everythin' we've done, an' it'll seem likely an' true to 'em. An' it is true—way down. I did help ye—somehow.

ABBIE: {*laying her head on his—sobbing*} No! I don't want yew t' suffer!

EBEN: I got t' pay fur my part o' the sin! An' I'd suffer wuss leavin' ye, goin' West, thinkin' o' ye day an' night, bein' out when yew was in—{*Lowering his voice*} 'r bein' alive when yew was dead. {*A pause*} I want t' share with ye, Abbie—prison 'r death 'r hell 'r anythin'! {*He looks into her eyes and forces a trembling smile*} If I'm sharin' with ye, I won't feel lonesome, leastways.

ABBIE: {*weakly*} Eben! I won't let ye! I can't let ye!

EBEN: {*kissing her—tenderly*} Ye can't help yerself. I got ye beat fur once!

ABBIE: {*forcing a smile—adoringly*} I hain't beat—s'long's I got ye!

EBEN: {*hears the sound of feet outside*} Ssshh! Listen! They've come t' take us!

ABBIE: No, it's him. Don't give him no chance to fight ye, Eben. Don't say nothin'—no matter what he says. An' I won't neither. {*It is* CABOT. *He comes up from the barn in a great state of excitement and strides into the house and then into the kitchen.* EBEN *is kneeling beside* ABBIE, *his arm around her, hers around him. They stare straight ahead*}

CABOT: {*stares at them, his face hard. A long pause—vindictively*} Ye makes a slick pair o' murderin' turtle doves! Ye'd ought t' be both hung on the same limb an' left thar t' swing in the breeze an' rot—a warnin' t' old fools like me t' b'ar their lonesomeness alone—an' fur young fools like ye t' hobble their lust. {*A pause. The excitement returns to his face, his eyes snap, he looks a bit crazy*} I couldn't work today. I couldn't take no interest. T' hell with the farm! I'm leavin' it! I've turned the cows an' other stock loose! I've druv 'em into the woods whar they kin be free! By freein' 'em, I'm freein' myself! I'm quittin' here today! I'll set fire t' house an' barn an' watch 'em burn, an I'll leave yer Maw t' haunt the ashes, an' I'll will the fields

back t' God, so that nothin' human kin never touch 'em! I'll be a-goin' to Californi-a—t' jine Simeon an' Peter—true sons o' mine if they be dumb fools—an' the Cabots'll find Solomon's Mines t'gether! {*He suddenly cuts a mad caper*} Whoop! What was the song they sung? "Oh, Californi-a! That's the land fur me." {*He sings this—then gets on his knees by the floor-board under which the money was hid*} An' I'll sail thar on one o' the finest clippers I kin find! I've got the money! Pity ye didn't know whar this was hidden so's ye could steal. . . . {*He has pulled up the board. He stares —feels—stares again. A pause of dead silence. He slowly turns, slumping into a sitting position on the floor, his eyes like those of a dead fish, his face the sickly green of an attack of nausea. He swallows painfully several times—forces a weak smile at last*} So—ye did steal it!

EBEN: {*emotionlessly*} I swapped it t' Sim an' Peter fur their share o' the farm—t' pay their passage t' Californi-a.

CABOT: {*with one sardonic*} Ha! {*He begins to recover. Gets slowly to his feet—strangely*} I calc'late God give it to 'em—not yew! God's hard, not easy! Mebbe they's easy gold in the West but it hain't God's gold. It hain't fur me. I kin hear His voice warnin' me agen t' be hard an' stay on my farm. I kin see his hand usin' Eben t' steal t' keep me from weakness. I kin feel I be in the palm o' His hand, His fingers guidin' me. {*A pause—then he mutters sadly*} It's a-goin' t' be lonesomer now than ever it war afore—an' I'm gittin' old, Lord—ripe on the bough. . . . {*Then stiffening*} Waal—what d'ye want? God's lonesome, hain't he? God's hard an' lonesome! {*A pause. The Sheriff with two men comes up the road from the left. They move cautiously to the door. The Sheriff knocks on it with the butt of his pistol*}

SHERIFF: Open in the name o' the law! {*They start*}

CABOT: They've come fur ye. {*He goes to the rear door*} Come in, Jim! {*The three men enter.* CABOT *meets them in doorway}* Jest a minit, Jim. I got 'em safe here. *{The Sheriff nods. He and his companions remain in the doorway}*

EBEN: *{suddenly calls}* I lied this mornin', Jim. I helped her to do it. Ye kin take me, too.

ABBIE: *{brokenly}* No!

CABOT: Take 'em both. *{He comes forward—stares at* EBEN *with a trace of grudging admiration}* Purty good—fur yew! Waal, I got t' round up the stock. Good-by.

EBEN: Good-by.

ABBIE: Good-by. *[*CABOT *turns and strides past the men—comes out and around the corner of the house, his shoulders squared, his face stony, and stalks grimly toward the barn. In the meantime the Sheriff and men have come into the room}*

SHERIFF: *{embarrassedly}* Waal—we'd best start.

ABBIE: Wait. *{Turns to* EBEN] I love ye, Eben.

EBEN: I love ye, Abbie. *{They kiss. The three men grin and shuffle embarrassedly.* EBEN *takes* ABBIE's *hand. They go out the door in rear, the men following, and come from the house, walking hand in hand to the gate.* EBEN *stops there and points to the sunrise sky}* Sun's a-rizin'. Purty, hain't it?

ABBIE: Ay-eh. *{They both stand for a moment looking up raptly in attitudes strangely aloof and devout}*

SHERIFF: *{looking around at the farm enviously—to his companion}* It's a jim-dandy farm, no denyin'. Wished I owned it!

CURTAIN

Thornton Wilder (1897–   )
THE SKIN OF OUR TEETH

CHARACTERS

(In the order of their appearance)

ANNOUNCER
SABINA
MR. FITZPATRICK
MRS. ANTROBUS
DINOSAUR
MAMMOTH
TELEGRAPH BOY
GLADYS
HENRY
MR. ANTROBUS
DOCTOR
PROFESSOR
JUDGE
HOMER

MISS E. MUSE
MISS T. MUSE
MISS M. MUSE
TWO USHERS
TWO DRUM MAJORETTES
FORTUNE TELLER
TWO CHAIR PUSHERS
SIX CONVEENERS
BROADCAST OFFICIALS
DEFEATED CANDIDATE
MR. TREMAYNE
HESTER
IVY
FRED BAILEY

ACT I. *Home, Excelsior, New Jersey.*

ACT II. *Atlantic City Boardwalk.*

ACT III. *Home, Excelsior, New Jersey.*

Act I

A projection screen in the middle of the curtain. The first lantern slide: the name of the theatre, and the words: NEWS EVENTS OF THE WORLD. An ANNOUNCER'S voice is heard.

ANNOUNCER: The management takes pleasure in bringing to you—The News Events of the World: {*Slide of the sun appearing above the horizon*}

Freeport, Long Island.

The sun rose this morning at 6:32 a.m. This gratifying event was first reported by Mrs. Dorothy Stetson of Freeport, Long Island, who promptly telephoned the Mayor.

The Society for Affirming the End of the World at once went into a special session and postponed the arrival of that event for TWENTY-FOUR HOURS.

All honor to Mrs. Stetson for her public spirit.

New York City: {*Slide of the front doors of the theatre in which this play is playing; three cleaning* WOMEN *with mops and pails*}

The X Theatre. During the daily cleaning of this theatre a number of lost objects were collected as usual by Mesdames Simpson, Pateslewski, and Moriarty.

Among these objects found today was a wedding ring, inscribed: To Eva from Adam. Genesis II:18.

The ring will be restored to the owner or owners, if their credentials are satisfactory.

Tippehatchee, Vermont: {*Slide representing a glacier*}

The unprecedented cold weather of this summer has produced a condition that has not yet been satisfactorily explained. There is a report that a wall of ice is moving southward across these counties. The disruption of communications by the cold wave now crossing the country has rendered exact information difficult, but little credence is given to the rumor that the ice has pushed the Cathedral of Montreal as far as St. Albans, Vermont.

For further information see your daily papers.

Excelsior, New Jersey: {*Slide of a modest suburban home*}

The home of Mr. George Antrobus, the inventor of the wheel. The discovery of the wheel, following so closely on the discovery of the lever, has centered the attention of the country on Mr. Antrobus of this attractive suburban residence district. This is his home, a commodious seven-room house, conveniently situated near a public school, a Methodist church, and a firehouse; it is right handy to an A. and P. {*Slide of* MR. ANTROBUS *on his front steps, smiling and lifting his straw hat. He holds a wheel*}

Mr. Antrobus, himself. He comes of very old stock and has made his way up from next to nothing.

It is reported that he was once a gardener, but left that situation under circumstances that have been variously reported.

Mr. Antrobus is a veteran of foreign wars, and bears a number of scars, front and back. {*Slide of* MRS. ANTROBUS, *holding some roses*}

This is Mrs. Antrobus, the charming and gracious president of the Excelsior Mothers' Club.

Mrs. Antrobus is an excellent needlewoman; it is she who invented the apron on which so many interesting changes have been rung since. {*Slide of the* FAMILY *and* SABINA]

Here we see the Antrobuses with their two children, Henry and Gladys, and friend. The friend in the rear, is Lily Sabina, the maid.

I know we all want to congratulate this typical American family on its enterprise. We all wish Mr. Antrobus a successful future. Now the management takes you to the interior of this home for a brief visit.

{*Curtain rises. Living room of a commuter's home.* SABINA—*straw-blonde, overrouged—is standing by the window back center, a feather duster under her elbow*}

SABINA: Oh, oh, oh! Six o'clock and the master not home yet.

Pray God nothing serious has happened to him crossing the Hudson River. If anything happened to him, we would certainly be inconsolable and have to move into a less desirable residence district.

The fact is I don't know what'll become of us. Here it is the middle of August and the coldest day of the year. It's simply freezing; the dogs are sticking to the sidewalks; can anybody explain that? No.

But I'm not surprised. The whole world's at sixes and sevens, and why the house hasn't fallen down about our ears long ago is a miracle to me. {*A fragment of the right wall leans precariously over the stage.* SABINA *looks at it nervously and it slowly rights itself*}

Every night this same anxiety as to whether the master will get home safely: whether he'll bring home anything to eat. In the midst of life we are in the midst of death, a truer word was never said. {*The fragment of scenery flies up into the lofts.* SABINA *is struck dumb with surprise, shrugs her shoulders and starts dusting* MR. ANTROBUS' *chair, including the under side*}

Of course, Mr. Antrobus is a very fine man, an excellent husband and father, a pillar of the church, and has all the best interests of the community at heart. Of course, every muscle goes tight every time he passes a policeman; but what I think is that there are certain charges that ought not to be made, and I think I may add, ought not to be allowed to be made; we're all human; who isn't? {*She dusts* MRS. ANTROBUS' *rocking chair*}

Mrs. Antrobus is as fine a woman as you could hope to see. She lives only for her children; and if it would be any benefit to her children she'd see the rest of us stretched out dead at her feet without turning a hair,—that's the truth. If you want to know anything more about Mrs. Antrobus, just go and look at a tigress, and look hard.

As to the children—

Well, Henry Antrobus is a real, clean-cut American boy. He'll graduate from High School one of these days, if they make the alphabet any easier.—Henry, when he has a stone in his hand, has a perfect aim; he can hit anything from a bird to an older brother—Oh! I didn't mean to say that!—but it certainly was an unfortunate accident, and it was very hard getting the police out of the house.

Mr. and Mrs. Antrobus' daughter is named Gladys. She'll make some good man a good wife some day, if he'll just come down off the movie screen and ask her.

So here we are!

We've managed to survive for some time now, catch as catch can, the fat and the lean, and if the dinosaurs don't trample us to death, and if the grasshoppers don't eat up our garden, we'll all live to see better days, knock on wood.

Each new child that's born to the Antrobuses seems to them to be sufficient reason for the whole universe's being set in motion; and each new child that dies seems to them to have been spared a whole world of sorrow, and what the end of it will be is still very much an open question.

We've rattled along, hot and cold, for some time now—{A portion of the wall above the door, right, flies up into the air and disappears}—and my advice to you is not to inquire into why or whither, but just enjoy your ice cream while it's on your plate,—that's my philosophy.

Don't forget that a few years ago we came through the depression by the skin of our teeth! One more tight squeeze like that and where will we be? {This is a cue line. SABINA looks angrily at the kitchen door and repeats:} . . . we came through the depression by the skin of our teeth; one more tight squeeze like that and where will we be? {Flustered, she looks through the opening in the right wall; then goes to the window and reopens the Act}

Oh, oh, oh! Six o'clock and the master not home yet. Pray God nothing has happened to him crossing the Hudson. Here it is the middle of August and the coldest day of the year. It's simply freezing; the dogs are sticking. One more tight squeeze like that and where will we be?

VOICE: {off stage} Make up something! Invent something!

SABINA: Well . . . uh . . . this certainly is a fine American home . . . and —uh . . . everybody's very happy . . . and—uh . . . {Suddenly flings pretense

to the winds and coming downstage says with indignation:}

I can't invent any words for this play, and I'm glad I can't. I hate this play and every word in it.

As for me, I don't understand a single word of it, anyway,—all about the troubles the human race has gone through, there's a subject for you.

Besides, the author hasn't made up his silly mind as to whether we're all living back in caves or in New Jersey today, and that's the way it is all the way through.

Oh—why can't we have plays like we used to have—*Peg o' My Heart*, and *Smilin' Thru*, and *The Bat*—good entertainment with a message you can take home with you?

I took this hateful job because I had to. For two years I've sat up in my room living on a sandwich and a cup of tea a day, waiting for better times in the theatre. And look at me now: I—I who've played *Rain* and *The Barretts of Wimpole Street* and *First Lady*—God in Heaven! {The STAGE MANAGER puts his head out from the hole in the scenery}

MR. FITZPATRICK: Miss Somerset!! Miss Somerset!

SABINA: Oh! Anyway!—nothing matters! It'll all be the same in a hundred years. {Loudly}

We came through the depression by the skin of our teeth,—that's true!—one more tight squeeze like that and where will we be? {Enter MRS. ANTROBUS, a mother}

MRS. ANTROBUS: Sabina, you've let the fire go out.

SABINA: {In a lather} One-thing-and-another; don't - know - whether -- my - wits - are - upside - or - down; might - as - well - be - dead - as - alive - in - a - house - all - sixes - and - sevens. . . .

MRS. ANTROBUS: You've let the fire go out. Here it is the coldest day of the year right in the middle of August, and you've let the fire go out.

SABINA: Mrs. Antrobus, I'd like to give my two weeks' notice, Mrs. Antrobus. A girl like I can get a situation in a home where they're rich enough to have a fire in every room, Mrs. Antrobus, and a girl don't have to carry the responsibility of the whole house on her two shoulders. And a home without children, Mrs. Antrobus, because children are a thing only a parent can stand, and a truer word was never said; and a home, Mrs. Antrobus, where the master of the house don't pinch decent, self-respecting girls when he meets them in a dark corridor. I mention no names and make no charges. So you have my notice, Mrs. Antrobus. I hope that's perfectly clear.

MRS. ANTROBUS: You've let the fire go out!—Have you milked the mammoth?

SABINA: I don't understand a word of this play.—Yes, I've milked the mammoth.

MRS. ANTROBUS: Until Mr. Antrobus comes home we have no food and we have no fire. You'd better go over to the neighbors and borrow some fire.

SABINA: Mrs. Antrobus! I can't! I'd die on the way, you know I would. It's worse than January. The dogs are sticking to the sidewalks. I'd die.

MRS. ANTROBUS: Very well, I'll go.

SABINA: *{Even more distraught, coming forward and sinking on her knees}* You'd never come back alive; we'd all perish; if you weren't here, we'd just perish. How do we know Mr. Antrobus'll be back? We don't know. If you go out, I'll just kill myself.

MRS. ANTROBUS: Get up, Sabina.

SABINA: Every night it's the same thing. Will he come back safe, or won't he? Will we starve to death, or freeze to death, or boil to death or will we be killed by burglars? I don't know why we go on living. I don't know why we go on living at all. It's easier being dead. *{She flings her arms on the table and buries her head in them. In each of the succeeding speeches she flings her head up— and sometimes her hands—then quickly buries her head again}*

MRS. ANTROBUS: The same thing! Al-ways throwing up the sponge, Sabina. Always announcing your own death. But give you a new hat—or a plate of ice cream—or a ticket to the movies, and you want to live forever.

SABINA: You don't care whether we live or die; all you care about is those children. If it would be any benefit to them you'd be glad to see us all stretched out dead.

MRS. ANTROBUS: Well, maybe I would.

SABINA: And what do they care about? Themselves—that's all they care about. *{Shrilly}* They make fun of you behind your back. Don't tell me: they're ashamed of you. Half the time, they pretend they're someone else's children. Little thanks you get from them.

MRS. ANTROBUS: I'm not asking for any thanks.

SABINA: And Mr. Antrobus—you don't understand *him*. All that work he does—trying to discover the alphabet and the multiplication table. Whenever he tries to learn anything you fight against it.

MRS. ANTROBUS: Oh, Sabina, I know you.

When Mr. Antrobus raped you home from your Sabine hills, he did it to insult me.

He did it for your pretty face, and to insult me.

You were the new wife, weren't you?

For a year or two you lay on your bed all day and polished the nails on your hands and feet.

You made puff-balls of the combings of your hair and you blew them up to the ceiling.

And I washed your underclothes and I made you chicken broths.

I bore children and between my very groans I stirred the cream that you'd put on your face.

But I knew you wouldn't last.

You didn't last.

SABINA: But it was I who encouraged Mr. Antrobus to make the alphabet. I'm sorry to say it, Mrs. Antrobus, but you're not a beautiful woman, and you can never know what a man could do if he tried. It's girls like I who inspire the multiplication table.

I'm sorry to say it, but you're not a beautiful woman, Mrs. Antrobus, and that's the God's truth.

MRS. ANTROBUS: And you didn't last —you sank to the kitchen. And what do you do there? *You let the fire go out!*

No wonder to you it seems easier being dead.

Reading and writing and counting on your fingers is all very well in their way,—but I keep the home going.

MRS. ANTROBUS: —There's that dinosaur on the front lawn again.—Shoo! Go away. Go away. *{The baby DINO-SAUR puts his head in the window}*

DINOSAUR: It's cold.

MRS. ANTROBUS: You go around to the back of the house where you belong.

DINOSAUR: It's cold.

{The DINOSAUR disappears. MRS. AN-TROBUS goes calmly out. SABINA slowly raises her head and speaks to the audience. The central portion of the center wall rises, pauses, and disappears into the loft}

SABINA: Now that you audience are listening to this, too, I understand it a little better.

I wish eleven o'clock were here; I don't want to be dragged through this whole play again. *{The TELEGRAPH BOY is seen entering along the back wall of the stage from the right. She catches sight of him and calls:}*

Mrs. Antrobus! Mrs. Antrobus! Help! There's a strange man coming to the house. He's coming up the walk, help! *{Enter MRS. ANTROBUS in alarm, but efficient}*

MRS. ANTROBUS: Help me quick! *{They barricade the door by piling the furniture against it}*

Who is it? What do you want?

TELEGRAPH BOY: A telegram for Mrs. Antrobus from Mr. Antrobus in the city.

SABINA: Are you sure, are you sure? Maybe it's just a trap!

MRS. ANTROBUS: I know his voice, Sabina. We can open the door. *{Enter*

the TELEGRAPH BOY, 12 years old, in uniform. The DINOSAUR and MAMMOTH slip by him into the room and settle down front right} I'm sorry we kept you waiting. We have to be careful, you know. *{To the ANIMALS]*

Hm! . . . Will you be quiet? *{They nod}*

Have you had your supper? *{They nod}*

Are you ready to come in? *{They nod}*

Young man, have you any fire with you? Then light the grate, will you? *{He nods, produces something like a briquet; and kneels by the imagined fireplace, footlights center. Pause}*

What are people saying about this cold weather? *{He makes a doubtful shrug with his shoulders}*

Sabina, take this stick and go and light the stove.

SABINA: Like I told you, Mrs. Antrobus; two weeks. That's the law. I hope that's perfectly clear. *{Exit}*

MRS. ANTROBUS: What about this cold weather?

TELEGRAPH BOY: *{Lowered eyes}* Of course, I don't know anything . . . but they say there's a wall of ice moving down from the North, that's what they say. We can't get Boston by telegraph, and they're burning pianos in Hartford.

. . . It moves everything in front of it, churches and post offices and city halls.

I live in Brooklyn myself.

MRS. ANTROBUS: What are people doing about it?

TELEGRAPH BOY: Well . . . uh . . . Talking, mostly.

Or just what you'd do a day in February.

There are some that are trying to go South and the roads are crowded; but you can't take old people and children very far in a cold like this.

MRS. ANTROBUS: —What's this telegram you have for me?

TELEGRAPH BOY: *{Fingertips to his forehead}*

If you wait just a minute; I've got to remember it. *{The ANIMALS have left their corner and are nosing him. Pre-*

sently they take places on either side of him, leaning against his hips, like heraldic beasts} This telegram was flashed from Murray Hill to University Heights! And then by puffs of smoke from University Heights to Staten Island.

And then by lantern from Staten Island to Plainfield, New Jersey. What hath God wrought! *{He clears his throat}*

"To Mrs. Antrobus, Excelsior, New Jersey:

My dear wife, will be an hour late. Busy day at the office.

Don't worry the children about the cold just keep them warm burn everything except Shakespeare." *{Pause}*

MRS. ANTROBUS: Men!—He knows I'd burn ten Shakespeares to prevent a child of mine from having one cold in the head. What does it say next? *{Enter* SABINA]

TELEGRAPH BOY: "Have made great discoveries today have separated em from en."

SABINA: I know what that is, that's the alphabet, yes it is. Mr. Antrobus is just the cleverest man. Why, when the alphabet's finished, we'll be able to tell the future and everything.

TELEGRAPH BOY: Then listen to this: "Ten tens make a hundred semi-colon consequences far-reaching." *{Watches for effect}*

MRS. ANTROBUS: The earth's turning to ice, and all he can do is to make up new numbers.

TELEGRAPH BOY: Well, Mrs. Antrobus, like the head man at our office said: a few more discoveries like that and we'll be worth freezing.

MRS. ANTROBUS: What does he say next?

TELEGRAPH BOY: I . . . I can't do this last part very well. *{He clears his throat and sings}*

"Happy w'dding ann'vers'ry to you, Happy ann'vers'ry to you—" *{The* ANIMALS *begin to howl soulfully;* SABINA *screams with pleasure}*

MRS. ANTROBUS: Dolly! Frederick! Be quiet.

TELEGRAPH BOY: *{Above the din}* "Happy w'dding ann'vers'ry, dear Eva; happy w'dding ann'vers'ry to you."

MRS. ANTROBUS: Is that in the telegram? Are they singing telegrams now? *{He nods}*

The earth's getting so silly no wonder the sun turns cold.

SABINA: Mrs. Antrobus, I want to take back the notice I gave you. Mrs. Antrobus, I don't want to leave a house that gets such interesting telegrams and I'm sorry for anything I said. I really am.

MRS. ANTROBUS: Young man, I'd like to give you something for all this trouble; Mr. Antrobus isn't home yet and I have no money and no food in the house—

TELEGRAPH BOY: Mrs. Antrobus . . . I don't like to . . . appear to . . . ask for anything, but . . .

MRS. ANTROBUS: What is it you'd like?

TELEGRAPH BOY: Do you happen to have an old needle you could spare? My wife just sits home all day thinking about needles.

SABINA: *{Shrilly}* We only got two in the house. Mrs. Antrobus, you know we only got two in the house.

MRS. ANTROBUS: *{After a look at* SABINA *taking a needle from her collar}* Why yes, I can spare this.

TELEGRAPH BOY: *{Lowered eyes}* Thank you, Mrs. Antrobus. Mrs. Antrobus, can I ask for something else? I have two sons of my own; if the cold gets worse, what should I do?

SABINA: I think we'll all perish, that's what I think. Cold like this in August is just the end of the whole world. *{Silence}*

MRS. ANTROBUS: I don't know. After all, what does one do about anything? Just keep as warm as you can. And don't let your wife and children see that you're worried.

TELEGRAPH BOY: Yes . . . Thank you, Mrs. Antrobus. Well, I'd better be going.—Oh, I forgot! There's one more sentence in the telegram. "Three cheers have invented the wheel."

MRS. ANTROBUS: A wheel? What's a wheel?

TELEGRAPH BOY: I don't know. That's what it said. The sign for it is like this. Well, goodbye. *{The* WOMEN *see him to the door, with goodbyes and injunctions to keep warm}*

SABINA: *{Apron to her eyes, wailing}* Mrs. Antrobus, it looks to me like all the nice men in the world are already married; I don't know why that is. *{Exit}*

MRS. ANTROBUS: *{Thoughtful; to the* ANIMALS*}* Do you ever remember hearing tell of any cold like this in August? *{The* ANIMALS *shake their heads}*

From your grandmothers or anyone? *{They shake their heads}*

Have you any suggestions? *{They shake their heads. She pulls her shawl around, goes to the front door and opening it an inch calls:}*

HENRY. GLADYS. CHILDREN. Come right in and get warm. No, no, when mamma says a thing she means it. Henry! HENRY. Put down that stone. You know what happened last time. *{Shriek}*

HENRY! Put down that stone!

Gladys! Put down your dress! Try and be a lady. *{The* CHILDREN *bound in and dash to the fire. They take off their winter things and leave them in heaps on the floor}*

GLADYS: Mama, I'm hungry. Mama, why is it so cold?

HENRY: *{At the same time}* Mama, why doesn't it snow? Mama, when's supper ready?

Maybe, it'll snow and we can make snowballs.

GLADYS: Mama, it's so cold that in one more minute I just couldn't of stood it.

MRS. ANTROBUS: Settle down, both of you, I want to talk to you. *{She draws up a hassock and sits front center over the orchestra pit before the imaginary*

fire. *The* CHILDREN *stretch out on the floor, leaning against her lap. Tableau by Raphael. The* ANIMALS *edge up and complete the triangle}*

It's just a cold spell of some kind. Now listen to what I'm saying:

When your father comes home I want you to be extra quiet. He's had a hard day at the office and I don't know but what he may have one of his moods.

I just got a telegram from him very happy and excited, and you know what that means. Your father's temper's uneven; I guess you know that. *{Shriek}* Henry! Henry!

Why—why can't you remember to keep your hair down over your forehead? You must keep that scar covered up. Don't you know that when your father sees it he loses all control over himself? He goes crazy. He wants to die. *{After a moment's despair she collects herself decisively, wets the hem of her apron in her mouth and starts polishing his forehead vigorously}*

Lift your head up. Stop squirming. Blessed me, sometimes I think that it's going away—and then there it is: just as red as ever.

HENRY: Mama, today at school two teachers forgot and called me by my old name. They forgot, Mama. You'd better write another letter to the principal, so that he'll tell them I've changed my name. Right out in class they called me: Cain.

MRS. ANTROBUS: *{Putting her hand on his mouth, too late; hoarsely}*

Don't say it. *{Polishing feverishly}*

If you're good they'll forget it. Henry, you didn't hit anyone . . . today, did you?

HENRY: Oh . . . no-o-o!

MRS. ANTROBUS: *{Still working, not looking at Gladys}* And, Gladys, I want you to be especially nice to your father tonight. You know what he calls you when you're good—his little angel, his little star. Keep your dress down like a little lady. And keep your voice nice and low. Gladys Antrobus. What's that red stuff you have on your face? {*Slaps her*}

You're a filthy detestable child! {*Rises in real, though temporary, repudiation and despair*}

Get away from me, both of you! I wish I'd never seen sight or sound of you. Let the cold come! I can't stand it. I don't want to go on. {*She walks away*}

GLADYS: {*Weeping*} All the girls at school do, Mama.

MRS. ANTROBUS: {*Shrieking*} I'm through with you, that's all!—Sabina! Sabina!—Don't you know your father'd go crazy if he saw that paint on your face? Don't you know your father thinks you're perfect? Don't you know he couldn't live if he didn't think you were perfect?—Sabina! {*Enter* SABINA}

SABINA: Yes, Mrs. Antrobus!

MRS. ANTROBUS: Take this girl out into the kitchen and wash her face with the scrubbing brush.

MR. ANTROBUS: {*Outside, roaring*} "I've been working on the railroad, all the livelong day . . . etc." {*The* ANIMALS *start running around in circles, bellowing.* SABINA *rushes to the window*}

MRS. ANTROBUS: Sabina, what's that noise outside?

SABINA: Oh, it's a drunken tramp. It's a giant, Mrs. Antrobus. We'll all be killed in our beds, I know it!

MRS. ANTROBUS: Help me quick. Quick. Everybody. {*Again they stack all the furniture against the door.* MR. ANTROBUS *pounds and bellows*} Who is it? What do you want?—Sabina, have you any boiling water ready?—Who is it?

MR. ANTROBUS: Broken-down camel of a pig's snout, open this door.

MRS. ANTROBUS: God be praised! It's your father.—Just a minute, George! —Sabina, clear the door, quick. Gladys, come here while I clean your nasty face!

MR. ANTROBUS: She-bitch of a goat's gizzard, I'll break every bone in your body. Let me in or I'll tear the whole house down.

MRS. ANTROBUS: Just a minute, George, something's the matter with the lock.

MR. ANTROBUS: Open the door or I'll tear your livers out. I'll smash your brains on the ceiling, and Devil take the hindmost.

MRS. ANTROBUS: Now you can open the door, Sabina. I'm ready. {*The door is flung open. Silence.* MR. ANTROBUS— *face of a Keystone Comedy Cop—stands there in fur cap and blanket. His arms are full of parcels, including a large stone wheel with a center in it. One hand carries a railroad man's lantern. Suddenly he bursts into joyous roar*}

MR. ANTROBUS: Well, how's the whole crooked family? {*Relief. Laughter. Tears. Jumping up and down.* ANIMALS *cavorting.* ANTROBUS *throws the parcels on the ground. Hurls his cap and blanket after them. Heroic embraces. Melee of* HUMANS *and* ANIMALS, SABINA *included*} I'll be scalded and tarred if a man can't get a little welcome when he comes home. Well, Maggie, you old gunny-sack, how's the broken down old weather hen?—Sabina, old fishbait, old skunkpot.—And the children,—how've the little smellers been?

GLADYS: Papa, Papa, Papa, Papa.

MR. ANTROBUS: How've they been, Maggie?

MRS. ANTROBUS: Well, I must say, they've been as good as gold. I haven't had to raise my voice once. I don't know what's the matter with them.

ANTROBUS: {*Kneeling before* GLADYS} Papa's little weasel, eh?— Sabina, there's some food for you.— Papa's little gopher?

GLADYS: {*Her arm around his neck*} Papa, you're always teasing me.

ANTROBUS: And Henry? Nothing rash today, I hope. Nothing rash?

HENRY: No, Papa.

ANTROBUS: {*Roaring*} Well that's good, that's good—I'll bet Sabina let the fire go out.

SABINA: Mr. Antrobus, I've given my

notice. I'm leaving two weeks from to-day. I'm sorry, but I'm leaving.

ANTROBUS: {*Roar*} Well, if you leave now you'll freeze to death, so go and cook the dinner.

SABINA: Two weeks, that's the law. {*Exit*}

ANTROBUS: Did you get my telegram?

MRS. ANTROBUS: Yes.—What's a wheel? {*He indicates the wheel with a glance.* HENRY *is rolling it around the floor. Rapid, hoarse interchange:* MRS. ANTROBUS: *What does this cold weather mean? It's below freezing.* ANTROBUS: *Not before the children!* MRS. ANTROBUS: *Shouldn't we do something about it?—start off, move?* ANTROBUS: *Not before the children!!!* He gives HENRY *a sharp slap*}

HENRY: Papa, you hit me!

ANTROBUS: Well, remember it. That's to make you remember today. Today. The day the alphabet's finished; and the day that we *saw* the hundred—the hundred, the hundred, the hundred, the hundred, the hundred—there's no end to 'em.

I've had a day at the office!

Take a look at that wheel, Maggie—when I've got that to rights: you'll see a sight.

There's a reward there for all the walking you've done.

MRS. ANTROBUS: How do you mean?

ANTROBUS: {*On the hassock looking into the fire; with awe*} Maggie, we've reached the top of the wave. There's not much more to be done. We're there!

MRS. ANTROBUS: {*Cutting across his mood sharply*} And the ice?

ANTROBUS: The ice!

HENRY: {*Playing with the wheel*} Papa, you could put a chair on this.

ANTROBUS: {*Broodingly*} Ye-e-s, any booby can fool with it now,—but I thought of it first.

MRS. ANTROBUS: Children, go out in the kitchen. I want to talk to your father alone. {*The* CHILDREN *go out.* ANTROBUS *has moved to his chair up left. He takes the goldfish bowl on his lap; pulls the canary cage down to the level of his face. Both the* ANIMALS *put their paws up on the arm of his chair.* MRS. ANTROBUS *faces him across the room, like a judge*}

MRS. ANTROBUS: Well?

ANTROBUS: {*Shortly*} It's cold.—How things been, eh? Keck, keck, keck.—And you, Millicent?

MRS. ANTROBUS: I know it's cold.

ANTROBUS: {*To the canary*} No spilling of sunflower seed, eh? No singing after lights-out, y'know what I mean?

MRS. ANTROBUS: You can try and prevent us freezing to death, can't you? You can do something? We can start moving. Or we can go on the animals' backs?

ANTROBUS: The best thing about animals is that they don't talk much.

MAMMOTH: It's cold.

ANTROBUS: Eh, eh, eh! Watch that!—
—By midnight we'd turn to ice. The roads are full of people now who can scarcely lift a foot from the ground. The grass out in front is like iron,—which reminds me, I have another needle for you.—The people up north—where are they?

Frozen . . . crushed. . . .

MRS. ANTROBUS: Is that what's going to happen to us?—Will you answer me?

ANTROBUS: I don't know. I don't know anything. Some say that the ice is going slower. Some say that it's stopped. The sun's growing cold. What can I do about that? Nothing we can do but burn everything in the house, and the fence-posts and the barn. Keep the fire going. When we have no more fire, we die.

MRS. ANTROBUS: Well, why didn't you say so in the first place? [MRS. ANTROBUS *is about to march off when she catches sight of two* REFUGEES, *men, who have appeared against the back wall of the theatre and who are soon joined by others*}

REFUGEES: Mr. Antrobus! Mr. Antrobus! Mr. An-nn-tro-bus!

MRS. ANTROBUS: Who's that? Who's that calling you?

ANTROBUS: *{Clearing his throat guiltily}* Hm—let me see. *{Two* REFUGEES *come up to the window}*

REFUGEE: Could we warm our hands for a moment, Mr. Antrobus. It's very cold, Mr. Antrobus.

ANOTHER REFUGEE: Mr. Antrobus, I wonder if you have a piece of bread or something that you could spare. *{Silence. They wait humbly.* MRS. ANTROBUS *stands rooted to the spot. Suddenly a knock at the door, then another hand knocking in short rapid blows}*

MRS. ANTROBUS: Who are these people? Why, they're all over the front yard. What have they come *here* for? *{Enter* SABINA]

SABINA: Mrs. Antrobus! There are some tramps knocking at the back door.

MRS. ANTROBUS: George, tell these people to go away. Tell them to move right along. I'll go and send them away from the back door. Sabina, come with me. *{She goes out energetically}*

ANTROBUS: Sabina! Stay here! I have something to say to you. *{He goes to the door and opens it a crack and talks through it}* Ladies and gentlemen! I'll have to ask you to wait a few minutes longer. It'll be all right . . . while you're waiting you might each one pull up a stake of the fence. We'll need them all for the fireplace. There'll be coffee and sandwiches in a moment. [SABINA *looks out door over his shoulder and suddenly extends her arm pointing, with a scream}*

SABINA: Mr. Antrobus, what's that?? —that big white thing? Mr. Antrobus, it's ICE. It's ICE!!

ANTROBUS: Sabina, I want you to go in the kitchen and make a lot of coffee. Make a whole pail full.

SABINA: Pail full!!

ANTROBUS: *{With gesture}* And sandwiches . . . piles of them . . . like this.

SABINA: Mr. An . . . !! *{Suddenly she drops the play, and says in her own per-* son *as* MISS SOMERSET, *with surprise}* Oh, *I* see what this part of the play means now! This means refugees. *{She starts to cross to the proscenium}*

Oh, I don't like it. I don't like it. *{She leans against the proscenium and bursts into tears}*

ANTROBUS: Miss Somerset! *{Voice of the* STAGE MANAGER] Miss Somerset!

SABINA: *{Energetically, to the audience}* Ladies and gentlemen! Don't take this play serious. The world's not coming to an end. You know it's not. People exaggerate! Most people really have enough to eat and a roof over their heads. Nobody actually starves—you can always eat grass or something. That icebusiness—why, it was a long, long time ago. Besides they were only savages. Savages don't love their families—not like we do.

ANTROBUS *and* STAGE MANAGER: Miss Somerset!! *{There is renewed knocking at the door}*

SABINA: All right. I'll say the lines, but I won't think about the play. *{Enter* MRS. ANTROBUS]

SABINA: *{Parting thrust at the audience}* And I advise *you* not to think about the play, either. *{Exit* SABINA]

MRS. ANTROBUS: George, these tramps say that you asked them to come to the house. What does this mean? *{Knocking at the door}*

ANTROBUS: Just . . . uh . . . there are a few friends, Maggie, I met on the road. Real nice, real useful people. . . .

MRS. ANTROBUS: *{Back to the door}* Now don't you ask them in! George Antrobus, not another soul comes in here over my dead body.

ANTROBUS: Maggie, there's a doctor there. Never hurts to have a good doctor in the house. We've lost a peck of children, one way and another. You can never tell when a child's throat will get stopped up. What you and I have seen—!!! *{He puts his fingers on his throat and imitates diphtheria}*

MRS. ANTROBUS: Well, just one person then, the Doctor. The others can go right along the road.

ANTROBUS: Maggie, there's an old man, particular friend of mine.

MRS. ANTROBUS: I won't listen to you.

ANTROBUS: It was he that really started off the A.B.C.'s.

MRS. ANTROBUS: I don't care if he perishes. We can do without reading or writing. We can't do without food.

ANTROBUS: Then let the ice come!! Drink your coffee!! I don't want any coffee if I can't drink it with some good people.

MRS. ANTROBUS: Stop shouting. Who else is out there trying to push us off the cliff?

ANTROBUS: Well, there's the man . . . who makes all the laws. Judge Moses!

MRS. ANTROBUS: Judges can't help us now.

ANTROBUS: And if the ice melts? . . . and if we pull through? Have you and I been able to bring up Henry? What have we done?

MRS. ANTROBUS: Who are those old women?

ANTROBUS: *{Coughs}* Up in town there are nine sisters. There are three or four of them here. They're sort of music teachers . . . and one of them recites and one of them—

MRS. ANTROBUS: That's the end. A singing troupe! Well, take your choice, live or die. Starve your own children before your face.

ANTROBUS: *{Gently}* These people don't take much. They're used to starving.

They'll sleep on the floor.

Besides, Maggie, listen: no, listen: Who've we got in the house, but Sabina? Sabina's always afraid the worst will happen. Whose spirits can she keep up? Maggie, these people never give up. They think they'll live and work forever.

MRS. ANTROBUS: *{Walks slowly to the middle of the room}*

All right, let them in. Let them in. You're master here. *{Softly}*—But these animals must go. Enough's enough. They'll soon be big enough to push the walls down, anyway. Take them away.

ANTROBUS: *{Sadly}* All right. The dinosaur and mammoth—! Come on, baby, come on Frederick. Come for a walk. That's a good little fellow.

DINOSAUR: It's cold.

ANTROBUS: Yes, nice cold fresh air. Bracing. *{He holds the door open and the* ANIMALS *go out. He beckons to his friends. The* REFUGEES *are typically elderly out-of-works from the streets of New York today.* JUDGE MOSES *wears a skull cap.* HOMER *is a blind beggar with a guitar. The seedy crowd shuffles in and waits humbly and expectantly.* ANTROBUS *introduces them to his wife who bows to each with a stately bend of her head}*

Make yourself at home, Maggie, this the doctor . . . m . . . Coffee'll be here in a minute. . . . Professor, this is my wife. . . . And: . . . Judge . . . Maggie, you know the Judge. *{An old blind man with a guitar}* Maggie, you know . . . you know Homer?—Come right in, Judge.—

Miss Muse—are some of your sisters here? Come right in. . . .

Miss E. Muse; Miss T. Muse, Miss M. Muse.

MRS. ANTROBUS: Please to meet you. Just . . . make yourself comfortable. Supper'll be ready in a minute. *{She goes out, abruptly}*

ANTROBUS: Make yourself at home, friends. I'll be right back. *{He goes out.*

The REFUGEES *stare about them in awe. Presently several voices start whispering "Homer! Homer!" All take it up.* HOMER *strikes a chord or two on his guitar, then starts to speak:}*

HOMER: Μῆνιν ἄειδε, θεὰ, Πηληϊάδεω Ἀχιλῆος, οὐλομένην, ἣ μυρί' Ἀχαιοῖς ἄλγε' ἔθηκεν, πολλὰς δ' ἰφθίμους Ψυχὰς— [HOMER's *face shows he is lost in thought and memory and the words die away on his lips. The* REFUGEES *likewise nod in dreamy recollection. Soon the whisper "Moses, Moses!" goes around. An aged Jew parts his beard and recites dramatically:}*

MOSES:

בְּרֵאשִׁית בָּרָא אֱלֹהִים אֵת הַשָּׁמַיִם וְאֵת הָאָרֶץ:
וְהָאָרֶץ הָיְתָה תֹהוּ וָבֹהוּ וְחֹשֶׁךְ עַל־פְּנֵי תְהוֹם
וְרוּחַ אֱלֹהִים מְרַחֶפֶת עַל־פְּנֵי הַמָּיִם:

{The same dying away of the words takes place, and on the part of the REFUGEES *the same retreat into recollection. Some of them murmur, "Yes, yes."*

The mood is broken by the abrupt entrance of MR. *and* MRS. ANTROBUS *and* SABINA *bearing platters of sandwiches and a pail of coffee.* SABINA *stops and stares at the guests}*

MR. ANTROBUS: Sabina, pass the sandwiches.

SABINA: I thought I was working in a respectable house that had respectable guests. I'm giving my notice, Mr. Antrobus: two weeks, that's the law.

MR. ANTROBUS: Sabina! Pass the sandwiches.

SABINA: Two weeks, that's the law.

MR. ANTROBUS: There's the law. That's Moses.

SABINA: *{Stares}* The Ten Commandments — faugh!! — *{To Audience}* That's the worst line I've ever had to say on any stage.

ANTROBUS: I think the best thing to do is just not to stand on ceremony, but pass the sandwiches around from left to right.—Judge, help yourself to one of these.

MRS. ANTROBUS: The roads are crowded, I hear?

THE GUESTS: *{All talking at once}* Oh, ma'am, you can't imagine. . . . You can hardly put one foot before you . . . people are trampling one another. *{Sudden silence}*

MRS. ANTROBUS: Well, you know what I think it is,—I think it's sunspots!

THE GUESTS: *{Discreet hubbub}* Oh, you're right, Mrs. Antrobus . . . that's what it is. . . . That's what I was saying the other day. *{Sudden silence}*

ANTROBUS: Well, I don't believe the whole world's going to turn to ice. *{All eyes are fixed on him, waiting}*

I can't believe it, Judge! Have we worked for nothing? Professor! Have we just failed in the whole thing?

MRS. ANTROBUS: It is certainly very strange—well fortunately on both sides of the family we come of very hearty stock.—Doctor, I want you to meet my children. They're eating their supper now. And of course I want them to meet you.

MISS M. MUSE: How many children have you, Mrs. Antrobus?

MRS. ANTROBUS: I have two,—a boy and a girl.

MOSES: *{Softly}* I understood you had two sons, Mrs. Antrobus. [MRS. ANTROBUS *in blind suffering; she walks toward the footlights}*

MRS. ANTROBUS: *{In a low voice}* Abel, Abel, my son, my son, Abel, my son, Abel, Abel my son. *{The* REFUGEES *move with a few steps toward her as though in comfort murmuring words in Greek, Hebrew, German, et cetera.*

A piercing shriek from the kitchen,— SABINA's *voice. All heads turn}*

ANTROBUS: What's that? [SABINA *enters, bursting with indignation, pulling on her gloves}*

SABINA: Mr. Antrobus—that son of yours, that boy Henry Antrobus—I don't stay in this house another moment!—He's not fit to live among respectable folks and that's a fact.

MRS. ANTROBUS: Don't say another word, Sabina. I'll be right back. *{Without waiting for an answer she goes past her into the kitchen}*

SABINA: Mrs. Antrobus, Henry has thrown a stone again and if he hasn't killed the boy that lives next door, I'm very much mistaken. He finished his supper and went out to play; and I heard such a fight; and then I saw it. I saw it with my own eyes. And it looked to me like stark murder. [MRS. ANTROBUS *appears at the kitchen door, shielding* HENRY *who follows her. When she steps aside, we see on* HENRY's *forehead a large ochre and scarlet scar in the shape of a C.* MR. ANTROBUS *starts toward him. A pause.* HENRY *is heard saying under his breath:}*

HENRY: He was going to take the wheel away from me. He started to throw a stone at me first.

MRS. ANTROBUS: George, it was just a boyish impulse. Remember how young he is. *{Louder, in an urgent wail}* George, he's only four thousand years old.

SABINA: And everything was going along so nicely! *{Silence.* ANTROBUS *goes back to the fireplace}*

ANTROBUS: Put out the fire! Put out all the fires. *{Violently}* No wonder the sun grows cold. *{He starts stamping on the fireplace}*

MRS. ANTROBUS: Doctor! Judge! Help me!—George, have you lost your mind?

ANTROBUS: There is no mind. We'll not try to live. *{To the guests}* Give it up. Give up trying. [MRS. ANTROBUS *seizes him}*

SABINA: Mr. Antrobus! I'm downright ashamed of you.

MRS. ANTROBUS: George, have some more coffee.—Gladys! Where's Gladys gone? [GLADYS *steps in, frightened}*

GLADYS: Here I am, mama.

MRS. ANTROBUS: Go upstairs and bring your father's slippers. How could you forget a thing like that, when you know how tired he is? [ANTROBUS *sits in his chair. He covers his face with his hands.* MRS. ANTROBUS *turns to the* REFUGEES:] Can't some of you sing? It's your business in life to sing, isn't it? Sabina! *{Several of the women clear their throats tentatively, and with frightened faces gather around* HOMER's *guitar. He establishes a few chords. Almost inaudibly they start singing, led by* SABINA.

"Jingle Bells." MRS. ANTROBUS *continues to* ANTROBUS *in a low voice, while taking off his shoes:}* George, remember all the other times. When the volcanoes came right up in the front yard. And the time the grasshoppers ate every single leaf and blade of grass, and all the grain and spinach you'd grown with your own hands. And the summer there were earthquakes every night.

ANTROBUS: Henry! Henry! *{Puts his hand on his forehead}* Myself. All of us, we're covered with blood.

MRS. ANTROBUS: Then remember all the times you were pleased with him and when you were proud of yourself. —Henry! Henry! Come here and recite to your father the multiplication table that you do so nicely. [HENRY *kneels on one knee beside his father and starts whispering the multiplication table}*

HENRY: *{Finally}* Two times six is twelve; three times six is eighteen—I don't think I know the sixes. *[Enter* GLADYS *with the slippers.* MRS. ANTROBUS *makes stern gestures to her: Go in there and do your best. The* GUESTS *are now singing "Tenting Tonight."}*

GLADYS: *{Putting slippers on his feet}* Papa . . . Papa . . . I was very good in school today. Miss Conover said right out in class that if all the girls had as good manners as Gladys Antrobus, that the world would be a very different place to live in.

MRS. ANTROBUS: You recited a piece at assembly, didn't you? Recite it to your father.

GLADYS: Papa, do you want to hear what I recited in class? *{Fierce directional glance from her mother}* "THE STAR" by Henry Wadsworth LONGFELLOW.

MRS. ANTROBUS: Wait!!! The fire's going out. There isn't enough wood! Henry, go upstairs and bring down the chairs and start breaking up the beds. *{Exit* HENRY. *The singers return to "Jingle Bells," still very softly}*

GLADYS: Look, Papa, here's my report

card. Lookit. Conduct A! Look, Papa. Papa, do you want to hear the Star, by Henry Wadsworth Longfellow? Papa, you're not mad at me, are you?—I know it'll get warmer. Soon it'll be just like spring, and we can go to a picnic at the Hibernian Picnic Grounds like you always like to do, don't you remember? Papa, just look at me once. *{Enter* HENRY *with some chairs}*

ANTROBUS: You recited in assembly, did you? *{She nods eagerly}* You didn't forget it?

GLADYS: No!!! I was perfect. *{Pause. Then* ANTROBUS *rises, goes to the front door and opens it. The* REFUGEES *draw back timidly; the song stops; he peers out of the door, then closes it}*

ANTROBUS: *{With decision, suddenly}* Build up the fire. It's cold. Build up the fire. We'll do what we can. Sabina, get some more wood. Come around the fire, everybody. At least the young ones may pull through. Henry, have you eaten something?

HENRY: Yes, papa.

ANTROBUS: Gladys, have you had some supper?

GLADYS: I ate in the kitchen, papa.

ANTROBUS: If you do come through this—what'll you be able to do? What do you know? Henry, did you take a good look at that wheel?

HENRY: Yes, papa.

ANTROBUS: *{Sitting down in his chair}* Six times two are—

HENRY: —twelve; six times three are eighteen; six times four are—Papa, it's hot and cold. It makes my head all funny. It makes me sleepy.

ANTROBUS: *{Gives him a cuff}* Wake up. I don't care if your head is sleepy. Six times four are twenty-four. Six times five are—

HENRY: Thirty. Papa!

ANTROBUS: Maggie, put something into Gladys' head on the chance she can use it.

MRS. ANTROBUS: What do you mean, George?

ANTROBUS: Six times six are thirty-six. Teach her the beginning of the Bible.

GLADYS: But, Mama, it's so cold and close. [HENRY *has all but drowsed off. His father slaps him sharply and the lesson goes on}*

MRS. ANTROBUS: "In the beginning God created the heavens and the earth; and the earth was waste and void; and the darkness was upon the face of the deep—" *{The singing starts up again louder.* SABINA *has returned with wood}*

SABINA: *{After placing wood on the fireplace comes down to the footlights and addresses the audience:}* Will you please start handing up your chairs? We'll need everything for this fire. Save the human race.—Ushers, will you pass the chairs up here? Thank you.

HENRY: Six times nine are fifty-four; six times ten are sixty. *{In the back of the auditorium the sound of chairs being ripped up can be heard.* USHERS *rush down the aisles with chairs and hand them over}*

GLADYS: "And God called the light Day and the darkness he called Night."

SABINA: Pass up your chairs, everybody. Save the human race.

CURTAIN

Act II

Toward the end of the intermission, though with the houselights still up, lantern slide projections begin to appear on the curtain. Timetables for trains leaving Pennsylvania Station for Atlantic City. Advertisements of Atlantic City hotels, drugstores, churches, rug merchants; fortune tellers, Bingo parlors.

When the houselights go down, the voice of an ANNOUNCER *is heard.*

ANNOUNCER: The Management now brings you the News Events of the World. Atlantic City, New Jersey: *{Projection of a chrome postcard of the waterfront, trimmed in mica with the legend: FUN AT THE BEACH}* This great convention city is playing host this week to the anniversary convocation of that great fraternal order,—the Ancient and Honorable Order of Mammals, Subdivision Humans. This great fraternal, militant and burial society is celebrating on the Boardwalk, ladies and gentlemen, its six hundred thousandth Annual Convention.

It has just elected its president for the ensuing term,—*{Projection of* MR. *and* MRS. ANTROBUS *posed as they will be shown a few moments later}* Mr. George Antrobus of Excelsior, New Jersey. We show you President Antrobus and his gracious and charming wife, every inch a mammal. Mr. Antrobus has had a long and chequered career. Credit has been paid to him for many useful enterprises including the introduction of the lever, of the wheel and the brewing of beer. Credit has been also extended to President Antrobus's gracious and charming wife for many practical suggestions, including the hem, the gore, and the gusset; and the novelty of the year,—frying in oil. Before we show you Mr. Antrobus accepting the nomination, we have an important announcement to make. As many of you know, this great celebration of the Order of the Mammals has received delegations from the other rival Orders,—or shall we say: esteemed concurrent Orders: the WINGS, the FINS, the SHELLS, and so on. These Orders are holding their conventions also, in various parts of the world, and have sent representatives to our own, two of a kind.

Later in the day we will show you President Antrobus broadcasting his words of greeting and congratulation to the collected assemblies of the whole natural world.

Ladies and Gentlemen! We give you President Antrobus! *{The screen becomes a Transparency.* MR. ANTROBUS *stands beside a pedestal;* MRS. ANTROBUS *is seated wearing a corsage of orchids.* ANTROBUS *wears an untidy Prince Albert; spats; from a red rosette in his buttonhole hangs a fine long purple ribbon of honor. He wears a gay lodge hat,—something between a fez and a legionnaire's cap}*

ANTROBUS: Fellow-mammals, fellow-vertebrates, fellow-humans, I thank you. Little did my dear parents think,—when they told me to stand on my own two feet,—that I'd arrive at this place.

My friends, we have come a long way.

During this week of happy celebration it is perhaps not fitting that we dwell on some of the difficult times we have been through. The dinosaur is extinct—*{Applause}*—the ice has retreated; and the common cold is being pursued by every means within our power. [MRS. ANTROBUS *sneezes, laughs prettily, and murmurs: "I beg your pardon"}* In our memorial service yesterday we did honor to all our friends and relatives who are no longer with us, by reason of cold, earthquakes, plagues and . . . and . . . *{Coughs}* differences of opinion.

As our Bishop so ably said . . . uh . . . so ably said. . . .

MRS. ANTROBUS: *{Closed lips}* 'Gone, but not forgotten.'

ANTROBUS: 'They are gone, but not forgotten.'

I think I can say, I think I can prophesy with complete . . . uh . . . with complete. . . .

MRS. ANTROBUS: Confidence.

ANTROBUS: Thank you, my dear,—With complete lack of confidence, that a new day of security is about to dawn.

The watchword of the closing year was: Work. I give you the watchword for the future: Enjoy Yourselves.

MRS. ANTROBUS: George, sit down!

ANTROBUS: Before I close, however, I wish to answer one of those unjust and malicious accusations that were brought against me during this last electoral campaign.

Ladies and gentlemen, the charge was made that at various points in my career I leaned toward joining some of the rival orders,—that's a lie.

As I told reporters of the *Atlantic City Herald*, I do not deny that a few months before my birth I hesitated between . . . uh . . . between pinfeathers and gillbreathing,—and so did many of us here,—but for the last million years I have been viviparous, hairy and diaphragmatic. *{Applause. Cries of 'Good old Antrobus,' 'The Prince chap!' 'Georgie,' etc.}*

ANNOUNCER: Thank you. Thank you very much, Mr. Antrobus.

Now I know that our visitors will wish to hear a word from that gracious and charming mammal, Mrs. Antrobus, wife and mother,—Mrs. Antrobus! *{*MRS. ANTROBUS *rises, lays her program on her chair, bows and says:}*

MRS. ANTROBUS: Dear friends, I don't really think I should say anything. After all, it was my husband who was elected and not I. Perhaps, as president of the Women's Auxiliary Bed and Board Society,—I had some notes here, oh, yes, here they are:—I should give a short report from some of our committees that have been meeting in this beautiful city.

Perhaps it may interest you to know that it has at last been decided that the tomato is edible. Can you all hear me? The tomato *is* edible.

A delegate from across the sea reports that the thread woven by the silkworm gives a cloth . . . I have a sample of it here . . . can you see it? smooth, elastic. I should say that it's rather attractive,—though personally I prefer less shiny surfaces. Should the windows of a sleeping apartment be open or shut? I know all mothers will follow our debates on this matter with close interest. I am sorry to say that the most expert authorities have not yet decided. It does seem to me that the night air would be bound to be unhealthy for our children,

but there are many distinguished authorities on both sides. Well, I could go on talking forever,—as Shakespeare says: a woman's work is seldom done; but I think I'd better join my husband in saying thank you, and sit down. Thank you. *{She sits down}*

ANNOUNCER: Oh, Mrs. Antrobus!

MRS. ANTROBUS: Yes?

ANNOUNCER: We understand that you are about to celebrate a wedding anniversary. I know our listeners would like to extend their felicitations and hear a few words from you on that subject.

MRS. ANTROBUS: I have been asked by this kind gentleman . . . yes, my friends, this Spring Mr. Antrobus and I will be celebrating our five thousandth wedding anniversary.

I don't know if I speak for my husband, but I can say that, as for me, I regret every moment of it. *{Laughter of confusion}* I beg your pardon. What I *mean* to say is that I do not regret one moment of it. I hope none of you catch my cold. We have two children. We've always had two children, though it hasn't always been the same two. But as I say, we have two fine children, and we're very grateful for that. Yes, Mr. Antrobus and I have been married five thousand years. Each wedding anniversary reminds me of the times when there were no weddings. We had to crusade for marriage. Perhaps there are some women within the sound of my voice who remember that crusade and those struggles; we fought for it, didn't we? We chained ourselves to lampposts and we made disturbances in the Senate,—anyway, at last we women got the ring.

A few men helped us, but I must say that most men blocked our way at every step: they said we were unfeminine.

I only bring up these unpleasant memories, because I see some signs of backsliding from that great victory.

Oh, my fellow mammals, keep hold of that.

My husband says that the watchword

for the year is Enjoy Yourselves. I think that's very open to misunderstanding.

My watchword for the year is: Save the Family. It's held together for over five thousand years: Save it! Thank you.

ANNOUNCER: Thank you, Mrs. Antrobus. *{The transparency disappears}*

We had hoped to show you the Beauty Contest that took place here today.

President Antrobus, an experienced judge of pretty girls, gave the title of Miss Atlantic City 1942, to Miss Lily-Sabina Fairweather, charming hostess of our Boardwalk Bingo Parlor.

Unfortunately, however, our time is up, and I must take you to some views of the Convention City and conveeners,—enjoying themselves.

{A burst of music; the curtain rises. The Boardwalk. The audience is sitting in the ocean. An handrail of scarlet cord stretches across the front of the stage. A ramp—also with scarlet hand rail—descends to the right corner of the orchestra pit where a great scarlet beach umbrella or a cabana stands. Front and right stage left are benches facing the sea; attached to each bench is a street-lamp.

The only scenery is two cardboard cutouts six feet high, representing shops at the back of the stage. Reading from left to right they are: SALT WATER TAFFY: FORTUNE TELLER; then the blank space; BINGO PARLOR; TURKISH BATH. They have practical doors, that of the Fortune Teller's being hung with bright gypsy curtains.

By the left proscenium and rising from the orchestra pit is the weather signal; it is like the mast of a ship with cross bars. From time to time black discs are hung on it to indicate the storm and hurricane warnings. Three roller chairs, pushed by melancholy NEGROES, file by empty. Throughout the act they traverse the stage in both directions.

From time to time, CONVEENERS, dressed like MR. ANTROBUS, cross the stage. Some walk sedately by; others engage in inane horseplay. The old gypsy FORTUNE TELLER *is seated at the door of her shop, smoking a corncob pipe.*

From the Bingo Parlor comes the voice of the CALLER]

BINGO CALLER: A-Nine; A-Nine. C-Twenty-six; C-Twenty-six. A-Four; A-Four, B-Twelve.

CHORUS: *{Back-stage}* Bingo!!! *{The front of the Bingo Parlor shudders, rises a few feet in the air and returns to the ground trembling}*

FORTUNE TELLER: *{Mechanically, **to** the unconscious back of a passerby, pointing with her pipe}* Bright's disease! Your partner's deceiving you in that Kansas City deal. You'll have six grandchildren. Avoid high places. *{She rises and shouts after another:}* Cirrhosis of the liver! [SABINA *appears at the door of the Bingo Parlor. She hugs about her a blue raincoat that almost conceals her red bathing suit. She tries to catch the* FORTUNE TELLER's *attention}*

SABINA: Ssssst! Esmeralda! Sssssst!

FORTUNE TELLER: Keck!

SABINA: Has President Antrobus come along yet?

FORTUNE TELLER: No, no, no. Get back there. Hide yourself.

SABINA: I'm afraid I'll miss him. Oh, Esmeralda, if I fail in this, I'll die; I know I'll die. President Antrobus!!! And I'll be his wife! If it's the last thing I'll do, I'll be Mrs. George Antrobus.—Esmeralda, tell me my future.

FORTUNE TELLER: Keck!

SABINA: All right, I'll tell *you* my future. *{Laughing dreamily and tracing it out with one finger on the palm of her hand}* I've won the Beauty Contest in Atlantic City,—well, I'll win the Beauty Contest of the whole world. I'll take President Antrobus away from that wife of his. Then I'll take every man away from his wife. I'll turn the whole earth upside down.

FORTUNE TELLER: Keck!

SABINA: When all those husbands just think about me they'll get dizzy. They'll faint in the streets. They'll have to lean against lampposts.—Esmeralda, who was Helen of Troy?

FORTUNE TELLER: *{Furiously}* Shut your foolish mouth. When Mr. Antrobus comes along you can see what you can do. Until then,—go away. [SABINA *laughs. As she returns to the door of her Bingo Parlor a group of* CONVEENERS *rush over and smother her with attentions: "Oh, Miss Lily, you know me. You've known me for years."}*

SABINA: Go away, boys, go away. I'm after bigger fry than you are.—Why, Mr. Simpson! How *dare* you!! I expect that even you nobodies must have girls to amuse you; but where you find them and what you do with them, is of absolutely no interest to me. *{Exit. The* CONVEENERS *squeal with pleasure and stumble in after her.*

The FORTUNE TELLER *rises, puts her pipe down on the stool, unfurls her voluminous skirts, gives a sharp wrench to her bodice and strolls toward the audience, swinging her hips like a young woman}*

FORTUNE TELLER: I tell the future. Keck. Nothing easier. Everybody's future is in their face. Nothing easier.

But who can tell your past,—eh? Nobody!

Your youth,—where did it go? It slipped away while you weren't looking. While you were asleep. While you were drunk? Puh! You're like our friends, Mr. and Mrs. Antrobus; you lie awake nights trying to know your past. What did it mean? What was it trying to say to you?

Think! Think! Split your heads. I can't tell the past and neither can you. If anybody tries to tell you the past, take my word for it, they're charlatans! Charlatans! But I can tell the future. *{She suddenly barks at a passing chairpusher}* Apoplexy! *{She returns to the audience}* Nobody listens.—Keck! I see a face among you now—I won't embarrass him by pointing him out, but, listen, it may be you: Next year the watchsprings inside you will crumple up. Death by regret,—Type Y. It's in

the corners of your mouth. You'll decide that you should have lived for pleasure, but that you missed it. Death by regret,—Type Y. . . . Avoid mirrors. You'll try to be angry,—but no!—no anger. *{Far forward, confidentially}* And now what's the immediate future of our friends, the Antrobuses? Oh, you've seen it as well as I have, keck,—that dizziness of the head; that Great Man dizziness? The inventor of beer and gunpowder. The sudden fits of temper and then the long stretches of inertia? "I'm a sultan; let my slave-girls fan me?"

You know as well as I what's coming. Rain. Rain. Rain in floods. The deluge. But first you'll see shameful things— shameful things. Some of you will be saying: "Let him drown. He's not worth saving. Give the whole thing up." I can see it in your faces. But you're wrong. Keep your doubts and despairs to yourselves.

Again there'll be the narrow escape. The survival of a handful. From destruction,—total destruction. *{She points sweeping with her hand to the stage}*

Even of the animals, a few will be saved: two of a kind, male and female, two of a kind. *{The heads of* CONVEENERS *appear about the stage and in the orchestra pit, jeering at her}*

CONVEENERS: Charlatan! Madam Kill-Joy! Mrs. Jeremiah! Charlatan!

FORTUNE TELLER: And *you!* Mark my words before it's too late. Where'll *you* be?

CONVEENERS: The croaking raven. Old dust and ashes. Rags, bottles, sacks.

FORTUNE TELLER: Yes, stick out your tongues. You can't stick your tongues out far enough to lick the death-sweat from your foreheads.

It's too late to work now—bail out the flood with your soup spoons. You've had your chance and you've lost.

CONVEENERS: Enjoy yourselves!!! *{They disappear. The* FORTUNE TELLER *looks off left and puts her finger on her lips}*

FORTUNE TELLER: They're coming—

the Antrobuses. Keck. Your hope. Your despair. Your selves. *{Enter from the left,* MR. *and* MRS. ANTROBUS *and* GLADYS]*

MRS. ANTROBUS: Gladys Antrobus, stick your stummick in.

GLADYS: But it's easier this way.

MRS. ANTROBUS: Well, it's too bad the new president has such a clumsy daughter, that's all I can say. Try and be a lady.

FORTUNE TELLER: Aijah! That's been said a hundred billion times.

MRS. ANTROBUS: Goodness! Where's Henry? He was here just a minute ago. Henry! *{Sudden violent stir. A roller-chair appears from the left. About it are dancing in great excitement* HENRY *and a* NEGRO CHAIR-PUSHER]*

HENRY: *{Slingshot in hand}* I'll put your eye out. I'll make you yell, like you never yelled before.

NEGRO: *{At the same time}* Now, I warns you. I warns you. If you make me mad, you'll get hurt.

ANTROBUS: Henry! What is this? Put down that slingshot.

MRS. ANTROBUS: *{At the same time}* Henry! HENRY! Behave yourself.

FORTUNE TELLER: That's right, young man. There are too many people in the world as it is. Everybody's in the way, except one's self.

HENRY: All I wanted to do was— have some fun.

NEGRO: Nobody can't touch my chair, nobody, without I allow 'em to. You get clean away from me and you get away fast. *{He pushes his chair off, muttering}*

ANTROBUS: What were you doing, Henry?

HENRY: Everybody's always getting mad. Everybody's always trying to push you around. I'll make him sorry for this; I'll make him sorry.

ANTROBUS: Give me that slingshot.

HENRY: I won't. I'm sorry I came to this place. I wish I weren't here. I wish I weren't anywhere.

MRS. ANTROBUS: Now, Henry, don't get so excited about nothing. I declare I don't know what we're going to do with you. Put your slingshot in your pocket, and don't try to take hold of things that don't belong to you.

ANTROBUS: After this you can stay home. I wash my hands of you.

MRS. ANTROBUS: Come now, let's forget all about it. Everybody take a good breath of that sea air and calm down. *{A passing* CONVEENER *bows to* ANTROBUS *who nods to him}* Who was that you spoke to, George?

ANTROBUS: Nobody, Maggie. Just the candidate who ran against me in the election.

MRS. ANTROBUS: The man who ran against you in the election!! *{She turns and waves her umbrella after the disappearing* CONVEENER]* My husband didn't speak to you and he never will speak to you.

ANTROBUS: Now, Maggie.

MRS. ANTROBUS: After those lies you told about him in your speeches! Lies, that's what they were.

GLADYS AND HENRY: Mama, everybody's looking at you. Everybody's laughing at you.

MRS. ANTROBUS: If you must know, my husband's a SAINT, a downright SAINT, and you're not fit to speak to him on the street.

ANTROBUS: Now, Maggie, now, Maggie, that's enough of that.

MRS. ANTROBUS: George Antrobus, you're a perfect worm. If you won't stand up for yourself, I will.

GLADYS: Mama, you just act awful in public.

MRS. ANTROBUS: *{Laughing}* Well, I must say I enjoyed it. I feel better. Wish his wife had been there to hear it. Children, what do you want to do?

GLADYS: Papa, can we ride in one of those chairs? Mama, I want to ride in one of those chairs.

MRS. ANTROBUS: No, sir. If you're tired you just sit where you are. We have no money to spend on foolishness.

ANTROBUS: I guess we have money enough for a thing like that. It's one of the things you do at Atlantic City.

MRS. ANTROBUS: Oh, we have? I tell you it's a miracle my children have shoes to stand up in. I didn't think I'd ever live to see them pushed around in chairs.

ANTROBUS: We're on a vacation, aren't we? We have a right to some treats, I guess. Maggie, some day you're going to drive me crazy.

MRS. ANTROBUS: All right, go. I'll just sit here and laugh at you. And you can give me my dollar right in my hand. Mark my words, a rainy day is coming. There's a rainy day ahead of us: I feel it in my bones. Go on, throw your money around. I can starve. I've starved before. I know how. {*A* CONVEENER *puts his head through Turkish Bath window, and says with raised eyebrows:*}

CONVEENER: Hello, George. How are ya? I see where you brought the WHOLE family along.

MRS. ANTROBUS: And what do you mean by that? [CONVEENER *withdraws head and closes window*}

ANTROBUS: Maggie, I tell you there's a limit to what I can stand. God's Heaven, haven't I worked *enough?* Don't I get *any* vacation? Can't I even give my children so much as a ride in a roller-chair?

MRS. ANTROBUS: {*Putting out her hand for raindrops*} Anyway, it's going to rain very soon and you have your broadcast to make.

ANTROBUS: Now, Maggie, I warn you. A man can stand a family only just so long. I'm warning you. {*Enter* SABINA *from the Bingo-Parlor. She wears a flounced red silk bathing suit, 1905. Red stockings, shoes, parasol. She bows demurely to* ANTROBUS *and starts down the ramp.* ANTROBUS *and the children stare at her.* ANTROBUS *bows gallantly*}

MRS. ANTROBUS: Why, George Antrobus, how can you say such a thing! You have the best family in the world.

ANTROBUS: Good morning, Miss Fairweather. [SABINA *finally disappears behind the beach umbrella or in a cabana in the orchestra pit*}

MRS. ANTROBUS: Who on earth was that you spoke to George?

ANTROBUS: {*Complacent; mock-modest*} Hm . . . m . . . Just a . . . solambaka keray.

MRS. ANTROBUS: What? I can't understand you.

GLADYS: Mama, wasn't she beautiful?

HENRY: Papa, introduce her to me.

MRS. ANTROBUS: Children, will you be quiet while I ask your father a simple question?—Who did you say it was, George?

ANTROBUS: Why-uh . . . a friend of mine. Very nice refined girl.

MRS. ANTROBUS: I'm waiting.

ANTROBUS: Maggie, that's the girl I gave the prize to in the beauty contest,—that's Miss Atlantic City 1942.

MRS. ANTROBUS: Hm! She looked like Sabina to me.

HENRY: {*At the railing*} Mama, the lifeguard knows her, too. Mama, he knows her well.

ANTROBUS: Henry, come here.—She's a very nice girl in every way and the sole support of her aged mother.

MRS. ANTROBUS: So was Sabina, so was Sabina; and it took a wall of ice to open your eyes about Sabina.—Henry, come over and sit down on this bench.

ANTROBUS: She's a very different matter from Sabina. Miss Fairweather is a college graduate, Phi Beta Kappa.

MRS. ANTROBUS: Henry, you sit here by mama. Gladys—

ANTROBUS: {*Sitting*} Reduced circumstances have required her taking a position as hostess in a Bingo Parlor; but there isn't a girl with higher principles in the country.

MRS. ANTROBUS: Well, let's not talk about it.—Henry, I haven't seen a whale yet.

ANTROBUS: She speaks seven languages and has more culture in her little finger than you've acquired in a lifetime.

MRS. ANTROBUS: {*Assumed amiability*} All right, all right, George. I'm glad to know there are such superior girls in the Bingo Parlors.—Henry, what's that?

{Pointing at the storm signal, which has one black disk}

HENRY: What is it, Papa?

ANTROBUS: What? Oh, that's the storm signal. One of those black disks means bad weather; two means storm; three means hurricane; and four means the end of the world. *{As they watch it a second black disk rolls into place}*

MRS. ANTROBUS: Goodness! I'm going this very minute to buy you all some raincoats.

GLADYS: *{Putting her cheek against her father's shoulder}* Mama, don't go yet. I like sitting this way. And the ocean coming in and coming in. Papa, don't you like it?

MRS. ANTROBUS: Well, there's only one thing I lack to make me a perfectly happy woman: I'd like to see a whale.

HENRY: Mama, we saw two. Right out there. They're delegates to the convention. I'll find you one.

GLADYS: Papa, ask me something. Ask me a question.

ANTROBUS: Well . . . how big's the ocean?

GLADYS: Papa, you're teasing me. It's—three-hundred and sixty million square-miles — and — it — covers — three-fourths — of — the — earth's — surface — and — its — deepest-place — is — five — and — a — half — miles — deep — and — its — average — depth — is — twelve-thousand-feet. No, Papa, ask me something hard, real hard.

MRS. ANTROBUS: *{Rising}* Now I'm going off to buy those raincoats. I think that bad weather's going to get worse and worse. I hope it doesn't come before your broadcast. I should think we have about an hour or so.

HENRY: I hope it comes and zzzzzz everything before it. I hope it—

MRS. ANTROBUS: Henry!—George, I think . . . maybe, it's one of those storms that are just as bad on land as on the sea. When you're just as safe and safer in a good stout boat.

HENRY: There's a boat out at the end of the pier.

MRS. ANTROBUS: Well, keep your eye on it. George, you shut your eyes and get a good rest before the broadcast.

ANTROBUS: Thundering Judas, do I have to be told when to open and shut my eyes? Go and buy your raincoats.

MRS ANTROBUS: Now, children, you have ten minutes to walk around. Ten minutes. And Henry: control yourself. Gladys, stick by your brother and don't get lost. *{They run off}*

MRS. ANTROBUS: Will you be all right, George? [CONVEENERS suddenly *stick their heads out of the Bingo Parlor and Salt Water Taffy store, and voices rise from the orchestra pit}*

CONVEENERS: George, Geo-r-r-rge! George! Leave the old hen-coop at home, George. Do-mes-ticated Georgie!

MRS. ANTROBUS: *{Shaking her umbrella}* Low common oafs! That's what they are. Guess a man has a right to bring his wife to a convention, if he wants to. *{She starts off}* What's the matter with a family, I'd like to know. What else have they got to offer? *{Exit.* ANTROBUS *has closed his eyes. The* FORTUNE TELLER *comes out of her shop and goes over to the left proscenium. She leans against it watching* SABINA *quizzically}*

FORTUNE TELLER: Heh! Here she comes!

SABINA: *{Loud whisper}* What's he doing?

FORTUNE TELLER: Oh, he's ready for you. Bite your lips, dear, take a long breath and come on up.

SABINA: I'm nervous. My whole future depends on this. I'm nervous.

FORTUNE TELLER: Don't be a fool. What more could you want? He's forty-five. His head's a little dizzy. He's just been elected president. He's never known any other woman than his wife. Whenever he looks at her he realizes that she knows every foolish thing he's ever done.

SABINA: *{Still whispering}* I don't know why it is, but every time I start one of these I'm nervous. *{The* FORTUNE TELLER *stands in the center of the stage watching the following:}*

FORTUNE TELLER: You make me tired.

SABINA: First tell me my fortune. *{The* FORTUNE TELLER *laughs drily and makes the gesture of brushing away a nonsensical question.* SABINA *coughs and says:}* Oh, Mr. Antrobus,—dare I speak to you for a moment?

ANTROBUS: What?—Oh, certainly, certainly, Miss Fairweather.

SABINA: Mr. Antrobus . . . I've been so unhappy. I've wanted . . . I've wanted to make sure that you don't think that I'm the kind of girl who goes out for beauty contests.

FORTUNE TELLER: That's the way!

ANTROBUS: Oh, I understand. I understand perfectly.

FORTUNE TELLER: Give it a little more. Lean on it.

SABINA: I knew you would. My mother said to me this morning: Lily, she said, that fine Mr. Antrobus gave you the prize because he saw at once that you weren't the kind of girl who'd go in for a thing like that. But, honestly, Mr. Antrobus, in this world, honestly, a good girl doesn't know where to turn.

FORTUNE TELLER: Now you've gone too far.

ANTROBUS: My dear Miss Fairweather!

SABINA: You wouldn't know how hard it is. With that lovely wife and daughter you have. Oh, I think Mrs. Antrobus is the finest woman I ever saw. I wish I were like her.

ANTROBUS: There, there. There's . . . uh . . . room for all kinds of people in the world, Miss Fairweather.

SABINA: How wonderful of you to say that. How generous!—Mr. Antrobus, have you a moment free? . . . I'm afraid I may be a little conspicuous here . . . could you come down, for just a moment, to my beach cabana . . . ?

ANTROBUS: Why-uh . . . yes, certainly . . . for a moment . . . just for a moment.

SABINA: There's a deck chair there. Because: you know you *do* look tired. Just this morning my mother said to me: Lily, she said, I hope Mr. Antrobus is getting a good rest. His fine strong face has deep lines in it. Now isn't it true, Mr. Antrobus: you work too hard?

FORTUNE TELLER: Bingo! *{She goes into her shop}*

SABINA: Now you will just stretch out. No, I shan't say a word, not a word. I shall just sit there,—privileged. That's what I am.

ANTROBUS: *{Taking her hand}* Miss Fairweather . . . you'll . . . spoil me.

SABINA: Just a moment. I have something I wish to say to the audience.— Ladies and gentlemen. I'm not going to play this particular scene tonight. It's just a short scene and we're going to skip it. But I'll tell you what takes place and then we can continue the play from there on. Now in this scene—

ANTROBUS: *{Between his teeth}* But, Miss Somerset!

SABINA: I'm sorry. I'm sorry. But I have to skip it. In this scene, I talk to Mr. Antrobus, and at the end of it he decides to leave his wife, get a divorce at Reno and marry me. That's all.

ANTROBUS: Fitz!—Fitz!

SABINA: So that now I've told you we can jump to the end of it,—where you say: *{Enter in fury* MR. FITZPATRICK, *the stage manager}*

MR. FITZPATRICK: Miss Somerset, we insist on your playing this scene.

SABINA: I'm sorry, Mr. Fitzpatrick, but I can't and I won't. I've told the audience all they need to know and now we can go on. *{Other* ACTORS *begin to appear on the stage, listening}*

MR. FITZPATRICK: And *why* can't you play it?

SABINA: Because there are some lines in that scene that would hurt some people's feelings and I don't think the theatre is a place where people's feelings ought to be hurt.

MR. FITZPATRICK: Miss Somerset, you can pack up your things and go home. I shall call the understudy and I shall report you to Equity.

SABINA: I sent the understudy up to

the corner for a cup of coffee and if Equity tries to penalize me I'll drag the case right up to the Supreme Court. Now listen, everybody, there's no need to get excited.

MR. FITZPATRICK *and* ANTROBUS: Why can't you play it . . . what's the matter with the scene?

SABINA: Well, if you must know, I have a personal guest in the audience tonight. Her life hasn't been exactly a happy one. I wouldn't have my friend hear some of these lines for the whole world. I don't suppose it occurred to the author that some other women might have gone through the experience of losing their husbands like this. Wild horses wouldn't drag from me the details of my friend's life, but . . . well, they'd been married twenty years, and before he got rich, why, she'd done the washing and everything.

MR. FITZPATRICK: Miss Somerset, your friend will forgive you. We must play this scene.

SABINA: Nothing, nothing will make me say some of those lines . . . about "a man outgrows a wife every seven years" and . . . and that one about "the Mohammedans being the only people who looked the subject square in the face." Nothing.

MR. FITZPATRICK: Miss Somerset! Go to your dressing room. I'll *read* your lines.

SABINA: Now everybody's nerves are on edge.

MR. ANTROBUS: Skip the scene. [MR. FITZPATRICK *and the other* ACTORS *go off}*

SABINA: Thank you. I knew you'd understand. We'll do just what I said. So Mr. Antrobus is going to divorce his wife and marry me. Mr. Antrobus, you say: "It won't be easy to lay all this before my wife." *{The* ACTORS *withdraw.* ANTROBUS *walks about, his hand to his forehead muttering:}*

ANTROBUS: Wait a minute. I can't get back into it as easily as all that. "My wife is a very obstinate woman."

Hm . . . then you say . . . hm . . . Miss Fairweather, I mean Lily, it won't be easy to lay all this before my wife. It'll hurt her feelings a little.

SABINA: Listen, George: *other* people haven't got feelings. Not in the same way that we have,—we who are presidents like you and prize-winners like me. Listen, other people haven't got feelings; they just imagine they have. Within two weeks they go back to playing bridge and going to the movies.

Listen, dear: everybody in the world except a few people like you and me are just people of straw. Most people have no insides at all. Now that you're president you'll see that. Listen, darling, there's a kind of secret society at the top of the world,—like you and me,—that know this. The world was made for us. What's life anyway? Except for two things, pleasure and power, what is life? Boredom! Foolishness. You know it is. Except for those two things, life's nause-at-ing. So,—come here! *{She moves close. They kiss}* So.

Now when your wife comes, it's really very simple; just tell her.

ANTROBUS: Lily, Lily: you're a wonderful woman.

SABINA: Of course I am. *{They enter the cabana and it hides them from view. Distant roll of thunder. A third black disk appears on the weather signal. Distant thunder is heard.* MRS. ANTROBUS *appears carrying parcels. She looks about, seats herself on the bench left, and fans herself with her handkerchief. Enter* GLADYS *right, followed by two* CON-VEENERS. *She is wearing red stockings}*

MRS. ANTROBUS: Gladys!

GLADYS: Mama, here I am.

MRS. ANTROBUS: Gladys Antrobus!!! Where did you get those dreadful things?

GLADYS: Wha-a-t? Papa liked the color.

MRS. ANTROBUS: You go back to the hotel this minute!

GLADYS: I won't. I won't. Papa liked the color.

MRS. ANTROBUS: All right. All right. You stay here. I've a good mind to let your father see you that way. You stay right here.

GLADYS: I . . . don't want to stay if . . . if you don't think he'd like it.

MRS. ANTROBUS: Oh . . . it's all one to me. I don't care what happens. I don't care if the biggest storm in the whole world comes. Let it come. {*She folds her hands*} Where's your brother?

GLADYS: {*In a small voice*} He'll be here.

MRS. ANTROBUS: Will he? Well, let him get into trouble. I don't care. I don't know where your father is, I'm sure. {*Laughter from the cabana*}

GLADYS: {*Leaning over the rail*} I think he's . . . Mama, he's talking to the lady in the red dress.

MRS. ANTROBUS: Is that so? {*Pause*} We'll wait till he's through. Sit down here beside me and stop fidgeting . . . what are you crying about? {*Distant thunder. She covers* GLADYS'S *stockings with a raincoat*}

GLADYS: You don't like my stockings. {*Two* CONVEENERS *rush in with a microphone on a standard and various paraphernalia. The* FORTUNE TELLER *appears at the door of her shop. Other characters gradually gather*}

BROADCAST OFFICIAL: Mrs. Antrobus! Thank God we've found you at last. Where's Mr. Antrobus? We've been hunting everywhere for him. It's about time for the broadcast to the conventions of the world.

MRS. ANTROBUS: {*Calm*} I expect he'll be here in a minute.

BROADCAST OFFICIAL: Mrs. Antrobus, if he doesn't show up in time, I hope you will consent to broadcast in his place. It's the most important broadcast of the year. [SABINA *enters from cabana followed by* ANTROBUS}

MRS. ANTROBUS: No, I shan't. I haven't one single thing to say.

BROADCAST OFFICIAL: Then won't you help us find him, Mrs. Antrobus? A storm's coming up. A hurricane. A deluge!

SECOND CONVEENER: {*Who has sighted* ANTROBUS *over the rail*} Joe! Joe! Here he is.

BROADCAST OFFICIAL: In the name of God, Mr. Antrobus, you're on the air in five minutes. Will you kindly please come and test the instrument? That's all we ask. If you just please begin the alphabet slowly. [ANTROBUS, *with set face, comes ponderously up the ramp. He stops at the point where his waist is level with the stage and speaks authoritatively to the* OFFICIALS]

ANTROBUS: I'll be ready when the time comes. Until then, move away. Go away. I have something I wish to say to my wife.

BROADCAST OFFICIAL: {*Whimpering*} Mr. Antrobus! This is the most important broadcast of the year. {*The* OFFICIALS *withdraw to the edge of the stage.* SABINA *glides up the ramp behind* ANTROBUS]

SABINA: {*Whispering*} Don't let her argue. Remember arguments have nothing to do with it.

ANTROBUS: Maggie, I'm moving out of the hotel. In fact, I'm moving out of everything. For good. I'm going to marry Miss Fairweather. I shall provide generously for you and the children. In a few years you'll be able to see that it's all for the best. That's all I have to say.

BROADCAST OFFICIAL: Mr. Antrobus! I hope you'll be ready. This is the most important broadcast of the year.	BINGO ANNOUNCER: A—nine; A—nine. D—forty-two; D—forty-two. C—thirty; C—thirty. B—seventeen; B—seventeen. C—forty; C—forty.
GLADYS: What did Papa say, Mama? I didn't hear what Papa said.	CHORUS: Bingo!!

BROADCAST OFFICIAL: Mr. Antrobus. All we want to do is test your voice with the alphabet.

ANTROBUS: Go away. Clear out.

MRS. ANTROBUS: {*Composedly with lowered eyes*} George, I can't talk to you until you wipe those silly red marks off your face.

ANTROBUS: I think there's nothing to talk about. I've said what I have to say.

SABINA: Splendid!!

ANTROBUS: You're a fine woman, Maggie, but . . . but a man has his own life to lead in the world.

MRS. ANTROBUS: Well, after living with you for five thousand years I guess I have a right to a word or two, haven't I?

ANTROBUS: {*To* SABINA} What can I answer to that?

SABINA: Tell her conversation would only hurt her feelings. It's-kinder-in-the-long-run-to-do-it-short-and-quick.

ANTROBUS: I want to spare your feelings in every way I can, Maggie.

BROADCAST OFFICIAL: Mr. Antrobus, the hurricane signal's gone up. We could begin right now.

MRS. ANTROBUS: {*Calmly, almost dreamily*} I didn't marry you because you were perfect. I didn't even marry you because I loved you. I married you because you gave me a promise.

{*She takes off her ring and looks at it*}

That promise made up for your faults. And the promise I gave you made up for mine. Two imperfect people got married and it was the promise that made the marriage.

ANTROBUS: Maggie, . . . I was only nineteen.

MRS. ANTROBUS: {*She puts her ring back on her finger*} And when our children were growing up, it wasn't a house that protected them; and it wasn't our love, that protected them—it was that promise.

And when that promise is broken—this can happen! {*With a sweep of the hand she removes the raincoat from* GLADYS'S *stockings*}

ANTROBUS: {*Stretches out his arm, apoplectic*} Gladys!! Have you gone crazy? Has everyone gone crazy? {*Turning on* SABINA} You did this. You gave them to her.

SABINA: I never said a word to her.

ANTROBUS: {*To* GLADYS} You go back to the hotel and take those horrible things off.

GLADYS: {*Pert*} Before I go, I've got something to tell you,—it's about Henry.

MRS. ANTROBUS: {*Claps her hands peremptorily*} Stop your noise,—I'm taking her back to the hotel, George. Before I go I have a letter. . . . I have a message to throw into the ocean. {*Fumbling in her handbag*} Where is the plagued thing? Here it is. {*She flings something—invisible to us—far over the heads of the audience to the back of the auditorium*} It's a bottle. And in the bottle's a letter. And in the letter is written all the things that a woman knows.

It's never been told to any man and it's never been told to any woman, and if it finds its destination, a new time will come. We're not what books and plays say we are. We're not what advertisements say we are. We're not in the movies and we're not on the radio.

We're not what you're all told and what you think we are: We're ourselves. And if any man can find one of us he'll learn why the whole universe was set in motion. And if any man harm any one of us, his soul—the only soul he's got—had better be at the bottom of that ocean,—and that's the only way to put it. Gladys, come here. We're going back to the hotel. {*She drags* GLADYS *firmly off by the hand, but* GLADYS *breaks away and comes down to speak to her father*}

SABINA: Such goings-on. Don't give it a minute's thought.

GLADYS: Anyway, I think you ought to know that Henry hit a man with a stone. He hit one of those colored men that push the chairs and the man's very sick. Henry ran away and hid and some policemen are looking for him very hard. And I don't care a bit if you don't want to have anything to do with mama and me, because I'll never like you again and I hope nobody ever likes you again,—so there! *{She runs off.* ANTROBUS *starts after her}*

ANTROBUS: I . . . I have to go and see what I can do about this.

SABINA: You stay right here. Don't you go now while you're excited. Gracious sakes, all these things will be forgotten in a hundred years. Come, now, you're on the air. Just say anything,—it doesn't matter what. Just a lot of birds and fishes and things.

BROADCAST OFFICIAL: Thank you, Miss Fairweather. Thank you very much. Ready, Mr. Antrobus.

ANTROBUS: *{Touching the microphone}* What is it, what is it? Who am I talking to?

BROADCAST OFFICIAL: Why, Mr. Antrobus! To our order and to all the other orders.

ANTROBUS: *{Raising his head}* What are all those birds doing?

BROADCAST OFFICIAL: Those are just a few of the birds. Those are the delegates to our convention,—two of a kind.

ANTROBUS: *{Pointing into the audience}* Look at the water. Look at them all. Those fishes jumping. The children should see this!—There's Maggie's whales!! Here are your whales, Maggie!!

BROADCAST OFFICIAL: I hope you're ready, Mr. Antrobus.

ANTROBUS: And look on the beach! You didn't tell me these would be here!

SABINA: Yes, George. Those are the animals.

BROADCAST OFFICIAL: *{Busy with the apparatus}* Yes, Mr. Antrobus, those are the vertebrates. We hope the lion will have a word to say when you're through. Step right up, Mr. Antrobus, we're ready. We'll just have time before the storm. *{Pause. In a hoarse whisper:}* They're waiting. *{It has grown dark. Soon after he speaks a high whistling noise begins. Strange veering lights start whirling about the stage. The other characters disappear from the stage}*

ANTROBUS: Friends. Cousins. Four score and ten billion years ago our fore-father brought forth upon this planet the spark of life,—*{He is drowned out by thunder. When the thunder stops the* FORTUNE TELLER *is seen standing beside him}*

FORTUNE TELLER: Antrobus, there's not a minute to be lost. Don't you see the four disks on the weather signal? Take your family into that boat at the end of the pier.

ANTROBUS: My family? I have no family. Maggie! Maggie! They won't come.

FORTUNE TELLER: They'll come.— Antrobus! Take these animals into that boat with you. All of them,—two of each kind.

SABINA: George, what's the matter with you? This is just a storm like any other storm.

ANTROBUS: Maggie!

SABINA: Stay with me, we'll go . . . *{Losing conviction}* This is just another thunderstorm,—isn't it? Isn't it?

ANTROBUS: Maggie!!! [MRS. ANTROBUS *appears beside him with* GLADYS]

MRS. ANTROBUS: *{Matter-of-fact}* Here I am and here's Gladys.

ANTROBUS: Where've you been? Where have you been? Quick, we're going into that boat out there.

MRS. ANTROBUS: I know we are. But I haven't found Henry. *{She wanders off into the darkness calling "Henry!"}*

SABINA: *{Low urgent babbling, only occasionally raising her voice}* I don't believe it. I don't believe it's anything at all. I've seen hundreds of storms like this.

FORTUNE TELLER: There's no time to lose. Go. Push the animals along before you. Start a new world. Begin again.

SABINA: Esmeralda! George! Tell me,—is it really serious?

ANTROBUS: *{Suddenly very busy}* Elephants first. Gently, gently.—Look where you're going.

GLADYS: *{Leaning over the ramp and striking an animal on the back}* Stop it or you'll be left behind!

ANTROBUS: Is the Kangaroo there? *There* you are! Take those turtles in your pouch, will you? *{To some other animals, pointing to his shoulder}* Here! You jump up here. You'll be trampled on.

GLADYS: *{To her father, pointing below}* Papa, look,—the snakes!

MRS. ANTROBUS: I can't find Henry. Hen-ry!

ANTROBUS: Go along. Go along. Climb on their backs.—Wolves! Jackals —whatever you are,—tend to your own business!

GLADYS: *{Pointing, tenderly}* Papa,— look.

SABINA: Mr. Antrobus—take me with you. Don't leave me here. I'll work. I'll help. I'll do anything. [THREE CONVEENERS *cross the stage, marching with a banner}*

CONVEENERS: George! What are you scared of?—George! Fellas, it looks like rain.—"Maggie, where's my umbrella?" —George, setting up for Barnum and Bailey.

ANTROBUS: *{Again catching his wife's hand}* Come on now, Maggie,— the pier's going to break any minute.

MRS. ANTROBUS: I'm not going a step without Henry. Henry!

GLADYS: *{On the ramp}* Mama! Papa! Hurry. The pier's cracking, Mama. It's going to break.

MRS. ANTROBUS: Henry! Cain! CAIN! [HENRY *dashes into the stage and joins his mother}*

HENRY: Here I am, Mama.

MRS. ANTROBUS: Thank God!—now come quick.

HENRY: I didn't think you wanted me.

MRS. ANTROBUS: Quick! *{She pushes him down before her into the aisle}*

SABINA: *{All the* ANTROBUSES *are now in the theatre aisle.* SABINA *stands at the top of the ramp}* Mrs. Antrobus, take me. Don't you remember me? I'll work. I'll help. Don't leave me here!

MRS. ANTROBUS: *{Impatiently, but as though it were of no importance}* Yes, yes. There's a lot of work to be done. Only hurry.

FORTUNE TELLER: *{Now dominating the stage. To* SABINA *with a grim smile}* Yes, go—back to the kitchen with you.

SABINA: *{Half-down the ramp. To* FORTUNE TELLER] I don't know why my life's always being interrupted—just when everything's going fine!! *{She dashes up the aisle. Now the* CONVEENERS *emerge doing a serpentine dance on the stage. They jeer at the* FORTUNE TELLER]

CONVEENERS: Get a canoe—there's not a minute to be lost! Tell me my future, Mrs. Croaker.

FORTUNE TELLER: Paddle in the water, boys—enjoy yourselves.

VOICE FROM THE BINGO PARLOR: A-nine; A-nine. C-Twenty-four. C-Twenty-four.

CONVEENERS: Rags, bottles, and sacks.

FORTUNE TELLER: Go back and climb on your roofs. Put rags in the cracks under your doors.—Nothing will keep out the flood. You've had your chance. You've had your day. You've failed. You've lost.

VOICE FROM THE BINGO PARLOR: B-fifteen. B-Fifteen.

FORTUNE TELLER: *{Shading her eyes and looking out to sea}* They're safe. George Antrobus! Think it over! A new world to make.—think it over!

CURTAIN

Act III

Just before the curtain rises, two sounds are heard from the stage: a cracked bugle call.

The curtain rises on almost total darkness. Almost all the flats composing the walls of MR. ANTROBUS'S *house, as of Act I, are up, but they lean helter-skelter against one another, leaving irregular gaps. Among the flats missing are two in the back wall, leaving the frames of the window and door crazily out of line. Off stage, back right, some red Roman fire is burning. The bugle call is repeated. Enter* SABINA *through the tilted door. She is dressed as a Napoleonic camp follower, "la fille du regiment," in begrimed reds and blues.*

SABINA: Mrs. Antrobus! Gladys! Where are you?

The war's over. The war's over. You can come out. The peace treaty's been signed.

Where are they?—Hmph! Are they dead, too? Mrs. Annnntrobus! Glaaaadus! Mr. Antrobus'll be here this afternoon. I just saw him downtown. Huuuurry and put things in order. He says that now that the war's over we'll all have to settle down and be perfect. *{Enter* MR. FITZPATRICK, *the stage manager, followed by the whole company, who stand waiting at the edges of the stage.* MR. FITZPATRICK *tries to interrupt* SABINA]

MR. FITZPATRICK: Miss Somerset, we have to stop a moment.

SABINA: They may be hiding out in the back—

MR. FITZPATRICK: Miss Somerset! We have to stop a moment.

SABINA: What's the matter?

MR. FITZPATRICK: There's an explanation we have to make to the audience.—Lights, please. *{To the actor who plays* MR. ANTROBUS,] Will you explain the matter to the audience? *{The lights go up. We now see that a balcony or elevated runway has been erected at the back of the stage, back of the wall of the Antrobus house. From its extreme right and left ends ladder-like steps descend to the floor of the stage}*

ANTROBUS: Ladies and gentlemen, an unfortunate accident has taken place back stage. Perhaps I should say *another* unfortunate accident.

SABINA: I'm sorry. I'm sorry.

ANTROBUS: The management feels, in fact, we all feel that you are due an apology. And now we have to ask your indulgence for the most serious mishap of all. Seven of our actors have . . . have been taken ill. Apparently, it was something they ate. I'm not exactly clear what happened. *{All the* ACTORS *start to talk at once.* ANTROBUS *raises his hand}* Now, now—not all at once. Fitz, do you know what it was?

MR. FITZPATRICK: Why, it's perfectly clear. These seven actors had dinner together, and they ate something that disagreed with them.

SABINA: Disagreed with them!!! They have ptomaine poisoning. They're in Bellevue Hospital this very minute in agony. They're having their stomachs pumped out this very minute, in perfect agony.

ANTROBUS: Fortunately, we've just heard they'll all recover.

SABINA: It'll be a miracle if they do, a downright miracle. It was the lemon meringue pie.

ACTORS: It was the fish . . . it was the canned tomatoes . . . it was the fish.

SABINA: It was the lemon meringue pie. I saw it with my own eyes; it had blue mould all over the bottom of it.

ANTROBUS: Whatever it was, they're in no condition to take part in this performance. Naturally, we haven't enough understudies to fill all those roles; but we do have a number of splendid volunteers who have kindly consented to help us out. These friends have watched our rehearsals, and they assure me that they know the lines and the business very well. Let me introduce them to you—my dresser, Mr. Tremayne,—himself a distinguished Shakespearean actor for many years; our wardrobe mistress, Hester; Miss Somerset's maid, Ivy; and Fred Bailey, captain of the ushers in this theatre. *{These persons bow modestly.* IVY *and* HESTER *are colored girls}*

Now this scene takes place near the end of the act. And I'm sorry to say we'll need a short rehearsal, just a short run-through. And as some of it takes place in the auditorium, we'll have to keep the curtain up. Those of you who wish can go out in the lobby and smoke some more. The rest of you can listen to us, or . . . or just talk quietly among yourselves, as you choose. Thank you. Now will you take it over, Mr. Fitzpatrick?

MR. FITZPATRICK: Thank you.—Now for those of you who are listening perhaps I should explain that at the end of this act, the men have come back from the War and the family's settled down in the house. And the author wants to show the hours of the night passing by over their heads, and the planets crossing the sky . . . uh . . . over their heads. And he says—this is hard to explain—that each of the hours of the night is a philosopher, or a great thinker. Eleven o'clock, for instance, is Aristotle. And nine o'clock is Spinoza. Like that. I don't suppose it means anything. It's just a kind of poetic effect.

SABINA: Not mean anything! Why, it certainly does. Twelve o'clock goes by saying those wonderful things. I think it means that when people are asleep they have all those lovely thoughts, much better than when they're awake.

IVY: Excuse me, I think it means,— excuse me, Mr. Fitzpatrick—

SABINA: What were you going to say, Ivy?

IVY: Mr. Fitzpatrick, you let my father come to a rehearsal; and my father's a Baptist minister, and he said that the author meant that—just like the hours and stars go by over our heads at night, in the same way the ideas and thoughts of the great men are in the air around us all the time and they're working on us, even when we don't know it.

MR. FITZPATRICK: Well, well, maybe that's it. Thank you, Ivy. Anyway,—the hours of the night are philosophers. My friends, are you ready? Ivy, can you be eleven o'clock? "This good estate of the mind possessing its object in energy we call divine." Aristotle.

IVY: Yes, sir. I know that and I know twelve o'clock and I know nine o'clock.

MR. FITZPATRICK: Twelve o'clock? Mr. Tremayne, the Bible.

TREMAYNE: Yes.

MR. FITZPATRICK: Ten o'clock? Hester,—Plato? *{She nods eagerly}* Nine o'clock, Spinoza,—Fred?

BAILEY: Yes, sir. [FRED BAILEY *picks up a great gilded cardboard numeral IX and starts up the steps to the platform.* MR. FITZPATRICK *strikes his forehead}*

MR. FITZPATRICK: The planets!! We forgot all about the planets.

SABINA: O my God! The planets! Are they sick too? [ACTORS *nod}*

MR. FITZPATRICK: Ladies and gentlemen, the planets are singers. Of course, we can't replace them, so you'll have to imagine them singing in this scene. Saturn sings from the orchestra pit down here. The Moon is way up there. And Mars with a red lantern in his hand, stands in the aisle over there— Tz-tz-tz. It's too bad; it all makes a very fine effect. However! Ready—nine o'clock: Spinoza.

BAILEY: *{Walking slowly across the balcony, left to right}* "After experience had taught me that the common occurrences of daily life are vain and futile—"

FITZPATRICK: Louder, Fred, "And I saw that all the objects of my desire and fear—"

BAILEY: "And I saw that all the objects of my desire and fear were in themselves nothing good nor bad save insofar as the mind was affected by them—"

FITZPATRICK: Do you know the rest? All right. Ten o'clock. Hester. Plato.

HESTER: "Then tell me, O Critias, how will a man choose the ruler that shall rule over him? Will he not—"

FITZPATRICK: Thank you. Skip to the end, Hester.

HESTER: ". . . can be multiplied a thousand fold in its effects among the citizens."

FITZPATRICK: Thank you.—Aristotle, Ivy?

IVY: "This good estate of the mind possessing its object in energy we call divine. This we mortals have occasionally and it is this energy which is pleasantest and best. But God has it always. It is wonderful in us; but in Him how much more wonderful."

FITZPATRICK: Midnight. Midnight, Mr. Tremayne. That's right,—you've done it before.—All right, everybody. You know what you have to do.—Lower the curtain. House lights up. Act Three of THE SKIN OF OUR TEETH. {As the curtain descends he is heard saying:} You volunteers, just wear what you have on. Don't try to put on the costumes today. {House lights go down. The Act begins again. The Bugle call. Curtain rises. Enter SABINA}

SABINA: Mrs. Antrobus! Gladys! Where are you?

The war's over.—You've heard all this—{She gabbles the main points}

Where — are — they? Are — they — dead, too, et cetera.

I — just — saw — Mr. — Antrobus — down town, et cetera. {Slowing up:} He says that now that the war's over we'll all have to settle down and be perfect. They may be hiding out in the back somewhere. Mrs. An-tro-bus. {She wanders off. It has grown lighter. A trapdoor is cautiously raised and MRS. ANTROBUS emerges waist-high and listens. She is disheveled and worn; she wears a tattered dress and a shawl half covers her head. She talks down through the trapdoor}

MRS. ANTROBUS: It's getting light. There's still something burning over there—Newark, or Jersey City. What? Yes, I could swear I heard someone moving about up here. But I can't see anybody. I say: I can't see anybody. {She starts to move about the stage. GLADYS' head appears at the trapdoor. She is holding a BABY}

GLADYS: Oh, Mama. Be careful.

MRS. ANTROBUS: Now, Gladys, you stay out of sight.

GLADY: Well, let me stay here just a minute. I want the baby to get some of this fresh air.

MRS. ANTROBUS: All right, but keep your eyes open. I'll see what I can find. I'll have a good hot plate of soup for you before you can say Jack Robinson. Gladys Antrobus! Do you know what I think I see? There's old Mr. Hawkins sweeping the sidewalk in front of his A. and P. store. Sweeping it with a broom. Why, he must have gone crazy, like the others! I see some other people moving about, too.

GLADYS: Mama, come back, come back. [MRS. ANTROBUS returns to the trapdoor and listens}

MRS. ANTROBUS: Gladys, there's something in the air. Everybody's movement's sort of different. I see some women walking right out in the middle of the street.

SABINA'S VOICE: Mrs. An-tro-bus!

MRS. ANTROBUS AND GLADYS: What's that?!!

SABINA's VOICE: Glaaaadys! Mrs. An-tro-bus! {Enter SABINA}

MRS. ANTROBUS: Gladys, that's Sabina's voice as sure as I live.—Sabina! Sabina!—Are you alive?!!

SABINA: Of course, I'm alive. How've you girls been?—Don't try and kiss me. I never want to kiss another human being as long as I live. Sh-sh, there's nothing to get emotional about. Pull yourself together, the war's over. Take a deep breath,—the war's over.

MRS. ANTROBUS: The war's over!! I don't believe you. I don't believe you. I can't believe you.

GLADYS: Mama!

SABINA: Who's that?

MRS. ANTROBUS: That's Gladys and her baby. I don't believe you. Gladys, Sabina says the war's over. Oh, Sabina.

SABINA: {Leaning over the BABY} Goodness! Are there any babies left in the world! Can it see? And can it cry and everything?

GLADYS: Yes, he can. He notices everything very well.

SABINA: Where on earth did you get

it? Oh, I won't ask.—Lord, I've lived all these seven years around camp and I've forgotten how to behave.—Now we've got to think about the men coming home.—Mrs. Antrobus, go and wash your face, I'm ashamed of you. Put your best clothes on. Mr. Antrobus'll be here this afternoon. I just saw him downtown.

MRS. ANTROBUS AND GLADYS: He's alive!! He'll be here!! Sabina, you're not joking?

MRS. ANTROBUS: And Henry?

SABINA: *{dryly}* Yes, Henry's alive, too, that's what they say. Now don't stop to talk. Get yourself fixed up. Gladys, you look terrible. Have you any decent clothes? [SABINA *has pushed them toward the trapdoor}*

MRS. ANTROBUS: *{Half down}* Yes, I've something to wear just for this very day. But, Sabina,—who won the war?

SABINA: Don't stop now,—just wash your face. *{A whistle sounds in the distance}* Oh, my God, what's that silly little noise?

MRS. ANTROBUS: Why, it sounds like . . . it sounds like what used to be the noon whistle at the shoe-polish factory. *{Exit}*

SABINA: That's what it is. Seems to me like peacetime's coming along pretty fast—shoe polish!

GLADYS: *{Half down}* Sabina, how soon after peacetime begins does the milkman start coming to the door?

SABINA: As soon as he catches a cow. Give him time to catch a cow, dear. *{Exit* GLADYS. SABINA *walks about a moment, thinking}* Shoe polish! My, I'd forgotten what peacetime was like. *{She shakes her head, then sits down by the trapdoor and starts talking down the hole}* Mrs. Antrobus, guess what I saw Mr. Antrobus doing this morning at dawn. He was tacking up a piece of paper on the door of the Town Hall. You'll die when you hear: it was a recipe for grass soup, for a grass soup that doesn't give you the diarrhea. Mr. Antrobus is still thinking up new

things.—He told me to give you his love. He's got all sorts of ideas for peacetime, he says. No more laziness and idiocy, he says. And oh, yes! Where are his books? What? Well, pass them up. The first thing he wants to see are his books. He says if you've burnt those books, or if the rats have eaten them, he says it isn't worthwhile starting over again. Everybody's going to be beautiful, he says, and diligent, and very intelligent. *{A hand reaches up with two volumes}* What language is that? Pu-u-gh,—mold! And he's got such plans for you, Mrs. Antrobus. You're going to study history and algebra—and so are Gladys and I—and philosophy. You should hear him talk: *{Taking two more volumes}* Well, these are in English, anyway.—To hear him talk, seems like he expects you to be a combination, Mrs. Antrobus, of a saint and a college professor, and a dancehall hostess, if you know what I mean. *{Two more volumes}* Ugh. German! *{She is lying on the floor; one elbow bent, her cheek on her hand, meditatively}* Yes, peace will be here before we know it. In a week or two we'll be asking the Perkinses in for a quiet evening of bridge. We'll turn on the radio and hear how to be big successes with a new toothpaste. We'll trot down to the movies and see how girls with wax faces live—all *that* will begin again. Oh, Mrs. Antrobus, God forgive me but I enjoyed the war. Everybody's at their best in wartime. I'm sorry it's over. And, oh, I forgot! Mr. Antrobus sent you another message —can you hear me?—*{Enter* HENRY, *blackened and sullen. He is wearing torn overalls, but has one gaudy admiral's epaulette hanging by a thread from his right shoulder, and there are vestiges of gold and scarlet braid running down his left trouser leg. He stands listening}* Listen! Henry's never to put foot in this house again, he says. He'll kill Henry on sight, if he sees him.

You don't know about Henry??? Well, where have you been? What?

Well, Henry rose right to the top. Top of *what?* Listen, I'm telling you. Henry rose from corporal to captain, to major, to general.—I don't know how to say it, but the enemy is *Henry;* Henry *is* the enemy. Everybody knows that.

HENRY: He'll kill me, will he?

SABINA: Who are you? I'm not afraid of you. The war's over.

HENRY: I'll kill him so fast. I've spent seven years trying to find him; the others I killed were just substitutes.

SABINA: Goodness! It's Henry!—*{He makes an angry gesture}* Oh, I'm not afraid of you. The war's over, Henry Antrobus, and you're not any more important than any other unemployed. You go away and hide yourself, until we calm your father down.

HENRY: The first thing to do is to burn up those old books; it's the ideas he gets out of those old books that . . . that makes the whole world so you can't live in it. *{He reels forward and starts kicking the books about, but suddenly falls down in a sitting position}*

SABINA: You leave those books alone!! Mr. Antrobus is looking forward to them a-special.—Gracious sakes, Henry, you're so tired you can't stand up. Your mother and sister'll be here in a minute and we'll think what to do about you.

HENRY: What did they ever care about me?

SABINA: There's that old whine again. All you people think you're not loved enough, nobody loves you. Well, you start being lovable and we'll love you.

HENRY: *{Outraged}* I don't want anybody to love me.

SABINA: Then stop talking about it all the time.

HENRY: I *never* talk about it. The last thing I want is anybody to pay any attention to me.

SABINA: I can hear it behind every word you say.

HENRY: I want everybody to hate me.

SABINA: Yes, you've decided that's second best, but it's still the same thing.

—Mrs. Antrobus! Henry's here. He's so tired he can't stand up. [MRS. ANTROBUS *and* GLADYS, *with her* BABY, *emerge. They are dressed as in Act I.* MRS. ANTROBUS *carries some objects in her apron, and* GLADYS *has a blanket over her shoulder}*

MRS. ANTROBUS AND GLADYS: Henry! Henry! Henry!

HENRY: *{Glaring at them}* Have you anything to eat?

MRS. ANTROBUS: Yes, I have, Henry. I've been saving it for this very day,—two good baked potatoes. No! Henry! one of them's for your father. Henry!! Give me that other potato back this minute. [SABINA *sidles up behind him and snatches the other potato away}*

SABINA: He's so dog-tired he doesn't know what he's doing.

MRS. ANTROBUS: Now you just rest there, Henry, until I can get your room ready. Eat that potato good and slow, so you can get all the nourishment out of it.

HENRY: You all might as well know right now that I haven't come back here to live.

MRS. ANTROBUS: Sh. . . . I'll put this coat over you. Your room's hardly damaged at all. Your football trophies are a little tarnished, but Sabina and I will polish them up tomorrow.

HENRY: Did you hear me? I don't live here. I don't belong to anybody.

MRS. ANTROBUS: Why, how can you say a thing like that! You certainly do belong right here. Where else would you want to go? Your forehead's feverish, Henry, seems to me. You'd better give me that gun, Henry. You won't need that any more.

GLADYS: *{Whispering}* Look, he's fallen asleep already, with his potato half-chewed.

SABINA: Puh! The terror of the world.

MRS. ANTROBUS: Sabina, you mind your own business, and start putting the room to rights. [HENRY *has turned his face to the back of the sofa.* MRS. AN-

TROBUS *gingerly puts the revolver in her apron pocket, then helps* SABINA. SABINA *has found a rope hanging from the ceiling. Grunting, she hangs all her weight on it, and as she pulls the walls begin to move into their right places.* MRS. ANTROBUS *brings the overturned tables, chairs and hassock into the positions of Act I}*

SABINA: That's all we do—always beginning again! Over and over again. Always beginning again. *{She pulls on the rope and part of the wall moves into place. She stops. Meditatively:}* How do we know that it'll be any better than before? Why do we go on pretending? Some day the whole earth's going to have to turn cold anyway, and until that time all these other things'll be happening again: it will be more wars and more walls of ice and floods and earthquakes.

MRS. ANTROBUS: Sabina!! Stop arguing and go on with your work.

SABINA: All right. I'll go on just out of *habit,* but I won't believe in it.

MRS. ANTROBUS: *{Aroused}* Now, Sabina. I've let you talk long enough. I don't want to hear any more of it. Do I have to explain to you what everybody knows,—everybody who keeps a home going? Do I have to say to you what nobody should ever *have* to say, because they can read it in each other's eyes?

Now listen to me: [MRS. ANTROBUS *takes hold of the rope}* I could live for seventy years in a cellar and make soup out of grass and bark, without doubting that this world has a work to do and will do it.

Do you hear me?

SABINA: *{Frightened}* Yes, Mrs. Antrobus.

MRS. ANTROBUS: Sabina, do you see this house,—216 Cedar Street,—do you see it?

SABINA: Yes, Mrs. Antrobus.

MRS. ANTROBUS: Well, just to have known this house is to have seen the idea of what we can do someday if we keep our wits about us. Too many people have suffered and died for my children for us to start reneging now. So we'll start putting this house to rights. Now, Sabina, go and see what you can do in the kitchen.

SABINA: Kitchen! Why is it that however far I go away, I always find myself back in the kitchen? *{Exit}*

MRS. ANTROBUS: *{Still thinking over her last speech, relaxes and says with a reminiscent smile:}* Goodness gracious, wouldn't you know that my father was a parson? It was just like I heard his own voice speaking and he's been dead five thousand years. There! I've gone and almost waked Henry up.

HENRY: *{Talking in his sleep, indistinctly}* Fellows . . . what have they done for us? . . . Blocked our way at every step. Kept everything in their own hands. And you've stood it. When are you going to wake up?

MRS. ANTROBUS: Sh, Henry. Go to sleep. Go to sleep. Go to sleep.—Well, that looks better. Now let's go and help Sabina.

GLADYS: Mama, I'm going out into the backyard and hold the baby right up in the air. And show him that we don't have to be afraid any more. *{Exit* GLADYS *to the kitchen.* MRS. ANTROBUS *glances at* HENRY, *exits into kitchen.* HENRY *thrashes about in his sleep. Enter* ANTROBUS, *his arms full of bundles, chewing the end of a carrot. He has a slight limp. Over the suit of Act I he is wearing an overcoat too long for him, its skirts trailing on the ground. He lets his bundles fall and stands looking about. Presently his attention is fixed on* HENRY, *whose words grow clearer}*

HENRY: All right! What have you got to lose? What have they done for us? That's right—nothing. Tear everything down. I don't care what you smash. We'll begin again and we'll show 'em. [ANTROBUS *takes out his revolver and holds it pointing downwards. With his back towards the audience he moves toward the footlights.* HENRY'S *voice grows louder and he wakes with a start.*

They stare at one another. Then HENRY *sits up quickly. Throughout the following scene* HENRY *is played, not as a misunderstood or misguided young man, but as a representation of strong unreconciled evil}* All right! Do something. *{Pause}* Don't think I'm afraid of you, either. All right, do what you were going to do. Do it. *{Furiously}* Shoot me, I tell you. You don't have to think I'm any relation of yours. I haven't got any father or any mother, or brothers or sisters. And I don't want any. And what's more I haven't got anybody over me; and I never will have. I'm alone, and that's all I want to be: alone. So you can shoot me.

ANTROBUS: You're the last person I wanted to see. The sight of you dries up all my plans and hopes. I wish I were back at war still, because it's easier to fight you than to live with you. War's a pleasure—do you hear me?—War's a pleasure compared to what faces us now: trying to build up a peacetime with you in the middle of it. [ANTROBUS *walks up to the window}*

HENRY: I'm not going to be a part of any peacetime of yours. I'm going a long way from here and make my own world that's fit for a man to live in. Where a man can be free, and have a chance, and do what he wants to do in his own way.

ANTROBUS: *{His attention arrested; thoughtfully. He throws the gun out of the window and turns with hope}* . . . Henry, let's try again.

HENRY: Try what? Living *here?*—Speaking polite downtown to all the old men like you? Standing like a sheep at the street corner until the red light turns to green? Being a good boy and a good sheep, like all the stinking ideas you get out of your books? Oh, no. I'll make a world, and I'll show you.

ANTROBUS: *{Hard}* How can you make a world for people to live in, unless you've first put order in yourself? Mark my words: I shall continue fighting you until my last breath as long as you mix up your idea of liberty with your idea of hogging everything for yourself. I shall have no pity on you. I shall pursue you to the far corners of the earth. You and I want the same thing; but until you think of it as something that everyone has a right to, you are my deadly enemy and I will destroy you.—I hear your mother's voice in the kitchen. Have you seen her?

HENRY: I have no mother. Get it into your head. I don't belong here. I have nothing to do here. I have no home.

ANTROBUS: Then why did you come here? With the whole world to choose from, why did you come to this one place: 216 Cedar Street, Excelsior, New Jersey. . . . Well?

HENRY: What if I did? What if I wanted to look at it once more, to see if—

ANTROBUS: Oh, you're related, all right—When your mother comes in you must behave yourself. Do you hear me?

HENRY: *{Wildly}* What is this?—*must behave* yourself. Don't you say *must* to me.

ANTROBUS: Quiet! *{Enter* MRS ANTROBUS *and* SABINA]

HENRY: Nobody can say *must* to me. All my life everybody's been crossing me,—everybody, everything, all of you. I'm going to be free, even if I have to kill half the world for it. Right now, too. Let me get my hands on his throat. I'll show him. *{He advances toward* ANTROBUS. *Suddenly,* SABINA *jumps between them and calls out in her own person:}*

SABINA: Stop! Stop! Don't play this scene. You know what happened last night. Stop the play. *{The men fall back, panting.* HENRY *covers his face with his hands}* Last night you almost strangled him. You became a regular savage. Stop it!

HENRY: It's true. I'm sorry. I don't know what comes over me. I have nothing against him personally. I respect him very much . . . I . . . I admire him. But something comes over me. It's like I become fifteen years old again. I . . . I . . . listen; my own father used to whip me and lock me up every Saturday night. I never had enough to eat. He never let me have enough money to buy decent clothes. I was ashamed to go downtown. I never could go to the dances. My father and my uncle put rules in the way of everything I wanted to do. They tried to prevent my living at all.—I'm sorry. I'm sorry.

MRS. ANTROBUS: *{Quickly}* No, go on. Finish what you were saying. Say it all.

HENRY: In this scene it's as though I were back in High School again. It's like I had some big emptiness inside me,—the emptiness of being hated and blocked at every turn. And the emptiness fills up with the one thought that you have to strike and fight and kill. Listen, it's as though you have to kill somebody else so as not to end up killing yourself.

SABINA: That's not true. I knew your father and your uncle and your mother. You imagined all that. Why, they did everything they could for you. How can you say things like that? They didn't lock you up.

HENRY: They did. They did. They wished I hadn't been born.

SABINA: That's not true.

ANTROBUS: *{In his own person, with self-condemnation, but cold and proud}* Wait a minute. I have something to say, too. It's not wholly his fault that he wants to strangle me in this scene. It's my fault, too. He wouldn't feel that way unless there were something in me that reminded him of all that. He talks about an emptiness. Well, there's an emptiness in me, too. Yes,—work, work, work,—that's all I do. I've ceased to *live.* No wonder he feels that anger coming over him.

MRS. ANTROBUS: There! At least you've said it.

SABINA: We're all just as wicked as we can be, and that's the God's truth.

MRS. ANTROBUS: *{Nods a moment, then comes forward; quietly:}* Come. Come and put your head under some cold water.

SABINA: *{In a whisper}* I'll go with him. I've known him a long while. You have to go on with the play. Come with me. [HENRY *starts out with* SABINA, *but turns at the exit and says to* AN-TROBUS:]

HENRY: Thanks. Thanks for what you said. I'll be all right tomorrow. I won't lose control in that place. I promise. *{Exeunt* HENRY *and* SABINA. ANTROBUS *starts toward the front door, fastens it.* MRS. ANTROBUS *goes up stage and places the chair close to table}*

MRS. ANTROBUS: George, do I see you limping?

ANTROBUS: Yes, a little. My old wound from the other war started smarting again. I can manage.

MRS. ANTROBUS: *{Looking out of the window}* Some lights are coming on,—the first in seven years. People are walking up and down looking at them. Over in Hawkins' open lot they've built a bonfire to celebrate the peace. They're dancing around it like scarecrows.

ANTROBUS: A bonfire! As though they hadn't seen enough things burning.—Maggie,—the dog died?

MRS. ANTROBUS: Oh, yes. Long ago. There are no dogs left in Excelsior.—You're back again! All these years. I gave up counting on letters. The few that arrived were anywhere from six months to a year late.

ANTROBUS: Yes, the ocean's full of letters, along with the other things.

MRS. ANTROBUS: George, sit down, you're tired.

ANTROBUS: No, you sit down. I'm tired but I'm restless. *{Suddenly, as she comes forward:}* Maggie! I've lost it. I've lost it.

MRS. ANTROBUS: What, George? What have you lost?

ANTROBUS: The most important thing of all: The desire to begin again, to start building.

MRS. ANTROBUS: *{Sitting in the chair right of the table}* Well, it will come back.

ANTROBUS: *{At the window}* I've lost it. This minute I feel like all those people dancing around the bonfire—just relief. Just the desire to settle down; to slip into the old grooves and keep the neighbors from walking over my lawn.—Hm. But during the war,—in the middle of all that blood and dirt and hot and cold—every day and night, I'd have moments, Maggie, when I *saw* the things that we could do when it was over. When you're at war you think about a better life; when you're at peace you think about a more comfortable one. I've lost it. I feel sick and tired.

MRS. ANTROBUS: Listen! The baby's crying.

I hear Gladys talking. Probably she's quieting Henry again. George, while Gladys and I were living here—like moles, like rats, and when we were at our wits' end to save the baby's life—the only thought we clung to was that you were going to bring something good out of this suffering. In the night, in the dark, we'd whisper about it, starving and sick.—Oh, George, you'll have to get it back again. Think! What else kept us alive all these years? Even now, it's not comfort we want. We can suffer whatever's necessary; only give us back that promise. *{Enter* SABINA *with a lighted lamp. She is dressed as in Act I}*

SABINA: Mrs. Antrobus . . .

MRS. ANTROBUS: Yes, Sabina?

SABINA: Will you need me?

MRS. ANTROBUS: No, Sabina, you can go to bed.

SABINA: Mrs. Antrobus, if it's all right with you, I'd like to go to the bonfire and celebrate seeing the war's over. And, Mrs. Antrobus, they've opened the Gem Movie Theatre and they're giving away a hand-painted soup tureen to every lady, and I thought one of us ought to go.

ANTROBUS: Well, Sabina, I haven't any money. I haven't seen any money for quite a while.

SABINA: Oh, you don't need money. They're taking anything you can give them. And I have some . . . some . . . Mrs. Antrobus, promise you won't tell anyone. It's a little against the law. But I'll give you some, too.

ANTROBUS: What is it?

SABINA: I'll give you some, too. Yesterday I picked up a lot of . . . of beefcubes! [MRS. ANTROBUS *turns and says calmly:}*

MRS. ANTROBUS: But, Sabina, you know you ought to give that in to the Center downtown. They know who needs them most.

SABINA: *{Outburst}* Mrs. Antrobus, I didn't make this war. I didn't ask for it. And, in my opinion, after anybody's gone through what we've gone through, they have a right to grab what they can find. You're a very nice man, Mr. Antrobus, but you'd have got on better in the world if you'd realized that dog-eat-dog was the rule in the beginning and always will be. And most of all now. *{In tears}* Oh, the world's an awful place, and you know it is. I used to think something could be down about it; but I know better now. I hate it. I hate it. *{She comes forward slowly and brings six cubes from the bag}* All right. All right. You can have them.

ANTROBUS: Thank you, Sabina.

SABINA: Can I have . . . can I have one to go to the movies? [ANTROBUS *in silence gives her one}* Thank you.

ANTROBUS: Good night, Sabina.

SABINA: Mr. Antrobus, don't mind what I say. I'm just an ordinary girl, you know what I mean, I'm just an ordinary girl. But you're a bright man, you're a very bright man, and of course you invented the alphabet and the wheel, and, my God, a lot of things . . . and if you've got any other plans, my God, don't let me upset them. Only every now and then I've got to go to the movies. I mean my nerves can't stand it. But if you have any ideas about improving the crazy old world, I'm really with you. I really am. Because it's . . . it's . . . Good night. *{She goes out.* ANTROBUS *starts laughing softly with exhilaration}*

ANTROBUS: Now I remember what three things always went together when I was able to see things most clearly: three things. Three things: *{He points to where* SABINA *has gone out}* The voice of the people in their confusion and their need. And the thought of you and the children and this house. . . . And . . . Maggie! I didn't dare ask you: my books! They haven't been lost, have they?

MRS. ANTROBUS: No. There are some of them right here. Kind of tattered.

ANTROBUS: Yes.—Remember, Maggie, we almost lost them once before? And when we finally did collect a few torn copies out of old cellars they ran in everyone's head like a fever. They as good as rebuilt the world. *{Pauses, book in hand, and looks up}* Oh, I've never forgotten for long at a time that living is struggle. I know that every good and excellent thing in the world stands moment by moment on the razor-edge of danger and must be fought for— whether it's a field, or a home, or a country. All I ask is the chance to build new worlds and God has always given us that. And has given us *{Opening the book}* voices to guide us; and the memory of our mistakes to warn us. Maggie, you and I will remember in peacetime all the resolves that were so clear to us in the days of war. We've come a long way. We've learned. We're learning. And the steps of our journey are marked for us here. *{He stands by the table turning the leaves of a book}* Sometimes out there in the war,—standing all night on a hill—I'd try and remember some of the words in these books. Parts of them and phrases

would come back to me. And after a while I used to give names to the hours of the night. *{He sits, hunting for a passage in the book}* Nine o'clock I used to call Spinoza. Where is it: "After experience had taught me—" *{The back wall has disappeared, revealing the platform.* FRED BAILEY *carrying his numeral has started from left to right.* MRS. ANTROBUS *sits by the table sewing}*

BAILEY: "After experience had taught me that the common occurrences of daily life are vain and futile; and I saw that all the objects of my desire and fear were in themselves nothing good nor bad save insofar as the mind was affected by them; I at length determined to search out whether there was something truly good and communicable to man." *{Almost without break* HESTER, *carrying a large Roman numeral ten, starts crossing the platform.* GLADYS *appears at the kitchen door and moves towards her mother's chair}*

HESTER: "Then tell me, O Critias, how will a man choose the ruler that shall rule over him? Will he not choose a man who has first established order in himself, knowing that any decision that has its spring from anger or pride or vanity can be multiplied a thousand fold in its effects upon the citizens?" [HESTER *disappears and* IVY, *as eleven o'clock starts speaking}*

IVY: "This good estate of the mind possessing its object in energy we call divine. This we mortals have occasionally and it is this energy which is pleasantest and best. But God has it always. It is wonderful in us; but in Him how much more wonderful." *{As* MR. TREMAYNE *starts to speak,* HENRY *appears at the edge of the scene, brooding and unreconciled, but present}*

TREMAYNE: "In the beginning, God created the Heavens and the earth; And the Earth was waste and void; And the darkness was upon the face of the deep. And the Lord said let there be light and there was light." *{Sudden black-out and* *silence, except for the last strokes of the midnight bell. Then just as suddenly the lights go up, and* SABINA *is standing at the window, as at the opening of the play}*

SABINA: Oh, oh, oh. Six o'clock and the master not home yet. Pray God nothing serious has happened to him crossing the Hudson River. But I wouldn't be surprised. The whole world's at sixes and sevens, and why the house hasn't fallen down about our ears long ago is a miracle to me. *{She comes down to the footlights}*

This is where you came in. We have to go on for ages and ages yet.

You go home.

The end of this play isn't written yet.

Mr. and Mrs. Antrobus! Their heads are full of plans and they're as confident as the first day they began,—and they told me to tell you: good night.

POETRY

William Butler Yeats (1865–1939)

A PRAYER FOR MY DAUGHTER

Once more the storm is howling, and
  half hid
Under this cradle-hood and coverlid
My child sleeps on. There is no obstacle
But Gregory's wood and one bare hill
Whereby the haystack and roof-leveling
  wind   5
Bred on the Atlantic, can be stayed;
And for an hour I have walked and
  prayed
Because of the great gloom that is in my
  mind.

I have walked and prayed for this
  young child an hour
And heard the sea-wind scream upon
  the tower,   10
And under the arches of the bridge, and
  scream
In the elms above the flooded stream;
Imagining in excited reverie
That the future years had come,
Dancing to a frenzied drum,   15
Out of the murderous innocence of the
  sea.

May she be granted beauty, and yet not
Beauty to make a stranger's eye
  distraught,
Or hers before a looking-glass, for such,
Being made beautiful overmuch,   20

Consider beauty a sufficient end,
Lose natural kindness and maybe
The heart-revealing intimacy
That chooses right, and never find a
  friend.

Helen being chosen found life flat and
  dull   25
And later had much trouble from a fool,
While the great Queen, that rose out of
  the spray,
Being fatherless could have her way
Yet chose a bandy-legged smith for
  man.
It's certain that fine women eat   30
A crazy salad with their meat
Whereby the Horn of Plenty is undone.

In courtesy I'd have her chiefly learned;
Hearts are not had as a gift but hearts
  are earned
By those that are not entirely
  beautiful;   35
Yet many, that have played the fool
For beauty's very self, has charm made
  wise,
And many a poor man that has roved,
Loved and thought himself beloved,
From a glad kindness cannot take his
  eyes.   40

May she become a flourishing hidden
tree
That all her thoughts may like the
linnet be,
And have no business but dispensing
round
Their magnanimities of sound,
Nor but in merriment begin a chase,   45
Nor but in merriment a quarrel.
Oh, may she live like some green laurel
Rooted in one dear perpetual place.

My mind, because the minds that I have
loved,
The sort of beauty that I have
approved,   50
Prosper but little, has dried up of late,
Yet knows that to be choked with hate
May well be of all evil chances chief.
If there's no hatred in a mind
Assault and battery of the wind   55
Can never tear the linnet from the leaf.

An intellectual hatred is the worst,
So let her think opinions are accursed.
Have I not seen the loveliest woman
born
Out of the mouth of Plenty's horn,   60
Because of her opinionated mind

Barter that horn and every good
By quiet natures understood
For an old bellows full of angry wind?

Considering that, all hatred driven
hence,   65
The soul recovers radical innocence
And learns at last that it is self-
delighting
Self-appeasing, self-affrighting,
And that its own sweet will is Heaven's
will;
She can, though every face should
scowl   70
And every windy quarter howl
Or every bellows burst, be happy still.

And may her bridgegroom bring her to
a house
Where all's accustomed, ceremonious;
For arrogance and hatred are the
wares   75
Peddled in the thoroughfares.
How but in custom and in ceremony
Are innocence and beauty born?
Ceremony's a name for the rich horn,
And custom for the spreading laurel
tree.   80

THE SECOND COMING

Turning and turning in the widening
gyre
The falcon cannot hear the falconer;
Things fall apart; the centre cannot
hold;
Mere anarchy is loosed upon the world,
The blood-dimmed tide is loosed, and
everywhere   5
The ceremony of innocence is drowned;
The best lack all conviction, while the
worst
Are full of passionate intensity.

Surely some revelation is at hand;
Surely the Second Coming is at
hand: 10
The Second Coming! Hardly are those
words out
When a vast image out of *Spiritus
Mundi*
Troubles my sight: somewhere in sands
of the desert
A shape with lion body and the head of
a man,
A gaze blank and pitiless as the sun, 15

Is moving its slow thighs, while all
    about it
Reel shadows of the indignant desert
    birds.
The darkness drops again; but now I
    know
That twenty centuries of stony sleep

Were vexed to nightmare by a rocking
    cradle,   20
And what rough beast, its hour come
    round at last,
Slouches towards Bethlehem to be
    born?

THE LEADERS OF THE CROWD

They must to keep their certainty
    accuse
All that are different of a base intent;
Pull down established honor; hawk for
    news
Whatever their loose phantasy invent
And murmur it with bated breath, as
    though   5
The abounding gutter had been Helicon
Or calumny is a song. How can they
    know

Truth flourishes where the student's
    lamp has shone,
And there alone, that have no solitude?
So the crowd come they care not what
    may come.   10
They have loud music, hope every day
    renewed
And heartier loves; that lamp is from
    the tomb.

EASTER 1916

I have met them at close of day
Coming with vivid faces
From counter or desk among grey
Eighteenth-century houses.
I have passed with a nod of the head 5
Or polite meaningless words,
Or have lingered awhile and said
Polite meaningless words,
And thought before I had done
Of a mocking tale or a gibe   10
To please a companion
Around the fire at the club,
Being certain that they and I
But lived where motley is worn:
All changed, changed utterly: 15
A terrible beauty is born.

That woman's days were spent
In ignorant good will,
Her nights in argument
Until her voice grew shrill.   20
What voice more sweet than hers
When, young and beautiful,
She rode to harriers?
This man had kept a school
And rode our winged horse;   25
This other his helper and friend
Was coming into his force;
He might have won fame in the end,
So sensitive his nature seemed,
So daring and sweet his thought.   30
The other man I had dreamed
A drunken, vainglorious lout.

He had done most bitter wrong
To some who are near my heart,
Yet I number him in the song;   35
He, too, had resigned his part
In the causual comedy;
He, too, has been changed in his turn,
Transformed utterly:
A terrible beauty is born.   40

Hearts with one purpose alone
Through summer and winter seem
Enchanted to a stone
To trouble the living stream.
Tho horse that comes from the road,   45
The rider, the birds that range
From cloud to tumbling cloud,
Minute by minute they change;
A shadow of cloud on the stream
Changes minute by minute;   50
A horse-hoof slides on the brim,
And a horse splashes within it;
The long-legged moor-hens dive,
And hens to moor-cocks call;
Minute by minute they live: 55
The stone's in the midst of all.

Too long a sacrifice
Can make a stone of the heart.
O when may it suffice?
That is Heaven's part, our part   60
To mutter name upon name,
As a mother names her child
When sleep at last has come
On limbs that had run wild.
Was it but nightfall?   65
No, no, not night but death;
Was it needless death after all?
For England may keep faith
For all that is done and said.
We know their dreams; enough   70
To know they dreamed and are dead;
And what if excess of love
Bewildered them till they died?
I write it out in verse—
MacDonagh and MacBride   75
And Connolly and Pearse
Now and in time to be,
Wherever green is worn,
Are changed, changed utterly:
A terrible beauty is born.   80

SAILING TO BYZANTIUM

I

That is no country for old men. The young
In one another's arms, birds in the trees,
—Those dying generations—at their song,
The salmon-falls, the mackerel-crowded seas,
Fish, flesh, or foul, command all summer long   5
Whatever is begotten, born, and dies.
Caught in that sensual music all neglect
Monuments of unageing intellect.

II

An agèd man is but a paltry thing,
A tattered coat upon a stick, unless   10
Soul clap its hands and sing, and louder sing
For every tatter in its mortal dress,

Nor is there singing school but studying
Monuments of its own magnificence;
And therefore I have sailed the seas and come   15
To the holy city of Byzantium.

III

O sages standing in God's holy fire
As in the gold mosaic of a wall,
Come from the holy fire, perne in a gyre,
And be the singing-masters of my soul.   20
Consume my heart away; sick with desire
And fastened to a dying animal
It knows not what it is; and gather me
Into the artifice of eternity.

IV

Once out of nature I shall never take   25
My bodily form from any natural thing,
But such a form as Grecian goldsmiths make
Of hammered gold and gold enamelling
To keep a drowsy Emperor awake;
Or set upon a golden bough to sing   30
To lords and ladies of Byzantium
Of what is past, or passing, or to come.

Robert Frost (1874–1963)

THE TUFT OF FLOWERS

I went to turn the grass once after one
Who mowed it in the dew before the sun.

The dew was gone that made his blade so keen
Before I came to view the leveled scene.

I looked for him behind an isle of trees;   5
I listened for his whetstone on the breeze.

"The Tuft of Flowers," "The Star-splitter," "Acquainted with the Night," "Two Tramps in Mud Time," "Departmental," "The White-tailed Hornet," "There Are Roughly Zones," and "Design" from *Complete Poems of Robert Frost*. Copyright 1923, 1928 by Holt, Rinehart and Winston, Inc. Copyright 1936, 1951, © 1956 by Robert Frost. Copyright © 1964 by Lesley Frost Ballantine. Reprinted by permission of Holt, Rinehart and Winston, Inc.

But he had gone his way, the grass all mown,
And I must be, as he had been—alone,

"As all must be," I said within my heart,
"Whether they work together or apart."   10

But as I said it, swift there passed me by
On noiseless wing a bewildered butterfly,

Seeking with memories grown dim o'er night
Some resting flower of yesterday's delight.

And once I marked his flight go round and round,   15
As where some flower lay withering on the ground.

And then he flew as far as eye could see,
And then on tremulous wing came back to me.

I thought of questions that have no reply,
And would have turned to toss the grass to dry;   20

But he turned first, and led my eye to look
At a tall tuft of flowers beside a brook,

A leaping tongue of bloom the scythe had spared
Beside a reedy brook the scythe had bared.

The mower in the dew had loved them thus,   25
By leaving them to flourish, not for us,

Nor yet to draw one thought of ours to him,
But from sheer morning gladness at the brim.

The butterfly and I had lit upon,
Nevertheless, a message from the dawn,   30

That made me hear the wakening birds around,
And hear his long scythe whispering to the ground,

And feel a spirit kindred to my own;
So that henceforth I worked no more alone;

But glad with him, I worked as with his aid,   35
And weary, sought at noon with him the shade;

And dreaming, as it were, held brotherly speech
With one whose thought I had not hoped to reach

"Men work together," I told him from the heart,
"Whether they work together or apart."   40

THE STAR-SPLITTER

"You know Orion always comes up sideways.
Throwing a leg up over our fence of mountains,
And rising on his hands, he looks in on me
Busy outdoors by lantern-light with something
I should have done by daylight, and indeed,   5
After the ground is frozen, I should have done
Before it froze, and a gust flings a handful
Of waste leaves at my smoky lantern chimney
To make fun of my way of doing things,
Or else fun of Orion's having caught me.   10
Has a man, I should like to ask, no rights
These forces are obliged to pay respect to?"
So Brad McLaughlin mingled reckless talk
Of heavenly stars with hugger-mugger farming,
Till having failed at hugger-mugger farming,   15
He burned his house down for the first insurance
And spent the proceeds on a telescope
To satisfy a life-long curiosity
About our place among the infinities.

"What do you want with one of those blame things?"   20
I asked him well beforehand. "Don't you get one!"
"Don't call it blamed; there isn't anything
More blameless in the sense of being less
A weapon in our human fight," he said.
"I'll have one if I sell my farm to buy it."   25
There where he moved the rocks to plough the ground
And ploughed between the rocks he couldn't move,
Few farms changed hands; so rather than spend years
Trying to sell his farm and then not selling,
He burned his house down for the fire insurance   30
And bought the telescope with what it came to.
He had been heard to say by several:
"The best thing that we're put her for's to see;
The strongest thing that's given us to see with's
A telescope. Someone in every town   35
Seems to me owes it to the town to keep one.
In Littleton it may as well be me."
After such loose talk it was no surprise
When he did what he did and burned his house down.

Mean laughter went about town that day   40
To let him know we weren't the least imposed on,

And he could wait—we'd see to him tomorrow.
But the first thing next morning we reflected
If one by one we counted people out
For the least sin, it wouldn't take us long   45
To get so we had no one left to live with.
For to be social is to be forgiving.
Our thief, the one who does our stealing from us,
We don't cut off from coming to church suppers,
But what we miss we go to him and ask for.   50
He promptly gives it back, that is if still
Uneaten, unworn out, or undisposed of.
It wouldn't do to be too hard on Brad
About his telescope. Beyond the age
Of being given one for Christmas gift,   55
He had to take the best way he knew how
To find himself in one. Well, all we said was
He took a strange thing to be roguish over.
Some sympathy was wasted on the house,
A good old-timer dating back along;   60
But a house isn't sentient; the house
Didn't feel anything. And if it did,
Why not regard it as a sacrifice,
And an old-fashioned sacrifice by fire,
Instead of a new-fashioned one at auction?   65
Out of a house and so out of a farm
At one stroke (of a match), Brad had to turn
To earn a living on the Concord railroad,
As under-ticket-agent at a station
Where his job, when he wasn't selling tickets,   70
Was setting out up track 'and down, not plants
As on a farm, but planets, evening stars
That varied in their hue from red to green.

He got a good glass for six hundred dollars.
His new job gave him leisure for star-gazing.   75
Often he bid me come and have a look
Up the brass barrel, velvet black inside,
At a star quaking in the other end.
I recollect a night of broken clouds
And underfoot snow melted down to ice,   80
And melting further in the wind to mud.
Bradford and I had out the telescope.
We spread our two legs as we spread its three,
Pointed our thoughts the way we pointed it,
And standing at our leisure till the day broke,   85
Said some of the best things we ever said.
That telescope was christened the Star-splitter,
Because it didn't do a thing but split
A star in two or three the way you split
A globule of quicksilver in your hand   90
With one stroke of your finger in the middle.

It's a star splitter if there ever was one
And ought to do some good if splitting stars
'Sa thing to be compared with splitting wood.

We've looked and looked, but after all where are we?   95
Do we know any better where we are,
And how it stands between the night tonight
And a man with a smoky lantern chimney?
How different from the way it ever stood?

ACQUAINTED WITH THE NIGHT

I have been one acquainted with the
   night.
I have walked out in rain—and back in
   rain.
I have walked the furthest city light.
I have looked down the saddest city
   lane.
I have passed by the watchman on his
   beat.   5
And dropped my eyes, unwilling to
   explain.

I have stood still and stopped the sound
   of feet
When far away an interrupted cry
Came over houses from another street,

But not to call me back or say
   goodbye;   10
And further still at an unearthly height,
One luminary clock against the sky
Proclaimed the time was neither wrong
   nor right.
I have been one acquainted with the
   night.

TWO TRAMPS IN MUD TIME
or, A Full-time Interest

Out of the mud two strangers came
And caught me splitting wood in the
   yard.
And one of them put me off my aim
By hailing cheerily "Hit them hard!"
I knew pretty well what he had in
   mind: 5
He wanted to take my job for pay.

Good blocks of oak it was I split,
As large around as the chopping block;
And every piece I squarely hit
Fell splinterless as a cloven rock.   10

The blows that a life of self-control
Spares to strike for the common good
That day, giving a loose to my soul,
I spent on the unimportant wood.

The sun was warm but the wind was
   chill.   15
You know how it is with an April day
When the sun is out and the wind is
   still,
You're one month on in the middle of
   May.

But if you so much as dare to speak,
A cloud comes over the sunlit arch,   20
A wind comes off a frozen peak,
And you're two months back in the
    middle of March.

A bluebird comes tenderly up to alight
And turns to the wind to unruffle a
    plume
His song so pitched as not to excite   25
A single flower as yet to bloom.
It is snowing a flake: and he half knew
Winter was only playing possum.
Except in color he isn't blue.
But he wouldn't advise a thing to
    blossom.   30

The water for which we may have to
    look
In summertime with a witching-wand,
In every wheelrut's now a brook,
In every print of a hoof a pond.
Be glad of water, but don't forget   35
The lurking frost in the earth beneath
That will steal forth after the sun is set
And show on the water its crystal teeth.

The time when most I loved my task
These two must make me love it
    more   40
By coming with what they came to ask.
You'd think I never had felt before
The weight of an axe-head poised aloft,
The grip on earth of outspread feet.
The life of muscles rocking soft   45
And smooth and moist in vernal heat.

Out of the woods two hulking tramps
(From sleeping God knows where last
    night,
But not long since in the lumber
    camps).
They thought all chopping was theirs of
right.   50
Men of the woods and lumberjacks,
They judged me by their appropriate
tool.
Except as a fellow handled an axe,
They had no way of knowing a fool.

Nothing on either side was said.   55
They knew they had but to stay their
    stay
And all their logic would fill my head:
As that I had no right to play
With what was another man's work for
    gain.
My right might be love but theirs was
    need.   60
And where the two exist in twain
Theirs was the better right—agreed.

But yield who will to their separation,
My object in living is to unite
My avocation and my vocation   65
As my two eyes make one in sight.
Only where love and need are one,
And the work is play for mortal stakes,
Is the deed ever really done
For Heaven and the future's sakes.   70

DEPARTMENTAL
or, The End of My Ant Jerry

An ant on the tablecloth
Ran into a dormant moth
Of many times her size.
He showed not the least surprise.
His business wasn't with such.   5
He gave it scarcely a touch,

And was off on his duty run.
Yet if he encountered one
Of the hive's inquiry squad
Whose work is to find out God   10
And the nature of time and space,
He would put him on to the case.

Ants are a curious race;
One crossing with hurried tread
The body of one of their dead   15
Isn't given a moment's arrest—
Seems not even impressed.
But he no doubt reports to any
With whom he crosses antennae,
And they no doubt report   20
To the higher up at court.
Then word goes forth in Formic:
"Death's come to Jerry McCormic,
Our selfless forager Jerry.
Will the special Janizary   25
Whose office it is to bury
The dead of the commissary
Go bring him home to his people.

Lay him in state on a sepal.
Wrap him for shroud in a petal.   30
Embalm him with ichor of nettle.
This is the word of your Queen."
And presently on the scene
Appears a solemn mortician;
And taking formal position   35
With feelers calmly atwiddle,
Seizes the dead by the middle,
And heaving him high in air
Carries him out of there.
No one stands around to stare.   40
It is nobody else's affair.

It couldn't be called ungentle.
But how thoroughly departmental.

THE WHITE-TAILED HORNET

The white-tailed hornet lives in a balloon
That floats against the ceiling of the woodshed.
The exit he comes out at like a bullet
Is like the pupil of a pointed gun.
And having power to change his aim in flight,   5
He comes out more unerring than a bullet.
Verse could be written on the certainty
With which he penetrates my best defense
Of whirling hands and arms about the head
To stab me in the sneeze-nerve of a nostril.   10
Such is the instinct of it I allow.
Yet how about the insect certainty
That in the neighborhood of home and children
Is such an execrable judge of motives
As not to recognize in me the exception   15
I like to think I am in everything—
One who would never hang above a bookcase
His Japanese crepe-paper globe for trophy?
He stung me first and stung me afterward.
He rolled me off the field head over heels   20
And would not listen to my explanations.

That's when I went as visitor to his house.
As visitor at my house he is better.
Hawking for flies about the kitchen door,
In at one door perhaps and out another,   25
Trust him then not to put you in the wrong.

He won't misunderstand your freest movements.
Let him light on your skin unless you mind
So many prickly grappling feet at once.
He's after the domesticated fly   30
To feed his thumping grubs as big as he is.
Here he is at his best, but even here—
I watched him where he swooped, he pounced, he struck;
But what he found he had was just a nailhead.
He struck a second time. Another nailhead.   35
"Those are just nailheads. Those are fastened down."
Then disconcerted and not unannoyed,
He stooped and struck a little huckleberry
The way a player curls around a football.
"Wrong shape, wrong color, and wrong scent," I said.   40
The huckleberry rolled him on his head.
At last it was a fly. He shot and missed;
And the fly circled round him in derision.
But for the fly he might have made me think
He had been at his poetry, comparing   45
Nailhead with fly and fly with huckleberry:
How like a fly, how very like a fly.
But the real fly he missed would never do;
The missed fly made me dangerously skeptic.

Won't this whole instinct matter bear revision?   50
Won't almost any theory bear revision?
To err is human, not to, animal.
Or so we pay the compliment to instinct,
Only too liberal of our compliment.
That really takes away instead of gives.   55
Or worship, humor, conscièntiousness
Went long since to the dogs under the table.
And served us right for having instituted
Downward comparisons. As long on earth
As our comparisons were stoutly upward   60
With gods and angels, we were men at least,
But little lower than the gods and angels.
But once comparisons were yielded downward,
Once we began to see our images
Reflected in the mud and even dust,   65
'Twas disillusion upon disillusion.
We were lost piecemeal to the animals,
Like people thrown out to delay the wolves.
Nothing but fallibility was left us,
And this day's work made even that seem doubtful.   70

THERE ARE ROUGHLY ZONES

We sit indoors and talk of the cold outside.
And every gust that gathers strength and heaves
Is a threat to the house. But the house has long been tried.
We think of the tree. If it never again has leaves,
We'll know, we say, that this was the night it died. 5
It is very far north, we admit, to have brought the peach.
What comes over a man, is it soul or mind—
That to no limits and bounds he can stay confined?
You would say his ambition was to extend the reach
Clear to the Arctic of every living kind. 10
Why is his nature forever so hard to teach
That though there is no fixed line between wrong and right,
There are roughly zones whose laws must be obeyed?
There is nothing much we can do for the tree tonight,
But we can't help feeling more than a little betrayed 15
That the northwest wind should rise to such a height
Just when the cold went down so many below.
The tree has no leaves and may never have them again.
We must wait till some months hence in the spring to know.
But if it is destined never again to grow, 20
It can blame this limitless trait in the hearts of men.

DESIGN

I found a dimpled spider, fat and white,
On a white heal-all, holding up a moth
Like a white piece of rigid satin cloth—
Assorted characters of death and blight
Mixed ready to begin the morning
right, 5
Like the ingredients of a witches'
broth—
A snow-drop spider, a flower like a
froth,
And dead wings carried like a paper
kite.

What had the flower to do with being
white,
The wayside blue and innocent heal-
all? 10
What brought the kindred spider to
that height,
Then steered the white moth thither in
the night?
What but design of darkness to
appall?—
If design govern in a thing so small.

Carl Sandburg (1878–1967)

TO A CONTEMPORARY BUNKSHOOTER

You come along . . . tearing your shirt . . . yelling about Jesus.
Where do you get that stuff?
What do you know about Jesus?
Jesus had a way of talking soft and outside of a few bankers and higher-ups among
the con men of Jerusalem everybody liked to have this Jesus around because he
never made any fake passes and everything he said went and he helped the sick
and gave the people hope.
You come along squirting words at us, shaking your fist and call us all damn fools so
fierce the froth slobbers over your lips . . . always blabbing we're all going to
hell straight off and you know all about it.   5

I've read Jesus' words. I know what he said. You don't throw any scare into me. I've
got your number. I know how much you know about Jesus.
He never came near clean people or dirty people but they felt cleaner because he
came along. It was your crowd of bankers and business men and lawyers hired
the sluggers and murderers who put Jesus out of the running.
I say the same bunch backing you nailed the nails into the hands of this Jesus of
Nazareth. He had lined up against him the same crooks and strong-arm men
now lined up with you paying your way.

This Jesus was good to look at, smelled good, listened good. He threw out something
fresh and beautiful from the skin of his body and the touch of his hands
whereever he passed along.
You slimy bunkshooter, you put a smut on every human blossom in reach of your
rotten breath belching about hell-fire and hiccupping about this Man who lived
a clean life in Galilee.   10
When are you going to quit making the carpenters build emergency hospitals for
women and girls driven crazy with wrecked nerves from your gibberish about
Jesus?—I put it to you again: Where do you get that stuff? What do you know
about Jesus?

Go ahead and bust all the chairs you want to. Smash a whole wagon-load of furniture at every performance. Turn sixty somersaults and stand on your nutty
head. If it wasn't for the way you scare the women and kids I'd feel sorry for
you and pass the hat.
I like to watch a good four-flusher work, but not when he starts people puking and
calling for the doctors.
I like a man that's got nerve and can pull off a great original performance, but you—
you're only a bug-house pedlar of secondhand gospel—you're only shoving out
a phoney imitation of the goods this Jesus wanted free as air and sunlight.

You tell people living in shanties Jesus is going to fix it up all right with them by giving them mansions in the skies after they're dead and the worms have eaten 'em. 15

You tell $6 a week department store girls all they need is Jesus; you take a steel trust wop, dead without having lived, grey and shrunken at forty years of age, and you tell him to look at Jesus on the cross and he'll be all right.

You tell poor people they don't need any more money on pay day and even if it's fierce to be out of a job, Jesus'll fix that up all right, all right—all they gotta do is take Jesus the way you say.

I'm telling you Jesus wouldn't stand for the stuff you're handing out. Jesus played it different. The bankers and lawyers of Jerusalem got their sluggers and murderers to go after Jesus just because Jesus wouldn't play their game. He didn't sit in with the big thieves.

I don't want a lot of gab from a bunkshooter in my religion.

I won't take my religion from any man who never works except with his mouth and never cherishes any memory except the face of the woman on the American silver dollar. 20

I ask you to come through and show me where you're pouring out the blood of your life.

I've been to this suburb of Jerusalem they call Golgotha, where they nailed Him, and I know if the story is straight it was real blood ran from His hands and the nailholes, and it was real blood spurted in red drops where the spear of the Roman soldier rammed in between the ribs of this Jesus of Nazareth.

GRASS

Pile the bodies high at Austerlitz and
   Waterloo.
Shovel them under and let me work—
   I am the grass; I cover all.

And pile them high at Gettysburg
And pile them high at Ypres and
   Verdun.   5
Shovel them under and let me work.

Two years, ten years, and passengers
   ask the conductor:
What place is this?
Where are we now?

I am the grass.   10
Let me work.

SOUTHERN PACIFIC

Huntington sleeps in a house six feet
  long.
Huntington dreams of railroads he built
  and owned.
Huntington dreams of ten thousand
  men saying: Yes, sir.

Blithery sleeps in a house six feet long.

Blithery dreams of rails and ties he
  laid.
Blithery dreams of saying to
  Huntington: Yes, sir.

Huntington,
Blithery, sleep in houses six feet long.

D. H. Lawrence (1885–1930)
WEDDING MORN

The morning breaks like pomegranate
  In a shining crack of red;
Ah, when tomorrow the dawn comes
    late
  Whitening across the bed
It will find me at the marriage gate   5
  And waiting while light is shed
On him who is sleeping satiate
  With a sunk, unconscious head.

And when the drawn comes creeping in,
  Cautiously I shall raise   10
Myself to watch the daylight win
  On my first of days,
As it shows him sleeping a sleep he got
  With me, as under my gaze
He grows distinct, and I see his hot   15
  Face freed of the wavering blaze.

Then I shall know which image of God
  My man is made toward;
And I shall see my sleeping rod
  Or my life's reward;   20

And I shall count the stamp and worth
  Of the man I've accepted as mine,
Shall see an image of heaven or of earth
  On his minted metal shine.

Oh, I long to see him sleep   25
  In my power utterly;
So I shall know what I have to keep . . .
  I long to see
My love, that spinning coin, laid still
  And plain at the side of me   30
For me to reckon—for surely he will
  Be wealth of life to me.

And then he will be mine, he will lie
  Revealed to me;
Patent and open beneath my eye   35
  He will sleep of me;
He will lie negligent, resign
  His truth to me, and I
Shall watch the dawn light up for me
  This fate of mine.   40

And as I watch the wan light shine
  On his sleep that is filled of me,
On his brow where the curved wisps
    clot and twine
  Carelessly,

On his lips where the light breaths
    come and go   45
  Unconsciously,
On his limbs in sleep at last laid low
  Helplessly,
I shall weep, oh, I shall weep, I know
  For joy or for misery.   50

LOVE ON THE FARM

What large, dark hands are those at the window
Grasping in the golden light
Which weaves its way through the evening wind
  At my heart's delight?

Ah, only the leaves! But in the west   5
I see a redness suddenly come
Into the evening's anxious breast—
  'Tis the wound of love goes home!

The woodbine creeps abroad   10
Calling low to her lover:
  The sun-lit flirt who all the day
  Has poised above her lips in play
  And stolen kisses, shallow and gay
  Of pollen, now has gone away—
  She woos the moth with her sweet, low word;   15
And when above her his moth-wings hover
Then her bright breast she will uncover
And yield her honey-drop to her lover.

Into the yellow, evening glow
Saunters a man from the farm below;   20
Leans, and looks in at the low-built shed
Where the swallow has hung her marriage bed.
  The bird lies warm against the wall.
  She glances quick her startled eyes
  Towards him, then she turns away   25
  Her small head, making warm display
  Of red upon the throat. Her terrors sway
  Her out of the nest's warm, busy ball,
  Whose plaintive cry is heard as she flies
  In one blue stoop from out the sties   30
  Into the twilight's empty hall.
Oh, water-hen, beside the rushes,
Hide your quaintly scarlet blushes,

Still your quick tail, lie still as dead,
Till the distance folds over his ominous tread!　　　　　　　35

The rabbit presses back her ears,
Turns back her liquid, anguished eyes
And crouches low; then with wild spring
Spurts from the terror of his oncoming;
To be choked back, the wire ring　　　　　　　　　　　40
Her frantic effort throttling:
　　Piteous brown ball of quivering fears!
Ah, soon in his large, hard hand she dies,
Yet calm and kindly are his eyes
And ready to open in brown surprise　　　　　　　　45
Should I not answer to his talk
Or should he my tears surmise.

I hear his hand on the latch, and rise from my chair
Watching the door open; he flashes bare
His strong teeth in a smile, and flashes his eyes　　　50
In a smile like triumph upon me; then careless-wise
He flings the rabbit soft on the table board
And comes toward me: he! the uplifted sword
Of his hand against my bosom! and oh, the broad
Blade of his glance that asks me to applaud　　　　55
His coming! With his hand he turns my face to him
And caresses me with his fingers that still smell grim
Of rabbit's fur! God, I am caught in a snare!
I know not what fine wire is round my throat;
I only know I let him finger there　　　　　　　　60
My pulse of life, and let him nose like a stoat
Who sniffs with joy before he drinks the blood.

And down his mouth comes to my mouth! and down
His bright dark eyes come over me, like a hood
Upon my mind! his lips meet mine, and a flood　　　65
Of sweet fire sweeps across me, so I drown
Against him, die, and find death good.

SNAKE

A snake came to my water-trough
On a hot, hot day, and I in pyjamas for the heat,
To drink there.

In the deep, strange-scented shade of the great dark carob tree　　　5
I came down the steps with my pitcher
And must wait, must stand and wait, for there he was at the trough before me.

He reached down from a fissure in the earth-wall in the gloom
And trailed his yellow-brown slackness soft-bellied down, over the edge of the
   stone trough
And rested his throat upon the stone bottom,
And where the water had dripped from the tap, in a small clearness,   10
He sipped with his straight mouth
Softly drank through his straight gums, into his slack long body,
Silently.

Someone was before me at my water-trough,
And I, like a second-comer, waiting.   15

He lifted his head from his drinking, as cattle do,
And looked at me vaguely, as drinking cattle do,
And flicked his two-forked tongue from his lips, and mused a moment,

And stooped and drank a little more,
Being earth-brown, earth-golden from the burning bowels of the earth   20
On the day of Sicilian July, with Etna smoking.

The voice of my education said to me
He must be killed,
For in Sicily the black black snakes are innocent, the gold are venomous.

And voices in me said, If you were a man,   25
You would take a stick and break him now, and finish him off.

But must I confess how I liked him,
How glad I was he had come like a guest in quiet, to drink at my water-trough
And depart peaceful, pacified, and thankless
Into the buring bowels of this earth?   30

Was it cowardice, that I dared not kill him?
Was it perversity, that I longed to talk to him?
Was it humility, to feel so honoured?
I felt so honoured.

And yet those voices: 35
If you were not afraid, you would kill him!

And truly I was afraid, I was most afraid,
But even so, honoured still more
That he should seek my hospitality
From out the dark door of the secret earth.   40

He drank enough
And lifted his head, dreamily, as one who has drunken,

And flickered his tongue like a forked night on the air, so black,
Seeming to lick his lips,
And looked around like a god unseeing, into the air,   45

And slowly turned his head,
And slowly, very slowly, as if thrice adream
Proceeded to draw his slow length curving round
And climb again the broken bank of my wall-face.

And as he put his head into that dreadful hole,   50
And as he slowly drew up, snake-easing his shoulders, and entered further,
A sort of horror, a sort of protest against his withdrawing into that horrible
    black hole.
Deliberately going into the blackness, and slowly drawing himself after,
Overcame me now his back was turned.

I looked round, I put down by pitcher,   55
I picked up a clumsy log
And threw it at the water-trough with a clatter.

I think it did not hit him;
But suddenly that part of him that was left behind convulsed in undignified
    haste,
Writhed like lightning, and was gone   60
Into the black hole, the earth-lipped fissure in the wall-front
At which, in the intense still noon, I stared with fascination.

And immediately I regretted it.
I thought how paltry, how vulgar, what a mean act!
I despised myself and the voices of my accused human education.   65
And I thought of the albatross,
And I wished he would come back, my snake.

For he seemed to me again like a king,
Like a king in exile, uncrowned in the underworld,
Now due to be crowned again.   70
And so, I missed my chance with one of the lords
Of life.
And I have something to expiate:
A pettiness.

Wallace Stevens (1879–1955)
THE SNOW MAN

One must have a mind of winter
To regard the frost and the boughs
Of the pine-trees crusted with snow;

And have been cold a long time
To behold the junipers shagged with
   ice,   5
The spruces rough in the distant glitter
Of the January sun; and not to think
Of any misery in the sound of the wind,
In the sound of a few leaves,

Which is the sound of the land   10
Full of the same wind
That is blowing in the same bare place

For the listener, who listens in the
   snow,
And, nothing himself, beholds
Nothing that is not there and the
   nothing that is.   15

THE EMPEROR OF ICE-CREAM

Call the roller of big cigars,
The muscular one, and bid him whip
In kitchen cups concupiscent curds.
Let the wenches dawdle in such dress
As they are used to wear, and let the
   boys   5
Bring flowers in last month's
   newspapers.
Let be be finale of seem.
The only emperor is the emperor of ice-
   cream.

Take from the dresser of deal,
Lacking the three glass knobs, that
   sheet   10
On which she embroidered fantails
   once
And spread it so as to cover her face.
If her horny feet protrude, they come
To show how cold she is, and dumb.
Let the lamp affix its beam.   15
The only emperor is the emperor of ice-
   cream.

ANECDOTE OF THE JAR

I placed a jar in Tennessee,
And round it was, upon a hill.
It made the slovenly wilderness
Surround that hill.

The wilderness rose up to it,   5
And sprawled around, no longer wild.

The jar was round upon the ground
And tall and of a port in air.

It took dominion everywhere.
The jar was gray and bare.   10
It did not give of bird or brush,
Like nothing else in Tennessee.

William Carlos Williams (1883–1963)
TRACT

I will teach you my townspeople
how to perform a funeral
for you have it over a troop
of artists—
unless one should scour the world—   5
you have the ground sense necessary.

See! the hearse leads.
I begin with a design for a hearse.
For Christ's sake not black—
nor white either—and not polished!   10
Let it be weathered—like a farm
   wagon—
with gilt wheels (this could be
applied fresh at small expense)
or no wheels at all:
a rough day to drag over the ground.   15

Knock the glass out!
My God—glass, my townspeople!
For what purpose? Is it for the dead
to look out or for us to see   20
how well he is housed or to see

the flowers or the lack of them—
or what?
To keep the rain and snow from him?
He will have a heavier rain soon:
pebbles and dirt and what not.   25
Let there be no glass—
and no upholstery, phew!
and no little brass rollers
and small easy wheels on the bottom—
my townspeople what are you thinking
   of?   30

A rough plain hearse then
with gilt wheels and no top at all.
On this the coffin lies
by its own weight.

            No wreaths please—35
especially no hot house flowers.
Some common memento is better,
something he prized and is known by:
his old clothes—a few books perhaps—
God knows what! You realize   40

how we are about these things
my townspeople—
something will be found—anything
even flowers if he had come to that.
So much for the hearse.   45

For heaven's sake though see to the
    driver!
Take off the silk hat! In fact
that's no place at all for him—
up there unceremoniously
dragging our friend out to his own
    dignity!   50
Bring him down—bring him down!
Low and inconspicuous! I'd not have
    him ride
on the wagon at all—damn him—
the undertaker's understrapper!

Let him hold the reins   55
and walk at the side
and inconspicuously too!

Then briefly as to yourselves:
Walk behind—as they do in France,
seventh class, or if you ride   60
Hell take curtains! Go with some show
of inconvenience; sit openly—
to the weather as to grief.
Or do you think you can shut grief in?
What—from us? We who have
    perhaps   65
nothing to lose? Share with us
share with us—it will be money
in your pockets.
                              Go now
I think you are ready.   70

THE RED WHEELBARROW

so much depends
upon

a red wheel
barrow

glazed with rain   5
water

beside the white
chickens.

THE YACHTS

contend in a sea which the land partly encloses
shielding them from the too heavy blows
of an ungoverned ocean which when it chooses

tortures the biggest hulls, the best man knows
to pit against its beatings, and sinks them pitilessly.
Mothlike in mists, scintillant in the minute

brilliance of cloudless days, with broad bellying sails
they glide to the wind tossing green water
from their sharp prows while over them the crew crawls

ant like, solicitously grooming them, releasing,
making fast as they turn, lean far over and having
caught the wind again, side by side, head for the mark.

In a well guarded arena of open water surrounded by
lesser and greater craft which, sycophant, lumbering
and flittering follow them, they appear youthful, rare

as the light of a happy eye, live with the grace
of all that in the mind is feckless, free and
naturally to be desired. Now the sea which holds them

is moody, lapping their glossy sides, as if feeling
for some slightest flaw but fails completely.
Today no race. Then the wind comes again. The yachts

move, jockeying for a start, the signal is set and they
are off. Now the waves strike at them but they are too
well made, they slip through, though they take in canvas.

Arms with hands grasping seek to clutch at the prows.
Bodies thrown recklessly in the way are cut aside.
It is a sea of faces about them in agony, in despair

until the horror of the race dawns staggering the mind,
the whole sea becoming entanglement of water bodies
lost to the world bearing what they cannot hold. Broken,

beaten, desolate, reaching from the dead to be taken up
they cry out, failing, failing! their cries rising
in waves still as the skillful yachts pass over.

Ezra Pound (1885–1972)

PORTRAIT D'UNE FEMME

Your mind and you are our Sargasso
  Sea,
London has swept about you this score
  years
And bright ships left you this or that in
  fee:
Ideas, old gossip, oddments of all things,
Strange spars of knowledge and
  dimmed wares of price.   5
Great minds have sought you—lacking
  someone else.
You have been second always. Tragical?

No. You preferred it to the usual thing:
One dull man, dulling and uxorious,
One average mind—with one thought
   less, each year.   10
Oh, you are patient, I have seen you sit
Hours, where something might have
   floated up.
And now you pay one. Yes, you richly
   pay.
You are a person of some interest, one
   comes to you
And takes strange gain away: 15
Trophies fished up; some curious
   suggestion;
Fact that leads nowhere; and a tale or
   two,
Pregnant with mandrakes, or with
   something else
That might prove useful and yet never
   proves,

That never fits a corner or shows
   use,   20
Or finds its hours upon the loom of
   days:
The tarnished, gaudy, wonderful old
   work;
Idols and ambergris and rare inlays,
These are your riches, your great store;
   and yet
For all this sea-hoard of deciduous
   things,   25
Strange woods half sodden, and new
   brighter stuff:
In the slow float of differing light and
   deep,
No! there is nothing! In the whole and
   all,
Nothing that's quite your own.
        Yet this is you.   30

Robinson Jeffers (1887–1962)

THE PURSE-SEINE

Our sardine fishermen work at night in the dark of the moon; day-light or moonlight
They could not tell where to spread the net, unable to see the phosphorescence of
   the shoals of fish.
They work northward from Monterey, coasting Santa Cruz; off New Year's Point
   or off Pigeon Point
The look-out man will see some lakes of milk-color light on the sea's night-purple;
   he points, and the helmsman
Turns the dark prow, the motorboat circles the gleaming shoal and drifts out her
   seine-net. They close the circle   5
And purse the bottom of the net, then with great labor haul it in.

                                       I cannot tell you
How beautiful the scene is, and a little terrible, then, when the crowded fish
Know they are caught, and wildly beat from one wall to the other of their closing
   destiny the phosphorescent
Water to a pool of flame, each beautiful slender body sheeted with flame, like a
   live rocket   10

A comet's tail wake of clear yellow flame; while outside the narrowing
Floats and cordage of the net great sea-lions come up to watch, sighing in the
    dark; the vast walls of night
Stand erect to the stars.

                                    Lately I was looking from a night mountain-top
On a wide city, the colored splendor, galaxies of light: how could I help but recall
    the seine-net   15
Gathering the luminous fish? I cannot tell you how beautiful the city appeared, and
    a little terrible.
I thought, We have geared the machines and locked all together into interde-
    pendence; we have built the great cities; now
There is no escape. We have gathered vast populations incapable of free survival,
    insulated
From the strong earth, each person in himself helpless, on all dependent.
    The circle is closed, and the net   20
Is being hauled in. They hardly feel the cords drawing, yet they shine already.
    The inevitable mass-disasters
Will not come in our time nor in our children's, but we and our children
Must watch the net draw narrower, government take all powers—or revolution, and
    the new government
Take more than all, add to kept bodies kept souls—or anarchy, the mass-disasters.

                                            These things are Progress;   25
Do you marvel our verse is troubled or frowning, while it keeps its reason? Or it
    lets go, lets the mood flow
In the manner of the recent young men into mere hysteria, splintered gleams,
    crackled laughter. But they are quite wrong.
There is no reason for amazement; surely one always knew that cultures decay, and
    life's end is death.

MAY-JUNE 1940

Foreseen for so many years: these evils, this monstrous violence, these massive
    agonies: no easier to bear.
We saw them with slow stone strides approach, everyone saw them; we closed our
    eyes against them, we looked
And they had come nearer. We ate and drank and slept, they came nearer.
    Sometimes we laughed, they were nearer. Now
They are here. And now a blind man foresees what follows them: Degradation,
    famine, recovery and so forth, and the
Epidemic manias: but not enough death to serve us, not enough death. It would be
    better for men   5
To be few and live far apart, where none could infect another; then slowly the
    sanity of field and mountain
And the cold ocean and glittering stars might enter their minds.

Another

dream, another dream.
We shall have to accept certain limitations
In future, and abandon some humane dreams; only hard-minded, sleepless and
　realistic, can ride this rock-slide　　　　　　　　　　　　　　　　　　10
To new fields down the dark mountain; and we shall have to perceive that these
　insanities are normal;
We shall have to perceive that battle is a burning flower or like a huge music, and
　the dive-bomber's screaming orgasm
As beautiful as other passions; and that death and life are not serious alternatives.
　One has known all these things
For many years: there is greater and darker to know
In the next hundred.　　　　　　　　　　　　　　　　　　　　　　　15

　　　　　And why do you cry, my dear, why do you cry?
It is all in the whirling circles of time.
If millions are born millions must die,
If England goes down and Germany goes up
The stronger dog will still be on top,　　　　　　　　　　　　　　　　20
All in the turning of time.
If civilization goes down, that
Would be an event to contemplate.
It will not be in our time, alas, my dear,
It will not be in our time.　　　　　　　　　　　　　　　　　　　　25

Thomas Stearns Eliot (1888–1965)

THE LOVE SONG OF J. ALFRED PRUFROCK

S'io credesse che mia riposta fosse
A persona che mai tornasse al mondo,
Questa fiamma staria senza piu scosse.
Ma perciocche giammai di questo fondo
Non torno vivo alcun, s'i'odo il vero,
Senza tema d'infamia ti rispondo[1]

Let us go then, you and I,
When the evening is spread out against
　the sky
Like a patient etherised upon a table;
Let us go, through certain half-deserted
　streets,　　　　5
The muttering retreats
Of restless nights in one-night cheap
　hotels
And sawdust restaurants with oyster-
　shells:
Streets that follow like a tedious
　argument
Of insidious intent
To lead you to an overwhelming
　question . . .　　　　10
Oh, do not ask, "What is it?"
Let us go and make our visit.

"The Love Song of J. Alfred Prufrock" and "The Hollow Men" from *Collected Poems 1909-1962* by T. S. Eliot, copyright, 1936, by Harcourt Brace Jovanovich, Inc.; copyright, © 1963, 1964, by T. S. Eliot. Reprinted by permission of Harcourt Brace Jovanovich, Inc. and Faber & Faber Ltd.

[1] *Epigraph:* "If I thought my answer were to one who ever could return to the world, this flame should shake no more; but since no one did ever return alive from this depth, if what I hear be true, without fear of infamy I answer thee." (Dante, *Inferno*, XXVII, 61–66)

In the room the women come and go
Talking of Michelangelo.

The yellow fog that rubs its back upon
    the window-panes,   15
The yellow smoke that rubs its muzzle
    on the window-panes
Licked its tongue into the corners of the
    evening,
Lingered upon the pools that stand in
    drains,
Let fall upon its back the soot that falls
    from chimneys,
Slipped by the terrace, made a sudden
    leap,   20
And seeing that it was a soft October
    night,
Curled once about the house, and fell
    asleep.

And indeed there will be time
For the yellow smoke that slides along
    the street,
Rubbing its back upon the window-
    panes;   25
There will be time, there will be time
To prepare a face to meet the faces that
    you meet;
There will be time to murder and
    create,
And time for all the works and days of
    hands
That lift and drop a question on your
    plate;   30
Time for you and time for me,
And time yet for a hundred indecisions,
And for a hundred visions and
    revisions,
Before the taking of a toast and tea.

In the room the women come and
    go   35
Talking of Michelangelo.

And indeed there will be time
To wonder, "Do I dare?" and, "Do I
    dare?"
Time to turn back and descend the
    stair,

With a bald spot in the middle of my
    hair—   40
(They will say: "How his hair is
    growing thin!")
My morning coat, my collar mounting
    firmly to the chin,
My necktie rich and modest, but
    asserted by a simple pin—
(They will say: "But how his arms and
    legs are thin!")
Do I dare   45
Disturb the universe?
In a minute there is time
For decisions and revisions which a
    minute will reverse.

For I have known them all already,
    known them all:
Have known the evenings, mornings,
    afternoons,   50
I have measured out my life with coffee
    spoons;
I know the voices dying with a dying
    fall
Beneath the music from a farther room.
    So how should I presume?

And I have known the eyes already,
    known them all—   55
The eyes that fix you in a formulated
    phrase,
And when I am formulated, sprawling
    on a pin,
When I am pinned and wriggling on
    the wall,
Then how should I begin
To spit out all the butt-ends of my days
    and ways?   60
    And how should I presume?

And I have known the arms already,
    known them all—
Arms that are braceleted and white and
    bare
(But in the lamplight, downed with
    light brown hair!)
Is it perfume from a dress   65
That makes me so digress?
Arms that lie along a table, or wrap
    about a shawl.

And should I then presume?
And how should I begin?

. . .

Shall I say, I have gone at dusk through
   narrow streets   70
And watched the smoke that rises from
   the pipes
Of lonely men in shirt-sleeves, leaning
   out of windows? . . .

I should have been a pair of ragged
   claws
Scuttling across the floors of silent seas.

. . .

And the afternoon, the evening, sleeps
   so peacefully!   75
Smoothed by long fingers,
Asleep . . . tired . . . or it malingers,
Stretched on the floor, here beside you
   and me.
Should I, after tea and cakes and ices,
Have the strength to force the moment
   to its crisis?   80
But though I have wept and fasted,
   wept and prayed,
Though I have seen my head (grown
   slightly bald) brought in upon a
   platter,
I am no prophet—and here's no great
   matter;
I have seen the moment of my greatness
   flicker,
And I have seen the eternal Footman
   hold my coat, and snicker   85
And in short, I was afraid.

And would it have been worth it,
   after all,
After the cups, the marmalade, the tea,
Among the porcelain, among some talk
   of you and me,
Would it have been worth while,   90
To have bitten off the matter with a
   smile,
To have squeezed the universe into a
   ball
To roll it toward some overwhelming
   question,
To say: "I am Lazarus, come from the
   dead,

Come back to tell you all, I shall tell
   you all"—   95
If one, settling a pillow by her head,
   Should say: "That is not what I meant
   at all.
   That is not it, at all."

And would it have been worth it,
   after all,
Would it have been worth while,   100
After the sunsets and the dooryards and
   the sprinkled streets,
After the novels, after the teacups, after
   the skirts that trail along the
   floor—
And this, and so much more?—
It is impossible to say just what I mean!
But as if a magic lantern threw the
   nerves in patterns on a screen: 105
Would it have been worth while
If one, settling a pillow or throwing off
   a shawl,
And turning toward the window, should
   say:
   "That is not it at all,
   That is not what I meant, at all." 110

. . .

No! I am not Prince Hamlet, nor was
   meant to be:
Am an attendant lord, one that will do
To swell a progress, start a scene or two,
Advise the prince; no doubt, an easy
   tool,
Deferential, glad to be of use,   115
Politic, cautious, and meticulous;
Full of high sentence, but a bit obtuse;
At times, indeed, almost ridiculous—
Almost, at times, the Fool.

   I grow old. . . . I grow old . . .   120
I shall wear the bottoms of my trousers
   rolled.

   Shall I part my hair behind? Do I
   dare to eat a peach?
I shall wear white flannel trousers, and
   walk upon the beach.
I have heard the mermaids singing, each
   to each.

   I do not think that they will sing to
   me.   125

I have seen them riding seaward on
  the waves
Combing the white hair of the waves
  blown back
When the wind blows the water white
  and black.

We have lingered in the chambers of
  the sea
By sea-girls wreathed with seaweed red
  and brown   130
Till human voices wake us, and we
  drown.

THE HOLLOW MEN

Mistah Kurtz—he dead.
A penny for the Old Guy.

I

We are the hollow men
We are the stuffed men
Leaning together
Headpiece filled with straw. Alas!
Our dried voices, when   5
We whisper together
Are quiet and meaningless
As wind in dry grass
Or rats' feet over broken glass
In our dry cellar   10
Shape without form, shade without
  colour,
Paralysed force, gesture without
  motion;

Those who have crossed
With direct eyes, to death's other
  Kingdom
Remember us—if at all—not as lost   15
Violent souls, but only
As the hollow men
The stuffed men.

II

Eyes I dare not meet in dreams
In death's dream kingdom   20
These do not appear:
There, the eyes are

Sunlight on a broken column
There, is a tree swinging
And voices are   25
In the wind's singing
More distant and more solemn
Than a fading star.
Let me be no nearer
In death's dream kingdom   30
Let me also wear
Such deliberate disguises
Rat's coat, crowskin, crossed staves
In a field
Behaving as the wind behaves   35
No nearer—

Not that final meeting
In the twilight kingdom.

III

This is the dead land
This is cactus land   40
Here the stone images
Are raised, here they receive
The supplication of a dead man's hand
Under the twinkle of a fading star.

Is it like this   45
In death's other kingdom
Waking alone
At the hour when we are
Trembling with tenderness
Lips that would kiss   50
Form prayers to broken stone

IV

The eyes are not here
There are no eyes here
In this valley of dying stars
In this hollow valley   55
This broken jaw of our lost kingdoms.

In this last of meeting places
We grope together
And avoid speech
Gathered on this beach of the tumid
    river.   60

Sightless, unless
The eyes reappear
As the perpetual star
Multifoliate rose
Of death's twilight kingdom   65
The hope only
Of empty men.

V

Here we go round the prickly pear
Prickly pear prickly pear
Here we go round the prickly pear   70
At five o'clock in the morning.

Between the idea
And the reality
Between the motion
And the act   75
Falls the Shadow
    For Thine is the Kingdom

Between the conception
And the creation
Between the emotion   80
And the response
Falls the Shadow
    Life is very long

Between the desire
And the spasm   85
Between the potency
And the existence
Between the essence
And the descent
Falls the Shadow   90
    For Thine is the Kingdom

For Thine is
Life is
For Thine is the

This is the way the world ends   95
This is the way the world ends
This is the way the world ends
Not with a bang but a whimper.

John Crowe Ransom (1888–1974)

BELLS FOR JOHN WHITESIDE'S DAUGHTER

There was such speed in her little body,
And such lightness in her footfall,
It is no wonder that her brown study
Astonishes us all.

Her wars were bruited in our high
    window.   5
We looked among orchard trees and
    beyond,

Where she took arms against her
    shadow,
Or harried unto the pond

The lazy geese, like a snow cloud
Dripping their snow on the green
    grass,   10
Tricking and stopping, sleepy and
    proud,
Who cried in goose, Alas,

For the tireless heart within the little
Lady with rod that made them rise
From their noon apple-dreams, and
    scuttle   15
Goose-fashion under the skies!

But now go the bells, and we are ready;
In one house we are sternly stopped
To say we are vexed at her brown
    study,
Lying so primly propped.   20

DEAD BOY

The little cousin is dead, by foul subtraction,
A green bough from Virginia's aged tree,
And none of the country kin like the transaction,
Nor some of the world of outer dark, like me.

A boy not beautiful, nor good, nor clever,   5
A black cloud full of storms too hot for keeping,
A sword beneath his mother's heart—yet never
Woman bewept her babe as this is weeping.

A pig with a pasty face, so I had said,
Squealing for cookies, kinned by poor pretense   10
With a noble house. But the little man quite dead,
I see the forebears' antique lineaments.

The elder men have strode by the box of death
To the wide flag porch, and muttering low send round
The bruit of the day. O friendly waste of breadth! 15
Their hearts are hurt with a deep dynastic wound.

He was pale and little, the foolish neighbors say;
The first fruits, saith the preacher, the Lord hath taken;
But this was the old tree's late branch wrenched away,
Grieving the sapless limbs, the shorn and shaken.   20

Edna St. Vincent Millay (1892–1950)
JUSTICE DENIED IN MASSACHUSETTS

Let us abandon then our gardens and go
  home
And sit in the sitting-room.
Shall the larkspur blossom or the corn
  grow under this cloud?
Sour to the fruitful seed
Is the cold earth under this cloud,   5
Fostering quack and weed, we have
  marched upon but cannot conquer;
We have bent the blades of our hoes
  against the stalks of them.
Let us go home, and sit in the sitting-
  room.
Not in our day
Shall the cloud go over and the sun rise
  as before,   10
Beneficient upon us
Out of the glittering bay,
And the warm winds be blown inward
  from the sea
Moving the blades of corn
With a peaceful sound.   15
Forlorn, forlorn,
Stands the blue hay-rack by the empty
  mow.
And the petals drop to the ground,

Leaving the tree unfruited.
The sun that warmed our stooping
  backs and withered the weed
  uprooted—   20
We shall not feel it again.
We shall die in darkness, and be buried
  in the rain.

What from the splendid dead
We have inherited—
Furrows sweet to the grain, and the
  weed subdued—   25
See now the slug and the mildew
  plunder.
Evil does overwhelm
The larkspur and the corn;
We have seen them go under.
Let us sit here, sit still,   30
Here in the sitting-room until we die;
At the step of Death on the walk, rise
  and go;
Leaving to our children's children this
  beautiful doorway,
And this elm,
And a blighted earth to till   35
With a broken hoe.

WHAT LIPS MY LIPS HAVE KISSED

What lips my lips have kissed, and
  where, and why,
I have forgotten, and what arms have
  lain

Under my head till morning; but the
  rain
Is full of ghosts tonight, that tap and
  sigh

Upon the glass and listen for reply; 5
And in my heart there stirs a quiet pain
For unremembered lads that not again
Will turn to me at midnight with a cry.
Thus in the winter stands the lonely tree,
Nor knows what birds have vanished one by one, 10

Yet knows its boughs more silent than before:
I cannot say what loves have come and gone;
I only know that summer sang in me
A little while, that in me sings no more.

Archibald MacLeish (1892–   )

MEMORIAL RAIN

Ambassador Puser the ambassador
Reminds himself in French, felicitous tongue,
What these (young men no longer) lie here for
In rows that once, and somewhere else, were young . . .

All night in Brussels the wind had tugged at my door: 5
I had heard the wind at my door and the trees strung
Taut, and to me who had never been before
In that country it was a strange wind, blowing
Steadily, stiffening the walls, the floor,
The roof of my room. I had not slept for knowing 10
He too, dead, was a stranger in that land
And felt beneath the earth in the wind's flowing
A tightening of roots and would not understand,
Remembering lake winds in Illinois,
That strange wind. I had felt his bones in the sand 15
Listening.

      . . . Reflects that these enjoy
Their country's gratitude, that deep repose,
That peace no pain can break, no hurts destroy,
That rest, that sleep . . . 20

      At Ghent the wind rose.
There was a smell of rain and a heavy drag
Of wind in the hedges but not as the wind blows
Over fresh water when the waves lag
Foaming and the willows huddle and it will rain; 25
I felt him waiting.

...Indicates the flag
Which (may he say) enisles in Flanders' plain
This little field these happy, happy dead
Have made America ...

      In the ripe grain
The wind coiled glistening, darted, fled,
Dragging its heavy body: at Waereghem   30
The wind coiled in the grass above his head:
Waiting—listening . . .

      ...Dedicates to them
This earth their bones have hallowed, this last gift
A grateful country ...

      Under the dry grass stem   35
The words are blurred, are thickened, the words sift
Confused by the rasp of the wind, by the thin grating
Of ants under the grass, the minute shift
And tumble of dusty sand separating
From dusty sand. The roots of the grass strain,   40
  Tighten, the earth is rigid, waits—he is waiting—

  And suddenly, and all at once, the rain!

The living scatter, they run into houses, the wind
Is trampled under the rain, shakes free, is again
Trampled. The rain gathers, running in thinned   45
Spurts of water that ravel in the dry sand,
Seeping into the sand under the grass roots, seeping
Between cracked boards to the bones of a clenched hand:
The earth relaxes, loosens; he is sleeping,
He rests, he is quiet, he sleeps in a strange land.   50

E. E. Cummings (1894–1962)
POEM, OR BEAUTY HURTS MR. VINAL

take it from me kiddo
believe me
my country, 'tis of
you, land of the Cluett

Shirt Boston Garter and Spearmint   5
Girl With The Wrigley Eyes (of you
land of the Arrow Ide
and Earl &
Wilson
Collars) of you i   10
sing: land of Abraham Lincoln and Lydia E. Pinkham,
land above all of Just Add Hot Water And Serve—
from every B.V.D.

let freedom ring

amen. i do however protest, anent the un   15
-spontaneous and otherwise scented merde which
greets one (Everywhere Why) as divine poesy per
that and this radically defunct periodical. i would

suggest that certain ideas gestures
rhymes, like Gillette Razor Blades   20
having been used and reused
to the mystical moment of dullness emphatically are
Not To Be Resharpened. (Case in point

if we are to believe these gently O sweetly
melancholy trillers amid the thrillers   25
these crepuscular violinists among my and your
skyscrapers—Helen & Cleopatra were Just Too Lovely,
The Snail's On The Thorn enter Morn and God's
In His andsoforth

do you get me?)according   30
to such supposedly indigenous
throstles Art is O World O Life
a formula:example, Turn Your Shirttails Into
Drawers and If It Isn't An Eastman It Isn't A
Kodak therefore my friends let   35
us now sing each and all fortissimo A-
mer
i

ca, I
love,   40
You. And there're a
hun-dred-mil-lion-oth-ers, like
all of you successfully if
delicately gelded(or spaded)
gentlemen(and ladies)—pretty   45
littleliverpill-
hearted-Nujolneeding-There's-A-Reason
americans(who tensetendoned and with
upward vacant eyes, painfully

perpetually crouched, quivering, upon the 50
sternly allotted sandpile
—how silently
emit a tiny violetflavored nuisance:Odor?

ono.
comes out like a ribbon lies flat on the brush 55

LA GUERRE

I

the bigness of cannon
is skillful,

but i have seen
death's clever enormous voice
which hides in a fragility 5
of poppies. . . .

i say that sometimes
on these long talkative animals
are laid fists of huger silence

I have seen all the silence 10
filled with vivid noiseless boys

at Roupy
i have seen
between barrages,

the night utter ripe unspeaking girls. 15

II

O sweet spontaneous
earth how often have
the
doting

fingers of 20
prurient philosophers pinched
and
poked

thee
, has the naughty thumb 25
of science prodded
thy
        beauty   .how
often have the religions taken
thee upon their scraggy knees 30
squeezing and

buffeting thee that thou mightest con-
    ceive
gods
        (but
true 35

to the incomparable
couch of death thy
rhythmic
lover

        thou answerest 40

them only with
                spring)

PORTRAIT VIII

Buffalo Bill's
defunct
         who used to
         ride a watersmooth-silver
                              stallion   5
and break onetwothreefourfive pigeonsjustlikethat
                                        Jesus
he was a handsome man
                    and what i want to know is
how do you like your blueeyed boy
Mister death.

PITY THIS BUSY MONSTER, MANUNKIND

pity this busy monster, manunkind,

not. Progress is a comfortable disease:
your victim(death and life safely
   beyond)

plays with the bigness of his littleness
—electrons deify one razorblade   5
into a mountainrange; lenses extend

unwish through curving wherewhen till
   unwish
returns on its unself.

                    A world of made
is not a world of born—pity poor
   flesh   10

and trees,poor stars and stones,but
   never this
fine specimen of hypermagical

ultraomnipotence. We doctors know

a hopeless case if—listen:there's a hell
of a good universe next door; let's
   go   15

NEXT TO OF COURSE GOD

"next to of course god america i
love you land of the pilgrims' and so
  forth oh
say can you see by the dawn's early my
country 'tis of centuries come and go
and are no more what of it we should
  worry   5
in every language even deafanddumb
thy sons acclaim your glorious name by
  gorry
by jingo by gee by gosh by gum

why talk of beauty what could be more
  beaut-
iful than these heroic happy dead   10
who rushed like lions to the roaring
  slaughter
they did not stop to think they died
  instead
then shall the voice of liberty be
  mute?"

He spoke. And drank rapidly a glass of
  water.

MY FATHER MOVED THROUGH DOOMS OF LOVE

my father moved through dooms of
  love
through sames of am through haves of
  give,
singing each morning out of each night
my father moved through depths of
  height

this motionless forgetful where   5
turned at his glance to shining here;
that if (so timid air is firm)
under his eyes would stir and squirm

newly as from unburied which
floats the first who, his april touch   10
drove sleeping selves to swarm their
  fates
woke dreamers to their ghostly roots

and should some why completely weep
my father's fingers brought her sleep:
vainly no smallest voice might cry   15
for he could feel the mountains grow.

Lifting the valleys of the sea
my father moved through griefs of joy;
praising a forehead called the moon
singing desire into begin   20

joy was his song and joy so pure
a heart of star by him could steer
and pure so now and now so yes
the wrists of twilight would rejoice

keen as midsummer's keen beyond   25
conceiving mind of sun will stand,
so strictly (over utmost him
so hugely) stood my father's dream

his flesh was flesh his blood was blood:
no hungry man but wished him
  food;   30
no cripple wouldn't creep one mile
uphill to only see him smile.

Scorning the pomp of must and shall
my father moved through dooms of
  feel;
his anger was as right as rain   35
his pity was as green as grain

septembering arms of year extend
less humbly wealth to foe and friend
than he to foolish and to wise
offered immeasurable is   40

proudly and (by octobering flame
beckoned) as earth will downward
    climb,
so naked for immortal work
his shoulders marched against the dark

his sorrow was as true as bread: 45
no liar looked him in the head;
if every friend became his foe
he'd laugh and build a world with snow.

My father moved through theys of we,
singing each new leaf out of each
    tree   50
(and every child was sure that spring
danced when she heard my father sing)

then let men kill which cannot share,
let blood and flesh be mud and mire,
scheming images,passion willed,   55
freedom a drug that's bought and sold

giving to steal and cruel kind,
a heart to fear,to doubt a mind,
to differ a disease of same,
conform the pinnacle of am   60

though dull were all we taste as bright,
bitter all utterly things sweet,
maggoty minus and dumb death
all we inherit,all bequeath

and nothing quite so least as truth   65
—i say though hate were why men
    breathe—
because my father lived his soul
love is the whole and more than all

Robert Graves (1895–   )
RECALLING WAR

Entrance and exit wounds are silvered clean,
The track aches only when the rain reminds.
The only-legged man forgets his leg of wood,
The one-armed man his jointed wooden arm.
The blinded man sees with his ears and hands   5
As much or more than once with both his eyes.
Their war was fought these twenty years ago
And now assumes the nature-look of time,
As when the morning traveller turns and views
His wild night-stumbling carved into a hill.   10

What, then, was war? No mere discord of flags
But an infection of the common sky
That sagged ominously upon the earth
Even when the season was the airiest May.
Down pressed the sky, and we, oppressed, thrust out   15
Boastful tongue, clenched fist and valiant yard.
Natural infirmities were out of mode.
For Death was young again: patron alone
Of healthy dying, premature, fate-spasm.

Fear made fine bed-fellows. Sick with delight   20
At life's discovered transitoriness,
Our youth became all-fresh and waived the mind.
Never was such antiqueness of romance,
Such tasty honey oozing from the heart.
And old importance came swimming back—   25
Wine, meat, log-fires, a roof over the head,
A weapon at the thigh, surgeons at call.
Even there was a use again for God—
A word of rage in lack of meat, wine, fire,
In ache of wounds beyond all surgeoning.   30

War was return of earth to ugly earth,
War was foundering of sublimities,
Extinction of each happy art and faith
By which the world had still kept head in air,
Protesting logic or protesting love,   35
Until the unendurable moment struck—
The inward scream, the duty to run mad.

And we recall the merry ways of guns—
Nibbling the walls of factory and church
Like a child, piecrust; felling groves of trees   40
Like a child, dandelions with a switch.
Machine-guns rattle toy-like from a hill,
Down in a row the brave tin-soldiers fall:
A sight to be recalled in elder days
When learnedly the future we devote   45
To yet more boastful visions of despair.

WITH HER LIPS ONLY

This honest wife, challenged at dusk
At the garden gate, under a moon perhaps,
In scent of honeysuckle, dared to deny
Love to an urgent lover: with her lips only,
Not with her heart. It was no assignation;   5
Taken aback, what could she say else?
'For the children's sake,' she argued with her conscience.

Yet a mortal lie must follow before dawn:
Challenged as usual in her own bed,   10
She protests love to an urgent husband,
Not with her heart but with her lips only;
'For the children's sake,' she argues with her conscience,
'For the children'—turning suddenly cold towards them.

Stephen Vincent Benét (1898–1943)
NIGHTMARE NUMBER THREE

We had expected everything but revolt
And I kind of wonder myself when they started thinking—
But there's no dice in that now.
                       I've heard fellows say
They must have planned it for years and maybe they did.   5
Looking back, you can find little incidents here and there,
Like the concrete-mixer in Jersey eating the wop
Or the roto press that printed "Fiddle-dee-dee!"
In a three-color process all over Senator Sloop,
Just as he was making a speech. The thing about that   10
Was, how could it walk upstairs? But it was upstairs,
Clicking and mumbling in the Senate Chamber.
They had to knock out the wall to take it away
And the wrecking-crew said it grinned.
                       It was only the best   15
Machines, of course, the superhuman machines,
The ones we'd built to be better than flesh and bone,
But the cars were in it, of course . . .
                   and they hunted us
Like rabbits through the cramped streets on that Bloody Monday,   20
The Madison Avenue busses leading the charge.
The busses were pretty bad—but I'll not forget
The smash of glass when the Dusenberg left the show-room
And pinned three brokers to the Racquet Club steps
Or the long howl of the horns when they saw men run,   25
When they saw them looking for holes in the solid ground . . .

I guess they were tired of being ridden in
And stopped and started by pygmies for silly ends,
Of wrapping cheap cigarettes and bad chocolate bars   30
Collecting nickels and waving platinum hair
And letting six million people live in a town.
I guess it was that. I guess they got tired of us
And the whole smell of human hands.
                     But it was a shock   35
To climb sixteen flights of stairs to Art Zuckow's office
(Nobody took the elevators twice)
And find him strangled to death in a nest of telephones,

From: *The Selected Works of Stephen Vincent Benét.* Published by Holt, Rinehart and Winston, Inc. Copyright, 1940, by Stephen Benét. Copyright renewed © 1967, by Thomas C. Benét, Stephanie B. Mahin and Rachel Benét Lewis. Reprinted by permission of Brandt & Brandt.

The octopus-tendrils waving over his head,
And a sort of quiet humming filling the air . . .   40
Do they eat? . . . There was red . . . But I did not stop to look.
I don't know yet how I got to the roof in time
And it's lonely, here on the roof.
                        For a while, I thought
That window-cleaner would make it, and keep me company.   45
But they got him with his own hoist at the sixteenth floor
And dragged him in, with a squeal.
You see, they cooperate. Well, we taught them that
And it's fair enough, I suppose. You see, we built them.
We taught them to think for themselves.   50
It was bound to come. You can see it was bound to come.

And it won't be so bad, in the country. I hate to think
Of the reapers, running wild in the Kansas fields,
And the transport planes like hawks on a chickenyard,
But the horses might help. We might make a deal with the horses.   55
At least, you've more chance, out there.
                        And they need us, too.
They're bound to realize that when they once calm down.
They'll need oil and spare parts and adjustments and tuning up.
Slaves? Well, in a way, you know, we were slaves before.   60
There won't be so much real difference—honest, there won't.
(I wish I hadn't looked into that beauty-parlor
And seen what was happening there.
But those are female machines and a bit high-strung.)
Oh, settle down. We'll arrange it. We'll compromise.   65
It wouldn't make sense to wipe out the whole human race.
Why, I bet if I went to my old Plymouth now
(Of course you'd have to do it the tactful way)
And said, "Look here! Who got you the swell French horn?"   70
He wouldn't turn me over to those police cars;
At least I don't think he would.

                        Oh, it's going to be jake.
There won't be so much real difference—honest, there won't—
And I'd go down in a minute and take my chance—
I'm a good American and I always liked them—   75
Except for one small detail that bothers me
And that's the food proposition. Because, you see,
The concrete-mixer may have made a mistake,
And it looks like just high spirits.
But, if it's got so they like the flavor . . . well . . .   80

Hart Crane (1899–1932)
CHAPLINESQUE

We make our meek adjustments,
Contented with such random consolations
As the wind deposits
In slithered and too ample pockets.

For we can still love the world, who find   5
A famished kitten on the step, and know
Recesses for it from the fury of the street,
Or warm torn elbow coverts.

We will sidestep, and to the final smirk
Dally the doom of that inevitable thumb   10
That slowly chafes its puckered index toward us,
Facing the dull squint with what innocence
And what surprise!

And yet these fine collapses are not lies
More than the pirouettes of any pliant cane;   15
Our obsequies are, in a way, no enterprise.
We can evade you, and all else but the heart:
What blame to us if the heart live on.

The game enforces smirks; but we have seen
The moon in lonely alleys make   20
A grail of laughter of an empty ash can,
And through all sound of gaiety and quest
Have heard a kitten in the wilderness.

THE RIVER
(from *The Bridge*)

Stick your patent name on a signboard
brother—all over—going west—young man
Tintex—Japalac—Certain-teed Overalls ads
and lands sakes! under the new playbill ripped

in the guaranteed corner—see Bert Williams what?   5
Minstrels when you steal a chicken just
save me the wing, for if it isn't
Erie it ain't for miles around a
Mazda—and the telegrapic night coming on Thomas

a Ediford—and whistling down the tracks   10
a headlight rushing with the sound—can you
imagine—while an EXPRESS makes time like
SCIENCE—COMMERCE and the HOLYGHOST
RADIO ROARS IN EVERY HOME WE HAVE THE NORTHPOLE
WALLSTREET AND VIRGINBIRTH WITHOUT STONES OR   15
WIRES OR EVEN RUNNING brooks connecting ears
and no more sermon windows flashing roar
Breathtaking—as you like it . . . eh?

       So the 20th Century—so
whizzed the Limited—roared by and left   20
three men, still hungry on the tracks, ploddingly
watching the tail lights wizen and converge,
slipping gimleted and neatly out of sight.
The last bear, shot drinking in the Dakotas,
Loped under wires that span the mountain stream.   25
Keen instruments, strung to a vast precision
Bind town to town and dream to ticking dream.
But some men take their liquor slow—and count—
Though they'll confess no rosary nor clue—
The river's minute by the far brook's year.   30
Under a world of whistles, wires and steam
Caboose-like they go ruminating through
Ohio, Indiana—blind baggage—
To Cheyenne tagging . . . Maybe Kalamazoo.

Time's renderings, time's blendings they construe   35
As final reckonings of fire and snow;
Strange bird-wit, like the elemental gist
Of unwalled winds they offer, singing low
My Old Kentucky Home and *Casey Jones,*
Some Sunny Day. I heard a road-gang chanting so.   40
And afterwards, who had a colt's eyes—one said,
"Jesus! Oh I remember watermelon days!" And sped
High in a cloud of merriment, recalled
"—And when my Aunt Sally Simpson smiled," he drawled—
"It was almost Louisiana, long ago."   45

"There's no place like Booneville though, Buddy,"
One said, excising a last burr from his vest,
"—For early trouting." Then peering in the can,
"—But I kept on the tracks." Possessed, resigned,
He trod the fire down pensively and grinned,
Spreading dry shingles of a beard . . .   50

Behind

My father's cannery works I used to see
Rail-squatters ranged in nomad raillery,   55
The ancient men—wifeless or runaway
Hobo-trekkers that forever search
An empire wilderness of freight and rails.
Each seemed a child, like me, on a loose perch,
Holding to childhood like some termless play.   60
John, Jake, or Charley, hopping the slow freight
—Memphis to Tallahassee—riding the rods,
Blind fists of nothing, humpty-dumpty clods.

Yet they touch something like a key perhaps.
From pole to pole across the hills, the states   65
—They know a body under the wide rain;
Youngsters with eyes like fjords, old reprobates
With racetrack jargon,—dotting immensity
They lurk across her, knowing her yonder breast
Snow-silvered, sumac-stained or smoky blue,   70
Is past the valley-sleepers, south or west.
—As I have trod the rumorous midnight, too.

And past the circuit of the lamp's thin flame
(O Nights that brought me to her body bare!)
Have dreamed beyond the print that bound her name.   75
Trains sounding the long blizzards out—I heard
Wail into distances I knew were hers.
Papooses crying on the wind's long mane
Screamed redskin dynasties that fled the brain,
—Dead echoes! But I knew her body there   80
Time like a serpent down her shoulder dark,
And space, an eagle's wing, laid on her hair.

Under the Ozarks, domed by Iron Mountain,
The old gods of the rain lie wrapped in pools
Where eyeless fish curvet a sunken fountain   85
And re-descend with corn from querulous crows.
Such pilferings make up their timeless eatage,
Propitiate them for their timber torn
By iron, iron—always the iron dealt cleavage!
They doze now, below axe and powder horn.

And Pullman breakfasters glide glistening steel   90
From tunnel into field—iron strides the dew—
Straddles the hill, a dance of wheel on wheel.
You have a half-hour's wait at Siskiyou,
Or stay the night and take the next train through.
Southward, near Cairo passing, you can see   95
The Ohio merging,—borne down Tennessee;
And if it's summer and the sun's in dusk
Maybe the breeze will lift the River's musk
—As though the waters breathed that you might know
Memphis Johnny, Steamboat Bill, Missouri Joe.   100

Oh, lean from the window, if the train slows down,
As though you touched hands with some ancient clown,
—A little while gaze absently below
And hum *Deep River* with them while they go.

Yes, turn again and sniff once more—look see,   105
O Sheriff, Brakeman and Authority—
Hitch up your pants and crunch another quid,
For you, too, feed the River timelessly.
And few evade full measure of their fate;
Always they smile out eerily what they seem.   110
I could believe he joked at heaven's gate—
Dan Midland—jolted from the cold brake-beam.

Down, down—born pioneers in time's despite,
Grimed tributaries to an ancient flow—
They win no frontier by their wayward plight,   115
But drift in stillness, as from Jordan's brow.

You will not hear it as the sea; even stone
Is not more hushed by gravity . . . But slow,
As loth to take more tribute—sliding prone
Like one whose eyes were buried long ago   120

The River, spreading, flows—and spends your dream.
What are you, lost within this tideless spell?
You are your father's father, and the stream—
A liquid theme that floating niggers swell.

Damp tonnage and alluvial march of days—   125
Nights turbid, vascular with silted shale
And roots surrendered down of moraine clays:
The Mississippi drinks the farthest dale.

O quarrying passion, undertowed sunlight!
The basalt surface drags a jungle grace   130
Ochreous and lynx-barred in lengthening might;
Patience! and you shall reach the biding place!

Over De Soto's bones the freighted floors
Throb past the City storied of three thrones.
Down two more turns the Mississippi pours   135
(Anon tall ironsides up from salt lagoons)

And flows within itself, heaps itself free.
All fades but one thin skyline 'round . . . Ahead
No embrace opens but the stinging sea;
The River lifts itself from its long bed.   140

Poised wholly on its dream, a mustard glow,
Tortured with history, its one will—flow!
—The Passion spreads in wide tongues, choked and slow,
Meeting the Gulf, hosannas silently below.

E. B. White (1899–   )

I PAINT WHAT I SEE
A Ballad of Artistic Integrity

"What do you paint, when you paint a
    wall?"
    Said John D.'s grandson Nelson.
"Do you paint just anything there at all?
"Will there be any doves, or a tree in
    fall?
"Or a hunting scene, like an English
    hall?"   5

   "I paint what I see," said Rivera.

"What are the colors you use when you
    paint?"
    Said John D.'s grandson Nelson.
"Do you use any red in the beard of a
    saint?
"If you do, is it terribly red, or faint? 10
"Do you use any blue? Is it Prussian?"

   "I paint what I paint," said Rivera.

"Whose is that head that I see on my
    wall?"
    Said John D.'s grandson Nelson.
"Is it anyone's head whom we know, at
    all?   15
"A Rensselaer, or a Saltonstall?
"Is it Franklin D.? Is it Mordaunt Hall?
"Or is it the head of a Russian?"

   "I paint what I think," said Rivera.

*"I paint what I paint, I paint what I
    see,*   20
   "I paint what I think," said Rivera,
*"And the thing that is dearest in life to
    me*

"In a bourgeois hall is Integrity;
   "However . . .
*"I'll take out a couple of people
    drinkin'*   25
*"And put in a picture of Abraham
    Lincoln,*
*"I could even give you McCormick's
    reaper*
*"And still not make my art much
    cheaper.*
"But the head of Lenin has got to stay
*"Or my friends will give me the bird
    today*   30
   "The bird, the bird, forever."

"It's not good taste in a man like me,"
    Said John D.'s grandson Nelson,
"To question an artist's integrity
"Or mention a practical thing like a
    fee,   35
"But I know what I like to a large
    degree
   "Though art I hate to hamper;
"For twenty-one thousand conservative
    bucks
"You painted a radical. I say shucks,
   "I never could rent the offices—   40
   "The capitalistic offices.
"For this, as you know, is a public hall
"And people want doves, or a tree in
    fall,
"And though your art I dislike to
    hamper,
"I owe a *little* to God and Gramper,   45
   "And after all,
   "It's *my* wall . . ."

   "We'll see if it is," said Rivera.

Kenneth Fearing (1902–1961)
AMERICAN RHAPSODY (2)

First you bit your fingernails. And then you comb your hair again. And then you
wait. And wait.
(They say, you know, that first you lie. And then you steal, they say. And then, they
say, you kill.)

Then the doorbell rings. Then Peg drops in. And Bill. And Jane. And Doc.
And first you talk, and smoke, and hear the news and have a drink. Then you walk
down the stairs.
And you dine, then, and go to a show after that, perhaps, and after that a night
spot, and after that come home again, and climb the stairs again, and again go to
bed. 5

But first Peg argues, and Doc replies. First you dance the same dance and you drink
the same drink you always drank before.
And the piano builds a roof of notes above the world.
And the trumpet weaves a dome of music through space. And the drum makes a
ceiling over space and time and night.
And then the table-wit. And then the check. Then home again to bed.
But first, the stairs 10
And do you now, baby, as you climb the stairs, do you still feel as you felt back
there?
Do you feel again as you felt this morning? And the night before? And then the
night before that?

(They say, you know, that first you hear voices. And then you have visions, they
say. Then, they say, you kick and scream and rave.)
Or do you feel: What is one more night in a lifetime of nights?
What is one more death, or friendship, or divorce out of two, or three? Of four? Or
five? 15
One more face among so many, many faces, one more life among so many million
lives?

But first, baby, as you climb and count the stairs (and they total the same) did you,
sometime or somewhere, have a different idea?
Is this, baby, what you were born to feel, and do, and be?

"American Phapsody (2)" and "Dirge" from *New and Selected Poems* by Kenneth Fearing.
Reprinted by permission of Indiana University Press.

DIRGE

1-2-3 was the number he played but today the number came 3-2-1;
  bought his Carbide at 30 and it went to 29; had the favorite at Bowie but the
    track was slow—

O, executive type, would you like to drive a floating power, knee-action, silk-
    upholstered six? Wed a
Hollywood star? Shoot the course in 58? Draw to
the ace, king, jack?
O, fellow with a will who won't take no. watch out
for three cigarettes on the same, single match; O
democratic voter born in August under Mars, beware of liquidated rails—

Dénouement to dénouement, he took a personal pride in the certain, certain way he
    lived his own, private life,
  but nevertheless, they shut off his gas; nevertheless, the bank foreclosed;
    nevertheless, the landlord called; nevertheless, the radio broke,

And twelve o'clock arrived just once too often,
  just the same he wore one grey tweed suit, bought one straw hat, drank one
    straight Scotch, walked one short step, took one long look, drew one deep
    breath,
  just one too many,

And wow he died as wow he lived,
  going whop to the office and blooie home to sleep and biff got married and bam
    had children and oof got fired,
  zowie did he live and zowie did he die,

With who the hell are you at the corner of his casket, and where the hell we going
    on the right hand silver knob, and who the hell cares walking second from the
    end with an American Beauty wreath
  from why the hell not.

Very much missed by the circulation staff of the New York Evening Post; deeply,
  deeply mourned by the B.M.T.,

Wham, Mr. Roosevelt; pow, Sears Roebuck; awk, big dipper; bop, summer rain;
  bong, Mr., bong, Mr., bong, Mr., bong.

Countee Cullen (1903–1946)

SCOTTSBORO, TOO, IS WORTH ITS SONG
(A poem to American poets)

I said:
Now will the poets sing,—
Their cries go thundering
Like blood and tears
Into the nation's ears,
Like lightning dart.
Into the nation's heart.
Against disease and death and all things
    fell,
And war,
Their strophes rise and swell
To jar
The foe smug in his citadel.

Remembering their sharp pretty
Tunes for Sacco and Vanzetti,
I said:
Here too's a cause divinely spun
For those whose eyes are on the sun,
Here in epitome
Is all disgrace
And epic wrong,
Like wine to brace
The minstrel heart, and blare it into
    song.

Surely, I said,
Now will the poets sing.
    But they have raised no cry.
    I wonder why.

YET DO I MARVEL

I doubt not God is good, well-meaning,
    kind,
And did He stoop to quibble could tell
    why
The little buried mole continues blind,
Why flesh that mirrors Him must some
    day die,
Make plain the reason tortured Tantalus
Is baited by the fickle fruit, declare

If merely brute caprice dooms Sisyphus
To struggle up a never-ending stair.
Inscrutable His ways are, and immune
To catechism by a mind too strewn
With petty cares to slightly understand
What awful brain compels His awful
    hand.
Yet do I marvel at this curious thing:
To make a poet black, and bid him sing!

HERITAGE

(For Harold Jackman)

What is Africa to me:
Copper sun or scarlet sea,
Jungle star or jungle track,
Strong bronzed men, or regal black
Women from whose loins I sprang
When the birds of Eden sang?
One three centuries removed
From the scenes his fathers loved,
Spicy grove, cinnamon tree,
What is Africa to me?

So I lie, who all day long
Want no sound except the song
Sung by wild barbaric birds
Goading massive jungle herds,
Juggernauts of flesh that pass
Trampling tall defiant grass
Where young forest lovers lie,
Plighting troth beneath the sky.
So I lie, who always hear,
Though I cram against my ear
Both my thumbs, and keep them there,
Great drums throbbing through the air.
So I lie, whose fount of pride,
Dear distress, and joy allied,
Is my somber flesh and skin,
With the dark blood dammed within
Like great pulsing tides of wine
That, I fear, must burst the fine
Channels of the chafing net
Where they surge and foam and fret.

Africa? A book one thumbs
Listlessly, till slumber comes.
Unremembered are her bats
Circling through the night, her cats
Crouching in the river reeds,
Stalking gentle flesh that feeds
By the river brink; no more
Does the bugle-throated roar
Cry that monarch claws have leapt
From the scabbards where they slept.
Silver snakes that once a year
Doff the lovely coats you wear,

Seek no covert in your fear
Lest a mortal eye should see;
What's your nakedness to me?
Here no leprous flowers rear
Fierce corollas in the air;
Here no bodies sleek and wet,
Dripping mingled rain and sweat,
Tread the savage measures of
Jungle boys and girls in love.
What is last year's snow to me,
Last year's anything? The tree
Budding yearly must forget
How its past arose or set—
Bough and blossom, flower, fruit,
Even what shy bird with mute
Wonder at her travail there,
Meekly labored in its hair.
One three centuries removed
From the scenes his father loved,
Spicy grove, cinnamon tree,
What is Africa to me?

So I lie, who find no peace
Night or day, no slight release
From the unremittant beat
Made by cruel padded feet
Walking through my body's street.
Up and down they go, and back,
Treading out a jungle track.
So I lie, who never quite
Safely sleep from rain at night—
I can never rest at all
When the rain begins to fall;
Like a soul gone mad with pain
I must match its weird refrain;
Ever must I twist and squirm,
Writhing like a baited worm,
While its primal measures drip
Through my body, crying, "Strip!
Doff this new exuberance.
Come and dance the Lover's Dance!"
In an old remembered way
Rain works on me night and day.

Quaint, outlandish heathen gods
Black men fashion out of rods,
Clay, and brittle bits of stone,
In a likeness like their own,
My conversion came high-priced;
I belong to Jesus Christ,
Preacher of humility;
Heathen gods are naught to me.

Father, Son, and Holy Ghost,
So I make an idle boast;
Jesus of the twice-turned cheek,
Lamb of God, although I speak
With my mouth thus, in my heart,
Do I play a double part.
Ever at Thy glowing altar
Must my heart grow sick and falter,
Wishing He I served were black,
Thinking then it would not lack
Precedent of pain to guide it,
Let who would or might deride it;
Surely then this flesh would know
Yours had borne a kindred woe.

Lord, I fashion dark gods, too,
Daring even to give You
Dark despairing features where,
Crowned with dark rebellious hair,
Patience waves just so much as
Mortal grief compels, while touches
Quick and hot, of anger, rise
To smitten check and weary eyes.
Lord, forgive me if my need
Sometimes shapes a human creed.

All day long and all night through,
One thing only must I do:
Quench my pride and cool my blood,
Lest I perish in the flood.
Lest a hidden ember set
Timber that I thought was wet
Burning like the dryest flax,
Melting like the nearest wax,
Lest the grave restore its dead.
Not yet has my heart or head
In the least way realized
They and I are civilized.

C. Day Lewis (1904–1972)

NEWSREEL

Enter the dream-house, brothers and sisters, leaving
Your debts asleep, your history at the door:
This is the home for heroes, and this loving
Darkness a fur you can afford.

Fish in their tank electrically heated   5
Nose without envy the glass wall: for them
Clerk, spy, nurse, killer, prince, the great and the defeated,
Move in a mute day-deam.

Bathed in this common source, you gape incurious
At what your active hours have willed—   10
Sleep-walking on that silver wall, the furious
Sick shapes and pregnant fancies of your world.

"Newsreel" Copyright 1940, 1941 by C. Day Lewis. Reprinted by permission of Harold Matson Company, Inc.

There is the mayor opening the oyster season:
A society wedding: the autumn hats look well:
An old crock's race, and a politician   15
In fishing-waders to prove that all is well.

Oh, look at the warplanes! Sreaming hysteric treble
In the long power-dive, like gannets they fall steep.
But what are they to trouble—   20
These silver shadows to trouble your watery, womb-deep sleep?

See the big guns, rising, groping, erected
To plant death in your world's soft womb,
Fire-bud, smoke-blossom, iron seed projected—
Are these exotics? They will grow nearer home:

Grow nearer home—and out of the dream-house stumbling   25
One night into a strangling air and the flung
Rags of children and thunder of stone niagaras tumbling,
You'll know you slept too long.

Louis MacNeice (1907–1963)

from AUTUMN JOURNAL, 1938

Conferences, adjournments, ultimatums,
    Flights in the air, castles in the air,
The autopsy of treaties, dynamite under the bridges,
    The end of *laissez faire.*
After the warm days the rain comes pimpling   5
    The paving stones with white
And with the rain the national conscience, creeping,
    Seeping through the night.
And in the sodden park on Sunday protest
    Meetings assemble not, as so often, now   10
Merely to advertise some patent panacea
    But simply to avow
The need to hold the ditch; a bare avowal
    That may perhaps imply
Death at the doors in a week but perhaps in the long run   15
    Exposure of the lie.
Think of a number, double it, treble it, square it,
    And sponge it out
And repeat *ad lib.* and mark the slate with crosses;
    There is no time to doubt   20

"Autumn Journal, 1938" from *The Collected Poems of Louis MacNeice*, edited by E. R. Dodds. Copyright © The Estate of Louis MacNeice 1966. Reprinted by permission of Oxford University Press, Inc., and Faber & Faber Ltd.

If the puzzle really has an answer. Hitler yells on the wireless,
    The night is damp and still
And I hear dull blows on wood outside my window;
    They are cutting down the trees on Primrose Hill.
The wood is white like the roast flesh of chicken,   25
    Each tree falling like a closing fan;
No more looking at the view from seats beneath the branches,
    Everything is going to plan;
They want the crest of this hill for anti-aircraft,
    The guns will take the view   30
And searchlights probe the heavens for bacilli
    With narrow wands of blue.
And the rain came on as I watched the territorials
    Sawing and chopping and pulling on ropes like a team
In a village tug-of-war; and I found my dog had vanished   35
    And thought 'This is the end of the old regime,'
But found the police had got her at St. John's Wood station
    And fetched her in the rain and went for a cup
Of coffee to an all-night shelter and heard a taxi-driver
    Say 'It turns me up   40
When I see them soldiers in lorries'—rumble of tumbrils
    Drums in the trees
Breaking the eardrums of the ravished dryads—
    Its turns me up; a coffee, please.
And as I go out I see a windshield-wiper   45
    In an empty car
Wiping away like mad and I feel astounded
    That things have gone so far.
And I come back here to my flat and wonder whether
    From now on I need take   50
The trouble to go out choosing stuff for curtains
    As I don't know anyone to make
Curtains quickly. Rather one should quickly
    Stop the cracks for gas or dig a trench
And take one's paltry measures against the coming   55
    Of the unknown *Uebermensch.*
But one—meaning I—is bored, am bored, the issue
    Involving principle but bound in fact
To squander principle in panic and self-deception—
    Accessories after the act,   60
So that all we foresee is rivers in spate spouting
    With drowning hands
And men like dead frogs floating till the rivers
    Lose themselves in the sands.
And we who have been brought up to think of 'Gallant Belgium'   65
    As so much blague
Are now preparing again to essay good through evil
    For the sake of Prague;
And must, we suppose, become uncritical, vindictive,
    And must, in order to beat   70
The enemy, model ourselves upon the enemy,
    A howling radio for our paraclete.

The night continues wet, the axe keeps falling,
  The hill grows bald and bleak
No longer one of the sights of London but maybe   75
  We shall have fireworks here by this day week.

W. H Auden (1907–1973)

IN MEMORY OF SIGMUND FREUD

When there are so many we shall have to mourn,
When grief has been made so public, and exposed
    To the critique of a whole epoch
    The frailty of our conscience and anguish,

Of whom shall we speak? For every day they die   5
Among us, those who were doing us some good,
    And knew it was never enough but
    Hoped to improve a little by living.

Such was this doctor: still at eighty he wished
To think of our life, from whose unruliness   10
    So many plausible young futures
    With threats or flattery ask obedience.

But his wish was denied him; he closed his eyes
Upon that last picture common to us all,
    Of problems like relatives standing   15
    Puzzled and jealous about our dying.

For about him at the very end were still
Those he had studied, the nervous and the nights,
    And shades that still waited to enter
    The bright circle of his recognition   20

Turned elsewhere with their disappointment as he
Was taken away from his old interest
    To go back to the earth in London,
    An important Jew who died in exile.

                                                 25
Only Hate was happy, hoping to augment
His practice now, and his shabby clientele
    Who think they can be cured by killing
    And covering the gardens with ashes.

They are still alive but in a world he changed
Simply by looking back with no false regrets;   30
    All that he did was to remember
    Like the old and be honest like children.

He wasn't clever at all: he merely told
The unhappy Present to recite the Past
    Like a poetry lesson till sooner   35
    Or later it faltered at the line where

Long ago the accusations had begun,
And suddenly knew by whom it had been judged,
    How rich life had been and how silly,
    And was life-forgiven and most humble.   40

Able to approach the Future as a friend
Without a wardrobe of excuses, without
    A set mask of rectitude or an
    Embarrassing over-familiar gesture.

No wonder the ancient cultures of conceit   45
In his technique of unsettlement foresaw
    The fall of princes, the collapse of
    Their lucrative patterns of frustration.

If he succeeded, why, the Generalised Life
Would become impossible, the monolith   50
    Of State be broken and prevented
    The co-operation of avengers.

Of course they called on God: but he went his way,
Down among the Lost People like Dante, down
    To the stinking fosse where the injured   55
    Lead the ugly life of the rejected.

And showed us what evil is: not as we thought
Deeds that must be punished, but our lack of faith,
    Or dishonest mood of denial,
    The concupiscence of the oppressor.   60

And if something of the autocratic pose,
The paternal strictness he distrusted, still
    Clung to his utterance and features,
    It was a protective imitation

For one who lived among enemies so long;   65
If often he was wrong and at times absurd,
    To us he is no more a person
    Now but a whole climate of opinion,

Under whom we conduct our differing lives:
Like weather he can only hinder or help,   70
    The proud can still be proud but find it
    A little harder, and the tyrant tries

To make him do but doesn't care for him much.
He quietly surrounds all our habits of growth;
    He extends, till the tired in even
    The remotest most miserable dunchy   75

Have felt the change in their bones and are cheered,
And the child unlucky in his little State,
    Some hearth where freedom is excluded,
    A hive whose honey is fear and worry,   80

Feels calmer now and somehow assured of escape;
While as they lie in the grass of our neglect,
    So many long-forgotten objects
    Revealed by his undiscouraged shining

Are returned to us and made precious again;   85
Games we had thought we must drop as we grew up,
    Little noises we dared not laugh at,
    Faces we made when no one was looking.

But he wishes us more than this: to be free
Is often to be lonely; he would unite   90
    The unequal moieties fractured
    By our own well-meaning sense of justice.

Would restore to the larger the wit and will
The smaller possesses but can only use
    For arid disputes, would give back to   95
    The son the mother's richness of feeling.

But he would have us remembered most of all
To be enthusiastic over the night
    Not only for the sense of wonder
    It alone has to offer, but also   100

Because it needs our love: for with sad eyes
Its delectable creatures look up and beg
    Us dumbly to ask them to follow;
    They are exiles who long for the future

That lies in our power. They too would rejoice   105
If allowed to serve enlightment like him,
    Even to bear our cry of "Judas,"
    As he did and all must bear who serve it.

One rational voice is dumb: over a grave
The household of Impulse mourns one dearly loved.   110
    Sad is Eros, builder of cities,
    And weeping anarchic Aphrodite.

HERMAN MELVILLE

Towards the end he sailed into an extraordinary mildness,
And anchored in his home and reached his wife
And rode within the harbour of her hand,
And went across each morning to an office
As though his occupation were another island.   5

Goodness existed: that was the new knowledge.
His terror had to blow itself quite out
To let him see it; but it was the gale had blown him
Past the Cape Horn of sensible success
Which cries: "This rock is Eden. Shipwreck here."   10

But deafened him with thunder and confused with lightning:
—The maniac hero hunting like a jewel
The rare ambiguous monster that had maimed his sex,
Hatred for hatred ending in a scream,
The unexplained survivor breaking off the nightmare—   15
All that was intricate and false; the truth was simple.

Evil is unspectacular and always human,
And shares our bed and eats at our own table,
And we are introduced to Goodness every day,
Even in drawing-rooms among a crowd of faults;   20
He has a name like Billy and is almost perfect
But wears a stammer like a decoration:
And every time they meet the same thing has to happen;
It is the Evil that is helpless like a lover
And has to pick a quarrel and succeeds,   25
And both are openly destroyed before our eyes.

For now he was awake and knew
No one is ever spared except in dreams;
But there was something else the nightmare had distorted—
Even the punishment was human and a form of love: 30
The howling storm had been his father's presence
And all the time he had been carried on his father's breast.

Who now had set him gently down and left him.
He stood upon the narrow balcony and listened:
And all the stars above him sang as in his childhood   35
"All, all is vanity," but it was not the same;
For now the words descended like the calm of mountains—
—Nathaniel had been shy because his love was selfish—
But now he cried in exultation and surrender
"The Godhead is broken like bread. We are the pieces."   40

And sat down at his desk and wrote a story.

VOLTAIRE AT FERNEY

Perfectly happy now, he looked at his estate.
An exile making watches glanced up as he passed
And went on working; where a hospital was rising fast,
A joiner touched his cap; an agent came to tell
Some of the trees he'd planted were progressing well.   5
The white alps glittered. It was summer. He was very great.

Far off in Paris where his enemies
Whispered that he was wicked, in an upright chair
A blind old woman longed for death and letters. He would write,
"Nothing is better than life." But was it? Yes, the fight   10
Against the false and the unfair
Was always worth it. So was gardening. Civilize.

Cajoling, scolding, screaming, cleverest of them all,
He'd had the other children in a holy war
Against the infamous grown-ups; and, like a child, been sly   15
And humble, when there was occasion for
The two-faced answer or the plain protective lie,
But, patient like a peasant, waited for their fall.

And never doubted, like D'Alembert, he would win:
Only Pascal was a great enemy, the rest   20
Were rats already poisoned; there was much, though, to be done,
And only himself to count upon.
Dear Diderot was dull but did his best;
Rousseau, he'd always known, would blubber and give in.

Night fell and made him think of women: Lust   25
Was one of the great teachers; Pascal was a fool.
How Emilie had loved astronomy and bed;
Pimpette had loved him too, like scandal; he was glad.
He'd done his share of weeping for Jerusalem: As a rule,
It was the pleasure-haters who became unjust.   30

Yet, like a sentinel, he could not sleep. The night was full of wrong,
Earthquakes and executions: Soon he would be dead,
And still all over Europe stood the horrible nurses
Itching to boil their children. Only his verses
Perhaps could stop them: He must go on working: Overhead,   35
The uncomplaining stars composed their lucid song.

WHO'S WHO

A shilling life will give you all the facts:
How Father beat him, how he ran away,
What were the struggle of his youth,
  what acts
Made him the greatest figure of his day:
Of how he fought, fished, hunted,
  worked all night,   5
Though giddy, climbed new mountains;
  named a sea:
Some of the last researchers even write
Love made him weep his pints like you
  and me.

With all his honours on, he sighed for
  one
Who, say astonished critics, lived at
  home;   10
Did little jobs about the house with skill
And nothing else; could whistle; would
  sit still
Or potter round the garden; answered
  some
Of his long marvellous letters but kept
  none.

MUSÉE DES BEAUX ARTS

About suffering they were never wrong,
The Old Masters: how well they understood
Its human position; how it takes place
While someone else is eating or opening a window or just walking dully along;
How, when the aged are reverently, passionately waiting   5
For the miraculous birth, there always must be
Children who did not specially want it to happen, skating
On a pond at the edge of the wood:
They never forgot
That even the dreadful martyrdom must run its course   10
Anyhow in a corner, some untidy spot
Where the dogs go on with their doggy life and the torturer's horse
Scratches its innocent behind on a tree.

In Brueghel's *Icarus,* for instance: how everything turns away
Quite leisurely from the disaster; the ploughman may   15
Have heard the splash, the forsaken cry,
But for him it was not an important failure; the sun shone
As it had to on the white legs disappearing into the green
Water; and the expensive delicate ship that must have seen
Something amazing, a boy falling out of the sky,   20
Had somewhere to get to and sailed calmly on.

THE UNKNOWN CITIZEN

(To JS/07/M/378
This Marble Monument
Is Erected by the State)

He was found by the Bureau of Statistics to be
One against whom there was no official complaint,
And all the reports on his conduct agree
That, in the modern sense of an old-fashioned word, he was a saint,
For in everything he did he served the Greater Community.   5
Except for the War till the day he retired
He worked in a factory and never got fired,
But satisfied his employers, Fudge Motors Inc.
Yet he wasn't a scab or odd in his views,
For his Union reports that he paid his dues,   10
(Our report on his Union shows it was sound)
And our Social Psychology workers found
That he was popular with his mates and liked a drink.
The Press are convinced that he bought a paper every day   15
And that his reactions to advertisements were normal in every way.
Policies taken out in his name prove that he was fully insured,
And his Health-card shows he was once in hospital but left it cured.
Both Producers Research and High-Grade Living declare
He was fully sensible to the advantages of the Instalment Plan
And had everything necessary to the Modern Man,   20
A phonograph, a radio, a car and a frigidaire.
Our researchers into Public Opinion are content
That he held the proper opinions for the time of year;
When there was peace, he was for peace; when there was war, he went.
He was married and added five children to the population,   25
Which our Eugenist says was the right number for a parent of his generation,
And our teachers report that he never interfered with their education.
Was he free? Was he happy? The question is absurd:
Had anything been wrong, we should certainly have heard.

Drawing by Chas. Addams; © 1975 The New Yorker Magazine, Inc.

Stephen Spender (1909–   )

THE EXPRESS

After the first powerful plain manifesto
The black statement of pistons, without more fuss
But gliding like a queen, she leaves the station.
Without bowing and with restrained unconcern
She passes the houses which humbly crowd outside,   5
The gasworks and at last the heavy page
Of death, printed by gravestones in the cemetery.
Beyond the town 'there lies the open country
Where, gathering speed, she acquires mystery,
The luminous self-possession of ships on ocean.   10
It is now she begins to sing—at first quite low
Then loud, and at last with a jazzy madness—
The song of her whistle screaming at curves,
Of deafening tunnels, brakes, innumerable bolts.
And always light, aerial, underneath   15
Goes the elate meter of her wheels.
Steaming through metal landscape on her lines
She plunges new eras of wild happiness
Where speed throws up strange shapes, broad curves
And parallels clean like the steel of guns.   20
At last, further than Edinburgh or Rome,
Beyond the crest of the world, she reaches night
Where only a low streamline brightness
Of phosphorus on the tossing hills is white.
Ah, like a comet through flames she moves entranced   25
Wrapt in her music no bird song, no, nor bough
Breaking with honey buds, shall ever equal.

ULTIMA RATIO REGUM

The guns spell money's ultimate reason
In letters of lead on the spring hillside.
But the boy lying dead under the olive trees
Was too young and too silly
To have been notable to their important eye.   5
He was a better target for a kiss.

When he lived, tall factory hooters never summoned him.
Nor did restaurant plate-glass doors revolve to wave him in.
His name never appeared in the papers.
The world maintained its traditional wall   10
Round the dead with their gold sunk deep as a well,
Whilst his-life, intangible as a Stock Exchange rumour, drifted outside.

O too lightly he threw down his cap
One day when the breeze threw petals from the trees.
The unflowering wall sprouted with guns,   15
Machine-gun anger quickly scythed the grasses;
Flags and leaves fell from hands and branches;
The tweed cap rotted in the nettles.

Consider his life which was valueless
In terms of employment, hotel ledgers, news files.   20
Consider. One bullet in ten thousand kills a man.
Ask. Was so much expenditure justified
On the death of one so young and so silly
Lying under the olive trees, O world, O death?

The Triumph of Wit

3
UNDER THE VOLCANO
1939-1976

INTRODUCTION

A year that is memorable is 1939. John Steinbeck published *The Grapes of Wrath* and thus dramatized the human tragedy of the Great Depression in America. The Daughters of the American Revolution refused to allow the great black singer Marian Anderson to give a concert in Washington's Constitution Hall, and though Miss Anderson sang, on Easter Day, on the steps of the Lincoln Memorial, the atonement was hollow. Dr. Sigmund Freud died, and with his death scientists began to question the validity of his techniques and ideas, while the mass media began to popularize Freud's gospel in newspapers, movies, and ultimately television. Science and technology continued to transform the world: the first regular weekly North Atlantic air service was inaugurated; the first public television program was broadcast at the opening ceremonies of the New York World's Fair; and a letter from Albert Einstein to Franklin Delano Roosevelt noted: "Some recent work by E. Fermi and L. Szilard . . . leads me to expect that the element uranium may be turned into a new •and important source of energy in the immediate future. . . . This new phenomenon would lead also to the construction of bombs."

In 1939 the Great Depression, in America and abroad, was coming to an end, but even so 17 percent of the American work force was unemployed (compared with 5 percent in 1960 and 9 percent in 1975). The average weekly wage for American production workers—those lucky enough to have a job—was $25; and of the 130 million American citizens in 1939, 126 million had incomes under $2,000. An advertisement in New York City for twelve female laboratory assistants, at an annual salary of $960.00, brought 239 early applicants willing to wait through a February night in hopes of an interview the next morning. The federal government announced its budget for 1939 as some 9 billion dollars (compared to a 1975 "austerity" budget of more than 12 billion dollars for New York City alone).

Abroad, Germany's quest for "lebensraum" met its first significant opposition in 1939: on September 1 the German Army marched into Poland and in so doing precipitated World War II. With its lightning, mechanized attacks—which gave the word *blitzkrieg* to the English language—the German army swiftly overran most of Western Europe. The allied troops were routed. Only England seemed to stand between Hitler and total victory, and the defeat of the French and English armies was not altered by the rhetoric of Winston Churchill's speech "Dunkirk," with its magnificent peroration:

> Even though large tracts of Europe and many old and famous states have fallen or may fall into the grip of the Gestapo and all the odious apparatus of Nazi rule, we shall not flag or fail. We shall go on to the end, we shall fight in France, we shall fight on the seas and oceans, we shall fight with growing confidence and growing strength in the air, we shall defend our island, whatever the cost may be, we shall fight on the beaches, we shall fight on the landing grounds, we shall fight in the fields and in the streets, we shall fight in the hills; we shall never surrender, and even if, which I do not for a moment believe, this island or a large part of it were subjugated and starving, then our Empire beyond the seas, armed and guarded by the British Fleet, would carry on the struggle, until, in God's good time, the New World, with all its power and might steps forth to the rescue and the liberation of the old.

From this point, the high-water mark of the Axis cause, Winston Churchill sustained English hope and courage through the Battle of Britain until the New World did begin to pour its men and resources into the struggle. The American entrance into the war, abetted by Hitler's fatal miscalculation when he marched on Russia, ultimately led to the defeat of Germany and Italy. The third Axis nation, Japan, surrendered only after atomic bombs devastated two of its major cities. Although much of the world rejoiced in the Allied victory, atomic bombs became synonymous with visions of doom, and since their use, the world has been poised between the hope of cooperation embodied in the United Nations Charter and the fear of universal destruction.

After 1945 the British accelerated their withdrawal from their former colonies and haltingly moved toward an economy regulated by socialist concepts of income redistribution but weakened economically by the escalating demands of labor—demands that by 1975 had led to an annual inflation rate of approximately 25 percent. As England's global influence shrank, that of America and Russia grew, a fact that occasionally led to "cold war" confrontation. One consequence was that the American suspicion of communism intensified in the forties and fifties. Demagogues like Senator Joseph McCarthy fabricated dark Communist conspiracies and maligned private citizens and public servants indiscriminately. In some ways the "cold war" reached its climax during the presidency of John F. Kennedy, when Russia installed missile bases on Cuban soil and America threatened to retaliate. For a brief period the world toppled on the brink of nuclear confrontation. The very prospect, however, acted as an deterrent. Since then the two great world powers, though politically unreconciled, have achieved a limited "détente," most especially in economic and cultural ventures.

The "cold war" was further complicated by the emergence of China as a significant world force, and by the Vietnam war, which tested American power. During the war, some men called American actions in Vietnam "the arrogance of power," whereas others stressed American idealism. There is little doubt. however, that the American moral fiber, as well as its economic capabilities, were weakened in the struggle. Though the "peace" negotiated by Secretary of State Henry Kissinger was greeted with ambivalent emotions strengthened by North Vietnam's total victory over the South after American withdrawal, one thing seems certain: America will not again enter lightly into such military adventures.

The tensions of the "cold war" eased during the seventies, but others remained. By 1975 six nations had exploded nuclear bombs and joined the proliferating nuclear club. In Ireland the political, social, and religious conflicts between Catholics and Protestants escalated into terror and violence, and British troops intervened to prevent civil war. Israel and the Arab states quarreled over the rights of the Palestinian refugees to a homeland and the territorial integrity of the Jewish state. Their contention erupted into intermitten political terrorism and then exploded into warfare. From partisan stances Russia and America attempted to mediate the apparently irreconcilable dispute. Under the impetus of the Yom Kippur war between Israel and the Arab states in 1973, a number of Arab members of the Organization of Petroleum Exporting Countries (OPEC) imposed an embargo on oil export to countries supporting Israel, and the success of that political weapon led the oil cartel later on to raise the price of oil drastically. The effectiveness of this action led other underdeveloped nations with essential natural resources such as copper and bauxite to aspire to similar cartels and profits.

During the sixties two other horrors, to some extent exacerbated by the Vietnam war, emerged clearly: drug abuse and increasing violence. What began as debate between proponents of legalized marijuana and those who demanded harsh penalties for its use was made academic by the widespread use of hard drugs: LSD, and heroin. Though not peculiar to America, the drug problem is most intense there. In both England and America, however, the tolerance among the young of the use of drugs has led many of their elders to be skeptical of youthful idealism and morality. Statistics support, if not justify, the skepticism: between 1961 and 1975 the rate for all serious crimes in America has more than doubled; almost half of all arrests are of teenagers and young adults; and 44 percent of those arrested for murder are under the age of twenty-five, while 75 percent of those arrested for street crimes, excluding murder, are under twenty-five. Whatever accounts for these crimes, the streets of many large American cities have become canyons of fear largely deserted after dark.

In America, and to a lesser extent in England, the population explosion following World War II has led to demographic changes and innumerable modifications of standards and values. In 1950 there were 24 million Americans between the ages of fourteen and twenty-four; by 1960 that number had increased to 27 million and by 1970 to 44 million. This increase radically altered the proportion of the middle-aged (those between twenty-five and sixty-four) to the adolescent and young adult (those between fourteen and twenty-four) from three-to-one to two-to-one, and undoubtedly this demographic change, in part at least, has lessened parental authority and intensified the difficulty in the social assimilation of the young. In aspiring to be themselves many of the young have adopted unconventional modes of dress —jeans, bangles, T-shirts, and long hair and headbands—that symbolize the difference in life-styles, as well as the generation gap, between the "establishment" and the "counterculture."

Perhaps the greatest social revolution during the period between 1939 and 1975 was the modification of many sexual conventions. The availability of "the pill" and the changes in legal and moral attitudes toward abortion have enabled the young to accept premarital and extramarital sex with a casualness foreign to their elders. In addition, many women have demanded equality with men in everything from employment opportunities to military obligations. The National Organization for Women (NOW) has challenged, both in the courts and on the streets, masculine prerogatives from bars to baseball. In 1975 the United Nations' World Conference on Women, held in Mexico City, served as an international forum from which women could voice their claims for equal opportunities, equal respect and equal justice. Despite its idealism, the Conference exposed human and political frailties: when the wife of Israeli Premier Yitzhak Rabin rose to address the Conference, the delegates from the Arabian states streamed from the room.

In recent years England and America have been racked by racial conflict. Although in both countries laws ostensibly guarantee all races the same civil rights, it has been difficult to translate that legality into reality. Ironically, the murder of the Reverend Martin Luther King, Jr., whose entire life was a preachment against violence, set off in 1968 an orgy of looting and rioting in American cities, and in the nation's capital city, where the disorder was worst, federal troops patrolled the gates of the White House.

For some people, violation of the law has become rationalized into a mode of political protest. The Symbionese Liberation Army justified itself on "political" grounds when it kidnapped Patricia Hearst and forced her parents to provide more than a million dollars of food for the poor of California. The militancy of "activists" has reached all the way from college to prison. In the Attica Correctional Facility it produced violent confrontations between guards (mostly white) and inmates (mostly black). There is no clear resolution of racial tensions in sight. As the economic problems of America intensify, so does this agonizing struggle.

Finally, for many conservative Americans the seventies was a traumatic period, not only because of the humiliation of Vietnam and Cambodia but also because of the ineptness, pettiness, corruption, and immorality at the heart of a federal government whose leaders, from the Attorney General to the Vice-President to the President himself, had ironically proclaimed their belief not only in probity but also in law and order. The peculations that drove one Vice-President from office, and the hyprocrisy and mendacity that brought a President to resign under fear of impeachment, left many Americans disillusioned and enraged, wondering in what they could place their faith. In the Federal Bureau of Investigation—whose chief, J. Edgar Hoover, was rumored to have regaled American presidents with pornography? In the Central Intelligence Agency—with the rumors that it, with or without presidential knowledge and consent, might have plotted the assassination of foreign leaders such as Fidel Castro? In what? As the latter quarter of the twentieth century began, with the stock market uncertain and only rising taxes sure, good bourgeois Americans could hardly be censured for feeling, as that staunch conservative

William Butler Yeats had once put it, "Things fall apart; the centre cannot hold; mere anarchy is loosed upon the world . . ."

Much English and American literature after 1939 was preoccupied with war and survival. Edith Sitwell and Richard Eberhart responded to the horrors of aerial bombardment and atomic sunrises. In Wales, Dylan Thomas composed his poignant elegy refusing to mourn the fiery death of a London child. War seared the brains of the young and sensitive: the British poet Ted Hughes and his American wife Sylvia Plath saw the world as they do—full of savagery in nature and animalism in man, with violence everywhere—in part because of the horror they knew in youth.

In England the better poets after World War II (Thomas, Betjeman, Larkin) used conventional forms in their art, though Thomas' work seems more impassioned than does the wry, intellectual poetry of Betjeman and Larkin. In America the struggle between the academic poets and the poets of the streets—the combat between what Robert Lowell has called "cooked" verse and "raw" verse—has gained critical attention for the former and large sales and great notoriety for the latter. The language, for instance, of Ginsberg's poem "Howl" brought indignant outcries at police precincts and academic teas alike. Other modern poets belong to what M. L. Rosenthal has called the "confessional" school (Plath, Roethke, Sexton). A number (Hall, Simpson, Wright) whose poetry is more "cooked" than that of the "Beat" poets have won by simplicity, directness, and social convictions a considerable audience.

Robert Hayden and Gwendolyn Brooks, black poets and mature artists, have consistently placed their art above revolutionary rhetoric and adolescent vulgarities. Other black artists have used their anger effectively in their work. The depths and width of American black rage have been revealed as fully in the explosion of black poetry—by such writers as Raymond R. Patterson, LeRoi Jones, Clarence Major, and Nikki Giovanni—as in the riots of Watts, Detroit, and Washington.

In fiction the spiritual malaise of modern times has perturbed innumerable writers. More and more Americans, and Englishmen too, have questioned not only suburban, bourgeois values but also national mores. The motif of helplessness has obsessed many modern writers. We are all victims of the bingo game, Ralph Ellison implies in "The King of the Bingo Game," and even when we win, we lose. Yet the modern writer's quest for identity, purpose, and meaning in life remains. Metaphorically, John Cheever suggests this search in "The Swimmer" by his image of a man swimming through the pools of suburbia, and through his life as well, while Donald Barthelme in "Me and Miss Mandible" sends a thirty-five-year old man back to elementary school to learn the social lessons of conformity and hypocrisy he needs for survival. Whatever the image, the vision has less of hope than of despair. Even a religious writer like Flannery O'Connor emphasizes the mundane reality of the lack of faith in the modern world. The superficial, atheistic, intellectual Hulga, O'Connor insists, is a reality of our time.

In America the literature of ethnic minorities since World War II has become increasingly significant, and a number of ethnic writers have produced essays and fiction of the higher order. In "Back to Bachimba" Enrique Hank López explores the dilemma of the dangling man, between two cultures and never totally comfortable in either one, so that "Though my entire upbringing and education took place in the United States, I have never felt completely American, and when I am in Mexico, I sometimes feel like a displaced gringo with a curiously Mexican name. . . ." Similarly, James Alan McPherson, in his story "Of Cabbages and Kings," explores the tension in black men between brotherhood and separateness, between the irrational and the rational in man.

Modern fiction often uses symbolic and allegorical implications and mysterious, dreamlike, surrealistic overtones. "The Swimmer" and "Me and Miss Mandible" go beyond the natural world and into the inward truth of the human heart. In her story "Where Are You Going, Where Have You Been?" Joyce Carol Oates fuses the conscious and subconscious knowledge of an insecure, adolescent girl into her weird initiation into the meaning of evil. In a real world where helplessness and fear are dominant emotions, the story reflects one vision of the nightmare of life today. Yet another is Renata Adler's experimental story "Brownstone," with its iteration and reiteration of the isolated and disconnected existences of men and women living out their lives of quiet desperation in a New York City apartment.

Like the fiction and poetry, the drama since World War II echoes the despair and emptiness of contemporary life. Tennessee William's first important work was *The Glass Menagerie*, a "memory" play that dramatizes with wit and pathos the contrast between the dreams of the characters and the Darwinian fact that the weak perish and the strong survive. Dominating the play are the emotions of betrayal and guilt—most especially dramatized at the end of the play as the fragile Laura's "candles" die out and leave the stage in darkness—but the play's allusions to violent conquest and its antireligious imagery extend the betrayal and the guilt into a universe "lit by lightning" that goes far beyond the dreary tenement in which the Wing-fields exist.

Remarkably similar in concept, though not in treatment, to *The Glass Menagerie* is Jules Feiffer's *Little Murders*. In capturing the black humor of his world, however, Feiffer deserts reality entirely. By his dramatization of an il-logical and absurd universe in which violence is the norm, and psychopathic introversion, numbness, and indifference are the only defenses, he manifests, with both wit and depth, what such drama-tists of the absurd as Samuel Beckett and Eugene Ionesco had to teach the Amer-ican theater.

EXPOSITION AND ARGUMENT

E. B. White (1899–   )

THE SHAPE OF THE U.N.

Turtle Bay, December 1, 1956

My most distinguished neighbor in Turtle Bay, as well as my most peculiar one, is the U.N., over on the East River. Its fame has soared in the past month, on the wings of its spectacular deeds, and its peculiarities have become more and more apparent. Furthermore, the peculiarities have taken on an added importance, because of President Eisenhower's determination to make United States foreign policy jibe with the U.N. Charter. In many respects, I would feel easier if he would just make it jibe with the Classified Telephone Directory, which is clear and pithy.

The Charter was a very difficult document to draft and get accepted. The nations were still at war and the founding fathers were doubtful about whether a world organization could be made to work at all, so they inserted a clause or two to cover themselves in case it didn't. Every member went in with his fingers crossed, and the Charter reflects this. It derives a little from the Ten Commandments, a little from the Covenant of the League of Nations, and a little from the fine print on a bill of lading. It is high in purpose, low in calories. Portions of it are sheer double-talk and, as a result, support double-dealing, but membership in a league is an exercise in double-dealing anyway, because the stern fact is that each sovereign nation has one foot in, one foot out. When the United States, for example, found itself up to its neck in the Middle East dilemma, it subscribed to the Charter's pledge to suppress aggression in the common interest; it also issued an order to the commander of the 6th Fleet: "Take no guff from anyone!" You won't find such words in the Charter, but they are implicit in the Charter, and that is one of its peculiarities.

In shape the U.N. is like one of the very early flying machines—a breathtaking sight as it takes to the air, but full of bugs. It is obviously in the experimental stage, which is natural. Since many readers have probably never examined the Charter, I will give a quick rundown, covering merely the Preamble and Chapter One, where the gist of the political structure is to be found.

The Preamble awards honorable mention to the following: human rights, equal rights, justice, respect for treaties (the Charter itself is a treaty, so it is just whistling to keep up its courage here), tolerance, peace, neighborliness, economic and social advancement. The Preamble is *against*: war, and the use of armed force except in the common interest.

Chapter One deals with (1) Purposes, (2) Principles. The *purposes* are, in summarized form: to maintain peace; to suppress aggression; to develop friendly relations among nations on the principle of equal rights and self-determination (which I presume includes cannibalism); to cooperate; to harmonize actions of nations. The *principles* are: sovereign equality; members shall fulfill obligations in good faith; settle disputes by peaceful means; refrain from the threat or use of force against the territorial integrity or political independence of any state; cooperate; and never, never intervene in matters which are essentially within the domestic jurisdiction of any state.

As you can see, the thing has bugs. There are some truly comical ones, like Chapter 1, Article 2, Paragraph 5, which, if I interpret it correct, commands a member to help deliver a public whipping to himself. But I shall not dwell on the funny ones. Let us just stare for a few moments at two of the more serious bugs.

One: In a fluid world, the Charter affirms the *status quo*. By its use of the word "aggression" and by other devices it makes the *status quo* the test of proper international conduct.

Two: Aimed at building a moral community, of peace, order, and justice, the Charter fails to lay down rules of conduct as a condition of membership. Any nation can enjoy the sanctuary of the Charter while violating its spirit and letter. A member, for example, is not required to allow the organization to examine its internal activities. Mr. Shepilov can come to Turtle Bay, but can Mr. Hammarskjöld go to Budapest? The world waits to see. Even if he makes it he will arrive awfully late.

Despite its faults, the U.N. has just emerged from a great month in world history, and emerged all in one piece. It pulled England and France out of a shooting war and sent the constabulary to replace them in Egypt. It failed in Hungary, but in the General Assembly the Soviet Union took a rhetorical shellacking that really counted. The U.N. is our most useful international device, but it is built on old-fashioned ideas. The Charter is an extremely tricky treaty. Its trickiness is dangerous to the world because, for one thing, it leads idealistic nations like ours into situations that suddenly become sticky and queer. This very thing happened when, in order to "condemn aggression" in the Middle East, in conformity with our Charter obligations, we deserted England and France and took up with the dictator of the Arab world and his associate the Soviet Union.

Some people, perhaps most people, think words are not really important, but I am a word man and I attach the very highest importance to words. I even think it was dishonest to call the world organization the "United Nations," when everybody knew the name was a euphemism. Why start on a note of phonyness, or wistfulness? The newspapers, with their sloppy proofreading, sometimes call the world organization the United Notions, sometimes the Untied Nations. Neither of these typos would make a serviceable title, but curiously enough, both are pat. Dr. Luns, of the Netherlands, recently described the U.N. Charter as "the expression of an attitude of mind." He said some countries used it merely as a juke box—they put in their nickel and the box would light up and play. That is about it. The Charter is an accommodating box and can produce a remarkable variety of tunes.

When Hungary erupted, the world was shocked beyond measure at what was taking place. But under the Charter of the United Nations the Hungarian government was in a position to put up just as noisy an argument as the oppressed people who were in rebellion. "Nothing contained in the present Charter shall authorize the United Nations to intervene in matters which are essentially within the domestic jurisdiction of any state." (Chapter I, Article 2, Paragraph 7). And when the U.N. wanted to send observers in, it received a polite no. This is palpably ridiculous, and it boils down to a deficiency in the Charter, a deficiency that is in the nature of an eleven-year-old appeasement. The Charter says that a member shall encourage "respect for human rights." That is laudable but fluffy. One way a Charter can advance human rights is to insist that the rights themselves (such as they are) remain visible to the naked eye, remain open to inspection. One of the preconditions of membership in the United Nations should be that the member himself not shut his door in the face of the Club. If the member won't agree to that, let him look elsewhere, join some other club.

Many will argue that if you are dealing with Iron Curtain countries, you have to take them on their own terms or you don't get them at all. That may be true. But who agreed to that amount of appeasement in the first place? And were they right? The appeasement was agreed to eleven years ago by charter writers who were trying to put together a world organization while a world war was still in progress. Their eye was not always on the ball, and they were looking back more than ahead. They were playing with century-old ideas: nonaggression (which is undefinable), self-determination (which includes the determination to send people to the salt mines), sovereign equality (which means that all nations are equal in the sight of God but the big ones are equal in the Secur-

ity Council). The Charter bravely tries to keep these threadbare ideas alive, but they will not stay alive in the modern world of hydrogen and horror, and unless the Charter is brought up to date, it may fail us.

Much has happened in eleven years. Almost everything that has happened indicates that the United Nations should never have admitted the Communist nations on *their* terms; that is, freedom to operate behind a wall. If nations are to cooperate, the first condition must be that they have social and political intercourse. The Soviet Union held out for cooperation without intercourse, which is a contradiction in terms and which is as unworkable for nations as for spouses. A marriage can be annulled on the ground of denial of intercourse. A world organization can blow up on account of it.

The subtlest joker in the Charter is the word "aggression." There are other jokers, but none so far-reaching. When the United States was confronted with the Middle East crisis, it was surprised and bewildered to discover itself backing Nasser and Russia against France and England. One reason for this queer turn of events was that Britain and France had "aggressed," and therefore had violated the Charter of the United Nations. Actually, our government did not take its stand solely, or even principally, on the basis of its U.N. membership, but it did use its U.N. membership to justify its decision and lend it a high moral tone.

The word "aggression" pops up right at the very beginning of the Charter: Chapter I, Article 1, Paragraph 1. Aggression is the keystone of the Charter. It is what every member is pledged to suppress. It is also what nobody has been able to define. In 1945, the founding fathers agreed among themselves that it would be unwise to include a definition of aggression in the Charter, on the score that somebody would surely find a loophole in it. But in 1954 a special U.N. committee was appointed to see if it could arrive at a definition of aggression. The committee was called the United Nations Special Committee on the Question of Defining Aggression. It huffed and it puffed, but it did not come up with a definition, and around the first of last month it adjourned. So one of the great peculiarities of the Charter is that all nations are pledged to oppose what no nation is willing to have defined. I think it can fairly be said that the one subject the seventy-nine members of the United Nations are in silent agreement on is aggression: they are agreed that each nation shall reserve the right to its own interpretation, when the time comes.

This isn't surprising. To define aggression, it is necessary to get into the realm of right and wrong, and the Charter of the United Nations studiously avoids this delicate area. It is also necessary to go back a way. Webster says of aggression, "A first or unprovoked attack." And that, you see, raises the old, old question of which came first, the hen or the egg. What, we must ask, came first in the Middle East clash between Arab and Jew? You could go back two thousand years, if you wanted to. You could certainly go back beyond October 29, 1956, when the Israelis came streaming across the Sinai desert.

Not only has no member, in eleven years, accepted a definition of aggression, no member has admitted that it has committed an aggressive act, although many members have used arms to get their way and at least one member, the U.S.S.R., employs the threat of force as a continuing instrument of national policy. The Charter of the U.N. is a treaty signed by sovereign nations, and the effect of a treaty written around the concept of aggression is to equate the use of arms with

wrongdoing and to assume that the world is static, when, of course, that is not so—the world is fluid and (certainly at this point in history) riddled with revolutionary currents at work everywhere. The tendency of any document founded on the idea of non-aggression is to freeze the world in its present mold and command it to stand still.

The world has seen a lot happen lately; it hasn't been standing still. And you will get as many definitions of aggression as there are parties to the event. Ask the delegate of the Soviet Union what happened in Hungary and he will say, "Remnants of Fascist bands aggressed." And he will cite Chapter 1, Article 2, Paragraph 4: "All members shall refrain . . . from the threat or use of force against the territorial integrity or political independence of any state." Ask a citizen of Budapest what happened and he will say, "We couldn't take it any longer. We threw stones." And he will cite the Preamble on fundamental human rights and the dignity and worth of the human person. Under the Charter, it is possible to condemn both these aggressive acts—you just take your choice. Is the aggressor the man who throws stones at a tank; or is the aggressor the man who drives the tank into the angry crowd? The world was quick to form an opinion about this, but it got little help from the Charter. The Charter affirms the integrity of Hungary as a political entity, and officially designates both the Hungarian government and the Soviet government as "peace-loving." But that's not the way it looked to most of the world.

When the Israelis were asked what had happened, Eban replied, "The Israeli forces took security measures in the Sinai Peninsula in the exercise of Israel's inherent right of self-defense" (Chapter VII, Article 51). When the Arabs were asked what had happened, the heads of the Arab League issued a statement applauding Egypt's "glorious defense of the safety of her territories and sovereignty" (same chapter, same verse).

Neither England nor France has admitted to an aggression, although the two nations mounted an assault and carried it out—two permanent members of the Security Council shooting their way into Egypt before breakfast. It is, in fact, inconceivable that any nation will ever admit to having aggressed.

In the *Herald Tribune* the other morning, Walter Lippmann wrote, "In the past few days, the U.N. has been pushed into a position where its main function seems to be that of restoring conditions as they were before the explosion." That is certainly true, and one reason for it is that the Charter condemns aggression, sight unseen, and then turns over to the forum the task of studying the events leading up to the tragedy and the atmosphere in which it occurred. To condemn aggression is to decide *in advance of an event* the merits of the dispute. Since this is absurd, the subject of aggression should not be made part of a charter. The business of a charter is not to decide arguments in advance, it is to diagram the conditions under which it may be possible, with luck, to settle the argument when it arises. Surely one of those conditions is the right to observe at close hand.

Another peculiarity of the U.N. is its police. These are now famous, and rightly so. A couple of weeks ago, ninety-five Danish and Norwegian riflemen, wearing emergency blue, dropped out of the sky to keep the peace of the world. They were the advance unit of the United Nations Emergency Force. The men were reported looking "tired," and I should think they might. One editorial writer described them as "symbolic soldiers";

the label is enough in itself to tire a man. The *Times* correspondent in Abu Suweir, where the troops landed, described the policemen's task as "most delicate."

Their task is more than merely delicate; it is primeval. This force (it now numbers about two thousand) is the true dawn patrol, and these Scandinavian riflemen are dawn men. They are the police who are charged with enforcing the laws that do not yet exist. They are clothed with our universal good intentions, armed with the hopes and fears of all the years. They have been turned loose in a trouble spot with the instructions "Enforce the absence of law! Keep us all safe!" Behind them is the authority of the United Nations, all of whose members are "peace-loving" and some of whose members have just engaged in war. It is a confusing scene to a young policeman. It is confusing for people everywhere. One of the first things that happened on the arrival of UNEF was that General Burns, the commander, had to fly back to First Avenue to find out what the Chief of Police had in mind. Another thing that happened was that the Secretary General of the U.N. had to fly to Cairo to get permission from the Egyptian government to let the world be policed in its bailiwick.

It is confusing, but it is not hopeless. Police (so-called) have sometimes been known to antedate the laws that they enforce. It is again a case of the egg and the hen—law enforces preceding law itself, like the vigilantes of our frontier West.

The U.N. has from the very start stirred people's imaginations and hopes. There seems little doubt that the very existence of a world organization is a help. I read in the *Times* magazine section the other day a good analysis of the U.N. by Ambassador Henry Cabot Lodge, who praised it because it "mobilizes world opinion" and because it shows "midnight courage." All this is certainly true. The U.N. is the shaky shape of the world's desire for order. If it is to establish order, though, it will have to muster the right words as well as the midnight courage. The words of the Charter are soft and punky. The Charter makes "aggression" synonymous with "wrongdoing" but drops the matter there, as though everyone understood the nature of sin. Yet it would appear from recent events they are aggressing, and never admit they are. To simplify an idea this way is bad writing.

A league of sovereign nations—some of them much sovereigner than others—is not in a good position to keep order by disciplining a member in the middle of a fracas. Discipline can mean war itself, as we saw in Korea, and the U.N. is physically puny. But a league *is* in a position to do other things. One thing it can do is lay down conditions of membership. In its own house the U.N. has unlimited power and authority. Its by-laws should not appease anybody or make life easy for bad actors. The U.N. swings very little weight in Moscow or in Budapest, but it swings a lot of weight in Turtle Bay, and that's where it should start to bear down. Whether the U.N. could have been effective in Hungary is anybody's guess, but certainly its chances of operating effectively, for human rights and humankind, were diminished by the softness of the Charter and the eleven-year-old accommodation to the Communists, who from the very start showed that they intended to eat their forum and have it, too. Munich has nothing on San Francisco in this matter.

Ambassador Lodge, in his article, pointed out that the U.N., contrary to what a few Americans hope and a few Americans fear, is not a world government. He wrote, "As for the future, a world government which free men could accept is as far off as a worldwide common sense of justice—without which world government would be world tyranny."

True enough. And the world is a long way from a common sense of justice. But the way to cut down the distance is to get on the right track, use the right words. Our Bill of Rights doesn't praise free speech, it forbids Congress to make any law abridging it. The U.N. could profit from that kind of tight writing. The Charter sings the praises of the dignity of man, but what it lacks is a clause saying, "A member shall make no move abridging the right of the Secretary General to stop by for a drink at any hour of the day or night."

P.S. (May 1962). The Goa episode was a perfect demonstration of the pleasures and paradoxes of membership in a league of nations. When India, a peace-loving member, decided the time had come to tidy up its coastline, it took Goa from Portugal by force of arms, an operation that struck other members as in violation of the Charter (Chapter I, Article 2, Paragraph 4: "All Members shall refrain in their international relations from the threat or use of force against the territorial integrity or political independence of any State."). Mr. Nehru's explanation of the Goa adventure was that it was not an aggressive act, since it was "right"—an interesting new sidelight on the meaning of aggression. The Soviet Union, another peace-lover, came to India's defense; it said the seizure of Goa wasn't aggression because it was "inevitable," it was "historic." This left Western nations, including the United States, pointing to the simple words about not using arms. It also left them in bed with colonialism for a few moments, while India and Russia waved the anti-colonial flag and pretended they didn't smell gunsmoke.

Goa was "historic," all right. But everything that happens is historic, because everything that happens is a part of history. It is not unlikely that some similar episode, involving the use of guns by a lover of peace, will ignite the great fire of nuclear war. This may turn out to be so historic it won't even be remembered.

The United Nations has managed to survive for seventeen years. It is a more flexible organization than the old League—more accommodating, more ambitious, more daring. Under Dag Hammarskjöld it was sometimes breathtaking. Hammarskjöld was a sort of Paladin, roaming the world, doing good according to his lights, far, far from home. And behind it, it has a far stronger desire of people to cooperate for peace, a far greater sense of urgency. The U.N. was designed not to establish order but to prevent trouble and preserve peace. It is not, as some seem to believe, an embryo government; it is simply a pistol-packing trouble-shooter. Many groups, searching for an approach to world government, advocate "strengthening" the U.N., to make it a "limited world government," its function the control of arms; and, in a sense, this is now the avowed policy of the United States in its program for general and complete disarmament under a U.N. Peace Force. I think this is idle talk. Strengthening the U.N. would not turn it into a government. Short of knocking the whole thing apart and starting fresh, there would be, I think, no way to build the U.N. into a government, even if its members wanted that, and most of them don't.

Nevertheless, the U.N. is so useful, it should strive to strengthen itself and put its own house in better order, not in the hope of becoming a government but with the intention of improving its services, lessening its capacity to cause trouble, and promoting liberty. The Charter should be re-examined. The Charter is eloquent on the subject of human rights and fundamental freedoms, but it does not spell them out in the places where they would count, such as in Chapter II, where the question of membership is dealt with. Since 1945, the U.N. has almost doubled its membership, and the newly admitted states have been taken into the fold without presenting any credentials. They merely advertised themselves as "peace-loving" and were accepted as peace-loving by the others. Red China wants in, and the question of admitting China is as vexing as it is persistent. It would be a whole lot easier for the United States, for example, to make out a case against the admission of Red China if Chapter II offered any guidelines, but it doesn't.

Here are a few elementary matters that might well be considered for inclusion in the Charter. (1) A nation that jams the air shall not be eligible for membership. (2) A member of the U.N. that jams the air shall be expelled. (3) A nation that builds a wall to prevent people from leaving the country shall not be eligible for membership. (4) In the case of members whose press is run by the government, the privilege of using the forum shall carry with it the obligation to report fully the proceedings of the forum, in the home press. Failure to publish the proceedings revokes the privilege of the forum and is ground for suspension. (5) Member states shall grant the Secretary General and his aides free access to the country at all times.

To inject such democratic things into the Charter would require a two-thirds vote in the General Assembly. Moreover, even if an amendment that favored an open society over a closed society were to pass in the Assembly, it could be vetoed by any of the five permanent members of the Security Council. (Among its other defects, the Charter is virtually amendment-proof.)

The U.N. was, of course, not created to praise liberty; yet the lovers of liberty should occasionally try to write their love into the document. Amendments ought to be proposed from time to time, if only to place the proprietors of closed societies in the unwholesome and embarrassing position of having to stand up before the crowd and defend darkness. The U.N. should do more than try to preserve the peace. If it seriously hopes to save future generations from the scourge of war, it should come out in favor of light, in favor of openness, and get it into the Charter.

Loren C. Eiseley (1907–   )
THE BIRD AND THE MACHINE

I suppose their little bones have years ago been lost among the stones and winds of those high glacial pastures. I suppose their feathers blew eventually into the piles of tumbleweed beneath the straggling cattle fences and rotted there in the mountain snows, along with dead steers and all the other things that drift to an end in the corners of the wire. I do not quite know why I should be thinking of birds over the *New York Times* at breakfast, nor particularly of the birds of my youth half a continent away. It is a funny thing what the brain will do with memories and how it will treasure them and finally bring them into odd juxtapositions with other things, as though it wanted to make a design, or get some meaning out of them, whether you want it or not, or even see it.

It used to seem marvelous to me, but I read now that there are machines, that can do these things in a small way, machines that can crawl about like animals, and that it may not be long now until they do more things—maybe even make themselves—I saw that piece in the *Times* just now—and then they will, maybe—well, who knows—but you read about it more and more with no one making any protest, and already they can add better than we and reach up and hear things through the dark and finger the guns over the night sky.

This is the new world that I read about at breakfast. This is the world that confronts me in my biological books and journals, until there are times when I sit quietly in my chair and try to hear the little purr of the cogs in my head and the tubes flaring and dying as the messages go through them and the circuits snap shut or open. This is the great age, make no mistake about it; the robot has been born somewhat appropriately along with the atom bomb, and the brain they say now is just another type of more complicated feedback system. The engineers have its basic principles worked out; it's mechanical, you know; nothing to get superstitious about; and man can always improve on nature once he gets the idea. Well, he's got it all right and that's why, I guess, that I sit here in my chair, with the article crunched in my hand, remembering those two birds and that blue mountain sunlight. There is another magazine title on my desk that reads "Machines Are Getting Smarter Every Day." I don't deny it, but I'll stick with the birds. It's life I believe in, not machines.

Maybe you don't believe there is any difference. A skeleton is all joints and pulleys, I'll admit. And when man was in his simpler stages of machine building in the eighteenth century, he quickly saw the resemblances. "What," wrote Hobbes, "is the heart but a spring, and the nerves so many springs, and the joints but so many wheels, giving motion to the whole body?" Tinkering about in their shops it was inevitable in the end that men would see the world as a huge machine "subdivided into an infinite number of lesser machines."

The idea took on with a vengeance. Little automatons toured the country —dolls controlled by clockwork. Clocks described as little worlds were taken on tours by their designers. They were made up of moving figures, shifting scenes, and other remarkable devices. The life of the cell was unknown. Man, whether he was conceived as possessing a soul or not, moved and jerked about like these tiny puppets. A human being thought of himself in terms of his own tools and implements. He had been fashioned like the puppets he produced and was only a more clever model made by a great designer.

Then in the nineteenth century, the cell was discovered, and the single machine in its turn was found to be the product of millions of infinitesimal machines—the cells. Now, finally, the cell itself dissolves away into an abstract chemical machine—and that into some intangible, inexpressible flow of energy. The secret seems to lurk all about, the wheels get smaller and smaller, and they turn more rapidly, but when you try to seize it the life is gone—and so, it is popular to say, the life was never there in the first place. The wheels and the cogs are the secret and we can make them better in time —machines that will run faster and more accurately than real mice to cheese.

I have no doubt it can be done, though a mouse harvesting seeds on an autumn thistle is to me a fine sight and more complicated, I think, in his multiform activity, than a machine "mouse" running a maze. Also, I like to think of the possible shape of the future brooding in mice, just as it brooded once in a rather ordinary mousy insectivore who became a man. It leaves a nice fine indeterminate sense of wonder that even an electronic brain hasn't got, because you know perfectly well that if the electronic brain changes it will be because of something man has done to it. But what man will do to himself he doesn't really know. A certain scale of time and a ghostly intangible thing called change are ticking in him. Powers and potentialities like the oak in the seed, or a red and awful ruin. Either way, it's impressive; and the mouse has it, too—or those birds, I'll never forget those birds, though I learned the lesson of time first of all. I was young then and left alone in a great desert— part of an expedition that had scattered its men over several hundred miles in order to carry on research more effectively. I learned there that time is a series of planes existing superficially in the same universe. The tempo is a human illusion, a subjective clock ticking in our kind of protoplasm.

As the long months passed, I began to live on the slower planes and to observe more readily what passed for life there. I sauntered, I passed more and more slowly up and down the canyons in the dry baking heat of midsummer. I slumbered for long hours in the shade of huge brown boulders that had gathered in tilted companies out on the flats. I had forgotten the world of men and the world had forgotten me. Now and then I found a skull in the canyons and these justified my remaining there. I took a serene cold interest in these discoveries. I had come, like many a naturalist before me, to view life with a wary and subdued attention. I had grown to take pleasure in the divested bone.

I sat once on a high ridge that fell away before me into a waste of sand dunes. I sat through hours of a long afternoon. Finally glancing by my boot an indistinct configuration caught my eye. It was a coiled rattlesnake, a big one. How long he had sat with me I do not know. I had not frightened him. We were both locked in the sleep-walking tempo of the earlier world, baking in the same high air and sunshine. Perhaps he had been there when I came. He slept on as I left, his coils, so ill discerned by me, dissolving once more among the stones and gravel from which I had barely made him out.

Another time, I got on a higher ridge, among some tough little wind-warped pines half covered over with sand in a basin-like depression that caught everything carried by the air up to those heights. There were a few thin bones of birds, some cracked shells of indeterminable age, and the knotty fingers of pine roots bulged out of shape from their long and agonizing grasp upon the crevices of the rock. I lay under the pines in the sparse shade and went to sleep once more.

It grew cold finally, for autumn was in the air by then, and the few things that lived thereabouts were sinking down into an even chillier scale of time. In the moments between sleeping and waking I saw the roots about me and slowly, slowly, a foot in what seemed many centuries, I moved by sleep-stiffened hands over the scaling bark and lifted my numbed face after the vanishing sun. I was a great awkward thing of knots and aching limbs, trapped up there in some long

patient endurance that involved the necessity of putting living fingers into rock and by slow, aching expansion bursting those rocks asunder. I suppose, so thin and slow was the time of my pulse by then, that I might have stayed on to drift still deeper into the lower cadences of the frost, or the crystalline life that glisters pebbles or shines in a snow flake, or dreams in the meteoric iron between the worlds.

It was a dim descent but time was present in it. Somewhere far down in that scale the notion struck me that one might come the other way. Not many months thereafter, I joined some colleagues heading higher into a remote windy tableland where huge bones were reputed to protrude like boulders from the turf. I had drowsed with reptiles and moved with the century-long pulse of trees; now, lethargically, I was climbing back up some invisible ladder of quickening hours. There had been talk of birds in connection with my duties. Birds are intense, fast-living creatures—reptiles, I suppose one might say—that have escaped out of the heavy sleep of time, transformed fairy creatures dancing over sunlit meadows. It is a youthful fancy, no doubt, but because of something that happened up there among the escarpments of that range, it remains with me a life-long impression. I can never bear to see a bird imprisoned.

We came into that valley through the trailing mists of a spring night. It was a place that looked as though it might never have known the foot of man, but our scouts had been ahead of us and we knew all about the abandoned cabin of stone that lay far up on one hillside. It had been built in the land rush of the last century and then lost to the cattlemen again as the marginal soils failed to take to the plow.

There were spots like this all over that country. Lost graves marked by unlettered stones and old corroding rim-fire cartridge cases lying where somebody had made a stand among the boulders that rimmed the valley. They are all that remain of the range wars; the men are under the stones now. I could see our cavalcade winding in and out through the mist below us: torches, and lights reflected on collecting tins, and the far-off bumping of a loose dinosaur thigh bone in the bottom of a trailer. I stood on a rock a moment looking down and thinking what it cost in money and equipment to capture the past.

We had, in addition, instructions to lay hands on the present. The word had come through to get them alive, birds, reptiles, anything. A zoo somewhere abroad needed restocking. It was one of those reciprocal matters in which science involves itself. Maybe our museum needed a stray ostrich egg and this was the payoff. Anyhow, my job was to help capture some birds and that was why I was there before the trucks.

The cabin had not been occupied for years. We intended to clean it out and live in it, but there were holes in the roof and the birds had come in and were roosting in the rafters. You could depend on it in a place like this where everything blew away and even a bird needed some place out of the weather and away from coyotes. A cabin going back to nature in a wild place draws them till they come in, listening at the eaves, I imagine, pecking softly among the shingles till they find a hole and then suddenly the place is theirs and man is forgotten.

Sometimes of late years I find myself thinking the most beautiful sight in the world might be the birds taking over New York after the last man has run away to the hills. I will never live to see it, of course, but I know just how it will sound because I've lived up high and I know the sort of watch birds keep on us. I've listened to sparrows tapping tentatively on the tin of the air conditioners when they thought no one was listening, and I know how other birds test the vibrations that come up to them through the television aerials.

"Is he gone?" they ask, and the vibrations come up from below, "not yet, not yet."

Well, to come back, I got the door open softly and I had the spotlight all ready to turn on and blind whatever birds were there so they couldn't see to get out through the roof. I had a short piece of ladder to put against the far wall where there was a shelf on which I expected to make the biggest haul. I had all the information I needed just like any skilled assassin. I pushed the door open with the hinges only squeaking a little after the oil was put on them. A bird or so stirred—I could hear them—but nothing flew and there was a faint starshine through the holes in the roof.

I padded across the floor, got the ladder up, and the light ready, and slithered up the ladder till my head and arms were over the shelf. Everything was dark as pitch except for the starlight at a little place back of the shelf near the eaves. With the light to blind them, they'd never make it. I had them. I reached my arm carefully over in order to be ready to seize whatever was there and I put the flash on the edge of the shelf where it would stand by itself when I turned it on. That way I'd be able to use both hands.

Everything worked perfectly except for one detail—I didn't know what kind of birds were there. I never thought about it all and it wouldn't have mattered if I had. My orders were to get something interesting. I snapped on the flash and sure enough there was a great beating and feathers flying, but instead of my having them, they, or rather he, had me. He had my hand, that is, and for a small hawk not much bigger than my fist he was doing all right. I heard him give one short metallic cry when the light went on and my hand descended on the bird beside him; after that he was busy with his claws and his beak was sunk in my thumb. In the struggle I knocked the lamp over on the shelf and his mate got her sight back and whisked neatly through the hole in the roof, and off among the stars outside. It all happened in fifteen seconds and you might think I would have fallen down the ladder, but no, I had a professional assassin's reputation to keep up and the bird, of course, made the mistake of thinking the hand was the enemy and not the eyes behind it. He chewed my thumb up pretty effectively and lacerated my hand with his claws, but in the end I got him, having two hands to work with.

He was a sparrow hawk and a fine young male in the prime of life. I was sorry not to catch the pair of them, but as I dripped blood and folded his wings carefully, holding him by the back so he couldn't strike again, I had to admit the two of them might have been a little more than I could have handled under the circumstances. The little fellow had saved his mate by diverting me, and that was that. He was born to it, and made no outcry now, resting in my hand hopelessly, but peering toward me in the shadows behind the lamp with a fierce, almost indifferent glance. He neither gave nor expected mercy and something out of the air passed from him to me, stirring a faint embarrassment.

I quit looking into that eye and managed to get my huge carcass with its fist full of prey back down the ladder. I put the bird in a box too small to allow him to injure himself by struggle and walked out to welcome the arriving trucks. It had been a long day and camp was still to make in the darkness. In the morning that bird would be just another episode. He would go back with the bones in the truck to a small cage in a city where he would spend the rest of his life. And a good thing, too. I sucked my aching thumb and spat out some blood. An assassin has to get used to these things. I had a professional reputation to keep up.

In the morning with the change that comes on suddenly in that high country, the mist that had hovered below us in the valley was gone. The sky was a deep blue and one could see for miles over the high outcroppings of stone. I was up early and brought the box in which the little hawk was imprisoned out onto the grass where I was building a cage. A wind as cool as a mountain spring ran over the grass and stirred my hair. It was a fine day to be alive. I looked up and all around and at the hole in the cabin roof out of which the other little hawk had fled. There was no sign of her anywhere that I could see.

"Probably in the next county by now," I thought cynically, but before beginning work I decided I'd have a look at my last night's capture.

Secretively, I looked again all around the camp and up and down and opened the box. I got him right out in my hand with his wings folded properly and I was careful not to startle him. He lay limp in my grasp and I could feel his heart pound under the feathers but he only looked beyond me and up.

I saw him look that last look away beyond me into a sky so full of light that I could not follow his gaze. The little breeze flowed over me again, and nearby a mountain aspen shook all its tiny leaves. I suppose I must have had an idea about then of what I was going to do, but I never let it come up into consciousness. I just reached over and laid the hawk on the grass.

He lay there a long minute without hope, unmoving, his eyes still fixed on that blue vault above him. It must have been that he already was so far away in heart that he never felt the release from my hand. He never even stood. He just lay with his breast against the grass and my eye upon him.

In the next second after that long minute he was gone. Like a flicker of light, he had vanished with my eyes full on him, but without actually seeing even a premonitory wing beat. He was gone straight into that towering emptiness of light and crystal that my eyes could scarcely bear to penetrate. For another long moment there was silence. I could not see him. The light was too intense. Then from far up somewhere a cry came ringing down.

I was young then and had seen little of the world, but when I heard that cry my heart turned over. It was not the cry of the hawk I had captured; for, by shifting my position against the sun, I was now seeing further up. Straight out of the sun's eye, where she must have been soaring restlessly above us for untold hours, hurtled his mate. And from far up, ringing from peak to peak of the summits over us, came a cry of such unutterable and ecstatic joy that it sounds down across the years and tingles among the cups on my quiet breakfast table.

I saw them both now. He was rising fast to meet her. They met in a great soaring gyre that turned to a whirling circle and a dance of wings. Once more, just once, their two voices, joined in a harsh wild medley of question and response, struck and echoed against the pinnacles of the valley. Then they were gone forever some-

where into those upper regions beyond the eyes of men.

I am older now, and sleep less, and have seen most of what there is to see and am not very impressed any more, I suppose, by anything. "What Next in the Attributes of Machines?" my morning headline runs. "It Might be the Power to Reproduce Themselves."

I lay the paper down and across my mind a phrase floats insinuatingly: "It does not seem that there is anything in the construction, constituents, or behavior of the human being which it is essentially impossible for science to duplicate and synthesize. On the other hand . . ."

All over the city the cogs in the hard, bright mechanisms have begun to turn. Figures move through computers, names are spelled out, a thoughtful machine selects the fingerprints of a wanted criminal from an array of thousands. In the laboratory an electronic mouse runs swiftly through a maze toward the cheese it can neither taste nor enjoy. On the second run it does better than a living mouse.

"On the other hand . . ." Ah, my mind takes up, on the other hand the machine does not bleed, ache, hang for hours in the empty sky in a torment of hope to learn the fate of another machine, nor does it cry out with joy nor dance in the air with the fierce passion of a bird. Far off, over a distance greater than space, that remote cry from the heart of heaven makes a faint buzzing among my breakfast dishes and passes on and away.

Martin Luther King, Jr. (1929–1968)
LETTER FROM BIRMINGHAM JAIL

MARTIN LUTHER KING, JR.
Birmingham City Jail
April 16, 1963

Bishop C. C. J. CARPENTER
Bishop JOSEPH A. DURICK
Rabbi MILTON L. GRAFMAN
Bishop PAUL HARDIN
Bishop NOLAN B. HARMON
The Rev. GEORGE M. MURRAY
The Rev. EDWARD V. RAMAGE
The Rev. EARL STALLINGS

My dear Fellow Clergymen,

While confined here in the Birmingham City Jail, I came across your recent statement calling our present activities "unwise and untimely." Seldom, if ever, do I pause to answer criticism of my work and ideas. If I sought to answer all of the criticisms that cross my desk, my secretaries would be engaged in little else in the course of the day and I would have no time for constructive work. But since I feel that you are men of genuine good will and your criticisms are sincerely set forth, I would like to answer your statement in what I hope will be patient and reasonable terms.

I think I should give the reason for my being in Birmingham, since you have been influenced by the argument of "outsiders coming in." I have the honor of serving as president of the Southern Christian Leadership Conference, an organization operating in every Southern state with headquarters in Atlanta, Georgia. We have some eighty-five affiliate organizations all across the South—one being the Alabama Christian Movement for Human Rights. Whenever necessary and possible we share staff, educational, and financial resources with our affiliates. Several months ago our local affiliate here in Birmingham invited us to be on call to engage in a nonviolent direct action program if such were deemed necessary. We readily consented and when the hour came we lived up to our promises. So I am here, along with several members of my staff, because we were invited here. I am here because I have basic organizational ties here. Beyond this, I am in Birmingham because injustice is here. Just as the eighth century prophets left their little villages and carried their "thus saith the Lord" far beyond the boundaries of their home town, and just as the Apostle Paul left his little village of Tarsus and carried the gospel of Jesus Christ to practically every hamlet and city of the Graeco-Roman world, I too am compelled to carry the gospel of freedom beyond my particular home town. Like Paul, I must constantly respond to the Macedonian call for aid.

Moreover, I am cognizant of the interrelatedness of all communities and states. I cannot sit idly by in Atlanta and not be concerned about what happens in Birmingham. Injustice anywhere is a threat to justice everywhere. We are caught in an inescapable network of mutuality tied in a single garment of destiny. Whatever affects one directly affects all indirectly. Never again can we afford to live with the narrow, provincial "outside agitator" idea. Anyone who lives inside the United States can never be considered an outsider anywhere in this country.

You deplore the demonstrations that are presently taking place in Birmingham. But I am sorry that your statement did not express a similar concern for the conditions that brought the demonstrations into being. I am sure that each of you would want to go beyond the superficial social analyst who looks merely at effects, and does not grapple with underlying causes. I would not hesitate to say that it is unfortunate that so-called demonstrations are taking place in Birmingham at this time, but I would say in more emphatic terms that it is even more unfortunate that the white power structure of this city left the Negro community with no other alternative.

In any nonviolent campaign there are four basic steps: (1) collection of the facts to determine whether injustices are alive; (2) negotiation; (3) self-purification; and (4) direct action. We have gone through all of these steps in Birmingham. There can be no gainsaying of the fact that racial injustice engulfs this community. Birmingham is probably the most thoroughly segregated city in the United States. Its ugly record of police brutality is known in every section of this country. Its unjust treatment of Negroes in the courts is a notorious reality. There have been more unsolved bombings of Negro homes and churches in Birmingham than any city in this nation. These are the hard, brutal, and unbelievable facts. On the basis of these conditions Negro leaders sought to negotiate with the city fathers. But the political leaders consistently refused to engage in good faith negotiation.

Then came the opportunity last September to talk with some of the leaders of the economic community. In these negotiating sessions certain promises were made by the merchants —such as the promise to remove the humiliating racial signs from the stores. On the basis of these promises Rev. Shuttlesworth and the leaders of the Alabama Christian Movement for Human Rights agreed to call a moratorium on any type of demonstrations. As the weeks and months unfolded we realized that we were the victims of a broken promise. The signs remained. As in so many experiences of the past we were confronted with blasted hopes, and the dark shadow of a deep disappointment settled upon us. So we had no alternative except that of preparing for direct action, whereby we would present our very bodies as a means of laying our case before the conscience of the local and national community. We were not unmindful of the difficulties involved. So we decided to go through a process of self-purification. We started having workshops on nonviolence and repeatedly asked ourselves the questions, "Are you able to accept blows without retaliating?" "Are you able to endure the ordeals of jail?"

We decided to set our direct action program around the Easter season, realizing that with the exception of Christmas, this was the largest shopping period of the year. Knowing that a strong economic withdrawal program would be the by-product of direct action, we felt that this was the best time to bring pressure on the merchants for the needed changes. Then it occurred to us that the March election was ahead, and so we speedily decided to postpone action until after election day. When we discovered that Mr. Connor was in the run-off, we decided again to postpone action so that the demonstrations could not be used to cloud the issues.

At this time we agreed to begin our nonviolent witness the day after the run-off.

This reveals that we did not move irresponsibly into direct action. We too wanted to see Mr. Connor defeated; so we went through postponement after postponement to aid in this community need. After this we felt that direct action could be delayed no longer.

You may well ask, "Why direct action? Why sit-ins, marches, etc? Isn't negotiation a better path?" You are exactly right in your call for negotiation. Indeed, this is the purpose of direct action. Nonviolent direct action seeks to create such a crisis and establish such creative tension that a community that has constantly refused to negotiate is forced to confront the issue. It seeks so to dramatize the issue that it can no longer be ignored. I just referred to the creation of tension as a part of the work of the nonviolent resister. This may sound rather shocking. But I must confess that I am not afraid of the word tension. I have earnestly worked and preached against violent tension, but there is a type of constructive nonviolent tension that is necessary for growth. Just as Socrates felt that it was necessary to create a tension in the mind so that individuals could rise from the bondage of myths and half-truths to the unfettered realm of creative analysis and objective appraisal, we must see the need of having nonviolent gadflies to create the kind of tension in society that will help men rise from the dark depths of prejudice and racism to the majestic heights of understanding and brotherhood. So the purpose of the direct action is to create a situation so crisis-packed that it will inevitably open the door to negotiation. We, therefore, concur with you in your call for negotiation. Too long has our beloved Southland been bogged down in the tragic attempt to live in monologue rather than dialogue.

One of the basic points in your statement is that our acts are untimely. Some have asked, "Why didn't you give the new administration time to act?" The only answer that I can give to this inquiry is that the new administration must be prodded about as much as the outgoing one before it acts. We will be sadly mistaken if we feel that the election of Mr. Boutwell will bring the millennium to Birmingham. While Mr. Boutwell is much more articulate and gentle than Mr. Connor, they are both segregationists dedicated to the task of maintaining the status quo. The hope I see in Mr. Boutwell is that he will be reasonable enough to see the futility of massive resistance to desegregation. But he will not see this without pressure from the devotees of civil rights. My friends, I must say to you that we have not made a single gain in civil rights without determined legal and nonviolent pressure. History is the long and tragic story of the fact that privileged groups seldom give up their privileges voluntarily. Individuals may see the moral light and voluntarily give up their unjust posture; but as Reinhold Niebuhr has reminded us, groups are more immoral than individuals.

We know through painful experience that freedom is never voluntarily given by the oppressor; it must be demanded by the oppressed. Frankly I have never yet engaged in a direct action movement that was "well timed," according to the timetable of those who have not suffered unduly from the disease of segregation. For years now I have heard the word "Wait!" It rings in the ear of every Negro with a piercing familiarity. This "wait" has almost always meant "never." It has been a tranquilizing thalidomide, relieving the emotional stress for a moment, only to give birth to an ill-formed infant of frustration. We must come to see with the distinguished jurist of yesterday that "justice too long delayed is justice denied." We have waited for more than three hundred and forty years for our constitutional and God-given rights. The nations of Asia and Africa are moving with jet-like speed toward the goal of political independence, and we still creep at horse and buggy pace toward the gaining of a cup of coffee at a lunch counter.

I guess it is easy for those who have never felt the stinging darts of segregation to say wait. But when you have seen vicious mobs lynch your mothers and fathers at will and drown your sisters and brothers at whim; when you have seen hate filled policemen curse, kick, brutalize, and even kill your black brothers and sisters with impunity; when you see the vast majority of your twenty million Negro brothers smothering in an air-tight cage of poverty in the midst of an affluent society; when you suddenly find your tongue twisted and your speech stammering as you seek to explain to your six-year-old daughter why she can't go to the public amusement park that has just been advertised on television, and see tears welling up in her little eyes when she is told that Funtown is closed to colored children, and see the depressing clouds of inferiority begin to form in her little mental sky, and see her begin to distort her little personality by unconsciously developing a bitterness toward white people; when you have to concoct an answer for a five-year-old son asking in agonizing pathos: "Daddy, why do white people treat colored people so mean?"; when you take a cross country drive and find it necessary to sleep night after night in the uncomfortable corners of your automobile because no motel will accept you; when you are humiliated day in and day out by nagging signs reading "white" men and "colored"; when your first name becomes "nigger" and

your middle name becomes "boy" (however old you are) and your last name becomes "John," and when your wife and mother are never given the respected title "Mrs."; when you are harried by day and haunted by night by the fact that you are a Negro, living constantly a tip-toe stance never quite knowing what to expect next, and plagued with inner fears and outer resentments; when you are forever fighting a degenerating sense of "nobodiness";—then you will understand why we find it difficult to wait. There comes a time when the cup of endurance runs over, and men are no longer willing to be plunged into an abyss of injustice where they experience the bleakness of corroding despair. I hope, sirs, you can understand our legitimate and unavoidable impatience.

You express a great deal of anxiety over our willingness to break laws. This is certainly a legitimate concern. Since we so diligently urge people to obey the Supreme Court's decision of 1954 outlawing segregation in the public schools, it is rather strange and paradoxical to find us consciously breaking laws. One may well ask, "How can you advocate breaking some laws and obeying others?" The answer is found in the fact that there are two types of laws. There are *just* laws and there are *unjust* laws. I would be the first to advocate obeying just laws. One has not only a legal but moral responsibility to obey just laws. Conversely, one has a moral responsibility to disobey unjust laws. I would agree with Saint Augustine that "An unjust law is no law at all."

Now what is the difference between the two? How does one determine when a law is just or unjust? A just law is a man-made code that squares with the moral law or the law of God. An unjust law is a code that is out of harmony with the moral law. To put it in the terms of Saint Thomas Aquinas, an unjust law is a human law that is not rooted in eternal and natural law. Any law that uplifts human personality is just. Any law that degrades human personality is unjust. All segregation statues are unjust because segregation distorts the soul and damages the personality. It gives the segregator a false sense of superiority and the segregated a false sense of inferiority. To use the words of Martin Buber, the great Jewish philosopher, segregation substitutes an "I-it" relationship for the "I-thou" relationship, and ends up relegating persons to the status of things. So segregation is not only politically, economically, and sociologically unsound, but it is morally wrong and sinful. Paul Tillich has said that sin is separation. Isn't segregation an existential expression of man's tragic separation, an expression of his awful estrangement, his terrible sinfulness? So I can urge men to obey the 1954 decision of the Supreme Court because it is morally right, and I can urge them to disobey segregation ordinances because they are morally wrong.

Let us turn to a more concrete example of just and unjust laws. An unjust law is a code that a majority inflicts on a minority that is not binding on itself. This is *difference* made legal. On the other hand a just law is a code that a majority compels a minority to follow that is willing to follow itself. This is *sameness* made legal.

Let me give another explanation. An unjust law is a code inflicted upon a minority which that minority had no part in enacting or creating because they did not have the unhampered right to vote. Who can say the legislature of Alabama which set up the segregation laws was democratically elected? Throughout the state of Alabama all types of conniving methods are used to prevent Negroes from becoming registered voters and there are some counties without a single Negro registered to vote despite the fact that the Negro constitutes a majority of the population. Can any law set up in such a state be considered democratically structured?

These are just a few examples of unjust and just laws. There are some instances when a law is just on its face but unjust in its application. For instance, I was arrested Friday on a charge of parading without a permit. Now there is nothing wrong with an ordinance which requires a permit for a parade, but when the ordinance is used to preserve segregation and to deny citizens the First Amendment privilege of peaceful assembly and peaceful protest, then it becomes unjust.

I hope you can see the distinction I am trying to point out. In no sense do I advocate evading or defying the law as the rabid segregationist would do. This would lead to anarchy. One who breaks an unjust law must do it *openly, lovingly* (not hatefully as the white mothers did in New Orleans when they were seen on television screaming "nigger, nigger, nigger") and with a willingness to accept the penalty. I submit that an individual who breaks a law that conscience tells him is unjust, and willingly accepts the penalty by staying in jail to arouse the conscience of the community over its injustice, is in reality expressing the very highest respect for law.

Of course there is nothing new about this kind of civil disobedience. It was seen sublimely in the refusal of Shadrach, Meshach, and Abednego to obey the laws of Nebuchadnezzar because a higher moral law was involved. It was practiced superbly by the early Christians who were willing to face hungry lions and the excruciating pain of chopping blocks, before submitting to certain unjust laws of the Roman Empire. To a degree academic freedom is a reality today because Socrates practiced civil disobedience. We can never forget that everything Hitler did in Germany was "legal" and everything the Hungarian freedom fighters did in Hungary was "illegal." It was "illegal" to aid and comfort a Jew in Hitler's Germany. But I am sure that, if I had lived in Germany during that time, I would have aided and comforted my Jewish brothers even though it was illegal. If I lived in a communist country today where certain principles dear to the Christian faith are suppressed, I believe I would openly advocate disobeying these antireligious laws.

I must make two honest confessions to you, my Christian and Jewish brothers. First I must confess that over the last few years I have been gravely disappointed with the white moderate. I have almost reached the regrettable conclusion that the Negroes' great stumbling block in the stride toward freedom is not the White Citizens' "Counciler" or the Ku Klux Klanner, but the white moderate who is more devoted to "order" than to justice; who prefers a negative peace which is the absence of tension to a positive peace which is the presence of justice; who constantly says "I agree with you in the goal you seek, but I can't agree with your methods of direct action"; who paternalistically feels that he can set the time-table for another man's freedom; who lives by the myth of time and who constantly advises the Negro to wait until a "more convenient season." Shallow understanding from people of good will is more frustrating than absolute misunderstanding from people of ill will. Lukewarm acceptance is much more bewildering than outright rejection.

I had hoped that the white moderate would understand that law and order exist for the purpose of establishing justice, and that when they fail to do this they become the dangerously structured dams that block the flow of social progress. I had hoped that the white moderate would understand that the present tension in the South is merely a necessary phase of the transition from an obnoxious negative peace, where the Negro passively accepted his unjust plight, to a substance-filled positive peace, where all men will respect the dignity and worth of human personality. Actually, we who engage in non-violent direct action are not the creators of tension. We merely bring to the surface the hidden tension that is already alive. We bring it out in the open where it can be seen and dealt with. Like a boil that can never be cured as long as it is covered up but must be opened with all its pus-flowing ugliness to the natural medicines of air and light, injustice must likewise be exposed, with all of the tension its exposing creates, to the light of human conscience and the air of national opinion before it can be cured.

In your statement you asserted that our actions, even though peaceful, must be condemned because they precipitate violence. But can this assertion be logically made? Isn't this like condemning the robbed man because his possession of money precipitated the evil act of robbery? Isn't this like condemning Socrates because his unswerving commitment to truth and his philosophical delvings precipitated the misguided popular mind to make him drink the hemlock? Isn't this like condemning Jesus because His unique God-consciousness and never-ceasing devotion to His will precipitated the evil act of crucifixion? We must come to see, as federal courts have consistently affirmed, that it is immoral to urge an individual to withdraw his efforts to gain his basic constitutional rights because the quest precipitates violence. Society must protect the robbed and punish the robber.

I had also hoped that the white moderate would reject the myth of time. I received a letter this morning from a white brother in Texas which said: "All Christians know that the colored people will receive equal rights eventually, but is it possible that you are in too great of a religious hurry? It has taken Christianity almost 2000 years to accomplish what it has. The teachings of Christ take time to come to earth." All that is said here grows out of a tragic misconception of time. It is the strangely irrational notion that there is something in the very flow of time that will inevitably cure all ills. Actually time is neutral. It can be used either destructively or constructively. I am coming to feel that the people of ill will have to repent in this generation not merely for the vitriolic words and actions of the bad people, but for the appalling silence of the good people. We must come to see that human progress never rolls in on wheels of inevitability. It comes through the tireless efforts and persistent work of men willing to be co-workers with God, and without this hard work time itself becomes an ally of the forces of social stagnation.

We must use time creatively, and forever realize that the time is always ripe to do right. Now is the time to make real the promise of democracy, and transform our pending national elegy into a creative psalm of brotherhood. Now is the time to lift our national policy from the quicksand of racial injustice to the solid rock of human dignity.

You spoke of our activity in Birmingham as extreme. At first I was rather disappointed that fellow clergymen would see my nonviolent efforts as those of the extremist. I started thinking about the fact that I stand in the middle of two opposing forces in the Negro community. One is a force of complacency made up of Negroes who, as a result of long years of oppression, have been so completely drained of self-respect and a sense of "somebodiness" that they have adjusted to segregation, and of a few Negroes in the middle class who, because of a degree of academic and economic security, and because at points they profit by segregation, have unconsciously become insensitive to the problems of the masses. The other force is one of bitterness and hatred and comes perilously close to advocating violence. It is expressed in the various black nationalist groups that are springing up over the nation, the largest and best known being Elijah Muhammad's Muslim movement. This movement is nourished by the contemporary frustration over the continued existence of racial discrimination. It is made up of people who have absolutely repudiated Christianity, and who have concluded that the white man is an incurable "devil." I have tried to stand between these two forces saying that we need not follow the "do-nothingism" of the complacent or the hatred and despair of the black nationalist. There is the more excellent way of love and nonviolent protest. I'm grateful to God that, through the Negro church, the dimension of nonviolence entered our struggle. If this philosophy had not emerged I am convinced that by now many streets of the South would be flowing with floods of blood. And I am further convinced that if our white brothers dismiss us as "rabble rousers" and "outside agitators"—those of us who are working through the channels of nonviolent direct action—and refuse to support our nonviolent efforts, millions of Negroes, out of frustration and despair, will seek solace and security in black nationalist ideologies, a development that will lead inevitably to a frightening racial nightmare.

Oppressed people cannot remain oppressed forever. The urge for freedom will eventually come. This is what has happened to the American Negro. Something within has reminded him of his birthright of freedom; something without has reminded him that he can gain it. Consciously and unconsciously, he has been swept in by what the Germans call the *Zeitgeist,* and with his black brothers of Africa, and his brown and yellow brothers of Asia, South America, and the Caribbean, he is moving with a sense of cosmic urgency toward the promised land of racial justice. Recognizing this vital urge that has engulfed the Negro community, one should readily understand public demonstrations. The Negro has many pent-up resentments and latent frustrations. He has to get them out. So let him march sometime; let him have his prayer pilgrimages to the city hall; understand why he must have sit-ins and freedom rides. If his repressed emotions do not come out in these nonviolent ways, they will come out in ominous expressions of violence. This is not a threat; it is a fact of history. So I have not said to my people, "Get rid of your discontent." But I have tried to say that this normal and healthy discontent can be channeled through the creative outlet of nonviolent direct action. Now this approach is being dismissed as extremist. I must admit that I was initially disappointed in being so categorized.

But as I continued to think about the matter I gradually gained a bit of satisfaction from being considered an extremist. Was not Jesus an extremist in love? "Love your enemies, bless them that curse you, pray for them that despitefully use you." Was not Amos an extremist for justice—"Let justice roll down like waters and righteousness like a mighty stream." Was not Paul an extremist for the gospel of Jesus Christ—"I bear in my body the marks of the Lord Jesus." Was not Martin Luther an extremist—"Here I stand; I can do none other so help me God." Was not John Bunyan an extremist—"I will stay in jail to the end of my days before I make a butchery of my conscience." Was not Abraham Lincoln an extremist—"This nation cannot survive half slave and half

free." Was not Thomas Jefferson an extremist—"We hold these truths to be self evident, that all men are created equal." So the question is not whether we will be extremist but what kind of extremist will we be. Will we be extremists for hate or will we be extremists for love? Will we be extremists for the preservation of injustice—or will we be extremists for the cause of justice? In that dramatic scene on Calvary's hill three men were crucified. We must never forget that all three were crucified for the same crime—the crime of extremism. Two were extremists for immorality, and thus fell below their environment. The other, Jesus Christ, was an extremist for love, truth, and goodness, and thereby rose above His environment. So, after all, maybe the South, the nation, and the world are in dire need of creative extremists.

I had hoped that the white moderate would see this. Maybe I was too optimistic. Maybe I expected too much. I guess I should have realized that few members of a race that has oppressed another race can understand or appreciate the deep groans and passionate yearnings of those that have been oppressed, and still fewer have the vision to see that injustice must be rooted out by strong, persistent, and determined action. I am thankful, however, that some of our white brothers have grasped the meaning of this social revolution and committed themselves to it. They are still all too small in quantity, but they are big in quality. Some like Ralph McGill, Lillian Smith, Harry Golden, and James Dabbs have written about our struggle in eloquent, prophetic, and understanding terms. Others have marched with us down nameless streets of the South. They have languished in filthy, roach-infested jails, suffering the abuse and brutality of angry policemen who see them as "dirty nigger lovers." They, unlike so many of their moderate brothers and sisters, have recognized the urgency of the moment and sensed the need for powerful "action" antidotes to combat the disease of segregation.

Let me rush on to mention my other disappointment. I have been so greatly disappointed with the white Church and its leadership. Of course there are some notable exceptions. I am not unmindful of the fact that each of you has taken some significant stands on this issue. I commend you, Rev. Stallings, for your Christian stand on this past Sunday, in welcoming Negroes to your worship service on a non-segregated basis. I commend the Catholic leaders of this state for integrating Springhill College several years ago.

But despite these notable exceptions I must honestly reiterate that I have been disappointed with the Church. I do not say that as one of those negative critics who can always find something wrong with the Church. I say it as a minister of the gospel, who loves the Church; who was nurtured in its bosom; who has been sustained by its spiritual blessings and who will remain true to it as long as the cord of life shall lengthen.

I had the strange feeling when I was suddenly catapulted into the leadership of the bus protest in Montgomery several years ago that we would have the support of the white Church. I felt that the white ministers, priests, and rabbis of the South would be some of our strongest allies. Instead, some have been outright opponents, refusing to understand the freedom movement and misrepresenting its leaders; all too many others have been more cautious than courageous and have remained silent behind the anesthetizing security of stained glass windows.

In spite of my shattered dreams of the past, I came to Birmingham with the hope that the white religious leadership of this community would see the justice of our cause and, with deep moral concern, serve as the channel through which our just grievances could get to the power structure. I had hoped that each of you would understand. But again I have been disappointed.

I have heard numerous religious leaders of the South call upon their worshippers to comply with a desegregation decision because it is the law, but I have longed to hear white ministers say follow this decree because integration is morally right and the Negro is your brother. In the midst of blatant injustices inflicted upon the Negro, I have watched white churches stand on the sideline and merely mouth pious irrelevancies and sanctimonious trivialities. In the midst of a mighty struggle to rid our nation of racial and economic injustice, I have heard so many ministers say, "Those are social issues with which the Gospel has no real concern," and I have watched so many churches commit themselves to a completely otherworldly religion which made a strange distinction between body and soul, the sacred and the secular.

So here we are moving toward the exit of the twentieth century with a religious community largely adjusted to the status quo, standing as a tail light behind other community agencies rather than a headlight leading men to higher levels of justice.

I have travelled the length and breadth of Alabama, Mississippi, and all the other Southern states. On sweltering summer days and crisp autumn mornings I have looked at her beautiful churches with their spires pointing heavenward. I have beheld the impressive outlay of her massive religious education buildings. Over and over again I have found myself asking: "Who worships here? Who worships here? Who is their God? Where were their voices when the lips of Governor Barnett dripped with words of interposition and nullification? There were they when Governor Wallace gave the clarion call for defiance and hatred? Where were their voices of support when tired, bruised, and weary Negro men and women decided to rise from the dark dungeons of complacency to the bright hills of creative protest?"

Yes, these questions are still in my mind. In deep disappointment, I have wept over the laxity of the Church. But be assured that my tears have been tears of love. There can be no deep disappointment where there is not deep love. Yes, I love the Church; I love her sacred walls. How could I do otherwise? I am in the rather unique position of being the son, the grandson, and the great grandson of preachers. Yes, I see the Church as the body of Christ. But, oh! How we have blemished and scarred the body through social neglect and fear of being nonconformist.

There was a time when the Church was very powerful. It was during that period when the early Christians rejoiced when they were deemed worthy to suffer for what they believed. In those days the Church was not merely a thermometer that recorded the ideas and principles of popular opinion; it was a thermostat that transformed the mores of society. Wherever the early Christians entered a town the power structure got disturbed and immediately sought to convict them for being "disturbers of the peace" and "outside agitators." But they went on with the conviction that they were a "colony of heaven" and had to obey God rather than man. They were small in number but big in commitment. They were too God-intoxicated to be "astronomically intimidated." They brought an end to such ancient evils as infanticide and gladiatorial contest.

Things are different now. The contemporary Church is so often a weak, ineffectual voice with an uncertain sound. It is so often the arch-supporter of the status quo. Far from being disturbed by the presence of the Church, the power structure of the average community is consoled by the Church's silent and often vocal sanction of things as they are.

But the judgment of God is upon the Church as never before. If the Church of today does not recapture the sacrificial spirit of the early Church, it will lose its authentic ring, forfeit the loyalty of millions, and be dismissed as an irrelevant social club with no meaning for the twentieth century. I am meeting young people every day whose disappointment with the Church has risen to outright disgust.

Maybe again I have been too optimistic. Is organized religion too inextricably bound to the status quo to save our nation and the world? Maybe I must turn my faith to the inner spiritual Church, the church within the Church, as the true *ecclesia* and the hope of the world. But again I am thankful to God that some noble souls from the ranks of organized religion have broken loose from the paralyzing chains of conformity and joined us as active partners in the struggle for freedom. They have left their secure congregations and walked the streets of Albany, Georgia, with us. They have gone through the highways of the South on torturous rides for freedom. Yes, they have gone to jail with us. Some have been kicked out of their churches and lost the support of their bishops and fellow ministers. But they have gone with the faith that right defeated is stronger than evil triumphant. These men have been the leaven in the lump of the race. Their witness has been the spiritual salt that has preserved the true meaning of the Gospel in these troubled times. They have carved a tunnel of hope through the dark mountain of disappointment.

I hope the Church as a whole will meet the challenge of this decisive hour. But even if the Church does not come to the aid of justice, I have no despair about the future. I have no fear about the outcome of our struggle in Birmingham, even if our motives are presently misunderstood. We will reach the goal of freedom in Birmingham and all over the nation, because the goal of America is freedom. Abused and scorned though we may be, our destiny is tied up with the destiny of America. Before the pilgrims landed at Plymouth, we were here. Before the pen of Jefferson etched across the pages of history the majestic words of the Declaration of Independence, we were here. For more than two centuries our foreparents labored in this country without wages; they made cotton "king"; and they built the homes of their masters in the midst of brutal injustice and shameful humiliation—and yet out of a bottomless vitality they continued to thrive and develop. If the inexpressible cruelties of slavery could not stop us, the opposition we now face will surely fail. We will win our freedom because the sacred heritage of our nation and the eternal will of God are embodied in our echoing demands.

I must close now. But before closing I am impelled to mention one other point in your statement that troubled me profoundly. You warmly commended the Birmingham police force for keeping "order" and "preventing violence." I don't believe you would have so warmly commended the police force if you had seen its angry violent dogs literally biting six unarmed, nonviolent Negroes. I don't believe you would so quickly commend the policemen if you would observe their ugly and inhuman treatment of Negroes here in the city jail;

if you would watch them push and curse old Negro women and young Negro girls; if you would see them slap and kick old Negro men and young Negro boys; if you will observe them, as they did on two occasions, refuse to give us food because we wanted to sing our grace together. I'm sorry that I can't join you in your praise for the police department.

It is true that they have been rather disciplined in their public handling of the demonstrators. In this sense they have been rather publicly "nonviolent." But for what purpose? To preserve the evil system of segregation. Over the last few years I have consistently preached that nonviolence demands that the means we use must be as pure as the ends we seek. So I have tried to make it clear that it is wrong to use immoral means to attain moral ends. But now I must affirm that it is just as wrong, or even more so, to use moral means to preserve immoral ends. Maybe Mr. Connor and his policemen have been rather publicly nonviolent, as Chief Prichett was in Albany, Georgia, but they have used the moral means of nonviolence to maintain the immoral end of flagrant racial injustice. T. S. Eliot has said that there is no greater treason than to do the right deed for the wrong reason.

I wish you had commended the Negro sit-inners and demonstrators of Birmingham for their sublime courage, their willingness to suffer, and their amazing discipline in the midst of the most inhuman provocation. One day the South will recognize its real heroes. They will be the James Merediths, courageously and with a majestic sense of purpose, facing jeering and hostile mobs and the agonizing loneliness that characterizes the life of the pioneer. They will be old, oppressed, battered Negro women, symbolized in a seventy-two year old woman of Montgomery, Alabama   who rose up with a sense of dignity and with her people decided not to ride the segregated buses, and responded to one who inquired about her tiredness with ungrammatical profundity: "My feets is tired, but my soul is rested." They will be young high school and college students, young ministers of the gospel and a host of the elders, courageously and nonviolently sitting in at lunch counters and willingly going to jail for conscience sake. One day the South will know that when these disinherited children of God sat down at lunch counters they were in reality standing up for the best in the American dream and the most sacred values in our Judeo-Christian heritage, and thus carrying our whole nation back to great wells of democracy which were dug deep by the founding fathers in the formulation of the Constitution and the Declaration of Independence.

Never before have I written a letter this long (or should I say a book?). I'm afraid that it is much too long to take your precious time. I can assure you that it would have been much shorter if I had been writing from a comfortable desk, but what else is there to do when you are alone for days in the dull monotony of a narrow jail cell other than write long letters, think strange thoughts, and pray long prayers?

If I have said anything in this letter that is an overstatement of the truth and is indicative of an unreasonable impatience, I beg you to forgive me. If I have said anything in this letter that is an understatement of the truth and is indicative of my having a patience that makes me patient with anything less than brotherhood, I beg God to forgive me.

I hope this letter finds you strong in the faith. I also hope that circumstances will soon make it possible for me to meet each of you, not as an integrationist or a civil rights leader, but as a fellow clergyman and a Christian brother. Let us all hope that the dark clouds of racial prejudice will soon pass away and the deep fog of misunderstanding will be lifted from our fear-drenched communities and in some not too distant tomorrow the radiant stars of love and brotherhood will shine over our great nation with all of their scintillating beauty.

Yours for the cause of
Peace and Brotherhood

MARTIN LUTHER KING, JR.

Enrique Hank López (1920–   )

BACK TO BACHIMBA

I am a *pocho* from Bachimba, a rather small Mexican village in the state of Chihuahua, where my father fought with the army of Pancho Villa. He was, in fact, the only private in Villa's army.

Pocho is ordinarily a derogatory term in Mexico (to define it succinctly, a *pocho* is a Mexican slob who has pretensions of being a gringo sonofabitch), but I use it in a very special sense. To me that word has come to mean "uprooted Mexican," and that's what I have been all my life. Though my entire upbringing and education took place in the United States, I have never felt completely American, and when I am in Mexico, I sometimes feel like a displaced gringo with a curiously Mexican name—Enrique Preciliano López y Martínez de Sepulveda de Sapien de Quien-sabe-quien. One might conclude that I'm either a schizo-cultural Mexican or a cultured schizoid American.

In any event, the schizo-ing began a long time ago, when my father and many of Pancho Villa's troops fled across the border to escape the oncoming *federales* who eventually defeated Villa. My mother and I, traveling across the hot desert plains in a buckboard wagon, joined my father in El Paso, Texas, a few days after his hurried departure. With more and more Villistas swarming into El Paso every day, it was quickly apparent that jobs would be exceedingly scarce and insecure; so my parents packed our few belongings and we took the first available bus to Denver. My father had hoped to move to Chicago because the name sounded so Mexican, but my mother's meager savings were hardly enough to buy tickets for Colorado.

There we moved into a ghetto of Spanish-speaking residents who chose to call themselves Spanish Americans and resented the sudden migration of their brethren from Mexico, whom they sneeringly called *surumatos* (slang for "southerners"). These so-called Spanish Americans claimed direct descent from the original *conquistadores* of Spain. They also insisted that they had *never* been Mexicans, since their region of New Spain (later annexed to the United States) was never a part of Mexico. But what they claimed most vociferously—and erroneously—was an absence of Indian ancestry. It made no difference that any objective observer could see by

merely looking at them the results of considerable fraternization between the conquering Spaniards and the Comanche and Navaho women who crossed their paths. Still, these *manitos*, as they were snidely labeled by the *surumatos*, stubbornly refused to be identified with Mexico, and would actually fight anyone who called them Mexican. So intense was this intergroup rivalry that the bitterest "race riots" I have ever witnessed—and engaged in—were between the look-alike, talk-alike *surumatos* and *manitos* who lived near Denver's Curtis Park. In retrospect the harsh conflicts between us were all the more silly and self-defeating when one recalls that we were all lumped together as "spiks" and "greasers" by the Anglo-Saxon community.

Predictably enough, we *surumatos* began huddling together in a subneighborhood within the larger ghetto, and it was there that I became painfully aware that my father had been the only private in Pancho Villa's army. Most of my friends were the sons of captains, colonels, majors, and even generals, though a few fathers were admittedly mere sergeants and corporals. My father alone had been a lowly private in that famous Division del Norte. Naturally, I developed a most painful complex, which led me to all sorts of compensatory fibs. During one brief spell I fancied my father as a member of the dreaded *los dorados*, the "golden ones," who were Villa's favorite henchmen. (Later I was to learn that my father's cousin, Martin López, was a genuine and quite notorious *dorado*). But all my inventions were quickly un-invented by my very own father, who seemed to take a perverse delight in being Pancho's only private.

No doubt my chagrin was accentuated by the fact that Pancho Villa's exploits were a constant topic of conversation in our household. My entire childhood seems to be shadowed by his presence. At our dinner table, almost every night, we would listen to endlessly repeated accounts of this battle, that stratagem, or some great act of Robin Hood kindness by *el centauro del norte.* I remember how angry my parents were when they saw Wallace Beery in *Viva Villa!* "Garbage by stupid gringos," they called it. They were particularly offended by the sweaty, unshaven sloppiness of Beery's portrayal. "Pancho Villa was clean and orderly, no matter how much he chased after women. This man's a dirty swine."

As if to deepen our sense of *Villismo,* my parents also taught us "Adelita" and *"Se llevaron el cañon para Bachimba"* ("They took the cannons to Bachima"), the two most famous songs of the Mexican revolution. Some twenty years later (during my stint at Harvard Law School), while strolling along the Charles River, I would find myself softly singing *"Se llevaron el cañon para Bachimba, para Bachimba, para Bachimba"* over and over again. That's all I could remember of that poignant rebel song. Though I had been born there, I had always regarded "Bachimba" as a fictitious, made-up, Lewis Carroll kind of word. So that eight years ago, when I first returned to Mexico, I was literally stunned when I came to a crossroad south of Chihuahua and saw an old road marker: "Bachimba 18 km." Then it really exists—I shouted inwardly—Bachimba is a real town! Swinging onto the narrow, poorly paved road, I gunned the motor and sped toward the town I'd been singing about since infancy. It turned out to be a quiet, dusty village with a bleak worn-down plaza that was surrounded by nondescript buildings of uncertain vintage.

Aside from the songs about Bachimba and Adelita and all the folk tales about Villa's guerrilla fighters, my early years were strongly influenced by our neighborhood celebrations of Mexico's two most important patriotic events: Mexican Independence Day on September 16 and the anniversary of the battle of Puebla on May 5. On those two dates Mexicans all over the world are likely to become extremely chauvinistic. In Denver we would stage annual parades that included three or four floats skimpily decorated with crepe paper streamers, a small band, several adults in threadbare battle dress, and hundreds of kids marching in wild disorder. It was during one of these parades—I was ten years old then—that I was seized with acute appendicitis and had to be rushed to a hospital. The doctor subsequently told my mother that I had made a long, impassioned speech about the early revolutionist Miguel Hidalgo while the anesthetic was taking hold, and she explained with pardonable pride that it was the speech I was to make at Turner Hall that evening. Mine was one of the twenty-three *discursos* scheduled on the postparade program, a copy of which my mother still retains. My only regret was missing the annual *discurso* of Don Miguel Gómez, my god-father, a deep-throated orator who would always climax his speech by falling to his knees and dramatically kissing the floor, almost weeping as he loudly proclaimed: *"Ay, Mexico! Beso tu tierra, tu mero corazon"* ("Ah, Mexico! I kiss your sacred soil, the very heart of you"). He gave the same oration for seventeen years, word for word and gesture for gesture, and it never failed to bring tears to his eyes. But not once did he return to Chihuahua, even for a brief visit.

My personal Mexican-ness eventually produced serious problems for me. Upon entering grade school I learned English rapidly, and rather well, always ranking either first or second in my class; yet the hard core of me remained stubbornly Mexican. This chauvinism may have been a reaction to the constant racial prejudice we encountered on all sides. The neighborhood cops were always running us off the streets and calling us "dirty greasers," and most of our teachers frankly regarded us as totally inferior. I still remember the galling disdain of my sixth-grade teacher, whose constant mimicking of our heavily accented speech drove me to a desperate study of *Webster's Dictionary* in the hope of acquiring a vocabulary larger than hers. Sadly enough, I succeeded only too well, and for the next few years I spoke the most ridiculous high-flown rhetoric in the Denver public schools. One of my favorite words was "indubitably," and it must have driven everyone mad. I finally got rid of my accent by constantly reciting "Peter Piper picked a peck of pickled peppers" with little round pebbles in my mouth. Somewhere I had read about Demosthenes.

During this phase of my childhood the cultural tug of war known as "Americanization" almost pulled me apart. There were moments when I would identify completely with the gringo world (what could have been more American than my earnest high-voiced portrayal of George Washington, however ridiculous the cotton wig my mother had fashioned for me?); then quite suddenly I would feel so acutely Mexican that I would stammer over the simplest English phrase. I was so ready to take offense at the slightest slur against Mexicans that I would imagine prejudice where none existed. But on other occasions, in full confidence of my belonging, I would venture forth into social areas that I should have realized were clearly forbidden to little chicanos from Curtis Park. The inevitable rebuffs would leave me floundering in selfpity; it was small comfort to know that other minority groups suffered even worse rebuffs than we did.

The only non-Mexican boy on our street was a Negro named Leroy Logan, who was probably my closest childhood friend. Leroy was the best athlete, the best whistler, the best liar, the best horseshoe player, the best marble shooter, the best mumblety-pegger, and the best shoplifter in our neighborhood. He was also my "partner," and I thus entitled myself to a fifty-fifty share of all his large triumphs and petty thefts. Because he considered "Mexican" a derogatory word bordering on obscenity, Leroy would pronounce it "Mesican" so as to soften its harshness. But once in a while, when he'd get angry with me, he would call me a "lousy Mesican greasy spik" with the most extraordinarily effective hissing one can imagine. And I'm embarrassed to admit that I would retaliate by calling him "alligator bait." As a matter of fact, just after I had returned from the hospital, he came to visit me, and I thoughtlessly greeted him with a flippant, "Hi, alligator ba—" I never finished the phrase because Leroy whacked me on the stomach with a Ping-Pong paddle and rushed out of my house with great, sobbing anger.

Weeks later, when we had re-established a rather cool rapport, I tried to make up for my stupid insult by helping him steal cabbages from the vegetable trucks that rumbled through our neighborhood on their way to the produce markets. They would come down Larimer Street in the early dawn, and Leroy and I would sneak up behind them at the 27th Street stop sign, where they were forced to pause for cross traffic. Then Leroy, with a hooked pole he had invented, would stab the top cabbages and roll them off the truck. I would be waiting below to catch them with an open gunny sack. Our system was fabulously successful for a while, and we found a ready market for the stolen goods; but one morning, as I started to unfurl my sack, a fairly large cabbage conked me on the head. Screaming with pain, I lunged at Leroy and tried to bite him. He, laughing all the while—it was obviously a funny scene—glided out of my reach, and finally ran into a nearby alley. We never engaged in commercial affairs thereafter.

Still and all, I remember him with great affection and a touch of sadness. I say sadness because eventually Leroy was to suffer the misery of being an outsider in an already outside ghetto. As he grew older, it was apparent that he longed to be a Mexican, that he felt terribly dark and alone. "Sometimes," he would tell me, "I feel like my damn skin's too tight, like I'm gonna bust out of it." One cold February night I found him in the coal shed behind Pacheco's store, desperately scraping his forearm with sandpaper, the hurt tears streaming down his face. "I got to get this off, man. I can't stand all this blackness." We stood there quietly staring at the floor for a long, anguished moment, both of us miserable beyond word or gesture. Finally he drew a deep breath, blew his nose loudly, and mumbled half audibly, "Man, you sure lucky to be a Mexican."

Not long after this incident Leroy moved out of Denver to live with relatives in Georgia. When I saw him off at the bus station, he grabbed my shoulder and whispered huskily, "You gonna miss me, man. You watch what I tellya." "Indubitably," I said. "Aw, man, cut that stuff. You the most fancy-pants Mexican I know." Those were his last words to me, and they caused a considerable dent in my ego. Not enough, however, to diminish my penchant for fancy language. The dictionary continued to be my comic book well into high school.

Speaking of language, I am reminded of a most peculiar circumstance: almost every Mexican American lawyer that I've ever met speaks English with a noticeable Spanish accent, this despite the fact that they have all been born, reared, and educated exclusively in America. Of the forty-eight lawyers I have in mind, only three of us are free of any accent. Needless to say, our "cultural drag" has been weighty and persistent. And one must presume that our ethnic hyphens shall be with us for many years to come.

My own Mexican-ness, after years of decline at Harvard University, suddenly burst forth again when I returned to Chihuahua and stumbled on the town of Bachimba. I had long conversations with an uncle I'd never met before, my father's younger brother, Ramón. It was Tío Ramón who chilled my spine with eyewitness stories about Pancho Villa's legendary *dorados*, one of whom was Martin López. "He was your second cousin. The bravest young buck in Villa's army. And he became a *dorado* when he was scarcely seventeen years old because he dared to defy Pancho Villa himself. As your papa may have told you, Villa had a bad habit of burying treasure up in the mountains and also burying the man he took with him to dig the hole for it. Well, one day he chose Martin López to go with him. Deep in the mountains they went, near Parral. And when they got to a suitably lonely place, Pancho Villa told him to dig a hole with pick and shovel. Then, when Martin had dug down to his waist, Villa leveled a gun at the boy. "Say your prayers, *muchacho*. You shall stay here with the gold—forever." But Martin had come prepared. In his large right boot he had a gun, and when he rose from his bent position, he was pointing that gun at Villa. They stood there, both ready to fire, for several seconds, and finally Don Pancho started to laugh in that wonderful way of his. *"Bravo, bravo, muchacho!* You've got more guts than a man. Get out of that hole, boy. I need you for my *dorados."*

Tío Ramón's eyes were wet with

pride. "But what is more important, he died with great valor. Two years later, after he had terrorized the *federales* and Pershing's gringo soldiers, he was finally wounded and captured here in Bachimba. It was a bad wound in his leg, finally turning to gangrene. Then one Sunday morning they hauled Martín López and three other prisoners to the plaza. One by one they executed the three lesser prisoners against that wall. I was up on the church tower watching it all. Finally it was your uncle's turn. They dragged him off the buckboard wagon and handed him his crutches. Slowly, painfully, he hobbled to the wall and stood there. Very straight he stood. 'Do you have any last words?' asked the captain of the firing squad. With great pride Martin tossed his crutches aside and stood very tall on his one good leg. 'Give me, you yellow bastards, give me a gun—and I'll show you who is the man among . . .' Eight bullets crashed into his chest and face, and I never heard that final word. That was your second cousin. You would have been proud to know him."

As I listened to Tio Ramón's soft nostalgic voice that evening, there in the sputtering light of the kerosene lamp on his back patio, I felt as intensely Mexican as I shall ever feel.

But not for long. Within six weeks I was destined to feel *less* Mexican than I had ever felt. The scene of my trauma was the Centro Mexicano de Escritores, where the finest young writers of Mexico met regularly to discuss works in progress and to engage in erudite literary and philostphical discussions. Week after week I sat among them, dumbstruck by my inadequacy in Spanish and my total ignorance of their whole frame of reference. How could I have possibly imagined that I was Mexican? Those conversations were a dense tangle of local and private allusions, and the few threads I could grasp only magnified my ig-

norance. The novelist Juan Rulfo was then reading the initial drafts of his *Pedro Páramo,* later to be acclaimed the best avant-garde fiction in Mexican literature. Now that I have soaked myself in the *ambiance* of Mexico, Rulfo's novel intrigues me beyond measure; but when he first read it at the Centro, he might just as well have been reading "Jabberwocky" in Swahili for all I understood of it. And because all of the other Mexican writers knew and greatly appreciated *Páramo,* I could only assume that I was really "too gringo" to comprehend it. For this reason, I, a person with no great talent for reticence, never opened my mouth at the Centro. In fact, I was so shell-shocked by those sessions that I even found it difficult to converse with my housekeeper about such simple matters as dirty laundry or the loose doorknob in the bathroom.

Can any of us really go home again? I, for one, am convinced that I have no true home, that I must reconcile myself to a schizo-cultural limbo, with a mere hyphen to provide some slight cohesion between my split selves. This inevitable splitting is a plague and a pleasure. Some mornings as I glide down the Paseo de la Reforma, perhaps the most beautiful boulevard in the world, I am suddenly angered by the *machismo,* or aggressive maleness, of Mexican drivers who crowd and bully their screeching machines through dense traffic. What terrible insecurity, what awful dread of emasculation, produces such assertive bully-boy conduct behind a steering wheel? Whatever the reasons, there is a part of me that can never accept this much-celebrated *machismo.* Nor can I accept the exaggerated nationalism one so frequently encounters in the press, on movie screens, over the radio, in daily conversations—that shrill barrage of slogans proclaiming that "there is only one Mexico."

Recently, when I expressed these

views to an old friend, he smiled quite knowingly: "Let's face it, Hank, you're not really a Mexican—despite that long, comical name of yours. You're an American through and through." But that, of course, is a minority view and almost totally devoid of realism. One could just as well say that Martin Luther King was not a Negro, that he was merely an American. But the plain truth is that neither I nor the Martin Luther Kings of our land can escape the fact that we are Mexican and Negro with roots planted so deeply in the United States that we have grown those strong little hyphens that make us Mexican-American and Negro-American. This assertion may not please some idealists who would prefer to blind themselves to our obvious ethnic and racial differences, who are unwittingly patronizing when they insist that we are all alike and indistinguishable. But the politicians, undoubtedly the most pragmatic creatures in America, are completely aware that ethnic groups *do* exist and that they seem to huddle together, bitch together, and sometimes vote together.

When all is said and done, we hyphenated Americans are here to stay, bubbling happily or unhappily in the great non-melting pot. Much has been gained and will be gained from the multiethnic aspects of the United States, and there is no useful purpose in attempting to wish it away or to homogenize it out of existence. In spite of the race riots in Watts and ethnic unrest elsewhere, there would appear to be a kind of modus vivendi developing on almost every level of American life.

And if there are those of us who may never feel completely at home, we can always make the brief visit to Bachimba.

Edwin Newman (1919–   )

from STRICTLY SPEAKING

Can a *phrase* be repealed? I have in mind Y'know. The prevalence of Y'know is one of the most far-reaching and depressing development of our time, disfiguring conversation wherever you go. I attend meetings at NBC and elsewhere in which people of high rank and station, with salaries to match, say almost nothing else.

For a while I thought it clever to ask people who were spattering me with Y'knows why, if I knew, they were telling me? After having lunch alone with some regularity, I dropped the question. In Britain, a National Society for the Suppression of Y'know, Y'know, Y'know in the Diction of Broadcasters was organized in 1969. It put out a list of the broadcasters who were the worst offenders. Reporters then interviewed the offenders and quoted all the Y'knows in their answers when they were asked whether they really said Y'know that often. Nothing changed.

Once it takes its grip, Y'know is hard to throw off. Some people collapse into Y'know after giving up trying to say what they mean. Others scatter it broadside, these, I suspect, being for some reason embarrassed by a silence of any duration during which they might be suspected of thinking about what they were going to say next. It is not uncommon to hear Y'know used a dozen times in a minute.

We know less about the origin of Y'know than about the origin of Boola boola, but there is some reason to believe that in this country it began among poor blacks who, because of the various disabilities imposed on them, often did not speak well and for whom Y'know was a request for assurance that they had been understood. From that sad beginning it spread, among people who wanted to show themselves sympathetic to blacks, and among those who saw it as the latest thing and either could not resist or did not want to be left out.

Those who wanted to show that they were down to earth, and so not above using Y'know, or—much the same thing—telling you that somebody is like six feet tall, have been particularly influential. They include makers of television commercials who begin the sales pitch with Y'know, and so gain the confidence of the viewer, who realizes at once that the person doing the commercial is down to earth, regular, not stuck-up, and therefore to be trusted.

It also included, on May 1, 1970, the day after he announced the American and South Vietnamese invasion of Cambodia, President Nixon. To a gathering of employes at the Pentagon, he made these remarks about antiwar students at universities:

"You see these bums, you know, blowing up the campuses. Listen, the boys that are on the college campuses today are the luckiest people in the world, going to the greatest universities, and here they are burning up the books, storming around about this issue. You name it. Get rid of the war and there will be another one." The White House Watergate transcripts show Mr. Nixon to be fairly devoted to Y'know, even without one use deleted by the White House but shown in the House Judiciary Committee's version: "One of these blacks, y'know, goes in there and holds up a store with a Goddamn gun, and they give him two years and then probation afterward."

The technique might be extended to other fields, perhaps to make Shakespeare more popular in the schools.

> HAMLET: To be or not to be, that is the question. Y'know? Or: I pledge, y'know, allegiance to the flag, and to the y'know, republic for which it stands. One nation indivisible, like I mean with liberty and justice for all. Y'know?

The White House transcript did not show it, but the President also dropped the g at the end of some ing words, apparently to ensure that his down-to-earthness would be recognized.* The g at the end of ing words must be thought by politicians to have class connotations that may offend the masses of voters. For that reason it is often dropped in party songs. In 1960, for example, the Democrats' song was "Walkin' Down to Washington," and the Republicans had one about

* Mr. Nixon supplied another and even less graceful demonstration of how down to earth and regular he was when he was visited by a former prisoner of war who gave him an American flag he had made while he was in North Vietnam. The President asked about the man's wife and was told that she had divorced him during his stay in prison camp. Mr. Nixon assured the former prisoner that he would be popular at Washington dinner parties, and added, "Watch out for some of those dogs they have you sit by." Mr. Nixon quickly thought better of this and said, "No, there are some very nice girls in Washington."

"The Good Time Train," which was "a-waitin' at the station" in the first stanza and "a-waitin' for the nation" in the second.

To choose a lower order of speech is, I suppose, antiestablishment in motive and carries a certain scorn for organized, grammatical, and precise expression. Object to it and you are likely to be told that you are a pedant, a crank, an elitist, and behind the times. "Right on," "uptight," and "chicken out," to take only a few examples, are looked upon as vivid phrases that enrich and renew the language.

They do enrich it, but they are exhausted very rapidly by overuse. When that happens they wrinkle into clichés before our eyes. Nor does it matter where they come from. "Right on" was a black expression. "It's a new ball game" came from sports. "In orbit" came from the space program. Space was also indirectly responsible for "A nation that can put a man on the moon ought to be able to . . ." Since July 20, 1969, this has been popular with those urging the government to improve mass transit, take care of old people, take care of children, take care of the sick, win the Winter Olympics, win the Summer Olympics, build a nonpolluting automobile engine, see to it that meat in supermarkets is wrapped in packages transparent on both sides, and so on and so on. Those who say these things believe that they have put forward compelling ideas, and such pronouncements do often pass for thought. In reality they camouflage its absence.

Much written and spoken expression these days is equivalent to the background music that incessantly encroaches on us, in banks, restaurants, department stores, trains, shops, airports, airplanes, dentists' offices, hospitals, elevators, waiting rooms, hotel lobbies, pools, apartment building lobbies, bars, and, to my personal knowledge, at least one museum. It thumps and tinkles away, mechanical, without color, inflection, vigor, charm, or distinction. People who work in the presence of background music often tell you, and sometimes with pride, that they don't hear it anymore. The parallel with language is alarming.

Language, then, sets the tone of our society. Since we must speak and read, and spend much of our lives doing so, it seems sensible to get some pleasure and inspiration from these activities. The wisecrack is a wonderful thing, and the colorful phrase, and the flight of fancy. So is the accurate description of a place or an event, and so is the precise formulation of an idea. They brighten the world.

It need not be elaborate. In January, 1974, during the struggle over wages between the British miners' union and the government, there was speculation that Prime Minister Edward Heath would call an election. A BBC man went out to interview miners:

BBC MAN: Do you want an election?
MINER: Yes.
BBC MAN: Why?
MINER: To get the buggers out.

In March, 1958, I was in Tunis to cover a speech by President Bourguiba about Tunisian independence. I started to leave the building where the speech was being made, and a policeman told me that if I did, I could not get back in.

NEWMAN: Mais je suis journaliste.
POLICEMAN: Oui, monsieur, et moi, je suis policier.

I stayed.

In the summer of 1966 I attended a concert in the Alhambra in Granada as the guest of Andrés Segovia. A pianist played a Beethoven concerto with the Madrid Symphony and received polite applause. At once he sat down and played an encore. Segovia leaned over to me. "Too queeck," he said.

Maestro!

Most of us will never speak that succinctly or concretely. We may, however, aspire to. For direct and precise language, if people could be persuaded to try it, would make conversations more interesting, which is no small thing; it would help to substitute facts for bluster, also no small thing; and it would promote the practice of organized thought and even of occasional silence, which would be an immeasurable blessing.

I do not want to overstate the case. The rules of language cannot be frozen and immutable; they will reflect what is happening in society whether we want them to or not. Moreover, just as libraries, which are storehouses of wisdom, are also storehouses of unwisdom, so will good English, being available to all, be enlisted in evil causes. Still, it remains true that since nothing is more important to a society than the language it uses—there would be no society without it—we would be better off if we spoke and wrote with exactness and grace, and if we preserved, rather than destroyed, the value of our language.

It is not as complicated as it is sometimes made out to be. At an English girls' school one of the mistresses was asked whether the children were allowed to have comic books. She cited no studies, surveys, or research projects. "Oh, no," she said. "Such inferior language."

I speak, then, for a world from which the stilted and pompous phrase, the slogan and the cliché, have not been banished—that would be too much to hope for—but which they do not dominate. This book is intended to help bring about, good-naturedly, I hope (please, not hopefully), that outcome.

Elaine Morgan (1920–   )

from THE DESCENT OF WOMAN

The maternal relationship, then, seems to be offering less immediate biological reward to many women, largely because the environmental context is inimical to it.

But the opposite, surely, is true of her relations with the male. The actual performance of the sex act should be, and usually is, more pleasurable to her than it has been for her predecessors over a good many generations. She has been relieved of a good deal of the load of artificial and unnecessary shame and guilt associated with it, and the amount of attention concentrated recently on her own sensations and reactions and responses has been unprecedented. One might expect her to be overwhelmed with feelings of joyous gratitude for this. The whole relationship between men and women should by now be irradiated with a cordial new atmosphere of warmth and comradeship and mutual esteem.

In individual cases I have no doubt that this has happened. But only an optimist would maintain that the net result of recent developments has been to make men and women on the whole *like* each other any better than they did under earlier, less permissive regimes. There are plenty of signs that in many ways they have actually less liking and respect and admiration for one another than their great-grand-parents had in the old days when in the words of the old cliché men were men and women were glad of it; and chastity had not been outmoded; and sex was so hedged around with taboos that, as Thurber wrote, "It got so that in speaking of birth and other natural phenomena, women seemed often to be discussing something else, such as the Sistine Madonna or the aurora borealis."

We don't want to go back there. A lot of cant has been swept away, and the areas of human experience that could not be spoken of have drastically shrunk, and this cannot be anything but a solid gain. The only advantage of the old system was that in essentials it had been in operation for a pretty long time; people were used to it and knew where they were, and what roles they had to play, and to nine people out of ten this is always a great comfort.

The roles they played were based upon a script constructed around a few basic axioms. One was that men were created dominant and would always remain so because of their superior strength and superior wisdom, and because it was the will of God. (Milton: "He for God only, she for God in him.") But in a secular and mechanical age Milton's God is out of date, muscle power seems to have less and less relevance, and even the male's superior wisdom is not the self-evident proposition that it once was.

Another axiom was the division of labor. Woman was unfit to face the harsh realities of economic life, so her place was in the kitchen and in the nursery. As long as there was no way out of this, most women adapted themselves to it very well, and took a pride in it, and the nuclear family (based from the beginning far more on division of labor than on sex) continued to cohere. Nowadays most women for some part of their lives face the harsh realities of economic life, and find them far from intolerable. They have also discovered that male dominance was not so much based on the fact that he had more muscles and more wisdom, but on the fact that as long as she stayed in the kitchen he had *all* of the money.

An even more venerable axiom going right back to the Garden of Eden was: "In sorrow shalt thou bring forth." It was one of the eternal rules that any act of sexual intercourse was likely to be (inside marriage) "blessed," or (outside it) "punished," by pregnancy. Now, new contraceptive methods, though still comparatively in their infancy, have set a light to this one. It is burning its way along a long fuse, but the evolutionary bomb at the end of it has not yet gone off.

With so many bastions of his dominant status skidding out from under him, man hung on tight to the one symbol nobody could take away from him. He still, by God, had his penis. However cool and efficient and economically independent a female might be, if he ever had any tremor of doubt that he was worth three of her, he had only to remind himself that underneath that elegant exterior was a nude female with all the usual sexual appendages. If he was driven to ask himself what the position of women ought to be, he could always—if only in his mind—come up with Stokely Carmichael's answer: "Prone." (I have never been quite clear whether Mr. Carmichael had a sexual prejudice against the "missionary position," or whether he just didn't know the difference between prone and supine, but it was obvious to everybody what he meant.)

This reaction of course is not typical of all men, or even of most men. Most well-adjusted men, especially intelligent ones, have on the whole welcomed the emancipation of women, if only because they have to spend at least part of their time in the company of women in nonsexual contexts—even the marital context is nonsexual for most of the twenty-four hours—and it is less boring to talk to women since they have acquired a few more topics of conversation.

However, I think the reaction is one factor contributing to the astonishing boom in sex and pornography. The urge isn't new; it was always there, but the recent wave of obsession with it in Western countries seems to be new, and the women's liberation complaint that females are being regarded more and more as "sexual objects" has a lot of truth in it.

Only a very small minority of women as yet are "complaining." Most of them are rejoicing. Sex is nice; being looked at and admired and talked about is very nice; and the keen competition to be the sexiest among the local sex objects is worth millions to the manufacturers of cosmetics, perfumes, eyelashes, miniskirts, hot pants, and the pill.

Reactions to all these phenomena are sharply divided. Some people see the new attitudes toward sex as a tremendous liberation of benevolent life-enhancing forces once cruelly held in chains by sour-faced puritans. It is regarded by others as a Gadarene rush away from all standards of decency and morality down a muddy slope into filth and debauchery. One side sees it as an emergence into sanity and sunshine; the other as the crumbling away of the very foundations of order and civilization.

These reactions are both slightly hysterical, and accompanied by acute manifestations of mutual aggression, fear, hatred, and moral indignation, with each side totally convinced it has a monopoly of the only really moral morality.

They hurl atrocity stories at one another. One side weeps for "the youth pined away with desire and the pale virgin shrouded in snow," couples trapped in impossible marriages, unmarried mothers pilloried by prejudice, children tortured with guilt and fear because they'd been told masturbation was deadly sin and led to epilepsy and dementia; homosexuals hounded and persecuted simply because they loved one another; Marie Stopes pelted with filth and threatened with arson.

The other side points to soaring figures of venereal diseases, abortion, and drug deaths; to shattered children of homes broken by adultery, desertion, and divorce; to schoolgirls promiscuous at eleven and pregnant at twelve; to cynical commercial exploitations of pornography and exhibitionism and perversion driving family entertainment out of cinemas and theaters.

It is very unlikely that the net effect on the total of human happiness will be as great as either side believes. Some things become easier with greater "permissiveness," others become harder. People are less likely now to be embarrassed when a man says he loves another man, which would once have been shocking: they are more likely now to be embarrassed if he says he loves his mother, which would once have been commendable. It is easier for a young girl to kiss a young man in public; but a recent inquiry revealed that in many areas she would be chary of walking about with her arms around the waist of another girl—though ladies in the novels of Jane Austen and Dickens and Tolstoy do it constantly with complete lack of inhibition—because now she has heard of lesbianism and it has taught her a new taboo.

Guilt and anxiety are not being dispersed, only attached to different situations. There is less shame attached to losing one's virginity too soon, and more attached to keeping it too long. It is less taboo to say "shit," and more taboo to say "nigger." There is less fear that you can be unbalanced by masturbation, but a new conviction that you can be unbalanced by abstention. Less obloquy attaches to sleeping with a girl without giving her a wedding ring; but to do it without giving her an orgasm is a newly patented way of lousing up your self-esteem and peace of mind.

Tolerance is not really being enlarged: it is moving its targets. The woman who cuts loose from an unpleasant husband because she cannot bear to live with him is praised where once she was condemned. But the woman who hangs on to a reluctant husband because she cannot bear to live without him is condemned where once she was praised. Anyone who succumbs to alcoholism meets with less censure and more compassion than formerly ("it's an illness, really . . . perfectly understandable, the pressures are too great . . ."), but anyone who succumbs to obesity gets short shrift ("no excuse for it these days . . . only needs a bit of will power . . . *other* people manage not to let themselves go. . . ."). The total number of moral attitudes struck, the difficulty of trying to conform to them, and the weight of social disapproval visited on those who fail vary hardly at all.

As for the obsession with sex itself, it is partly a by-product of affluence. Less and less time and attention needs to be given to the gratification of other physical needs, so this one is thrown into prominence. Even in primitive societies sexual activity is heightened at periods when the community is more than usually well stocked up, so that there is feasting and no need to go foraging for several days.

For people with boring jobs whose work only demands a small fraction of their mental capacity—and there are more of these every year—sex provides them with something interesting to think about; for people starved for love or a sense of identity it ensures that at least one person will pay them close attention for a while; for those who win the rat race it is a trophy and for those who lose it, a consolation prize.

The trouble is that sex as a pastime, when divorced from love, has one serious drawback. Like many forms of physical gratification, it is subject to a law of diminishing returns. To a hungry man any food is delicious; to a not very hungry man only delicious food is delicious; to a sated man no food is delicious. It is very frustrating for a man with the means and the opportunity to satisfy an appetite when he finds the appetite itself is failing him.

In some of its more extreme aspects the sexual revolution seems to have passed the point of campaigning for the liberation of a natural appetite, and reached the vomitorial stage of trying to reactivate an exhausted one.

Up to a point, as any biologist knows, it is possible to achieve this. When a given stimulus, on account of repeated applications, ceases to elicit a given response, it is possible to reawaken the response by increasing the stimulus. The foster parents of the cuckoo's chick work themselves to skin and bone to rear their enormous changeling and let their own go hungry, because a large gaping beak is a stronger stimulus than a small one. Many birds will show a preference for trying to hatch a larger-than-life egg; a male butterfly will get besotted over an artificial female with larger-than-life spots on her wings.

In terms of human sex this technique can be applied in various ways

—cosmetic aids can supply redder lips, longer lashes, brighter hair, whiter teeth, larger breasts, or smaller waists as fashion may demand. There are, however, certain natural limits. Where the demand for increased stimulation centers on increased exposure it runs into a cul-de-sac, because you can't get nuder than nude. Once full frontal nakedness as a public spectacle has become another *déjà vu*, there is no further for it to go except into the nightmare of one cartoonist who drew a stripped striptease girl responding to the demand for more by gracefully, with an enticing smile, drawing out her entrails and displaying them to her avid audience.

Recently there have been some signs that the sex boom is running out of steam, and certainly in some areas it is encountering a vigorous backlash. Much of it has been due to a well-recognized syndrome known as "cultural shock." At least it is recognized by anthropologists, who know that primitive tribes have sometimes literally died of it. But at home many progressives, who are hotly indignant when ham-handed imperialists trample over the taboos of subject races, fail to see that their sexual iconoclasm is inflicting the same trauma on some of their fellow countrymen. This doesn't necessarily mean the process should be halted. It does mean it should be carried out non-aggressively, and the words "I believe you are shocked!" should be spoken not with derision but with concern, whether the shock was inflicted by defective electrical wiring or by a change in sexual mores.

How will all this finally affect the status of women? They will have some hard thinking to do and some careful adjustments to make if they are not to end up losers on the deal. Because what is happening is slackening of the rules. Some of them were bad rules; and I believe they will inevitably be replaced by new rules, because that is the nature of human society. Meanwhile, whenever you get a situation where the rules are temporarily suspended—as in the Wild West before the lawmen came—the effect is that the tough come to the top and the weakest go to the wall. And women, in the aggregate, are not the tougher sex.

Thus one effect is that there are rather fewer sexual problems for young men, as chastity gets outmoded; but a higher proportion of young women are faced with the still formidable crises of unsupported motherhood or abortion. Insofar as it is true that more men are content with casual sex and more women desire a permanent relationship, the males are now capturing the moral initiative; so that if a girl does want love and marriage, she can now sometimes be conned into actually feeling ashamed of wanting them, and denying with profuse apologies that she had any such unreasonable thought in her mind.

Males are capturing the hypochondriac initiative, too. In the old days it was the bride who had to be treated tenderly, with infinite tact and patience, if the relationship was to be a success. Now it is the groom whose delicate ego must be cosseted, because he has a more fragile piece of machinery there than was dreamed of in the old philosophy. To judge by the letters sent in to some male magazines, he spends half his life worrying because his ejaculations come too quickly or too infrequently or in highly specialized circumstances, just as mothers used to worry about similar aberrations in their babies' bowel movements, until Dr. Spock breezed along and posed the cosmic question: "So what?"

Despite all this there are some women's liberation types who are in the forefront of the sexual revolution and calling for more, on the grounds that marriage can be slavery, and sex is getting more democratic, or on the more general grounds that things have been so horrible up to now that they want to change everything. However, these are for the most part pretty tough babies who know they will survive even the most drastic upheavals. And even they don't find it too easy, because a sex-ridden society is always ready to resurrect the old slogan of "woman's place is on her back," and a man whose gaze is too avidly riveted on a woman's cleavage only gets irritated if he's asked to listen, really listen, to any words coming out of her mouth. . . .

Up to a few generations ago the decline of sexual attractiveness was still not hard to take. The change of role from blushing bride to full-time mother happened in a few short busy years, and most women after the first nine or ten pregnancies would be uttering fervent prayers for the whole business to be over and done with. Even Queen Victoria, a loving wife if ever there was one, grew to feel strongly that one could have altogether too much of a good thing. There would be all the children to be absorbed in and worried about, and then the arrival of the grandchildren, and then good night.

The shape of our lives is vastly different now. The children are fewer. They need *economic* support for a longer period than ever; but the actual physical chore of supervising the average two-point-something offspring after they have reached school age is simply not enough to absorb the energies of their mother for the rest of her (greatly extended) active life. As for grandmotherhood, which used to mean a resurgence of importance in a new, pleasant and well-nigh indispensable role, it is not what it used to be, certainly in the West. In a society where sex is king and youth at a premium, a forty-two-year-old granny has mixed feelings about laying claim to the title, and with more mobile populations and the fragmentation of the extended family it is a relationship increasingly conducted at long distance via phone calls, and birthday cards, rather than in the chimney corner with fairy tales and lullabies.

The net result is that a girl who plumps joyously at sixteen for being "strictly a female female," with her eyelashes all in curl, and her sights trained on the "career" of marriage, embarks on adult life looking sexy, having fun, and with everything going for her. Anyone who approaches her then and says, "It's all very well being beautiful, but keep pegging away at your math because you may need it yet," or "What about equal pay?" is going to get a very short answer. She knows that youth's a stuff will not endure, her status is as high as a baboon's in full estrus, she's hell-bent on falling in love, and being fallen in love with, and living happily ever after. Nobody can blame her. It's the way she's been conditioned to think.

Around thirty-five or thirty-six she looks over her shopping list one week and sees, with a comic ruefulness, that it includes a couple of items like anti-wrinkle cream and a new slightly more supportive foundation garment because a body stocking no longer quite fills the bill. Slowly, consciously or subconsciously, it gets borne in on her that from here on, for the strictly female female in a sex-obsessed society, the role gets tougher all the time.

This is where, in the more prosperous sections of society, all that famous neurosis begins to set in. If her husband is in the rat race she doesn't dare let up on looking sexy, because her husband's image suffers considerable damage if his wife isn't at least trying her best to be sexually attractive. It used to be okay if she was faithful and patient and competent, but now he has this thing about his virility, and the most sure-fire way of proving it is to have a woman in tow who makes the other chaps feel: "Boy, he's doing all right for himself there!" Moreover, marriage isn't as binding a bond as it used to be. If he feels she's seriously letting him down in this department, he's liable to look elsewhere for this status symbol, and possibly think about switching over in early middle age to a Mark II wife maybe ten or twelve years younger. Because the graph for a man doesn't follow the same curve. His status (sexual as well as social) depends to a much greater extent on factors that at thirty-five or forty are still on the upgrade—power, and knowhow, and money.

America is the place where these attitudes first appeared; they are not nearly as prevalent outside it. It is also the place where (no accident) women's liberation first began to make a real noise. And for most of the Western world, for good or ill, it seems to be the place the wind blows from where social changes of this kind are concerned. If they are, as they appear to be, consequences of increasing affluence and increasingly detaching the concept of sex from the concept of love, they are likely to spread.

"Matriarchy" is a word often applied to American life, but one of the best comments on this came from J. B. Priestley:

"If [American] women become aggressive, demanding, dictatorial, it is because they find themselves struggling to find satisfaction in a world that is not theirs. If they use sex as a weapon, it is because they so badly need a weapon. They are like the inhabitants of an occupied country. They are compelled to accept values and standards that are alien to their deepest nature. . . . A society in which a man takes his wife for a night out and they pay extra, out of their common stock of dollars, to see another woman undressing herself is a society in which the male has completely imposed his values." Woman "is compelled to appear not as her true self, but as the reflection of a man's immature, half-childish, half-adolescent fancies and dreams. Victorious woman forms a lasting relationship with a mature man. Defeated woman strips and teases." If these tendencies continue to spread we shall all be facing defeat.

No one can go on about a problem at the length I have been going on without raising the expectation that the last chapter will demand in ringing tones: "What then must we do to be saved?" and come up with a slick answer. Anyone who fails to do so may be accused of chickening out. I haven't got a slick answer, and I don't particularly mind being accused of chickening out. But since there are a few things I feel quite strongly we ought *not* to do, it might be a good idea to take a tentative stab at considering where we might go from here.

What we surely mustn't do is try to found a women's movement on a kind of pseudo-male bonding, alleging the whole male sex to be a ferocious leopard, and whipping up hatred against it. We mustn't do this for four good reasons.

1. In the words of Bertrand Russell: "To love is wise: to hate is foolish." Any damage it might do to the hated is nothing compared to the corrosive effect it has on the hater.

2. It is arrant nonsense to pretend that men are hateful. Not more than 2 or 3 percent of them are activated by malice against women. It's just that while things are in a state of flux they are just as confused about their role as we are about ours; most of them, if they see any advantage to be gained from the confusion, will attempt to cash in on it, and most women given the chance will do the same. It takes two to tango, and it takes two to make a woman into a sex object: at the time of going to press most women are

highly flattered to be so regarded, and would be insulted if their efforts to look sexy weren't rewarded with precisely this "tribute." If some women feel trapped by marriage, you can bet your bottom dollar that at least as many men feel trapped by it, and any woman feeling disenchanted by the status quo should pay heed to Thurber's heartfelt answer: "We're all disenchanted."

3. As a bonding mechanism it just won't work. Most women don't hallucinate that easily. You may raise the alarm and beat the drum, but when you point your finger at the enemy, most of them will say: "No, no, those aren't leopards. That's the postman, and that one is my son, and the one with the nice blue eyes is the one who was so kind to us last winter when there was all that snow." And they will be right.

4. Where a bonding mechanism doesn't work, more than half the steam that's been worked up gets diverted from the "enemy" and redirected against the "traitors." This we just can't afford. Most women have far too little self-confidence anyway, and when they start criticizing one another everything gets ten times worse. The nonworking wife gets on the defensive because she feels the working ones think she's turning into a vegetable; the working ones are on the defensive because they feel the full-time mothers think their kitchens are in a mess and their children neglected. Childless women write defensive letters to the papers, feeling they are being called selfish because they'd rather have their freedom and a new car or go on with their careers; mothers of five are on the defensive about the population problem. It is time we stopped all this nonsense.

The first of all the things women need to be liberated from is their chronic tendency to feelings (admitted, concealed, or aggressively overcompensated for) of guilt and inadequacy. A woman who feels bad because her house is in a mess is tempted to restore her self-esteem by sneering at her house-proud neighbor: but what on earth is wrong with being house-proud if that's what turns you on? Keeping a house beautiful is no more barren or "stultifying" a job than a professional gardener's keeping a garden beautiful.

Any attempt at "bonding" women into a cohort all facing one way is not only doomed to failure, but will result in undermining their self-esteem still further....

Out with the hate bit, then. I admit to feeling uneasy on this account about Kate Millett's *Sexual Politics*, as well as a few other liberationist writings along the same lines. It's a highly intelligent book meticulously analyzing the pornographic fantasies incorporated in the works of some high-rating and best-selling male authors. But what is Kate Millett's book *for*? What it is saying to women seems to be something like: "This is what men really think of us. It's pretty loathsome and insulting stuff. We do right to hate them."

I doubt it. I doubt whether this kind of writing has anything to do with politics, or with anything at all in the real world. Without having met the gentleman I would hazard a bet that not even Mr. Norman Mailer actually moves around the United States committing brutal sexual attacks on casually encountered females. Surely this is dream stuff, male soap-opera, and the women in it are dolls, not people. And in their waking moments the men who write it must be aware of this truth and act on it; otherwise they would be certifiable.

Let us grant that men, or some men, have some of this stuff fuming around in the bottom of their minds. It's been left there from a very long time ago; it's a little surprising it hasn't evaporated yet. But it has no more "political" significance than Jack and the Beanstalk. It shouldn't be too hard to verify this, for some women likewise have masochistic fantasies, and doubtless they form pair bonds with "sadistic" dreamers and play bedroom games together, as dramatized by John Osborne in one of his plays. The sixty-four-thousand-dollar question is whether the "submissive" partner in these capers is necessarily any more likely on that account to give way in the cold light of dawn over the color of the new drawing-room carpet, or anything else she feels strongly about. And I suspect not. Any more than the jackbooted "governess'-type prostitute could flog an extra thousand dollars out of her kinky clients with her whip. Dream worlds have no effect on where the real power lies.

If we don't go for hate, what should we go for? Two or three objectives seem fairly clear. First, as for any other ex-subject population, greater self-respect. I remember watching Pierre Trudeau in a confrontation with a group of young females, and he addressed them as "girls." They informed him that they had recently attained their majority, and so were no longer girls. This shook him somewhat and he floundered for a minute looking for another polite euphemism for what they were. "Er—ladies?" he hazarded. "We are women," they said, as if they were proud of it. It was like the first time somebody said right out loud: "Black is beautiful."

Second, economic independence; because until every woman feels confident that she can at need support herself we will never quite eradicate the male suspicion that when we say, "I want love. I want a permanent relationship," we really mean, "I want a meal ticket. I want you to work and support me for the rest of my life." It needn't mean the end, for everybody, of the division-of-labor family. If a man wants a wife who will stay home

and raise his children and finds a woman who wants to do just that, then that's fine; as long as he has paused to assure himself that it *is* what he wants and that like anything else it costs money; and as long as she has paused to ask herself the important question, "First I will raise our children— and *then what?*" Because the "then what" may last for forty years and she doesn't want it all to be anticlimax.

Third, the *certainty* of having no more children than she wants, and none at all if she doesn't want any. This is essential not only for women but for everybody, because every human being should have the inalienable right not to be born to a mother who doesn't want him. Once this is fully achieved it will be within the power of every woman to decide whether or not she wishes to have a child.

"Take what you want," said God in the old proverb, "and pay for it." If she wants this, one way or another she's got to pay for it, and it doesn't come cheap. She may do it by devoting a few years of her life to rearing it. She may do it by settling for at least a period of economic dependence (probably on a husband) while she's doing it. If she's very fiercely independent she may do it by settling for a period of comparative economic penury while she's doing it.

She may wish to have the child and get someone else to do most of the rearing, and this is fine if she's lucky enough to have sufficient capital or earning power or a rich enough husband. She has the right to shout and complain and move heaven and earth to try to get some public recognition that the job she's doing is important to society, and money should be expended on enabling her to do it better and more efficiently; and to combine with other women to set up play groups or anything else that will make things easier until such time as heaven and earth begin to listen to her. She has the right and duty to select a husband who also wants children, if she wants them herself; and to urge him to help her as far as he is able and willing.

What she will no longer have any right to do, once "accident" is altogether ruled out and every child is the result of conscious choice, is to give birth to it and then shortly afterward start raising the cry of "Will no one for Pete's sake come and take this kid off my back?" If we campaign for more efficient and foolproof contraception and free abortion on demand (as I believe we must), then we must face the moral consequence of this, which is that motherhood will be an option, not an imperative; that anyone who thinks the price too high needn't take up the option; and from that point on, where children are concerned, more inexorably than ever before, the buck stops here. On the distaff side. If we try to dodge that, we lose all credibility.

What about marriage? The more way-out liberationists seem to be hell-bent on destroying the institution. I can't quite see why there has to be a "policy" about this. When we're just getting loose of one lot of people laying down the law that we *must* get married, it's a bit rough to run head on into another lot telling us we mustn't. It is surely, as Oscar Wilde ruled about the tallness of aunts, a matter that a girl may be allowed to decide for herself.

Anyway, marriage is going to be with us for a long time yet. As Shulamith Firestone mourned: "Everybody debunks marriage, but everybody ends up married." And one of the most durable statements ever made about it was Dr. Johnson's: "Marriage is not commonly unhappy otherwise than as life is unhappy." It can sometimes be tough for two people of opposite sexes trying to live permanently at close quarters without driving each other up the wall. But it can be equally tough trying to do it with someone of the same sex, or with a child, or a parent, or a sibling, or a colleague; or with a succession of different partners; or with a commune (for the rate of failed communes is at least as high as the rate of failed marriages). And it can be toughest of all trying to live in an empty house or apartment quite alone.

Nor is there much fear that men, once sex is more freely available, will seriously seek to escape the "trap" of matrimony. Even on the physical level, there's nothing quite like having it on tap at home, without having to go out in all winds and weathers to chase after it. Besides, though they seldom admit it, their psychological need of a stable relationship is as great as ours, or greater. After studies carried out at the Mental Research Institute in Berkeley, California, a research group reported: "In accordance with the popular idea of marriage as a triumph for women and a defeat for men . . . we could expect to find those men who escaped marriage to be much better adjusted than those women who failed to marry. . . . The findings suggest the opposite. More single men are maladjusted than single women [as shown] particularly in indices of unhappiness, of severe neurotic tendencies and of antisocial tendencies."

So marriage (or something less legalistic but the same in essence) will certainly endure until the people who say it's a miserable institution can come up with a convincing answer to the question, "Compared to what?" I haven't been convinced by any of the answers yet.

But can marriage (or even sex) survive, once women have achieved equality and independence? The cichlid school of thought affects to have grave doubts about this. The cichlid is the fish that the "psychological castration" boys go on about. It appears that a female cichlid is incapable of mating with a male one unless he is aggressive, belligerent, and masterful; and a male cichlid is rendered impotent by a female who fails to put on a display of timorousness and subservience. Therefore, it is subtly implied, if women ever attain equality, then we will find to our horror that men are no longer men, and we will all heartily wish that we hadn't been so hasty.

What we are less often reminded of is that human beings are not fish, but mammals; that psychological castration is quite a common feature in many mammal societies also, but that in these cases the mechanism is totally different. In the vast majority of mammal species the only creature who can psychologically castrate a male mammal is *another* male mammal; and he does it quite simply by beating him in fair combat. This pattern is exemplified over and over again in studies of primate behavior, but the most classic and frequently quoted illustration of the process comes from cattle. There was this bull who was growing older and no longer able to service all the cows in the herd, so they brought in a couple of younger bulls to help him with the chore. He challenged them; he fought them; he defeated them. And not only were the defeated bulls psychologically castrated, but the victorious one had attained such an access of virility that he returned to his harem, serviced all his remaining wives, and snorted around for the rest of the season like Alexander looking for new worlds to conquer. Any man who insists on playing the cichlid game and complaining he's castrated because the little woman isn't being submissive enough shouldn't be surprised if she asks him what's going on at the office lately.

For the real answer to this we needn't go to the animal kingdom at all. In Soviet Russia, women have had economic equality for a long time now. Seventy-five percent of their doc-tors and teachers are women, and 58 percent of their technicians and a third of their engineers, and 63 percent of their economists, and nearly half their scientists and their lawyers, and all the women in all the jobs get equal pay. And while I have heard a lot of criticisms leveled in the West against the average Russian communist, I don't remember hearing anyone call him a sissy.

For a final speculative look into the future I would like to link together one of the earliest and one of the latest items in this history—Darwin, and the pill.

People have talked a good deal about the possible effects of the pill on society, and sexual relations, and the birth rate, and so on. There has been surprisingly little discussion about its possible genetic effects, and what there has been has been conducted mostly in 1984 terms, about the possibility of the state stepping in and stipulating which men and women should be allowed to breed and what type of citizen it wants to produce.

It is very unlikely to happen that way. Reproduction will continue to take place, as it has taken place since the days of the dinosaur and earlier, as a result of processes of natural selection. Only the pill will have thrown two monumental wrenches into the works. One thing it will mean is that the evolutionary effects of natural selection may in some directions be immeasurably speeded up. The other thing is that slightly different types of human beings will be "selected" as parents of the next generation.

Suppose that there is some genetic predisposition in certain women to be more favorably disposed than others to undertake the task of child-rearing. Such a predisposition has been treated in a previous chapter as a class and therefore a cultural difference, which to a great extent it probably is. But almost certainly there are also genetic factors involved. For instance, certain strains of poultry are more "maternally" inclined than others, and this tendency can be greatly increased by selective breeding. A farmer who has invested in an incubator, and doesn't want his hens to stop laying eggs in order to sit on a clutch of them, can breed out the "broodies" until he has eliminated this behavior pattern entirely. He could also do the opposite, if it were in his economic interest to do so.

Back in the jungle or the sea or the savannah, a woman who was deficient in maternal promptings would be less likely than the average to perpetuate her line. She would continue to produce infants but would have less interest in them, less patience with them, and tend to neglect them. More of them would die, and the ones who survived would be unlikely to become dominant and prolific, though some might be taken under the wing of other females and thrive. The mechanism would be weighted appreciably against this nonmaternal factor. It would not entirely die out, but its incidence would not increase.

In civilized society up to the last century the picture was different. Women who didn't want or like children continued to produce them quite prolifically because they fell in love, or because they wanted a home and security and marital status, and the children arrived as part of the package deal. The danger that they would actually die of neglect and starvation as a direct result of maternal indifference was less, and in the more prosperous sections of society where one woman produced the child and another woman reared it, it was nil. It was perfectly possible for a woman totally deficient in maternal promptings to produce a large, highly prosperous, and dominant line of progeny. Her kind would multiply, especially in the upper classes, and there is some reason to

believe that it did: as with the poultry, the "broodies" were increasingly bred out.

But if we arrive at a situation where a woman can have sex and security without having children, where children are a handicap to her in pursuing the objectives more important to her, where nannies are a rare and terribly expensive luxury, and where demographers are plugging childlessness as a benefaction to humanity, such a woman is increasingly likely to have very few children or none. She will select herself out. It will not be a painfully slow and gradual business, as evolutionary processes have hitherto been, powered only by the fact that certain genetic factors make their inheritors marginally more or marginally less likely to survive. It could come down like a guillotine. If we lost the tradition that there is some "status" involved in being a mother—it is a tradition beginning to falter and has recently for the first time ever been coming under direct fire—then the only women to have children would be the ones who cordially wanted them. The others would wipe themselves out in a generation.

It may well be that one hundred and fifty years hence people will read with astonishment of our fears that the net effect of the pill would be to defeminize women. Their own females will all be descendants of grandmothers and great-grandmothers so fizzing with estrogen that a baby meant more to them than almost any other objective in life.

Any selective effect on the males would be far less instantaneous. The impetuous sexy Don Juan character who once careered around stamping his image over large areas of the countryside cannot do so from now on. He may still career, and his animal magnetism may prove as irresistible, but his likeness will not appear in the cradles for very much longer. Whether his type will die out depends on whether there is a hereditary element in his behavior, or whether it is purely a psychological aberration, and we cannot be quite sure about this.

In the past husbands have been selected for a variety of reasons. Physical attractiveness is one, and fairly adaptive since it presupposes at least a degree of health and fitness. Being a "good provider" is another, also adaptive since it implies at least a degree of competence. In the aristocracy "breeding" has weighed heavily—genetically the worst bet of the lot since a noble name correlates neither with physical nor with mental viability. But the net genetic effect of all this in civilized society has been minimal, since unlike the gorilla and the baboon we have monogamy, and the prerogative of the "breeding male" is unknown. Fatherhood is not limited to the handsome, the intelligent, the noble, or the dominant, as long as nearly everybody in the end gets married and children "appear" as a consequence.

In future this may be slightly less true. The truly "proletarian" family (literally those for whom their children constitute their only wealth and for the female her only status) is on the way out, and the woman with the "lady's" attitude (that there are many other and easier ways of getting rewards out of life) is becoming the norm. In places where equality between the sexes has gone furthest, as for instance Moscow, the birth rate is going down fairly rapidly, not because of ecological exhortation by the state —the authorities are getting no joy out of the trend—but because more women have more options to choose from, and they make their own decisions on the matter.

Another tendency beginning to show itself in Russia and Scandinavia and other places is for girls of independent outlook to decide to have the baby without the husband. They obviously feel that the latter is a more bothersome thing to get saddled with than the former.

If both of these trends continue, then the process of husband-selecting might for the first time begin to have some genetic significance. The woman who decides to have a baby without a husband is making a cool and conscious choice anyway, and presumably doesn't select its father without thinking: "I should be well content if my child turned out to resemble him." And if, say, 15 percent of women decided in this way against marriage, the remaining 85 percent would have a wider choice and could afford to be more discriminating. Children are less likely to be the result of a woman's being "swept off her feet" by an excess of passion. She can afford to get swept off her feet with joyous abandon for a year or so and still wait, before cementing the bond with a couple of children, to see whether the partnership looks like settling down comfortably for a long run; and the qualifications for this are somewhat different. It calls for less of sexiness on the male's part and more of loving-kindness. Men who possess most of this quality will be the likeliest to perpetuate their kind and help to form their children's minds.

What it adds up to is that, with the advent of the pill, woman is beginning to get her finger on the genetic trigger. What she will do with it we cannot quite foresee. But it is a far cry from the bull who gets to be prolific just because he's tops at beating the daylights out of all the other bulls.

It may be that for Homo sapiens in the future, extreme manifestations of the behavior patterns of dominance and aggression will be evolutionarily at a discount; and if that happens he will begin to shed them as once, long ago, he shed his coat of fur.

He may feel a little odd for the first

few millennia because he is less accustomed to living without them than we are; but he has passed through more violent vicissitudes than this and survived. He is the most miraculous of all the creatures God ever made or the earth ever spawned. All we need to do is hold out loving arms to him and say:

"Come on in. The water's lovely."

Tom Wolfe (1931–   )
CLEAN FUN AT RIVERHEAD

The inspiration for the demolition derby came to Lawrence Mendelsohn one night in 1958 when he was nothing but a spare-ribbed twenty-eight-year-old stock-car driver halfway through his 10th lap around the Islip, L.I., Speedway and taking a curve too wide. A lubberly young man with a Chicago boxcar haircut came up on the inside in a 1949 Ford and caromed him 12 rows up into the grandstand, but Lawrence Mendelsohn and his entire car did not hit one spectator.

"That was what got me," he said, "I remember I was hanging upside down from my seat belt like a side of Jersey bacon and wondering why no one was sitting where I hit. 'Lousy promotion,' I said to myself.

"Not only that, but everybody who *was* in the stands forgot about the race and came running over to look at me gift-wrapped upside down in a fresh pile of junk."

At that moment occurred the transformation of Lawrence Mendelsohn, racing driver, into Lawrence Mendelsohn, promoter, and, a few transactions later, owner of the Islip Speedway, where he kept seeing more of this same underside of stock car racing that everyone in the industry avoids putting into words. Namely, that for every purist who comes to see the fine points of the race, such as who is going to win, there are probably five waiting for the wrecks to which stock car racing is so gloriously prone.

The pack will be going into a curve when suddenly two cars, three cars, four cars tangle, spinning and splattering all over each other and the retaining walls, upside down, right side up, inside out and in pieces, with the seams bursting open and discs, rods, wires and gasoline spewing out and yards of sheet metal shearing off like Reynolds Wrap and crumpling into the most baroque shapes, after which an ash-blue smoke starts seeping up from the ruins and a thrill begins to spread over the stands like Newburg sauce.

So why put up with the monotony between crashes?

Such, in brief, is the early history of what is culturally the most important sport ever originated in the United States, a sport that ranks with the gladiatorial games of Rome as a piece of national symbolism. Lawrence Mendelsohn had a vision of an automobile sport that would be all crashes. Not two cars, not three cars, not four cars, but 100 cars would be out in an arena doing nothing but smashing each other into shrapnel. The car that outrammed

Reprinted with the permission of Farrar, Straus & Giroux, Inc., from *The Kandy-Kolored Tangerine-Flake Streamline Baby* by Tom Wolfe.

and outdodged all the rest, the last car that could still move amid the smoking heap, would take the prize money.

So at 8:15 at night at the Riverhead Raceway, just west of Riverhead, L.I., on Route 25, amid the quaint tranquility of the duck and turkey flatlands of eastern Long Island, Lawrence Mendelsohn stood up on the back of a flat truck in his red neon warmup jacket and lectured his 100 drivers on the rules and niceties of the new game, the "demolition derby." And so at 8:30 the first 25 cars moved out onto the raceway's quarter-mile stock car track. There was not enough room for 100 cars to mangle each other. Lawrence Mendelsohn's dream would require four heats. Now the 25 cars were placed at intervals all about the circumference of the track, making flatulent revving noises, all headed not around the track but toward a point in the center of the infield.

Then the entire crowd, about 4,000, started chanting a countdown, "Ten, nine, eight, seven, six, five, four, three, two," but it was impossible to hear the rest because right after "two" half the crowd went into a strange whinnying wail. The starter's flag went up, and the 25 cars took off, roaring into second gear with no mufflers, all headed toward that same point in the center of the infield, converging nose on nose.

The effect was exactly what one expects that many simultaneous crashes to produce: the unmistakable tympany of automobiles colliding and cheapgauge sheet metal buckling; front ends folding together at the same cockeyed angles police photographs of night-time wreck scenes capture so well on grainy paper; smoke pouring from under the hoods and hanging over the infield like a howitzer cloud; a few of the surviving cars lurching eccentrically on bent axles. At last, after four heats, there were only two

cars moving through the junk, a 1953 Chrysler and a 1958 Cadillac. In the Chrysler a small fascia of muscles named Skip Ligon who smoked a cigar while he drove, had the Cadillac cornered up against a guard rail in front of the main grandstand. He dispatched it by swinging around and backing full throttle through the left side of its grille and radiator.

By now the crowd was quite beside itself. Spectators broke through a gate in the retaining screen. Some rushed to Spider Ligon's car, hoisted him to their shoulders and marched off the field, howling. Others clambered over the stricken cars of the defeated, enjoying the details of their ruin, and howling. The good, full cry of triumph and annihilation rose from Riverhead Raceway, and the demolition derby was over.

That was the 154th demolition derby in two years. Since Lawrence Mendelsohn staged the first one at Islip Speedway in 1961, they have been held throughout the United States at the rate of one every five days, resulting in the destruction of about 15,000 cars. The figures alone indicate a gluttonous appetite for the sport. Sports writers, of course, have managed to ignore demolition derbies even more successfully than they have ignored stock car racing and drag racing. All in all, the new automobile sports have shown that the sports pages, which on the surface appear to hum with life and earthiness, are at bottom pillars of gentility. This drag racing and demolition derbies and things, well, there are too many kids in it with sideburns, tight Levis and winkle-picker boots.

Yet the demolition derbies keep growing on word-of-mouth publicity. The "nationals" were held last month at Langhorne, Pa., with 50 cars in the finals, and demolition derby fans everywhere know that Don McTavish, of Dover, Mass., is the new world's champion. About 1,250,000 spectators have come to the 154 contests held so far. More than 75 per cent of the derbies have drawn full houses.

The nature of their appeal is clear enough. Since the onset of the Christian era, i.e., since about 500 A.D., no game has come along to fill the gap left by the abolition of the purest of all sports, gladiatorial combat. As late as 300 A.D. these bloody duels, usually between men but sometimes between women and dwarfs, were enormously popular not only in Rome but throughout the Roman Empire. Since then no game, not even boxing, has successfully acted out the underlying motifs of most sport, that is, aggression and destruction.

Boxing, of course, is an aggressive sport, but one contestant has actually destroyed the other in a relatively small percentage of matches. Other games are progressively more sublimated forms of sport. Often, as in the case of football, they are encrusted with oddments of passive theology and metaphysics to the effect that the real purpose of the game is to foster character, teamwork, stamina, physical fitness and the ability to "give-and-take."

But not even those wonderful clergymen who pray in behalf of Congress, expressway ribbon-cuttings, urban renewal projects and testimonial dinners for ethnic aldermen would pray for a demolition derby. The demolition derby is, pure and simple, a form of gladiatorial combat for our times.

As hand-to-hand combat has gradually disappeared from our civilization, even in wartime, and competition has become more and more sophisticated and abstract, Americans have turned to the automobile to satisfy their love of direct aggression. The mild-mannered man who turns into a bear behind the wheel of a car—i.e., who finds in the power of the automobile a vehicle for the release of his inhibitions—is part of American folklore. Among teen-agers the automobile has become

the symbol, and in part the physical means, of triumph over family and community restrictions. Seventy-five per cent of all car thefts in the United States are by teen-agers out for "joy rides."

The symbolic meaning of the automobile tones down but by no means vanishes in adulthood. Police traffic investigators have long been convinced that far more accidents are purposeful crashes by belligerent drivers than they could ever prove. One of the heroes of the era was the Middle Eastern diplomat who rammed a magazine writer's car from behind in the Kalorama embassy district of Washington two years ago. When the American bellowed out the window at him, he backed up and smashed his car again. When the fellow leaped out of his car to pick a fight, he backed up and smashed his car a third time, then drove off. He was recalled home for having "gone native."

The unabashed, undisguised, quite purposeful sense of destruction of the demolition derby is its unique contribution. The aggression, the battering, the ruination are there to be enjoyed. The crowd at a demolition derby seldom gasps and often laughs. It enjoys the same full-throated participation as Romans at the Colosseum. After each trial or heat at a demolition derby, two drivers go into the finals. One is the driver whose car was still going at the end. The other is the driver the crowd selects from among the 24 vanquished on the basis of his courage, showmanship or simply the awesomeness of his crashes. The numbers of the cars are read over loudspeakers, and the crowd chooses one with its cheers. By the same token, the crowd may force a driver out of competition if he appears cowardly or merely cunning. This is the sort of driver who drifts around the edge of the battle avoiding crashes with the hope that the other cars will eliminate one another. The umpire waves a yellow flag at him and he must crash into someone within 30 seconds or run the risk of being booed off the field in dishonor and disgrace.

The frank relish of the crowd is nothing, however, compared to the kick the contestants get out of the game. It costs a man an average of $50 to retrieve a car from a junk yard and get it running for a derby. He will only get his money back—$50— for winning a heat. The chance of being smashed up in the madhouse first 30 seconds of a round are so great, even the best of drivers faces long odds in his shot at the $500 first prize. None of that matters to them.

Tommy Fox, who is nineteen, said he entered the demolition derby because, "You know, it's fun. I like it. You know what I mean?" What was fun about it? Tommy Fox had a way of speaking that was much like the early Marlon Brando. Much of what he had to say came from the trapezii, which he rolled quite a bit, and the forehead, which he cocked, and the eyebrows, which he could bring together expressively from time to time. "Well," he said, "you know, like when you hit 'em, and all that. It's fun."

Tommy Fox had a lot of fun in the first heat. Nobody was bashing around quite like he was in his old green Hudson. He did not win, chiefly because he took too many chances, but the crowd voted him into the finals as the best showman.

"I got my brother," said Tommy. "I came in from the side and he didn't even see me."

His brother is Don Fox, thirty-two, who owns the junk yard where they both got their cars. Don likes to hit them, too, only he likes it almost too much. Don drives with such abandon, smashing into the first car he can get a shot at and leaving himself wide open, he does not stand much chance of finishing the first three minutes.

For years now sociologists have been calling upon one another to undertake a serious study of America's "car culture." No small part of it is the way the automobile has, for one very large segment of the population, become the focus of the same sort of quasi-religious dedication as art is currently for another large segment of a higher social order. Tommy Fox is unemployed, Don Fox runs a junk yard, Spider Ligon is a maintenance man for Brookhaven Naval Laboratory, but to categorize them as such is getting no closer to the truth than to have categorized William Faulkner in 1926 as a clerk at Lord & Taylor, although he was.

Tommy Fox, Don Fox and Spider Ligon are acolytes of the car culture, an often esoteric world of arts and sciences that came into its own after World War II and now has believers of two generations. Charlie Turbush, thirty-five, and his son, Buddy, seventeen, were two more contestants, and by no stretch of the imagination can they be characterized as bizarre figures or cultists of the death wish. As for the dangers of driving in a demolition derby, they are quite real by all physical laws. The drivers are protected only by crash helmets, seat belts and the fact that all glass, interior handles, knobs and fixtures have been removed. Yet Lawrence Mendelsohn claims that there have been no serious injuries in 154 demolition derbies and now gets his insurance at a rate below that of stock car racing.

The sport's future may depend in part on word getting around about its relative safety. Already it is beginning to draw contestants here and there from social levels that could give the demolition derby the cachet of respectability. In eastern derbies so far two doctors and three young men of more than passable connections in eastern society have entered under whimsical *noms de combat* and emerged neither scarred nor victorious. Bull fighting had to win the same social combat.

All of which brings to mind that fine afternoon when some high-born Roman women were out in Nero's box at the Colosseum watching this sexy Thracian carve an ugly little Samnite up into prime cuts, and one said, darling, she had an inspiration, and Nero, needless to say, was all for it. Thus began the new vogue of Roman socialites fighting as gladiators themselves, for kicks. By the second century A.D. even the Emperor Commodus was out there with a tiger's head as a helmet hacking away at some poor dazed fall guy. He did a lot for the sport. Arenas sprang up all over the empire like shopping center bowling alleys.

The future of the demolition derby, then, stretches out over the face of America. The sport draws no lines of gender, and post-debs may reach Lawrence Mendelsohn at his office in Deer Park.

Dwight D. Eisenhower et al.

THE VIETNAMIZATION OF VIETNAM: AN ORAL CHRONICLE

YOU HAVE A ROW OF DOMINOES SET UP, YOU KNOCK OVER
THE FIRST ONE, AND WHAT WILL HAPPEN TO THE LAST ONE
IS THE CERTAINTY THAT IT WILL GO OVER VERY QUICKLY.

—President Dwight D. Eisenhower explaining "the falling domino principle" at a news conference, April 1954

MY SOLUTIONS? TELL THE VIETNAMESE THEY'VE GOT
TO DRAW IN THEIR HORNS OR WE'RE GOING TO BOMB
THEM BACK INTO THE STONE AGE.

—Gen. Curtis E. LeMay, Air Force Chief of Staff, May 1964

BUT WE ARE NOT ABOUT TO SEND AMERICAN BOYS NINE
OR TEN THOUSAND MILES AWAY FROM HOME TO DO WHAT
ASIAN BOYS OUGHT TO BE DOING FOR THEMSELVES.

—President Lyndon B. Johnson, Akron, Ohio, October 1964

COME HOME WITH THAT COONSKIN ON THE WALL.

—President Johnson to commanders at Cam Ranh Bay, October 1966

I SEE LIGHT AT THE END OF THE TUNNEL.

—Walt W. Rostow, President Johnson's national security adviser, in *Look*, December 1967

WE HAD TO DESTROY IT IN ORDER TO SAVE IT.

—American officer at Ben Tre after Tet attack, February 1968

IN THE PATRIOTIC STRUGGLE AGAINST U.S. AGGRESSION, WE
SHALL HAVE INDEED TO UNDERGO MORE DIFFICULTIES AND
SACRIFICES, BUT WE ARE SURE TO WIN TOTAL VICTORY. THIS
IS AN ABSOLUTE CERTAINTY.

—The Last Testament of Ho Chi Minh, 1969

WE BELIEVE PEACE IS AT HAND.

—Henry A. Kissinger, President Richard M. Nixon's national security adviser, October 1972

THIS IS IT. EVERYBODY OUT.

—Word from the American embassy in Saigon to the last American evacuees from the city

Terror of War. Children flee from their village after South Vietnamese planes dropped Napalm on it by mistake during the Vietnamese war. *(Wide World Photos)*

FICTION

John Cheever (1912–   )

THE SWIMMER

It was one of those midsummer Sundays when everyone sits around saying: "I *drank* too much last night." You might have heard it whispered by the parishioners leaving church, heard it from the lips of the priest himself, struggling with his cassock in the *vestiarium,* heard it from the golf links and the tennis courts, heard it from the wild-life preserve where the leader of the Audubon group was suffering from a terrible hangover. "I *drank* too much," said Donald Westerhazy. "We all *drank* too much," said Lucinda Merill. "It must have been the wine," said Helen Westerhazy. "I *drank* too much of that claret."

This was at the edge of the Westerhazys' pool. The pool, fed by an artesian well with a high iron content, was a pale shade of green. It was a fine day. In the west there was a massive stand of cumulus cloud so like a city seen from a distance—from the bow of an approaching ship—that it might have had a name. Lisbon. Hackensack. The sun was hot. Neddy Merill sat by the green water, one hand in it, one around a glass of gin. He was a slender man—he seemed to have the especial slenderness of youth—and while he was far from young he had slid down his banister that morning and

given the bronze backside of Aphrodite on the hall table a smack, as he jogged toward the smell of coffee in his dining room. He might have been compared to a summer's day, particularly the last hours of one, and while he lacked a tennis racket or a sail bag the impression was definitely one of youth, sport, and clement weather. He had been swimming, and now he was breathing deeply, stertorously as if he could gulp into his lungs the components of that moment, the heat of the sun, the intenseness of his pleasure. It all seemed to flow into his chest. His own house stood in Bullet Park, eight miles to the south, where his four beautiful daughters would have had their lunch and might be playing tennis. Then it occurred to him that by taking a dogleg to the southwest he could reach his home by water.

His life was not confining and the delight he took in this observation could not be explained by its suggestion of escape. He seemed to see, with a cartographer's eye, that string of swimming pools, that quasi-subterranean stream that curved across the country. He had made a discovery, a contribution to modern geography; he would name the stream Lucinda after his wife. He was not a practical joker nor was he a fool but he was determinedly original and had a vague and modest idea of himself as a legendary figure. The day was beautiful and it seemed to him that a long swim might enlarge and celebrate its beauty.

He took off a sweater that was hung over his shoulders and dove in. He had an inexplicable contempt for men who did not hurl themselves into pools. He swam a choppy crawl, breathing either with every stroke or every fourth stroke and counting somewhere well in the back of his mind the one-two one-two of a flutter kick. It was not a serviceable stroke for long distances but the domestication of swimming had saddled the sport with some customs and in his part of the world a crawl was customary. To be embraced and sustained by the light green water was less a pleasure, it seemed, than the resumption of a natural condition, and he would have liked to swim without trunks, but this was not possible, considering his project. He hoisted himself up on the far curb —he never used the ladder—and started across the lawn. When Lucinda asked where he was going he said he was going to swim home.

The only maps and charts he had to go by were remembered or imaginary but these were clear enough. First there were the Grahams, the Hammers, the Lears, the Howlands, and the Crosscups. He would cross Ditmar Street to the Bunkers and come, after a short portage, to the Levys, the Welchers; and the public pool in Lancaster. Then there were the Hallorans, the Sachses, the Biswangers, Shirley Adams, the Gilmartins, and the Clydes. The day was lovely, and that he lived in a world so generously supplied with water seemed like a clemency, a beneficence. His heart was high and he ran across the grass. Making his way home by an uncommon route gave him the feeling that he was a pilgrim, an explorer, a man with a destiny, and he knew that he would find friends all along the way; friends would line the banks of the Lucinda River.

He went through a hedge that separated the Westerhazys' land from the Grahams', walked under some flowering apple trees, passed the shed that housed their pump and filter, and came out at the Grahams' pool. "Why Neddy," Mrs. Graham said, "what a marvelous surprise. I've been trying to get you on the phone all morning. Here let me get you a drink." He saw then, like any explorer, that the hospitable customs and traditions of the natives would have to be handled with diplomacy if he was ever going to reach his destination. He did not want to mystify or seem rude to the Grahams nor did he have the time to linger there. He swam the length of their pool and joined them in the sun and was rescued, a few minutes later, by the arrival of two car-loads of friends from Connecticut. During the uproarious reunions he was able to slip away. He went down by the front of the Grahams' house, stepped over a thorny hedge, and crossed a vacant lot to the Hammers'. Mrs. Hammer, looking up from her roses, saw him swim by although she wasn't quite sure who it was. The Lears heard him splashing past the open windows of their living room. The Howlands and the Crosscups were away. After leaving the Howlands' he crossed Ditmar Street and started for the Bunkers', where he could hear, even at that distance, the noise of a party.

The water refracted the sound of voices and laughter and seemed to suspend it in midair. The Bunkers' pool was on a rise and he climbed some stairs to a terrace where twenty-five or thirty men and women were drinking. The only person in the water was Rusty Towers, who floated there on a rubber raft. Oh how bonny and lush were the banks of the Lucinda River! Prosperous men and women gathered by the sapphire-colored waters while caterer's men in white coats passed them cold gin. Overhead a red de Haviland trainer was circling around and around and around in the sky with something like the glee of a child in a swing. Ned felt a passing affection for the scene, a tenderness for the gathering, as if it was something he might touch. In the distance he heard thunder. As soon as Enid Bunker saw him she began to scream: "Oh look who's here! What a marvelous surprise! When Lucinda said that you couldn't come I thought I'd *die.*" She made her way to him through the crowd, and when they had finished kissing she led him to the bar, a progress that was slowed by the fact that he stopped to kiss eight or ten other women and shake the hands of as many men. A smiling bartender he had seen at a hundred parties gave him a gin and tonic and he stood by the bar for a moment, anxious not to get stuck in any conversation that would delay his voyage. When he seemed about to be surrounded he dove in and swam close to the side to avoid colliding with Rusty's raft. At the far end of the pool he bypassed the Tomlinsons with a broad smile and jogged up the garden path. The gravel cut his feet but this was the only unpleasantness. The party was confined to the pool, and as he went toward the house he heard the brilliant, watery sound of voices fade, heard the noise of a radio from the Bunkers' kitchen, where someone was listening to a ballgame. Sunday afternoon. He made his way through the parked cars and down the grassy border of their driveway to Alewives' Lane. He did not want to be seen on the road in his bathing trunks but there was no traffic and he made the short distance to the Levys' driveway, marked with a private property sign and a green tube for the *New York Times.* All the doors and windows of the big house were open but there

were no signs of life; not even a dog barked. He went around the side of the house to the pool and saw that the Levys had only recently left. Glasses and bottles and dishes of nuts were on a table at the deep end, where there was a bathhouse or gazebo, hung with Japanese lanterns. After swimming the pool he got himself a glass and poured a drink. It was his fourth or fifth drink and he had swum nearly half the length of the Lucinda River. He felt tired, clean, and pleased at that moment to be alone; pleased with everything.

It would storm. The stand of cumulus cloud—that city—had risen and darkened, and while he sat there he heard the percussiveness of thunder again. The de Haviland trainer was still circling overhead and it seemed to Ned that he could almost hear the pilot laugh with pleasure in the afternoon; but when there was another peal of thunder he took off for home. A train whistle blew and he wondered what time it had gotten to be. Four! Five? He thought of the provincial station at that hour, where a waiter, his tuxedo concealed by a raincoat, a dwarf with some flowers wrapped in newspaper, and a woman who had been crying would be waiting for the local. It was suddenly growing dark; it was that moment when the pin-headed birds seem to organize their song into some acute and knowledgeable recognition of the storm's approach. Then there was a fine noise of rushing water from the crown of an oak at his back, as if a spigot there had been turned. Then the noise of fountains came from the crowns of all the tall trees. Why did he love storms, what was the meaning of his excitement when the door sprang open and the rain wind fled rudely up the stairs, why had the simple task of shutting the windows of an old house seemed fitting and urgent, why did the first watery notes of a storm wind have for him the unmistakable sound of good news, cheer, glad tidings? Then there was an explosion, a smell of cordite, and rain lashed the Japanese lanterns that Mrs. Levy had bought in Kyoto the year before last, or was it the year before that?

He stayed in the Levys' gazebo until the storm had passed. The rain had cooled the air and he shivered. The force of the wind had stripped a maple of its red and yellow leaves and scattered them over the grass and the water. Since it was midsummer the tree must be blighted, and yet he felt a peculiar sadness at this sign of autumn. He braced his shoulders, emptied his glass, and started for the Welchers' pool. This meant crossing the Lindleys' riding ring and he was surprised to find it over-grown with grass and all the jumps dismantled. He wondered if the Lindleys had sold their horses or gone away for the summer and put them out to board. He seemed to remember having heard something about the Lindleys and their horses but the memory was unclear. On he went, barefoot through the wet grass, to the Welchers', where he found their pool was dry.

This breach in his chain of water disappointed him absurdly, and he felt like some explorer who seeks a torrential headwater and finds a dead stream. He was disappointed and mystified. It was common enough to go away for the summer but no one ever drained his pool. The Welchers had definitely gone away. The pool furniture was folded, stacked, and covered with a tarpaulin. The bathhouse was locked. All the windows of the house were shut, and when he went around to the driveway in front he saw a for-sale sign nailed to a tree. When had he last heard from the Welchers—when, that is, had he and Lucinda last regretted an invitation to dine with them. It seemed only a week or so ago. Was his memory failing or had he

so disciplined it in the repression of unpleasant facts that he had damaged his sense of the truth? Then in the distance he heard the sound of a tennis game. This cheered him, cleared away all his apprehensions and let him regard the overcast sky and the cold air with indifference. This was the day that Neddy Merrill swam across the county. That was the day! He started off then for his most difficult portage.

Had you gone for a Sunday afternoon ride that day you might have seen him, close to naked, standing on the shoulders of route 424, waiting for a chance to cross. You might have wondered if he was the victim of foul play, had his car broken down, or was he merely a fool. Standing barefoot in the deposits of the highway—beer cans, rags, and blowout patches—exposed to all kinds of ridicule, he seemed pitiful. He had known when he started that this was a part of his journey—it had been on his maps—but confronted with the lines of traffic, worming through the summery light, he found himself unprepared. He was laughed at, jeered at, a beer can was thrown at him, and he had no dignity or humor to bring to the situation. He could have gone back, back to the Westerhazys', where Lucinda would still be sitting in the sun. He had signed nothing, vowed nothing, pledged nothing not even to himself. Why, believing as he did, that all human obduracy was susceptible to common sense, was he unable to turn back? Why was he determined to complete his journey even if it meant putting his life in danger? At what point had this prank, this joke, this piece of horseplay become serious? He could not go back, he could not even recall with any clearness the green water at the Westerhazys', the sense of inhaling the day's components, the friendly and relaxed voices saying that they had *drunk* too much. In the space of an hour, more or less, he had covered a distance that made his return impossible.

An old man, tooling down the highway at fifteen miles an hour, let him get to the middle of the road, where there was a grass divider. Here he was exposed to the ridicule of the northbound traffic, but after ten or fifteen minutes he was able to cross. From here he had only a short walk to the Recreation Center at the edge of the Village of Lancaster, where there were some handball courts and a public pool.

The effect of the water on voices, the illusion of brilliance and suspense, was the same here as it had been at the Bunkers' but the sounds here were louder, harsher, and more shrill, and as soon as he entered the crowded enclosure he was confronted with regimentation. "ALL SWIMMERS MUST TAKE A SHOWER BEFORE USING THE POOL. ALL SWIMMERS MUST USE THE FOOTBATH. ALL SWIMMERS MUST WEAR THEIR IDENTIFICATION DISKS." He took a shower, washed his feet in a cloudy and bitter solution and made his way to the edge of the water. It stank of chlorine and looked to him like a sink. A pair of lifeguards in a pair of towers blew police whistles at what seemed to be regular intervals and abused the swimmers through a public address system. Neddy remembered the sapphire water at the Bunkers' with longing and thought that he might contaminate himself—damage his own prosperousness and charm—by swimming in this murk, but he reminded himself that he was an explorer, a pilgrim, and that this was merely a stagnant bend in the Lucinda River. He dove, scowling with distaste, into the chlorine and had to swim with his head above water to avoid collisions, but even so he was bumped into, splashed and jostled. When he got to the shallow end both lifeguards were shouting at him; "Hey, you, you without the identification disk, get outa the water." He did, but they had no way of pursuing him and he went through the reek of suntan oil and chlorine out through the hurricane fence and passed the handball courts. By crossing the road he entered the wooded part of the Halloran estate. The woods were not cleared and the footing was treacherous and difficult until he reached the lawn and the clipped beech hedge that encircled their pool.

The Hallorans were friends, an elderly couple of enormous wealth who seemed to bask in the suspicion that they might be Communists. They were zealous reformers but they were not Communists, and yet when they were accused, as they sometimes were, of subversion, it seemed to gratify and excite them. Their beech hedge was yellow and he guessed this had been blighted like the Levys' maple. He called hullo, hullo, to warn the Hallorans of his approach, to palliate his invasion of their privacy. The Hallorans, for reasons that had never been explained to him, did not wear bathing suits. No explanations were in order, really. Their nakedness was a detail in their uncompromising zeal for reform and he stepped politely out of his trunks before he went through the opening in the hedge.

Mrs. Halloran, a stout woman with white hair and a serene face, was reading the *Times*. Mr. Halloran was taking beech leaves out of the water with a scoop. They seemed not surprised or displeased to see him. Their pool was perhaps the oldest in the county, a fieldstone rectangle, fed by a brook. It had no filter or pump and its waters were the opaque gold of the stream.

"I'm swimming across the county," Ned said.

"Why, I didn't know one could," exclaimed Mrs. Halloran.

"Well, I've made it from the Westerhazys'," Ned said. "That must be about four miles."

He left his trunks at the deep end, walked to the shallow end, and swam this stretch. As he was pulling himself out of the water he heard Mrs. Halloran say: "We've been *terribly* sorry to hear about all your misfortunes?" Neddy."

"My misfortunes?" Ned asked. "I don't know what you mean."

"Why, we heard that you'd sold the house and that your poor children . . ."

"I don't recall having sold the house," Ned said, "and the girls are at home."

"Yes," Mrs. Halloran sighed. "Yes . . ." Her voice filled the air with an unseasonable melancholy and Ned spoke briskly. "Thank you for the swim."

"Well, have a nice trip," said Mrs. Halloran.

Beyond the hedge he pulled on his trunks and fastened them. They were loose and he wondered if, during the space of an afternoon, he could have lost some weight. He was cold and he was tired and the naked Hallorans and their dark water had depressed him. The swim was too much for his strength but how could he have guessed this, sliding down the banister that morning and sitting in the Westerhazys' sun? His arms were lame. His legs felt rubbery and ached at the joints. The worst of it was the cold in his bones and the feeling that he might never be warm again. Leaves were falling down around him and he smelled woodsmoke on the wind. Who would be burning wood at this time of year?

He needed a drink. Whiskey would warm him, pick him up, carry him through the last of his journey, refresh his feeling that it was original and valorous to swim the county. Channel swimmers took brandy. He needed a stimulant. He crossed the lawn in front of the Hallorans' house and went down a little path to where they had built a house for their only daughter Helen and her husband Eric Sachs. The Sachses' pool was small and he found Helen and her husband there.

"Oh, *Neddy*," Helen said. "Did you lunch at Mother's?"

"Not *really*," Ned said. "I *did* stop to see your parents." This seemed to be explanation enough. "I'm terribly sorry to break in on you like this but I've taken a chill and I wonder if you'd give me a drink."

"Why, I'd *love* to," Helen said, "but there hasn't been anything in this house to drink since Eric's operation. That was three years ago."

Was he losing his memory, had his gift for concealing painful facts let him forget that he had sold his house, that his children were in trouble, and that his friend had been ill? His eyes slipped from Eric's face to his abdomen, where he saw three pale, sutured scars, two of them at least a foot long. Gone was his navel, and what, Neddy thought, would the roving hand, bed-checking one's gifts at 3 A.M. make of a belly with no navel, no link to birth, this breach in the succession?

"I'm sure you can get a drink at the Biswangers'," Helen said. "They're having an enormous do. You can hear it from here. Listen!"

She raised her head and from across the road, the lawns, the gardens, the woods, the fields, he heard again the brilliant noise of voices over water. "Well, I'll get wet," he said, still feeling that he had no freedom of choice about his means of travel. He dove into the Sachses' cold water and, gasping, close to drowning, made his way from one end of the pool to the other. "Lucinda and I want *terribly* to see you," he said over his shoulder, his face set toward the Biswangers'. "We're sorry it's been so long and we'll call you *very* soon."

He crossed some fields to the Biswangers' and the sounds of revelry there. They would be honored to give him a drink, they would be happy to give him a drink, they would in fact be lucky to give him a drink. The Biswangers invited him and Lucinda for dinner four times a year, six weeks in advance. They were always rebuffed and yet they continued to send out their invitations, unwilling to comprehend the rigid and undemocratic realities of their society. They were the sort of people who discussed the price of things at cocktails, exchanged market tips during dinner, and after dinner told dirty stories to mixed company. They did not belong to Neddy's set—they were not even on Lucinda's Christmas card list. He went toward their pool with feelings of indifference, charity, and some unease, since it seemed to be getting dark and these were the longest days of the year. The party when he joined it was noisy and large. Grace Biswanger was the kind of hostess who asked the optometrist, the veterinarian, the real-estate dealer and the dentist. No one was swimming and the twilight, reflected on the water of the pool, had a wintry gleam. There was a bar and he started for this. When Grace Biswanger saw him she came toward him, not affectionately as he had every right to expect, but bellicosely.

"Why, this party has everything," she said loudly, "including a gate crasher."

She could not deal him a social blow—there was no question about this and he did not flinch. "As a gate crasher," he asked politely, "do I rate a drink?"

"Suit yourself," she said. "You don't seem to pay much attention to invitations."

She turned her back on him and joined some guests, and he went to the bar and ordered a whiskey. The bartender served him but he served him rudely. His was a world in which the caterer's men kept the social score, and to be rebuffed by a part-time barkeep meant that he had suffered some loss of social esteem. Or perhaps the man was new and uninformed. Then he heard Grace at his back say: "They went for broke overnight—nothing but income —and he showed up drunk one Sunday and asked us to loan him five thousand dollars. . . ." She was always talking about money. It was worse than eating your peas off a knife. He dove into the pool, swam its length and went away.

The next pool on his list, the last but two, belonged to his old mistress, Shirley Adams. If he had suffered any injuries at the Biswangers' they would be cured here. Love—sexual rough-house in fact—was the supreme elixir, the painkiller, the brightly colored pill that would put the spring back into his step, the joy of life in his heart. They had had an affair last week, last month, last year. He couldn't remember. It was he who had broken it off, his was the upper hand, and he stepped through the gate of the wall that surrounded her pool with nothing so considered as self-confidence. It seemed in a way to be his pool as the lover, particularly the illicit lover, enjoys the possessions of his mistress with an authority unknown to holy matrimony. She was there, her hair the color of brass, but her figure, at the edge of the lighted, cerulean water, excited in him no profound memories. It had been, he thought, a lighthearted affair, although she had wept when he broke it off. She seemed confused to see him and he wondered if she was still wounded. Would she, God forbid, weep again?

"What do you want?" she asked.

"I'm swimming across the county."

"Good Christ. Will you ever grow up?"

"What's the matter?"

"If you've come here for money," she said, "I won't give you another cent."

"You could give me a drink."

"I could but I won't. I'm not alone."

"Well, I'm on my way."

He dove in and swam the pool, but when he tried to haul himself up onto the curb he found that the strength in his arms and his shoulders had gone, and he paddled to the ladder and climbed out. Looking over his shoulder he saw, in the lighted bathhouse, a young man. Going out onto the dark lawn he smelled chrysanthemums or marigolds—some stubborn autumnal fragrance—on the night air, strong as gas. Looking overhead he saw that the stars had come out, but why should he seem to see Andromeda, Cepheus, and Cassiopeia? What had become of the constellations of midsummer? He began to cry.

It was probably the first time in his adult life that he had ever cried, certainly the first time in his life that he had ever felt so miserable, cold, tired, and bewildered. He could not understand the rudeness of the caterer's barkeep or the rudeness of a mistress who had come to him on her knees and showered his trousers with tears. He had swum too long, he had been immersed too long, and his nose and his throat were sore from the water. What he needed then was a drink, some company, and some clean dry clothes, and while he could have cut directly across the road to his home he went on to the Gilmartins' pool. Here, for the first time in his life, he did not dive but went down the steps into the icy water and swam a hobbled side stroke that he might have learned as a youth. He staggered with fatigue on his way to the Clydes' and paddled the length of their pool, stopping again and again with his hand on the curb to rest. He climbed up the ladder and wondered if he had the strength to get home. He had done what he wanted, he had swum the county, but he was so stupefied with exhaustion that his triumph seemed vague. Stooped, holding onto the gateposts for support, he turned up the driveway of his own house.

The place was dark. Was it so late that they had all gone to bed? Had Lucinda stayed at the Westerhazys' for supper? Had the girls joined her there or gone someplace else? Hadn't they agreed, as they usually did on Sunday, to regret all their invitations and stay at home? He tried the garage doors to see what cars were in but the doors were locked and rust came off the handles onto his hands. Going toward the house, he saw that the force of the thunderstorm had knocked one of the rain gutters loose. It hung down over the front door like an umbrella rib, but it could be fixed in the morning. The house was locked, and he thought that the stupid cook or the stupid maid must have locked the place up until he remembered that it had been some time since they had employed a maid or a cook. He shouted, pounded on the door, tried to force it with his shoulder, and then, looking in at the windows, saw that the place was empty.

Ralph Ellison (1914–   )
KING OF THE BINGO GAME

The woman in front of him was eating roasted peanuts that smelled so good that he could barely contain his hunger. He could not even sleep and wished they'd hurry and begin the bingo game. There, on his right, two fellows were drinking wine out of a bottle wrapped in a paper bag, and he could hear soft gurgling in the dark. His stomach gave a low, gnawing growl. "If this was down South," he thought, "all I'd have to do is lean over and say, 'Lady, gimme a few of those peanuts, please ma'm,' and she'd pass me the bag and never think nothing of it." Or he could ask the fellows for a drink in the same way. Folks down South stuck together that way; they didn't even have to know you. But up here it was different. Ask somebody for something, and they'd think you were crazy. Well, I ain't crazy. I'm just broke, 'cause I got no birth certificate to get a job, and Laura 'bout to die cause we got no money for a doctor. But I ain't crazy. And yet a pinpoint of doubt was focused in his mind as he glanced toward the screen and saw the hero stealthily entering a dark room and sending the beam of a flashlight along a wall of bookcases. This is where he finds the trapdoor, he remembered. The man would pass abruptly through the wall and find the girl tied to a bed, her legs and arms spread wide, and her clothing torn to rags. He laughed softly to himself. He had seen the picture three times, and this was one of the best scenes.

On his right the fellow whispered wide-eyed to his companion, "Man, look a-yonder!"

"Damn!"

"Wouldn't I like to have her tied up like that . . ."

"Hey! That fool's letting her loose!"

"Aw, man, he loves her."

"Love or no love!"

The man moved impatiently beside him, and he tried to involve himself in the scene. But Laura was on his mind. Tiring quickly of watching the picture he looked back to where the white beam filtered from the projection room above the balcony. It started small and grew large, specks of dust dancing in its whiteness as it reached the screen. It was strange how the beam always landed right on the screen and didn't mess up and fall somewhere else. But they had it all fixed. Everything was fixed. Now suppose when they showed that girl with her dress torn the girl started taking off the rest of her clothes, and when the guy came in he didn't untie her but kept her there and went

to taking off his own clothes? *That* would be something to see. If a picture got out of hand like that those guys up there would go nuts. Yeah, and there'd be so many folks in here you couldn't find a seat for nine months! A strange sensation played over his skin. He shuddered. Yesterday he'd seen a bedbug on a woman's neck as they walked out into the bright street. But exploring his thigh through a hole in his pocket he found only goose pimples and old scars.

The bottle gurgled again. He closed his eyes. Now a dreamy music was accompanying the film and train whistles were sounding in the distance, and he was a boy again walking along a railroad trestle down South, and seeing the train coming, and running back as fast as he could go, and hearing the whistle blowing, and getting off the trestle to solid ground just in time, with the earth trembling beneath his feet, and feeling relieved as he ran down the cinderstrewn embankment onto the highway, and looking back and seeing with terror that the train had left the track and was following him right down the middle of the street, and all the white people laughing as he ran screaming . . .

"Wake up there, buddy! What the hell do you mean hollering like that? Can't you see we trying to enjoy this here picture?"

He stared at the man with gratitude. "I'm sorry, old man," he said. "I musta been dreaming."

"Well, here, have a drink. And don't be making no noise like that, damn!"

His hands trembled as he tilted his head. It was not wine, but whiskey. Cold rye whiskey. He took a deep swoller, decided it was better not to take another, and handed the bottle back to its owner.

"Thanks, old man," he said.

Now he felt the cold whiskey breaking a warm path straight through the middle of him, growing hotter and sharper as it moved. He had not eaten all day, and it made him light-headed. The smell of the peanuts stabbed him like a knife, and he got up and found a seat in the middle aisle. But no sooner did he sit than he saw a row of intense-faced young girls, and got up again, thinking, "You chicks musta been Lindy-hopping somewhere." He found a seat several rows ahead as the lights came on, and he saw the screen disappear behind a heavy red and gold curtain; then the curtain rising, and the man with the microphone and a uniformed attendant coming on the stage.

He felt for his bingo cards, smiling. The guy at the door wouldn't like it if he knew about his having *five* cards. Well, not everyone played the bingo game; and even with five cards he didn't have much of a chance. For Laura, though, he had to have faith. He studied the cards, each with its different numerals, punching the free center hole in each and spreading them neatly across his lap, and when the lights faded he sat slouched in his seat so that he could look from his cards to the bingo wheel with but a quick shifting of his eyes.

Ahead, at the end of the darkness, the man with the microphone was pressing a button attached to a long cord and spinning the bingo wheel and calling out the number each time the wheel came to rest. And each time the voice rang out his finger raced over the cards for the number. With five cards he had to move fast. He became nervous; there were too many cards, and the man went too fast with his grating voice. Perhaps he should just select one and throw the others away. But he was afraid. He became warm. Wonder how much Laura's doctor would cost? Damn that, watch the cards! And with despair he heard the man call three in a row which he missed on all five cards. This way he'd never win . . .

When he saw the row of holes punched across the third card, he sat paralyzed and heard the man call three more numbers before he stumbled forward, screaming,

"Bingo! Bingo!"

"Let that fool up there," someone called.

"Get up there, man!"

He stumbled down the aisle and up the steps to the stage into a light so sharp and bright that for a moment it blinded him, and he felt that he had moved into the spell of some strange, mysterious power. Yet it was as familiar as the sun, and he knew it was the perfectly familiar bingo.

The man with the microphone was saying something to the audience as he held out his card. A cold light flashed from the man's finger as the card left his hand. His knees trembled. The man stepped closer, checking the card against the numbers chalked on the board. Suppose he had made a mistake? The pomade on the man's hair made him feel faint, and he backed away. But the man was checking the card over the microphone now, and he had to stay. He stood tense, listening.

"Under the O, forty-four," the man chanted. "Under the I, seven. Under the G, three. Under the B, ninety-six. Under the N, thirteen!"

His breath came easier as the man smiled at the audience.

"Yessir, ladies and gentlemen, he's one of the chosen people!"

The audience rippled with laughter and applause.

"Step right up to the front of the stage."

He moved slowly forward, wishing that the light was not so bright.

"To win tonight's jackpot of $36.90 the wheel must stop between the double zero, understand?"

He nodded, knowing the ritual from the many days and nights he had watched the winners march across the stage to press the button that controlled the spinning wheel and receive the prizes. And now he followed the instructions as though he'd crossed the slippery stage a million prize-winning times.

The man was making some kind of a joke, and he nodded vacantly. So tense had he become that he felt a sudden desire to cry and shook it away. He felt vaguely that his whole life was deter-minded by the bingo wheel; not only that which would happen now that he was at last before it, but all that had gone before, since his birth, and his mother's birth and the birth of his father. It had always been there, even though he had not been aware of it, handing out the unlucky cards and numbers of his days. The feeling per-sisted, and he started quickly away. I better get down from here before I make a fool of myself, he thought.

"Here, boy," the man called. "You haven't started yet."

Someone laughed as he went hesi-tantly back.

"Are you all reet?"

He grinned at the man's jive talk, but no words would come, and he knew it was not a convincing grin. For sud-denly he knew that he stood on the slippery brink of some terrible embar-rassment.

"Where are you from, boy?" the man asked.

"Down South."

"He's from down South, ladies and gentlemen," the man said. "Where from? Speak right into the mike."

"Rocky Mont," he said. "Rock' Mont, North Car'lina."

"So you decided to come down off that mountain to the U.S.," the man laughed. He felt that the man was mak-ing a fool of him, but then something cold was placed in his hand, and the lights were no longer behind him.

Standing before the wheel he felt alone, but that was somehow right, and he remembered his plan. He would give the wheel a short quick twirl. Just a touch of the button. He had watched it many times, and always it came close to

double zero when it was short and quick. He steeled himself; the fear had left, and he felt a profound sense of promise, as though he were about to be repaid for all the things he'd suffered all his life. Trembling, he pressed the but-ton. There was a whirl of lights, and in a second he realized with finality that though he wanted to, he could not stop. It was as though he held a high-powered line in his naked hand. His nerves tightened. As the wheel increased its speed it seemed to draw him more and more into its power, as though it held his fate; and with it came a deep need to submit, to whirl, to lose himself in its swirl of color. He could not stop it now, he knew. So let it be.

The button rested snuggly in his palm where the man had placed it. And now he became aware of the man beside him, advising him through the microphone, while behind the shadowy audience hummed with noisy voices. He shifted his feet. There was still that feel-ing of helplessness within him, making part of him desire to turn back, even now that the jackpot was right in his hand. He squeezed the button until his fist ached. Then, like the sudden shriek of a subway whistle, a doubt tore through his head. Suppose he did not spin the wheel long enough? What could he do, and how could he tell? And then he knew, even as he won-dered, that as long as he pressed the button, he could control the jackpot. He and only he could determine whether or not it was to be his. Not even the man with the microphone could do anything about it now. He felt drunk. Then, as though he had come down from a high hill into a valley of people, he heard the audience yelling.

"Come down from there, you jerk!"

"Let somebody else have a chance..."

"Ole Jack thinks he done found the end of the rainbow..."

The last voice was not unfriendly, and he turned and smiled dreamily into the yelling mouths. Then he turned his back squarely on them.

"Don't take too long, boy," a voice said.

He nodded. They were yelling behind him. Those folks did not understand what had happened to him. They had been playing the bingo game day in and night out for years, trying to win rent money or hamburger change. But not one of those wise guys had discovered this wonderful thing. He watched the wheel whirling past the numbers and experienced a burst of exaltation: This is God! This is the really truly God! He said it aloud, "This is God!"

He said it with such absolute conviction that he feared he would fall fainting into the footlights. But the crowd yelled so loud that they could not hear. Those fools, he thought. I'm here trying to tell them the most wonderful secret in the world, and they're yelling like they gone crazy. A hand fell upon his shoulder.

"You'll have to make a choice now, boy. You've taken too long."

He brushed the hand violently away. "Leave me alone, man. I know what I'm doing!"

The man looked surprised and held on to the microphone for support. And because he did not wish to hurt the man's feelings he smiled, realizing with a sudden pang that there was no way of explaining to the man just why he had to stand there pressing the button forever.

"Come here," he called tiredly.

The man approached, rolling the heavy microphone across the stage.

"Anybody can play this bingo game, right?" he said.

"Sure, but . . ."

He smiled, feeling inclined to be patient with this slick looking white man with his blue sport shirt and his sharp gabardine suit.

"That's what I thought," he said. "Anybody can win the jackpot as long as they get the lucky number, right?"

"That's the rule, but after all . . ."

"That's what I thought," he said. "And the big prize goes to the man who knows how to win it?"

The man nodded speechlessly.

"Well then, go on over there and watch me win like I want to. I ain't going to hurt nobody," he said "and I'll show you how to win. I mean to show the whole world how it's got to be done."

And because he understood, he smiled again to let the man know that he held nothing against him for being white and impatient. Then he refused to see the man any longer and stood pressing the button, the voices of the crowd reaching him like sounds in distant streets. Let them yell. All the Negroes down there were just ashamed because he was black like them. He smiled inwardly, knowing how it was. Most of the time he was ashamed of what Negroes did himself. Well, let them be ashamed for something this time. Like him. He was like a long thin black wire that was being stretched and wound upon the bingo wheel; wound until he wanted to scream; wound, but this time himself controlling the winding and the sadness and the shame, and because he did, Laura would be all right. Suddenly the lights flickered. He staggered backwards. Had something gone wrong? All this noise. Didn't they know that although he controlled the wheel, it also controlled him, and unless he pressed the button forever and forever and ever it would stop, leaving him high and dry, dry and high on this hard high slippery hill and Laura dead? There was only one chance; he had to do whatever the wheel demanded. And gripping the button in despair, he discovered with surprise that it imparted a nervous energy. His spine tingled. He felt a certain power.

Now he faced the raging crowd with defiance, its screams penetrating his eardrums like trumpets shrieking from a jukebox. The vague faces glowing in the bingo lights gave him a sense of himself that he had never known before. He was running the show, by God! They had to react to him, for he was their luck. This is *me*, he thought. Let the bastards yell. Then someone was laughing inside him, and he realized that somehow he had forgotten his own name. It was a sad, lost feeling to lose your name, and a crazy thing to do. That name had been given him by the white man who had owned his grandfather a long lost time ago down South. But maybe those wise guys knew his name.

"Who am I?" he screamed.

"Hurry up and bingo, you jerk!"

They didn't know either, he thought sadly. They didn't even know their own names, they were all poor nameless bastards. Well, he didn't need that old name; he was reborn. For as long as he pressed the button he was The-man-who-pressed-the-button-who-held-the-prize-who-was-the-King-of Bingo. That was the way it was, and he'd have to press the button even if nobody understood, even though Laura did not understand.

"Live!" he shouted.

The audience quieted like the dying of a huge fan.

"Live, Laura, baby. I got holt of it now, sugar. Live!"

He screamed it, tears streaming down his face. "I got nobody but YOU!"

The screams tore from his very guts. He felt as though the rush of blood to his head would burst out in baseball seams of small red droplets, like a head beaten by police clubs. Bending over he saw a trickle of blood splashing the toe of his shoe. With his free hand he felt that the whole audience had somehow entered him and was stamping its feet in his stomach, and he was unable to throw them out. They wanted the prize, that was it. They wanted the secret for themselves. But they'd never get it; he would keep the bingo wheel whirling forever, and Laura would be safe in the wheel. But would she? It had to be, because if she were not safe the wheel would cease to turn; it could not go on. He had to get away, *vomit* all, and his mind formed an image of himself running with Laura in his arms down the tracks of the subway just ahead of an A train, running desperately *vomit* with people screaming for him to come out but knowing no way of leaving the tracks because to stop would bring the train crushing down upon him and to attempt to leave across the other tracks would mean to run into a hot third rail as high as his waist which threw blue sparks that blinded his eyes until he could hardly see.

He heard singing and the audience was clapping its hands.

Shoot the liquor to him, Jim, boy!
Clap-clap-clap
Well a-calla the cop
He's blowing his top!
Shoot the liquor to him, Jim, boy!

Bitter anger grew within him at the singing. They think I'm crazy. Well let 'em laugh. I'll do what I got to do.

He was standing in an attitude of intense listening when he saw that they were watching something on the stage behind him. He felt weak. But when he turned he saw no one. If only his thumb did not ache so. Now they were applauding. And for a moment he thought that the wheel had stopped. But that was impossible, his thumb still pressed the button. Then he saw them. Two men in uniform beckoned from the end of the stage. They were coming toward him, walking in step, slowly, like a tapdance team returning for a third encore. But their shoulders shot forward, and he backed away, looking wildly about. There was nothing to fight them with. He had only the long black cord which led to a plug somewhere back stage, and he couldn't use that because it operated the bingo wheel. He backed slowly, fixing the men with his eyes as his lips stretched over his teeth in a tight, fixed grin; moved toward the end of the stage and realizing that he couldn't go much further, for suddenly the cord became taut and he couldn't afford to break the cord. But he had to do something. The audience was howling. Suddenly he stopped dead, seeing the men halt, their legs lifted as in an interrupted step of a slow-motion dance. There was nothing to do but run in the other direction and he dashed forward, slipping and sliding. The men fell back, surprised. He struck out violently going past.

"Grab him!"

He ran, but all too quickly the cord tightened, resistingly, and he turned and ran back again. This time he slipped them, and discovered by running in a circle before the wheel he could keep the cord from tightening. But this way he had to flail his arms to keep the men away. Why couldn't they leave a man alone? He ran, circling.

"Ring down the curtain," someone yelled. But they couldn't do that. If they did the wheel flashing from the projection room would be cut off. But they had him before he could tell them so, trying to pry open his fist, and he was wrestling and trying to bring his knees into the fight and holding on to the button, for it was his life. And now he was down, seeing a foot coming down, crushing his wrist cruelly, down, as he saw the wheel whirling serenely above.

"I can't give it up," he screamed. Then quietly, in a confidential tone, "Boys, I really can't give it up."

It landed hard against his head. And in the blank moment they had it away from him, completely now. He fought them trying to pull him up from the stage as he watched the wheel spin slowly to a stop. Without surprise he saw it rest a double-zero.

"You see," he pointed bitterly.

"Sure, boy, sure, it's O.K.," one of the men said smiling.

And seeing the man bow his head to someone he could not see, he felt very, very happy; he would receive what all the winners received.

But as he warmed in the justice of the man's tight smile he did not see the man's slow wink, nor see the bow-legged man behind him step clear of the swiftly descending curtain and set himself for a blow. He only felt the dull pain exploding in his skull, and he knew even as it slipped out of him that his luck had run out on the stage.

Bernard Malamud (1914–   )

THE MAGIC BARREL

Not long ago there lived in uptown New York, in a small, almost meager room, though crowded with books, Leo Finkle, a rabbinical student in the Yeshivah University. Finkle, after six years of study, was to be ordained in June and had been advised by an acquaintance that he might find it easier to win himself a congregation if he were married. Since he had no present prospects of marriage, after two tormented days of turning it over in his mind, he called in Pinye Salzman, a marriage broker whose two-line advertisement he had read in the *Forward*.

The matchmaker appeared one night out of the dark fourth-floor hallway of the graystone rooming house where Finkle lived, grasping a black, strapped portfolio that had been worn thin with use. Salzman, who had been long in the business, was of slight but dignified build, wearing an old hat, and an overcoat too short and tight for him. He smelled frankly of fish, which he loved to eat, and although he was missing a few teeth, his presence was not displeasing, because of an amiable manner curiously contrasted with mournful eyes. His voice, his lips, his wisp of beard, his bony fingers were animated, but give him a moment of repose and his mild blue eyes revealed a depth of sadness, a characteristic that put Leo a little at ease although the situation, for him, was inherently tense.

He at once informed Salzman why he had asked him to come, explaining that his home was in Cleveland, and that but for his parents, who had married comparatively late in life, he was alone in the world. He had for six years devoted himself almost entirely to his studies, as a result of which, understandably, he had found himself without time for a social life and the company of young women. Therefore he thought it the better part of trial and error—of embarrassing fumbling—to call in an experienced person to advise him on these matters. He remarked in passing that the function of the marriage broker was ancient and honorable, highly approved in the Jewish community, because it made practical the necessary without hindering joy. Moreover, his own parents had been brought together by a matchmaker. They had made, if not a financially profitable marriage—since neither had possessed any worldly goods to speak of —at least a successful one in the sense of their everlasting devotion to each other. Salzman listened in embarrassed surprise, sensing a sort of apology. Later, however, he experienced a glow of pride in his work, an emotion that had left him years ago, and he heartily approved of Finkle.

The two went to their business. Leo had led Salzman to the only clear place in the room, a table near a window that overlooked the lamp-lit city. He seated himself at the matchmaker's side but facing him, attempting by an act of will to suppress the unpleasant tickle in his throat. Salzman eagerly unstrapped his portfolio and removed a loose rubber band from a thin packet of much-handled cards. As he flipped through them, a gesture and sound that physically hurt Leo, the student pretended not to see and gazed steadfastly out the window. Although it was still February, winter was on its last legs, signs of which he had for the first time in years begun to notice. He now observed the round white moon, moving high in the sky through a cloud menagerie, and watched with half-open mouth as it penetrated a huge hen, and dropped out of her like an egg laying itself. Salzman, though pretending through eyeglasses he had just slipped on, to be engaged in scanning the writing on the cards, stole occasional glances at the young man's distinguished face, noting with pleasure the long, severe scholar's nose, brown eyes heavy with learning, sensitive yet ascetic lips, and a certain, almost hollow quality of the dark cheeks. He gazed around at shelves upon shelves of books and let out a soft, contented sigh.

When Leo's eyes fell upon the cards, he counted six spread out in Salzman's hand.

"So few?" he asked in disappointment.

"You wouldn't believe me how much cards I got in my office," Salzman replied. "The drawers are already filled to the top, so I keep them now in a barrel, but is every girl good for a new rabbi?"

Leo blushed at this, regretting all he had revealed of himself in a curriculum vitae he had sent to Salzman. He had thought it best to acquaint him with his strict standards and specifications, but in having done so, felt he had told the marriage broker more than was absolutely necessary.

He hesitantly inquired, "Do you keep photographs of your clients on file?"

"First comes family, amount of dowry, also what kind promises," Salzman replied, unbuttoning his tight coat and settling himself in the chair. "After comes pictures, rabbi."

"Call me Mr. Finkle. I'm not yet a rabbi."

Salzman said he would, but instead called him doctor, which he changed to rabbi when Leo was not listening too attentively.

Salzman adjusted his horn-rimmed spectacles, gently cleared his throat and read in an eager voice the contents of the top card:

"Sophie P. Twenty four years. Widow one year. No children. Educated high school and two years college. Father promises eight thousand dollars. Has wonderful wholesale business. Also real estate. On the mother's side comes teachers, also one actor. Well known on Second Avenue."

Leo gazed up in surprise. "Did you say a widow?"

"A widow don't mean spoiled, rabbi. She lived with her husband maybe four months. He was a sick boy she made a mistake to marry him."

"Marrying a widow has never entered my mind."

"This is because you have no experience. A widow, especially if she is young and healthy like this girl, is a wonderful person to marry. She will be thankful to you the rest of her life. Believe me, if I was looking now for a bride, I would marry a widow."

Leo reflected, then shook his head.

Salzman hunched his shoulders in an almost imperceptible gesture of disappointment. He placed the card down on the wooden table and began to read another:

"Lily H. High school etacher. Regular. Not a substitute. Has savings and new Dodge car. Lived in Paris one year. Father is successful dentist thirty-five years. Interested in professional man. Well Americanized family. Wonderful opportunity.

"I knew her personally," said Salzman. "I wish you could see this girl. She is a doll. Also very intelligent. All day you could talk to her about books and theyater and what not. She also knows current events."

"I don't believe you mentioned her age?"

"Her age?" Salzman said, raising his brows. "Her age is thirty-two years."

Leo said after a while. "I'm afraid that seems a little too old."

Salzman let out a laugh. "So how old are you, rabbi?"

"Twenty-seven."

"So what is the difference, tell me, between twenty-seven and thirty-two? My own wife is seven years older than me. So what did I suffer?—Nothing. If Rothschild's a daughter wants to marry you, would you say on account her age, no?"

"Yes," Leo said dryly.

Salzman shook off the no in the yes. "Five years don't mean a thing. I give you my word that when you will live with her for one week you will forget her age. What does it mean five years— that she lived more and knows more than somebody who is younger? On this girl, God bless her, years are not wasted. Each one that it comes makes better the bargain."

"What subject does she teach in high school?"

"Languages. If you heard the way she speaks French, you will think it is music. I am in the business twenty-five years, and I recommend her with my whole heart. Believe me, I know what I'm talking, rabbi."

"What's on the next card?" Leo said abruptly.

Salzman reluctantly turned up the third card:

"Ruth K. Nineteen years. Honor student. Father offers thirteen thousand cash to the right bridegroom. He is a medical doctor. Stomach specialist with marvelous practice. Brother in law owns own garment business. Particular people."

Salzman looked as if he had read his trump card.

"Did you say nineteen?" Leo asked with interest.

"On the dot."

"Is she attractive?" He blushed. "Pretty?"

Salzman kissed his finger tips. "A little doll. On this I give you my word. Let me call the father tonight and you will see what means pretty."

But Leo was troubled. "You're sure she's that young?"

"This I am positive. The father will show you the birth certificate."

"Are you positive there isn't something wrong with her?" Leo insisted.

"Who says there is wrong?"

"I don't understand why an American girl her age should go to a marriage broker."

A smile spread over Salzman's face. "So for the same reason you went, she comes."

Leo flushed. "I am pressed for time."

Salzman, realizing he had been tactless, quickly explained. "The father came, not her. He wants she should have the best, so he looks around himself. When we will locate the right boy he will introduce him and encourage. This makes a better marriage than if a young girl without experience takes for herself. I don't have to tell you this."

"But don't you think this young girl believes in love?" Leo spoke uneasily.

Salzman was about to guffaw but caught himself and said soberly, "Love comes with the right person, not before."

Leo parted dry lips but did not speak. Noticing that Salzman had snatched a glance at the next card, he cleverly asked. "How is her health?"

"Perfect," Salzman said, breathing with difficulty. "Of course, she is a little lame on her right foot from an auto accident that it happened to her when she was twelve years, but nobody notices on account she is so brilliant and also beautiful."

Leo got up heavily and went to the window. He felt curiously bitter and up-braided himself for having called in the marriage broker. Finally, he shook his head.

"Why not?" Salzman persisted, the pitch of his voice rising.

"Because I detest stomach specialists."

"So what do you care what is his business? After you marry her do you need him? Who says he must come every Friday night in your house?"

Ashamed of the way the talk was going, Leo dismissed Salzman, who went home with heavy, melancholy eyes.

Though he had felt only relief at the marriage broker's departure, Leo was in low spirits the next day. He explained it as arising from Salzman's failure to produce a suitable bride for him. He did not care for his type of clientele. But when Leo found himself hesitating whether to seek out another matchmaker, one more polished than Pinye, he wondered if it could be—his protestations to the contrary, and although he honored his father and mother—that he did not, in essence, care for the matchmaking institution? This thought he quickly put out of mind yet found himself still upset. All day he ran around in the woods—missed an important appointment, forgot to give out his laundry, walked out of a Broadway cafeteria without paying and had to run back with the ticket in his hand; had even not recognized his landlady in the street when she passed with a friend and courteously called out, "A good evening to you, Doctor Finkle." By nightfall, however, he had regained sufficient calm to sink his nose into a book and there found peace from his thoughts.

Almost at once there came a knock on the door. Before Leo could say enter, Salzman, commercial cupid, was standing in the room. His face was gray and meager, his expression hungry, and he looked as if he would expire on his feet. Yet the marriage broker managed, by some trick of the muscles, to display a broad smile.

"So good evening. I am invited?"

Leo nodded, disturbed to see him again, yet unwilling to ask the man to leave.

Beaming still, Salzman laid his portfolio on the table. "Rabbi, I got for you tonight good news."

"I've asked you not to call me rabbi. I'm still a student."

"Your worries are finished. I have for you a first-class bride."

"Leave me in peace concerning this subject." Leo pretended lack of interest.

"The world will dance at your wedding."

"Please, Mr. Salzman, no more."

"But first must come back my strength," Salzman said weakly. He fumbled with the portfolio straps and took out of the leather case an oily paper bag, from which he extracted a hard, seeded roll and a small, smoked white fish. With a quick motion of his hand he stripped the fish out of its skin and began ravenously to chew. "All day in a rush," he muttered.

Leo watched him eat.

"A sliced tomato you have maybe?" Salzman hesitantly inquired.

"No."

The marriage broker shut his eyes and ate. When he had finished he carefully cleaned up the crumbs and rolled up the remains of the fish, in the paper bag. His spectacled eyes roamed the room until he discovered, amid some piles of books, a one-burner gas stove. Lifting his hat he humbly asked, "A glass tea you got, rabbi?"

Conscience-stricken, Leo rose and brewed the tea. He served it with a chunk of lemon and two cubes of lump sugar, delighting Salzman.

After he had drunk his tea, Salzman's strength and good spirits were restored.

"So tell me, rabbi," he said amiably, "you considered some more the three clients I mentioned yesterday?"

"There was no need to consider."

"Why not?"

"None of them suits me."

"What then suits you?"

Leo let it pass because he could give only a confused answer.

Without waiting for a reply, Salzman asked, "You remember this girl I talked to you—the high school teacher?"

"Age thirty-two?"

But surprisingly, Salzman's face lit in a smile. "Age twenty-nine."

Leo shot him a look. "Reduced from thirty-two?"

"A mistake," Salzman avowed. "I talked today with the dentist. He took me to his safety deposit box and showed me the birth certificate. She was twenty-nine years last August. They made her a party in the mountains where she went for her vacation. When her father spoke to me the first time I forgot to write the age and I told you thirty-two, but now I remember this was a different client, a widow."

"The same one you told me about? I thought she was twenty-four?"

"A different. Am I responsible that the world is filled with widows?"

"No, but I'm not interested in them, nor for that matter, in school teachers."

Salzman pulled his clasped hands to his breast. Looking at the ceiling he devoutly exclaimed, "Yiddishe kinder, what can I say to somebody that he is not interested in high school teachers? So what then you are interested?"

Leo flushed but controlled himself.

"In what else will you be interested," Salzman went on, "if you not interested in this fine girl that she speaks four languages and has personally in the bank ten thousand dollars? Also her father guarantees further twelve thousand. Also she has a new car, wonderful clothes, talks on all subjects, and she will give you a first-class home and children. How near do we come in our life to paradise?"

"If she's so wonderful, why wasn't she married ten years ago?"

"Why?" said Salzman with a heavy laugh. "—Why? Because she is *partiki-ler*. This is why. She wants the *best*."

Leo was silent, amused at how he had entangled himself. But Salzman had aroused his interest in Lily H., and he began seriously to consider calling on her. When the marriage broker observed how intently Leo's mind was at work on the facts he had supplied, he felt certain they would soon come to an agreement.

Late Saturday afternoon, conscious of Salzman, Leo Finkle walked with Lily Hirschorn along Riverside Drive. He walked briskly and erectly, wearing with distinction the black fedora he had that morning taken with trepidation out of the dusty hat box on his closet shelf, and the heavy black Saturday coat he had thoroughly whisked clean. Leo also owned a walking stick, a present from a distant relative, but quickly put temptation aside and did not use it. Lily, petite and not unpretty, had on something signifying the approach of spring. She was au courant, animatedly, with all sorts of subjects, and he weighed her words and found her surprisingly sound—score another for Salzman, whom he uneasily sensed to be somewhere around, hiding perhaps high in a tree along the street, flashing the lady signals with a pocket mirror; or perhaps a cloven-hoofed Pan, piping nuptial ditties as he danced his

invisible way before them, strewing wild buds on the walk and purple grapes in their path, symbolizing fruit of a union, though there was of course still none.

Lily startled Leo by remarking, "I was thinking of Mr. Salzman, a curious figure, wouldn't you say?"

Not certain what to answer, he nodded.

She bravely went on, blushing, "I for one am grateful for his introducing us. Aren't you?"

He courteously replied, "I am."

"I mean," she said with a little laugh—and it was all in good taste, or at least gave the effect of being not in bad—"do you mind that we came together so?"

He was not displeased with her honesty, recognizing that she meant to set the relationship aright, and understanding that it took a certain amount of experience in life, and courage, to want to do it quite that way. One had to have some sort of past to make that kind of beginning.

He said that he did not mind. Salzman's function was traditional and honorable—valuable for what it might achieve, which, he pointed out, was frequently nothing.

Lily agreed with a sigh. They walked on for a while and she said after a long silence, again with a nervous laugh, "Would you mind if I asked you something a little bit personal? Frankly, I find the subject fascinating." Although Leo shrugged, she went on half embarrassedly, "How was it that you came to your calling? I mean was it a sudden passionate inspiration?"

Leo, after a time, slowly replied, "I was always interested in the Law."

"You saw revealed in it the presence of the Highest?"

He nodded and changed the subject. "I understand that you spent a little time in Paris, Miss Hirschorn?"

"Oh, did Mr. Salzman tell you, Rabbi Finkle?" Leo winced but she went on,

"It was ages ago and almost forgotten. I remember I had to return for my sister's wedding."

And Lily would not be put off. "When," she asked in a trembly voice, "did you become enamored of God?"

He stared at her. Then it came to him that she was talking not about Leo Finkle, but of a total stranger, some mystical figure, perhaps even passionate prophet that Salzman had dreamed up for her—no relation to the living or dead. Leo trembled with rage and weakness. The trickster had obviously sold her a bill of goods, just as he had him, who'd expected to become acquainted with a young lady of twenty-nine, only to behold, the moment he laid eyes upon her strained and anxious face, a woman past thirty-five and aging rapidly. Only his self control had kept him this long in her presence.

"I am not," he said gravely, "a talented religious person," and in seeking words to go on, found himself possessed by shame and fear. "I think," he said in a strained manner, "that I came to God not because I loved Him, but because I did not."

This confession he spoke harshly because its unexpectedness shook him.

Lily wilted. Leo saw a profusion of loaves of bread go flying like ducks high over his head, not unlike the winged loaves by which he had counted himself to sleep last night. Mercifully, then, it snowed, which he would not put past Salzman's machinations.

He was infuriated with the marriage broker and swore he would throw him out of the room the minute he reappeared. But Salzman did not come that night, and when Leo's anger had subsided, an unaccountable despair grew in its place. At first he thought this was caused by his disappointment in Lily, but before long it became evident that he had involved himself with Salzman without a true knowledge of his own intent. He gradually realized—with an emptiness that seized him with six hands—that he had called in the broker to find him a bride because he was incapable of doing it himself. This terrifying insight he had derived as a result of his meeting and conversation with Lily Hirschorn. Her probing questions had somehow irritated him into revealing—to himself more than her—the true nature of his relationship to God, and from that it had come upon him, with shocking force, that apart from his parents, he had never loved anyone. Or perhaps it went the other way, that he did not love God so well as he might, because he had not loved man. It seemed to Leo that his whole life stood starkly revealed and he saw himself for the first time as he truly was—unloved and loveless. This bitter but somehow not fully unexpected revelation brought him to a point of panic, controlled only by extraordinary effort. He covered his face with his hands and cried.

The week that followed was the worst of his life. He did not eat and lost weight. His beard darkened and grew ragged. He stopped attending seminars and almost never opened a book. He seriously considered leaving the Yeshivah, although he was deeply troubled at the thought of the loss of all his years of study—saw them like pages torn from a book, strewn over the city—and at the devastating effect of this decision upon his parents. But he had lived without knowledge of himself, and never in the Five Books and all the Commentaries—mea culpa—had the truth been revealed to him. He did not know where to turn, and in all this desolating loneliness there was no *to whom*, although he often thought of Lily but not once could bring himself to go downstairs and make the call. He became touchy and irritable, especially with his landlady, who asked him all manner of personal questions; on the other hand, sensing his own disagreeableness, he waylaid her on the stairs

and apologized abjectly, until mortified, she ran from him. Out of this,
however, he drew the consolation that
he was a Jew and that a Jew suffered.
But gradually, as the long and terrible
week drew to a close, he regained his
composure and some idea of purpose in
life: to go on as planned. Although he
was imperfect, the ideal was not. As for
his quest of a bride, the thought of continuing afflicted him with anxiety and
heartburn, yet perhaps with this new
knowledge of himself he would be more
successful than in the past. Perhaps love
would now come to him and a bride to
that love. And for this sanctified seeking who needed a Salzman?

The marriage broker, a skeleton with
haunted eyes, returned that very night.
He looked, withal, the picture of frustrated expectancy—as if he had steadfastly waited the week at Miss Lily
Hirschorn's side for a telephone call
that never came.

Casually coughing, Salzman came
immediately to the point: "So how did
you like her?"

Leo's anger rose and he could not
refrain from chiding the matchmaker:
"Why did you lie to me, Salzman?"

Salzman's pale face went dead white,
the world had snowed on him.

"Did you not state that she was
twenty-nine?" Leo insisted.

"I give you my word—"

"She was thirty-five, if a day. *At
least* thirty-five."

"Of this don't be too sure. Her father
told me—"

"Never mind. The worst of it was
that you lied to her."

"How did I lie to her, tell me?"

"You told her things about me that
weren't true. You made me out to be
more, consequently less than I am. She
had in mind a totally different person, a
sort of semi-mystical Wonder Rabbi."

"All I said, you was a religious man."

"I can imagine."

Salzman sighed. "This is my weakness that I have," he confessed. "My

wife says to me I shouldn't be a salesman, but when I have two fine people
that they would be wonderful to be
married, I am so happy that I talk too
much." He smiled wanly. "This is why
Salzman is a poor man."

Leo's anger left him. "Well, Salzman,
I'm afraid that's all."

The marriage broker fastened hungry
eyes on him.

"You don't want any more a bride?"

"I do," said Leo, "but I have decided
to seek her in a different way. I am no
longer interested in an arranged marriage. To be frank, I now admit the
necessity of premarital love. That is, I
want to be in love with the one I
marry."

"Love?" said Salzman, astounded.
After a moment he remarked, "For us,
our love is our life, not for the ladies. In
the ghetto they—"

"I know, I know," said Leo. "I've
thought of it often. Love, I have said to
myself, should be a by-product of living
and worship rather than its own end.
Yet for myself I find it necessary to
establish the level of my need and fulfill
it."

Salzman shrugged but answered,
"Listen, rabbi, if you want love, this I
can find for you also. I have such beautiful clients that you will love them the
minute your eyes will see them."

Leo smiled unhappily. "I'm afraid
you don't understand."

But Salzman hastily unstrapped his
protfolio and withdrew a manila packet
from it.

"Pictures," he said, quickly laying
the envelope on the table.

Leo called after him to take the pictures away, but as if on the wings of
the wind, Salzman had disappeared.

March came. Leo had returned to his
regular routine. Although he felt not
quite himself yet—lacked energy—he
was making plans for a more active
social life. Of course it would cost
something, but he was an expert in cutting corners; and when there were no

corners left he would make circles rounder. All the while Salzman's pictures had lain on the table, gathering dust. Occasionally as Leo sat studying, or enjoying a cup of tea, his eyes fell on the manila envelope, but he never opened it.

The days went by and no social life to speak of developed with a member of the opposite sex—it was difficult, given the circumstances of his situation. One morning Leo toiled up the stairs to his room and stared out the window at the city. Although the day was bright his view of it was dark. For some time he watched the people in the street below hurrying along and then turned with a heavy heart to his little room. On the table was the packet. With a sudden relentless gesture he tore it open. For a half-hour he stood by the table in a state of excitement, examining the photographs of the ladies Salzman had included. Finally, with a deep sigh he put them down. There were six, of varying degrees of attractiveness, but look at them long enough and they all became Lily Hirschorn: all past their prime, all starved behind bright smiles, not a true personality in the lot. Life, despite their frantic yoohooings, had passed them by; they were pictures in a brief case that stank of fish. After a while, however, as Leo attempted to return the photographs into the envelope, he found in it another, a snapshot of the type taken by a machine for a quarter. He gazed at it a moment and let out a cry.

Her face deeply moved him. Why, he could at first not say. It gave him the impression of youth—spring flowers, yet age—a sense of having been used to the bone, wasted; this came from the eyes, which were hauntingly familiar, yet absolutely strange. He had a vivid impression that he had met her before, but try as he might he could not place her although he could almost recall her name, as if he had read it in her own handwriting. No, this couldn't be; he would have remembered her. It was not, he affirmed, that she had an extraordinary beauty—no, though her face was attractive enough; it was that *something* about her moved him. Feature for feature, even some of the ladies of the photographs could do better; but she leaped forth to his heart—had *lived,* or wanted to—more than just wanted, perhaps regretted how she had lived—had somehow deeply suffered: it could be seen in the depths of those reluctant eyes, and from the way the light enclosed and shone from her, and within her, opening realms of possibility: this was her own. Her he desired. His head ached and eyes narrowed with the intensity of his gazing, then as if an obscure fog had blown up in the mind, he experienced fear of her and was aware that he had received an impression, somehow, of evil. He shuddered, saying softly, it is thus with us all. Leo brewed some tea in a small pot and sat sipping it without sugar, to calm himself. But before he had finished drinking, again with excitement he examined the face and found it good: good for Leo Finkle. Only such a one could understand him and help him seek whatever he was seeking. She might, perhaps, love him. How she had happened to be among the discards in Salzman's barrel he could never guess, but he knew he must urgently go find her.

Leo rushed downstairs, grabbed up the Bronx telephone book, and searched for Salzman's home address. He was not listed, nor was his office. Neither was he in the Manhattan book. But Leo remembered having written down the address on a slip of paper after he had read Salzman's advertisement in the "personals" column of the *Forward.* He ran up to his room and tore through his papers, without luck. It was exasperating. Just when he needed the matchmaker he was nowhere to be found. Fortunately Leo remembered to look in his wallet. There on a card he found his name written and a Bronx address. No phone number was listed, the reason—Leo now recalled—he had originally communicated with Salzman by letter. He got on his coat, put a hat on over his skull cap and hurried to the subway station. All the way to the far end of the Bronx he sat on the edge of his seat. He was more than once tempted to take out the picture and see if the girl's face was as he remembered it, but he refrained, allowing the snapshot to remain in his inside coat pocket, content to have her so close. When the train pulled into the station he was waiting at the door and bolted out. He quickly located the street Salzman had advertised.

The building he sought was less than a block from the subway, but it was not an office building, nor even a loft, nor a store in which one could rent office space. It was a very old tenement house. Leo found Salzman's name in pencil on a soiled tag under the bell and climbed three dark flights to his apartment. When he knocked, the door was opened by a thin, asthmatic, gray-haired woman, in felt slippers.

"Yes?" she said, expecting nothing. She listened without listening. He could have sworn he had seen her, too, before but knew it was an illusion.

"Salzman—does he live here? Pinye Salzman," he said, "the matchmaker?"

She stared at him a long minute. "Of course."

He felt embarrassed. "Is he in?"

"No." Her mouth, though left open, offered nothing more.

"The matter is urgent. Can you tell me where his office is?"

"In the air." She pointed upward.

"You mean he has no office?" Leo asked.

"In his socks."

He peered into the apartment. It was sunless and dingy, one large room divided by a half-open curtain, beyond which he could see a sagging metal bed. The near side of the room was crowded with rickety chairs, old bureaus, a three-legged table, racks of cooking utensils, and all the apparatus of a kitchen. But there was no sign of Salzman or his magic barrel, probably also a figment of the imagination. An odor of frying fish made Leo weak to the knees.

"Where is he?" he insisted. "I've got to see your husband."

At length she answered, "So who knows where he is? Every time he thinks a new thought he runs to a different place. Go home, he will find you."

"Tell him Leo Finkle."

She gave no sign she had heard.

He walked downstairs, depressed.

But Salzman, breathless, stood waiting at his door.

Leo was astounded and overjoyed. "How did you get here before me?"

"I rushed."

"Come inside."

They entered. Leo fixed tea, and a sardine sandwich for Salzman. As they were drinking he reached behind him for the packet of pictures and handed them to the marriage broker.

Salzman put down his glass and said expectantly, "You found somebody you like?"

"Not among these."

The marriage broker turned away.

"Here is the one I want." Leo held forth a snapshot.

Salzman slipped on his glasses and took the picture into his trembling hand. He turned ghastly and let out a groan.

"What's the matter?" cried Leo.

"Excuse me. Was an accident this one—wild, without shame. This is not a picture. She isn't for you."

Salzman frantically shoved the manila packet into his protfolio. He thrust the snapshot into his pocket and fled down the stairs.

Leo, after momentary paralysis, gave chase and cornered the marriage broker in the vestibule. The landlady made hysterical outcries but neither of them listened.

"Give me back the picture, Salzman."

"No." The pain in his eyes was terrible.

"Tell me who she is then."

"This I can't tell you. Excuse me."

He made to depart, but Leo, forgetting himself, seized the matchmaker by his tight coat and shook him frenziedly.

"Please," sighed Salzman. *"Please."*

Leo ashamedly let him go. "Tell me who she is," he begged. "It's very important for me to know."

"She is not for you. She is a wild bride for a rabbi."

"What do you mean wild?"

"Like an animal. Like a dog. For her to be poor was a sin. This is why to me she is dead now."

"In God's name, what do you mean?"

Her I can't introduce to you," Salzman cried.

"Why are you so excited?"

"Why, he asks," Salzman said, bursting into tears. "This is my baby, my Stella, she should burn in hell."

Leo hurried up to bed and hid under the covers. Under the covers he thought his life through. Although he soon fell asleep he could not sleep her out of his mind. He woke, beating his breast. Though he prayed to be rid of her, his prayers went unanswered. Through days of torment he endlessly struggled not to love her; fearing success, he escaped it. He then concluded to convert her to goodness, himself to God. The idea alternately nauseated and exalted him.

He perhaps did not know he had come to a final decision until he encountered Salzman in a Broadway cafeteria. He was sitting alone at a rear table, sucking the bony remains of a fish. The marriage broker appeared haggard, and transparent to the point of vanishing.

Salzman looked up at first without recognizing him. Leo had grown a pointed beard and his eyes were weighted with wisdom.

"Salzman," he said, "love has at last come to my heart."

"Who can love from a picture?" mocked the marriage broker.

"It is not impossible."

"If you can love her, then you can love anybody. Let me show you some new clients that they just sent me their photographs. One is a little doll."

"Just her I want," Leo murmured.

"Don't be a fool, doctor. Don't bother with her."

"Put me in touch with her, Salzman," Leo said humbly. "Perhaps I can be of service."

Salzman had stopped eating and Leo understood with emotion that it was now arranged.

Leaving the cafeteria, he was, however, afflicted by a tormenting suspicion that Salzman had planned it all to happen this way.

Leo was informed by letter that she would meet him on a certain corner, and she was there one spring night, waiting under a street lamp. He appeared, carrying a small bouquet of violets and rosebuds. Stella stood by the lamp post, smoking. She wore white with red shoes, which fitted his expectations, although in a troubled moment he had imagined the dress red, and only the shoes white. She waited uneasily and shyly. From afar he saw that her eyes—clearly her father's—were filled with desperate innocence. He pictured, in her, his own redemption. Violins and lit candles revolved in the sky. Leo ran forward with flowers outthrust.

Around the corner, Salzman, leaning against a wall, chanted prayers for the dead.

Flannery O'Connor (1925–1964)
GOOD COUNTRY PEOPLE

Besides the neutral expression that she wore when she was alone, Mrs. Freeman had two others, forward and reverse, that she used for all her human dealings. Her forward expression was steady and driving like the advance of a heavy truck. Her eyes never swerved to left or right but turned as the story turned as if they followed a yellow line down the center of it. She seldom used the other expression because it was not often necessary for her to retract a statement, but when she did, her face came to a complete stop, there was an almost imperceptible movement of her black eyes, during which they seemed to be receding, and then the observer would see that Mrs. Freeman, though she might stand there as real as several grain sacks thrown on top of each other, was no longer there in spirit. As for getting anything across to her when this was the case, Mrs. Hopewell had given it up. She might talk her head off. Mrs. Freeman could never be brought to admit herself wrong on any point. She would stand there and if she could be brought to say anything, it was something like, "Well, I wouldn't of said it was and I wouldn't of said it wasn't," or letting her gaze range over the top kitchen shelf where there was an assortment of dusty bottles, she might remark, "I see you ain't ate many of them figs you put up last summer."

They carried on their most important business in the kitchen at breakfast. Every morning Mrs. Hopewell got up at seven o'clock and lit her gas heater and Joy's. Joy was her daughter, a large blonde girl who had an artificial leg. Mrs. Hopewell thought of her as a child though she was thirty-two years old and highly educated. Joy would get up while her mother was eating and lumber into the bathroom and slam the door, and before long, Mrs. Freeman would arrive at the back door. Joy would hear her mother call, "Come on in," and then they would talk for a while in low voices that were indistinguishable in the bathroom. By the time Joy came in, they had usually finished the weather report and were on one or the other of Mrs. Freeman's daughters, Glynese or Carramae. Joy called them Glycerin and Caramel. Glynese, a redhead, was eighteen and had many admirers; Carramae, a blonde, was only fifteen but already married and pregnant. She could not keep anything on her stomach. Every morning Mrs. Freeman told Mrs. Hopewell how many times she had vomited since the last report.

Mrs. Hopewell liked to tell people that Glynese and Carramae were two of the finest girls she knew and that Mrs. Freeman was a *lady* and that she was never ashamed to take her anywhere or introduce her to anybody they might meet. Then she would tell how she had happened to hire the Freemans in the first place and how they were a godsend to her and how she had had them four years. The reason for her keeping them so long was that they were not trash. They were good country people. She had telephoned the man whose name they had given as a reference and he had told her that Mr. Freeman was a good farmer but that his wife was the nosiest woman ever to walk the earth. "She's got to be into everything," the man said. "If she don't get there before the dust settles, you can bet she's dead, that's all. She'll want to know all your business. I can stand him real good," he had said, "but me nor my wife neither could have stood that woman one more minute on this place." That had put Mrs. Hopewell off for a few days.

She had hired them in the end because there were no other applicants but she had made up her mind beforehand exactly how she would handle the woman. Since she was the type who had to be into everything, then, Mrs. Hopewell had decided, she would not only let her be into everything, she would *see to it* that she was into everything—she would give her the responsibility of everything, she would put her in charge. Mrs. Hopewell had no bad qualities of her own but she was able to use other people's in such a constructive way that she never felt the lack. She had hired the Freemans and she had kept them four years.

Nothing is perfect. This was one of Mrs. Hopewell's favorite sayings. Another was: that is life! And still another, the most important, was: well, other people have their opinions too. She would make these statements, usually at the table, in a tone of gentle insistence as if no one held them but her, and the large hulking Joy, whose constant outrage had obliterated every expression from her face, would stare just a little to the side of her, her eyes icy blue, with the look of someone who has achieved blindness by an act of will and means to keep it.

When Mrs. Hopewell said to Mrs. Freeman that life was like that, Mrs. Freeman would say, "I always said so myself." Nothing had been arrived at by anyone that had not first been arrived at by her. She was quicker than

Mr. Freeman. When Mrs. Hopewell said to her after they had been on the place a while, "You know, you're the wheel behind the wheel," and winked, Mrs. Freeman had said, "I know it. I've always been quick. It's some that are quicker than others."

"Everybody is different," Mrs. Hopewell said.

"Yes, most people is," Mrs. Freeman said.

"It takes all kinds to make the world."

"I always said it did myself."

The girl was used to this kind of dialogue for breakfast and more of it for dinner; sometimes they had it for supper too. When they had no guest they ate in the kitchen because that was easier. Mrs. Freeman always managed to arrive at some point during the meal and to watch them finish it. She would stand in the doorway if it were summer but in the winter she would stand with one elbow on top of the refrigerator and look down on them, or she would stand by the gas heater, lifting the back of her skirt slightly. Occasionally she would stand against the wall and roll her head from side to side. At no time was she in any hurry to leave. All this was very trying on Mrs. Hopewell but she was a woman of great patience. She realized that nothing is perfect and that in the Freemans she had good country people and that if, in this day and age, you get good country people, you had better hang onto them.

She had had plenty of experience with trash. Before the Freemans she had averaged one tenant family a year. The wives of these farmers were not the kind you would want to be around you for very long. Mrs. Hopewell, who had divorced her husband long ago, needed someone to walk over the fields with her; and when Joy had to be impressed for these services, her remarks were usually so ugly and her face so glum that Mrs. Hopewell would say, "If you can't come pleasantly, I don't want you at all," to which the girl, standing square and rigid-shouldered with her neck thrust slightly forward, would reply, "If you want me, here I am—LIKE I AM."

Mrs. Hopewell excused this attitude because of the leg (which had been shot off in a hunting accident when Joy was ten). It was hard for Mrs. Hopewell to realize that her child was thirty-two now and that for more than twenty years she had had only one leg. She thought of her still as a child because it tore her heart to think instead of the poor stout girl in her thirites who had never danced a step or had any *normal* good times. Her name was really Joy but as soon as she was twenty-one and away from home, she had had it legally changed. Mrs. Hopewell was certain that she had thought and thought until she had hit upon the ugliest name in any language. Then she had gone and had the beautiful name, Joy, changed without telling her mother until after she had done it. Her legal name was Hulga.

When Mrs. Hopewell thought the name, Hulga, she thought of the broad blank hull of a battleship. She would not use it. She continued to call her Joy to which the girl responded but in a purely mechanical way.

Hulga had learned to tolerate Mrs. Freeman who saved her from taking walks with her mother. Even Glynese and Carramae were useful when they occupied attention that might otherwise have been directed at her. At first she had thought she could not stand Mrs. Freeman for she had found that it was not possible to be rude to her. Mrs. Freeman would take on strange resentments and for days together she would be sullen but the source of her displeasure was always obscure; a direct attack, a positive leer, blatant ugliness to her face—these never touched her. And without warning one day, she began calling her Hulga.

She did not call her that in front of Mrs. Hopewell who would have been incensed but when she and the girl happened to be out of the house together, she would say something and add the name Hulga to the end of it, and the big spectacled Joy-Hulga would scowl and redden as if her privacy had been intruded upon. She considered the name her personal affair. She had arrived at it first purely on the basis of its ugly sound and then the full genius of its fitness had struck her. She had a vision of the name working like the ugly sweating Vulcan who stayed in the furnace and to whom, presumably, the goddess had to come when called. She saw it as the name of her highest creative act. One of her major triumphs was that her mother had not been able to turn her dust into Joy, but the greater one was that she had been able to turn it herself into Hulga. However, Mrs. Freeman's relish for using the name only irritated her. It was as if Mrs. Freeman's beady steel-pointed eyes had penetrated far enough behind her face to reach some secret fact. Something about her seemed to fascinate Mrs. Freeman and then one day Hulga realized that it was the artificial leg. Mrs. Freeman had a special fondness for the details of secret infections, hidden deformities, assaults upon children. Of diseases, she preferred the lingering or incurable. Hulga had heard Mrs. Hopewell give her the details of the hunting accident, how the leg had been literally blasted off, how she had never lost consciousness. Mrs. Freeman could listen to it any time as if it had happened an hour ago.

When Hulga stumped into the kitchen in the morning (she could walk without making the awful noise but she made it—Mrs. Hopewell was certain—because it was ugly-sounding), she glanced at them and did not speak. Mrs. Hopewell would be in her red kimono with her hair tied around her head in rags. She would be sitting at the table, finishing her breakfast and

Mrs. Freeman would be hanging by her elbow outward from the refrigerator, looking down at the table. Hulga always put her eggs on the stove to boil and then stood over them with her arms folded, and Mrs. Hopewell would look at her—a kind of indirect gaze divided between her and Mrs. Freeman—and would think that if she would only keep herself up a little, she wouldn't be so bad looking. There was nothing wrong with her face that a pleasant expression wouldn't help. Mrs. Hopewell said that people who looked on the bright side of things would be beautiful even if they were not.

Whenever she looked at Joy this way, she could not help but feel that it would have been better if the child had not taken the Ph.D. It had certainly not brought her out any and now that she had it, there was no more excuse for her to go to school again. Mrs. Hopewell thought it was nice for girls to go to school to have a good time but Joy had "gone through." Anyhow, she would not have been strong enough to go again. The doctors had told Mrs. Hopewell that with the best of care, Joy might see forty-five. She had a weak heart. Joy had made it plain that if it had not been for this condition, she would be far from these red hills and good country people. She would be in a university lecturing to people who knew what she was talking about. And Mrs. Hopewell could very well picture her there, looking like a scarecrow and lecturing to more of the same. Here she went about all day in a six-year-old skirt and a yellow sweat shirt with a faded cowboy on a horse embossed on it. She thought this was funny; Mrs. Hopewell thought it was idiotic and showed simply that she was still a child. She was brilliant but she didn't have a grain of sense. It seemed to Mrs. Hopewell that every year she grew less like other people and more like herself—bloated, rude, and squint-eyed. And she said such strange things! To her own mother she had said—without warning, without excuse, standing up in the middle of a meal with her face purple and her mouth half full—"Woman! do you ever look inside? Do you ever look inside and see what you are *not?* God!" she had cried sinking down again and staring at her plate, "Malebranche was right: we are not our own light. We are not our own light!" Mrs. Hopewell had no idea to this day what brought that on. She had only made the remark, hoping Joy would take it in, that a smile never hurt anyone.

The girl had taken the Ph.D. in philosophy and this left Mrs. Hopewell at a complete loss. You could say, "My daughter is a nurse," or "My daughter is a school teacher," or even, "My daughter is a chemical engineer." You could not say, "My daughter is a philosopher." That was something that had ended with the Greeks and Romans. All day Joy sat on her neck in a deep chair, reading. Sometimes she went for walks but she didn't like dogs or cats or birds or flowers or nature or nice young men. She looked at nice young men as if she could smell their stupidity.

One day Mrs. Hopewell had picked up one of the books the girl had just put down and opening it at random, she read, "science, on the other hand, has to assert its soberness and seriousness afresh and declare that it is concerned solely with what-is. Nothing—how can it be for science anything but a horror and a phantasm? If science is right, then one thing stands firm: science wishes to know nothing of nothing. Such is after all the strictly scientific approach to Nothing. We know it by wishing to know nothing of Nothing." These words had been underlined with a blue pencil and they worked on Mrs. Hopewell like some evil incantation in gibberish. She shut the book quickly and went out of the room as if she were having a chill.

This morning when the girl came in, Mrs. Freeman was on Carramae. "She thrown up four times after supper," she said, "and was up twict in the night after three o'clock. Yesterday she didn't do nothing but ramble in the bureau drawer. All she did. Stand up there and see what she could run up on."

"She's got to eat," Mrs. Hopewell muttered, sipping her coffee, while she watched Joy's back at the stove. She was wondering what the child had said to the Bible salesman. She could not imagine what kind of a conversation she could possibly have had with him.

He was a tall gaunt hatless youth who had called yesterday to sell them a Bible. He had appeared at the door, carrying a large black suitcase that weighted him so heavily on one side that he had to brace himself against the door facing. He seemed on the point of collapse but he said in a cheerful voice, "Good morning, Mrs. Cedars!" and set the suitcase down on the mat. He was not a bad-looking young man though he had on a bright blue suit and yellow socks that were not pulled up far enough. He had prominent face bones and a streak of sticky-looking brown hair falling across his forehead.

"I'm Mrs. Hopewell," she said.

"Oh!" he said, pretending to look puzzled but with his eyes sparkling, "I saw it said 'The Cedars,' on the mailbox so I thought you was Mrs. Cedars!" and he burst out in a pleasant laugh. He picked up the satchel and under cover of a pant, he fell forward into her hall. It was rather as if the suitcase had moved first, jerking him after it. "Mrs. Hopewell!" he said and grabbed her hand. "I hope you are well!" and he laughed again and then all at once his face sobered completely. He paused and gave her a straight earnest look and said, "Lady, I've come to speak of serious things."

"Well, come in." she muttered, none too pleased because her dinner was almost ready. He came into the parlor and sat down on the edge of a straight chair and put the suitcase between his feet and glanced around the room as if he were sizing her up by it. Her silver gleamed on the two sideboards; she decided he had never been in a room as elegant as this.

"Mrs. Hopewell," he began, using her name in a way that sounded almost intimate, "I know you believe in Chrustian service."

"Well yes," she murmured.

"I know," he said and paused, looking very wise with his head cocked on one side, "that you're a good woman. Friends have told me.

Mrs. Hopewell never liked to be taken for a fool. "What are you selling?" she asked.

"Bibles," the young man said and his eye raced around the room before he added, "I see you have no family Bible in your parlor, I see that is the one lack you got!"

Mrs. Hopewell could not say, "My daughter is an atheist and won't let me keep the Bible in the parlor." She said, stiffening slightly, "I keep my Bible by my bedside." This was not the truth. It was in the attic somewhere.

"Lady," he said, "the word of God ought to be in the parlor."

"Well, I think that's a matter of taste," she began. "I think . . ."

"Lady," he said, "for a Chrustian, the word of God ought to be in every room in the house besides in his heart. I know you're a Chrustian because I can see it in every line of your face."

She stood up and said, "Well, young man, I don't want to buy a Bible and I smell my dinner burning."

He didn't get up. He began to twist his hands and looking down at them, he said softly, "Well lady, I'll tell you the truth—not many people want to buy one nowadays and besides, I know I'm real simple. I don't know how to say a thing but to say it. I'm just a country boy." He glanced up into her unfriendly face, "People like you don't like to fool with country people like me!"

"Why!" she cried, "good country people are the salt of the earth! Besides, we all have different ways of doing, it takes all kinds to make the world go 'round. That's life!"

"You said a mouthful," he said.

"Why, I think there aren't enough good country people in the world!" she said, stirred. "I think that's what's wrong with it!"

His face had brightened. "I didn't inraduce myself," he said. "I'm Manley Pointer from out in the country around Willohobie, not even from a place, just from near a place."

"You wait a minute," she said. "I have to see about my dinner." She went out to the kitchen and found Joy standing near the door where she had been listening.

"Get rid of the salt of the earth," she said, "and let's eat."

Mrs. Hopewell gave her a pained look and turned the heat down under the vegetables. "*I* can't be rude to anybody," she murmured and went back into the parlor.

He had opened the suitcase and was sitting with a Bible on each knee.

"You might as well put those up," she told him. "I don't want one."

"I appreciate your honesty," he said. "You don't see any more real honest people unless you go way out in the country."

"I know," she said, "real genuine folks!" Through the crack in the door she heard a groan.

"I guess a lot of boys come telling you they're working their way through college," he said, "but I'm not going to tell you that. Somehow," he said, "I don't want to go to college. I want to devote my life to Chrustian service. See," he said, lowering his voice, "I got this heart condition. I may not live long, well then, lady . . ." He paused, with his mouth open, and stared at her.

He and Joy had the same condition! She knew that her eyes were filling with tears but she collected herself quickly and murmured, "Won't you stay for dinner? We'd love to have you!" and was sorry the instant she heard herself say it.

"Yes mam," he said in an abashed voice, "I would sher love to do that!"

Joy had given him one look on being introduced to him and then throughout the meal had not glanced at him again. He had addressed several remarks to her, which she had pretended not to hear. Mrs. Hopewell could not understand deliberate rudeness, although she lived with it, and she felt she had always to overflow with hospitality to make up for Joy's lack of courtesy. She urged him to talk about himself and he did. He said he was the seventh child of twelve and that his father had been crushed under a tree when he himself was eight year old. He had been crushed very badly, in fact, almost cut in two and was practically not recognizable. His mother had got along the best she could by hard working and she had always seen that her children went to Sunday School and that they read the Bible every evening. He was now nineteen year old and he had been selling Bibles for four months. In that time he had sold seventy-seven Bibles and had the promise of two more sales. He wanted to become a missionary because he thought that was the way you could do most for people. "He who losest his life shall find it," he said simply and he was so sincere, so genuine and earnest that Mrs. Hopewell would not for the world have smiled. He prevented his peas from sliding onto the table by blocking them with a piece of bread which he later cleaned his plate with. She could see Joy observing sidewise how he handled his knife and fork and she saw too that every few minutes, the boy would dart a keen appraising glance at the girl as if he were trying to attract her attention.

After dinner Joy cleared the dishes

off the table and disappeared and Mrs. Hopewell was left to talk with him. He told her again about his childhood and his father's accident and about various things that had happened to him. Every five minutes or so she would stifle a yawn. He sat for two hours until finally she told him she must go because she had an appointment in town. He packed his Bibles and thanked her and prepared to leave, but in the door way he stopped and wrung her hand and said that not on any of his trips had he met a lady as nice as her and he asked if he could come again. She had said she would always be happy to see him.

Joy had been standing in the road, apparently looking at something in the distance, when he came down the steps toward her, bent to the side with his heavy valise. He stopped where she was standing and confronted her directly. Mrs. Hopewell could not hear what he said but she trembled to think what Joy would say to him. She could see that after a minute Joy said something and that then the boy began to speak again, making an excited gesture with his free hand. After a minute Joy said something else at which the boy began to speak once more. Then to her amazement, Mrs. Hopewell saw the two of them walk off together, toward the gate. Joy had walked all the way to the gate with him and Mrs. Hopewell could not imagine what they had said to each other, and she had not yet dared to ask.

Mrs. Freeman was insisting upon her attention. She had moved from the refrigerator to the heater so that Mrs. Hopewell had to turn and face her in order to seem to be listening. "Glynese gone out with Harvey Hill again last night," she said. "She had this sty."

"Hill," Mrs. Hopewell said absently, "is that the one who works in the garage?"

"Nome, he's the one that goes to chiropracter school," Mrs. Freeman said.

"She had this sty. Been had it two days. So she says when he brought her in the other night he says, 'Lemme get rid of that sty for you,' and she says, 'How?' and he says, 'You just lay yourself down acrost the seat of that car and I'll show you.' So she done it and he popped her neck. Kept on a-popping it several times until she made him quit. This morning," Mrs. Freeman said, "she ain't got no sty. She ain't got no traces of a sty."

"I never heard of that before," Mrs. Hopewell said.

"He ast her to marry him before the Ordinary," Mrs. Freeman went on," and she told him she wasn't going to be married in no *office*."

"Well, Glynese is a fine girl," Mrs. Hopewell said. "Glynese and Carramae are both fine girls."

"Carramae said when her and Lyman was married Lyman said it sure felt sacred to him. She said he said he wouldn't take five hundred dollars for being married by a preacher."

"How much would he take?" the girl asked from the stove.

"He said he wouldn't take five hundred dollars," Mrs. Freeman repeated.

"Well we all have work to do," Mrs. Hopewell said.

"Lyman said it just felt more sacred to him," Mrs. Freeman said. "The doctor wants Carramae to eat prunes. Says instead of medicine. Says them cramps is coming from pressure. You know where I think it is?"

"She'll be better in a few weeks," Mrs. Hopewell said.

"In the tube," Mrs. Freeman said. "Else she wouldn't be as sick as she is."

Hulga had cracked her two eggs into a saucer and was bring them to the table along with a cup of coffee that she had filled too full. She sat down carefully and began to eat, meaning to keep Mrs. Freeman there by questions if for any reason she showed an inclination to leave. She could perceive her mother's eye on her. The first round-about question would be about the Bible salesman and she did not wish to bring it on. "How did he pop her neck?" she asked.

Mrs. Freeman went into a description of how he had popped her neck. She said he owned a '55 Mercury but that Glynese said she would rather marry a man with only a '36 Plymouth who would be married by a preacher. The girl asked what if he had a '32 Plymouth and Mrs. Freeman said what Glynese had said was a '36 Plymouth.

Mrs. Hopewell said there were not many girls with Glynese's common sense. She said what she admired in those girls was their common sense. She said that reminded her that they had had a nice visitor yesterday, a young man selling Bibles. "Lord," she said, "he bored me to death but he was so sincere and genuine I couldn't be rude to him. He was just good country people, you know," she said, "—just the salt of the earth."

"I seen him walk up," Mrs. Freeman said, "and then later—I seen him walk off," and Hulga could feel the slight shift in her voice, the slight insinuation, that he had not walked off alone, had he? Her face remained expressionless but the color rose into her neck and she seemed to swallow it down with the next spoonful of egg. Mrs. Freeman was looking at her as if they had a secret together.

"Well, it takes all kinds of people to make the world go 'round," Mrs. Hopewell said. "It's very good we aren't all alike."

"Some people are more alike than others," Mrs. Freeman said.

Hulga got up and stumped, with about twice the noise that was necessary, into her room and locked the door. She was to meet the Bible salesman at ten o'clock at the gate. She had thought about it half the night. She had started thinking of it as a great joke and then she had begun to see profound implications in it. She had lain in bed

imagining dialogues for them that were insane on the surface but that reached below to depths that no Bible salesman would be aware of. Their conversation yesterday had been of this kind.

He had stopped in front of her and had simply stood there. His face was bony and sweaty and bright, with a little pointed nose in the center of it, and his look was different from what it had been at the dinner table. He was gazing at her with open curiosity, with fascination, like a child watching a new fantastic animal at the zoo, and he was breathing as if he had run a great distance to reach her. His gaze seemed somehow famliiar but she could not think where she had been regarded with it before. For almost a minute he didn't say anything. Then on what seemed an insuck of breath, he whispered, "You ever ate a chicken that was two days old?"

The girl looked at him stonily. He might have just put this question up for consideration at the meeting of a philosophical association. "Yes," she presently replied as if she had considered it from all angles.

"It must have been mighty small!" he said triumphantly and shook all over with little nervous giggles, getting very red in the face, and subsiding finally into his gaze of complete admiration, while the girl's expression remained exactly the same.

"How old are you?" he asked softly.

She waited some time before she answered. Then in a flat voice she said, "Seventeen."

His smiles came in succession like waves breaking on the surface of a little lake. "I see you got a wooden leg." he said. "I think you're real brave. I think you're real sweet."

The girl stood blank and solid and silent.

"Walk to the gate with me," he said. "You're a brave sweet little thing and I liked you the minute I seen you walk in the door."

Hulga began to move forward.

"What's your name?" he asked, smiling down on the top of her head.

"Hulga," she said.

"Hulga," he murmured, "Hulga. Hulga. I never heard of anybody name Hulga before. You're shy, aren't you, Hulga?" he asked.

She nodded, watching his large red hand on the handle of the giant valise.

"I like girls that wear glasses," he said. "I think a lot. I'm not like these people that a serious thought don't ever enter their heads. It's because I may die."

"I may die too," she said suddenly and looked up at him. His eyes were very small and brown, glittering feverishly.

"Listen," he said, "don't you think some people was meant to meet on account of what all they got in common and all? Like they both think serious thoughts and all?" He shifted the valise to his other hand so that the hand nearest her was free. He caught hold of her elbow and shook it a little. "I don't work on Saturday," he said. "I like to walk in the woods and see what Mother Nature is wearing. O'er the hills and far away. Pic-nics and things. Couldn't we go on a pic-nic tomorrow? Say yes, Hulga," he said and gave her a dying look as if he felt his insides about to drop out of him. He had even seemed to sway slightly toward her.

During the night she had imagined that she seduced him. She imagined that the two of them walked on the place until they came to the storage barn beyond the two back fields and there, she imagined, that things came to such a pass that she very easily seduced him and than then, of course, she had to reckon with his remorse. True genius can get an idea across even to an inferior mind. She imagined that she took his remorse in hand and changed it into something useful.

She set off for the gate at exactly ten o'clock, escaping without drawing Mrs.

Hopewell's attention. She didn't take anything to eat, forgetting that food is usually taken on a picnic. She wore a pair of slacks and a dirty white shirt, and as an afterthought, she had put some Vapex on the collar of it since she did not own any perfume. When she reached the gate no one was there.

She looked up and down the empty highway and had the furious feeling that she had been tricked, that he had only meant to make her walk to the gate after the idea of him. Then suddenly he stood up, very tall, from behind a bush on the opposite embankment. Smiling, he lifted his hat which was new and wide-brimmed. He had not worn it yesterday and she wondered if he had bought if for the occasion. It was toast-colored with a red and white band around it and was slightly too large for him. He stepped from behind the bush still carrying the black valise. He had on the same suit and the same yellow socks sucked down in his shoes from walking. He crossed the highway and said, "I knew you'd come!"

The girl wondered acidly how he had known this. She pointed to the valise and asked, "Why did you bring your Bibles?"

He took her elbow, smiling down on her as if he could not stop. "You can never tell when you'll need the word of God, Hulga," he said. She had a moment in which she doubted that this was actually happening and then they began to climb the embankment. They went down into the pasture toward the woods. The boy walked lightly by her side, bouncing on his toes. The valise did not seem to be heavy today; he even swung it. They crossed half the pasture without saying anything and then, putting his hand easily on the small of her back, he asked softly, "Where does your wooden leg join on?"

She turned an ugly red and glared at him and for an instant the boy looked abashed. "I didn't mean you no harm," he said. "I only meant you're so brave and all. I guess God takes care of you."

"No," she said, looking forward and walking fast, "I don't even believe in God."

At this he stopped and whistled. "No!" he exclaimed as if he were too astonished to say anything else.

She walked on and in a second he was bouncing at her side, fanning with his hat. "That's very unusual for a girl," he remarked, watching her out of the corner of his eye. When they reached the edge of the wood, he put his hand on her back again and drew her against him without a word and kissed her heavily.

The kiss, which had more pressure than feeling behind it, produced that extra surge of adrenalin in the girl that enables one to carry a packed trunk out of a burning house, but in her, the power went at once to the brain. Even before he released her, her mind, clear and detached and ironic anyway, was regarding him from a great distance, with amusement but with pity. She had never been kissed before and she was pleased to discover that it was an unexceptional experience and all a matter of the mind's control. Some people might enjoy drain water if they were told it was vodka. When the boy, looking expectant but uncertain, pushed her gently away, she turned and walked on, saying nothing as if such business, for her, were common enough.

He came along panting at her side, trying to help her when he saw a root that she might trip over. He caught and held back the long swaying blades of thorn vine until she had passed beyond them. She led the way and he came breathing heavily behind her. Then they came out on a sunlit hillside, sloping softly into another one a little smaller. Beyond, they could see the rusted top of the old barn where the extra hay was stored.

The hill was sprinkled with small pink weeds. "Then you ain't saved?" he asked suddenly, stopping.

The girl smiled. It was the first time she had smiled at him at all. "In my economy," she said, "I'm saved and you are damned but I told you I didn't believe in God."

Nothing seemed to destroy the boy's look of admiration. He gazed at her now as if the fantastic animal at the zoo had put its paw through the bars and given him a loving poke. She thought he looked as if he wanted to kiss her again and she walked on before he had the chance.

"Ain't there somewheres we can sit down sometime?" he murmured, his voice softening toward the end of the sentence.

"In that barn," she said.

They made for it rapidly as if it might slide away like a train. It was a large two-story barn, cool and dark inside. The boy pointed up the ladder that led into the loft and said, "It's too bad we can't go up there."

"Why can't we?" she asked.

"Yer leg," he said reverently.

The girl gave him a contemptuous look and putting both hands on the ladder, she climbed it while he stood below, apparently awestruck. She pulled herself expertly through the opening and then looked down at him and said, "Well, come on if you're coming," and he began to climb the ladder, awkwardly bringing the suitcase with him.

"We won't need the Bible," she observed.

"You never can tell," he said, panting. After he had got into the loft, he was a few seconds catching his breath. She had sat down in a pile of straw. A wide sheath of sunlight, filled with dust particles, slanted over her. She lay back against a bale, her face turned away, looking out the front opening of the barn where hay was thrown from a wagon into the loft. The two pink-speckled hillsides lay back against a dark ridge of woods. The sky was cloudless and cold blue. The boy dropped down by her side and put one arm under her and the other over her and began methodically kissing her face, making little noises like a fish. He did not remove his hat but it was pushed far enough back not to interfere. When her glasses got in his way, he took them off of her and slipped them into his pocket.

The girl at first did not return any of the kisses but presently she began to and after she had put several on his cheek, she reached his lips and remained there, kissing him again and again as if she were trying to draw all the breath out of him. His breath was clear and sweet like a child's and the kisses were sticky like a child's. He mumbled about loving her and about knowing when he first seen her that he loved her, but the mumbling was like the sleepy fretting of a child being put to sleep by his mother. Her mind, throughout this, never stopped or lost itself for a second to her feelings. "You ain't said you loved me none," he whispered finally pulling back from her. "You got to say that."

She looked away from him off into the hollow sky and then down at a black ridge and then down farther into what appeared to be two green swelling lakes. She didn't realize he had taken her glasses but this landscape could not seem exceptional to her for she seldom paid any close attention to her surroundings.

"You got to say it," he repeated. "You got to say you love me."

She was always careful how she committed herself. "In a sense," she began, "if you use the word loosely, you might say that. But it's not a word I use. I don't have illusions. I'm one of those people who see *through* to nothing."

The boy was frowning. "You got to say it. I said it and you got to say it," he said.

The girl looked at him almost tenderly. "You poor baby," she murmured. "It's just as well you don't understand," and she pulled him by the neck, face-

down, against her. "We are all damned," she said, "but some of us have taken off our blindfolds and see that there's nothing to see. It's a kind of salvation."

The boy's astonished eyes looked blankly through the ends of her hair. "Okay," he almost whined, "but do you love me or don'tcher?"

"Yes," she said and added, "in a sense. But I must tell you something. There mustn't be anything dishonest between us." She lifted his head and looked him in the eye. "I am thirty years old," she said. "I have a number of degrees."

The boy's look was irritated but dogged. "I don't care," he said. "I don't care a thing about what all you done. I just want to know if you love me or don'tcher?" and he caught her to him and wildly planted her face with kisses until she said, "Yes, yes."

"Okay then," he said, letting her go. "Prove it."

She smiled, looking dreamily out on the shifty landscape. She had seduced him without even making up her mind to try. "How?" she asked, feeling that he should be delayed a little.

He leaned over and put his lips to her ear. "Show me where your wooden leg joins on," he whispered.

The girl uttered a sharp little cry and her face instantly drained of color. The obscenity of the suggestion was not what shocked her. As a child she had sometimes been subject to feelings of shame but education had removed the last traces of that as a good surgeon scrapes for cancer; she would no more have felt it over what he was asking than she would have believed in his Bible. But she was as sensitive about the artificial leg as a peacock about his tail. No one ever touched it but her. She took care of it as someone else would his soul, in private and almost with her own eyes turned away. "No," she said.

"I known it," he muttered, sitting up. "You're just playing me for a sucker."

"Oh no no!" she cried. "It joins on at the knee. Only at the knee. Why do you want to see it?"

The boy gave her a long penetrating look. "Because," he said, "it's what makes you different. You ain't like anybody else."

She sat staring at him. There was nothing about her face or her round freezing-blue eyes to indicate that this had moved her; but she felt as if her heart had stopped and left her mind to pump her blood. She decided that for the first time in her life she was face to face with real innocence. This boy, with an instinct that came from beyond wisdom, had touched the truth about her. When after a minute, she said in a hoarse high voice, "All right," it was like surrendering to him completely. It was like losing her own life and finding it again, miraculously, in his.

Very gently he began to roll the slack leg up. The artificial limb, in a white sock and brown flat shoe, was bound in a heavy material like canvas and ended in an ugly jointure where it was attached to the stump. The boy's face and his voice were entirely reverent as he uncovered it and said, "Now show me how to take it off and on."

She took it off for him and put it back on again and then he took it off himself, handling it as tenderly as if it were a real one. "See!" he said with a delighted child's face. "Now I can do it myself!"

"Put it back on," she said. She was thinking that she would run away with him and that every night he would take the leg off and every morning put it back on again. "Put it back on," she said.

"Not yet," he murmured, setting it on its foot out of her reach. "Leave it off for a while. You got me instead."

She gave a little cry of alarm but he pushed her down and began to kiss her again. Without the leg she felt entirely dependent on him. Her brain seemed to have stopped thinking altogether and to be about some other function that it was not very good at. Different expressions raced back and forth over her face. Every now and then the boy, his eyes like two steel spikes, would glance behind him where the leg stood. Finally she pushed him off and said, "Put it back on me now."

"Wait," he said. He leaned the other way and pulled the valise toward him and opened it. It had a pale blue spotted lining and there were only two Bibles in it. He took one of these out and opened the cover of it. It was hollow and contained a pocket flask of whiskey, a pack of cards, and a small blue box with printing on it. He laid these out in front of her one at a time in an evenly-spaced row, like one presenting offerings at the shrine of a goddess. He put the blue box in her hand. THIS PRODUCT TO BE USED ONLY FOR THE PREVENTION OF DISEASE, she read, and dropped it. The boy was unscrewing the top of the flask. He stopped and pointed, with a smile, to the deck of cards. It was not an ordinary deck but one with an obscene picture on the back of each card. "Take a swig," he said, offering her the bottle first. He held it in front of her, but like one mesmerized, she did not move.

Her voice when she spoke had an almost pleading sound. "Aren't you, she murmured, "aren't you just good country people?"

The boy cocked his head. He looked as if he were just beginning to understand that she might be trying to insult him. "Yeah," he said, curling his lip slightly, "but it ain't held me back none. I'm as good as you any day in the week."

"Give me my leg," she said.

He pushed it farther away with his foot. "Come on now, let's begin to have us a good time," he said coaxingly. "We ain't got to know one another good yet."

"Give me my leg!" she screamed and tried to lunge for it but he pushed her down easily.

"What's the matter with you all of a sudden?" he asked, frowning as he screwed the top on the flask and put it quickly back inside the Bible. "You just a while ago said you didn't believe in nothing. I thought you was some girl!"

Her face was almost purple. "You're a Christian!" she hissed. "You're a fine Christian! You're just like them all—say one thing and do another. You're a perfect Christian, you're . . ."

The boy's mouth was set angrily. "I hope you don't think," he said in a lofty indignant tone, "that I believe in that crap! I may sell Bibles but I know which end is up and I wasn't born yesterday and I know where I'm going!"

"Give me my leg!" she screeched. He jumped up so quickly that she barely saw him sweep the cards and the blue box back into the Bible and throw the Bible into the valise. She saw him grab the leg and then she saw it for an instant slanted forlornly across the inside of the suitcase with a Bible at either side of its opposite ends. He slammed the lid shut and snatched up the valise and swung it down the hole and then stepped through himself.

When all of him had passed but his head, he turned and regarded her with a look that no longer had any admiration in it. "I've gotten a lot of interesting things," he said. "One time I got a woman's glass eye this way. And you needn't to think you'll catch me because Pointer ain't really my name. I use a different name at every house I call at and don't stay nowhere long. And I'll tell you another thing, Hulga," he said, using the name as if he didn't think much of it, "you ain't so smart. I been believing in nothing ever since I was born!" and then the toast-colored hat disappeared down the hole and the girl was left, sitting on the straw in the dusty sunlight. When she turned her churning face toward the opening, she saw his blue figure struggling successfully over the green speckled lake.

Mrs. Hopewell and Mrs. Freeman, who were in the back pasture, digging up onions, saw him emerge a little later from the woods and head across the meadow toward the highway. "Why, that looks like that nice dull young man that tried to sell me a Bible yesterday," Mrs. Hopewell said, squinting. "He must have been selling them to the Negroes back in there. He was so simple," she said, "but I guess the world would be better off if we were all that simple."

Mrs. Freeman's gaze drove forward and just touched him before he disappeared under the hill. Then she returned her attention to the evil-smelling onion shoot she was lifting from the ground. "Some can't be that simple," she said. "I know I never could."

A GOOD MAN IS HARD TO FIND

for Sally and Robert Fitzgerald

The dragon is by the side of the road, watching those who pass. Beware lest he devour you. We go to the father of souls, but it is necessary to pass by the dragon.

ST. CYRIL OF JERUSALEM

The grandmother didn't want to go to Florida. She wanted to visit some of her connections in east Tennessee and she was seizing at every chance to change Bailey's mind. Bailey was the son she lived with, her only boy. He was sitting on the edge of his chair at the table, bent over the orange sports section of the *Journal.* "Now look here, Bailey," she said, "see here, read this," and she stood with one hand on her thin hip and the other rattling the newspaper at his bald head. "Here this fellow that calls himself The Misfit is aloose from the Federal Pen and headed toward Florida and you read here what it says he did to these people. Just you read it. I wouldn't take my children in any direction with a criminal like that aloose in it. I couldn't answer to my conscience if I did."

Bailey didn't look up from his reading so she wheeled around then and faced the children's mother, a young woman in slacks, whose face was as broad and innocent as a cabbage and was tied around with a green headkerchief that had two points on the top like a rabbit's ears. She was sitting on the sofa, feeding the baby his apricots out of a jar. "The children have been to Florida before," the old lady said. "You all ought to take them somewhere else for a change so they would see

different parts of the world and be broad. They never have been to east Tennessee."

The children's mother didn't seem to hear her but the eight-year-old boy, John Wesley, a stocky child with glasses, said, "If you don't want to go to Florida, why dontcha stay at home?" He and the little girl, June Star, were reading the funny papers on the floor.

"She wouldn't stay at home to be queen for a day," June Star said without raising her yellow head.

"Yes and what would you do if this fellow, the Misfit, caught you?" the grandmother asked.

"I'd smack his face," John Wesley said.

"She wouldn't stay at home for a million bucks," June Star said. "Afraid she'd miss something. She has to go everywhere we go."

"All right, Miss," the grandmother said. "Just remember that the next time you want me to curl your hair."

June Star said her hair was naturally curly.

The next morning the grandmother was the first one in the car, ready to go. She had her big black valise that looked like the head of a hippopotamus in one corner, and underneath it she was hiding a basket with Pitty Sing, the cat, in it. She didn't intend for the cat to be left alone in the house for three days because he would miss her too much and she was afraid he might brush against one of the gas burners and accidentally asphyxiate himself. Her son, Bailey, didn't like to arrive at a motel with a cat.

She sat in the middle of the back seat with John Wesley and June Star on either side of her. Bailey and the children's mother and the baby sat in front and they left Atlanta at eight forty-five with the mileage on the car at 55890. The grandmother wrote this down because she thought it would be interesting to say how many miles they had been when they got back. It took them twenty minutes to reach the outskirts of the city.

The old lady settled herself comfortably, removing her white cotton gloves and putting them up with her purse on the shelf in front of the back window. The children's mother still had on slacks and still had her head tied up in a green kerchief, but the grandmother had on a navy blue straw sailor hat with a bunch of white violets on the brim and a navy blue dress with a small white dot in the print. Her collars and cuffs were white organdy trimmed with lace and at her neckline she had pinned a purple spray of cloth violets containing a sachet. In case of an accident, anyone seeing her dead on the highway would know at once that she was a lady.

She said she thought it was going to be a good day for driving, neither too hot nor too cold, and she cautioned Bailey that the speed limit was fifty-five miles an hour and that the patrolmen hid themselves behind billboards and small clumps of trees and sped out after you before you had a chance to slow down. She pointed out interesting details of the scenery: Stone Mountain; the blue granite that in some places came up to both sides of the highway; the brilliant red clay banks slightly streaked with purple; and the various

crops that made rows of green lacework on the ground. The trees were full of silver-white sunlight and the meanest of them sparkled. The children were reading comic magazines and their mother had gone back to sleep.

"Let's go through Georgia fast so we won't have to look at it much," John Wesley said.

"If I were a little boy," said the grandmother, "I wouldn't talk about my native state that way. Tennessee has the mountains and Georgia has the hills."

"Tennessee is just a hillbilly dumping ground," John Wesley said, "and Georgia is a lousy state too."

"You said it," June Star said.

"In my time," said the grandmother, folding her thin veined fingers, "children were more respectful of their native states and their parents and everything else. People did right then. Oh look at the cute little pickaninny!" she said and pointed to a Negro child standing in the door of a shack. "Wouldn't that make a picture, now?" she asked and they all turned and looked at the little Negro out of the back window. He waved.

"He didn't have any britches on," June Star said.

"He probably didn't have any," the grandmother explained. "Little niggers in the country don't have things like we do. If I could paint, I'd paint that picture," she said.

The children exchanged comic books.

The grandmother offered to hold the baby and the children's mother passed him over the front seat to her. She set him on her knee and bounced him and told him about the things they were passing. She rolled her eyes and screwed up her mouth and stuck her leathery thin face into his smooth bland one. Occasionally he gave her a faraway smile. They passed a large cotton field with five or six graves fenced in the middle of it, like a small island. "Look at the graveyard!" the grandmother said, pointing it out. "That was the old family burying ground. That belonged to the plantation."

"Where's the plantation?" John Wesley asked.

"Gone With the Wind," said the grandmother. "Ha. Ha."

When the children finished all the comic books they had brought, they opened the lunch and ate it. The grandmother ate a peanut butter sandwich and an olive and would not let the children throw the box and the paper napkins out the window. When there was nothing else to do they played a game by choosing a cloud and making the other two guess what shape it suggested. John Wesley took one the shape of a cow and June Star guessed a cow and John Wesley said, no, an automobile, and June Star said he didn't play fair, and they began to slap each other over the grandmother.

The grandmother said she would tell them a story if they would keep quiet. When she told a story, she rolled her eyes and waved her head and was very dramatic. She said once when she was a maiden lady she had been courted by a Mr. Edgar Atkins Teagarden from Jasper, Georgia. She said he was a very good-looking man and a gentleman and that he brought her a watermelon every Saturday afternoon with his initials cut in it, E. A. T. Well, one Saturday, she said, Mr. Teagarden brought the watermelon and there was nobody at home and he left it on the front porch and returned in his buggy to Jasper, but she never got the watermelon, she said, because a nigger boy ate it when he saw the initials, E. A. T.! This story tickled John Wesley's funny bone and he giggled and giggled but June Star didn't think it was any good. She said she wouldn't marry a man that just brought her a watermelon on Saturday. The grandmother said she would have done well to marry Mr. Teagarden because he was a gentleman and had bought Coca-Cola stock when it first

came out and that he had died only a few years ago, a very wealthy man.

They stopped at The Tower for barbecued sandwiches. The Tower was a part stucco and part wood filling station and dance hall set in a clearing outside of Timothy. A fat man named Red Sammy Butts ran it and there were signs stuck here and there on the building and for miles up and down the highway saying, TRY RED SAMMY'S FAMOUS BARBECUE. NONE LIKE FAMOUS RED SAMMY'S! RED SAM! THE FAT BOY WITH THE HAPPY LAUGH. A VETERAN! RED SAMMY'S YOUR MAN!

Red Sammy was lying on the bare ground outside The Tower with his head under a truck while a gray monkey about a foot high, chained to a small chinaberry tree, chattered nearby. The monkey sprang back into the tree and got on the highest limb as soon as he saw the children jump out of the car and run toward him.

Inside, The Tower was a long dark room with a counter at one end and tables at the other and dancing space in the middle. They all sat down at a board table next to the nickelodeon and Red Sam's wife, a tall burnt-brown woman with hair and eyes lighter than her skin, came and took their order. The children's mother put a dime in the machine and played "The Tennessee Waltz," and the grandmother said that tune always made her want to dance. She asked Bailey if he would like to dance but he only glared at her. He didn't have a naturally sunny disposition like she did and trips made him nervous. The grandmother's brown eyes were very bright. She swayed her head from side to side and pretended she was dancing in her chair. June Star said play something she could tap to so the children's mother put in another dime and played a fast number and June Star stepped out onto the dance floor and did her tap routine.

"Ain't she cute?" Red Sam's wife

said, leaning over the counter. "Would you like to come be my little girl?"

"No I certainly wouldn't," June Star said. "I wouldn't live in a broken-down place like this for a million bucks!" and she ran back to the table.

"Ain't she cute?" the woman repeated, stretching her mouth politely.

"Aren't you ashamed?" hissed the grandmother.

Red Sam came in and told his wife to quit lounging on the counter and hurry up with these people's order. His khaki trousers reached just to his hip bones and his stomach hung over them like a sack of meal swaying under his shirt. He came over and sat down at a table nearby and let out a combination sigh and yodel. "You can't win," he said. "You can't win," and he wiped his sweating red face off with a gray handkerchief. "These days you don't know who to trust," he said. "Ain't that the truth?"

"People are certainly not nice like they used to be," said the grandmother.

"Two fellers come in here last week," Red Sammy said, "driving a Chrysler. It was a old beat-up car but it was a good one and these boys looked all right to me. Said they worked at the mill and you know I let them fellers charge the gas they bought? Now why did I do that?"

"Because you're a good man!" the grandmother said at once.

"Yes'm, I suppose so," Red Sam said as if he were struck with this answer.

His wife brought the orders, carrying the five plates all at once without a tray, two in each hand and one balanced on her arm. "It isn't a soul in this green world of God's that you can trust," she said. "And I don't count nobody out of that, not nobody," she repeated, looking at Red Sammy.

"Did you read about that criminal, The Misfit, that's escaped?" asked the grandmother.

"I wouldn't be a bit surprised if he didn't attact this place right here," said the woman. "If he hears about it being here, I wouldn't be none surprised to see him. If he hears it's two cent in the cash register, I wouldn't be a tall surprised if he . . ."

"That'll do," Red Sam said. "Go bring these people their Co'-Colas," and the woman went off to get the rest of the order.

"A good man is hard to find," Red Sammy said. "Everything is getting terrible. I remember the day you could go off and leave your screen door unlatched. Not no more."

He and the grandmother discussed better times. The old lady said that in her opinion Europe was entirely to blame for the way things were now. She said the way Europe acted you would think we were made of money and Red Sam said it was no use talking about it, she was exactly right. The children ran outside into the white sunlight and looked at the monkey in the lacy chinaberry tree. He was busy catching fleas on himself and biting each one carefully between his teeth as if it were a delicacy.

They drove off again into the hot afternoon. The grandmother took cat naps and woke up every few minutes with her own snoring. Outside of Toombsboro she woke up and recalled an old plantation that she had visited in this neighborhood once when she was a young lady. She said the house had six white columns across the front and that there was an avenue of oaks leading up to it and two little wooden trellis arbors on either side in front where you sat down with your suitor after a stroll in the garden. She recalled exactly which road to turn off to get to it. She knew that Bailey would not be willing to lose any time looking at an old house, but the more she talked about it, the more she wanted to see it once again and find out if the little twin arbors were still standing. "There was a secret panel in this house," she said craftily, not telling the truth but wishing that she were, "and the story went that all the family silver was hidden in it when Sherman came through but it was never found . . ."

"Hey!" John Wesley said. "Let's go see it! We'll find it! We'll poke all the woodwork and find it! Who lives there? Where do you turn off at? Hey Pop, can't we turn off there?"

"We never have seen a house with a secret panel!" June Star shrieked. "Let's go to the house with the secret panel! Hey Pop, can't we go see the house with the secret panel!"

"It's not far from here, I know," the grandmother said. "It wouldn't take over twenty minutes."

Bailey was looking straight ahead. His jaw was as rigid as a horseshoe. "No," he said.

The children began to yell and scream that they wanted to see the house with the secret panel. John Wesley kicked the back of the front seat and June Star hung over her mother's shoulder and whined desperately into her ear that they never had any fun even on their vacation, that they could never do what THEY wanted to do. The baby began to scream and John Wesley kicked the back of the seat so hard that his father could feel the blows in his kidney.

"All right!" he shouted and drew the car to a stop at the side of the road. "Will you all shut up? Will you all just shut up for one second? If you don't shut up, we won't go anywhere."

"It would be very educational for them," the grandmother murmured.

"All right," Bailey said, "but get this: this is the only time we're going to stop for anything like this. This is the one and only time."

"The dirt road that you have to turn down is about a mile back," the grandmother directed. "I marked it when we passed."

"A dirt road," Bailey groaned.

After they had turned around and were headed toward the dirt road, the grandmother recalled other points about the house, the beautiful glass over the front doorway and the candle-lamp in the hall. John Wesley said that the secret panel was probably in the fireplace.

"You can't go inside this house," Bailey said. "You don't know who lives there."

"While you all talk to the people in front, I'll run around behind and get in a window," John Wesley suggested.

"We'll all stay in the car," his mother said.

They turned onto the dirt road and the car raced roughly along in a swirl of pink dust. The grandmother recalled the times when there were no paved roads and thirty miles was a day's journey. The dirt road was hilly and there were sudden washes in it and sharp curves on dangerous embankments. All at once they would be on a hill, looking down over the blue tops of trees for miles around, then the next minute, they would be in a red depression with the dust-coated trees looking down on them.

"This place had better turn up in a minute," Bailey said, "or I'm going to turn around."

The road looked as if no one had traveled on it in months.

"It's not much farther," the grandmother said and just as she said it, a horrible thought came to her. The thought was so embarrassing that she turned red in the face and her eyes dilated and her feet jumped up, upsetting her valise in the corner. The instant the valise moved, the newspaper top she had over the basket under it rose with a snarl and Pitty Sing, the cat, sprang onto Bailey's shoulder.

The children were thrown to the floor and their mother, clutching the baby, was thrown out the door onto the ground; the old lady was thrown into the front seat. The car turned over once and landed right-side-up in a gulch off the side of the road. Bailey remained in the driver's seat with the cat—gray-striped with a broad white face and an orange nose—clinging to his neck like a caterpillar.

As soon as the children saw they could move their arms and legs, they scrambled out of the car, shouting, "We've had an ACCIDENT!" The grandmother was curled up under the dashboard, hoping she was injured so that Bailey's wrath would not come down on her all at once. The horrible thought she had had before the accident was that the house she had remembered so vividly was not in Georgia but in Tennessee.

Bailey removed the cat from his neck with both hands and flung it out the window against the side of a pine tree. Then he got out of the car and started looking for the children's mother. She was sitting against the side of the red gutted ditch, holding the screaming baby, but she only had a cut down her face and a broken shoulder. "We've had an ACCIDENT!" the children screamed in a frenzy of delight.

"But nobody's killed," June Star said with disappointment as the grandmother limped out of the car, her hat still pinned to her head but the broken front brim standing up at a jaunty angle and the violet spray hanging off the side. They all sat down in the ditch, except the children, to recover from the shock. They were all shaking.

"Maybe a car will come along," said the children's mother hoarsely.

"I believe I have injured an organ," said the grandmother, pressing her side, but no one answered her. Bailey's teeth were clattering. He had on a yellow sport shirt with bright blue parrots designed in it and his face was as yellow as the shirt. The grandmother decided that she would not mention that the house was in Tennessee.

The road was about ten feet above and they could see only the tops of the trees on the other side of it. Behind the ditch they were sitting in there were more woods, tall and dark and deep. In a few minutes they saw a car some distance away on top of a hill, coming slowly as if the occupants were watching them. The grandmother stood up and waved both arms dramatically to attract their attention. The car continued to come on slowly, disappeared around a bend and appeared again, moving even slower, on top of the hill they had gone over. It was a big black battered hearse-like automobile. There were three men in it.

It came to a stop just over them and for some minutes, the driver looked down with a steady expressionless gaze to where they were sitting, and didn't speak. Then he turned his head and muttered something to the other two and they got out. One was a fat boy in black trousers and a red sweat shirt with a silver stallion embossed on the front of it. He moved around on the right side of them and stood staring, his mouth partly open in a kind of loose grin. The other had on khaki pants and a blue striped coat and a gray hat pulled down very low, hiding most of his face. He came around slowly on the left side. Neither spoke.

The driver got out of the car and stood by the side of it, looking down at them. He was an older man than the other two. His hair was just beginning to gray and he wore silver-rimmed spectacles that gave him a scholarly look. He had a long creased face and didn't have on any shirt or undershirt. He had on blue jeans that were too tight for him and was holding a black hat and a gun. The two boys also had guns.

"We've had an ACCIDENT!" the children screamed.

The grandmother had the peculiar feeling that the bespectacled man was someone she knew. His face was as familiar to her as if she had known him all her life but she could not recall who he was. He moved away from the car and began to come down the embankment, placing his feet carefully so that he wouldn't slip. He had on tan and white shoes and no socks, and his ankles were red and thin. "Good afternoon," he said. "I see you all had you a little spill."

"We turned over twice!" said the grandmother.

"Oncet," he corrected. "We seen it happen. Try their car and see will it run, Hiram," he said quietly to the boy with the gray hat.

"What you got that gun for?" John Wesley asked. "Whatcha gonna do with that gun?"

"Lady," the man said to the children's mother, "would you mind calling them children to sit down by you? Children make me nervous. I want all you all to sit down right together there where you're at."

"What are you telling US what to do for?" June Star asked.

Behind them the line of woods gaped like a dark open mouth. "Come here," said their mother.

"Look here now," Bailey began suddenly, "we're in a predicament! We're in . . ."

The grandmother shrieked. She scrambled to her feet and stood staring. "You're The Misfit!" she said. "I recognized you at once!"

"Yes'm," the man said, smiling slightly as if he were pleased in spite of himself to be known, "but it would have been better for all of you, lady, if you hadn't of reckernized me."

Bailey turned his head sharply and said something to his mother that shocked even the children. The old lady began to cry and The Misfit reddened.

"Lady," he said, "don't you get upset. Sometimes a man says things he don't mean. I don't reckon he meant to talk to you thataway."

"You wouldn't shoot a lady, would you?" the grandmother said and removed a clean handkerchief from her cuff and began to slap at her eyes with it.

The Misfit pointed the toe of his shoe into the ground and made a little hole and then covered it up again. "I would hate to have to," he said.

"Listen," the grandmother almost screamed, "I know you're a good man. You don't look a bit like you have common blood. I know you must come from nice people!"

"Yes mam," he said, "finest people in the world." When he smiled he showed a row of strong white teeth. "God never made a finer woman than my mother and my daddy's heart was pure gold," he said. The boy with the red sweat shirt had come around behind them and was standing with his gun at his hip. The Misfit squatted down on the ground. "Watch them children, Bobby Lee," he said. "You know they make me nervous." He looked at the six of them huddled together in front of him and he seemed to be embarrassed as if he couldn't think of anything to say. "Ain't a cloud in the sky," he remarked, looking up at it. "Don't see no sun but don't see no cloud neither."

"Yes, it's a beautiful day," said the grandmother. "Listen," she said, "you shouldn't call yourself The Misfit because I know you're a good man at heart. I can just look at you and tell."

"Hush!" Bailey yelled. "Hush! Everybody shut up and let me handle this!" He was squatting in the position of a runner about to sprint forward but he didn't move.

"I pre-chate that, lady," The Misfit said and drew a little circle in the ground with the butt of his gun.

"It'll take a half a hour to fix this here car," Hiram called, looking over the raised hood of it.

"Well, first you and Bobby Lee get him and that little boy to step over yonder with you," The Misfit said, pointing to Bailey and John Wesley. "The boys want to ast you something," he said to Bailey. "Would you mind stepping back in them woods there with them?"

"Listen," Bailey began, "we're in a terrible predicament! Nobody realizes what this is," and his voice cracked. His eyes were as blue and intense as the parrots in his shirt and he remained perfectly still.

The grandmother reached up to adjust her hat brim as if she were going to the woods with him but it came off in her hand. She stood staring at it and after a second she let it fall on the ground. Hiram pulled Bailey up by the arm as if he were assisting an old man. John Wesley caught hold of his father's hand and Bobby Lee followed. They went off toward the woods and just as they reached the dark edge, Bailey turned and supporting himself against a gray naked pine trunk, he shouted, "I'll be back in a minute, Mamma, wait on me!"

"Come back this instant!" his mother shrilled but they all disappeared into the woods.

"Bailey Boy!" the grandmother called in a tragic voice but she found she was looking at The Misfit squatting on the ground in front of her. "I just know you're a good man," she said desperately. "You're not a bit common!"

"Nome, I ain't a good man," The Misfit said after a second as if he had considered her statement carefully, "but I ain't the worst in the world neither. My daddy said I was a different breed of dog from my brothers and sisters. 'You know,' Daddy said, 'it's some that can live their whole life out without asking about it and it's others has to know why it is, and this boy is one of the latters. He's going to be into everything!'" He put on his black hat and looked up suddenly and then away deep into the woods as if he were embarrassed again. "I'm sorry I don't have on a shirt before you ladies," he said, hunching his shoulders slightly. "We buried our clothes that we had on when we escaped and we're just making do until we can get better. We borrowed these from some folks we met," he explained.

"That's perfectly all right," the grandmother said. "Maybe Bailey has an extra shirt in his suitcase."

"I'll look and see terrectly," The Misfit said.

"Where are they taking him?" the children's mother screamed.

"Daddy was a card himself," The Misfit said. "You couldn't put anything over on him. He never got in trouble with the Authorities though. Just had the knack of handling them."

"You could be honest too if you'd only try," said the grandmother. "Think how wonderful it would be to settle down and live a comfortable life and not have to think about somebody chasing you all the time."

The Misfit kept scratching in the ground with the butt of his gun as if he were thinking about it. "Yes'm, somebody is always after you," he murmured.

The grandmother noticed how thin his shoulder blades were just behind his hat because she was standing up looking down on him. "Do you every pray?" she asked.

He shook his head. All she saw was the black hat wiggle between his shoulder blades. "Nome," he said.

There was a pistol shot from the woods, followed closely by another. Then silence. The old lady's head jerked around. She could hear the wind move through the tree tops like a long satisfied insuck of breath. "Bailey Boy!" she called.

"I was a gospel singer for a while," The Misfit said. "I been most everything. Been in the arm service, both land and sea, at home and abroad, been twict married, been an undertaker, been with the railroads, plowed Mother Earth, been in a tornado, seen a man burnt alive oncet," and he looked up at the children's mother and the little girl who were sitting close together, their faces white and their eyes glassy; "I even seen a woman flogged," he said.

"Pray, pray," the grandmother began, "pray, pray . . ."

"I never was a bad boy that I remember of," The Misfit said in an almost dreamy voice, "but somewheres along the line I done something wrong and got sent to the penitentiary. I was buried alive," and he looked up and held her attention to him by a steady stare.

"That's when you should have started to pray," she said. "What did you do to get sent to the penitentiary that first time?"

"Turn to the right, it was a wall," The Misfit said, looking up again at the cloudless sky. "Turn to the left, it was a wall. Look up it was a ceiling, look down it was a floor. I forget what I done, lady. I set there and set there, trying to remember what it was I done and I ain't recalled it to this day. Oncet in a while, I would think it was coming to me, but it never come."

"Maybe they put you in by mistake," the old lady said vaguely.

"Nome," he said. "It wasn't no mistake. They had the papers on me."

"You must have stolen something," she said.

The Misfit sneered slightly. "Nobody had nothing I wanted," he said. "It was a head-doctor at the penitentiary said what I had done was kill my daddy but I known that for a lie. My daddy died in nineteen ought nineteen of the epidemic flu and I never had a thing to do with it. He was buried in the Mount Hopewell Baptist churchyard and you can go there and see for yourself."

"If you would pray," the old lady said, "Jesus would help you."

"That's right," The Misfit said.

"Well then, why don't you pray?" she asked trembling with delight suddenly.

"I don't want no hep," he said. "I'm doing all right by myself."

Bobby Lee and Hiram came ambling back from the woods. Bobby Lee was dragging a yellow shirt with bright blue parrots in it.

"Thow me that shirt, Bobby Lee," The Misfit said. The shirt came flying at him and landed on his shoulder and he put it on. The grandmother couldn't name what the shirt reminded her of. "No, lady," The Misfit said while he was buttoning it up, "I found out the crime don't matter. You can do one thing or you can do another, kill a man or take a tire off his car, because sooner or later you're going to forget what it was you done and just be punished for it."

The children's mother had begun to make heaving noises as if she couldn't get her breath. "Lady," he asked, "would you and that little girl like to step off yonder with Bobby Lee and Hiram and join your husband?"

"Yes, thank you" the mother said faintly. Her left arm dangled helplessly and she was holding the baby, who had gone to sleep, in the other. "Hep that lady up, Hiram," The Misfit said as she struggled to climb out of the ditch, "and Bobby Lee, you hold onto that little girl's hand."

"I don't want to hold hands with him," June Star said. "He reminds me of a pig."

The fat boy blushed and laughed and caught her by the arm and pulled her off into the woods after Hiram and her mother.

Alone with The Misfit, the grandmother found that she had lost her voice. There was not a cloud in the sky nor any sun. There was nothing around her but woods. She wanted to tell him that he must pray. She opened and closed her mouth several times before anything came out. Finally she found herself saying, "Jesus, Jesus," meaning, Jesus will help you, but the way she was saying it, it sounded as if she might be cursing.

"Yes'm," The Misfit said as if he agreed. "Jesus thown everything off balance. It was the same case with Him as with me except He hadn't committed any crime and they could prove I had committed one because they had the papers on me. Of course," he said, "they never shown me my papers.

That's why I sign myself now. I said long ago, you get you a signature and sign everything you do and keep a copy of it. Then you'll know what you done and you can hold up the crime to the punishment and see do they match and in the end you'll have something to prove you ain't been treated right. I call myself The Misfit," he said, "because I can't make what all I done wrong fit what all I gone through in punishment."

There was a piercing scream from the woods, followed closely by a pistol report. "Does it seem right to you, lady, that one is punished a heap and another ain't punished at all?"

"Jesus!" the old lady cried. "You've got good blood! I know you wouldn't shoot a lady! I know you come from nice people! Pray! Jesus, you ought not to shoot a lady. I'll give you all the money I've got!"

"Lady," The Misfit said, looking beyond her far into the woods, "there never was a body that give the undertaker a tip."

There were two more pistol reports and the grandmother raised her head like a parched old turkey hen crying for water and called, "Bailey Boy, Bailey Boy!" as if her heart would break.

"Jesus was the only One that ever raised the dead," The Misfit continued, "and He shouldn't have done it. He thown everything off balance. If He did what He said, then it's nothing for you to do but thow away everything and follow Him, and if He didn't, then it's nothing for you to do but enjoy the few minutes you got left the best way you can—by killing somebody or burning down his house or doing some other meanness to him. No pleasure but meanness," he said and his voice had become almost a snarl.

"Maybe He didn't raise the dead," the old lady mumbled, not knowing what she was saying and feeling so dizzy that she sank down in the ditch with her legs twisted under her.

"I wasn't there so I can't say He didn't," The Misfit said. "I wisht I had of been there," he said, hitting the ground with his fist. "It ain't right I wasn't there because if I had of been there I would of known. Listen lady," he said in a high voice, "if I had of been there I would of known and I wouldn't be like I am now." His voice seemed about to crack and the grandmother's head cleared for an instant. She saw the man's face twisted close to her own as if he were going to cry and she murmured, "Why you're one of my babies. You're one of my own children!" She reached out and touched him on the shoulder. The Misfit sprang back as if a snake had bitten him and shot her three times through the chest. Then he put his gun down on the ground and took off his glasses and began to clean them.

Hiram and Bobby Lee returned from the woods and stood over the ditch, looking down at the grandmother who half sat and half lay in a puddle of blood with her legs crossed under her like a child's and her face smiling up at the cloudless sky.

Without his glasses, The Misfit's eyes were red-rimmed and pale and defenseless-looking. "Take her off and thow her where you thown the others," he said, picking up the cat that was rubbing itself against his leg.

"She was a talker, wasn't she?" Bobby Lee said, sliding down the ditch with a yodel.

"She would of been a good woman," The Misfit said, "if it had been somebody there to shoot her every minute of her life."

"Some fun!" Bobby Lee said.

"Shut up, Bobby Lee," The Misfit said. "It's no real pleasure in life."

Donald Barthelme (1933–   )
ME AND MISS MANDIBLE

13 September

Miss Mandible wants to make love to me but she hesitates because I am officially a child; I am, according to the records, according to the gradebook on her desk, according to the card index in the principal's office, eleven years old. There is a misconception here, one that I haven't quite managed to get cleared up yet. I am in fact thirty-five, I've been in the Army, I am six feet one, I have hair in the appropriate places, my voice is a baritone, I know very well what to do with Miss Mandible if she ever makes up her mind.

In the meantime we are studying common fractions. I could, of course, answer all the questions, or at least most of them (there are things I don't remember). But I prefer to sit in this too-small seat with the desktop cramping my thighs and examine the life around me. There are thirty-two in the class, which is launched every morning with the pledge of allegiance to the flag. My own allegiance, at the moment, is divided between Miss Mandible and Sue Ann Brownly, who sits across the aisle from me all day long and is, like Miss Mandible, a fool for love. Of the two I prefer, today, Sue Ann; although between eleven and eleven and a half (she refuses to reveal her exact age) she is clearly a woman, with a woman's disguised aggression and woman's peculiar contradictions. Strangely neither she nor any of the other children seem to see any incongruity in my presence here.

15 September

Happily our geography text, which contains maps of all the principal landmasses of the world, is large enough to conceal my clandestine journal-keeping, accomplished in an ordinary black composition book. Every day I must wait until Geography to put down such thoughts as I may have had during the morning about my situation and my fellows. I have tried writing at other times and it does not work. Either the teacher is walking up and down the aisles (during this period, luckily, she sticks close to the map rack in the front of the room) or Bobby Vanderbilt, who sits behind me, is punching me in the kidneys and wanting to know what I am doing. Vanderbilt, I have found out from certain desultory conversations on the playground, is hung up on sports cars, a veteran consumer of *Road & Track*. This explains the continual roaring sounds which seem to emanate from his desk; he is reproducing a record album called *Sounds of Sebring*.

19 September

Only, I, at times (only at times), understand that somehow a mistake has been made, that I am in a place where I don't belong. It may be that Miss Mandible also knows this, at some level, but for reasons not fully understood by me she is going along with the game. When I was first assigned to this room I wanted to protest, the error seemed obvious, the stupidest principal could have seen it; but I have come to believe it was deliberate, that I have been betrayed again.

Now it seems to make little difference. This life-role is as interesting as my former life-role, which was that of a claims adjuster for the Great Northern Insurance Company, a position which compelled me to spend my time amid the debris of our civilization: rumpled fenders, roofless sheds, gutted warehouses, smashed arms and legs. After ten years of this one has a tendency to see the world as a vast junkyard, looking at a man and seeing only his (potentially) mangled parts, entering a house only to trace the path of the inevitable fire. Therefore when I was installed here, although I knew an error had been made, I countenanced it, I was shrewd; I was aware that there might well be some kind of advantage to be gained from what seemed a disaster. The role of The Adjuster teaches one much.

22 September

I am being solicited for the valleyball team. I decline, refusing to take unfair profit from my height.

23 September

Every morning the roll is called: Bestvina, Bokenfohr, Broan, Brownly, Cone, Coyle, Crecelius, Darin, Durbin, Geiger, Guiswite, Heckler, Jacobs, Kleinschmidt, Lay, Logan, Masei, Mitgang, Pfeilsticker. It is like the litany chanted in the dim miserable dawns of Texas by the cadre sergeant of our basic training company.

In the Army, too, I was ever so slightly awry. It took me a fantastically long time to realize what the others grasped almost at once: that much of what we were doing was absolutely pointless, to no purpose. I kept wondering why. Then something happened that proposed a new question. One day we were commanded to whitewash, from the ground to the topmost leaves, all of the trees in our training area. The corporal who relayed the order was nervous and apologetic. Later an off-duty captain sauntered by and watched us, white-splashed and totally weary, strung out among the freakish shapes we had created. He walked away swearing. I understood the principle (orders are orders), but I wondered: Who decides?

29 September

Sue Ann is a wonder. Yesterday she viciously kicked my ankle for not paying attention when she was attempting to pass me a note during History. It is swollen still. But Miss Mandible was watching me, there was nothing I could do. Oddly enough Sue Ann reminds me of the wife I had in my former role, while Miss Mandible seems to be a child. She watches me constantly, trying to keep sexual significance out of her look; I am afraid the other children have noticed. I have already heard, on that ghostly frequency that is the medium of classroom communication, the words *"Teacher's pet!"*

2 October

Sometimes I speculate on the exact nature of the conspiracy which brought me here. At times I believe it was instigated by my wife of former days, whose name was . . . I am only pretending to forget. I know her name very well, as well as I know the name of my former motor oil (Quaker State) or my old Army serial number (US 54109268). Her name was Brenda, and the conversation I recall best, the one which makes me suspicious now, took place on the day we parted. "You have the soul of a whore," I said on that occasion, stating nothing less than literal, unvarnished fact. "You," she replied, "are a pimp, a poop, and a child. I am leaving you forever and I trust that without me you will perish of your own inadequacies. Which are considerable."

I squirm in my seat at the memory of this conversation, and Sue Ann watches me with malign compassion. She has noticed the discrepancy between the size of my desk and my own size, but apparently sees it only as a token of my glamour, my dark man-of-the-worldness.

7 October

Once I tiptoed up to Miss Mandible's desk (when there was no one else in the room) and examined its surface. Miss Mandible is a clean-desk teacher, I discovered. There was nothing except her gradebook (the one in which I exist as a sixth-grader) and a text, which was open at a page headed *Making the Processes Meaningful.* I read: "Many pupils enjoy working fractions when they understand what they are doing. They have confidence in their ability to take the right steps, and to obtain correct answers. However, to give the subject full social significance, it is necessary that many realistic situations requiring the processes be found. Many interesting and lifelike problems involving the use of fractions should be solved . . ."

8 October

I am not irritated by the feeling of having been through all this before. Things are done differently now. The children, moreover, are in some ways different from those who accompanied me on my first voyage through the elementary schools: *"They have confidence in their ability to take the right steps and to obtain correct answers."* This is surely true. When Bobby Vanberbilt, who sits behind me and has the great tactical advantage of being able to maneuver in my disproportionate shadow, wishes to bust a classmate in the mouth he first asks Miss Mandible to lower the blind, saying that the sun hurts his eyes. When she does so, *bip!* My generation would never have been able to con authority so easily.

13 October

It may be that on my first trip through the schools I was too much under the impression that what the authorities (who decides?) had ordained for me was right and proper, that I confused authority with life itself. My path was not particularly of my own choosing. My career stretched out in front of me like a paper chase, and my role was to pick up the clues. When I got out of school, the first time, I felt that this estimate was substantially correct, and eagerly entered the hunt. I found clues abundant: diplomas, membership cards, campaign buttons, a marriage license, insurance forms, discharge papers, tax returns, Certificates of Merit. They seemed to prove, at the very least, that I was *in the running.* But that was before my tragic mistake on the Mrs. Anton Bichek claim.

I misread a clue. Do not misunderstand me: it was a tragedy only from the point of view of the authorities. I conceived that it was my duty to obtain satisfaction for the injured, for this elderly lady (not even one of our policy-holders, but a claimant against Big Ben Transfer & Storage, Inc.) from the company. The settlement was $165,000; the claim, I still believe, was just. But without my encouragement Mrs. Bichek would never have had the self-love to prize her injury so highly. The company paid, but its faith in me, in my efficacy in the role, was broken. Henry Goodykind, the district manager, expressed this thought in a few not altogether unsympathetic words, and told me at the same time that I was to have a new role. The next thing I knew I was here, at Horace Greeley Elementary, under the lubricious eye of Miss Mandible.

17 October

Today we are to have a fire drill. I know this because I am a Fire Marshal, not only for our room but for the entire right wing of the second floor. This distinction, which was awarded shortly after my arrival, is interpreted by some as another mark of my somewhat dubious relations with our teacher. My armband, which is red and decorated with white felt letters reading FIRE, sits on the little shelf under my desk, next to the brown paper bag containing the lunch I carefully make for myself each morning. One of the advantages of packing my own lunch (I have no one to pack it for me) is that I am able to fill it with things I enjoy. The peanut butter sandwiches that my mother made in my former existence, many years ago, have been banished in favor of ham and cheese. I have found that my diet has mysteriously adjusted to my new situation; I no longer drink, for instance, and when I smoke, it is in the boys' john, like everybody else. When school is out I hardly smoke at all. It is only in the matter of sex that I feel my own true age; this is apparently something that, once learned, can never be forgotten. I live in fear that Miss Mandible will one day keep me after school, and when we are alone, create a compromising situation. To avoid this I have become a model pupil: another reason for the pronounced dislike I have encountered in certain quarters. But I cannot deny that I am singled by those long glances from the vicinity of the chalkboard; Miss Mandible is in many ways, notably about the bust, a very tasty piece.

24 October

There are isolated challenges to my largeness, to my dimly realized position in the class as Gulliver. Most of my classmates are polite about this matter, as they would be if I had only one eye, or wasted, metal-wrapped legs. I am viewed as a mutation of some sort but essentially a peer. However Harry Broan, whose father has made himself rich manufacturing the Broan Bath-

room Vent (with which Harry is frequently reproached; he is always being asked how things are in Ventsville), today inquired if I wanted to fight. An interested group of his followers had gathered to observe this suicidal undertaking. I replied that I didn't feel quite up to it, for which he was obviously grateful. We are now friends forever. He has given me to understand privately that he can get me all the bathroom vents I will ever need, at a ridiculously modest figure.

25 October

"*Many interesting and lifelike problems involving the use of fractions should be solved . . .*" The theorists fail to realize that everything that is either interesting or lifelike in the classroom proceeds from what they would probably call interpersonal relations: Sue Ann Brownly kicking me in the ankle. How lifelike, how womanlike, is her tender solicitude after the deed! Her pride in my newly acquired limp is transparent; everyone knows that she has set her mark upon me, that it is a victory in her unequal struggle with Miss Mandible for my great, overgrown heart. Even Miss Mandible knows, and counters in perhaps the only way she can, with sarcasm. "Are you wounded, Joseph?" Conflagrations smolder behind her eyelids, yearning for the Fire Marshal clouds her eyes. I mumble that I have bumped my leg.

30 October

I return again and again to the problem of my future.

4 November

The underground circulating library has brought me a copy of *Movie—TV Secrets*, the multicolor cover blazoned with the headline. "Debbie's Date Insults Liz!" It is a gift from Frankie Randolph, a rather plain girl who until today has had not one word for me, passed on via Bobby Vanderbilt. I nod and smile over my shoulder in acknowledgment; Frankie hides her head under her desk. I have seen these magazines being passed around among the girls (sometimes one of the boys will condescend to inspect a particularly lurid cover). Miss Mandible confiscates them whenever she finds one. I leaf through *Movie—TV Secrets* and get an eyeful. "The exclusive picture on these pages isn't what it seems. We know how it looks and we know what the gossipers will do. So in the interests of a nice guy, we're publishing the facts first. Here's what really happened!" The picture shows a rising young movie idol in bed, pajama-ed and bleary-eyed, while an equally blowzy young woman looks startled beside him. I am happy to know that the picture is not really what it seems; it seems to be nothing less than divorce evidence.

What do these hipless eleven-year-olds think when they come across, in the same magazine, the full-page ad for Maurice de Paree, which features "Hip Helpers" or what appear to be padded rumps? ("A real undercover agent that adds appeal to those hips and derriere, both!") If they cannot decipher the language the illustrations leave nothing to the imagination. "Drive him frantic . . ." the copy continues. Perhaps this explains Bobby Vanderbilt's preoccupation with Lancias and Maseratis; it is a defense against being driven frantic.

Sue Ann has observed Frankie Randolph's overture, and catching my eye, she pulls from her satchel no less then seventeen of these magazines, thrusting them at me as if to prove that anything any of her rivals has to offer, she can top. I shuffle through them quickly, noting the broad editorial perspective:

"Debbie's Kids Are Crying"
"Eddie Asks Debbie. Will You . . .?"
"The Nightmares Liz Has About Eddie!"

"The Things Debbie Can Tell About Eddie"
"The Private Life of Eddie and Liz"
"Debbie Gets Her Man Back?"
"A New Life for Liz"
"Love Is a Tricky Affair"
"Eddie's Taylor-Made Love Nest"
"How Liz Made a Man of Eddie"
"Are They Planning to Live Together?"
"Isn't It Time to Stop Kicking Debbie Around?"
"Debbie's Dilemma"
"Eddie Becomes a Father Again"
"Is Debbie Planning to Re-wed?"
"Can Liz Fulfill Herself?"
"Why Debbie Is Sick of Hollywood"

Who are these people, Debbie, Eddie, Liz, and how did they get themselves in such a terrible predicament? Sue Ann knows, I am sure; it is obvious that she has been studying their history as a guide to what she may expect when she is suddenly freed from this drab, flat classroom.

I am angry and I shove the magazines back at her with not even a whisper of thanks.

5 November

The sixth grade at Horace Greeley Elementary is a furnace of love, love, love. Today it is raining, but inside the air is heavy and tense with passion. Sue Ann is absent; I suspect that yesterday's exchange has driven her to her bed. Guilt hangs about me. She is not responsible, I know, for what she reads, for the models proposed to her by a venal publishing industry; I should not have been so harsh. Perhaps it is only the flu.

Nowhere have I encountered an atmosphere as charged with aborted sexuality as this. Miss Mandible is helpless; nothing goes right today. Amos Darin has been found drawing a dirty picture in the cloakroom. Sad and inac- ·curate, it was offered not as a sign of something else but as an act of love in itself. It has excited even those who have not seen it, even those who saw but understood only that it was dirty. The room buzzes with imperfectly comprehended titillation. Amos stands by the door, waiting to be taken to the principal's office. He wavers between fear and enjoyment of his temporary celebrity. From time to time Miss Mandible looks at me reproachfully, as if blaming me for the uproar. But I did not create this atmosphere, I am caught in it like all the others.

8 November
Everything is promised my classmates and I, most of all the future. We accept the outrageous assurances without blinking.

9 November
I have finally found the nerve to petition for a larger desk. At recess I can hardly walk; my legs do not wish to uncoil themselves. Miss Mandible says she will take it up with the custodian. She is worried about the excellence of my themes. Have I, she asks, been receiving help? For an instant I am on the brink of telling her my story. Something, however, warns me not to attempt it. Here I am safe, I have a place; I do not wish to entrust myself once more to the whimsy of authority. I resolve to make my themes less excellent in the future.

11 November
A ruined marriage, a ruined adjusting career, a grim interlude in the Army when I was almost not a person. This is the sum of my existence to date, a dismal total. Small wonder that re-education seemed my only hope. It is clear even to me that I need reworking in some fundamental way. How efficient is the society that provides thus for the salvage of its clinkers!
Plucked from my unexamined life among other pleasant, desperate, money-making young Americans, thrown back-

ward in space and time, I am beginning to understand how I went wrong, how we all go wrong. (Although this was far from the intention of those who sent me here; they require only that I *get right*.)

14 November
The distinction between children and adults, while probably useful for some purposes, is at bottom a specious one, I feel. There are only individual egos, crazy for love.

15 November
The custodian has informed Miss Mandible that our desks are all the correct size for sixth-graders, as specified by the Board of Estimate and furnished the schools by the Nu-Art Educational Supply Corporation of Englewood, California. He has pointed out that if the desk size is correct, then the pupil size must be incorrect. Miss Mandible, who has already arrived at this conclusion, refuses to press the matter further. I think I know why. An appeal to the administration might result in my removal from the class, in a transfer to some sort of setup for "exceptional children." This would be a disaster of the first magnitude. To sit in a room with child geniuses (or, more likely, children who are "retarded") would shrivel me in a week. Let my experience here be that of the common run, I say; let me be, please God, typical.

20 November
We read signs as promises. Miss Mandible understands by my great height, by my resonant vowels, that I will one day carry her off to bed. Sue Ann interprets these same signs to mean that I am unique among her male acquaintances, therefore most desirable, therefore her special property as is everything that is Most Desirable. If neither of these propositions work out then life has broken faith with them.

I myself, in my former existence, read the company motto ("Here to Help in Time of Need") as a description of the duty of the adjuster, drastically mislocating the company's deepest concerns. I believed that because I had obtained a wife who was made up of wife-signs (beauty, charm, softness, perfume, cookery) I had found love. Brenda, reading the same signs that have now misled Miss Mandible and Sue Ann Brownly, felt she had been promised that she would never be bored again. All of us, Miss Mandible, Sue Ann, myself, Brenda, Mr. Goodykind, still believe that the American flag betokens a kind of general righteousness.

But I say, looking about me in this incubator of future citizens, that signs are signs, and that some of them are lies. This is the great discovery of my time here.

23 November

It may be that my experience as a child will save me after all. If only I can remain quietly in this classroom, making my notes while Napoleon plods through Russia in the droning voice of Harry Broan, reading aloud from our History text. All of the mysteries that perplexed me as an adult have their origins here, and one by one I am numbering them, exposing their roots.

2 December

Miss Mandible will refuse to permit me to remain ungrown. Her hands rest on my shoulders too warmly, and for too long.

7 December

It is the pledges that this place makes to me, pledges that cannot be redeemed, that confuse me later and make me feel I am not *getting anywhere*. Everything is presented as the result of some knowable process; if I wish to arrive at four I get there by way of two and two. If I wish to burn

Moscow the route I must travel has already been marked out by another visitor. If, like Bobby Vanderbilt, I yearn for the wheel of the Lancia 2.4-liter coupé, I have only to go through the appropriate process, that is, get the money. And if it is money itself that I desire, I have only to make it. All of these goals are equally beautiful in the sight of the Board of Estimate; the proof is all around us, in the no-nonsense ugliness of this steel and glass building, in the straightline matter-of-factness with which Miss Mandible handles some of our less reputable wars. Who points out that arrangements sometimes slip, that errors are made, that signs are misread? *"They have confidence in their ability to take the right steps and to obtain correct answers."* I take the right steps, obtain correct answers, and my wife leaves me for another man.

8 December

My enlightenment is proceeding wonderfully.

9 December

Disaster once again. Tomorrow I am to be sent to a doctor, for observation. Sue Ann Brownly caught Miss Mandible and me in the cloakroom, during recess, and immediately threw a fit. For a moment I thought she was actually going to choke. She ran out of the room weeping, straight for the principal's office, certain now which of us was Debbie, which Eddie, which Liz. I am sorry to be the cause of her disillusionment, but I know that she will recover. Miss Mandible is ruined but fulfilled. Although she will be charged with contributing to the delinquency of a minor, she seems at peace; *her* promise has been kept. She knows now that everything she has been told about life, about America, is true.

I have tried to convince the school authorities that I am a minor only in a very special sense, that I am in fact mostly to blame—but it does no good. They are as dense as ever. My contemporaries are astounded that I present myself as anything other than an innocent victim. Like the Old Guard marching through the Russian drifts, the class marches to the conclusion that truth is punishment.

Bobby Vanderbilt has given me his copy of *Sounds of Sebring*, in farewell.

Joyce Carol Oates (1938–   )

WHERE ARE YOU GOING, WHERE HAVE YOU BEEN?

for Bob Dylan

Her name was Connie. She was fifteen and she had a quick, nervous giggling habit of craning her neck to glance into mirrors or checking other people's faces to make sure her own was all right. Her mother, who noticed everything and knew everything and who hadn't much reason any longer to look at her own face, always scolded Connie about it. "Stop gawking at yourself. Who are you? You think you're so pretty?" she would say. Connie would raise her eyebrows at these familiar old complaints and look right through her mother, into a shadowy vision of herself as she was right at that moment: she knew she was pretty and that was everything. Her mother had been pretty once too, if you could believe those old snapshots in the album, but now her looks were gone and that was why she was always after Connie.

"Why don't you keep your room clean like your sister? How've you got your hair fixed—what the hell stinks? Hair spray? You don't see your sister using that junk."

Her sister June was twenty-four and still lived at home. She was a secretary in the high school Connie attended, and if that wasn't bad enough—with her in the same building—she was so plain and chunky and steady that Connie had to hear her praised all the time by her mother and her mother's sisters. June did this, June did that, she saved money and helped clean the house and cooked and Connie couldn't do a thing, her mind was all filled with trashy daydreams. Their father was away at work most of the time and when he came home he wanted supper and he read the newspaper at supper and after supper he went to bed. He didn't bother talking much to them, but around his bent head Connie's mother kept picking at her until Connie wished her mother was dead and she herself was dead and it was all over. "She makes me want to throw up sometimes," she complained to her friends. She had a high, breathless, amused voice that made everything she said sound a little forced, whether it was sincere or not.

There was one good thing: June went places with girl friends of hers, girls who were just as plain and steady as she, and so when Connie wanted to do that her mother had no objections. The father of Connie's best girl friend drove the girls the three miles to town and left them at a shopping plaza so they could walk through the stores or go to a movie, and when he came to pick them up again at eleven he never bothered to ask what they had done.

They must have been familiar sights, walking around the shopping plaza in their shorts and flat ballerina slippers that always scuffed the sidewalk, with charm bracelets jingling on their thin wrists; they would lean together to whisper and laugh secretly if someone passed who amused or interested them. Connie had long dark blond hair that drew anyone's eye to it, and she wore part of it pulled up on her head and puffed out and the rest of it she let fall down her back. She wore a pull-over jersey blouse that looked one way when she was at home and another way when she was away from home. Everything about her had two sides to it, one for home and one for anywhere that was not home: her walk, which could be childlike and bobbing, or languid enough to make anyone think she was hearing music in her head; her mouth, which was pale and smirking most of the time, but bright and pink on these evenings out; her laugh, which was cynical and drawling at home—"Ha, ha, very funny,"—but high-pitched and nervous anywhere else, like the jingling of the charms on her bracelet.

Sometimes they did go shopping or to a movie, but sometimes they went across the highway, ducking fast across the busy road, to a drive-in restaurant where older kids hung out. The restaurant was shaped like a big bottle, though squatter than a real bottle, and on its cap was a revolving figure of a grinning boy holding a hamburger aloft. One night in midsummer they ran across, breathless with daring, and right away someone leaned out a car window and invited them over, but it was just a boy from high school they didn't like. It made them feel good to be able to ignore him. They went up through the maze of parked and cruising cars to the bright-lit, fly-infested restaurant, their faces pleased and expectant as if they were entering a sacred building that loomed up out of the night to give them what haven and blessing they yearned for. They sat at the counter and crossed their legs at the ankles, their thin shoulders rigid with excitement, and listened to the music that made everything so good: the music was always in the background, like music at a church service; it was something to depend upon.

A boy named Eddie came in to talk with them. He sat backwards on his stool, turning himself jerkily around in semicircles and then stopping and turning back again, and after a while he asked Connie if she would like something to eat. She said she would and so she tapped her friend's arm on her way out—her friend pulled her face up into a brave, droll look—and Connie said she would meet her at eleven, across the way. "I just hate to leave her like that," Connie said earnestly, but the boy said that she wouldn't be alone for long. So they went out to his car, and on the way Connie couldn't help but let her eyes wander over the windshields and faces all around her, her face gleaming with a joy that had nothing to do with Eddie or even this place; it might have been the music. She drew her shoulders up and sucked in her breath with the pure pleasure of being alive, and just at that moment she happened to glance at a face just a few feet from hers. It was a boy with shaggy black hair, in a convertible jalopy painted gold. He stared at her and then his lips widened into a grin. Connie slit her eyes at him and turned away, but she couldn't help glancing back and there he was, still watching her. He wagged a finger and laughed and said, "Gonna get you, baby," and Connie turned away again without Eddie noticing anything.

She spent three hours with him, at the restaurant where they ate hamburgers and drank Cokes in wax cups that were always sweating, and then down an alley a mile or so away, and when he left her off at five to eleven only the movie house was still open at the plaza. Her girl friend was there, talking with a boy. When Connie came up, the two girls smiled at each other and Connie said, "How was the movie?" and the girl said, "*You* should know." They rode off with the girl's father, sleepy and pleased, and Connie couldn't help but look back at the darkened shopping plaza with its big empty parking lot and its signs that were faded and ghostly now, and over at the drive-in restaurant where cars were still circling tirelessly. She couldn't hear the music at this distance.

Next morning June asked her how the movie was and Connie said, "So-so."

She and that girl and occasionally another girl went out several times a week, and the rest of the time Connie spent around the house—it was summer vacation—getting in her mother's way and thinking, dreaming about the boys she met. But all the boys fell back and dissolved into a single face that was not even a face but an idea, a feeling, mixed up with the urgent insistent pounding of the music and the humid night air of July. Connie's mother kept dragging her back to the daylight by finding things for her to do or saying suddenly, "What's this about the Pettinger girl?"

And Connie would say nervously, "Oh, her. That dope." She always drew thick clear lines between herself and such girls, and her mother was simple and kind enough to believe it. Her mother was so simple, Connie thought, that it was maybe cruel to fool her so much. Her mother went scuffling around the house in old bedroom slippers and complained over the telephone to one sister about the other, then the other called up and the two of them complained about the third one. If June's name was mentioned her mother's tone was approving, and if Connie's name was mentioned it was disapproving. This did not really mean she disliked Connie, and actually Connie thought that her mother preferred her to June just because she was prettier, but the two of them kept up a pretense of exasperation, a sense that they were tugging and struggling over something of little value to either of them. Sometimes, over coffee, they were almost friends, but something would come up—some vexation that was like a fly buzzing suddenly around their heads—and their faces went hard with contempt.

One Sunday Connie got up at eleven —none of them bothered with church —and washed her hair so that it could dry all day long in the sun. Her parents and sister were going to a barbecue at an aunt's house and Connie said no, she wasn't interested, rolling her eyes to let her mother know just what she thought of it. "Stay home alone then," her mother said sharply. Connie sat out back in a lawn chair and watched them drive away, her father quiet and bald, hunched around so that he could back the car out, her mother with a look that was still angry and not at all softened through the windshield, and in the back seat poor old June, all dressed up as if she didn't know what a barbecue was, with all the running yelling kids and the flies. Connie sat with her eyes closed in the sun, dreaming and dazed with the warmth about her as if this were a kind of love, the caresses of love, and her mind slipped over onto thoughts of the boy she had been with the night before and how nice he had been, how sweet it always was, not the way someone like June would suppose but sweet, gentle, the way it was in movies and promised in songs; and when she opened her eyes she hardly knew where she was, the back yard ran off into weeds and a fence-like line of trees and behind it the sky was perfectly blue and still. The asbestos "ranch house" that was now three years old startled her—it looked small. She shook her head as if to get awake.

It was too hot. She went inside the house and turned on the radio to drown out the quiet. She sat on the edge of her bed, barefoot, and listened for an hour and a half to a program called XYZ Sunday Jamboree, record after record of hard, fast, shrieking songs she sang along with, interspersed by exclamations from "Bobby King": "An' look here, you girls at Napoleon's—Son and Charley want you to pay real close attention to this song coming up!"

And Connie paid close attention herself, bathed in a glow of slow-pulsed joy that seemed to rise mysteriously out of the music itself and lay languidly about the airless little room, breathed in and breathed out with each gentle rise and fall of her chest.

After a while she heard a car coming up the drive. She sat up at once, startled, because it couldn't be her father so soon. The gravel kept crunching all the way in from the road—the driveway was long—and Connie ran to the window. It was a car she didn't know. It was an open jalopy, painted a bright gold that caught the sunlight opaquely. Her heart began to pound and her fingers snatched at her hair, checking it, and she whispered, "Christ. Christ," wondering how bad she looked. The car came to a stop at the side door and the horn sounded four short taps, as if this were a signal Connie knew.

She went into the kitchen and approached the door slowly, then hung out the screen door, her bare toes curling down off the step. There were two boys in the car and now she recognized the driver: he had shaggy, shabby black hair that looked crazy as a wig and he was grinning at her.

"I ain't late, am I?" he said.

"Who the hell do you think you are?" Connie said.

"Toldja I'd be out, didn't I?"

"I don't even know who you are."

She spoke sullenly, careful to show no interest or pleasure, and he spoke in a fast, bright monotone. Connie looked past him to the other boy, taking her time. He had fair brown hair, with a lock that fell onto his forehead. His sideburns gave him a fierce, embarrassed look, but so far he hadn't even bothered to glance at her. Both boys wore sunglasses. The driver's glasses were metallic and mirrored everything in miniature.

"You wanta come for a ride?" he said.

Connie smirked and let her hair fall loose over one shoulder.

"Don'tcha like my car? New paint job," he said. "Hey."

"What?"

"You're cute."

She pretended to fidget, chasing flies away from the door.

"Don'tcha believe, me, or what?" he said.

"Look, I don't even know who you are," Connie said in disgust.

"Hey, Ellie's got a radio, see. Mine broke down." He lifted his friend's arm and showed her the little transistor radio the boy was holding, and now Connie began to hear the music. It was the same program that was playing inside the house.

"Bobby King?" she said.

"I listen to him all the time. I think he's great."

"He's kind of great," Connie said reluctantly.

"Listen, that guy's *great*. He knows where the action is."

Connie blushed a little, because the glasses made it impossible for her to see just what this boy was looking at. She couldn't decide if she liked him or if he was just a jerk, and so she dawdled in the doorway and wouldn't come down or go back inside. She said, "What's all that stuff painted on your car?"

"Can'tcha read it?" He opened the door very carefully, as if he were afraid it might fall off. He slid out just as carefully, planting his feet firmly on the ground, the tiny metallic world in his glasses slowing down like gelatine hardening, and in the midst of it Connie's bright green blouse. "This here is my name, to begin with," he said. ARNOLD FRIEND was written in tarlike black letters on the side, with a drawing of a round, grinning face that reminded Connie of a pumpkin, except it wore sunglasses. "I wanta introduce myself, I'm Arnold Friend and that's my real name and I'm gonna be your friend, honey, and inside the car's Ellie Oscar, he's kinda shy." Ellie brought his transistor radio up to his shoulder and balanced it there. "Now, these numbers are a secret code, honey," Arnold Friend explained. He read off the numbers 33, 19, 17 and raised his eyebrows at her to see what she thought of that, but she didn't think much of it. The left rear fender had been smashed and around it was written, on the gleaming gold background: DONE BY CRAZY WOMAN DRIVER. Connie had to laugh at that. Arnold Friend was pleased at her laughter and looked up at her. "Around the other side's a lot more— you wanta come and see them?"

"No."

"Why not?"

"Why should I?"

"Don'tcha wanta see what's on the car? Don'tcha wanta go for a ride?"

"I don't know." "Why not?"

"I got things to do."

"Like what?"

"Things."

He laughed as if she had said something funny. He slapped his thighs. He was standing in a strange way, leaning back against the car as if he were balancing himself. He wasn't tall, only an inch or so taller than she would be if she came down to him. Connie liked the way he was dressed, which was the way all of them dressed: tight faded jeans stuffed into black, scuffed boots, a belt that pulled his waist in and showed how lean he was, and a white pull-over shirt that was a little soiled and showed the hard small muscles of his arms and shoulders. He looked as if he probably did hard work, lifting and carrying things. Even his neck looked muscular. And his face was a familiar face, somehow: the jaw and chin and cheeks slightly darkened because he hadn't shaved for a day or two, and the nose long and hawklike, sniffing as if she were a treat he was going to gobble up and it was all a joke.

"Connie, you ain't telling the truth. This is your day set aside for a ride with me and you know it," he said, still laughing. The way he straightened and recovered from his fit of laughing showed that it had been all fake.

"How did you know what my name is?" she said suspiciously.

"It's Connie."

"Maybe and maybe not."

"I know my Connie," he said, wagging his finger. Now she remembered him even better, back at the restaurant, and her cheeks warmed at the thought of how she had sucked in her breath just at the moment she passed him— how she must have looked to him. And he had remembered her. "Ellie and I come out here especially for you," he said. "Ellie can sit in back. How about it?"

"Where?"

"Where what?"

"Where're we going?"

He looked at her. He took off the sunglasses and she saw how pale the skin around his eyes was, like holes that were not in shadow but instead in light. His eyes were like chips of broken glass that catch the light in an amiable way. He smiled. It was as if the idea of going for a ride somewhere, to someplace, was a new idea to him.

"Just for a ride, Connie sweetheart."

"I never said my name was Connie," she said.

"But I know what it is. I know your name and all about you, lots of things,"

Arnold Friend said. He had not moved yet but stood still leaning back against the side of his jalopy. "I took a special interest in you, such a pretty girl, and found out all about you—like I know your parents and sister are gone somewheres and I know where and how long they're going to be gone, and I know who you were with last night, and your best girl friend's name is Betty. Right?"

He spoke in a simple lilting voice, exactly as if he were reciting the words to a song. His smile assured her that everything was fine. In the car Ellie turned up the volume on his radio and did not bother to look around at them.

"Ellie can sit in the back seat," Arnold Friend said. He indicated his friend with a casual jerk of his chin, as if Ellie did not count and she should not bother with him.

"How'd you find out all that stuff?" Connie said.

"Listen: Betty Schultz and Tony Fitch and Jimmy Pettinger and Nancy Pettinger," he said in a chant. "Raymond Stanley and Bob Hutter—"

"Do you know all those kids?"

"I know everybody."

"Look, you're kidding. You're not from around here."

"Sure."

"But—how come we never saw you before?"

"Sure you saw me before," he said. He looked down at his boots, as if he were a little offended. "You just don't remember."

"I guess I'd remember you," Connie said.

"Yeah?" He looked up at this, beaming. He was pleased. He began to mark time with the music from Ellie's radio, tapping his fists lightly together. Connie looked away from his smile to the car, which was painted so bright it almost hurt her eyes to look at it. She looked at that name, ARNOLD FRIEND. And up at the front fender was an expression that was familiar—MAN THE FLYING SAUCERS. It was an expression kids had used the year before but didn't use this year. She looked at it for a while as if the words meant something to her that she did not yet know.

"What're you thinking about? Huh?" Arnold Friend demanded. "Not worried about your hair blowing around in the car, are you?"

"No."

"Think I maybe can't drive good?"

"How do I know?"

"You're a hard girl to handle. How come?" he said. "Don't you know I'm your friend? Didn't you see me put my sign in the air when you walked by?"

"What sign?"

"My sign." And he drew an X in the air, leaning out toward her. They were maybe ten feet apart. After his hand fell back to his side the X was still in the air, almost visible. Connie let the screen door close and stood perfectly still inside it, listening to the music from her radio and the boy's blend together. She stared at Arnold Friend. He stood there so stiffly relaxed, pretending to be relaxed, with one hand idly on the door handle as if he were keeping himself up that way and had no intention of ever moving again. She recognized most things about him, the tight jeans that showed his thighs and buttocks and the greasy leather boots and the tight shirt, and even that slippery friendly smile of his, that sleepy dreamy smile that all the boys used to get across ideas they didn't want to put into words. She recognized all this and also the singsong way he talked, slightly mocking, kidding, but serious and a little melancholy, and she recognized the way he tapped one fist against the other in homage to the perpetual music behind him. But all these things did not come together.

She said suddenly, "Hey, how old are you?"

His smile faded. She could see then that he wasn't a kid, he was much older

—thirty, maybe more. At this knowledge her heart began to pound faster.

"That's a crazy thing to ask. Can'tcha see I'm your own age?"

"Like hell you are."

"Or maybe a coupla years older. I'm eighteen."

"Eighteen?" she said doubtfully.

He grinned to reassure her and lines appeared at the corners of his mouth. His teeth were big and white. He grinned so broadly his eyes became slits and she saw how thick the lashes were, thick and black as if painted with a black tarlike material. Then, abruptly, he seemed to become embarrassed and looked over his shoulder at Ellie. "*Him,* he's crazy," he said. "Ain't he a riot? He's a nut, a real character." Ellie was still listening to the music. His sunglasses told nothing about what he was thinking. He wore a bright orange shirt unbuttoned halfway to show his chest, which was a pale, bluish chest and not muscular like Arnold Friend's. His shirt collar was turned up all around and the very tips of the collar pointed out past his chin as if they were protecting him. He was pressing the transistor radio up against his ear and sat there in a kind of daze, right in the sun.

"He's kinda strange," Connie said.

"Hey, she says you're kinda strange! Kinda strange!" Arnold Friend cried. He pounded on the car to get Ellie's attention. Ellie turned for the first time and Connie saw with shock that he wasn't a kid either—he had a fair, hairless face, cheeks reddened slightly as if the veins grew too close to the surface of his skin, the face of a forty-year-old baby. Connie felt a wave of dizziness rise in her at this sight and she stared at him as if waiting for something to change the shock of the moment, make it all right again. Ellie's lips kept shaping words, mumbling along with the blasting in his ear.

"Maybe you two better go away," Connie said faintly.

"What? How come?" Arnold Friend cried. "We come out here to take you for a ride. It's Sunday." He had the voice of the man on the radio now. It was the same voice, Connie thought. "Don'tcha know it's Sunday all day? And honey, no matter who you were with last night, today you're with Arnold Friend and don't you forget it! Maby you better step out here," he said, and this last was in a different voice. It was a little flatter, as if the heat was finally getting to him.

"No. I got things to do."

"Hey."

"You two better leave."

"We ain't leaving until you come with us."

"Like hell I am—"

"Connie, don't fool around with me. I mean—I mean, don't fool *around,*" he said, shaking his head. He laughed incredulously. He placed his sunglasses on top of his head, carefully, as if he were indeed wearing a wig, and brought the stems down behind his ears. Connie stared at him, another wave of dizziness and fear rising in her so that for a moment he wasn't even in focus but was just a blur standing there against his gold car, and she had the idea that he had driven up the driveway all right but had come from nowhere before that and belonged nowhere and that everything about him and even about the music that was so familiar to her was only half real.

"If my father comes and sees you—"

"He ain't coming. He's at a barbecue."

"How do you know that?"

"Aunt Tillie's. Right now they're—uh—they're drinking. Sitting around," he said vaguely, squinting as if he were staring all the way to town and over to Aunt Tillie's back yard. Then the vision seemed to get clear and he nodded energetically. "Yeah. Sitting around. There's your sister in a blue dress, huh? And high heels, the poor sad bitch—nothing like you, sweetheart! And your mother's helping some fat woman with the corn, they're cleaning the corn—husking the corn—"

"What fat woman?" Connie cried.

"How do I know what fat woman, I don't know every goddamn fat woman in the world!" Arnold Friend laughed.

"Oh, that's Mrs. Hornsby. . . . Who invited her?" Connie said. She felt a little lightheaded. Her breath was coming quickly.

"She's too fat. I don't like them fat. I like them the way you are, honey," he said, smiling sleepily at her. They stared at each other for a while through the screen door. He said softly, "Now, what you're going to do is this: you're going to come out that door. You're going to sit up front with me and Ellie's going to sit in the back, the hell with Ellie, right? This isn't Ellie's date. You're my date. I'm your lover, honey."

"What? You're crazy—"

"Yes, I'm your lover. You don't know what that is but you will," he said. "I know that too. I know all about you. But look: it's real nice and you couldn't ask for nobody better than me, or more polite. I always keep my word. I'll tell you how it is, I'm always nice at first, the first time. I'll hold you so tight you won't think you have to try to get away or pretend anything because you'll know you can't. And I'll come inside you where it's all secret and you'll give in to me and you'll love me—"

"Shut up! You're crazy!" Connie said. She backed away from the door. She put her hand up against her ears as if she'd heard something terrible, something not meant for her. "People don't talk like that, you're crazy," she muttered. Her heart was almost too big now for her chest and its pumping made sweat break out all over her. She looked out to see Arnold Friend pause and then take a step toward the porch, lurching. He almost fell. But, like a clever drunken man, he managed to catch his balance. He wobbled in his high boots and grabbed hold of one of the porch posts.

"Honey?" he said. "You still listening?"

"Get the hell out of here!"

"Be nice, honey. Listen."

"I'm going to call the police—"

He wobbled again and out of the side of his mouth came a fast spat curse, an aside not meant for her to hear. But even this "Christ!" sounded forced. Then he began to smile again. She watched this smile come, awkward as if he were smiling from inside a mask. His whole face was a mask, she thought wildly, tanned down to his throat but then running out as if he had plastered make-up on his face but had forgotten about his throat.

"Honey—? Listen, here's how it is. I always tell the truth and I promise you this: I ain't coming in that house after you."

"You better not! I'm going to call the police if you—if you don't—"

"Honey," he said, talking right through her voice, "honey, I'm not coming in there but you are coming out here. You know why?"

She was panting. The kitchen looked like a place she had never seen before, some room she had run inside but that wasn't good enough, wasn't going to help her. The kitchen window had never had a curtain, after three years, and there were dishes in the sink for her to do—probably—and if you ran your hand across the table you'd probably feel something sticky there.

"You listening, honey? Hey?"

"—going to call the police—"

"Soon as you touch the phone I don't need to keep my promise and can come inside. You won't want that."

She rushed forward and tried to lock the door. Her fingers were shaking. "But why lock it," Arnold Friend said gently, talking right into her face. "It's just a screen door. It's just nothing." One of his boots was at a strange angle, as if his foot wasn't in it. It pointed out to the left, bent at the ankle. "I mean, anybody can break through a screen door and glass and wood and iron or anything else if he needs to, anybody at all, and especially Arnold Friend. If the place got lit up with a fire, honey, you'd come runnin' out into my arms, right into my arms an' safe at home—like you knew I was your lover and'd stopped fooling around. I don't mind a nice shy girl but I don't like no fooling around." Part of those words were spoken with a slight rhythmic lilt, and Connie somehow recognized them—the echo of a song from last year, about a girl rushing into her boy friend's arms and coming home again—

Connie stood barefoot on the linoleum floor, staring at him. "What do you want?" she whispered.

"I want you," he said.

"What?"

"Seen you that night and thought, that's the one, yes sir. I never needed to look anymore."

"But my father's coming back. He's coming to get me. I had to wash my hair first—" She spoke in a dry, rapid voice, hardly raising it for him to hear.

"No, your daddy is not coming and yes, you had to wash your hair and you washed it for me. It's nice and shining and all for me. I thank you sweetheart," he said with a mock bow, but again he almost lost his balance. He had to bend and adjust his boots. Evidently his feet did not go all the way down; the boots must have been stuffed with something so that he would seem taller. Connie stared out at him and behind him at Ellie in the car, who seemed to be looking off toward Connie's right, into nothing. This Ellie said, pulling the words out of the air one after another as if he were just discovering them, "You want me to pull out the phone?"

"Shut your mouth and keep it shut," Arnold Friend said, his face red from bending over or maybe from embarrassment because Connie had seen his boots. "This ain't none of your business."

"What—what are you doing? What do you want?" Connie said. "If I call the police they'll get you, they'll arrest you—"

"Promise was not to come in unless you touch that phone, and I'll keep that promise," he said. He resumed his erect position and tried to force his shoulders back. He sounded like a hero in a movie, declaring something important. But he spoke too loudly and it was as if he were speaking to someone behind Connie. "I ain't made plans for coming in that house where I don't belong but just for you to come out to me, the way you should. Don't you know who I am?"

"You're crazy," she whispered. She backed away from the door but did not want to go into another part of the house, as if this would give him permission to come through the door. "What do you . . . you're crazy, you. . . ."

"Huh? What're you saying, honey?"

Her eyes darted everywhere in the kitchen. She could not remember what it was, this room.

"This is how it is, honey: you come out and we'll drive away, have a nice ride. But if you don't come out we're gonna wait till your people come home and then they're all going to get it."

"You want that telephone pulled out?" Ellie said. He held the radio away from his ear and grimaced, as if without the radio the air was too much for him.

"I toldja shut up, Ellie," Arnold Friend said, "you're deaf, get a hearing aid, right? Fix yourself up. This little girl's no trouble and's gonna be nice to me, so Ellie keep to yourself, this ain't your date—right? Don't hem in on me, don't hog, don't crush, don't bird dog, don't trail me," he said in a rapid, meaningless voice, as if he were running through all the expressions he'd learned but was no longer sure which of them was in style, then rushing on to new ones, making them up with his eyes closed. "Don't crawl under my fence, don't squeeze in my chipmunk hole, don't sniff my glue, suck my popsicle, keep your own greasy fingers on yourself!" He shaded his eyes and peered in at Connie, who was backed against the kitchen table. "Don't mind him, honey, he's just a creep. He's a dope. Right? I'm the boy for you and like I said, you come out here nice like a lady and give me your hand, and nobody else gets hurt, I mean, your nice old baldheaded daddy and your mummy and your sister in her high heels. Because listen: why bring them in this?"

"Leave me alone," Connie whispered.

"Hey, you know that old woman down the road, the one with the chickens and stuff—you know her?"

"She's dead!"

"Dead? What? You know her?" Arnold Friend said.

"She's dead—"

"Don't you like her?"

"She's dead—she's—she isn't here any more—"

"But don't you like her, I mean, you got something against her? Some grudge or something?" Then his voice dipped as if he were conscious of a rudeness. He touched the sunglasses perched up on top of his head as if to make sure they were still there. "Now, you be a good girl."

"What are you going to do?"

"Just two things, or maybe three," Arnold Friend said. "But I promise it won't last long and you'll like me the way you get to like people you're close to. You will. It's all over for you here, so come on out. You don't want your people in any trouble, do you?"

She turned and bumped against a chair or something, hurting her leg, but she ran into the back room and picked up the telephone. Something roared in her ear, a tiny roaring, and she was so sick with fear that she could do nothing but listen to it—the telephone was clammy and very heavy and her fingers groped down to the dial but were too weak to touch it. She began to scream into the phone, into the roaring. She

cried out, she cried for her mother, she felt her breath start jerking back and forth in her lungs as if it were some thing Arnold Friend was stabbing her with again and again with no tenderness. A noisy sorrowful wailing rose all about her and she was locked inside it the way she was locked inside this house.

After a while she could hear again. She was sitting on the floor with her wet back against the wall.

Arnold Friend was saying from the door, "That's a good girl. Put the phone back."

She kicked the phone away from her.

"No, honey. Pick it up. Put it back right."

She picked it up and put it back. The dial tone stopped.

"That's a good girl. Now, you come outside."

She was hollow with what had been fear but what was now just an emptiness. All that screaming had blasted it out of her. She sat, one leg cramped under her, and deep inside her brain was something like a pinpoint of light that kept going and would not let her relax. She thought, I'm not going to see my mother again. She thought, I'm not going to sleep in my bed again. Her bright green blouse was all wet.

Arnold Friend said, in a gentle-loud voice that was like a stage voice, "The place where you came from ain't there any more, and where you had in mind to go is cancelled out. This place you are now—inside your daddy's house—is nothing but a cardboard box I can knock down any time. You know that and always did know it. You hear me?"

She thought, I have got to think. I have got to know what to do.

"We'll go out to a nice field, out in the country here where it smells so nice and it's sunny," Arnold Friend said. "I'll have my arms tight around you so you won't need to try to get away and I'll show you what love is like, what it does. The hell with this house! It looks solid all right," he said. He ran a fingernail down the screen and the noise did not make Connie shiver, as it would have the day before. "Now, put your hand on your heart, honey. Feel that? That feels solid too but we know better. Be nice to me, be sweet like you can because what else is there for a girl like you but to be sweet and pretty and give in?—and get away before her people come back?"

She felt her pounding heart. Her hand seemed to enclose it. She thought for the first time in her life that it was nothing that was hers, that belonged to her, but just a pounding, living thing inside this body that wasn't really hers either.

"You don't want them to get hurt," Arnold Friend went on. "Now, get up, honey. Get up all by yourself."

She stood.

"Now, turn this way. That's right. Come over here to me.—Ellie, put that away, didn't I tell you? You dope. You miserable creepy dope," Arnold Friend said. His words were not angry but only part of an incantation. The incantation was kindly. "Now, come out through the kitchen to me, honey, and let's see a smile, try it, you're a brave, sweet little

girl and now they're eating corn and hot dogs cooked to bursting over an outdoor fire, and they don't know one thing about you and never did and honey, you're better than them because not a one of them would have done this for you."

Connie felt the linoleum under her feet; it was cool. She brushed her hair back out of her eyes. Arnold Friend let go of the post tentatively and opened his arms for her, his elbows pointing in toward each other and his wrists limp, to show that this was an embarrassed embrace and a little mocking, he didn't want to make her self-conscious.

She put out her hand against the screen. She watched herself push the door slowly open as if she were back safe somewhere in the other doorway, watching this body and this head of long hair moving out into the sunlight where Arnold Friend waited.

"My sweet little blue-eyed girl," he said in a half-sung sigh that had nothing to do with her brown eyes but was taken up just the same by the vast sun-lit reaches of the land behind him and on all sides of him—so much land that Connie had never seen before and did not recognize except to know that she was going to it.

Renata Adler (1938–   )
BROWNSTONE

The camel, I had noticed, was passing, with great difficulty, through the eye of the needle. The Apollo flight, the four-minute mile, Venus in Scorpio, human records on land and at sea—these had been events of enormous importance. But the camel, practicing in near obscurity for almost two thousand years,

was passing through. First the velvety nose, then the rest. Not many were aware. But if the lead camel and then perhaps the entire caravan could make it, the thread, the living thread of camels, would exist, could not be lost. No one could lose the thread. The prospects of the rich would be enhanced.

"Ortega tells us that the business of philosophy," the professor was telling his class of indifferent freshmen, "is to crack open metaphors which are dead."

"I shouldn't have come," the Englishman said, waving his drink and breathing so heavily at me that I could feel my bangs shift. "I have a terrible cold."

"He would probably have married her," a voice across the room said, "with the exception that he died."

"Well, I am a personality that prefers not to be annoyed."

"We should all prepare ourselves for this eventuality."

A six-year-old was passing the hors d'oeuvres. The baby, not quite steady on his feet, was hurtling about the room.

"He's following me," the six-year-old said, in despair.

"Then lock yourself in the bathroom, dear," Inez replied.

"He always waits outside the door."

"He loves you, dear."

"Well, I don't like it."

"How I envy you," the minister's wife was saying to a courteous, bearded boy, "reading 'Magic Mountain' for the first time."

The homosexual across the hall from me always takes Valium and walks his beagle. I borrow Valium from him from time to time, and when he takes a holiday the dog is left with me. On our floor of this brownstone, we are friends. Our landlord, Roger Somerset, was murdered last July. He was a kind and absentminded man, and on the night when he was stabbed there was a sort of requiem for him in the heating system. There is a lot of music in this building anyway. The newlyweds on the third floor play Bartók on their stereo. The couple on the second floor play clarinet quintets; their kids play rock. The girl on the fourth floor, who has been pining for two months, plays Judy Collins' "Maid of Constant Sorrow" all day long. We have a kind of orchestra in here. The ground floor is a shop. The owner of the shop speaks of our landlord's murder still. Shaking his head, he says that he suspects "foul play." We all agree with him. We changed our locks. But "foul play" seems a weird expression for the case.

It is all weird. I am not always well. One block away (I often think of this), there was ten months ago an immense crash. Water mains broke. There were small rivers in the streets. In a great skyscraper that was being built, something had failed. The newspapers reported the next day that by some miracle only two people had been "slightly injured" by ten tons of falling steel. The steel fell from the eighteenth floor. The question that preoccupies me now is how, under the circumstances, slight injuries could occur. Perhaps the two people were grazed in passing by. Perhaps some fragments of the sidewalk ricocheted. I knew a deliverer of flowers who, at Sixty-ninth and Lexington, was hit by a flying suicide. Situations simply do not yield to the most likely structures of the mind. A "self-addressed envelope," if you are inclined to brood, raises deep questions of identity. Such an envelope, immutably itself, is always precisely where it belongs. "Self-pity" is just sadness, I think, in the pejorative. But "joking with nurses" fascinates me in the press. Whenever someone has been quite struck down, lost faculties, members of his family, he is said to have "joked with his nurses" quite a lot. What a mine of humor every nurses's life must be.

The St. Bernard at the pound on Ninety-second Street was named Bonnie and would have cost five dollars. The attendant held her tightly on a leash of rope. "Hello, Bonnie," I said. Bonnie growled.

"I wouldn't talk to her if I was you," the attendant said.

I leaned forward to pat her ear. Bonnie snarled. "I wouldn't touch her if I was you," the attendant said. I held out my hand under Bonnie's jowls. She strained against the leash, and choked and coughed. "Now cut that out, Bonnie," the attendant said.

"Could I just take her for a walk around the block," I said, "before I decide?" "Are you out of your mind?" the attendant said. Aldo patted Bonnie, and we left.

I have a job, of course. I have had several jobs. I've had our paper's gossip column since last month. It is egalitarian. I look for people who are quite obscure, and report who is breaking up with whom and where they go and what they wear.

The person who invented this new form for us is on antidepressants now. He lives in Illinois. He says there are people in southern Illinois who have not yet been covered by the press. I often write about families in Queens. Last week, I went to a dinner party on Park Avenue. After 1 A.M., something called the Alive or Dead Game was being played. Someone would mention an old character from Tammany or Hollywood. "Dead," "Dead," "Dead," everyone would guess. "No, no. Alive. I saw him walking down the street just yesterday," or "Yes. Dead. I read a little obituary Notice about him last year." One of the little truths people can subtly enrage or reassure each other with is who—when you have looked away a month, a year—is still around.

DEAR TENANT:

We have reason to believe that there are impostors posing as Con Ed repairmen and inspectors circulating in this area.

Do not permit any Con Ed man to enter your premises or the building, if possible.

THE PRECINCT

My cousin, who was born on February 29th, became a veterinarian. Some years ago, when he was twenty-eight (seven, by our childhood birthday count), he was drafted, and sent to Malaysia. He spent most of his military service there, assigned to the zoo. He operated on one tiger, which, in the course of abdominal surgery, began to wake up and wag its tail. The anesthetist grabbed the tail, and injected more sodium pentothal. That tiger survived. But two flamingos, sent by the city of Miami to Kuala Lumpur as a token of good will, could not bear the trip or the climate and, in spite of my cousin's efforts, died. There was also a cobra—the largest anyone in Kuala Lumpur could remember having seen. An old man had brought it, in an immense sack, from somewhere in the countryside. The zoo director called my cousin at once, around dinnertime, to say that an unprecedented cobra had arrived. Something quite drastic, however, seemed wrong with its neck. My cousin, whom I have always admired—for his leap-year birthday, for his pilot's license, for his presence of mind—said that he would certainly examine the cobra in the morning but that the best thing for it after its long journey must be a good night's rest. By morning, the cobra was dead.

My cousin is well. The problem is this. Hardly anyone about whom I deeply care at all resembles anyone else I have ever met, or heard of, or read about in the literature. I know an Israeli general who, in 1967, retook the Mitla Pass but who, since his mandatory retirement from military service at fifty-five, has been trying to repopulate the Ark. He asked me, over breakfast at the Drake, whether I knew any owners of oryxes. Most of the vegetarian species he has collected have already multiplied enough, since he has found and cared for them, to be permitted to run wild. The carnivorous animals, though, must still be kept behind barbed wire—to keep them from stalking the rarer vegetarians. I know a group that studies Proust one Sunday afternoon a month, and an analyst, with that Exeter laugh (embittered mooing noises, and mirthless heaving of the shoulder blades), who has the most remarkable terrorist connections in the Middle East.

The New York Chinese cabdriver lingered at every corner and at every traffic light, to read his paper. I wondered what the news was. I looked over his shoulder. The illustrations and the type were clear enough: newspaper print, pornographic fiction. I leaned back in my seat. A taxi-driver who happened to be Oriental with a sado-masochistic cast of mind was not my business. I lit a cigarette, looked at my bracelet. I caught the driver's eyes a moment in the rearview mirror. He picked up his paper. "I don't think you ought to read," I said, "while you are driving." Traffic was slow. I saw his mirrored eyes again. He stopped his reading. When we reached my address, I did not tip him. Racism and prudishness, I thought, and reading over people's shoulders.

But there are moments in this place when everything becomes a show of force. He can read what he likes at home. Tipping is still my option. Another newspaper event, in our brownstone. It was a holiday. The superintendent normally hauls the garbage down and sends the paper up, by dumbwaiter, each morning. On holidays, the garbage stays upstairs, the paper on the sidewalk. At 8 A.M., I went downstairs. A ragged man was lying across the little space that separates the inner door, which locks, from the outer door, which doesn't. I am not a news addict. I could have stepped over the sleeping man, picked up my *Times*, and gone upstairs to read it. Instead, I knocked absurdly from inside the door, and said, "Wake up. You'll have to leave now." He got up, lifted the flattened cardboard he had been sleeping on, and walked away,

mumbling and reeking. It would have been kinder, certainly, to let the driver read, the wino sleep. One simply cannot bear down so hard on all these choices.

What is the point. That is what must be borne in mind. Sometimes the point is really who wants what. Sometimes the point is what is right or kind. Sometimes the point is a momentum, a fact, a quality, a voice, an intimation, a thing said or unsaid. Sometimes it's who's at fault, or what will happen if you do not move at once. The point changes and goes out. You cannot be forever watching for the point, or you lose the simplest thing: being a major character in your own life. But if you are, for any length of time, custodian of the point—in art, in court, in politics, in lives, in rooms—it turns out there are rearguard actions everywhere. Now and then, a small foray is worthwhile. Just so that being constantly, complacently, thoroughly wrong does not become the safest position of them all. The point has never quite been entrusted to me.

The conversation of "The Magic Mountain" and the unrequited love of six-year-olds occurred on Saturday, at brunch. "Bring someone new," Inez had said. "Not queer. Not married, maybe separated. John and I are breaking up." The invitation was not of a kind that I had heard before. Aldo, who lives with me between the times when he prefers to be alone, refused to come. He despises brunch. He detests Inez. I went, instead, with a lawyer who has been a distant, steady friend but who, ten years ago, when we first came to New York, had once put three condoms on the night table beside the phone. We both had strange ideas then about New York. Aldo is a gentle, orderly, soft-spoken man, slow to conclude. I try to be tidy when he is here, but I have often made his cigarettes, and once his manuscript, into the bed. Our paper's publisher is an intellectual from Baltimore. He has read Wittgenstein; he's always making unimpeachable remarks. Our music critic throws a tantrum every day, in print. Our book reviewer is looking for another job. He found that the packages in which all books are mailed could not, simply could not, be opened without doing considerable damage—through staples, tape, wire, fluttering gray stuff, recalcitrance—to the reviewer's hands. He felt it was a symptom of some kind—one of those cases where incompetence at every stage, across the board, acquired a certain independent force. Nothing to do with books, he thought, worked out at all. We also do the news. For horoscopes, there are the ladies' magazines. We just cannot compete.

My late landlord was from Scarsdale. The Maid of Constant Sorrow is from Texas. Aldo is from St. Louis. Inez's versions vary about where she's from. I grew up in a New England mill town, where, in the early thirties, all the insured factories burned down. It has been difficult to get fire insurance in that region ever since. The owner of a hardware store, whose property adjoined an insured factory at the time, lost everything. Afterward, he walked all day along the railroad track, waiting for a train to run him down. Railroad service has never been very good up there. No trains came. His children own the town these days, for what it's worth. The two cobbled streets where black people always lived have been torn up and turned into a public park since a flood that occurred some years ago. Unprecedented rains came. Retailers had to destroy their sodden products for fear of contamination. And the black section was torn up and seeded over in the town's rezoning project. No one knows where the blacks live now. But there are Negroes in the stores and schools, and on the football team. It is assumed that the park integrated the town. Those black families

must be living somewhere. It is a mystery.

The host, for some reason, was taking Instamatic pictures of his guests. It was not clear whether he was doing this in order to be able to show, at some future time, that there had been this gathering in his house. Or whether he thought of pictures in some voodoo sense. Or whether he found it difficult to talk. Or whether he was bored. Two underground celebrities—one of whom had become a sensation by never generating or exhibiting a flicker of interest in anything, the other of whom was known mainly for hanging around the first—were taking pictures, too. I was there with a movie star I've known for years. He had already been received in an enormous embrace by an Eastern European poet, whose hair was cut too short but who was neither as awkwardly spontaneous nor as drunk as he cared to seem. The party was in honor of the poet, who celebrated the occasion by insulting everyone and being fawned upon, by distinguished and undistinguished writers alike. "This group looks as through someone had torn up a few guest lists and floated the pieces on the air," somebody said.

Paul: "Two diamonds."

Inez: "Two hearts."

Mary: "Three clubs."

John: "Four kings."

Inez: "Darling, you know you can't just bid four kings."

John: "I don't see why. I might have been bluffing."

Inez: "No, darling. That's poker. This is bridge. And even in poker you can't just bid four kings."

John: "No. Well, I guess we'd better deal another hand."

The friend of the underground sensation walked up to the actor and me and said hello. Then, in a verbal seizure of some sort, he began muttering obscenities. The actor said a few calming things that didn't work. He finally put his finger on the mutterer's lips. The mutterer bit that finger extremely hard, and walked away. The actor wrapped his finger in a paper napkin, and got himself another drink. We stayed till twelve.

I went to a women's college. We had distinguished faculty in everything, digs at Nuoro and Mycenae. We had a quality of obsession in our studies. For professors who had quarrelled with their wives at breakfast, those years of bright-eyed young women, never getting any older, must have been a trial. The head of the history department once sneezed into his best student's honors thesis. He slammed it shut. It was ultimately published. When I was there, a girl called Cindy Melchior was immensely fat. She wore silk trousers and gilt mules. One day, in the overheated classroom, she laid aside her knitting and lumbered to the window, which she opened. Then she lumbered back. "Do you think," the professor asked, "you are so graceful?" He somehow meant it kindly. Cindy wept. That year, Cindy's brother Melvin phoned me. "I would have called you sooner," he said, "but I had the most terrible eczema." All the service staff on campus in those days were black. Many of them were followers of Father Divine. They took new names in the church. I remember the year when a maid called Serious Heartbreak married a janitor called Universal Dictionary. At a meeting of the faculty last fall, the college president, who is new and male, spoke of raising money. A female professor of Greek was knitting—and working on Linear B, with an abacus before her. In our time, there was a vogue for madrigals. Some of us listened, constantly, to a single record. There was a phrase we could not decipher. A professor of symbolic logic, a French Canadian, had sounds that matched but a meaning that seemed unlikely: Sheep are no angels; come upstairs. A countertenor

explained it, after a local concert: She'd for no angel's comfort stay. Not so likely, either.

The Maid of Constant Sorrow said our landlord's murder marked a turning point in her analysis. "I don't feel guilty. I feel hated," she said. It is true, for a time, we all wanted to feel somehow a part—if only because violence offset the boredom of our lives. My grandfather said that some people have such extreme insomnia that they look at their watches every hour after midnight, to see how sorry they ought to be feeling for themselves. Aldo says he does not care what my grandfather said. My grandmother refused to concede that any member of the family died of natural causes. An uncle's cancer in middle age occurred because all the suitcases fell off the luggage rack onto him when he was in his teens, and so forth. Death was an acquired characteristic. My grandmother, too, used to put other people's ailments into the diminutive: strokelets were what her friends had. Aldo said he was bored to tearsies by my grandmother's diminutives.

When I worked, for a time, in the infirmary of a branch of an up-state university, it was becoming more difficult with each passing semester, except in the most severe cases, to determine which students had mental or medical problems. At the clinic, young men with straggly beards and stained bluejeans wept alongside girls in jeans and frayed sweaters—all being fitted with contact lenses, over which they then wore granny glasses. There was no demand for prescription granny glasses at all. For the severely depressed, the paranoids, and the hallucinators, our young psychiatrists prescribed "mood elevators," pills that were neither uppers nor downers but which affected the bloodstream in such a way that within three to five weeks many sad outpatients became very cheerful, and several saints and historical figures became again Midwestern graduate students under tolerable stress. On one, not unusual, morning, the clinic had a call from an instructor in political science. "I am in the dean's office," he said. "My health is quite perfect. They want me to have a checkup."

"Oh?" said the doctor on duty. "Perhaps you could come in on Friday."

"The problem is," the voice on the phone said, "I have always thought myself, and been thought by others, a Negro. Now, through research, I have found that my family on both sides have always been white."

"Oh," the doctor on duty said. "Perhaps you could just take a cab and come over."

Within twenty minutes, the political-science instructor appeared at the clinic. He was black. The doctor said nothing, and began a physical examination. By the time his blood pressure was taken, the patient confided that his white ancestors were, in fact, royal. The mood elevators restored him. He and the doctor became close friends besides. A few months later, the instructor took a job with the government in Washington. Two weeks after that, he was calling the clinic again. "I have found new documentation," he said. "All eight of my great-grandparents were pure-blooded Germans—seven from Prussia, one from Alsace. I thought I should tell you, dear friend." The doctor suggested he come for the weekend. By Sunday afternoon, a higher dose of the pill had had its effect. The problem has not since recurred.

"All babies are natural swimmers," John said, lowering his two-year-old son gently over the side of the rowboat, and smiling. The child thrashed and sank. Aldo dived in and grabbed him. The baby came up coughing, not crying, and looked with pure fear at his father. John looked with dismay at his son. "He would have come up in a minute," John said to Aldo, who was dripping and rowing. "You have to give nature a chance."

"Reservations are still busy. Thank you for your patience," the voice of the airline kept saying. It was a recording. After it had said the same thing thirty-two times, I hung up. Scattered through the two cars of the Brewster-New York train last week were adults with what seemed to be a clandestine understanding of some sort. They did not look at each other. They stared out the windows, or read. "Um," sang a lady at our fourth stop on the way to Grand Central. She appeared to be reading the paper. She kept singing her "Um," as one who is getting the pitch. A young man had already been whistling "Frère Jacques" for three stops. When the "Um" lady found her pitch and began to sing the national anthem, he looked at her with rage. The conductor passed through, punching tickets in his usual fashion, not in the aisle but directly over people's laps. Every single passenger was obliged to flick the tiny punched part of the ticket from his lap onto the floor. Conductors have this process as their own little show of force. The whistler and the singer were in a dead heat when we reached the city. The people with the clandestine understanding turned out to be inmates from an upstate asylum, now on leave with their families, who met them in New York.

I don't think much of writers in whom nothing is at risk. It is possible, though, to be too literal-minded about this question.

"$3000 for First Person Articles," for example:

> An article for this series must be a true, hitherto unpublished narrative of an unusual personal experience. It may be dramatic, inspirational, or humorous, but it must have, in the opinion of the editors, a quality of narrative and interest comparable to "How I Lost My

Eye" (June '72) and "Attacked by a Killer Shark" (April '72). Contributions must be typewritten, preferably *double-spaced* . . .

I particularly like where the stress, the italics, goes.

In Corfu, I once met a polo-playing Argentine Existential psychiatrist who had lived for months in a London commune. He said that on days when the ordinary neurotics in the commune were getting on each other's nerves the few psychopaths and schizophrenics in their midst retired to their rooms and went their version of berserk, alone. On days when the neurotics got along, the psychopaths calmed down, tried to make contact, cooked meals. It was, he said, as though the sun came out for them. I hope that's true. Although altogether too much of life is mood. I receive communications almost every day from an institution called the Center for Short-Lived Phenomena. They have reporting sources all over the world, and an extensive correspondence. Under the title "Type of Event: Biological," I have received postcards about the progress of the Dormouse Invasion of Formentera ("Apart from population density, the Dormouse of Formentera had a peak of reproduction in 1970. All females checked were pregnant, and perhaps this fact could have been the source of the idea of an 'invasion'"), and the Northwest Atlantic Puffin Decline. I have followed the Tanzanian Army Worm Outbreak; the San Fernando Earthquake; the Green Pond Fish Kill ("80% of the numbers involved," the Center's postcard reports, "were mummichogs"); the Samar Spontaneous Soil Burn; the Hawaiian Monk Seal Disappearance; and, also, the Naini Tal Sudden Sky Brightening.

Those are accounts of things that do not last long, but if you become famous for a single thing in this country, and just endure, it is certain you will recur enlarged. Of the eighteen men who were indicted for conspiracy to murder Schwerner, Goodman, and Chaney, seven were convicted by a Mississippi jury—a surprising thing. But then a year later, a man was wounded and a woman killed in a shootout while trying to bomb the house of some Mississippi Jews. It turned out that the informer, the man who had helped the bombers, and led the F.B.I. to them, was one of the convicted seven—the one, in fact, who was alleged to have killed two of the three boys who were found in that Mississippi dam. And what's more, and what's more, the convicted conspirator, alleged double killer, was paid thirty-six thousand dollars by the F.B.I. for bringing the bombers in. Yet the wave of anti-Semitic bombings in Mississippi stopped after the shootout. I don't know what it means. I am in this brownstone.

Last year, Aldo moved out and went to Los Angeles on a story. I called him to ask whether I could come. He said, "Are you going to stay this time?" I said I wasn't sure. I flew out quite early in the morning. On the plane, there was the most banal, unendurable pickup, lasting the whole flight. A young man and a young woman—he was Italian, I think; she was German— had just met, and settled on French as their only common language. They asked each other where they were from, and where they were going. They posed each other riddles. He took out a pencil and paper and sketched her portrait. She giggled. He asked her whether she had ever considered a career as a model. She said she had considered it but she feared that all men in the field were after the same thing. He agreed. He began to tell slightly off-color stories. She laughed and reproached him. It was like that. I wondered whether these things were always, to captive eavesdroppers, so dreary.

When I arrived at Aldo's door, he met me with a smile that seemed surprised, a little sheepish. We talked awhile. Sometimes he took, sometimes I held, my suitcase. I tried, I thought, a joke. I asked whether there was already a girl there. He said there was. He met me in an hour at the corner drugstore for a cup of coffee. We talked. We returned to the apartment. We had Scotch. That afternoon, quite late, I flew home. I called him from time to time. He had his telephone removed a few days later. Now, for a while, he's here again. He's doing a political essay. It begins, "Some things cannot be said too often, and some can." That's all he's got so far.

We had people in for drinks one night last week. The cork in the wine bottle broke. Somebody pounded it into the bottle with a chisel and a hammer. We went to a bar. I have never understood the feeling men seem to have for bars they frequent. A fine musician who was with us played Mozart, Chopin, and Beethoven on the piano. It seemed a great, impromptu occasion. Then he said, we thought, "I am now going to play some Yatz." From what he played, it turned out he meant jazz. He played it badly.

We had driven in from another weekend in the country while it was still daylight. Lots of cars had their headlights on. We weren't sure whether it was for or against peace, or just for highway safety. Milly, a secretary in a brokerage office, was married in our groundfloor shop that evening. She cried hysterically. Her mother and several people from her home town and John, whose girl she had been before he married Inez, thought it was from sentiment or shyness, or some conventional reason. Milly explained it to Aldo later. She and her husband had really married two years before—the week they met, in fact—in a chapel in Las Vegas. They hadn't wanted to tell their parents, or anybody, until he finished law school. They had torn up their Las Vegas license. She had been crying out of some legal fear of being married

twice, it turned out. Their best man, a Puerto Rican doctor, said his aunt had been mugged in a cemetery in San Juan by a man on horseback. She thought it was her husband, returned from the dead. She had required sedation. We laughed. My friend across the hall, who owns the beagle, looked very sad all evening. He said, abruptly, that he was cracking up, and no one would believe him. There were sirens in the street. Inez said she knew exactly what he meant: she was cracking up also. Her escort, an Italian jeweller, said, "I too. I too have it. The most terrible anguishes, anguishes all in the night."

Inez said she knew the most wonderful man for the problem. "He may strike you at first as a phony," she said, "but then, when you're with him, you find yourself naturally screaming. It's such a relief. And he teaches you how you can practice at home." Milly said she was not much of a screamer—had never, in fact, screamed in her life. "High time you did, then," Inez said. Our sportswriter said he had recently met a girl whose problem was stealing all the suéde garments of house guests, and another, in her thirties, who cried all the time because she had not been accepted at Smith. We heard many more sirens in the streets. We all went home.

At 4 A.M., the phone rang about fifty times. I did not answer it. Aldo suggested that we remove it. I took three Valium. The whole night was sirens, then silence. The phone rang again. It is still ringing. The paper goes to press tomorrow. It is possible that I know who killed our landlord. So many things point in one direction. But too strong a case, I find, is often lost. It incurs doubts, suspicions. Perhaps I do not know. Perhaps it doesn't matter. I think it does, though. When I wonder what it is that we are doing—in this brownstone, on this block, with this paper—the truth is probably that we are fighting for our lives.

James Alan McPherson (1943–)
OF CABBAGES AND KINGS

I

Claude Sheats had been in the Brotherhood all his life and then he had tried to get out. Some of his people and most of his friends were still in the Brotherhood and were still very good members but Claude was no longer a good member because he had tried to get out after over twenty years. To get away from the Brotherhood and all his friends who were still active in it he moved to Washington Square, and took to reading about being militant. But, living there, he developed a craving for whiteness the way a nicely broke-in virgin craves sex. In spite of this he maintained a steady black girl, whom he saw at least twice a month to keep up appearances and once he took both of us with him when he visited his uncle in Harlem who was still in the Brotherhood.

"She's a nice girl, Claude," his uncle's wife had told him that night because the girl, besides being attractive, had some very positive ideas about the Brotherhood. Her name was Marie, she worked as a secretary in my office and it was on her suggestion that I had moved in with Claude Sheats.

"I'm glad to see you don't waste your time on hippies," the uncle had said. "All our young men are selling out these days."

The uncle was the kind of fellow who had played his cards right. He was much older than his wife, and I had the impression, that night, that he must have given her time to experience enough and to become bored enough before he overwhelmed her with his success. He wore glasses and combed his hair back and had that oily kind of composure that made me think of a waiter waiting to be tipped. He was very proud of his English, I observed, and how he always ended his words with just the right sound. He must have felt superior to people who didn't. He must have felt superior to Claude because he was still with the Brotherhood and Claude had tried to get out.

Claude did not like him and always seemed to feel guilty whenever we visited his uncle's house. "Don't mention any of my girls to him," he told me after our first visit.

"Why would I do that?" I said.

"He'll try to psych you into telling him."

"Why should he suspect you? He never comes over to the apartment."

"He just likes to know what I'm doing. I don't want him to know about my girls."

"I won't say anything," I promised.

He was almost twenty-three and had no steady girls, except for Marie. He was well built, so that he had no trouble in the Village area. It was like going to the market for him. During my first days in the apartment the process had seemed like a game. And once, when he was going out, I said: "Bring back two."

Half an hour later he came back with two girls. He got their drinks and then he called me into his room to meet them.

"This is Doris," he said, pointing to the smaller one, "and I forgot your name," he said to the big blonde.

"Jane," she said.

"This is Howard," he told her.

"Hi," I said. Neither one of them smiled. The big blonde in white pants sat on the big bed and the little one sat on a chair near the window. He had given them his worst bourbon.

"Excuse me a minute," Claude said to the girls. "I want to talk to Howard for a minute." He put on a record before we went outside into the hall between our rooms. He was always extremely polite and gentle, and very soft-spoken in spite of his size.

"Listen," he said to me outside, "you can have the blonde."

"What can I do with that amazon?"

"I don't care. Just get her out of the room."

"She's dirty," I said.

"So you can give her a bath."

"It wouldn't help much."

"Well just take her out and talk to her," he told me. "Remember, you asked for her."

We went back in. "Where you from?" I said to the amazon.

"Brighton."

"What school?"

"No. I just got here."

"From where?"

"*Brighton!*"

That's not so far," I said.

"*England*," she said. She looked very bored. Claude Sheats looked at me.

"How did you find Washington Square so fast?"

"I got friends."

She was very superior about it all and seemed to look at us with the same slightly patient irritation of a professional theater critic waiting for a late performance to begin. The little one sat on the chair, her legs crossed, looking up at the ceiling. Her white pants were dirty too. They looked as though they would have been very relieved if we had taken off our clothes and danced for them around the room and across the bed, and made hungry sounds in our throats with our mouths slightly opened.

I said that I had to go out to the drugstore and would be back very soon; but once outside, I walked a whole hour in one direction and then I walked back. I passed them a block away from our apartment. They were walking fast and did not slow down or speak when I passed them.

Claude Sheats was drinking heavily when I came into the apartment.

"What the hell are you trying to pull?" he said.

"I couldn't find a drugstore open."

He got up from the living room table and walked toward me. "You should have asked me," he said. "I got more than enough."

"I wanted some mouthwash too," I said.

He fumed a while longer, and then told me how I had ruined his evening because the amazon would not leave the room to wait for me and the little one would not do anything with the amazon around. He suddenly thought about going down and bringing them back; and he went out for a while. But he came back without them, saying that they had been picked up again.

"When a man looks out for you, you got to look out for him," he warned me.

"I'm sorry."

"A hell of a lot of good *that* does. And that's the last time I look out for *you*, baby," he said. "From now on it's *me* all the way."

"Thanks," I said.

"If she was too much for you I could of taken the amazon."

"It didn't matter that much," I said.

"You could of had Doris if you couldn't handle the amazon."

"They were both too much," I told him.

But Claude Sheats did not answer. He just looked at me.

II

After two months of living with him I concluded that Claude hated whites as much as he loved them. And he hated himself with the very same passion. He hated the country and his place in it and he loved the country and his place in it. He loved the Brotherhood and all that being in it had taught him and he still believed in what he had been taught, even after he had left it and did not have to believe in anything.

"This Man is going *down*, Howard," he would announce with conviction.

"Why?" I would ask.

"Because it's the Black Man's time to rule again. They had five thousand years, now we get five thousand years."

"What if I don't *want* to rule?" I asked. "What happens if I don't want to take over?"

He looked at me with pity in his face. "You go down with the rest of the country."

"I guess I wouldn't mind much anyway," I said. "It would be a hell of a place with nobody to hate."

But I could never get him to smile about it the way I tried to smile about it. He was always serious. And, once, when I questioned the mysticism in the teachings of the Brotherhood, Claude almost attacked me. "Another man might kill you for saying that," he had said. "Another man might not let you get away with saying something like that." He was quite deadly and he stood over me with an air of patient superiority. And because he could afford to be generous and forgiving, being one of the saved, he sat down at the table with me under the single light bulb and began to teach me. He told me the stories about how it was in the beginning before the whites took over, and about all the little secret significances of black, and about the subtle infiltration of white superiority into everyday objects.

"You've never seen me eat white bread or white sugar, have you?"

"No," I said. He used brown bread and brown sugar.

"Or use bleached flour or white rice?"

"No."

"You know why, don't you?" He waited expectantly.

"No," I finally said. "I don't know why."

He was visibly shocked, so much so that he dropped that line of instruction and began to draw on a pad before him on the living room table. He moved his big shoulders over the yellow pad to conceal his drawings and looked across the table at me. "Now I'm going to tell you something that white men have paid thousands of dollars to learn," he said. "Men have been killed for telling this but I'm telling you for nothing. I'm warning you not to repeat it because if the whites find out you know, you could be killed too."

"You know me," I said. "I wouldn't repeat any secrets."

He gave me a long thoughtful look.

I gave him back a long, eager, honest look.

Then he leaned across the table and whispered: "Kennedy isn't buried in this country. He was the only President who never had his coffin opened during the funeral. The body was in state all that time and they never opened the coffin once. You know why?"

"No."

"Because he's not *in it!* They buried an empty coffin. Kennedy was a Thirty-third Degree Mason. His body is in Jerusalem right now."

"How do you know?" I asked.

"If I told you it would put your life in danger."

"Did his family know about it?"

"No. His lodge kept it secret."

"No one knew?"

"I'm telling you, *no!*"

"Then how did you find out?"

He sighed, more from tolerance than from boredom with my inability to comprehend the mysticism of pure reality in its most unadulterated form. Of course I could not believe him and we argued about it, back and forth, but to absolutely cap all my uncertainties he drew the thirty-three degree circle, showed me the secret signs that men had died to learn, and spoke about the time when our black ancestors chased an evil genius out of their kingdom and across a desert and onto an island somewhere in the sea; from which, hundreds of years later, this same evil genius sent forth a perfected breed of white-skinned and evil creatures who, through trickery, managed to enslave for five thousand years the onetime Black Masters of the world. He further explained the significance of the East and why all the saved must go there once during their lifetimes, and possibly be buried there, as Kennedy had been.

It was dark and late at night, and the glaring bulb cast his great shadow into the corners so that there was the sense of some outraged spirit, fuming in the halls and dark places of our closets, waiting to extract some terrible and justifiable revenge from him for disclosing to me, an unbeliever, the closest-kept of secrets. But I was aware of them only for an instant, and then I did not believe him again.

The most convincing thing about it all was that he was very intelligent and had an orderly, well regimented lifestyle, and yet *he* had no trouble with believing. He believed in the certainty of statistical surveys, which was his work; the nutritional value of wheat germ sprinkled on eggs; the sensuality of gin; and the dangers inherent in smoking. He was stylish in that he did not believe in God, but he was extremely moral and warm and kind; and I wanted sometimes to embrace him for his kindness and bigness and gentle manners. He lived his life so carefully that no matter what he said, I could not help but believe him sometimes. But I did not want to, because I knew that once I started I could not stop; and then there would be no purpose to my own beliefs and no real conviction or direction in my own efforts to achieve when always in the back of my regular thoughts, there would be a sense of futility and a fear of the un-

known all about me. So, for the sake of necessity, I chose not to believe him.

He felt that the country was doomed and that the safe thing to do was to make enough money as soon as possible and escape to the Far East. He forecast summer riots in certain Northern cities and warned me, religiously, to avoid all implicating ties with whites so that I might have a chance to be saved when that time came. And I asked him about *his* ties, and the girls, and how it was never a movie date with coffee afterwards but always his room and the cover-all blanket of Motown sounds late into the night.

"A man has different reasons for doing certain things," he had said.

He never seemed to be comfortable with any of the girls. He never seemed to be in control. And after my third month in the apartment I had concluded that he used his virility as a tool and forged, for however long it lasted, a little area of superiority which could never, it seemed, extend itself beyond the certain confines of his room, no matter how late into the night the records played. I could see him fighting to extend the area, as if an increase in the number of girls he saw could compensate for what he had lost in duration. He saw many girls: curious students, unexpected bus-stop pickups, and assorted other one-nighters. And his rationalizations allowed him to believe that each one was an actual conquest, a physical affirmation of a psychological victory over all he hated and loved and hated in the little world of his room.

But then he seemed to have no happiness, even in this. Even here I sensed some intimations of defeat. After each girl, Claude would almost immediately come out of his room, as if there was no need for aftertalk; as if, after it was over, he felt a brooding, silent emptiness that quickly intensified into nervousness and instantaneous shyness and embarrassment so that the cold which sets in after that kind of emotional drain came in very sharp against his skin, and he could not bear to have her there any longer. And when the girl had gone, he would come into my room to talk. These were the times when he was most like a little boy; and these were the times when he really began to trust me.

"That bitch called me everything but the son of God," he would chuckle. And I would put aside my papers brought home from the office, smile at him, and listen.

He would always eat or drink afterwards and in those early days I was glad for his companionship and the return of his trust, and sometimes we drank and talked until dawn. During these times he would tell me more subtleties about the Man and would re-predict the fall of the country. Once, he warned me, in a fatherly way, about reading life from books before experiencing it; and another night he advised me on how to schedule girls so that one could run them without being run in return. These were usually good times of good-natured arguments and predictions; but as we drank more often he tended to grow more excited and quick-tempered, especially after he had just entertained. Sometimes he would seethe hate, and every drink he took gave life to increasingly bitter condemnations of the present system and our place in it. There were actually flying saucers, he told me once, piloted by things from other places in the universe which would eventually destroy the country for what it had done to the black man. He had run into his room, on that occasion, and had brought out a book by a man who maintained that the government was deliberately withholding from the public overwhelming evidence of flying saucers and strange creatures from other galaxies that walked among us every day. Claude emphasized the fact that the writer was a Ph.D. who must know what he was talking about, and insisted that the politicians withheld the information because they knew

that their time was almost up and if they made it public the black man would know that he had outside friends who would help him take over the world again. Nothing I said could make him reconsider the slightest bit of his information.

"What are we going to use for weapons when we take over?" I asked him once.

"We've got atomic bombs stockpiled and waiting for the day."

"How can you believe that crap?"

He did not answer, but said instead: "You are the living example of what the Man has done to my people."

"I just try to think things out for myself," I said.

"You can't think. The handkerchief over your head is too big."

I smiled.

"I know," he continued. "I know all there is to know about whites because I've been studying them all my life."

I smiled some more.

"I ought to know," he said slowly. "I have supernatural powers."

"I'm tired," I told him. "I want to go to sleep now."

Claude started to leave the room, then he turned. "Listen," he said at the door. He pointed his finger at me to emphasize the gravity of his pronouncement. "I predict that within the next week something is going to happen to this country that will hurt it even more than Kennedy's assassination."

"Goodnight," I said as he closed the door.

He opened it again. "Remember that I predicted it when it happens," he said. For the first time I noticed that he had been deadly serious all along.

Two days later several astronauts burned to death in Florida. He raced into my room hot with the news.

"Do you believe me *now?*" he said. "Just two days and look what happened."

I tried to explain, as much to myself as to him, that in any week of the year something unfortunate was bound to occur. But he insisted that this was only part of a divine plan to bring the country to its knees. He said that he intended to send a letter off right away to Jeanne Dixon in D.C. to let her know that she was not alone because he also had the same power. Then he thought that he had better not because the FBI knew that he had been active in the Brotherhood before he got out.

At first it was good fun believing that someone important cared enough to watch us. And sometimes when the telephone was dead a long time before the dial tone sounded, I would knock on his door and together we would run through our telephone conversations for that day to see if either of us had said anything implicating or suspect, just in case were listening. This feeling of persecution brought us closer together and soon the instruction sessions began to go on almost every night. At this point I could not help but believe him a little. And he began to trust me again, like a tolerable little brother, and even confided that the summer riots would break out simultaneously in Harlem and Watts during the second week in August. For some reason, something very difficult to put into words, I spent three hot August nights on the streets of Harlem, waiting for the riot to start.

In the seventh month of our living together, he began to introduce me to his girls again when they came in. Most of them came only once, but all of them received the same mechanical treatment. He only discriminated with liquor, the quality of which improved with the attractiveness or reluctance of the girl: gin for slow starters, bourbon for momentary strangers, and the scotch he reserved for those he hoped would come again. There was first the trek into his room, his own trip out for the ice and glasses while classical music was played within; then after a while the classical piece would be replaced by several Motowns. Finally, there was her

trip to the bathroom, his calling a cab in the hall, and the sound of both their feet on the stairs as he walked her down to the cab. Then he would come to my room in his red bathrobe, glass in hand, for the aftertalk.

Then in the ninth month the trouble started. It would be very easy to pick out one incident, one day, one area of misunderstanding in that month and say: "That was where it began." It would be easy, but not accurate. It might have been one instance or a combination of many. It might have been the girl who came into the living room, when I was going over the proposed blueprints for a new settlement house, and who lingered too long outside his room in conversation because her father was a builder somewhere. Or it might have been nothing at all. But after that time he warned me about being too friendly with his company.

Another night, when I was leaving the bathroom in my shorts, he came out of his room with a girl who smiled.

"Hi," she said to me.

I nodded hello as I ducked back into the bathroom.

When he had walked her down to the door he came to my room and knocked. He did not have a drink.

"Why didn't you speak to my company?" he demanded.

"I was in my shorts."

"She felt bad about it. She asked what the hell was wrong with you. What could I tell her—'He got problems'?"

"I'm sorry," I said. "But I didn't want to stop in my shorts."

"I see through you, Howard," he said. "You're just jealous of me and try to insult my girls to get to me."

"Why should I be jealous of you?"

"Because I'm a man and you're not."

"What makes a man anyway?" I said. "Your fried eggs and wheat germ? Why should I be jealous of you *or* what you bring in?"

"Some people don't need a reason. You're a black devil and you'll get yours. I predict that you'll get yours."

"Look," I told him, "I'm sorry about the girl. Tell her I'm sorry when you see her again."

"You treated her so bad she probably won't come back."

I said nothing more and he stood there silently for a long time before he turned to leave the room. But at the door he turned again and said: "I see through you, Howard. You're a black devil."

It should have ended there and it might have with anyone else. I took great pains to speak to his girls after that, even though he tried to get them into the room as quickly as possible. But a week later he accused me of walking about in his room after he had gone out, some two weeks before.

"I swear I wasn't in your room," I protested.

"I saw your shadow on the blinds from across the street at the bus stop," he insisted.

"I've *never* been in your room when you weren't there," I told him.

"I *saw* you!"

We went into his room and I tried to explain how, even if he could see the window from the bus stop, the big lamp next to the window prevented any shadow from being cast on the blinds. But he was convinced in his mind that at every opportunity I plundered his closets and drawers. He had no respect for simple logic in these matters, no sense of the absurdity of his accusations, and the affair finally ended with my confessing that I might have done it without actually knowing; and if I had, I would not do it again.

But what had been a gesture for peace on my part became a vindication for him, proof that I *was* a black devil, capable of lying and lying until he confronted me with the inescapable truth of the situation. And so he persisted in creating situations from which, if he in-

sisted on a point long enough and with enough self-righteousness, he could draw my inevitable confession.

And I confessed eagerly, goaded on by the necessity of maintaining peace. I confessed to mixing white sugar crystals in with his own brown crystals so that he could use it and violate the teachings of the Brotherhood; I confessed to cleaning the bathroom all the time merely because I wanted to make him feel guilty for not having ever cleaned it. I confessed to telling the faithful Marie, who brought a surprise dinner over for him, that he was working late at his office in order to implicate him with the girls who worked there. I confessed to leaving my papers about the house so that his company could ask about them and develop an interest in me. And I pleaded guilty to a record of other little infamies, which multiplied into countless others, and again subdivided into hundreds of little subtleties until my every movement was a threat to him. If I had a girlfriend to dinner, we should eat in my room instead of at the table because he had to use the bathroom a lot and, besides not wanting to seem as if he were making a pass at my girl by walking through the room so often, he was genuinely embarrassed to be seen going to the bathroom.

If I protested he would fly into a tantrum and shake his big finger at me vigorously. And so I retreated, step by step, into my room, from which I emerged only to go to the bathroom or kitchen or out of the house. I tried to stay out on nights when he had company. But he had company so often that I could not always help being in my room after he had walked her to the door. Then he would knock on my door for his talk. He might offer me a drink, and if I refused, he would go to his room for a while and then come back. He would pace about for a while, like a big little boy who wants to ask for money over his allowance. At these times my mind would move feverishly over all our contacts for as far back as I could make it reach, searching and attempting to pull out that one incident which would surely be the point of his attack. But it was never any use; it might have been anything.

"Howard, I got something on my chest and I might as well get it off."

"What is it?" I asked from my bed.

"You been acting strange lately. Haven't been talking to me. If you got something on your chest, get if off now."

"I have nothing on my chest," I said.

"Then why don't you talk?"

I did not answer.

"You hardly speak to me in the kitchen. If you have something against me, tell me now."

"I have nothing against you."

"Why don't you talk, then?" He looked directly at me. "If a man doesn't talk, you think *something's* wrong!"

"I've been nervous lately, that's all. I got problems and I don't want to talk."

"Everybody's got problems. That's no reason for going around making a man feel guilty."

"For God's sake, I don't want to talk."

"I know what's wrong with you. Your conscience is bothering you. You're so evil that your conscience is giving you trouble. You got everybody fooled but *me*. I know you're a black devil."

"I'm a black devil," I said. "Now will you let me sleep?"

He went to the door. "You dish it out but you can't take it," he said. "That's *your* trouble."

"I'm a black devil," I said.

I lay there, after he left, hating myself but thankful that he hadn't called me into his room for the fatherly talk as he had done another time. That was the worst. He had come to the door and said: "Come out of there, I want to talk to you." He had walked ahead of me into his room and had sat down in his big leather chair next to the lamp with

his legs spread wide and his big hands in his lap. He had said: "Don't be afraid. I'm not going to hurt you. Sit down. I'm not going to argue. What are you so nervous about? Have a drink," in his kindest, most fatherly way, and that had been the worst of all. That was the time he had told me to eat in my room. Now I could hear him pacing about in the hall and I knew that it was not over for the night. I began to pray that I could sleep before he came and that he would not be able to wake me, no matter what he did. I did not care what he did as long as I did not have to face him. I resolved to confess to anything he accused me of if it would make him leave sooner. I was about to go out into the hall for my confession when the door was kicked open and he charged into the room.

"You black son-of-a-bitch!" he said. "I ought to *kill* you." He stood over the bed in the dark room and shook his big fist over me. And I lay there hating the overpowering cowardice in me, which kept my body still and my eyes closed, and hoping that he would kill all of it when his heavy fist landed.

"First you insult a man's company, then you ignore him. I been *good* to you. I let you live here, I let you eat my uncle's food, and I taught you things. But you're a ungrateful motherfucker. I ought to *kill* you right now!"

And I still lay there, as he went on, not hearing him, with nothing in me but a loud throbbing which pulsed through the length of my body and made the sheets move with its pounding. I lay there secure and safe in cowardice for as long as I looked up at him with my eyes big and my body twitching and my mind screaming out to him that it was all right, and I thanked him, because now I truly believed in the new five thousand years of Black Rule.

It is night again. I am in bed again, and I can hear the new blonde girl closing the bathroom door. I know that in a minute he will come out in his red robe and call a cab. His muffled voice through my closed door will seem very tired, but just as kind and patient to the dispatcher as it is to everyone, and as it was to me in those old times. I am afraid because when they came up the stairs earlier they caught me working at the living room table with my back to them. I had not expected him back so soon; but then I should have known that he would not go out. I had turned around in the chair and she smiled and said hello and I said "Hi" before he hurried her into the room. I *did* speak and I know that she heard. But I also know that I must have done something wrong; if not to her, then to him earlier today or yesterday or last week, because he glared at me before following her into the room and he almost paused to say something when he came out to get the glasses and ice. I wish that I could remember just where it was. But it does not matter. I *am* guilty and he knows it.

Now that he knows about me I am afraid. I could move away from the apartment and hide my guilt from him, but I know that he would find me. The brainwashed part of my mind tells me to call the police while he is still busy with her, but what could I charge him with when I know that he is only trying to help me. I could move the big, ragged yellow chair in front of the door, but that would not stop him, and it might make him impatient with me. Even if I pretended to be asleep and ignored him, it would not help when he

comes. He has not bothered to knock for weeks.

In the black shadows over my bed and in the corners I can sense the outraged spirits who help him when they hover about his arms as he gestures, with his lessons, above my bed. I am determined now to lie here and take it. It is the price I must pay for all the black secrets I have learned, and all the evil I have learned about myself. I *am* jealous of him, of his learning, of his girls. I am not the same handkerchief-head I was nine months ago. I have Marie to thank for that, and Claude, and the spirits. They know about me, and perhaps it is they who make him do it and he cannot help himself. I believe in the spirits now, just as I believe most of the time that I am a black devil.

They are going down to the cab now.

I will not ever blame him for it. He is helping me. But I blame the girls. I blame them for not staying on afterwards, and for letting all the good nice happy love talk cut off automatically after it is over. *I* need to have them there, after it is over. And he needs it; he needs it much more and much longer than they could ever need what he does for them. He should be able to teach them, as he has taught me. And he should have their appreciation, as he has mine. I blame them. I blame them for letting him try and try and never get just a little of the love there is left in the world.

I can hear him coming back from the cab.

DRAMA

Tennessee Williams (1914–   )

THE GLASS MENAGERIE

THE CHARACTERS

AMANDA WINGFIELD (*the mother*)

A little woman of great but confused vitality clinging frantically to another time and place. Her characterization must be carefully created, not copied from type. She is not paranoiac, but her life is paranoia. There is much to admire in Amanda, and as much to love and pity as there is to laugh at. Certainly she has endurance and a kind of heroism, and though her foolishness makes her unwittingly cruel at times, there is tenderness in her slight person.

LAURA WINGFIELD (*her daughter*)

Amanda, having failed to establish contact with reality, continues to live vitally in her illusions, but Laura's situa-tion is even graver. A childhood illness has left her crippled, one leg slightly shorter than the other, and held in a brace. This defect need not be more than suggested on the stage. Stemming from this, Laura's separation increases till she is like a piece of her own glass collection, too exquisitely fragile to move from the shelf.

TOM WINGFIELD (*her son*)

And the narrator of the play. A poet with a job in a warehouse. His nature is not remorseless, but to escape from a trap he has to act without pity.

JIM O'CONNOR (*the gentleman caller*)

A nice, ordinary, young man.

SCENE

AN ALLEY IN ST. LOUIS

PART I. Preparation for a Gentleman Caller.

PART II. The Gentleman calls.

Time: Now and the Past.

Scene I

The Wingfield apartment is in the rear of the building, one of those vast hive-like conglomerations of cellular living-units that flower as warty growths in overcrowded urban centers of lower middle-class population and are symptomatic of the impulse of this largest and fundamentally enslaved section of American society to avoid fluidity and differentiation and to exist and function as one interfused mass of automatism.

The apartment faces an alley and is entered by a fire-escape, a structure whose name is a touch of accidental poetic truth, for all of these huge buildings are always burning with the slow and implacable fires of human desperation. The fire-escape is included in the set—that is, the landing of it and steps descending from it.

The scene is memory and is therefore nonrealistic. Memory takes a lot of poetic license. It omits some details; others are exaggerated, according to the emotional value of the articles it touches, for memory is seated predominantly in the heart. The interior is therefore rather dim and poetic.

At the rise of the curtain, the audience is faced with the dark, grim rear wall of the Wingfield tenement. This building, which runs parallel to the footlights, is flanked on both sides by dark, narrow alleys which run into murky canyons of tangled clotheslines, garbage cans and the sinister latticework of neighboring fire-escapes. It is up and down these side alleys that exterior entrances and exits are made, during the play. At the end of TOM'S *opening commentary, the dark tenement wall slowly reveals (by means of a transparency) the interior of the ground floor Wingfield apartment.*

Downstage is the living room, which also serves as a sleeping room for LAURA, *the sofa unfolding to make her bed. Upstage, center, and divided by a wide arch or second proscenium with transparent faded portieres (or second curtain), is the dining room. In an old-fashioned what-not in the living room are seen scores of transparent glass animals. A blown-up photograph of the father hangs on the wall of the living room, facing the audience, to the left of the archway. It is the face of a very handsome young man in a doughboy's First World War cap. He is gallantly smiling, ineluctably smiling, as if to say, "I will be smiling forever."*

The audience hears and sees the opening scene in the dining room through both the transparent fourth wall of the building and the transparent gauze portieres of the diningroom arch. It is during this revealing scene that the fourth wall slowly ascends, out of sight. This transparent exterior wall is not brought down again until the very end of the play, during TOM'S *final speech.*

The narrator is an undisguised convention of the play. He takes whatever license with dramatic convention as is convenient to his purposes.

TOM *enters dressed as a merchant sailor from alley, stage left, and strolls across the front of the stage to the fire-escape. There he stops and lights a cigarette. He addresses the audience.*

TOM

Yes, I have tricks in my pocket, I have things up my sleeve. But I am the opposite of a stage magician. He gives you illusion that has the appearance of truth. I give you truth in the pleasant disguise of illusion.

To begin with, I turn back time. I reverse it to that quaint period, the thirties, when the huge middle class of America was matriculating in a school for the blind. Their eyes had failed them, or they had failed their eyes, and so they were having their fingers pressed forcibly down on the fiery Braille alphabet of a dissolving economy.

In Spain there was revolution. Here there was only shouting and confusion.

In Spain there was Guernica. Here there were disturbances of labor, sometimes pretty violent, in otherwise peaceful cities such as Chicago, Cleveland, Saint Louis . . .

This is the social background of the play.

(MUSIC.)

The play is memory.

Being a memory play, it is dimly lighted, it is sentimental, it is not realistic.

In memory everything seems to happen to music. That explains the fiddle in the wings.

I am the narrator of the play, and also a character in it.

The other characters are my mother, Amanda, my sister, Laura, and a gentleman caller who appears in the final scenes.

He is the most realistic character in the play, being an emissary from a world of reality that we were somehow set apart from.

But since I have a poet's weakness for symbols, I am using this character also as a symbol; he is the long delayed but always expected something that we live for.

There is a fifth character in the play who doesn't appear except in this larger-than-life-size photograph over the mantel.

This is our father who left us a long time ago.

He was a telephone man who fell in love with long distances; he gave up his job with the telephone company and skipped the light fantastic out of town . . .

The last we heard of him was a picture post-card from Mazatlan, on the Pacific coast of Mexico, containing a message of two words—

"Hello— Good-bye!" and no address.

I think the rest of the play will explain itself. . . .

(AMANDA's *voice becomes audible through the portieres.*)

(LEGEND ON SCREEN: "OU SONT LES NEIGES.")

(*He divides the portieres and enters the upstage area.*)

(AMANDA *and* LAURA *are seated at a drop-leaf table. Eating is indicated by gestures without food or utensils.* AMANDA *faces the audience.* TOM *and* LAURA *are seated in profile.*)

(*The interior has lit up softly and through the scrim we see* AMANDA *and* LAURA *seated at the table in the upstage area.*)

AMANDA
(*Calling*)

Tom?

TOM

Yes, Mother.

AMANDA

We can't say grace until you come to the table!

TOM

Coming, Mother. (*He bows slightly and withdraws, reappearing a few moments later in his place at the table.*)

AMANDA
(*To her son*)

Honey, don't *push* with your *fingers.* If you have to push with something, the thing to push with is a crust of bread. And chew—chew! Animals have sections in their stomachs which enable them to digest food without mastication, but human beings are supposed to chew their food before they swallow it down. Eat food leisurely, son, and really enjoy it. A well-cooked meal has lots of delicate flavors that have to be held in the mouth for appreciation. So chew your food and give your salivary glands a chance to function!

(TOM *deliberately lays his imaginary fork down and pushes his chair back from the table.*)

TOM

I haven't enjoyed one bite of this dinner because of your constant directions on how to eat it. It's you that make me rush through meals with your hawk-like attention to every bite I take. Sickening—spoils my appetite—all this discussion of—animals' secretion—salivary glands—mastication!

AMANDA
(*Lightly*)

Temperament like a Metropolitan star! (*He rises and crosses downstage*) You're not excused from the table.

TOM
I'm getting a cigarette.

AMANDA
You smoke too much.
(LAURA *rises.*)

LAURA
I'll bring in the blanc mange.
(*He remains standing with his cigarette by the portieres during the following.*)

AMANDA
(*Rising*)

No, sister, no, sister—you be the lady ' this time and I'll be the darky.

LAURA
I'm already up.

AMANDA
Resume your seat, little sister—I want you to stay fresh and pretty—for gentlemen callers!

LAURA
I'm not expecting any gentlemen callers.

AMANDA
(*Crossing out to kitchenette. Airily*)

Sometimes they come when they are least expected! Why, I remember one Sunday afternoon in Blue Mountain—(*Enters kitchenette.*)

TOM
I know what's coming!

LAURA
Yes. But let her tell it.

TOM
Again?

LAURA
She loves to tell it.
(AMANDA *returns with bowl of dessert.*) ·

AMANDA
One Sunday afternoon in Blue Mountain—your mother received—*seventeen!* —gentlemen callers! Why, sometimes there weren't chairs enough to accommodate them all. We had to send the nigger over to bring in folding chairs from the parish house.

TOM
(*Remaining at portieres*)

How did you entertain those gentlemen callers?

AMANDA
I understood the art of conversation!

TOM
I bet you could talk.

AMANDA
Girls in those days *knew* how to talk, I can tell you.

TOM
Yes?
(IMAGE: AMANDA AS A GIRL ON A PORCH, GREETING CALLERS.)

AMANDA
They knew how to entertain their gentlemen callers. It wasn't enough for a girl to be possessed of a pretty face and a graceful figure—although I wasn't slighted in either respect. She also needed to have a nimble wit and a tongue to meet all occasions.

TOM
What did you talk about?

AMANDA
Things of importance going on in the world! Never anything coarse or common or vulgar. (*She addresses* TOM *as though he were seated in the vacant chair at the table though he remains by portieres. He plays this scene as though he held the book*) My callers were gentlemen—all! Among my callers were

some of the most prominent young planters of the Mississippi Delta—planters and sons of planters!

(TOM *motions for music and a spot of light on* AMANDA.)

(*Her eyes lift, her face glows, her voice becomes rich and elegiac.*)

(SCREEN LEGEND: "OU SONT LES NEIGES.")

There was young Champ Laughlin who later became vice-president of the Delta Planters Bank.

Hadley Stevenson who was drowned in Moon Lake and left his widow one hundred and fifty thousand in Government bonds.

There were the Cutrere brothers, Wesley and Bates. Bates was one of my bright particular beaux! He got in a quarrel with that wild Wainwright boy. They shot it out on the floor of Moon Lake Casino. Bates was shot through the stomach. Died in the ambulance on his way to Memphis. His widow was also well-provided for, came into eight or ten thousand acres, that's all. She married him on the rebound—never loved her—carried my picture on him the night he died!

And there was that boy that every girl in the Delta had set her cap for! That beautiful, brilliant young Fitzhugh boy from Greene County!

TOM

What did he leave his widow?

AMANDA

He never married! Gracious, you talk as though all of my old admirers had turned up their toes to the daisies!

TOM

Isn't this the first you've mentioned that still survives?

AMANDA

That Fitzhugh boy went North and made a fortune—came to be known as the Wolf of Wall Street! He had the Midas touch, whatever he touched turned to gold!

And I could have been Mrs. Duncan J. Fitzhugh, mind you! But—I picked your *father!*

LAURA

(*Rising*)

Mother, let me clear the table.

AMANDA

No, dear, you go in front and study your typewriter chart. Or practice your shorthand a little. Stay fresh and pretty! —It's almost time for our gentlemen callers to start arriving. (*She flounces girlishly toward the kitchenette*) How many do you suppose we're going to entertain this afternoon?

(TOM *throws down the paper and jumps up with a groan.*)

LAURA

(*Alone in the dining room*)

I don't believe we're going to receive any, Mother.

AMANDA

(*Reappearing, airily*)

What? No one—not one? You must be joking! (LAURA *nervously echoes her laugh. She slips in a fugitive manner through the half-open portieres and draws them gently behind her. A shaft of very clear light is thrown on her face against the faded tapestry of the curtains.* MUSIC: "THE GLASS MENAGERIE" UNDER FAINTLY. *Lightly*) Not one gentleman caller? It can't be true! There must be a flood, there must have been a tornado!

LAURA

It isn't a flood, it's not a tornado, Mother. I'm just not popular like you were in Blue Mountain. . . . (TOM *utters another groan.* LAURA *glances at him with a faint, apologetic smile. Her voice catching a little*) Mother's afraid I'm going to be an old maid.

THE SCENE DIMS OUT WITH "GLASS MENAGERIE" MUSIC

Scene II

"Laura, Haven't You Ever Liked Some Boy?"
On the dark stage the screen is lighted with the image of blue roses.
Gradually LAURA'S *figure becomes apparent and the screen goes out.*
The music subsides.
LAURA *is seated in the delicate ivory chair at the small clawfoot table.*
She wears a dress of soft violet material for a kimono—her hair tied back from her forehead with a ribbon.
She is washing and polishing her collection of glass.
AMANDA *appears on the fire-escape steps. At the sound of her ascent,* LAURA *catches her breath, thrusts the bowl of ornaments away and seats herself stiffly before the diagram of the typewriter keyboard as though it held her spellbound.*
Something has happened to AMANDA. *It is written in her face as she climbs to the landing: a look that is grim and hopeless and a little absurd.*
She has on one of those cheap or imitation velvety-looking cloth coats with imitation fur collar. Her hat is five or six years old, one of those dreadful cloche hats that were worn in the late twenties and she is clasping an enormous black patent-leather pocketbook with nickel clasps and initials. This is her full-dress outfit, the one she usually wears to the D.A.R.
Before entering she looks through the door.
She purses her lips, opens her eyes very wide, rolls them upward and shakes her head. Then she slowly lets herself in the door. Seeing her mother's expression LAURA *touches her lips with a nervous gesture.*

LAURA

Hello, Mother, I was— (*She makes a nervous gesture toward the chart on the wall.* AMANDA *leans against the shut door and stares at* LAURA *with a martyred look.*)

AMANDA

Deception? Deception? (*She slowly removes her hat and gloves, continuing the sweet suffering stare. She lets the hat and gloves fall on the floor—a bit of acting.*)

LAURA
(*Shakily*)

How was the D.A.R. meeting? (AMANDA *slowly opens her purse and removes a dainty white handkerchief which she shakes out delicately and delicately touches to her lips and nostrils*) Didn't you go to the D.A.R. meeting, Mother?

AMANDA
(*Faintly, almost inaudibly*)

—No.—No. (*Then more forcibly*) I did not have the strength—to go to the D.A.R. In fact, I did not have the courage! I wanted to find a hole in the ground and hide myself in it forever! (*She crosses slowly to the wall and removes the diagram of the typewriter keyboard. She holds it in front of her for a second, staring at it sweetly and sorrowfully—then bites her lips and tears it in two pieces.*)

LAURA
(*Faintly*)

Why did you do that, Mother? (AMANDA *repeats the same procedure with the chart of the Gregg Alphabet*) Why are you—

AMANDA

Why? Why? How old are you, Laura?

LAURA

Mother, you know my age.

AMANDA

I thought that you were an adult; it seems that I was mistaken. (*She crosses slowly to the sofa and sinks down and stares at* LAURA.)

LAURA

Please don't stare at me, Mother.
(AMANDA *closes her eyes and lowers her head. Count ten.*)

AMANDA

What are we going to do, what is going to become of us, what is the future?
(*Count ten.*)

LAURA

Has something happened, Mother?
(AMANDA *draws a long breath and takes out the handkerchief again. Dabbing process*) Mother has—something happened?

AMANDA

I'll be all right in a minute, I'm just bewildered—(*Count five*)—by life. . . .

LAURA

Mother, I wish that you would tell me what's happened!

AMANDA

As you know, I was supposed to be inducted into my office at the D.A.R. this afternoon. (IMAGE: A SWARM OF TYPEWRITERS) But I stopped off at Rubicam's business college to speak to your teachers about your having a cold and ask them what progress they thought you were making down there.

LAURA

Oh. . . .

AMANDA

I went to the typing instructor and introduced myself as your mother. She didn't know who you were. Wingfield, she said. We don't have any such student enrolled at the school!
I assured her she did, that you had been going to classes since early in January.
"I wonder," she said, "if you could be talking about that terribly shy little girl who dropped out of school after only a few days' attendance?"
"No," I said, "Laura, my daughter,

has been going to school every day for the past six weeks!"
"Excuse me," she said. She took the attendance book out and there was your name, unmistakably printed, and all the dates you were absent until they decided that you had dropped out of school.
I still said, "No, there must have been some mistake! There must have been some mix-up in the records!"
And she said, "No—I remember her perfectly now. Her hands shook so that she couldn't hit the right keys! The first time we gave a speed-test, she broke down completely—was sick at the stomach and almost had to be carried into the wash-room! After that morning she never showed up any more. We phoned the house but never got any answer—while I was working at Famous and Barr, I suppose, demonstrating those—Oh!"
I felt so weak I could barely keep on my feet!
I had to sit down while they got me a glass of water!
Fifty dollars' tuition, all of our plans—my hopes and ambitions for you—just gone up the spout, just gone up the spout like that.
(LAURA *draws a long breath and gets awkwardly to her feet. She crosses to the victrola and winds it up.*)
What are you doing?

LAURA

Oh! (*She releases the handle and returns to her seat.*)

AMANDA

Laura, where have you been going when you've gone out pretending that you were going to business college?

LAURA

I've just been going out walking.

AMANDA

That's not true.

LAURA

It is. I just went walking.

AMANDA

Walking? Walking? In winter? Deliberately courting pneumonia in that light coat? Where did you walk to, Laura?

LAURA

All sorts of places—mostly in the park.

AMANDA

Even after you'd started catching that cold?

LAURA

It was the lesser of two evils, Mother. (IMAGE: WINTER SCENE IN PARK) I couldn't go back up. I—threw up—on the floor!

AMANDA

From half past seven till after five every day you mean to tell me you walked around in the park, because you wanted to make me think that you were still going to Rubicam's Business College?

LAURA

It wasn't as bad as it sounds. I went inside places to get warmed up.

AMANDA

Inside where?

LAURA

I went in the art museum and the bird-houses at the Zoo. I visited the penguins every day! Sometimes I did without lunch and went to the movies. Lately I've been spending most of my afternoons in the Jewel-box, that big glass house where they raise the tropical flowers.

AMANDA

You did all this to deceive me, just for deception? (LAURA *looks down*) Why?

LAURA

Mother, when you're disappointed, you get that awful suffering look on your face, like the picture of Jesus' mother in the museum!

AMANDA

Hush!

LAURA

I couldn't face it.
(*Pause. A whisper of strings.*)
(LEGEND: "THE CRUST OF HUMILITY.")

AMANDA

(*Hopelessly fingering the huge pocketbook*)

So what are we going to do the rest of our lives? Stay home and watch the parades go by? Amuse ourselves with the glass menagerie, darling? Eternally play those worn-out phonograph records your father left as a painful reminder of him?

We won't have a business career—we've given that up because it gave us nervous indigestion! (*Laughs wearily*) What is there left but dependency all our lives? I know so well what becomes of unmarried women who aren't prepared to occupy a position. I've seen such pitiful cases in the South—barely tolerated spinsters living upon the grudging patronage of sister's husband or brother's wife!—stuck away in some little mouse-trap of a room—encouraged by one in-law to visit another—little birdlike women without any nest—eating the crust of humility all their life!

Is that the future that we've mapped out for ourselves?

I swear it's the only alternative I can think of!

It isn't a very pleasant alternative, is it?

Of course—some girls *do marry*.
(LAURA *twists her hands nervously*.)
Haven't you ever liked some boy?

LAURA

Yes. I liked one once. (*Rises*) I came across his picture a while ago.

AMANDA

(*With some interest*)

He gave you his picture?

LAURA

No, it's in the year-book.

AMANDA
(*Disappointed*)

Oh—a high-school boy.
(SCREEN IMAGE: JIM AS HIGH-SCHOOL HERO BEARING A SILVER CUP.)

LAURA

Yes. His name was Jim. (LAURA *lifts the heavy annual from the claw-foot table*) Here he is in *The Pirates of Penzance.*

AMANDA
(*Absently*)

The what?

LAURA

The operetta the senior class put on. He had a wonderful voice and we sat across the aisle from each other Mondays, Wednesdays and Fridays in the Aud. Here he is with the silver cup for debating! See his grin?

AMANDA
(*Absently*)

He must have had a jolly disposition.

LAURA

He used to call me—Blue Roses.
(IMAGE: BLUE ROSES.)

AMANDA

Why did he call you such a name as that?

LAURA

When I had that attack of pleurosis —he asked me what was the matter when I came back. I said pleurosis—he thought that I said Blue Roses! So that's what he always called me after that. Whenever he saw me, he'd holler,

"Hello, Blue Roses!" I didn't care for the girl that he went out with. Emily Meisenbach. Emily was the best-dressed girl at Soldan. She never struck me, though, as being sincere . . . It says in the Personal Section—they're engaged. That's—six years ago! They must be married by now.

AMANDA

Girls that aren't cut out for business careers usually wind up married to some nice man. (*Gets up with a spark of revival*) Sister, that's what you'll do!
(LAURA *utters a startled, doubtful laugh. She reaches quickly for a piece of glass.*)

LAURA

But, Mother—

AMANDA

Yes? (*Crossing to photograph.*)

LAURA
(*In a tone of frightened apology*)

I'm—crippled!
(IMAGE: SCREEN.)

AMANDA

Nonsense! Laura, I've told you never, never to use that word. Why, you're not crippled, you just have a little defect— hardly noticeable, even! When people have some slight disadvantage like that, they cultivate other things to make up for it—develop charm—and vivacity— and—*charm!* That's all you have to do! (*She turns again to the photograph*) One thing your father had *plenty of*— was *charm!*
(TOM *motions to the fiddle in the wings.*)

THE SCENE FADES OUT WITH MUSIC

Scene III

LEGEND ON SCREEN: "AFTER THE FIASCO—"
TOM *speaks from the fire-escape landing.*

TOM

After the fiasco at Rubicam's Business College, the idea of getting a gentle-man caller for Laura began to play a more and more important part in Mother's calculations.

It became an obsession. Like some archetype of the universal unconscious, the image of the gentleman caller haunted our small apartment. . . .

(IMAGE: YOUNG MAN AT DOOR WITH FLOWERS.)

An evening at home rarely passed without some allusion to this image, this spectre, this hope. . . .

Even when he wasn't mentioned, his presence hung in Mother's preoccupied look and in my sister's frightened, apologetic manner—hung like a sentence passed upon the Wingfields!

Mother was a woman of action as well as words.

She began to take logical steps in the planned direction.

Late that winter and in the early spring—realizing that extra money would be needed to properly feather the nest and plume the bird—she conducted a vigorous campaign on the telephone, roping in subscribers to one of those magazines for matrons called *The Home-maker's Companion*, the type of journal that features the serialized sublimations of ladies of letters who think in terms of delicate cup-like breasts, slim, tapering waists, rich, creamy thighs, eyes like wood-smoke in autumn, fingers that soothe and caress like strains of music, bodies as powerful as Etruscan sculpture.

(SCREEN IMAGE: GLAMOR MAGA-ZINE COVER.)

(AMANDA *enters with phone on long extension cord. She is spotted in the dim stage.*)

AMANDA

Ida Scott? This is Amanda Wingfield!

We *missed* you at the D.A.R. last Monday!

I said to myself: She's probably suffering with that sinus condition! How is that sinus condition?

Horrors! Heaven have mercy!— You're a Christian martyr, yes, that's what you are, a Christian martyr!

Well, I just now happened to notice that your subscription to the *Com-panion's* about to expire! Yes, it expires with the next issue, honey!—just when that wonderful new serial by Bessie Mae Hopper is getting off to such an exciting start. Oh, honey, it's something that you can't miss! You remember how *Gone With the Wind* took everybody by storm? You simply couldn't go out if you hadn't read it. All everybody *talked* was Scarlett O'Hara. Well, this book is a book that critics already compare to *Gone With the Wind*. It's the *Gone With the Wind* of the post-World War generation!—What?— Burning?— Oh, honey, don't let them burn, go take a look in the oven and I'll hold the wire! Heavens—I think she's hung up!

DIM OUT

(LEGEND ON SCREEN: "YOU THINK I'M IN LOVE WITH CON-TINENTAL SHOEMAKERS?")

(*Before the stage is lighted, the violent voices of* TOM *and* AMANDA *are heard.*)

(*They are quarreling behind the portieres. In front of them stands* LAURA *with clenched hands and panicky expression.*)

(*A clear pool of light on her figure throughout this scene.*)

TOM

What in Christ's name am I—

AMANDA

(*Shrilly*)

Don't you use that—

TOM

Supposed to do!

AMANDA

Expression! Not in my—

TOM

Ohhh!

AMANDA

Presence! Have you gone out of your senses?

TOM

I have, that's true, *driven* out!

AMANDA

What is the matter with you, you—
big—big—IDIOT!

TOM

Look!—I've got *no thing*, no single
thing—

AMANDA

Lower your voice!

TOM

In my life here that I can call my
OWN! Everything is—

AMANDA

Stop that shouting!

TOM

Yesterday you confiscated my books!
You had the nerve to—

AMANDA

I took that horrible novel back to the
library—yes! That hideous book by that
insane Mr. Lawrence. (TOM *laughs
wildly*) I cannot control the output of
diseased minds or people who cater to
them— (TOM *laughs still more wildly*)
BUT I WON'T ALLOW SUCH FILTH
BROUGHT INTO MY HOUSE! No, no,
no, no, no!

TOM

House, house! Who pays rent on it,
who makes a slave of himself to—

AMANDA

(*Fairly screeching*)
Don't you DARE to—

TOM

No, no, *I* mustn't say things! *I've* got
to just—

AMANDA

Let me tell you—

TOM

I don't want to hear any more! (*He
tears the portieres open. The upstage
area is lit with a turgid smoky red
glow.*)
(AMANDA's *hair is in metal curlers
and she wears a very old bathrobe,*

*much too large for her slight figure,
a relic of the faithless Mr. Wingfield.*)
(*An upright typewriter and a wild
disarray of manuscripts is on the
drop-leaf table. The quarrel was
probably precipitated by* AMANDA's
*interruption of his creative labor.
A chair lying overthrown on the
floor.*)
(*Their gesticulating shadows are
cast on the ceiling by the fiery
glow.*)

AMANDA

You *will* hear more, you—

TOM

No, I won't hear more, I'm going out!

AMANDA

You come right back in—

TOM

Out, out, out! Because I'm—

AMANDA

Come back here, Tom Wingfield!
I'm not through talking to you!

TOM

Oh, go—

LAURA

(*Desperately*)
—Tom!

AMANDA

You're going to listen, and no more
insolence from you! I'm at the end of
my patience!
(*He comes back toward her.*)

TOM

What do you think I'm at? Aren't I
supposed to have any patience to reach
the end of, Mother? I know, I know.
It seems unimportant to you, what I'm
doing—what I *want* to do—having a
little *difference* between them! You
don't think that—

AMANDA

I think you've been doing things that
you're ashamed of. That's why you act

like this. I don't believe that you go every night to the movies. Nobody goes to the movies night after night. Nobody in their right minds goes to the movies as often as you pretend to. People don't go to the movies at nearly midnight, and movies don't let out at two A.M. Come in stumbling. Muttering to yourself like a maniac! You get three hours' sleep and then go to work. Oh, I can picture the way you're doing down there. Moping, doping, because you're in no condition.

TOM
(*Wildly*)
No, I'm in no condition!

AMANDA
What right have you got to jeopardize your job? Jeopardize the security of us all? How do you think we'd manage if you were—

TOM
Listen! You think I'm crazy *about* the *warehouse*? (*He bends fiercely toward her slight figure*) You think I'm in love with the Continental Shoemakers? You think I want to spend fifty-five *years* down there in that—*celotex interior!* with—*fluorescent—tubes!* Look! I'd rather somebody picked up a crowbar and battered out my brains—than go back mornings! I *go!* Every time you come in yelling that God damn *"Rise and Shine!" "Rise and Shine!"* I say to myself, "How *lucky dead* people are!" But I get up. I *go!* For sixty-five dollars a month I give up all that I dream of doing and being *ever!* And you say self —*self's* all I ever think of. Why, listen, if self is what I thought of, Mother, I'd be where he is—GONE! (*Pointing to father's picture*) As far as the system of transportation reaches! (*He starts past her. She grabs his arm*) Don't grab at me, Mother!

AMANDA
Where are you going?

TOM
I'm going to the *movies!*

AMANDA
I don't believe that lie!

TOM
(*Crouching toward her, overtowering her tiny figure. She backs away, gasping*)
I'm going to opium dens! Yes, opium dens, dens of vice and criminals' hangouts, Mother. I've joined the Hogan gang, I'm a hired assassin, I carry a tommy-gun in a violin case! I run a string of cat-houses in the Valley! They call me Killer, Killer Wingfield, I'm leading a double-life, a simple, honest warehouse worker by day, by night a dynamic *czar* of the *underworld, Mother*. I go to gambling casinos, I spin away fortunes on the roulette table! I wear a patch over one eye and a false mustache, sometimes I put on green whiskers. On those occasions they call me—*El Diablo!* Oh, I could tell you things to make you sleepless! My enemies plan to dynamite this place. They going to blow us all sky-high some night! I'll be glad, very happy, and so will you! You'll go up, up on a broomstick, over Blue Mountain with seventeen gentlemen callers! You ugly—babbling old—*witch*. . . . (*He goes through a series of violent, clumsy movements, seizing his overcoat, lunging to the door, pulling it fiercely open. The women watch him, aghast. His arm catches in the sleeve of the coat as he struggles to pull it on. For a moment he is pinioned by the bulky garment. With an outraged groan he tears the coat off again, splitting the shoulder of it, and hurls it across the room. It strikes against the shelf of* LAURA's *glass collection, there is a tinkle of shattering glass.* LAURA *cries out as if wounded.*)
(MUSIC. LEGEND: "THE GLASS MENAGERIE.")

LAURA
(*Shrilly*)
My glass!—menagerie. . . . (*She covers her face and turns away.*)
(*But* AMANDA *is still stunned and*

stupefied by the "ugly witch" so that she barely notices this occurrence. Now she recovers her speech.)

AMANDA
(*In an awful voice*)

I won't speak to you—until you apologize! (*She crosses through portieres and draws them together behind*

her. TOM *is left with* LAURA. LAURA *clings weakly to the mantel with her face averted.* TOM *stares at her stupidly for a moment. Then he crosses to shelf. Drops awkwardly on his knees to collect the fallen glass, glancing at* LAURA *as if he would speak but couldn't.*)

"The Glass Menagerie" steals in as

THE SCENE DIMS OUT

Scene IV

The interior is dark. Faint light in the alley.
A deep-voiced bell in a church is tolling the hour of five as the scene commences.
TOM *appears at the top of the alley. After each solemn boom of the bell in the tower, he shakes a little noise-maker or rattle as if to express the tiny spasm of man in contrast to the sustained power and dignity of the Almighty. This and the unsteadiness of his advance make it evident that he has been drinking.*
As he climbs the few steps to the fire-escape landing light steals up inside. LAURA *appears in night-dress, observing* TOM'S *empty bed in the front room.*
TOM *fishes in his pockets for door-key, removing a motley assortment of articles in the search, including a perfect shower of movie-ticket stubs and an empty bottle. At last he finds the key, but just as he is about to insert it, it slips from his fingers. He strikes a match and crouches below the door.*

TOM
(*Bitterly*)

One crack—and it falls through!
(LAURA *opens the door.*)

LAURA

Tom! Tom, what are you doing?

TOM

Looking for a door-key.

LAURA

Where have you been all this time?

TOM

I have been to the movies.

LAURA

All this time at the movies?

TOM

There was a very long program. There was a Garbo picture and a Mickey Mouse and a travelogue and a newsreel and a preview of coming attractions. And there was an organ solo and a collection for the milk-fund—simultan-

eously—which ended up in a terrible fight between a fat lady and an usher!

LAURA
(*Innocently*)

Did you have to stay through everything?

TOM

Of course! And, oh, I forgot! There was a big stage show! The headliner on this stage show was Malvolio the Magician. He performed wonderful tricks, many of them, such as pouring water back and forth between pitchers. First it turned to wine and then it turned to beer and then it turned to whiskey. I know it was whiskey it finally turned into because he needed somebody to come up out of the audience to help him, and I came up—both shows! It was Kentucky Straight Bourbon. A very generous fellow, he gave souvenirs. (*He pulls from his back pocket a shimmering rainbow-colored scarf*) He gave me this. This is his magic scarf. You can have it, Laura. You wave it over a canary cage and you get a bowl of gold-fish. You wave it over the gold-fish bowl and they fly away canaries. . . . But the wonderfullest trick of all was the coffin trick. We nailed him into a coffin and he got out of the coffin without removing one nail. (*He has come inside*) There is a trick that would come in handy for me—get me out of this 2 by 4 situation! (*Flops onto bed and starts removing shoes.*)

LAURA

Tom—Shhh!

TOM

What're you shushing me for?

LAURA

You'll wake up Mother.

TOM

Goody, goody! Pay 'er back for all those "Rise an' Shines." (*Lies down, groaning*) You know it don't take much intelligence to get yourself into a nailed-up coffin, Laura. But who in hell ever got himself out of one without removing one nail?
(*As if in answer, the father's grinning photograph lights up.*)
SCENE DIMS OUT
(*Immediately following: The church bell is heard striking six. At the sixth stroke the alarm clock goes off in* AMANDA's *room, and after a few moments we hear her calling: "Rise and Shine! Rise and Shine! Laura, go tell your brother to rise and shine!"*)

TOM

(*Sitting up slowly*)
I'll rise—but I won't shine.
(*The light increases.*)

AMANDA

Laura, tell your brother his coffee is ready.
(LAURA *slips into front room.*)

LAURA

Tom!—It's nearly seven. Don't make Mother nervous. (*He stares at her stupidly. Beseechingly*) Tom, speak to Mother this morning. Make up with her, apologize, speak to her!

TOM

She won't to me. It's her that started not speaking.

LAURA

If you just say you're sorry she'll start speaking.

TOM

Her not speaking—is that such a tragedy?

LAURA

Please—please!

AMANDA

(*Calling from kitchenette*)
Laura, are you going to do what I asked you to do, or do I have to get dressed and go out myself?

LAURA

Going, going—soon as I get on my coat! (*She pulls on a shapeless felt hat with nervous, jerky movement, pleadingly glancing at* TOM. *Rushes awkwardly for coat. The coat is one of* AMANDA's, *inaccurately made-over, the sleeves too short for* LAURA) Butter and what else?

AMANDA

(*Entering upstage*)
Just butter. Tell them to charge it.

LAURA

Mother, they make such faces when I do that.

AMANDA

Sticks and stones can break our bones, but the expression on Mr. Garfinkel's face won't harm us! Tell your brother his coffee is getting cold.

LAURA

(*At door*)
Do what I asked you, will you, will you, Tom?
(*He looks sullenly away.*)

AMANDA

Laura, go now or just don't go at all!

LAURA

(*Rushing out*)

Going—going! (*A second later she cries out.* TOM *springs up and crosses to door.* AMANDA *rushes anxiously in.* TOM *opens the door.*)

TOM

Laura?

LAURA

I'm all right. I slipped, but I'm all right.

AMANDA

(*Peering anxiously after her*)

If anyone breaks a leg on those fire-escape steps, the landlord ought to be sued for every cent he possesses! (*She shuts door. Remembers she isn't speaking and returns to other room*)

(*As* TOM *enters listlessly for his coffee, she turns her back to him and stands rigidly facing the window on the gloomy gray vault of the areaway. Its lights on her face with its aged but childish features is cruelly sharp, satirical as a Daumier print.*)

(MUSIC UNDER: "AVE MARIA.")

(TOM *glances sheepishly but sullenly at her averted figure and slumps at the table. The coffee is scalding hot; he sips it and gasps and spits it back in the cup. At his gasp,* AMANDA *catches her breath and half turns. Then catches herself and turns back to window.*)

(TOM *blows on his coffee, glancing sidewise at his mother. She clears her throat.* TOM *clears his. He starts to rise. Sinks back down again, scratches his head, clears his throat again.* AMANDA *coughs.* TOM *raises his cup in both hands to blow on it, his eyes staring over the rim of it at his mother for several moments. Then he slowly sets the cup down and awkwardly and hesitantly rises from the chair.*)

TOM

(*Hoarsely*)

Mother. I—I apologize, Mother. (AMANDA *draws a quick, shuddering breath. Her face works grotesquely. She breaks into childlike tears*) I'm sorry for what I said, for everything that I said, I didn't mean it.

AMANDA

(*Sobbingly*)

My devotion has made me a witch and so I make myself hateful to my children!

TOM

No, you *don't*.

AMANDA

I worry so much, don't sleep, it makes me nervous!

TOM

(*Gently*)

I understand that.

AMANDA

I've had to put up a solitary battle all these years. But you're my right-hand bower! Don't fall down, don't fail!

TOM

(*Gently*)

I try, Mother.

AMANDA

(*With great enthusiasm*)

Try and you will SUCCEED! (*The notion makes her breathless.*) Why, you—you're just *full* of natural endowments! Both of my children—they're *unusual* children! Don't you think I know it? I'm so—*proud!* Happy and—feel I've—so much to be thankful for but— Promise me one thing, Son!

TOM

What, Mother?

AMANDA

Promise, son, you'll—never be a drunkard!

TOM

(*Turns to her grinning*)

I will never be a drunkard, Mother.

AMANDA

That's what frightened me so, that you'd be drinking! Eat a bowl of Purina!

TOM

Just coffee, Mother.

AMANDA

Shredded wheat biscuit?

TOM

No. No, Mother, just coffee.

AMANDA

You can't put in a day's work on an empty stomach. You've got ten minutes —don't gulp! Drinking too-hot liquids makes cancer of the stomach. . . . Put cream in.

TOM

No, thank you.

AMANDA

To cool it.

TOM

No! No, thank you, I want it black.

AMANDA

I know, but it's not good for you. We have to do all that we can to build ourselves up. In these trying times we live in, all that we have to cling to is—each other. . . . That's why it's so important to— Tom, I— I sent out your sister so I could discuss something with you. If you hadn't spoken I would have spoken to you. (*Sits down.*)

TOM
(*Gently*)

What is it, Mother, that you want to discuss?

AMANDA

Laura!
(TOM *puts his cup down slowly.*)
(LEGEND ON SCREEN: "LAURA.")
(MUSIC: "THE GLASS MENAGERIE.")

TOM

—Oh.—Laura . . .

AMANDA
(*Touching his sleeve*)

You know how Laura is. So quiet but —still water runs deep! She notices things and I think she—broods about them. (TOM *looks up*) A few days ago I came in and she was crying.

TOM

What about?

AMANDA

You.

TOM

Me?

AMANDA

She has an idea that you're not happy here.

TOM

What gave her that idea?

AMANDA

What gives her any idea? However, you do act strangely. I—I'm not criticizing, understand *that!* I know your ambitions do not lie in the warehouse, that like everybody in the whole wide world —you've had to—make sacrifices, but— Tom—Tom—life's not easy, it calls for —Spartan endurance! There's so many things in my heart that I cannot describe to you! I've never told you but I—*loved* your father. . . .

TOM
(*Gently*)

I know that, Mother.

AMANDA

And you—when I see you taking after his ways! Staying out late—and—well, you *had* been drinking the night you were in that—terrifying condition! Laura says that you hate the apartment and that you go out nights to get away from it! Is that true, Tom?

TOM

No. You say there's so much in your heart that you can't describe to me. That's true of me, too. There's so much

in my heart that I can't describe to *you!*
So let's respect each other's—

AMANDA

But, why—*why*, Tom—are you always so *restless?* Where do you *go* to,
nights?

TOM

I—go to the movies.

AMANDA

Why do you go to the movies so
much, Tom?

TOM

I go to the movies because—I like
adventure. Adventure is something I
don't have much of at work, so I go to
the movies.

AMANDA

But, Tom, you go to the movies *entirely* too *much!*

TOM

I like a lot of adventure.
(AMANDA *looks baffled, then hurt.
As the familiar inquisition resumes
he becomes hard and impatient
again.* AMANDA *slips back into her
querulous attitude toward him.*)
(IMAGE ON SCREEN: SAILING
VESSEL WITH JOLLY ROGER.)

AMANDA

Most young men find adventure in
their careers.

TOM

Then most young men are not employed in a warehouse.

AMANDA

The world is full of young men employed in warehouses and offices and
factories.

TOM

Do all of them find adventure in
their careers?

AMANDA

They do or they do without it! Not
everybody has a craze for adventure.

TOM

Man is by instinct a lover, a hunter,
a fighter, and none of those instincts are
given much play at the warehouse!

AMANDA

Man is by instinct! Don't quote instinct to me! Instinct is something that
people have got away from! It belongs
to animals! Christian adults don't want
it!

TOM

What do Christian adults want, then,
Mother?

AMANDA

Superior things! Things of the mind
and the spirit! Only animals have to
satisfy instincts! Surely your aims are
somewhat higher than theirs! Than
monkeys—pigs—

TOM

I reckon they're not.

AMANDA

You're joking. However, that isn't
what I wanted to discuss.

TOM
(*Rising*)
I haven't much time.

AMANDA
(*Pushing his shoulders*)
Sit down.

TOM

You want me to punch in red at the
warehouse, Mother?

AMANDA

You have five minutes. I want to talk
about Laura.
(LEGEND: "PLANS AND PROVI-
SIONS.")

TOM

All right! What about Laura?

AMANDA

We have to be making some plans
and provisions for her. She's older than
you, two years, and nothing has happened. She just drifts along doing

nothing. It frightens me terribly how she just drifts along.

TOM

I guess she's the type that people call home girls.

AMANDA

There's no such type, and if there is, it's a pity! That is unless the home is hers, with a husband!

TOM

What?

AMANDA

Oh, I see the handwriting on the wall as plain as I see the nose in front of my face! It's terrifying!

More and more you remind me of your father! He was out all hours without explanation!—Then *left! Good-bye!*

And me with the bag to hold. I saw that letter you got from the Merchant Marine. I know what you're dreaming of. I'm not standing here blindfolded.

Very well, then. Then *do* it!

But not till there's somebody to take your place.

TOM

What do you mean?

AMANDA

I mean that as soon as Laura has got somebody to take care of her, married, a home of her own, independent—why, then you'll be free to go wherever you please, on land, on sea, whichever way the wind blows you!

But until that time you've got to look out for your sister. I don't say me because I'm old and don't matter! I say for your sister because she's young and dependent.

I put her in business college—a dismal failure! Frightened her so it made her sick at the stomach.

I took her over to the Young People's League at the church. Another fiasco. She spoke to nobody, nobody spoke to her. Now all she does is fool with those pieces of glass and play those worn-out records. What kind of a life is that for a girl to lead?

TOM

What can I do about it?

AMANDA

Overcome selfishness!

Self, self, self is all that you ever think of!

(TOM *springs up and crosses to get his coat. It is ugly and bulky. He pulls on a cap with earmuffs.*)

Where is your muffler? Put your wool muffler on!

(*He snatches it angrily from the closet and tosses it around his neck and pulls both ends tight.*)

Tom! I haven't said what I had in mind to ask you.

TOM

I'm too late to—

AMANDA

(*Catching his arm—very importunately. Then shyly*)

Down at the warehouse, aren't there some—nice young men?

TOM

No!

AMANDA

There *must* be—*some* . . .

TOM

Mother—

(*Gesture.*)

AMANDA

Find out one that's clean-living—doesn't drink and—ask him out for sister!

TOM

What?

AMANDA

For *sister!* To *meet!* Get *acquainted!*

TOM

(*Stamping to door*)

Oh, my *go-osh!*

AMANDA

Will you? (*He opens door. Imploringly*) Will you? (*He starts down*) Will you? *Will* you, dear?

TOM
(*Calling back*)

YES!

(AMANDA *closes the door hesitantly and with a troubled but faintly hopeful expression.*)
SCREEN IMAGE: GLAMOR MAGAZINE COVER.
Spot AMANDA *at phone.*

AMANDA

Ella Cartwright? This is Amanda Wingfield!

How are you, honey?

How is that kidney condition?
(*Count five.*)

Horrors!
(*Count five.*)

You're a Christian martyr, yes, honey, that's what you are, a Christian martyr!

Well, I just now happened to notice in my little red book that your subscription to the *Companion* has just run out! I knew that you wouldn't want to miss out on the wonderful serial starting in this new issue. It's by Bessie Mae Hopper, the first thing she's written since *Honeymoon for Three.*

Wasn't that a strange and interesting story? Well, this one is even lovelier, I believe. It has a sophisticated, society background. It's all about the horsey set on Long Island!

FADE OUT

Scene V

LEGEND ON SCREEN: "ANNUNCIATION." *Fade with music.*
It is early dusk of a spring evening. Supper has just been finished in the Wingfield apartment. AMANDA *and* LAURA *in light-colored dresses are removing dishes from the table, in the upstage area, which is shadowy, their movements formalized almost as a dance or ritual, their moving forms as pale and silent as moths.*
TOM, *in white shirt and trousers, rises from the table and crosses toward the fire-escape.*

AMANDA
(*As he passes her*)
Son, will you do me a favor?

TOM

What?

AMANDA

Comb your hair! You look so pretty when your hair is combed! (TOM *slouches on sofa with evening paper. Enormous caption "Franco Triumphs"*) There is only one respect in which I would like you to emulate your father.

TOM

What respect is that?

AMANDA

The care he always took of his appearance. He never allowed himself to look untidy. (*He throws down the paper and crosses to fire-escape*) Where are you going?

TOM

I'm going out to smoke.

AMANDA

You smoke too much. A pack a day at fifteen cents a pack. How much would that amount to in a month? Thirty times fifteen is how much, Tom? Figure it out and you will be astounded at what you could save. Enough to give you a night-school course in accounting at Washington U! Just think what a wonderful thing that would be for you, Son!

(TOM *is unmoved by the thought.*)

TOM

I'd rather smoke. *He steps out on landing, letting the screen door slam.*)

AMANDA
(*Sharply*)

I know! That's the tragedy of it. . . .
(*Alone, she turns to look at her husband's picture.*)
(DANCE MUSIC: "ALL THE WORLD IS WAITING FOR THE SUNRISE!")

TOM
(*To the audience*)

Across the alley from us was the Paradise Dance Hall. On evenings in spring the windows and doors were open and the music came outdoors. Sometimes the lights were turned out except for a large glass sphere that hung from the ceiling. It would turn slowly about and filter the dusk with delicate rainbow colors. Then the orchestra played a waltz or a tango, something that had a slow and sensuous rhythm. Couples would come outside, to the relative privacy of the alley. You could see them kissing behind ash-pits and telephone poles.

This was the compensation for lives that passed like mine, without any change or adventure.

Adventure and change were imminent in this year. They were waiting around the corner for all these kids.

Suspended in the mist over Berchtesgaden, caught in the folds of Chamberlain's umbrella—

In Spain there was Guernica!

But here there was only hot swing music and liquor, dance halls, bars, and movies, and sex that hung in the gloom like a chandelier and flooded the world with brief, deceptive rainbows. . . .

All the world was waiting for bombardments!

(AMANDA *turns from the picture and comes outside.*)

AMANDA
(*Sighing*)

A fire-escape landing's a poor excuse for a porch. (*She spreads a newspaper on a step and sits down, gracefully and demurely as if she were settling into a* swing on a Mississippi veranda) What are you looking at?

TOM

The moon.

AMANDA

Is there a moon this evening?

TOM

It's rising over Garfinkel's Delicatessen.

AMANDA

So it is! A little silver slipper of a moon. Have you made a wish on it yet?

TOM

Um-hum.

AMANDA

What did you wish for?

TOM

That's a secret.

AMANDA

A secret, huh? Well, I won't tell mine either. I will be just as mysterious as you.

TOM

I bet I can guess what yours is.

AMANDA

Is my head so transparent?

TOM

You're not a sphinx.

AMANDA

No, I don't have secrets. I'll tell you what I wished for on the moon. Success and happiness for my precious children! I wish for that whenever there's a moon, and when there isn't a moon, I wish for it, too.

TOM

I thought perhaps you wished for a gentleman caller.

AMANDA

Why do you say that?

TOM

Don't you remember asking me to fetch one?

AMANDA

I remember suggesting that it would be nice for your sister if you brought home some nice young man from the warehouse. I think that I've made that suggestion more than once.

TOM

Yes, you have made it repeatedly.

AMANDA

Well?

TOM

We are going to have one.

AMANDA

What?

TOM

A gentleman caller!
(THE ANNUNCIATION IS CELE-BRATED WITH MUSIC.)
(AMANDA *rises.*)
(IMAGE ON SCREEN: CALLER WITH BOUQUET.)

AMANDA

You mean you have asked some nice young man to come over?

TOM

Yep. I've asked him to dinner.

AMANDA

You really did?

TOM

I did!

AMANDA

You did, and did he—*accept?*

TOM

He did!

AMANDA

Well, well—well, well! That's—lovely!

TOM

I thought that you would be pleased.

AMANDA

It's definite, then?

TOM

Very definite.

AMANDA

Soon?

TOM

Very soon.

AMANDA

For heaven's sake, stop putting on and tell me some things will you?

TOM

What things do you want me to tell you?

AMANDA

Naturally I would like to know when he's *coming!*

TOM

He's coming tomorrow.

AMANDA

Tomorrow?

TOM

Yep. Tomorrow.

AMANDA

But, Tom!

TOM

Yes, Mother?

AMANDA

Tomorrow gives me no time!

TOM

Time for what?

AMANDA

Preparations! Why didn't you phone me at once, as soon as you asked him, the minute that he accepted? Then, don't you see, I could have been getting ready!

TOM

You don't have to make any fuss.

AMANDA

Oh, Tom, Tom, Tom, of course I have to make a fuss! I want things nice, not sloppy! Not thrown together. I'll certainly have to do some fast thinking, won't I?

TOM

I don't see why you have to think at all.

AMANDA

You just don't know. We can't have a gentleman caller in a pig-sty! All my wedding silver has to be polished, the monogrammed table linen ought to be laundered! The windows have to be washed and fresh curtains put up. And how about clothes? We have to *wear* something, don't we?

TOM

Mother, this boy is no one to make a fuss over!

AMANDA

Do you realize he's the first young man we've introduced to your sister?

It's terrible, dreadful, disgraceful that poor little sister has never received a single gentleman caller! Tom, come inside! (*She opens the screen door.*)

TOM

What for?

AMANDA

I want to ask you some things.

TOM

If you're going to make such a fuss, I'll call it off, I'll tell him not to come!

AMANDA

You certainly won't do anything of the kind. Nothing offends people worse than broken engagements. It simply means I'll have to work like a Turk! We won't be brilliant, but we will pass inspection. Come on inside. (TOM *follows, groaning*) Sit down.

TOM

Any particular place you would like me to sit?

AMANDA

Thank heavens I've got that new sofa! I'm also making payments on a floor lamp I'll have sent out! And put the chintz covers on, they'll brighten things up! Of course I'd hoped to have

these walls re-papered. . . . What is the young man's name?

TOM

His name is O'Connor.

AMANDA

That, of course, means fish—tomorrow is Friday! I'll have that salmon loaf—with Durkee's dressing! What does he do? He works at the warehouse?

TOM

Of course! How else would I—

AMANDA

Tom, he—doesn't drink?

TOM

Why do you ask me that?

AMANDA

Your father *did!*

TOM

Don't get started on that!

AMANDA

He *does* drink, then?

TOM

Not that I know of!

AMANDA

Make sure, be certain! The last thing I want for my daughter's a boy who drinks!

TOM

Aren't you being a little bit premature? Mr. O'Connor has not yet appeared on the scene!

AMANDA

But will tomorrow. To meet your sister, and what do I know about his character? Nothing! Old maids are better off than wives of drunkards!

TOM

Oh, my God!

AMANDA

Be still!

TOM

(*Leaning forward to whisper*)

Lots of fellows meet girls whom they don't marry!

AMANDA

Oh, talk sensibly, Tom—and don't be sarcastic! (*She has gotten a hairbrush.*)

TOM

What are you doing?

AMANDA

I'm brushing that cow-lick down!
What is this young man's position at the warehouse?

TOM

(*Submitting grimly to the brush and the interrogation*)
This young man's position is that of a shipping clerk, Mother.

AMANDA

Sounds to me like a fairly responsible job, the sort of a job *you* would be in if you just had more *get-up.*
What is his salary? Have you any idea?

TOM

I would judge it to be approximately eighty-five dollars a month.

AMANDA

Well—not princely, but—

TOM

Twenty more than I make.

AMANDA

Yes, how well I know! But for a family man, eighty-five dollars a month is not much more than you can just get by on. . . .

TOM

Yes, but Mr. O'Connor is not a family man.

AMANDA

He might be, mightn't he? Some time in the future?

TOM

I see. Plans and provisions.

AMANDA

You are the only young man that I know of who ignores the fact that the future becomes the present, the present the past, and the past turns into everlasting regret if you don't plan for it!

TOM

I will think that over and see what I can make of it.

AMANDA

Don't be supercilious with your mother! Tell me some more about this —what do you call him?

TOM

James D. O'Connor. The D. is for Delaney.

AMANDA

Irish on *both* sides! *Gracious!* And doesn't drink?

TOM

Shall I call him up and ask him right this minute?

AMANDA

The only way to find out about those things is to make discreet inquiries at the proper moment. When I was a girl in Blue Mountain and it was suspected that a young man drank, the girl whose attentions he had been receiving, if any girl *was*, would sometimes speak to the minister of his church, or rather her father would if her father was living, and sort of feel him out on the young man's character. That is the way such things are discreetly handled to keep a young woman from making a tragic mistake!

TOM

Then how did you happen to make a tragic mistake?

AMANDA

That innocent look of your father's had everyone fooled!
He *smiled*—the world was *enchanted!*
No girl can do worse than put herself at the mercy of a handsome appearance!
I hope that Mr. O'Connor is not too good-looking.

TOM

No, he's not too good-looking. He's covered with freckles and hasn't too much of a nose.

AMANDA

He's not right-down homely, though?

TOM

Not right-down homely. Just medium homely, I'd say.

AMANDA

Character's what to look for in a man.

TOM

That's what I've always said, Mother.

AMANDA

You've never said anything of the kind and I suspect you would never give it a thought.

TOM

Don't be so suspicious of me.

AMANDA

At least I hope he's the type that's up and coming.

TOM

I think he really goes in for self-improvement.

AMANDA

What reason have you to think so?

TOM

He goes to night school.

AMANDA

(*Beaming*)

Splendid! What does he do, I mean study?

TOM

Radio engineering and public speaking!

AMANDA

Then he has visions of being advanced in the world!

Any young man who studies public speaking is aiming to have an executive job some day!

And radio engineering? A thing for the future!

Both of these facts are very illuminating. Those are the sort of things that a mother should know concerning any young man who comes to call on her daughter. Seriously or—not.

TOM

One little warning. He doesn't know about Laura. I didn't let on that we had dark ulterior motives. I just said, why don't you come and have dinner with us? He said okay and that was the whole conversation.

AMANDA

I bet it was! You're eloquent as an oyster.

However, he'll know about Laura when he gets here. When he sees how lovely and sweet and pretty she is, he'll thank his lucky stars he was asked to dinner.

TOM

Mother, you mustn't expect too much of Laura.

AMANDA

What do you mean?

TOM

Laura seems all those things to you and me because she's ours and we love her. We don't even notice she's crippled any more.

AMANDA

Don't say crippled! You know that I never allow that word to be used!

TOM

But face facts, Mother. She is and—that's not all—

AMANDA

What do you mean "not all"?

TOM

Laura is very different from other girls.

AMANDA

I think the difference is all to her advantage.

TOM

Not quite all—in the eyes of others—strangers—she's terribly shy and lives in a world of her own and those things make her seem a little peculiar to people outside the house.

AMANDA

Don't say peculiar.

TOM

Face the facts. She is.
(THE DANCE-HALL MUSIC
CHANGES TO A TANGO THAT HAS
A MINOR AND SOMEWHAT OMIN-
OUS TONE.)

AMANDA

In what way is she peculiar—may I
ask?

TOM
(*Gently*)

She lives in a world of her own—a
world of—little glass ornaments, Mother.
. . . (*Gets up.* AMANDA *remains holding
brush, looking at him, troubled*) She
plays old phonograph records and—
that's about all— (*He glances at himself
in the mirror and crosses to door.*)

AMANDA
(*Sharply*)

Where are you going?

TOM

I'm going to the movies. (*Out screen
door.*)

AMANDA

Not to the movies, every night to the
movies! (*Follows quickly to screen door*)
I don't believe you always go to the
movies! (*He is gone.* AMANDA *looks
worriedly after him for a moment. Then
vitality and optimism return and she
turns from the door. Crossing to por-*

tieres) Laura! Laura! (LAURA *answers
from kitchenette.*)

LAURA

Yes, Mother.

AMANDA

Let those dishes go and come in front!
(LAURA *appears with dish towel. Gaily*)
Laura, come here and make a wish on
the moon!
(SCREEN IMAGE: MOON.)

LAURA
(*Entering*)

Moon—moon?

AMANDA

A little silver slipper of a moon.
Look over your left shoulder, Laura,
and make a wish!
(LAURA *looks faintly puzzled as if
called out of sleep.* AMANDA *seizes
her shoulders and turns her at an
angle by the door.*)
Now!
Now, darling, *wish!*

LAURA

What shall I wish for, Mother?

AMANDA
(*Her voice trembling and her eyes
suddenly filling with tears*)
Happiness! Good fortune!
(*The violin rises and the stage
dims out.*)

CURTAIN

Scene VI

IMAGE: HIGH SCHOOL HERO.

*And so the following evening I brought Jim home to dinner. I had known Jim
slightly in high school. In high school Jim was a hero. He had tremendous Irish good
nature and vitality with the scrubbed and polished look of white chinaware. He
seemed to move in a continual spotlight. He was a star in basketball, captain of the
debating club, president of the senior class and the glee club and he sang the male
lead in the annual light operas. He was always running or bounding, never just
walking. He seemed always at the point of defeating the law of gravity. He was
shooting with such velocity through his adolescence that you would logically expect
him to arrive at nothing short of the White House by the time he was thirty.
But Jim apparently ran into more interference after his graduation from Soldan.*

His speed had definitely slowed. Six years after he left high school he was holding a job that wasn't much better than mine.
(IMAGE: CLERK.)

He was the only one at the warehouse with whom I was on friendly terms. I was valuable to him as someone who could remember his former glory, who had seen him win basketball games and the silver cup in debating. He knew of my secret practice of retiring to a cabinet of the wash-room to work on poems when business was slack in the warehouse. He called me Shakespeare. And while the other boys in the warehouse regarded me with suspicious hostility, Jim took a humorous attitude toward me. Gradually his attitude affected the others, their hostility wore off and they also began to smile at me as people smile at an oddly fashioned dog who trots across their path at some distance.

I knew that Jim and Laura had known each other at Soldan, and I had heard Laura speak admiringly of his voice. I didn't know if Jim remembered her or not. In high school Laura had been as unobtrusive as Jim had been astonishing. If he did remember Laura, it was not as my sister, for when I asked him to dinner, he grinned and said, "You know, Shakespeare, I never though of you as having folks!"

He was about to discover that I did. . . .

(LIGHT UP STAGE.)
(LEGEND ON SCREEN: "THE ACCENT OF A COMING FOOT.")
(*Friday evening. It is about five o'clock of a late spring evening which comes "scattering poems in the sky."*)
(*A delicate lemony light is in the Wingfield apartment.*)
(AMANDA *has worked like a Turk in preparation for the gentleman caller. The results are astonishing. The new floor lamp with its rose-silk shade is in place, a colored paper lantern conceals the broken light fixture in the ceiling, new billowing white curtains are at the windows, chintz covers are on chairs and soft, a pair of new sofa pillows make their initial appearance.*)
(*Open boxes and tissue paper are scattered on the floor.*)
(LAURA *stands in the middle with lifted arms while* AMANDA *crouches before her, adjusting the hem of the new dress, devout and ritualistic. The dress is colored and designed by memory. The arrangement of*

LAURA's *hair is changed; it is softer and more becoming. A fragile, unearthly prettiness has come out in* LAURA: *she is like a piece of translucent glass touched by light, given a momentary radiance, not actual, not lasting.*)

AMANDA
(*Impatiently*)
Why are you trembling?

LAURA
Mother, you've made me so nervous!

AMANDA
How have I made you nervous?

LAURA
By all this fuss! You make it seem so important!

AMANDA
I don't understand you, Laura. You couldn't be satisfied with just sitting home, and yet whenever I try to arrange something for you, you seem to resist it.
(*She gets up.*)
Now take a look at yourself.
No, wait! Wait just a moment—I have an idea!

LAURA

What is it now?

(AMANDA *produces two powder puffs which she wraps in handkerchiefs and stuffs in* LAURA's *bosom.*)

LAURA

Mother, what are you doing?

AMANDA

They call them "Gay Deceivers"!

LAURA

I won't wear them!

AMANDA

You will!

LAURA

Why should I?

AMANDA

Because, to be painfully honest, your chest is flat.

LAURA

You make it seem like we were setting a trap.

AMANDA

All pretty girls are a trap, a pretty trap, and men expect them to be.

(LEGEND: "A PRETTY TRAP.")

Now look at yourself, young lady. This is the prettiest you will ever be!

I've got to fix myself now! You're going to be surprised by your mother's appearance! (*She crosses through portieres, humming gaily.*)

(LAURA *moves slowly to the long mirror and stares solemnly at herself.*)

(*A wind blows the white curtains inward in a slow, graceful motion and with a faint, sorrowful sighing.*)

AMANDA

(*Off stage*)

It isn't dark enough yet. (*She turns slowly before the mirror with a troubled look.*)

(LEGEND ON SCREEN: "THIS IS MY SISTER: CELEBRATE HER WITH STRINGS!" MUSIC.)

AMANDA

(*Laughing, off*)

I'm going to show you something. I'm going to make a spectacular appearance!

LAURA

What is it, Mother?

AMANDA

Possess your soul in patience—you will see!

Something I've resurrected from that old trunk! Styles haven't changed so terribly much after all. . . .

(*She parts the portieres.*)

Now just look at your mother!

(*She wears a girlish frock of yellowed voile with a blue silk sash. She carries a bunch of jonquils —the legend of her youth is nearly revived. Feverishly.*)

This is the dress in which I led the cotillion. Won the cakewalk twice at Sunset Hill, wore one spring to the Governor's ball in Jackson!

See how I sashayed around the ballroom, Laura?

(*She raises her skirt and does a mincing step around the room.*)

I wore it on Sundays for my gentlemen callers! I had it on the day I met your father—

I had malaria fever all that spring. The change of climate from East Tennessee to the Delta—weakened resistance—I had a little temperature all the time—not enough to be serious— just enough to make me restless and giddy!—Invitations poured in—parties all over the Delta!—"Stay in bed," said Mother, "you have fever!"—but I just wouldn't.—I took quinine but kept on going, going!—Evenings, dances!— Afternoons, long, long rides! Picnics— lovely!—So lovely, that country in May. —All lacy with dogwood, literally flooded with jonquils!—That was the spring I had the craze for jonquils. Jonquils became an absolute obsession. Mother said, "Honey, there's no more room for jonquils." And still I kept on bringing in more jonquils. Whenever, wherever I saw them, I'd say, "Stop! Stop! I see jonquils!" I made the young men help me gather the jonquils! It was a joke, Amanda and her jonquils! Finally there were no more vases to hold them, every available space was filled with jonquils. No vases to hold them? All right, I'll hold them myself! And then I—(*She stops in front of the picture.* MUSIC) met your father!

Malaria fever and jonquils and then —this—boy. . . .

(*She switches on the rose-colored lamp.*)

I hope they get here before it starts to rain.

(*She crosses upstage and places the jonquils in bowl on table.*)

I gave your brother a little extra change so he and Mr. O'Connor could take the service car home.

LAURA
(*With altered look*)
What did you say his name was?

AMANDA
O'Connor.

LAURA
What is his first name?

AMANDA
I don't remember. Oh, yes, I do. It was—Jim!

(LAURA *sways slightly and catches hold of a chair.*)

(LEGEND ON SCREEN: "NOT JIM!")

LAURA
(*Faintly*)
Not—Jim!

AMANDA
Yes, that was it, it was Jim! I've never known a Jim that wasn't nice!

(MUSIC: OMINOUS.)

LAURA
Are you sure his name is Jim O'Connor?

AMANDA
Yes. Why?

LAURA
Is he the one that Tom used to know in high school?

AMANDA
He didn't say so. I think he just got to know him at the warehouse.

LAURA
There was a Jim O'Connor we both knew in high school—(*Then, with effort*) If that is the one that Tom is bringing to dinner—you'll have to excuse me, I won't come to the table.

AMANDA
What sort of nonsense is this?

LAURA
You asked me once if I'd ever liked a boy. Don't you remember I showed you this boy's picture?

AMANDA
You mean the boy you showed me in the year book?

LAURA
Yes, that boy.

AMANDA
Laura, Laura, were you in love with that boy?

LAURA
I don't know, Mother. All I know is I couldn't sit at the table if it was him!

AMANDA
It won't be him! It isn't the least bit likely. But whether it is or not, you will come to the table. You will not be excused.

LAURA
I'll have to be, Mother.

AMANDA
I don't intend to humor your silliness, Laura. I've had too much from you and your brother, both!

So just sit down and compose your-self till they come. Tom has forgotten his key so you'll have to let them in, when they arrive.

LAURA
(*Panicky*)
Oh, Mother—*you* answer the door!

AMANDA
(*Lightly*)
I'll be in the kitchen—busy!

LAURA
Oh, Mother, please answer the door, don't make me do it!

AMANDA
(*Crossing into kitchenette*)
I've got to fix the dressing for the salmon. Fuss, fuss—silliness!—over a gentleman caller!

(*Door swings shut.* LAURA *is left alone.*)
(LEGEND: "TERROR!")
(*She utters a low moan and turns off the lamp—sits stiffly on the edge of the sofa, knotting her fingers together.*)
(LEGEND OF SCREEN: "THE OPEN-ING OF A DOOR!")
(TOM *and* JIM *appear on the fire-escape steps and climb to landing. Hearing their approach,* LAURA *rises with a panicky gesture. She retreats to the portieres.*)
(*The doorbell.* LAURA *catches her breath and touches her throat. Low drums.*)

AMANDA
(*Calling*)
Laura, sweetheart! The door!
(LAURA *stares at it without mov-ing.*)

JIM
I think we just beat the rain.

TOM
Uh-huh. (*He rings again, nervously.* JIM *whistles and fishes for a cigarette.*)

AMANDA
(*Very, very gaily*)
Laura, that is your brother and Mr. O'Connor! Will you let them in, darling?
(LAURA *crosses toward kitchenette door.*)

LAURA
(*Breathlessly*)
Mother—you go to the door!
(AMANDA *steps out of kitchenette and stares furiously at* LAURA. *She points imperiously at the door.*)

LAURA
Please, please!

AMANDA
(*In a fierce whisper*)
What is the matter with you, you silly thing?

LAURA
(*Desperately*)
Please, you answer it, *please!*

AMANDA
I told you I wasn't going to humor you, Laura. Why have you chosen this moment to lose your mind?

LAURA
Please, please, please, you go!

AMANDA
You'll have to go to the door because I can't!

LAURA
(*Despairingly*)
I can't either!

AMANDA
Why?

LAURA
I'm *sick!*

AMANDA
I'm sick, too—of your nonsense! Why can't you and your brother be normal people? Fantastic whims and behavior!
(TOM *gives a long ring.*)
Preposterous goings on! Can you give

me one reason—(*Calls out lyrically*) COMING! JUST ONE SECOND!—why you should be afraid to open a door? Now you answer it, Laura!

LAURA

Oh, oh, oh . . . (*She returns through the portieres. Darts to the victrola and winds it frantically and turns it on.*)

AMANDA

Laura Wingfield, you march right to that door!

LAURA

Yes—yes, Mother!
(*A faraway, scratchy rendition of "Dardanella" softens the air and gives her strength to move through it. She slips to the door and draws it cautiously open.*)
(TOM *enters with the caller,* JIM O'CONNOR.)

TOM

Laura, this is Jim. Jim, this is my sister, Laura.

JIM
(*Stepping inside*)
I didn't know that Shakespeare had a sister!

LAURA
(*Retreating stiff and trembling from the door*)
How—how do you do?

JIM
(*Heartily extending his hand*)
Okay!
(LAURA *touches it hesitantly with hers.*)

JIM

Your hand's *cold*, Laura!

LAURA

Yes, well—I've been playing the victrola. . . .

JIM

Must have been playing classical music on it! You ought to play a little hot swing music to warm you up!

LAURA

Excuse me—I haven't finished playing the victrola. . . . (*She turns awkwardly and hurries into the front room. She pauses a second by the victrola. Then catches her breath and darts through the portieres like a frightened deer.*)

JIM
(*Grinning*)
What was the matter?

TOM

Oh—with Laura? Laura is—terribly shy.

JIM

Shy, huh? It's unusual to meet a shy girl nowadays. I don't believe you ever mentioned you had a sister.

TOM

Well, now you know. I have one. Here is the *Post Dispatch*. You want a piece of it?

JIM

Uh-huh.

TOM

What piece? The comics?

JIM

Sports! (*Glances at it*) Ole Dizzy Dean is on his bad behavior.

TOM
(*Disinterest*)
Yeah? (*Lights cigarette and crosses back to fire-escape door.*)

JIM

Where are *you* going?

TOM

I'm going out on the terrace.

JIM
(*Goes after him*)
You know, Shakespeare—I'm going to sell you a bill of goods!

TOM

What goods?

JIM

A course I'm taking.

TOM

Huh?

JIM

In public speaking! You and me, we're not the warehouse type.

TOM

Thanks—that's good news.
But what has public speaking got to do with it?

JIM

It fits you for—executive positions!

TOM

Awww.

JIM

I tell you it's done a helluva lot for me.
(IMAGE: EXECUTIVE AT DESK.)

TOM

In what respect?

JIM

In every! Ask yourself what is the difference between you an' me and men in the office down front? Brains?—No! —Ability?—No! Then what? Just one little thing—

TOM

What is that one little thing?

JIM

Primarily it amounts to—social poise! Being able to square up to people and hold your own on any social level!

AMANDA
(Off stage)

Tom?

TOM

Yes, Mother?

AMANDA

Is that you and Mr. O'Connor?

TOM

Yes, Mother.

AMANDA

Well, you just make yourselves comfortable in there.

TOM

Yes, Mother.

AMANDA

Ask Mr. O'Connor if he would like to wash his hands.

JIM

Aw, no—no—thank you—I took care of that at the warehouse. Tom—

TOM

Yes?

JIM

Mr. Mendoza was speaking to me about you.

TOM

Favorably?

JIM

What do you think?

TOM

Well—

JIM

You're going to be out of a job if you don't wake up.

TOM

I am waking up—

JIM

You show no signs.

TOM

The signs are interior.
(IMAGE ON SCREEN: THE SAILING VESSEL WITH JOLLY ROGER AGAIN.)

TOM

I'm planning to change. (*He leans over the rail speaking with quiet exhilaration. The incandescent marquees and signs of the first-run movie houses light his face from across the alley. He looks like a voyager*) I'm right at the point of committing myself to a future that doesn't include the warehouse of Mr. Mendoza or even a night-school course in public speaking.

JIM

What are you gassing about?

TOM

I'm tired of the movies.

JIM

Movies!

TOM

Yes, movies! Look at them—(*A wave toward the marvels of Grand Avenue*) All of those glamorous people —having adventures—hogging it all, gobbling the whole thing up! You know what happens? People go to the *movies* instead of *moving!* Hollywood characters are supposed to have all the adventures for everybody in America, while everybody in America sits in a dark room and watches them have them! Yes, until there's a war. That's when adventure becomes available to the masses! *Everyone's* dish, not only Gable's! Then the people in the dark room come out of the dark room to have some adventures themselves—Goody, goody!—It's our turn now, to go to the South Sea Island —to make a safari—to be exotic, far-off!—But I'm not patient. I don't want to wait until then. I'm tired of the *movies* and I am *about* to *move!*

JIM
(*Incredulously*)

Move?

TOM

Yes.

JIM

When?

TOM

Soon!

JIM

Where? Where?
(THEME THREE MUSIC SEEMS TO ANSWER THE QUESTION, WHILE TOM THINKS IT OVER. HE SEARCHES AMONG HIS POCKETS.)

TOM

I'm starting to boil inside. I know I seem dreamy, but inside—well, I'm boiling!—Whenever I pick up a shoe, I shudder a little thinking how short life is and what I am doing!—Whatever that means, I know it doesn't mean shoes —except as something to wear on a traveler's feet! (*Finds paper*) Look—

JIM

What?

TOM

I'm a member.

JIM
(*Reading*)

The Union of Merchant Seamen.

TOM

I paid my dues this month, instead of the light bill.

JIM

You will regret it when they turn the lights off.

TOM

I won't be here.

JIM

How about your mother?

TOM

I'm like my father. The bastard son of a bastard! See how he grins? And he's been absent going on sixteen years!

JIM

You're just talking, you drip. How does your mother feel about it?

TOM

Shhh!—Here comes Mother! Mother is not acquainted with my plans!

AMANDA
(*Enters portieres*)

Where are you all?

TOM

On the terrace, Mother.
(*They start inside. She advances to them.* TOM *is distinctly shocked at her appearance. Even* JIM *blinks a little. He is making his first contact with girlish Southern vivacity and in spite of the night-school course in public speaking is somewhat thrown off the beam by the unexpected outlay of social charm.*)
(*Certain responses are attempted by* JIM *but are swept aside by*

AMANDA's *gay laughter and chatter.* TOM *is embarrassed but after the first shock* JIM *reacts very warmly. Grins and chuckles, is altogether won over.*)

(IMAGINE: AMANDA AS A GIRL).

AMANDA

(Coyly smiling, shaking her girlish ringlets)

Well, well, well, so this is Mr. O'Connor. Introductions entirely unnecessary. I've heard so much about you from my boy. I finally said to him, Tom—good gracious!—why don't you bring this paragon to supper? I'd like to meet this nice young man at the warehouse! —Instead of just hearing him sing your praises so much!

I don't know why my son is so standoffish—that's not Southern behavior!

Let's sit down and—I think we could stand a little more air in here! Tom, leave the door open. I felt a nice fresh breeze a moment ago. Where has it gone to?

Mmm, so warm already! And not quite summer, even. We're going to burn up when summer really gets started.

However, we're having—we're having a very light supper. I think light things are better fo' this time of year. The same as light clothes are. Light clothes an' light food are what warm weather calls fo'. You know our blood gets so thick during th' winter—it takes a while fo' us to *adjust* ou'selves!— when the season changes . . .

It's come so quick this year. I wasn't prepared. All of a sudden—heavens! Already summer!—I ran to the trunk an' pulled out this light dress— Terribly old! Historical almost! But feels so good—so good an' co-ol, y' know. . . .

TOM

Mother—

AMANDA

Yes, honey?

TOM

How about—supper?

AMANDA

Honey, you go ask Sister if supper is ready! You know that Sister is in full charge of supper!

Tell her you hungry boys are waiting for it.

(*To* JIM.)

Have you met Laura?

JIM

She—

AMANDA

Let you in? Oh, good, you've met already! It's rare for a girl as sweet an' pretty as Laura to be domestic! But Laura is, thank heavens, not only pretty but also very domestic. I'm not at all. I never was a bit. I never could make a thing but angel-food cake. Well, in the South we had so many servants. Gone, gone, gone. All vestiges of gracious living! Gone completely! I wasn't prepared for what the future brought me. All of my gentlemen callers were sons of planters and so of course I assumed that I would be married to one and raise my family on a large piece of land with plenty of servants. But man proposes—and woman accepts the proposal!—To vary that old, old saying a little bit— I married no planter! I married a man who worked for the telephone company! —That gallantly smiling gentleman over there! (*Points to the picture*) A telephone man who—fell in love with long-distance!—Now he travels and I don't even know where!—But what am I going on for about my—tribulations? Tell me yours—I hope you don't have any!

Tom?

TOM

(Returning)

Yes, Mother?

AMANDA

Is supper nearly ready?

TOM

It looks to me like supper is on the table.

AMANDA

Let me look— (*She rises prettily and looks through portieres*) Oh, lovely!— But where is Sister?

TOM

Laura is not feeling well and she says that she thinks she'd better not come to the table.

AMANDA

What?— Nonsense!— Laura? Oh, Laura!

LAURA

(*Off stage, faintly*)
Yes, Mother.

AMANDA

You really must come to the table. We won't be seated until you come to the table!

Come in, Mr. O'Connor. You sit over there, and I'll—

Laura? Laura Wingfield!

You're keeping us waiting, honey! We can't say grace until you come to the table!

(*The back door is pushed weakly open and* LAURA *comes in. She is obviously quite faint, her lips trembling, her eyes wide and staring. She moves unsteadily toward the table.*)

(LEGEND: "TERROR!")

(*Outside a summer storm is coming abruptly. The white curtains billow inward at the windows and there is a sorrowful murmur and deep blue dusk.*)

(LAURA *suddenly stumbles—she catches at a chair with a faint moan.*)

TOM

Laura!

AMANDA

Laura!

(*There is a clap of thunder.*)
(LEGEND: "AH!")
(*Despairingly*)

Why, Laura, you *are* sick, darling! Tom, help your sister into the living room, dear!

Sit in the living room, Laura—rest on the sofa.

Well!

(*To the gentleman caller.*)

Standing over the hot stove made her ill!—I told her that it was just too warm this evening, but—

(TOM *comes back in.* LAURA *is on the sofa.*)

Is Laura all right now?

TOM

Yes.

AMANDA

What *is* that? Rain? A nice cool rain has come up!

(*She gives the gentleman caller a frightened look.*)

I think we may—have grace— now . . .

(TOM *looks at her stupidly.*)

Tom, honey—you say grace!

TOM

Oh . . .

"For these and all thy mercies—"

(*They bow their heads,* AMANDA *stealing a nervous glance at* JIM. *In the living room* LAURA, *stretched on the sofa, clenches her hand to her lips, to hold back a shuddering sob.*)

God's Holy Name be praised—

THE SCENE DIMS OUT

Scene VII

A Souvenir.

Half an hour later. Dinner is just being finished in the upstage area which is concealed by the drawn portieres.

As the curtain rises LAURA *is still huddled upon the sofa, her feet drawn under her, her head resting on a pale blue pillow, her eyes wide and mysteriously watchful. The new floor lamp with its share of rose-colored silk gives a soft, becoming light to her face, bringing out the fragile, unearthly prettiness which usually escapes attention. There is a steady murmur of rain, but it is slackening and stops soon after the scene begins; the air becomes pale and luminous as the moon breaks out. A moment after the curtain rises, the lights in both rooms flicker and go out.*

JIM

Hey, there, Mr. Light Bulb!
  (AMANDA *laughs nervously.*)
  (LEGEND: "SUSPENSION OF A
PUBLIC SERVICE.")

AMANDA

Where was Moses when the lights went out? Ha-ha. Do you know the answer to that one, Mr. O'Connor?

JIM

No, Ma'am, what's the answer?

AMANDA

In the dark!
  (JIM *laughs appreciatively.*)
Everybody sit still. I'll light the candles. Isn't it lucky we have them on the table? Where's a match? Which of you gentlemen can provide a watch?

JIM

Here.

AMANDA

Thank you, sir.

JIM

Not at all, Ma'am!

AMANDA

I guess the fuse has burnt out. Mr. O'Connor, can you tell a burnt-out fuse? I know I can't and Tom is a total loss when it comes to mechanics.
  (SOUND: GETTING UP: VOICES
RECEDE A LITTLE TO KITCHEN-
ETTE.)
Oh, be careful you don't bump into something. We don't want our gentle-man caller to break his neck. Now wouldn't that be a fine howdy-do?

JIM

Ha-ha!
Where is the fuse-box?

AMANDA

Right here next to the stove. Can you see anything?

JIM

Just a minute.

AMANDA

Isn't electricity a mysterious thing?
Wasn't it Benjamin Franklin who tied a key to a kite?
We live in such a mysterious universe, don't we? Some people say that science clears up all the mysteries for us. In my opinion it only creates more!
Have you found it yet?

JIM

No, Ma'am. All these fuses look okay to me.

AMANDA

Tom!

TOM

Yes, Mother?

AMANDA

That light bill I gave you several days ago. The one I told you we got the notices about?
  (LEGEND: "HA!")

TOM

Oh.—Yeah.

AMANDA

You didn't neglect to pay it by any chance?

TOM

Why, I—

AMANDA

Didn't! I might have known it!

JIM

Shakespeare probably wrote a poem on that light bill, Mrs. Wingfield.

AMANDA

I might have known better than to trust him with it! There's such a high price for negligence in this world!

JIM

Maybe the poem will win a ten-dollar prize.

AMANDA

We'll just have to spend the remainder of the evening in the nineteenth century, before Mr. Edison made the Mazda lamp!

JIM

Candlelight is my favorite kind of light.

AMANDA

That shows you're romantic! But that's no excuse for Tom.

Well, we got through dinner. Very considerate of them to let us get through dinner before they plunged us into everlasting darkness, wasn't it, Mr. O'Connor?

JIM

Ha-ha!

AMANDA

Tom, as a penalty for your carelessness you can help me with the dishes.

JIM

Let me give you a hand.

AMANDA

Indeed you will not!

JIM

I ought to be good for something.

AMANDA

Good for something? (*Her tone is rhapsodic.*)

You? Why, Mr. O'Connor, nobody, *nobody's* given me this much entertainment in years—as you have!

JIM

Aw, now, Mrs. Wingfield!

AMANDA

I'm not exaggerating, not one bit! But Sister is all by her lonesome. You go keep her company in the parlor!

I'll give you this lovely old candelabrum that used to be on the altar at the church of the Heavenly Rest. It was melted a little out of shape when the church burnt down. Lightning struck it one spring. Gypsy Jones was holding a revival at the time and he intimated that the church was destroyed because the Episcopalians gave card parties.

JIM

Ha-ha.

AMANDA

And how about you coaxing Sister to drink a little wine? I think it would be good for her! Can you carry both at once?

JIM

Sure. I'm Superman!

AMANDA

Now, Thomas, get into this apron!
(*The door of kitchenette swings closed on* AMANDA's *gay laughter; the flickering light approaches the portieres.*)
(LAURA *sits up nervously as he enters. Her speech at first is low and breathless from the almost intolerable strain of being alone with a stranger.*)
(THE LEGEND: "I DON'T SUPPOSE YOU REMEMBER ME AT ALL!")
(*In her first speeches in this scene, before* JIM's *warmth overcomes her paralyzing shyness,* LAURA's *voice is thin and breathless as though she has just run up a steep flight of stairs.*)
(JIM's *attitude is gently humorous. In playing this scene it should be stressed that while the incident is apparently unimportant, it is to* LAURA *the climax of her secret life.*)

JIM

Hello, there, Laura.

LAURA

(*Faintly*)

Hello. (*She clears her throat.*)

JIM
How are you feeling now? Better?

LAURA
Yes. Yes, thank you.

JIM
This is for you. A little dandelion wine. (*He extends it toward her with extravagant gallantry.*)

LAURA
Thank you.

JIM
Drink it—but don't get drunk!
(*He laughs heartily.* LAURA *takes the glass uncertainly; laughs shyly.*)
Where shall I set the candles?

LAURA
Oh—oh, anywhere . . .

JIM
How about here on the floor? Any objections?

LAURA
No.

JIM
I'll spread a newspaper under to catch the drippings. I like to sit on the floor. Mind if I do?

LAURA
Oh, no.

JIM
Give me a pillow?

LAURA
What?

JIM
A pillow!

LAURA
Oh . . . (*Hands him one quickly.*)

JIM
How about you? Don't you like to sit on the floor?

LAURA
Oh—yes.

JIM
Why don't you, then?

LAURA
I—will.

JIM
Take a pillow! (LAURA *does. Sits on the other side of the candelabrum.* JIM *crosses his legs and smiles engagingly at her*) I can't hardly see you sitting way over there.

LAURA
I can—see you.

JIM
I know, but that's not fair, I'm in the limelight. (LAURA *moves her pillow closer*) Good! Now I can see you! Comfortable?

LAURA
Yes.

JIM
So am I. Comfortable as a cow! Will you have some gum?

LAURA
No, thank you.

JIM
I think that I will indulge, with your permission. (*Musingly unwraps it and holds it up*) Think of the fortune made by the guy that invented the first piece of chewing gum. Amazing, huh? The Wrigley Building is one of the sights of Chicago.—I saw it summer before last when I went up to the Century of Progress. Did you take in the Century of Progress?

LAURA
No, I didn't.

JIM
Well, it was quite a wonderful exposition. What impressed me most was the Hall of Science. Gives you an idea of what the future will be in America, even more wonderful than the present time is! (*Pause. Smiling at her*) Your brother tells me you're shy. Is that right, Laura?

LAURA
I—don't know.

JIM

I judge you to be an old-fashioned type of girl. Well, I think that's a pretty good type to be. Hope you don't think I'm being too personal—do you?

LAURA

(*Hastily, out of embarrassment*)
I believe I *will* take a piece of gum, if you—don't mind. (*Clearing her throat*) Mr. O'Connor, have you—kept up with your singing?

JIM

Singing? Me?

LAURA

Yes. I remember what a beautiful voice you had.

JIM

When did you hear me sing?
(VOICE OFF STAGE IN THE PAUSE.)

VOICE

O blow, ye winds, heigh-ho,
A-roving I will go!
I'm off to my love
With a boxing glove—
Ten thousand miles away!

JIM

You say you've heard me sing?

LAURA

Oh, yes! Yes, very often . . . I—don't suppose—you remember me—at all?

JIM

(*Smiling doubtfully*)
You know I have an idea I've seen you before. I had that idea soon as you opened the door. It seemed almost like I was about to remember your name. But the name that I started to call you —wasn't a name! And so I stopped myself before I said it.

LAURA

Wasn't it—Blue Roses?

JIM

(*Springs up. Grinning*)
Blue Roses!—My gosh, yes—Blue Roses!
That's what I had on my tongue when you opened the door!

Isn't it funny what tricks your memory plays? I didn't connect you with high school somehow or other.

But that's where it was; it was high school. I didn't even know you were Shakespeare's sister!
Gosh, I'm sorry.

LAURA

I didn't expect you to. You—barely knew me!

JIM

But we did have a speaking acquaintance, huh?

LAURA

Yes, we—spoke to each other.

JIM

When did you recognize me?

LAURA

Oh, right away!

JIM

Soon as I came in the door?

LAURA

When I heard your name I thought it was probably you. I knew that Tom used to know you a little in high school. So when you came in the door—
Well, then I was—sure.

JIM

Why didn't you *say* something, then?

LAURA

(*Breathlessly*)
I didn't know what to say, I was— too surprised!

JIM

For goodness' sakes! You know, this sure is funny!

LAURA

Yes! Yes, isn't it, though . . .

JIM

Didn't we have a class in something together?

LAURA

Yes, we did.

JIM

What class was that?

LAURA

It was—singing—Chorus!

JIM

Aw!

LAURA

I sat across the aisle from you in the Aud.

JIM

Aw.

LAURA

Mondays, Wednesdays and Fridays.

JIM

Now I remember—you always came in late.

LAURA

Yes, it was so hard for me, getting upstairs. I had that brace on my leg—it clumped so loud!

JIM

I never heard any clumping.

LAURA

(*Wincing at the recollection*)
To me it sounded like—thunder!

JIM

Well, well, well, I never even noticed.

LAURA

And everybody was seated before I came in. I had to walk in front of all those people. My seat was in the back row. I had to go clumping all the way up the aisle with everyone watching!

JIM

You shouldn't have been selfconscious.

LAURA

I know, but I was. It was always such a relief when the singing started.

JIM

Aw, yes, I've placed you now! I used to call you Blue Roses. How was it that I got started calling you that?

LAURA

I was out of school a little while with pleurosis. When I came back you asked me what was the matter. I said I had pleurosis—you thought I said Blue Roses. That's what you always called me after that!

JIM

I hope you didn't mind.

LAURA

Oh, no—I liked it. You see, I wasn't acquainted with many—people. . . .

JIM

As I remember you sort of stuck by yourself.

LAURA

I—I—never have had much luck at—making friends.

JIM

I don't see why you wouldn't.

LAURA

Well, I—started out badly.

JIM

You mean being—

LAURA

Yes, it sort of—stood between me—

JIM

You shouldn't have let it!

LAURA

I know, but it did, and—

JIM

You were shy with people!

LAURA

I tried not to be but never could—

JIM

Overcome it?

LAURA

No, I—I never could!

JIM

I guess being shy is something you have to work out of kind of gradually.

LAURA

(*Sorrowfully*)
Yes—I guess it—

JIM

Takes time!

LAURA

Yes—

JIM

People are not so dreadful when you know them. That's what you have to remember! And everybody has problems. Not just you, but practically everybody has got some problems.

You think of yourself as having the only problems, as being the only one who is disappointed. But just look around you and you will see lots of people as disappointed as you are. For instance, I hoped when I was going to high school that I would be further along at this time, six years later, than I am now— You remember that wonderful write-up I had in *The Torch?*

LAURA

Yes! (*She rises and crosses to table.*)

JIM

It said I was bound to succeed in anything I went into! (LAURA *returns with the annual*) Holy Jeez! *The Torch!* (*He accepts it reverently. They smile across it with mutual wonder.* LAURA *crouches beside him and they begin to turn through it.* LAURA's *shyness is dissolving in his warmth.*)

LAURA

Here you are in *The Pirates of Penzance!*

JIM

(*Wistfully*)

I sang the baritone lead in that operetta.

LAURA

(*Raptly*)

So—*beautifully!*

JIM

(*Protesting*)

Aw—

LAURA

Yes, yes—beautifully—beautifully!

JIM

You heard me?

LAURA

All three times!

JIM

No!

LAURA

Yes!

JIM

All three performances?

LAURA

(*Looking down*)

Yes.

JIM

Why?

LAURA

I—wanted to ask you to—autograph my program.

JIM

Why didn't you ask me to?

LAURA

You were always surrounded by your own friends so much that I never had a chance to.

JIM

You should have just—

LAURA

Well, I—thought you might think I was—

JIM

Thought I might think you was—what?

LAURA

Oh—

JIM

(*With reflective relish*)

I was beleaguered by females in those days.

LAURA

You were terribly popular!

JIM

Yeah—

LAURA

You had such a—friendly way—

JIM

I was spoiled in high school.

LAURA

Everybody—liked you!

JIM

Including you?

LAURA

I—yes, I—I did, too— (*She gently closes the book in her lap*)

JIM

Well, well, well!—Give me that program, Laura. (*She hands it to him. He signs it with a flourish*) There you are—better late than never!

LAURA

Oh, I—what a—surprise!

JIM

My signature isn't worth very much right now.

But some day—maybe—it will increase in value!

Being disappointed is one thing and being discouraged is something else. I am disappointed but I am not discouraged.

I'm twenty-three years old.

How old are you?

LAURA

I'll be twenty-four in June.

JIM

That's not old age!

LAURA

No, but—

JIM

You finished high school?

LAURA

(*With difficulty*)

I didn't go back.

JIM

You mean you dropped out?

LAURA

I made bad grades in my final examinations. (*She rises and replaces the book and the program. Her voice strained*) How is—Emily Meisenbach getting along?

JIM

Oh, that kraut-head!

LAURA

Why do you call her that?

JIM

That's what she was.

LAURA

You're not still—going with her?

JIM

I never see her.

LAURA

It said in the Personal Section that you were—engaged!

JIM

I know, but I wasn't impressed by that—propaganda!

LAURA

It wasn't—the truth?

JIM

Only in Emily's optimistic opinion!

LAURA

Oh—

(LEGEND: "WHAT HAVE YOU DONE SINCE HIGH SCHOOL?")

(JIM *lights a cigarette and leans indolently back on his elbows smiling at* LAURA *with a warmth and charm which lights her inwardly with altar candles. She remains by the table and turns in her hands a piece of glass to cover her tumult.*)

JIM

(*After several reflective puffs on a cigarette*)

What have you done since high school? (*She seems not to hear him*) Huh? (LAURA *looks up*) I said what have you done since high school, Laura?

LAURA
Nothing much.

JIM
You must have been doing something these six long years.

LAURA
Yes.

JIM
Well, then, such as what?

LAURA
I took a business course at business college—

JIM
How did that work out?

LAURA
Well, not very—well—I had to drop out, it gave me—indigestion—
(JIM *laughs gently.*)

JIM
What are you doing now?

LAURA
I don't do anything—much. Oh, please don't think I sit around doing nothing! My glass collection takes up a good deal of time. Glass is something you have to take good care of.

JIM
What did you say—about glass?

LAURA
Collection I said—I have one— (*She clears her throat and turns away again, acutely shy.*)

JIM
You know what I judge to be the trouble with you?
Inferiority complex! Know what that is? That's what they call it when some-one low-rates himself!
I understand it because I had it, too. Although my case was not so aggravated as yours seems to be. I had it until I took up public speaking, developed my voice, and learned that I had an apti-tude for science. Before that time I never thought of myself as being out-standing in any way whatsoever!

Now I've never made a regular study of it, but I have a friend who says I can analyze people better than doctors that make a profession of it. I don't claim that to be necessarily true, but I can sure guess a person's psychology, Laura! (*Takes out his gum*) Excuse me, Laura. I always take it out when the flavor is gone. I'll use this scrap of paper to wrap it in. I know how it is to get it stuck on a shoe.

Yep—that's what I judge to be your principal trouble. A lack of confidence in yourself as a person. You don't have the proper amount of faith in yourself. I'm basing that fact on a number of your remarks and also on certain observations I've made. For instance that clumping you thought was so awful in high school. You say that you even dreaded to walk into class. You see what you did? You dropped out of school, you gave up an education because of a clump, which as far as I know was practically non-existent! A little physical defect is what you have. Hardly noticeable even! Mag-nified thousands of times by imagination!

You know what my strong advice to you is? Think of yourself as *superior* in some way!

LAURA
In what way would I think?

JIM
Why, man alive, Laura! Just look about you a little. What do you see? A world full of common people! All of 'em born and all of 'em going to die!

Which of them has one-tenth of your good points! Or mine! Or anyone else's, as far as that goes—Gosh!

Everybody excels in some one thing. Some in many!
(*Unconsciously glances at himself in the mirror.*)
All you've got to do is discover in *what!*

Take me, for instance.
(*He adjusts his tie at the mirror.*)

My interest happens to lie in electro-dynamics. I'm taking a course in radio engineering at night school, Laura, on top of a fairly responsible job at the warehouse. I'm taking that course and studying public speaking.

LAURA

Ohhhh.

JIM

Because I believe in the future of television!

(*Turning back to her.*)

I wish to be ready to go up right along with it. Therefore I'm planning to get in on the ground floor. In fact I've already made the right connections and all that remains is for the industry itself to get under way! Full steam—

(*His eyes are starry.*)

Knowledge — Zzzzzp! *Money* — *Zzzzzzp!* — *Power!*

That's the cycle democracy is built on!

(*His attitude is convincingly dynamic.* LAURA *stares at him, even her shyness eclipsed in her absolute wonder. He suddenly grins.*)

I guess you think I think a lot of myself!

LAURA

No—o-o-o, I—

JIM

Now how about you? Isn't there something you take more interest in than anything else?

LAURA

Well, I do—as I said—have my—glass collection—

(*A peal of girlish laughter from the kitchen.*)

JIM

I'm not right sure I know what you're talking about.

What kind of glass is it?

LAURA

Little articles of it, they're ornaments mostly!

Most of them are little animals made out of glass, the tiniest little animals in the world. Mother calls them a glass menagerie!

Here's an example of one, if you'd like to see it!

This one is one of the oldest. It's nearly thirteen.

(MUSIC: "THE GLASS MENAGERIE.")

(*He stretches out his hand.*)

Oh, be careful—if you breathe, it breaks!

JIM

I'd better not take it. I'm pretty clumsy with things.

LAURA

Go on, I trust you with him!

(*Places it in his palm*)

There now—you're holding him gently!

Hold him over the light, he loves the light! You see how the light shines through him?

JIM

It sure does shine!

LAURA

I shouldn't be partial, but he is my favorite one.

JIM

What kind of a thing is this one supposed to be?

LAURA

Haven't you noticed the single horn on his forehead?

JIM

A unicorn, huh?

LAURA

Mmm-hmmm!

JIM

Unicorns, aren't they extinct in the modern world?

LAURA

I know!

JIM

Poor little fellow, he must feel sort of lonesome.

LAURA
(*Smiling*)
Well, if he does he doesn't complain about it. He stays on a shelf with some horses that don't have horns and all of them seem to get along nicely together.

JIM
How do you know?

LAURA
(*Lightly*)
I haven't heard any arguments among them!

JIM
(*Grinning*)
No arguments, huh? Well, that's a pretty good sign!
Where shall I set him?

LAURA
Put him on the table. They all like a change of scenery once in a while!

JIM
(*Stretching*)
Well, well, well, well—
Look how big my shadow is when I stretch!

LAURA
Oh, oh, yes—it stretches across the ceiling!

JIM
(*Crossing to door*)
I think it's stopped raining. (*Opens fire-escape door*) Where does the music come from?

LAURA
From the Paradise Dance Hall across the alley.

JIM
How about cutting the rug a little, Miss Wingfield?

LAURA
Oh, I—

JIM
Or is your program filled up? Let me have a look at it. (*Grasps imaginary card*) Why, every dance is taken! I'll

just have to scratch some out. (WALTZ MUSIC: "LA GOLONDRINA") Ahhh, a waltz! (*He executes some sweeping turns by himself then holds his arms toward* LAURA.)

LAURA
(*Breathlessly*)
I—can't dance!

JIM
There you go, that inferiority stuff!

LAURA
I've never danced in my life!

JIM
Come on, try!

LAURA
Oh, but I'd step on you!

JIM
I'm not made out of glass.

LAURA
How—how—how do we start?

JIM
Just leave it to me. You hold your arms out a little.

LAURA
Like this?

JIM
A little bit higher. Right. Now don't tighten up, that's the main thing about it—relax.

LAURA
(*Laughing breathlessly*)
It's hard not to.

JIM
Okay.

LAURA
I'm afraid you can't budge me.

JIM
What do you bet I can't. (*He swings her into motion.*)

LAURA
Goodness, yes, you can!

JIM

Let yourself go, now, Laura, just let yourself go.

LAURA

I'm—

JIM

Come on!

LAURA

Trying!

JIM

Not so stiff— Easy does it!

LAURA

I know but I'm—

JIM

Loosen th' backbone! There now, that's a lot better.

LAURA

Am I?

JIM

Lots, lots better! (*He moves her about the room in a clumsy waltz.*)

LAURA

Oh, my!

JIM

Ha-ha!

LAURA

Oh, my goodness!

JIM

Ha-ha-ha! (*They suddenly bump into the table.* JIM *stops*) What did we hit on?

LAURA

Table.

JIM

Did something fall off it? I think—

LAURA

Yes.

JIM

I hope that it wasn't the little glass horse with the horn!

LAURA

Yes.

JIM

Aw, aw, aw. Is it broken?

LAURA

Now it is just like all the other horses.

JIM

It's lost its—

LAURA

Horn!
It doesn't matter. Maybe it's a blessing in disguise.

JIM

You'll never forgive me. I bet that that was your favorite piece of glass.

LAURA

I don't have favorites much. It's no tragedy, Freckles. Glass breaks so easily. No matter how careful you are. The traffic jars the shelves and things fall off them.

JIM

Still I'm awfully sorry that I was the cause.

LAURA
(*Smiling*)

I'll just imagine he had an operation. The horn was removed to make him feel less—freakish!
(*They both laugh.*)
Now he will feel more at home with the other horses, the ones that don't have horns. . .

JIM

Ha-ha, that's very funny!
(*Suddenly serious.*)
I'm glad to see that you have a sense of humor.
You know—you're—well—very different!
Surprisingly different from anyone else I know!
(*His voice becomes soft and hesitant with a genuine feeling.*)
Do you mind me telling you that?
(LAURA *is abashed beyond speech.*)
I mean it in a nice way . . .
(LAURA *nods shyly, looking away.*)

You make me feel sort of—I don't know how to put it!

I'm usually pretty good at expressing things, but—

This is something that I don't know how to say!

(LAURA *touches her throat and clears it—turns the broken unicorn in her hands.*)

(*Even softer.*)

Has anyone ever told you that you were pretty?

(PAUSE: MUSIC.)

(LAURA *looks up slowly, with wonder, and shakes her head.*)

Well, you are! In a very different way from anyone else.

And all the nicer because of the difference, too.

(*His voice becomes low and husky.* LAURA *turns away, nearly faint with the novelty of her emotions.*)

I wish that you were my sister. I'd teach you to have some confidence in yourself. The different people are not like other people, but being different is nothing to be ashamed of. Because other people are not such wonderful people. They're one hundred times one thousand. You're one times one! They walk all over the earth. You just stay here. They're common as—weeds, but—you—well, you're—*Blue Roses!*

(IMAGE ON SCREEN: BLUE ROSES.)

(MUSIC CHANGES.)

LAURA

But blue is wrong for—roses . . .

JIM

It's right for you!—You're—pretty!

LAURA

In what respect am I pretty?

JIM

In all respects—believe me! Your eyes—your hair—are pretty! Your hands are pretty!

(*He catches hold of her hand.*)

You think I'm making this up because I'm invited to dinner and have to be nice. Oh, I could do that! I could put on an act for you, Laura, and say lots of things without being very sincere. But this time I am. I'm talking to you sincerely. I happened to notice you had this inferiority complex that keeps you from feeling comfortable with people. Somebody needs to build your confidence up and make you proud instead of shy and turning away and—blushing—

Somebody—ought to—

Ought to—*kiss* you, Laura!

(*His hand slips slowly up her arm to her shoulder.*)

(MUSIC SWELLS TUMULTOUSLY.)

(*He suddenly turns her about and kisses her on the lips.*)

(*When he releases her,* LAURA *sinks on the sofa with a bright, dazed look.*)

(JIM *backs away and fishes in his pocket for a cigarette.*)

(LEGEND ON SCREEN: "SOUVE-NIR.")

Stumble-john!

(*He lights the cigarette, avoiding her look.*)

(*There is a peal of girlish laughter from* AMANDA *in the kitchen.*)

(LAURA *slowly raises and opens her hand. It still contains the little broken glass animal. She looks at it with a tender, bewildered expression.*)

Stumble-john!

I shouldn't have done that— That was way off the beam.

You don't smoke, do you?

(*She looks up, smiling, not hearing the question.*)

(*He sits beside her a little gingerly. She looks at him speechlessly—waiting.*)

(*He coughs decorously and moves a little farther aside as he considers the situation and senses her feelings, dimly, with perturbation.*)

(*Gently.*)

Would you—care for a—mint?

(*She doesn't seem to hear him but her look grows brighter even.*)

Peppermint—Life-Saver?

My pocket's a regular drug store—
wherever I go . . .

(*He pops a mint in his mouth.
Then gulps and decides to make a
clean breast of it. He speaks slowly
and gingerly.*)

Laura, you know, if I had a sister like
you, I'd do the same thing as Tom. I'd
bring out fellows and—introduce her to
them. The right type of boys of a type
to—appreciate her.

Only—well—he made a mistake
about me.

Maybe I've got no call to be saying
this. That may not have been the idea
in having me over. But what if it was?

There's nothing wrong about that.
The only trouble is that in my case—
I'm not in a situation to—do the right
thing.

I can't take down your number and
say I'll phone.

I can't call up next week and—ask for
a date.

I thought I had better explain the
situation in case you—misunderstood it
and—hurt your feelings. . . .

(*Pause.*)

(*Slowly, very slowly, LAURA's look
changes, her eyes returning slowly
from his to the ornament in her
palm.*)

(AMANDA *utters another gay laugh
in the kitchen.*)

LAURA
(*Faintly*)
You—won't—call again?

JIM
No, Laura, I can't.

(*He rises from the sofa.*)

As I was just explaining, I've—got
strings on me.

Laura, I've—been going steady!

I go out all of the time with a girl
named Betty. She's a home-girl like you,
and Catholic, and Irish, and in a great
many ways we—get along fine.

I met her last summer on a moonlight boat trip up the river to Alton,
on the *Majestic*.

Well—right away from the start it
was—love!

(LEGEND: LOVE!)

(LAURA *sways slightly forward and
grips the arm of the sofa. He fails
to notice, now enrapt in his own
comfortable being.*)

Being in love has made a new man
of me!

(*Leaning stiffly forward, clutching
the arm of the sofa,* LAURA *struggles
visibly with her storm. But* JIM *is
oblivious, she is a long way off.*)

The power of love is really pretty
tremendous!

Love is something that—changes the
whole world, Laura!

(*The storm abates a little and*
LAURA *leans back. He notices her
again.*)

It happened that Betty's aunt took
sick, she got a wire and had to go to
Centralia. So Tom—when he asked me
to dinner—I naturally just accepted the
invitation, not knowing that you—that
he—that I—

(*He stops awkwardly.*)

Huh—I'm a stumble-john!

(*He flops back on the sofa.*)

(*The holy candles in the altar of*
LAURA's *face have been snuffed out.
There is a look of almost infinite
desolation.*)

(JIM *glances at her uneasily.*)

I wish that you would—say something. (*She bites her lip which was
trembling and then bravely smiles. She
opens her hand again on the broken
glass ornament. Then she gently takes
his hand and raises it level with her own.
She carefully places the unicorn in the
palm of his hand, then pushes his fingers
closed upon it*) What are you—doing
that for? You want me to have him?—
Laura? (*She nods*) What for?

LAURA
A—souvenir . . .

(*She rises unsteadily and crouches
beside the victrola to wind it up.*)

(LEGEND ON SCREEN: "THINGS

HAVE A WAY OF TURNING OUT
SO BADLY!")
(OR IMAGE: "GENTLEMAN CALLER
WAVING GOOD-BYE!—GAILY.")
(*At this moment* AMANDA *rushes
brightly back in the front room.
She bears a pitcher of fruit punch
in an old-fashioned cut-glass pitcher
and a plate of macaroons. The plate
has a gold border and poppies
painted on it.*)

AMANDA

Well, well, well! Isn't the air delight-
ful after the shower?
I've made you children a little liquid
refreshment.
(*Turns gaily to the gentleman
caller*)
Jim, do you know that song about
lemonade?
"Lemonade, lemonade
Made in the shade and stirred
with a spade—
Good enough for any old maid!"

JIM
(*Uneasily*)
Ha-ha! No—I never heard it.

AMANDA

Why, Laura! You look so serious!

JIM

We were having a serious conversation.

AMANDA

Good! Now you're better acquainted!

JIM
(*Uncertainly*)
Ha-ha! Yes.

AMANDA

You modern young people are much
more serious-minded than my generation. I was so gay as a girl!

JIM

You haven't changed, Mrs. Wingfield.

AMANDA

Tonight I'm rejuvenated! The gaiety
of the occasion, Mr. O'Connor!

(*She tosses her head with a peal
of laughter. Spills lemonade.*)
Oooo! I'm baptizing myself!

JIM

Here—let me—

AMANDA
(*Setting the pitcher down*)
There now. I discovered we had some
maraschino cherries. I dumped them in,
juice and all!

JIM

You shouldn't have gone to that
trouble, Mrs. Wingfield.

AMANDA

Trouble, trouble? Why, it was loads
of fun!
Didn't you hear me cutting up in the
kitchen? I bet your ears were burning!
I told Tom how outdone with him I
was for keeping you to himself so long
a time! He should have brought you
over much, much sooner! Well, now
that you've found your way, I want you
to be a very frequent caller! Not just
occasional but all the time.
Oh, we're going to have a lot of gay
times together! I see them coming!
Mmm, just breathe that air! So fresh,
and the moon's so pretty!
I'll skip back out—I know where my
place is when young folks are having
a—serious conversation!

JIM

Oh, don't go out, Mrs. Wingfield. The
fact of the matter is I've got to be going.

AMANDA

Going, now? You're joking! Why, it's
only the shank of the evening, Mr.
O'Connor!

JIM

Well, you know how it is.

AMANDA

You mean you're a young working-
man and have to keep workingmen's
hours. We'll let you off early tonight.
But only on the condition that next time
you stay later.

What's the best night for you? Isn't Saturday night the best night for you workingmen?

JIM

I have a couple of time-clocks to punch, Mrs. Wingfield. One at morning, another one at night!

AMANDA

My, but you *are* ambitious! You work at night, too?

JIM

No, Ma'am, not work but—Betty! (*He crosses deliberately to pick up his hat. The band at the Paradise Dance Hall goes into a tender waltz.*)

AMANDA

Betty? Betty? Who's—Betty!
(*There is an ominous cracking sound in the sky.*)

JIM

Oh, just a girl. The girl I go steady with! (*He smiles charmingly. The sky falls.*)
(LEGEND: "THE SKY FALLS.")

AMANDA

(*A long-drawn exhalation*)
Ohhhh . . . Is it a serious romance, Mr. O'Connor?

JIM

We're going to be married the second Sunday in June.

AMANDA

Ohhhh—how nice!
Tom didn't mention that you were engaged to be married.

JIM

The cat's not out of the bag at the warehouse yet.
You know how they are. They call you Romeo and stuff like that.
(*He stops at the oval mirror to put on his hat. He carefully shapes the brim and the crown to give a discreetly dashing effect.*)
It's been a wonderful evening, Mrs. Wingfield. I guess this is what they mean by Southern hospitality.

AMANDA

It really wasn't anything at all.

JIM

I hope it don't seem like I'm rushing off. But I promised Betty I'd pick her up at the Wabash depot, an' by the time I get my jalopy down there her train'll be in. Some women are pretty upset if you keep 'em waiting.

AMANDA

Yes, I know— The tyranny of women!
(*Extends her hand.*)
Good-bye, Mr. O'Connor.
I wish you luck—and happiness—and success! All three of them, and so does Laura!—Don't you, Laura?

LAURA

Yes!

JIM

(*Taking her hand*)
Good-bye, Laura. I'm certainly going to treasure that souvenir. And don't you forget the good advice I gave you.
(*Raises his voice to a cheery shout.*)
So long, Shakespeare!
Thanks again, ladies— Good night!
(*He grins and ducks jauntily out.*)
(*Still bravely grimacing, AMANDA closes the door on the gentleman caller. Then she turns back to the room with a puzzled expression. She and LAURA don't dare to face each other. LAURA crouches beside the victrola to wind it.*)

AMANDA

(*Faintly*)
Things have a way of turning out so badly.
I don't believe that I would play the victrola.
Well, well—well—
Our gentleman caller was engaged to be married!
Tom!

TOM
(*From back*)
Yes, Mother?

AMANDA
Come in here a minute. I want to tell you something awfully funny.

TOM
(*Enters with macaroon and a glass of the lemonade*)
Has the gentleman caller gotten away already?

AMANDA
The gentleman caller has made an early departure.
What a wonderful joke you played on us!

TOM
How do you mean?

AMANDA
You didn't mention that he was engaged to be married.

TOM
Jim? Engaged?

AMANDA
That's what he just informed us.

TOM
I'll be jiggered! I didn't know about that.

AMANDA
That seems very peculiar.

TOM
What's peculiar about it?

AMANDA
Didn't you call him your best friend down at the warehouse?

TOM
He is, but how did I know?

AMANDA
It seems extremely peculiar that you wouldn't know your best friend was going to be married!

TOM
The warehouse is where I work, not where I know things about people!

AMANDA
You don't know things anywhere! You live in a dream; you manufacture illusions!
(*He crosses to door.*)
Where are you going?

TOM
I'm going to the movies.

AMANDA
That's right, now that you've had us make such fools of ourselves. The effort, the preparations, all the expense! The new floor lamp, the rug, the clothes for Laura! All for what? To entertain some other girl's fiancé!
Go to the movies, go! Don't think about us, a mother deserted, an unmarried sister who's crippled and has no job! Don't let anything interfere with your selfish pleasure!
Just go, go, go—to the movies!

TOM
All right, I will! The more you shout about my selfishness to me the quicker I'll go, and I won't go to the movies!

AMANDA
Go, then! Then go to the moon—you selfish dreamer!
(TOM *smashes his glass on the floor. He plunges out on the fire-escape, slamming the door.* LAURA *screams—cut by door.*)
(*Dance-hall music up.* TOM *goes to the rail and grips it desperately, lifting his face in the chill white moonlight penetrating the narrow abyss of the alley.*)
(LEGEND ON SCREEN: "AND SO GOOD-BYE . . .")
(TOM's *closing speech is timed with the interior pantomime. The interior scene is played as though viewed through soundproof glass.* AMANDA *appears to be making a comforting speech to* LAURA *who is huddled upon the sofa. Now that we cannot hear the mother's speech, her silliness is gone and she has dignity and tragic beauty.* LAURA's *dark hair hides her face until at the*

end of the speech she lifts it to smile at her mother. AMANDA's *gestures are slow and graceful, almost dancelike, as she comforts the daughter. At the end of her speech she glances a moment at the father's picture—then withdraws through the portieres. At close of* TOM's *speech,* LAURA *blows out the candles, ending the play.*)

TOM

I didn't go to the moon, I went much further—for time is the longest distance between two places—

Not long after that I was fired for writing a poem on the lid of a shoe-box.

I left Saint Louis. I descended the steps of this fire-escape for a last time and followed, from then on, in my father's footsteps, attempting to find in motion what was lost in space—

I traveled around a great deal. The cities swept about me like dead leaves, leaves that were brightly colored but torn away from the branches.

I would have stopped, but I was pursued by something.

It always came upon me unawares, taking me altogether by surprise. Perhaps it was a familiar bit of music. Perhaps it was only a piece of transparent glass—

Perhaps I am walking along a street at night, in some strange city, before I have found companions. I pass the lighted window of a shop where perfume is sold. The window is filled with pieces of colored glass, tiny transparent bottles in delicate colors, like bits of a shattered rainbow.

Then all at once my sister touches my shoulder. I turn around and look into her eyes . . .

Oh, Laura, Laura, I tried to leave you behind me, but I am more faithful than I intended to be!

I reach for a cigarette, I cross the street, I run into the movies or a bar, I buy a drink, I speak to the nearest stranger—anything that can blow your candles out!

(LAURA *bends over the candles.*)

—for nowadays the world is lit by lightning! Blow out your candles, Laura—and so good-bye. . . .

(*She blows the candles out.*)

THE SCENE DISSOLVES

Jules Feiffer (1929–   )
LITTLE MURDERS

"Two, four, six, eight—who do we assassinate?"
—*New York children's street chant, circa 1964*

CHARACTERS

MARJORIE NEWQUIST	PATSY NEWQUIST	REVEREND DUPAS
KENNY NEWQUIST	ALFRED CHAMBERLAIN	ASSORTED WEDDING GUESTS
CAROL NEWQUIST	JUDGE STERN	LIEUTENANT PRACTICE

Synopsis of Scenes

Act I

SCENE I *The Newquist apartment*
SCENE II *The Newquist apartment, one month later*
SCENE III *The Newquist apartment, two months later*

Act II

SCENE I *The Newquist apartment, four hours later*
SCENE II *The Newquist apartment, six months later*

Act I

SCENE ONE

A view of the Newquist apartment. The living room, dining area, foyer and front door slowly fade into view (by means of a scrim or any other workable method), in sync with the rising sound of city street noises. The apartment is typically Upper West Side, dominated by overstuffed furniture, enormous multipaned windows and walls with too much molding. At the moment, mid-morning, it is empty. As the apartment fades into view the level of noise rises—morning noises: construction, traffic and helicopters. In the next few minutes both light and noise change: shadows shift, lengthen and darken in sync with the fading of construction sounds, replaced by the late afternoon cries of children at play. This too fades into the quieter monotone of early evening traffic.

The apartment darkens accordingly and we may even see the setting sun as reflected in the apartment windows across the street. (The only view of the world outside is of other buildings, other windows.) What we see is comparable to a stop-motion camera's view of the apartment, from mid-morning to dusk. Throughout, a steady patina of soot has drifted in through one of the half-open windows, and specks of plaster may now and then drop from the ceiling. The telephone rings. Other sounds: police sirens, fire engines, etc. The front door unlocks; this takes time, since there are two double locks on the door. The door slowly pushes open, revealing two enormous shopping bags. Almost completely hidden behind them is MARJORIE, *small, energetic, in her fifties. She switches on the foyer light with an elbow and bustles across to the kitchen.*

MARJORIE: Don't let a draft in! *{As she disappears through the swinging door that leads to the kitchen,* KENNY *enters reading a paperback. He is list-less, in his early twenties. Leaving the door open he starts slowly across the room, engrossed in his reading. On the return swing of the kitchen door,* MAR-JORIE *reappears sans coat and shopping bags, this time carrying a folded table-cloth and a large sponge}* I'm going to need your help, young man. *[*KENNY *enters the bathroom, closes door loudly}* Don't dawdle! *[*MARJORIE *runs sponge across dining-room table. It comes up pitch black}* Filth! *{She unfolds table-cloth in one motion. It falls perfectly into place}* They'll be here any minute, Kenny!

{She disappears into kitchen with sponge, reappears on return swing of door with serving cart piled high with dishes and silver. She is about to set table when an explosion of automobile horns drives her to window, which she slams shut with great effort. She hastens to other window and switches on air conditioner—a loud hum. CAROL *enters, carrying brief case. He is a short, thick-set, energetic man in his fifties, about* MARJORIE'S *size}*

CAROL: What the hell is that for? This is February!

{Switches off air conditioner}

MARJORIE: *{A cheerful but unin-terested hug}* It drowns out the traffic.

CAROL: *{Slips out of embrace}* All right, when we don't have guests. We don't want people to think we're crazy. Did the liquor come?

MARJORIE: It came. *{Suspicious}* Why are you so interested in liquor?

CAROL: Don't worry. You've got nothing to worry about.

MARJORIE: You called up twice from the office to ask about the liquor.

CAROL: That's all right. That's perfectly all right. *{Evades her stare}* You can find out a lot more about somebody, you know, when he's a little—

{He flutters his hand to indicate tipsiness}

MARJORIE: *{Shocked}* Carol, you're not going to get that poor boy *drunk!*

CAROL: That poor boy wants to marry my Patsy! And don't call me *Carol!*

{Sounds of toilet flush and door slam. KENNY *enters from bathroom, reading}*

MARJORIE: But—dear—you haven't even met him!

KENNY: *{Matter-of-fact}* He's an artsyfartsy photographer. Patsy says he's thirty-six, but I know he's forty.

CAROL: *{To* KENNY*}* Are you *reading* again? *{He grabs paperback}* Harlots of Venus! Is that what I spent seven thousand a year on graduate school for? Get dressed!

KENNY: You lost my place!

*[*KENNY *exits}*

CAROL: Why is she doing this to me?

MARJORIE: He'll be a fine boy. I know it in my bones.

CAROL: What are you talking about? Do you have the slightest idea what you're talking about? She's only known him three weeks! I bet he's a fag!

MARJORIE: Carol!

CAROL: *{Vicious}* I *hate* that name! I told you never to call me that name. You deliberately do that to annoy me! *{Shouts}* Call me *dear! {Subsides}* You refuse to look at the facts. This whole family. That's the trouble with it. I'm the only one who looks at the facts. What was the name of that interior decorator she went to Europe with?

MARJORIE: Howard. He was—delicate.

CAROL: Swish! And that *actor,* the one who she went camping up in Maine with?

MARJORIE: Roger. He was very muscular.

CAROL: Swish! And the musician. And the stockbroker. And the Jewish novelist!

MARJORIE: Oh, *they're* not like that—

CAROL: Swish! Swish! Swish! I can spot 'em a mile away. She draws 'em like flies. Too strong for real men. Too much stuff! *{Proudly}* She's got *too much stuff!* Wait, you'll see. This new one—what's his name?

MARJORIE: Alfred.

CAROL: A swish name if I ever heard one. You'll see. He'll come in. Be very polite. Very charming. Look handsome. Well dressed. Have a strong handshake. Look me right in the eye. Smile a lot. Have white teeth. Shiny hair. Look very regular. But after two or three drinks—look at his wrists—he'll have trouble keeping 'em straight. Watch his lips. He'll start smacking his lips with his tongue. Watch his eyes. He'll start rolling his eyes. And his legs will go from being crossed like this—*{Wide-legged}* to this.—*{Closed-legged}* And when he gets up to start walking—*{He is about to mimick walk. Offstage sound of shots.* CAROL *and* MARJORIE *rush to window. He struggles, but can't get it open}* Damn! Goddamn!

MARJORIE: Hurry! *{Shots fade. Offstage siren, loud, then fading}* They're miles away by now. You take forever.

{Doorbell}

PATSY'S VOICE: Hey, everybody!

*[*CAROL *outpaces* MARJORIE *to door.* PATSY *and* ALFRED *enter. Much excitement, laughter.* CAROL *is more involved with his daughter than* MARJORIE, *who is just a touch restrained.* PATSY *is all-consuming. Tall, blond, vibrant, the All-American Girl.* ALFRED *is big, heavyset and quite dour. He is in his middle thirties. Two cameras hangs from straps around his neck.* PATSY, MARJORIE *and* CAROL *speak in unison. None of the following is intelligible}*

PATSY: Daddy, Mother, I love your hair! Daddy, you're putting on weight, Mother, Daddy.

MARJORIE: Hello, dear, how are you, what's wrong with my hair, you're putting on weight.

CAROL: Patsy, Patsy, my little girl! My baby girl, you look like a million dollars! I'll tell the world.

PATSY: This is Alfred!

CAROL: *{Ignoring* ALFRED, *to* PATSY] Hey, you weren't in that business down there?

PATSY: What business?

CAROL: Well, from now on just be more careful.

MARJORIE: *{Her eyes on* ALFRED] I don't think we need worry any longer, dear. Patsy's finally got herself a *man!*

[CAROL *scowls}*

PATSY: Where's my Kenny?

{Offstage sound of toilet flush and door slam. KENNY *enters, adjusting trousers.* PATSY *swoops down on him.* PATSY *and* KENNY *speak in unison. None of the following is intelligible}*

PATSY: Kenny! My baby brother! Isn't he the absolute cutest? I could eat him alive! Kenny!

KENNY: Ah, come on, cut it out! Quit all the hugging! Quit it! Boy, oboy, oboy.

MAJORIE: *{Somewhat catty}* Alfred, have you ever seen such a madhouse?

[ALFRED *smiles diffidently}*

CAROL: He's in the house for three minutes and she's already putting him on the spot. Have you ever seen anything like it, Alfred?

[ALFRED *smiles diffidently}*

PATSY: Kenny! You're so handsome! I can't get over it! *{To* ALFRED] I've always had a mad thing on my kid brother! [KENNY *clowns embarrassment,* PATSY *and* MARJORIE *laugh,* ALFRED *smiles diffidently,* CAROL *looks annoyed. To* ALFRED] He breaks me up!

CAROL: *{Nastily}* Kenny's the *comedian* around here. [KENNY *sobers immediately. To* ALFRED] What's your pleasure, young fellow?

PATSY: Mother, what have you done to this room?

{Lights flicker and black out in apartment, and in windows across the street}

MARJORIE: *{Lighting candles}* Nothing special. A little bit of this. A little bit of that.

{Offstage sirens begin}

CAROL: *{Self-pityingly}* If you bothered to come here more often—

MARJORIE: *{Studying* PATSY'S *face by candlelight}* I don't like your looks.

CAROL: *{Studying* PATSY] What's the matter? The day that girl doesn't look like a million dollars—

MARJORIE: You've got black rings under your eyes.

PATSY: Mother, that's eyeliner.

MARJORIE: Makes you look exhausted.

KENNY: *{Studying* PATSY] I like it.

MARJORIE: Always together!

CAROL: Do you have the slightest idea what you're talking about? She looks like a million dollars!

MARJORIE: I know. It's what they're wearing today. I'm out of step. As usual.

{Lights come back on. MARJORIE *blows out candle}*

CAROL: *{A little nervous. To* ALFRED] What's your pleasure, young fellow?

MARJORIE: *{Critical}* Why don't you wear your other outfit?

PATSY: What other outfit?

CAROL: Will you stop criticizing?

PATSY: What other outfit, Mother?

MARJORIE: I can't be expected to remember everything. It's not as if you still lived here.

KENNY: Hey, Al, want to see Patsy's old room?

PATSY: *Alfred,* Kenny. And he's not interested in that!

KENNY: I bet he is! Want to?

ALFRED: Maybe later.

KENNY: *{Rejected}* Why should I care?

CAROL: *{To* KENNY] He doesn't want to! Stop acting silly! *{To* ALFRED] What's your pleasure, young fellow?

MARJORIE: Alfred, may I shake your hand? My mother taught us that you could tell a lot about a person by the way he shakes hands. *{Shakes his hand}* You have a good hand. *{Flirtatious}* Better look out, Patsy! I'll steal your boy friend! *{Releases* ALFRED'S *hand. Short laugh. To* ALFRED] I'm only joking.

KENNY: Let me try. *{Shakes* ALFRED'S *hand}* You don't squeeze so hard. *{Disengaged}* Dad?

CAROL: This is the silliest business I've ever heard of! I think we all need drinks. What's your pleasure, young fellow?

MARJORIE: Alfred, is something the matter with your face?

ALFRED: {*To* PATSY] Is there?

PATSY: {*Subdued annoyance*} Just the usual assortment of bruises, Mother.

MARJORIE: What kind of talk is that? Modern talk?

PATSY: {*Not overjoyed to be on the subject*} Alfred is always getting beat up, Mother. At least once a week. {*To* ALFRED] Or is it more?

ALFRED: {*Shakes his head to indicate it is not more*} I don't get hurt.

MARJORIE: You don't get hurt? Carol, look at that boy! His face is a mass of bruises!

CAROL: I have asked you repeatedly never to call me Carol. {*To* PATSY] I hate that name Carol!

MARJORIE: I have to call you something, dear.

CAROL: I don't care what you call me. Just don't call me Carol!

KENNY: Call him Harriet! {*Laughs*} Harriet! Harriet! *Yoohoo!* Harriet! {*Convulses himself*}

PATSY: You're not being funny, Kenny. {*He sobers immediately*} I love your name. I know lots of men named Carol.

KENNY: Sure. Sure. Name one.

[CAROL *glares at him*}

PATSY: {*Thinking*} Carol—

KENNY: *Chessman* {*Screams with laughter*}

PATSY: King Carol of Rumania!

CAROL: That's right! King Carol! Damn it, that's right! Say, I feel like a drink. Anyone join me?

MARJORIE: I want to know why Alfred gets into these fights. I don't think that's the least bit funny.

PATSY: {*Resigned*} Ask him!

ALFRED: {*Not interested but making an effort, mindful that this is his first attempt at conversation*} Look. {*Long pause. Others stir uncomfortably*} There are lots of little people who like to start fights with big people. They hit me for a couple of minutes, they see I'm not going to fall down, they get tired and they go away.

MARJORIE: {*After an embarrassed pause*} So much tension. Rush. Rush. Rush. My mother taught me to take dainty, little steps. She'd *kill* me if she saw the stride on Patsy.

CAROL: {*Puzzled. The beginnings of contempt*} Don't you defend yourself?

ALFRED: I ask them not to hit my cameras. They're quite good about that. {*Cheerful*} Surprising!

CAROL: Let me get this straight. You just stand there and let these hooligans do whatever they want to you?

ALFRED: I'm quite strong, so you needn't worry about it. At the risk of sounding arrogant, this has been going on for ten years and I've yet to be knocked unconscious.

CAROL: But why don't you fight back?

ALFRED: I don't want to.

CAROL: Christ Jesus, you're not a pacifist?

PATSY: {*Warning*} Daddy—

ALFRED: {*Slowly shakes his head*} An apathist. {*Blank stares from* CAROL *and* MARJORIE] I want to do what I want to do, not what *they* want me to do.

CAROL: So you just stand there.

ALFRED: It doesn't hurt.

CAROL: Getting your face beat in doesn't hurt?

ALFRED: Not if you daydream. I daydream all through it. About my work. I imagine myself standing there, in the same spot, clicking off roll after roll of film, humming to myself with pleasure. I hum to myself when I work. There are times when I get so carried away that I think I'm actually doing what I'm only dreaming I'm doing. Muggers tend to get very depressed when you hum all the while they're hitting you. It's not something I choose to happen. It's just one of those things you learn to live with.

PATSY: {*To family*} Look, this is an

old argument and it doesn't really concern you. Why don't we get on something else?

CAROL: *{Indignant}* It certainly does concern me, young lady!

PATSY: *{Placating}* Oh, Daddy—

CAROL: I want you to know it concerns me very much. *{To ALFRED}* How do you get into these things? You must do something to get them mad—

ALFRED: No—

CAROL: Well, Goddamnit, you're getting me mad!

MARJORIE: *{Taking the heat off}* Alfred, do you try *talking* to them?

ALFRED: *{The patient old pro}* There's no way of talking someone out of beating you up if that's what he wants to do.

KENNY: *{To PATSY}* This guy's a riot!

{She slaps at him. He playfully eludes her}

PATSY: Haven't we had enough of this? I'm going to make some drinks.

KENNY: Vodka and tonic.

MARJORIE: Just *one*, young man.

CAROL: I'll make them!

PATSY: No, Daddy. I want to get my hands busy. Alfred?

ALFRED: Nothing right now.

CAROL: You don't drink either. Is that right?

ALFRED: I drink beer.

CAROL: Get him a beer, Kenny.

KENNY: Why is it always my turn?

ALFRED: Not now, thanks.

CAROL: He doesn't drink.

ALFRED: I'll drink later.

CAROL: You don't drink. You don't fight.

PATSY: I fight, Daddy!

MARJORIE: Carol, leave the poor boy alone.

CAROL: *{Shouts}* How many times do I have to tell you—

MARJORIE: *{Hurt}* I'm sorry. Whatever I do is wrong.

KENNY: *{Doing Bogart}* Hey. What's dat? Dat my best goil talking? Hey.

{He hugs her from behind}

MARJORIE: *{Kittenish}* Kenny! What will Alfred think? He'll think you're always making love to your mother!

CAROL: *{Sourly}* He *is* always making love to his mother.

MARJORIE: Well, someone has to— *{She smiles into CAROL's glare}* dear.

PATSY: *{Serving drinks}* What's this? What's this? I thought I was your best girl, Kenny?

[KENNY *tries to release* MARJORIE *and go to* PATSY. *She grabs his arms and holds on}*

MARJORIE: *{To* ALFRED] When Patsy lived at home we used to go on like this all the time.

KENNY: *{Whining}* Let go, Mom!

CAROL: Stop all this silliness and drink your liquor!

[MARJORIE *releases* KENNY, *who goes over to* PATSY]

MARJORIE: *{Flirtatious}* You're an intelligent-sounding man, Alfred. I would think if you spoke to these people quietly and sensibly they'd realize the sort of person you were and go away.

ALFRED: What can you say that's sensible to a drunk who you haven't been staring at, when he shoves you in the chest and says, "Who do you think you're staring at, fatface?" If you deny you've been staring at him, you've as much as called him a liar. For that you get hit. If you stutter in confusion, you've as much as admitted your guilt. For that you get hit. If you tell him you were staring at him because he reminds you of a kid you went to school with in Chicago, he turns out to *hate* Chicago. And for that you get hit.

MARJORIE: *{To* PATSY] I didn't know he went to school in Chicago. Nobody tells me anything. *{To* ALFRED] We went to Chicago in 1946. Whereabout did you live in Chicago, Alfred?

ALFRED: The South Side.

MARJORIE: I'm not comfortable eating away from home. Well, that's another story. Does your family still live there?

ALFRED: I don't know.

CAROL: You don't know! What kind of answer is that? You don't know! That's the silliest answer I've ever heard!

ALFRED: I haven't kept up contact. [CAROL *frowns, disapproving*]

MARJORIE: There seems to be so little cohesiveness in families today. *We* never went anywhere. We were too unsophisticated to know that home wouldn't serve. *{At* PATSY] Today they run off here, they run off there—

KENNY: *{Hugs her}* I'll never leave you, Mom.

CAROL: Will you two break it up? How about another round? Name your poison, Alfred.

MAJORIE: *{Sadly}* We've had our share of tragedy—

PATSY: *{Warning}* Mother—

{Phone rings. CAROL *starts for it.* MARJORIE *beats him to it}*

MARJORIE: Let me, dear. It's never for you. Hello. *{Amplified sound of heavy breathing}* Hello. Hello. Who is this? Hello. [PATSY *starts toward her}* The most curious business. Hello.

[PATSY *takes phone, listens and hangs up}*

PATSY: *{To* MARJORIE] You get it too.

CAROL: What? [PATSY *looks toward* MARJORIE, *who smiles but does not answer}* What?

MARJORIE: Never mind, dear. It's not important.

[CAROL *frustrated.* PATSY *goes to him}*

PATSY: The Breather, Daddy. Do you get many of these, Mother?

MARJORIE: He's the pleasantest of the lot. You should hear the ones who *talk!* I grit my teeth, turn my ears *right* off, and wait politely for them till they've finished their business.

CAROL: *{Exasperated}* Will somebody please explain to me—

PATSY: I get them every night. You know, Daddy—these oddballs who call you up at all hours and just *breathe* at you.

CAROL: *{Appalled}* Late at night? They breathe at you? *{To* ALFRED} And you don't fight back?!

{Doorbell}

MARJORIE: I'll get it! *{She crosses to door and opens peephole}* Who is it? I'm sorry, I can't understand you! Will you please stand closer to the peephole? I can't see you—take your hand off the peephole. I warn you, I'm calling the doorman! [PATSY *starts for door.* MARJORIE *shuts peephole and intercepts her. She returns, musing}* If it happens once, it happens a dozen times a day. And we gave that doorman fifteen dollars for Christmas.

[PATSY *protectively puts her arms around her.* MARJORIE *lightly shrugs it off}*

CAROL: *{To* ALFRED] *What are you going to do if you're on the street with my daughter?*

PATSY: Don't be silly, Daddy. I'm quite capable of taking care of myself.

KENNY: *{Proudly}* She's as strong as an ox. When we were kids we used to wrestle all the time. I always lost.

PATSY: *{Enjoying herself}* Daddy, I assure you, no one's going to pick on me. I'm a big, strapping girl! I don't daydream, and I *do* hit back. When I take Alfred home every night, I guarantee you there's no trouble.

CAROL: You let *her* take you home?

PATSY: He doesn't *let* me. He doesn't have anything to say about it. Every time I leave him alone somebody in this crazy city mugs him. Once I have him safely married, [CAROL *and* KENNY *wince}* I won't let him out of my sight for five minutes. *{Pinches* ALFRED} He's too cute to get beat up—by anyone but me.

{She throws a playful but entirely masculine punch at ALFRED. *He smiles happily as it connects.* KENNY *exits. Offstage door slam}*

MARJORIE: Aren't they adorable?

CAROL: *{Quietly to* MARJORIE} What did I tell you about him, huh? Didn't I predict?

MARJORIE: I think he's very sweet.

CAROL: That's a sure sign. You think they're *all* sweet. I'll be damned *{Louder}* if I'd let myself stand by and let a woman fight my battles for me.

PATSY: *{Hugging* CAROL *from behind}* They don't make frontier fighters like my father any more.

MARJORIE: *{Looks about}* Kenny! *{Shakes her head in exasperation and smiles seductively at* ALFRED] Alfred, would you mind giving me a hand?

{They exit}

CAROL: *{Delighted}* Come on. Stop being silly. Cut it out.

PATSY: *{Playful, squeezing tighter}* Let's see how good you are, tiger. Break my grip! Come on!

{Momentary look of panic in CAROL'S *eyes.* PATSY *releases him. They laugh}*

CAROL: *{Slaps her cheek playfully}* Who's my baby girl, eh? *{Suddenly serious}* I wish you had as much brains as you have brawn.

PATSY: You don't like him, do you, Daddy?

CAROL: Don't put words in my mouth.

PATSY: Then you *do* like him?

CAROL: I want to know more about him before I make up my mind—

PATSY: Not to like him.

CAROL: Don't bully me, young lady. You know I don't like it when you bully me.

PATSY: You *love* it when I bully you.

CAROL: *{Chuckles}* You're too damned fast for the old man. *{Slaps her cheek playfully}* But I know a thing or two. *{Deadly serious}* Never settle for less.

PATSY: Daddy, I'm *not!*

CAROL: Never sell yourself short.

PATSY: Oh, Daddy, when have I ever—

CAROL: The right man will come along.

PATSY: Daddy, I'm twenty-seven. The right men all got married two years ago. They won't get their first divorce for another five years, and I just don't have the time, the inclination, or the kind of looks that can afford to wait.

CAROL: I don't want to hear you knocking yourself. You've got ten people working under you! *{Proudly}* You're five-foot eight!

PATSY: After a while it doesn't *matter* that you can do everything better than everyone else. I've been the best for years now, and all it comes down to is that I'm efficient.

CAROL: You don't know what you're talking about. You're very popular.

PATSY: When you want a woman they can collapse without shame in front of—they come to me.

CAROL: Why not? You're trusted!

PATSY: Oh, to meet a man who *is* ashamed to collapse in front of me! Daddy, I get dizzy spells from being so strong; I get migraine from being so damnably dependable. I'm tired of being Mother Earth! Daddy, Alfred's the *only* man I know who isn't waiting for me to save him. Don't you know how that makes me feel? God help me, I've got to save him!

{She embraces CAROL, *who blissfully returns embrace.* ALFRED *enters uncorking the wine and surveys scene.* CAROL *quickly disengages}*

MARJORIE: *{Enters wheeling serving cart}* Come an' git it! *{To* ALFRED *as she starts serving}* My mother always used to say that to us children at mealtimes. I've always found it a charming family tradition. So I say, "Come an' git it!" to our children. I dream of the day when I can hear Patsy say, "Come an' git it!" to her children. *{To* KENNY, *who is offstage}* Kenny! Didn't you hear me say come an' git it, or do you need a special invitation?

KENNY: *{Still offstage}* In a minute!

MARJORIE: Not a minute, young man! Right now! *{To* ALFRED] It's so stuffy in here. Alfred, would you open a window like a good fellow? *{Sounds of toilet flush, offstage door slam.* CAROL *rises}* No, I asked Alfred, dear.

[KENNY *enters with paperback,*

passes CAROL, *who outpaces* ALFRED *to window}*

CAROL: *{Struggling with window}* It's all right. It's perfectly all right. *{Gives up} Son of a bitch! {To AL-FRED]* The son of a bitch refuses to open!

[ALFRED *gives strong jerk. Window opens. Traffic, construction and airplane noise}*

MARJORIE: Thank you, Alfred. *{To* CAROL] You see, I had my reasons.

{Light film of soot wafts through window}

CAROL: I loosened it!

KENNY: He loosened it! That's a riot!

{Convulses himself}

CAROL: *{Slams window shut. To* KENNY] Now *you* open it! [KENNY *airily dismisses him}* No, you're the smart one around here! Let's see you open it!

MARJORIE: I spent the whole day cooking. Can't we eat now and open and close windows later?

CAROL: It won't take a second. Well, young man, are you going to try or are you just going to sit back and laugh at the earnest efforts of your betters? [KENNY, *with arrogant mockery, rises, tries and fails to open window. He shrugs, smiles, and ambles back to table.* ALFRED *and* CAROL *follow. All sit}* You're not so smart now, are you?

MARJORIE: Will someone please open the window? [PATSY *leaps up before* ALFRED *can rise, strides to window, kicks off heels, jerks window open. Noise and dust.* KENNY *and* CAROL *bend over their plates, embarrassed.* PATSY *returns to table}* When Patsy lived at home I always knew I had someone to do my heavy lifting for me. I was always too petite. [PATSY *shrinks over her plate. All quietly eat}* You don't know what a pleasure it is to have my family all together this way. *{Lights flicker and black out, as before. Sounds of eating}* Do you know that in the *big* power failure some people stood in the sub-

ways, in total darkness, for as long as four hours without bringing their newspapers down from in front of their faces? *{Long silence. Eating sounds.* MARJORIE *lights candles}* It would be nice if someone else, on occasion, would think of lighting the candles. Kenny, come back here! *{Offstage door slam.* KENNY *returns carrying paperback}* I'm the watchdog around here, Alfred. I can imagine what Patsy must have told you about me.

PATSY: *{Bored}* Must you, Mother?

{They exchange long stares. MAR-JORIE *rises and exits. Door slam. Lights go on}*

CAROL: *{Up quickly}* I'm going to make myself another drink.

KENNY: Make me one.

PATSY: Me too.

ALFRED: Scotch neat.

CAROL *stops, stares at him, goes over to bar, grinning. Offstage sounds of toilet flush, door slam}*

MARJORIE: *{Enters carrying photographs}* It's gotten a little chilly in here . . . [KENNY *up before anyone can move. He slams down window.* CAROL *serves drinks}* That's your second tonight, isn't it? And I suppose you're still smoking as much? [PATSY *salutes with glass. Drains it}* Drinks like a fish. Smokes like a chimney. [PATSY *has mock cough spasm}* It's the ones who think they're indestructible who do the most damage to themselves. Kenny, is that a new drink? [KENNY *bolts drink.* MARJORIE *shakes head, looks warily at* CAROL. *He bolts drink, scratches his hand nervously. To* ALFRED, *with photographs}* You're a photographer, Alfred, so I thought you'd be interested in seeing these pictures of Patsy's dead brother, Steve.

[PATSY *covers her face with her hands}*

ALFRED: He looks very handsome in his swimsuit.

MARJORIE: He won five gold cups. He was ten years older than Patsy.

KENNY: Fifteen years older than me.

ALFRED: He look very handsome in his baseball uniform.

MARJORIE: He only pitched no-hitters.

ALFRED: *{Handing back pictures}* Thank you for letting me see them.

MARJORIE: This one was taken after he came home from the war, a hero.

ALFRED: He looks very handsome in his uniform. What do these double bars signify?

MARJORIE: He was a captain. A hero. He bombed Tokyo. When his country called on him to serve again he bombed Korea. A brilliant future in electronics, not an enemy in the world, whoever dreamed he'd be shot down in his tracks on the corner of Ninety-seventh Street and Amsterdam Avenue. *{Gathers up pictures}* But I won't bore you with our tragedy.

PATSY: *{Explodes}* Damn it, Mother! Must I go through this every time I bring a man home to dinner? [MARJORIE *sobs, rushes off. Door slam}* Patsy's done it again!

KENNY: *{Admiring}* Boy, I'd be killed if I ever talked like that.

CAROL: I don't approve of your behavior, young lady. Your mother worked long and hard and imaginatively over this dinner. [PATSY *puts a cigarette in her mouth}* And she's right about your smoking too much, Goddamnit!

[PATSY *turns to* CAROL, *cigarette in mouth, waiting for a light. He resists for a moment, then lights it}*

PATSY: *{In command}* Thank you. [CAROL *scratches his hand. Softly to* ALFRED] I'm sorry you had to be subjected to this honey, *{To* CAROL, *taking his hand, placating}* Alfred knows all about Steve, Daddy.

[CAROL *revives}*

ALFRED: They still don't have any idea who did it?

CAROL: That's all right. The boys down at Homicide have worked long and hard and imaginatively on this case. *{With pride}* Many have become close personal friends.

{Toilet flush, door slam. MARJORIE *enters, eyes red but smiling. She is clutching a handkerchief.* KENNY *rises and exits in her direction. Door slam}*

MARJORIE: *{At serving cart}* We can't disappoint our guest with only one helping.

ALFRED: No, thank you, Mrs. Newquist. I've had plenty.

PATSY: *{Ingratiating}* It was delicious, Mother!

CAROL: It was delicious!

MARJORIE: Kenny! Where are you?

KENNY: *{Offstage, muffled}* It was delicious!

MARJORIE: *{To* ALFRED] A big man like you. Now, don't just stand on politeness—

ALFRED: No. I'm really quite stuffed, thank you.

MARJORIE: *{To* PATSY} Well, then I'll have to turn to my best customer.

PATSY: I couldn't eat another bite, Mother. It was delicious.

CAROL: I couldn't eat another bite. It was delicious.

KENNY: *{Offstage, muffled}* I couldn't eat another bite. It was delicious! *{Toilet flush. Door slam. He enters carrying paperback}* I could use another drink, though.

{He detours on his way back from bar to surreptitiously pick up PATSY'S *heels in front of window. Takes them to his seat}*

CAROL: *{Rises}* I think I'll have another. *{At the bar}* Patsy?

PATSY: *{Rises}* Leave out the water this time.

{She goes to bar}

ALFRED: Scotch neat.

MARJORIE: *{Not really approving}* Well, it's a special occasion.

PATSY: *{Looks around}* Where the devil did I leave my shoes?

[KENNY *looks away}*

MARJORIE: *{Gathering photographs from table}* I'd better put these in a safe place before someone spills liquor on them. I'm sorry to have taken your time, Alfred. Knowing you were a photographer I thought you'd be interested. *{Waits for response; there is none}* Exactly what sort of work do you do? Portraits?

ALFRED: No.

PATSY: *{Returns protectively. Hands* ALFRED *drink}* Stop cross-examining him, Mother.

MARJORIE: I don't know why everything I do is wrong. Alfred, do you object to my asking you about your work?

ALFRED: It's not all that interesting, actually.

MARJORIE: You don't do portraits?

ALFRED: No.

MARJORIE: Do you do magazine photography?

ALFRED: No.

PATSY: Has somebody got a cigarette?

MARJORIE: *{To* PATSY*}* Must you? Can't you give in to me just this once? [CAROL *sits, hands* PATSY *cigarette.* KENNY *lights it. Barely in control, to* ALFRED] Advertising photography?

ALFRED: Well, I used to. I don't any more.

CAROL: Fashion photography?

{He nudges KENNY*}*

KENNY: *{Rolls his eyes}* Woo! Woo!

[CAROL *and* KENNY *exchange joyful glances. Stifle laughs}*

ALFRED: It's sort of complicated. Are you sure you want to hear?

PATSY: *{Resigned}* You may as well—

ALFRED: Well, I began as a commercial photographer—

PATSY: He began as a painter.

ALFRED: A very bad painter.

PATSY: Says you!

CAROL: *For Christ sakes, will you let the boy finish!*

{All, including CAROL, *are surprised by outburst}*

ALFRED: I began as a commercial photographer, and was doing sort of well at it.

PATSY: *Sort of* well! You should see his portfolio. He's had work in *Holiday, Esquire, The New Yorker, Vogue*—

CAROL: *Vogue!*

KENNY: *{Rolls his eyes}* Woo! Woo!

{He and CAROL *exchange nudges, joyful glances.* PATSY *glares. They subside}*

ALFRED: It's an overrated business. But after a couple of years of doing sort of well [PATSY *slaps his hand lightly}* at it, things began to go wrong. I began losing my people. Somehow I got my heads chopped off. Or out of focus. Or *terrible* expressions on my models. I'd have them examining a client's product like this *{Expression of distaste}*— the agencies began to wonder if I didn't have some editorial motive in mind. Well, it wasn't true. But once they'd *planted* the idea—I couldn't help thinking of plane crashes every time I shot an airline ad, or deaths on the highway everytime I shot an automobile ad, or price-rigging every time I shot a pharmaceutical ad—and power failures when I shot Con Edison ads.

{Lights go out}

MARJORIE: I don't mean to interrupt, dear. *{Lights match and candles}* "How far better it is to light a match than curse the darkness." My mother told us that. Go on.

ALFRED: Well, my career suffered. But there was nothing I could do about it. The harder I tried to straighten out, the fuzzier my people got and the clearer my objects. Soon my people disappeared entirely, they just somehow never came out. But the objects I was shooting—brilliantly clear. *{Snaps fingers. Lights come back on}* So I began to do a lot of catalogue work. [MARJORIE *blows out candles}* Pictures of medical instruments, things like that. There was—well, the best way to describe it is—a *seductiveness* I was able to draw out of inanimate things that other photographers didn't seem to be able to get. I suppose the real break came with the I.B.M. show. They had me shoot thirty of their new models. They hired a gallery and had a computer show. One hundred and twenty color pictures of computers. It got some very strange *{Whimsical smile}* notices, the upshot of which was that the advertising business went "thing" crazy, and I became commercial again.

MARJORIE: You must be extremely talented.

ALFRED: *{More to himself than to family}* I got *sick* of it! Where the hell are standards? That's what I kept asking myself. Those people will take anything! Hell, if I gave them a picture of *shit* they'd give me an award for it!

{All stiffen. PATSY looks wary}

MARJORIE: Language, young man!

ALFRED: Hm? So that's what I do now.

CAROL: *{Hesitantly}* What?

ALFRED: Take pictures of shit.

MARJORIE: Language! Language! This is *my* table!

ALFRED: I don't mean to offend you, Mrs. Newquist. I've been shooting shit for a year now, and I've already won a half-dozen awards.

MARJORIE: *{Slowly thaws}* Awards?

ALFRED: And *Harper's Bazaar* wants me to do its spring issue.

KENNY: *{Rolling his eyes}* Woo! Woo!

CAROL: *{Angry, to KENNY]* Don't kid!

MARJORIE: That's a very respectable publication. *{Rises shakily, gathers up dishes}* It all sounds very impressive.

{She exits with serving cart}

CAROL: *{Up quickly, about to speak, when phone rings. He goes for it, all the while glaring at ALFRED]* Hello. *{Amplified breathing}* Look, I don't know who you are, but you're not dealing with helpless women now! *You people!* You young people today! Destroy! Destroy! When are you going to find time to build? In my day we couldn't afford telephones to breathe in! You ought to get down on your hands and knees and be grateful! Why isn't anybody GRATEFUL—[PATSY takes *receiver away, hangs up}* Excuse me.

{He exits}

PATSY: Kenny, would you mind—

KENNY: *{Grins}* It's my house.

PATSY: *{Threatening}* Kenny! [PATSY *starts for him. He jumps up from table grabbing his drink, and runs out. He has on* PATSY'S *heels. Door slams. Offstage sound of distant sirens}* Well, my friend—

ALFRED: They asked me what I did for a living.

{Shrugs}

PATSY: *{Gives him a long stare}* I don't know what to do with you. You're the toughest reclamation job *I've* ever had.

ALFRED: You might try retiring on your laurels. You've reformed five fags in a row, why press your luck with a nihilist?

PATSY: *Because you're wrong! {Calms herself}* Alfred, *every* age has problems. And people somehow manage . . . *to be happy!* I'm sorry, I don't mean to bully you . . . Yes, I do mean to bully you. Alfred, do you know how I wake up every morning of my life? With a smile on my face! And for the rest of the day I come up against an unending series of challenges to wipe that smile off my face. The Breather calls . . . ex-boy friends call to tell me they're getting married . . . someone tries to break into the apartment while I'm dressing . . . there's a drunk asleep in the elevator . . . three minutes after I'm out on the street my camel coat turns brown . . . the subway stalls . . . the man standing next to me presses his body against mine . . . the up elevator jams . . . rumors start buzzing around the office that we're about to be automated . . . the down elevator jams . . . all the taxis are off-duty . . . the air on Lexington Avenue is purple . . . a man tries to pick me up on the bus . . . another man follows me home . . . I step in the door and the Breather's on the phone . . . isn't that enough to wipe the smile off anybody's face? Well, it doesn't wipe it off *mine!* Because for every bad thing there are two good things—no—*four* good things! There are friends . . . and a wonderful job . . . and tennis . . . and skiing . . . and traveling . . . and musicals . . .

and driving in the country . . . and flying your own airplane . . . and staying up all night to see the sun rise. [ALFRED *goes into his daydream}* Alfred, come back here! *{Long pause}* Alfred, if everything is so hopeless—why do anything?

ALFRED: Okay.

PATSY: That's why you don't hit back.

ALFRED: There isn't much point, is there?

PATSY: *{Explodes}* *Do you know what you're talking about? Do you have the slightest idea {Catches herself, shakes her head}*—I always talk like my father when I'm in this house. Alfred . . . if you feel that way about things . . . why get *married?*

ALFRED: You said you wanted to.

PATSY: *{Turns away}* I find this a very unpleasant conversation.

ALFRED: *{Dryly}* Patsy, let's not turn this into a "critical conversation," just because you're not getting your way. *I'm* for getting married.

PATSY: *{Dryly}* Thanks.

ALFRED: *{After a long, tense pause}* So it is a "critical conversation."

{He starts off}

PATSY: Where do you think you're going? *{He exits}* Alfred! *{Starts after him, muttering to herself}* He doesn't know how to fight; *that's* why I'm not winning. *{Exits and brings him back}* Damn it! Aren't you willing to battle over *anything?* Even *me?*

{She anticipates what he is about to say}

ALFRED *and* PATSY: There isn't much point, is there?

{She bear-hugs him}

PATSY: At least say you love me.

ALFRED AND PATSY: I'm not sure I know what love is.

PATSY: *{Slaps him in the stomach}* Okay. The gauntlet's flung! You've had it, buster! I'm going to marry you, make you give me a house, entrap you into a half-dozen children, and seduce you into a life so remorselessly satisfying that within two years under my management you'll come to me with a camera full of baby pictures and say: "Life can be beautiful!"

ALFRED: And ugly. More often ugly.

PATSY: You'll give me a piano to sing around. And a fireplace to lie in front of. And each and every Christmas we will send our *personalized Christmas* cards—with a group family portrait on the front—taken by *Alfred Chamberlain.* Daddy! Mother! I have an announcement! [CAROL *and* MARJORIE *rush in. Sounds of toilet flush, door slam.* KENNY *rushes in, adjusting his trousers}* Alfred and I are getting married! [CAROL *and* KENNY *freeze}* Next week!

[CAROL *sits down heavily}*

MARJORIE: *{Beaming}* I've always dreamed of a wedding in my living room! Oh, there's so much to do. *{Kisses them}* You've got yourself a fine young man. And so accomplished! We'll have to let Dr. Paterson know right away—

ALFRED: *{To* PATSY] Who?

PATSY: The minister, dopey.

ALFRED: *{To* MARJORIE, *picking up phone}* Mrs. Newquist—*{Sound of amplified breathing.* MARJORIE *quickly hangs up. Picks up again and begins to dial}* Mrs. Newquist, when you speak to the minister, you'd better tell him—we don't want any mention of God in the ceremony.

CAROL: I'm going to have him arrested.

{All freeze, stare at ALFRED. *Blackout. Street noises, sirens, etc.}*

SCENE TWO

The Newquist apartment, one month later. ALFRED, PATSY, CAROL *and* MARJORIE *sit quietly.* CAROL *looks at his watch, rises, begins to pace.* PATSY *places a calming hand on* ALFRED'S *arm.* MARJORIE, *the only one unperturbed, smiles gamely. Doorbell.* CAROL *crosses to door.*

MARJORIE: Ask who it is first!

[CAROL *opens door. The* JUDGE *enters, a portly, well-dressed man of about* CAROL'S *age}*

CAROL: *{Softly, as if at a wake}* Jerry. You don't know how I appreciate this.

{The JUDGE *nods, accepts* CAROL'S *handshake, looks at his watch}*

JUDGE: *{Softly}* Nice to see you again, Mrs. Newquist. Are these the youngsters? [CAROL *nods}* No God in the ceremony. Does she live away from home? [CAROL *nods}* It begins there.

MARJORIE: *{Softly}* You'll have to pardon the mess, Judge Stern.

JUDGE: You have a second girl, don't you, Carol?

CAROL: A boy.

JUDGE: A son!

CAROL: A boy.

MARJORIE: *{To* PATSY *and* ALFRED] Children, this is—

CAROL: I'll do it! Judge Jerome M. Stern, one of my oldest and dearest—

JUDGE: I don't have much time. If the grownups will please excuse us—

{Looks to CAROL *and* MARJORIE, *who reluctantly start to exit as* KENNY *enters}*

MARJORIE: Out, young man!

KENNY: Why can't I—

[MARJORIE *shoves him. They exit together}*

JUDGE: *{Stares at* ALFRED *and* PATSY *for a long moment}* Sit down please. *{They remain standing}* I can't talk unless I'm the tallest. [PATSY *sits, and eases* ALFRED *down beside her}* No God in the ceremony, mm? Getting a lot of turndowns, aren't you? Surprising, isn't it, how the name of God is still respected in this town. *{Studies* PATSY] Carol Newquist's daughter. *{Sighs}* Your father and me go back a long ways, young lady. He's done me a lot of favors. Got me tickets to shows—*{Sighs. Shakes his head}* I'd *like* to help him out *{Shakes his head}*—My mother, thank God she's not alive today, landed in this country sixty-five years ago. Four infants in her arms. Kissed the side-

walk the minute she got off the boat, she was so happy to be out of Russia alive. Across the ocean alive. More dead than alive, if you want to know the truth. Sixteen days in the steerage. Fifteen people got consumption. Five died. My father, thank God he's not alive today, came over two years earlier, sixty-seven years ago. Worked like a son of a bitch to earn our passage *{To* PATSY]—Pardon my French. You don't want God in the ceremony, so you're probably familiar with it. My father worked fourteen hours a day in a sweatshop on lower Broadway. Number three-fifteen. Our first apartment was a five-flight walk-up, four-and-a-half-room cold-water flat. With the bathtub in the kitchen and the toilet down the hall. One-forty-two Hester Street. Three families used the toilet. An Italian family. A colored family. A Jewish family. Three families with different faiths, but one thing each of those families had in common. They had in common the sacrifices each of them had to make to get where they were. What they had in common was *persecution.* So they weren't so *glib* about God. God was in my mother's every conversation about how she got her family out of Russia, thank God, in one piece. About the pogroms. The steerage. About those who *didn't* make it. Got sick and died. Who could they ask for help? If not God, then *who? The Great Society? The Department of Welfare? Travelers Aid?* Mind you, I'm a good Democrat, I'm not knocking these things. Although sometimes—there weren't any handouts in those days. This city was a—a—*concrete jungle* to the families that came here. They had to carve homes and lives out of *concrete*—cold *concrete!* You think they didn't call on God, these poor suffering greenhorns? You see the suit I'm wearing? Expensive? Custommade? My father, thank God he's not alive today, worked sixteen hours a day in a shop on Broome Street, and his artistry for a tenth of what you pay today makes meat loaf out of this suit. One-forty-five dash one-forty-seven Broome Street. So tired, so broken in spirit, when he climbed the six flights of stairs each night to the three-room unheated cold-water flat the five of us were crowded in—one-seventy-one Attorney Street—that he did not have the strength to eat. *The man did not have the strength to eat.* Turning thinner and yellower by the day for lack of *what?* A well-balanced diet? Too much choles-terol? Too many carbohydrates and starchy substances in his blood? Not on your sweet *life!* For lack of *everything!* What was God to my father? I'll tell you—sit down, I'm not finished!—I'll tell you what God was to my father! God got my father up those six and a half flights of stairs, not counting the stoop, every night. God got my mother, worn gray from lying to her children about a better tomorrow she didn't be-lieve in, up each morning with enough of the failing strength that finally de-serted her last year in Miami Beach at the age of ninety-one, to face another day of hopelessness and despair. Thirty-one-thirty-five Biscayne Boulevard. God. Do you know how old I was when I first had to go out and work? Look at these hands? The hands of a professional man? Not on your sweet life! The hands of a *worker!* I *worked!* These hands toiled from the time I was nine—strike that, *seven*. Every morning up at five, dressing in the pitch black to run down seven flights of stairs, thirteen steps to a flight—I'll never forget them—to run five blocks to the Wash-ington market, unpacking crates for seventy-five cents a week. A dollar if I worked Sundays. Maybe! Based on the goodness of the bosses' heart. Where was my God then? Where, on those bit-ter cold mornings, with my hands so blue with frostbite they looked like ladies' gloves, was God? Here! In my heart! Where He was, has been, will al-ways be! Till the day they carry me feet first out of these chambers—knock wood, God grant it's soon. My first murder trial—where are you going? I'm not finished!

ALFRED: *{At the door}* You're not going to marry us.

JUDGE: I'm not finished! Don't be a smart punk! [Alfred *exits}* You're a know-it-all wise guy smart punk, aren't you? I've seen your kind! *You'll come up before me again!* [PATSY *exits.* CAROL *and* MARJORIE *enter. The* JUDGE *looks at his watch. Very coldly, after a long pause}* He made me very late.

BLACKOUT

SCENE THREE

The lights come up. The Newquist apartment is decorated for a wedding. The guests are gathered around the wedding cake, having their picture taken. Ad lib laughter on the camera flash. Two gunshots are heard coming from the window. The guests rush to the window.

FIRST GUEST: Where is it—

SECOND GUEST: Up there!

THIRD GUEST: Where?

FOURTH GUEST: There!

SECOND GUEST: He's got a rifle!

FIFTH GUEST: Somebody call the police!

SECOND GUEST: He's only a kid!

THIRD GUEST: Kids can kill.

FOURTH GUEST: I think somebody should call the police!

FIFTH GUEST: I think Carol should call the police.

SIXTH GUEST: An old lady got mur-dered in my building in front of thirty witnesses.

THIRD GUEST: And everybody just stood there, right?

FIRST GUEST: Call the police.

{Guests have begun to drift away from the window. Two more gunshots, which they ignore}

THIRD GUEST: I learned to kill with the edge of a rolled-up newspaper.

FIRST GUEST: I carry a hunting knife.

{The family enters and the guests applaud}

CAROL: *{To* FIRST GUEST*}* Nothing like a little excitement—

{Loses smile as he watches PATSY *cross to* ALFRED *and hug him. Scattered cheers, drinks raised in toast}*

MARJORIE: *{To* SECOND GUEST*}* Aren't they an attractive couple? He's so big. It's wonderful to marry a big man. There are so many complications when you marry a man shorter than yourself.

CAROL: *{To* THIRD GUEST*}* I gave them twenty-five hundred. It's just a token.

MARJORIE: *{To* SECOND GUEST*}* And she's so big herself. Many's the time I gave up hope she'd find a man bigger than she is.

CAROL: *{To* FOURTH GUEST*}* Twenty-five hundred—

MARJORIE: *{To* SECOND GUEST*}* Or heavier. It's always amazed me the size of her. I've always been such a little peanut.

ALFRED: *{To* FIFTH GUEST*}* No. My family's not here.

MARJORIE: *{To* SECOND GUEST*}* You'd think almost anybody I'd married would have to be bigger than me; well, that's the way life works out.

KENNY: *{To* SIXTH GUEST*}* I haven't made up my mind. I may go into teaching.

MARJORIE: *{To* THIRD GUEST*}* He's a world-famous photographer, you know. He does collages for *Harper's Bazaar. {General laughter.* MARJORIE *looks around to see what she's missing}* And he's terribly independent. I always thought Patsy was independent, but this time I think she's met her match.

PATSY: *{To* SECOND GUEST*}* Well, the first year at least we'll live at my place.

MARJORIE: *{To* THIRD GUEST*}* No God in the ceremony, he says. Yes, God in the ceremony, she says. Well, you see who won that one.

CAROL: Twenty-five hundred—

ALFRED: *{To* FIRST GUEST*}* No. My family isn't here.

MARJORIE: *{To* THIRD GUEST*}* I would never have the nerve to stand up to her. Her father has never stood up to her. Her brother has never stood up to her. But this time she didn't get her way. *{Gaily}* There's not going to be any God in the ceremony.

KENNY: *{To* SECOND GUEST*}* What I really want to do is direct films.

MARJORIE: *{To* FOURTH GUEST*}* Poor children, these past few weeks they've really had a rough time of it. Nobody wanted to marry them. Even the state of New York has God in the ceremony. They looked everywhere.

ALFRED: *{To* SECOND GUEST*}* No My family's not here.

MARJORIE: *{To* FOURTH GUEST*}* Ethical Culture told them they didn't have to have God in the ceremony, but they had to have clinical culture in the ceremony.

PATSY: *{To* FIRST GUEST*}* I plan to go on working into my eighth month.

MARJORIE: *{To* FOURTH GUEST*}* Finally, they found this man *{Doorbell. All pause tensely.* CAROL *checks peephole, unlocks door.* DUPAS *enters}*—there he is now—Alfred found him, really—Reverend Dupas. *{Pronounced Doo-pah}*

ALFRED: *{Escorting* PATSY *over to* DUPAS*}* Henry.

{Mimed greetings and handshakes}

MARJORIE: *{To* FOURTH GUEST*}* He doesn't have much of a handshake, but Alfred says he's very well established in Greenwich Village. He's pastor of the First Existential Church—the one that has that sign in front that says—

DUPAS: *{To* ALFRED*}* My bike wouldn't start up.

MARJORIE: *{To* FOURTH GUEST, *quoting}* "Christ died for our sins. Dare we make his martyrdom meaningless by not committing them?"

CAROL: *{To* DUPAS, *with feigned good cheer}* No atheists in foxholes these days, eh, Reverend? They've all gone into the ministry.

MARJORIE: *{To* FOURTH GUEST]* Two Sundays ago he gave a sermon on the moral affirmation in Alfred's photographs.

CAROL: Can I see you for a minute in private, Reverend?

{He leads him off}

KENNY: *{Starts off}* Hey, that's *my* room!

PATSY: *{Looking after them, puzzled}* They'll be right out.

MARJORIE: They'll be right out, dear.

KENNY: How do they know I don't have to go in there? *{Starts off.* MARJORIE *blocks his way}* I need a *handkerchief! {Tries to get around her but is blocked}* I've got a right to go into my own room!

MARJORIE: *{Conciliatory}* Why don't you go into the bathroom, dear?

KENNY: *{To* PATSY]* Why can't you do your things in your own room?

PATSY: Kenny—*{Reaches for him. He turns away}* Why are you mad at me?

[KENNY *storms away. The phone rings.* KENNY *gets it. Amplified breathing}*

KENNY: *{Into phone}* Faggot!

{Hangs up. Sound of gunshots. All ignore them. CAROL *enters with his arm around* DUPAS, *who disengages and crosses to* ALFRED]

DUPAS: *{To* ALFRED}* Your father-in-law wants me to sneak the deity into the ceremony.

ALFRED: What did you tell him?

DUPAS: He offered me a lot of money. I told him I'd make my decision in a few minutes. [DUPAS *checks* CAROL'S *whereabouts. He is across room being congratulated, scratching his hand and staring intently at* DUPAS] If it's all right with you I'd like to take the money, and then *not* mention the deity. First Existential can use the money.

ALFRED: He'll stop the check.

DUPAS: I thought he might. Still, it would serve as a lesson . . .

ALFRED: I don't know what to tell you, Henry.

DUPAS: Well, we'll see.

{He crosses over to CAROL. *They exit}*

KENNY: *{Starts off}* I need something out of my bedroom.

MARJORIE: Kenny! *{Blocks his way.* KENNY *tries to charge past her. She intercepts and they begin to struggle. With forced gaiety}* Ha! Ha! Look, everybody! We're dancing!

[CAROL *and* DUPAS *enter—wrestling match breaks up.* CAROL, *hiding triumph, crosses over to* ALFRED]

CAROL: *{Slaps him on back}* Nervous, young fellow? [ALFRED *turns to look for* PATSY. CAROL *takes him by the arm}* I've been looking forward to this day for a long, long time. It would only take one thing more to make it perfect. [ALFRED *smiles politely, looks for* PATSY. CAROL *squeezes his arm}* To hear you call me Dad.

ALFRED: I didn't call my own father Dad.

CAROL: What did you call him?

ALFRED: I didn't call him anything. The occasion never came up. *{Amiably}* I could call you Carol.

CAROL: *{Winces}* Look, if it's this God business that's bothering you, I'm willing to be open-minded. I wouldn't let this on to Marjorie or the kids— *{Winks}* I don't believe in God. But to me it's not a matter of belief in God. It's a matter of belief in institutions. I have great belief in institutions. You couldn't concede me *one* Dad? *{No response}* Not all the time—but every once in a while, "Hello, Dad," "How are you, Dad?"

DUPAS: May we proceed?

CAROL: "You like some of my tobacco, Dad?" [ALFRED *tries to free his arm.* CAROL *hangs on, hisses}* I want an *answer!* [PATSY *crosses, kisses* CAROL, *takes* ALFRED *away. All take their positions for the ceremony}*

DUPAS: *{In a gentle, folksy manner}*
You all know why we're here. There is
often so much sham about this business
of marriage. Everyone accepts it. Ritual.
They's why I was so heartened when
Alfred asked me to perform this ceremony. He has certain beliefs that I
assume you all know. He is an atheist,
which is perfectly all right. Really it is. I
happen not to be, but inasmuch as this
ceremony connotates an abandonment
of ritual in the search for truth, I agreed
to perform it. First, let me state frankly
to you, Alfred, and to you, Patricia, that
of the two hundred marriages I have
performed, all but seven have failed. So
the odds are not good. We don't like to
admit it, especially at the wedding ceremony, but it's in the back of all our
minds, isn't it? How long will it last?
We all think that, don't we? We don't
like to bring it out in the open, but we
all think that. Well, I say why *not* bring
it out in the open? *Why* does one decide
to marry? Social pressure? Boredom?
Loneliness? Sexual appeasement? Um,
Love? I do not put any of these reasons
down. Each, in its own way, is adequate.
Each is all right. I married a musician
last year who wanted to get married in
order to stop masturbating. *{Guests
stir}* Please don't be startled. I am not
putting it down. That marriage did not
work. But the man tried. Now the man
is separated, and still masturbating—
but he is at peace with himself. He tried
society's way. So you see, it was not a
mistake, it turned out all right. Last
month I married a novelist to a painter,
with everyone at the wedding under the
influence of hallucinogenic drugs. The
drug quickened our mental responses
but slowed our physical responses. It
took two days to perform the ceremony.
But never had the words so much meaning. *That* marriage should last. Still, if
it does not—well, that will be all right.
For, don't you see, *any* step that one
takes is useful, is positive, *has* to be positive, because it is part of life. And nega-
tion of the previously taken step is
positive. It too is part of life. And in this
light, and *only* in this light, should marriage be regarded. As a small, single
step. If it works—fine! If it fails—fine!
Look elsewhere for satisfaction. Perhaps
to more marriages—fine! As many as
one likes—fine! To homosexuality—
fine! To drug addiction—I won't put it
down. Each of these is an *answer*—for
somebody. For Alfred, today's answer is
Patsy. For Patsy, today's answer is
Alfred. I won't put them down for that.
So what I implore you both, Alfred and
Patricia, to dwell on as I ask the questions required by the State of New York
in order to legally bind you—sinister
phrase, that—is that not only are the
legal questions I ask you meaningless
but so, too, are those *inner* questions
you ask of yourselves meaningless. Failing one's partner does *not* matter. Sexual disappointment does *not* matter.
Nothing can hurt if we do not see it as
hurtful. Nothing can destroy if we will
not see it as destructive. It is all part of
life. Part of what we are. So now,
Alfred. Do you take Patricia as your
lawfully wedded wife, to love—whatever *that* means—to honor—but is not
dishonor, in a sense, a *form* of honor?—
to keep her in sickness, in health, in
prosperity and adversity—what nonsense!— Forsaking all others—what a
shocking invasion of privacy! Rephrase
that to more sensibly say: if you *choose*
to have affairs you won't feel guilty
about them—as long as you both shall
live—or as long as you're not bored
with each other?

ALFRED: *{Numb}* I do.

DUPAS: So. Patricia. Do you take
Alfred here as your lawfully wedded
husband, to love—that harmful word—
can't we more wisely say: communicate?—to honor—meaning, I suppose,
you won't cut his balls off. Yet some
men like that. And to obey—well, my
very first look at you told me you were
not the type to obey, so I went through
the thesaurus and came up with these
alternatives: to be loyal, to show fealty,
to show devotion, to answer the helm—
general enough, I would think, and still

leave plenty of room to dominate, in sickness, in health, and all the rest of that gobbledegook, as long as you both shall live?

PATSY: *{Struggling to suppress her fury}* I do.

DUPAS: Alfred and Patsy. I know now that whatever you do will be all right. And Patsy's father, Carol Newquist— I've never heard that name on a man before, but I'm sure it's all right—I ask you, sir, not to feel guilt over the $250 check you gave me to mention the deity in this ceremony. What you have done is all right. It is part of what you are, what we all are. And I beg you not to be overly perturbed when I do not mention the deity in this ceremony. Betrayal, too, is all right. It is part of what we all

are. And Patsy's brother Kenneth Newquist, in whose bedroom I spent a few moments earlier this afternoon and whose mother proudly told me the decoration was by your hand *entirely:* I beg of you to feel no shame; homosexuality is all right—

[KENNY and CAROL, followed by MARJORIE and GUESTS, charge DUPAS. Outraged screams and cries as they mob and beat him. PATSY staggers off as DUPAS, crying "It's all right, it's all right," is driven out the door. CAROL turns on ALFRED and begins to slug away at his body. ALFRED, unflinching, begins to hum}

CURTAIN

Act II

SCENE ONE

Four hours later. The Newquist apartment is strewn with wedding litter. ALFRED and CAROL have not moved since last scene. They stand in half dark, CAROL sluggishly pounding away at ALFRED, who is humming obviously in a dream world. The phone rings several times. PATSY enters, answers phone—amplified breathing.

PATSY: *{Into phone}* You're all we need today. *{Hangs up. To CAROL]* Daddy, you've been at it for hours. Will you please come away from there? *{She helps CAROL off. ALFRED doesn't move. She reenters, stares a long while at him}* Mother's hysterical, Daddy's collapsed and Kenny's disappeared with my wardrobe. I hope you're pleased with your day's work. *{She goes to him}* You can stop daydreaming, Alfred. Nobody's hitting—

{Stops. Takes off wedding glove. Cocks back fist. Holds, undecided. Distant gunshot}

ALFRED: *{Coming out of trance}* I thought it was a very nice ceremony. *{She drops fist}* A little hokey—

PATSY: *{Controlling herself}* Alfred? *{Waves hand in front of his face}* What's going to become of us if you go on this way? Weren't you *there?*

Weren't you *listening?* I wanted a *wedding!* What in God's name do you use for feelings?

ALFRED: I feel.

PATSY: You don't feel.

ALFRED: Have it your way.

PATSY: There you go again! You won't fight!

ALFRED: You knew I wouldn't fight before you married me. I didn't realize it was a prerequisite.

PATSY: Well, maybe it is. More and more I think it is. If you don't fight you don't feel. If you don't feel you don't love.

ALFRED: I don't know—

PATSY: *{Finishing his sentence}* What love is. Of course you don't know! Because you don't feel.

ALFRED: I feel what I want to feel.

PATSY: *{An impulsive kiss}* It's like kissing white bread. You *don't* feel!

Alfred, what is it with you? It gets worse instead of better! I've never had a man do this to me before. It's not just pain you don't feel, you don't feel *pleasure!*

ALFRED: I do feel pleasure.

PATSY: About what?

ALFRED: A lot of things.

PATSY: Name one.

ALFRED: {*Pause*} My work.

PATSY: Name another.

ALFRED: {*Pause*} Sleeping.

PATSY: Work and sleeping! That's just great! What about sex?

ALFRED: {*Pause*} It helps you sleep better.

PATSY: Alfred, do you mean half the things you say? You *must* feel something! {*No response. Snaps her fingers in his face. No response. Holds her head*} Jesus Christ! {*Very tired*} Alfred, why did you marry me?

ALFRED: {*Pause*} You're comfortable.

PATSY: *I've never made men comfortable!* I'm popular because I make them *uncertain. You don't understand the first thing about me!*

ALFRED: Patsy, you're screaming.

PATSY: *Screaming! You son of a bitch, I'll tear you limb from limb! I married you because I wanted to mold you. I love the man I wanted to mold you into! But you're not even there! How can I mold you if you're not there?*

ALFRED: Everything I say makes you unhappy. We used to get along so well—

PATSY: Because *I* did all the talking! My God! That's why you were always so quiet! You weren't listening—

ALFRED: Sure I was.

PATSY: Don't lie, Alfred. I used to stare into those eyes of yours, so warm, so complete with understanding—and now I remember where I've seen those eyes since—When my father was hitting you! *That's* the way you look when you're daydreaming!

ALFRED: You don't get hurt that way.

PATSY: Honey, I don't want to hurt you. I want to change you. I want to make you see that there is some value

in life, that there is some beauty, some tenderness, some things *worth* reacting to. Some things *worth* feeling {*Snaps finger in front of his eyes*}—Come back here! I swear, Alfred, *nobody* is going to kill you. {*Distant gunshots*} But you've got to take some *chances* some time! What do you want out of life? Just *survival?*

ALFRED: {*Nods*} And to take pictures.

PATSY: Of shit? It's not enough! It's not, not, not enough! I'm not going to have a surviving marriage, I'm going to have a flourishing marriage! I'm a *woman!* Or, by Jesus, it's about time I became one. I want a *family!* Oh, Christ, Alfred, this is my wedding day. {*Pause. Regains composure*} I want—I want to be married to a big, strong, protective, vital, virile, self-assured man. Who I can protect and take care of. Alfred, honey, you're the first man I've ever gone to bed with where I didn't feel *he* was a lot more likely to get pregnant than I was. {*Desperate*} You owe me something! I've invested everything I believe in you. You've *got* to let me mold you. *Please* let me mold you. {*Regains control*} You've got me begging. You've got me whining, begging and crying. I've never behaved like this in my life. Will you look at this? {*Holds out finger*} That's a tear. I never cried in my life.

ALFRED: Me neither.

PATSY: You never cried because you were too terrified of everything to let yourself *feel!* You'd have to learn crying from a manual! Chop onions! I never cried because I was too tough—but I felt *everything.* Every slight, every pressure, every vague competition—but I *fought.* And I *won!* There hasn't been a battle since I was five that I haven't won! And the people I fought were happy that I won! Happy! After a while. Alfred, do you have any idea how many people in this town *worship* me? {*To herself, quickly*} Maybe that's the attraction—you don't worship me. Maybe I'd quit loving you if you *did* worship me. Maybe I'd lose all respect for you if you did all the things I want you to do.

{Thinks about it} Alfred, you've got to change! *{Regains calm}* Listen . . . I'm not saying I'm better or stronger than you are. It's just that we—you and I—have different temperaments. *{Explodes} And my temperament is better and stronger than yours! {No reaction}* You're a wall! *{Circles around him}* You don't fight! You hardly even listen! Dear God, will somebody please explain to me why I think you're so beautiful? *{Phone rings. She picks it up. Amplified breathing}* Leave me alone! What do you want out of me? Will you please leave me alone?

[ALFRED, *startled by outburst, takes phone away.* PATSY *buries her head in her hands}*

ALFRED: *{Into phone}* She can't talk now.

{Hangs up. Distant siren. PATSY *brings hands down from her face: all life has been drained out of it}*

PATSY: *{Empty}* Alfred, it's all shit. How come I never noticed before?

ALFRED: Patsy—

PATSY: *{Empty}* You were right. I'm just dense. *I'm* the one who doesn't feel. It's all terrible. Terrible. Terrible.

ALFRED: Come on, Patsy.

PATSY: *{Empty}* No more reason for *anything.*

ALFRED: *{Uncomfortable, weakly}* Mrs. Newquist!

PATSY: *{Flat}* The only true feeling is no feeling. The only way to survive. You're one hundred percent right. Hold my hand. [ALFRED *backs away.* PATSY *drops hand}* I'm sorry. I'm not this weak, really. You know how tough I am. I'll be just as tough again, I promise. I just have to learn to be tough about shit. And I will.

[ALFRED *backs off to a chair}*

ALFRED: I feel weak.

PATSY: *{Flat}* Alfred, we can't both feel weak at the same time.

ALFRED: Patsy, you're beginning to get me nervous. You have to listen to me for a minute—

PATSY: *{Flat}* You're right. I'm wrong. Everything is the way you say.

{Begins to withdraw} You sit. *{Sits}* You get old. *{Freezes}* You die.

{Stares as if in one of ALFRED's *day-dreams.* ALFRED *goes to her. Touches her head. No reaction. Lifts her arm. It drops limply to her side. He stares at her horri-fied, then goes into his daydream stare. He slides into the chair opposite hers. Both stare blankly into space. Phone rings. Many rings.* ALFRED *finally rises, crosses to phone, numbly lifts it. Ampli-fied breathing}*

ALFRED: *{Dazed, into phone}* Thanks. I'm up. *{Hangs up. Stares thoughtfully at* PATSY. *Then, slowly, deliberately}* During Korea—I was in school then—the government couldn't decide whether I was a security risk or not—I wore a beard—so they put a mail check on me. *{Passes a hand in front of her eyes. No reaction}* Every day the mail would come later and later. And it would be bent. Corners torn. Never sealed cor-rectly. Like they didn't give a damn whether I knew they were reading my mail or not. I was more of a militant in those days, so I decided to fight fire with fire. I began writing letters to the guy who was reading my mail. I addressed them to myself, of course, but inside they went something like: "Dear Sir: I am not that different from you. All men are brothers. Tomorrow, instead of read-ing my mail in that dark, dusty hall, why not bring it upstairs where we can check it out together." I never got an answer. So I wrote a second letter. "Dear Sir: There are no heroes, no villains, no good guys, no bad guys. The world is more complicated than that. Come on up where we can open a couple of beers and talk it all out." *{Checks* PATSY. *No reac-tion}* Again no answer. So then I wrote: "Dear Sir: I've been thinking too much of my own problems, too little of yours. Yours cannot be a happy task—reading another man's mail. It's dull, unimagina-tive. A job—and let's not mince words —for a hack. Yet, I wonder—can this be the way you see yourself? Do you see yourself as a hack? Do you see yourself as the office slob? Have you ever *wondered* why they stuck *you* with *this* particular job, instead of others who have *less* seniority? Or was it, do you think, that your supervisor looked around the office to see who he'd stick for the job, saw *you* and said, 'No one will miss *him* for a month!' " *{Checks* PATSY] *That* letter never got delivered to me. So *then* I wrote: "Dear Friend: Just a note to advise—you may retain my letters as long as you deem fit. Reread them. Study them. Think them out. Who back at the home office is *out to get you?* Who, at this *very* moment, is sitting at *your* desk, reading *your* mail? I do not say this to be cruel, but because I am the only one left you can *trust*—" No answer. *But,* the next day a man, saying he was from the telephone company, showed up—no complaint had been made—to check the phone. Shaky hands. Bloodshot eyes. A small quaver in the voice. And as he dismembered my phone he said, "Look. What nobody understands is that everybody has his job to do. I got my job. In this case it's repairing telepones. I like it or I don't like it, but it's my job. If I had another job—say, for example, with the F.B.I. or someplace, putting in a wiretap, for example, or reading a guy's mail—*like it or don't like it, it would be my job!* Has anyone got the right to *destroy* a man for doing his job?" I wrote one more letter—expressing my deep satisfaction that he and I had at last made contact, and informing him that the next time he came, say, to read the meter, I had valuable information, photostats, recordings, names and dates, about the conspiracy against him. This letter showed up a week after I mailed it, in a crumpled, grease-stained, and Scotch-taped envelope. The letter itself was torn in half and then clumsily glued together again. In the margin, on the bottom, in large, shaky letters was written the word: "Please!" I wasn't bothered again. It was after this that I began to wonder: If they're *that* unformidable, why bother to fight back? *{*PATSY *stirs}* It's very dangerous to challenge a system unless you're completely at peace with the thought that you're not going to miss it when it collapses. Patsy—You can't be the one to change. *{*PATSY *stares, uncomprehending}* I'm the one who has to change.

PATSY: *{Tired}* Alfred, what are you talking about?

ALFRED: When I first met you I remember thinking, this is the most formidable person I have ever known. I don't stand a chance! I'll try to stay the way I am. I'll try desperately! *{Happily}* But I don't stand a chance! It's only a matter of time. Very soon now I'll be *{Smiles}*—different. I'll be able to look at half-empty glasses of water and say, This glass isn't half empty. This glass is half *full! You* can't be the one to sell out. *I* was supposed to sell out. *{Stares miserably at the disheveled, slumped-over* PATSY *he's created}* Why doesn't somebody beat me up now? *{Starts off}* I'm going out to Central Park!

{He exits}

PATSY: *{Watches him go. Slowly straightens}* Alfred—*Come back here! {A long pause, then* ALFRED *enters, uncertain}* You see what happens when you start fooling around with the rules? *{Recovering, holds out her arms}* It begins with weddings and it ends with —well, there's no telling where it ends. *{More affirmative}* There are reasons for doing things the old way. *{With growing assurance she takes his hands}* Don't look for trouble and trouble won't look for you. *{Very strong}* I don't say there aren't problems but you have to fight. You are going to fight. *{Squeezes her arms around him}* Starting now. Is that right? *{Pause. Finally he nods}* And you are going to feel. Starting right now. Is that right? *{Pause. He finally nods}* I don't want a nod. I want an answer. Say, "Yes, Patsy."

ALFRED: Yes, Patsy.

PATSY: Yes, Patsy, what?

ALFRED: Yes, Patsy—I'm going to feel.

PATSY: Starting when?

ALFRED: Starting as soon as I can manage it.

PATSY: Starting *when?*

ALFRED: Starting now.

PATSY: And what's your first feeling?

ALFRED: It's sort of distant.

PATSY: Don't be ashamed of it.

ALFRED: It's worship.

PATSY: Of God?

ALFRED: Of you.

PATSY: You're doing fine. *{Kisses him. Puts her arms around him}* My lover. *{Kisses him}* My hero! *{Kisses him.* ALFRED *tentatively responds. Em-brace builds.* CAROL *and* MARJORIE *enter. React with warm surprise. They put their arms around each other}*

MARJORIE: Aren't they an attractive couple?

{Sound of gunshot. Window shatters. Explosion of blood as PATSY's *hand flies up to her head. She drops.* CAROL *and* MARJORIE *freeze.* ALFRED *stares down at* PATSY, *then melting into his daydream pose, slowly turns away. The street noise is loud through the shattered window}*

BLACKOUT

SCENE TWO

The Newquist apartment, six months later. There have been changes. Heavy blackout drapes cover the windows. Large photographic blowups of PATSY'S *eyes, nose, hair, smiling lips and teeth are hung unframed on the walls, and are in evidence in several two- and three-foot high stacks on the floor. (These pictures can be premounted on the reverse sides of the molded sections of the walls and pivoted about during the scene change.)*

ALFRED *is bent over a small photo stand, shooting away with a camera, humming to himself. He looks happy. Sporadic gunfire is heard in the background. He pays no attention. Doorbell.* ALFRED *takes a quick last look at the work on the stand, goes to the door, detouring past the couch to pick up a long cardboard carton and shove it out of sight under the couch. He has the beginning of a black eye.*

ALFRED: One minute. *{He checks through keyhole and unlocks door. There are now four different kinds of locks and bolts on door, including a police bar}* One more minute. *{Opens Door}* Hi, Dad!

CAROL: *{Enters carrying bulging brief case}* It's murder out there.

[ALFRED *tries to relieve him of brief case.* CAROL *brusquely pushes him aside}*

ALFRED: Hey, Dad, you're limping!

CAROL: *{Shouts} How many times have I told you not to call me Dad!*

ALFRED: I can't call you "Dad." I can't call you "Carol." What can I call you? "Dear"?

{Long exchange of stares, ALFRED's *good-humored,* CAROL's *sullen}*

CAROL: Call me "Mr. Newquist."

ALFRED: You're just in a bad mood, Dad. Let me fix you a drink.

{Crosses to bar}

CAROL: *{Sits}* I don't want you to fix me— Bourbon.

ALFRED: *{Serving drink}* The family that drinks together sinks together.

CAROL: *{Drinks}* Maybe I'd feel better if you turned on the air conditioner. It blots out the sound of the shooting. Agh, the hell with it. It's here to stay. I might as well get used to it. *{Conspiratorial}* I dropped by police headquarters this afternoon. That's why I'm late.

ALFRED: Are you late?

CAROL: *{Annoyed} Yes, I'm late!* I'm four hours late. I told you I'd be finished with my deliveries at one. Any calls?

ALFRED: The Breather, once or twice. He's picking up the pace again.

CAROL: *{Mutters}* Asthmatic bastard!

ALFRED: I never told you, but the day

after Patsy died he rang up. I went a little crazy—I started screaming, "Didn't you hear the news? No need to call any more! Patsy's dead!" In no more than ten seconds, he called back. And he *spoke!* He said, "I don't know what to say. I'm terribly sorry." And then before hanging up he said, "What can we do? The world's gone crazy!" Not another breath out of him until this week. In mourning, I suppose.

CAROL: You sure it's the same one?

ALFRED: You think we're on a mailing list? God, I *hope* it's the same one.

CAROL: This damned business! *{Conspiratorial}* Keep this under your hat—but I paid an unexpected call on police headquarters this afternoon.

ALFRED: I'm surprised they didn't shoot you.

CAROL: They did shoot me. *{Rubs his leg}* It was my own damned fault. I didn't give the password. *{Hands empty glass to ALFRED, who pours drink}* I feel sorry for those poor bastards. I know a lot of them by their first names. I call them Jimmy, and Mac and Phil. They call me Carol. *{Quickly}* It sounds different when *they* say it. I had a fifteen-minute talk with Lieutenant Practice. Busy as hell but he found fifteen minutes to talk to me. He's convinced they're closing in on the conspiracy.

ALFRED: What conspiracy?

CAROL: Three hundred and forty-five unsolved murders in six months. There's got to be a conspiracy! [ALFRED *shrugs}* There's *got* to be some logic behind all this. Any other calls?

ALFRED: You mean orders? No.

CAROL: I have to admit to you these new pictures are really catching on! Fifty orders of Patsy Number Seven last week, ten orders so far this week of Patsy Number Eight and Fifteen, and five orders from an uptown gallery for the entire Patsy series. *{Thickly}* We wouldn't have come through this without you, Alfred.

ALFRED: *{Shrugs}* I had to do *something* after I abandoned my shit series.

CAROL: *{Emotional}* But you didn't have to put *me* to work. Nobody asked. *{Suddenly defensive}* I didn't ask—

ALFRED: You're a topnotch salesman, Dad.

CAROL: I'm an order taker and a messenger boy. But when I get back on my feet—

ALFRED: It'll be no time.

CAROL: Who knows if they'll even want me back at the office. Six months —*{Shakes his head}* You've been very good—to us.

ALFRED: Forget it.

CAROL: *{Nods}* I'll do that. *{A pained sign}* I wish I resented you less.

ALFRED: Keep up the fight, tiger.

CAROL: *{Sadly}* Patsy used to call me tiger. Everything you say these days reminds me of Patsy.

ALFRED: *{Thoughtful, a little sad}* I owe Patsy a lot. *{Cheerful again}* Why shouldn't I talk like her?

CAROL: Just as long as you don't dress like her. Where's Kenny?

ALFRED: In her closet.

CAROL: Little son of a bitch! Christ, I hope it's only a phase. I don't see where that Doctor Harm is helping any—

ALFRED: Doctor Good.

CAROL: Yeah? Well, I suppose he must be good. Otherwise he'd take a hell of a kidding. *{Depressed}* Agh—I don't understand anything any more. You know how I get through the day?— don't say a word of this to Marjorie— in planned segments. I get up in the morning and I think, Okay, a sniper didn't get me for breakfast, let's see if I can go for my morning walk without being mugged. Okay, I finish my walk, let's see if I can make it back home without having a brick dropped on my head from the top of a building. Okay, I'm safe in the lobby, let's see if I can go up in the elevator without getting a knife in my ribs. Okay, I made it to the front door, let's see if I can open it without finding burglars in the hall. Okay, I made it to the hall, let's see if I can walk into the living room and not find the rest of my family dead. *This Goddamned city!*

ALFRED: *{With sympathy}* Got to fight, tiger.

CAROL: You do enough fighting for one family. Where'd you get that eye?

{He indicates ALFRED's *mouse}*

ALFRED: Some kid was staring at me in the park. I hit him.

CAROL: *{Tired}* Another fight?

ALFRED: What could I do? The little bastard was *staring* at me! [CAROL *turns away in disgust. Placating}* I beat the crap out of him—[CAROL *reluctantly smiles.* ALFRED *starts to spar with him}* Let's go a couple of quick ones, tiger.

CAROL: *{Retreating}* Come on. Cut it out. Cut it out.

ALFRED: *{Sparring}* Pow! Pow! Pow! Boy if Patsy could have only been there! *{Mimes a wicked kick}* And she said I didn't feel. Every time I get into one of these things, I think of her—I think of her alive and me coming home weary, every night—you know, after I beat somebody up, and she meets me at the door, looking up at me with eyes full of pride, and she takes my swollen fists in her hands, and she kisses my knuckles —what a dream. Why is it we only learn when it's too late? *{Spars}* Pow! Pow! It was my fourth fight this week. I suppose all the euphoria takes something out of you. Anyhow, I got very faint, so I sat down on a park bench to rest—and I found *this* lying there.

{He holds up the Daily News]

CAROL: *{Reading}* "Hippie Minister Slain at Church Happening." They're sure giving that son of a bitch a hell of a lot of free publicity!

ALFRED: It wasn't so much the story that interested me. I don't have the patience for facts, or any of that nonsense any more. What interested me was *{Shows* CAROL *newspaper}* this photograph of the body—what does it look like?

CAROL: That son of a bitch. With his eyes closed.

ALFRED: *{Excited}* No! Look closer!

{He raises newspaper to CAROL's *face}*

CAROL: What do I want to look for? This is the silliest—

ALFRED: Don't you see the dots?

CAROL: What dots?

ALFRED: Here! The little black dots that make up the photograph. Use your eyes, Dad!

CAROL: *{Pushes paper away}* Okay. I see them! So what!

ALFRED: Keep staring at them. *{Raises paper closer to* CAROL's *face}* You see how they slowly begin to move? *{Takes paper away from* CAROL] I was sitting on the park bench looking at this photograph of the body and the little black dots began to break apart—they began detaching themselves from the body— the dots that make up his eyes—the little black dots that make up his mouth —and the top of his head—they just lifted off his body—and broke apart. Until it wasn't the body of Henry Dupas I was staring at, but millions of little black dots coming at me until I thought I was going to be sucked in alive. I panicked! I wanted to close off! But then I thought, Wait a minute, that's the *old* you, the *pre-Patsy* you. So I let go and I was swallowed. Into a free-floating constellation of dots. Fantastic! I swung my eyes away from the photograph—I looked up at a tree. Do you know how many trillions of dots there are in one Central Park tree? And then the dots that made up the tree merged with the dots that made up the sky merged with the dots that made up the park bench and the grass and the dirt path and the three colored kids walking toward me carrying bicycle chains. Do you know the wild arrangement of dots that's made everytime you punch somebody out? Those poor kids must've thought I was crazy—humming as I beat their heads against the sidewalk. [*Offstage muffled shot}* I've been studying this newspaper for hours now trying to figure out a way of decomposing everything into dots.

CAROL: I don't know why you want

to fool around. We're doing *extremely* well with our current line.

ALFRED: There gets to be something ultimately stifling about taking photographs of old photographs.

CAROL: *{Reasonably}* You enlarge them.

ALFRED: It's limited! I want to do *life!* If I could somehow make people see themselves as trillions upon trillions of free-wheeling, interchanging dots— *{Loses himself in thought.* CAROL *shakes his head, says nothing. Doorbell.* ALFRED *puts an arm on* CAROL's *shoulder and goes to door}* One minute. *{Looks through peephole. Begins the process of unlocking the door}* One more minute.

MARJORIE: *{Enters, flushed, carrying leaking shopping bag}* Will you look at this mess? They shot a hole in my shopping bag.

CAROL: *{Stricken}* You could have been killed!

MARJORIE: *{Annoyed}* I get shot at every day. We all do, Carol. Don't make more of it than it is. *{To* ALFRED*}* I saw that nice Lieutenant Practice in the lobby. He looks simply awful. I invited him up for coffee just as soon as he gets finished investigating the new murder.

CAROL: What new murder?

MARJORIE: *{Bored}* I don't know. It's in the other wing. [ALFRED *reaches under couch and slides out long carton he concealed at start of scene. It is not the box he intended to pull out. He slides it back and reaches for a smaller box, which he hands to* MARJORIE]

ALFRED: Mom.

MARJORIE: *{Opens box}* Alfred. Oh, Alfred! *{Removes flowers}* Aren't they beautiful! Look, Carol, they're flowers! *{Clutches them to her. Cries}* I'm sorry —there is so little thought left of giving today that I've forgotten how to receive. *{Drops flowers. Rushes offstage, holding her hands to her face. Offstage}* Kenny! Let me in there!

{Offstage toilet flush, door slams. KENNY *camps in, wearing dark glasses,*

carrying *Vogue.* CAROL, *who cannot look at him, exits.* KENNY *sees flowers on floor. He picks them up}*

ALFRED: You want 'em?

KENNY: *{Drops flowers}* What do I want with your fruity flowers?

(ALFRED *returns to camera stand.* MARJORIE *enters}*

MARJORIE: *{Staring down at flowers}* Alfred, you are a love. [ALFRED, *distracted, waves from camera stand}* When I was twelve-and-a-half my mother and father would cart the whole pack of us out to the country and we would always picnic near the flowers. There were so many more flowers in those days. We'd pick every last one and bring it back to the city. *{To* KENNY *as she stoops for flowers}* No one does the cleaning up around here except me. *{Doorbell.* KENNY *starts for door}* I'll get it. [KENNY *spots protruding edge of the carton under the couch}* Who is it? Will you step a little closer and turn your face into the light please?

{She checks peephole, starts to unlock door. KENNY *slides out carton, is about to lift lid}*

ALFRED: *{Still peering into camera on stand}* That's—not—a—good—idea—

KENNY: *{Whirls}* Who died and made you boss? *{Shot splinters window near* KENNY's *head just as* LIEUTENANT PRACTICE *enters.* KENNY *shakes fist at window, screams}* Fags!

MARJORIE: *{To* PRACTICE*}* You'll have to pardon the mess.

CAROL: *{Enters, glances over to* KENNY *at window, hurries over to* PRACTICE, *shakes his hand}* Well, well, well. This is an unexpected pleasure. Alfred, look who's decided to pay us a visit. Lieutenant Practice! [ALFRED, *at work, gives a perfunctory wave of hand.* CAROL *whispers}* He's working. Goes on day and night. It's no accident he's successful.

PRACTICE: And I'm not. Is that it?

CAROL: *{Takes his arm}* I didn't mean that. You're making great strides.

Nobody expects very much anyway. [PRACTICE *draws arm away}* Nobody's complaining.

MARJORIE: *{Cheerful}* We certainly haven't complained. And if anyone has a right to—

PRACTICE: *{Sad}* Can I please have a glass of milk, Mrs. Newquist?

{He sits down}

MARJORIE: Of course, dear.

PRACTICE: And a cookie. Jeez, I'm depressed. There's got to be some logical explanation to all of this.

[MARJORIE exits}

CAROL: You've got nothing to be ashamed of. You'll figure it out.

PRACTICE: *{Hands* CAROL *envelope}* I really stopped by to return this. I don't know what got into me this afternoon.

CAROL: *{Looks nervously around}* It's all right. It's yours! Forget it!

PRACTICE: I *can't* accept a $250 check. I know your heart was in the right place, Mr. Newquist, but believe me, it's not gonna make us find your daughter's murderer any quicker.

CAROL: Keep it! Keep it! You never can tell—

MARJORIE: *{Enters with glass of milk}* Drink this. You'll feel better. Carol, are you giving money away again? You know, Lieutenant, every time we pass a policeman he hands him five dollars.

CAROL: I just want the boys on the beat to know somebody still has faith in them.

PRACTICE: *{Drinks}* I needed this. [ALFRED *slides carton back under couch;* KENNY *watches with interest.* PRACTICE *examines hand holding glass. It has a tremor}* I wasn't like this when I met you six months ago, was I? Wasn't I a lot more self-confident? Jeez, the way I used to enter the scene of a crime! Like I owned the Goddamned world! Can you put a little Scotch in this milk, please? And a piece of cheese on this cookie? There's going to be a shakeup, you know. When there are three hun-

dred and forty-five murders and none of them get solved. *{Angry}* Somebody has to be elected fall guy! *{Accepts drink}* Thank you. Maybe a piece of ice like a good fellow. *{Hands drink back}* Somewhere there's a logical pattern to this whole business. There *has* to be. *{Accepts cookie}* I didn't ask for butter on the cookie, just cheese. *{Hands cookie back}* Thank you. And these damned vigilante groups—they're not helping matters. Black against white. White against black. What ever became of human dignity? *{Accepts drink}* Oh, for Christ sakes, only *one* piece of ice? Let's get it right, huh? Say, what kind of cheese is this? Sharp cheddar? You ought to know by now with my stomach I can't take sharp cheddar! Come on! *Will you shape up?* *{Reflective}* Sooner or later there's a pattern. Sooner or later everything falls into place. I believe that. If I didn't believe that I wouldn't want to wake up to see the sun tomorrow morning. [CAROL *and* MARJORIE *scrambling from different directions with drink and cheese}* Is *this* what I asked for? Goddamnit. *I want some cooperation! {A shot—milk glass explodes in his hand. All except* PRACTICE *stare toward window. He stares at remnant of glass in his hand}* Every crime has its own pattern of logic. Everything has an order. If we can't find that order it's not because it doesn't exist, but only because we've incorrectly observed some vital piece of evidence. Let us examine the evidence. *{Places glass in handkerchief, handkerchief in pocket}* Number one. In the last six months three hundred and forty-five homicides have been committed in this city. The victims have ranged variously in sex, age, social status and color. Number two. In none of the three hundred and forty-five homicides have we been able to establish motive. Number three. All three hundred and forty-five homicides remain listed on our books as unsolved. So much for the evidence. A subtle pattern begins to emerge. What is this pattern? What is it that each of these three hundred and forty-five homicides have in common? They have in common three things: a) that they have nothing in common; b) that they have no motive; c) that, consequently, they remain unsolved. The pattern becomes clearer. Orthodox police procedure dictates that the basic question you ask in all such investigations is: I) who has the most to gain? What could possibly be the single unifying motive behind three hundred and forty-five unconnected homicides? When a case does not gel it is often not because we lack the necessary facts, but because we have observed our facts incorrectly. In each of these three hundred and forty-five homicides we observed our facts incorrectly. Following normal routine we looked for a cause. And we could find no cause. Had we looked for effect we would have had our answer that much sooner. What is the effect of three hundred and forty-five unsolved homicide cases? The effect is loss of faith in law-enforcement personnel. That is our motive. The pattern is complete. We are involved here in a far-reaching conspiracy to undermine respect for our basic beliefs and most sacred institutions. Who is behind this conspiracy? Once again ask the question: Who has the most to gain? People in high places. Their names would astound you. People in low places. Concealing their activities beneath a cloak of poverty. People in all walks of life. Left wing and right wing. Black and white. Students and scholars. A conspiracy of such ominous proportions that we may not know the whole truth in our lifetime, and we will never be able to reveal all the facts. We are readying mass arrests. *{Rises to leave}* I'm going to try my best to see that you people get every possible break. If there is any information you wish to volunteer at this time it will be held in the strictest confidence. *{Waits for response.*

There is none. Crosses to door and opens it} I strongly advise against any of you trying to leave town.

{Quickly exits}

CAROL: *{Gradually exploding}* What's left? What's there left? I'm a reasonable man. Just explain to me what I have left to believe in. I swear to God the tide's rising! Two hundred and fifty dollars. Gimme, gimme. We need honest cops! People just aren't being protected any more! We need a revival of honor. And trust! We need the Army! We need a giant fence around every block in the city. An electrically charged fence. And everyone who wants to leave the block has to have a pass. And a hair cut. And can't talk with a filthy mouth! We need respect for a man's reputation. TV cameras! That's what we need! In every building lobby, in every elevator, in every apartment, in every room. Public servants who *are* public servants! And if they catch you doing anything funny— to yourself, or anybody—they break down the door and beat the living— A return to common sense! We have to have lobotomies for anyone who earns less than ten thousand a year. I don't like it but it's an emergency. Our side needs weapons too. Is it fair that they should have all the weapons? We've got to train ourselves! And steel ourselves! It's freedom I'm talking about! There's a fox loose in the chicken coop! *Kill him!* I want my *freedom!*

{He collapses}

ALFRED: Let's get him inside.

[ALFRED *and* MARJORIE *carry* CAROL *off.* KENNY *watches after them, quickly crosses to box, slides it out and lifts lid as* MARJORIE *enters.* KENNY *slams down lid.* MARJORIE *grabs bottle from bar and exits.* KENNY *lifts rifle out of box, goes to window, parts curtain slightly, aims* —ALFRED *enters.* KENNY, *startled, holds rifle out to him}*

KENNY: I thought it was more flowers.

ALFRED: Use it.

KENNY: What do I want to use it for?

I've only been in analysis four months. I've never fired one of these in my life.

ALFRED: Me too.

KENNY: *{Suspicious}* Why'd you get it?

ALFRED: *{Shrugs}* It was on sale. [Stares at rifle in KENNY's *hands. Goes to door, relocks it. To* KENNY] Put it away—[KENNY *begins to}* No. [ALFRED *crosses to* KENNY, *takes rifle, studies it}* You notice, if you stare at it long enough it breaks into dots?

KENNY: *{Studies rifle}* No—

ALFRED: *{Turns rifle in his hand}* Trillions of dots—*{Pulls trigger. A loud click}* It's not loaded.

{Puts it down}

KENNY: Why don't you load it?

ALFRED: I don't know how.

{Hands rifle to KENNY, *who backs away from it}*

KENNY: *{Shakes his head}* The Army rejected me four times. The fifth time they said if I ever came around again they'd have me arrested. *{Reaches into box. Takes out instruction booklet, turns page, reads}* "Nomenclature." *{Turns page}* "Trigger housing group." *{Turns page}* "To load: hold the weapon by the forearm of the stock with left hand. Rotate the safety to its 'on' position. Lock the bolt open. With right hand insert the magazine into the magazine opening and push up."

MARJORIE: *{Enters. Looks over* ALFRED's *shoulder as he struggles to insert magazine clip}* I don't know about these things, dear, but I found the best way to deal with the unfamiliar is to think things back to their source. *{She takes rifle out of his hands}* Now, it would seem to me that *this* goes in— *{Struggles.* CAROL *enters. Observes}* Damn it! They must have given you the wrong—[CAROL *takes rifle out of her hands, expertly loads it, tosses it to* ALFRED. MARJORIE *is very impressed}* Dear!

ALFRED: *{Hands rifle back to* CAROL] Go on, Dad. You loaded it. You go first.

CAROL: *{Solemnly hands rifle back}* It's yours.

KENNY: Where'd you learn that, Dad? It's a trick, right?

[CAROL *stares scornfully at* KENNY, *takes rifle.* ALFRED *parts curtains}*

ALFRED: Can you see well enough?

[CAROL *aims, fires}*

KENNY: I think you got somebody.

MARJORIE: Let me see! I never can see! [ALFRED *boosts her}* Yes! Yes! Somebody's lying there!

CAROL: *{To* ALFRED] Why don't you try *your* luck?

{Hands over rifle}

ALFRED: *{Hands rifle to* KENNY] You first, Kenny.

KENNY: Gee.

ALFRED: *{Reassuring}* I'll go right after you.

[KENNY *quickly gets up with rifle. Fires out window}*

CAROL: Miss!

KENNY: You made me nervous! You were *looking!*

CAROL: *{Takes rifle}* It's Alfred's turn.

KENNY: No fair! You shook my arm.

ALFRED: Let him have another shot.

[KENNY *aims carefully, fires}*

CAROL: *{Looking into street. Very proud}* Son of a bitch!

MARJORIE: *{Hugs him}* You did it! You did it!

[CAROL *reloads, hands rifle to* ALFRED]

KENNY: *{Cool, manly}* Dad and I got *our* two.

[CAROL *puts his arm around* KENNY's *shoulder.* ALFRED *aims out window, fires}*

CAROL: You know who I think he got?

MARJORIE: Lieutenant Practice!

{All jump up and down in self-congratulations—ad lib shouts, Texas yells. ALFRED, CAROL *and* KENNY *in unison; none of the following is intelligible}*

ALFRED: Fantastic! What a picture! Unbelievable! Fantastic! What a picture!

CAROL: Some hell of a team, eh, boys! Now we're moving! Now we'll show 'em! Show the whole Goddamn world!

KENNY: Son of a bitch! Bastard! See me, Dad? Goddamn! Son of a bitch! Goddamn! See me, Alfred?

{During all of this MARJORIE *has made a sprightly exit, instantly reentering, wheeling serving cart. She lights candles on dining-room table}*

MARJORIE: Come an' git it!

{The others, wrestling, horsing around, move slowly toward table}

MARJORIE: Boys!

{Amidst great noise, bustle, serving of drinks, they finally sit. More ad lib cries, friendly shoving}

ALFRED: *{Over the others}* Hey, how about Mom trying her luck after dinner?

{Cheers, ad lib agreement}

MARJORIE: *{Serving}* It's so nice to have my family laughing again. You know, for a while I was really worried.

{General merriment}

CURTAIN

POETRY

Edith Sitwell (1887–1964)

DIRGE FOR THE NEW SUNRISE

(Fifteen minutes past eight o'clock,
on the morning of Monday,
the 6th of August, 1945.)

Bound to my heart as Ixion to the
  wheel,
Nailed to my heart as the Thief upon
  the Cross,
I hang between our Christ and the gap
  where the world was lost

And watch the phantom Sun in Famine
  Street—
The ghost of the heart of man . . . red
  Cain,   5
And the more murderous brain
Of Man, still redder Nero that
  conceived the death
Of his mother Earth, and tore
Her womb, to know the place where he
  was conceived.

But no eyes grieved—   10
For none were left for tears:
They were blinded as the years
Since Christ was born. Mother or
  Murderer, you have given or taken
  life—
Now all is one!
There was a morning when the holy
  Light   15
Was young . . . The beautiful First
  Creature came
To our water-springs, and thought us
  without blame.

Our hearts seemed safe in our breasts
  and sang to the Light—
The marrow in the bone
We dreamed was safe . . . the blood in
  the veins, the sap in the tree   20
Were springs of Deity.
But I saw the little Ant-men as they ran
Carrying the world's weight of the
  world's filth
And the filth in the heart of Man—
Compressed till those lusts and greeds
  had a greater heat than that of the
  Sun.   25

And the ray from that heat came
  soundless, shook the sky
As if in search for food, and squeezed
  the stems
Of all that grows on the earth till they
  were dry—
And drank the marrow of the bone:
The eyes that saw, the lips that kissed,
  are gone—   30
Or black as thunder lie and grin at the
  murdered Sun.

The living blind and seeing Dead
  together lie
As if in love . . . There was no more
  hating then,
And no more love: Gone is the heart of
  Man.

"Dirge for the New Sunrise" from *Collected Poems* by Dame Edith Sitwell, published by Vanguard. Reprinted by permission of David Higham Associates, Ltd.

Marianne Moore (1887–1972)
POETRY

I, too, dislike it: there are things that are important beyond all this
    fiddle.
  Reading it, however, with a perfect contempt for it, one discovers in
  it after all, a place for the genuine.
      Hands that can grasp, eyes
      that can dilate, hair that can rise   5
        if it must, these things are important not because a

high-sounding interpretation can be put upon them but because they
    are
  useful. When they become so derivative as to become unintelligible,
  the same thing may be said for all of us, that we
      do not admire what   10
      we cannot understand: the bat
        holding on upside down or in quest of something to

eat, elephants pushing, a wild horse taking a roll, a tireless wolf under
  a tree, the immovable critic twitching his skin like a horse that feels
  a flea, the base-
  ball fan, the statistician—   15
      nor is it valid
        to discriminate against 'business documents and

school-books'; all these phenomena are important. One must make a
    distinction
  however: when dragged into prominence by half poets, the result is
  not poetry,
  nor till the poets among us can be   20
    'literalists of
      the imagination'—above
        insolence and triviality and can present

for inspection, 'imaginary gardens with real toads in them', shall we
    have
  it. In the meantime, if you demand on the one hand,   25
  the raw material of poetry in
    all its rawness and
      that which is on the other hand
        genuine, you are interested in poetry.

  Reprinted with permission of Macmillan Publishing Co., Inc., from *Collected Poems* by
Marianne Moore. "Poetry" (copyright 1935 by Marianne Moore, renewed © 1963 by
Marianne Moore and T. S. Eliot) and "The Steeple-Jack" (copyright 1951 by Marianne
Moore).

THE STEEPLE-JACK

Dürer would have seen a reason for living
   in a town like this, with eight stranded whales
to look at; with the sweet sea air coming into your house
on a fine day, from water etched
   with waves as formal as the scales   5
on a fish.

One by one in two's and three's, the seagulls keep
   flying back and forth over the town clock,
or sailing around the light house without moving their wings—
rising steadily with a slight   10
   quiver of the body—or flock
mewing where

a sea the purple of the peacock's neck is
   paled to greenish azure as Dürer changed
the pine green of the Tyrol to peacock blue and guinea   15
gray. You can see a twenty-five-
   pound lobster; and fish nets arranged
to dry. The

whirlwind fife-and-drum of the storm bends the salt
   marsh grass, disturbs stars in the sky and the   20
star on the steeple; it is a privilege to see so
much confusion. Disguised by what
   might seem the opposite, the sea-
side flowers and

trees are favored by the fog so that you have   25
   the tropics at first hand: the trumpet vine,
foxglove, giant snapdragon, a salpiglossis that has
spots and stripes; morning-glories, gourds,
   or moon-vines trained on fishing twine
at the back door: 30

cattails, flags, blueberries and spiderwort,
   striped grass, lichens, sunflowers, asters, daisies—
yellow and crab-claw ragged sailors with green bracts—toad-plant,
petunias, ferns; pink lilies, blue
   ones, tigers; poppies, black sweet-peas.   35
The climate

is not right for the banyan, frangipani, or
   jack-fruit trees; or for exotic serpent
life. Ring lizard and snakeskin for the foot, if you see fit;

but here they've cats, not cobras, to
   keep down the rats. The diffident
little newt   40

with white pin-dots on black horizontal spaced-
   out bands lives here; yet there is nothing that
ambition can buy or take away. The college student   45
named Ambrose sits on the hillside
   with his not-native books and hat
and sees boats

at sea progress white and rigid as if in
   a groove. Liking an elegance of which   50
the source is not bravado, he knows by heart the antique
sugar-bowl shaped summerhouse of
   interlacing slats, and the pitch
of the church

spire, not true, from which a man in scarlet lets   55
   down a rope as a spider spins a thread;
he might be part of a novel, but on the sidewalk a
sign says C. J. Poole, Steeple Jack,
   in black and white; and one in red
and white says   60

Danger. The church portico has four fluted
   columns, each a single piece of stone, made
modester by whitewash. This would be a fit haven for
waifs, children, animals, prisoners,
   and presidents who have repaid   65
sin-driven

senators by not thinking about them. The
   place has a schoolhouse, a post-office in a
store, fish-houses, hen-houses, a three masted schooner on
the stocks. The hero, the student,   70
   the steeple jack, each in his way,
is at home.

It could not be dangerous to be living
   in a town like this, of simple people,
who have a steeple-jack placing danger signs by the church   75
while he is gilding the solid-
   pointed star, which on a steeple
stands for hope.

Langston Hughes (1902–1967)
THEME FOR ENGLISH B

The instructor said,

> *Go home and write*
> *a page tonight.*
> *And let that page come out of you—*
> *Then, it will be true.*

I wonder if it's that simple?   5

I am twenty-two, colored, born in Winston-Salem.
I went to school there, then Durham, then here
to this college on the hill above Harlem.
I am the only colored student in my class.   10
The steps from the hill lead down into Harlem,
through a park, then I cross St. Nicholas,
Eighth Avenue, Seventh, and I come to the Y,
the Harlem Branch Y, where I take the elevator   15
up to my room, sit down, and write this page:

It's not easy to know what is true for you or me
at twenty-two, my age. But I guess I'm what
I feel and see and hear, Harlem, I hear you:
hear you, here me—we two—you, me, talk on this page.
(I hear New York, too) Me—who?   20
Well, I like to eat, sleep, drink, and be in love.
I like to work, read, learn, and understand life.
I like a pipe for a Christmas present,
or records—Bessie, bop, or Bach.
I guess being colored doesn't make me *not* like   25
the same things other folks like who are other races.
So will my page be colored that I write?

Being me, it will not be white.
But it will be
a part of you, instructor.   30
You are white—
yet a part of me, as I am a part of you.
That's American.
Sometimes perhaps you don't want to be a part of me.
Nor do I often want to be a part of you.   35
But we are, that's true!

From *Montage of a Dream Deferred* by Langston Hughes. Reprinted by permission of Harold Ober Associates Incorporated. Copyright 1951 by Langston Hughes.

As I learn from you,
I guess you learn from me—
although you're older—and white—
and somewhat more free.   40

This is my page for English B.

THE NEGRO SPEAKS OF RIVERS

(To W. E. B. DuBois)

I've known rivers:
I've known rivers ancient as the world and older than the flow of human blood
    in human veins.

My soul has grown deep like the rivers.

I bathed in the Euphrates when dawns were young.
I built my hut near the Congo and it lulled me to sleep.
I looked up the Nile and raised the pyramids above it.
I heard the singing of the Mississippi when Abe Lincoln went down to New
    Orleans, and I've seen its muddy bosom turn all golden in the sunset.

I've known rivers:
Ancient, dusky rivers.

My soul has grown deep like the rivers.

DINNER GUEST: ME

I know I am   To probe in polite way
The Negro Problem   The why and wherewithal
Being wined and dined,   Of darkness U.S.A.—
Answering the usual questions   Wondering how things got this way
That come to white mind   In current democratic night,
Which seeks demurely   Murmuring gently

Over *fraises du bois*,
"I'm so ashamed of being white."

The lobster is delicious,
The wine divine,
And center of attention

At the damask table, mine.
To be a Problem on
Park Avenue at eight
Is not so bad.
Solutions to the Problem,
Of course, wait.

HARLEM

What happens to a dream deferred?

Does it dry up
like a raisin in the sun?
Or fester like a sore —
And then run?   5
Does it stink like rotten meat?

Or crust and sugar over —
like a syrupy sweet?

Maybe it just sags
like a heavy load.   10

Or does it explode?

Richard Eberhart (1904–   )
THE FURY OF AERIAL BOMBARDMENT

You would think the fury of aerial
    bombardment
Would rouse God to relent; the infinite
    spaces
Are still silent. He looks on shock-pried
    faces.
History, even, does not know what is
    meant.

You would feel that after so many
    centuries   5
God would give man to repent; yet he
    can kill
As Cain could, but with multitudinous
    will,
No farther advanced than in his ancient
    furies.

Was man made stupid to see his own
    stupidity?
Is God by definition indifferent, beyond
    us all?   10
Is the eternal truth man's fighting soul
Wherein the Beast ravens in its own
    avidity?

Of Van Wettering I speak, and Averill,
Names on a list, whose faces I do not
    recall
But they are gone to early death, who
    late in school   15
Distinguished the belt feed lever from
    the belt holding pawl.

ON SHOOTING PARTICLES BEYOND THE WORLD

"White Sands, N.M., Dec. 18 (U. P.).
'We first throw a little something into
the skies,' Zwicky said. 'Then a little
more, then a shipload of instruments,
then ourselves.' "

On this day man's disgust is known
Incipient before but now full blown
With minor wars of major consequence,
Duly building empirical delusions.

Now this little creature in a rage   5
Like new-born infant screaming
    compleat angler
Objects to the whole globe itself
And with a vicious lunge he throws

Metal particles beyond the orbit of
    mankind.
Beethoven shaking his fist at death,   10
A giant dignity in human terms,
Is nothing to this imbecile metal fury.

The world is too much for him. The
    green
Of earth is not enough, love's deities.
Peaceful intercourse, happiness of
    nations,   15
The wild animals dazzled on the desert.

If the maniac would only realize
The comforts of his padded cell
He would have penetrated the
Impenetrability of the spiritual.   20
It is not intelligent to go too far.
How he frets that he can't go too!
But his particles would maim a star,
His free-floating bombards rock the
    moon.

Good Boy! We pat the baby to
    eructate,   25
We pat him then for eructation.
Good Boy Man! Your innards are put
    out,
From now all space will be your
    vomitorium.

The atom bomb accepted this world,
Its hatred of man blew death in his
    face.   30
But not content, he'll send slugs
    beyond,
His particles of intellect will spit on the
    sun.

Not God he'll catch, in the mystery of
    space.
He flaunts his own out-cast state
As he throws his imperfections outward
    bound   35
And his shout that gives a hissing
    sound.

John Betjeman (1906–   )
IN WESTMINSTER ABBEY

Let me take this other glove off
  As the *vox humana* swells,
And the beauteous fields of Eden
  Bask beneath the Abbey bells.
Here, where England's statesmen lie,   5
Listen to a lady's cry.

Gracious Lord, oh bomb the Germans.
  Spare their women for Thy Sake,
And if that is not too easy
  We will pardon Thy Mistake.   10
But, gracious Lord, whate'er shall be,
Don't let anyone bomb me.

Keep our Empire undismembered
  Guide our Forces by Thy Hand,
Gallant blacks from far Jamaica,   15
  Honduras and Togoland;
Protect them Lord in all their fights,
And, even more, protect the whites.

Think of what our Nation stands for,
  Books from Boots' and country
    lanes,   20
Free speech, free passes, class
  distinction,

Democracy and proper drains.
Lord, put beneath Thy special care
One-eighty-nine Cadogan Square.

Although dear Lord I am a sinner,   25
  I have done no major crime;
Now I'll come to Evening Service
  Whensoever I have the time.
So, Lord, reserve for me a crown,
And do not let my shares go down.   30

I will labour for Thy Kingdom,
  Help our lads to win the war,
Send white feathers to the cowards
  Join the Women's Army Corps,
Then wash the Steps around Thy
    Throne   35
In the Eternal Safety Zone.

Now I feel a little better,
  What a treat to hear Thy Word,
Where the bones of leading statesmen,
  Have so often been interr'd.   40
And now, dear Lord, I cannot wait
Because I have a luncheon date.

SLOUGH

Come, friendly bombs, and fall on
    Slough
It isn't fit for humans now,
There isn't grass to graze a cow
  Swarm over, Death!

Come, bombs, and blow to
    smithereens   5
Those air-conditioned, bright canteens.
Tinned fruit, tinned meat, tinned milk,
    tinned beans
  Tinned minds, tinned breath.

"In Westminster Abbey" and "Slough" from *Collected Poems* by John Betjeman. Reprinted by permission of John Murray, Ltd.

Mess up the mess they call a town—
A house for ninety-seven down   10
And once a week a half-a-crown
   For twenty years,

And get that man with double chin
Who'll always cheat and always win,
Who washes his repulsive skin   15
   In women's tears,

And smash his desk of polished oak
And smash his hands so used to stroke
And stop his boring dirty joke
   And make him yell.   20

But spare the bald young clerks who
   add
The profits of the stinking cad;
It's not their fault that they are mad,
   They've tasted Hell.

It's not their fault they do not know   25
The birdsong from the radio,
It's not their fault they often go
   To Maidenhead

And talk of sports and makes of cars
In various bogus Tudor bars   30
And daren't look up and see the stars
   But belch instead.

In labour-saving homes, with care
Their wives frizz out peroxide hair
And dry it in synthetic air   35
   And paint their nails.

Come, friendly bombs, and fall on
   Slough
To get it ready for the plough.
The cabbages are coming now:
   The earth exhales.   40

Theodore Roethke (1908–1963)

OPEN HOUSE

My secrets cry aloud.
I have no need for tongue.
My heart keeps open house,
My doors are widely swung.
An epic of the eyes   5
My love, with no disguise.

My truths are all foreknown,
This anguish self-revealed.
I'm naked to the bone,

With nakedness my shield,   10
Myself is what I wear:
I keep the spirit spare.
The anger will endure,
The deed will speak the truth
In language strict and pure.   15
I stop the lying mouth:
Rage warps my clearest cry
To witless agony.

MY PAPA'S WALTZ

The whiskey on your breath
Could make a small boy dizzy;
But I hung on like death:
Such waltzing was not easy.

We romped until the pans   5
Slid from the kitchen shelf;
My mother's countenance
Could not unfrown itself.

The hand that held my wrist
Was battered on one knuckle;   10
At every step you missed
My right ear scraped a buckle.

You beat time on my head
With a palm caked hard by dirt,
Then waltzed me off to bed   15
Still clinging to your shirt.

HIGHWAY: MICHIGAN

Here from the field's edge we survey
The progress of the jaded. Mile
On mile of traffic from the town
Rides by, for at the end of day
The time of workers is their own.   5

They jockey for position on
The strip reserved for passing only.
The drivers from production lines
Hold to advantage dearly won.
They toy with death and traffic
     fines.   10

Acceleration is their need:
A mania keeps them on the move
Until the toughest nerves are frayed.
They are the prisoners of speed
Who flee in what their hands have
     made.   15

The pavement smokes when two cars
     meet
And steel rips through conflicting steel.
We shiver at the siren's blast.
One driver, pinned beneath the seat,
Escapes from the machine at last.   20

LULL

(November, 1939)

The winds of hatred blow
Cold, cold across the flesh
And chill the anxious heart;
Intricate phobia grow
From each malignant wish   5
To spoil collective life.
Now each man stands apart.
We watch opinion drift,
Think of our separate skins,
On well-upholstered bums   10

The generals cough and shift
Playing with painted pins.
The arbitrators wait;
The newsmen suck their thumbs.
The mind is quick to turn   15
Away from simple faith
To the cant and fury of
Fools who will never learn;
Reason embraces death,
While out of frightened eyes   20
Still stares the wish to love.

BALLAD OF THE CLAIRVOYANT WIDOW

A kindly Widow Lady, who lived upon a hill,
Climbed to her attic window and gazed across the sill.

  "Oh tell me, Widow Lady, what is it that you see,
  As you look across my city, in God's country?"

"I see ten million windows, I see ten thousand streets,   5
I see the traffic doing miraculous feats.

The lawyers all are cunning, the business men are fat,
Their wives go out on Sunday beneath the latest hat.

The kids play cops and robbers, the kids play mumbley-peg,
Some learn the art of thieving, and some grow up to beg;   10

The rich can play at polo, the poor can do the shag,
Professors are condoning the cultural lag.

I see a banker's mansion with twenty wood-grate fires,
Alone, his wife is grieving for what her heart desires.

Next door there is a love-nest of plaster board and tin,   15
The rats soon will be leaving, the snow will come in."

"Clairvoyant Widow Lady, with an eye like a telescope,
Do you see any sign or semblance of that thing called 'Hope'?"

"I see the river harbor, alive with men and ships,
A surgeon guides a scalpel with thumb and finger-tips.   20

I see grandpa surviving a series of seven strokes,
The unemployed are telling stale unemployment jokes.

The gulls ride on the water, the gulls have come and gone,
The men on rail and roadway keep moving on and on.

The salmon climb the rivers, the rivers nudge the sea,   25
The green comes up forever in the fields of our country."

Karl Shapiro (1913–   )
HOLLYWOOD

Farthest from any war, unique in time
Like Athens or Baghdad, this city lies
Between dry purple mountains and the sea.
The air is clear and famous, every day
Bright as a postcard, bringing bungalows   5
    And sights. The broad nights advertise
For love and music and astronomy.

Heart of a continent, the hearts converge
On open boulevards where palms are nursed
With flare-pots like a grove, on villa roads   10
Where castles cultivated like a style
Breed fabulous metaphors in foreign stone,
    And on enormous movies lots
Where history repeats its vivid blunders.

Alice and Cinderella are most real.   15
Here may the tourist, quite sincere at last,
Rest from his dream of travels. All is new,
No ruins claim his awe, and permanence,
Despised like customs, fails at every turn.
    Here where the eccentric thrives,   20
Laughter and love are leading industries.

Luck is another. Here the body-guard,
The parasite, the scholar are well paid,
The quack erects his alabaster office,
The moron and the genius are enshrined,   25
And the mystic makes a fortune quietly;
   Here all superlatives come true
And beauty is marketed like a basic food.

O can we understand it? Is it ours,
A crude whim of a beginning people,   30
A private orgy in a secluded spot?
Or alien like the word *harem,* or true
Like hideous Pittsburgh or depraved Atlanta?
   Is adolescence just as vile
As this its architecture and its talk?   35

Or are they parvenus, like boys and girls?
Or ours and happy, cleverest of all?
Yes. Yes. Though glamorous to the ignorant
This is the simplest city, a new school.
What is more nearly ours? If soul can mean   40
   The civilization of the brain,
This is a soul, a possibly proud Florence.

THE CONSCIENTIOUS OBJECTOR

The gates clanged and they walked you into jail
More tense than felons but relieved to find
The hostile world shut out, the flags that dripped
From every mother's windowpane, obscene
The bloodlust sweating from the public heart,   5
The dog authority slavering at your throat.
A sense of quiet, of pulling down the blind
Possessed you. Punishment you felt was clean.

The decks, the catwalks, and the narrow light
Composed a ship. This was a mutinous crew   10
Troubling the captains for plain decencies,
A *Mayflower* brim with pilgrims headed out
To establish new theocracies to west,
A Noah's ark coasting the topmost seas
Ten miles above the sodomites and fish.   15
These inmates loved the only living doves.

Like all men hunted from the world you made
A good community, voyaging the storm
To no safe Plymouth or green Ararat;
Trouble or calm, the men with Bibles prayed,   20

The gaunt politicals constructed our hate.
The opposite of all armies, you were best
Opposing uniformity and yourselves;
Prison and personality were your fate.

You suffered not so physically but knew   25
Maltreatment, hunger, ennui of the mind.
Well might the soldier kissing the hot beach
Erupting in his face damn all your kind.
Yet you who saved neither yourselves nor us
Are equally with those who shed the blood   30
The heroes of our cause. Your conscience is
What we come back to in the armistice.

UNIVERSITY

To hurt the Negro and avoid the Jew
Is the curriculum. In mid-September
The entering boys, identified by hats,
Wander in a maze of mannered brick
     Where boxwood and magnolia brood   5
     And columns with imperious stance
     Like rows of anti-bellum girls
          Eye them, outlanders.

In whited cells, on lawns equipped for peace,
Under the arch, and lofty banister,   10
Equals shake hands, unequals blankly pass;
The exemplary weather whispers, "Quiet, quiet"
     And visitors on tiptoe leave
     For the raw North, the unfinished West,
     As the young, detecting an advantage,   15
          Practice a face.

Where, on their separate hill, the colleges,
Like manor houses of an older law,
Gaze down embankments on a land in fee,
The Deans, dry spinsters over family plate,   20
     Ring out the English name like coin,
     Humor the snob and lure the lout.
     Within the precincts of this world
          Poise is a club.

But on the neighboring range, misty and high,   25
The past is absolute: some luckless race
Dull with inbreeding and conformity

Wears out its heart, and comes barefoot and bad
    For charity or jail. The scholar
    Sanctions their obsolete disease;   30
    The gentleman revolts with shame
    At his ancestor.

    And the true nobleman, once a democrat,
Sleeps on his private mountain. He was one
Whose thought was shapely and whose dream was broad;   35
This school he held his art and epitaph.
    But now it takes from him his name,
    Falls open like a dishonest look,
    And shows us, rotted and endowed,
        Its senile pleasure.   40

DRUG STORE

I do remember an apothecary,
And hereabouts 'a dwells—

It baffles the foreigner like an idiom,
And he is right to adopt it as a form
Less serious than the living-room or bar;   5
    For it disestablishes the café,
Is a collective, and on basic country.

Not that it praises hygiene and corrupts
The ice-cream parlor and the tobacconist's
Is it a center; but that the attractive symbols   10
    Watch over puberty and leer
Like rubber bottles waiting for sick-use.

Youth comes to jingle nickels and crack wise;
The baseball scores are his, the magazines
Devoted to lust, the jazz, the Coca-Cola,   15
    The lending-library of love's latest.
He is the customer; he is heroized.

And every nook and cranny of the flesh
Is spoken to by packages with wiles,
"Buy me, buy me," they whimper and cajole;   20
    The hectic range of lipstick pouts,
Revealing the wicked and the simple mouth.

With scarcely any evasion in their eye
They smoke, undress their girls, exact a stance;
But only for a moment. The clock goes round;   25
    Crude fellowships are made and lost;
They slump in booths like rags, not even drunk.

THE HUMANITIES BUILDING

All the bad Bauhaus comes to a head
In this gray slab, this domino, this plinth
Standing among the olives or the old oak trees,
As the case may be and whatever the clime.
No bells, no murals, no gargoyles,
But rearing like a fort, with slits of eyes
Suspicious in the aggregate, its tons
Of concrete—glaciers of no known color—
Gaze down upon us. St. Thomas More,
Behold the Humanities Building!
                              On the top floor
Are one and a half professors of Greek,
Kicked upstairs but with the finest view,
Two philosophers, and assorted Slavics;
Then stacks of languages coming down,
Mainly the mother tongue and its dissident children
(History has a building all its own),
To the bottom level with its secretaries,
Advisers, blue-green photographic light
Of many precious copying machines;
All is bathed in cool fluorescence
From top to bottom, justly distributed:
Light, Innovation, Progress, Equity—
Though in my cell I hope and pray
Not to be confronted by
A student with a gun or a nervous breakdown,
Or a girl who closes the door as she comes in.

The Old Guard sits in judgment and wears ties,
Eying the New in proletarian drag,
And the Assistant with one lowered eyelid
Plots against Tenure, dreaming of getting it,

And in the lobby, under the bulletin boards,
The Baudelairean forest of posters
For Transcendental Meditation, Audubon Group,
"The Hunchback of Notre Dame," Scientology,
Arab Students Co-op, "Case of the Curious Bride,"
Two students munch upon a single sandwich.

Robert E. Hayden (1913–   )
FREDERICK DOUGLASS

When it is finally ours, this freedom, this liberty, this beautiful
and terrible thing, needful to man as air,
usable as earth; when it belongs at last to all,
when it is truly instinct, brain matter, diastole, systole,
reflex action; when it is finally won; when it is more   5
than the gaudy mumbo jumbo of politicians:
this man, this Douglass, this former slave, this Negro
beaten to his knees, exiled, visioning a world
where none is lonely, none hunted, alien,
this man, superb in love and logic, this man   10
shall be remembered. Oh, not with statutes' rhetoric,
not with legends and poems and wreaths of bronze alone,
but with the lives grown out of his life, the lives
fleshing his dream of the beautiful, needful thing.

RUNAGATE RUNAGATE

I.

Runs fall rises stumbles on from darkness into darkness
and the darkness thickened with shapes of terror
and the hunters pursuing and the hounds pursuing
and the night cold and the night long and the river
to cross and the jack-muh-lanterns beckoning beckoning   5
and blackness ahead and when shall I reach that somewhere
morning and keep on going and never turn back and keep on going

      Runagate
           Runagate
                  Runagate   10

Many thousands rise and go
many thousands crossing over

O mythic North
O star-shaped yonder Bible city

Some go weeping and some rejoicing   15
some in coffins and some in carriages
some in silks and some in shackles

     Rise and go or fare you well

No more auction block for me
no more driver's lash for me   20

    If you see my Pompey, 30 yrs of age,
    new breeches, plain stockings, negro shoes;
    if you see my Anna, likely young mulatto
    branded E on the right cheek, R on the left,
    catch them if you can and notify subscriber.   25
    Catch them if you can, but it won't be easy.
    They'll dart underground when you try to catch them,
    plunge into quicksand, whirlpools, mazes,
    turn into scorpions when you try to catch them.

And before I'll be a slave   30
I'll be buried in my grave

    North star and bonanza gold
    I'm bound for the freedom, freedom-bound
    and oh Susyanna don't you cry for me

           Runagate   35
              Runagate

II.

Rises from their anguish and their power,

    Harriet Tubman,

    woman of earth, whipscarred,
    a summoning, a shining   40

Mean to be free

    And this was the way of it, brethren brethren,
    way we journeyed from Can't to Can.
    Moon so bright and no place to hide,
    the cry up and the patterollers riding,   45
    hound dogs belling in bladed air.
    And fears starts a-murbling, Never make it,
    we'll never make it. *Hush that now,*

and she's turned upon us, levelled pistol
glinting in the moonlight: 50
Dead folks can't jaybird-talk, she says;
you keep on going now or die, she says.
Wanted   Harriet Tubman   alias The General
alias Moses   Stealer of Slaves

In league with Garrison   Alcott   Emerson   55
Garrett   Douglass   Thoreau   John Brown

Armed and known to be Dangerous

Wanted   Reward   Dead or Alive

Tell me, Ezekiel, oh tell me do you see
mailed Jehovah coming to deliver me?   60

Hoot-owl calling in the ghosted air,
five times calling to the hants in the air.
Shadow of a face in the scary leaves,
shadow of a voice in the talking leaves:

come ride-a my train   65

Oh that train, ghost-story train
through swamp and savanna movering movering,
over trestles of dew, through caves of the wish,
Midnight Special on a sabre track movering movering,
first stop Mercy and the last Hallelujah.   70

Come ride-a my train

Mean mean mean to be free.

"SUMMERTIME AND THE LIVING . . ."

Nobody planted roses, he recalls,
but sunflowers gangled there sometimes,
tough-stalked and bold
and like the vivid children there unplanned.
There circus-poster horses curveted   5
in trees of heaven
above the quarrels and shattered glass,
and he was bareback rider of them all.

No roses there in summer—
oh, never roses except when people died— 10
and no vacations for his elders,
so harshened after each unrelenting day
that they were shouting-angry.
But summer was, they said, the poor folks' time
of year. And he remembers 15
how they would sit on broken steps amid

The fevered tossings of the dusk, the dark,
wafting hearsay with funeral-parlor fans
or making evening solemn by
their quietness. Feels their Mosaic eyes 20
upon him, though the florist roses
that only sorrow could afford
long since have bidden them Godspeed.

Oh, summer summer summertime—

Then grim street preachers shook 25
their tambourines and Bibles in the face
of tolerant wickedness;
then Elks parades and big splendiferous
Jack Johnson in his diamond limousine
set the ghetto burgeoning 30
with fantasies
of Ethiopia spreading her gorgeous wings.

TOUR 5

The road winds down through autumn hills
in blazonry of farewell scarlet
and recessional gold,
past cedar groves, through static villages
whose names are all that's left 5
of Choctaw, Chickasaw.

We stop a moment in a town
watched over by Confederate sentinels,
buy gas and ask directions of a rawboned man
whose eyes revile us as the enemy. 10

Shrill gorgon silence breathes behind
his taut civility
and in the ever-tautening air,

dark for us despite its Indian summer glow.
We drive on, following the route   15
of highwaymen and phantoms,

Of slaves and armies.
Children, wordless and remote,
wave at us from kindling porches.
And now the land is flat for miles,   20
the landscape lush, metallic, flayed,
its brightness harsh as bloodstained swords.

Randall Jarrell (1914–1965)

A CAMP IN THE PRUSSIAN FOREST

I walk beside the prisoners to the road.
Load on puffed load,
Their corpses, stacked like sodden
     wood,
Lie barred or galled with blood

By the charred warehouse. No one
     comes today   5
In the old way
To knock the fillings from their teeth;
The dark, coned, common wreath

Is plaited for their grave—a kind of
     grief.
The living leaf   10
Clings to the planted profitable
Pine if it is able;

The boughs sigh, mile on green, calm,
     breathing mile,
From this dead file
The planners ruled for them. . . . One
     year   15
They sent a million here:

Here men were drunk like water, burnt
     like wood.
The fat of good
And evil, the breast's star of hope
Were rendered into soap.   20

I paint the star I sawed from yellow
     pine—
And plant the sign
In soil that does not yet refuse
Its usual Jews

Their first asylum. But the white,
     dwarfed star—   25
This dead white star—
Hides nothing, pays for nothing; smoke
Fouls it, a yellow joke,

The needles of the wreath are chalked
     with ash,   30
A filmy trash
Litters the black woods with the death
Of men; and one last breath

Curls from the monstrous chimney.
     . . . I laugh aloud
Again and again;   35
The star laughs from its rotting shroud
Of flesh. O star of men!

"A Camp in the Prussian Forest" reprinted by permission of Mrs. Randall Jarrell.

THE DEATH OF THE BALL TURRET GUNNER

From my mother's sleep I fell into the State,
And I hunched in its belly till my wet fur froze.
Six miles from earth, loosed from its dream of life,
I woke to black flak and the nightmare fighters.
When I died they washed me out of the turret with a hose.   5

A GIRL IN A LIBRARY

An object among dreams, you sit here with your shoes off
and curl your legs up under you; your eyes
Close for a moment, your face moves toward sleep . . .
You are very human.
                    But my mind, gone out in tenderness,   5
Shrinks from its object with a thoughtful sigh.
This is a waist the spirit breaks its arm on.
The gods themselves, against you, struggle in vain.
This broad low strong-boned brow; these heavy eyes;
These calves, grown muscular with certainties;   10
This nose, three medium-sized pink strawberries
—But I exaggerate. In a little you will leave:
I'll hear, half squeal, half shriek, your laugh of greeting—
Then, *decrescendo,* bars of that strange speech
In which each sound sets out to seek each other,   15
Murders its own father, marries its own mother,
And ends as one grand transcendental vowel.

(Yet for all I know, the Egyptian Helen spoke so.)
As I look, the world contracts around you:
I see Brünnhilde has brown braids and glasses   20
She used for studying; Salome straight brown bangs,
A calf's brown eyes, and sturdy light-brown limbs
Dusted with cinnamon, an apple-dumpling's . . .
Many a beast has gnawn a leg off and got free,
Many a dolphin curved up from Necessity—   25
The trap has closed about you, and you sleep.
If someone questioned you, *What doest thou here?*

You'd knit your brows like an orangoutang
(But not so sadly; not so thoughtfully)
And answer with a pure heart, guilelessly: 30
I'm studying. . . .
              If only you were not!
Assignments,
        recipes,
              the *Official Rulebook*   35
Of Basketball—ah, let them go; you needn't mind.
The soul has no assignments, neither cooks
Nor referees: it wastes its time.
                 It wastes its time.
Here in this enclave there are centuries   40
For you to waste: the short and narrow stream
Of Life meanders into a thousand valleys
Of all that was, or might have been, or is to be.
The books, just leafed through, whisper endlessly . . .
Yet it is hard. One sees in your blurred eyes   45
The "uneasy half-soul" Kipling saw in dogs'.
One sees it, in the glass, in one's own eyes.
In rooms alone, in galleries, in libraries,
In tears, in searchings of the heart, in staggering joys
We memorize once more our old creation,   50
Humanity: with what yawns the unwilling
Flesh puts on its spirit, O my sister!

So many dreams! And not one troubles
Your sleep of life? no self stares shadowily
From these worn hexahedrons, beckoning   55
With false smiles, tears? . . .
               Meanwhile Tatyana
Larina (gray eyes nickel with the moonlight
That falls through the willows onto Lensky's tomb;
Now young and shy, now old and cold and sure)   60
Asks, smiling: "But what is she dreaming of, fat thing?"
I answer: She's not fat. She isn't dreaming.
She purrs or laps or runs, all in her sleep;
Believes, awake, that she is beauiful;
She never dreams.   65
            Those sunrise-colored clouds
Around man's head—that inconceivable enchantment
From which, at sunset, we come back to life
To find our graves dug, families dead, selves dying:
Of all this, Tanya, she is innocent.   70
For nineteen years she's faced reality:
They look alike already.
              They say, man wouldn't be
The best thing in this world—and isn't he?—
If he were not too good for it. But she   75
—She's good enough for it.
             And yet sometimes

Her sturdy form, in its pink strapless formal,
Is as if bathed in moonlight—modulated
Into a form of joy, a Lydian mode; 80
This Wooden Mean's a kind, furred animal
That speaks, in the Wild of things, delighting riddles
To the soul that listens, trusting . . .
     Poor senseless Life:
When, in the last light sleep of dawn, the messenger 85
Comes with his message, you will not awake.
He'll give his feathery whistle, shake you hard,
You'll look with wide eyes at the dewy yard
And dream, with calm slow factuality:
"Today's Commencement. My bachelor's degree 90
In Home Ec., my doctorate of philosophy
In Phys. Ed.
   [Tanya, they won't even *scan*}
Are waiting for me. . . ."
     Oh, Tatyana, 95
The Angel comes: better to squawk like a chicken
Than to say with truth, "But I'm a *good* girl,"
And Meet his Challenge with a last firm strange
Uncomprehending smile; and —then, then!—see
The blind date that has stood you up; your life. 100
(For all this, if it isn't, perhaps, life,
Has yet, at least, a language of its own
Different from the books'; worse than the books'.)
And yet, the ways we miss our lives are life.
Yet . . . yet . . . 105
    to have one's life add up to *yet!*
You sigh a shuddering sigh. Tatyana murmurs,
"Don't cry, little peasant"; leaves us with a swift
"Good-bye, good-bye . . . Ah, don't think ill of me . . ."
Your eyes open: you sit here thoughtlessly. 110
I love you—and yet—and yet—I love you.

Don't cry, little peasant. Sit and dream.
One comes, a finger's width beneath your skin,
To the braided maidens singing as they spin;
There sound the shepherd's pipe, the watchman's rattle 115
Across the short dark distance of the years.
I am a thought of yours: and yet, you do not think . . .
The firelight of a long, blind, dreaming story
Lingers upon your lips; and I have seen
Firm, fixed forever in your closing eyes, 120
The Corn King beckoning to his Spring Queen.

THE OLD AND THE NEW MASTERS

About suffering, about adoration, the old masters
Disagree. When someone suffers, no one else eats
Or walks or opens the window—no one breathes
As the sufferers watch the sufferer.
In *St. Sebastian Mourned by St. Irene*   5
The flame of one torch is the only light.
All the eyes except the maidservant's (she weeps
And covers them with a cloth) are fixed on the shaft
Set in his chest like a column; St. Irene's
Hands are spread in the gesture of the Madonna,   10
Revealing, accepting, what she does not understand
Her hands say: "Lo! Behold!"
Beside her a monk's hooded head is bowed, his hands
Are put together in the work of mourning.
It is as if they were still looking at the lance   15
Piercing the side of Christ, nailed on his cross.
The same nails pierce all their hands and feet, the same
Thin blood, mixed with water, trickles from their sides.
The taste of vinegar is on every tongue
That gasps, "My God, my God, why hast Thou forsaken me?" 20
They watch, they are, the one thing in the world.

So, earlier, everything is pointed
In Van der Goes' *Nativity,* toward the naked
Shining baby, like the needle of a compass.
The different orders and sizes of the world:

The angels like Little People, perched in the rafters
Or hovering in mid-air like hummingbirds;
The shepherds, so big and crude, so plainly adoring;
The medium-sized donor, his little family,
And their big patron saints; the Virgin who kneels 30
Before her child in worship; the Magi out in the hills
With their camels—they ask directions, and have pointed out
By a man kneeling, the true way; the ox
And the donkey, two heads in the manger
So much greater than a human head, who also adore; 35
Even the offerings, a sheaf of wheat,
A jar and a glass of flowers, are absolutely still
In natural concentration, as they take their part
In the salvation of the natural world.

The time of the world concentrates 40
On this one instant; far off in the rocks
You can see Mary and Joseph and their donkey
Coming to Bethlehem; on the grassy hillside
Where their flocks are grazing, the shepherds gesticulate
In wonder at the star; and so many hundreds 45
Of years in the future, the donor, his wife,
And their children are kneeling, looking: everything
That was or will be in the world is fixed
On its small, helpless, human center.

After a while the masters show the crucifixion 50
In one corner of the canvas: the men come to see
What is important, see that it is not important.
The new masters paint a subject as they please,
And Veronese is prosecuted by the Inquisition
For the dogs playing at the feet of Christ, 55
The earth is a plant among galaxies.
Later Christ disappears, the dogs disappear: in abstract
Understanding, without adoration, the last master puts
Colors on canvas, a picture of the universe
In which a bright spot somewhere in the corner 60
Is the small radioactive planet men called Earth.

GUNNER

Did they send me away from my cat and my wife
To a doctor who poked me and counted my teeth,
To a line on a plain, to a stove in a tent?
Did I nod in the flies of the schools?

And the fighters rolled into the tracer like rabbits, 5
The blood froze over my splints like a scab—
Did I snore, all still and grey in the turret,
Till the palms rose out of the sea with my death?

And the world ends here, in the sand of a grave,
All my wars over? . . . It was easy as that! 10
Has my wife a pension of so many mice?
Did the medals go home to my cat?

Henry Reed (1914–   )
LESSONS OF THE WAR

To Alan Michell

Vixi duellis nuper idoneus
Et militavi non sine gloria

1. NAMING OF PARTS

Today we have naming of parts. Yesterday,
We had daily cleaning. And tomorrow morning,
We shall have what to do after firing. But today,
Today we have naming of parts. Japonica
Glistens like coral in all of the neighbouring gardens,   5
    And today we have naming of parts.

This is the lower sling swivel. And this
Is the upper sling swivel, whose use you will see,
When you are given your slings. And this is the piling swivel,
Which in your case you have not got. The branches   10
Hold in the gardens their silent, eloquent gestures,
    Which in our case we have not got.

This is the safety-catch, which is always released
With an easy flick of the thumb. And please do not let me
See anyone using his finger. You can do it quite easy   15

If you have any strength in your thumb. The blossoms
Are fragile and motionless, never letting anyone see
    Any of them using their finger.

And this you can see is the bolt. The purpose of this
Is to open the breech, as you see. We can slide it   20
Rapidly backwards and forwards: we call this
Easing the spring. And rapidly backwards and forwards
The early bees are assaulting and fumbling the flowers:
    They call it easing the Spring.

They call it easing the Spring: it is perfectly easy   25
If you have any strength in your thumb: like the bolt,
And the breech, and the cocking-piece, and the point of balance,
Which in our case we have not got; and the almond-blossom
Silent in all of the gardens and the bees going backwards and forwards,
    For today we have naming of
    parts.   30

Dylan Thomas (1914–1953)

A REFUSAL TO MOURN THE DEATH, BY FIRE, OF A CHILD IN LONDON

Never until the mankind making
Bird beast and flower
Fathering and all humbling darkness
Tells with silence the last light breaking
And the still hour   5
Is come of the sea tumbling in harness

And I must enter again the round
Zion of the water bead
And the synagogue of the ear of corn
Shall I let pray the shadow of a
    sound   10
Or sow my salt seed
In the least valley of sackcloth to mourn

The majesty and burning of the child's
    death.

I shall not murder
The mankind of her going with a grave
    truth   15
Nor blaspheme down the stations of the
breath
With any further
Elegy of innocence and youth.

Deep with the first dead lies London's
    daughter,
Robed in the long friends,   20
The grains beyond age, the dark veins
    of her mother
Secret by the unmourning water
Of the riding Thames.
After the first death, there is no other.

FERN HILL

Now as I was young and easy under the
    apple boughs
About the lilting house and happy as
    the grass was green,
    The night above the dingle starry,
        Time let me hail and climb
    Golden in the heydays of his eyes,   5
And honoured among wagons I was
    prince of the apple towns

And once below a time I lordly had the
    trees and leaves
    Trail with daisies and barley
    Down the rivers of the windfall light.

And as I was green and carefree,
        famous among the barns   10
    About the happy yard and singing as
        the farm was home,

In the sun that is young once only,
   Time let me play and be
Golden in the mercy of his means,
And green and golden I was huntsman
    and herdsman, the calves   15
Sang to my horn, the foxes on the hills
   barked clear and cold,
    And the sabbath rang slowly
In the pebbles of the holy streams.

All the sun long it was running, it was
   lovely, the hay-
Fields high as the house, the tunes from
   the chimneys, it was air   20
  and playing, lovely and watery
    And fire green as grass.
  And nightly under the simple stars
As I rode to sleep the owls were bearing
   the farm away,
All the moon long I heard, blessed
   among stables, the night-jars   25
  Flying with the ricks, and the horses
  Flashing into the dark.

And then to awake, and the farm, like a
   wanderer white
With the dew, come back, the cock on
   his shoulder: it was all
  Shining, it was Adam and
    maiden,   30
   The sky gathered again
And the sun grew round that very
   day.
So it must have been after the birth of
   the simple light

In the first, spinning place, the
    spellbound horses walking warm
  Out of the whinnying green
    stable   35
  On to the fields of praise.

And honoured among foxes and
   pheasants by the gay house
Under the new made clouds and happy
   as the heart was long,
  In the sun born over and over,
   I ran my heedless ways,   40
  My wishes raced through the house-
   high hay
And nothing I cared, at my sky blue
   trades, that time allows
In all his tuneful turning so few and
   such morning songs
  Before the children green and golden
   Follow him out of grace,   45

Nothing I cared, in the lamb white days,
   that time would take me
Up to the swallow thronged loft by the
   shadow of my hand,
  In the moon that is always rising,
   Nor that riding to sleep
  I should hear him fly with the high
   fields   50
And wake to the farm forever fled from
   the childless land.
Oh as I was young and easy in the
   mercy of his means,
   Time held me green and dying
  Though I sang in my chains like the
  sea.

AMONG THOSE KILLED IN THE DAWN RAID WAS A MAN AGED ONE HUNDRED

When the morning was waking over the
  war
He put on his clothes and stepped out
  and he died,
The locks yawned loose and a blast
  blew them wide,

He dropped where he loved on the
  burst pavement stone
And the funeral grains of the
  slaughtered floor.   5
Tell his street on its back he stopped a
  sun

And the craters of his eyes grew
  springshoots and fire
When all the keys shot from the locks,
  and rang.

Dig no more for the chains of his grey
  haired heart.
The heavenly ambulance drawn by a
  wound   10

Assembling waits for the spades' ring
  on the cage.
O keep his bones away from that
  common cart,
The morning is flying on the wings of
  his age
And a hundred storks perch on the
  sun's right hand.

IN MY CRAFT OR SULLEN ART

In my craft or sullen art
Exercised in the still night
When only the moon rages
And the lovers lie abed
With all their griefs in their arms,   5
I labour by singing light
Not for ambition or bread
Or the strut and trade of charms
On the ivory stages
But for the common wages   10
Of their most secret heart.

Not for the proud man apart
From the raging moon I write
On these spindrift pages
Not for the towering dead   15
With their nightingales and psalms
But for the lovers, their arms
Round the griefs of the ages,
Who pay no praise or wages
Nor heed my craft or art.   20

Margaret Walker (1915–   )

FOR ANDY GOODMAN—
MICHAEL SCHWERNER—
AND JAMES CHANEY

*(Three Civil Rights Workers
Murdered in Mississippi on June 21, 1964)*

(Written After Seeing the Movie, Andy in A.M.*)*

Three faces . . .
  mirrored in the muddy streams
    of living . . .
young and tender like

quiet beauty of still water,
sensitive as the mimosa leaf,
  intense as the stalking cougar
  and impassive as the face of rivers;

The sensitive face of Andy
The intense face of Michael
The impassive face of Chaney.

Three leaves . . .
   Floating in the melted snow
   Flooding the Spring
   oak leaves
   one by one
   moving like a barge
   across the seasons
   moving like a breeze across the
      window pane
   winter . . . summer . . . spring
When is the evil year of the cricket?
When comes the violent day of
   the stone?
In which month
do the dead ones appear at the cistern?

Three lives . . .
   turning on the axis of our time
   Black and white together
   turning on the wheeling compass
   of a decade and a day
   The concerns of a century of time
   . . . an hourglass of destiny

Three lives . . .
   ripe for immortality of daisies
      and wheat
   for the simple beauty of a humming
      bird
   and dignity of a sequoia
   of renunciation and
   resurrection
For the Easter morning of our Meridians.

Why should another die for me?
Why should there be a calvary
A subterranean hell for three?
In the miry clay?
In the muddy stream?
In the red misery?
In mutilating hatred and in fear?
The brutish and the brazen

without brain
without blessing
without beauty . . .
They have killed these three.
They have killed them for me

Sunrise and sunset . . .
Spring rain and winter window pane . . .
I see the first leaves budding
The green Spring returning
I mark the falling
of golden Autumn leaves
and three lives floating down the
      quiet stream
Till they come to the surging falls . . .

The burned blossoms of the dogwood
      tree
tremble in the Mississippi morning
The wild call of the cardinal bird
troubles the Mississippi morning
I hear the morning singing
larks, robins, and the mocking bird
while the mourning dove
broods over the meadow
Summer leaf falls never turning brown
Deep in a Mississippi thicket
I hear that mourning dove
Bird of death singing in the swamp
Leaves of death floating in their
      watery grave

Three faces turn their ears and eyes
sensitive
intense
impassive
to see the solemn sky of summer
to hear the brooding cry
of the mourning dove

Mississippi bird of sorrow
O mourning bird of death
Sing their sorrow
Mourn their pain
And teach us death,
To love and live with them again!

John Ciardi (1916–   )
ELEGY FOR G. B. SHAW

"If I survive this, I shall be immortal."

Administrators of minutes into hours,
Hours into ash, and ash to its own wedding
At the edge of fire and air—here's time at last
To make an ash of Shaw, who in his time
Survived his times, retired, and for a hobby   5
Bred fire to fire as one breeds guinea pigs.

In time, one can imagine, schoolchildren
Will confuse him as a contemporary of Socrates.
For a time, the fact is, he confused us:
We half believed he really had lived forever.   10
Sometimes, perhaps, a man can. That is to say,
Civilization is one man at a time,

And that forever, and he was that man.
For this we will not forgive him. Neither
The ape in me nor the ape in you, tenants   15
Of the flag-flying tree and drinkers of blood in season.
We meant to resemble the agonies of statues:
He left us only a treadmill in a cage.

Consider his crimes: He would not commit our diet.
He opened our tombs. He sold his medals for cash.   20
His laughter blew out our anthems. He wiped his nose
On the flags we die for—a crazy Irishman
Who looked like a goat and would not be serious.
But when we are finished, he will be our times.

And all times will be nothing in his eye.   25
All marshals, kings, and presidents we obey.
His presence in men's minds is contempt of court,
Of congress, and of flags. So must we pray
That he be born again, anarch and rare,
The race we are not in the race we are.   30

ON A PHOTO OF SGT. CIARDI A YEAR LATER

The sgt. stands so fluently in leather,
So poster-holstered and so newsreel-jawed
As death's costumed and fashionable brother,
My civil memory is overawed.

Behind him see the circuses of doom   5
Dance a finale chorus on the sun.
He leans on gunsights, doesn't give a damn
For dice or stripes, and waits to see the fun.

The cameraman whose ornate public eye
Invented that fine bravura look of calm   10
At murderous clocks hung ticking in the sky
Palmed the deception off without a qualm.

Even the camera, focused and exact
To a two dimensional conclusion,
Uttered its formula of physical fact   15
Only to lend data to illusion.

The camera always lies. By a law of perception
The obvious surface is always an optical ruse.
The leather was living tissue in its own dimension,
The holsters held benzedrine tablets, the guns were no use.   20

The careful slouch and dangling cigarette
Were always superstitious as Amen.
The shadow under the shadow is never caught;
The camera photographs the cameraman.

CHORUS

They were singing Old MacDonald in the schoolbus
With a *peep peep* here and a *peep peep* there after
Margie Littenach had been delivered to the right mailbox
And the gears had gnashed their teeth uphill to the Cliff House
Where the driver, shifting gears, honked at the countergirls,   5
And the tourists turned from panorama all smiles
To remember schooldays, long curls, hooky, and how

The view had always stretched for miles and miles
Where the gentle cumulus puffed small in gentle weather
Putting a cottonfluff roof on the green world leaning down hill   10
To the bluelevelfield of sea, and all together
With an *oink oink* here and a *moo moo* there the children
Were singing Old MacDonald in the schoolbus

When a bolt fell from the compound interest problem,
A rod broke in the third chapter of the Civicsbook   15
Where the country had no money for inspection in the first place
                                        and
Momentum had no brakes, but with a *honk honk* here
And a *honk honk* there went sidewise over tirescreech
Downturning in round air away from panorama where   20
Even the tourists could tell sea didn't measure each
Stone falling, or button, or bolt, or Caroline Helmhold,
Nor anywhere its multitudinous self incarnadine, but only swallowed
What books, belts, lunchpails, pity
Spilled over the touristfaredge of the world and Old MacDonald   25

A THOUSANDTH POEM FOR DYLAN THOMAS

Waking outside his Babylonia binge
    in the wet and cramp of morningstone, the sot
begins his daily death. A first stiff wince
    numbers his bones, each like a tooth of God.

Where did night end? Girlies in a red flame   5
    squeal through his broken memory like pigs;
Hell's barnyard burning or the zoo of days,
    stampeded shapes exploded from their skins.

He tastes again the ooze of a first sigh
    dead in his throat; his mouth, a rotten fig;   10
his sex, a broken glue-pot in the thighs;
    his breath, a shudder from below the will.

Sooner or later he must break an eye
    to look at what he sees of what he is.
An angel beating at the trap of time?   15
    A bird-heart pulsing in an idiot's fist?

Both. Either. Floated open from its muds,
   that moment in the clear, the sot's eye sees
as much as saints could bear of the fireblood
   God's heart pumps in its seizure of the skies.   20

Then how the man could sing his ghost to tears,
   there in God's eye and blood, for that lost place
where he was innocent, before his need
   changed to a thirst inside the worm of waste.

He pours his celebration of regret,   25
   tormented joyous from the throat of mud,
hawk-hearted as Augustine in his sweat,
dove-eyed as Francis' bridal with the wood.

It is the age of sots. Our holiness
   wakens outside the minareted fronts   30
of a jazzy, airless, and expensive hell.
   He sings our wish. He drinks his death for us

Who have no throats to die of or to sing.
   He is Saint Binge at death in his own meat,
the blaze meant in the char we make of things,   35
   our addict, and our angel of defeat.

Peter Viereck (1916–   )

KILROY

Also Ulysses once—that other war.
       (Is it because we find his scrawl
       Today on every ivy door
       That we forget his ancient role?)
Also was there—he did it for the wages—   5
When a Cathay-drunk Genoese set sail.
Whenever "longen folk to goon on pilgrimages,"
Kilroy is there;
         he tells The Miller's Tale.

At times he seems a paranoiac king   10
Who stamps his crest on walls and says "My Own!"
But in the end he fades like a lost tune,
Tossed here and there, whom all the breezes sing.

  "Kilroy" first appeared in *Terror & Decorum*, out of print, recipient of Pulitzer Prize for poetry in 1949. Reprinted in Peter Viereck's *New and Selected Poems*, Bobbs-Merrill Co., N.Y.C., 1967.

"Kilroy was here"; these words sound wanly gay,
       Haughty yet tired with long marching.   15
He is Orestes—guilty of what crime?—
       For whom the Furies still are searching;
       When they arrive, they find their prey
(Leaving his name to mock them) went away.
Sometimes he does not flee from them in time: 20
"Kilroy was—"
         with his blood a dying man
       Wrote half the phrase out in Bataan.

Kilroy, beware. "HOME" is the final trap
That lurks for you in many a wily shape: 25
In pipe-and-slippers plus a Loyal Hound
       Or fooling around, just fooling around.
Kind to the old (their warm Penelope)
But fierce to boys,
       Thus "home" becomes that sea,   30
Horribly disguised, where you were always drowned—
       (How could suburban Crete condone
The yarns you would have V-mailed from the sun?)—
And folksy fishes sip Icarian tea.

One stab of hopeless wings imprinted your   35
       Exultant Kilroy-signature
Upon sheer sky for all the world to stare:
       "I was there! I was there! I was there!"

God is like Kilroy. He, too, sees it all;
That's how He knows of every sparrow's fall;   40
That's why we prayed each time the tightropes cracked
On which our loveliest clowns contrived their act,
The G. I. Faustus who was
           everywhere
Strolled home again. "What was it like outside?"   45
Asked Can't, with his good neighbors Ought and But
And pale Perhaps and grave-eyed Better Not;
For "Kilroy" means: the world is very wide.
       He was there, he was there, he was there!

And in the suburbs Can't sat down and cried.   50

"Fresh, spirited American troops, flushed with victory, are bringing in thousands of hungry, ragged, battle-weary prisoners . . ." (News item)

Gwendolyn Brooks (1917–   )

THE CHICAGO DEFENDER SENDS A MAN TO LITTLE ROCK

Fall, 1957

In Little Rock the people bear
Babes, and comb and part their hair
And watch the want ads, put repair
To roof and latch. While wheat toast burns
A woman waters multiferns.   5

Time upholds or overturns
The many, tight, and small concerns.

In Little Rock the people sing
Sunday hymns like anything,
Through Sunday pomp and polishing.   10

And after testament and tunes,
Some soften Sunday afternoons
With lemon tea and Lorna Doones.

I forecast
and I believe   15
Come Christmas Little Rock will cleave
To Christmas tree and trifle, weave,
From laugh and tinsel, texture fast.

In Little Rock is baseball; Barcarolle.
That hotness in July . . . the uniformed figures raw and implacable
And not intellectual,   20
Batting the hotness or clawing the suffering dust.
The Open Air Concert, on the special twilight green . . .
When Beethoven is brutal or whispers to lady-like air.
Blanket-sitters are solemn, as Johann troubles to lean   25
To tell them what to mean. . . .

There is love, too, in Little Rock. Soft women softly
Opening themselves in kindness,
Or, pitying one's blindness,

Awaiting one's pleasure   30
In azure
Glory with anguished rose at the root . . .
To wash away old semi-discomfitures.

They re-teach purple and unsullen blue.
The wispy soils go. And uncertain   35
Half-havings have they clarified to sures.
In Little Rock they know
Not answering the telephone is a way of rejecting life,
That it is our business to be bothered, is our business
To cherish bores or boderom, be polite   40
To lies and love and many-faceted fuzziness.

I scratch my head, massage the hate-I-had.
I blink across my prim and pencilled pad.
The saga I was sent for is not down.
Because there is a puzzle in this town.   45
The biggest News I do not dare
Telegraph to the Editor's chair:
"They are like people everywhere."

The angry Editor would reply
In hundred harryings of Why.   50

And true, they are hurling spittle, rock,
Garbage and fruit in Little Rock.
And I saw coiling storm a-writhe
On bright madonnas. And a scythe
Of men harassing brownish girls.   55
(The bows and barrettes in the curls
And braids declined away from joy.)

I saw a bleeding brownish boy. . . .

The lariat lynch-wish I deplored.

The loveliest lynchee was our Lord.   60

the preacher: ruminates behind the sermon

I think it must be lonely to be God.
Nobody loves a master. No. Despite
The bright hosannas, bright dear-Lords,
   and bright
Determined reverence of Sunday eyes.

Picture Jehovah striding through the
   hall   5
Of His importance, creatures running
   out
From servant-corners to acclaim, to
   shout
Appreciation of His merit's glare.

But who walks with Him?—dares to
   take His arm,
To slap Him on the shoulder, tweak His
   ear,   10
Buy Him a Coca-Cola or a beer,
Pooh-pooh His politics, call Him a fool?

Perhaps—who knows?—He tires of
   looking down.
Those eyes are never lifted. Never
   straight.
Perhaps sometimes He tires of being
   great   15
In solitude. Without a hand to hold.

my dreams, my works, must wait till after hell

I hold my honey and I store my bread
In little jars and cabinets of my will.
I label clearly, and each latch and lid
I bid, Be firm till I return from hell.
I am very hungry. I am incomplete.   5
And none can tell when I may dine again.
No man can give me any word but Wait,
The puny light. I keep eyes pointed in;
Hoping that, when the devil days of my hurt
Drag out to their last dregs and I resume   10
On such legs as are left me, in such heart
As I can manage, remember to go home,
My taste will not have turned insensitive
To honey and bread old purity could love.

Robert Lowell (1917–   )

FALL 1961

Back and forth, back and forth
goes the tock, tock, tock
of the orange, bland, ambassadorial
face of the moon
on the grandfather clock.   5

All autumn, the chafe and jar
of nuclear war;
we have talked our extinction to death.
I swim like a minnow
behind my studio window.   10

Our end drifts nearer,
the moon lifts,
radiant with terror.
The state
is a diver under a glass bell.   15

A father's no shield
for his child.
We are like a lot of wild
spiders crying together,
but without tears.   20

Nature holds up a mirror.
One swallow makes a summer.
It's easy to tick
off the minutes,
but the clockhands stick.   25

Back and forth!
Back and forth, back and forth—
my one point of rest
is the orange and black oriole's
    swinging nest!

THE QUAKER GRAVEYARD IN NANTUCKET

(For Warren Winslow, Dead at Sea)

*Let man have dominion over the fishes of the sea and the fowls
of the air and the beasts and the whole earth, and every
creature that moveth upon the earth.*

I

A brackish reach of shoal off Madaket,—
The sea was still breaking violently and night
Had steamed into our North Atlantic Fleet,
When the drowned sailor clutched the drag-net. Light
Flashed from his matted head and marble feet,   5

He grappled at the net
With the coiled, hurdling muscles of his thighs:
The corpse was bloodless, a botch of reds and whites,
Its open staring eyes
Were lusterless dead-lights   10
Or cabin-windows on a stranded hulk
Heavy with sand. We weight the body, close
Its eyes and heave it seaward whence it came,
Where the heel-headed dogfish barks its nose
On Ahab's void and forehead; and the name   15
Is blocked in yellow chalk.
Sailors, who pitch this portent at the sea
Where dreadnaughts shall confess
Its hell-bent deity,
When you were powerless   20
To sand-bag the Atlantic bulwark, faced
By the earth-shaker, green, unwearied, chaste
In his steel scales: ask for no Orphean lute
To pluck life back. The guns of the steeled fleet
Recoil and then repeat   25
The hoarse salute.

II

Whenever winds are moving and their breadth
Heaves at the roped-in bulwarks of this pier,
The terns and sea-gulls tremble at your death
In these home waters. Sailor, can you hear   30
The Pequod's sea wings, beating landward, fall
Headlong and break on our Atlantic wall
Off 'Sconset, where the yawning S-boats splash
The bellbuoy, with ballooning spinnakers,
As the entangled, screeching mainsheet clears   35
The blocks: off Madaket, where lubbers lash
The heavy surf and throw their long lead squids
For blue-fish? Sea-gulls blink their heavy lids
Seaward. The winds' wings beat upon the stones,
Cousin, and scream for you and the claws rush   40
At the sea's throat and wring it in the slush
Of this old Quaker graveyard where the bones
Cry out in the long night for the hurt beast
Bobbing by Ahab's whaleboats in the East.

III

All you recovered from Poseidon died   45
With you, my cousin, and the harrowed brine
Is fruitless on the blue beard of the god,
Stretching beyond us to the castles in Spain,

Nantucket's westward haven. To Cape Cod
Guns, cradled on the tide, 50
Blast the eelgrass about a waterclock
Of bilge and backwash, roil the salt and sand
Lashing earth's scaffold, rock
Our warships on the hand
Of the great God, where time's contrition blues 55
Whatever it was these Quaker sailors lost
In the mad scramble of their lives. They died
When time was open-eyed,
Wooden and childish; only bones abide
There, in the nowhere, where their boats were tossed 60
Sky-high, where mariners had fabled news
Of IS, the whited monster. What it cost
Them is their secret. In the sperm-whale's slick
I see the Quakers drown and hear their cry:
"If God himself had not been on our side, 65
If God himself had not been on our side,
When the Atlantic rose against us, why,
Then it had swallowed us up quick."

IV

This is the end of the whaleroad and the whale
Who spewed Nantucket bones on the thrashed swell 70
And stirred the troubled waters to whirlpools
To send the Pequod packing off to hell:
This is the end of them, three-quarters fools,
Snatching at straws to sail
Seaward and seaward on the turntail whale, 75
Spouting out blood and water as it rolls,
Sick as a dog to these Atlantic shoals:
Clamavimus, O depths. Let the sea-gulls wail
For water, for the deep where the high tide
Mutters to its hurt self, mutters and ebbs. 80
Waves wallow in their wash, go out and out,
Leave only the death-rattle of the crabs,
The beach increasing, its enormous snout
Sucking the ocean's side.
This is the end of running on the waves; 85
We are poured out like water. Who will dance
The mast-lashed master of Leviathans
Up from this field of Quakers in their unstoned graves?

V

When the whale's viscera go and the roll
Of its corruption overruns this world 90
Beyond tree-swept Nantucket and Wood's Hole
And Martha's Vineyard, Sailor, will your sword

Whistle and fall and sink into the fat?
In the great ash-pit of Jehoshaphat
The bones cry for the blood of the white whale,   95
The fat flukes arch and whack about its ears,
The death-lance churns into the sanctuary, tears
The gun-blue swingle, heaving like a flail,
And hacks the coiling life out: it works and drags
And rips the sperm-whale's midriff into rags,   100
Gobbets of blubber spill to wind and weather,
Sailor, and gulls go round the stoven timbers
Where the morning stars sing out together
And thunder shakes the white surf and dismembers
The red flag hammered in the mast-head. Hide,   105
Our steel, Jonas Messias, in Thy side.

VI
OUR LADY OF WALSINGHAM

There once the penitents took off their shoes
And then walked barefoot the remaining mile;
And the small trees, a stream and hedgerows file
Slowly along the munching English lane,   110
Like cows to the old shrine, until you lose
Track of your dragging pain.
The stream flows down under the druid tree,
Shiloh's whirlpools gurgle and make glad
The castle of God. Sailor, you were glad   115
And whistled Sion by that stream. But see:

Our Lady too small for her canopy,
Sits near the altar. There's no comeliness
At all or charm in that expressionless
Face with its heavy eyelids. As before,   120
This face, for centuries a memory,
Non est species, neque decor,
Expressionless, expresses God: it goes
Past castled Sion. She knows what God knows,
No Calvary's Cross nor crib at Bethlehem   125
Now, and the world shall come to Walsingham.

VII

The empty winds are creaking and the oak
Splatters and splatters on the cenotaph,
The boughs are trembling and a gaff
Bobs on the untimely stroke   130
Of the greased wash exploding on a shoal-bell
In the old mouth of the Atlantic. It's well;

Atlantic, you are fouled with the blue sailors,
Sea-monsters, upward angel, downward fish:
Unmarried and corroding, spare of flesh   135
Mart once of supercilious, wing'd clippers,
Atlantic, where your bell-trap guts its spoil
You could cut the brackish winds with a knife
Here in Nantucket, and cast up the time
When the Lord God formed man from the sea's slime   140
And breathed into his face the breath of life,
And blue-lung'd combers lumbered to the kill.
The Lord survives the rainbow of His will.

MR. EDWARDS AND THE SPIDER

I saw the spiders marching through the air,
Swimming from tree to tree that mildewed day
    In latter August when the hay
    Came creaking to the barn. But where
        The wind is westerly,   5
Where gnarled November makes the spiders fly
Into the apparitions of the sky,
They purpose nothing but their ease and die
Urgently beating east to sunrise and the sea;

What are we in the hands of the great God?   10
It was in vain you set up thorn and briar
    In battle array against the fire
    And treason crackling in your blood;
        For the wild thorns grow tame
And will do nothing to oppose the flame;   15
Your lacerations tell the losing game
You play against a sickness past your cure.
How will the hands be strong? How will the heart endure?
A very little thing, a little worm,
Or hourglass-blazoned spider, it is said,   20
    Can kill a tiger. Will the dead
    Hold up his mirror and affirm
        To the four winds the smell
And flash of his authority? It's well
If God who holds you to the pit of hell,   25
Much as one holds a spider, will destroy,
Baffle and dissipate your soul. As a small boy

On Windsor Marsh, I saw the spider die
When thrown into the bowels of fierce fire:
    There's no long struggle, no desire   30
    To get up on its feet and fly—

It stretches out its feet
And dies. This is the sinner's last retreat;
Yes, and no strength exerted on the heat
Then sinews the abolished will, when sick   35
And full of burning, it will whistle on a brick.

But who can plumb the sinking of that soul?
Josiah Hawley, picture yourself cast
   Into a brick-kiln where the blast
   Fans your quick vitals to a coal—   40
      If measured by a glass,
How long would it seem burning! Let there pass
A minute, ten, ten trillion; but the blaze
Is infinite, eternal: this is death,
To die and know it. This is the Black Widow, death.   45

Lawrence Ferlinghetti (1919–   )
Dada would have liked a day like this

Dada would have liked a day like this
                          with its various very realistic
             unrealities
                          each about to become
   too real for its locality   5
                          which is never quite remote enough
       to be Bohemia
Dada would have loved a day like this
                          with its light-bulb sun
      which shines so differently   10
                          for different people
   but which still shines the same
                          on everyone
             and on everything
                          such as   15
       a bird on a bench about to sing
                          a plane in a gilded cloud
a dishpan hand
             waving at a window
                          or a phone about to ring   20
       or a mouth about to give up
                          smoking

        or a new newspaper
                        with its new news story
                                        of a cancerous dancer   25
Yes Dada would have died for a day like this
                                        with its sweet street carnival
            and its too real funeral
                        just passing thru it
                with its real dead dancer   30
                                so beautiful and dumb
                in her shroud
                                and her last lover lost
                in the unlonely crowd
                                        and its dancer's darling baby 35
            about to say Dada
                        and its passing priest
                about to pray
                        Dada
                                and offer his so transcendental   40
                apologies
Yes Dada would have loved a day like this
                                        with its not so accidental
                apologies
                analogies

Howard Nemerov (1920–   )
BOOM!

SEES BOOM IN RELIGION, TOO

Atlantic City, June 23, 1957 (AP).—President Eisenhower's pastor said tonight that Americans are living in a period of "unprecedented religious activity" caused partially by paid vacations, the eight-hour day and modern conveniences.

"These fruits of material progress," said the Rev. Edward L. R. Elson of the National Presbyterian Church, Washington, "have provided the leisure, the energy, and the means for a level of human and spiritual values never before reached."

Here at the Vespasian-Carlton, it's just one
religious activity after another; the sky
is constantly being crossed by cruciform
airplanes, in which nobody disbelieves
for a second, and the tide, the tide   5
of spiritual progress and prosperity
miraculously keeps rising, to a level
never before attained. The churches are full,

"Boom" reprinted by permission of Margot Johnson Agency.

the beaches are full, and the filling-stations
are full, God's great ocean is full   10
of paid vacationers praying an eight-hour day
to the human and spiritual values, the fruits,
the leisure, the energy, and the means, Lord,
the means for the level, the unprecedented level,
and the modern conveniences, which also are full.   15
Never before, O Lord, have the prayers and praises
from belfry and phonebooth, from ballpark and barbecue
the sacrifices, so endlessly ascended.

It was not thus when Job in Palestine
sat in the dust and cried, cried bitterly;   20
when Damien kissed the lepers on their wounds
it was not thus; it was not thus
when Francis worked a fourteen-hour day
strictly for the birds; when Dante took
a week's vacation without pay and it rained   25
part of the time, O Lord, it was not thus.

But now the gears mesh and the tires burn
and the ice chatters in the shaker and the priest
in the pulpit, and Thy Name, O Lord,
is kept before the public, while the fruits   30
ripen and religion booms and the level rises
and every modern convenience runneth over,
that it may never be with us as it hath been
with Athens and Karnak and Nagasaki,
nor Thy sun for one instant refrain from shining   35
on the rainbow Buick by the breezeway
or the Chris Craft with the uplift life raft;
that we may continue to be the just folks we are,
plain people with ordinary superliners and
disposable diaperliners, people of the stop'n'shop   40
'n' pray as you go, of hotel, motel, boatel,
the humble pilgrims of no deposit no return
and please adjust thy clothing, who will give to Thee,
if Thee will keep us going, our annual
Miss Universe, for Thy Name's Sake, Amen.   45

Richard Wilbur (1921–   )

ADVICE TO A PROPHET

When you come, as you soon must, to the streets of our city,
Mad-eyed from stating the obvious,
Not proclaiming our fall but begging us
In God's name to have self-pity,

Spare us all word of the weapons, their force and range,   5
The long numbers that rocket the mind;
Our slow, unreckoning hearts will be left behind,
Unable to fear what is too strange.

Nor shall you scare us with talk of the death of the race.
How should we dream of this place without us?—
The sun mere fire, the leaves untroubled about us,
A stone look on the stone's face?

Speak of the world's own change. Though we cannot conceive
Of an undreamt thing, we know to our cost
How the dreamt cloud crumbles, the vines are blackened by frost,   15
How the view alters. We could believe,

If you told us so, that the white-tailed deer will slip
Into perfect shade, grown perfectly shy,
The lark avoid the reaches of our eye,
The jack-pine lose its knuckled grip   20

On the cold ledge, and every torrent burn
As Xanthus once, its gliding trout
Stunned in a twinkling. What should we be without
The dolphin's arc, the dove's return,

These things in which we have seen ourselves and spoken?   25
Ask us, prophet, how we shall call
Our natures forth when that live tongue is all
Dispelled, that glass obscured or broken

In which we have said the rose of our love and the clean
Horse of our courage, in which beheld   30
The singing locust of the soul unshelled,
And all we mean or wish to mean.

Ask us, ask us whether with the worldless rose
Our hearts shall fail us; come demanding
Whether there shall be lofty or long standing 35
When the bronze annals of the oak-tree close.

Philip Larkin (1922–   )
CHURCH GOING

Once I am sure there's nothing going on
I step inside, letting the door thud shut.
Another church: matting, seats, and stone,
And little books; sprawlings of flowers, cut
For Sunday, brownish now; some brass and stuff 5
Up at the holy end; the small neat organ;
And a tense, musty, unignorable silence,
Brewed God knows how long. Hatless, I take off
My cycle-clips in awkward reverence,

Move forward, run my hand around the font. 10
From where I stand, the roof looks almost new—
Cleaned, or restored? Someone would know: I don't.
Mounting the lectern, I peruse a few
Hectoring large-scale verses, and pronounce
"Here endeth" much more loudly than I'd meant. 15
The echoes snigger briefly. Back at the door
I sign the book, donate an Irish sixpence,
Reflect the place was not worth stopping for.

Yet stop I did: in fact I often do,
And always end much at a loss like this, 20
Wondering what to look for; wondering, too,
When churches fall completely out of use
What we shall turn them into, if we shall keep
A few cathedrals chronically on show,
Their parchment, plate and pyx in locked cases, 25
And let the rest rent-free to rain and sheep.
Shall we avoid them as unlucky places?

Or after dark, will dubious women come
To make their children touch a particular stone;
Pick simples for a cancer; or on some 30
Advised night see walking a dead one?

"Church Going," "I Remember, I Remember," and "Reasons for Attendance" by Philip Larkin are reprinted from *The Less Deceived* by permission of The Marvell Press, Hessle, Yorkshire, England.

Power of some sort or another will go on
In games, in riddles, seemingly at random;
But superstition, like belief, must die,
And what remains when disbelief has gone?   35
Grass, weedy pavement, brambles, buttress, sky,

A shape less recognizable each week,
A purpose more obscure. I wonder who
Will be the last, the very last, to seek
This place for what it was; one of the crew   40
That tap and jot and know what rood-lofts were?
Some ruin-bibber, randy for antique,
Or Christmas-addict, counting on a whiff
Of gown-and-bands and organ-pipes and myrrh?
Or will he be my representative,   45

Bored, uninformed, knowing the ghostly silt
Dispersed, yet tending to this cross of ground
Through suburb scrub because it held unspilt
So long and equably what since is found
Only in separation—marriage, and birth,   50
And death, and thoughts of these—for which was built
This special shell? For, though I've no idea
What this accoutred frowsty barn is worth,
It pleases me to stand in silence here;

A serious house on serious earth it is,   55
In whose blent air all our compulsions meet,
Are recognized, and robed as destinies.
And that much never can be obsolete,
Since someone will forever be surprising
A hunger in himself to be more serious,   60
And gravitating with it to this ground,
Which, he once heard, was proper to grow wise in,
If only that so many dead lie round.

MCMXIV

Those long uneven lines
Standing as patiently
As if they were stretched outside
The Oval or Villa Park,
The crowns of hats, the sun   5
On moustached archaic faces
Grinning as if it were all
An August Bank Holiday lark;

And the shut shops, the bleached
Established names on the sunblinds,   10
The farthings and sovereigns,
And dark-clothed children at play
Called after kings and queens,
The tin advertisements
For cocoa and twist, and the pubs   15
Wide open all day;

And the countryside not caring:
The place-names all hazed over
With flowering grasses, and fields
Shadowing Domesday lines   20
Under wheat's restless silence;
The differently-dressed servants
With tiny rooms in huge houses,
The dust behind limousines;

Never such innocence,   25
Never before or since,
As changed itself to past
Without a word—the men
Leaving the gardens tidy,
The thousands of marriages   30
Lasting a little while longer:
Never such innocence again.

I REMEMBER, I REMEMBER

Coming up England by a different line
For once, early in the cold new year,
We stopped, and, watching men with number-plates
Sprint down the platform to familiar gates,
"Why, Coventry!" I exclaimed, "I was born here."   5

I leant far out, and squinnied for a sign
That this was still the town that had been "mine"
So long, but found I wasn't even clear
Which side was which. From where those cycle-crates
Were standing, had we annually departed   10

For all those family hols? . . . A whistle went:
Things moved. I sat back, staring at my boots.
"Was that," my friend smiled, "where you 'have your roots'?"
No, only where my childhood was unspent,
I wanted to retort, just where I started: 15

By now I've got the whole place clearly charted.
Or garden, first: where I did not invent
Blinding theologies of flowers and fruits,
And wasn't spoken to by an old hat.
And here we have that splendid family   20

I never ran to when I got depressed,
The boys all biceps and the girls all chest,
Their comic Ford, their farm where I could be
"Really myself." I'll show you, come to that,
The bracken where I never trembling sat,   25

Determined to go through with it; where she
Lay back, and "all became a burning mist."
And, in those offices, my doggerel
Was not set up in blunt ten-point, nor read
By a distinguished cousin of the mayor,   30

Who didn't call and tell my father *There*
Before us, had we the gift to see ahead—
"You look as if you wished the place in Hell,"
My friend said, "judging from your face." "Oh well,
I suppose it's not the place's fault," I said,   35
"Nothing, like something, happens anywhere."

REASONS FOR ATTENDANCE

The trumpet's voice, loud and
    authoritative,
Draws me a moment to the lighted glass
To watch the dancers—all under
    twenty-five—
Shifting intently, face to flushed face,
Solemnly on the beat of happiness.   5

—Or so I fancy, sensing the smoke and
    sweat,
The wonderful feel of girls. Why be out
    here?
But then, why be in there? Sex, yes, but
    what
Is sex? Surely, to think the lion's share
Of happiness is found by couples—
    sheer   10

Inaccuracy, as far as I'm concerned.
What calls me is that lifted, rough-
    tongued bell
(Art, if you like) whose individual
    sound
Insists I too am individual.
It speaks; I hear; others may hear as
    well;   15

But not for me, nor I for them; and so
With happiness. Therefore I stay
    outside,
Believing this; and they maul to and fro,
Believing that; and both are satisfied,
If no one has misjudged himself. Or
    lied.   20

Anthony Hecht (1923–   )
THE DOVER BITCH

A Criticism of Life

So there stood Matthew Arnold and this girl
With the cliffs of England crumbling away behind them,
And he said to her, "Try to be true to me,
And I'll do the same for you, for things are bad

All over, etc., etc."   5
Well now, I knew this girl. It's true she had read
Sophocles in a fairly good translation
And caught that bitter allusion to the sea,
But all the time he was talking she had in mind
The notion of what his whiskers would feel like   10
On the back of her neck. She told me later on
That after a while she got to looking out
At the lights across the channel, and really felt sad,
Thinking of all the wine and enormous beds
And blandishments in French and the perfumes.   15
And then she got really angry. To have been brought
All the way down from London, and then be addressed
As a sort of mournful cosmic last resort
Is really tough on a girl, and she was pretty.
Anyway, she watched him pace the room   20
And finger his watch-chain and seem to sweat a bit,
And then she said one or two unprintable things.
But you mustn't judge her by that. What I mean to say is,
She's really all right. I still see her once in a while
And she always treats me right. We have a drink   25
And I give her a good time, and perhaps it's a year
Before I see her again, but there she is,
Running to fat, but dependable as they come.
And sometimes I bring her a bottle of *Nuit d'Amour.*

"MORE LIGHT! MORE LIGHT!"

Composed in the Tower before his execution
These moving verses, and being brought at that time

Painfully to the stake, submitted, declaring thus:
"I implore my God to witness that I have made no crime"

Nor was he forsaken of courage, but the death was horrible,   5
The sack of gunpowder failing to ignite.
His legs were blistered sticks on which the black sap
Bubbled and burst as he howled for the Kindly Light.

And that was but one, and by no means one of the worst;
Permitted at least his pitiful dignity;   10
And such as were made prayers in the names of Christ,
That shall judge all men, for his soul's tranquillity.

We move now to outside a German wood.
Three men are there commanded to dig a hole
In which the two Jews are ordered to lie down   15
And be buried alive by the third, who is a Pole.

Not light from the shrine at Weimar beyond the hill
Nor light from heaven appeared. But he did refuse.
A Lüger settled back deeply in its glove.
He was ordered to change places with the Jews.   20

Much casual death had drained away their souls.
The thick dirt mounted toward the quivering chin.
When only the head was exposed the order came
To dig him out again and to get back in.

No light, no light in the blue Polish eye.   25
When he finished a riding boot packed down the earth.
The Lüger hovered lightly in its glove.
He was shot in the belly and in three hours bled to death.

No prayers or incense rose up in those hours
Which grew to be years, and every day came mute   30
Thousands sifting down through the crisp air
And settled upon his eyes in a black soot.

Ruth Ann Lief (1923–   )

EVE'S DAUGHTERS

The old masters of subordination, were
   they right?
Superior by testicle to this weak vessel
   with plentiful hair?
When Nora got liberated, where did she
   go, you want to know.
Where? Here and there like her captors
   to register title
On erasable slate to traits flesh was heir
   to. Did she learn   5
More than an embrace is an embrace,
   and when the cords
Strained with intolerable rage in her
   neck
Drink and sex were ways, thinking was
   another?

And of course she poetastered, Mr.
   Pope.
Her plight was intricate, implicit with
   sins   10
Perpetuate in her and her mother. On
   the whole
Little help from the men, who had a
   tendency
To trace the causes of her malady to a
   curable
Itch in the crotch, with which she was
   more seldom
Afflicted than her doctors. Oh well, in
   another hundred years   15
She should be human. Then what shall
   we do for difference

"Eve's Daughters" reprinted by permission of *The Kenyon Review* and Ruth Ann Lief. "Astronautics" and "Sailing for Oblivion" reprinted by permission of Ruth Ann Lief.

ASTRONAUTICS

You who eat stars for breakfast
And again at noon
And digest them by evening
When the local moon
Settles time around you like a
    comforter   5
Less warm than the supple aluminum
    womb
In which you bathed weightless
Umbilically related to the cloud-drifted
    mother,
Already God-filled
The livingroom of heaven shifts   10
To admit history

With overflow of anaerobic
    populations.

Ubiquitous colonist,
Hazard will not fail
Like fuel or boosters in the final
    stage.   15
Hazard in our grave
Gazes Venusward
Drinking continents actualized
By graduates in Advanced Infinity.

Unimpressed by gravity   20
Or lack of it,
Hazard will not fail.

SAILING FOR OBLIVION

This is no world for old girls.
The thread of generation snaps and stings their womb.
Umbilicals shrivel in their scrapbooks.
They are due from gynecology to pass
Into the hands of the internist soon.   5
What will he find to keep his interest in the species
Alive?

Inoperable clots. Daughter begotten
Prodigal of promise (is she honest?
Madam, do you really want to hear?)   10
Son come a cropper, supervised
By prognoses of fear.
Last egg spermed by elderly sire
Poses possible malignancy.

Starting with the head, then the heart—   15
The tender parts—the slender teeth have eaten
And the permanent now gnaw with all reasonable speed

Intestine, gizzard, et cetera.
Will it profit (bright little teeth
Flashing in lightless nest of consumption)—   20
Will it get all the protein it needs?

There are parent study groups
In the schools of the world,
But there are no good places
For the old girls. . . .   25

Louis Simpson (1923–   )

WALT WHITMAN AT BEAR MOUNTAIN

*. . . life which does not give the
preference to any other life, of any
previous period, which therefore
prefers its own existence . . .*
                    —Ortega y Gasset

Neither on horseback nor seated,
But like himself, squarely on two feet,
The poet of death and lilacs
Loafs by the footpath. Even the bronze
    looks alive
Where it is folded like cloth. And he
    seems friendly.   5

"Where is the Mississippi panorama
And the girl who played the piano?
Where are you, Walt?
The Open Road goes to the used-car lot.

"Where is the nation you promised?   10
These houses built of wood sustain
Colossal snows,
And the light above the street is sick to
    death.

"As for the people—see how they
    neglect you!
Only a poet pauses to read the
    inscription."   15

"I am here," he answered.
"It seems you have found me out.
Yet, I did not warn you that it was
    Myself
I advertised? Were my words not
    sufficiently plain?

"I gave no prescriptions,   20
And those who have taken my moods
    for prophecies
Mistake the matter."
Then, vastly amused—"Why do you
    reproach me?
I freely confess I am wholly
    disreputable.
Yet I am happy, because you have
    found me out."   25

A crocodile in wrinkled metal
    loafing . . .

Then all the realtors,
Pickpockets, salesmen, and the actors
    performing

"Walt Whitman at Bear Mountain" and "My Father in the Night Commanding No" from *At the End of the Open Road*, by Louis Simpson, copyright © 1960. Reprinted by permission of Wesleyan University Press.

Official scenarios,
Turned a deaf ear, for they had
    contracted   30
American dreams.

But the man who keeps a store on a
    lonely road,
And the housewife who knows she's
    dumb,
And the earth, are relieved.

All that grave weight of America   35
Cancelled! Like Greece and Rome.
The future in ruins!
The castles, the prisons, the cathedrals
Unbuilding, and roses
Blossoming from the stones that are not
    there . . .   40

The clouds are lifting from the high
    Sierras,
The Bay mists clearing;
And the angel in the gate, the flowering
    plum,
Dances like Italy, imagining red.

MY FATHER IN THE NIGHT COMMANDING NO

My father in the night commanding No
Has work to do. Smoke issues from his lips;
    He reads in silence.
The frogs are croaking and the streetlamps glow.

And then my mother winds the gramophone;   5
The Birds of Lammermoor begins to shriek—
    Or reads a story
About a prince, a castle and a dragon.

The moon is glittering above the hill.
I stand before the gateposts of the King—   10
    So runs the story—
Of Thule, at midnight when the mice are still.

And I have been in Thule! It has come true—
The journey and the danger of the world,
    All that there is   15
To bear and to enjoy, endure and do.

Landscapes, seascapes . . . where have I been led?
The names of cities—Paris, Venice, Rome—
    Held out their arms.
A feathered god, seductive, went ahead.   20

Here is my house. Under a red rose tree
A child is swinging; another gravely plays.
    They are not surprised
That I am here; they were expecting me.

And yet my father sits and reads in silence,   25
My mother sheds a tear, the moon is still,
   And the dark wind
Is murmuring that nothing ever happens.

Beyond his jurisdiction as I move
Do I not prove him wrong? And yet, it's true   30
   They will not change
There, on the stage of terror and of love.

The actors in that playhouse always sit
In fixed positions—father, mother, child
   With painted eyes.   35
How sad it is to be a little puppet!

Their heads are wooden. And you once pretended
To understand them! Shake them as you will,
   They cannot speak.
Do what you will, the comedy is ended.   40

Father, why did you work? Why did you weep,
Mother, Was the story so important?
   "Listen!" the wind
Said to the children, and they fell asleep.

James Dickey (1923–   )

THE HEAVEN OF ANIMALS

Here they are. The soft eyes open.
If they have lived in a wood
It is a wood.
If they have lived on plains
It is grass rolling   5
Under their feet forever.

Having no souls, they have come,
Anyway, beyond their knowing.
Their instincts wholly bloom
And they rise.   10
The soft eyes open.

To match them, the landscape flowers,
Outdoing, desperately
Outdoing what is required:
The richest wood,   15
The deepest field.

For some of these,
It could not be the place
It is, without blood.
These hunt, as they have done,   20
But with claws and teeth grown perfect,

More deadly than they can believe.
They stalk more silently,
And crouch on the limbs of trees,
And their descent   25
Upon the bright backs of their prey

May take years
In a sovereign floating of joy.
And those that are hunted
Know this as their life,   30
Their reward: to walk

Under such trees in full knowledge
Of what is in glory above them,
And to feel no fear,
But acceptance, compliance.   35
Fulfilling themselves without pain

At the cycle's center,
They tremble, they walk
Under the tree,
They fall, they are torn,   40
They rise, they walk again.

Allen Ginsberg (1926–   )

A SUPERMARKET IN CALIFORNIA

What thoughts I have of you tonight, Walt Whitman, for I walked down the side-
streets under the trees with a headache self-conscious looking at the full moon.
In my hungry fatigue, and shopping for images, I went into the neon fruit supermarket, dreaming of your enumerations!
What peaches and what penumbras! Whole families shopping at night! Aisles   5
full of husbands! Wives in the avocados, babies in the tomatoes!—and you,
Garcia Lorca, what were you doing down by the watermelons?

I saw you, Walt Whitman, childless, lonely old grubber, poking among the meats
in the refrigerator and eyeing the grocery boys.
I heard you asking questions of each: Who killed the pork chops? What price   10
bananas? Are you my Angel?
I wandered in and out of the brilliant stacks of cans following you, and followed
in my imagination by the store detective.
We strode down the open corridors together in our solitary fancy tasting arti-
chokes, possessing every frozen delicacy, and never passing the cashier.   15

Where are we going, Walt Whitman? The doors close in an hour. Which way
does your beard point tonight?
(I touch your book and dream of our odyssey in the supermarket and feel
absurd.)
Will we walk all night through solitary streets? The trees add shade to shade, 20
lights out in the houses, we'll both be lonely.

Will we stroll dreaming of the lost America of love past blue automobiles
in driveways, home to our silent cottage?
Ah, dear father, graybeard, lonely old courage-teacher, what America did you have
when Charon quit poling his ferry and you got out on a smoking bank and   25
stood watching the boat disappear on the black waters of Lethe?

AMERICA

America I've given you all and now I'm nothing.
America two dollars and twenty-seven cents January 17, 1956.
I can't stand my own mind.
America when will we end the human war?
Go fuck yourself with your atom bomb   5
I don't feel good don't bother me.
I won't write my poem till I'm in my right mind.
America when will you be angelic?
When will you take off your clothes?
When will you look at yourself through the grave?   10
When will you be worthy of your million Trotskyites?
America why are your libraries full of tears?
America when will you send your eggs to India?
I'm sick of your insane demands.
When can I go into the supermarket and buy what I need with my good looks?   15
America after all it is you and I who are perfect not the next world.
Your machinery is too much for me.
You made me want to be a saint.
There must be some other way to settle this argument.
Burroughs is in Tangiers I don't think he'll come back it's sinister.   20
Are you being sinister or is this some form of practical joke?
I'm trying to come to the point.
I refuse to give up my obsession.
America stop pushing I know what I'm doing.
America the plum blossoms are falling.   25
I haven't read the newspapers for months, everyday somebody goes on trial for
    murder.
America I feel sentimental about the Wobblies.
America I used to be a communist when I was a kid I'm not sorry.
I smoke marijuana every chance I get.
I sit in my house for days on end and stare at the roses in the closet.   30
When I go to Chinatown I get drunk and never get laid.
My mind is made up there's going to be trouble.
You should have seen me reading Marx.
My psychoanalyst thinks I'm perfectly right.
I won't say the Lord's Prayer.   35
I have mystical visions and cosmic vibrations.
America I still haven't told you what you did to Uncle Max after he came over
    from Russia.

I'm addressing you.
Are you going to let our emotional life be run by Time Magazine?
I'm obsessed by Time Magazine.   40
I read it every week.
Its cover stares at me every time I slink past the corner candystore.

I read it in the basement of the Berkeley Public Library.
It's always telling me about responsibility. Businessmen are serious. Movie
    producers are serious. Everybody's serious but me.   45
It occurs to me that I am America.
I am talking to myself again.

Asia is rising against me.
I haven't got a chinaman's chance.
I'd better consider my national resources.   50
My national resources consist of two joints of marijuana millions of genitals an
    unpublishable private literature that goes 1400 miles and hour and
    twentyfivethousand mental institutions.
I say nothing about my prisons nor the millions of underprivileged who live in
    my flowerpots under the light of five hundred suns.
I have abolished the whorehouses of France, Tangiers is the next to go.
My ambition is to be President despite the fact that I'm a Catholic.

America how can I write a holy litany in your silly mood?   55
I will continue like Henry Ford my strophes are as individual as his automobiles
    more so they're all different sexes.
America I will sell you strophes $2500 apiece $500 down on your old strophe
America free Tom Mooney
America save the Spanish Loyalists
America Sacco & Vanzetti must not die   60
America I am the Scottsboro boys.
America when I was seven momma took me to Communist Cell meetings they
    sold us garbanzos a handful per ticket a ticket costs a nickel and the
    speeches were free everybody was angelic and sentimental about the
    workers it was all so sincere you have no idea what a good thing the party
    was in 1935 Scott Nearing was a grand old man a real mensch Mother
    Bloor made me cry I once saw Israel Amter plain. Everybody must have
    been a spy.
America you don't really want to go to war.
America it's them bad Russians.
Them Russians them Russians and them Chinamen. And them Russians.   65
The Russia wants to eat us alive. The Russia's power mad. She wants to take our
    cars from out our garages.
Her wants to grab Chicago. Her needs a Red Reader's Digest. Her wants our auto
    plants in Siberia. Him big bureaucracy running our fillingstations.
That no good. Ugh. Him make Indians learn read. Him need big black niggers.
    Hah. Her make us all work sixteen hours a day. Help.
America this is quite serious.
America this is the impression I get from looking in the television set.   70
America is this correct?
I'd better get right down to the job.
It's true I don't want to join the Army or turn lathes in precision parts factories,
    I'm nearsighted and psychopathic anyway.
America I'm putting my queer shoulder to the wheel.

SUNFLOWER SUTRA

I walked on the banks of the tincan banana dock and sat down under the huge shade of a Southern Pacific locomotive to look at the sunset over the box house hills and cry.

Jack Kerouac sat beside me on a busted rusty iron pole, companion, we thought the same thoughts of the soul, bleak and blue and sad-eyed, surrounded by the gnarled steel roots of trees of machinery.

The oily water on the river mirrored the red sky, sun sank on top of final Frisco peaks, no fish in that stream, no hermit in those mounts, just ourselves rheumy-eyed and hungover like old bums on the riverbank, tired and wily.

Look at the Sunflower, he said, there was a dead gray shadow against the sky, big as a man, sitting dry on top of a pile of ancient sawdust—

—I rushed up enchanted—it was my first sunflower, memories of Blake—my visions—Harlem

and Hells of the Eastern rivers, bridges clanking Joes Greasy Sandwiches, dead baby carriages, black treadless tires forgotten and unretreaded, the poem of the river-bank, condoms & pots, steel knives, nothing stainless, only the dank muck and the razor sharp artifacts passing into the past—

and the gray Sunflower poised against the sunset, cracky bleak and dusty with the smut and smog and smoke of olden locomotives in its eye—

corolla of bleary spikes pushed down and broken like a battered crown, seeds fallen out of its face, soon-to-be-toothless mouth of sunny air, sunrays obliterated on its hairy head like a dried wire spiderweb,

leaves stuck out like arms out of the stem, gestures from the sawdust root, broke pieces of plaster fallen out of the black twigs, a dead fly in its ear,

Unholy battered old thing you were, my sunflower O my soul, I loved you then!

The grime was no man's grime but death and human locomotives,

all that dress of dust, that veil of darkened railroad skin, that smog of cheek, that eyelid of black mis'ry, that sooty hand or phallus or protuberance of artificial worse-than-dirt—industrial—modern—all that civilization spotting your crazy golden crown—

and those blear thoughts of death and dusty loveless eyes and ends and withered roots below, in the home-pile of sand and sawdust, rubber dollar bills, skin of machinery, the guts and innards of the weeping coughing car, the empty lonely tincans with their rusty tongues alack, what more could I name, the smoked ashes of some cock cigar, the cunts of wheelbarrows and the milky breasts of cars, worn-out asses out of chairs & sphincters of dynamos—all these

entangled in your mummied roots—and you there standing before me in the sunset, all your glory in your form!

A perfect beauty of a sunflower! a perfect excellent lovely sunflower existence! a sweet natural eye to the new hip moon, woke up alive and excited grasping in the sunset shadow sunrise golden monthly breeze!

How many flies buzzed round you innocent of your grime, while you cursed the heavens of the railroad and your flower soul?

Poor dead flower? when did you forget you were a flower? when did you look at

your skin and decide you were an impotent dirty old locomotive? the ghost of
a locomotive? the specter and shade of a once powerful mad American locomotive?
You were never no locomotive, Sunflower, you were a sunflower!
And you Locomotive, you are a locomotive, forget me not!
So I grabbed up thet skeleton thick sunflower and stuck it at my side like a scepter.
and deliver my sermon to my soul, and Jack's soul too, and anyone who'll listen,
—We're not our skin of grime, we're not our dread bleak dusty imageless locomotive, we're all beautiful golden sunflowers inside, we're blessed by our own seed
& golden hairy naked accomplishment—bodies growing into mad black formal
sunflowers in the sunset, spied on by our eyes under the shadow of the mad
locomotive riverbank sunset Frisko hilly tincan evening sitdown vision.

Robert Bly (1926–   )

WATCHING TELEVISION

Sounds are heard too high for ears,
From the body cells there is an answering bay;
Soon the inner streets fill with a chorus of barks.

We see the landing craft coming in,
The black car sliding to a stop,   5
The Puritan killer loosening his guns.

Wild dogs tear off noses and eyes
And run off with them down the street—
The body tears off its own arms and throws them into the air.

The detective draws fifty-five million people into his revolver,   10
Who sleep restlessly as in an air raid in London;
Their backs become curved in the sloping dark.

The filaments of the soul slowly separate:
The spirit breaks, a puff of dust floats up,
Like a house in Nebraska that suddenly explodes.   15

THOSE BEING EATEN BY AMERICA

The cry of those being eaten by America,
Others pale and soft being stored for later eating

And Jefferson
Who saw hope in new oats

The wild houses go on   5
With long hair growing from between their toes
The feet at night get up
And run down the long white roads by themselves

The dams reverse themselves and want to go stand alone in the desert

Ministers who dive headfirst into the earth   10
The pale flesh
Spreading guiltily into new literatures

That is why these poems are so sad
The long dead running over the fields

The mass sinking down   15
The light in children's faces fading at six or seven

The world will soon break up into small colonies of the saved

COUNTING SMALL-BONED BODIES

Let's count the bodies over again.

If we could only make the bodies smaller,
The size of skulls,
We could make a whole plain white with skulls in the moonlight!

If we could only make the bodies smaller,   5
Maybe we could get
A whole year's kill in front of us on a desk!

If we could only make the bodies smaller,
We could fit
A body into a finger-ring, for a keepsake forever.   10

Charles Tomlinson (1927–   )
POEM

Upended, it crouches on broken limbs
About to run forward. No longer
   threatened
But surprised into this vigilance
It gapes enmity from its hollowed core.

Moist woodflesh, softened to a paste   5
Of marl and white splinter, dangles
Wherever overhead the torn root
Casts up its wounds in a ragged orchis.

The seasons strip, but do not tame you.
I grant you become more smooth   10
As you are emptied and where the
   heart shreds
The gap mouths a more practiced silence.

You would impress, but merely startle.
   Your accomplice
Twilight is dragging its shadows here
Deliberate and unsocial: I leave you   15
To your own meaning, yourself alone.

RETURN TO HINTON

Written on the author's return to Hinton
Blewett from the United States

Ten years
   and will you be
      a footnote, merely,
England
   of the Bible   5
      open at Genesis
on the parlour table?
   "God
      saw the light
that it was good."   10
   It falls
      athwart the book
through window-lace
   whose shadow
      decorates the sheets   15

of "The Bridal March"—
   a square of white
      above the keyboard
and below
   a text which is a prayer.   20
      The television box
is one,
   the mullions and flagged floor
      of the kitchen
through an open door   25
   witness a second
      world in which
beside the hob
   the enormous kettles'
      blackened bellies ride—   30

"Poem" reprinted by permission of the author. "Return to Hinton" from *A Peopled Land-scape* by Charles Tomlinson, published by Oxford University Press and reprinted with their permission.

as much the tokens of an order as
    the burnished brass.
        You live
between the two
    and, ballasted against   35
        the merely new, the tide
and shift of time
    you wear
        your widow's silk
your hair   40
    plaited, as it has been
        throughout those years
whose rime it bears.
    A tractor
        mounts the ramp of stones 45
into the yard:
    a son surveys
        the scenes
that occupied a father's days.
    Proud of his machine,   50
        will he transmit
that more than bread
    that leaves you undisquieted?
        This house
is poorer by a death   55
    than last I saw it
        yet
who may judge
    as poverty that
        sadness without bitterness 60
those sudden tears
    that your composure
        clears, admonishes?
Your qualities
    are like the land   65
        —inherited:
but you
    have earned
        your right to them
have given   70
    grief its due
        and, on despair,
have closed your door
    as the gravestones tell you to.
        Speak   75
your composure and you share
    the accent of their rhymes
        express

won readiness
    in a worn dress   80
        of chapel gospel.
Death's
    not the enemy
        of you nor of your kind:
a surer death   85
    creeps after me
        out of that generous
rich and nervous land
    where, buried by
        the soft oppression of
prosperity,   90
locality's mere grist
    to build
        the even bed
of roads that will not rest
    until they lead   95
        into a common future
rational
    and secure
        that we must speed
by means that are not either.   100
    Narrow
        your farm-bred certainties
I do not hold:
    I share
        your certain enemy.   105
For we who write
    the verse you do not read
        already plead your cause
before
    that cold tribunal   110
        while you're unaware
they hold their session.
    Our language is our land
        that we'll
not waste or sell   115
    against a promised mess
        of pottage that we may not
taste.
For who has known
    the seasons' sweet succession
        and would still   120
exchange them for a whim, a wish
    or swim into
        a mill-race for an unglimpsed
fish?

James Wright (1927–   )
THE REVELATION

Stress of his anger set me back
To musing over time and space.
The apple branches dripping black
Divided light across his face.
Towering beneath the broken tree,   5
He seemed a stony shade to me.
He spoke no language I could hear
For long with my distracted ear.

Between his lips and my delight
In blowing wind, a bird-song rose.   10
And soon in fierce, blockading light
The planet's shadow hid his face.
And all that strongly molded bone
Of chest and shoulder soon were gone,
Devoured among the soiled shade.   15
Assured his angry voice was dead,

And satisfied his judging eyes
Had given over plaguing me,
I stood to let the darkness rise—
My darkness, gathering in the tree,   20
The field, the swollen shock of hay,
Bank of the creek half washed away.
Lost in my self, and unaware
Of love, I took the evening air.

I blighted, for a moment's length,   25
My father out of sight and sound;
Prayed to annihilate his strength,
The proud legs planted on the ground.

Why should I hear his angry cry
Or bear the damning of his eye?   30
Anger for anger I could give,
And murder for my right to live.
The moon rose. Lucidly the moon
Ran skimming shadows off the trees,
To strip all shadow but its own   35
Down to the perfect mindlessness.
Yet suddenly the moon light caught
My father's fingers reaching out,
The strong arm begging me for love,
Loneliness I knew nothing of.   40

And weeping in the nakedness
Of moonlight and of agony,
His blue eyes lost their barrenness
And bore a blossom out to me
And as I ran to give it back,   45
The apple branches, dripping black,
Trembled across the lunar air
And dropped white petals on his hair.

COMPLAINT

She's gone. She was my love, my moon or more.
She chased the chickens out and swept the floor,
Emptied the bones and nut-shells after feasts,
And smacked the kids for leaping up like beasts.

Now morbid boys have grown past awkwardness;   5
The girls let stitches out, dress after dress,
To free some swinging body's riding space
And form the new child's unimagined face.
Yet, while vague nephews, spitting on their curls,
Amble to pester winds and blowsy girls,   10
What arm will sweep the room, what hand will hold
New snow against the milk to keep it cold?
And who will dump the garbage, feed the hogs,
And pitch the chickens' heads to hungry dogs?
Not my lost hag who dumbly bore such pain: 15
Childbirth and midnight sassafras and rain.
New snow against her face and hands she bore,
And now lies down, who was my moon or more.

TWO POEMS ABOUT PRESIDENT HARDING
ONE: HIS DEATH

In Marion, the honey locust trees are falling.
Everybody in town remembers the white hair,
The campaign of a lost summer, the front porch
Open to the public, and the vaguely stunned smile
Of a lucky man.   5

"Neighbor, I want to be helpful," he said once.
Later, "You think I'm honest, don't you?"
Weeping drunk.

I am drunk this evening in 1961,
In a jog for my countryman,   10
Who died of crab meat on the way back from Alaska.
Everyone knows that joke.

How many honey locusts have fallen,
Pitched rootlong into the open graves of strip mines,
Since the First World War ended   15
And Wilson the gaunt deacon jogged sullenly
Into silence?
Tonight,
The cancerous ghosts of old con men
Shed their leaves.   20
For a proud man,
Lost between the turnpike near Cleveland
And the chiropractors' signs looming among dead mulberry trees,
There is no place left to go
But home.   25

"Warren lacks mentality," one of his friends said.
Yet he was beautiful, he was the snowfall
Turned to white stallions standing still
Under dark elm trees.

He died in public. He claimed the secret right   30
To be ashamed.

TWO: HIS TOMB IN OHIO

. . . he died of a busted gut.
                    —Mencken, on Bryan

A hundred slag piles north of us,
At the mercy of the moon and rain,
He lies in his ridiculous
Tomb, our fellow citizen.   35
No, I have never seen that place,
Where many shadows of faceless
    thieves
Chuckle and stumble and embrace
On beer cans, stogie butts, and graves.

One holiday, one rainy week   40
After the country fell apart,
Hoover and Coolidge came to speak
And snivel about his broken heart.
His grave, a huge absurdity,
Embarrassed cops and visitors.   45
Hoover and Coolidge crept away
By night, and women closed their doors.

Now junkmen call their children in
Before they catch their death of cold;
Young lovers let the moon begin   50
Its quick spring; and the day grows old;
The mean one-legger who rakes up
    leaves
Has chased the loafers out of the park;
Minnegan Leonard half-believes   55
In God, and the poolroom goes dark;

America goes on, goes on
Laughing, and Harding was a fool.
Even his big pretentious stone
Lays him bare to ridicule.   60
I know it. But don't look at me.
By God, I didn't start this mess.
Whatever moon and rain may be,
The hearts of men are merciless.

EISENHOWER'S VISIT TO FRANCO, 1959

... we die of cold, and not
of darkness.—Unamuno

The American hero must triumph over
The forces of darkness.
He has flown through the very light of
   heaven
And come down in the slow dusk
Of Spain.   5

Franco stands in a shining circle of
   police.
His arms open in welcome.
He promises all dark things
Will be hunted down.

State police yawn in the prisons.   10
Antonio Machado follows the moon
Down a road of white dust,
To a cave of silent children

Under the Pyrenees.
Wine darkens in stone jars in
   villages.   15
Wine sleeps in the mouths of old men,
   it is a dark red color.

Smiles glitter in Madrid.
Eisenhower has touched hands with
   Franco, embracing
In a glare of photographers.
Clean new bombers from America
   muffle their engines   20
And glide down now.

Their wings shine in the searchlights
Of bare fields,
In Spain.

Galway Kinnell (1927–   )

THE CORRESPONDENCE SCHOOL INSTRUCTOR
SAYS GOODBYE TO HIS POETRY STUDENTS

Goodbye, lady in Bangor, who sent me
snapshots of yourself, after definitely hinting
you were beautiful; goodbye,
Miami Beach urologist, who enclosed plain
brown envelopes for the return of your very   5
"Clinical Sonnets"; goodbye, manufacturer
of brassieres on the Coast, whose eclogues
give the fullest treatment in literature yet
to the sagging breast motif; goodbye, you in San Quentin,
who wrote, "Being German my hero is Hitler,"   10

"The Correspondence School Instructor Says Goodbye to His Poetry Students" from Kinnell's *Body Rags.* Copyright © 1965, 1966, 1967, by Galway Kinnell. Reprinted by permission of the publisher, Houghton Mifflin Co.

instead of "Sincerely yours," at the end of a long,
neat-scripted letters demolishing
the pre-Raphaelites:

I swear to you, it was just my way   15
of cheering myself up, as I licked
the stamped, self-addressed envelopes,
the game I had
of trying to guess which one of you, this time,
had poisoned his glue. I did care.   20
I did read each poem entire.
I did say what I thought was the truth
in the mildest words I knew. And now,

in this poem, or chopped prose, not any better,
I realize, than those troubled lines   25
I kept sending back to you,
I have to say I am relieved it is over:
at the end I could feel only pity
for that urge toward more life
your poems kept smothering in words, the smell   30
of which, days later, would tingle
in your nostrils as new, God-given impulses
to write.

Goodbye,
you who are, for me, the postmarks again
of shattered towns—Xenia, Burnt Cabins, Hornell—   35
their loneliness
given away in poems, only their solitude kept.

Bink Noll (1927–   )

THE LOCK

remembers the first door, on which
it was the first bolt shot forward
and declares "You are somewhat bad,
Mankind." And I say "These are mine."

She calls down "Have you locked the door?"   5
Habit, same as owning a moat:
"Have you filled the moat?"

Originally published by *The Virginia Quarterly Review*, September 1971. Used by permission of Bink Noll.

                              Two or three
bad men pollute the neighborhood—
pillage, arson, mutilation, rape—   10
and round us the stagnant moat.

And the stranger locked out who could
help himself to fruit and a drink,
nap on the couch, walk off with a spoon.
Of course I've locked the door.   15

                              But think:
those raised floors—pavillions sideless
and grass-roofed—where villages sleep
without knowing they own so much
that Want prowls forward through the murk.   20
O Happy Savages!

                              But we
northern men for ten thousand years
have bred attack into the dogs
that sleep by our fires, leap and SNAP!   25
like the more recent, more certain lock.

O Efficacious Lock! your wedge,
your spring, your admirable wards,
your keyhold and my key and this,
your inside bolt, and all is safe.   30
Stranger Want does not hear your snap
but expects you, your counter force,
my door stubborn as a policeman
with prudence on its side, and law.

Philip Levine (1928–   )

THEY FEED THEY LION

Out of burlap sacks, out of bearing butter,
Out of black bean and wet slate bread,
Out of the acids of rage, the candor of tar,
Out of creosote, gasoline, drive shafts, wooden dollies,
They Lion grow.   5

"They Feed They Lion" and "Coming Home, Detroit, 1968" from *They Feed They Lion* by Philip Levine. Copyright © 1968, 1972 by Philip Levine. Reprinted by permission of Atheneum Publishers. "They Feed They Lion" appeared originally in *Kayak*; "Coming Home" appeared originally in *The Hudson Review*.

Out of the gray hills
Of industrial barns, out of rain, out of bus ride,
West Virginia to Kiss My Ass, out of buried aunties,
Mothers hardening like pounded stumps, out of stumps,
Out of the bones' need to sharpen and the muscles' to stretch,   10
They Lion grow.

Earth is eating trees, fence posts,
Gutter cars, earth is calling in her little ones,
"Come home, Come home!" From pig balls,
From the ferocity of pig driven to holiness,   15
From the furred ear and the full jowl come
The repose of the hung belly, from the purpose
They Lion grow.

From the sweet glues of the trotters
Come the sweet kinks of the fist, from the full flower   20
Of the hams the thorax of caves,
From "Bow Down" come "Rise Up,"
Come they Lion from the reeds of shovels,
The grained arm that pulls the hands,
They Lion grow.   25

From my five arms and all my hands,
From all my white sins forgiven, they feed,
From my car passing under the stars,
They Lion, from my children inherit,
From the oak turned to a wall, they Lion,   30
From the sack and they belly opened
And all that was hidden burning on the oil-stained earth
They feed they Lion and he comes.

COMING HOME, *Detroit*, 1968

A winter Tuesday, the city pouring fire,
Ford Rouge sulfurs the sun, Cadillac, Lincoln,
Chevy gray. The fat stacks
of breweries hold their tongues. Rags,
papers, hands, the stems of birches   5
dirtied with words.
Near the freeway
you stop and wonder what came off,
recall the snowstorm where you lost it all,
the wolverine, the northern bear, the wolf   10
caught out, ice and steel raining
from the foundries in a shower
of human breath. On sleds in the false sun
the new material rests. One brown child
stares and stares into your frozen eyes   15

until the lights change and you go
forward to work. The charred faces, the eyes
boarded up, the rubble of innards, the cry
of wet smoke hanging in your throat,
the twisted river stopped at the color of iron.   20
We burn this city every day.

Donald Hall (1928–   )
THE BODY POLITIC

I shot my friend to save my country's
    life,
And when the happy bullet struck him
    dead,
I was saluted by the drum and fife
Corps of a high school, while the traitor
    bled.

I never thought until I pulled the
    trigger   5
But that I did the difficult and good.
I thought republics stood for something
    bigger,
For the mind of man, as Plato said they
    stood.

So when I heard the duty they assigned,
Shooting my friend seemed only
    sanity;   10
To keep disorder from the state of mind
Was mental rectitude, it seemed to me.

The audience dispersed. I felt
    depressed.
I went to where my orders issued from,
But the right number on the street was
    just   15
A vacant lot. Oh, boy, had I been
    dumb!

I tried to find the true address, but
    where?
Nobody told me what I had to know,
And secretaries sent me here and there
To other secretaries, just for show.   20

Poor Fred. His presence will be greatly
    missed
By children and by cronies by the score.
The State (I learn too late) does not
    exist;
Man lives by love, and not by
    metaphor.

Anne Sexton (1928–1974)
THE WEDDING NIGHT

There was this time in Boston
before spring was ready—a short
  celebration—
and then it was over.
I walked down Marlborough Street the
  day you left me
under branches as tedious as leather,   5
under branches as stiff as driver's
  gloves.
I said, (but only because you were gone)
"Magnolia blossoms have rather a
  southern sound,
so unlike Boston anyhow,"
and whatever it was that happened, all
  that pink,   10
and for so short a time,
was unbelievable, was pinned on.

The magnolias had sat once, each in a
  pink dress,
looking, of course, at the ceiling.
For weeks the buds had been as sure-
  bodied   15
as the twelve-year-old flower girl I was
at Aunt Edna's wedding.
Will they bend, I had asked,
as I walked under them toward you,
bend two to a branch,   20
cheek, forehead, shoulder to the floor?
I could see that none were clumsy.
I could see that each was tight and firm.
Not one of them had trickled blood—
waiting as polished as gull beaks,   25
as closed as all that.

I stood under them for nights,
  hesitating,
and then drove away in my car.
Yet one night in the April night
someone (someone!) kicked each bud
  open—   30
to disprove, to mock, to puncture!
The next day they were all hot-colored,
moist, not flawed in fact.
Then they no longer huddled.
They forgot how to hide.   35
Tense as they had been,
they were flags, gaudy, chafing in the
  wind.
There was such abandonment in all
  that!
Such entertainment
in their flaring up.   40

After that, well—
like faces in a parade,
I could not tell the difference between
  losing you
and losing them.
They dropped separately after the
  celebration,   45
handpicked,
one after the other like artichoke leaves.
After that I walked to my car
  awkwardly
over the painful bare remains on the
  brick sidewalk,
knowing that someone had, in one
  night,   50
passed roughly through,
and before it was time.

THE ADDICT

Sleepmonger,
deathmonger,
with capsules in my palms each night,
eight at a time from sweet
    pharmaceutical bottles
I make arrangements for a pint-sized
    journey.   5
I'm the queen of this condition.
I'm an expert on making the trip
and now they say I'm an addict.
Now they ask why.
Why!   10

Don't they know
that I promised to die!
I'm keeping in practice.
I'm merely staying in shape.
The pills are a mother, but better,   15
every color and as good as sour balls.
I'm on a diet from death.

Yes, I admit
it has gotten to be a bit of a habit—
blows eight at a time, socked in the
    eye,   20
hauled away by the pink, the orange,
the green and the white goodnights.
I'm becoming something of a chemical
mixture
That's it!   25

My supply
of tablets
has got to last for years and years.
I like them more than I like me.
Stubborn as hell, they won't let go.   30

It's a kind of marriage.
It's a kind of war
where I plant bombs inside
of myself.

Yes   35
I try
to kill myself in small amounts,
an innocuous occupation.
Actually I'm hung up on it.
But remember I don't make too much
    noise.   40
And frankly no one has to lug me out

and I don't stand there in my winding
    sheet.
I'm a little buttercup in my yellow
    nightie
eating my eight loaves in a row
and in a certain order as in   45
the laying on of hands
or the black sacrament.

It's a ceremony
but like any other sport
it's full of rules.   50
It's like a musical tennis match where
my mouth keeps catching the ball.
Then I lie on my altar
elevated by the eight chemical kisses.

What a lay me down this is   55
with two pink, two orange,
two green, two white goodnights.
Fee-fi-fo-fum—
Now I'm borrowed.
Now I'm numb.   60

"The Wedding Night" and "The Addict," reprinted by permission of Houghton Mifflin Company.

ALL MY PRETTY ONES

> *All my pretty ones?*
> *Did you say all? O hell-kite! All?*
> *What! all my pretty chickens and their dam*
> *At one fell swoop? . . .*
> *I cannot but remember such things were,*
> *That were most precious to me.*   MACBETH

Father, this year's jinx rides us apart
where you followed our mother to her cold slumber,
a second shock boiling its stone to your heart,
leaving me here to shuffle and disencumber
you from the residence you could not afford: 5
a gold key, your half of a woollen mill,
twenty suits from Dunne's, an English Ford,
the love and legal verbiage of another will,
boxes of pictures of people I do not know.
I touch their cardboard faces. They must go.   10

But the eyes, as thick as wood in this album,
hold me. I stop here, where a small boy
waits in a ruffled dress for someone to come . . .
for this soldier who holds his bugle like a toy   15
or for this velvet lady who cannot smile.
Is this your father's father, this commodore
in a mailman suit? My father, time meanwhile
has made it unimportant who you are looking for..
I'll never know what these faces are all about.
I lock them into their book and throw them out.   20

This is the yellow scrapbook that you began
the year I was born; as crackling now and wrinkly
as tobacco leaves: clippings where Hoover outran
the Democrats, wriggling his dry finger at me
and Prohibition; news where the *Hindenburg* went   25
down and recent years where you went flush
on war. This year, solvent but sick, you meant
to marry that pretty widow in a one-month rush.
But before you had that second chance, I cried
on your fat shoulder. Three days later you died.   30

These are the snapshots of marriage, stopped in places.
Side by side at the rail toward Nassau now;
here, with the winner's cup at the speedboat races,
here, in tails at the Cotillion, you take a bow.
here, by our kennel of dogs with their pink eyes,   35
running like show-bred pigs in their chain-link pep;
here, at the horseshow where my sister wins a prize;
and here, standing like a duke among groups of men.
Now I fold you down, my drunkard, my navigator,
my first lost keeper, to love or look at later.   40

I hold a five-year diary that my mother kept
for three years, telling all she does not say
of your alcoholic tendency. You overslept,
she writes. My God, father, each Christmas Day
with your blood, will I drink down your glass   45
of wine? The diary of your hurly-burly years
goes to my shelf to wait for my age to pass.
Only in this hoarded span will love persevere.
Whether you are pretty or not, I outlive you,
bend down my strange face to yours and forgive you.   50

Thom Gunn (1929–   )

ON THE MOVE

'Man, you gotta Go.'

The blue jay scuffling in the bushes follows
Some hidden purpose, and the gust of birds
That spurts across the field, the wheeling swallows,
Have nested in the trees and undergrowth.
Seeking their instinct, or their poise, or both,   5
One moves with an uncertain violence
Under the dust thrown by a baffled sense
Or the dull thunder of approximate words.

On motorcycles, up the road, they come:
Small, black, as flies hanging in heat, the Boys,   10
Until the distance throws them forth, their hum
Bulges to thunder held by calf and thigh.
In goggles, donned impersonality,
In gleaming jackets trophied with the dust,
They strap in doubt—by hiding it, robust—   15
And almost hear a meaning in their noise.

Reprinted by permission of Faber & Faber, Ltd. from *The Sense of Movement*.

Exact conclusion of their hardiness
Has no shape yet, but from known whereabouts
They ride, direction where the tires press.
They scare a flight of birds across the field: 20
Much that is natural, to the will must yield.
Men manufacture both machine and soul,
And use what they imperfectly control
To dare a future from the taken routes.

It is a part solution, after all.   25
One is not necessarily discord
On earth; or damned because, half animal,
One lacks direct instinct, because one wakes
Afloat on movement that divides and breaks.
One joins the movement in a valueless world,   30
Choosing it, till, both hurler and the hurled,
One moves as well, always toward, toward.

A minute holds them, who have come to go:
The self-defined, astride the created will
They burst away; the towns they travel through   35
Are home for neither bird nor holiness,
For birds and saints complete their purposes.
At worse, one is in motion; and at best,
Reaching no absolute, in which to rest,
One is always nearer by not keeping still.   40

Raymond R. Patterson (1929–   )

AT THAT MOMENT

(For Malcolm X)

When they shot Malcolm Little down
On the stage of the Audubon Ballroom,
When his life ran out through bullet holes
(Like the people running out when the murder began)
His blood soaked the floor
One drop found a crack through the stark
Pounding thunder—slipped under the stage and began
Its journey: burrowed through concrete into the cellar,
Dropped down darkness, exploding like quicksilver
Pellets of light, panicking rats, paralyzing cockroaches—
Tunneled through rubble and wrecks of foundations,

The rocks that buttress the bowels of the city, flowed
Into pipes and powerlines, the mains and cables of the city:
A thousand fiery seeds.
At that moment,
Those who drank water where he entered . . .
Those who cooked food where he passed . . .
Those who burned light while he listened . . .
Those who were talking as he went, knew he was water
Running out of faucets, gas running out of jets, power
Running out of sockets, meaning running along taut wires—
To the hungers of their living. It is said
Whole slums of clotted Harlem plumbing groaned
And sundered free that day, and disconnected gas and light
Went on and on and on. . . .
They rushed his riddled body on a stretcher
To the hospital. But the police were too late.
It had already happened.

Jon Silkin (1930–   )

FURNISHED LIVES

I have been walking today
Where the sour children of London's poor sleep
  Pressed close to the unfrosted glare
Torment lying closed in to tenement,
Of the clay fire; I   5
Have watched their whispering souls fly straight to God:

"O Lord, please give to us
A dinner-service, austere, yet gay: like snow
  When swans are on it; Bird
Unfold your wings until like a white smile   10
  You fill this mid-white room."
I have balanced myself on this meagre Strand where

Each man and woman turn
On the deliberate hour of the cock,
  As if two new risen souls,   15
Through the cragged landscape of each other's eyes.
  But where lover upon lover
Should meet—where sheet, and pillow, and eiderdown

Should frolic and crisp,
As dolphins on the stylized crown of the sea   20
    Their pale cerements lie.
They tread with chocolate souls and paper hands;
    They walk into that room
Your gay and daffodil smile has never seen:

    Not to love's pleasant feast   25
They go, in the mutations of the night,
    But to their humiliations
Paled as a swan's dead feather scorched in the sun.
    I have been walking today
Among the newly paper-crowned, among those   30

    Whose casual, paper body
Is crushed between fate's fingers and the platter;
    But Sir, their perpetual fire
Was not stubbed out, folded on brass or stone
    Extinguished in the dark,   35
But burns with the drear dampness of cut flowers.

    I cannot hear their piped
Cry. These souls have no players. They have resigned
    The vivid performance of their world.
        And your world, Lord,   40
            Has now become
Like a dumb winter show, held in one room,

    Which must now reek of age
Before you have retouched its lips with such straight fire
    As through your stony earth   45
Burns with ferocious tears in the world's eyes:
Church-stone, door-knocker and polished railway lines
    Move in their separate dumb way
        So why not these lives;
I ask you often, but you never say?   50

Ted Hughes (1930–   )

THE HAWK IN THE RAIN

I drown in the drumming ploughland, I drag up
Heel after heel from the swallowing of the earth's mouth,
From clay that clutches my each step to the ankle
With the habit of the dogged grave, but the hawk

Effortlessly at height hangs his still eye.   5
His wings hold all creation in a weightless quiet,
Steady as a hallucination in the streaming air.
While banging wind kills these stubborn hedges,

Thumbs my eyes, throws my breath, tackles my heart,
And rain hacks my head to the bone, the hawk hangs   10
The diamond point of will that polestars
The sea drowner's endurance: and I,

Bloodily grabbed dazed last-moment-counting
Morsel in the earth's mouth, strain towards the master-
Fulcrum of violence where the hawk hangs still.   15
That maybe in his own time meets the weather

Coming the wrong way, suffers the air, hurled upside down,
Fall from his eye, the ponderous shires crash on him,
The horizon trap him; the round angelic eye
Smashed, mixed his heart's blood with the mire of the land.   20

THE JAGUAR

The apes yawn and adore their fleas in the sun.
The parrots shriek as if they were on fire, or strut
Like cheap tarts to attract the stroller with the nut.
Fatigued with indolence, tiger and lion

Lie still as the sun. The boa-constrictor's coil   5
Is a fossil. Cage after cage seems empty, or
Stinks of sleepers from the breathing straw.
It might be painted on a nursery wall.

But who runs like the rest past these arrives
At a cage where the crowd stands, stares, mesmerized,
As a child at a dream, at a jaguar hurrying enraged
Through prison darkness after the drills of his eyes

10

On a short fierce fuse. Not in boredom—
The eye satisfied to be blind in fire,
By the bang of blood in the brain deaf the ear—
He spins from the bars, but there's no cage to him

15

More than to the visionary his cell:
His stride is wildernesses of freedom:
The world rolls under the long thrust of his heel.
Over the cage floor the horizons come.

20

CROW'S FIRST LESSON

God tried to teach Crow how to talk.
"Love," said God. "Say, Love."
Crow gaped, and the white shark crashed into the sea
And went rolling downwards, discovering its own depth.

"No, no," said God. "Say Love. Now try it. LOVE."
Crow gaped, and a bluefly, a tsetse, a mosquito
Zoomed out and down
To their sundry flesh-pots.

5

"A final try," said God. "Now, LOVE."
Crow convulsed, gaped, retched and
Man's bodiless prodigious head
Bulbed out onto the earth, with swivelling eyes,
Jabbering protest —

10

And Crow retched again, before God could stop him.
And woman's vulva dropped over man's neck and tightened.
The two struggled together on the grass.
God struggled to part them, cursed, wept—

15

Crow flew guiltily off.

CROW'S THEOLOGY

Crow realized God loved him—
Otherwise, he would have dropped dead.
So that was proved.
Crow reclined, marvelling, on his heart-beat.

And he realized that God spoke Crow—   5
Just existing was His revelation.

But what
Loved the stones and spoke stone?
They seemed to exist too.
And what spoke that strange silence   10
After his clamour of caws faded?

And what loved the shot-pellets
That dribbled from those strung-up mummifying crows?
What spoke the silence of lead?

Crow realized there were two Gods—   15

One of them much bigger than the other
Loving his enemies
And having all the weapons.

Barry Spacks (1931–   )
FRESHMEN

My freshmen
settle in. Achilles
sulks; Pascal consults
his watch; and true
Cordelia—with her just-washed hair,   5
stern-hearted princess, ready to defend
the meticulous garden of truths in her
   high-school notebook—
uncaps her ballpoint pen.
And the corridors drum:
give us a flourish, fluorescence of light,
   for the teachers come,   10

green and seasoned, bearers
of the Word, who differ
like its letters; there are some
so wise their eyes
are birdbites; one   15

a mad, grinning gent with a golden
     tooth, God knows
he might be Pan, or the sub-
custodian; another
is a walking podium, dense
with his mystery—high   20

priests and attachés
of the ministry; kindly
old women, like unfashionable watering
     places;
and the assuming young, rolled tight as
     a City
umbrella;   25

thought-salesmen with samples cases,
and saints upon whom
merely to gaze is like Sunday—
their rapt, bright,
cat-licked faces!   30

And the freshmen wait;
wait bristling, acned, glowing like a
     brand,
or easy, chatting, munching, muscles
     lax,
each in his chosen corner, and in each
a chosen corner.   35

Full of certainties and reasons,
or uncertainties and reasons.
full of reasons as a conch contains the
     sea,

they wait: for the term's first bell;
for another mismatched wrestle through
     the year;   40

for a teacher who's religious in his art,
a wizard of a sort, to call the roll
and from mere names
cause people
to appear.   45

The best look like the swinging door
to the opera just before
the Marx Brothers break through.
The worst—debased,
on the back row,   50

as far as one can go
from speech—
are walls where childish scribbling's
     been erased;
are stones
to teach.   55

And I am paid to ask them questions:
Dare man proceed by need alone?
Did Esau like
his pottage?
Is any heart in order after Belsen?   60

And when one stops to think, I'll catch
     his heel,
put scissors to him, excavate his chest!
Watch, freshmen, for my words about
     the past
can make you turn your back. I wait to
     throw,
most foul, most foul, the future in your
     face.   65

Sylvia Plath (1932–1963)
DADDY

You do not do, you do not do
Any more, black shoe
In which I have lived like a foot
For thirty years, poor and white,
Barely daring to breathe or Achoo.   5

Daddy, I have had to kill you.
You died before I had time—
Marble-heavy, a bag full of God,
Ghastly statue with one grey toe
Big as a Frisco seal   10

And a head in the freakish Atlantic
Where it pours bean green over blue
In the waters off beautiful Nauset.
I used to pray to recover you.
Ach, du.   15

In the German tongue, in the Polish
    town
Scraped flat by the roller
Of wars, wars, wars.
But the name of the town is common.
My Polack friend   20

Says there are a dozen or two
So I never could tell where you
Put your foot, your root,
I never could talk to you.
The tongue stuck in my jaw.   25

It stuck in a barb wire snare.
Ich, ich, ich, ich,
I could hardly speak.
I thought every German was you.
And the language obscene   30

An engine, an engine
Chuffing me off like a Jew.
A Jew to Dachau, Auschwitz, Belsen.
I began to talk like a Jew.
I think I may well be a Jew.   35

The snows of the Tyrol, the clear beer
    of Vienna
Are not very pure or true.
With my gypsy ancestress and my
    weird luck
And my Taroc pack and my Taroc pack
I may be a bit of a Jew.   40

I have always been scared of *you*,
With your Luftwaffe, your
    gobbledygoo.
And your neat moustache
And your Aryan eye, bright blue.
Panzer-man, panzer-man, O You—   45

Not God but a swastika
So black no sky could squeak through.
Every woman adores a Fascist,
The boot in the face, the brute
Brute heart of a brute like you.   50

You stand at the blackboard, daddy,
In the picture I have of you,
A cleft in your chin instead of your foot
But no less a devil for that, no not
Any less the black man who   55

Bit my pretty red heart in two.
I was ten when they buried you.
At twenty I tried to die
And get back, back, back to you.
I thought even the bones would do.   60

But they pulled me out of the sack,
And they stuck me together with glue.
And then I knew what to do.
I made a model of you,
A man in black with a Meinkampf
   look   65

And a love of the race and the screw.
And I said I do, I do.
So daddy, I'm finally through.
The black telephone's off at the root,
The voices just can't worm through.   70

If I've killed one man, I've killed two—
The vampire who said he was you
And drank my blood for a year,
Seven years, if you want to know.
Daddy, you can lie back now.   75

There's a stake in your fat black heart
And the villagers never liked you
They are dancing and stamping on you.
They always *knew* it was you.
Daddy, daddy, you bastard, I'm
   through.   80

THE APPLICANT

First, are you our sort of a person?
Do you wear
A glass eye, false teeth or a crutch,
A brace or a hook,
Rubber breasts or a rubber crotch,   5

Stitches to show something missing?
   No, no? Then
How can we give you a thing?
Stop crying.
Open your hand.
Empty? Empty. Here is a hand   10

To fill it and willing
To bring teacups and roll away
   headaches
And do whatever you tell it.
Will you marry it?
It is guaranteed   15

To thumb shut your eyes at the end
And dissolve of sorrow.
We make new stock from the salt.
I notice you are stark naked.
How about this suit—   20

Black and stiff, but not a bad fit.
Will you marry it?
It is waterproof, shatterproof, proof
Against fire and bombs through the roof.
Believe me, they'll bury you in it.   25

Now your head, excuse me, is empty.
I have the ticket for that.
Come here, sweetie, out of the closet.
Well, what do you think of *that*?
Naked as paper to start   30

But in twenty-five years she'll be silver,
In fifty, gold
A living doll, everywhere you look.
It can sew, it can cook,
It can talk, talk, talk.   35

It works, there is nothing wrong with it.
You have a hole, it's a poultice.
You have an eye, it's an image.
My boy, it's your last resort.
Will you marry it, marry it, marry it.   40

JULES FEIFFER

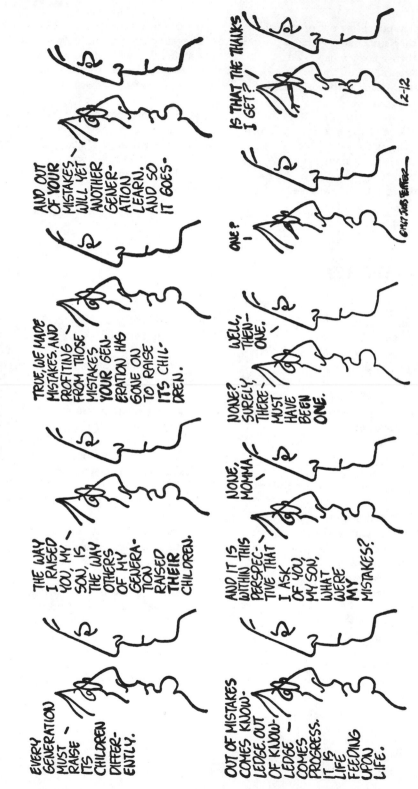

A LIFE

Touch it: it won't shrink like an eyeball,
This egg-shaped bailiwick, clear as a tear.
Here's yesterday, last year—
Palm-spear and lily distinct as flora in the vast
Windless threadwork of a tapestry.   5

Flick the glass with your fingernail:
It will ping like a Chinese chime in the slightest air stir
Though nobody in there looks up or bothers to answer.
The inhabitants are light as cork,
Every one of them permanently busy.   10

At their feet, the sea waves bow in single file.
Never trespassing in bad temper:
Stalling in midair,
Short-reined, pawing like paradeground horses.
Overhead, the clouds sit tasseled and fancy   15

As Victorian cushions. This family
Of valentine faces might please a collector:
They ring true, like good china.
Elsewhere the landscape is more frank.
The light falls without letup, blindingly.   20

A woman is dragging her shadow in a circle
About a bald hospital saucer
It resembles the moon, or a sheet of blank paper
And appears to have suffered a sort of private blitzkrieg.
She lives quietly   25

With no attachments, like a foetus in a bottle,
The obsolete house, the sea, flattened to a picture
She has one too many dimensions to enter.
Grief and anger, exorcised,
Leave her alone now.   30

The future is a grey seagull
Tattling in its cat-voice of departure, departure.
Age and terror, like nurses, attend her,
And a drowned man, complaining of the great cold,
Crawls up out of the sea.   35

LADY LAZARUS

I have done it again.
One year in every ten
I manage it——

A sort of walking miracle, my skin
Bright as a Nazi lampshade,   5
My right foot

A paperweight,
My face a featureless, fine
Jew linen.

Peel off the napkin   10
O my enemy.
Do I terrify?——

The nose, the eye pits, the full set
   of teeth?
The sour breath
Will vanish in a day.   15

Soon, soon the flesh
The grave cave ate will be
At home on me

And I a smiling woman.
I am only thirty.   20
And like the cat I have nine times
   to die.

This is Number Three.
What a trash
To annihilate each decade.

What a million filaments.   25
The peanut-crunching crowd
Shoves in to see

Them unwrap me hand and foot——
The big strip tease.
Gentlemen, ladies   30

These are my hands
My knees.
I may be skin and bone,

Nevertheless, I am the same, identical
   woman.
The first time it happened I was ten.   35
It was an accident.

The second time I meant
To last it out and not come back at all.
I rocked shut

As a seashell.   40
They had to call and call
And pick the worms off me like
   sticky pearls.

Dying
Is an art, like everything else.
I do it exceptionally well.   45

I do it so it feels like hell.
I do it so it feels real.
I guess you could say I've a call.

It's easy enough to do it in a cell.
It's easy enough to do it and stay put   50
It's the theatrical

Come back in broad day
To the same place, the same face,
   the same brute
Amused shout:

"A miracle!"   55
That knocks me out.
There is a charge

For the eyeing of my scars, there is a
   charge
For the hearing of my heart——
It really goes.   60

And there is a charge, a very large charge
For a word or a touch
Or a bit of blood

Or a piece of my hair or my clothes.
So, so, Herr Doktor.   65
So, Herr Enemy.

I am your opus,
I am your valuable,
The pure gold baby

That melts to a shriek.   70
I turn and burn.
Do not think I underestimate your
  great concern.

Ash, ash—
You poke and stir.
Flesh, bone, there is nothing
  there——   75

A cake of soap,
A wedding ring,
A gold filling.

Herr God, Herr Lucifer
Beware   80
Beware.

Out of the ash
I rise with my red hair
And I eat men like air.

Imamu Amiri Baraka (LeRoi Jones) (1934–   )
IN MEMORY OF RADIO

Who has ever stopped to think of the divinity of Lamont Cranston?
(Only Jack Kerouac, that I know of: & me.
The rest of you probably had on WCBS and Kate Smith,
Or something equally unattractive.)

What can I say?   5
It is better to have loved and lost
Than to put linoleum in your living rooms?

Am I a sage or something?
Mandrake's hypnotic gesture of the week?
(Remember, I do not have the healing powers of Oral Roberts . . .   10
I cannot, like F. J. Sheen, tell you how to get saved & *rich!*
I cannot even order you to gaschamber satori like Hitler or Goody Knight

& Love is an evil word.
Turn it backwards/see, what I mean?
An evol word. & besides   15
Who understands it?
I certainly wouldn't like to go out on that kind of limb.

Saturday mornings we listened to *Red Lantern* & his undersea folk.
At 11, *Let's Pretend*/& we did/& I, the poet, still do, Thank God!
What was it he used to say (after the transformation, when he was safe   **20**
& invisible & the unbelievers couldn't throw stones?) "Heh, heh, heh,
Who knows what evil lurks in the hearts of men? The Shadow knows."

O, yes he does
O, yes he does.
An evil word it *is*,   **25**
This Love.

POEM FOR HALF WHITE COLLEGE STUDENTS

Who are you, listening to me, who are you
listening to yourself? Are you white or
black, or does that have anything to do
with it? Can you pop your fingers to no
music, except those wild monkies go on   **5**
in your head, can you jerk, to no melody,
except finger poppers get it together
when you turn from starchecking to checking
yourself. How do you sound, your words, are they
yours? The ghost you see in the mirror, is it really   **10**
you, can you swear you are not an imitation greyboy,
can you look right next to you in that chair, and swear,
that the sister you have your hand on is not really
so full of Elizabeth Taylor, Richard Burton is
coming out of her ears. You may even have to be Richard   **15**
with a white shirt and face, and four million negroes
think you cute, you may have to be Elizabeth Taylor, old lady,
if you want to sit up in your crazy spot dreaming about dresses,
and the sway of certain porters' hips. Check yourself, learn who it is
speaking, when you make some ultrasophisticated point, check yourself,   **20**
when you find yourself gesturing like Steve McQueen, check it out, ask
in your black heart who it is you are, and is that image black or white,
you might be surprised right out the window, whistling dixie on the way in

Clarence Major (1936–   )
SOMETHING IS EATING ME UP INSIDE

I go in & out a thousand times a day
& the round fat women with black velvet skin
expressions sit out on the
front steps, watching—"where does he go
so much" as if the knowledge could give meaning to   5
a hood from the 20s I look like in
my pocket black shirt button-down collar & black ivy
league. In & out to break the
agony in the pit of skull of fire for a drink a
cigarette bumming it anything the floor is   10
too depressing. I turn around inside the closet to search
the floor for a dime/ a nickel

this is from time & drunks of time again nights when
the pants pockets turned
inside turned   15
out but seriously something is
eating me up inside I don't
believe in anything anymore, science, magic—
in tape worms inside philosophy inside
I go outside   20

maybe inside you but not anybody else but
in the middle of going like
it's an inscrutable (what

ever
that   25
is)
something getting itself in deeper in. In,
time I mean pushing in against
my ear drums my time

—this is what I move full of.   30
slow young strong & sure of nothing myself a gangster
of the sunshine the sun is blood in my guts:
moving me from gin highs to lakesides to sit down
beside reasons for being in
the first place   35
in the second place looking
outward to definitions for definitions like

a formal ending would be unlawful unfair

Dick Allen (1939–   )

OH, ROUSSEAU, ROUSSEAU

—for David and Susan

Our friends are moving back
  to small lonesome towns,
are building porches back
  on half-ruined dwellings.

Evenings, they watch   5
  cities through their television sets,
grow marijuana in
  their outlandish backyards,

or slowly carpenter
  grandfather clocks—   10
like ancestors turning
  their lives into fixtures.

And I had thought
  the future was space
travel and tubes,   15
  and aphrodisiac culture.

Who could predict
  their faces grown stern,
this strict new religion
  of seasons and walls?   20

As we drive upstate
  into the valleys,
we pass the statues of
  colonial soldiers

whose economic war   25
  seems sensible again.
We stop at a cluttered
ramshackle store

and spend too much
  for a lovely glass deer,   30
a pink and blue vase,
  uncertainly china.

Lately, I've noticed,
  we are choosing gifts
smaller and smaller   35
  as if we have sensed

or accepted, perhaps,
  a world of miniatures,
each of us one
  microscopic circuit   40

through which the energy
  of life must be routed
if anything is to work,
  find salvation, or fail.

But for reasons beyond us   45
  our friends are scattering
and it may mean, at last,
  our civilization machine—

its unknown job being done—
  may now be deserted   50
and we are finally free
  to begin to go home,

collect green bottles, shop
  at the General Store;
think no more   55
  of strange lives stranger than ours.

THEORY OF THE ALTERNATE UNIVERSE

Another world lies tangent to our
   own—
where everything is whackeyed. You
wear purple skirts; you leave
the dustcloth on translucent shelves;
the sun   5
is slightly green.
I sculpture wood and plastic, talk
about the rain.
          You take
swigs from bottles of intense
   champagne.   10
To everything there is
"a touch of strange."
When you go out of sight
you're walking down a lamplit street
and in your place   15
the woman I embrace
writes strange lovephrases on my
   cellophane
skin.

   The worlds
slide in and out. They look   20
like time-exposure pictures of the moon
passed through eclipse
or our child's bronze
toy of spiral rings
resting at the bottom of the stairs.   25
And there's no stopping this
constant alternation of ourselves—
no steady state
         One moment you
are X, the other you're X-1.   30
Only in your death
when both your bodies lie
stupid and nonplused as iron machines
will you be
         like those   35
who live in one world, spend
their lives explaining why they cannot
   change,
hanging portraits in their oval frames.

Nikki Giovanni (1943–)

FOR SAUNDRA

i wanted to write
a poem
that rhymes
but revolution doesn't lend
itself to be-bopping

then my neighbor
who thinks i hate
asked—do you ever write
tree poems—i like trees

so i thought
i'll write a beautiful green tree poem
peeked from my window
to check the image

noticed the school yard was covered
with asphalt
no green—no trees grow
in manhattan

then, well, i thought the sky
i'll do a big blue sky poem
but all the clouds have winged
low since no-Dick was elected

so i thought again
and it occurred to me

maybe i shouldn't write
at all
but clean my gun
and check my kerosene supply

perhaps these are not poetic
times
at all

EGO TRIPPING
(there may be a reason why)

I was born in the congo
I walked to the fertile crescent and built
   the sphinx
I designed a pyramid so tough that a star
   that only glows every one hundred years falls   5
   into the center giving divine perfect light
I am bad

I sat on the throne
   drinking nectar with allah
I got hot and sent an ice age to europe   10
   to cool my thirst
My oldest daughter is nefertiti
   the tears from my birth pains
   created the nile
I am a beautiful woman   15

I gazed on the forest and burned
   out the sahara desert
   with a packet of goat's meat
   and a change of clothes
I crossed it in two hours   20
I am a gazelle so swift
   so swift you can't catch me

For a birthday present when he was three
I gave my son hannibal an elephant
   He gave me rome for mother's day   25
My strength flows ever on

My son noah built new/ark and
I stood proudly at the helm
   as we sailed on a soft summer day
I turned myself into myself and was
   jesus
   men intone my loving name
   All praises All praises
I am the one who would save

I sowed diamonds in my back yard
My bowels deliver uranium
   the filings from my fingernails are
   semi-precious jewels
   On a trip north
I caught a cold and blew
My nose giving oil to the arab world
I am so hip even my errors are correct
I sailed west to reach east and had to round off
   the earth as I went
   The hair from my head thinned and gold was laid
across three continents

I am so perfect so divine so ethereal so surreal
I cannot be comprehended
   except by my permission

I mean . . . I . . . can fly
   like a bird in the sky . . .

APPENDIX

INTRODUCTION TO THE FORMS OF DISCOURSE

Some men read a great deal, others read a moderate amount, and still others read hardly at all. Those who do read—and they number most of the influential men of any society—do so to be entertained or informed, and occasionally they may be emotionally moved or mentally persuaded as well. In their quest for the enriched life that literature can bring, men read both creative and discursive writing, and what they read has traditionally been classified into four categories. These rhetorical divisions, usually called the forms of discourse, are description, narration, exposition, and argumentation. It is useful for anyone who wishes to read or to write well to be familiar with these categories; for by seeing the distinctiveness of each form, as well as the ways in which all the forms work cooperatively with each other to achieve intellectual and emotional communication, the good student can see the methods by which writers achieve their purposes. From such perception, intelligent readers and effective writers are made.

Imaginative description is seldom written for its own sake alone (save, possibly, in such freshman writing assignments as "My Room" or "The Beach at Night"), but, instead, enriches the other forms of discourse. Unlike scientific description (which is a form of exposition), imaginative description is less concerned with the precision and the colorlessness of denotative words and objective truths than with creating a vivid impression of a person, place, or object by a careful selection and orderly presentation of a number of visual and other sensual details. To capture with words the full picture of some subject, the writer draws upon the suggestiveness of connotative language; the vividness of the senses of sight, taste, touch, smell, and hearing; and the truthfulness of memorable comparisons. To organize his picture, the writer often presents his material in some logical spatial arrangement, as from left to right, from top to bottom, or from near to far. Usually in such an organization, the writer establishes a point of view—that is, an angle of vision from which the picture is being viewed—and the logic of that point of view dictates the order in which the parts of the picture come into view. At times, too, the writer may wish to communicate a dominant emotional impression—that is, to emphasize one basic truth about a person or a place—and to do so selects his details and charges his language to insist upon that psychological reality. In the following passage from Mark Twain's *Life on the Mississippi,* the point of view is that of an unsophisticated, adolescent boy as he at first looks down from the pilot house; then looks around the interior of the pilot house; and finally wanders about a steamboat. The dominant impression upon the mind of the boy (though not necessarily upon the mature Twain) is that of the grandeur of the boat. Note the simplicity of the language, the connotative diction, the word pictures, and the naturalness of the similes (that is, images drawn by the comparison of two dissimilar objects through the use of "like" or "as").

My chief was presently hired to go on a big New Orleans boat, and I packed my satchel and went with him. She was a grand affair. When I stood in the pilot house I was so far above the water that I seemed perched on a mountain; and her decks stretched so far away, fore and aft below me, that I wondered how I could ever have considered the *Paul Jones* a large craft. There were other differences, too. The *Paul Jones's* pilot house was a cheap, dingy, battered rattle trap, cramped for room; but here was a sumptuous glass temple; room enough to have a dance in; showy red and gold window-curtains; an imposing sofa; leather cushions and a back to the high bench where visiting pilots sit, to spin yarns and "look at the river"; bright, fanciful "cuspidores," instead of a broad wooden box filled with sawdust; nice new oilcloth on the floor; a hospitable stove for winter; a wheel as high as my head, costly with inlaid work; a wire tiller-rope; bright brass knobs for the bells; and a tidy, white-aproned, black "texas-tender," to bring up tarts and ices and coffee during mid-watch, day and night. Now this was "something like"; and so I began to take heart once more to believe that piloting was a romantic sort of occupation after all. The moment we were under way I began to prowl about the great steamer and fill myself with joy. She was as clean and as dainty as a drawing room; when I looked down her long, gilded saloon, it was like gazing through a splendid tunnel; she had an oil-picture, by some gifted sign-painter, on every stateroom door; she glittered with no end of prism-fringed chandeliers; the clerk's office was elegant, the bar was marvelous, and the bar-keeper had been barbered and upholstered at incredible cost. The boiler deck (*i.e.,* the second story of the boat, so to speak) was as spacious as a church, it seemed to me; so with the forecastle; and there was no pitiful handful of deck-hands, firemen, and roustabouts down there, but a whole battalion of men. The furnaces were fiercely glaring from a long row of furnaces, and over them were eight huge boilers! This was unutterable pomp.

In the following passage, from Frank Norris' novel *The Octopus,* the point of view is that of a young man named Vanamee, something of a romantic and mystic, who looks, at daybreak, at the land around him after a recent rain. The description captures a dominant impression through an analogy—that is, an extended comparison—of the fruitfulness of the land to the fertility of a woman.

The day was fine. Since the first rain of the season, there had been no other. Now the sky was without a cloud, pale, blue, delicate, luminous, scintillating with morning. The great brown earth turned a huge flank to it, exhaling the moisture of the early dew. The atmosphere, washed clean of dust and mist, was as translucent as crystal . . . . All about between the horizons, the carpet of the land unrolled itself to infinity. But now it was no longer parched with heat, cracked and warped by a merciless sun, powdered with dust. The rain had done its work; not a clod that was not swollen with fertility, not a fissure that did not exhale the sense of fecundity. One could not take a dozen steps upon the ranches without the brusque sensation that underfoot the land was alive, roused at last from its sleep, palpitating with the desire of reproduction. Deep down there in the recesses of the soil the great heart throbbed once more, thrilling with passion, vibrating with desire, offering itself to the caress of the plow, insistent, eager, impervious. Dimly one felt the deep-seated trouble of the earth, the uneasy agitation of its members, the hidden tumult of its womb, demanding to be fruitful, to reproduce, to disengage the eternal renascent germ of life that stirred and struggled in its loins.

Narration, a second form of discourse, ranges from the short anecdote (a simple bit of action told to make a point) to the long novel, but narratives are all organized in a time pattern; they are all interested (unlike most histories and biographies) in action for its own sake rather than as an excuse for analysis and interpretation; and they all gain effectiveness, or lack of it, from the way in which they tease their readers into wanting to answer the question, "What happens next?" Simple narratives tend toward a straightforward sequence of time, while more complex narratives (discussed in detail later in the Appendix) often manipulate their chronology for artistic effectiveness. Where the action of the simple narrative may begin with A, the first event in time, and continue consecutively on to G, the last event in the action, the complex narrative may look more like this: C D E A B F G.

Because narration dramatizes events, depicts the conflicts and motives of people, is easy to follow, and has strong emotional appeal, writers of exposition and argumentation often introduce their ideas and reinforce their points by appropriate bits of narrative. For instance, John Woolman, the American Quaker, in his remarkable *Journal,* remembers a childhood event in order to make a religious point:

> . . . once . . . I saw . . . a robin sitting on her nest; and as I came near she went off, but having young ones flew about, and with many cries expressed her concern for them. I stood and threw stones at her, till one striking her, she fell down dead. At first I was pleased with the exploit; but after a few minutes was seized with horror, having in a sportive way, killed an innocent creature while she was careful for her young. I beheld her lying dead, and thought these young ones, for which she was so careful, must now perish for want of their dam to nourish them; and after some painful considerations on the subject, I climbed up the tree, took all the young birds, and killed them—supposing that better than to leave them to pine away and die miserably; and believed, in this case, that Scripture proverb was fulfilled, "The tender mercies of the wicked are cruel." I then went on my errand, but, for some hours, could think of little else but the cruelties I had committed, and was much troubled.

The eighteenth-century American patriot and propagandist Tom Paine often argued for an immediate declaration of American independence from Great Britain; and in one of his *Crisis* papers he invented an anecdote to refute a common objection to such a declaration.

> I once felt all that kind of anger, which a man ought to feel, against the mean principles that are held by tories: A noted one who kept a tavern at Amboy, was standing at his door, with as pretty a child in his hand, about eight or nine years old, as ever I saw, and after speaking his mind as freely as he thought was prudent, finished with the unfatherly expression, "Well! give me peace in my day." Not a man lives on the continent but fully believes that a separation must some time or other finally take place, and a generous parent should have said, *"If there must be trouble, let it be in my day, that my child may have peace."*

The most common form of discourse— the one by which the practical everyday concerns of life are largely carried on—is exposition. Concerned primarily with ideas rather than with action or sensory impressions, exposition explains the logical relationships of things. When exposition is well written, it reveals the connection of a number of parts to one unified whole. Though exposition may make use of the other forms of discourse, its master is not the clock or the senses but the intellect, and when exposition does employ the devices of narration and description, it does so better to fulfill its primary obligation: to explain, clearly and interestingly, the logical nature of something.

If he is to explain an expository topic well, the writer must think effectively about the logical connections of the parts of his subject before he begins to write, so that he can show with organization and clarity the relationship of each part of his material to the whole subject. In addition he should remember that a good expository paragraph does two further things: it states, or implies, a general concept (often called a topic statement); and it proves, in sufficient detail to make the case, the truth of that topic statement. As in a lawyer's brief, the general statement should be neither too broad to be proved convincingly nor too narrow to lack opportunity for discussion; and the proof itself should be sufficiently detailed to be convincing but not so overly developed as to become repetitious and uninteresting.

Whether he is writing a paragraph, an article, or a book, the writer must never forget the importance of unity, coherence, and emphasis—elements necessary to all good writing but more often lacking in exposition than in description or narration—and if he is writing a work of some length and complexity, he may find it useful to make an outline before he begins. By so doing, he may avoid the temptation to stray from the one subject to which he is committed (a violation of unity); to omit connections between the parts of his subject (a violation of coherence); or to give inadequate space to a major idea or excessive attention to a minor one (a violation of emphasis). Note the way in which the paragraph on page 748 (from Henry David Thoreau's *Civil Disobedience*) clings to one idea (as stated in the topic sentence that opens the passage and that limits the concept to be developed); makes appropriate connections from the paragraph preceding it and between the sentences within the paragraph; and makes emphatic the one idea of the paragraph by adequate development and vivid language. (The editors have underlined the principal connective devices and made, to the sides, editorial comments on these transitions.)

In the paragraph on page 748, Thoreau develops his material by the use of *comparison and contrast,* but this method of development is only one of numerous ways by which topic ideas may be resolved and illuminated. In another paragraph from *Civil Disobedience* Thoreau develops his material by *definition* (technically definition by exclusion) when he tells of all the things that government does not do (and men can do) and thus makes his point that government is merely a recent, useless, and relatively unprincipled tradition:

This American government,—what is it but a tradition, though a recent one, endeavoring to transmit itself unimpaired to posterity, but each instant losing some of its integrity? It has not the vitality and force of a single living man; for a single man can bend it to his will. It is a sort of wooden gun to the people themselves. But it is not the less necessary for this; for the people must have some complicated machinery or other, and hear its din, to satisfy that idea of government which they have. Governments show thus how successfully men can be imposed on, even impose on themselves, for their own advantage. It is excellent, we must all allow. Yet this government never of itself furthered any enterprise, but by the alacrity with which it got out of its way. *It* does not keep the country free. *It* does not settle the West. *It* does not educate. The character inherent in the American people has done all that has been accomplished; and it would have done somewhat more, if the government had not sometimes got in its way. For government is an expedient by which men would fain succeed in letting one another alone; and, as has been said, when it is most expedient, the governed are most let alone by it. Trade and commerce, if they were not made of india-rubber, would never manage to bounce over the obstacles which legislators are continually putting in their way; and, if one were to judge these men wholly by the effects of their actions and not partly by their intentions, they would deserve to be classed and punished with those mis-

chievous persons who put obstructions on the railroads.

Thomas Henry Huxley uses yet another common method of development of expository material when, in "The Method of Scientific Investigation," he uses an *illustration* to aid him in showing the relationship of scientific thought to everyday reasoning:

A very trivial circumstance will serve to exemplify this [the similarity between scientific thought and everyday reasoning]. Suppose you go into a fruiterer's shop, wanting an apple. You take up one, and on biting it you find it is sour; you look at it and see that it is hard and green. You take up another one, and that too is hard, green, and sour. The shopman offers you a third; but before biting it you examine it and find that is is hard and green, and you immediately say that you will not have it, as it must be sour like those that you have already tried.

Nothing can be more simple than that, you think; but if you will take the trouble to analyze and trace out into its logical elements what has been done by the mind, you will be greatly surprised. In the first place you have performed the operation of induction. You found that in two experiences hardness and greenness in apples go together with sourness. It was so in the first case, and it was confirmed by the second. True, it is a very small basis, but still it is enough to make an induction from; you generalize the facts, and you expect to find sourness in apples where you get hardness and greenness. You found upon that a general law that all hard and green apples are sour; and that, so far as it goes, is a perfect induction. Well, having got your natural law in this way, when you are offered another apple which you find is hard and green, you say, "All hard and green apples are sour; this apple is hard and green; therefore this apple is sour." That train of reasoning is what logicians call a syllogism and has all its various parts and terms—its major premise, its minor premise, and its conclusion. And by the help of further reasoning, which if drawn out would have to be exhibited in two or three other syllogisms, you arrive at your final determination, "I will not have that apple."

To these common methods of expository development—by comparison and contrast, by definition, and by illustration—many more could be added, but it is the

The opening sentence or generalization limiting the development of the paragraph contrasts the way men actually serve the state (as mere machines) with the implied way they might serve the state (as more than machines).

The word "they" is, of course, a pronoun, and since pronouns, by definition, refer backward to an antecedent, ideally a single unambiguous one, they are effective transitional devices.

Soon afterward Thoreau repeats his key word "men" and makes the contrast between what "men" often are, wooden creatures with no more humanity than a machine, and what "men" should be, thinking creatures with a moral sense; and Thoreau constantly uses his key word, or synonyms for it, to insist upon this contrast.

"The state" is another key phrase that is repeated constantly, and it is contrasted, as the master of unthinking men, with real thinking men of conscience who should be master of the state.

The mass of men serve the state thus, not as men mainly, but as machines, with their bodies. They are the standing army, and the militia, jailers, constables, *posse comitatus,* etc. In most cases there is no free exercise whatever of the judgment or of the moral sense; but they put themselves on a level with wood and earth and stones; and wooden men can perhaps be manufactured that will serve the purpose as well. Such [men] command no more respect than men of straw or a lump of dirt. They have the same sort of worth only as horses and dogs. Yet such [men] as these even are commonly esteemed good citizens. Others [other men]—as most legislators, politicians, lawyers, ministers, and office-holders—serve the state chiefly with their heads; and, as they rarely make any moral distinctions, they are as likely to serve the Devil without *intending* it, as God. A very few [men],—as heroes, patriots, martyrs; reformers in the great sense, and *men*—serve the state with their consciences also, and so necessarily resist it for the most part; and they are commonly treated as enemies by it. A wise man will only be useful as a man, and will not submit to be "clay," and "stop a hole to keep the wind away," but leave that office to his dust at least:—

"I am too high-born to be propertied,
To be a secondary at control,
Or useful serving-man and
  instrument
To any soverign state throughout
  the world."

The transitional word "thus" (or "it follows therefore") shows the logical connection between this paragraph and the one preceding it.

"In most cases" refers to the key concept of the paragraph (that most men serve the state as mere machines), and that concept is held constantly before the reader.

The word "yet" serves here as a conjunction, in the sense of "nevertheless"; and conjunctions are, of course, joining words whose primary duty is to connect—usually, as with the conjunction "and," in the sense of continuity, but often, as with the conjunction "but," in the sense of contrast, of "on the other hand."

Finally, in his last sentence, Thoreau shifts from his key word, "men" to a logical limitation of that word in defining one basic quality of "a wise man": he will not submit to being dead clay while he is alive, and he will not accept his own murder, for the service of the state, without protest.

material that should determine the method of development. The important thing is that ideas, to be of any significance, must be effectively developed. An idea without development is like a tadpole that never grew to be a frog. To put it another way, the secret of good writing—if there is a single secret—is effective development; and the secret of effective development is not only for the writer to have information about his subject but also to have the wisdom to communicate fully and clearly the knowledge that he has.

The last of the conventional forms of discourse is argumentation. Since an effective argument inevitably demands a considerable amount of explanation, argumentation is similar to exposition; but the ultimate aim of argument is less to analyze and explain than it is to convince and persuade. The contrast between the two is clearly illustrated by the difference between Huxley's "The Method of Scientific Investigation," which aims to define and clarify a mode of human thought, and Thoreau's "Civil Disobedience," which aims to persuade Americans that they must not only cease to support the American government but must actively attempt to prevent its orderly functioning.

In fulfilling his purpose, the writer of an argument may follow some of the more useful conventions of argumentation. He may, for instance, begin his essay by defining and limiting the terms and scope of the argument and by considering the past history and present importance of his subject. Next, he will probably make the best case he can for the side of the question to which he is committed. Then he may recognize the most compelling arguments of the opposition in order to refute them as convincingly as he can. Finally, he may summarize his position, and if the topic is appropriate, request a call for action.

The most important aspect of the argument is, of course, the effectiveness with which the writer persuades his audience to agree with his position. In making his case, the writer may appeal to the emotions or the intellect, or he may, in different degrees, make both kinds of appeals. When he flatters his audience, for instance, by telling each of its members that they are honorable men, all honorable men, he is appealing to emotion, not intellect.

One of the great American writers to use emotional appeals was Tom Paine. In the first paper of the *Crisis,* Paine argued effectively for a continuation of the American Revolution; and perhaps because he had relatively few points that were intellectually convincing, he emphasized such emotional appeals as the concept that God was on the American side; as name calling; as threats of physical violence aimed at those Tories who would not change their ways; and as tearful pictures of helpless little children who depended upon the selflessness of their parents for their future freedom and salvation. At the end of his essay Paine imagines the future if the English were to conquer the American patriots, and the imagery of his vision suggests the extent to which emotional appeals may be carried:

> By perseverance and fortitude we [Americans] have the prospect of a glorious issue; by cowardice and submission, the sad choice of a variety of evils—a ravaged country and depopulated city—habitations without safety, and slavery without hope—our homes turned into barracks and bawdy-houses for Hessians, and a future race to provide for, whose fathers we shall doubt of. Look on this picture and weep over it! and if there yet remains one thoughtless wretch who believes it not, let him suffer it unlamented.

When they have, or think they have, facts and logic on their side, most writers prefer to direct their appeals to the head rather than the heart. Doing so, they tend to argue from one or more particular facts (the evidence) to a general conclusion (argument by induction), or from general premises (major and minor) to a particular conclusion deduced from them (argument by deduction). The first kind of reasoning brings conclusions that are probabilities (the dependableness of the probability varying with the extent of the evidence), while the second kind, when the premises are sound and the reasoning valid, brings logical certainty.

The distinction between these two basic kinds of argument (of which all other types are merly variants) can be seen by comparing Darwin's essay on "Natural Selection" (from his long argument *On*

The Origin of Species) with Thoreau's essay "Civil Disobedience." In the first, a scientist, on the basis of the evidence of accumulated observations, argues that over the centuries, changes in the conditions of life have resulted in changes in organic beings; and since some of these changes, according to the evidence of history, have been retained in various species, while other mutations have been eliminated, Darwin theorizes that those modifications that aid the preservation of a species have been retained, while those modifications that are injurious have been destroyed. Darwin summarizes his argument by stating:

> It may metaphorically be said that natural selection is daily and hourly scrutinizing, throughout the world, the slightest variations; rejecting those that are bad, preserving and adding up all that are good; silently and insensibly working, *whenever and wherever opportunity offers,* at the improvement of each organic being in relation to its organic and inorganic conditions of life. We see nothing of these slow changes in progress, until the hand of time has marked the lapse of ages, and then so imperfect is our view into long-past geological ages, that we see only that the forms of life are now different from what they formerly were. . . .

Thoreau, on the other hand, does not pile up evidence based on observation to bring himself to a conclusion. Instead, he argues from a conviction that the American government of his time is morally evil and, therefore, an honorable man cannot support it. Thoreau's argument is based on deduction, and the steps in his logic can be shown by the syllogistic form especially associated with deductive logic.

Major premise:—A morally evil government can be supported only by immoral men.

Minor premise:—The present American government is morally evil.

Conclusion:—Therefore, the present American government can be supported only by immoral men.

By the same kind of logic, Thoreau later attempts to refute the argument that a man must obey the commands of the govern-

ment if he is to avoid punishment. He does so by claiming that the essential part of a man is not his body but his mind; and the government, in its blindness, imprisons the body (the animal part of man) but leaves the essential quality of a man (his mind) unfettered and unpunished. Syllogistically, Thoreau's argument runs as follows:

> The mind is the essential element in a man.
> Government cannot imprison (and punish) the mind.
> Therefore, government cannot imprison (and punish) the essential part of a man.

Mechanically, the first of Thoreau's arguments is valid (though not necessarily factually accurate), and the second is invalid. The first is valid for the same reason that a marble that is put in a hatbox that is put in a barrel is not only in the hatbox but also in the barrel. Note how Thoreau's argument against support of the American government might be diagramed:

On the other hand, Thoreau's second argument is mechanically invalid (though the conclusion might be truthful), for though there seem three terms in the argument (and there must always be three terms in a valid syllogism), there are actually only two because "the mind" and "the essential element in man" are stated to be the same thing.

The second of Thoreau's arguments could, therefore, be attacked on the basis of the fallibility of its reasoning, but a critic who wished to attack Thoreau's first argument would have to quarrel with his premises, not his reasoning. Thus the minor premise—that "the present American government is morally evil"—might be attacked by defending the morality of both the Mexican War and the institution of slavery. If such an attack on the minor premise seemed weak, the critic might quarrel with the major premise—possibly by claiming, as does the philosopher Thomas Hobbes, that moral men can support immoral governments because even the worst of governments is better than the anarchy unloosed by no government at all.

An argument, of course, is only as effective as the weight of its evidence and the validity of its reasoning, and many arguments are founded on insufficient evidence and invalid reasoning. A few common fallacies in the use of inductive logic are the following:

1. *Hasty generalizations: in which a general conclusion is based on inadequate evidence.*

Example: "Negroes have no respect for law and order." "Why do you say that?" "Look at what they did in Newark and Watts." Or more obviously: "That teacher should be fired." "Why?" "One of his students says he's ignorant and unfair."

2. *Faulty sampling: in which a general conclusion is based on an unrepresentative body of evidence.*

Example: "On the whole, a large majority of Americans approves the idea of a national lottery." "What makes you think so?" "I took a poll of the fellows in the pool hall, and . . ." Or on the other hand: "Most American strongly disapprove of drinking." "You don't say." "Yes, I do. I was talking to the girls in my sewing circle, and . . ."

3. *Faulty analogy: in which vivid comparisons imply that because two things are alike in one way they are necessarily similar in other (possibly quite dissimilar) ways.*

Example: "I'm going to vote for the president." "Why?" "Because I think it's just too dangerous right now to change horses in the middle of a stream." (There is a great deal more difference than similarity between the need for a wise president in a period of peril and the need for caution in a time of physical

danger. And, of course, it is possible that it is more dangerous to stay on a dying horse than to change to a healthy one.) More obvious example: "So what if Jones's political opponent called him a liar and a Communist. If Jones didn't like the heat, he shouldn't have come into the kitchen." (The similarity between the concepts is forced, for certainly there is more difference than similarity between political morality and physical comfort.)

4. Post hoc, ergo propter hoc: *in which a time sequence (after this; therefore because of this) is taken to prove a cause-effect relationship.*

Example: "That men's hair tonic sure does work." "What makes you think so?" "Well, I started using it last month, and already I've gotten a dozen new hairs." (Maybe there is a causal connection, but more evidence is needed under scientifically controlled conditions. How can we be sure that it was the hair tonic, and not some other circumstances, that caused the hair to grow?) More obvious example: "Boy, I'll never walk under another ladder." "Why not?" "Well, I did this morning, and I think I've lost a dollar somewhere."

In addition to these fallacies in the use of inductive logic, there are two fallacies, each with innumerable variations, of deductive logic. These flaws in logic are called material fallacies (or flaws in the premises on which an argument is based) and formal fallacies (or flaws in the validity of the reasoning from the premises). The following *enthymeme* (or syllogism in which one or two of the parts is implied) illustrates one kind of material fallacy: "I know he murdered his wife." "What makes you so sure?" "Well, I heard them quarreling constantly, and so did everybody else that was friendly with them." When the three parts of this implied syllogism are stated, the absurdity of the major premise (unstated in the *enthymeme*) becomes clear:

All men who quarrel with their wives murder them.

John quarreled with his wife before she was murdered.

Therefore, John murdered his wife.

Another kind of material fallacy is "begging the question," in which one assumes in the premises what is supposed to be proved in the conclusion—as, for instance, in the following statement: "Books like *Lady Chatterley's Lover* and *The Catcher in the Rye*—obscene, immoral books—should be banned from the library, and that's what I'm proposing right now." The flaw, of course (if we grant that immoral books should be banned from the library), is that two "immoral" books have been named; and they deserve to be convicted by proof, not assumption, of immorality before being banned. In syllogistic form, the argument, with the debatable minor premise, would obviously run:

All immoral books should be banned.

Lady Chatterley *and* The Catcher *are immoral books.*

Therefore, Lady Chatterley *and* The Catcher *should be banned.*

The second type of deductive error is the formal fallacy that leads to *non sequiturs* (or conclusions that do not follow from the premises). The most common of the formal fallacies is that in which the middle term (or term that appears in both the major and minor premise but not in the conclusion) is left "undistributed" (so that the middle term does not truly mediate between the other two terms). An obvious example of the undistributed middle can be seen in this formal fallacy.

$$A = B$$
All men are mammals.

$$C = B$$
All women are mammals.

$$A = C$$
Therefore, all men are women.

The flaw, of course, is in the fact that "men" should be the middle term, not "mammals." The error can be shown by diagram:

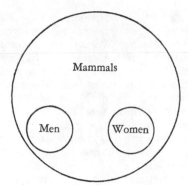

The correct form might read:

$$A = B$$
All men are mammals.

$$C = A$$
John is a man.

$$C = B$$
Therefore, John is a mammal.

A less obvious example of the undistributed middle might be the following—fairly common—fallacious argument:

$$A = B$$
All Communists advocate radical changes in American government.

$$C = B$$
John advocates radical changes in American government.

$$C = A$$
Therefore, John is a Communist.

A second formal fallacy is that of the ambiguous middle term, in which the meaning of the middle term shifts from the major premise to the minor premise. The following syllogism illustrates an ambiguous middle term (in the vagueness of the clause "acts that help a democratic society to function smoothly"):

All acts that help a democratic society to function smoothly are the acts of a good citizen.

Betting on the races brings in taxes that help the smooth functioning of government.

Therefore, betting on the races is the act of a good citizen.

The logical fallacy is obvious here, as is usually true when a writer or speaker abruptly changes the meaning of a word or phrase. When an argument, however, becomes complex, it is relatively easy, after a few pages of argumentation, to shift the meanings of abstract terms, so that the word "socialist," for instance, changes its definition from "one who believes in a social system in which society owns the means of production," to "one who advocates planned economy," to "one who believes in socialized medicine," to "one who believes in government dictatorship," to "anyone who disagrees with me."

Beyond these errors in the use of inductive and deductive logic there are a few common fallacies that have little to do with formal logic but do often occur in argument. These may be briefly noted:

1. Argument from degree: in which it is argued that there is no essential difference between two things because they do not differ in kind. Thus, it might be argued, robbery is a crime and murder is also a crime; and since murderers and robbers are both criminals, they deserve similar punishment. Less obviously fallacious might be the argument that the treatment of Negroes in South Africa is no more immoral than the treatment of Negroes in America, for in both places there is considerable violation of the civil rights of Negroes.
2. Argument from authority: in which the influence of an expert in one field is illegitimately brought into another area. Thus a medical doctor has no more right to testify on military tactics than an army general has to give advice upon how best to treat childhood diseases.
3. Argument *ad hominem* and *ad populum:* in which the self-interest of a particular individual *(ad hominem)* or a particular group *(ad populum)* becomes the origin of the point to be made. Thus a group of American millionaires would probably have no great objection to an appeal for lower income taxes, while they might be considerably more skeptical about the need for all adult American citizens to have a guaranteed income.
4. Argument off the question: in which the topic of controversy is gradually shifted in order to evade or obscure the problem. Thus a lawyer who is defending his client upon a charge of murder may, especially if he feels his defense is weak, insist on noting that his client is married, has three beautiful children, and has always been an excellent father and husband.

With all this said, the most important thing yet remains to be noted. That is, that an effective argument is only effective if it persuades as well as convinces its audience. And persuasion, like love, arises from a host of intangibles that go beyond logic. Perhaps most of all, an audience is persuaded by a well-chosen tone—one that is appropriate for that particular audience at that particular time. Thus a modest tone may be effective on most occasions, but it is possible that on other occasions a tone of boldness and certitude may be even more appropriate. At times it may be wise to seem a seeker of truth, and at other times it may be even wiser to assume the posture of one who knows the truth. The mark of the mature writer of argument is the fact that he has the intelligence to recognize the slightest differentiation in tones and the wisdom to use the right one at the right time.

INTRODUCTION TO THE SHORT STORY

The short story may be identified simply as a brief narrative—but not so lacking in development as to be merely an anecdote—that aims at unity of impression.

Early, though relatively crude, examples may be found in episodes from the Bible (such as the New Testament parable of The Prodigal Son), *The Arabian Nights* (the tale of Ali Baba), and *The Canterbury Tales* (The Nun's Priest's Tale). Not until the nineteenth century, however, did writers begin to reflect upon the form, and it did not really come of age until Edgar Allan Poe rationalized his own artistic practices into a theory of the short story. For Poe, the short story, in its ideal form, could be read at a single sitting of an hour or so. In that time the author had the opportunity to make one vivid, uninterrupted impression upon the reader. Reviewing Nathaniel Hawthorne's tales, Poe generalized:

> A skillful literary artist has contructed a tale. If wise, he has not fashioned his thoughts to accommodate his incidents; but having conceived, with deliberate care, a certain unique or single *effect* to be wrought out, he then invents such incidents—he then combines such events as may best aid him in establishing this preconceived effect. If his very initial sentence tend not to the outbringing of this effect then he has failed in his first step. In the whole composition there should be no word written, of which the tendency, direct or indirect, is not to the one pre-established design. . . . The idea of the tale has been presented unblemished, because undisturbed, and this is an end unattainable by the novel. Undue brevity is just as exceptionable here as in the poem; but undue length is yet more to be avoided.

Though the short story differs, most obviously so in length, from such longer narrative forms as the novel and the *nouvelle,* the short story also has much in common with them. To discuss any form of fiction effectively, one must understand some of the rudiments of setting, plot, character, and theme. At times, setting is relatively unimportant, most especially so when an implied point in the tale is in its universality, in the fact that the action could occur anywhere and the characters live in any epoch. At other times, setting may be extremely important—as, for instance, when the author of a tale of local color wants to capture the language, appearance, and mentality of people who live in a particular place at a specific moment in history; or when the author wishes to capture a mood, as Poe often does in his tales of the supernatural and irrational; or when the writer desires to filter setting through a character's mind so that the time and place reflect the mood of the character as much as actual physical reality; or, finally, when the author conceives of nature as hostile, indifferent, or benign and reflects his philosophical conviction in one dominating impression. In the first group of short stories in *The Modern Age,* an understanding of the significance of the setting will illuminate much of the meaning of the story. What does Stephen Crane gain thematically by setting "The Bride Comes to Yellow Sky" in the American West? Why does Joyce contrast Dublin with London in "A Little Cloud," and why is the appearance of "grimy children" important?

Plot, a second basic element of narrative fiction, may be defined as the writer's dramatic manipulation of the events of his tale for the maximum artistic effect. Usually the writer of a modern short story (or play) will observe the unities of time, place, and action—the narrative will cover a short period of time, will occur in a limited area of space, and will be limited to a single dramatic event—and will tell his story in a straightforward chronological manner. Sometimes, however, the writer may violate the unities of time and place (though seldom, in short fiction, of action) and may choose to violate conventional chronology. Occasionally, especially if the story covers a lengthy period of time, the writer may begin his tale in the middle of the action (*in medias res*) and later on convey the necessary information preceding the initial action by summary exposition or by dramatic flashbacks. Whichever way he chooses to tell his story, the action (as distinct from the plot) covers the chronological sequence of events, from the first event in time until the last; and the reader should see the action clearly before he begins to ponder the significance of any of the author's variations from straightforward chronological narration.

In an effective plot there is a conflict that arouses suspense concerning the victor by pitting two relatively equal powers (an irrestible force meeting an immovable object) in a meaningful struggle. Four major kinds of conflict deserve to be noted. The most obvious is the struggle of man against man, as in Stephen Crane's "The Bride Comes to Yellow Sky" when the old gun-slinger, Scratchy Wilson, confronts the town marshal with drawn gun and the marshal attempts to persuade his old antagonist that the ritual gun duel must be foregone. A second conflict is man against nature. In Lawrence's "The Horse Dealer's Daughter," Dr. Fergusson rescues Mabel from the pond in which she has attempted suicide, but in doing so (since he cannot swim), he struggles fearfully against the "deep, soft clay" which seems to pull him down, and the "foul earthy water" which he feels is "hideous" and "cold." Still another is the conflict of the individual against society, as in E. M. Forster's "The Machine Stops," in which the youth Kuno violates the laws of his state in order to escape his warm, secure home (or womb) and see and explore the dangerous outer world of nature. Finally, the most common of conflicts is that of man against himself, as revealed in "The Horse Dealer's Daughter" when Doctor Fergusson, at the insistence of the girl whom he has rescued from suicide, must decide between life (and the pains of love) and death (and its chill "freedom") for Mabel (literally) and for himself (symbolically). The latter kind of conflict can be extremely subtle, as well as psychologically illuminating, but some critics have objected to what they consider excesses of this kind of drama (or lack of drama). To one such critic, Henry James responded, in "The Art of Fiction," by proclaiming:

> Mr. Henry Besant does not, to my sense, light up the subject by intimating that a story must, under penalty of not being a story, consist of "adventures." Why of adventures more than of green spectacles? He mentions a category of impossible things, and among them he places "fiction without adventure." . . . And what *is* adventure, when it comes to that, and by what sign is the listening pupil to recognize it? . . . A psychological reason [or conflict] is, to my imagination, an object adorably pictorial; to catch the tint of its complexion—I feel as if that idea might inspire me to Titianesque efforts.

The intelligent student of fiction, of course, recognizes that it is less important to perceive a general area of conflict than it is to see how any conflict manifests itself in a particular situation (one individual with a unique problem that he must attempt to solve). What is more, a single work of fiction may embody a variety of conflicts. "The Machine Stops," for instance, dramatizes the conflict of man against himself (in Kuno's efforts to train his body and his mind to survive without the machine); of man against man (in Kuno's attempt to persuade his mother to approve his rebellion); of man against his society (in Kuno's determination to escape the machine and the people it enslaves and the machine's opposition to anything save conformity and submission); and of man against nature (in Kuno's efforts to breathe without mechanical assistance when he briefly escapes the machine). Finally, it is wise to remember that conflict, especially the climax, or highest intensity of conflict, is usually, in artistically serious stories, more important in illuminating the meaning of the story than in merely satisfying the curiosity of the reader as to the victor in the struggle.

A third fundamental aspect of fiction is character. Though it is critically useful to discuss action and character separately, it is also wise to remember that the two are really merely different sides of the same coin. In "The Art of Fiction," Henry James made this point when he noted:

> What is character but the determination of incident? What is incident but the illustration of character? . . . It is an incident for a women to stand with her hand resting on a table and look out at you in a certain way. . . . At the same time it is an expression of character.

In depicting their characters, authors use various techniques. At times an author may speak directly in his own voice to tell how a character is to be seen—as miserly, generous, or sadistic. Occasionally the author may describe his characters physically and imply a connection between the physical appearance and the internal reality. (In nineteenth-century melodramas it was an easy task to discover the villain because he always wore a mustache.) At other times, the author may illuminate his characters by things they say about themselves or things others say about them. (Of course the reader should be wary about accepting such evidence at face value.) Most often, however, the modern author will illuminate his characters through what they do—for it is action that makes for drama—so that a character who speaks benevolently and acts tyranically may be correctly adjudged to be not only a tyrant but a hypocrite.

Since verisimilitude (or the feeling of believableness) is important to any piece of fiction, characters should be consistent (or consistently inconsistent) in their behavior, and they should act with sufficient motivation. The more complicated the character, the more complex his motivations may be; but the reader should probe what a character thinks and does in order to find the answer to what he ultimately *is*. By continual questioning, the reader can often find in serious fiction, where there is usually more order and reason than in life itself, an illumination not only of the superficial causes, but even of the deepest roots of human action. In such a story as Graham Greene's "The Basement Room," the author suggests, by dramatizing an event of a child's life, a reason for a man's total withdrawal from the realities of existence; and though Greene's explanation may be something of a Freudian oversimplification, he does give a plausible explanation for a profound mystery of human behavior. A psychologist might even be able to suggest an explanation for The Misfit's action in "A Good Man Is Hard to Find," but perhaps Flannery O'Connor's decision to minimize psychological explanations and to emphasize religious choices ultimately makes for a more disturbing story about the inexplicableness of evil than might otherwise have been true.

The perceptive reader not only searches for the reasons characters act as they do, but is also aware that characters may change, at least in small ways, in the course of a short story. A character that develops in the course of the narrative may be called dynamic, while a character that stays the same may be termed static. Sometimes characters develop through changes in, or modifications of, personality traits. More often in modern stories, characters develop through gaining, for a moment at least, greater awareness of the truth about life and about themselves. These delicate, evanescent moments, these "showings forth" of the nature of reality, occur often in the stories of Katherine Mansfield and James Joyce. One of these "epiphanies," as Joyce called these radiant illuminations, occurs in Joyce's story "A Little Cloud" when the major character sees the truth of the dull reality of his life, as apart from the romantic dreams in which he indulges, and feels "He couldn't do anything. . . . He was a prisoner for life."

In developing his characters, an author may, especially in longer fiction, attempt to capture a rounded personality, full of the complexities of a real human being. Such a person is unique, an individual character. If, however, the author desires to satirize a particular category of people —say the conventional businessman or the female flirt—he may draw a flat, uncomplicated, universal type. One of the limitations of short fiction is that it is impossible, because of the brevity of the story, to delineate a fully rounded being. This does not, however, mean that the short-story writer is doomed to depicting only familiar types. What he is confined to is selectivity, the depiction of limited aspects (and possibly only one aspect) of his major characters (one of whom usually dominates the story). Thus, James Joyce, in "A Little Cloud," leads toward his epiphany by confining his story to events that arouse his protagonist's daydreams, discontent, and eventual frustrated outbreak. By limiting his events and characters, Joyce focuses sharply; and though he does not capture the wholeness of his protagonist, he depicts one essential part so well that he implies much of the whole. That kind of suggestivity is a major aspect of an effective modern short story.

The last of the fundamental elements of the short story is theme or meaning. Though some escapist works have little or no meaning (horror stories, for instance, may have the sole purpose of arousing a shudder), the theme is, perhaps, the most important aspect of a serious work of art. The reason for this is simply that serious writers want to say something about the nature of man and the purpose (or lack of it) of life itself. To do so, they have chosen a more indirect method of statement than that of the formal essay; but they, like poets, are as concerned as philosophers and scientists with presenting a truth (which is not to be confused with the kind of factual truth that scientists seek) that is important to them. In dramatizing his ideas, the writer may draw upon sociology or history or psychology, and in attempting to persuade his readers toward has own convictions, he may become propagandistic; but the reality of his "truth" is dependent only upon the power with which he creates and populates his world.

Whether the theme of a piece of fiction is extremely simple or exceedingly complex, one of the first duties of the intelligent reader on completing the story is to formulate a hypothesis about the dominant idea (as distinct from subordinate themes) of the work. In doing so, he should remember Poe's injunction that "there should be no word written, of which the tendency, direct or indirect, is not to the one pre-established design." With that advice in mind, he should test the validity of his attempt to state the story's central idea, and if he finds his tentative theme unable to withstand analysis, he should modify or alter his concept. Doing so, he will continually attempt to sharpen his statement, so that it is not so broad as to be meaningless (" 'The Magic Barrel' is about love."); so partial or so obsessed by the attempt to find a "moral" moral as to distort the uniqueness of the work (" 'Good Country People' proves that highly educated people who have lost their Christian faith may not be so smart as they think they are."); or so much a meaningless cliché as to offend intelligence (" 'Thus I Refute Beelzy' demonstrates that there is more on heaven and earth than many people dream of.").

In justifying the theme of a story, the scholar may find it wise to go beyond the four fundamental elements of fiction. Point of view, or the angle of vision from which a story is told, may well illuminate meaning. (The fact that "The Open Boat" varies the point of view from the limited perceptions of the people in the boat ["None of them knew the color of the sky."] to the broader perception of an objective onlooker of the scene ultimately has thematic implications.)

There are numerous variations in point of view (and one should not confuse this technical element of fiction with the author's attitudes, or "point of view"),

but the most important categories are first person, third person, omniscient, and dramatic. In the first-person point of view, the "I" who tells the story may be the major character or an interested observer who may or may not participate in a subordinate way in the action. The writer who uses the first person tends for the most part to limit himself to what his narrator sees and knows about the actions and characters of whom he writes, but since this can often be confining, the author may occasionally go beyond his narrator's first-hand knowledge—as, for instance, when Nick Carraway, the narrator of Fitzgerald's novel *The Great Gatsby,* imagines what might have occurred at certain times. The third-person point of view may be quite limited (as when the author confines himself to the thoughts and perceptions of one character), or it may be extremely broad (as when the author decides to reveal the inward world of all his major characters). The author who writes from the omniscient point of view (which is seldom used in contemporary short fiction) takes a god-like stance, in which he knows all and reveals what he wishes, and at times the omniscient narrator may go beyond revealing the inward worlds of his characters and enter the narrative himself by commenting upon the action and its actors. Directly opposed to the omniscient viewpoint is the dramatic angle of vision, in which the author deliberately refrains from entering the minds of any of his characters and tells his tale as though it were a play taking place before his eyes. Each of these viewpoints, and their variations, has narrative strengths and weaknesses, and often a reader may find his analysis of a story deepened by pondering such problems as what Barthelme may have gained by the particular variation of the first-person viewpoint that he uses in his story "Me and Miss Mandible."

The reader of serious prose fiction, most especially of that of the twentieth century, should also be aware of, though not obsessed by, the significance of symbols in literature. A symbol is something that casts meanings beyond its factual reality—as, for instance, the color white may symbolize purity in one story and sterility in another; or it may, as it does in the whiteness of the whale in *Moby Dick*, suggest a complex range of concepts from the beauty to the horror to the blankness of the whale and nature and divinity. Through the use of symbols the author can achieve indirection (and most modern writers dislike bluntness of any kind); compression (for the symbol implies but does not develop meanings); and genuine emotion (if the artist is very good or very lucky). Almost anything in the story—action, setting, particular objects—may become symbolic if the author wishes to make it so by either hinting or insisting (through imagery, repetition, connotative language, or other artistic devices) that the material means more than it literally does; but it is wise to remember that excessive symbol hunting can be both juvenile and misleading, and that symbolic interpretations of a whole story, or any of its parts, must be defended through evidence of symbolic intentions within the story itself. When a literary symbol, however, does exist and does reinforce the meaning and deepen the emotions inherent in a story, it is myopic to overlook it and folly to insist that those who have better eyesight are imagining the things they see. In "The Basement Room," for instance, Graham Greene makes it clear that the Meccano set that the young boy never uses after his traumatic childhood experience is symbolic of the lack of creativity, the wasted life, that results from the boy's mental wound suffered in childhood; and probing deeper, a good reader should see that the basement room where much of the action takes place is filled with Freudian overtones that indicate that this setting implies more than a mere physical locale. Similarly, some stories are so charged with suggestive meanings that any attempt to understand them without probing the symbolic overtones is doomed. Such a story is D. H. Lawrence's "The Horse Dealer's Daughter," where the atmosphere of heightened meanings pervades all things, from the tone set by the heavy dullness of the beginning, to the imagery surrounding the brackish pond, to the movement from death toward life in the acceptance (reluctant as it may be on the man's part) of the delights, torments, and obligations of love.

The style and tone of any literary work

also merit analysis. Though the discussion of the style of a work or of a writer may become almost as complicated as the psychological analysis of a human personality, the most important thing to remember about style is that it is the revelation of individuality, whether of an artist (the Hemingway style), a period (literary style in the fifteenth century), a place (American literary style), or a genre (the style of naturalism). A writer reveals his uniqueness through the peculiar manner of his expression (as opposed to the variety of his thoughts), and though it is as easy to feel the stylistic differences between writers as to sense the differences in the personalities of Arthur Miller and Allen Ginsberg, it is necessary in analyzing literary style to consider such things as the writer's preferences in diction, in figures of speech (such as simile, metaphor, irony, and allusion), in sentence variety and rhythms, and in rhetorical devices for gaining emphasis.

The tone of a particular work is one aspect of the artist's style, and like a man's tone of voice, it suggests the writer's attitude—angry, ironic, humorous, whatever—toward his material. Through the use of connotative words, for instance, the writer may slant his presentation of an action or a character so that his readers are persuaded toward an emotion (possibly of admiration or contempt); and by the manipulation of his audience's feelings the writer implies not only his judgment of his own world and its inhabitants but also his evaluation of the larger universe that his art reflects.

In his fantasy "The Machine Stops," E. M. Forster uses a narrator who seems identical with the author, and the narrator makes Forster's tone clear from the very beginning. In the narrator's "meditation" (to use his word for his apocalyptic vision), each person in the future will live in "a small room . . . like the cell of a bee," and this charged image dramatizes the narrator's attitude, or tone, which implies that the quality of life in the new civilization will be restricted, cramped, and dehumanized. In the room, the "soft radiance" of the light (which owes nothing to natural sunlight), the freshness of the air (which comes elsewhere than from natural ventilation), and the melodious, uninterrupted throbbing (which bears no resemblance to the sounds of life on earth)—all these selective details insist upon the unnaturalness of "life" in this air-conditoned womb.

The attitude of the narrator toward his material is made even more clear by the tone with which he describes his first character. Apparently a typical citizen of this new civilization, she is a "swaddled lump of flesh," and her face—"as white as a fungus"—shows that she is more a parasite than a human being. Later on when this dependent thing hears the noise of something resembling a telephone, the narrator notes: "She knew several thousand people; in certain directions human intercourse had advanced enormously." The sentence, of course, drips with irony, for much more is meant than is said and much of what is meant—as is usually true of irony—is exactly the opposite of what is said. In truth, irony is the dominant aspect of the tone of "The Machine Stops," for more than anything else the story is an attack upon modern "progress," which, Forster says, is leading men to ever greater dependence upon, and worship of, machines, and is contributing to a constant weakening of the links that join man to man and man to nature. By the end of his vision, Forster has used his tone to persuade his audience to fear the machine and to detest life in a civilization lived under the rule of the machine. Obviously, he means his statement to apply to life during the twentieth century even more than to life in some "utopia" of a distant time.

One last note. Ideally, intelligent analysis (which does not mean interminable attention to pedantic minutiae) should deepen the pleasure of reading, just as understanding the logistics of the construction of the Brooklyn Bridge intensifies the awe with which we view the structure. Through effective reading, the reader becomes a lesser creator, for in probing a work of art, he not only opens intercourse with the great and original minds of all times but he challenges the depths of his own mind. There is joy in that.

An Analysis of "Thus I Refute Beelzy"

Since man began to communicate in more complicated ways than grunts, some men have pondered the question of reality, and some have been so tormented by the problem of what is really "real" and what is merely appearance that they have spent much of their lives investigating that branch of philosophy, metaphysics, that probes the ultimate nature of reality. John Collier, in his story "Thus I Refute Beelzy," dramatizes, in a small way, the conflict between two philosophical positions, and at the same time indicates his own stance—that there is more to reality than near-sighted fools can see.

To make his point, Collier has devised a plot that is straightforward in construction and, save for its fantastic conclusion, realistic in technique. The dominant conflict of the narrative is that between a father, Big Simon, and his son, Little Simon. The son is addicted to daydreams, and the father, Mr. Carter, attempts to convince him that the imaginative world is one of lies, while the material world is one of truth. Mr. Carter's arguments, however, do not persuade the child. Even when the father squeezes the boy's shoulder—in order, through pain, to demonstrate the difference between something you can see and feel and something that has no sensual reality—the boy persists in claiming that his world of make-believe, and his imaginative friend "Beelzy," is the real world, while the pretend world is that of Big Simon and Little Simon. His son's defiance enrages Mr. Carter, and he sends Little Simon to his room with the threat to punish the child. Little Simon claims that his defender, his friend Beelzy, will not allow him to be punished, and soon afterward Mr. Carter goes upstairs to refute the claim. Shortly thereafter, Mrs. Carter and her friend

Betty hear a scream, and when they investigate it, they discover the remnants of Mr. Carter—one shoe "with the man's foot still in it, like that last morsel of a mouse which sometimes falls from the jaws of a hasty cat." The victor in the conflict, therefore, seems to be Little Simon, and his claim that "Beelzy" exists seems to be valid. In making that assertion, the narrative implies the "reality" of a world of the supernatural (where the devil Beelzebub is a fact), and indicates that philosophically John Collier believes more in the complex "reality" of Bishop Berkeley (who posited the existence of "facts" beyond sensory perception) than he does in the simple "reality" of the writer Samuel Johnson (who, on one occasion, indicated his contempt for the theories of Berkeley by kicking a large rock and proclaiming: "Thus I refute Berkeley.").

In drawing his two major characters, Collier uses dramatic contrast to reveal his theme. Mr. Carter is, above all, a "reasonable" man of the modern age, but the tone with which he is depicted shows Collier's contempt for the kind of person that he represents. As a dentist, Mr. Carter is associated with science, though more a science with practical applications than one involved in realms of theory. From his profession, he has picked up the habit of continually washing his hands and thus forever attempting, at least symbolically, to wash away the invisible world of microscopic germs. As a contemporary man living in a conventionally furnished modern house—even to its Van Gogh reproduction—Mr. Carter can explain all elements of the complexity of human beings through the jargon of psychiatry—"fantasy," "guilt feelings," "defense mechanisms"—and can insist that men learn only through experience: "the new way." To his son's assertion that learning can be gained beyond experience—" 'I have learned,' the boy said, speaking like an old, tired man"—Mr. Carter has no sympathy; for to him "doing nothing" can lead neither to wealth nor knowledge.

Throughout the story, Mr. Carter proclaims that his six-year-old son "is a reasonable being" and must, therefore, be allowed to "choose for himself"; but ironically Mr. Carter insists that the boy choose "reasonably"—that is, as reasonably as the father wishes him to choose. The irony implies the weakness of Mr. Carter, and many scientifically oriented men, as a human being: He has no sympathy for, and no conception of, any thought other than his own. Because of this he is, as his overbearing pattern of speech suggests, an autocrat who breeds fear and contempt from those over whom he tyrannizes. When he arrives home, his wife merely says "You! . . . Home already!" but the exclamation marks have a world of meaning. By his self-centered blindness and tyranny, he invites his own destruction, if not by supernatural forces, then by the hatred (the lion or tiger) he arouses within others or by the confinement he places upon his own mentality.

Unlike his father, Little Simon is associated with the world of the supernatural. He has discontinued his normal social life and spends most of his time playing alone in his "retreat." There he mouths "solemn mumbo-jumbo" and performs "ritual sweeps and scratchings"—all of his actions suggestive of black magic—and his faith in the reality of the world he conjures up is so great that his father's threats cannot frighten him into accepting the material, sensory world at the price of denying the validity of the supernatural one. His childish faith that Beelzy will protect him from his father is comparable to the religious beliefs—beyond reason—that have often sustained Christians through times of trial; and his claim that Big Simon and Little Simon inhabit the pretend world, not the real one, echoes the Puritan contention that this world is mere appearance and we humans are but walking shadows.

Ironically, however, the creature whom Little Simon loves is not Christ but Beelzebub. The reason for this is that Beelzebub cares enough to come when Little Simon makes his ritual pass with his stick. From Beelzebub the child gets the one thing for which most men are willing to sell their souls—love. Little Simon desperately wants such love (and psychologically, therefore, it is plausible that he should create Beelzy), for it is totally lacking in his father and the chill rationality—the new way—that he represents. If it is the devil who responds to the silent cry for help that comes from the child—then he belongs to

Beelzebub. The important thing is that Beelzy comes when Little Simon calls. There is no question, as is supposed to be true of those who make their choice for Christ, of whether Little Simon has chosen Beelzy of his own free will. No, Beelzy comes on call. What he brings is love and protection—the things a child needs much more than the free choice Mr. Carter forces upon Little Simon before he is ready to make small decisions for play (as opposed to naps) or large ones for Christ (as opposed to Beelzebub).

Through his fantastic end, John Collier shocks his readers with the suggestion that a little child, weak and irrational as he may be, may be wiser than his parents. Whether the reader accepts or rejects the plausibility of Beelzy, Collier's skepticism about "the new way" may encourage the reader toward the kind of examination that leads toward wisdom. That is what Mr. Carter lacks, and that is why his son is justified in calling him a fool. In the son's indictment is Collier's condemnation of some elements of our day: its excessive practicality; its worship of the superficially scientific at the expense of the profoundly mysterious; and its chill, inhuman, arrogant assumption that there is but one truth and that experimental science (founded on experience rather than intuition) has uncovered, or can reveal, all that man needs to know about the nature of himself and his universe. Don't believe it, says Collier, for if you do, you may, in your shallowness and certainties, so limit your mind as to become nothing more than the remaining flesh left in a shoe after a busy devil has fed.

INTRODUCTION TO DRAMA

A play is meant to be seen, not read. Why then do we bother reading plays? Apart from the impossibility of seeing all the plays now in print—the cost alone would be staggering—there is profit as well as pleasure in reading plays. The profit comes from studying the play's literary values, many of the same values discussed in the section on fiction in this book. The pleasure depends to some extent on one's ability to imagine the play on a stage with actors speaking the lines that appear in print. The decision to produce a play—that is, actually put it on the stage—begins with a reading. Dramatic potential can be gleaned by a skilled reader from a text alone; but the fact that most plays do not succeed, either financially or esthetically, indicates that regardless of how expert the reader is, the text of a play is not the final test. Only the stage, with its actors, its sets, its lighting, and a director who develops and coordinates the whole, can provide the final testing ground.

Drama, therefore, is the only literary form that requires more than a writer and a reader. When the story writer finishes his short story or novel, he is finished. He will receive his rewards or punishments from his readers; nothing stands in the way. But when a modern playwright finishes the text of a play, he has just begun his job. Then comes the equally difficult task of putting it into production, of having many people interpret and shape the text, of changing it, of making numerous revisions before it reaches its audience. The differences between the first finished version of a play and its opening-night version can be enormous. What we do when we read a play, therefore, is second best. The ideal is to see a play, then read it, then study it.

Playwriting requires a special literary skill. A fine poet or novelist is not necessarily a good playwright. Shelley, Henry James, Thomas Wolfe, Ernest Hemingway—to mention a few—all tried their hands at playwriting and failed. James, in particular, tried again and again to mount a successful play but never did. The detailed reasons for these failures are not our business here. They merely indicate that drama demands a gift for constructing plots and a felicity in dialogue peculiar to itself as a distinct literary genre.

The essence of successful drama, ancient or modern, as Aristotle observed long ago, is action, an action that brings a protagonist in conflict with the world, with destiny, or with himself. The conflict may be external (one person against another, one group against another), or it may be internal (one person debating with himself). In classical tragedy—*Oedipus Rex,* for example—the conflict is largely internal. Although Oedipus debates with Teiresias, who warns him of his destructive course, the conflict takes place within Oedipus himself as he draws nearer and nearer to his own doom, sees that he is doing so, yet chooses, with dramatic irony, to ignore clear warnings. Because classical tragedy usually does not reveal physical conflict on the stage, the focus is on the internal struggle.

Shakespearean tragedy similarly portrays much of its conflict internally. Macbeth, Lear, Hamlet, and Othello all must resolve conflicts within themselves that arise from the drama of struggles without. We feel the tension of Hamlet's pursuit of Claudius, but the enigma of Hamlet is locked within himself, and this enigma carries much of the dramatic impact. Hamlet's "To be or not to be" speech remains a dramatic highlight precisely because it expounds a purely internal conflict. Indeed, the purpose of the soliloquy—that is, the speech given by one character when he is alone on stage—is to get inside the character's mind, to project his thoughts in dramatic utterance. And more often than not the thoughts thus projected center about some conflict.

Modern drama, while rarely using the soliloquy, has its own devices for articulating conflict. *Desire Under the Elms* portrays a psychological struggle between father and son, the struggle for possession of a woman and for possession of the land. It occurs outwardly as the verbal and physical struggle between two men and as something intangible but ubiquitous, filling the stage and creating tension even when no explicit conflict is taking place.

In this play the stark setting of the New England farmland and its associations with a life as hard as the soil also contribute to the sense of foreboding, of inherent disaster.

In the comic *Little Murders,* however, the conflict exists throughout society. No one is immune from the mutilation so that murder itself becomes a sport, a "little" act. And at the end when Alfred has killed Lieutenant Practice everyone is jubilant, and Marjorie says, "It's so nice to have my family laughing again."

The action of a particular play dictates its structure. A play generally unfolds its action in such a way that the audience, despite the best playbill in the world, will not understand it until the characters on stage explain not only who they are but the situation in which they find themselves. That which explains what has gone on before the opening of the play is called the exposition. The best kind of exposition does not call attention to itself. It comes out in dialogue and action that are appropriate to the tone of the play. Take, for example, the opening scene in *Major Barbara.* Lady Britomart Undershaft is discussing family finances with her son Stephen, a reluctant discussant. She asks for his help with the girls:

STEPHEN: But the girls are all right. They are engaged.

LADY BRITOMART: *{Complacently}* Yes: I have made a very good match for Sarah. Charles Lomax will be a millionaire at thirty-five. But that is ten years ahead; and in the meantime his trustees cannot under the terms of his father's will allow him more than £ 800 a year.

STEPHEN: But the will says also that if he increases his income by his own exertions, they may double the increase.

LADY BRITOMART: Charles Lomax's exertions are much more likely to decrease his income than to increase it. Sarah will have to find at least another £ 800 a year for the next ten years; and even then they will be as poor as church mice. And what about Barbara? I thought Barbara was going to make the most brilliant career of all of you. And what does she do? Joins the Salvation Army; discharges her maid; lives on a pound a week; and walks in one evening with a professor of Greek whom she has picked up in the street, and who pretends to be a Salvationist, and actually plays the big drum for her in public because he has fallen head over ears in love with her.

What the audience has learned from the brief exchange is not only the identification of the leading characters but also the chief topic with which the play deals: money. Lady Britomart wants money for her children and for herself. Barbara thinks she wants to live on one pound a week but soon finds that when money runs out there is no salvation for anyone. Even her philosopher husband, after accepting a job with Undershaft, says:

I think all power is spiritual: these cannons will not go off by themselves. I have tried to make spiritual power by teaching Greek. But the world can never be really touched by a dead language and a dead civilization. . . .

So he turns to the business of making guns and, of course, money. Undershaft, on the other hand, suffers no illusions about the money. It saves souls, he says, from the seven deadly sins: "Food, clothing, firing, rent, taxes, respectability and children. Nothing can lift those seven millstones from Man's neck but money; and the spirit cannot soar until the millstones are lifted." And in the final moment, at least according to one critical interpretation, it is Undershaft who triumphs.

Not all plays are constructed like *Major Barbara,* where there is a considerable amount of important exposition and it is revealed early in the play. In *Desire under the Elms,* O'Neill creates a strong sense of inevitability, of destructive forces at large that will culminate in catastrophe. Even before the appearance of Abbie, who acts as a catalyst, Eben appears in conflict not only with his father but with his half brothers, who tease him for being too easy and timid. His father also taunts him for being soft, as his mother was, rather than like the land, which is rocky and hard. Eben clearly identifies with his mother and denies, in a conversation with his brothers, that Ephraim is his father. Unlike his father and half brothers, Simeon and Peter, who are gruff and simplistic, Eben is brooding and introspective. He is tormented by his hatred of his father, whom he blames for having worked his mother to death. When Ephraim brings home a young wife, the con-

flict between father and son is intensified. Now there is rivalry over Abbie as there had been over the second Mrs. Cabot, Eben's mother. The love affair between Eben and Abbie, a love affair twisted as the two elms that "brood oppressively over the house," seems to grow inevitably from the climate of frustration, envy, and antipathy in which those related by no bonds but the arbitrary bonds of blood have to live. O'Neill thus fulfills the expectation he creates in his audience by bringing the lovers together, as he does in the "courting" scene that takes place in the family parlor. It is toward the union of the doomed lovers that everything else in the play tends, and it is from this union that the catastrophe springs.

The mounting tension of *Desire under the Elms* is not sought in Tennessee Williams' *The Glass Menagerie.* Instead the audience is moved by various artistic devices that emphasize the fact that this is a "memory" play: the poetic passages with which the play begins and ends, the recurring musical theme, the shades of lighting from soft purple to harsh white, the transparent gauze veil behind which the opening scene is played, and the symbolic glass menagerie. Even more the audience is held by a gradually increasing interest in the characters, the environment, and the themes of the play. Set in the 1930s, the drama illuminates a milieu in which the great depression was the prevailing American problem, and the rising surge of fascism was the dominant international reality. These facts, and the tensions consequent upon them, are never far from the surface of *The Glass Menagerie,* but they serve primarily as complementary reflections of the truth illustrated by the drama of the Wingfield family. That truth is simple: in this Darwinistic world the strong survive and the weak perish. Christ, in the imagery of the play, becomes only a greater magician, and his magic is a fraud; the gentleman caller of whom we dream brings not salvation but only greater despair. There is no salvation and no escape.

The conflict of the play, then, is less that between individuals (though the quarrels of Tom Wingfield and his mother are both humorous and pathetic) than between images and concepts: between visions of light and images of darkness, between the Christian faith and the Darwinistic fact, between the urge for peace and static beauty and the drive toward adventure and continual change. At the end of the play when the heroine, Laura, blows her "candles" out and the stage—the world—is left in darkness, the victor in this conflict is memorably apparent.

In the last analysis the mystery of dramatic success eludes solution. No single technique, whether it be Shaw's skill in creating reversal of attitudes in *Major Barbara*, Feiffer's ability to make comic what is potentially tragic in *Little Murders*, or Williams' use of a Darwinian action complemented by antireligious imagery in *The Glass Menagerie*, provides an infallible clue to the mystery. But certainly the stage illusion is woven by the actors, costumes, sound effects, lighting, and sets. All of these are manipulated by a director inspired by the latent possibilities of the playwright's text, and this complex manipulation is responsible for creating in the spectators the illusion of a living action in which (despite theatrical artifice and paradoxically because of that artifice) they participate.

An Analysis of "The Skin of Our Teeth"

Thornton Wilder won his second Pulitzer Prize for drama with *The Skin of Our Teeth,* which was first performed in New Haven Connecticut, on October 15, 1942, and had its New York opening on November 18 of the same year. The roles of Sabina and Mr. and Mrs. Antrobus were played respectively by Tallulah Bankhead, Fredric March, and Florence Eldridge, and the opening-night audience must have been aware from the very beginning of the play that it was in for an unusual evening. The opening scene was of a news broadcast, and in it pertinent lantern slides were flashed on the theater curtain. The first slide was of the sun rising above the horizon, and of this slide the news broadcaster commented: "The sun rose this morning at 6:32 A.M. This gratifying event was first reported by Mrs. Dorothy Stetson of Freeport, Long Island, who promptly telephoned the Mayor. The Society for Affirming the End of the World at once went into a special session and postponed the arrival of that event for TWENTY-FOUR HOURS. All honor to Mrs. Stetson for her public spirit."

Eccentric though such an opening may have seemed, it wasn't long before the audience was not only aware of its perfect relevance—for the play is concerned basically with the survival of man and his universe—but was also aware that the open-ing was only one of many playwriting eccentricities through which Wilder made his own dramatic points and at the same time spoofed conventional dramatic form. Among these eccentricities are scenery that seems always ready to fall, and when it does, falls upward instead of down; a dinosaur and a mammoth who are apparently the family pets of the Antrobus family; two characters named Homer and Moses who sing Greek and Jewish songs; a character who is the baby of the Antrobus family and at the beginning of the play is "only four thousand years old"; and another character, Sabina, who at one point refuses to play a sexual scene because she's afraid it will offend a friend of hers in the audience, and at another interrupts the play to tell the audience of her disgust with it: "I can't invent any words for this play, and I'm glad I can't. I hate this play and every word in it. As for me, I don't understand a single word of it, anyway—all about the troubles the human race has gone through, there's a subject for you. Besides, the author hasn't made up his silly mind as to whether we're all living back in caves or in New Jersey today, and that's the way it is all the way through." The reason for such dramatic idiosyncrasy was Wilder's unhappiness with the conventional box-set, picture-window staging that dominated nineteenth-

and twentieth-century drama and that emphasized a particular time and place—partially doing so by an elaborate use of scenery—in an attempt to achieve verisimilitude. Because he was "unable to lend credence to such childish attempts to be 'real'" and because he felt that such a technique produced plays in which "the characters are all dead from the start," Wilder began to write plays in which he tried "to capture not verisimilitude but reality."

To put it simply, the eccentricity of *The Skin of Our Teeth* is an example of controlled chaos in art, an aspect that probably, as much as anything else, led to a senseless furore, shortly after the play opened, in which the play was charged with being plagiarized from Joyce's highly unintelligible *Finnegans Wake*. (Wilder suggested, quite seriously, that he thought he was more indebted to *Hellzapoppin* than to *Finnegans Wake*.) Undoubtedly the dominating singularity of the play is the one that disgusts Sabina—the dislocation of time and space. The cause for this dislocation is, of course, Wilder's insistence upon the universal, but that does not alleviate a confusion in which the first act seems to be taking place in both modern New Jersey and in the time of the ice age; in which the second act seems to be set both at a modern convention meeting in Atlantic City and in the days of the flood and Noah's Ark; and in which the third act is set after a war—any war—while at the end of the act the hours of the night (named for such philosophers as Aristotle and Spinoza) pass by in their eternal wisdom, their eternal orbits, cycle upon cycle upon cycle. In insisting upon this dislocation of time and space, Wilder affirms his belief that the external events of most men's lives make what he calls "repetitive patterns," and this concept dramatically affirms his belief, as he once stated it, that "Literature is the orchestration of platitudes." The duty of the dramatist is to use an individual experience to indicate a general truth. To fuse the two truths is the obligation of the worthwhile dramatist, because, as Wilder says, "The theatre is admirably fitted to tell both truths. It has one foot planted firmly in the particular, since each actor before us (even when he wears a mask!) is indubi-

tably a living breathing 'one'; yet it tends and strains to exhibit a general truth. . . . It is through the theatre's power to raise the exhibited individual action into the realm of idea and type and universal that it is able to evoke our belief."

The conflict of *The Skin of Our Teeth* is the eternal one of man for survival. The conflict has two facets: that of man with his environment and that of man with the evil in himself. The conflict is seen through the struggle for survival of the Antrobus family and their servant Sabina, or in biblical, and universal, terms, the family of man as embodied in the figures of Adam, Eve, Cain, and Lilith. The first facet of the conflict dominates the first act, and it is of man against an ever hostile environment. Constantly through the first act the family is trying to gain warmth, and at the end of the act Sabina is pleading with the audience to pass up their seats in order to fuel the fire that will "save the human race." Constantly, too, in this act there are telegraph reports from the office of Mr. Antrobus to his home. These reports expand the specific conflict against the cold and ice to a general one of man with his external environment, for the reports bring news of how Mr. Antrobus is engaged in works that will aid human survival, of how he has invented the wheel and formulated the alphabet and the multiplication table. When he comes home from the office, however, Mr. Antrobus brings with him some characters that suggest the need of man in life for more than mere animal survival. What Mr. Antrobus brings home are a doctor, Judge Moses, and the nine sisters called the Muses. Mrs. Antrobus calls the whole horde tramps, especially objecting to the Muses—"That's the end," she says, "A singing troupe!"—but Mr. Antrobus insists on giving shelter to the entire group. As he says to Mrs. Antrobus, "I don't want any coffee if I can't drink it with some good people."

Apparently the opening-night audience —as well as later ones—contributed enough fuel to save the race, for the Antrobuses, as typical representatives of the human race, survive into the second act. By this time the couple have been married five thousand years, and in the act Mr. Antrobus and his charming wife—

"every inch a mammal"—are at Atlantic City for the convention of the "Ancient and Honorable Order of Mammals, Subdivision Humans." The basic conflict of the action is still over survival, but now there is a perfect fusion between the two possible causes for the destruction of man. Destruction by the environment overshadows the act, for thunder and lightning intermittently occur, and a weather indicator rises straight up from the orchestra pit. One black disk on the indicator indicates bad weather; two, storm; three, hurricane; and four, the end of the world. As the act progresses the disks multiply, and at the end they indicate the end of the world. At that time, in the midst of thunder and lightning, Mr. Antrobus—like Noah before him—hurries his family, and the animals of the earth, two by two, into a boat. A Cassandra-like fortune teller, who has earlier in the act foretold the future doom of man, watches the Antrobuses depart; and as they do, she mutters, "They're safe. George Antrobus! Think it over! A new world to make—think it over!'

As important as the conflict with the environment is the conflict within man, for the carnival, convention atmosphere suggests the evil that God ended when he caused the flood to cover the earth. This kind of evil now exists in Mr. Antrobus, for he has been elected President of the Mammals and has caught what the fortune teller calls the "great man" dizziness. In his speech to the convention Mr. Antrobus shows how far he has degenerated in his humanity, for he ends his speech with the Dionysian injunction: "I give you the watchword for the future: Enjoy yourselves." In pursuit of this aim Mr. Antrobus begins an affair with Sabina—who in this act has become Miss Atlantic City, 1942, and who dreams of taking Mr. Antrobus "away from that wife of his. Then I'll take every man away from his wife. I'll turn the whole earth upside down." The affair is going well, and Mr. Antrobus is pretty well convinced of the truth, evil though it is, of the philosophy that Sabina espouses: ". . . everybody in the world except a few people like you and me are just people of straw . . . there's a kind of secret society at the top of the world,—like you and me,—that know

this. The world was made for us." However, before Mr. Antrobus—and the human race—are doomed, Mrs. Antrobus, the maternal preserver of family ties, appears. To her husband she shows the essential Sabina, vulgar and common, in his own daughter, Gladys. At the same time, Mr. Antrobus becomes reawakened to the potential Cain in his son Henry. The realization of the evil strains in his children leads him to forsake Sabina, to proclaim, "I . . . I have to go and see what I can do about this." In leaving Sabina and her philosophy of selfishness, Mr. Antrobus preserves the human race again—at least into the third act.

In the last act the essential conflict is of man against himself, but that conflict also has two facets. One is of man against man; the other is the internal one of man within himself. The first facet is dramatized by the quarrel within the family of man as implied in the conflict between Mr. Antrobus and his son Henry. The two have returned from the war—any war—with hatred for each other in their hearts, each still desirous of totally destroying the other. The reason for this hatred is, as Sabina proclaims, that Mr. Antrobus has discovered during the war that "the enemy is *Henry;* Henry *is* the enemy. Everybody knows that." Why Henry is the enemy is revealed by the omnipresent allusion to him, from the first act on, as not only Henry but Cain. As Henrycain or Cainhenry—one word in either spelling—Henry stands for two kinds of evil, either of which has the potential of destroying the world. The first facet of his evil is his opposition to his father's desire to build a better world for all. What Henry wants is a better world for Henry; and the conflict between father and son, within the family of man, will never end, as Mr. Antrobus says, "as long as you [Henry] mix up your idea of liberty with your idea of hogging everything for yourself." Henry, however, also suggests a second kind of conflict. He cannot stand authority, and this inability to control, to discipline, himself leads to violent acts and violent results for which even Henry is sorry. Thus Henry advances upon his father ready to kill, screaming, "Let me get my hands on his throat." At this point Sabina interrupts the action, saying that the scene must not be played because at the previous night's performance Henry had almost strangled his father. The two men, the two actors, then halt and Henry apologizes, saying, "I don't know what comes over me." Mr. Antrobus does, however, for Henry is the spoiled child, perhaps made so by the father, but no matter where the fault lies the conclusion is the same: "How can you make a world for people to live in, unless you've first put order in yourself?" The answer is, you cannot; and at the end of the play Henry, "brooding and unreconciled," as the stage directions note, reappears at the edge of the scene, and in him reappears the most important threat—especially so today when man has largely conquered his environment—to the survival of man.

Little remains to be said, but one cannot leave the play without commenting upon the voices of the night that appear at the end of the last act. The appearance of the voices is foreshadowed at the beginning of the third act when the stage manager interrupts the action to explain that a number of the actors have suddenly been taken ill. These actors were to have played the voices—"a kind of poetic effect of the author," says the stage manager—and since there are no understudies for these minor roles, it is necessary that there be a short rehearsal with some volunteers who have agreed to play the voices. While the rehearsal is taking place, it is suggested that the audience smoke in the lobby, or chat quietly in their seats, or even watch the rehearsal. For the latter, the stage manager explains that each of the voices is a philosopher. To this, one of the volunteers adds that "just like the hours and stars go by over our heads at night, in the same way the ideas and thoughts of the great men are in the air around us all the time and they're working on us, even when we don't know it." At the end of the play, then, the voices reappear—nine o'clock, Spinoza; ten o'clock, Plato; eleven o'clock, Aristotle; and twelve o'clock, the Bible. Spinoza asserts the need of the wise to search for the good in man; Plato, the need of man to establish order in himself; Aristotle, the energy of God and man (the one greater, the other lesser), so that man through energy, by work, best reflects God; and the Bible, the creation of the universe: "And the Lord said let there be light and there was light."

The play ends, or almost ends, upon this religious note, and what that note implies is an optimistic, theological commonplace. That is, that God created the universe, but he left it up to man to make his own destiny. That destiny may be an earthly paradise—achieved by man's constant working toward the betterment of existence—or it may be man's own destruction. Whatever the result, God is not the cause. He may know the final answer, but He does not predestine it; man makes his own fate, and in the making of that fate is his glory or his shame.

What that fate may be is still undecided, for at the end of the play Sabina reappears voicing again her first lines of the play, "Oh, oh, oh. Six o'clock and the master not home yet." Then Sabina comes down to the footlights and addresses the audience: "This is where you came in. We have to go on for ages and ages yet. You go home."

The end of the play does undoubtedly suggest that man's fate is still in doubt, but an audience seeing the play does not really believe the assertion. Perhaps the reason is that there is too much stage trickery constantly going on in the play and too much homespun Pollyanna philosophy being mouthed in the course of the action. Because of these qualities, Wilder leaves his audience not basically disturbed, as it should be, but complacent and consoled. Perhaps this is why Wilder was so popular in Germany shortly after World War II. It was a psychological necessity for the Germans to feel that the evil they had lived with was but part of a continual cycle, for if they could feel so, they could live with themselves. It was also necessary for them to feel that soon life would go on as it had before—and Wilder told them that, too. Finally Wilder told them, and us too, that man has been left to make his own destiny, either to survive and even prevail, or to work his own destruction.

Perhaps, however, what man needs—and what the greatest playwrights give him—is less consolation and ego satisfaction and more realization of his human weakness and potential depravity. That is what the great tragic playwrights give us in their greatest works, and the lack of this in Wilder's plays makes them best described as amusements—well done, but, nevertheless, amusements. They should be judged on that basis, and on that level they are successful art.

INTRODUCTION TO POETRY

Poetry is difficult to define. William Wordsworth said it was "the spontaneous overflow of powerful feelings recollected in tranquility." Edgar Allan Poe called it "the rhythmical creation of beauty." And Robert Frost, in apparent desperation, said that "Poetry is what poets write." Regardless of the precise or "poetical" definition, however, most people, at one time or another, do read poetry, and one derives more pleasure from his reading if he understands the nature of poetry and the skills that go into its creation. Poetry is an art—it has form and meaning that enable it to survive. However casual and spontaneous a poem may seem, it has not just "happened." Milton referred to his great epic *Paradise Lost* as "unpremeditated verse"; but obviously he did not simply toss off twelve books of distinguished poetry. Milton meant that divine inspiration rather than pure intellect had moved him to write. But whether divine inspiration or rationality or both are the sources of great poetry, the poetic work is language molded into a form, and one that edifies and delights.

Traditionally, poetry has been categorized as epic (which celebrates a figure of heroic proportions doing deeds that illuminate the history and character of a nation); as dramatic (which tells or implies a story involving dramatic tensions); and as lyric (which melodiously emphasizes the personal emotions of the poet). But whatever type of poetry we read, it is the language of the poem that first attracts us. Technical details such as meter and rhyme are important parts of poetry; yet long before we learn about these we must concentrate on what words mean, what they suggest, and how they are used in their poetic context. It is possible, of course, to know the dictionary definition of each word and yet fail to understand a poem; but not to know what the words mean is a guarantee of such failure.

Consider the poor student who guesses at the meaning of "bootless" in Shakespeare's line "And trouble deaf Heaven with my bootless cries." The word in question obviously does not mean "shoeless"; yet the "cries" are not ordinary "cries" and the adjective that tells about them cannot be guessed at or ignored. In this particular context, "bootless" means "fruitless" and therefore describes the frustration of the supplication to Heaven.

Or take these lines from "The Eve of St. Agnes" by John Keats:

Full on this casement shone the wintry moon,
And threw warm gules on Madeline's fair breast

The intended sensuality of the scene is lost unless one knows that the "warm gules" are the red shades of light caused by the moon's rays passing through the stained-glass casement windows. In the same poem we learn that the Beadsman's fingers were numb "while he told/ His rosary . . ." We know the usual meaning of "told," but in this context the usual meaning is wrong. The Beadsman, who is paid to recite prayers for the dead, is not telling his rosary anything; he is instead "telling" or "numbering" his prayers.

Examples of the importance of meaning are endless, and they exist in prose as well as in poetry. Most students, however, are uninhibited by prose, which they see and read almost daily, but avoid poetry, partly because in addition to looking strange on the page, a poem uses language in unusual and challenging ways. One of the notable characteristics of poetry is, for example, compression. Prose paraphrases of good poems are usually longer than the poems themselves; for good poetry distills experience and emotion. One word does the work of several, and a single phrase condenses a whole train of thought.

Compression is achieved by a number of devices, one of which is metaphor. T. S. Eliot's J. Alfred Prufrock describes his genteel, meaningless existence in metaphoric language: "I have measured out my life with coffee spoons." Because everything about Prufrock (except his thoughts and dreams) is small and trivial, coffee spoons are appropriate measuring devices. His life has dribbled away in actions no more distinguished than sugaring coffee. Much as Prufrock longs for it, there is no epic role for him to play among the "tea and cakes and ices." Prufrock's awareness of his own inconsequence and his longing to escape from human sentience and suffering are expressed in his wish to be "a pair of ragged claws," merely a crab on the ocean floor. "Coffee spoons" and "ragged claws" say in four words what would take hundreds of words in prose.

In "To an Athlete Dying Young," Housman describes fame as a "garland briefer than a girl's." Two ideas are compressed in this one phrase: Fame is slighter and more fragile than a garland, and fame is less enduring than a floral wreath. In the same poem the runner is "chaired" through town, that is, carried in triumph on his comrades' shoulders. This same athlete, however, is "carried shoulder-high" by the pallbearers after his early death. The ironical parallel between victory and death is thus economically expressed.

An even greater degree of compression is achieved in the sustained metaphor of Emily Dickinson's "I Like to See It Lap the Miles." Here a train is seen as a rambunctious, playful, yet threatening horse. It laps, licks, feeds, steps, peers, crawls, complains, neighs—but finally, "punctual as a star," it stops at "its own stable door." The star, usually symbolic of a distant goal, has no such romantic connotations here. It is instead an astronomical phenomenon of dependability and accuracy. The poem then concerns itself with the relationship of the manmade and the godlike, and the underlying irony that something man devised should ever compete with cosmic "punctuality."

In Whitman's lyrical tribute to intuitive knowledge, "When I Heard the Learn'd Astronomer," he has the persona of the poem (that is, the character that the poet creates for the purposes of his poem) leave the lecture of "the learn'd astronomer" out of disgust with the superficiality of the factual knowledge the astronomer purveys. Then, in the open air, the persona looks up in "perfect silence at the stars." In these terms the stars express, symbolically, exalted height and eternal beauty, but even more they suggest the existence of a transcendent mystery beyond the perception of such "learned" scientists as the astronomer.

A symbol may be any object from man's perceptual reality—a star, a road, a rose—that suggests and comes to stand for something that is not palpable in the real world—a goal, a choice, a rare beauty. In each stanza of "In Time of 'The Breaking of Nations' " by Thomas Hardy, something eternal is symbolized—man working the earth; the home fire; the young lovers. Each represents something permanent or continual that will be present long after "War's annals . . . fade." At the time of World War I, Hardy expressed, symbolically, the hope that despite the wracking of nations, the old patterns of work, home, and love would endure.

A metaphor is an implied comparison. Two dissimilar things are compared on the basis of one or more features they have in common. In "A Narrow Fellow in the Grass," Emily Dickinson calls the straightened body of the snake a "spotted shaft." Like an arrow, the snake is tapered, assumes direction, and moves swiftly. When the snake uncoils, she calls it "a whiplash/ Unbraiding"; and when it contracts muscularly for movement, she says it "wrinkled, and was gone." Here the snake's appearance and movement are described by an implied comparison with leather and fabric. In the same poem the observer, using simile, reports, "The grass divides as with a comb." A simile is a direct comparison using "like" or "as." "My luve is like a red, red rose," writes Robert Burns. Like the metaphor, a simile suggests the similarity in things that appear dissimilar and compresses into a single figure several ideas. In "Fern Hill," Dylan Thomas describes a boy who was "happy as the grass was green." Logically, happiness has nothing to do with the color of grass. In the poem, however, the simile stresses the eternal color of grass and the lastingly intense quality of a boy's happiness.

Just as words may be used figuratively or connotatively, they may be used to evoke images, to present imaginatively an appeal to one of our senses. In "The Love Song of J. Alfred Prufrock," the mood of the evening is set by being compared to "a patient etherized upon a table." This kinesthetic image suggests a state of suspended animation, of immobility, of something deathlike. Later in the poem a visual image intensifies the gloom:

The yellow fog that rubs its back upon
the window-panes,
The yellow smoke that rubs its muzzle on
the window-panes. . . .

Metaphorically these lines suggest the cat-like stealth of the fog. We can visualize its disagreeable assault upon city buildings. In addition we respond to the tactile suggestion of dampness, slime, and industrial grit, and the noiseless advance of the fog and smoke creates an auditory image that strikes us as ominous.

Auditory images are forcibly assisted by the sounds of words in themselves. In "A Prayer for My Daughter" by William Butler Yeats, a father hears a storm and imagines the years to come:

Dancing to a frenzied drum,
Out of the murderous innocence of the
sea.

The generally low vowels, the heavy, thudding "d's" in "dancing," "frenzied," "drum," and "murderous," and the recurrent nasal consonants in "dancing," "frenzied drum," and "murderous innocence" reinforce the auditory image of the storm and suggest the tumultuous crisis of the father's thoughts. The ponderous, snarling sounds also strengthen the threat to innocence, beauty, and graciousness implicit in human nature as it aproaches the dangers of a chaotic future.

Thomas Hardy's "Darkling Thrush" offers a variety of images that create the bleakness of a winter landscape. The frost is "spectre-gray"; the sun is the "weakening eye of day." These grim visual images cause us not only to "see" the thin light and shrouded surfaces but to "feel" the bitter cold. The thermal image of cold is intensified by the lines that close the first stanza:

And all mankind that haunted nigh
Had sought their household fires.

Hardy next transfers to the century just completed the features of this winter landscape, as though they were the "Century's corpse outleant." The era is dead and buried and with it, seemingly, all the hopes and promises men believed it contained. The wind sings its "death-lament," and the pulse of life seems frozen eternally. Suddenly, the silence is broken by a sound that possibly offers hope: the song of an "aged thrush" in "blast-be-ruffled plume." Ironically, however, there is still nothing to sing about, and even if there were, even if—contrary to what we know—the bird had divine insight, man himself remains "unaware" of the "cause for carolings/ Of such ecstatic sound." Hardy, therefore, uses language imaginatively to affect our sensory perceptions; that is, he evokes images. But these images do not stand in isolation. They serve to heighten the irony, the intellectual wit of the poem. The poem works on two levels: the sensory and the intellectual.

A comparable use of figurative language and irony is found in Wilfred Owen's "Arms and the Boy." By personifying items in the arsenal of the modern world, Owen makes vivid the latent hostility of weapons and the vulnerability of young flesh. The steel of the bayonet is "cold" and "keen with hunger of blood"; it is "Blue with all malice" and "famishing for flesh." The bulletheads, "blind," that is, indiscriminating, as they are, "long to nuzzle in the hearts of lads." The cartridges, like predators, have sharp "teeth." The personified weapons are thus endowed with malignant purpose, and by implication the boy who is to embrace them will fondle them with naïve admiration and anticipation. The advice to allow him to do so, of course, is given as a warning and hence is meant ironically: If the boy embraces these "arms," he will embrace death. Yet, to compound the irony, the weapons are the only real defense the boy has. He has teeth, but they are meant "for laughing round an apple." His fingers lack claws, and, God-created though he is, he has "no talons at his heels/ Nor antlers through the thickness of his curls." We infer that what God intended for him was not battle, for which he needs artificial means, but happiness in a Garden of Eden where an apple was once his symbolic downfall. The allusion in the final stanza of the poem to the fateful apple underscores man's propensity for disobeying the will of his creator.

Another poetic allusion occurs when J. Alfred Prufrock says, "I have heard the mermaids singing each to each." The sirens of legend sang to lure men to their destruction, and for a moment Prufrock stands ready to be moved by some overwhelming passion. He concludes, however, that they will not sing to him. His death will be as undramatic as his life. He personifies death as an "Eternal Footman," decorous, prosaic, and obsequious.

In addition to meaning, of course, poetry has sound and movement. No one who remembers his elementary school days can forget the pupil who, falling into the predominant meter of a poem, read it so mechanically that he destroyed it forever. It is difficult, for example, to read the opening line of Poe's "The Raven" without smiling: "Once upon a midnight dreary, while I pondered, weak and weary." There is nothing amusing about the meaning of the line, but there is something funny about the metrical possibilities. The consistent pattern of trochaic feet (metrical units in which the first syllable receives strong stress, the second a weak stress as in "midnight") tempts one into a singsong. When the meter is perfectly regular, one must be careful not to be swept along oblivious to the meaning of the lines. Or take Byron's "The Destruction of the Sennacherib":

The Assyrian came down like the wolf on
  the fold,
And his cohorts were gleaming in purple
  and gold,

Here the meter, which is anapestic (that is, every third syllable is stressed: "And his cohorts"), nearly overwhelms the lines.

These examples illustrate a feature that some people think of as the most essential, or at least most characteristic, feature of poetry: metrical pattern. Although it is true that most poems have meter, metrical regularity is usually not as pronounced as it is in the aforementioned examples. Meter exists as a part of the total fabric of a poem; and, even though it may be isolated for study, its function can be understood only in relation to other poetic elements.

In Housman's poem "To an Athlete Dying Young," the basic meter is iambic: every other syllable, beginning with the second, is stressed. The iambic pattern is unbroken until the third stanza. There, the speaker addresses the dead athlete directly with the epithet "Smart lad." These two equally stressed syllables form the metrical foot we call a "spondee." When such a substitute foot obtrudes upon the basic meter, it metrically calls attention to the words or syllables so stressed.

In "The Second Coming" by William Butler Yeats, the meter is also basically iambic, but the first line begins with substitute feet: "Turning and turning in the widening gyre." Here a dactyl (a stressed syllable followed by two unstressed ones), followed by a trochaic and then a pyrrhic foot (a metrical unit of two unstressed syllables), makes for strong initial stresses that simulate the impulse, and lightly accented syllables that simulate the spinning. The final line of the poem also illustrates the contribution of metrical irregularity to total effect. The line "Slouches toward Bethlehem to be born" slouches much in the manner of the beast who comes to destroy. The breakdown of rhythm in this line ramifies the falling apart of "things" feared in the first stanza.

A poem written in free verse lacks both metrical pattern and rhyme scheme. In W. H. Auden's "Musée des Beaux Arts," for example, the very absence of the poetic artifices of meter and rhyme enables Auden to establish a casual conversational tone, a manner of offhand observation, which ironically underplays the tragic topic of human mortality. The understatement, assisted by natural speech rhythms, heightens the terror of the scene in Brueghel's painting by adopting the very detachment and indifference that characterize the world's reaction to individual suffering. How well such "Old Masters" as Brueghel understood that human suffering must be done in isolation!

An Analysis of "Anthem for Doomed Youth"

Although no poetic analysis, however accurate and complete, is a substitute for the poem itself, the following analysis of Wilfred Owen's "Anthem for Doomed Youth" is intended to illustrate some of the characteristics that have been discussed.

Anthem for Doomed Youth

What passing-bells for these who die as
    cattle?
Only the monstrous anger of the guns.
Only the stuttering rifles' rapid rattle
Can patter out their hasty orisons.
No mockeries for them; no prayers nor
    bells,
Nor any voice of mourning save the
    choirs,—
The shrill, demented choirs of wailing
    shells;
And bugles calling for them from sad
    shires.

What candles may be held to speed them
    all?
Not in the hands of boys, but in their
    eyes
Shall shine the holy glimmers of good-
    byes.
The pallor of girls' brows shall be their
    pall;
Their flowers the tenderness of patient
    minds,
And each slow dusk, a drawing-down of
    blinds.

A quick reading of this poem indicates that it is about the inhumanity of war. Young men die on the battlefield, and no one formally mourns them. Although inspired by the events of World War I, the poem just as easily could have been written about any war since the invention of the rifle. The idea is not new; the poetic expression of the idea, however, is unique.

Wilfred Owen chose as his form the sonnet, a poem of fourteen lines in a basic meter of iambic pentameter. The rhyme scheme is that of an English (as opposed to an Italian, or Petrarchan) sonnet; that is, the first and third lines rhyme in each four-line unit or quatrain. The poem also ends, as English sonnets do, with a rhymed couplet, a two-line rhyme. A special form of the lyric, the sonnet is well suited for brief expressions of joy or grief, love or hate, for which the restraint of a prescribed form is appropriate.

The sonnet is organized around two related questions, the first in line one, the second in line nine. The first question explicitly compares the youths who die to cattle. By implication, of course, these youths are led to slaughter as a herd would be, dumbly, not knowing they will die. The only mourning sound is the "monstrous anger of the guns." In the absence of human voices and sentiments, the guns are personified as outraged. We feel the bitter irony that the guns, actually the unwitting instruments of this slaughter, alone commemorate the deaths audibly.

In the third line the alliterative "r's" and "t's" in "stuttering rifles' rapid rattle" simulate onomatopoetically the sound described by the words. This quick, light (perhaps because distant) sound "patters out" mechanically the prayers of the dying. Again, it is the sound of weapons rather than human utterance we are made aware of. The irony of these lines is strengthened by the linking in rhyme of the key words "guns" and "orisons."

The next four lines particularize the answer to the opening question and develop an unexpected irony. Since "prayers" or "bells" for the dead in a public display of sorrow would be inapt for "cattle" and mere hypocrisy in the official realm that sanctioned the battle in which the youth were "doomed," they are mourned by "shrill, demented choirs of wailing shells" rather than by the solemn harmony of human voices in a church. The instruments of death are again personified as agents, here not only mad ("demented") but paradoxically lamenting ("wailing"). These "voices" are joined by bugle calls coming from the localities bereaved by the death of their young men, the "sad shires." The repeated "s's" here suggest the hush of these villages. Ironically, the bugle still summons young men to battle. The rhyme of "bells" and "shells" not only unifies the quatrain but stresses the military "music" that accompanies the dying.

The second question of the sonnet, in line nine, turns attention to the specifically human response: what "candles," what memorial services will "speed" or help the dead men on their way? In an inversion of normal word order that places the subject ("the holy glimmers of good-byes") in an emphatic position at the end of the two-line sentence, the speaker predicts again no formal ostentation of sorrow for the dead but something more touching, meaningful, and sacred: the tears in the eyes of boys, or, with a less literalistic reading of the verb "shall shine," perhaps a light or a radiance that signifies remembrance. Notably, Owen does not paint the hackneyed picture of the mothers' grief but directs attention to the boys and girls who survive their only slightly older brothers and friends, for they are members of a depleted generation and their remembrance is the most poignant. The "pallor of girls' brows" is expressive, of course, of the unblemished white of young skin, but the word "pallor" also suggests the fading of healthy color under oppressive conditions of sadness or sickness. The pining, the silent mourning of maidens, then, shall be the "pall" for the doomed youth. The obvious play on the words "pallor" and "pall" draws together the meanings of the words. The dictionary meaning of a pall is either a coffin or a square of heavy cloth placed over the coffin. Of these two meanings, the second seems metaphorically more apt to the context. The coffins of the dead will be, in effect, not adorned literally. But a third dictionary meaning of "pall" is "something that covers or conceals; *esp:* an overspreading element that produces an effect of gloom." The paleness of the girls, then, will silently express their mourning, just as their "flowers," presumably laid memorially on the soldiers' graves, will express the "tenderness of patient minds." It is interesting that the words that describe in these lines a wordless mourning are characterized by low vowels, an absence of abrupt stop consonants, and a predominance of sibilants, aspirates, and liquids. The last line of the sonnet illustrates the influence of metrical variation upon pace. The spondee "slow dusk" brings together three equally stressed monosyllables: "each slow dusk" slows the line to suggest the tedious passage of time for those who remain alive and who at evening shut out the dusk by a "drawing-down of blinds." The drawing-down of blinds may also be understood metaphorically as a shutting out of light once the light, here suggesting hope, has vanished. It in this sense reminds us of the eternal darkness of the buried and at the same time the despair of the living. The repeated "*d's*" weight the line to assist the notion of heaviness and hopelessness.

The implicit irony of the sonnet is clear. No human ceremony marks the death throes on the battlefield. The men who ostensibly fought for human values die without even completing their prayers. The sound of mourning comes from weapons, not from human voices. The grief of the survivors is expressed in personal suffering, not formal tributes.

SELECTIVE GLOSSARY OF LITERARY TERMS*

AESTHETIC DISTANCE—critical or creative disinterestedness; the ability to regard an artistic object without prejudice or preconception; the power to objectify fully in artistic form the emotion or experience which requires expression.

ALLEGORY—a literary mode in which characters, events, and settings are of interest not only in themselves but in their power to imply a set of meanings over and beyond themselves. This second level of meanings may be religious, political, or philosophical. Characters

* Cross-references are shown in italics; so also are a number of literary terms not given entries of their own.

are frequently personifications of abstract qualities or conditions of being. Thus Gulliver is the credulous traveller through whose eyes Jonathan Swift ironically surveys the follies and vices of mankind; Christian, the hero of John Bunyan's *Pilgrim's Progress,* allegorically undertakes the journey from religious indifference to spiritual dedication. *The Faerie Queene* by Edmund Spenser, the most complex, ambitious allegory in the English language, sustains the adventures of its characters, on the level of *chivalric romance,* for the sake of illustrating specific Christian virtues and the obstacles to their attainment. For example, the Red Crosse Knight, whose quest is holiness, must overcome such adversaries as Archimago (the arch-deceiver) and Duessa (duplicity). He must protect Una (truth) and liberate her parents, whose kingdom (the true church) has lain in captivity.

ALLITERATION—the repetition of initial consonant or vowel sounds to effect a reinforcement of meaning or mood, as in Emily Dickinson's phrase "horrid, hooting," which suggests in its very sound the hollow "complaining" of the train in "I Like to See It Lap the Miles."

ALLUSION—an indirect reference to a literary, mythical, or historical context. When T. S. Eliot's Prufrock confesses he has seen his head "brought in upon a platter," he alludes to St. John the Baptist, to whom he bears no resemblance: "I am no prophet."

AMBIGUITY—a term which designates the presence of more than one meaning in a word or a more extended literary passage. Although the term may be applied to unintentionally imprecise expression, functional ambiguity in literature is a device to gain compression and multiplicity of meaning. Wilfred Owen intends ambiguity in "Arms and The Boy" (the word "arms" in the title, for example, is deliberately ambiguous). Although the advice in the poem seems to be ironic (the "arms" would seem to be the vulnerable boy's worst enemy), a further *irony* lies in the possibility of an equally possible, more cynical interpretation: the boy in his innocence, lacking "claws" and "teeth" as natural means

of defense, would do well to embrace artificial means against his enemies.

ANAPEST—a metric foot of two unaccented syllables followed by one accented syllable (◡◡/).

ANTAGONIST—a term designating the one opposed to the *hero* or *protagonist* in dramatic conflict.

ANTICLIMAX—the arranging of material in order of decreasing emphasis or interest; a rhetorical weakness unless used deliberately for humorous effect, in which case the effect is *bathetic* (from the noun "bathos").

ANTIHERO—As rather loosely distinguished from a *hero,* the antihero is a protagonist, of relatively modern origin, whose thoughts and actions—whose very being—seems ironically to mock the idea of the heroic. (In common usage the *hero,* or *heroine,* of a tale is the *protagonist*—that is the major character of the narrative—and thus, paradoxically, an antihero may often be described quite accurately as a "hero.")

ANTITHESIS—a rhetorical device in which strongly contrasting terms or ideas are structurally balanced against each other for emphasis or *paradox,* as in Robert Frost's description in "Two Tramps in Mud Time": "The sun was warm but the wind was chill. . . ."

APOSTROPHE—direct address to a person or a personified entity, usually absent, as though present. In "Kilroy" the poet addresses that "G. I. Faustus who was everywhere" when he warns: "Kilroy, beware. 'HOME' is the final trap/that lurks for you in many a wily shape. . . ."

ARCHETYPE—A critical term used by the psychologist Carl G. Jung (and popularized by such archetypal critics as Northrop Frye), archetypes, according to Jung, are "racial memories" deep in the "collective unconscious" of all men. These archetypes may manifest themselves in dreams and *myths,* and literary artists who draw upon such materials have the potential of stirring readers and audiences beyond their rational existence, deep down into their bones and their unconscious being.

ASSONANCE—the repetition of similar vowel sounds within a poetic line (or lines) or at the end of a line in place of end rime. See Dylan Thomas's "Fern

Hill": "Now as I was yOUng and Easy Under the *A*pple boughs/ About the lilting ho*u*se and h*A*ppy *A*s the gr*A*ss was grEen. . . ."

ATMOSPHERE—the dominant mood, often descriptively established, of a literary work; for example, Joyce Carol Oates creates an atmosphere at once sensuous and foreboding in her story "Where Are You Going, Where Have You Been?"

BALLAD—a form of narrative originating among people with little or no literary sophistication, intended to be sung or recited and dealing generally with a single strong emotion or elemental situation, such as betrayal, heroism, love, heartbreak, or untimely death. The characters, sometimes legendary, are simply characterized, perhaps merely by an epithet, and the action is adumbrated rather than detailed. The narrator may leap over some steps in the action and linger descriptively at points of emotional crisis. The literary ballad, written deliberately to simulate the folk ballad, borrows its form and devices (incremental repetition, use of dialogue and the supernatural) but yields a meaning which transcends the story it tells. (See Theodore Roethke, "Ballad of the Clairvoyant Widow.")

BLANK VERSE—unrhymed *iambic pentameter*. It was put to best use in Elizabethan drama and in epic poetry by John Milton in *Paradise Lost*. Since then it has been used in idylls, lyrics, and an occasional play, such as T. S. Eliot's *The Cocktail Party*. Stephen Spender employs it in his poem "The Express."

BURLESQUE—exaggeration, often preposterous, for comic or satiric effect. In "The Love Song of J. Alfred Prufrock" Prufrock sees himself as a burlesque Hamlet. Although he wrestles with a decision, his problem, unlike Hamlet's, is "no great matter." One of the most renowned burlesques is Cervantes's *Don Quixote*, in which the form of the medieval romance encompasses the ridiculous tilting of the celebrated Don. Often burlesque employs a deliberately inappropriate style, as in *The Importance of Being Earnest*, where, for all their glossy manners and affectations, the upper classes deal with nothing more important than cucumber sandwiches and where being earnest substitutes for being sensible.

CARICATURE—a deliberate distortion, in drawing or in writing, which exaggerates specific features of a person or animal for satiric purposes. Max Beerbohm's "Self-Caricature 1897" highlights the playboy dandy of the turn-of-the-century to the exclusion of other realistic features. Emily Dickinson caricatures gentlewomen in "What Soft, Cherubic Creatures."

CATHARSIS—the purgation of strong feeling aroused by a dramatic situation through identification with its characters, a process alleged to take place with the resolution of conflict.

CLICHÉ—an overworked, consequently stale, expression; a stereotype. In "I Paint What I See," E. B. White balances Rivera's assertion antithetically with Nelson Rockefeller's "I know what I like" to suggest the discrepancy between a fresh vision in the painter and a hackneyed reaction in the millionaire.

CLIMAX—the arrangement of elements in ascending order of importance; the culmination of episodes in a story or novel; the point of greatest emotional intensity. In drama, a "turning point" in the action which reverses the course of the protagonist and makes his destiny clear.

COMEDY—as opposed to tragedy, that form of drama in which *conflict* is resolved short of death, and the continuance of life is insured by the temporary removal or overcoming of obstacles for its chief characters. Modern comedy frequently suggests that all is not well that ends well; the mere preservation of life is not synonymous with its renewal. Such "comedy" may seem sadder than tragedy.

COMPLICATION—in the action of a story or drama, the embroiling of characters in an increasingly complex fabric of *conflict*, leading up to the climax and resolved in the *dénouement*.

CONCEIT—originally synonymous with "idea" or "conception," the term has come to designate an elaborate, contrived, or intellectually ingenious metaphor, a farfetched comparison of unlike things. In "Freshmen" Barry Spacks describes the look of alert apprehension in the "best" students by comparing it to "the swinging door/ to the opera just before/ the Marx Brothers break through." This "conceit" presupposes subtlety of perception as well as specialized cinematic experience in the reader. The "conceits" of the so-called metaphysical poets as a rule are more detailed and sustained than those of modern poets.

CONNOTATION—as opposed to the *denotation* of a word, the suggestions a word makes or the associations it evokes; the emotional charge of a word as distinct from its dictionary definition. Gwendolyn Brooks in "The Chicago Defender Sends a Man to Little Rock" writes: "they are hurling spittle." The word "spittle" denotes "saliva," but conjures up repellent connotations of disease, senility, or sheer vulgarity.

CONSONANCE—at the end of poetic lines, half rime or slant rime; stressed syllables of the same final consonant but unlike vowel sounds, a device common in the poetry of Emily Dickinson, who rhymes "pearl" with "alcohol" in "I Taste a Liquor Never Brewed." Within a line consonance contributes sound effects which may reinforce meaning. In the line "Where all's accustomed, ceremonious" the consonance of the nasal *m*'s and *n* lends a measure, weight, and continuity to Yeats's meaning in "A Prayer for My Daughter."

COUPLET—two successive rhymed lines of identical meter.

DACTYL—a metric foot of one accented syllable followed by two unaccented syllables ($/\,\cup\cup$).

DECORUM—appropriateness or propriety in the treatment of literary subjects; the avoidance of the incongruous, incredible, or obscene.

DENOTATION—the literal or dictionary meaning of a word.

DENOUEMENT—that point in the action of a play or narrative at which everything in the plot is made clear and explained. In *Major Barbara,* for example, the dénouement begins when Undershaft explains his ideas on society and convinces Barbara, who has previously preached Christian salvation, to join him in the munitions business.

DEUS EX MACHINA—literally, "god from the machine"; metaphorically, any arbitrary action from outside the main action which resolves dramatic problems. The term originated with the Greek theatre, especially with the plays of Euripides, where the actors who played gods were lowered onto the stage by a crane or machine. Their role was to set situations right. In modern times such devices as the arrival of the cavalry to rescue beleaguered forces just in the nick of time, or the discovery of a birthmark which identifies the protagonist as a prince instead of a pauper, are instances of this artificial device. Often regarded as the failure of a writer to control his plot, this device is burlesqued in *Tom Jones.*

DRAMATIC MONOLOGUE—a lyric poem in which one character only speaks and reveals himself and his inner thoughts. Robert Browning brought the form into popular acclaim, and several twentieth-century poets, including T. S. Eliot in "The Love Song of J. Alfred Prufrock," have used it.

ELEGY—a dignified, meditative poem occasioned by the thought of death or the death of a particular person, for example, Walt Whitman's "When Lilacs Last in the Dooryard Bloom'd" or John Ciardi's "Elegy for G. B. Shaw."

EMPATHY—"feeling into"; in the reading of literature, the involuntary identification of the reader with fictitious characters; the vicarious "living" of their created lives.

END-STOPPED LINES—poetic lines in which the completion of syntax and meaning coincide with the end of the line.

ENJAMBEMENT—a device by which the syntax and meaning of one poetic line is carried to the succeeding line, or lines, without a break.

EPIC—a lengthy narrative poem concerning characters of heroic proportions in an action which has worldly or universal significance. The epic style is elevated and characterized by formal rhetorical devices such as the invocation of the Muse, the roll call of heroes past and present, extended *similes, apostrophes,* and *antitheses.* Beginning at a crucial point midway in the total action to be narrated, the epic author works forward and backward in time, incorporating accounts of battles, councils, and single combats between great contestants that are tangential to the main action. Gods as well as men take part in these actions, and the outcome affects not only the epic hero but his people, his nation, or mankind itself, as Adam's fall does in John Milton's *Paradise Lost.* Milton, like Virgil in *The Aeneid,* patterned his epic upon those of his famous Greek predecessor Homer: *The Iliad* and *The Odyssey.*

EPIGRAM—a pointed saying, characterized by elegance, terseness, and wit.

EPILOGUE—a section appended to a literary work; in drama, a short speech delivered by a performer directly to the audience at the conclusion of the play.

EULOGY—a piece, written or oral, in praise of a person or thing.

EUPHEMISM—an innocuous term substituted for a socially offensive one, such as "passing away" for "dying" or "perspiring" for "sweating."

EXPOSITION—that material in a story or play which gives information antecedent to the action proper but essential to understanding the present action or fictional situation. In *Desire Under the Elms,* for instance, the relationship of Eben Cabot's dead mother to her son and her husband is vital to understanding either the action or the meaning of the play.

EXPRESSIONISM—a movement of late-nineteenth-century and early-twentieth-century artists who proposed to objectify inner states of feeling in unconventional ways. By saying he has measured out his life in coffee spoons, T. S. Eliot's Prufrock presents directly, in an image of triviality, the tedium and inconsequence of his days and hours.

FABLE—a short tale with a moral, didactic in nature, and frequently endowing animals with human attributes to show men's absurdities and vices. Aesop's well-known beast fables gain political dimension in the modern fable *Animal Farm* by George Orwell.

FALLING ACTION—the resolution of dramatic action after the climax.

FIGURE OF SPEECH—a word or words used to give forceful, imaginative expression to something other than their literal meaning. Words so used undergo either a shift in meaning (as when Sylvia Plath metaphorically calls her father a "black shoe") or a shift for the sake of rhetorical emphasis, as in *apostrophe* and *antithesis.*

FLASHBACK—a break in narrative sequence for the sake of recounting what has happened prior to the present action. Willy Loman's dramatized memories of early days with his sons are flashbacks in Arthur Miller's *Death of a Salesman.*

FOOT—a metrical unit such as the *iamb* (◡/), *trochee* (/◡), *anapest* (◡◡/), and *dactyl* (/◡◡).

FORESHADOWING—the preparation of expectations for what is to come in a story or drama by means of setting; speeches which appear significant only in the light of later developments; images or symbols which adumbrate central ideas or future crises.

FREE VERSE—verse which relies for its effects on devices other than meter and rhyme.

GENRE—a literary type, as well as a subdivision of such kinds; for example, the novel is a genre distinct from the fable or the short story, as the picaresque novel is a genre distinct from the historical novel.

GOTHIC—a term applied to elements in a literary work which introduce the supernatural (rather than the spiritual), the extravagant, the grotesque, or the exotic for the sake of creating atmosphere. The stories of Edgar Allan Poe and the cartoons of Charles Addams (for quite different purposes) employ Gothic features: live burial, torture chambers, predatory birds, ghosts, clanking chains, cobwebs, hanging moss, castles, monsters, fiends, and hags. The term Gothic originally designated the barbaric and crude as opposed to the classical in art, architecture, and literature.

HEROIC COUPLET—two successive lines of rhymed iambic pentameter.

HUBRIS—the *tragic flaw* of many classical protagonists: the excessive pride which goes before their fall.

HYPERBOLE—an exaggeration, for rhetorical effect, which proposes a literal impossibility or improbability; for example, "I'll die if I don't pass English."

IAMB—a poetic foot in which an unaccented syllable is followed by an accented one. The following line is written in iambs and consists of four iambic feet:

I lĭke tŏ sée ĭt láp thĕ míles.

Technically the line is, therefore, written in iambic (∪/) tetrameter (four feet to the line).

IMAGERY—the use of verbal sensory appeals to stimulate the imagination and at times to suggest by indirection the major elements in the intellectual content of a literary work. The most common of the sensory appeals is visual, but the other senses—hearing, taste, touch and smell, as well as the sense of movement—are often used effectively, sometimes in complexly mingled fashions, by the sophisticated writer. Figures of speech such as the simile and the metaphor often make vivid use of images, and individual images may be made symbolic by artistic manipulation (often through repetition) in the course of a literary work. In Housman's "Loveliest of Trees" the cherry tree "Wearing white for Eastertide" makes a memorable image which ultimately goes beyond the white color to the concept of purity and then to the yearly resurrection of nature.

IMPRESSIONISM—a literary term drawn from a school of nineteenth-century French painting (Claude Monet was among its leaders) which attempted to demonstrate, through its depiction of the changing effects of light, that even in the external world "objective reality" was varied. In literaure the term is associated with the concept that subjective reality is more "true" than objective facts. Thus the author may emphasize (as James Joyce often does) the inward world of his characters to the neglect of the external environment, or he may (as Eugene O'Neill often does) use distortions of reality (the sailor's quarters in a ship may be made to seem like a cage for animals) to communicate "truths" that realistic treatment cannot capture. In his poem "On a Photo of Sgt. Ciardi a Year Later" John Ciardi

espouses the impressionistic credo when he writes: "The camera always lies. By a law of perception/ The obvious surface is always an optical ruse."

INEVITABILITY—the mood created by an author to dramatize the concept that lives are predestined and events are fated. For the ancient Greek playwrights the inevitability of dramatic actions often sprang from a concept of man's relationship to the gods; thus Oedipus, in Sophocles' play *Oedipus Rex,* tries to elude the fulfillment of the prophesy of the Oracle (that Oedipus would kill his own father and marry his own mother) and succeeds only in exposing his own flaw of *hubris* (or excessive pride). In modern drama, as in O'Neill's plays *Desire Under the Elms* and *Mourning Becomes Electra,* the feeling of the inevitability of events flows from inward compulsions of the characters (often based on such Freudian concepts as the Oedipal complex) which cannot be successfully resisted.

INFORMAL ESSAY—a short literary composition. As contrasted to the formal essay, the informal (or personal or familiar) essay is subjective and individualistic, disposed more toward the illumination of personal feelings and opinions than toward the teaching of facts and the expounding of ideas. Though the distinction between the formal and informal essay is often imprecise, Huxley's "The Method of Scientific Investigation" exemplifies the formal essay while F. Scott Fitzgerald's "Early Success" and George Orwell's "Shooting an Elephant" are undoubtedly informal.

INVOCATION—an author's plea to the gods (most especially the Greek muses) to bring him inspiration, divine powers, in the creation of his art. The epic poem customarily begins with an invocation to Calliope, the muse of epic poetry.

IRONY—a literary device which especially involves contrast in meaning and indirection in technique. Two significant forms of irony are the irony of words and the irony of events. The first especially involves a contrast between what is said and what is meant; the second usually involves a contrast between what one expects to result from an action and what actually occurs. A simple example of verbal irony may be seen in the title of T. S. Eliot's poem "The Love Song of J. Alfred Prufrock" (for the poem mocks Prufrock's capacity for both life and love); an example of the irony of events may be seen in *The Glass Menagerie* (where the Wingfield family seeks a gentleman caller for the heroine, Laura, but when he arrives, he ultimately brings not salvation, but only greater despair).

LYRIC—in Greek poetry, a poem to be sung to the accompaniment of a lyre, but now a short poem with strong musical and subjective elements.

MELODRAMA—a type of play, most popular in the late nineteenth century, which exploits extreme (and improbable) situations involving simple black and white characters (villains and heroes) to come to a resolution in which evil is overcome and virtue triumphantly prevails.

METAPHOR—Among the most common forms of figurative language, the metaphor implies a comparison, without the use of like or as, between two dissimilar objects by stating that the two are identical. By asserting the identity of the two, a literal impossibility, the writer forces the audience to probe for a way in which the assertion may be valid in respect to some essential similarity between the objects compared. A simple metaphor is the statement, "America is an insane asylum."

METER—in English poetry, the basic rhythmic pattern of stressed (/) and unstressed (◡) syllables in a line of verse. The most common metrical patterns are *iambic* (◡/), *trochaic* (/◡), *anapestic* (◡◡/), and *dactylic* (/◡◡). Most poetry, especially modern poetry, makes use of considerable metrical variation in order to avoid monotonous regularity.

MOTIVATION—the reasons, largely psychological, that a character acts in certain ways in particular situations. When a character acts in ways inappropriate to the personality he has established, his actions become implausible and the narrative becomes unbelievable.

MYTH—in the traditional sense, a fictitious narrative usually involving supernatural beings; revealing popular ideas about the mysteries of natural phenomena and their explanation; and dramatically symbolizing some of the more profound beliefs of a particular culture. These primitive legends have, for such writers as Sigmund Freud and Carl Jung, been seen as similar to dreams in that they may be used as sources for symbolic revelations of the deeper truths of individuals and civilizations. Carl Jung's theory of *archetypal* memories posits a racial "collective unconscious," a common mental inheritance, that "remembers" at the deepest level of being such repeated racial experiences and events as those of birth and death. These ideas have been used by such critics as Leslie Fiedler and Northrop Frye to serve as the foundation of a critical system involving archetypes (what Jung calls "primordial images") in literature. Modern poets and novelists such as T. S. Eliot and James Joyce have made much use of myth in such primary works of the twentieth century as *The Wasteland* and *Ulysses*.

NATURALISM—Sometimes defined as "realism on all fours," naturalism emphasizes the physical, brute, instinctive nature of man (the "natural" man) rather than the mental abilities (such as the skill of reading) and spiritual aspirations (toward morality) which differentiate man from a purely animal being. The generally acknowledged "father" of realism was the French writer Émile Zola, and in *Le roman expérimental* ("The Experimental Novel") he insisted that the novelist should be, like the scientist, a dispassionate observer whose "experiments" revealed the "law" by which men's actions and lives were determined by heredity and environment. These kinds of determinism—biological determinism, which implies man is what he must be because of his genes, and environmental determinism, which insists that a man is what he is because of where he is nurtured—are, perhaps, the dominant traits of naturalism. Its other qualities often include a tendency towards great detail (in an effort to tell the whole truth); towards the depiction of lower life (in an attempt to depict the animal source of man); towards presenting an unplotted "slice of life" (in an effort to suggest the purposeless chaos of existence); and towards implying a Darwinistic, evolutionary philosophy (in an effort to dramatize the thesis that force is the ultimate law in a world dominated by the struggle for survival).

ODE—A formal lyric characterized by extended length, elevated language, exalted emotion, and a serious and dignified theme, the ode was originally a precise choral form (divided, in the Pindaric ode, into strophe, antistrophe, and epode) and was used in such Greek dramas as *Oedipus Rex;* now the ode, when written at all, is usually an intellectual, introspective meditation, not conceived for public performance but to aid self understanding.

ONOMATOPEIA—the use of words whose very sound ("buzz," "bang") implies their meanings. In the hands of a subtle poet individual lines or even complete stanzas may so manipulate sound as to imply the event by the sound itself; note, for instance, how Matthew Arnold, at the end of the first stanza of "Dover Beach," captures by his manipulation of sound the movement of water against shore.

PARADOX—a statement which seems on superficial examination to be either absurd or contradictory but which on closer inspection reveals its own validity. Like *irony,* paradox implies contrast, and some critics (especially among those categorized as New Critics) see irony and paradox (as well as indirection generally) as the particular language appropriate to poetry (as opposed to the factual, explicit language appropriate to science).

PARODY—a humorous mockery, usually by exaggerated stylistic and thematic imitation, of another piece of work. Anthony Hecht's "The Dover Bitch" is in part a parody of Matthew Arnold's "Dover Beach."

PATHETIC FALLACY—a phrase first used by John Ruskin to categorize that tendency of impassioned writers to ascribe human emotions to inanimate objects.

In his *Modern Painters* (1856), Ruskin quotes the passage:

They rowed her in across the rolling foam—
The cruel, crawling foam.

Then Ruskin comments:

The foam is not cruel, neither does it crawl. The state of mind which attributes to it these characters of a living creature is one in which the reason is unhinged by grief. All violent feelings have the same effect. They produce in us a falseness in all our impressions of external things, which I would generally characterize as the "pathetic fallacy."

PERSONA—in one sense the character or characters (personae) in a work, most especially a play. In a second sense the voice (or mask) through which the author speaks in a particular artistic work. Thus Mark Twain uses Huckleberry Finn as his persona in *The Adventures of Huckleberry Finn,* but Mark Twain is obviously not Huckleberry Finn even though Twain may have drawn upon his own experiences and emotions to give *verisimilitude* to his narrative.

PERSONIFICATION—a figure of speech in which non-human objects and ideas are treated as if they possessed human attributes. Edna St. Vincent Millay in "Justice Denied in Massachusetts" personifies death in the lines:

Let us sit here, sit still,
Here in the sitting-room until we die;
At the step of Death on the walk,
rise and so; . . .

PICARESQUE NOVEL—an episodic narrative, realistic in its language and details, in which the central figure (or picaro) wanders from place to place and undergoes a series of adventures which in large part satirize the follies of various social classes, most especially the bourgeoisie. Originating in Spain as a burlesque of chivalric romances (as was Cervantes' *Don Quixote),* the form, with considerable modification, has been employed effectively by novelists as diverse as Daniel Defoe *(Moll Flanders),* Mark Twain *(The Adventures of Huckleberry Finn),* and Saul Bellow *(The Adventures of Augie March).*

PLOT—a series of causally related events

(the second arising from the first, the third from the second) with a clearly discernible beginning, middle, and end and involving a *conflict* of forces which ultimately comes to a *climax*. The plot may differ from the action of a story, for the plot is the author's arrangement of events to gain the highest dramatic effect (often ignoring chronological sequence), while the *action* is the chronological ordering of the events. In his *Poetics,* Aristotle insists on the necessity of *unity* in plot; thus by his test no event in the plot can be omitted or rearranged without altering the whole.

POINT OF VIEW—the angle of vision from which a story is told. The basic points of view are the first person and the third person. In the first person the story is told by "I," and "I" may be the major actor in the story, a minor participant, or merely someone who observes what occurs or narrates what he has heard from others. The third person narrator ("he"), may be omniscient (that is, he knows everything about all his characters, including their thoughts, and tells anything which he desires); may have selective omniscience (in which case the author limits what his narrator knows); or may merely see, like an audience at a play, what takes place before his eyes (the objective or dramatic point of view). The particular point of view of any story may be highly complex, for in any story there may be considerable overlapping in point of view, and there are innumerable variations of both the first and third person angles of vision.

PUN (or PARONOMASIA)—word play in which differences in meaning in a single word, or similarities in sound between two words with different meanings are manipulated for humorous or thematic effects. That the pun is not always the lowest form of humor is proved by one of the greatest of punsters, Shakespeare, as, for instance, in his play upon the word "dust" in the following lines: "Golden lads and girls all must/ As chimney sweepers, come to dust."

QUATRAIN—a *stanza* of four lines of either rhymed or unrhymed verse.

REALISM—Historically a mode of writing especially associated with the nineteenth century, realism may generally be defined as a literary mode which emphasizes fact or reality and rejects the impractical or visionary. William Dean Howells, sometimes called the "Father" of American realism, defined the mode as "nothing more and nothing less than the truthful treatment of materials"; in his own realistic credo he insisted upon the primacy of the ordinary and the commonplace and upon the duty of the realist "to front the every-day world and catch the charm of its work-worn, care-worn, brave, kindly face." Realists such as John W. De Forest, W. D. Howells, and Henry James often satirize the excesses of romantic overstatement and idealization, and they generally avoid the tendency of naturalists towards deterministic philosophies. In their treatment of ordinary materials, the realists tend towards precision and understatement, towards simple, even colloquial, expression, and towards minimizing of rhetorical language and symbolic suggestion.

RHYME—the repetition of similar patterns of sound (cat: rat) in verse. The most common place where rhyme occurs is at the end of a poetic line (end rhyme), but internal rhyme (in which the rhyming syllable or syllables come after the beginning and before the end of a line) is common, and beginning rhyme (in which the rhyming syllable or syllables occur at the beginning of a line) is occasionally practiced. Masculine (or single) rhyme is the correspondence of final syllables (time: crime; decay: portray); feminine (or double) rhyme is the correspondence of the last two syllables (lending: bending); and polysyllabic rhyme is the correspondence of three or more syllables (Victorian: Praetorian). Approximate rhyme (or *slant* or *half rhyme*) occurs when the similarity of sounds is imperfect (steel: tell). The *rhyme scheme* of a poem is the pattern of the end rhymes in the work. A common pattern for a Petrarchan sonnet is as follows: abbaabbacdcdcd; the repetition of the various letters indicates the pattern of repetition in the rhyme scheme.

RHYTHM—the general quality of the rise

and fall of emphasis which exists with relative looseness in prose and relative rigidity in poetry. Broader in concept than meter, rhythm is, nevertheless, closely associated with *meter* in verse, save that the regularity of metrical stresses is not the sole determinant of the rhythm of a poem. In *free verse,* which lacks metrical symmetry, rhythm exists but it is less rigidly organized than in metrical poetry.

RISING ACTION—that part of the action of a dramatic narrative which proceeds from the *complication* (in which opposition to the protagonist first becomes evident in the plot) through the development of the *conflict* to the *climax* (in which the dramatic tension is at its height). The falling action follows the climax and leads ultimately to the *dénouement.*

ROMANTICISM—in English and American literature a movement of the late eighteenth century which was in large part a revolt against neo-classic formalism as well as a reaction against artistic, political, and religious orthodoxy. Often used as a term in contrast to *realism* or *classicism,* romanticism in art emphasizes the individualistic, the spontaneous, the emotional, and the imaginative, but the vagueness of the term, the imprecision of its definition, has led some scholars such as Professor A. O. Lovejoy to complain that the confusion over the meaning of romanticism is a literary "scandal" and to insist that the varied, and often conflicting, senses of the term imply that there is no such thing as "romanticism" but only a diversity of "romanticisms." Be that as it may, certain characteristics in art are generally recognized as "romantic" (though the possession of any one or more of them does not mean that the writer possessing these characteristics is necessarily a "romantic" writer). Among these qualities is a tendency towards introspection; the worship of nature; an interest in the foreign, the mysterious, and the exotic; a tendency to adulate childhood and the "natural" in any form; an obsession with, and a quest for, absolute truth; an enthusiasm for unique, experimental styles; and a fondness for *symbols* which emphasize and

yet illuminate the mystery of existence. Among modern writers whose art, as well as their lives, exemplify important aspects of romanticism are Dylan Thomas and F. Scott Fitzgerald. Though few writers can be said to be wholly romantic (or *realistic* or *naturalistic*)— Hemingway, with different parts of himself, is all three—it can be said that the art of most writers is such that they can be conveniently categorized; it is important to remember, however, that the art, not the label, is what matters most.

RUN-ON-LINE—as opposed to an *end-stopped* line, a run-on or *enjambed* line is a poetic line in which there is no pause, either in sense or grammatic structure, from one line to the succeeding one.

SATIRE—a humorous indictment of human vices, frailties, and foibles, usually with the intent of reforming either man or society or both. Among classical Roman writers Horace mocked, with relative gentleness, the vices of his society, while Juvenal was more bitter and personal in his attacks upon the frailties and foibles of man; the most common differentiation of satire, into Horatian and Juvenalian, springs from this distinction. "The Machine Stops," in its indictment of various tendencies of modern technology, would properly be classified as Horatian satire.

SENTIMENTALISM—generally emotional self-indulgence stemming from a disproportion between an emotional response and the cause for that reaction. In another sense sentimentalism refers to a general philosophic outlook which denies the existence of evil and simplifies man into a creature that is essentially virtuous and benevolent.

SETTING—the physical details—most especially as to place and time—which illuminate the external (and sometimes the internal) background in which a story takes place. Often the setting of a story is extremely important in illuminating aspects of meaning in a narrative, and occasionally the primacy of setting in a story (such as Poe's "Fall of the House of Usher") may lead critics to refer to it as a story of setting.

SIMILE—a comparison, usually by the use

of "like" or "as," between two essentially dissimilar things. The following simile, from D. H. Lawrence's "Wedding Morn," makes an effective comparison:

The morning breaks like pomegranate
In a shining crack of red;

In addition, however, the simile suggests the sexual psychology and imagery of the poem as a whole. In doing so, the simile becomes not only ornamentative but functional.

SONNET—characteristically a fourteen line poem written in *iambic pentameter.* The most common kinds of sonnets are *Petrarchan* (or Italian) and *Shakespearean* (or English). The former takes its name from a great fourteenth-century Italian sonnet writer, and is characterized by a rhyme scheme in which the first eight lines (or *octet)* are regularly rhymed abbaabba; the last six lines (or *sestet)* are usually rhymed cde cde, but common variants of the sestet are such rhyme schemes as cd cd cd, cde edc, and cde dce. Typically the pattern of thought of the Petrarchan sonnet corresponds to the twofold division of the rhyme, so that the octet poses a question or suggests a psychological dilemma and the sestet asserts a possible resolution. The Shakespearean sonnet takes its name from the greatest practitioner of this modified form of the Petrarchan sonnet. In it the rhyme scheme is abab cdcd efef gg, that is, three quatrains followed by a rhymed couplet. Often the pattern of thought follows the four-fold pattern of the rhyme, with possibly the first three parts of the poem being three different images making a single thematic point and the whole summarized epigrammatically by the end couplet. A common practise, however, is to break the pattern of thought into a twofold one similar to the pattern of the Petrarchan sonnet, with the division being between the first eight lines and the last six. In addition to these common forms of the sonnet, a third form, irregular, is often practised. The variants in rhyme and meter in the irregular sonnet are innumerable, and twelve, sixteen, and twenty line sonnets are not unknown. Numerous writers have also written *sonnet sequences,* in which a series of sonnets are linked to each other by their treatment of a unified topic. Among the most celebrated sonnet sequences are Mrs. Elizabeth Barrett Browning's "Sonnets from the Portuguese," W. H. Auden's "The Quest," and Dylan Thomas's "Altarwise by Owl-light."

SPONDEE—in poetry, two long or accented syllables in succession.

STANZA—a poetic unit, usually similar in pattern to other such units in a single poem, and comparable, when short, to a prose sentence or, when long, to a prose paragraph. Among the more common stanzaic forms are the *couplet* (two lines), *terza rima* (three lines), *quatrain* (four lines), *rime royal* (seven lines), *ottava rima* (eight lines), and *Spenserian* (nine lines).

STREAM-OF-CONSCIOUSNESS—a type of psychological *realism* which uses the mind as the dominant force behind the form of the work. In using the technique the author attempts to capture the flux of a character's thought, often chaotic and disconnected, as it flows from different levels of consciousness and unconsciousness. Among the great novels to use this fictional technique are James Joyce's *Ulysses* and William Faulkner's *The Sound and the Fury.*

STYLE—When used in reference to literary style (as distinct from, say, a painting style or a life style), style is the use of language in all its variety—from diction to sentence patterns to imagery to symbolism—in a way that best expresses the artistic intent and the unique individuality of a particular author. There are, of course, an infinite number of styles, some of them named after authors *(Miltonic, Ciceronian, Euphuistic),* some after literary periods *(neoclassic, naturalistic),* some after particular professions *(journalistic, legalistic),* but these categories, though convenient, are only the beginning of saying anything truly intelligent about a particular writer's style.

SUSPENSE—the uncertainty and anxiety, especially appropriate to drama and fiction, which teases the reader or audience into excited anticipation of what will occur next.

SYMBOLISM—the conscious use in literature of things (events, images, objects) which are not only themselves but also stand for things (that is, become symbols that symbolize concepts) that extend beyond themselves. In his practise of symbolism, the symbolist may use natural symbols (the ebb and flow of the tide to suggest the ebb and flow of life), conventional symbols (white as suggestive of purity), Freudian symbols (a gun as symbolic of masculine sexuality), or private symbols (which he or a select circle of friends may alone know). Often the symbolist, by his use of symbols, attempts to suggest an unseen reality, an absolute truth, behind what he may conceive to be the veil of appearances. This attempt to hint rather than to state, to imply mysteries rather than assert facts, is to be found in many of the great writers of the *Symbolist Movement* (among them Rimbaud, Mallarmé, and Valéry) which flourished in France in the latter part of the nineteenth century.

THEME—generally speaking, the central meaning, either directly or indirectly expressed by the author, in a serious literary work. On occasions the dominant theme of a work is obvious; on others, it is elusive. In either case it is probably true that all else in a serious work—setting, plot, character, tone, whatever—will help to illuminate theme.

TONE—the emotional coloring of a piece of writing which suggests the author's attitude towards his material—tender, passionate, ironic—much as the tone of voice of a speaker implies part of the total meaning of what he says.

TRAGEDY—As distinct from *comedy*, tragedy uses dignified language to deal with a subject of high importance; dramatizes characters of some importance whose fate is of more than mere personal sig-

nificance; and ends with the destruction, either physically or spiritually, of the hero. Aristotle in his *Poetics* insisted that the hero of a tragedy should not be either evil or stupid; thus his downfall arises through a *tragic flaw (hamartia)* in himself with which the audience can sympathize. The ultimate effect of tragedy, according to Aristotle, is to arouse the emotions of pity and fear in order to effect a *catharsis* in the audience—that is, to produce in them a purgation, or possibly a purification, of their emotions. For Aristotle, *Oedipus Rex* is the perfect example of tragedy. In our time few dramatists have attempted to write classical tragedy, and some critics have claimed that such art is inappropriate to the temper of man and society in the modern age.

UNITY—that quality in literature by which the variety of the parts in a work is directed towards a single effect, so that all parts of the whole serve a function, and no part seems unnecessary or out of place. Aristotle insisted in his *Poetics* that a play should have unity of action, and Renaissance critics extended his theory to a deification of the *unities* of time (the action of the play should cover no more than twenty-four hours), place (the action should be set in one locale), and action (there should be only one narrative line). Partly as a reaction to such limitations, some critics and artists (among them Coleridge and Emerson) preached the doctrine of organic unity (or organic form), by which the work of art was compared to a living thing which grows from within itself rather than is shaped by rigid man-made laws.

VERISIMILITUDE—the feeling of truth achieved in a literary work by the use of details that are, or seem to be, drawn from reality.

INDEX